W9-CQS-050

INTERNATIONAL
BUSINESS

INTERNATIONAL
BUSINESS

THIRD EDITION

Michael R. Czinkota
Georgetown University

Ilkka A. Ronkainen
Georgetown University

Michael H. Moffett
Oregon State University

The Dryden Press
Harcourt Brace College Publishers
Fort Worth   Philadelphia   San Diego   New York   Orlando   Austin   San Antonio
Toronto   Montreal   London   Sydney   Tokyo

Publisher: Liz Widdicombe
Acquisitions Editor: Ruth Rominger
Developmental Editor: Carla Houx

Project Management: Elm Street Publishing Services, Inc.
Compositor: York Graphic Services, Inc.
Text Type: 10/12 Garamond

Cover Image ©Roy Wiemann, Image Bank

Address for Editorial Correspondence
The Dryden Press, 301 Commerce Street, Suite 3700, Fort Worth, TX 76102

Address for Orders
The Dryden Press, 6277 Sea Harbor Drive, Orlando, FL 32887
1-800-782-4479, or 1-800-433-0001 (in Florida)

ISBN: 0-03-097646-4

Library of Congress Catalogue Number: 93–2282

Printed in the United States of America

4   5   6   7   8   9   0   1   2   032   9   8   7   6   5   4   3   2

The Dryden Press
Harcourt Brace College Publishers

To all the Czinkotas: Ilona, Ursula, Mihaly, and Thomas—MRC
To Sirkka and Alpo Ronkainen—IAR
To Bennie Ruth and Hoy Moffett—MHM

THE DRYDEN PRESS SERIES IN MANAGEMENT

Anthony, Perrewe, and Kacmar
Strategic Human Resource Management

Bartlett
Cases in Strategic Management for Business

Bedeian
Management
Third Edition

Bedeian and Zammuto
Organizations: Theory and Design

Bereman and Lengnick-Hall
Compensation Decision Making: A Computer-Based Approach

Boone and Kurtz
Contemporary Business
Seventh Edition

Bowman and Branchaw
Business Report Writing
Second Edition

Bracker, Montanari, and Morgan
Cases in Strategic Management

Calvasina and Barton
Chopstick Company: A Business Simulation

Costin
Readings in Total Quality Management

Czinkota, Ronkainen, and Moffett
International Business
Third Edition

Daft
Management
Third Edition

Eckert, Ryan, and Ray
Small Business: An Entrepreneur's Plan
Third Edition

Etienne-Hamilton
Operations Strategies for Competitive Advantage: Text and Cases

Foegen
Business Planning Guide
Second Edition

Gaither
Production and Operations Management
Sixth Edition

Gatewood and Harris
Human Resource Selection
Third Edition

Gold
Exploring Organizational Behavior: A Management Challenge Readings, Cases, Experiences

Greenhaus
Career Management
Second Edition

Harris and DeSimone
Human Resource Development

Higgins and Vincze
Strategic Management: Text and Cases
Fifth Edition

Hills, Bergmann, and Scarpello
Compensation Decision Making
Second Edition

Hodgetts
Management: Theory, Process, and Practice

Hodgetts
Modern Human Relations at Work
Fifth Edition

Hodgetts and Kroeck
Personnel and Human Resource Management

Hodgetts and Kuratko
Effective Small Business Management
Fourth Edition

Hodgetts and Kuratko
Management
Third Edition

Holley and Jennings
The Labor Relations Process
Fifth Edition

Huseman, Lahiff, and Penrose
Business Communication: Strategies and Skills
Fourth Edition

Jauch and Coltrin
The Managerial Experience: Cases and Exercises
Sixth Edition

Kemper
Experiencing Strategic Management

Kuehl and Lambing
Small Business: Planning and Management
Third Edition

Kuratko and Hodgetts
Entrepreneurship: A Contemporary Approach
Second Edition

Kuratko and Welsch
Entrepreneurial Strategies: Text and Cases

Lewis
Io Enterprises Simulation

Luthans and Hodgetts
Business
Second Edition

McMullen and Long
Developing New Ventures: The Entrepreneurial Option

Matsuura
International Business: A New Era

Mauser
American Business: An Introduction
Sixth Edition

Montanari, Morgan, and Bracker
Strategic Management: A Choice Approach

Northcraft and Neale
Organizational Behavior: A Management Challenge
Second Edition

Penderghast
Entrepreneurial Simulation Program

Sandburg
Career Design Software

Sawyer
Business Policy and Strategic Management: Planning, Strategy, and Action

Schoderbek
Management
Second Edition

Schwartz
Introduction to Management: Principles, Practices, and Processes
Second Edition

Varner
Contemporary Business Report Writing
Second Edition

Vecchio
Organizational Behavior
Second Edition

Walton
Corporate Encounters: Law, Ethics, and the Business Environment

Wolford and Vanneman
Business Communication

Wolters and Holley
Labor Relations: An Experiential and Case Approach

Zikmund
Business Research Methods
Fourth Edition

The Harcourt Brace College Outline Series

Pentico
Management Science

Pierson
Introduction to Business Information Systems

Sigband
Business Communication

PREFACE

In a highly competitive book market, few books progress to a third edition. It is our market which has made that progress possible and we are grateful for the encouragement. By the same token, we are taking the mandate from the market very seriously by concentrating our energies on strengthening our leadership position. We present this third edition as another step up in the teaching and learning of international business.

Here are the reasons why this book is special: The text reflects the realities of educational and marketplace needs. It goes beyond a discussion of the glamorous operations of the multinational corporations and includes the operational concerns of small and medium-sized firms. International business is examined from a truly global perspective rather than just the view from the United States. The reality of the interplay between business and government is specifically addressed by presenting business as well as policy concerns. The important societal dimensions of ethics and the environment are fully integrated into the material. The text retains a strong theory base but at the same time reflects the managerial concerns of those who work on the front lines of the business world. To enhance the "tool" value of the text, improvements in pedagogy, presentation, and writing continue to make this book fun to teach with and learn from.

CHANGES IN THE THIRD EDITION

The key change in this edition is the addition of a new co-author, Dr. Michael H. Moffett. His expertise in the areas of international finance and economics measurably strengthens and refines many areas of the book. Furthermore, major efforts were undertaken to improve the timeliness of the information provided, the business relevance of the material taught, and the reader friendliness of the book. Chapter content reflects the newest advances in both research and practice. All tables and figures were updated to present the latest available data. The Global Perspectives featured in each chapter present the most recent business activities and best business practices. Sixty percent of the cases are either new or revised, and the use of video cases has been greatly expanded. The use of new technology and full-color printing allowed us to include text-specific maps and better graphics in each chapter. Our overall goal was to make the task of the instructor easier and to make learning more efficient and fun.

Part 1 has been extensively updated with new data. A more comprehensive integration of classical and modern international trade theory and thought have been added. This introductory part is followed by two cases, one of which includes a video presentation.

Part 2 now highlights the contemporary issues in international trade and capital flows. New sections are devoted to the effect of the continuing rise of the Japanese yen, as well as the structure and performance of the European Monetary system and its single-currency ambitions as set forth in the Maastricht Treaty. The emergence of trading blocs is analyzed in more detail together with the newest thinking on export promotion and trade policy. Increased emphasis has been placed on the managerial concerns resulting from all these changes.

Part 3 reflects the geo-political changes of the 1990s. Lobbying and environmental responsiveness are addressed specifically. The need for business to adjust to a rapidly shifting economic environment in the former Eastern Europe and Soviet Union are also highlighted. The process of privatization is discussed, and the corporate response to these shifts is analyzed.

Part 4 now includes explicit treatment of strategic alliances, the interaction between marketing and environmental concerns, and the emergence of the Euromanager. This part stresses the progress of international expansion and the effect of different strategies on corporate competitiveness. For example, different areas of accounting treatment across countries are detailed together with their effect on the operations of firms in international markets. The chapters also benefit from a strong increase in managerial emphasis. The implications of terms of shipment and sale are also discussed as well as the need for market-based financial management of risk. In addition, more attention has been paid to the implementation of global programs.

SPECIAL FEATURES

Art and Photo Program

In order to inspire the student's imagination, full-color photographs have been included in this edition. Throughout the text, concepts are visually depicted through tables, figures, and graphics. Artwork is designed to reiterate key concepts as well as provide a pleasing format for student learning.

Organization

The text is divided into four parts. The first part introduces the basic concepts of international business activity and theory. The second focuses on the economic and financial environment, reviews institutions and markets, and delineates trade policy issues. Part 3 concentrates on the business-government interface, with special attention given to emerging market economies and state-owned enterprises. Part 4 is devoted to strategic management issues.

Coverage

The text covers the international business activities of small and medium-sized firms that are new to the international arena as well as those of giant multinational corporations. It also provides thorough coverage of the policy aspects of international business, reflecting the concerns of the U.S. government, foreign governments, and international institutions.

The text consistently adopts a truly global approach. International business is covered from the viewpoint of the U.S. firm and the U.S. government, but the views and goals of foreign businesses and governments are represented as well. Attention is given to topics that are critical to the international manager yet so far have eluded other international texts. This coverage includes chapters on countertrade, logistics, international service trade, and doing business with newly emerging market economies under conditions of privatization.

Maps

To increase the geographic literacy of students, each chapter has a specific full-color map. They provide the instructor with the means visually to demonstrate concepts such as political blocs, socioeconomic variables, and transportation routes.

Contemporary Realism

Each chapter offers a number of Global Perspectives that describe actual contemporary business situations. They are intended to serve as reinforcing examples, or mini-cases. As such, they will assist the instructor in stimulating class discussion and aid the student in understanding and absorbing the text material.

Research Emphasis

A special effort has been made to provide current research information. Chapter notes are augmented by lists of relevant recommended readings. These materials will enable the instructor and the student to go beyond the text whenever time permits.

Cases and Video Support

All sections of the text are followed by cases, many written especially for this book. Eight cases are also supported by video materials available to the instructor. Challenging questions accompany each case. They encourage in-depth discussion of the material covered in the chapters and allow students to apply the knowledge they have gained.

Pedagogy

A textbook is about teaching and we have made a major effort to strengthen the pedagogical value of this book.

- The use of full-color printing makes it easier to differentiate sections and improves the presentation of graphs and figures.
- The design of maps specific to chapters adds a visual dimension to the verbal explanation.
- The Global Perspectives bring concrete examples from the business world into the classroom.
- The video support materials enable better and more efficient instruction.
- A glossary has been provided for the student's benefit. Each key term is bold-faced and defined in the text where it first appears. A complete glossary has also been provided at the end of the text.

COMPREHENSIVE LEARNING PACKAGE

Instructor's Manual, Test Bank, and Transparency Masters

The text is accompanied by an *Instructor's Manual* designed to provide in-depth assistance to the professor. For this edition, this manual has been thoroughly revised, updated, and expanded. For each chapter of the text, the manual provides suggested teaching notes, possible group projects, an overview of the chapter's objectives, and answers to all end-of-chapter Review and Discussion Questions. Answers are provided for all the questions that follow the end-of-part cases, and video teaching notes are provided for each video case that appears in the text. In addition, an annotated list of suggested films and videos is provided. The *Test Bank* portion of the manual provides a range of over 1,000 incisive true/false, multiple choice, short answer, and essay questions for each chapter. The manual also includes more than 60 transparency masters for use in the classroom.

Computerized Test Bank and RequesTest

All the questions in the printed Test Bank are available on computer diskette in IBM- and Macintosh-compatible form. Adopters also can request customized tests with Dryden's special service, RequesTest. By simply calling our toll-free number, Dryden will compile test questions according to a requestor's criteria and then either mail or fax the test master to the user within 48 hours. The number to call is 1-800-447-9457.

Study Guide

A complete *Study Guide,* written by Rajib N. Sanyal of Trenton State College, is available to students. It contains application exercises, self-test questions, and chapter reviews that will enable students to obtain the maximum benefit from the course.

Acetate Package

Transparency acetates are now available from the text art and maps. Acetates are accompanied by detailed teaching notes that include summaries of key concepts.

Computerized Instructor's Manual

A computer disk that contains most elements of the *Instructor's Manual* will be available to text adopters.

ACKNOWLEDGMENTS

We are grateful to a number of reviewers for their imaginative comments and criticisms and for showing us how to get it even more right:

Kamal M. Abouzeid
Lynchburg College
Riad Ajami
The Ohio State University
Joe Anderson
Northern Arizona University
Robert Aubey
University of Wisconsin–Madison
David Aviel
California State University

Julius M. Blum
University of South Alabama
Sharon Browning
Northwest Missouri State University
Ellen Cook
University of San Diego
Gary N. Dicer
The University of Tennessee
Massoud Farahbaksh
Salem State College

Anne-Marie Francesco
Pace University–New York
Esra F. Gencturk
University of Texas–Austin
Debra Glassman
University of Washington–Seattle
Raul de Gouvea Neto
University of New Mexico
Antonio Grimaldi
Rutgers, The State University of New Jersey
Basil J. Janavaras
Mankato State University
Michael Kublin
University of New Haven
Jan B. Luytjes
Florida International University
David McCalman
Indiana University–Bloomington
James Neelankavil
Hofstra University
Moonsong David Oh
California State University–Los Angeles
Diane Parente
State University of New York–Fredonia
Jesus Ponce de Leon
Southern Illinois University–Carbondale

Jerry Ralston
University of Washington–Seattle
William Renforth
Florida International University
Martin E. Rosenfeldt
The University of North Texas
Tagi Sagafi-nejad
Loyola College
Rajib N. Sanyal
Trenton State College
Ulrike Schaede
University of California–Berkeley
John Stanbury
Indiana University–Kokomo
John Thanopoulos
University of Akron
Douglas Tseng
Portland State University
Heidi Vernon-Wortzel
Northeastern University
Steve Walters
Davenport College
James O. Watson
Millikin University
George H. Westacott
SUNY–Binghamton

Many thanks to those faculty members and students who helped us in sharpening our thinking by cheerfully providing challenging comments and questions. Several individuals had particular long-term impact on our thinking. These are Professor Bernard LaLonde, of the Ohio State University, a true academic mentor; the late Professor Robert Bartels, also of Ohio State; Professor Arthur Stonehill, of Oregon State University; Professor James H. Sood, of American University; Professor Arch G. Woodside, of Tulane University; Professor David Ricks, of Thunderbird; Professor Brian Toyne, of St. Mary's University; and Professor John Darling, of Mississippi State University. They are our academic ancestors.

Many colleagues, friends, and business associates graciously gave their time and knowledge to clarify concepts; provide us with ideas, comments, and suggestions; and deepen our understanding of issues. Without the direct links to business and policy that you have provided, this book could not offer its refreshing realism. In particular, we are grateful to Secretaries Malcolm Baldrige, C. William Verity, Clayton Yeutter, and William Brock for the opportunity to gain international business policy experience and to William Morris, Paul Freedenberg, H. P. Goldfield, and J. Michael Farrell for enabling its implementation. We also thank William Casselman of Popham Haik, Robert Conkling of Conkling Associates, Lew Cramer of US WEST, Robert Keezer of Comsat, Joseph Lynch of ADI, and Reijo Luostarinen of HSE.

Valuable research assistance was provided by Joanne Schwartz as well as LuAnn Hartley and Jennifer Smith, all of Georgetown University. We appreciate all of your work!

A very special word of thanks to the people at The Dryden Press. Ruth Rominger and Carla Houx made the lengthy process of writing a text bearable with their enthusiasm, creativity, and constructive feedback. Major assistance was also provided by the friendliness, expertise, and help of Elm Street Publishing Services.

Foremost, we are grateful to our families, who have had to tolerate late-night computer noises, weekend library absences, and curtailed vacations. The support and love of Ilona Vigh-Czinkota, Susan and Sanna Ronkainen, and Megan Murphy, gave us the energy, stamina, and inspiration to write this book.

Michael R. Czinkota
Ilkka A. Ronkainen
Michael H. Moffett
September 1993

ABOUT THE AUTHORS

MICHAEL R. CZINKOTA

Michael R. Czinkota is on the faculty of marketing and international business of the Graduate School and the School of Business Administration at Georgetown University. From 1981 to 1986 he was the Chairman of the National Center for Export-Import Studies at the university.

From 1986 to 1989 Dr. Czinkota served in the U.S. government as Deputy Assistant Secretary of Commerce. He was responsible for macro trade analysis, departmental support of international trade negotiations and retaliatory actions, and policy coordination for international finance, investment, and monetary affairs. He also served as Head of the U.S. Delegation to the OECD Industry Committee in Paris and as Senior Trade Advisor for Export Controls.

Dr. Czinkota's background includes eight years of private sector business experience as a partner in an export-import firm and in an advertising agency and twelve years of research and teaching in the academic world. He has been the recipient of research grants from various organizations, including the National Science Foundation, the National Commission of Jobs and Small Business, and the Organization of American States. He was listed as one of the three most prolific contributors to international business research in the *Journal of International Business Studies* and has written several books including *International Marketing, Export Policy,* and *Unlocking Japan's Market.*

Dr. Czinkota served on the Board of Directors of the American Marketing Association and is on the Board of Governors of the Academy of Marketing Science and the editorial boards of the *Journal of Business Research, Journal of International Business Studies, International Marketing Review and Asian Journal of Marketing.* In 1991, he was named a Distinguished Fellow of the Academy of Marketing Science.

Dr. Czinkota has served as advisor to a wide range of individuals and institutions in the United States and abroad. He has worked with corporations such as AT&T, IBM, GE, and Nestlé and has assisted various governmental organizations in the structuring of effective trade promotion policies.

Dr. Czinkota was born and raised in Germany and educated in Austria, Scotland, Spain, and the United States. He studied law and business administration at the University of Erlangen-Nürnberg and was awarded a two-year Fulbright Scholarship. He holds an MBA in international business and a Ph.D. in marketing from The Ohio State University. He and his wife, Ilona, live in Luray, located in Virginia's Shenandoah Valley.

ILKKA A. RONKAINEN

Ilkka A. Ronkainen is a member of the faculty of marketing and international business at the School of Business Administration at Georgetown University. From 1981 to 1986 he served as Associate Director and from 1986 to 1987 as Chairman of the National Center for Export-Import Studies.

Dr. Ronkainen serves as docent of international marketing at the Helsinki School of Economics. He was visiting professor at HSE during the 1987–1988 and 1991–1992 academic years and continues to teach in its Executive MBA, International MBA, and International BBA programs. Dr. Ronkainen holds a Ph.D and a master's degree from the University of South Carolina as well as an M.S. (Economics) degree from the Helsinki School of Economics.

Dr. Ronkainen has published extensively in academic journals and the trade press. He is a co-author of *International Marketing*. He serves on the review boards of the *Journal of Business Research, International Marketing Review,* and *Journal of International Business Studies.* He served as the North American coordinator for the European Marketing Academy 1986–1990. He was a member of the board of the Washington International Trade Association from 1981 to 1986 and started the association's newsletter, Trade Trends.

Dr. Ronkainen has served as a consultant to a wide range of U.S. and international institutions. He has worked with entities such as IBM, the Rank Organization, and the Organization of American States. He maintains close relations with a number of Finnish companies and their internationalization and educational efforts.

MICHAEL H. MOFFETT

Michael H. Moffett is currently Associate Professor of Finance and International Business at Oregon State University. Dr. Moffett has a B.A. in Economics from the University of Texas at Austin (1977), an M.S. in Resource Economics from Colorado State University (1979), and M.A. and Ph.D. in International Economics from the University of Colorado, Boulder (1985).

Dr. Moffett has lectured at a number of universities around the world, including the Aarhus School of Business (Denmark), the Helsinki School of Economics and Business Administration (Finland), the Norwegian School of Economics (Norway), and the University of Ljubljana (Slovenia). Dr. Moffett has also lectured at a number of universities in the United States including Trinity College, Washington D.C., and the University of Colorado, Boulder. He is a former visiting research fellow at the Brookings Institution and he recently completed a two-year visiting professorship in the Department of International Business at the University of Michigan, Ann Arbor.

Michael Moffett's research publications have appeared in a number of academic journals, including the *Journal of International Money and Finance, the Journal of Financial and Quantitative Analysis, Contemporary Policy Issues,* and the *Journal of International Financial Management and Accounting.* He is co-author of *Multinational Business Finance,* sixth edition, 1992, with David Eiteman and Arthur Stonehill, as well as co-editor with Arthur Stonehill of *Transnational Financial Management* for the United Nations Centre for Transnational Corporations, 1993. He is a continuing contributor to numerous collective works in the fields of international finance and international business. Dr. Moffett has also consulted with a number of private firms both in the United States and Europe.

BRIEF CONTENTS

CONTENTS

PART 3

International Business and the Nation-State

PART 4

International Business Strategy and Operations

MAPS

The study of maps can be fascinating to any reader, especially to the student of international business. Throughout history, people have sought to chart the course of discovery and world events through the medium of maps, and maps continue to be a valuable instrument for establishing perspective on developments in an ever-changing world.

International managers must constantly deal with demographics, politics, economics, and culture. The maps in *International Business,* Third Edition, present the type of information managers must confront and analyze every day in the process of planning, forecasting, and managing international operations. Each map reflects an important chapter topic as well, and should aid you in understanding the material. We hope you enjoy using the maps in your study of international business, and that they help you to better understand the global links that affect us all.

Note: National divisions in the former Yugoslavia are as accurate as possible at the time of publication, but may change due to unrest.

Introduction to International Business Theory and Practice

Changes in the world environment are bringing totally new opportunities and threats to firms and individuals. The challenge is to compete successfully in the global marketplace as it exists today and develops tomorrow.

Part 1 sets the stage and then provides theoretical background for international trade and investment activities. Key classical concepts such as absolute and comparative advantage are explained and expanded to include modern-day realities. The intent is to enable the reader to understand both the theoretical and practical rationale for international business activities.

The International Business Imperative

LEARNING OBJECTIVES

1. To understand the history and importance of international business.

2. To learn the definition of international business.

3. To recognize the growth of global linkages today.

4. To understand the U.S. position in world trade and the impact international business has on the country.

5. To appreciate the opportunity offered by international business.

On the Importance of International Trade and Investment

Does foreign trade really matter much? You bet it does. The $580 billion of goods and services the United States exported in 1991 represented a bigger part of the $5.7 trillion American economy than car production and home building combined. Exports account for 20 percent of the profits of American corporations and one in every six American manufacturing jobs. They are good jobs, too. Lawrence Summers, chief economist at the World Bank, calculates that workers in export-extensive industries make 12 percent more than average. Furthermore, the increase in exports accounts for most of the nation's economic growth in 1990 and 1991.

But let's hear it for imports, too. Global sourcing of components has become so widespread that barriers to imports can be suicidal. Says Jeffrey Schott at the Institute for International Economics in Washington, D.C.: "If you want to be a world-class exporter, you need access to world-class suppliers." Imports are also the hallmark of a high standard of living for consumers, who will have more choices at competitive prices.

Not to forget foreign investments. American corporations have huge investments in plants and operations overseas. Sales from these amounted to $1.48 trillion in 1990, nearly three times exports. Similarly, foreign companies have major investments in the United States. These investments bring new money, new production, new tax revenues, and new jobs into the country, and the overseas connection is likely to lead to new exports, too.

Source: Brian O'Reilly, "How to Keep Exports on a Roll," *Fortune,* October 19, 1992:68–72.

THE NEED FOR INTERNATIONAL BUSINESS

You are about to begin an exciting, important, and necessary task: the exploration of international business. International business is exciting because it combines the science and the art of business with many other disciplines, such as economics, anthropology, geography, history, language, jurisprudence, statistics, and demography. International business is important and necessary because economic isolationism has become impossible. Failure to become a part of the global market assures a nation of declining economic influence and a deteriorating standard of living for its citizens. Successful participation in international business, however, holds the promise of improved quality of life and a better society, even leading, some believe, to a more peaceful world. International business offers companies new markets. Since the 1950s, growth of international trade and investment has been substantially larger than the growth of domestic economies. International business, therefore, presents more opportunities for expansion, growth, and income than does domestic business alone. International business causes the flow of ideas, services, and capital across the world. As a result, innovations can be developed and disseminated more rapidly, human capital can be used better, and financing can take place more quickly. International business also offers consumers new choices. It can permit the acquisition of a wider variety of products, both in terms of quantity and quality, and do so at prices that are reduced through international competition. Therefore, both as an opportunity and a challenge, international business is important to countries, companies, and individuals.

A DEFINITION OF INTERNATIONAL BUSINESS

International business consists of transactions that are devised and carried out across national borders to satisfy the objectives of individuals and organizations. In its many forms international business ranges from export-import trade to licensing, joint ventures, wholly owned subsidiaries, turnkey operations, and management contracts. As the definition indicates, the basic business tenet of "satisfaction" is retained. The fact that the transactions are *across national borders* highlights the difference

The collapse of the former Soviet Union created a new array of trading and investment partners eager for business with the West. But the removal of central authority also opened the way for ethnic strife that can undermine these favorable new conditions.

Source: Yisum/Gerd Ludwig.

between domestic and international business. The international executive is subject to a new set of macroenvironmental factors, to different constraints, and to quite frequent conflicts resulting from different laws, cultures, and societies. The basic principles of business still apply, but their application, complexity, and intensity may vary substantially.

The definition also focuses on international *transactions.* The use of this term recognizes that doing business internationally is an activity. Subject to constant change, international business is as much an art as a science. Yet success in the art depends on a firm grounding in the scientific aspects. Individual consumers, policymakers, and business executives with an understanding of both aspects will be able to incorporate international business considerations into their thinking and planning. They will be able to consider international issues and repercussions and make decisions related to questions such as these:

- How will my idea, product, or service fit into the international market?
- What adjustments are or will be necessary?
- What threats from global competition should I expect?
- How can these threats be counteracted?
- What are my strategic global alternatives?

When management integrates these issues into each decision, international markets can provide growth, profit, and needs satisfaction not available to firms that limit their activities to the domestic marketplace. To aid in this decision process is the purpose of this book.

A Brief History

Ever since the first national borders were formed, international business has been conducted by nations and individuals. In many instances, international business itself has been a major force in shaping borders and changing world history.

As an example, international business played a vital role in the formation and decline of the Roman Empire, whose impact on thought, knowledge, and development can still be felt today. Although we read about the marching of the Roman legions, it was not through military might that the empire came about. The Romans used as a major stimulus the **Pax Romana,** or Roman peace. This ensured that merchants were able to travel safely on roads built, maintained, and protected by the Roman legions and their affiliated troops. A second stimulus was the use of common coinage, which enabled business transactions to be carried out and easily compared throughout the empire. In addition, Rome developed a systematic law, central market locations through the founding of cities, and a communication system resembling an early version of the Pony Express; all of these actions contributed to the functioning of the marketplace and a reduction of business uncertainty.

International business flourished within the empire, and the improved standard of living within the empire became apparent to those outside. Soon city-nations and tribes that were not part of the empire decided to join as allies. They agreed to pay tribute and taxes because the benefits were greater than the drawbacks.

Thus the immense growth of the Roman Empire occurred mainly through the linkages of business. Of course, substantial effort was needed to preserve this favorable environment. When pirates threatened the seaways, for example, Pompeius sent out a large fleet to subdue them. Once this was accomplished, the cost of international distribution within the empire dropped substantially because fewer shipments were lost at sea. Goods could be made available at lower prices, which in turn translated into larger demand.

The fact that international business was one of the primary factors that held the empire together can also be seen in the decline of Rome. When "barbaric" tribes overran the empire, again it was not mainly through war and prolonged battles that Rome lost ground. Rather, outside tribes were attacking an empire that was already substantially weakened at its foundations because of internal infighting and increasing decadence. The Roman peace was no longer enforced, the use and acceptance of the common coinage had declined, and communications no longer worked as well. Therefore, affiliation with the empire no longer offered the benefits of the past. Former allies, no longer seeing any benefits in their association with Rome, willingly cooperated with invaders rather than face prolonged battles.

The withholding of the benefits of international business has also long been seen as a national policy tool. The use of economic coercion by nations or groups of nations, for example, can be traced back to the time of the Greek city-states and the Peloponnesian War. In the Napoleonic wars, combatants used naval blockades to achieve their goal of "bringing about commercial ruin and shortage of food by dislocating trade."[1] Similarly, during the Civil War period in the United States, the North consistently pursued a strategy of denying international business opportunities to the South in order to deprive it of needed export revenues. More recently, the United Nations imposed a trade embargo against Iraq for its invasion and subsequent occupation of Kuwait in an attempt to force it back to its original national boundaries. Even though the measure itself was ultimately not effective in achieving withdrawal, the fact that Iraq's isolation from the trade community was seen as a major policy action demonstrates the importance of international business.

The importance of international business was also highlighted during the 1930s. At that time, the **Smoot-Hawley Act** raised import duties to reduce the volume of goods coming into the United States. The act was passed in the hope that it would restore domestic employment. The result, however, was retaliation by most trading partners. The ensuing worldwide depression and the collapse of the world financial system were instrumental in bringing about the events that led to World War II.

World trade and investment have assumed a heretofore unknown importance to the global community. In past centuries trade was conducted internationally, but not at the level or with the impact on nations, firms, and individuals that it has recently achieved. In the past 20 years alone, the volume of international trade has expanded from $200 billion to more than $4 trillion. During the same time, foreign direct investment grew from $211 billion to more than $1.8 trillion in 1991.[2] Multinational corporations emerged in countries around the globe, with more than 800 of them having sales above $1 billion. Countries that have never been thought of as major participants have emerged as major economic powers. Individuals and firms have come to recognize that they are competing not only domestically but in a global marketplace.

GLOBAL LINKAGES TODAY

International business has forged a network of **global linkages** around the world that binds us all—countries, institutions, and individuals—much closer than ever before. These linkages tie together trade, financial markets, technology, and living standards in an unprecedented way. They were first widely recognized during the worldwide oil shock of the 1970s and have been apparent since then. A drought in Brazil and its effect on coffee production are felt around the world. The global crash of 1987 reverberated in financial quarters all around the globe. Iraq's invasion of Kuwait and the subsequent war affected oil prices, stock markets, and trade and travel flows in all corners of the earth.

The Balance of Visible Trade Based on Imports and Exports of Raw Materials and Manufactures

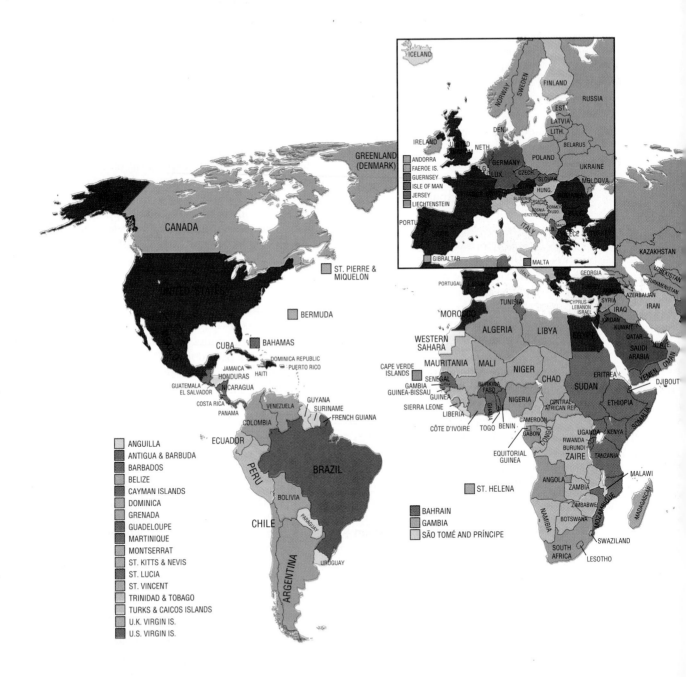

National divisions in the former Yugoslavia are as accurate as possible at the time of publication, but may change due to unrest.

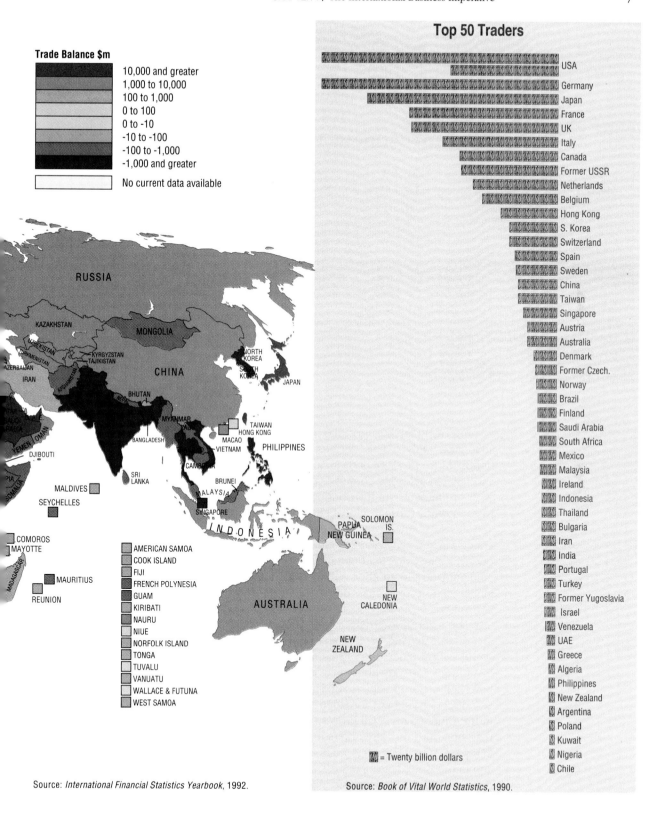

Trade Balance $m

	10,000 and greater
	1,000 to 10,000
	100 to 1,000
	0 to 100
	0 to -10
	-10 to -100
	-100 to -1,000
	-1,000 and greater
	No current data available

Top 50 Traders

USA
Germany
Japan
France
UK
Italy
Canada
Former USSR
Netherlands
Belgium
Hong Kong
S. Korea
Switzerland
Spain
Sweden
China
Taiwan
Singapore
Austria
Australia
Denmark
Former Czech.
Norway
Brazil
Finland
Saudi Arabia
South Africa
Mexico
Malaysia
Ireland
Indonesia
Thailand
Bulgaria
Iran
India
Portugal
Turkey
Former Yugoslavia
Israel
Venezuela
UAE
Greece
Algeria
Philippines
New Zealand
Argentina
Poland
Kuwait
Nigeria
Chile

= Twenty billion dollars

Source: *Book of Vital World Statistics*, 1990.

Source: *International Financial Statistics Yearbook*, 1992.

Global Perspective

1.1
Coal Investment Produces Trees

Applied Energy Services (AES), an independent power company in the United States, decided to plant 52 million trees in Guatemala. Growing trees absorb carbon dioxide. These trees will offset the gas produced by a coal-fired plant the company had just opened in Connecticut. It does not matter, says AES President Dennis Bakke, if carbon dioxide is produced in one country and mopped up in another. The effect on the atmosphere is the same.

A few other companies have done the same. New England Electric is paying for forest management in Malaysia. In Holland, the state-owned electricity-generating board has set up a foundation called FACE that will channel one guilder (58 cents) a year from every household's electricity bill into carbon-offset projects. FACE is helping to plant 25,000 hectares of trees in Malaysia and 16,000 hectares in Slovakia.

Such deals may backfire if the trees displace small farmers in poor countries. The Global Environment Facility, a body funded by the World Bank to run international greenery, may be able to help. It is looking at ways to steer private cash into offsetting carbon-dioxide output by spotting likely projects, helping to design schemes, or by chipping in its own cash to make borderline projects pay. To work on a large scale, greenery needs to be profitable as well as virtuous.

Source: "Plant a Tree," *The Economist,* October 24, 1992: 74

International business has also brought a global reorientation in production strategies. Only a few decades ago, for example, it would have been thought impossible to produce parts for a car in more than one country, assemble it in another, and sell it in yet other countries around the world. Yet such global strategies, coupled with production and distribution sharing, are common today. Firms are also linked to each other through global supply agreements and joint undertakings in research and development. Firms and governments are recognizing production's worldwide effects on the environment common to all. For example, high acid production in one area may cause acid rain in another. Pollution in one country may result in water contamination in another. As Global Perspective 1.1 shows, these concerns result in global action by some firms and heightened awareness by governments and consumers.

The level of international investment is at an unprecedented high. The United States, after having been a net creditor to the world for many decades, has been a world debtor since 1985. This means that the United States owes more to foreign institutions and individuals than they owe to U.S. entities. The shifts in financial flows have had major effects on international direct investment into plants as well. While U.S. direct investment abroad in 1991 was more than $450 billion, foreign investment in the United States had grown to $408 billion.[3] As Table 1.1 shows, currently more than one-third of the workers in the U.S. chemical industry toil for foreign owners. Many U.S. office buildings are held by foreign landlords. The opening of plants abroad and in the United States increasingly takes the place of trade. All these developments make us more and more dependent on one another.

This interdependence, however, is not stable. On virtually a daily basis realignments take place on both micro and macro levels that make past orientations at least partially obsolete. For example, for its first 200 years, the United States looked

	Millions of Dollars		Affiliate as a Percentage of All Business
Product Categories	**Affiliates***	**All Business**	
Stone, clay, glass products	24,825	59,414	41.8
Chemicals and allied products	135,842	325,370	41.7
Rubber and plastics	15,536	56,305	27.6
Primary metals	29,195	101,707	28.7
Petroleum and coal	68,236	339,451	20.1
Fabricated metals	19,858	94,213	21.1
Electric and electronic equip.	41,967	204,294	20.5
Printing and publishing	26,162	155,635	16.8
Machinery (excluding electrical)	32,434	267,543	12.1
Paper and allied products	9,811	117,335	8.4
Instruments and related products	10,609	114,718	9.2
Textile products	3,464	41,147	8.4
Transportation equipment	15,038	328,951	4.6
All manufacturing	489,753	2,629,458	18.6

TABLE 1.1
Total Assets of U.S. Affiliates of Foreign Corporations and of All U.S. Business in Manufacturing (1991)

*Affiliates are U.S. companies owned 10 percent or more by foreigners

Source: *Survey of Current Business,* U.S. Department of Commerce, Government Printing Office, May 1993, p. 8

to Europe for markets and sources of supply. Despite the maintenance of this orientation by many individuals, firms, and policymakers, the reality of trade relationships is gradually changing. U.S. two-way trade across the Pacific totalled $311 billion in 1990, $64 billion more than trade across the Atlantic.

At the same time, entirely new areas for international business activities have opened up. While the East-West juxtaposition had for more than 40 years effectively separated the "Western" economies from the centrally planned ones, the lifting of the Iron Curtain has suddenly presented a new array of trading and investment partners. As a result, trade and investment flows may again be realigned in different directions. Already, new products and services are being exchanged, and the volume is likely to increase. Global Perspective 1.2 provides an example of both trade and investment success.

Concurrently, an increasing regionalization is taking place around the world, resulting in the split-up of countries in some areas of the world and the development of country and trading blocs in others. Over time, firms may find that the free flow of goods, services, and capital encounters more impediments as regions become more inward-looking.

Not only is the environment changing, but the pace of change is accelerating. "A boy who saw the Wright brothers fly for a few seconds at Kitty Hawk in 1903 could have watched the Apollo II land on the moon in 1969. The first electronic computer was built in 1946; today the world rushes from the mechanical into the electronic age. The double helix was first unveiled in 1953; today biotechnology threatens to remake mankind."[4]

These changes and the speed with which they come about significantly affect both corporations and individuals. During the past few decades, the United States was seen as the hub of world trade. While the United States is still the locomotive that drives market flows, its participation in world trade measured as a portion of world market share has declined drastically. In the early 1950s, the United States accounted for nearly 25 percent of world trade flows; by 1991, this figure had

Global Perspective

1.2
New Markets Become New Suppliers

In 1984 a few computer whizzes from Communist Hungary attended a trade fair in western Europe, where they caught the eye of talent scouts from Apple Computer Inc. After some discussions, Apple gave the promising Hungarians two computers, a couple thousand dollars, and a challenge to develop world-class software. Apple's investment behind the then Iron Curtain led to the emergence of Graphisoft, a Hungarian software company that went on to create a popular software program for computer-aided design. Graphisoft, whose sleek offices in a renovated Budapest mansion bear all the trademarks of Silicon Valley–style success, is an example of the commercialization of a major asset in struggling eastern Europe: brains.

Just like its niche market, Graphisoft is small, with just $5 million in 1990 sales. But Imre Pakozdi, a vice president of Graphisoft, believes that Hungarian software developers now are as good as their Western competitors. The firm says its software, targeted for architects who use Apple's Macintosh computers, has gained a 50 percent market share in western Europe and 10 percent in the United States.

Source: Peter Maass, "The Little Computer Company That Could," *The Washington Post,* February 20, 1992: D11,D13

FIGURE 1.1
**The Changing U.S.
Share of World Trade**

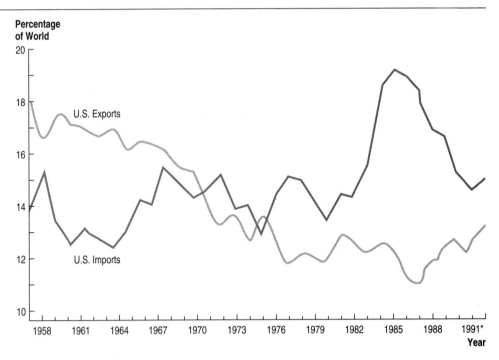

Source: International Monetary Fund (IMF), "International Financial Statistics," February 1992. U.S. Department of Commerce, Office of Import/Export Statistics. *Estimates, based on partial year data for world trade.

declined to 12 percent. Figure 1.1 shows how over time, U.S. exports as a share of world trade have declined, while imports have risen. As a result, from a global perspective, the United States has lost some of its importance as a supplier to the world but has gained importance as a market for the world.

THE CURRENT U.S. INTERNATIONAL TRADE POSITION

U.S. exports have not actually dropped over the years. On the contrary, exports have grown rapidly and successfully. Table 1.2 lists the top U.S. exporters and shows the large volume of their international sales. However, rather than standing still, the firms in the wartorn economies following World War II gradually reestablished themselves and aggressively obtained a share of the growing world trade for themselves. U.S. export growth was not able to keep pace with total growth of world exports.

U.S. exports as a share of the GNP have grown substantially in recent years. However, this increase pales when compared with the international trade performance of other nations. Germany, for example, has consistently maintained an export share of more than 20 percent of GNP. Japan, in turn, which so often is maligned as the export problem child in the international trade arena, exports only about 10 percent of its GNP. Exports across countries in terms of percentage of GNP can be seen in Table 1.3.

A Diagnosis of the U.S. Trade Position

The lack of international business participation by the United States immediately fosters the question, How did this happen? Merely citing temporary factors such as the value of exchange rates or unfair trade barriers abroad is not enough. A further search is needed to find the root causes of the decline in U.S. international competitiveness.

Since World War II it had been ingrained in the minds of U.S. policymakers that their country led in world power and world business. This perception was accompanied by the belief that the United States had an obligation to help other countries with their trade performance because, without American assistance, they would not be able to play a meaningful role in the world economy. At the same time, due to strong domestic growth, the importance of international business and its impact on jobs available to U.S. workers could be overlooked in the effort to achieve other major national policy goals. Many of these goals grew out of national security concerns related to a continuing struggle against political adversaries.

The measures taken seemed reasonable in light of continuous worldwide admiration for "Yankee ingenuity." U.S. firms were viewed as the most entrepreneurial, the most innovative, and the most aggressive in the world. U.S. policymakers firmly believed that the U.S. private sector did not need any help in its international business efforts.

Because the policies established were so successful, no one wished to tamper with them. They continued, even though the global environment changed. U.S. encouragement in the 1950s and 1960s succeeded in making other nations again full partners in the world economy. The same policies, when continued into the late 1970s, placed U.S. firms at a distinct disadvantage.

U.S. governmental actions were accompanied by assurances to U.S. firms that "because of its size and the diversity of its resources the American economy can satisfy consumer wants and national needs with a minimum of reliance on foreign trade."[5] U.S. firms simply did not feel a compelling need to seek business beyond national borders. Subsequently, the perception emerged within the private sector that doing business abroad was "too risky, complicated, and [therefore] not worth it."[6]

TABLE 1.2 Top 50 U.S. Exporters

Rank 1991		Major Exports	Exports 1991 $ millions	As % of Total sales %	RANK	Total Sales 1991 $ millions
1	BOEING Seattle	Commercial and military aircraft	17,856.0	60.9	1	29,314.0
2	GENERAL MOTORS Detroit	Motor vehicles, parts	11,284.7	9.1	39	123,780.1
3	GENERAL ELECTRIC Fairfield, Conn.	Jet engines. turbines, plastics, medical systems	8,614.0	14.3	25	60,236.0
4	INTERNATIONAL BUSINESS MACHINES Armonk, N.Y.	Computers, related equipment	7,668.0	11.8	31	64,792.0
5	FORD MOTOR Dearborn, Mich	Motor vehicle, parts	7,340.0[1]	8.3	41	88,962.8
6	CHRYSLER Highland Park, Mich.	Motor vehicles, parts	6,168.0	21.0	12	29,370.0
7	MCDONNELL DOUGLAS St. Louis	Aerospace products, missiles, electronic systems	6,160.0	32.9	5	18,718.0
8	E.I. DU PONT DE NEMOURS Wilmington, Del.	Specialty chemicals	3,812.0	10.0	34	38,031.0
9	CATERPILLAR Peoria, Ill.	Heavy machinery, engines, turbines	3,710.0	36.4	4	10,182.0
10	UNITED TECHNOLOGIES Hartford	Jet engines, helicopters, cooling equipment	3,587.0	16.9	15	21,262.0
11	HEWLETT-PACKARD Palo Alto, Calif.	Measurement and computation products and systems	3,223.0	22.2	11	14,541.0
12	PHILIP MORRIS New York	Tobacco, beverages, food products	3,061.0	6.4	46	48,109.0
13	EASTMAN KODAK Rochester, N.Y.	Imaging, chemicals, health products	3,020.0	15.4	21	19,649.0
14	MOTOROLA Schaumburg, Ill	Communication equipment, cellular phones, semiconductors	2,928.0	25.8	8	11,341.0
15	ARCHER-DANIELS-MIDLAND Decatur, Ill.	Protein meals, vegetable oils, flour, grain	2,600.0[2]	30.3	6	8,567.7
16	DIGITAL EQUIPMENT Maynard, Mass.	Computers, related equipment	2,200.0	15.7	19	14,024.2
17	INTEL Santa Clara, Calif.	Microcomputer components, modules, systems	1,929.0	40.4	3	4,778.6
18	ALLIED-SIGNAL Morristown, N.J.	Aircraft and automotive parts, chemicals	1,729.0	14.6	23	11,882.0
19	SUN MICROSYSTEMS Mountain View, Calif.	Computers, related equipment	1,606.0	49.3	2	3,259.8
20	UNISYS Blue Bell, Pa.	Computers, related equipment	1,598.0	18.4	13	8,696.1
21	RAYTHEON Lexington, Mass.	Electronics, environmental systems, aircraft products	1,556.0	16.6	17	9,355.5
22	WEYERHAEUSER Tacoma	Pulp, paper, logs, lumber	1,550.0	17.8	14	8,701.6
23	DOW CHEMICAL Midland, Mich.	Chemicals, plastics, consumer specialties	1,376.0	7.1	44	19,305.0
24	GENERAL DYNAMICS St. Louis	Tanks, aircraft, missiles, gun systems	1,370.0	14.3	24	9,548.0
25	MERCK Rahway, N.J.	Health products, specialty chemicals	1,342.0	15.6	20	8,602.7

Rank 1991		Major Exports	Exports 1991 $ millions	As % of Total sales		Total Sales 1991 $ millions
				%	RANK	
26	MINNESOTA MINING & MANUFACTURING St. Paul	Industrial, electronic, and health products	1,275.0	9.6	36	13,340.0
27	INTERNATIONAL PAPER Purchase, N.Y.	Pulp, paperboard, wood products	1,200.0	9.4	37	12,703.0
28	UNION CARBIDE Danbury, Conn.	Chemicals, plastics	1,200.0	16.3	18	7,346.0
29	TEXTRON Providence	Aerospace and consumer products	1,171.0	14.9	22	7,840.1
30	HOECHST CELANESE Bridgewater, N.J.	Chemicals, plastics, fibers, pharmaceuticals	1,158.0	16.9	16	6,856.0
31	WESTINGHOUSE ELECTRIC Pittsburgh	Electrical products, electronic systems	1,141.0	8.9	40	12,794.0
32	MONSANTO St. Louis	Herbicides, chemicals, pharmaceuticals	1,128.0	12.6	30	8,929.0
33	XEROX Stamford,Conn.	Copiers, printers, document processing services	1,040.0	5.8	47	17,830.0
34	ALUMINUM CO. OF AMERICA Pittsburgh	Aluminum products	967.0	9.7	35	9,981.2
35	ABBOTT LABORATORIES Abbot Park, Ill.	Drugs, diagnostic equipment	957.0	13.8	27	6,921.7
36	OCCIDENTAL PETROLEUM Los Angeles	Agricultural products, coal	951.0	9.2	38	10,304.8
37	COMPAQ COMPUTER Houston	Computers, related equipment	950.0[3]	29.0	7	3,271.4
38	FMC Chicago	Armored military vehicles, chemicals	913.0	23.2	10	3,931.5
39	MILES Pittsburgh	Chemicals, health and imaging products	877.0[4]	14.2	26	6,197.4
40	COOPER INDUSTRIES Houston	Petroleum and industrial equipment, electrical products	835.0	13.5	28	6,162.6
41	ROCKWELL INTERNATIONAL El Segundo, Calif.	Electronics, automotive parts	828.0	6.9	45	12,027.9
42	HONEYWELL Minnesota	Building, industry, and aviation control systems	808.0	13.0	29	6,220.9
43	BRISTOL-MYERS SQUIBB New York	Drugs, medical devices, consumer products	807.0	7.1	43	11,298.0
44	LOCKHEED Calabasas, Calif.	Aerospace products, electronics, missile systems	794.0	8.1	42	9,809.0
45	EXXON Irving, Texas	Petroleum, chemicals	744.0	0.7	50	103,242.0
46	DEERE Moline, Ill.	Farm and industrial equipment	713.0	10.1	33	7,055.2
47	AMOCO Chicago	Chemicals	712.0	2.8	49	25,604.0
48	TENNECO Houston	Farm, construction, and auto equipment	692.0	4.9	48	14,035.0
49	ETHYL Richmond	Specialty and petroleum chemicals	655.0	25.4	9	2,574.8
50	REYNOLDS METALS Richmond	Aluminum, aluminum and plastic products	603.0	10.4	32	5,784.5
	TOTALS		130,406.7			987,755.1

[1]Excludes some U.S. export figures.   [2]Includes sales value of grain merchandise; 1990 figure did not.   [3]Includes Canadian exports.   [4]A wholly owned subsidiary of Bayer AG, Germany

Source: FORTUNE, June 29, 1992, p.95. © 1992. Time Inc. All Rights Reserved.

Period	United States	France	Germany	Italy	Netherlands	United Kingdom	Japan	Canada
1980	8.1	17.5	23.6	17.1	43.7	20.5	12.2	24.6
1981	7.7	18.2	25.7	18.4	48.5	19.8	13.0	23.5
1982	6.7	17.5	26.8	18.2	48.0	20.0	12.8	22.6
1983	5.9	18.0	25.7	17.5	48.3	19.9	12.4	22.3
1984	5.8	19.5	27.6	17.7	52.4	21.6	13.5	25.2
1985	5.3	19.3	29.1	18.4	53.7	22.0	13.2	24.9
1986	5.1	17.2	27.1	16.1	45.4	19.1	10.7	23.7
1987	5.4	16.8	26.1	14.7	43.4	19.3	9.5	22.6
1988	6.6	17.5	26.7	15.4	45.6	17.3	9.2	23.7
1989	7.0	18.7	28.3	16.3	48.3	18.1	9.7	22.5
1990	7.2	17.8	27.2	15.8	47.0	18.8	9.7	22.8
1991	7.4	18.1	27.8	14.7	46.7	19.2	13.3	21.7
1992	7.5	17.9	24.1	14.5	43.0	15.5	8.9	23.0

[a]Gross domestic product for France, Italy, and Canada.

Sources: U. S. Department of Commerce, *International Economic Indicators*, March 1993, 35; IMF, *International Financial Statistics*, January 1993; OECD, *Quarterly National Accounts*, No. 2, 1993; *Bank of Canada Review*, January 1993; *Japan Economic Statistics Monthly*, November 1993; Reihe 4, *Saisonbereinigte Wirtschaftzahlen*, December 1993 (Statistische Beihefte zu den Monatsberichten der Deutschen Bundesbank). Economic Intelligence Unit Country Reports.

TABLE 1.4
Exports and Imports
per Capita for Selected
Countries (1992)

Country	Exports per Capita	Imports per Capita
United States	$1,750	$2,080
Canada	4,760	4,470
France	4,100	4,170
Germany	5,370	5,090
Netherlands	9,200	8,840
United Kingdom	3,250	3,844
Japan	2,660	1,690

Source: U.S. Department of Commerce, *FT 900*; OECD, *Main Economic Indicators*, December 1993; CIA, *World Factbook 1993*; IMF, *International Financial Statistics*, 1993 Yearbook. Economic Intelligence Unit Country Reports.

As a result of delayed adjustments in policy outlook, inadequate information, ignorance of where and how to do business internationally, unfamiliarity with foreign market conditions, and complicated trade regulations, the U.S. private sector became unwilling to participate in and fearful of international business. Table 1.4 shows the degree to which the United States "underparticipates" in international business on a per capita basis, particularly on the export side.

The Impact of International Business on the United States

Why should we worry about all of this unwillingness and fear? Why not simply concentrate on the large domestic market and get on with it? Why should it bother us that the largest portion of U.S. exports is attributed to only 2,500 companies? Why should it be of concern that the Department of Commerce estimates that tens of thousands of U.S. manufacturing firms are believed to be capable of exporting but do not do so?

U.S. international business outflows are important on the **macroeconomic level** in terms of balancing the trade account. Lack of U.S. export growth has resulted in merchandise-trade deficits that grew from the mid-1970s to the late 1980s. In 1983, imports of products into the United States exceeded exports by more than $70 billion. This deficit rose by 1987 to $171 billion. In the ensuing years, the merchandise-trade deficit was alleviated by a spurt in U.S. exports and decreased to $102 billion by 1992. Yet ongoing annual trade deficits in this range are still unsupportable in the long run. Such deficits add to the U.S. international debt, which must be serviced and eventually repaid. Exports therefore continue to be a major concern, particularly since one billion dollars' worth of exports creates, on average, 22,800 jobs.[7] Exporting is not only good for the international trade picture but also a key factor in increasing employment.

On the **microeconomic level,** participation in international business can help firms achieve economies of scale that cannot be achieved in domestic markets. Addressing a global market simply adds to the number of potential customers. Increasing production also lets firms climb the learning curve more quickly and therefore makes goods available more cheaply at home. Finally, and perhaps most important, international business permits firms to hone their competitive skills abroad by meeting the challenge of foreign products. By going abroad U.S. firms can learn from their foreign competitors, challenge them on their ground, and translate the absorbed knowledge into productivity improvements back home. Firms that operate only in the domestic market are at risk of being surprised by the onslaught of foreign competition and thus seeing their domestic market share threatened.

The United States as a nation and as individuals must therefore seek more involvement in the global market. The degree to which Americans can successfully do business abroad will be indicative of their competitiveness and so help to determine their future standard of living.

Individual firms and entire industries are coming to recognize that, in today's trade environment, isolation is no longer possible. Both the willing and unwilling are becoming participants in global business affairs. Most U.S. firms are affected directly or indirectly by economic and political developments in the international

McDonald's is one example of a U.S. business organization that realized early the opportunities available through international activities. McDonald's actively continues expansion. The company has restaurants in 66 countries with a total of 13,000 restaurants worldwide: 9,000 domestically and 4,000 internationally.

Source: © 1987 David Pollack/The Stock Market.

marketplace. Firms that refuse to participate actively are relegated to reacting to the global economy. Consider how the industrial landscape in the United States has been restructured in the past decade as a result of international trade.

Some industries are now beginning to experience the need for international adjustments. U.S. farmers, because of high prices, increased international competition, trade-restricting government actions, and unfair foreign trade practices, have increasingly lost world market share. U.S. firms in technologically advanced industries, such as semiconductor producers, saw the prices of their products drop precipitously and their sales volumes shrink by half in a two-year period because of foreign competition.

Other industries that were exposed early to foreign competition have partially adjusted, but with great pain. Examples abound in the steel, automotive, and textile sectors of the U.S. economy.

Still other U.S. industries never fully recognized what had happened and, therefore, in spite of attempts to adjust, were not successful and have ceased to exist. VCRs are no longer produced domestically. Only a small percentage of motorcycles are produced in the United States. The shoe industry is in its death throes.

These developments demonstrate that it has become virtually impossible to disregard the powerful impact that world trade now has on all of us. Temporary isolation may be possible and delay tactics may work for a while, but the old adage applies: You can run, but you cannot hide. Participation in the world market has become truly imperative.

Global activities offer many additional opportunities to business firms. Market saturation can be delayed by lengthening or rejuvenating the life of products in other countries. Sourcing policies that once were inflexible may suddenly become variable, because plants can be shifted from one country to another, and suppliers can be found on every continent. Cooperative agreements can be formed that enable each party to bring its major strength to the table and emerge with better products, services, and ideas than it could on its own. Firms and consumers all over the world can select from among a greater variety of products at lower prices, which enables them to improve their productivity and lifestyles, as Global Perspective 1.3 shows.

All of these opportunities need careful exploration if they are to be realized. What is needed is an awareness of global developments, an understanding of their meaning, and a development of the capability to adjust to change. Judging by the global linkages found in today's market and the rapid changes taking place, a background in international business is highly desirable for business students seeking employment. Globalization is the watchword which "describes the need for companies and their employees, if they are to prosper, to treat the world as their stage."[8]

THE STRUCTURE OF THE BOOK

This book is intended to enable you to become a better, more successful participant in the global business place. It is written for both those who want to attain more information about what is going on in international markets in order to be more well-rounded and better educated and for those who wish to translate their knowledge into successful business transactions. The text melds theory and practice in order to provide a balance between conceptual understanding and knowledge of day-to-day realities. The book therefore addresses the international concerns of both beginning internationalists and multinational corporations.

Global Perspective

1.3
The Sweet Taste of Success

Coming to Japan in the late 1960s a young American soldier immediately noticed that the Japanese have a remarkably sweet tooth. You couldn't walk a block without passing at least one pastry shop or candy store. He also noticed that many American images held a potent appeal for the Japanese. Those first impressions stayed with Joseph Dunkle, and he returned to civilian life convinced they were the keys to a promising opportunity.

Coming back to Japan in 1973, Dunkle set out to make his fortune in an ice cream joint venture with the Seibu Saison Group. His judgment proved right on the mark, but as international heavyweights targeted Japan in the early 1980s, success began to melt away. Undeterred, the American entrepreneur looked for a new concept.

As with so many good ideas, the answer lay close to home. Drifting through sweet memories of childhood, Dunkle recalled the special aroma of fresh-baked cookies emanating from his Aunt Stella's farm kitchen in Pennsylvania's rustic Amish country. The concept was complete in a flash: He would market the image, the taste, the aroma, the wholesome goodness of an earlier America where "kinder and gentler" were the norm.

Today, Dunkle, 46, is the president of Roly Doll Inc., operator and franchisor of fresh-baked cookie shops across Japan. Aunt Stella, meanwhile, has found posthumous fame far from home: Her name and smile beam from the logo on 62 Aunt Stella outlets.

Stella's nephew heads a company that has grown from sales of ¥1.9 billion in fiscal 1985 to more than ¥5 billion in 1990. Roly Doll has 40 directly managed stores and 22 franchised outlets in department stores and train stations.

Behind Dunkle's success lies a keen ability to identify appealing images from abroad and package them to suit Japanese tastes. "The Japanese have many perceptions of America," he says, "several of which are linked to the streetwise style of New York or L.A. But there's also an awareness of a simpler, more wholesome America: the land that produced my Aunt Stella."

Retailing at ¥450 per 100 grams or in gift packages priced from ¥ 1,000 to ¥ 24,000, Aunt Stella's cookies are clearly aimed at an upscale market. "We're targeting the Japanese woman over 35 who has an eye for quality," Dunkle says. "I believe you have to aim up-market because the middle will follow. Start at the middle, and the higher end isn't going to follow you down."

In keeping with utilitarian Amish ways—and a more modern environmental consciousness—Roly Doll has tried to minimize the elaborate but wasteful packaging often found in Japanese stores. Gift packages are reusable and labeled with pleas for recycling. These efforts have earned Aunt Stella Japan's Ecomark symbol of environmental approval.

Roly Doll further promotes the rural image by distributing monthly newsletters and calendars to some 400,000 customers. The identity is also being leveraged for new retail concepts. A chain of "Pennsylvania Home" dessert shops now features an extended range of homemade cookies and cakes. And, in an entirely new direction, a line of Early American wooden furniture and a collection of natural-fiber children's clothing are being launched through Seibu department stores.

Source: "Aunt Stella's Sweet Success: Roly Doll Inc.," *Focus Japan,* December 1990, 8.

The beginning international manager will need to know the answer to basic, yet important, questions: How can I find out whether demand for my product exists abroad? What must I do to get ready to market it? These issues are also relevant for managers in multinational corporations, but the questions they consider are often much more sophisticated. Of course, the resources available to address them are also much greater.

Throughout the book, public policy concerns are included in discussions of business activities. In this way, you are exposed to both macro and micro issues. Part 1 of the book serves as an introduction to the field of international business, stressing its importance and theoretical foundation. Part 2 then focuses on the international business environment and institutions, with particular emphasis on the financial dimensions. Part 3 discusses the interaction between international business and the nation-state and addresses policy, political, legal, and cultural issues. Part 4 presents international business management issues from a strategic perspective.

The authors hope that upon finishing the book, you will not only have completed another academic subject, but will also be well versed in the theoretical, policy, and strategic aspects of international business and therefore able to contribute to the attainment of improved international competitiveness.

SUMMARY

International business has been conducted ever since national borders were formed and has played a major role in shaping world history. Growing in importance over the past three decades, it has shaped an environment that, due to economic linkages, today presents us with a global marketplace.

In the past two decades, world trade has expanded from $200 billion to more than $4 trillion while international direct investment has grown from $211 billion to $1.8 trillion. The growth of both has been more rapid than the growth of most domestic economies. As a result, nations are much more affected by international business than in the past. Global linkages have made possible investment strategies and business alternatives that offer tremendous opportunities. Yet these changes and the speed of change also can represent threats to nations and firms.

Over the past 30 years, the dominance of the U.S. international trade position has been gradually eroded. Increasingly, new participants in international business compete fiercely for world market share, and U.S. firms have fallen behind in their global competitiveness. Apart from changes in the world environment, this development is mainly the result of delays in policy adjustments and an unwillingness by the U.S. private sector to participate in international business.

Yet times are changing. Individuals, corporations, and policymakers have awakened to the fact that international business is a major imperative and opportunity for future growth and prosperity. International business offers access to new customers, affords economies of scale, and permits the honing of competitive skills. Performing well in global markets is the key to improved standards of living, higher profits, and the continued leadership of the United States in the world. Knowledge about international business is therefore important to everyone, whether it is used to compete with foreign firms or simply to add to an understanding of the world around us.

Key Terms and Concepts

Pax Romana	macroeconomic level
Smoot-Hawley Act	microeconomic level
global linkages	

Questions for Discussion

1. Will future expansion of international business be similar to that in the past?
2. Discuss the reasons for the decline in the U.S. world trade market share.
3. Does increased international business mean increased risk?

4. Is it beneficial for nations to become dependent on one another?

5. With wages in some countries at one-tenth of U.S. wages, how can America compete?

6. Compare and contrast domestic and international business.

7. Why do more firms in other countries enter international markets than do firms in the United States?

8. What is needed to maintain U.S. competitiveness?

Recommended Readings

Dudley, James W. *1992 Strategies for the Single Market.* London: Kogan Page, 1989.

Halberstam, David. *The Reckoning.* New York: William Morrow, 1986.

Ohmae, Kenichi. *Triad Power: The Coming Shape of Global Competition.* New York: The Free Press, 1985.

Porter, Michael E. *The Competitive Advantage of Nations.* New York: The Free Press, 1990.

Reich, Robert B. *The Work of Nations: Preparing Ourselves for 21st-Century Capitalism.* New York: Random House, 1992.

Ryans, John K., Jr., and Pradeep A. Rau. *Marketing Strategies for the New Europe: A North American Perspective on 1992.* Chicago: American Marketing Association, 1990.

Tyson, Laura D. *Who's Bashing Whom? Trade Conflict in High-Technology Industries.* Washington, D.C.: Institute for International Economics, 1992.

Waldmann, Raymond J. *Managed Trade: The Competition between Nations.* Cambridge, Mass.: Ballinger, 1986.

Wolf, Charles, Jr. *Linking Economic Policy and Foreign Policy.* New Brunswick, N.J.: Transaction Publishers, 1991.

Notes

1. Margaret P. Doxey, *Economic Sanctions and International Enforcement* (New York: Oxford University Press, 1980), 10.
2. John Rutter, *Recent Trends in International Direct Investment* (Washington, D.C.: U.S. Department of Commerce), 1992.
3. *Survey of Current Business* (Washington, D.C.: U.S. Department of Commerce), August 1992.
4. Arthur M. Schlesinger, Jr., *The Cycles of American History* (Boston: Houghton Mifflin, 1986), XI.
5. Mordechai E. Kreinin, *International Economics: A Policy Approach* (New York: Harcourt Brace Jovanovich, 1971), 142.
6. House Subcommittee of the Committee on Government Operations, hearings on *Commerce and State Department's Export Promotion Programs,* March 22–23, 1977, 66.
7. Lester A. Davis, *Contribution of Exports to U.S. Employment: 1980–87* (Washington, D.C.: Government Printing Office, 1989).
8. "Management Education," *The Economist,* March 2, 1991, 7.

The Theory of International Trade and Investment

LEARNING OBJECTIVES

1. To understand the traditional arguments as to how and why international trade improves the welfare of all countries.

2. To review the history and compare the implications of trade theory from the original work of Adam Smith to the contemporary theories of Michael Porter.

3. To examine the criticisms of classical trade theory and examine alternative viewpoints of what business and economic forces determine trade patterns between countries.

4. To understand how the trade in goods is directly related to issues of international investment.

The North American Free Trade Agreement

WASHINGTON, February 2—The first comprehensive assessment of the North American Free Trade Agreement by a Federal agency has found that the pact will help overall American economic output and employment slightly, while producing job losses in the auto, household appliance and apparel manufacturing industries.

The study by the International Trade Commission, an independent Federal agency, buttresses claims made for the agreement by the Bush Administration and rebuts some of the criticism from labor unions and some members of Congress who have predicted huge job losses.

The report provides little ammunition for critics who have called for extensive renegotiation of the agreement. If approved by Congress, the trade agreement would eliminate—over the next 15 years—virtually all import-export barriers among the United States, Canada and Mexico.

The International Trade Commission's report concluded that if the North American pact was approved by Congress, employment would eventually drop by up to 5 percent in the automotive and apparel industries and up to 15 percent in the major household appliance, glass and ceramic tiles industries. The report attributed the job losses to extra competition from Mexican imports and the construction of new factories there.

Economic studies have consistently predicted that the pact would have the greatest effect on Mexico because its economy is only one-twentieth of the size of the United States economy, and because Mexico already relies heavily on trade with the United States.

Source: Keith Bradsher, Abstracted from "Study Says Trade Pact Will Aid U.S. Economy," *The New York Times*, Wednesday, February 3, 1993, sec. C, 1, 14.

International trade is expected to improve the productivity of industry and the welfare of consumers. The North American Free Trade Agreement is a step toward increasing the amount of trade among the United States, Canada, and Mexico, hopefully to achieve these benefits.

International trade is one of the oldest and most fundamental concepts in business or economics. Attempts to understand the nature of international trade—how it changes over time and how it affects the societies participating—prompted Adam Smith to write *The Wealth of Nations* in 1776. Although international trade theory precedes even the work of Smith, many of the concepts first elaborated by Smith still dominate trade theory and policy today, such as the formation of the North American Free Trade Area.

THE AGE OF MERCANTILISM

In the centuries leading up to the Industrial Revolution of the late 1770s and early 1800s, international commerce was largely conducted under the authority of governments. The goals of trade were, therefore, the goals of governments. The major European nations of the time were absorbed with supporting and expanding great colonial possessions around the world. These colonial possessions required fleets, armies, food, and all other resources the nations could muster. Trade was therefore conducted in a fashion that would fill the government's coffers, its treasuries, to provide the wealth necessary to purchase the resources needed. This was **Mercantilism.**

The conduct of trade under a Mercantilist philosophy was quite simple: export more than you import, and collect the excess in gold or silver. Governments actively encouraged the industries of export, sometimes even subsidizing their growth, while restricting the quantity of imports. Countries raised duties, implemented quotas, and applied restrictions, taking all measures practical to minimize imports. Laws were passed making it illegal to take gold or silver out of the country, even if, as was argued by merchants, they needed to purchase imports in order to produce their own products for export.

Obviously, the focus of international trade in this age of Mercantilism was not the needs, desires, or consumptive pleasures of the general population. Society's welfare was secondary to the needs of government,[1] It is really this point that differentiates Mercantilism from the times that followed, and not its emphasis on the accumulation of gold and silver. For it was the increasing growth of industry, largely private industry, that came to dominate and move world trade. This said, this still does not preclude policies of governments today from restricting trade for the pursuit of domestic political, social, or even supposed economic goals.[2]

CLASSICAL TRADE THEORY

Why Do Countries Trade?   Although seemingly a simple question, it has proven to be a quite complex one. Since the latter half of the 18th century, academicians have been not only struggling to understand what are the motivations and benefits of international trade, but also attempting to identify the causes of why some countries grow faster and wealthier than others through trade.

Figure 2.1 provides an overview of the path of evolution of international trade theory. Although somewhat simplified, it shows the line of development of the major theories put forward over the past two centuries. The line of evolution, which began with the work of Adam Smith and David Ricardo, has continued to advance understanding significantly. The trade theories up through those of Eli Heckscher and Bertil Ohlin were theories of national competition. More recent developments, however, have focused on the industry, the products, and how it may influence which country holds the advantage at certain points in time.

The Theory of Absolute Advantage

Generally considered the father of economics, Adam Smith published *The Wealth of Nations* in 1776 in London. In this book Smith attempted to explain the process by which markets and production actually operate in society. His studies led him to a number of striking results. Smith's two main areas of contribution **absolute advantage** and the **division of labor,** were fundamental to trade theory.

Production, the creation of a product for exchange, always requires the use of society's primary element of value, human labor. Smith noted that some countries, owing to the skills of their workers or the quality of their natural resources, could produce the same products as others with fewer labor-hours. He termed this efficiency absolute advantage.

Adam Smith observed the production processes of the early stages of the Industrial Revolution in England and recognized the fundamental change that had occurred in production. In previous states of society, a worker performed all stages of a production process, with resulting output that was little more than sufficient for the worker's own needs. The factories of the industrializing world were, however, separating the production process into distinct stages, in which each stage would be performed exclusively by one individual. Smith termed this the division of labor. This specialization increased the production of workers and industries. Smith's description of the pin factory has long been considered the recognition of one of the most significant principles of the industrial age.

FIGURE 2.1
The Evolution of
International Trade
Theory

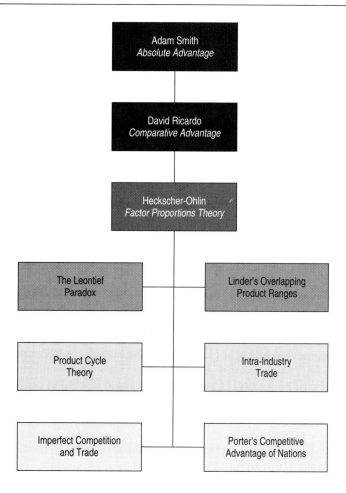

To take an example, therefore, from a very trifling manufacture; but one in which the division of labour has been very often taken notice of the trade of the pin-maker; a workman not educated to this business . . . could scarce, perhaps, with his utmost industry, make one pin in a day, and certainly could not make twenty. But in a way in which this business is now carried on, not only the whole work is a peculiar trade, but it is divided in to a number of branches, of which the greater part are likewise peculiar trades. One man draws out the wire, another straights it, a third cuts it, a fourth points it, a fifth grinds it at the top for receiving the head; to make the head requires two or three distinct operations; to put it on is a peculiar business . . . I have seen a small manufactory of this kind where ten men only were employed, and where some of them consequently performed two or three distinct operations. But though they were very poor, and therefore but indifferently accommodated with the necessary machine, they could, when they exerted themselves, make among them about twelve pounds of pins in a day. There are in a pound upwards of four thousand pins of a middling size.[3]

Adam Smith then extended his division of labor in the production process to a division of labor and specialized product across countries. Each country would specialize in a product that it was uniquely suited for. More would be produced for less. Thus, by each country specializing in products for which it possessed absolute advantage, countries could produce more in total and exchange products—trade—for goods that were cheaper in price than those produced at home.

The Theory of Comparative Advantage

Although Smith's work was instrumental in the development of economic theories about trade and production, it did not answer some fundamental questions about trade. First, Smith's trade relied on a country possessing absolute advantage in production but did not explain what caused the production advantages. Secondly, if a country did not possess absolute advantage in any product, could it (or would it) trade?

David Ricardo, in his work entitled *On the Principles of Political Economy and Taxation* published in 1819, sought to take the basic ideas set down by Adam Smith a few logical steps further. Ricardo noted that even if a country possessed absolute advantage in the production of two products, it must still be relatively more efficient than the other country in one good's product than the other. Ricardo termed this the **comparative advantage.** Each country would then possess comparative advantage in the production of one of the two products, and both countries would then benefit by specializing completely in one product and trading for the other.

A Numerical Example of Classical Trade

To fully understand the theories of absolute advantage and comparative advantage, consider the following example. Two countries, France and England, produce only two products, wheat and cloth (or beer and pizza, guns and butter, and so forth). The relative efficiency of each country in the production of the two products is measured by comparing the number of labor-hours needed to produce one unit of each product. Table 2.1 provides an efficiency comparison of the two countries.

England is obviously more efficient in the production of wheat. Whereas it takes France 4 labor-hours to produce one unit of wheat, it takes England only 2 hours to produce the same unit of wheat. France therefore takes twice as many labor-hours to produce the same output. England therefore has absolute advantage in the production of wheat. France needs 2 labor-hours to produce a unit of cloth that it takes England 4 labor-hours to produce. England therefore requires 2 more labor-hours than France to produce the same unit of cloth. France therefore has absolute

	Country	Wheat	Cloth
TABLE 2.1 **Absolute Advantage and Comparative Advantage***	England	2	4
	France	4	2

- England has absolute advantage in the production of wheat. It requires fewer labor hours (2 being less than 4) for England to produce one unit of wheat.
- France has absolute advantage in the production of cloth. It requires fewer labor hours (2 being less than 4) for France to produce one unit of cloth.
- England has comparative advantage in the production of wheat. If England produces one unit of wheat, it is foregoing the production of 2/4 (0.50) of a unit of cloth. If France produces one unit of wheat, it is foregoing the production of 4/2 (2.00) of a unit of cloth. England therefore has the lower opportunity cost of producing wheat.
- France has comparative advantage in the production of cloth. If England produces one unit of cloth, it is foregoing the production of 4/2 (2.00) of a unit of wheat. If France produces one unit of cloth, it is foregoing the production of 2/4 (0.50) of a unit of wheat. France therefore has the lower opportunity cost of producing cloth.

*Labor hours per unit of output.

advantage in the production of cloth. The two countries are exactly opposite in relative efficiency of production.

David Ricardo took this logic of absolute advantages in production one step further in order to explain how countries could exploit their own advantages and gain from international trade. Ricardo pointed out that both countries would be better off if they specialized in what they did best, and exchanged the resulting products for what they wished to consume. Ricardo emphasized what he termed the comparative advantages of each nation.

Comparative advantage, according to Ricardo, was based on what was given up or traded-off in producing one product instead of the other. In this numerical example England needs only 2/4 as many labor-hours to produce a unit of wheat as France, while France needs only 2/4 as many labor-hours to produce a unit of cloth. England therefore has comparative advantage in the production of wheat, while France has comparative advantage in the production of cloth. A country cannot possess comparative advantage in the production of both products, so each country has an economic role to play in international trade.

National Production Possibilities

If the total labor-hours available for production within a nation were devoted to the full production of either product, wheat or cloth, the production possibilities frontiers of each country can be constructed. Assuming both countries possess the same number of labor-hours, for example 100, the production possibilities frontiers for each country can be graphed as in Figure 2.2. If England devotes all labor-hours (100) to the production of wheat (which requires 2 labor-hours per unit produced), it can produce a maximum of 50 units of wheat. If England devotes all labor to the production of cloth instead, the same 100 labor-hours can produce a maximum of 25 units of cloth (100 hours/4 hours per unit of cloth). If England did not trade with any other country, it could only consume the products which it produced itself. England would therefore probably produce and consume some combination of wheat and cloth such as point A in Figure 2.2 (15 units of cloth, 20 units of wheat).

France's production possibilities frontier is constructed in the same way. If France devotes all 100 labor-hours to the production of wheat, it can produce a maximum of 25 units (100 labor hours/4 hours per unit of wheat). If France devotes all 100 labor-hours to cloth, the same 100 labor-hours can produce a maximum of 50 units of cloth (100 labor hours/2 hours per unit of cloth). If France did not trade with other countries, it would produce and consume at some point such as point D in Figure 2.2 (20 units of cloth, 15 units of wheat).

These frontiers depict what each country could produce in isolation—without trade (sometimes referred to as **autarky**). The slope of the production possibility frontier of a nation is a measure of how one product is traded-off in production with the other (moving up the frontier, England is choosing to produce more wheat and less cloth). The slope of the frontier reflects the "trade-off" of producing one product over the other; these trade-offs represent prices, or opportunity costs. Opportunity cost is the foregone value of a factor of production in its next best use. If England chooses to produce more units of wheat (in fact, produce only wheat), moving from point A to point B along the production possibilities frontier, it is giving up producing cloth to produce only wheat. The "cost" of the additional wheat is the loss of cloth. The slope of the production possibilities frontier is the ratio of product prices (opportunity costs). The slope of the production possibilities frontier for England is

FIGURE 2.2   **Production Possibility Frontiers, Specialization of Production, and the Benefits of Trade**

England

1. Initially produces and consumes at point A.
2. England chooses to specialize in the production of wheat, and shifts production from point A to point B.
3. England now exports the unwanted wheat (30 units) in exchange for imports of cloth (30 units) from France.
4. England is now consuming at point C, where it is consuming the same amount of wheat, but 15 more units of cloth than at original point A.

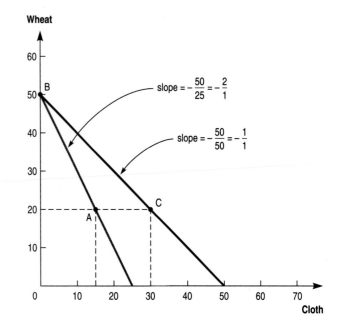

France

1. Initially produces and consumes at point D.
2. France chooses to specialize in the production of cloth, and shifts production from point D to point E.
3. France now exports the unwanted cloth (30 units) in exchange for imports of wheat (30 units) from England.
4. France is now consuming at point F, where it is consuming the same amount of cloth, but 15 more units of wheat than at original point D.

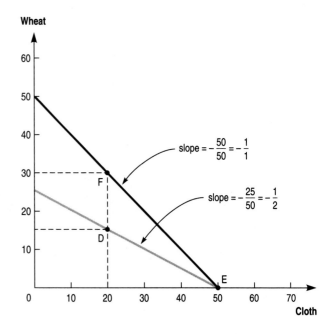

$-50/25$, or -2.00. The slope of the production possibilities frontier for France is flatter, $-25/50$ or -0.50.

These relative prices of products also provide an alternative way of seeing comparative advantage. The flatter slope of the French production possibilities frontier means that to produce more wheat (move up the frontier), France would have to give up the production of relatively more units of cloth than would England, with its steeper-sloped production possibilities frontier.

The Gains from International Trade

Continuing with Figure 2.2, if England were originally not trading with France (the only other country), and it was producing at its own maximum possibilities (on the frontier and not inside the line), it would probably be producing at some point A. Since it was not trading with another country, whatever it was producing it must be using itself—consuming. So England could be said to be consuming at point A also. Therefore, without trade, you consume what you produce.

If, however, England recognized that it has comparative advantage in the production of wheat, it should, according to the theory of comparative advantage, move production from point A to point B. England should specialize completely in the production of the product which it does best. Because it does not wish to consume only wheat, however, it would take the wheat it has produced which it does not want for its own consumption, and trade with France. For example, England may only wish to consume 20 units of wheat, as it did at point A. It is now producing 50 units, and therefore has 30 units of wheat which it can sell or export to France. If England could export 30 units of wheat in exchange for imports of 30 units of cloth (a 1/1 ratio of prices), England would clearly be better off than before. The new consumption point would be point C, where it is consuming the same amount of wheat as point A, but is now consuming 30 units of cloth instead of just 15. More is better; England would have benefitted from international trade.

France, following the same principle of completely specializing in the product of its comparative production advantage, moves production from point D to point E, producing 50 units of cloth. If France now exported the unwanted cloth, for example 30 units, and exchanged the cloth with England for imports of 30 units of

Heckscher and Ohlin noted that countries are endowed with varying degrees of productive resources and contended that the production of goods is a function of the most intensive use of these resources. Dekalb Genetics Corporation, an international marketer of seed products, is the leading supplier of corn, grain sorghum, and sunflower seeds to Argentina, where the growing season is the opposite of the United States'. Seasonal conditions are a significant factor in the high volume of corn production in Argentina.

Source: Courtesy of DeKalb Genetics Corporation.

Manufacturing: A Major Factor in Gross Domestic Product

Manufacturing as a Percent of GDP

> 30%
20 to 30%
10 to 20%
0 to 10%
No current data available

Source: *Europa World Yearbook*, 33 Ed., 1992; *Book of Vital World Statistics*, 1990.

wheat (note that England's exports are France's imports), France too is better off as a result of international trade. Each country would do what it does best, exclusively, and then trade for the other product.

But at what prices will the two countries trade? Since each country's production possibilities frontier has a different slope (different relative product prices), the two countries can determine a set of prices between the two domestic prices. In the above example, England's price ratio was $-2/1$, while France's domestic price ratio was $-1/2$. Trading 30 units of wheat for 30 units of cloth is a price ratio of $-1/1$, a slope or set or prices between the two domestic price ratios. The dashed line in Figure 2.2 illustrates this set of trade prices.

But are both countries better off as a result of trade? Yes. The final step to understanding the benefits of classical trade is to note that the point where a country produces (point B for England and point E for France in Figure 2.2) and the point where it consumes are now different. This allows each country to now consume beyond their own production possibilities frontier.

This final point is what the work of Adam Smith and David Ricardo was in many ways all about. Society's welfare, which is normally measured in its ability to consume more wheat, cloth, or any other goods or services is increased through trade. More is better, and trade provides more.

Concluding Points about Classical Trade Theory

Classical trade theory contributed much to the understanding of how production and trade operates in the world economy. Although like all economic theories they are often criticized for being unrealistic or out of date, the purpose of a theory is clearly to simplify reality so that the basic elements of the logic can be seen. Several of these simplifications have continued to provide insight in understanding international business.

- **Division of Labor.** Adam Smith's explanation of how industrial societies can increase output using the same labor-hours as in pre-industrial society is fundamental to our thinking even today. Smith extended this specialization of the efforts of a worker to the specialization of a nation.

- **Comparative Advantage.** David Ricardo's extension of Smith's work for the first time explained how countries that seemingly had no obvious reason for trade could individually specialize in whichever production they "did best," and trade for the product they did not produce.

- **Gains from Trade.** The theory of comparative advantage argued that nations could improve the welfare of their populations through international trade. A nation could actually achieve consumption levels beyond what it could produce by itself. To this day this is one of the fundamental principles underlying the arguments for all countries to strive to expand and "free" world trade.

FACTOR PROPORTIONS TRADE THEORY

Trade theory, like all of economic theory, changed drastically in the first half of the 20th century. The theory developed by the Swedish economist Eli Heckscher and later expanded by his former graduate student Bertil Ohlin formed the major theory of international trade that is still widely accepted today, **factor proportions theory**.

Factor proportions theory, also termed Heckscher-Ohlin theory, was based on a more modern concept of production, one that raised capital to the same level of importance as labor.

Factor Intensity in Production

This theory considered two **factors of production,** labor and capital. Technology determines the way they combine to form a product. Different products required different proportions of the two factors of production.

Figure 2.3 illustrates what it means to describe a product by its "factor proportions." The production of one unit of good X requires 4 units of labor and 1 unit of capital. At the same time, to produce 1 unit of good Y requires 4 units of labor and 2 units of capital. Good X therefore requires more units of labor per unit of capital (4 to 1) relative to Y (4 to 2). X is therefore classified as a "relatively labor-intensive" product, and Y is "relatively capital-intensive." These **factor intensities** or **proportions** are truly relative and are determined only on the basis of what product X requires relative to product Y and not to the specific numbers of labor to capital.

It is easy to see how the factor proportions of how a good is produced differ substantially across goods. For example, the manufacturing of leather footwear is still a relatively labor-intensive process, even with the most sophisticated leather-treatment and patterning machinery. Other goods, such as computer memory chips, however, although requiring some highly skilled labor, require massive quantities of capital for production. These large capital requirements include the enormous sums needed for research and development and the manufacturing facilities needed for clean production to ensure the extremely high quality demanded in the industry. The concept of factor proportions is very useful in the comparison of the production processes of goods.

According to factor proportions theory, factor intensities depend on the state of technology, the current method of manufacturing a product. The theory assumed that the same technology of production would be used for the same goods in all countries. It is not, therefore, differences in the efficiency of production that will determine trade between countries as it did in classical theory. Classical theory

FIGURE 2.3
Factor Proportions in Production

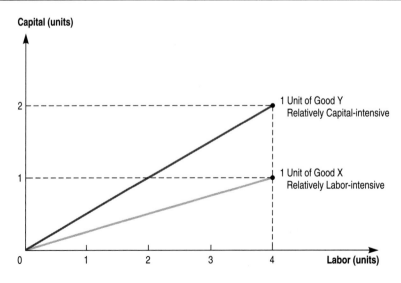

implicitly assumed that technology or the productivity of labor is different across countries. Otherwise, there would be no logical explanation as to why one country requires more units of labor to produce a unit of output than another country. Factor proportions theory assumes no such productivity differences.

Factor Endowments, Factor Prices, and Comparative Advantage

If there is no difference in technology or productivity of factors across the countries, what then determines comparative advantage in production and export? The answer is that factor prices determine cost differences. And these prices are determined by the endowments of labor and capital the country possesses. The theory assumes that labor and capital are immobile, meaning they cannot move across country borders. Therefore, the country's endowment determines the relative costs of labor and capital as compared to other countries.

Each country is defined or measured by the amount of labor and capital that it possesses. If a country has, when compared with other countries, more labor and less capital, it would be characterized as relatively labor-abundant. That which is more plentiful is cheaper; a labor-abundant country would therefore have relatively cheap labor.

For example, a country such as China possesses a relatively large endowment of labor and a relatively smaller endowment of capital. At the same time, Japan is a relatively capital-abundant country, with a relatively smaller endowment of labor. China possesses relatively cheaper labor and should therefore specialize in the production and export of labor-intensive products (such as good X in Figure 2.3). Japan possesses relatively cheap capital and should specialize in the production and export of capital-intensive products (such as good Y in Figure 2.3). Comparative advantage is derived not from the productivity of a country, but from the relative abundance of its factors of production.

Using these assumptions, factor proportions theory stated that a country should specialize in the production and export of those products that use intensively its relatively abundant factor.

- A country that is relatively labor-abundant should specialize in the production of relatively labor-intensive goods. It should then export these labor-intensive goods in exchange for capital-intensive goods.

- A country that is relatively capital-abundant should specialize in the production of relatively capital-intensive goods. It should then export these capital-intensive goods in exchange for labor-intensive goods.

Assumptions of the Factor Proportions Theory

Because of the increasing level of theoretical complexity of the factor proportions theory compared with the classical trade theory, the number of assumptions necessary for the theory to "hold" was large. It is important to take a last look at these assumptions before proceeding on to the theoretical and empirical research conducted in international trade in the latter half of the 20th century.

1. The theory assumes two countries, two products, and two factors of production, the so-called $2 \times 2 \times 2$ assumption. Note that if both countries were producing all of the output they could and trading only between themselves (only two countries), both countries would have to have balances in trade!

2. The markets for the inputs and the outputs are perfectly competitive. The factors of production, labor, and capital were exchanged in markets that paid them only what they were worth. Similarly, the trade of the outputs (the international trade between the two countries) was competitive so that one country had no market power over the other.

3. Increasing production of a product experiences diminishing returns. This meant that as a country increasingly specialized in the production of one of the two outputs, it would require more and more inputs per unit of output. For example there would no longer be the constant "labor-hours per unit of output" as assumed under the classical theory. This mean that the production possibilities frontiers would no longer be straight lines, but concave in shape. The result was that complete specialization would no longer occur under factor proportions theory.

4. Both countries were using identical technologies. Each product was produced in the same way in both countries. This meant the only way that a good could be more cheaply produced in one country than in the other was if the factors of production used (labor and capital) were cheaper.

Although there were a number of additional technical assumptions necessary, these four highlight the very specialized set of conditions needed in order to explain international trade with factor proportions theory. This modern theory of international trade has continued to develop in its sophistication over the past 50 years. Of particular note is that the theory of demand, the consumption preferences of society, has been expanded to a level of sophistication approaching that of the production theories of these traditional ideas. Demand can also affect the relative prices of the products and influence international trade patterns.

The Leontief Paradox

One of the most famous tests of any economic or business theory occurred in 1950, when economist Wassily Leontief tested whether the factor proportions theory could be used to explain the types of goods the United States imported and exported. Leontief's premise was the following.

> A widely shared view on the nature of the trade between the United States and the rest of the world is derived from what appears to be a common sense assumption that this country has a comparative advantage in the production of commodities which require for their manufacture large quantities of capital and relatively small amounts of labor. Our economic relationships with other countries are supposed to be based mainly on the export of such "capital intensive" goods in exchange for foregoing products which—if we were to make them at home—would require little capital but large quantities of American labor. Since the United States possesses a relatively large amount of capital—so goes this oft repeated argument—and a comparatively small amount of labor, direct domestic production of such "labor intensive" products would be uneconomical; we can much more advantageously obtain them from abroad in exchange for our capital intensive products.[4]

Leontief first had to devise a method to determine the relative amounts of labor and capital in a product. His solution, known as **input-output analysis,** was an accomplishment on its own. Input-output analysis is a technique of decomposing a product into the values and quantities of the labor, capital, and other potential factors employed in the product's manufacture. Leontief then used this methodology to analyze the labor and capital content of all U.S. merchandise imports and exports. The hypothesis was relatively straightforward: U.S. exports should be relatively capital-intensive (use more units of capital relative to labor) than U.S. imports. Leontief's results were, however, a bit of a shock.

Leontief found that the products that U.S. firms exported were relatively more labor-intensive than the products the United States imported.[5] It seemed that if the factor proportions theory were true, the United States is a relatively labor-abundant country! Alternatively, the theory could be wrong. Neither interpretation of the results was acceptable to many in the field of international-trade research.

A variety of explanations and continuing studies have attempted to solve what has become known as the **Leontief Paradox.** At first, it was thought to have been simply a result of the specific year (1947) that the data were for. However, the same results were found with different years and data sets. Secondly, it was noted that Leontief did not really analyze the labor and capital contents of imports, but rather the labor and capital contents of the domestic equivalents of these imports. It was possible that the United States was actually producing these products in a more capital-intensive fashion than were the countries from which it also imported these manufactured goods.[6] Finally, the debate turned to the need to distinguish different types of labor and capital. For example, several studies attempted to separate labor factors into skilled labor and unskilled labor. These studies have continued to show results more consistent with what the factor proportions theory would predict for country trade patterns. Finally, in the 1970s a number of studies expanded the factors of production to include energy, particularly oil, as a factor of production that would explain the paradox. The results to date have been mixed at best.

Linder's Overlapping Product Ranges Theory

The difficulties in empirically validating the factor proportions theory led many in the 1960s and 1970s to search for new explanations of the determinants of trade between countries. The work of Staffan Burenstam Linder focused not on the production or supply-side, but instead on the preferences of consumers, the demand-side. Linder acknowledged that in the natural resource–based industries, trade was indeed determined by relative costs of production and factor endowments. This was consistent with the previous factor proportions theory.

But, Linder argued, trade in manufactured goods was dictated not by cost concerns but rather by the similarity in product demands across countries. Linder's was a significant departure from previous theory. His theory was based on two principles:

1. As income rises, or more precisely per capita income, the complexity and quality level of the products demanded by the country's residents also rises. The total range of product sophistication demanded by a country's residents is largely determined by its level of income.

2. The entrepreneurs directing the firms that produce society's needs are more knowledgeable about their own domestic market than about foreign markets. An entrepreneur could not be expected to effectively service a foreign market that is significantly different from the domestic market be-cause competitiveness comes from experience. A logical pattern would be for an entrepreneur to gain success and market share at home first, then expand to foreign markets that are similar in their demands or tastes.

International trade in manufactured goods would then be influenced by similarity of demands. The countries that would see the most intensive trade are those with similar per capita income levels for they would possess greater likelihood of overlapping product demands.

So where does trade come in? According to Linder, the overlapping ranges of product sophistication represent the products that entrepreneurs would know well from their home markets and could therefore potentially export and compete in foreign markets. For example, the United States and Canada have almost parallel sophistication ranges, implying they would have a lot of "common ground," overlapping product ranges, for intensive international trade and competition. They are quite similar in their per capita income levels. But Mexico and the United States, or Mexico and Canada, would not. Mexico has a significantly different product sophistication range as a result of a different per capita income level.

The conclusions drawn from Linder's overlapping product ranges are strikingly different than from the traditional cost-oriented trade theory preceding it. First, the most intensive trade, according to Linder, would exist between countries of the same income or industrialization levels, not dissimilar levels as often concluded from previous theory. Second, the theory implied a large part of international trade would consist of the exchange of similar or slightly differentiated goods. Commonly referred to as intra-industry trade, the exchange of essentially identical goods between countries raised questions as to why consumers would import a product seemingly identical to the one they were often working to produce and export from their own country.

The overlapping product ranges described by Linder would today be termed market segments. Linder's work was not only instrumental in extending trade theory beyond cost considerations, but it has also found a place in the field of international marketing. As illustrated in the theories following the work of Linder, many of the questions that his work raised were the focus of considerable attention in the following decades.

INTERNATIONAL INVESTMENT AND PRODUCT CYCLE THEORY

A very different path was taken by Raymond Vernon in 1966 with what is now termed **product cycle theory.** Diverging significantly from traditional approaches, Vernon focused on the product (rather than the country and the technology of its manufacture), not its factor proportions. But most striking was the appreciation of the role of information, knowledge, and the costs and power that go hand in hand with knowledge.

> . . . we abandon the powerful simplifying notion that knowledge is a universal free good, and introduce it as an independent variable in the decision to trade or to invest.

Using many of the same basic tools and assumptions of factor proportions theory, Vernon added two technology-based premises to the factor-cost emphasis of existing theory:

1. Technical innovations leading to new and profitable products require large quantities of capital and highly skilled labor. These factors of production are predominantly available in highly industrialized capital-intensive countries.
2. These same technical innovations, both the product itself and more importantly the methods for its manufacture, go through three stages of maturation as the product becomes increasingly commercialized. As the manufacturing process becomes more standardized and low-skill labor-intensive, the comparative advantage in its production and export shifts across countries.

The Stages of the Product Cycle

Product cycle theory is both supply-side (cost of production) and demand-side (income levels of consumers) in its orientation. Each of these three stages that Vernon described combines differing elements of each.

Stage I: The New Product

Innovation requires highly skilled labor and large quantities of capital for research and development. The product will normally be most effectively designed and initially manufactured near the parent firm and therefore is a highly industrialized market due to the need for proximity to information; the need for communication between the many different skilled-labor components required.

In this development stage, the product is nonstandardized. The production process requires a high degree of flexibility (meaning continued use of highly skilled labor). Costs of production are therefore quite high.

The innovator at this stage is a monopolist and therefore enjoys all of the benefits of monopoly power, including the high profit margins required to repay the high development costs and expensive production process. Price elasticity of demand at this stage is low; high-income consumers buy it regardless of cost.

Stage II: The Maturing Product

As production expands, its process becomes increasingly standardized. The need for flexibility in design and manufacturing declines, and therefore the demand for highly skilled labor declines. The innovating country increases its sales to other countries. Competitors with slight variations develop, putting downward pressure on prices and profit margins. Production costs are an increasing concern.

As competitors increase, as well as their pressures on price, the innovating firm faces critical decisions as to how to maintain market share. Vernon argues that the firm faces a critical decision at this stage, to either lose market share to foreign-based manufacturers utilizing lower-cost labor or for the firm itself to invest abroad to maintain its market share by exploiting the comparative advantages of factor costs in other countries. This is one of the first theoretical explanations of how trade and investment become increasingly intertwined.

Stage III: The Standardized Product

In this final stage, the product is completely standardized in its manufacture. Thus, with access to capital on world capital markets, the country of production is simply the one with the cheapest unskilled labor. Profit margins are thin, and competition is fierce. The product has largely run its course in terms of profitability for the innovating firm.

The country of comparative advantage has therefore shifted as the technology of the product's manufacture has matured. The same product shifts in its location of production. The country possessing the product during that stage enjoys the benefits of net trade surpluses. But such advantages are fleeting, according to Vernon. As knowledge and technology continually change, so does the country of that product's comparative advantage.

Trade Implications of the Product Cycle

Product cycle theory shows how specific products were first produced and exported from one country, but through product and competitive evolution, shifted their location of production and export to other countries over time. Figure 2.4 illustrates

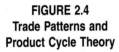

**FIGURE 2.4
Trade Patterns and
Product Cycle Theory**

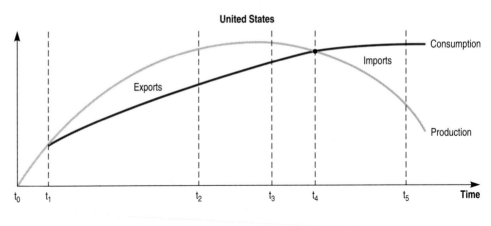

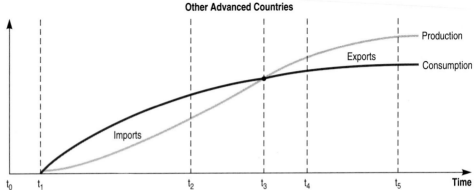

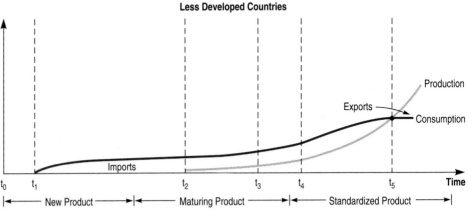

Source: Raymond Vernon, "International Investment and International Trade in the Product Cycle," *Quarterly Journal of Economics,* May 1966, p. 199.

the trade patterns that Vernon visualized as resulting from the maturing stages of a specific product's cycle. As the product and the market for the product mature and change, the countries of its production and export shift.

The product is initially designed and manufactured in the United States. In its early stages (from time t_0 to t_1), the United States is the only country producing and consuming the product. Production is highly capital-intensive and skilled labor–intensive at this time. At time t_1 the United States begins exporting the product to Other Advanced Countries, as Vernon classified them. These countries possessed the income to purchase the product in its still New Product Stage, in which it was relatively high-priced. These Other Advanced Countries also commence their own production at time t_1, but continue to be net importers. A few exports, however, do find their way to the Less Developed Countries at this time as well.

As product moves into the second stage, the Maturing Product Stage, production capability expands rapidly in the Other Advanced Countries. Competitive variations begin to appear as the basic technology of the product becomes more widely known, and the need for skilled labor in its production declines. These countries eventually also become net exporters of the product near the end of the stage (time t_3). At time t_2 the Less Developed Countries begin their own production, although they continue to be net importers. Meanwhile, the lower cost production from these growing competitors turns the United States into a net importer by time t_4. The competitive advantage for production and export is clearly shifting across countries at this time.

The third and final stage, the Standardized Product Stage, sees the comparative advantage of production and export now shifting to the Less Developed Countries. The product is now a relatively mass-produced product that can be produced with increasingly less-skilled labor. The United States continues to reduce domestic production and increase imports. The Other Advanced Countries continue to produce and export, although exports peak as the Less Developed Countries expand production and become net exporters themselves. The product has run its course or life cycle in reaching time t_5.

A final point. Note that throughout this product cycle, the countries of production, consumption, export, and import are identified by their labor and capital levels, not firms. Vernon noted that it could very well be the same firms that are moving production from the United States to Other Advanced Countries to Less Developed Countries. The shifting location of production was instrumental in the changing patterns of trade, but not necessarily in the loss of market share, profitability, or competitiveness of the firms. The country of comparative advantage changes.

The Contributions of Product Cycle Theory

Although interesting in its own right for increasing emphasis on technology's impact on production costs, product cycle theory was most important because it explained international investment. Not only did the theory recognize the mobility of capital across countries (breaking the traditional assumption of factor immobility), it shifted the focus from the country to the product. This made it important to match the product by its maturity stage with its production location to examine competitiveness.

Of course product cycle theory has many limitations. It is obviously most appropriate for technology-based products. These are the products that are most likely to experience the changes in production process as they grow and mature. Other products, either resource-based (like minerals and other commodities) or services (which employ capital but mostly in the form of human capital), are not so easily characterized by stages of maturity. And product cycle theory is most relevant to products that eventually fall victim to mass production and therefore cheap labor forces. But, all things considered, product cycle theory served to breach a wide gap between the trade theories of old and the intellectual challenges of a new more globally competitive market in which capital, technology, information, and firms themselves were more mobile.

THE NEW TRADE THEORY

The 1980s brought many of the questions regarding the validity of modern trade theory to the surface. The rapid growth of world trade, coupled with the sudden expansion of the U.S. merchandise trade deficit in the 1980s, forced many academics and policy-makers to take another look at the determinants of international trade. The issues included:

- Continuing frustration in verifying the factor proportions theory of international trade. Although tests continued, the results were still unconvincing in proving the basic theory to be sound.
- The inability of the theory to explain **intra-industry trade,** the two-way exchange of the same goods. For example, the United States exporting automobiles to Europe, and at the same time Europe exporting automobiles to the United States. Either they were not actually the same product, or there were factors in trade that could not be explained by theories of relative prices.
- The demonstrated ability of governments to influence positively and negatively the competitiveness of specific trade sectors of their economies. For example, a number of newly industrializing countries in the Asian Pacific had successfully nurtured industries purely for export purposes, some with great success.

There were two major developments in the 1980s largely in response to these and other issues: First, the work of many trade theorists like Paul Krugman at MIT in analyzing international trade for real-world economies, economies that do not possess perfect competition, free trade, or unregulated markets; and second, the works of people like Michael Porter at Harvard, who attempted to examine the competitiveness of industries on a global basis rather than relying on country-specific factors to determine their competitiveness, the so-called **competitive advantage.**

Intra-Industry Trade

All of the theories of international trade discussed so far have described factors or conditions leading to a firm either exporting or importing a specific product, but not both importing and exporting the same product. Intra-industry trade is the case in which a country seems to do both. First and foremost, why does intra-industry trade exist? If a country has comparative advantage in the production of a product, it should be exporting the product, not exporting and importing the same product.

There have been a variety of attempted explanations for the existence of intra-industry trade. The first explanation is that it is really just a data and definition problem. Although it may appear by statistical measures that the same product is being exported and imported, for example passenger automobiles, it may be they are not really the same product. If the classifications of passenger automobiles were narrowed down to distinguish price ranges, quality differences, options packages, it can be argued that one product is being exported and a different product is being imported. The puzzle of intra-industry trade is then "solved" by concluding that the level of data (product) aggregation is too high, and more specific data and product distinctions would show intra-industry trade to be an inconsequential issue. This argument can also be extended by realizing that in many markets today, consumers prefer variety for variety's sake. If that is the case, **product differentiation,** even if essentially cosmetic, is justified.

A second, more production-based explanation for intra-industry trade is that firms and industries expand at different rates in different countries. If the same product is being produced in different countries before trade is truly opened between countries, cost differences will likely exist. As trade increases between the two countries, a period of adjustment and product-production cost changes occur. But they occur at different rates in the two countries. One may expand and enjoy **economies of scale** (lower average costs per unit as a result of producing large quantities) much sooner than the other. In the period of time before one country achieves "advantage," both may be importing and exporting the same product.

Intra-industry trade is normally measured with the Grubel-Lloyd Index. The index is simply a ratio of how many imports and exports of the same product are occurring between two trading nations. It is calculated as follows:

$$IIT_i = 1 - \frac{|X_i - M_i|}{(X_i + M_i)}$$

where i is the product category and $|X_i - M_i|$ is the absolute value of net exports. For example, if U.S. imports of heavy bulldozers from Japan were 100 and at the same time the United States was exporting a value of 80, the intra-industry trade (IIT) index would be:

$$IIT_i = 1 - \frac{|80 - 100|}{(80 + 100)} = 1 - .1111 = .89.$$

The closer the index value to 1, the higher the level of intra-industry trade in that product category. The closer to 0, the more one-way the trade between the countries exists as traditional trade theory would predict.

A recent study of intra-industry trade between the United States and Japan revealed that two-way trade seems to be growing across all product categories. Figure 2.5 illustrates average IIT index values for three different trade years for three different product categories. The product categories reflect the theories of international trade previously presented in this chapter.

1. Ricardian: goods that are primarily commodity-based, involving natural-resource or agricultural components.
2. Heckscher-Ohlin: goods whose competitiveness in the marketplace is thought to rely primarily on factor costs (labor and capital).
3. Product Cycle: goods that are essentially technologically based, with the nature of the product and the market evolving over time with the maturity of the technology.

The results indicate that the general level of intra-industry trade across all categories was rising for the study years (1970, 1977, 1984). In fact, the average index values of .35 for the 1984 trade year are, for averages, quite high. Although these results do not support any one theory of why intra-industry trade occurs, they do indicate that two-way trade is not rare, and it appears to be increasing between two of the world's largest international traders. As Global Perspective 2.1 points out, intra-industry trade is one indicator of the openness of international trade between countries.

Imperfect Competition, Markets, and Trade

The Ricardian and factor proportions trade theories assumed that markets were open and competitive. In fact that is not always the case. For whatever reasons, many

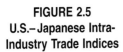

FIGURE 2.5
U.S.–Japanese Intra-Industry Trade Indices

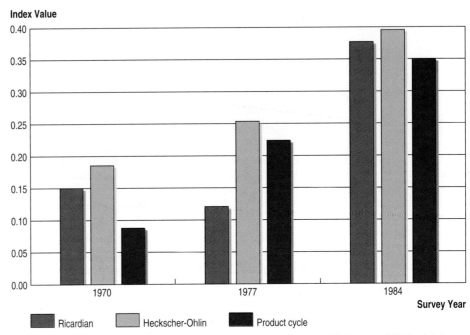

Source: Adapted from Keith E. Maskus, Deborah Battles, and Michael H. Moffett, "Determinants of the Structure of U.S. Manufacturing Trade with Japan and Korea, 1970–1984," in *The Internationalization of U.S. Markets*, NYU Press, 1989, 97–122.

industries in many countries are not operating in perfectly competitive markets. The market power gained by firms operating in imperfectly competitive markets (monopolists, oligopolists, and so forth) may allow those firms to "best" international rivals in foreign markets. When this is true, international trade does not necessarily make both countries and their citizens better off.

Although there is limited evidence to indicate that such **market imperfections** are a significant threat to the general benefits of world trade, research is continuing to examine the possible impacts of such imperfect competition and possible scale-economy advantages some firms may enjoy in international markets. As seen in the later discussion of commercial policies (**tariffs, quotas,** and other governmental restrictions on international trade), governments are well aware of the potential threats to all concerned if imperfectly competitive markets are allowed to persist or expand.

The Competitive Advantage of Nations

In many ways the study of international trade has come full circle. The focus of early trade theory was on the country or nation and its inherent, natural, or endowment characteristics that may give rise to increasing competitiveness. As trade theory evolved, it shifted its focus to the industry and product level, leaving the national-level competitiveness question somewhat behind. Recently, many have turned their attention to the question of how countries, governments, and even private industry can alter the conditions within a country to aid the competitiveness of its firms.

The leader in this area of research has been Michael Porter of Harvard. As he states:

Global Perspective

2.1
"Who's Bashing Whom: Trade Conflicts in High-Technology Industries"

Between 1987 and 1990, Japan's trade surplus with the U.S. declined by more than $15 billion, and American exports to Japan expanded by 72%. In 1990, Japan imported a record $30.9 billion of manufactured goods from the U.S., up from only $16.3 billion in 1987. Do numbers like these mean that we have seen the last of the so-called "Japan problem?" If so, why does trade friction persist between the U.S. and Japan, and why is it now heating up between Japan and several of its European trading partners?

Certainly, some of Japan's ongoing troubles with its trading partners are the predictable and unfortunate result of its astonishing successes. There is an instinctive protectionist response to these successes in both the U.S. and Europe. For the U.S., the growing ascendance of Japan in technology-intensive industries is a particular cause for concern. Although the overall trade deficit with Japan has improved markedly since 1987, the improvement has been mainly in low-technology areas. Indeed, the imbalance in high-technology industries has actually increased despite the appreciation of the yen. Japanese producers continue to gain market share in the world telecommunications and computer markets at the expense of American producers. Given current trends, the Japanese share will surpass the American share of the global computer market sometime this decade, mimicking a similar development in the world semiconductor markets during the 1980s.

Although protectionist impulses are sometimes part of the story of trade friction with Japan, they are not the whole story. Another part of the story concerns the openness or accessibility of the Japanese market to foreign products and producers. In recent years, a number of serious scholarly studies have confirmed what the world business community has known for years: the Japanese market remains significantly more closed than the markets of most of the other advanced industrial nations.

The relative closure of the Japanese market shows up in a variety of indicators. First, Japan engages in comparatively little intra-industry trade, and the level of such trade has failed to rise over time as it has in the other industrial countries. Put simply, Japan tends not to import very much in industries in which it is a significant exporter. Second, market closure also shows up in prices. A study completed as part of the so-called "Structural Impediments Initiative" between the U.S. and Japan found that prices of many foreign products are significantly higher in Japan than in world markets. Finally, despite the recent explosion of imports of manufactured goods into Japan, the ratio of such imports to GNP, although increasing from 2.7% in 1986 to 3.7% by 1989, remains significantly lower in Japan than in the other advanced industrial countries.

Source: Excerpted from "Managing Trade by Rules and Outcomes," by Laura D'Andrea Tyson, *California Management Review*, Fall 1991, pp. 115-143. The article itself is adapted from Laura D'Andrea Tyson, *Who's Bashing Whom: Trade Conflicts in High-Technology Industries*, Institute for International Economics, Washington, D.C., 1992. Laura D'Andrea Tyson was appointed Chairman of the President's Council of Economic Advisors in 1993.

National prosperity is created, not inherited. It does not grow out of a country's natural endowments, its labor pool, its interest rates, or its currency's values, as classical economics insists.

A nation's competitiveness depends on the capacity of its industry to innovate and upgrade. Companies gain advantage against the world's best competitors because of pressure and challenge. They benefit from having strong domestic rivals, aggressive home-based suppliers, and demanding local customers.

In a world of increasingly global competition, nations have become more, not less, important. As the basis of competition has shifted more and more to the creation and assimilation of knowledge, the role of the nation has grown. Competitive advantage is created and sustained through a highly localized process. Differences in national values, culture, economic structures, institutions, and histories all contribute to competitive success. There are striking differences in the patterns of competitiveness in every country;

no nation can or will be competitive in every or even most industries. Ultimately, nations succeed in particular industries because their home environment is most forward-looking, dynamic, and challenging.[7]

Porter argued innovation is what drives and sustains competitiveness. A firm must avail itself of all dimensions of competition, which he categorized into four major components of "the diamond of national advantage":

1. Factor Conditions: the appropriateness of the nation's factors of production compete successfully in a specific industry. Porter notes that although these factor conditions are very important in the determination of trade, they are not the only source of competitiveness as suggested by the classical or factor proportions theories of trade. Most importantly for Porter, it is the ability of a nation to continually create, upgrade, and deploy its factors (such as skilled labor) that is important, not the initial endowment.

2. Demand Conditions: the degree of health and competition the firm must face in its original home market. Firms that can survive and flourish in highly competitive and demanding local markets are much more likely to gain the competitive edge. Porter notes that it is the character of the market, not its size, that is paramount in promoting the continual competitiveness of the firm. And Porter translates *character* as demanding customers.

3. Related and Supporting Industries: the competitiveness of all related industries and suppliers to the firm. A firm that is operating within a mass of related firms and industries gains and maintains advantages through close working relationships, proximity to suppliers, and timeliness of product and information flows. The constant and close interaction is successful if it occurs not only in terms of physical proximity but also through the willingness of firms to work at it.

4. Firm Strategy, Structure, and Rivalry: the conditions in the home-nation that either hinder or aid in the firm's creation and sustaining international competitiveness. Porter notes that no one managerial, ownership, or operational strategy is universally appropriate. It depends on the fit and flexibility of what works for that industry in that country at that time.

These four, as illustrated in Figure 2.6, constitute what nations and firms must strive to "create and sustain through a highly localized process" to ensure themselves of success.

The work of Porter is in many ways a synthesis of all that came before it. The emphasis on innovation as the source of competitiveness reflects the increased focus on the industry and product that we have seen in the past three decades. The acknowledgement that the nation is "more, not less, important" is to many eyes a welcome return to a positive role for government and even national-level private industry in encouraging international competitiveness. Including factor conditions as a cost component, demand conditions as a motivator of firm actions, and competitiveness all combine to include the elements of classical, factor proportions, product cycle, and imperfect competition theories in a pragmatic approach to the challenges that the global markets of the 21st century present the firms of today.

THE THEORY OF INTERNATIONAL INVESTMENT

To understand international investment, its motivation, process, and implications, we return to the basic premise of international trade.[8] Trade is the production of a good or service in one country and its sale to a buyer in another country. In fact,

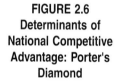

FIGURE 2.6 Determinants of National Competitive Advantage: Porter's Diamond

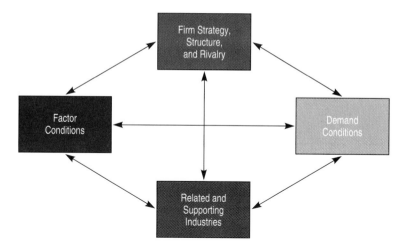

we specifically note that it is a firm (not a country) and a buyer (not a country) that are the subjects of trade, domestically or internationally. A firm therefore is attempting to access a market and its buyers. The producing firm wants to utilize its competitive advantage for growth and profit.

Although this sounds easy enough, consider any of the following potholes on this smooth freeway to investment success. Any of the following potholes may be avoided by producing within another country.

- Sales to some countries are difficult because of tariffs imposed on your product when it is entering. If you were producing within the country, your product would no longer be an import.

- Your product requires natural resources that are available only in certain areas of the world. It is therefore imperative that you have access to these natural resources. You can buy them from that country and bring them to your production process (import) or simply take the production to them.

- Competition is constantly pushing you to improve efficiency and decrease the costs of producing your product. You therefore may wish to produce where it will be cheaper—cheaper capital, cheaper energy, cheaper natural resources, or cheaper labor. Many of these factors are still not mobile, and therefore you will go to them instead of bringing them to you.

There are thousands of reasons why a firm may want to produce in another country, and not necessarily the country that is cheapest for production or the country where the final product is sold. And there are many shades of gray between the black and white of exporting or investing directly in the foreign country.

The subject of international investment arises from one basic idea: the mobility of capital. Although many of the traditional trade theories assumed the immobility of the factors of production, it is the movement of capital that has allowed **foreign direct investments** across the globe. If there is a competitive advantage to be gained, capital can get there.

The Foreign Direct Investment Decision

Consider a firm that wants to exploit its competitive advantage by accessing foreign markets as illustrated in the decision-sequence tree of Figure 2.7.

FIGURE 2.7   **The Direct Foreign Investment Decision Sequence**

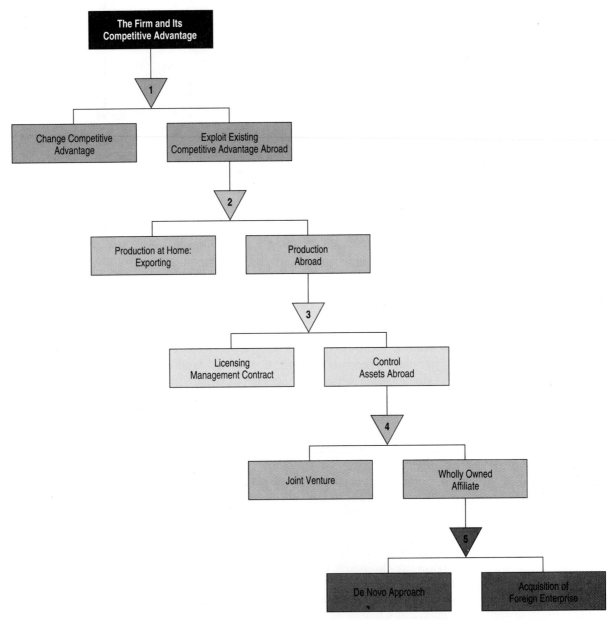

Source: Adapted from Gunter Dufey and R. Mirus, "Foreign Direct Investment: Theory and Strategic Considerations," unpublished, University of Michigan, May 1985.

The first choice is whether to exploit the existing competitive advantage in new foreign markets or to concentrate resources in the development of new competitive advantages in the domestic market. Although many firms may choose to do both as resources will allow, more and more firms are choosing to go international as at least part of their expansion strategies.

Secondly, should the firm produce at home and export to the foreign markets or produce abroad? Customarily, the firm will choose the path that will allow it to access the resources and markets it needs to exploit its existing competitive advantage. That is the minimum requirement. But it also should consider two additional dimensions of each foreign-investment decision: (1) the degree of control over assets, technology, information, and operations and (2) the magnitude of capital that the firm must risk. Each decision increases the firm's control at the cost of increased capital outlays.

For some reason, possibly one of the potholes described previously, the firm decides to produce abroad. There are, however, many different ways to produce abroad. The distinctions between different kinds of foreign direct investment (branch 3 and downward in Figure 2.7), licensing agreements to de novo construction (building a new facility from the ground up), vary by degrees of ownership. The licensing management contract is by far the simplest and cheapest way to produce abroad; another firm is actually doing the production, but with your firm's technology and know-how. The question for most firms is whether the reduced capital investment of simply licensing the product to another manufacturer is worth the risk of loss of control over the product and technology.

The firm that wants direct control over the foreign production process next determines the degree of equity control, to own the firm outright or as a joint investment with another firm. Trade-offs with shared ownership continue the debate over control of assets and other sources of the firm's original competitive advantage. Many countries, trying to ensure the continued growth of local firms and investors, may require that foreign firms operate jointly with local firms.

The final decision branch between a de novo investment, sometimes referred to as "greenfield," and the purchase of an existing firm is often a question of cost. A de novo investment is usually the most expensive of all foreign-investment alternatives. The acquistion of an existing firm is often lower in initial cost but may also contain a number of "customizing and adjustment costs" that are not apparent at the inital purchase. The purchase of a going concern may also have substantial benefits if the existing business possesses substantial customer and supplier relationships that can be utilized by the new owner in the pursuit of its own product line.

The Theory of Foreign Direct Investment

What motivates a firm to go beyond exporting or licensing? What benefits does the multinational firm expect to achieve by establishing a physical presence in other countries? These are the questions that the Theory of Foreign Direct Investment has sought to answer. As with trade theory, the questions have remained largely the same over time while the answers have continued to change. With hundreds of countries, thousands of firms, and millions of products and services, there is no question that the answer to such an enormous question will likely get messy.

The following overview of investment theory has many similarities to the preceding discussion of international trade. The theme is a global business environment that continues to attempt to satisfy increasingly sophisticated consumer demands, while the means of production, resources, skills, and technology needed become more complex and competitive. A more detailed analysis of foreign direct investment theory is presented in Chapter 12.

Firms as Seekers

There is no question that much of the initial foreign direct investment of the 18th and 19th centuries was the result of firms' seeking unique and valuable natural

In keeping with its global strategy to seek large, "children-oriented" markets, Toys "R" Us has recently opened two of a projected 100 stores in Japan and eight stores in Spain. Opening the first stores required three years of negotiation.

Source: Courtesy of Toys "R" Us.

resources for their products. Whether it be the copper resources of Chile, the linseed oils of Indonesia, or the petroleum resources spanning the Middle East, firms established permanent presences around the world to get access to the resources at the core of their business. The 20th century has seen the expansion of this activity combined with a number of other objectives sought by multinationals.

The resources needed for production are often combined with other advantages that may be inherent in the country of production. The same low-cost labor that was used as the source of international competitiveness in labor-intensive products according to factor proportions trade theory provides incentives for firms to move production to countries possessing these factor advantages. And, consistent with the principles of Vernon's product cycle, the same firms may move their own production to locations of factor advantages as the products and markets mature.

Seeking may also include the search for knowledge. Firms may attempt to acquire firms in other countries for the technical or competitive skills they may possess. Alternatively, companies may locate in and around centers of industrial enterprise unique to their specific industry, such as the footwear industry of Milan or the semiconductor industry of the Silicon Valley of California.

Firms continue to move internationally as they seek political stability or security. The massive outflow of capital and industry now occurring from Hong Kong is a striking example of how firms attempt to find new locations that will allow them to continue to operate and grow unfettered by the Chinese takeover of Hong Kong scheduled for 1997. Mexico has experienced a significant increase in the level of foreign direct investment as a result of the increasing political stability of the post-1985 government and the tacit support of the United States and Canada reflected by the North American Free Trade Agreement.

Finally, firms may seek markets. The ability to gain and maintain access to markets is of paramount importance to multinational firms. The need to grow beyond the domestic market is central to all of international trade and business theory (see Global Perspective 2.2). Whether following the principles of Linder, in which firms learn

Global Perspective

2.2
An Open Letter to the American Consumer to Encourage Foreign Investment

BRITISH AIRWAYS

75-20 Astoria Boulevard
Jackson Heights, NY 11370

November 25, 1992

Dear Traveler:

Between now and December 24th the Department of Transportation will make an historic decision that will significantly impact your choices for future travel.

I would like to take this opportunity to present the facts on our proposed $750 million investment in USAir and what this alliance means to you.

This alliance, between two publicly traded companies, is perfectly legal under U.S. and U.K. law.

The alliance will ensure continued, strong U.S. domestic competition giving you, the traveler, more choice, lower fares, more destinations and better service, which is what the airline business should be all about—serving the customer better. Even after the formation of this alliance, the three largest American carriers will still have three times as many non-stop transatlantic flights a week from the U.S. as we will.

This alliance is an investment—not an acquisition or takeover. British Airways will not control USAir. The truth is, the investment will ensure the long-term viability of USAir and its 47,000 employees.

America was built on private investment and we have grown our business here by investing in America's growth over 46 years. As of today, British Airways has over $6.5 billion in firm orders for Boeing aircraft—the largest of any foreign airline—and a major investment in American jobs. In addition, over the next 5 years we have another $8.5 billion of planned expenditures into the U.S. economy.

We're proud, as our advertising says, to be "The world's favourite airline." Perhaps our competitors are a bit afraid that with this USAir alliance, more of the American public will find out why.

Have a Happy Thanksgiving.

Sincerely,

Sir Colin Marshall
Deputy Chairman and Chief Executive.

British Airways Plc.
Registered office:
Speedbird House
Heathrow Airport (London)
Hounslow TW6 2JA.
Registered in England No. 1777777

Source: *The Wall Street Journal*, November 25, 1992. Courtesy of British Airways.

from their domestic market and use that information to go international, or the principles of Porter, which emphasized the character of the domestic market as dictating international competitiveness, foreign-market access is necessary. As governments have become more intertwined in the business affairs of their constituents, multinational firms have often been forced to position themselves against the potential loss of market access by establishing permanent physical presence. The reaction of North American and East Asian firms to the Single European Market pushed forward in 1986 was to increase their level of investment in the European Community to ensure that they would not fall victim to a "Fortress Europe" if it were to arise (it did not).

Firms as Exploiters of Imperfections

Much of the investment theory developed in the past three decades has focused on the efforts of multinational firms to exploit the imperfections in factor and product markets created by governments. The work of Stephen Hymer (1960), Charles Kindleberger (1969), and Richard Caves (1971) noted that many of the policies of governments create imperfections. These market imperfections cover the entire range of supply- and demand-related principles of the market: trade policy (tariffs and quotas), tax policies and incentives, preferential purchasing arrangements established by the governments themselves, and financial restrictions on the access of foreign firms to domestic capital markets. As illustrated in Global Perspective 2.3, government policies are currently used to manipulate foreign investment.

For example, many of the world's developing countries have long sought to create domestic industry by restricting imports of competitive products in order to allow smaller, less competitive domestic firms to grow and prosper—so-called **import substitution** policies. Multinational firms have sought to maintain their access to these markets by establishing their own production presence within the country, effectively bypassing the tariff restriction but at the same time fulfilling the country's desire to stimulate domestic industrial production (and employment) in that area.

Other multinational firms have exploited the same sources of comparative advantage identified throughout this chapter: the low cost resources or factors often located in less-developed countries or countries with restrictions in place on the mobility of labor and capital. It should once again be noted that it is mobility of capital, international investment and foreign direct investment, that is the topic. The combining of the mobility of capital with the immobility of low-cost labor has characterized much of the foreign investment seen throughout the developing world over the past 30 years.

The ability of multinational firms to exploit or at least manage these imperfections will still rely on their ability to gain an advantage. Market advantages or powers are seen in international markets in the same way as in domestic markets: cost advantages, economies of scale and scope, product differentiation, managerial or marketing technique and knowledge, financial resources and strength. All are the things that competitive dreams are made of. The multinational needs to find these in some form or another to justify the added complexities and costs of international investments.

Firms as Internalizers

The question that has plagued the field of foreign direct investment is why can't all of the advantages and imperfections mentioned above be achieved through management contracts or licensing agreements (the choice available to the

Global Perspective

2.3
"Open for Offers"

This place seems to have everything: 6,600 hectares of land, a deep-water port, ship-repair facilities, a big airport and a nice resort island. It also has a live volcano nearby.

Welcome to Subic Bay, the Philippine naval base that the U.S. is due to give up by November 24. Manila hopes to convert the $8 billion complex into a business center that will attract foreign investors. The ultimate goal: to turn the base into the Philippines' version of Taiwan's Kaohsiung or China's Schenzhen special economic zone. "It will be the country's engine of growth," declares Richard Gordon, administrator of the Subic Bay Metropolitan Authority.

Maybe, but there are plenty of obstacles. The risk is that Manila's failure to realize its ambitions would bolster foreign perceptions that the Philippines once again has thrown away an opportunity because of government inefficiency and political squabbles. "It will be a fundamental test whether this country—its new government, its politicians, its business sector—can all get their act together," says an Asian diplomat.

No one could accuse the Philippines of not trying. The country has lavished a lot of goodies on investors who set up in Subic Bay. In March, Congress created a free-port zone consisting of the naval base and the adjacent Olongapo City and Subic town. Export and import of goods will be duty-free. A single 5% business tax will be imposed, much lower than the 35% corporate income tax in the rest of the country. The Philippines promises there will be no foreign-currency restrictions, and foreigners investing a minimum of $250,000 will receive permanent resident status in the zone.

Nonetheless, it will not be easy creating a business center out of a military base. And it certainly does not help matters to have a volcano 32 kilometers away. Mount Pinatubo blew its top in June 1991, covering Subic with ashes and damaging several buildings. Fortunately, a mountain range protects the complex from the mudflows that continue to ravage most of central Luzon, but scientists have not ruled out another eruption.

Gordon does not seem worried. The Subic conversion program will indeed turn out to test that faith. Perhaps most of all, the project will be a test of the Philippines' ability to attract—and keep—foreign investors.

Source: Adapted from "Open for Offers: Subic Bay Will Test Philippine Attractions for Investors," by Rigoberto Tiglao, *Far Eastern Economic Review*, October 15, 1992, pp. 62, 64.

international investor at step 3 in Figure 2.7). Why is it necessary for the firm itself to establish a presence in the country? What pushes the multinational firm further down the investment-decision tree?

The research and writings of Peter Buckley and Mark Casson (1976) and John Dunning (1977) have attempted to answer these questions by focusing on nontransferable sources of competitive advantage—proprietary information possessed by the firm and its people. Many of the true advantages possessed by firms center on their hands-on knowledge of producing a product or providing a service. By establishing their own multinational operations, they can **internalize** the production, keep the information within the firm that is at the core of the firm's competitiveness. Internalization is preferable to the use of arm's-length investment arrangements, such as management contracts or licensing agreements. They either do not allow the effective transmission of the knowledge or represent too serious a threat to the loss of the knowledge to allow the firm to achieve the benefits of international investment.

As stated, these are theories. The synthesis of motivations provided by Dunning and others has only sought to partially explain, in the manner of Porter, many of the facts and forces leading firms to pursue international investment. To date there is scant empirical evidence to support or refute these theories.

SUMMARY

The theory of international trade has changed drastically from that first put forward by Adam Smith. The classical theories of Adam Smith and David Ricardo focused on the abilities of countries to produce goods more cheaply than other countries. The earliest production and trade theories saw labor as the major factor expense that went into any product. If a country could pay that labor less, and if that labor could produce more physically than labor in other countries, the country might obtain an absolute or comparative advantage in trade.

Subsequent theoretical development led to a more detailed understanding of production and its costs. Factors of production are now believed to include labor (skilled and unskilled), capital, natural resources, and other potentially significant commodities that are difficult to reproduce or replace, such as energy. Technology, once assumed to be the same across all countries, is now seen as one of the premier driving forces in determining who holds the competitive edge or advantage. International trade is now seen as a complex combination of thousands of products, technologies, and firms that are constantly innovating to either keep up with or get ahead of the competition.

Modern trade theory has looked beyond production cost to analyze how the demands of the marketplace alter who trades with whom and which firms survive domestically and internationally. The abilities of firms to adapt to foreign markets, both in the demands and the competitors that form the foreign markets, have required much of international trade and investment theory to search out new and innovative approaches to what determines success and failure.

Finally, as world economies have grown and the magnitude of world trade increased, the simplistic ideas that guided international trade and investment theory have had to grow with them. The choices that many firms face today require them to directly move their capital, technology, and know-how to countries that possess other unique factors or market advantages that will help the firm keep pace with market demands.

Key Terms and Concepts

mercantilism	product cycle theory
absolute advantage	intra-industry trade
division of labor	competitive advantage
comparative advantage	product differentiation
production possibilities frontier	economies of scale
autarky	market imperfections
opportunity cost	tariffs
factor proportions theory	quotas
factors of production	foreign direct investment
factor intensities	import substitution
input-output analysis	internalization
Leontief Paradox	

Questions for Discussion

1. According to the Theory of Comparative Advantage as explained by Ricardo, why is trade always possible between two countries, even when one is absolutely inefficient compared to the other?

2. The factor proportions theory of international trade assumes that all countries produce the same product the same way. Would international competition cause or prevent this from happening?

3. What in your opinion were the constructive impacts on trade theory resulting from the empirical research of Wassily Leontief?

4. Product cycle theory has always been a very "attractive theory" to many students. Why do you think that is?

5. If the product cycle theory were accepted for the basis of policy-making in the United States, what should the U.S. government do to help U.S. firms exploit the principles of the theory?

6. Many trade theorists argue that the primary contribution of Michael Porter has been to repopularize old ideas, in new, more applicable ways. To what degree do you think Porter's ideas are new or old?

7. How would you analyze the statement that "international investment is simply a modern extension of classical trade"?

8. Why would a firm like British Airways try to convince the American traveler that it only wants to invest in USAir, not control it?

Recommended Readings

Buckley, Peter J., and Mark Casson, *The Future of the Multinational Enterprise*. London: Macmillan, 1976.

Caves, Richard E., "International Corporations: The Industrial Economics of Foreign Investment," *Economica*, February 1971, 1–27.

Dunning, John H., "Trade Location of Economic Activity and the MNE: A Search for an Eclectic Approach," in *The International Allocation of Economic Activity*, Bertil Ohlin, Per-Ove Hesselborn, and Per Magnus Wijkman, editors, New York: Homes and Meier, 1977, 395–418.

Heckscher, Eli, "The Effect of Foreign Trade on the Distribution of Income," in *Readings in International Trade*, Howard S. Ellis and Lloyd A. Metzler, editors, Philadelphia: The Blakiston Company, 1949.

Husted, Steven, and Michael Melvin, *International Economics*. New York: Harper & Row, 1990.

Hymer, Stephen H., *The International Operations of National Firms: A Study of Direct Foreign Investment*. Cambridge, Mass.: MIT Press, 1976.

Linder, Staffan Burenstam, *An Essay on Trade and Transformation*. New York: John Wiley & Sons, 1961.

Maskus, Keith E., Deborah Battles, and Michael H. Moffett, "Determinants of the Structure of U.S. Manufacturing Trade with Japan and Korea, 1970–1984," in *The Internationalization of U.S. Markets*, David B. Audretch and Michael P. Claudon, editors, New York: New York University Press, 1989, 97–122.

Ohlin, Bertil, *Interregional and International Trade*. Boston: Harvard University Press, 1933.

Porter, Michael, "The Competitive Advantage of Nations," *Harvard Business Review*, March-April, 1990.

Ricardo, David, *The Principles of Political Economy and Taxation*. Cambridge. United Kingdom: Cambridge University Press, 1981.

Root, Franklin R. *International Trade and Investment*, sixth edition. Chicago: South-Western Publishing, 1990.

Smith, Adam, *The Wealth of Nations*. New York: The Modern Library, 1937.

Vernon, Raymond, "International Investment and International Trade in the Product Cycle," *Quarterly Journal of Economics*, 1966, 190–207.

Wells, Louis T., Jr., "A Product Life Cycle for International Trade?" *Journal of Marketing*, Vol. 22, July 1968, 1–6.

NOTES

1. Adam Smith noted the misplacement of society's desires for accumulation of specie (gold and silver) when he quoted John Locke in *The Wealth of Nations* (p. 376): "Money, on the contrary, is a steady friend, which, though it may travel from hand to hand, yet if it can be kept from going out of the country, is not very liable to be wasted or consumed." Smith wished to point out that what was more important was what gold would buy, buy for human needs, and not simply for the purpose of its accumulation.

2. A number of countries in the world economy today continue to follow neo-mercantilism, in many ways no different from that of the distant past. Countries like Taiwan, for example, actively pursue policies that will ensure net trade surpluses and simultaneously accumulate foreign-currency reserves, including gold, which will allow them to further public-sector goals.

3. Adam Smith, *An Inquiry into the Nature and Causes of the Wealth of Nations*, E.P. Dutton & Company, Inc., New York, 1937, 4–5.

4. Wassily Leontief, "Domestic Production and Foreign Trade: the American Capital Position Re-Examined," *Proceedings of the American Philosophical Society*, vol. 97, no. 4, September 1953, as reprinted in *Input-Output Economics*, Wassily Leontief, Oxford University Press, New York, 1966, 69–70.

5. In Leontief's own words: "These figures show that an average million dollars' worth of our exports embodies considerably less capital and somewhat more labor than would be required to replace from domestic production an equivalent amount of our competitive imports. . . . The widely held opinion that—as compared with the rest of the world—the United States' economy is characterized by a relative surplus of capital and a relative shortage of labor proves to be wrong. As a matter of fact, the opposite is true." Leontief, 1953, 86.

6. If this was true of course, it would defy one of the basic assumptions of the factor proportions theory, that all products are manufactured with the same technology (and therefore same proportions of labor and capital) across countries. However, continuing studies have found this to be quite possible in our imperfect world.

7. Michael E. Porter, "The Competitive Advantage of Nations," *Harvard Business Review*, March-April 1990, 73–74.

8. The term "international investment" will be used in this chapter to refer to all non-financial investment. International financial investment includes a number of forms beyond the concerns of this chapter, such as the purchase of bonds, stocks, or other securities issued outside the domestic economy.

P A R T

1

Cases

America for Sale

During the late 1980s and early 1990s, it appeared that the United States had become a country for sale. For the first time in decades, total foreign direct investment in the United States exceeded U.S. direct investment abroad. Purchases by foreign investors included Columbia Pictures, Carnation Foods, Allied Stores, Chesebrough-Ponds, Firestone Tire and Rubber, Exxon's headquarters in Manhattan's Rockefeller Center, and a major portion of the Watergate complex in Washington, D.C.

By the end of the 1980s, foreign investors owned more than half of the commercial real estate in downtown Los Angeles, more than one-third of Alaska's $680 million seafood-packaging industry, more than half of the hotels along Hawaii's Waikiki Beach, and four of the ten largest banks in California.

Japanese foreign direct investment has increased more than investment by any other country. Although Britain holds approximately twice as many investments in the United States as Japan, the Japanese increased their foreign direct investment in the United States more than 18-fold during the 1980s, by far the largest increase. Furthermore, American direct investment in Japan is only one-fourth of Japanese investment in the United States.

There are a number of reasons behind the rapid growth in foreign investment in the United States. First, U.S. businesses and properties are selling for low prices because of the plunge in the value of the dollar during the middle and late 1980s. A Japanese real estate investor visiting Manhattan noted, "Everything here is so cheap!" While prices seemed high to Americans, they seemed enticingly low to an investor holding yen or marks, both of which appreciated by about 40 percent relative to the dollar during the mid-1980s. Second, many foreign investors were flush with cash to invest. This was the result of both high savings rates in many other countries and the persistent U.S. current account deficits, which had transferred billions of dollars abroad. A third factor is that foreign investors were attracted to America's stable political climate and the open nature of its economy and capital markets.

Source: Hobart Rowen, "Dispelling Some Myths about Foreign Investment," *The Washington Post,* March 18, 1990, H1; John Burgess,"Foreigners Keep Investing in the U.S.—But with American Loans," *The Washington Post,* January 22, 1991, D1; "For Sale: America," *Time,* September 14, 1987, 52–62; "Unwelcome Mat," *The Wall Street Journal,* July 24, 1987, 1; "Distant Deals," *The Wall Street Journal,* February 24, 1988, 1; "The Selling of America," *Fortune,* December 22, 1986, 43–56; "As Foreign Investment Increases, So Do Concerns about Its Impact," *The Washington Post,* February 21, 1988, H1; "Most Americans Favor Laws to Limit Foreign Investment in U.S., Poll Finds," *The Wall Street Journal,* March 8, 1988, 60.

Historically, the United States has allowed capital to flow freely across its borders, and many argue that this is how it should be. "This is in everybody's interests, just as trade is in everybody's interests," said Robert Ortner, undersecretary for economic affairs at the Commerce Department. Proponents argue that the world is in the process of integration, and the United States should not stand in the way. Freedom of investment promotes efficiency in allocation of capital, according to most economists. "We get the jobs, we get the production," argues Ortner. "And for that matter, we are beginning to get the exports," he says, referring to an announcement by Japanese companies that they planned to export some of their U.S.-made cars to Japan.

Other benefits of foreign direct investment in the United States have also been apparent. Many industrial cities in the United States have been unable to attract American investors. For these cities, foreign investment that has come in to reopen plants has resulted in employment and growth. Foreign investment is also likely to reduce the United States' reliance on imports, because many of the goods previously imported are now manufactured in the United States. Another benefit is that foreign investment brings not only money but managerial talent, innovation, and technology.

Despite the obvious benefits, however, a number of observers have pointed out that there are corresponding costs. Lawrence Brainard, chief international economist for Bankers Trust, said, "By the end of the century the United States will have the most modern manufacturing sector in the world, but it won't own it." A Texas congressman has said, "America has been selling its family jewels to pay for a night on the town, and we don't know enough about the proud new owners."

Some observers are skeptical about the claim that foreign investment increases employment. A study by the United Auto Workers concluded the opposite: For every job created, the study claimed, three are destroyed because the foreign-owned operations import so many of their components. Further, because many foreign companies are nonunion, they may have cost advantages over their American competitors. Other studies, however, have disputed the claim that foreign investment reduces employment.

Some of the opposition to growth in direct investment in the United States is rooted in issues of national pride and security. In fighting to prevent a takeover by a British firm, a major textbook publisher argued that foreigners were unfit to publish textbooks for American schoolchildren. The Pentagon has objected to proposed purchases of defense contractors, such as Fairchild Semiconductors, arguing that national-security interests were at stake.

Foreign ownership in America is likely to be a burning political issue during the next decade, and a number of questions are likely to be addressed. How does foreign investment affect America's ability to compete? What, if any, controls should be placed on foreign investment? What are the economic effects of the growth in foreign direct investment? Finally, there are social and cultural implications of the growth in direct investment. Said a Japanese banker in Tokyo: "We are amazed at the way Americans are willing to sell out. In Japan, owners of companies hold on for life."

Surveys have found that the general public is alarmed about the extent of foreign investment in the United States. Some people believe that (1) foreign investment causes America to have less control over the economy, (2) foreign investors might pull their money out at any time, and (3) laws should limit the extent of foreign ownership of American business and real estate.

Questions for Discussion

1. Do you think foreign investors should be limited in their ability to acquire (a) U.S. farmland or (b) majority ownership in defense-related industries? Why or why not?

2. Direct foreign investment may take place through either the acquisition of existing facilities or the building of new ones. From the perspective of the host country, which do you think is preferable? Why?

3. Some observers have argued that foreign direct investment in developing countries should be limited so that the countries may develop their own industries. What is your opinion?

Music: America's Booming Export

As described in Chapter 1, international trade is imperative in today's world because the global nature of today's economy makes economic isolationism impossible. Failure to participate successfully in the global market will reduce a nation's economic influence and standard of living. Full participation can improve the quality of life.

While U.S. exports have not dropped in recent years, U.S. export growth has not kept pace with the total growth of world exports. Firms in economies torn by World War II have reestablished themselves and have obtained a share of the growing world trade for themselves.

Not all news about the U.S. trade position is bad news. An exception to the reduction in demand for American automobiles, steel, and television sets is the world's insatiable appetite for American entertainment. Some estimate that it is the country's second largest export behind aircraft, but ahead of such staples as soybeans and coal.

Foreign sales account for two-thirds of the music market, and there is plenty of room for growth. Deregulation of broadcasting in Europe and around the world is expected to open up new outlets for music to air, and presumably, young consumers will rush to the nearest record store with open wallets.

The industry is particularly interested in the former Soviet Union and China. Michael Jackson's album "Bad" sold half a million albums in China, a figure that looks very attractive to the music industry. The head of a major record company was asked why recorded America sells so well. "If you had an on-street interview any place in the world, and you asked the kid or the 25-year-old to name the first 10 artists that come to mind, I think that at least 6 of those 10 are going to be artists that had their beginnings in the United States," said Robert Summer, president of CBS Records International.

This broad appeal is not just for consumption. It also is attracting foreign companies to purchase U.S. record companies. Bertelsmann, a giant German conglomerate, owns RCA Records. Sony paid $2 billion for CBS Records. Thorn-EMI, which owns Capital Records, is British, and so is Polygram. Only two of the six major record companies are U.S.–owned, MCA and Warner. And while the music industry searches out its next batch of superstars, some worry that those stars and the companies that earn money from them will be foreign. Entertainment executives were asked: will the United States let this business slip offshore as so many other businesses have or is there something uniquely American about this product that will preclude imitations?

"I don't think the creative edge is going to be taken over until our cultural appeal worldwide is superseded," commented Sam Holdsworth, president of Billboard Entertainment Group.

Robert Huziak, president of RCA records, added "I don't think that the United States will ever be without that creative motivation for the young people and hence, we will always be able to continue to grow."

This case was drawn from the Public Broadcasting System's television program "Adam Smith," which aired on March 10, 1989. Producer: Alvin H. Perlmutter,Inc.

Joe Smith, president of Capital-EMI Music, was more pessimistic. He predicted a wave of Russian rock and roll to surface sometime before the end of this century. "Then those guys that make these VCRs and the television sets are soon going to turn creative, and one day somebody in China is going to say 'let's rock'n roll too.' I don't believe we can keep the edge unless we continue to develop our talent and do it," he said. "And that's my concern about the corporatization of rock and roll."

When asked whether the purchase of American record companies by Japanese and German firms will have an impact on the quality of the product, Smith said it depends on the dedication of the companies. "It won't have a great impact on our music unless they squeeze down on us and say, 'Well, don't sign so many new acts next year.' You only keep the edge by signing new talent, by mining what is the best in the country," said Smith. "In this country, a combination of blues and country and rock and roll got started here. We've still got the edge, but we can lose it because all that is very copyable."

"Somebody just with a headset and a CD can pick up every rift that Chuck Berry ever played or Joe Walsh, or Clapton," Smith said. "They can pick all that stuff up very quickly."

Questions for Discussion

1. How can the world demand for U.S.–produced entertainment, particularly in the music industry, have an effect on a macroeconomic level? On a microeconomic level? In your answer, define these two terms.

2. Explain the concept of "global linkages." Describe linkages that could be tied to the music industry on an international basis.

3. Should the United States be concerned about an increasing foreign presence within the American music industry? Why or why not? Will it affect the quality of the product? Explain.

4. What changes have occurred in the U.S. music industry since this PBS program was aired?

P A R T

2

The International Business Environment and Institutions

Operating internationally requires both firms and managers to be aware of a highly complex environment. Domestic and international environmental factors and their interaction have to be recognized and understood. In addition, ongoing changes in these environments have to be appreciated. Furthermore, the international manager must be acquainted with the purpose and activities of major international institutions.

Part 2 delineates the macroenvironmental factors and institutions affecting international business. It also highlights the increasing trend toward economic integration and its effect on international business operations. Finally, it discusses the policy concerns raised by today's changing international environment and institutions.

The International Economic Activity of the Nation: The Balance of Payments

LEARNING OBJECTIVES

1. To understand the fundamental principles of how countries measure international business activity, the Balance of Payments.

2. To examine the similarities of the current and capital accounts of the Balance of Payments.

3. To understand the critical differences between trade in merchandise and services, and why international investment activity has recently been controversial in the United States.

4. To review the mechanical steps of how exchange rate changes are transmitted into altered trade prices and eventually trade volumes.

"U.S. Excels in Service Productivity Poll"

WASHINGTON—U.S. workers in major service industries are more productive than their counterparts overseas—except in restaurants, where the French excel.

A new study by an affiliate of McKinsey & Co., a management consulting firm, concludes that the U.S. edge largely reflects both the way management organizes operations and the degree to which government allows competition to force businesses to be efficient. Workers' skills and the amount of financial investment make surprisingly little difference.

The report by the McKinsey Global Institute was prepared with advice from several economists, including Nobel laureate Robert Solow of the Massachusetts Institute of Technology. The study concludes that "the U.S. has a slightly higher level of overall productivity than Germany and France and a significantly higher level than Japan and the U.K."

Productivity, a measure of how much output is produced for an hour of work, is the key to rising standards of living.

In service industries, which represent a growing share of world employment, productivity is notoriously difficult to measure. The McKinsey report took a case-study approach to evaluate airlines, banks, and restaurants, as well as retailing and telecommunications industries. Japan was included in only the last two categories; Europe was included in all five.

The study urges governments to lower barriers so that new companies can more easily enter service industries; encourage foreign investment, particularly in airlines; relax regulations that prevent firms from laying off workers when technologies or markets change; and aggressively combat anti-competitive practices.

Source: Abstracted from "U.S. Excels in Service Productivity Poll," by David Wesser, *The Wall Street Journal,* October 13, 1992.

International business transactions occur in many different forms over the course of a year. The measurement of all international economic transactions between the residents of a country and foreign residents is called the **Balance of Payments (BOP).**[1] Government policy-makers need such measures of economic activity in order to evaluate the general competitiveness of domestic industry, set exchange-rate or interest-rate policies or goals, and for many other purposes. Individuals and businesses use various BOP measures to gauge the growth and health of specific types of trade or financial transactions by country and regions of the world with the home country.

International transactions take many forms. Each of the following examples is an international economic transaction that is counted and captured in the U.S. balance of payments.

- U.S imports of Honda automobiles, which are manufactured in Japan.
- A U.S.-based firm, Bechtel, is hired to manage the construction of a major water treatment facility in the Middle East.
- The U.S. subsidiary of a French firm, Saint Gobain, pays profits (dividends) back to the parent firm in Paris.
- Daimler-Benz, the well-known German automobile manufacturer, purchases a small automotive-parts manufacturer outside Chicago, Illinois.
- An American tourist purchases a hand-blown glass figurine in Venice, Italy.
- The U.S. government provides grant-financing of military equipment for its NATO (North Atlantic Treaty Organization) military ally, Turkey.
- A Canadian dentist purchases a U.S. Treasury Bill through an investment broker in Cleveland, Ohio.

These are just a small sample of the hundreds of thousands of international transactions that occur each year. The Balance of Payments provides a systematic method for the classification of all of these transactions. There is one rule of thumb that will always aid in the understanding of BOP accounting: watch the direction of the movement of money.

The Balance of Payments is composed of a number of subaccounts that are watched quite closely by investors on Wall Street, farmers in Iowa, politicians on Capitol Hill, and in boardrooms across America. These groups track and analyze the two major subaccounts, the **current account** and the **capital account,** on a continuing basis. Before describing these two subaccounts and the Balance of Payments as a whole, it is necessary to understand the rather unusual features of how Balance of Payments accounting is conducted.

FUNDAMENTALS OF BALANCE OF PAYMENTS ACCOUNTING

The Balance of Payments must balance. If it does not, something has not been counted or counted properly. It is therefore improper to state that the BOP is in disequilibrium. It cannot be. The supply and demand for a country's currency may be imbalanced, but that is not the same thing. Subaccounts of the BOP, such as the merchandise trade balance, may be imbalanced, but the entire BOP of a single country is always balanced.

There are three main elements to the process of measuring international economic activity: (1) identifying what is and is not an international economic transaction; (2) understanding how the flow of goods, services, assets, and money creates debits and credits to the overall BOP; and (3) understanding the bookkeeping procedures for BOP accounting, called double-entry.

Defining International Economic Transactions

Identifying international transactions is ordinarily not difficult. The export of merchandise, goods such as trucks, machinery, computers, telecommunications equipment, and so forth, is obviously an international transaction. Imports such as French wine, Japanese cameras, and German automobiles are also clearly international transactions. But this merchandise trade is only a portion of the thousands of different international transactions that occur in the United States or any other country each year.

Many international transactions are not so obvious. The purchase of a glass figure in Venice, Italy, by an American tourist is classified as a U.S. merchandise import. In fact, all expenditures made by American tourists around the globe that are for goods or services (meals, hotel accommodations, and so forth) are recorded in the U.S. Balance of Payments as imports of travel services in the current account. The purchase of a U.S. Treasury bill by a foreign resident is an international financial transaction and is dutifully recorded in the capital account of the U.S. Balance of Payments.

The BOP as a Flow Statement

The BOP is often misunderstood because many people believe it to be a balance sheet, rather than a cash-flow statement. By recording all international transactions over a period of time, it is tracking the continuing flow of purchases and payments between a country and all other countries. It does not add up the value of all assets and liabilities of a country like a balance sheet does for an individual firm.

There are two types of business transactions that dominate the Balance of Payments:

1. Real Assets. The exchange of goods (for example, automobiles, computers, watches, textiles) and services (for example, banking services, consulting services, travel services) for other goods and services (barter) or for the more common type of payment, money.

2. Financial Assets. The exchange of financial claims (for example, stocks, bonds, loans, purchases or sales of companies) in exchange for other financial claims or money.

Although assets can be separated as to whether they are real or financial, it is often easier to simply think of all assets as being goods that can be bought and sold. An American tourist's purchase of a hand-woven area rug in a shop in Bangkok is not all that different from a Wall Street banker buying a British government bond for investment purposes.

BOP Accounting: Double-Entry Bookkeeping

The Balance of Payments employs an accounting technique called **double-entry bookkeeping.** Double-entry bookkeeping is the age-old method of accounting in which every transaction produces a debit and a credit of the same amount. Simultaneously. It has to. A debit is created whenever an asset is increased, a liability is decreased, or an expense is increased. Similarly, a credit is created whenever an asset is decreased, a liability is increased, or an expense is decreased.

An example clarifies this process. A U.S. retail store imports from Japan $2 million worth of consumer electronics. A negative entry is made in the merchandise-import subcategory of the current account in the amount of $2 million. Simultaneously, a positive entry of the same $2 million is made in the capital account for the transfer of a $2 million bank account to the Japanese manufacturer. Obviously the result of hundreds of thousands of such transactions and entries should theoretically result in a perfect balance.

That said, it is now a problem of application, and a problem it is. The measurement of all international transactions in and out of a country over a year is a daunting task. Mistakes, errors, and statistical discrepancies will occur. The primary problem is that although double-entry bookkeeping is employed in theory, the individual transactions are recorded independently. Current and capital account entries are recorded independently of one another, not together as double-entry bookkeeping would prescribe. It must then be recognized that there will be serious discrepancies (to use a nice term for it) between debits and credits, and the possibility in total that the balance of payments may not balance!

THE ACCOUNTS OF THE BALANCE OF PAYMENTS

In addition to the BOP's two primary subaccounts, the current account and the capital account, the official reserves account tracks government currency transactions, and a fourth statistical subaccount is produced to preserve the balance in the BOP, the net errors and omissions account.

THE CURRENT ACCOUNT

The current account includes all international economic transactions with income or payment flows occurring within the year, the current period. The current account consists of four subcategories:

1. Merchandise Trade. This is the export and import of goods. **Merchandise trade** is the oldest and most traditional form of international economic activity. Although many countries depend on imports of many goods (as they should according to the theory of comparative advantage), they also normally work to preserve either a balance of merchandise trade or even a surplus. As illustrated in Table 3.1, the United States had a deficit of more than $73 billion in merchandise trade in 1991. Even though this is a considerable sum, it is a distinct improvement over the merchandise-trade deficits experienced between 1985 and 1990.

2. Service Trade. This is the export and import of services. Common international services include financial services provided by banks to foreign importers and exporters, travel services of airlines, and construction services of U.S. firms building pipelines or bridges in other countries. For the major industrial countries, this subaccount has shown the fastest growth in the past decade. The United States had gross exports of **service trade** of $163 billion in 1991, service imports of $118 billion, with a balance on service trade of a surplus of $45 billion. The service sector, both in domestic trade and international trade, continues to be a major growth sector for the U.S. economy.

3. Investment Income. This is the current income associated with investments that were made in previous periods. If a U.S. firm created a subsidiary in South Korea to produce metal parts in a previous year, the proportion of net income that is paid back to the parent company this year (the dividend) constitutes current **investment income.** The United States enjoyed a $16 billion surplus in income receipts on prior investments in 1991.

TABLE 3.1
The U.S. Current Account, 1991 (billions of U.S. dollars)

Current Account	1991
Exports of merchandise	416.0
Imports of merchandise	−489.4
Trade balance	−73.4
Exports of services	163.6
Imports of services	−118.3
Service trade balance	45.3
Income receipts on investments	125.3
Income payments on investments	−108.9
Income balance	16.4
Net unilateral transfers	8.0
Balance on current account	−3.7

Source: The International Monetary Fund, *Balance of Payments Statistics Yearbook*, 1992, p. 742.

4. Unilateral Transfers. Any transfer between countries which is one-way, a gift or grant, is termed a **unilateral transfer.** A common example of a uni-lateral transfer would be funds provided by the U.S. government to aid in the development of a less-developed nation. The surplus of $8 billion in unilateral transfers in 1991 is the first surplus in many years in this category of international transactions. The 1991 surplus is primarily a result of payments made by U.S. allies to the United States as a result of the Persian Gulf War.

All countries possess some amount of trade, most of which is merchandise. Many smaller and less-developed countries have little service trade and may also have very little international financial transactions that would be classified under the capital account.

The current account is typically dominated by the first component described, the export and import of merchandise. For this reason, the Balance of Trade (BOT), which is so widely quoted in the business press in most countries, refers specifically to the balance of exports and imports of merchandise trade only. For larger industrialized countries, however, the BOT is somewhat misleading in that service trade is not included, and that trade may actually be fairly large as well. Although the merchandise-trade deficit has been a continuing source of concern for the United States since the early 1980s, the other three major subaccounts of the Current Account should not be ignored. The total Current Account balance, a deficit of $3.7 billion, is a great improvement over what it was in the latter-half of the 1980s.

Merchandise Trade

Figure 3.1 places the current account values of 1991 in perspective over time by dividing the current account into its two major components: (1) merchandise trade and (2) services trade and investment income. The first and most striking message is the suddenness and magnitude with which the merchandise-trade deficit increased beginning in 1982. The balance on services and income, although not large in comparison to net merchandise trade, has with few exceptions run a surplus over the past two decades. The merchandise-trade deficit of the United States hit an all-time high of $160 billion in 1987. The 1988–1991 period, however, has shown a remarkable improvement as U.S. exports have grown at a much more rapid pace than U.S. merchandise imports. The post-1987 period has also seen a surge in the service-trade surplus and net income receipts. By 1991, the U.S. current account was the closest to balanced that it has been since the late 1970s.

The merchandise-trade deficits of the past decade have been an area of considerable concern for the United States, in both the public and private sectors. Merchandise trade is the original core of international trade. The manufacturing of goods was the basis of the Industrial Revolution and the focus of the theory of international trade described in the previous chapter. Manufacturing is traditionally the sector of the economy that employs most of a country's workers. The merchandise-trade deficit of the 1980s saw the decline in traditional heavy industries in the United States, industries that have historically employed many of America's workers. Declines in the net trade balance in areas such as steel, automobiles, automotive parts, textiles, shoe manufacturing, and others have caused massive economic and social disruption. The problems of dealing with these shifting trade balances will be discussed in detail in a later chapter.

The Balance of Payments Based on Components of the Current Account

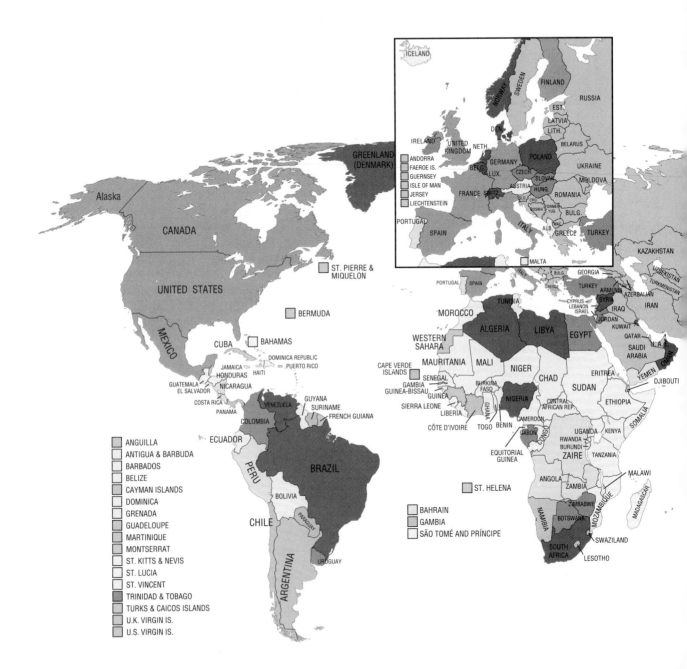

Source: *International Financial Statistics Yearbook*, 1992.

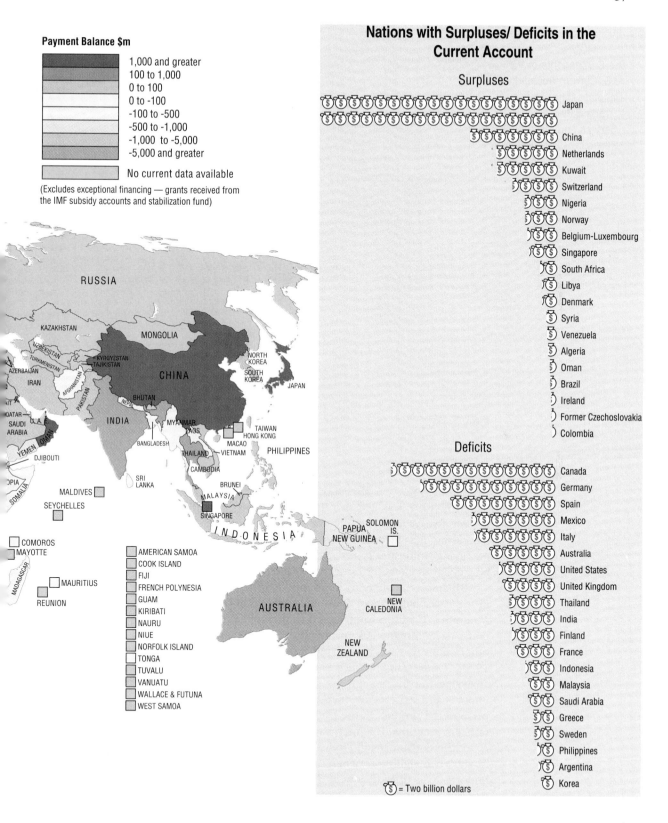

Payment Balance $m

- 1,000 and greater
- 100 to 1,000
- 0 to 100
- 0 to -100
- -100 to -500
- -500 to -1,000
- -1,000 to -5,000
- -5,000 and greater
- No current data available

(Excludes exceptional financing — grants received from the IMF subsidy accounts and stabilization fund)

Nations with Surpluses/ Deficits in the Current Account

Surpluses

Japan, China, Netherlands, Kuwait, Switzerland, Nigeria, Norway, Belgium-Luxembourg, Singapore, South Africa, Libya, Denmark, Syria, Venezuela, Algeria, Oman, Brazil, Ireland, Former Czechoslovakia, Colombia

Deficits

Canada, Germany, Spain, Mexico, Italy, Australia, United States, United Kingdom, Thailand, India, Finland, France, Indonesia, Malaysia, Saudi Arabia, Greece, Sweden, Philippines, Argentina, Korea

$ = Two billion dollars

FIGURE 3.1
The Components of the U.S. Current Account Balance: Merchandise Trade Balance and Service and Income Receipts, 1970–1991

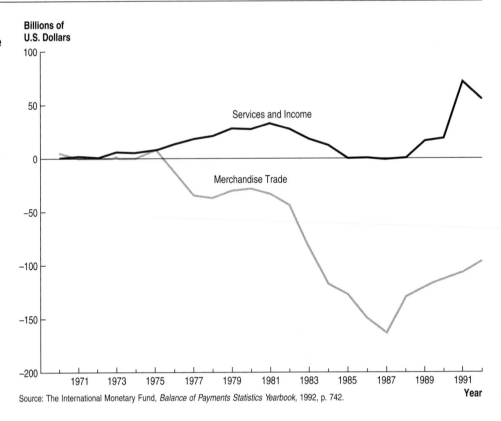

Billions of U.S. Dollars

Source: The International Monetary Fund, *Balance of Payments Statistics Yearbook*, 1992, p. 742.

But as Figure 3.1 also illustrates, all is not negative. First, the merchandise-trade deficit in 1991 was less than half what it was in 1987, an enormous improvement in only five years. Secondly, the resurgence of the U.S. service-sector surplus and increasing net investment-income receipts show internationally what has been occurring domestically for many years, the restructuring of U.S. society from the blue-collar manufacturing sector to the white-collar service sector.[2]

The most encouraging news for U.S. manufacturing trade is the growth of exports in the latter half of the 1980s and early years of the 1990s as shown in Figure 3.2. A number of factors contributed to the growth of U.S. exports, such as the weaker dollar (which made U.S. manufactured goods cheaper in terms of the currencies of other countries) and more rapid economic growth in Europe in the latter part of the 1980s. Understanding merchandise import-and-export performance is much like analyzing the market for any single product. The demand factors that drive both imports and exports are income, the economic growth rate of the buyer, and the price of the product in the eyes of the consumer after passing through an exchange rate. For example, U.S. merchandise imports reflect the income level and growth of American consumers and industry. As income rises, so does the demand for imports. As shown in Figure 3.2, when the United States came out of the 1981–1982 recession, imports rose dramatically as the U.S. economy recovered. Of course supply-side factors, such as the cost of production and the eventual cost of the product, are also important. Many experts argue that in the early to middle 1980s the U.S. economy

FIGURE 3.2
U.S. Merchandise
Imports and Exports,
1970–1991

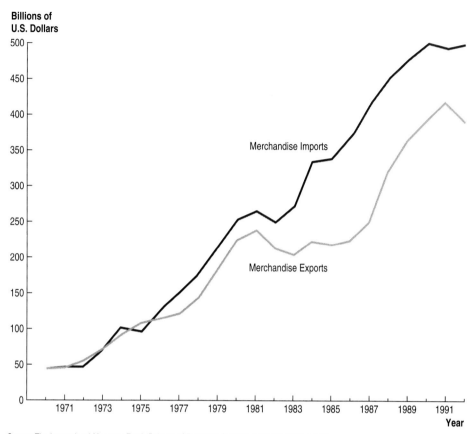

Source: The International Monetary Fund, *Balance of Payments Statistics Yearbook,* 1992, p. 742.

had no reasonably priced competitive products for much of the merchandise that was imported in larger and larger volumes.

Exports follow the same principles but in the reversed position. U.S. manufacturing exports depend not on the incomes of U.S. residents, but on the incomes of buyers of U.S. products in all other countries. The major markets for U.S. exports are the industrialized nations such as Canada, Japan, and western Europe. When these economies are growing, the demand for U.S. products rises. The rapid growth of the western European economies in the later 1980s, as well as the falling dollar making U.S. products relatively cheaper to European consumers, aided greatly in the growth of U.S. merchandise exports beginning in 1987.

The merchandise exports of the United States are normally subdivided into agricultural products and nonagricultural products. In 1991, more than $40 billion worth of exports, approximately 10 percent, were agricultural products. Agricultural and nonagricultural exports are separated for a variety of reasons. First, agricultural exports have been a strength of the U.S. economy for a very long time. The agricultural sector was probably the most "internationalized" sector of the U.S. economy. Secondly, because agricultural products are subject to random supply-side disturbances, such as the impact of weather on crop production, these products experience very volatile price movements from year to year, month to month, and

**FIGURE 3.3
U.S. Imports and
Exports of Services**

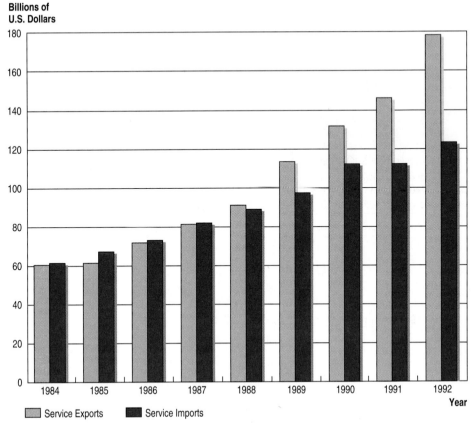

Source: The International Monetary Fund, *Balance of Payments Statistics Yearbook*, 1992, p. 742.

even day to day. Nonagricultural merchandise exports are industrial and consumer goods. This sector has suffered the majority of the declines in relative competitiveness and trade balance in the past decade.

U.S. merchandise imports are subdivided into petroleum products and non-petroleum products. For example, in 1991 the U.S. imported $51.2 billion worth of petroleum products (10 percent of total merchandise imports) while non-petroleum products totaled $438 billion. Petroleum imports are kept track of separately because of the impact this one commodity has on U.S. imports as a whole. The fact that U.S. consumption of petroleum and petroleum products is insensitive to price changes, its so-called price inelasticity, makes the distinction between petroleum imports and all other imports important for government policy-makers.

The service component of the U.S. current account is one of mystery to many. Figure 3.3 shows the recent growth in total U.S. service imports and exports, but also the much-appreciated increasing surplus in the U.S. service-trade balance. The major categories of services include travel and passenger fares, transportation services, expenditures by U.S. students abroad and foreign students pursuing studies in the United States, telecommunications services, and financial services.

The remaining components of the current account, net investment income and unilateral transfers, both enjoyed net surpluses in 1991. As detailed in Global

Global Perspective

3.1
Unilateral Transfers and the Persian Gulf War

The United States has for many years run a net deficit in unilateral transfers. This is mostly a result of military and development aid in the form of gifts and grants made to foreign governments. Operation Desert Storm, the war in the Persian Gulf which started with a military build-up by the United States in September 1990 and culminated with the initiation of hostilities in January 1991, represented an enormous expenditure by the U.S. government. As part of their support for the anti-Iraqi coalition, the countries of Kuwait, Saudi Arabia, the United Arab Emirates, Japan, Germany, Korea, Belgium, and Norway contributed more than $17 billion in the first quarter of 1991 alone. This was the first net surplus in unilateral transfers in more than two decades.

Source: Abstracted from "U.S. International Transactions, Fourth Quarter and Year 1991," *Survey of Current Business*, March 1992, p. 67.

TABLE 3.2
The U.S. Capital Account, 1991 (billions of U.S. dollars)

Capital Account	1991
Direct investment in United States	11.50
Direct investment abroad	−27.15
Net direct investment	−15.65
Net portfolio investment	5.44
Other long-term and short-term capital	
	−7.56
Balance on capital account	−17.77

Source: The International Monetary Fund, *Balance of Payments Yearbook*, 1992, p. 742.

Perspective 3.1, the net surplus on unilateral transfers was primarily a result of payments from U.S. allies for expenses incurred in the Persian Gulf War.

THE CAPITAL ACCOUNT

The Capital Account of the balance of payments measures all international transactions of financial assets. Financial assets can be classified in a number of different ways, including the length of the life of the asset (its maturity), by nature of the ownership (public or private), or by the degree of control over assets or operations that the claim represents (portfolio, with no control, or direct investment, with some degree of control).

Table 3.2 shows the major subcategories of the U.S. Capital Account balance for 1991, **direct investment, portfolio investment,** and other long-term and short-term capital.

1. Direct Investment. This is the net balance of capital that flows out of and into the United States for the purpose of exerting control over assets. For example, if a U.S. firm either builds a new automotive-parts facility in another country (Ford built a fuel-handling-part facility in Hungary) or pur-

Direct investments are those of an expected maturity value exceeding one year, with an investor ownership of at least 10 percent. The Sony Corporation's 1989 purchase of Columbia Pictures Entertainment Inc., producers of the hit movie *A Few Good Men,* represented a $3.4 billion investment in a U.S.–owned corporation by the Japanese firm.

Source: Columbia Tristar Film/Shooting Star.

chases a company in another country, this would fall under direct investment. When the capital flows out of the United States, as in the two examples just used, it enters the Balance of Payments as a negative cash flow. If, however, foreign firms purchase firms in the United States (for example, Sony of Japan purchased Columbia Pictures in 1989), it is a capital inflow and enters the Balance of Payments positively. Whenever 10 percent or more of the voting shares in a U.S. company are held by foreign investors, the company is classified as the U.S. affiliate of a foreign company and a foreign direct investment. Similarly, if U.S. investors hold 10 percent or more of the control in a company outside the United States, that company is considered the foreign affiliate of a U.S. company. The United States experienced a deficit of $15.65 billion in direct investment in 1991.

2. Portfolio Investment. This is net balance of capital that flows in and out of the United States but that does not reach the 10 percent ownership threshold of direct investment. If a U.S. resident purchases shares in a Japanese firm but does not attain the 10 percent threshold, it is considered a portfolio investment (and in this case an outflow of capital). The purchase or sale of debt securities (like U.S. Treasury Bills or bonds) across borders is always classified as portfolio investment because debt securities by definition do not provide the buyer with ownership or control. Net portfolio investment for the United States was a positive $5.44 billion in 1991.

3. Other Long-Term and Short-Term Capital. This category consists of various bank loans extended by U.S. resident banking operations as well as net borrowing by U.S. firms from financial institutions outside the United States. The net balance on other long-term capital in 1991 was $13.15 billion, with net deficit on other short-term capital of $20.71 billion.

Direct Investment

Figure 3.4 shows how the two major subaccounts of the U.S. capital account, net direct investment and portfolio investment, have changed since 1980. Net direct investment started the 1980s with a slight deficit in 1980 but showed a surplus every year between 1981 and 1990. The balance on net direct investment went negative

FIGURE 3.4   **U.S. Capital Account Components, 1974–1991: Net Direct Investment and Net Portfolio Investment**

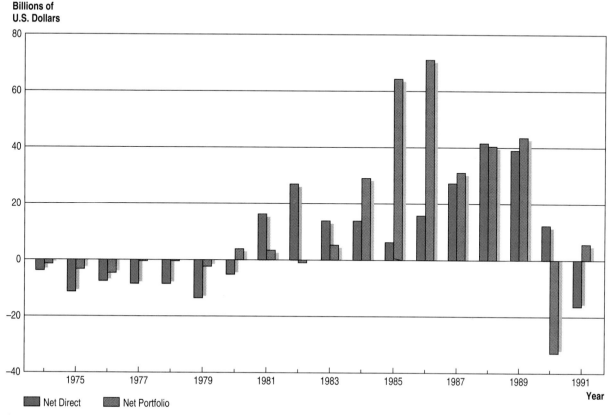

Source: The International Monetary Fund, *Balance of Payments Statistics Yearbook*, 1992, p. 742.

in 1991 for the first time in a decade. It appears the world's enthusiasm for the acquisition of U.S. firms and other foreign-controlled investment (direct investment) in the United States has waned.

The boom in foreign investment in the United States during the 1980s was, however, extremely controversial. Historically it has typically been the case that U.S. firms invested abroad. The rapid growth of the U.S. economy and the expansion of many U.S. firms to build manufacturing, mining, refining, and many other industrial facilities around the world had become the norm. With the 1980s came a complete reversal in the direction of these net capital flows. Foreign investors were pouring more long-term capital into the United States than U.S. firms invested abroad. Many Americans worried about this increasing foreign presence in the U.S. marketplace, not just in selling products to U.S. consumers as has become so common with merchandise imports, but with foreign investors actually exercising significant control over U.S. firms, U.S. workers, and U.S. assets.

The source of concern over foreign investment in any country, including the United States, normally focuses on one of two major topics, control and profit. Most countries have restrictions on what foreigners may own. This is based on the premise that domestic land, assets, and industry in general should be held by residents of the

Global Perspective

3.2
"They Don't Let Just Anyone Buy a Defense Contractor"

Alain Gomez, the dapper chairman of France's Thomson-CSF, lined up some of the best string-pullers money can buy to help acquire bankrupt LTV Corp.'s missile business. The defense-electronics giant, 58%-owned by the French government, joined with the Carlyle Group, a well-connected Washington investment bank whose vice-chairman is former Defense Secretary Frank C. Carlucci. For public relations, Gomez tapped Carter Administration Press Secretary Jody Powell's high-powered spin-ship, Powell Tate, as well as a legion of K Street lawyers.

But the pricey talent couldn't overcome the volatile politics of selling sensitive U.S. defense assets to foreigners, particularly in an election year. On July 5, Thomson withdrew its $450 million joint bid with Carlyle to buy LTV's missile and aircraft businesses. Small wonder. The U.S. defense establishment carried out a blistering behind-the-scenes assault on Thomson over its status as a French government holding and its past business dealings with Iraq.

Even if Thomson can pull together a new proposal, it will still face heated opposition from Martin Marietta Corp. and Lockheed Corp., whose rival $385 million offer lost out to the French in April. Martin Marietta Chairman Norman R. Augustine objects to Thomson's taking even a minority stake. Augustine has friends in high places: He was on Bush's short list of potential Defense Secretaries back in 1988.

Ironically, Thomson's association with the Carlyle Group also hurt the deal. Roughly one-third of the $150 million Carlyle planned to put up for LTV's aircraft unit was bankrolled by state-backed Credit Lyonnais. So the group was viewed as "a front" for the French government, says an Administration source. Such rough treatment speaks volumes about the U.S. defense industry's inevitable post-cold-war consolidation. Foreigners serious about buying their way in had better be combat-ready.

Source: "They Don't Let Just Anyone Buy A Defense Contractor," by Brian Bremner, Seth Payne, and Jonathan B. Levine, *Business Week,* July 20, 1992, pp. 41-42.

country. For example, until 1990 it was not possible for a foreign firm to own more than 20 percent of any company in Finland. And this is the norm, rather than the exception. The United States has traditionally had few restrictions on what foreign residents or firms can own or control in the United States, with most restrictions remaining today being related to national-security concerns (as illustrated in Global Perspective 3.2). As opposed to many of the traditional debates over whether international trade should be free or not, there is not the same consensus for unrestricted international investment. This is a question that is still very much a domestic political concern first and an international economic issue second.

The second major source of concern over foreign direct investment is who ultimately receives the profits from the enterprise. Foreign companies owning firms in the United States will ultimately profit from the activities of the firms, or put another way, from the efforts of American workers. In spite of evidence that indicates foreign firms in the United States reinvest most of the profits in the United States (in fact, at a higher rate than domestic firms), the debate has continued on possible profit drains. Regardless of the choices made, workers of any nation usually feel the profits of their work should remain in the hands of their own countrymen. Once again, this is in many ways a political and emotional concern more than an economic one.

A final note regarding the massive capital inflows into the United States in the 1980s. The choice of which words are used to describe this increasing foreign investment can alone influence public opinion. If these massive capital inflows are described as "capital investments from all over the world showing their faith in the future of American industry," the net capital surplus is represented as decidedly positive. If, however, the net capital surplus is described as resulting in "the United States as the world's largest debtor nation," the negative connotation is obvious. But which, if either, is correct? The answer is actually quite simple. Capital, whether short-term or long-term, flows to where it believes it can earn the greatest return for the level of risk. And although in an accounting sense this is "international debt," when the majority of the capital inflow is in the form of direct investment, a long-term commitment to jobs, production, services, technological, and other competitive investments, the competitiveness of American industry (industry located within the United States) is increased. The "net debtor" label is also misleading in that it invites comparison with large "debtor-nations" like Mexico and Brazil. But unlike Mexico and Brazil, the majority of this foreign investment is not bank loans that will have to be paid back in regular installments over 8 to 10 years, and it is not bank loans denominated in a currency that is foreign. Mexico and Brazil owe U.S. dollars; the United States "owes" U.S. dollars. Therefore, the profitability of the industry and the economy in the United States will be the source of repaying the investments.

Portfolio Investment

Portfolio investment is capital that is invested in activities that are purely profit-motivated (return), rather than ones made in the prospect of controlling or managing or directing the investment. Investments that are purchases of debt securities, bonds, interest-bearing bank accounts, and the like are only intended to earn a return. They provide no vote or control over the party issuing the debt. Purchase of debt issued by the U.S. government, U.S. Treasury Bills, notes, and bonds, by foreign investors constitute net portfolio investment in the United States.

As illustrated in Figure 3.4 portfolio investment has shown a similar pattern to net direct investment over the past decade. Many U.S. debt securities, such as U.S. Treasury securities and corporate bonds, were in high demand throughout the 1980s. The primary reason for the surge in net portfolio investment resulted from two different forces, return and risk.

In the early 1980s, interest rates were quite high in the United States, the result of high inflation in the late 1970s and the "tight money policy" (slow money-supply growth) of the U.S. Federal Reserve. The rate of inflation fell rapidly in the early 1980s, while interest rates did not. This resulted in very high "real rates" of interest (interest less inflation), which was much higher than what could be earned in many other nations. Capital flowed into the U.S. economy in order to take advantage of these relatively high **real returns.**

At the same time, many of the major industrial countries were suffering prolonged recessions or very slow economic growth. This meant that profitable investments for capital were hard to find. And many of the major borrower countries, like Mexico and Brazil, were turning out to be bad borrowers, unable to repay their debts. Capital was therefore looking for a **safe haven,** a place where the political and economic systems were dependable and secure. The safe haven for world capital in the early to middle 1980s was the United States.

As shown in Figure 3.4, the balance on portfolio investment was positive for every year between 1980 and 1989, except for a slight deficit in 1982. The net surplus

Global Perspective

3.3
Bilateral Trade and Investment: The United States and Japan

The poor merchandise-trade performance of the United States combined with the enormous merchandise-trade surplus of Japan in the 1980s created a very precarious relationship between the two industrial powers. The world economy performs much in the same fashion as a large plumbing system, recirculating the water or money of the system continuously. Trade and capital are the manifestations of money flows. While Japan ran substantial merchandise-trade surpluses with the United States in the 1980s, Japan also "recirculated" much of the capital by investing the U.S. dollar earnings back into the U.S. economy. These capital flows dried up in 1990 and 1991 as Japanese capital was needed at home to meet new bank capital requirements and to support firms with declining earnings.

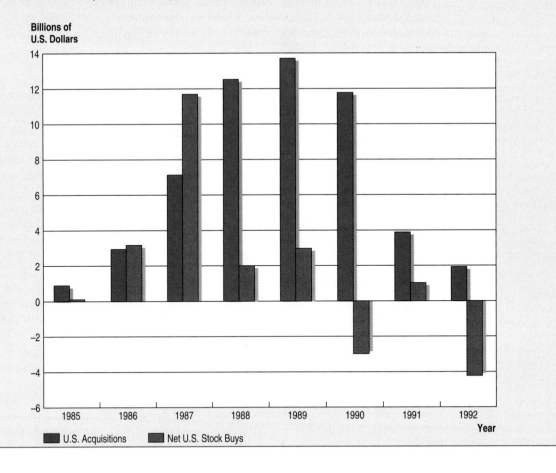

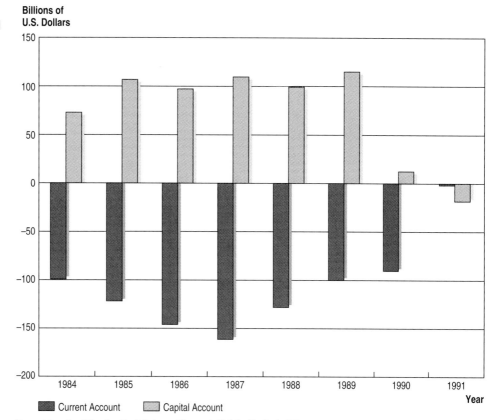

Source: International Monetary Fund, *Balance of Payments Statistics Yearbook,* 1992, p. 742.

Japan's Current and
Capital Account
Balances, 1984–1991
(billions of U.S. dollars)

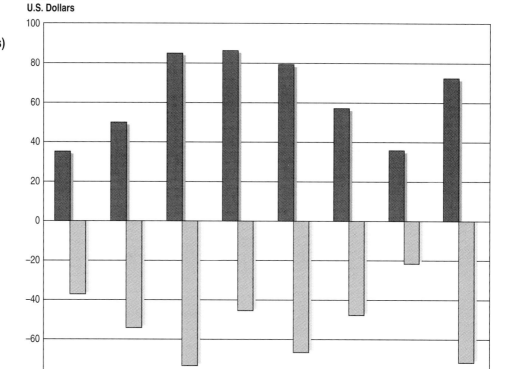

Source: The International Monetary Fund, *Balance of Payments Statistics Yearbook,* 1992, p. 365.

of portfolio investment peaked in 1986 at more than $70 billion. By 1990, however, interest rates and other motivations for portfolio investment in the United States had waned, as did the flow of portfolio investment. The balance on portfolio investment in 1990 saw a massive shift to the negative, with a net outflow of capital of approximately $30 billion. In 1991 it returned to a slight surplus once again, this time approximately $5 billion. Global Perspective 3.3 provides one bilateral example of how portfolio investment changes over time; in this case between the United States and Japan.

Current and Capital Account-Balance Relationships

Figure 3.5 illustrates the current and capital account balances for both the United States and Japan in recent years. What the figure shows is one of the basic economic and accounting relationships of the Balance of Payments: the inverse relation between the current and capital accounts. This inverse relationship is not accidental. The methodology of the Balance of Payments, double-entry bookkeeping, requires that the current and capital accounts be offsetting.

The U.S. current account deficits of the 1980s, resulting primarily from massive merchandise-trade deficits, were "financed" by equally large surpluses in the capital account. This is the typical way it is represented: current account activities cause capital account entries. There are experts who believe, however, that it could very well be the other way around. The truth is probably some combination of the two.

The last year for which Balance of Payments data are available, 1991, shows a return to the magnitudes more common in the 1970s, when net capital and current account balances were roughly zero. Japan, however, experienced the opposite combination: a surplus current account balance with a deficit capital account balance.

NET ERRORS AND OMISSIONS

As noted before, because current account and capital account entries are collected and recorded separately, errors or statistical discrepancies will occur. The net errors and omissions account (the title used by the International Monetary Fund) makes sure that the BOP actually balances.

For the United States the size of the net errors and omissions account has varied substantially over recent times. The United States recorded surpluses in "errors" of $27 billion and $20 billion in 1984 and 1985, but in the years following fell to substantially smaller amounts. However, 1990 saw a sudden net surplus again in "errors" of more than $47 billion. There are a variety of potential explanations for this, including underreporting of exports and the underground or illegal economy's impacts on the flows of asset values across borders.

OFFICIAL RESERVES ACCOUNT

The **official reserves account** is the total currency and metallic reserves held by official monetary authorities within the country. These reserves are normally composed of the major currencies used in international trade and financial transactions (so-called "hard currencies" like the U.S. dollar, German mark, Japanese yen, British pound, Swiss franc, French franc, and Canadian dollar) and gold.

The significance of official reserves depends generally on whether the country is operating under a fixed-exchange-rate regime or a floating-exchange-rate system. If a country's currency is fixed, this means that the government of the country officially declares that the currency is convertible into a fixed amount of some other currency. For example, for many years the South Korean won was fixed to the U.S. dollar at 484 won equal to 1 U.S. dollar. If the exchange rate is fixed, the government accepts responsibility for maintaining this fixed rate (also called parity rate). If for some reason there is an excess of Korean won on the currency market, to prevent the value of the won from falling, the South Korean government must "support the won." Supporting a currency is identical to supporting any price, to push a price up you must increase demand. Under these conditions the South Korean government would go to the currency markets and purchase its own currency until it eliminated the excess supply. But what does the South Korean government use to purchase South Korean won? Other major currencies like the dollar, the mark, the yen, or even gold. Therefore, in order for a country with a fixed exchange rate to be able to support its own currency, the country needs to maintain substantial reserves of foreign currencies and gold, official reserves.

As will be discussed in Chapters 4 and 5, many countries still use fixed-exchange-rate systems. For them it is still critically important to maintain official reserves in sufficient quantity to support their own currencies in case of need. However, many of the major industrial countries, such as the United States and Japan, no longer operate under fixed exchange rates. For these countries, holdings of official reserves are not as critically important and have, in fact, declined substantially over the past two decades in proportion to the volume of international trade and investment.

In 1991 the United States and several other major countries agreed that their holdings of foreign currencies were excessive and agreed to reduce them. The United States reduced the level of its official foreign reserves by buying dollars with these foreign currencies.

THE BALANCE OF PAYMENTS IN TOTAL

Table 3.3 provides the official Balance of Payments as presented by the International Monetary Fund (IMF), the multinational organization which collects these statistics for over 160 countries. Now that the individual accounts and the relationships between the accounts have been discussed, Table 3.3 allows an overview of how the individual accounts are combined to create useful summary measures.

The current account (line A in Table 3.3) and the long-term capital account (line B in Table 3.3) together constitute the **basic balance.** This is one of the most frequently used summary measures of the BOP to describe the international economic activity of the nation which is determined by market forces, and not by government decisions (such as currency market intervention). The United States basic balance deficit totaled only −$.75 billion in 1991 (current account balance of −$3.69 billion plus a long-term capital account balance of +$2.94 billion). Compared to the basic balances for the previous years (1990, −$88.46 billion; 1989, −$15.62 billion), this was a remarkable improvement.

A second summary measure is the overall balance, or **official settlements balance** as it is often termed. The overall balance is the sum of the current account (line A in Table 3.3), capital accounts (short-term and long-term, lines B and C), and net errors and omissions accounts (line D). The United States' overall balance in 1991 was a deficit of $22.58 billion. This is an obvious change from the basic balance, the

TABLE 3.3

TABLE 3.3 — The U.S. Balance of Payments: Aggregated Presentation, Transactions Data, 1984–1991*

	1984	1985	1986	1987	1988	1989	1990	1991
A. Current Account, excl. Group E	−98.99	−122.25	−145.42	−160.20	−126.37	−101.20	−90.46	−3.69
Merchandise: exports f.o.b.	219.90	215.93	223.36	250.28	320.34	361.67	388.71	415.96
Agricultural products	*38.40*	*29.57*	*27.36*	*29.55*	*38.25*	*42.19*	*40.18*	*40.13*
Other	*181.50*	*186.36*	*196.00*	*220.73*	*282.09*	*319.48*	*348.53*	*375.83*
Merchandise: imports f.o.b.	−332.41	−338.09	−368.41	−409.77	−447.31	−477.38	−497.55	−489.40
Petroleum and related products	*−57.32*	*−50.39*	*−34.39*	*−42.94*	*−39.63*	*−50.92*	*−62.30*	*−51.18*
Other	*−275.09*	*−287.70*	*−334.02*	*−366.83*	*−407.68*	*−426.46*	*−435.25*	*−438.22*
Trade balance	−112.51	−122.16	−145.05	−159.49	−126.97	−115.71	−108.84	−73.44
Services: credit	60.79	61.86	72.26	81.81	91.50	113.91	132.02	145.71
Services: debit	−62.11	−67.06	−73.20	−82.66	−89.06	−97.69	−112.35	−113.21
Income: credit	98.66	88.35	88.34	99.71	121.63	153.88	160.15	143.25
Reinvested earnings	*17.22*	*14.11*	*10.02*	*19.71*	*13.33*	*14.77*	*19.48*	*17.89*
Other investment income	*75.73*	*68.16*	*70.95*	*70.82*	*97.32*	*125.93*	*124.08*	*107.44*
Other	*5.71*	*6.08*	*7.37*	*9.18*	*10.98*	*13.18*	*16.59*	*17.92*
Income: debit	−71.21	−67.76	−71.88	−85.24	−108.42	−129.98	−128.50	−113.99
Reinvested earnings	*−2.91*	*1.37*	*2.30*	*.86*	*−2.82*	*8.52*	*16.28*	*20.05*
Other investment income	*−66.66*	*−67.51*	*−72.30*	*−83.79*	*−102.51*	*−134.87*	*−140.54*	*−128.92*
Other	*−1.64*	*−1.62*	*−1.88*	*−2.31*	*−3.09*	*−3.63*	*−4.24*	*−5.12*
Total: goods, services, and income	−86.38	−106.77	−129.53	−145.87	−111.32	−75.59	−57.52	−11.68
Private unrequited transfers	−1.77	−2.06	−1.86	−1.84	−1.76	−12.32	−12.39	−12.99
Total, excl. official unrequited transfers	−88.15	−108.83	−131.39	−147.71	−113.08	−87.91	−69.91	−24.67
Official unrequited transfers	−10.84	−13.42	−14.03	−12.49	−13.29	−13.29	−20.55	20.98
Grants (excluding military)	*−8.68*	*−11.28*	*−11.87*	*−10.28*	*−10.74*	*−10.77*	*−21.86*	*−18.08*
Other	*−2.16*	*−2.14*	*−2.16*	*−2.21*	*−2.55*	*−2.52*	*1.31*	*39.06*
B. Direct Investment and Other Long-Term Capital, excl. Groups E through G	29.94	78.32	81.86	57.52	93.48	85.58	2.00	2.94
Direct investment	13.97	5.86	15.39	27.10	41.54	38.87	12.45	−15.65
In United States	*25.55*	*19.03*	*34.08*	*58.14*	*59.42*	*67.87*	*45.14*	*11.50*
Abroad	*−11.58*	*−13.17*	*−18.69*	*−31.04*	*−17.88*	*−29.00*	*−32.69*	*−27.15*
Portfolio investment	28.76	64.43	71.60	31.06	40.31	43.50	−33.00	5.44

*In billions of U.S. dollars.

Source: The International Monetary Fund, *Balance of Payments Statistics Yearbook,* 1992, p. 742.

majority of the increased deficit resulting from the balance on short-term capital, which was at a deficit of $20.71 billion in 1991.

The remaining accounts of the Balance of Payments—exceptional financing ("E"), liabilities constituting foreign authorities' reserves ("F"), and U.S. reserves ("G")—are largely measures of official government transactions. Because these balances and values are largely a result of public policy, and do not necessarily reflect the economic forces at work upon a nation's international economic activity, they are not used as frequently to characterize a country's BOP.

The meaning of "the Balance of Payments" has changed over the past 25 years. As long as most of the major industrial countries were still operating under fixed exchange rates, the interpretation of the BOP was relatively straightforward. A surplus in the BOP implied that the demand for the country's currency exceeded the supply, and the government should either allow the currency value to increase (revalue) or intervene and accumulate additional foreign currency reserves in the Official Reserves Account. This would occur as the government sold its own currency in exchange for other currencies, thus building up its stores of hard currencies. A deficit in the BOP implied an excess supply of the country's currency on world markets, and the government would then either devalue the currency or expend its official reserves to support its value.

		1984	1985	1986	1987	1988	1989	1990	1991
	Other long-term capital								
	Resident official sector	−4.25	−.97	−.47	−1.26	1.05	2.43	3.70	6.45
	Disbursements on loans extended	−7.80	−5.90	−7.14	−4.85	−5.82	−3.93	−6.65	−10.11
	Repayments on loans extended	4.07	4.30	5.65	7.19	9.92	6.29	10.36	16.04
	Other	−.52	.63	1.02	−3.60	−3.05	.07	−.01	.52
	Deposit money banks	−8.54	9.00	−4.66	.62	10.58	.78	18.85	6.70
	Other sectors	—	—	—	—	—	—	—	—
	Total, Groups A plus B	−69.05	−43.93	−63.56	−102.68	−32.89	−15.62	−88.46	−.75
C.	Other Short-Term Capital, excl. Groups E								
	through G	42.58	29.86	13.92	52.54	5.75	30.12	11.19	−20.71
	Residential official sector	1.57	−1.44	−.52	−1.96	−.15	1.80	3.77	−.71
	Deposit money banks	27.54	24.30	26.76	45.88	5.49	10.91	−1.05	−14.81
	Other sectors	13.47	7.00	−12.32	8.62	.41	17.41	8.47	−5.19
D.	Net Errors and Omissions	27.19	19.87	15.86	−6.72	−9.13	2.43	47.46	−1.12
	Total, Groups A through D	.72	5.80	−33.78	−56.86	−36.27	16.93	−29.81	−22.58
E.	Exceptional Financing	—	—	—	—	—	—	—	—
	Total, Groups A through E	.72	5.80	−33.78	−56.86	−36.27	16.93	−29.81	−22.58
F.	Liabilities Constituting Foreign Authorities'								
	Reserves	2.41	−1.96	33.46	47.72	40.19	8.34	32.04	16.82
	Total, Groups A through F	3.13	3.84	−.32	−9.14	3.92	25.27	2.23	−5.76
G.	Reserves	−3.13	−3.84	.32	9.14	−3.92	−25.27	−2.23	5.76
	Monetary gold	—	.01	.01	—	—	.01	—	—
	SDRs	−.98	−.90	−.25	−.51	.13	−.53	−.20	−.18
	Reserve position in the Fund	−1.00	.91	1.50	2.07	1.02	.47	.66	−.37
	Foreign exchange assets	−1.15	−3.86	−.94	7.58	−5.07	−25.22	−2.70	6.31
	Other claims	—	—	—	—	—	—	—	—
	Use of Fund credit and loans	—	—	—	—	—	—	—	—
	Memorandum items								
	Total change in reserves	−.97	−8.21	−5.11	2.58	−1.79	−26.81	−8.68	5.61
	of which: revaluations	2.15	−4.37	−5.43	−6.56	2.13	−1.55	−6.45	−.15

But the major industrial nations such as Japan, the United States, and Germany are no longer operating in a world of fixed exchange rates. Now major industrial governments and other authorities no longer refer to the Balance of Payments for their country, but instead monitor and measure balances on trade, current account, net direct and portfolio investments, and sometimes basic balances.

BALANCE OF PAYMENTS DYNAMICS

The two major subaccounts of the BOP, the current and capital accounts, are watched individually for the magnitude of their imbalances, if imbalanced. However, it is not at all clear that they should be balanced individually or that a balance in either (actually if one is balance the other must be) is desirable.

Although economists do not really agree on what is best or what is sustainable, the bilateral relationship between the United States and Japan serves to demonstrate the trade-offs. The United States ran substantial current-account deficits and capital-account surpluses throughout the 1980s. Japan ran sizable current-account surpluses and capital-account deficits over the same period. And much of these respective imbalances were with each other (bilateral). But which is better off? There is no clear answer to this. Many have argued that the U.S. current-account deficit, more specifically the U.S. merchandise-trade deficit, was unsustainable. But this also allowed massive capital inflows into the United States aiding in the expansion and modernization of many industries.

Merchandise-Trade and Exchange-Rate Dynamics

Merchandise trade, exports and imports, is sensitive to exchange-rate changes. Many countries in the not too distant past have intentionally devalued their currencies to make their export products more competitive on world markets. These competitive devaluations, however, are normally considered self-destructive because although they do make export products relatively cheaper, they also make imports relatively more expensive. So what is the logic of intentionally devaluing the domestic currency to improve the trade balance?

A country typically devalues its currency as a result of persistent and sizable trade deficits. Economic analysis has usually characterized the trade-balance-adjustment process as occurring in three stages: (1) the currency-contract period, (2) the pass-through period, and (3) the quantity-adjustment period.

In the first period, a sudden unexpected devaluation of the domestic currency has a somewhat uncertain impact, simply because all of the contracts for exports and imports are already in effect. Firms operating under these agreements are required to fulfill their obligations, regardless of whether they profit or suffer losses. If the United States experienced a sudden fall in the value of the U.S. dollar (as occurred in the 1985–1987 period) and most exports were priced in U.S. dollars but most imports were contracts denominated in foreign currency, the result of a sudden depreciation would be an increase in the size of the trade deficit. This is because the cost to U.S. importers of "paying their bills" would rise (as they spent more and more dollars to buy the foreign currency they needed), while the revenues earned by U.S. exporters would remain unchanged. Although this is the commonly cited scenario regarding trade-balance adjustment, there is little reason to believe that most U.S. imports are denominated in foreign currency and most exports in U.S. dollars.

Global Perspective

3.4
A Rose by Any Other Name: The Terminology of the BOP

Measures of the international economic activity of the nation have been known to go by a variety of aliases. The two major institutions that measure the international transactions of the United States, the International Monetary Fund and the U.S. Department of Commerce, use very different names for the same measurements.

International Monetary Fund

Balance of Payments
Errors and Omissions
Balance on International Indebtness

U.S. Department of Commerce

Balance on International Transactions
Statistical Discrepancy
International Investment Position of the U.S.

The second period of the trade-balance adjustment process is termed the pass-through period. As exchange rates change, importers and exporters eventually must **pass** these exchange-rate changes **through** to their own product prices. For example, a foreign producer selling to the U.S. market after a major fall in the value of the U.S. dollar will have to cover its own domestic costs of production. This will require that the firm charge higher dollar prices in order to earn its own local currency in large enough quantities. The firm must raise its prices in the U.S. market. Import prices rise substantially, eventually passing through the full exchange-rate changes into prices. American consumers see higher import-product prices on the shelf. Similarly, the U.S. export prices are now cheaper compared to foreign competitors' because the dollar is cheaper. Unfortunately for U.S. exporters, many of their inputs may be imported, causing them also to suffer slightly rising prices after the fall of the dollar.

The third and final period, the quantity-adjustment period, achieves the balance of trade adjustment that is expected from a domestic currency devaluation or depreciation. As the import and export prices change as a result of the pass-through period, consumers both in the United States and in the U.S. export markets adjust their demands to the new prices. Imports are relatively more expensive, therefore the quantity demanded decreases. Exports are relatively cheaper, and therefore the quantity of exports rises. The balance of trade, the expenditures on exports less the expenditures on imports, improves.

Unfortunately these three adjustment periods do not occur overnight. Countries like the United States that have experienced major exchange-rate changes also have seen this adjustment take place over a prolonged period. Often, before the adjustment is completed, new exchange-rate changes occur, frustrating the total adjustment process. Trade adjustment to exchange-rate changes does not occur in a sterile laboratory environment, but in the messy and complex world of international business and economic events. And as detailed in Global Perspective 3.4, even the terminology of BOP accounting is a mess.

SUMMARY

The Balance of Payments is the summary statement of all international transactions between one country and all other countries. The Balance of Payments is a flow statement, summarizing all the international transactions that occur across the geographic boundaries of the nation over a period of time, typically a year. Because of its use of double–entry bookkeeping, the BOP must always balance in theory, though in practice there are substantial imbalances as a result of statistical errors and misreporting of current account and capital account flows.

The two major subaccounts of the Balance of Payments, the current account and the capital account, summarize the current trade and international capital flows of the country. Because of the method of accounting, double-entry bookkeeping, the current account and capital account are always inverse on balance, one in surplus while the other experiences deficit. Although most nations strive for current account surpluses, it is not clear that a balance on current or capital account, or a surplus on current account, is either sustainable or desirable. The monitoring of the various subaccounts of a country's Balance-of-Payments activity is helpful to decision-makers and policy-makers at all levels of government and industry in detecting the underlying trends and movements of fundamental economic forces driving a country's international economic activity.

Key Terms and Concepts

Balance of Payments (BOP)

current account

capital account

double-entry bookkeeping

merchandise trade

service trade

unilateral transfer

direct investment

portfolio investment account

safe haven

official reserves account

basic balance

official settlements balance

Questions for Discussion

1. Why must a country's Balance of Payments always be balanced in theory?
2. What is the difference between the Merchandise Trade Balance (BOT) and the Current Account balance?
3. What is service trade?
4. Why is foreign direct investment so much more controversial than foreign portfolio investment?
5. Should the fact that the United States may be the world's largest net debtor nation be a source of concern for government policy-makers?
6. While the United States "suffered" a Current Account deficit and a Capital Account surplus in the 1980s, what were the respective balances of Japan doing?
7. What does it mean for the United States to be one of the world's largest indebted countries?
8. How do exchange-rate changes alter trade so that the trade balance actually improves when the domestic currency depreciates?

Recommended Readings

Agenor, Pierre-Richard, Jagdeep S. Bhandari, and Robert P. Flood, "Speculative Attacks and Models of Balance of Payments Crises," *International Monetary Fund Staff Papers,* Vol. 39, Issue 2, June 1992, 357–394.

Bank for International Settlements, *62nd Annual Report,* Basle, Switzerland, June 15, 1992.

Bergsten, C. Fred, editor, *International Adjustment and Financing: The Lessons of 1985–1991.* Washington, D.C.: Institute for International Economics, 1991.

Evans, John S., *International Finance: A Markets Approach.* New York: Dryden Press, 1992.

Grabbe, J. Orlin, *International Financial Markets,* second edition. New York: Elsevier, 1991.

Husted, Steven, and Michael Melvin, *International Economics.* New York: Harper & Row, 1990.

International Monetary Fund, *IMF Balance of Payments Yearbook,* Washington, D.C., annually.

Root, Franklin R., *International Trade and Investment,* sixth edition. Chicago: SouthWestern Publishing, 1990.

United Nations, *Handbook of International Trade and Development Statistics,* New York, 1989.

Notes

1. The official terminology used throughout this chapter unless otherwise noted is that of the International Monetary Fund (IMF). Since the IMF is the primary source of similar statistics for Balance of Payments and economic performance worldwide, it is more general than other terminology forms, such as that employed by the U.S. Department of Commerce.

2. In January 1993, the United States employed more workers in the white-collar service sector than in the blue-collar manufacturing sector for the first time in history. It was also noted that there were three times as many lawyers in America as there were firemen.

4

The International Monetary System: Principles and History

LEARNING OBJECTIVES

1. To define what an exchange rate is and what its value should be.

2. To review the history of the international monetary system of the twentieth century in order to understand why the major world currencies are floating today.

3. To compare fixed and floating exchange rates.

4. To understand the purpose, mechanics, and future ambitions of the European Monetary System.

5. To examine the linkage between exchange rates and the debt crisis of the 1980s.

"It Pays to Be Jailed in Switzerland"

ZURICH, Switzerland—Drug smugglers have discovered a novel and lucrative form of employment—getting themselves arrested and imprisoned in Switzerland.

Swiss jails have long been held up as models of progressive enlightenment where prisoners are paid for their labors. While the rate is low by Swiss standards—around 23 Swiss Francs ($15) per day—it's attractive to South American drug couriers.

During the average 3 1/2-year sentence, a smuggler can earn about 28,000 francs ($18,480). Convicts can send checks to support their families or take lump sums on release.

The jails are clean, modern, and furnished with one-man cells. They provide three meals a day and health care. Despite the forced confinement, some offenders find the environment preferable to drug-running. Officials said one smuggler flew back to Switzerland after having been deported to poverty in Colombia, asking to be returned to his cell.

Prosecutor Marcel Bebie, who feels the prison system is being abused, wants prison pay linked to the cost of living in the offender's country. "Drug smugglers earn far more in a Swiss jail than a policeman in Colombia or Bolivia," he said. "To earn 20 or 25 francs a day may be punishment for the Swiss, but it is heaven on earth for these people."

Bebie's district handles drug-runners caught at or near Zurich Airport. Regensdorf Prison now houses 120 men arrested for smuggling at the airport last year.

An Interior Ministry spokesman defended the prison-pay policy. "Eventually these people have to reintegrate into society, so it is better to give them something to do while they are in jail," he said. He added that many Third World drug-runners were pushed into crime because they had families.

"If they have young children, it is very beneficial that they are able to send some money back home."

Source: "It Pays to Be Jailed in Switzerland," Birna Helgadottir, *The European*, distributed by Insight News.

What is a currency worth? Answer: whatever it will buy. A currency can buy goods, services, assets, or even other currencies. Actually, the larger problem is not really what it will buy today, but what a currency will buy tomorrow.

If exchange rates are set by market forces, and market forces are thought to be efficient, how can exchange rates change over such wide ranges? How can it actually be cheaper to be jailed in Switzerland than to work in Bolivia? Exchange rates and currency markets have long been a mystery to many people. This chapter provides an overview of the basic economic principles of exchange rates and a brief history of the recent **international monetary system.** Chapter 5 provides a more detailed description of the mechanics of exchange-rate markets today. The first problem, however, is to understand what purpose these exchange rates have for people and firms in international business.

THE PURPOSE OF EXCHANGE RATES

If countries are to trade, they must be able to exchange currencies. In order to buy wheat, or corn, or videocassette recorders, the buyer must first have the currency in which the product is sold. An American firm purchasing consumer electronic products manufactured in Japan must first exchange its U.S. dollars for Japanese yen, then purchase the products. And each country has its own currency.[1] The exchange of one country's currency for another should be a relatively simple transaction, but it's not.

What Is a Currency Worth?

At what rate should one currency be exchanged for another currency? For example, what should the exchange rate be between the U.S. dollar and the Japanese yen? The simplest answer is that the exchange rate should equalize purchasing power. For example, if the price of a movie ticket in the United States is $6, the "correct" exchange rate would be one that exchanges $6 for the amount of Japanese yen it would take to purchase a movie ticket in Japan. If ticket prices are ¥750 (a common symbol for the yen is ¥) in Japan, then the exchange rate that would equalize purchasing power would be:

$$\frac{¥750}{\$6} = ¥125/\$.$$

Therefore if the exchange rate between the two currencies was ¥125/$, regardless of which country the movie-goer was in, they could purchase a ticket. This is the theory of **purchasing power parity (PPP),** generally considered the definition of what exchange rates should ideally be. The purchasing power parity exchange rate is simply the rate that equalizes the price of the identical product or service in two different currencies:

$$\text{Price in Japan} = \text{Exchange rate} \times \text{Price in U.S.}$$

If the price of the same product in each currency is $P^¥$ and $P^\$$, and the spot exchange rate between the Japanese yen and the U.S. dollar is $S^{¥/\$}$, the price in yen is simply the price in dollars multiplied by the spot exchange rate,

$$P^¥ = S^{¥/\$} \times P^\$.$$

If this is rearranged (dividing both sides by $P^\$$), the spot exchange rate between the Japanese yen and the U.S. dollar is the ratio of the two product prices,

$$S^{¥/\$} = \frac{P^¥}{P^\$}.$$

These prices could be the price of just one good or service, like the movie ticket mentioned previously, or they could be price indices for each country that cover many different goods and services. Either form is an attempt to find comparable products in different countries (and currencies) in order to determine an exchange rate based on purchasing power parity. The question then is whether this logical approach to exchange rates actually works in practice.

The Law of One Price

The version of purchasing power parity that estimates the exchange rate between two currencies using just one good or service as a measure of the proper exchange for all goods and services is called the **Law of One Price** (for obvious reasons). To apply the theory to actual prices across countries, we need to select a product that is identical in quality and content in every country. To be truly theoretically correct, we would want such a product to be produced entirely domestically, so that there are no imported factors in its construction.

Where would one find such a perfect product? McDonald's. Table 4.1 presents what *The Economist* magazine calls the "Big Mac Index of Currencies." What it pro-

TABLE 4.1 Big Mac Currencies: The Hamburger Standard	Country	Big Mac price in local currency	Implied PPP of the dollar	Actual exchange rate 4/10/92	% over(+) or under(−) valuation of dollar
	Argentina	Peso 3.30	1.51	0.99	−34
	Australia	$A 2.54	1.16	1.31	+13
	Belgium	BF 108	49.32	33.55	−32
	Brazil	Cz$ 3,800	1,735	2,153	+24
	Britain	£ 1.74	0.79	0.57	−28
	Canada	C$ 2.76	1.26	1.19	−6
	China	Yuan 6.30	2.88	5.44	+89
	Denmark	DKr 27.25	12.44	6.32	−49
	France	F 18.10	8.26	5.55	−33
	Germany	DM 4.50	2.05	1.64	−20
	Holland	Fl 5.35	2.44	1.84	−24
	Hong Kong	HK$ 8.90	4.06	7.73	+91
	Hungary	Forint 133	60.73	79.70	+31
	Ireland	I£ 1.45	0.66	0.61	−8
	Italy	L 4,100	1,872	1,233	−34
	Japan	¥ 380	174	133	−24
	Russia	Ruble 58	26.48	98.95	+273
	Singapore	S$ 4.75	2.17	1.65	−24
	South Korea	Won 2,300	1,050	778	−26
	Spain	Pta 315	144	102	−29
	Sweden	Skr 25.50	11.64	5.93	−49
	United States	$2.19	———	———	———
	Venezuela	B 170	77.63	60.63	−22

Notes: Purchasing power parity is the local price divided by dollar price. Price for the United States is the average of New York, Chicago, San Francisco, and Atlanta.

Source: *The Economist,* April 18, 1992, p. 81.

vides is a product that is essentially the same the world over and is produced and consumed entirely domestically.

The Big Mac Index compares the actual exchange rate with the exchange rate implied by the purchasing power parity measurement of comparing Big Mac prices across countries. For example, the average price of a Big Mac in the United States was $2.19. On the same date, the price of a Big Mac in Canada, in Canadian dollars, was C$2.76. This is then used to calculate the PPP exchange rate as before:

$$\frac{\text{C\$2.76 per Big Mac}}{\text{\$2.19 per Big Mac}} = \text{C\$1.26/\$.}$$

The exchange rate between the Canadian dollar and the U.S. dollar should be C$1.26/$ according to a PPP comparison of Big Mac prices. The actual exchange rate on the date of comparison (April 10, 1992) was C$1.19/$. This means that each U.S. dollar was actually worth 1.19 Canadian dollars, when the index indicates that each U.S. dollar should have been worth 1.26 Canadian dollars. Therefore, if one is to believe in the Big Mac index, the U.S. dollar was being "undervalued" on the markets by about 6 percent.

Not simply entertaining, the Big Mac index is actually an excellent example of how purchasing power parity should work in determining exchange rates. There are few products that are not only identical across so many countries, but also produced completely within that country. Note that for most currencies listed, the Big Mac index implies an exchange rate that is not that distant from the actual rate. It is also interesting to note that two of the largest differences between the Big Mac exchange rate and the actual exchange rates are China and Russia. The reasons for these large discrepancies are to a large degree a result of the elemental stages of market economies in these countries, combined with the fact that the Chinese yuan and the Russian ruble were at this time not freely tradable currencies (the governments of these two countries control the trading of their currencies, restricting their exchange values artificially).

What should one conclude from this example of purchasing power parity? Although there are many valid criticisms of the Big Mac index (for example, local taxes, property values, tariffs, and so forth all affecting the prices in each country), it does serve as a measure of what currencies should be worth. Any single product could be similarly criticized, and the alternative method of comparing consumer or producer price indices across countries may actually be worse, considering how few products actually meet the requirements so clearly fulfilled by the Big Mac. One could do worse!

Qualities Desired in an Exchange Rate

The theory of purchasing power parity provides a measure or rule of the goal in the exchange of currencies between countries. It provides a focus for the value desired. But what other qualities are desired in an exchange rate?

First and foremost, stability. Currencies are only a medium of exchange, a store of value, a unit of account. They are money. The purpose of money is to facilitate business and commerce. Prices play a critical role in how goods are allocated between buyers and sellers, consumers and producers. If the prices of products across borders are more volatile or unpredictable than the prices within borders, international trade and commerce is more difficult and the benefits of trade pointed out in Chapter 2 are not fully realized. Regardless of how it is achieved, a stable and predictable currency value is conducive to international trade. Trade is easier when the price of a foreign product or asset, at least as affected by exchange rates, will be the same tomorrow and the day after as it is today.

Secondly, a system or regime (as exchange-rate systems are often referred to) is generally more dependable if it is "self-directing." This means a system or device that operates properly and dependably on its own, without the interference or direction of authorities like governments or groups of governments. The self-correcting properties of markets is one of the dominant features of the market economy as opposed to other forms, such as directed economies.

The major exchange-rate regimes discussed in the following sections all employ slightly different methods, rules, and agreements in attempting to achieve these goals. Some have worked better than others, but much of what has worked in the past will not work in the future because, literally, times change.

INTERNATIONAL MONETARY SYSTEMS OF THE 20TH CENTURY

The exchange rate system we see today is the latest stage in a world of continuing change. The systems that have preceded the present floating-exchange-rate system varied between gold-based standards in which currencies were nothing other than lightweight replacements for gold and complex systems in which the U.S. dollar was considered "good as gold." To understand why major world currencies like the dollar and yen are floating today, it is necessary to return to the (pardon the pun) "golden oldies."

A few words of caution are in order, however, before proceeding with a discussion of the modern history of exchange rates.

- History as conveyed in books tends to focus on outcomes, not processes. Very often the outcome is more a combination of principles or procedures or both, rather than the dominance of one idea or set of ideas. The most important lesson is the cause of change, not the result.
- Agreements between participants such as governments can be either formal or informal. The procedures or rules of a system may be laid down specifically in written articles, which are then signed and confirmed by all members, or totally informal in structure where all participants play by the same rules—they are just not written down or stated in an agreed-upon document or setting. An agreement is only as good as the adherence of all parties to it and not to the level of detail spelled out in its formalized rules. It is actions that count most.
- Finally, times change. The political and economic powers of the world change and evolve, and some systems or rules of markets may have to change with them.

The following discussion of the major international monetary systems of the 20th century will continually return to these three points: the causes of change, the actions of participants rather than the stated rules of the system, and finally the changing world economic conditions that have driven the global trading system from a standard based on gold to one based on faith.

THE GOLD STANDARD

Although there is no official starting date, the **gold standard** as we know it extended from the 1880s to the outbreak of World War I in 1914. History has looked on the gold standard with generally favorable recollections, although its success may be attributed to the relatively simpler economic world in which it existed and the fact that this era was one of few international wars or crises. The gold standard had three major features that are important to gain an understanding of why it did work and also why it may never work again.

1. It established a system of fixed exchange rates between participating countries. Stable exchange rates were considered a necessary ingredient to increase trade among nations.
2. The gold standard limited the rate of growth in a country's money supply. This was due to the fact that all "money" must be backed by gold, and the supply of gold in the world increased quite slowly during this period in history.
3. Gold served as an automatic adjustment tool for countries experiencing Balance of Payments problems. If a country was running a Balance of Payments deficit, gold would, by market forces, flow out of the country, decreasing economic activity and pushing the Balance of Payments back toward balance.

Fixed Exchange Parity Rates

The mechanics of the gold-standard system were actually quite simple. Each country's currency was set in value per ounce of gold. For example, the U.S. dollar was defined as being $20.67/oz. of gold,[2] while the British pound sterling, the dominant world currency at this time, was £4.2474/oz. The obvious benefit of this fixing to gold weight was that if each currency maintained its value relative to gold, then each currency was in effect fixed to every other currency. For example, with the dollar and the pound fixed at $20.67/oz. and £4.2474/oz., the dollar-pound exchange rate was fixed at

$$\frac{\$20.67/oz. \ of \ gold}{£4.2474/oz. \ of \ gold} = \$4.8665/£.$$

Although most countries followed the same basic set of principles, this "system" was not formalized to any great degree between countries. It worked because most governments followed, of their own accord, the same sets of rules. But, first and foremost, the gold standard established relatively fixed exchange rates.

These **par values,** or parity rates as they were known, were established on the basis of purchasing power parity, similar to that described in the previous section (although obviously not on the basis of the Big Mac). The selection of gold as the core element was more a result of historical tradition rather than anything particularly unique about gold itself. Gold was durable and divisible, although gold itself is a relatively soft metal. The most significant factor in favor of the use of gold was that it had been in relatively short supply for most of human history. Gold was generally accepted in all countries as a means of payment.

But establishing the system was only the first step. For the gold standard to work, the countries participating in such a system had to follow certain rules. The first and foremost **"rule of the game"** was that a currency was indeed valued as its parity rate with gold. The only way this could be proven was if the government stood ready, willing, and able to buy or sell gold at the stated parity rate. For example, the Bank of England assured both the British public and foreign public that the pound sterling was worth £4.2474 per ounce of gold by selling gold to anyone wanting it at that price. Whenever there was doubt in the minds of the public, the government would sell gold in return for the paper pounds. If for some reason the public believed that the pound sterling was worth more, again, the British government and the Bank of England would buy gold on the open market at the stated price of £4.2474 per ounce and stabilize the price.

Secondly, governments had to "let the gold flow." This meant that countries had to allow gold to move freely in and out of the country in order to earn the continued faith in the currency's worth. For example, a British citizen holding Federal Reserve Notes issued by the U.S. Treasury was assured by the U.S. government that 20.67 one-dollar bills were worth one ounce of gold. If the British citizen or anyone else outside the United States holding U.S. dollar bills had doubts, the U.S. Treasury assured all such people that they could exchange the paper for gold. If everyone believe it, no one really needed to exchange the paper for the more unwieldy gold. But of course in the case of doubt, and there are always doubters, they must be able to convert paper for gold to maintain the integrity of the system.

Restriction on Money-Supply Growth

In addition to implicitly establishing fixed exchange rates, the gold standard had a very powerful impact on the monetary policy of the participating countries. Because each unit of currency was backed by gold, the supply of money in the country could not increase faster than the amount of gold, and the supply of gold in the world was expanding quite slowly at this time. This meant that government authorities in charge of monetary policy were restricted in how fast they could increase the money supply.

This automatic restraint was distinctly anti-inflationary, and historical evidence, although inconclusive, suggests that average inflation rates were lower during the time of the gold standard than they have been since. However, this system prevents governments from deciding their own independent monetary policies. Some scholars have argued that it is illogical to allow the world supply of a metal to dictate policy as important as the quantity of money available to society.

Automatic Balance of Payments Adjustment

The third and final feature of the gold standard also relied on the ability of the gold to flow. Rapid growth, particularly in imports, could push the Balance of Payments into deficit (outflows of money and currency exceeding inflows). Because the system relied on fixed exchange rates and **convertibility** of currencies for gold, anyone not wanting to be paid in paper currency could essentially demand gold bullion. Thus, if there was reason to doubt the value of the currency, the government would allow gold to flow, in this case to flow out of the country.

The gold flow out of the country reduced the supply of money (remember the fixed link of paper money to gold), pushing the system back into balance. Having less money in the country's economy would slow business and economic activity. The slowed activity would return the country to a Balance of Payments.

Regardless of the strengths of the gold standard, the first world war effectively halted the free flow of gold across borders, and the world's currency markets were in substantial turmoil until 1919. The United States returned to the gold standard in

The London financial district flourished during the decades prior to World War I when the British pound sterling was the dominant world currency and when most currencies were based on the gold standard.

Source: The Bettmann Archive

June 1919. Great Britain did not return to the standard until 1925, and its term even then proved short-lived.

THE INTERWAR YEARS, 1919–1939

The 1920s and 1930s were a tumultuous period for the international monetary system. The British pound sterling, prior to World War I the world's dominant currency, survived the war but in a greatly weakened state. Inflation in England during and after the war threatened the stability of the British economy. In a desperate move to return to times of relative calm, the Bank of England once more established the British pound at its prewar parity of £4.2474 per ounce of gold.

It should be noted that one of Britain's leading economists of the time, John Maynard Keynes, was vehemently opposed to the return of the pound sterling to the gold standard. The advocates of the gold standard were led by Winston Churchill, then chancellor of the exchequer, and they held the day. But the pound was not what it had been, and continued runs on the stock of gold held by the Bank of England finally forced the abandonment of the gold standard again in 1931. As seen in Figure 4.1, this caused an enormous fall in the value of the pound in 1931 and 1932.

The U.S. dollar returned to the gold standard at the end of the war in June 1919. For the United States, which had suffered none of the physical destruction of the war and which had also not seen many of the inflationary pressures, the return to gold was much simpler. It was not until the bank runs and subsequent "holidays" of 1933 that the U.S. was forced to abandon gold convertibility again.

There is no question that the decade of the 1930s was a dark period for world trade and currency markets. With the onslaught of the Depression, many countries, including the United States, resorted to isolationist policies and protectionism. Mar-

FIGURE 4.1
The Dollar-Pound Exchange Rate Since World War I

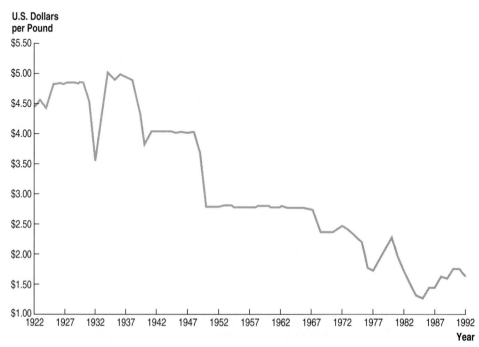

Source: *Federal Reserve Bulletin,* Board of Governors of the Federal Reserve System, monthly, 1919–1993.

kets were closed to foreign producers. In the international markets that did remain open, exporting countries tried to undercut each other through continual currency devaluations. These **competitive devaluations** only succeeded in pushing many of the world's currencies below their true values and increasing the pressures for further nationalistic protectionist policies to shield domestic firms from unfair foreign competition. By the early days of World War II, international trade had ground to a halt.

THE BRETTON WOODS AGREEMENT	The governments of the Allied powers knew that the devastating impacts of World War II would require swift and decisive policies. Therefore, a full year before the end of the war, representatives of 44 nations met in the summer of 1944 in Bretton Woods, New Hampshire. Their purpose was to plan the postwar international monetary system. It was a difficult process, and the final synthesis of viewpoints was shaded by pragmatism and significant doubt.[3]

Although the conference was attended by more than 40 nations, the leading policy-makers at Bretton Woods were the British and the Americans. The British delegation was led by Lord John Maynard Keynes, termed "Britain's economic heavyweight."[4] The British argued for a postwar system that would be decidedly more flexible than the various gold standards used before the second world war. Keynes argued, as he had after World War I, that attempts to tie currency values to gold would create pressures for deflation (a general fall in the level of prices in a country) in many of the war-ravaged economies. And these economies were faced with enormous reindustrialization needs that would likely cause inflation, not deflation.

The American delegation was led by the director of the U.S. Treasury's monetary research department, Harry D. White, and the U.S. Secretary of the Treasury, Henry Morgenthau, Jr. The American delegation argued for the need for stability (fixed rates) but not a return to the gold standard itself. In fact, although the United States at that time held most of the gold of the Allied powers, the U.S. delegates argued that currencies should be fixed in parities but redemption of gold should occur only between official authorities (central banks of governments).

On the more pragmatic side, all parties agreed that a postwar system would be stable and sustainable only if there was sufficient credit available for countries to defend their currencies in the event of Balance of Payments imbalances, which they knew to be inevitable in a reconstructing world order.

The conference divided up into three commissions for weeks of negotiation. One commission, led by U.S. Treasury Secretary Henry Morgenthau, was charged with the organization of a fund of capital to be used for exchange-rate stabilization. A second commission, chaired by Britain's Lord Keynes, was charged with the organization of a second "bank" whose purpose would be for long-term reconstruction and development. The third commission was to hammer out details such as what role silver would have in any new system.

The Agreement

After weeks of meetings, the participants finally came to a three-part **Bretton Woods Agreement** for the structure of the postwar international monetary system. The plan called for:

1. Fixed exchange rates, termed an "adjustable peg" among members;
2. A fund of gold and constituent currencies available to members for stabilization of their respective currencies, called the **International Monetary Fund (IMF);** and
3. A bank for financing long-term development projects.

Although the third component, what became known as the World Bank, was not integral to the operation of the system, the adjustable peg and the stabilization fund were to work hand in hand.

The Adjustable Peg

All currencies were to establish par values defined in terms of gold. However, unlike the gold standard prior to World War I, there was little if any convertibility of currencies for gold. Each government was responsible for monitoring its currency value to ensure that it varied by less than 1 percent from its par value. If a country experienced a **fundamental disequilibrium** in its Balance of Payments, it could alter its peg by up to 10 percent from its initial par value without approval from the IMF. But, as with any fixed-price system, the goal of the system was not to change the par value. The "adjustment" part of the peg was to be kept to a minimum.[5] A country experiencing significant problems could therefore apply to the IMF for temporary loans of gold or convertible currencies for the purpose of defending its par value and adjusting the Balance of Payments back toward equilibrium.

The one currency that was convertible to gold was the U.S. dollar. The dollar was pegged at $1 = 1/35 ounce of gold, or $35 per ounce. The U.S. Treasury would, however, convert U.S. dollars for gold only with foreign governments, not with private individuals, domestic or foreign. This was a significant reduction in convertibility compared to that of the old gold standard. But with all currencies pegged to gold, and the dollar convertible to gold, even if only with official authorities, the dollar was considered "good as gold." This was the feature of the system that brought 25 years of success, as well as its eventual collapse.

For example, a country experiencing a Balance of Payments deficit would normally experience devaluation pressure on its currency value. The country's authorities, normally the central bank, would defend its currency by using its foreign currency reserves, primarily U.S. dollars, to purchase its own currency on the open market to push its value back up and preserve its par value. Once a country used up a large proportion of its currency reserves, it could apply to the IMF for additional funds to stabilize its currency value. Similarly, if the country was experiencing a Balance of Payments surplus and associated upward pressure on its currency, it could sell additional currency on the open market and accept payment in major convertible currencies like the U.S. dollar. Since the dollar was convertible for gold, the U.S. dollar was quite acceptable.

The International Monetary Fund

The International Monetary Fund was created to provide funds to countries in need of additional assistance for economic stabilization. It was initially funded through the contributions from all members. Each country was given a quota in the original agree-

TABLE 4.2
Initial IMF Quotas

County	Quota
United States	$2,750,000,000
Great Britain	$1,300,000,000
Russia	$1,200,000,000
China	$ 550,000,000
France	$ 450,000,000
Total	$8,500,000,000

Source: "Rivalries Beset Monetary Pact," *Business Week*, Number 776, July 15, 1944, pp. 15–16.

ment at Bretton Woods. Quotas were established on the basis of the size and estimated strengths at the end of the second world war, in addition to the size of foreign trade the country demonstrated prior to the war.[6] Table 4.2 lists the agreed-upon quotas of the original members. The quotas once paid would establish the pool of capital available to the IMF for its economic stabilization lending.

Each quota was payable 25 percent in gold, and the remaining 75 percent in the country's own currency.[7] Since most countries possessed currencies that were obviously not convertible and therefore of little value, it was the gold portion of the quota that was considered the true resource of the IMF's lending capabilities.

A final feature of the IMF, not added until the mid-1960s, was the creation of an index of currencies, the **Special Drawing Right (SDR).** The SDR was intended as an artificial reserve asset for member countries, representing the resources available to each member in the event it were to draw upon IMF funds. The fund of SDRs would represent currency credits between central banks and would aid a country in the management of temporary Balance-of-Payments problems. The value of the SDR was originally calculated as the average of 16 different world currencies but was later reduced to five major currencies.

The International Bank for Reconstruction and Development

The third and final part of the Bretton Woods Agreement was the formation of the **International Bank for Reconstruction and Development,** or World Bank. As opposed to the other two elements, which were focused on exchange-rate stabilization, the World Bank was intended for reconstruction and development. Although initially focused on lending for the reconstruction of the war-torn country members, the World Bank quickly found its focus shifting toward the developing countries of Africa, Asia, the Middle East, and South America.

Even in the early stages of the Bretton Woods negotiations, the World Bank was considered the most politically acceptable portion of the three-part agreement. As noted by *Business Week* in July 1944, "the process of lending money is a fairly simple operation. Congress and the country find it easier to understand than currency stabilization. Hence, the bank might get approval as a rehabilitation measure when the currency plan would be smothered in economic debate."[8]

The Experience Under Bretton Woods, 1946–1971

The best indication of the success or failure of the Bretton Woods Agreement is the flat line in Figure 4.1 between 1949 and 1967. Although this is the U.S. dollar–British pound exchange rate only, the stability of the rate and the length of time of such stability was unparalleled before or after Bretton Woods. The U.S. economy was the foundation for the system. The fact that the U.S. economy had survived the war physically unscathed allowed the United States to emerge in the postwar world as the dominant economic power.

The 1950s were characterized by a dollar shortage on world markets as the United States ran Balance of Payments surpluses, primarily as a result of the strength of U.S. exports, as opposed to predicted deficits. As countries struggled to obtain the U.S. dollars needed for their currency reserves, the balances on trade and capital accounts slowly shifted as the European and Japanese economies recuperated from the devastation of World War II.

By the late 1960s the adjustable-peg exchange-rate system was showing signs of stress. As the United States continued to run larger and larger Balance of Payments deficits, many countries were being forced to intervene to preserve fixed parities. They bought dollars to keep the dollar from falling and their own currencies from rising. But imbalances on world currency markets persisted, and the fixed parities of member nations started changing at an alarming rate: on November 19, 1967, the British pound sterling was devalued 14.3 percent; on August 8, 1969, the French franc was devalued 11.1 percent; on October 24, 1969, the West German mark was revalued 9.3 percent. Canada simply allowed the Canadian dollar to float on May 31, 1970, with no specific plans to return to a fixed parity. By May 1971, the system was in turmoil. The major European currency exchanges closed the week of May 5, 1971. The German mark and Dutch guilder were floated and revalued, the Swiss franc was revalued 7.1 percent, and even the Austrian shilling was revalued 5.05 percent against the dollar.

The continued defense of the dollar left central banks around the world with massive quantities of U.S. dollars. These countries, knowing that the dollars they held were in fact convertible into gold with the U.S. Treasury, attempted to hold back demanding gold in exchange. These central banks knew that if they did demand gold in exchange for the paper balances they held, it could very well send the international monetary system into a tailspin. Yet, it became painfully clear in 1971 that the U.S. dollar was overvalued, and devaluation of the dollar versus gold was inevitable. More and more central banks began presenting U.S. dollar balances to the U.S. Treasury for conversion to gold. The United States allowed the gold to flow, and it flowed out of the Treasury coffers at an alarming rate.

Collapse and Transition, 1971–1973

On August 15, 1971, President Richard M. Nixon announced that "I have instructed [Treasury] Secretary [John B.] Connally to suspend temporarily the convertibility of the dollar into gold or other assets." With this simple statement, President Nixon effectively ended the fixed exchange rates established at Bretton Woods, New Hampshire, more than 25 years earlier.

The closing of the "gold window" by President Nixon was in fact not a major surprise to world currency markets. The events of the previous months and years had foretold the need for the dollar to fall. The real question was what would come next? What would the international monetary system look like now? In September 1970, almost a full year previous, the International Monetary Fund had completed an in-depth study of the possibility that the world monetary system would move to a full and permanent floating-rate basis. The report had been met with a deafening silence.

In the weeks and months following the August announcement, world currency markets devalued the dollar, although the United States had only ended gold convertibility, not officially declared the dollar's values to be less. The **Group of Ten** finance ministers met at the Smithsonian Institution in Washington, D.C., in December 1971 to patch the faltering system.[9] The resulting **Smithsonian Agreement** attempted to preserve the fixed parities without gold convertibility with three principal actions. First, the U.S. dollar was officially devalued to $38 an ounce of gold (although this was on paper only). Secondly, other major Group of Ten currencies were revalued versus the dollar in varying percentages. And finally, the percentage by which a currency would be allowed to deviate from its fixed parity rate was expanded to 2.25 percent, a sizable increase from the previous 1 percent.

Without convertibility of one of the member currencies to gold, the system was doomed from the start. Currencies continually surpassed their allotted plus 2.25 percent versus the dollar, so that by mid-1972, the central banks simply gave up. The British pound was floated in June 1972, the Swiss franc in January 1973. On February 12, 1973, the U.S. dollar was once again officially devalued versus gold, this time to $42.22 per ounce. After the system ground to a complete halt in March 1973, when major currency markets were closed for more than two weeks, most major currencies were simply allowed to float. The last vestiges of fixed rates sank with this final float.

In January 1976 the members of the Group of Ten met in Jamaica to formalize the new floating system. The **Jamaica Agreement** freed countries to float their currencies "legally," managing their currencies' values through various forms of intervention if they deemed it appropriate. Gold was officially demonetized as a reserve asset. This meant that the original gold quotas used in the financing of the International Monetary Fund were returned to members. The resources of the IMF itself, however, were increased to provide additional aid to countries needing assistance in the management of their Balance of Payments. The IMF, an original institution of the Bretton Woods Agreement, was not to die with the agreement. In fact, the IMF's role in the international monetary system would only grow over the coming decade.

FLOATING EXCHANGE RATES, 1973–PRESENT

A floating-exchange-rate system poses many new and different problems for participants. The biggest is the most obvious: the lack of certainty as to what rate currencies will be exchanged at a year, a month, or a day from now. However, firms worldwide have learned to live and deal with these price-risk issues relatively quickly. A larger crisis in the eyes of many major countries is that floating exchange rates do not allow the same degree of economic-policy isolation that they previously enjoyed.

Under the previous fixed-exchange-rate regime, governments could conduct relatively independent monetary policy. The central bank of a country would normally increase the country's money supply at rates consistent with domestic economic-policy goals. If interest rates rose or fell, although they may attract capital into or cause it to flow out of the country, government intervention in the foreign-exchange markets could offset negative exchange-rate effects. Governments enjoyed this degree of independence; the ability to self-determine domestic economic policy is one of the ways a country might define sovereignty. Floating exchange rates changed all of that. A country's domestic economic policies now translated into immediate impacts on its external relations, its currency's exchange value. There is no better example of this than the events in the United States beginning in 1979.

The Rise of the Dollar, 1980–1985

The United States suffered increasing rates of inflation throughout the 1970s. By 1979, the annual rate of inflation was approaching 12 percent, and the U.S. economy was continuing to suffer both inflation and stagnant economic growth. Paul Volker, the newly named chairman of the U.S. Federal Reserve system, implemented a strict new monetary policy in the late summer of 1979.[10] The policy was intended to end, once and for all, the inflationary expectations imbedded in the U.S. economy. Volker instituted a tight "monetary-growth rule." This meant the Federal Reserve would increase the money supply of the United States at a steady, but slow rate, regardless of economic conditions. Interest rates would, therefore, not be the focus of monetary policy, and within weeks interest rates in the United States rose precipitously. Over the following years the United States suffered a modest recession (1980) and then a severe recession (1981–1982). Inflation was purged slowly from the U.S. economy, but at the cost of increased unemployment and slow economic growth.

The eventual rebound of the U.S. economy in 1983 and 1984 was also characterized by a rapidly rising dollar. The relatively rapid economic growth of the United States compared to other industrial countries, the falling rate of inflation, the still extremely high real rates of interest available in the United States, and the role of the country as a "safe haven" in a world of increasing risk all contributed to the rise of the dollar. Depending on which currencies are used for measurement, the dollar rose roughly 45 percent against currencies of other major industrial countries between the spring of 1980 and early 1985. As illustrated in Figure 4.2, the rate of the dollar's rise was matched by the speed of its fall.

Although the dollar rose as a result of many forces, many of which were signs of relative economic health, the degree of the dollar's rise was not healthy for anyone inside or out of the United States. The strong dollar resulted in extreme U.S. purchasing power abroad, which led to rising import bills, while U.S. exports languished. American product prices were increasingly uncompetitive on world markets as a result of the dollar. Before you could buy an American product, you had to buy a dollar. And dollars were very expensive.

The single most powerful argument against freely floating exchange rates has always been the uncertainty it introduces into international commerce. Although the dollar had floated relatively freely throughout the 1970s, the volatility of its movements had not been an insurmountable problem for firms or governments. The first half of the 1980s, however, confronted policymakers around the world with the very thing they had always feared: massive exchange-rate movement over a very short period of time. Someone needed to do something.

Intervention in the 1980s: Expectations and Coordination

The intervention of a government in a foreign-exchange market has traditionally referred to the actual buying and selling of the country's own currency on the open market. If the magnitude of government sales or purchases relative to the total size

FIGURE 4.2

The U.S. Dollar Under Floating Exchange Rates(Morgan Index, foreign currency per U.S. dollar)

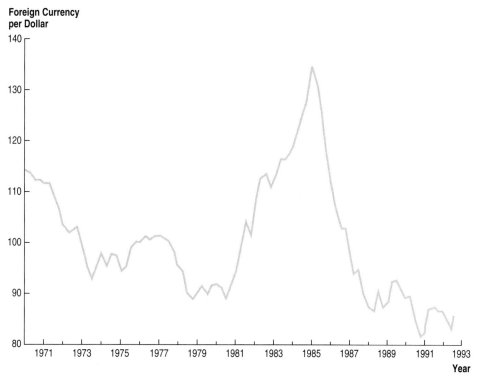

Foreign Currency per Dollar

Source: Derived by authors from *World Financial Markets,* Morgan Guaranty, New York, various issues. The Morgan 15 country nominal index is calculated using trade weights of the 15 largest bilateral trading partners of the United States. 1980–1982 average = 100.

of the market at the time of the trades is substantial, the government can literally alter the exchange rate on its own. However, while the world's currency markets grew in size over the 1960s, 1970s, and into the 1980s, the amount of official reserves (major currencies and gold) held by governments did not. It therefore became increasingly difficult for an individual government to intervene successfully.

A government attempting to move its currency in the opposite direction of its current trend is termed "leaning into the wind," while attempting to accelerate or perpetuate the current trend is termed "leaning with the wind." "Leaning into the wind," as it implies, is very difficult to do successfully. When major industrial countries attempted to move their own exchange rates, they found their efforts increasingly futile and quite expensive.

By the mid-1980s, it was clear that major world currencies like the U.S. dollar, the German mark, or the Japanese yen could only be managed by the coordination of policies among the industrial countries. Successful policy would also include much more than simply direct intervention. Coordination would have to also include the monetary and interest-rate policies of the individual countries, as well as general economic beliefs of the countries themselves. It became necessary to act on the factors causing currency movements. Intervention through simply buying and selling, acting as part of the market, was no longer enough.

Governments realized that one of their most powerful tools was their ability to influence the expectations of the market. Currency traders, international speculators, and investors are all moving the world's capital into currencies and assets that they expect to yield the relatively higher returns. Therefore, government economic policies with respect to monetary policy, anti-inflammatory measures, stimulus measures, and so forth alter the actual yields that these investors pursue. If a government can alter what investors believe, it may successfully influence the supply-and-demand forces for its currency—in theory.

The countries meeting at the Plaza Hotel in New York in 1985 were well aware of the inability of any one individual country to "talk the dollar down," so they proposed to do it as a group.

The Plaza Agreement, September 1985

Although the U.S. dollar peaked in its rise against most currencies in February 1985, it was September before the **Group of Five,** or G5 countries (United States, Japan, West Germany, United Kingdom, France), could meet to discuss the issue. Meeting at the Plaza Hotel in New York, the members convened to discuss the recent declines in the dollar, to reach some consensus on where they might like the dollar to fall to, and to decide what actions they might take to move the dollar. The rapidly deteriorating U.S. trade balance had caused a surge of protectionist sentiment in the United States. This renewed call for protection from imports—imports from Japan and Germany—prompted the meeting to aid in the dollar's fall to competitiveness.

The meeting of the G5 on Sunday, September 22, 1985, was a complex one. Although preliminary and background studies had been circulated before the meeting, there was little agreement going in. After all was said and done, the communique issued stated that "some further orderly appreciation of the main non-dollar currencies is desirable." The message to the world's financial markets was clear: the G5 countries wanted the dollar to fall, and they intended to work cooperatively toward that end. What the communique of the **Plaza Agreement** did not state was what measures would actually be taken or how far the dollar was intended to fall versus the Japanese yen and German mark.[11] In fact, after the finance ministers returned home, continuing statements and actions indicated little real action. It was generally concluded that the countries other than the United States needed to stimulate their own economies (and possibly raise their interest rates relative to dollar rates), and the United States in turn needed to work toward lowering interest rates through concerted efforts to reduce the ballooning U.S. government budget deficit. Although it is difficult to find true coordination of the policies following the Plaza meeting, the dollar did fall considerably over the following 18 months.

The Louvre Accord, February 1987

By February 1987 the dollar was thought to have fallen far enough. A meeting of the **Group of Seven,** or G7, was held February 21–22 at the Louvre Museum in Paris to consider the immediate prospects of the international monetary system.[12] The U.S. representative, Treasury Secretary James Baker, proposed the establishment of **"reference zones,"** in which exchange rates would be allowed to fluctuate over a specified range. If the dollar, mark, and yen were to move out of these ranges, coordinated intervention and macroeconomic policies would be utilized to push them back in line.

The response to Secretary Baker's proposal was noncommittal. West Germany's finance minister, Gerhard Stoltenberg, was interested only in short-term agreements on desirable currency values. Germany was not interested in any longer-term commitments on coordinated intervention or policies. Japanese Finance Minister Kiichi

Miyazawa, when asked about "reference zones," responded only that "the word is unfamiliar to me." The results of the Louvre meeting were obviously weak, with the concluding communique stating that the dollar's present level against the Japanese yen and German mark was "about right." There was also an informal agreement, the details of which were not made public, that coordinated intervention (buying and selling) would be forthcoming if the dollar were to fall significantly further. After all, the Louvre meetings were intended to put a floor under the dollar, to stop its precipitous fall.

Less than a month later, the dollar was indeed falling further. By the end of March 1987, the U.S. dollar was hitting record lows against the Japanese yen (approximately ¥148/$). Coordinated intervention by all major central banks did succeed in stabilizing the dollar's value over the next few months. Although the degree of coordinated policy was relatively short-lived, the events following the **Louvre Accord** demonstrated that coordinated policy among industrial countries could gain some degree of success in managing exchange rates. The real question was whether domestically oriented macroeconomic policies (such as government spending, taxation, monetary policy) would be subservient to international policies in controlling exchange rates.

Endaka

The U.S. dollar's rise and fall in the 1980s were not consistent across all major currencies. The Japanese yen, as illustrated in Figure 4.3, saw only momentary pauses in its continual appreciation in value versus the dollar over the past two decades.

**FIGURE 4.3
Endaka:
The Appreciation of the
Japanese Yen**

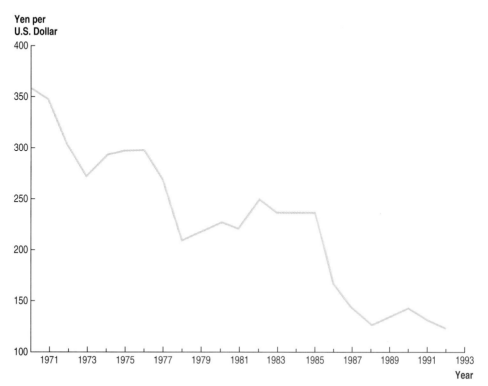

Source: *Federal Reserve Bulletin.* Average annual spot exchange rate.

Although the dollar did rise dramatically against all major European currencies between 1980 and 1985, it gained relatively little over this same period against the yen. Yet, the dollar fell like a rock against the yen after February 1985. As illustrated in Figure 4.3, the dollar fell in value from ¥250/$ to ¥125/$ in a two-year period, termed the Endaka in Japan.

There are many different reasons given for the astounding rise in the Japanese yen in the middle to late 1980s. The continued rapid growth of the Japanese economy, the continuing doubts regarding the prospects for growth in the American and European economies, the deregulation of the Japanese financial markets, the rapid growth in Japanese land values and share prices all are considered to have contributed to the rapidly growing demand for Japanese yen on world currency markets. Although the yen has seemingly stabilized since the 1987–1988 peak against the dollar, it is once again showing the same strength that has recently sent it to all-time highs against the U.S. dollar of ¥119/$.

Recent Currency Movements

As illustrated in Figure 4.4, the movements of the U.S. dollar, Japanese yen, and German mark have been stable since 1987. Yet, this is a "relative stability," given that

---

FIGURE 4.4   **The Recent Movements of the Dollar, Yen, and Mark (monthly, 1987–1992)**

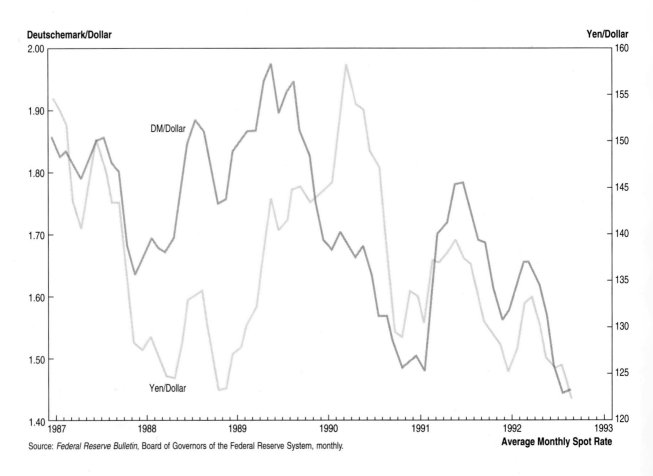

Source: *Federal Reserve Bulletin*, Board of Governors of the Federal Reserve System, monthly.

Average Monthly Spot Rate

these three currency values still have varied over large ranges in short periods of time. There has been little additional discussion of increased macroeconomic coordination among the major industrial powers, although the European currency crisis of 1992 (discussed in the following section) may eventually lead to renewed efforts for coordinated actions among countries.

EUROPEAN EXCHANGE RATES: THE MONETARY SYSTEM	In the week following the suspension of dollar convertibility to gold to 1971, the finance ministers of a number of the major countries of western Europe discussed how they might maintain the fixed parities of their currencies independently of the U.S. dollar. By April 1972, they had concluded an agreement that was termed the "snake within the tunnel." The member countries agreed to fix parity rates between currencies with allowable trading bands of 2.25 percent variance. As a group they would allow themselves to vary by 4.5 percent versus the U.S. dollar. Although the effort was well-intentioned, the various pressures and crises that rocked international economic order in the 1970s, such as the OPEC price shock of 1974, resulted in a relatively short life for the "snake."

The European Monetary System

In 1979 a much more formalized structure was put in place among many of the major members of the European Community. The **European Monetary System (EMS)** officially began operation in March 1979 and once again established a grid of fixed parity rates among member currencies. The EMS was a much more elaborate system for the management of exchange rates than its predecessor "snake." The EMS consisted of three different components that would work in concert to preserve fixed parities (also termed central rates).

First, all countries that were committing their currencies and their efforts to the preservation of fixed exchange rates entered the **Exchange-Rate Mechanism (ERM).** Although all the currencies of the countries of the European Community would be used in the calculation of important indices for management purposes, several countries chose not to be ERM participants. Participation meant the country would commit itself to the preservation of the agreed-upon grid of fixed rates, and several of the member countries were not yet willing to do so. Participation in the ERM technically required that countries accept bilateral responsibility of maintaining the fixed rates. If, for example, the German mark were to start rising to the limits of its allowed band versus another currency, such as the French franc, it would be the responsibility of both countries to undertake actions to preserve the rate. The coordinated-bilateral responsibility might include foreign-exchange-market intervention and possibly monetary-policy actions altering interest rates. In the event that the rate was considered to be unsustainable, the ERM allowed necessary realignments of the parity rates.

The second element of the European Monetary System was the actual grid of bilateral exchange rates with their specified band limits. As under the Smithsonian Agreement and the former snake, member currencies were allowed to deviate $+/- 2.25$ percent from their parity rate. Some currencies, however, such as the Italian lira, were originally allowed larger bands (10 percent variance) due to their more characteristic volatility.

The third and final element of the European Monetary System was the creation of the European Currency Unit (ECU). As illustrated in Figure 4.5, the ECU is a

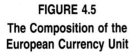

FIGURE 4.5
The Composition of the
European Currency Unit

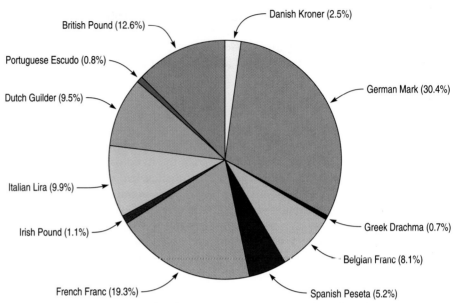

Source: "The ECU and Its Role in the Process Towards Monetary Union," *European Economy,* No. 48, September 1991, p. 125.

weighted average index of the currencies that are members of the EMS. Each currency is weighted by a value reflecting the relative size of that country's trade and gross domestic product. This allows each individual currency to be defined in units per ECU. The ECU can also serve as a method of value accounting between EMS members without showing preference by using one individual currency.

Events and Performance of the EMS

The need for fixed exchange rates within Europe is clear. The countries of western Europe trade amongst themselves to a degree approaching interstate commerce in the United States. It is therefore critical to the economies and businesses of Europe that exchange rates be as stable as possible. Although it has its critics, the EMS has been generally successful in providing exchange-rate stability. Between March 1979 and August 1992, there were 11 realignments of central rates, with most occurring in the earlier years.

The EMS, however, suffered several setbacks beginning in September 1992. A number of the political and economic forces that had driven European economies in the past decade started to put new and exceptional pressures on the EMS.

- Deutschemark dominance. Most EMS realignments have resulted in the revaluation of the German mark and the devaluation of most other member currencies. The rapid growth of German industry and trade has resulted in the deutschemark growing in its proportion of world currency trading. The EMS is often now referred to as the "DMZ" or "DM Zone."

- EMS membership expansion. Although not formally a part of the European Community, the EMS is a parallel organization in terms of membership. As the EC has expanded to include Greece (1981) and Portugal and Spain (1986), so has the EMS. The British pound has long been included in the calculation of the ECU, but it was not until the fall of 1990 that Great

FIGURE 4.6   The Single-Currency Provisions of the Maastricht Treaty

Stage 1: ERM Membership (July 1, 1990)

- The goals for Stage 1 were the full membership of all 12 EC countries within the Exchange-Rate Mechanism (ERM) of the European Monetary System (EMS).
- The only remaining countries outside the ERM are Greece and Portugal.

Stage 2: Transitional Adjustment (January 1, 1994)

- This will be a transitional period in which all member nations will begin adjustment to the primary criteria necessary for the EMU to be successful.
- The monitoring of compliance with economic criteria will be done by the newly created European Monetary Institute (EMI). The EMI will become the European Central Bank (ECB) at the end of the second-stage period in preparation for full EMU.

Stage 3: Economic and Monetary Union (Earliest January 1, 1997; Latest January 1, 1999)

- The primary condition for this transition to the third and final stage is that the majority of the EC countries meet the necessary conditions.

1.	Inflation	A country's rate of inflation cannot exceed that of the EC countries with the lowest rate by more than 1.5 percentage points.
2.	Interest Rates	A country's long-term interest rates cannot exceed those of the best performing countries by more than 2 percentage points.
3.	Exchange Rates	A country's currency shall have been devalued for at least the last two years prior to EMU.
4.	Government Budgets	A country's government deficit may not exceed 3 percent of gross domestic product and gross government debt (outstanding) may not exceed 60 percent of GDP.

- After conditions are judged to have been met, the ECU members will by qualified vote decide whether the move to Stage 3 will be made and a date set for it to start. The ECU basket will be frozen. The possibility of realignment of exchange rates will still exist in Stages 1 and 2.
- If unanimity is not reached or conditions not met, Stage 3 will commence on January 1, 1999, for all participating countries. On that date all participants will adopt a single currency.
- The European Central Bank (ECB) will begin operations in Stage 3. The ECB will be "fairly independent"; the Ministries of Finance of the members establishing broad outlines for monetary and exchange rate policy.
  1. The ECB will be responsible for monetary policy and the stability of the financial system.
  2. The main aim of monetary policy will be to maintain price stability.

Source: Adapted from "Timetable for Economic and Monetary Union Decided Upon at Maastricht," *Economic Review,* 1992-1, Kansallis-Osake-Pankki, Finland, p. 59.

Britain joined the ERM. Although all countries are not ERM participants, the expansion of more countries, economies, and their currencies into the EMS has introduced considerable pressure on the system.

- German reunification. The merging of West Germany and East Germany in 1989 increased inflationary and budget pressures in Germany significantly. The West German currency, the deutschemark, was exchanged for the East German, the ostmark, at fixed rates that were artificially high for the ostmark. This caused major monetary-policy actions that threatened the internal stability of the EMS as the dominance of the deutschemark within the EMS was only seen to increase.

● Maastricht and a single currency for Europe. The continuing movements toward European integration (the **Maastricht Treaty**) have resulted in a specific time schedule for the eventual creation of a single currency to replace the individual currencies of the EMS/EC members. The financial crisis of September 1992, which definitely set back much of financial integration, will likely have a lasting impact on the accomplishment of a single currency for Europe.

Single Europe and the Maastricht Treaty

The passage of the Single European Act in 1986 was the first step toward the creation of a true single currency for Europe. Through the implementation of 286 EC directives, the European Community successfully eliminated many of the internal barriers that remained between the countries of the EC. Many of the barriers that were eliminated by December 31, 1992, were remaining restrictions on capital flows between countries. Capital was now free to move across borders, and therefore across currencies, with the various financial incentives provided by competitive markets.

In December 1991, in an attempt to maintain the momentum of European integration, the members of the European Community concluded the Maastricht Treaty. The treaty, besides laying out long-term goals of harmonized social and welfare policies in the Community, specified a timetable for the adoption of a single currency to replace all individual currencies. This was a very ambitious move. As described in Figure 4.6, the Maastricht Treaty called for the integration and coordination of economic and monetary policy so that few financial differences would exist by the time of currency unification in 1997. For a single currency to work, there would be only one monetary policy across all countries. Otherwise, different monetary policies would lead to different interest rates. Differences in interest rates often lead to

Global Perspective

4.1
"Forex Dealers 'Idiots' Ex-German Chancellor Says"

Paris, Reuter — Former West German Chancellor Helmut Schmidt, in an interview published on Monday, blamed television for turning politicians into shallow showmen and said foreign exchange markets were made up of idiots. Television was changing the world as much as printing had 400 years ago, he told the French newspaper *Le Monde*.

"In a televised society, personalities are much more important than ideologies," he said. Schmidt accused foreign-exchange dealers of fomenting economic disorder, calling them "petty bank clerks only responding to the moment's mood and their pals' stories" and "idiots."

Source: Reuters News Service, January 12, 1993.

large capital flows. In fact, not even Germany would at the time of the signing of the treaty have met all the required criteria for economic performance.

The first major hurdle for the single currency was the acceptance of the treaty. Denmark had been successful in gaining the right to conduct a popular vote of its citizens to determine whether the degree of integration described by Maastricht was indeed desirable. In May 1992, the Danes voted "nej" (no). The Irish and French immediately scheduled popular votes in their own countries. The Irish vote resulted in a relatively strong show of support, while the French vote conducted on September 20 was an extremely narrow yes vote. The French result was immediately dubbed "le petit oui."

The EMS Crisis of September 1992

The inflationary pressures of absorbing, employing, and redeveloping the former East Germany led the German central bank, the Bundesbank, to tighten monetary policy in 1992. As interest rates rose in Germany over the summer of 1992, capital continued to flow out of other major European currencies into deutschemarks. Several EMS currencies experienced downward pressure to the point they were hitting their allowed bands versus the deutschemark. Although the Bundesbank was well aware of its tight money policy's impact on the exchange markets, its primary responsibility was preserving price stability in Germany, not exchange-rate stability.

Even after raising interest rates several times in attempts to defend their currencies, both Italy and Great Britain withdrew their currencies from the ERM the week of September 14, 1992. It was a devastating setback for the European Monetary System. The Spanish peseta and the Portuguese escudo were devalued officially within the EMS grid, although they were able to remain in the ERM. As the lira and pound then floated free of the EMS, their values dropped significantly as the downward pressures on currency values were given free rein. It is not expected that either currency will likely rejoin the ERM before 1994. The status of a single currency for Europe is therefore on hold. As the following section describes, the fundamental financial forces that drive exchange-rate movements are known, but the inherent conflict between domestic economic goals and international economic goals continues to plague the world's monetary system.

EXCHANGE RATES, INTEREST RATES, AND ECONOMIC POLICY

The international monetary system of the 1990s is a significantly different one than any of the past. The capital markets of major industrialized countries are now linked so closely that significant economic or financial events that used to be "isolated" can now affect capital flows worldwide in minutes. For those who believe in the efficiency of unregulated markets, the trend toward more open financial markets worldwide is a good one. But open markets and freely flowing markets also come at a cost. The cost is the ability of a country to define and determine its domestic economic and monetary policies independently of world markets. As Global Perspective 4.1 illustrates, many present and former government policymakers do not always approve of what the markets do or think.

As noted in the previous section, currencies respond to interest-rate movements. Assuming all markets and currencies are relatively stable and secure, a country that can lower its domestic interest rates to encourage growth may at the same time find its currency under downward pressure as capital flows out in search of higher interest. This poses a serious problem for the country. If it believes in open and free markets, government policymakers do not wish to restrict capital flows. Yet, most countries prefer stable exchange rates. So what is the government to do?

This is the problem now confronting the members of the European Community. Simply put, internal goals and external goals are in direct conflict. The conflict arises from the following three financial policies:

1. Fixed Exchange Rates. A fixed exchange rate is best for the conduct of international commerce. The stability it provides in pricing helps a country's importers and exporters to manage sourcing and sales without dealing with large currency risks.

2. Freedom of Capital Flows. Not only within the European Community, but throughout the world, countries are deregulating financial markets. Capital flows between countries and major financial markets are increasing. As capital moves more freely, it can move in larger quantities and more quickly to take advantage of higher returns (such as higher interest rates). If economic and monetary policies are roughly the same across countries, there is little reason to exchange currency in an attempt to escape inflation or seek out higher interest rates.

3. Independent Monetary Policies. Every country wants to conduct its own economic policy. This means the ability to utilize fiscal-policy measures (government spending and taxation) and monetary-policy measures (money-supply growth, interest-rate restricting or **pegging**) to manage domestic economic needs.

The result is that a country can have two of these, but not all three. If capital is allowed to move freely, and monetary policy utilized for domestic goals regardless of how it compares to other economies, fixed exchange rates are difficult to achieve (or maintain in the recent EMS crisis). The authors of the Maastricht Treaty recognized this when they designed a system that would have fixed exchange rates, free capital flows, but one single monetary policy for all countries. It seems that the internal-versus-external crisis hit the system in its early stages of transition. Exchange rates were fixed, but capital-flow freedom moved forward much faster than any harmonization of monetary policy.

THE DEBT CRISIS AND CURRENCY EARNINGS

The flow of capital across borders and currencies can have a number of positive and negative impacts, some of which were not intended. The difficulty in repayment of much of the capital that flowed into the world's developing countries in the late 1970s and early 1980s created a continuing series of severe problems for borrower and lender alike in the past decade. There have been many different individual "debt crises" over the past 40 years, in which countries could not repay the debt they had borrowed from others, but the difficulties of several major Latin American and South American countries beginning in 1982 are the focus of what is commonly termed the debt crisis.

The "debt" of the debt crisis was capital acquired by government borrowers primarily from large international banking syndicates worldwide. Throughout the 1970s and early 1980s, many Latin American and South American national governments (and other governmental units, such as states or provinces, national oil companies, railroads, and utilities) borrowed large quantities of capital to aid in the industrialization of their economies. Many of these countries possessed massive quantities of natural resources and other factors that would aid in rapid development, and the access to more capital was thought to constitute a sound policy for more rapid economic growth. At the same time, slower economic growth among the major industrial countries had produced large quantities of capital that could not find profitable uses.[13] The developing countries wanted to borrow, and the international banks wanted to lend. It was thought to be a profitable arrangement for both sides.

Debt, and the ability to repay or "service" debt, is normally not a particularly difficult problem. The proceeds of commerce produce the cash flows necessary for an individual, a firm, or even a country through its taxation to repay the debt. But what if the debt and its repayment are denominated in a foreign currency, such as the U.S. dollar? How does a country such as Mexico acquire U.S. dollars to repay debt in dollars? Simply exchanging the domestic currency like the Mexico peso for U.S. dollars will not work for the quantities needed. Attempts to exchange massive quantities of pesos for foreign currencies would quickly drive the value of the peso down to virtual worthlessness.

The answer is that a country obtains foreign currency only one way, by exporting. When Mexico or Brazil or Argentina exports products to world markets, it can request payment in a currency that is readily convertible on world markets, such as the U.S. dollar, German mark, or Japanese yen (often referred to as hard currencies). The country must not only export large quantities of goods to earn sufficient currency, but it also must not spend much of what it earns for imports. Only by running a trade surplus can a country such as Mexico hope to earn the hard currency needed for debt repayment.

Friday, August 13, 1982: The Crisis

On Friday, August 13, 1982, the finance minister of Mexico, Silva Herzog, called the U.S. secretary of the Treasury to inform him that Mexico would be unable to meet major debt-service payments due to banks on the following Monday. Mexico was requesting the aid of the United States and the other major industrial countries in finding solutions to the problem. Although the economic forces that produced this crisis had been in motion for years, it is this date that is often termed the "beginning of the Latin American debt crisis."[14]

Mexico, like Brazil, Argentina, Peru, Ecuador, and many other Latin American countries, had borrowed large amounts of capital on the assumption that its export earnings would continue to grow rapidly as they had throughout the 1970s. But the worldwide recession of 1980–1982 had slowed economies to the point that no one was buying, and the export earnings of the debtor countries dropped precipitously. The exports of these countries were primarily commodities. More than 70 percent of Mexico's export earnings came from the production and sale of one product, oil. However, oil prices had dropped from more than $30 a barrel in late 1979 to less than $20 a barrel in 1982. Other countries, like Brazil and Argentina, were heavily dependent on the exports of agricultural and timber products, all of which had experienced substantial declines in price and sales in the depressed world economy.

The debtor countries were unable to obtain the currencies they needed for debt service. It is estimated that more than 90 percent of all Latin American debt was dollar-denominated. It was only a matter of weeks before Mexico's debt-service difficulties spread to Brazil and Argentina, the countries with the largest and third-largest debts. The crisis took on epic proportions.

Due to the scale of the problem, both in terms of the magnitude of debt and the number of individual banks and institutions with which renegotiations and debt restructurings needed to take place, the IMF took on an increasingly central role in the debt crisis. In addition to providing much of the bailout lending throughout 1983 and 1984, the IMF also served as chief negotiator and manager of much of the debt restructurings through agreements with the international banks and their home governments. This constituted a significant increase in the power and visibility of the IMF, originally constructed only as a source of lending for countries with short-term Balance of Payments problems (which of course the debtor countries were experiencing).

By the mid-1980s, as the costs of the debt crisis continued to mount, the IMF came under increasing criticism from debtor countries for the economic policies the IMF required for the debtors to qualify for continuing capital. IMF conditionality is the set of prescribed economic and monetary polices deemed necessary for the individual countries to regain economic growth. Many of the most heavily indebted countries have continued to suffer high rates of inflation and slow or negative economic growth. But, unfortunately, most policies necessary for long-term economic stability (the reduction of inflation, reduced government deficits, and exchange-rate stability) cause increases in unemployment and reductions in the standard of living of the lower-income groups. It is hoped that the costs of these policies will be short-lived.

Solutions to the Debt Crisis

Solutions to the crisis have been both short- and long-term. First, the debtor countries needed additional capital immediately in order to avoid defaulting on the existing loans. Additional credit was immediately provided by international organizations such as the International Monetary Fund, the Bank for International Settlements (BIS), and individual loans or advance export purchases by industrial governments like the United States.[15]

The continuing management of the debt-service problems of the heavily indebted countries has gone through four stages of evolution. Each can be seen as a response to the economic pressures of the time, the successes and failures of previous stages, and the philosophy and capabilities of the individuals leading the debate.

Stage 1: Bailout Lending   The immediate liquidity aid provided by the IMF, BIS, and others was only a temporary fix, and all parties knew that true solutions would require the restructuring of the existing debt. This meant providing grace periods before additional debt-service payments were required, lower interest rates, and extended maturities for repayment. Although all agreed these measures were necessary, it was critical that the debtor countries be provided with short-term capital, so-called bailout lending, to see them through the time required for renegotiating the hundreds of loans. Much of the management during this period, 1982 and 1983, was simply the consolidation of debt that was coming due or already in arrears.

Stage 2: Multiyear-Restructuring Agreements   Once consolidation had taken place, immediate concern was to ensure some minimal continuing flow of capital to these heavily indebted countries. In 1983 and 1984 all parties entered into continuing renegotiations to attempt to restructure the debt to alleviate some of the burden on the debtors. Little real progress was made, however, as many of the renegotiations continued to be pursued on an individual basis, each country having to negotiate with the multitude of the banks and organizations holding their debt. It has also been argued that one of the reasons little progress was made in this period was the

The World's Most Severely Indebted Countries
(billions of United States dollars)

Source: *World Debt Tables, 1991-92.* Note: The World Bank defines *external debt* as the sum of portfolio investments by nonresidents and other long-term capital inflows by nonresidents. It does not include foreign direct investment by nonresidents; the category of international investment which leads to the classification of the United States as the "world's largest debtor nation."

burden of blame was concentrated on the borrowers, with little blame and burden accepted by the banking institutions, which, in the eyes of many, had been overly zealous in their lending practices.

Stage 3: The Baker Plan   When James Baker took over as secretary of the Treasury at the start of the second Reagan Administration, major initiatives were put forward to solve the ever-worsening debt crisis. Secretary Baker and the U.S. administration, in a complete reversal of previous policy, now wished to take a larger and more active hand in solving the crisis. The Baker Plan, as first presented at the IMF meetings in Seoul, Korea, in October 1985, had three elements: (1) recognition of realistic limits to the austerity measures being imposed from outside and inside on the debtor countries; (2) solutions to the continuing crisis required not only debt reduction but positive measures of promoting economic growth in the debtor countries; and (3) the need for renewed lending by private banking institutions to the developing countries.

Stage 4: The Brady Plan   With a new U.S. secretary of the Treasury, Nicholas Brady, came a new plan in March 1989. The Brady Plan differed markedly from previous strategies, given its adoption of ideas promoted the previous year by the Japanese finance minister, Kiichi Miyazawa. Miyazawa's plan was to focus multilateral efforts on debt reduction, not debt service. Debt reduction was to be accomplished by dividing the outstanding debt of several indebted countries into two parts, one part for debt reduction, the other for debt-interest-payment guarantees. Multilateral institutions like the IMF and World Bank would guarantee the interest payments on the second portion of the outstanding debt, thus shifting credit risk from the borrower countries to the institutions. Japan itself also served as a major source of the capital necessary for much of this debt-reduction policy. In addition, many of the debt-swap programs (debt for equity, debt for environment, debt for development, and so forth) that involve the substitution of local-currency debt for dollar debt were pushed forward.

The debt crisis is still far from over. Continued efforts at debt reduction and debt management are ongoing as many of the most severely indebted countries still struggle under the burden of servicing their obligations.

Recent Debt Levels and Economic Performance

It is important to note that many of the world's largest indebted countries are African and Eastern European; Latin America has no monopoly on debt. Brazil, Mexico, and Argentina are still the three most severely indebted countries, although Poland's debt levels have continued to rise. Nigeria, Venezuela, and Algeria, all exporters of oil, are also suffering under a burden of costly debt.

Figure 4.7 illustrates key debt-burden ratios for these same countries. Although the map on page 113 demonstrates who owes the most, the ratio of total external debt to the country's Gross National Product (GNP), is indicative of the relative burden. In 1990, two of the countries shown, Nigeria and Ivory Coast, both had debt levels that exceeded the entire annual output of their economies (Nigeria, 117.9 percent; Ivory Coast, 203.9 percent). Of more immediate concern with external debt, however, is the amount of export earnings that are required to service the debt in the current year. The ratios of interest expenses to export earnings also shown in Figure 4.7 indicate a number of countries are over 15 percent and approaching 20 percent of their total export revenues needed for debt service, income that is in effect already spent.

FIGURE 4.7   Relative Debt Burdens of the Most Severely Indebted Countries % (percent)

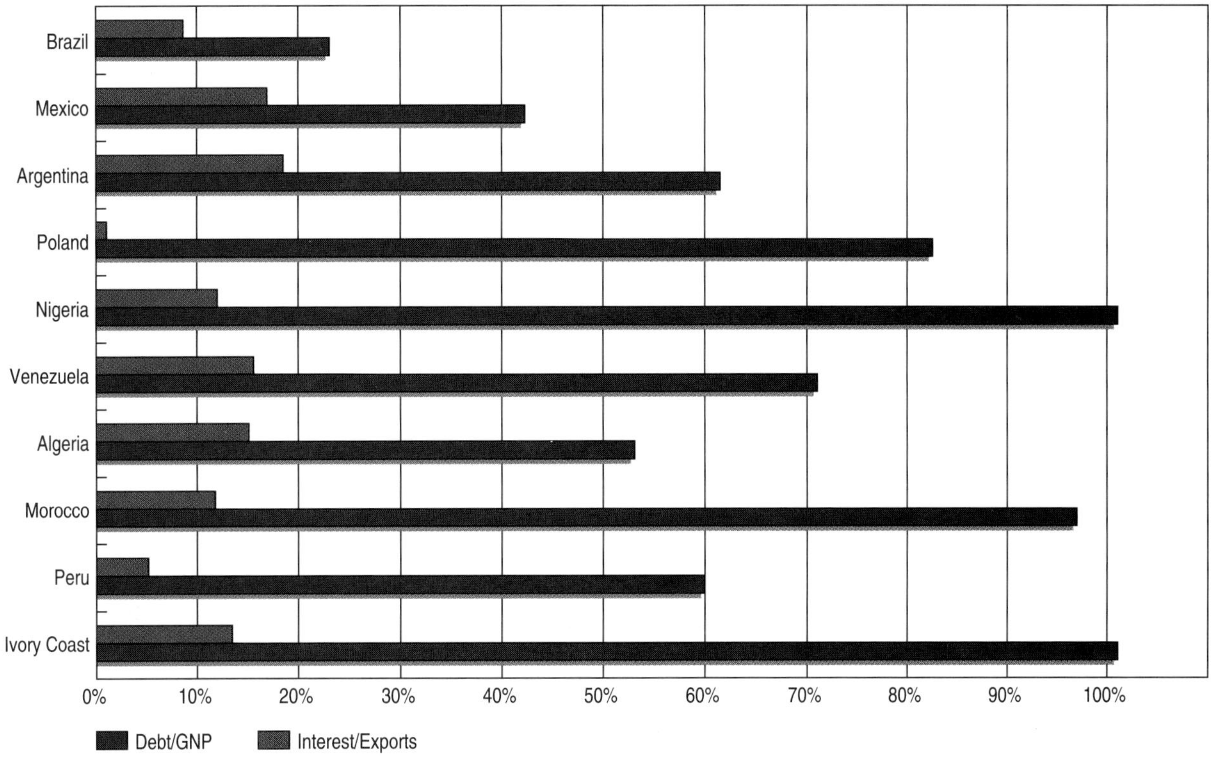

Note: Debt as a percentage of total Gross National Product (GNP) and interest expenses as a percentage of total export earnings are frequently used indicators of the burden of foreign currency–denominated debt.
Source: *World Debt Tables, 1991–92,* The World Bank, Washington, D.C., 1992, p. 25.

SUMMARY

The exchange of currency is necessary for international trade and commerce. The purpose of exchange-rate systems is to provide a free and liquid market for the world's currencies while providing some degree of stability and predictability to currency values. The modern history of the international monetary system has seen periods of success and failure in the accomplishments of this purpose.

The gold standard, which was in wide use during the early years of the 20th century, was a highly restrictive system. The ability to convert currency to gold imposed restrictions on the ability of countries to run inflationary monetary policies or conduct imbalanced trade for substantial periods of time. But the gold standard was also inflexible, and many have argued that it slowed economic growth unduly by limiting the amount of money that could be put into growing economies.

The Bretton Woods Agreement signed in 1944, in anticipation of the reconstruction of the world economy after World War II, was an international monetary system in which the U.S. dollar was the centerpiece, and literally "good as gold." Although working well for 25 years, it too saw its natural decline as the world economy changed and world currency markets needed to change with it. The result, the floating-exchange-rate system in use today, reflects the dominance of market economies, market forces, and the growth in international commerce. Two of the most influential multilateral institutions in operation today, the International Monetary Fund and the World Bank, arose from the Bretton Woods Agreement.

The international flow of capital, introduced in Chapter 2 and detailed in Chapter 3, is not without its dangers. Countries with large foreign-currency debts have continued to be burdened with the servicing of their debts. The ability of countries to generate sufficient hard-currency earnings is still dependent on export earnings. The stability of currency markets, the need for continued free-flowing international trade and export earnings, is integral to the continued health and growth of the world economy.

Key Terms and Concepts

international monetary system	Group of Ten
purchasing power parity (PPP)	Smithsonian Agreement
Law of One Price	Jamaica Agreement
gold standard	Group of Five
par value	Plaza Agreement
rules of the game	Group of Seven
convertibility	reference zone
competitive devaluation	Louvre Accord
Bretton Woods Agreement	European Monetary System (EMS)
International Monetary Fund (IMF)	Exchange Rate Mechanism (ERM)
fundamental disequilibrium	Maastricht Treaty
Special Drawing Right (SDR)	pegging
International Bank for Reconstruction and Development (World Bank)	

Questions for Discussion

1. Why has the gold standard always been considered such a solid and dependable system?
2. Why was it so important that the U.S. dollar be convertible to gold for the Bretton Woods system to operate effectively?
3. Why did the major world currencies move from a fixed- to a floating-exchange-rate system in the 1970s?
4. How has foreign-exchange-market intervention changed in the past two decades? Why is it that direct intervention no longer works?
5. Why have the currencies of the European Community countries remained relatively fixed, while the U.S. and Japanese currencies have continued to float?
6. Why is it necessary for the European Community to form a single banking system with a single monetary policy before it can adopt a single currency?
7. What caused the British pound to be withdrawn from the ERM in September 1992?
8. What is the relationship between exchange rates and the debt crisis?

Recommended Readings

Business Week, "Rivalries Beset Monetary Pact," Number 776, July 15, 1944, 15–16.

Business Week, "The New Trade Strategy," October 7, 1985, 90–93.

Business Week, "The Paris Pact May Not Buoy the Dollar for Long," March 9, 1987, 40–41.

Commission of the European Communities. "The ECU and Its Role in the Process Towards Monetary Union," *European Economy,* No. 48, September 1991, 121–138.

Dewey, Davis Rich, *Financial History of the United States,* Second Edition. New York: Longmans, Green, and Company, 1903.

Driscoll, David D., *What Is the International Monetary Fund?* Washington, D.C.: External Relations Department, International Monetary Fund, November 1992.

The Economist, "Black Wednesday: The Campaign for Sterling," January 9, 1993, 52, 54.

Evans, John S., *International Finance.* Ft. Worth, Tex.: Dryden Press, 1992.

Federal Reserve Bulletin, "Treasury and Federal Reserve Foreign Exchange Operations," October 1971, 783–814.

Funabashi, Yuichi, *Managing the Dollar: From the Plaza to the Louvre.* Washington, D.C.: Institute of International Economics, 1988.

Morgan Guaranty, *World Financial Markets,* New York, various issues.

O'Cleireacain, Seamus, *Third World Debt and International Public Policy.* New York: Praeger, 1990.

Ungerer, Horst, Jouko J. Hauvonen, Augusto Lopez-Claros, and Thomas Mayer, *The European Monetary System: Developments and Perspectives.* Washington, D.C.: International Monetary Fund, 1990.

Van Dormael, Armand, *Bretton Woods.* New York: Holmes & Meier, 1978.

The World Bank, *World Debt Tables, 1991–92,* Washington, D.C., 1992.

Notes

1. Actually there are a few exceptions. Panama has used the U.S. dollar as its currency for many years.

2. The U.S. dollar was actually stated as being officially worth $20.67 per ounce of gold from 1837 to 1914, although there were many periods in which the United States backed its money with both gold and silver and many periods in which it was very difficult to say that the paper currency was indeed redeemable for gold.

3. The student is always led to believe in the study of historical events that policies or laws or decisions were achieved so clearly or with little question or doubt. *Business Week*'s issue of July 8, 1944, in its regular editorial news on "The War and Business Abroad" led with the following statement:

    The world is watching the monetary conference at Bretton Woods for the first clews to the way the United Nations are prepared to cooperate in shaping the peace—and the results inevitably will be disappointing.

    Although the Bretton Woods Agreement eventually worked well for over 20 years, there was considerable debate regarding its prospects in 1944. And yes, the word was spelled "clews" and not "clues."

4. *Business Week,* July 15, 1944, p. 15.

5. The participants at Bretton Woods specifically wanted to avoid the devaluation problems experienced on world markets in the 1930s. The competitive devaluations that dominated that period proved disastrous to world trade and economic stability as governments continually attempted to devalue to keep exports cheaper than foreign competitors'. The point of the adjustable peg was ultimately not to have to adjust it.

6. The meetings at Bretton Woods had hardly begun when the delegation from the Soviet Union objected to its preliminary quota as being too small! Soviet delegates argued that prewar trade was not representative of the true size and strength of the Soviet economy, and the postwar era would see a much more powerful trading nation. The quotas were read-

justed, with the Soviet quota rising from about $800 million to $1.2 billion.

7. The original proposal was to contribute 25 percent of its quota in gold or 10 percent of its domestic gold stock, whichever the country chose. The Soviet Union as well as a number of other countries opposed this. Everyone was actually quite happy to eliminate the choice and choose the 25 percent of quota approach since it generally required a significantly smaller contribution of gold.

8. *Business Week,* "Rivalries Beset Monetary Pact," July 15, 1944, p. 16.

9. The Group of Ten, or G-10 Countries, consists of the United States, Canada, Great Britain, France, Germany, Italy, Belgium, the Netherlands, Sweden, and Japan.

10. Paul Volker was not new to the Federal Reserve or to world currency markets. It was Paul Volker, then Under Secretary of the U.S. Treasury, who had flown to London in August 1971 to explain President Nixon's closing of the gold window to European currency authorities.

11. Yuichi Funabashi, in *Managing the Dollar: From the Plaza to the Louvre,* provides an enlightening discussion of the rounds of private negotiation regarding the level of intervention each individual G5 member would be committed to under the Plaza Agreement. Although each country is believed to have committed itself to significant intervention, it is not believed that the levels discussed ever took place.

12. The Group of Seven is composed of the United States, Japan, Germany, France, Great Britain, Canada, and Italy. The Italian delegation withdrew from the meetings the first day, however, in protest over being excluded from a G5 (G7 less Canada and Italy) state dinner the evening before. So the meetings may actually have been classified as the G6.

13. The large increases in the price of oil instituted by the Organization of Petroleum Exporting Countries (OPEC) in 1974 and 1979 had also resulted in enormous quantities of capital that needed to be invested in profitable ventures. Because oil is priced and sold on world markets in U.S. dollars, this accumulation of capital, OPEC dollars, provided an enormous supply of one specific currency.

14. Mexico was indeed in crisis. In August 1982 Mexico devalued the peso 30 percent versus the U.S. dollar, instituted a two-tier exchange-rate system, froze dollar-denominated bank accounts in Mexico, and on August 12 announced the total embargo of U.S. dollars crossing the U.S.-Mexico border (on their way out). On Wednesday, September 1, President Jose Lopez Portillo announced the nationalization of Mexico's private banks.

15. One example of this is the advance payment to Mexico by the United States (specifically the Department of Energy) for $1 billion worth of oil. The United States purchased the oil for the government's strategic petroleum reserves. At the time of payment, however, the oil was still in the ground in Mexico.

International Financial Markets

LEARNING OBJECTIVES

1. To understand how currencies are traded and quoted on world financial markets.

2. To examine the linkages between interest rates and exchange rates.

3. To understand the similarities and differences between domestic sources of capital and international sources of capital.

4. To examine how the needs of individual borrowers have changed the nature of the instruments traded on world financial markets in the past decade.

"The Days Are Numbered For Secret Accounts"

What's a money launderer to do? If you've got millions in ill-gotten gains to stash, you'll probably want to steer clear of Swiss banks from now on.

In the latest step in a long campaign to drive out dirty money, Switzerland on May 3 abolished its most secret of accounts—the ones that permit depositors to hide their names even from their most trusted bankers by using lawyers or other agents as fronts.

The Swiss have been acting less for domestic reasons than for international ones. With their domestic market cooling, the Swiss have invested billions of dollars in expansion abroad. The country's three big banks—Union Bank of Switzerland, Credit Suisse, and Swiss Bank—now own large brokerage houses in London and New York. They also manage hundreds of billions of dollars in corporate pension funds worldwide. Thus, the Swiss have concluded, they can no longer afford to risk retaliation by governments angered at the prospect of Swiss banks hiding dirty cash.

The Swiss move also stems from several hot-money affairs that have tarnished the country's image in recent years. In 1986, Zurich's Bank Leu found itself entangled in the Securities & Exchange Commission's insider-trading investigation of Wall Street investment banker Dennis B. Levine. In 1989, Justice Minister Elisabeth Kopp was forced to resign after allegedly tipping her husband off that the company he worked for was under investigation in a $1 billion Lebanese money-laundering scandal. She was later cleared of wrongdoing.

Since the Kopp affair, Switzerland has made insider trading and money laundering illegal. It voluntarily froze Iraqi assets and blocked the secret accounts of former Philippines dictator Ferdinand Marcos and deposed Haitian ruler Jean-Claude Duvalier. Central Bank President Markus Lusser argues that refusing to adopt the same tough banking standards other countries use would be "extremely detrimental to Switzerland's international credibility."

Source: Abstracted from "The Days Are Numbered For Secret Accounts," *Business Week,* May 20, 1991, p. 122.

International financial markets serve as links between the financial markets of each individual country and as independent markets outside the jurisdiction of any one country. The market for currencies is the heart of this international financial market. International trade and investment are often denominated in a foreign currency, so the purchase of the currency precedes the purchase of goods, services, or assets.

This chapter provides a detailed guide to the structure and functions of the foreign-currency markets, the international money markets, and the international securities markets. All firms striving to attain or preserve competitiveness will need to work with and within these international financial markets in the 1990s.

THE MARKET FOR CURRENCIES

The price of one country's currency in terms of another country's currency is called a foreign-currency-exchange rate. For example, the exchange rate between the U.S. dollar (USD) and the German mark (deutschemark, or DEM) may be "1.5 marks per dollar," or simply abbreviated DEM 1.5000/USD. This is the same exchange rate as when it is stated USD 1.00 = DEM 1.50. Since most international business activities require at least one of the two parties to first purchase the country's currency before purchasing any good, service, or asset, a proper understanding of exchange rates and exchange-rate markets is very important to the conduct of international business.

A word on symbols. As already noted, the symbols USD and DEM are often used as the symbols for the U.S. dollar and the German mark. The field of international finance suffers, however, from a lack of common agreement when it comes to currency abbreviations. This chapter will use the computer symbols utilized by the Telerate news service for the sake of consistency (although any other set would work just as well). But as a practitioner of international finance, as with all fields, stay on

Foreign-exchange traders like these at Republic National Bank of New York can move millions of dollars, yen, or marks around the world with a few keystrokes on their networked computer terminals. In addition to technological advances in communications and data processing, the deregulation of international capital flows also contributes to faster, cheaper transactions in currency markets.

Source: Courtesy of Republic National Bank of New York: Photo by William Taufic.

your toes. Every market, every country, every firm, has its own set of symbols. For example, the symbol for the British pound sterling can be £ (the pound symbol), GBP (Great Britain pound), STG (sterling), or UKL (United Kingdom pound).

Exchange-Rate Quotations and Terminology

The order in which the foreign-exchange (FX) rate is stated is sometimes confusing to the uninitiated. For example, when the rate between the U.S. dollar and the German mark was stated above, a **direct quotation** on the German mark was used. This is simultaneously an **indirect quotation** on the U.S. dollar. The direct quote on any currency is the form when that currency is stated first; an indirect quotation refers to when the subject currency is stated second. Figure 5.1 illustrates both forms, direct and indirect quotations, for major world currencies on Friday, January 8, 1993. These are the most commonly seen set of exchange-rate quotations in use today, the daily currency quotations from *The Wall Street Journal.*

Most of the quotations listed in Figure 5.1 are **spot rates.** A spot transaction is the exchange of currencies for immediate delivery. Although it is defined as immediate, in practice, settlement actually occurs two business days following the agreed-upon exchange. The other time-related quotations listed in Figure 5.1 are the **forward rates.** Forward exchange rates are contracts that provide for two parties to exchange currencies on a future date at an agreed-upon exchange rate. Forwards are typically traded for the major-volume currencies for maturities of 30, 90, 120, 180, and 360 days (from the present date). The forward, like the basic spot exchange, can be for any amount of currency. Forward contracts serve a variety of purposes, but their primary purpose is to allow a firm to lock in a future rate of exchange. This is a valuable tool in a world of continually changing exchange rates.

The quotations listed will also occasionally indicate if the rate is applicable to business-trade, the commercial rate, or for financial-asset purchases or sales, the financial rate. Countries that have government regulations regarding the exchange or their currency may post official rates, while the markets operating outside their jurisdiction will list a floating rate. In this case any exchange of currency that is not under the control of that government is interpreted as a better indication of the currency's true market value.

FIGURE 5.1 **Exchange Rate Quotations**

Friday, January 8, 1993

The New York foreign exchange selling rates below apply to trading among banks in amounts of $1 million and more, as quoted at 3 p.m. Eastern time by Bankers Trust Co., Telerate and other sources. Retail transactions provide fewer units of foreign currency per dollar.

Country	U.S. $ equiv. Fri.	U.S. $ equiv. Thurs.	Currency per U.S. $ Fri.	Currency per U.S. $ Thurs.
Argentina (Peso)	1.01	1.01	.99	.99
Australia (Dollar)	.6728	.6698	1.4863	1.4930
Austria (Schilling)	.08640	.08681	11.57	11.52
Bahrain (Dinar)	2.6522	2.6522	.3771	.3771
Belgium (Franc)	.02955	.02967	33.84	33.70
Brazil (Cruzeiro)	.0000795	.0000804	12584.01	12439.05
Britain (Pound)	1.5325	1.5325	.6525	.6525
30-Day Forward	1.5272	1.5272	.6548	.6548
90-Day Forward	1.5181	1.5181	.6587	.6587
180-Day Forward	1.5075	1.5079	.6633	.6632
Canada (Dollar)	.7798	.7813	1.2823	1.2800
30-Day Forward	.7774	.7787	1.2864	1.2842
90-Day Forward	.7729	.7742	1.2938	1.2917
180-Day Forward	.7620	.7681	1.3123	1.3019
Czechoslovakia (Koruna)				
Commercial rate	.0350754	.0350631	28.5100	28.5200
Chile (Peso)	.002689	.002687	371.82	372.13
China (Renminbi)	.171233	.171233	5.8400	5.8400
Colombia (Peso)	.001612	.001612	620.50	620.50
Denmark (Krone)	.1573	.1581	6.3563	6.3248
Ecuador (Sucre)				
Floating rate	.000554	.000554	1806.00	1806.00
Finland (Markka)	.18214	.18539	5.4902	5.3939
France (Franc)	.17873	.17969	5.5950	5.5650
30-Day Forward	.17742	.17825	5.6365	5.6100
90-Day Forward	.17510	.17578	5.7110	5.6890
180-Day Forward	.17279	.17331	5.7875	5.7700
Germany (Mark)	.6079	.6107	1.6450	1.6375
30-Day Forward	.6051	.6078	1.6526	1.6452
90-Day Forward	.6004	.6030	1.6656	1.6585
180-Day Forward	.5948	.5974	1.6813	1.6740
Greece (Drachma)	.004551	.004572	219.75	218.70
Hong Kong (Dollar)	.12916	.12917	7.7425	7.7420
Hungary (Forint)	.0120700	.0120861	82.8500	82.7400
India (Rupee)	.03482	.03482	28.72	28.72
Indonesia (Rupiah)	.0004843	.0004843	2065.00	2065.00
Ireland (Punt)	1.5970	1.6049	.6262	.6231
Israel (Shekel)	.3659	.3670	2.7328	2.7249
Italy (Lira)	.0006626	.0006616	1509.30	1511.42
Japan (Yen)	.007974	.007984	125.40	125.25
30-Day Forward	.007971	.007980	125.46	125.31
90-Day Forward	.007968	.007979	125.49	125.34
180-Day Forward	.007974	.007986	125.41	125.23
Jordan (Dinar)	1.4789	1.4789	.6762	.6762
Kuwait (Dinar)	3.2927	3.2927	.3037	.3037
Lebanon (Pound)	.000544	.000544	1838.00	1838.00
Malaysia (Ringgit)	.3851	.3852	2.5970	2.5960
Malta (Lira)	2.6525	2.6525	.3770	.3770
Mexico (Peso)				
Floating rate	.3206156	.3206156	3.12	3.12
Netherland (Guilder)	.5410	.5434	1.8486	1.8401
New Zealand (Dollar)	.5103	.5089	1.9596	1.9650
Norway (Krone)	.1422	.1421	7.0299	7.0372
Pakistan (Rupee)	.0390	.0390	25.62	25.62
Peru (New Sol)	.6235	.6216	1.60	1.61
Philippines (Peso)	.04082	.04082	24.50	24.50
Poland (Zloty)	.00006550	.00006612	15268.01	15123.01
Portugal (Escudo)	.006770	.006801	147.72	147.05
Saudi Arabia (Riyal)	.26665	.26665	3.7503	3.7503
Singapore (Dollar)	.6015	.6026	1.6625	1.6595
South Africa (Rand)				
Commercial rate	.3235	.3260	3.0913	3.0678
Financial rate	.2045	.2079	4.8900	4.8100
South Korea (Won)	.0012628	.0012641	791.90	791.10
Spain (Peseta)	.008561	.008610	116.81	116.15
Sweden (Krona)	.1345	.1357	7.4354	7.3688
Switzerland (Franc)	.6667	.6696	1.5000	1.4935
30-Day Forward	.6652	.6681	1.5032	1.4968
90-Day Forward	.6627	.6655	1.5090	1.5026
180-Day Forward	.6603	.6630	1.5145	1.5082
Taiwan (Dollar)	.039746	.039746	25.16	25.16
Thailand (Baht)	.03917	.03917	25.53	25.53
Turkey (Lira)	.0001157	.0001161	8645.06	8616.00
United Arab (Dirham)	.2723	.2723	3.6725	3.6725
Uruguay (New Peso)				
Financial	.000277	.000277	3611.00	3611.00
Venezuela (Bolivar)				
Floating rate	.01269	.01271	78.78	78.70
SDR	1.36664	1.37202	.73172	.72885
ECU	1.19180	1.19730		

Special Drawing Rights (SDR) are based on exchange rates for the U.S., German, British, French and Japanese currencies. Source: International Monetary Fund.

European Currency Unit (ECU) is based on a basket of community currencies.

Source: *The Wall Street Journal*, January 11, 1993, p. C 15.

Direct and Indirect Quotations

The Wall Street Journal quotations list the rates of exchange between major currencies, both in direct and indirect forms. The exchange rate for the German mark versus U.S. dollar, in the third column shown, is DEM 1.6450/USD. This is a direct quote on the German mark or indirect quote on the U.S. dollar. The inverse of this spot rate is listed in the first column, the indirect quote on the German mark or direct quote on the U.S. dollar, USD .6079/DEM. The two forms of the exchange rate are of course equal, one being the inverse of the other.[1]

$$\frac{1}{\text{DEM } 1.6450/\text{USD}} = \text{USD } .6079/\text{DEM}$$

Luckily, the world foreign-currency markets do follow some conventions to minimize confusion. With only a few exceptions, most currencies are quoted in direct quotes versus the U.S. dollar (DEM/USD, YEN/USD, FFR/USD), also known as European terms. The major exceptions are currencies at one time or another associated with the British Commonwealth, including the Australian dollar and of course the British pound sterling. These are customarily quoted as USD per pound sterling or USD per Australian dollar, known as American terms. Once again, it makes no real difference whether one quotes U.S. dollars per Japanese yen or Japanese yen per U.S. dollar, as long as one knows which is being used for the transaction.

Cross Rates

Although it is common among exchange traders worldwide to quote currency values against the U.S. dollar, it is not necessary. Any currency's value can be stated in terms of any other currency. When the exchange rate for a currency is stated without using the U.S. dollar as a reference, it is referred to as a **cross rate.** For example, the German mark and Japanese yen are both quoted on Friday, January 8, 1993, versus the U.S. dollar: DEM 1.6450/USD and YEN 125.40/USD. But if the YEN/DEM cross rate is needed, it is simply a matter of division:

$$\frac{\text{YEN } 125.40/\text{USD}}{\text{DEM } 1.6450/\text{USD}} = \text{YEN } 76.231/\text{DEM}$$

The YEN/DEM cross rate of 76.231 is the third leg of the triangle, which must be true if the first two exchange rates are known. If one of the exchange rates changes due to market forces, the others must adjust for the three exchange rates to all be aligned once again. If they are out of alignment, it would be possible to make a profit simply by exchanging one currency for a second, the second for a third, and the third back to the first. This is known as triangular arbitrage. Besides the potential profitability of arbitrage that may occasionally occur, cross rates have become increasingly common in a world of rapidly expanding trade and investment. The world's financial markets no longer revolve about the U.S. dollar.

Percentage Change Calculations

The quotation form is important when calculating the percentage change in an exchange rate. For example, if the spot rate between the Japanese yen and the U.S. dollar changed from YEN 125/USD to YEN 150/USD, the percentage change in the value of the Japanese yen is

$$\frac{\text{YEN } 125/\text{USD} - \text{YEN } 150/\text{USD}}{\text{YEN } 150/\text{USD}} \times 100 = -16.67\%$$

The Japanese yen has declined in value versus the U.S. dollar by 16.67 percent. This is consistent with the intuition that it now requires more yen (150) to buy a dollar than it used to (125).

The same percentage change result can be achieved by using the inverted forms of the same spot rates (indirect quotes on the Japanese yen) if care is taken to also "invert" the basic percentage-change calculation. Using the inverse of YEN 125/USD (USD 0.0080/YEN) and the inverse of YEN 150/USD (USD 0.0067/YEN), the percentage change is still -16.67 percent:

$$\frac{\text{USD } 0.0067/\text{YEN} - \text{USD } 0.0080/\text{YEN}}{\text{USD } 0.0080/\text{YEN}} \times 100 = -16.67\%$$

If the percentage changes calculated are not identical, it is normally the result of rounding errors introduced when inverting the spot rates. Both methods are identical, however, when calculated properly.

Foreign-Currency-Market Structure

The market for foreign currencies is a worldwide market that is informal in structure. This means that it has no central place, pit, or floor like the floor of the New York Stock Exchange, where the trading takes place. The "market" is actually the thousands of telecommunications links between financial institutions around the globe, and it is open 24 hours a day. Someone, somewhere, is nearly always open for business.

The structure of the foreign-currency market leads to some interesting problems. For example, since there is no one exchange, no one floor, no world central bank, is there a single exchange rate? The answer is no, there is no single agreed-upon rate of exchange for all financial institutions. Since all the banks and financial institutions that are trading the currencies are calling and communicating with dozens or hundreds of banks all over the world, they are all seeing or hearing slightly different rates.

For example, Table 5.1 reproduces a computer screen from one of the major international financial information news sources, Reuters. This is the spot-exchange screen, called FXFX, which is available to all subscribers to the Reuters news network. The screen serves as a bulletin board, where all financial institutions wanting to buy or sell foreign currencies can post representative prices. Although the rates quoted on these computer screens are indicative of current prices, due to the rapid movement of rates worldwide, the buyer is still referred to the individual bank for the latest quotation. And there are obviously hundreds of banks operating in the markets at any moment that are not listed on the brief sample of Reuters FXFX page.[2] The speed with which this market moves and the multitude of players playing on a field that is open 24 hours long and the circumference of the earth wide produce many different "single prices." A good example of this lack of one price is to look back at Figure 5.1. The explanation of the exchange-rate quotes states:

> The New York foreign exchange selling rates below apply to trading among banks in amounts of $1 million and more, as quoted at 3 p.m. Eastern time by Bankers Trust Co., Telerate and other sources. Retail transactions provide fewer units of foreign currency per dollar.

TABLE 5.1
Typical Foreign-Currency Quotations on a Reuters Screen

13:07	CCY	Page	Name	*Reuters Spot Rates* CCY		HI* Euro**	Lo FXFX
13.06	DEM	DGXX	DG BANK	FFT	1.8528/33 * DEM	1.8538	1.8440
13.06	GBP	AIBN	AL IRISH	N.Y.	1.7653/63 * GBP	1.7710	1.7630
13.06	CHF	CITX	CITYBANK	ZUR	1.5749/56 * CHF	1.5750	1.5665
13.06	JPY	CHNY	CHEMICAL	N.Y.	128.53/58 * JPY	128.70	128.23
13.07	FRF	MGFX	MORGAN	LDN	6.3030/60 * FRF	6.3080	6.2750
13.06	NLG	MGFX	MORGAN	LDN	2.0920/30 * NLG	2.0925	2.0815
13.00	ITL	MGFX	MORGAN	LDN	1356.45/6.58 * ITL	1356.45	1349.00
13.02	XEV	PRBX	PRIVAT	COP	1.1259/68 * XEV	1.1304	1.1255

Column 1:   Time of entry of the latest quote to the nearest minute (British Standard time)
Column 2:   Currency of quotation (bilateral with the U.S. dollar); quotes are currency per USD, except for the British pound sterling (dollars per unit of pound) and the European Currency Unit (dollars per unit of XEV). The currency symbols are as follows: DEM — German mark; GBP — British pound sterling; CHF — Swiss franc; JPY — Japanese yen; FRF — French franc; NGL— Netherlands guilder; ITL — Italian lira; XEV — European Currency Unit.
Column 3:   Mnemonic of inputting bank. Allows the individual trader to dial up the correct page (by this mnemonic) where the trader could see the full set of spot and forward quotes for this and other currencies being offered by this bank.
Column 4:   Name of the inputting bank.
Column 5:   Branch location of that bank from which the quote has emanated (so that an inquiring trader can telephone the correct branch); FFT — Frankfurt, N.Y. — New York, ZUR — Zurich, LDN — London, COP — Copenhagen.
Column 6:   Spot exchange-rate quotation, bid quote, then offer quote.
Column 7:   Recent high price for this specific quote.
Column 8:   Recent low price for this specific quote.
Source: Adapted from Goodhart, C. A. E., and L. Figliuoli, "Every Minute Counts in Financial Markets," *Journal of International Money and Finance*, 10, 1991, pp 23-52.

Those are pretty specific prices! The rates quoted are the FX rates as seen by only one or a few members of the world of participants and at a specific point in time (3 p.m. Eastern time). The rates are obviously "wholesale rates," applicable to large-scale trading, and will therefore be better than one might trade at in an airport when exchanging currencies on international trips.

One way to put this ever-changing market in perspective is to think of the FX market as a never-ending horse race. The winner is whoever is ahead at one point on the track, at one point in time, from the viewpoint of where in the stands the audience is sitting. The markets continue, as would the theoretical horses, forever. The rates quoted by Bankers Trust or Telerate are therefore only daily snapshots of the race, the daily photo-finish from the individual bank's seat in the stands.

Currency Bid and Offer Quotes

The individual spot quotes shown in Table 5.1 have both bid and offer quotations for the currencies listed. For example, DG Bank (Deutsche Bank) in Frankfurt, Germany, posted a spot quote on the German mark (DEM) of 1.8528/33 at 13:07 (1:07 p.m. London time). These bid and offer quotes are for either the purchase (bid) or sale (offer) of German marks in exchange for U.S. dollars.

Bid:	DEM 1.8528/USD	The spot rate of exchange at which the bank is willing to purchase U.S. dollars, or sell German marks
Offer:	DEM 1.8533/USD	The spot rate of exchange at which the bank is willing to sell U.S. dollars, or buy German marks.

The quote is stated with only the last two digits of the offer rate listed separately. Every exchange rate has a customary number of digits used. In the case of the DEM/USD, all quotes are carried to the fourth decimal place. These are referred to as "basis points" or "pips."[3] The individual bank makes its profit on a single trade on the **spread,** the difference between the bid and offer quotes (if it simultaneously bought and sold dollars for marks at the quoted rates).

Market Size and Composition

Until recently there was little data on the actual volume of trading on world foreign-currency markets. Starting in the spring of 1986, however, the Federal Reserve Bank of New York, along with other major industrial countries' central banks through the auspices of the Bank for International Settlements (BIS), started surveying the activity of currency trading every three years. Some of the principal results are shown in Figure 5.2.

Growth in foreign-currency trading has been nothing less than astronomical. The survey results for the month of April 1992 indicate that daily foreign-currency trading on world markets exceeded $1,000,000,000,000 (a trillion with a "t"). In comparison, the annual (not daily) U.S. government budget deficit has never exceeded $300 billion, and the U.S. merchandise-trade deficit has never topped $200 billion.

There are three reasons typically given for the enormous growth in foreign-currency trading:

FIGURE 5.2
Daily Foreign-Currency Trading on World Markets
(billions of U.S. dollars)

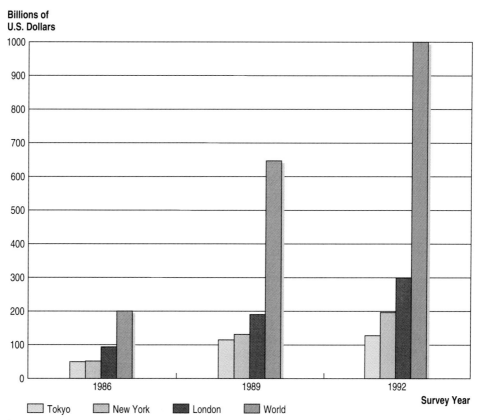

Source: Adapted by authors from the Federal Reserve Bank of New York's *Summary of Results of the U.S. Foreign Exchange Market Turnover Survey,* April 1992, and the Bank for International Settlements *60th Annual Report.*

Deregulation of International Capital Flows   It is now easier than ever to move currencies and capital around the world without major governmental restrictions. Much of the deregulation that has characterized government policy in the United States, Japan, and the European Community over the past 10 to 15 years has focused on financial deregulation.

Gains in Technology and Transaction Cost Efficiency   It is now faster, easier, and cheaper to move millions of dollars, yen, or marks around the world than ever before. Technological advancements in not only the dissemination of information, but also in the conduct of exchange or trading, have added greatly to the ability of individuals working in these markets to conduct instantaneous arbitrage (some would say speculation).

The World Is a Risky Place   Many argue that the financial markets have become increasingly volatile over recent years, with larger and faster swings in financial variables like stock values and interest rates adding to the motivations for moving more capital at faster rates.

It is obvious that the majority of the world's trading in foreign currencies is still taking place in the cities where international financial activity is centered: London, New York, and Tokyo. The recent survey by the U.S. Federal Reserve of currency trading by financial institutions and independent brokers in New York reveals additional information of interest. Approximately 66 percent of currency trading occurs in the morning hours (Eastern Standard Time), with 29 percent between noon and 4 p.m., and the remaining 5 percent between 4 p.m. and 8 a.m. the next day. The average size of a single spot currency trade in New York in April 1992 was $4 million.

The currency composition of the New York spot market is shown in Figure 5.3. Although there is some cross-currency trading (non-U.S. dollar), the vast majority of transactions involve the U.S. dollar. In fact the U.S. dollar was involved in 89 percent of all currency trades in New York, with the German mark being involved in an additional 10 percent (of which the U.S. dollar was not part). Although there may be at least 160 currencies listed around the world according to the International Monetary Fund, the U.S. dollar still dominates currency trading, at least in New York. The U.S. dollar versus the German mark, Japanese yen, and British pound sterling accounted for nearly 65 percent of all transactions at the time of the April 1992 New York survey.

Which Currencies Float?

The exchange-rate regimes in use around the world today cover the full spectrum between rigidly fixed to freely floating. The statement that "we live in a world of floating exchange rates" is, however, a misrepresentation of the world markets in general.

Table 5.2 summarizes world currency arrangements as of September 30, 1992. All currencies listed (members of the International Monetary Fund) are first classified in general categories of "currency pegged to," "flexibility limited in terms of a single currency or group of currencies," and "more flexible." The results are quite striking. Of the 167 individual currencies listed, 26 currencies were pegged to the U.S. dollar, 14 to the French franc, and 31 were pegged to a currency composite of the country's choosing (an index). The European Monetary System's members are

FIGURE 5.3   **Currency Composition of Spot Trades, New York, April 1992**

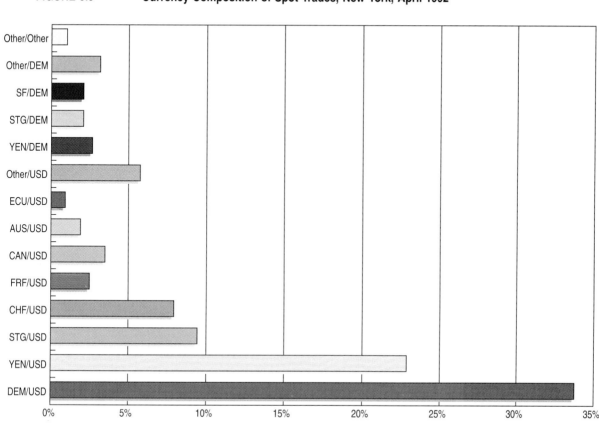

Source: Federal Reserve Bank of New York, *Summary of Results of the U.S. Foreign Exchange Market Turnover Survey,* April 1992, p. 9.

included within the "limited flexibility/cooperative arrangements" category. The only other countries listed in this category are four Middle Eastern countries that are economically intertwined. The third category, "more flexible," lists 22 countries of managed floating and 41 countries that are independently floating.

The world's currency markets cannot be classified with a blanket statement of fixed or floating exchange rates. In fact, only 67 of the listed 167 country currencies are either independently floating or managed floats (sometimes referred to as dirty floats). The remaining 100 currencies are pegged to one specific currency, such as the U.S. dollar, or are operating within a strict system of fixed exchange rates, such as the European Monetary System. A more detailed look at the world's currency markets supports the need to avoid generalizations when discussing international business and economics in today's world.

THE EUROPEAN MONETARY SYSTEM

The European Monetary System commenced operations in March 1979. As explained in Chapter 4, the EMS was formed by the countries of the European Community to construct an island of fixed exchange rates for themselves in an ocean of major floating currencies, such as the U.S. dollar and Japanese yen. This was particularly important since each of the individual countries relied so heavily on trade with its

TABLE 5.2 Exchange Rate Arrangements[1]

	Currency Pegged to					Flexibility Limited in Terms of a Single Currency or Group of Currencies		Adjusted according to a set of indicators[5]	More Flexible	
U.S. Dollar	French franc	Russian ruble	Other currency	SDR	Other composite[2]	Single currency[3]	Cooperative arrangements[4]		Other managed floating	Independently floating
Angola	Benin	Armenia	Bhutan (Indian rupee)	Iran, I.R. of	Algeria	Bahrain	Belgium	Chile	China, P.R.	Afghanistan
Antigua & Barbuda	Burkina Faso	Belarus		Libya	Austria	Qatar	Denmark	Colombia	Egypt	Albania
Argentina	Cameroon	Georgia	Estonia (deutsche mark)	Myanmar	Bangladesh	Saudi Arabia	France	Madagascar	Greece	Australia
Bahamas, The	C. African Rep.	Kyrgyzstan		Rwanda	Botswana	United Arab Emirates	Germany	Zambia	Guinea	Bolivia
Barbados	Chad	Moldova		Seychelles	Burundi		Ireland		Guinea-Bissau	Brazil
Belize	Comoros		Kiribati (Australian dollar)		Cape Verde		Luxembourg		India	Bulgaria
Djibouti	Congo				Cyprus		Netherlands		Indonesia	Canada
Dominica	Equatorial Guinea				Czechoslovakia		Portugal		Israel	Costa Rica
Ecuador	Gabon		Lesotho (South African rand)		Fiji		Spain		Korea	Dominican Rep.
Ethiopia	Ivory Coast				Hungary				Lao P.D. Rep	El Salvador
Grenada	Mali		Namibia (South African rand)		Iceland				Maldives	Finland
Iraq	Niger				Jordan				Mexico	Gambia, The
Liberia	Senegal				Kenya				Pakistan	Ghana
Marshall Islands	Togo				Kuwait				Poland	Guatemala
Mongolia					Malawi				Sao Tome & Principe	Guyana
Nicaragua			Swaziland (South African rand)		Malaysia				Singapore	Haiti
Oman					Malta				Somalia	Honduras
Panama					Mauritania				Sri Lanka	Italy
St. Kitts & Nevis					Mauritius				Tunisia	Jamaica
St. Lucia					Morocco					

	Currency Pegged to				Flexibility Limited in Terms of a Single Currency or Group of Currencies				Adjusted according to a set of indicators[5]	More Flexible	
	U.S. Dollar	French franc	Russian ruble	Other currency	SDR	Other composite[2]	Single currency[3]	Cooperative arrangements[4]		Other managed floating	Independently floating
	St. Vincent and the Grenadines					Nepal				Turkey	Japan
	Suriname					Norway				Uruguay	Latvia
	Syrian Arab Rep.					Papua New Guinea				Viet Nam	Lebanon
	Trinidad and Tobago					Solomon Islands					Lithuania
	Yemen, Republic of					Sweden					Mozambique
											New Zealand
	Yugoslavia					Tanzania					Nigeria
						Thailand					Paraguay
						Tonga					Peru
						Vanuatu					Philippines
						Western Saoma					Romania
						Zimbabwe					Russia
											Sierra Leone
											South Africa
											Sudan
											Switzerland
											Uganda
											Ukraine
											United Kingdom
											United States
											Venezuela
											Zaïre

Excluding the currency of Cambodia, for which no current information is available. For members with dual or multiple exchange markets, the arrangement shown is that in the major market.
Comprises currencies which are pegged to various "baskets" of currencies of the members' own choice, as distinct from the SDR basket.
Exchange rates of all currencies have shown limited flexibility in terms of the U.S. dollars.
Refers to the cooperative arrangement maintained under the European Monetary System.
Includes exchange arrangements under which the exchange rate is adjusted at relatively frequent intervals, on the basis of indicators determined by the respective member countries.
Source: International Monetary Fund, *International Financial Statistics*, December 1992, p. 6.

fellow EC members. But unlike the fixed exchange-rate systems of the past (the gold standard or the Bretton Woods system), the EMS is a highly intricate system of fixed central exchange rates and bilateral responsibilities.

The EMS Grid

The core of the EMS lies in the specification of central rates. The first row of Table 5.3 shows the central rates per currency in effect in the EMS preceding the crisis of September 1992. For example, the central rate for the German mark was DEM 2.05586/ECU. (Note that the currency symbols now used are the official symbols of the EMS, which of course differ from those used anywhere else!) The central rate of the Belgian franc is BFR 42.4032/ECU. Since both currencies are defined in terms of the same unit (the ECU), a central cross rate is then calculated:

$$\frac{\text{DEM } 2.05586/\text{ECU}}{\text{BFR } 42.4032/\text{ECU}} = \text{DEM } 0.048484/\text{BFR}$$

By this method, all EMS currencies can be stated in central-rate values of all other currencies. This forms "the grid" as shown in Table 5.3.

The purpose of the grid is twofold. First, as just described, it provides a method for the calculation of the central rates, sometimes called parity rates, among all member currencies. These are the "fixed rates" that are the focus of why the EMS exists. Secondly, however, these central rates are used to determine the allowable ranges over which the individual exchange rates may move. These upper and lower values, called intervention points, are also shown in Table 5.3. These intervention points are found by calculating movements of +/−2.25 percent from the central rate.[4]

The meaning of these intervention points is literal. For example, the central rate between the German mark and the French franc shown in Table 5.3 is DEM 0.298164/FF. The band of +/−2.25 percent is set at DEM 0.219500/FF (strong mark and weak franc) and DEM 0.304950/FF (weak mark and strong franc). Intervention is required if the German mark appreciates versus the French franc to the point where it takes only 0.2195 German marks to purchase a French franc.[5] At this point, it is the responsibility of both countries to undertake policies to keep the exchange rate within the band. These policies may include foreign currency intervention (buying and selling the currencies on the open market), interest-rate policies (usually raising interest rates to "support" the domestic currency by attracting capital), and even monetary policies affecting inflation and economic growth if needed. It is this bilateral responsibility that has allowed the EMS to achieve most of its goals, currency stability and economic growth of its member currencies and countries, over time.

Realignments of the EMS Grid

Times and economic conditions change. The EMS has been forced to realign central rates more than 12 times over its history. This has usually been the result of a number of factors such as the growth of one country's share of European trade, the relatively healthy growth of the country's economy, the stability and security of the country's currency, and so forth. All of these factors are the economic justifications for why the world demands more of one currency and less of another. The "popular currency" is eventually revalued in the EMS grid, and the "unpopular currency" (usually described as being under attack) is devalued.

The German mark is the one currency of the EMS that has seen continual revaluation during the past decade. The mark's original central rate was DEM 2.51064/ECU

TABLE 5.3 The European Monetary System Grid: Central Rates and Intervention Points

	German mark	British pound	French franc	Italian lira	Spanish peseta	Belgian franc	Dutch guilder	Danish krone	Irish pound	Portuguese escudo
ECU Central Rate	2.05586	0.696904	6.89509	1538.24	133.631	42.4032	2.31643	7.84195	0.767417	178.735
1 DM		0.31928	3.27920	731.5700	61.217	20.1655	1.1017	3.7300	0.3650	81.900
		0.33898	3.35386	748.2170	65.000	20.6255	1.1267	3.8144	0.3733	86.939
		0.35997	3.43050	765.4000	69.017	21.0950	1.1524	3.9016	0.3818	92.336
1 UKL	2.7780		9.31800	2078.79	180.59	57.3035	3.13050	10.5976	1.03710	241.545
	2.9500		9.89389	2207.25	191.75	60.8451	3.32389	11.2526	1.10118	256.470
	3.1320		10.50550	2343.62	203.60	64.6050	3.52950	11.9479	1.16920	272.320
1 FF	0.291500	0.09519		218.130	18.2530	6.0130	0.32848	1.1120	0.1088	24.4130
	0.298164	0.10107		223.091	19.3806	6.1498	0.33595	1.1373	0.1113	25.9291
	0.304950	0.10732		228.170	20.5780	6.2897	0.34360	1.1632	0.1138	27.5240
1 LIT	0.001307	.0004267	.0043830		0.081820	0.026953	.0014725	0.004985	.0004878	0.010943
	0.001337	.0004531	.0044825		0.086873	0.027566	.0015059	0.005098	.0004989	0.011619
	0.001367	.0004811	.0045845		0.092240	0.028193	.0015400	0.005214	.0005102	0.012338
1 PTA	0.014490	.0049116	0.048595	10.8410		0.298850	0.016325	0.05526	.0054086	1.25970
	0.015385	.0052151	0.051598	11.5111		0.317316	0.017335	0.05868	.0057428	1.33753
	0.016330	.0055374	0.054785	12.2230		0.336930	0.018405	0.06231	.0060977	1.42020
1 BFR	0.047400	.0154790	0.158990	35.4690	2.96802		0.053415	0.18083	0.017695	3.96980
	0.048484	.0164352	0.162608	36.2764	3.15143		0.054629	0.18494	0.018098	4.21513
	0.049590	.0174510	0.166310	37.1020	3.34619		0.055870	0.18914	0.018510	4.47560
1 DFL	0.86780	0.283340	2.91040	649.280	54.3310	17.8985		3.3102	0.32394	72.6700
	0.88753	0.300853	2.97661	664.053	57.6883	18.3054		3.3854	0.33129	77.1597
	0.90770	0.319450	3.04440	679.120	61.2530	18.7215		3.4624	0.33887	81.9000
1 DKR	0.25630	0.083697	0.859700	191.790	16.0490	5.2870	0.288825		0.095683	21.4660
	0.26216	0.088869	0.879257	196.154	17.0405	5.4072	0.295389		0.097860	22.7922
	0.26810	0.094361	0.899250	200.620	18.0940	5.5300	0.302100		0.100087	24.2010
1 IRL	2.61900	0.855260	8.7850	1959.84	163.997	54.0250	2.9510	9.9913		219.350
	2.67894	0.908116	8.9848	2004.43	174.131	55.2545	3.0185	10.2186		232.905
	2.74000	0.964240	9.1890	2050.03	184.892	56.5115	3.0870	10.4511		247.299
1 ESC	0.010830	.0036722	0.036332	0.081050	0.704130	0.223435	0.012210	0.041321	.0040437	
	0.011502	.0038991	0.038577	0.086063	0.747649	0.237241	0.012960	0.043875	.0042936	
	0.012210	.0041400	0.040961	0.091380	0.793850	0.251900	0.013760	0.046586	.0045590	

Source: Adapted from *European Economy*, No. 4, September 1991, p. 125.

(March 1979). As of August 1992, the mark had risen to DEM 2.05586/ECU. It continues to be the currency carrying the largest weight and the greatest long-term stability within the EMS.

As briefly described in Chapter 4, the **European Monetary System** has recently experienced its greatest crisis with the turmoil of September 1992. The British pound and the Italian lira both withdrew from the Exchange-Rate Mechanism in September 1992. The problems were compounded with the devaluations in the following months of the Spanish peseta, Portuguese escudo, and eventually the Irish pound (also called the punt). The expectations for the achievement of monetary unification for all of the EMS must realistically be postponed at the least. The withdrawal of the British pound and the Italian lira suspends responsibility for maintaining the currency value between the intervention points shown in Table 5.3; the currencies remain members of the EMS, mostly in spirit.

INTERNATIONAL MONEY MARKETS

A money market is traditionally defined as a market for deposits, accounts, or securities that have maturities of one year or less. The international money markets, often termed the Eurocurrency markets, constitute an enormous financial market that is in many ways outside the jurisdiction and supervision of world financial and governmental authorities.

Eurocurrency Markets

A **Eurocurrency** is any foreign currency–denominated deposit or account at a financial institution outside the country of the currency's issuance. For example, U.S. dollars that are held on account in a bank in London are termed **Eurodollars.** Similarly, Japanese yen held on account in a Parisian financial institution would be classified as Euroyen. The Euro prefix does not mean these currencies or accounts are only European, as German marks on account in Singapore would also be classified as a Eurocurrency, a Euromark account.

Eurocurrency Interest Rates

What is the significance of these foreign currency–denominated accounts? Simply put, the purity of value that comes from no governmental interference or restrictions with their use. Because Eurocurrency accounts are not controlled or managed by governments (for example, the Bank of England has no control over Eurodollar accounts), the financial institutions pay no deposit insurance, hold no reserve requirements, and are normally not subject to any interest-rate restrictions with respect to these accounts. Eurocurrencies are one of the purest indicators of what these currencies should yield in terms of interest. Sample Eurocurrency interest rates for 1993 are shown in Table 5.4.

There are hundreds of different major interest rates around the globe, but the international financial markets focus on a very few, the interbank interest rates. Interbank rates charged by banks to banks in the major international financial centers such as London, Frankfurt, Paris, New York, Tokyo, Singapore, and Hong Kong are generally regarded as "the interest rate" in the respective market. The interest rate that is used most often in international loan agreements is the Eurocurrency interest rate on U.S. dollars (Eurodollars) in London between banks: the London Interbank Offer Rate (LIBOR). Because it is a Eurocurrency rate, it floats freely without

		United States dollar	German mark	Japan yen
Eurocurrency deposit rate	Spot rate	—	1.6420	125.38
	1 month	3.1250	8.5000	3.8438
London rates	3 months	3.2500	8.3125	3.7188
(bid rates)	6 months	3.5000	8.0000	3.5938
	12 months	3.9375	7.3750	3.5000

TABLE 5.4
Eurocurrency Interest Rates
(percent per annum)

Source: *Harris Bank Foreign Exchange Weekly Review*, Harris Trust and Savings Bank, Chicago, January 8, 1993.

regard to governmental restrictions on reserves or deposit insurance or any other regulation or restriction that would add expense to transactions using this capital. The interbank rates for other currencies in other markets are often named similarly, PIBOR (Paris interbank offer rate), MIBOR (Madrid interbank offer rate), HIBOR (either Hong Kong or Helsinki interbank offer rate), SIBOR (Singapore interbank offer rate). While LIBOR is the offer rate, the cost of funds "offered" to those acquiring a loan, the equivalent deposit rate in the **Euromarkets** is LIBID, the London Inter-Bank Bid Rate, the rate of interest other banks can earn on Eurocurrency deposits.

How do these international Eurocurrency and interbank interest rates differ from domestic rates? Answer: not by much. They generally move up and down in unison, by currency, but often differ by the percent by which the restrictions alter the rates of interest in the domestic markets. For example, because the Euromarkets have no restrictions, the spread between the offer rate and the bid rate (the loan rate and the deposit rate) is substantially smaller than in domestic markets. This means the loan rates in international markets are a bit lower than domestic-market loan rates, and deposit rates are a bit higher in the international markets than in domestic markets. This is, however, only a big-player market. Only well-known international firms, financial or nonfinancial, have access to the quantities of capital necessary to operate in the Euromarkets. But as described in the following sections on international debt and equity markets, more and more firms are gaining access to the Euromarkets to take advantage of deregulated capital flows.

Linking Eurocurrency Interest Rates and Forward Exchange Rates

Eurocurrency interest rates also play a large role in the foreign-exchange markets themselves. They are, in fact, the interest rates used in the calculation of the forward rates we noted earlier (for examples of forward rate quotes refer back to Figure 5.1). Recall that a forward rate is a contract for a specific amount of currency to be exchanged for another currency at a future date, usually 30, 60, 90, 180, or even 360 days in the future. Forward rates are calculated from the spot rate in effect on the day the contract is written along with the respective Eurocurrency interest rates for the two currencies.

For example, to determine the 90-day forward rate on Friday, January 8, 1993, multiply the spot rate on that date by the ratio of the two Eurocurrency interest rates. Note that it is important to adjust the interest rates for the actual period of time needed, 90 days (3 months) of a 360-day financial year:

$$\text{90-Day Forward} = \text{Spot} \times \left[\frac{1 + i_{90}^{\text{DEM}}\left(\frac{90}{360}\right)}{1 + i_{90}^{\text{USD}}\left(\frac{90}{360}\right)} \right]$$

Now, plugging in the spot exchange rate of DEM 1.6420/USD (note that this Chicago spot rate is slightly different from the New York spot rate quoted in Figure 5.1 even though they are for the same day) and the two 90-day (3-month) Eurocurrency interest rates from Table 5.4 (3.2500 percent for the dollar and 8.3125 percent for the mark), the 90-day forward exchange rate is:

$$\text{DEM } 1.6420/\text{USD} \times \left[\frac{1 + .083125\left(\frac{90}{360}\right)}{1 + .032500\left(\frac{90}{360}\right)} \right] = \text{DEM } 1.6626/\text{USD}.$$

The forward rate of DEM 1.6626/USD is a "weaker rate" for the German mark than the spot rate. This is because one dollar is worth 1.6420 marks spot, but the forward rate states that one dollar will be exchanged for 1.6626 marks in 90 days according to the provisions of the contract. The German mark is **"selling forward at a discount,"** meaning that the forward contract has a rate for purchasing marks that is cheaper than the present spot rate. But why is this the case? The reason is interest rates on German marks are higher than U.S. interest rates. If the above forward rate were calculated with U.S. Eurocurrency interest rates that are higher than German Eurocurrency interest rates, the result would be the opposite. The German mark would be "selling forward at a premium," meaning more expensive versus the dollar than the present spot rate. The forward rates quoted in the foreign-exchange markets simply reflect the interest differentials between the two currencies.

Businesses frequently use forward-exchange-rate contracts to manage their exposure to currency risk. As Chapter 18 will show in detail, corporations use many other financial instruments and techniques beyond forward contracts to manage currency risk, but forwards are still the mainstay of industry.

INTERNATIONAL CAPITAL MARKETS

Just as with the money markets, the international capital markets serve as links between the capital markets of the individual countries, as well as constituting a separate market of its own, the capital that flows into the Euromarkets. Firms can now raise capital, debt or equity, fixed or floating interest rates, in any of a dozen currencies, for maturities ranging from one month to 30 years, in the international capital markets. Although the international capital markets have traditionally been dominated by debt instruments, international equity markets have shown considerable growth in recent years.

The international financial markets can be subdivided in a number of different ways. The following sections will describe the international debt and equity markets for securitized and nonsecuritized capital. This is capital which is separable and tradable, like a bond or a stock. Nonsecuritized, a fancy term for bank loans, was really the original source of international capital (as well as the international debt crisis).

Defining International Financing

The definition of what constitutes an international financial transaction is dependent on two fundamental characteristics: (1) whether the borrower is domestic or foreign and (2) whether the borrower is raising capital denominated in the domestic currency or a foreign currency. These two characteristics form four categories of financial transactions.

Category 1: Domestic Borrower/Domestic Currency   This is a traditional domestic-financial-market activity. A borrower that is resident within the country raises capital from domestic financial institutions denominated in local currency. For example, if a U.S. firm such as General Motors issues a bond in the United States, raising $100 million, the transaction would be classified as purely domestic. All countries with basic market economies have their own domestic financial markets, some large and some quite small. This is still by far the most common type of financial transaction.

Category 2: Foreign Borrower/Domestic Currency   This is when a foreign borrower enters another country's financial market and raises capital denominated in the local currency. For example, if a large foreign firm such as the German automaker BMW comes to the United States and issues a bond, raising $50 million in capital, it is conducting a Category 2 financial transaction. The international dimension of this transaction is only who the borrower is. This is a relatively common type of financial transaction. Many borrowers, both public and private, increasingly go to the world's largest financial markets to raise capital for their enterprises. The ability of a foreign firm to raise capital in another country's financial market is sometimes limited by government restrictions on who can borrow, as well as the market's willingness to lend to foreign governments and companies that it may not know as well as domestic borrowers.

Category 3: Domestic Borrower/Foreign Currency   Many borrowers in today's international markets need capital denominated in a foreign currency. A domestic firm may actually issue a bond to raise capital in its local market where it is known quite well, but raise the capital in the form of a foreign currency. For example, if a large British firm such as Allied-Lyons issued a bond in London to raise US$40 million, it would be classified as a domestic borrower of a foreign currency. This type of financial transaction occurs less often than the previous two types because it requires a local market in foreign currencies, a Eurocurrency market. A number of countries such as the United States highly restrict the amount and types of financial transactions in foreign currency. International financial centers such as London and Zurich have been the traditional centers of these types of transactions.

Category 4: Foreign Borrower/Foreign Currency   This is the strictest form of the traditional Eurocurrency financial transaction, a foreign firm borrowing foreign currency. For example, a French firm that issues a U.S. dollar–denominated bond in London would be issuing a Eurodollar bond. Once again, this type of activity may be restricted by which borrowers are allowed into a country's financial markets and which currencies are available. This type of financing dominates the activities of many banking institutions in the **offshore banking** market.

Using this classification system, it is possible to categorize any individual international financial transaction. For example, the distinction between an international bond and a Eurobond is simply that of a Category 2 transaction (foreign borrower in a domestic currency market) and a Category 3 or 4 transaction (foreign currency denominated in a single local market or many markets).

Driving Forces in the International Financial Markets

The rapid growth of the international financial markets over the past 30 years is the result of four different but complementary forces: deregulation, innovation, **securitization,** and internationalization. Although one normally thinks of the world's largest industrial countries when describing financial markets, all four forces are visible in differing degrees the world over. In fact, the newly opened economies of the former eastern European bloc such as Czechoslovakia (now split into the Czech Republic and Slovakia), Hungary, Poland, and many others are now seeing the impacts of these four forces at something approaching the speed of light.

Deregulation is the first and most important force in opening financial markets. As governments continue to allow foreign firms to enter their markets for the buying and selling of goods, they have also become more willing to allow foreign firms to participate in their local financial markets. Financial deregulation, however, usually lags behind the deregulation of trade markets by long periods of time. The deregulation of domestic markets for domestic firms itself has been important. For example, the distinction as to which types of financial institutions can undertake which types of financial transactions (accept deposits; pay interest; make consumer, industrial, or mortgage loans; underwrite and syndicate securities, and so forth) is very important to the growth of financial markets.

One of the major areas still restricted by many governments is the ability to conduct financial transactions in foreign currencies. Only the true international financial centers like London allow the types of transactions described in Categories 3 and 4, Euromarket transactions. The reason for the slow deregulation of foreign-currency transactions is that government authorities are charged with maintaining the security and stability of their own financial institutions. Since the quantities and values of foreign currency are beyond their control, they are hesitant to allow their own financial institutions to undertake significant activity in these currencies. Even in the case of traditional international financial centers such as London or Hong Kong, the government creates regulatory walls between local and foreign currencies.

Innovation has been the second major driving force. While product markets have grown increasingly competitive, so has the market for financial services. Financial institutions worldwide continue to innovate new and more efficient and effective services for their public and private clients alike. The creation of new types of financial instruments, like floating-rate loans and notes and bonds in the 1970s, was a logical market reaction to a world in which inflation was generally rising across all countries and currencies. Floating interest rates allowed lenders like banks to shift more of the risk of rising interest rates to the borrowers of capital while still allowing the markets to operate and provide much-needed financing for growth.

Securitization has been a remarkably important force in just the past decade. Securitization is the process of turning an illiquid loan into a tradable, asset-backed security. For example, a bank loan is a highly customized contract between a bank and a borrower. Because each loan is so different, it is difficult for the bank to sell its loans, even though it may want to in order to free up more lending capacity. Securitization is the process of creating new ways to make these types of financial agreements liquid (salable in a secondary market) so that the values of these transactions can be more easily identified.

Many firms have shifted away from traditional bank-loan markets to securitized-debt markets. Large firms in the United States, for example, used to acquire most of the long- and short-term capital from banks. As bond markets have grown in size, however, corporations have started funding their long-term capital needs through bonds, debt securities. In the past 20 years, many of America's largest firms have acquired more of their short-term capital from securitized markets, such as the commercial paper market. These long-term and short-term securitization forces are now spreading to many national and international markets.

Locations of the World's Most Important Financial Centers

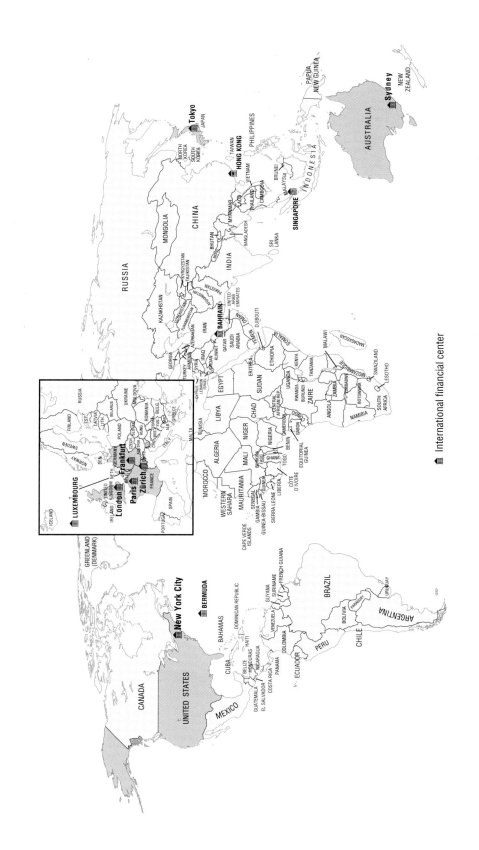

■ International financial center

Sources: *Financial Market Trends*, Oct. 1992; *Fortune*, July 30, 1990.

The fourth and final force is what this book is all about, internationalization. More than a buzzword, internationalization of business activity has forced many firms to acquire capital in many different markets in many different currencies. The growth of the multinational firm, a firm with subsidiaries and affiliates in 10, 20, or 30 countries, has provided an incentive for domestic financial markets to deregulate, innovate, and even securitize financial transactions to compete. Financial services in today's technologically sophisticated information age are considered by many to be more competitive than any product market. Capital today can move around the globe in seconds at practically zero cost.

INTERNATIONAL BANKING AND BANK LENDING

Banks have existed in different forms and roles since the Middle Ages. Bank loans provided nearly all of the debt capital needed by industry since the start of the Industrial Revolution. Even in this age in which securitized debt instruments (bonds, notes, and other types of tradable paper) are growing as sources of capital for firms worldwide, banks still perform a critical role by providing capital for medium and smaller firms, which dominate all economies.

Structure of International Banking

Similar to the direct-foreign-investment-decision sequence discussed in Chapter 2, banks can expand their cross-border activities in a variety of ways. Like all decisions involving exports and direct investment, increasing the level of international activity and capability normally requires placing more capital and knowledge at risk to be able to reap the greater benefits of expanding markets.

A bank that wants to conduct business with clients in other countries but does not want to open a banking operation in that country can do so through **correspondent banks** or **representative offices.** A correspondent bank is an unrelated bank (by ownership) based in the foreign country. By the nature of its business, it has knowledge of the local market and access to clients, capital, and information, which a foreign bank does not. For example, a U.S. bank may maintain correspondent bank relationships with several banks in every other major industrial country. This would require that the U.S. bank keep a small amount of capital on deposit at the individual banks, as would the foreign banks with the U.S. bank. No personnel or investment in other resources would be maintained in the other country. If there are financial services to be provided in the foreign country, the U.S. bank would communicate by phone, telex, or fax the appropriate directions and transactions to be undertaken.

A second way that banks may access foreign markets without actually opening a banking operation is through representative offices. A representative office is basically a sales office for a bank. It provides information regarding the financial services of the bank, but it cannot deliver the services itself. It cannot accept deposits or make loans. The foreign representative office of a U.S. bank will typically sell the bank's services to local firms that may need banking services for trade or other transactions in the United States.

If a bank wants to conduct banking business within the foreign country, it may open a branch banking office, banking affiliate, or even a wholly owned banking subsidiary. A branch banking office is an extension of the parent bank and is not independently financed from the parent. Because the branch office is not independently incorporated, it is commonly restricted in the types of banking activities that it may conduct. Any business conducted by the branch office is a legal liability of the parent bank. Branch banking is by far the most common form of international banking structure used by banks, particularly by banks based in the United States. Although branches are commonly limited in their capabilities due to the restrictions placed upon them by local governments (local governments have little control over the parent of the branch and therefore will limit the services and activities of the branch), they are also relatively cheap ways of accessing foreign markets.

A foreign banking affiliate or banking subsidiary is a locally and separately incorporated bank from the parent bank. If the local bank is wholly owned by the parent, it is a subsidiary; if only partially owned, it is an affiliate. Because these are for all intents and purposes local banks, they normally can provide all the same financial services just like any other banks in that country. Despite this freedom, many foreign banking subsidiaries find it difficult to compete with true local banks due to long-standing business relationships and corporate-banking ties that may date back decades or longer. Among the major industrial countries today, however, many foreign banking affiliates and subsidiaries are so highly integrated into local financial markets that they are indistinguishable from local banks.

Offshore Banking

Most governments regulate the degree of financial activity in a foreign currency that can take place. This has encouraged the growth of what is generally referred to as offshore banking. Offshore banking is the name given to Category 4 transactions, foreign borrowers of foreign currencies.

The primary motivation of offshore banking is avoiding regulation. Because governments do not normally regulate banking activity that does not affect their domestic markets, countries that have historically allowed unregulated foreign-banking activity have been the centers of offshore banking. Many tropical islands, such as the Caymans, the Bahamas, and the Netherlands Antilles, have been the center of much of offshore-banking activity, although countries such as Luxembourg and Switzerland have also provided many of the same services. Although these transactions are officially "booked" through these offshore centers, most of the activity is on paper or telex only as most of the capital never reaches these remote locales.

Because most of the appeal in these offshore centers has been avoiding taxes on income earned abroad, these offshore-banking centers have often been referred to as "tax havens." These centers can shield income from taxes because capital can be held unbeknownst to the owner's national tax authorities. For the most part, these "Wild West" days of international finance are past, and it is generally no longer possible to shield income in tax havens. More and more of the world's banking and financial authorities have increased their cooperation and harmonization of regulatory and supervisory policies. Taxes, as in the old expression, are indeed as unavoidable as death.

One of the most visible actions taken by an individual government to slow or stop the growth of offshore-banking activity was the creation of the **International Banking Facility (IBF)** by the United States in 1981. The IBF was a separate office with a separate set of asset and liability accounts, in which banks in the United States could hold deposits and make loans denominated in foreign currency—a type of onshore offshore Eurocurrency market. The major qualifying restriction on IBFs was that all deposits had to be held by nonresidents and all loans and investments made by the IBFs had to be also extended to nonresidents. In addition to the absence of Federal Deposit Insurance Corporation (FDIC) taxes and reserve requirements, several states, including New York, exempted income generated by IBFs from state and local taxes. Although the IBF attracted more than $300 million in capital within the first two or three years, it has never eliminated the offshore-banking institutions it was created to compete with. The Japanese government in a similar move created the Japanese Offshore Market (JOM) in 1986. The JOM has had similar success in attracting capital, but the same failure in eliminating offshore-banking activity.

International Bank Lending

Bank lending internationally consists of two types of financial credits: (1) loans extended by a single bank, and (2) loans extended by a collection or syndicate of banks. These loans are international loans if they are extended to a foreign borrower or are denominated in a foreign currency. Figure 5.4 illustrates total net international bank lending from 1981 through 1990, as well as the gross amounts of new syndicated loans made annually over the same period. The data given are "net lending," meaning that gross loans made are reduced by the amounts of loans repaid during the year. This is all the more astonishing given net lending of more than $450 billion in 1990.

FIGURE 5.4   International Bank Lending (billions of U.S. dollars)

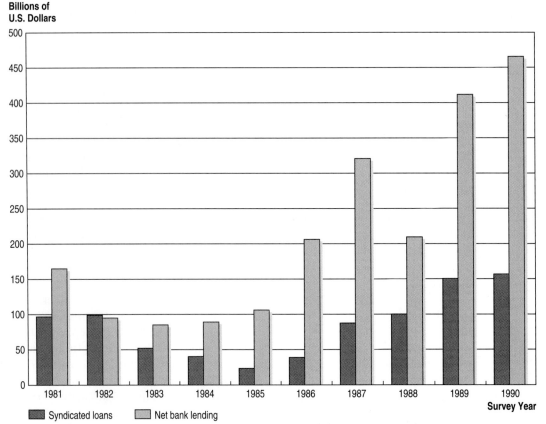

Source: Constructed by authors from data presented in *Bank for International Settlements Annual Reports,* 1983–1992. Syndicated loans are announced new gross issuances.

International bank lending has grown significantly since the early 1980s when net lending was dominated by syndicated loans extended to developing countries. After the decline of the syndicated-loan market in 1983–1986, the growth in international bank lending was in the more traditional form of a simple loan arranged between a single bank and a corporate (not government) borrower. As demonstrated in the following sections, only the international bond markets have grown to near the magnitude of international bank lending. There is no question that international bank lending continues to grow at a very rapid rate.

Syndicated Loans

A **syndicated loan,** sometimes called a syndicated credit, is an arrangement in which between 20 and 50 banks in many different countries contribute to the funding of a single large loan. Most syndicated loans are variable-rate loans with a fixed spread or premium added to a standard variable-rate base. Many of the loans to South American countries in the late 1970s and early 1980s were syndicated loans. A typical Brazilian loan made in 1981 was eight years in maturity, with a premium of 2 1/2 percent added to the six-month LIBOR (London Interbank Offer Rate) interest-rate base. One of the primary advantages of the syndicated loan was the ability of a banking institution to participate in a large loan but not be solely responsible for its funding. Similarly, the borrower could acquire very large amounts of capital in a single loan arrangement, thereby reducing the fees and other expenses associated with many individual loans.[6]

The syndicated-loan market was the source of the debt in the debt crisis. Figure 5.4 shows how the size of new syndicated-loan financing has changed since 1981. Total new loans totaled nearly $100 billion annually in 1981 and 1982 at the height of the lending to many of the now severely indebted countries of South and Latin America. With the onset of the debt crisis in 1982, the market essentially shut down, reaching barely $50 billion in 1983, and eventually falling to only $20 billion in 1985. Since 1985, the syndicated-loan market has once again grown rapidly, reaching nearly $160 billion in 1990.

However, the syndicated-loan market has returned with a different face. Originally a market that transferred capital from the richer industrial countries to the less-developed countries in need of development capital, the market has changed to one that recycles capital among the industrial countries. The market now focuses on lending not to less-developed country governments, but to corporate bodies in primarily two countries, the United States and the United Kingdom. And the capital is no longer targeted at long-term development projects, but rather for the financing of a large proportion of the merger and acquisition financing needed for corporate takeovers in the United States and the United Kingdom. As mergers and acquisitions slowed in the early 1990s, so did the lending activity in the syndicated-loan market.

INTERNATIONAL SECURITY MARKETS

Although banks continue to provide a large portion of the international financial needs of government and business, it is the international debt-securities markets that have experienced the greatest growth in the past decade. The international debt-securities market is composed of the **Euronote** market and the **international-bond** market. Figure 5.5 provides a summary of the degree of each market's growth since 1981.

FIGURE 5.5   **The Growth in International Debt Securities**

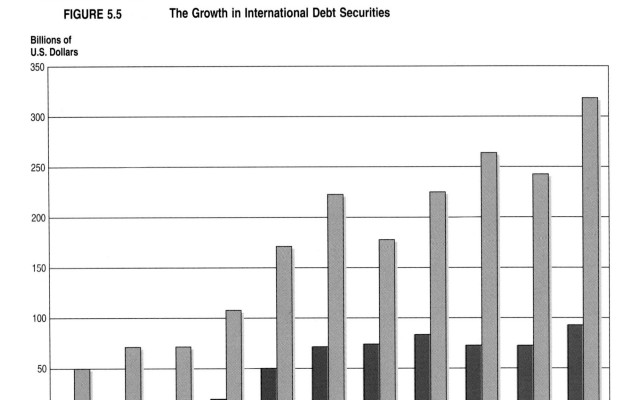

Note: Values are announced new gross issuances.
Source: Bank for International Settlements, *Annual Report,* annually, 1984–1992.

The Euronote Market

The Euronote market is a collective term for a variety of short- to medium-term types of financing. With the demise of the syndicated-loan market in the early 1980s, a gap resulted in the sources of capital for borrowers seeking medium-term financing. The original types of financing were termed note-issuance facilities (NIFs) and revolving-underwriting facilities (RUFs). These "facilities" were arrangements that would allow a firm to borrow capital as needed but at a predetermined rate of interest through notes that were guaranteed to be purchased by a group of financial institutions. These note-issuance facilities were so successful in their early years that many financial institutions competing in the market nearly competed themselves out of business with overly aggressive cut-rate financing. As demonstrated in Figure 5.6, the Euronote market peaked in 1986 and has continued to decline since then.

The true source of sustained financing in the Euronote market came from a financial export of the United States, commercial paper (CP). Commercial paper is a short-term note, typically 30, 60, 90, or 180 days in maturity, sold directly into the financial markets by large corporations. The market originated in the United States in the 1970s when a number of major firms realized they were actually larger and

**FIGURE 5.6
The Growth and
Composition of the
Euronote Market**

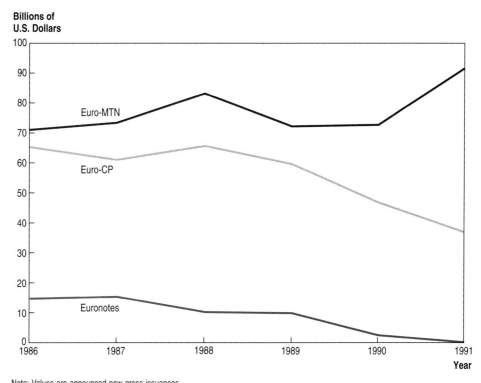

Billions of
U.S. Dollars

Euro-MTN

Euro-CP

Euronotes

1986   1987   1988   1989   1990   1991

Year

Note: Values are announced new gross issuances.
Source: Bank for International Settlements, *Annual Report,* annually, 1984–1992.

more creditworthy than many of the banks they were borrowing from. The solution was to sell their own debt notes directly to the market and bypass the costs of banks. These notes were called commercial paper.

The international version, **Euro–commercial paper (ECP),** arrived in the European markets with a splash in the early 1980s. One of the primary reasons for its rapid growth was the lack of anything similar in most national financial markets. Domestic-commercial-paper markets were legalized in many major countries only in the middle to late 1980s: France in 1985, the United Kingdom in 1986, Japan in 1987, Belgium in 1990, and Germany in 1991. But before the domestic markets arose, the Euro–CP market served most of the large industrial borrowers. Although the growth of domestic CP markets has taken a little steam out of the Euro–CP market of late, it has continued to provide the majority of the financing in the general Euronote market since the mid-1980s.

Figure 5.7 is the announcement of a recent Euro–CP issuance or programme. This announcement form, common to all security issues domestically and internationally, is called a tombstone. This issuance, a $700 million programme for a German firm's financial subsidiary, is sold by major investment banks throughout the world, such as Deutsche Bank, Chase, Citicorp, and Union Bank of Switzerland.

The third and final type of financing available in the Euronote market is the Euro-Medium-Term Note (EMTN). Another export of the rapidly innovating financial markets in the United States, the EMTN is the Euromarket version of a method of selling short- to medium-maturity bonds when needed. Unlike a bond issue, which is the sale of a large quantity of long-term debt all at one time, medium-term notes can be

FIGURE 5.7
Tombstone for
Euro–Commercial Paper
Issue

Source: *International Financing Review,* Issue 960, December 19, 1992, p. 11.

sold gradually into the market as the firm decides it needs additional debt financing. This is the result of having a "shelf-registration," in which the government authorities (in the United States the Securities and Exchange Commission) allow a large quantity of debt (the notes) to be registered but to be held "on the shelf" and sold as needed by the firm. The MTN has filled a maturity gap in debt-security issuance between the short-term commercial paper and the traditional longer maturities of bonds. The Euromarket version, the EMTN, has been just as successful for the very same reasons. Figure 5.6 clearly indicates the rapid growth of the EMTN market, reaching more than $50 billion in new issuances in 1991 alone.

The International Bond Market

Even with all these strange and innovative ways of raising capital in the international financial markets, it is still the international bond market that provides the bulk of financing. Figure 5.8 illustrates the growth and composition of the international bond market over the past decade. Amounting to only $50 billion in 1981, the international bond market grew to more than $300 billion in new gross financing in 1991. The market has shown little hesitation in its growth, pausing only briefly with the international debt crises and doubts of the early 1980s.

The four categories of international-debt financing discussed previously particularly apply to the international bond markets. Foreign borrowers have been using the large, well-developed capital markets of countries like the United States and the United Kingdom for many years. These issues are classified generally as foreign bonds as opposed to Eurobonds. Each has gained its own pet-name for foreign bonds issued in that market. For example, foreign bond issues in the United States are called Yankee bonds, in the United Kingdom Bulldogs, in the Netherlands Rembrandt bonds, and in Japan they are called Samurai bonds. When bonds are issued by foreign borrowers in these markets, they are subject to the same restrictions that apply to all domestic borrowers. If a Japanese firm issues a bond in the United States, it still must comply with all rules of the U.S. Securities and Exchange Commission, including the fact that they must be dollar-denominated.

**FIGURE 5.8
The Growth and
Composition of the
International Bond
Market**

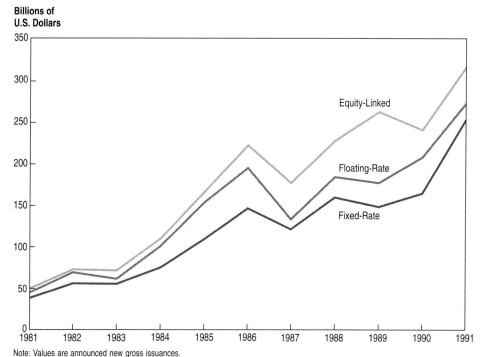

Note: Values are announced new gross issuances.
Source: Bank for International Settlements, *Annual Report,* annually, 1984–1992.

Bonds that fall into Categories 3 and 4 are termed **Eurobonds**. The primary characteristic of these instruments is that they are denominated in a currency other than that of the country where they are sold. For example, many U.S. firms may issue Euro-yen bonds on world markets. These bonds are sold in international financial centers such as London or Frankfurt, but they are denominated in Japanese yen. Because these Eurobonds are scattered about the global markets, most are a type of bond known as a bearer bond. A bearer bond is typically owned officially by whoever is holding it, with no master registration list being held by government authorities who then track who is earning interest income from bond investments.[7] Bearer bonds have a series of small coupons that border the bond itself. On an annual basis, one of the coupons is cut or "clipped" from the bond and taken to a banking institution that is one of the listed paying agents. The bank will pay the holder of the coupon the interest payment due, and no official records of payment are normally kept. As one might predict, these bonds have historically been a very attractive investment for individuals who want to keep interest earnings away from the eyes of tax authorities.[8] Besides the form of the bond issued having tax implications, the location of the enterprise actually issuing the bond has tax implications. Global Perspective 5.1 describes one of the traditional tax-advantaged locations for U.S. corporations.

Aside from the foreign bond–Eurobond distinction, international bonds are also classified by the way the buyer is repaid: (1) straight or fixed-rate bonds, (2) floating-rate bonds, and (3) bonds with equity links. As in any domestic market, the type of bond issued reflects what the firm thinks is the type that will be most acceptable to the market and easiest for the firm to repay.

5.1
Taxes, Eurobonds, and the
Netherlands Antilles

Until 1984, U.S. corporations found themselves at a distinct disadvantage in their ability to sell bonds to the international markets. The U.S. government required taxes of 20 percent be withheld from all interest payments to nonresidents of the United States. This meant that investors outside the United States would have a significant portion of their interest earnings withheld, and they did not intend to file tax returns in the United States in an attempt to have the tax refunded. This effectively shut out U.S. corporations from issuing international bonds and tapping the world's capital markets (at lower rates). That was until the discovery of the Caribbean tax loophole.

It seems that the United States had signed a very unusual tax treaty with a chain of islands in the Caribbean that had formerly been Dutch territories, the Netherlands Antilles. The treaty's primary provision of interest was that subsidiaries of U.S. corporations located in the Netherlands Antilles were free to issue bonds to the international capital markets without withholding taxes. And the proceeds of the issues could then be re-loaned to the parent corporation in the United States.

The results were predictable. Hundreds of U.S. firms incorporated financial subsidiaries in the Netherlands Antilles (usually on Curacao or Aruba). Each of these subsidiaries in turn issued debt to the international markets and then funneled the cheaper capital back to its U.S. parent. It is estimated that by 1984 there was more than $32 billion in debt outstanding that was issued through these islands off the Venezuelan coast. The result was a slight detour in the way capital flowed from the European markets to the United States. The capital would take a legal trip through a few small desert islands in the south Caribbean on its way to the U.S. mainland. Finally in May 1984 the United States repealed the withholding tax on interest payments to foreign investors. The Netherlands Antilles' brief period of time at center stage among the world's financial centers was over.

The majority of bonds issued internationally are still the traditional fixed-rate bond. This is a debt issuance typically between 4 and 10 years in maturity with a fixed coupon payment (interest payment) to the buyer of the bond annually. Because the timing and amount of all interest and principal repayments are known at the time of sale, the fixed-rate issue is always considered a solid and attractive investment. The continued growth of the international bond market is dependent on the continued use of the fixed-rate issue.

The second type of international bond, the floating-rate bond or floating-rate note (FRN), continues to make up a small but stable portion of the total market. The floating-rate note is structured so that its interest payments to the holders of the bonds are adjusted on an annual or semiannual basis with current market conditions. This type of floating rate is mostly a product of the time of great fear about inflation and inflation's impact on interest rates. Although a nice feature for investors who purchase the notes expecting interest rates to rise, the issuers do not welcome interest-rate risk, and that is the primary reason most bond issuers stick with the fixed-rate form.

The third type of international bond that has had some degree of success in the late 1980s is the equity-linked bond. There are two major types of equity-linked bonds: (1) convertible bonds and (2) bonds with equity warrants. An equity-linked bond is convertible into the common stock of the company issuing it. The conversion rate is usually set at a stock price 20 to 30 percent above the stock price at the time of issue. This provides the buyer of the bond two ways to achieve a return: the interest payment that the bond will still guarantee over its life, the coupon; and the possibility of converting the bond into common stock (equity) if the firm's stock price rises far enough to make the conversion worthwhile. The major advantage to the issuer of such a convertible bond is that the coupon that must be promised to investors is smaller when convertibility is present.

The bond with equity-warrant attached is much the same. A warrant is an option given to the buyer (literally attached to the bond) to purchase shares in the firm at a specified price. Like the convertible bond, the price is normally 20 to 30 percent higher than the price when issued. If the stock price does rise substantially over the coming years, the warrant would allow the investor to buy a share of the stock at the specified price, which would then be cheaper than the market price. Once again, attaching the warrant to the bond allows the issuer to save by promising a lower interest rate than without the warranty.

The equity-linked market has probably already seen the height of its popularity come and go. In 1989, more than half of all equity-linked international bond issues, about $45 billion worth, were by Japanese corporations (many of which were banks). The reason was actually quite simple. The Tokyo Stock Exchange saw an extremely rapid rise in 1988 and into 1989. The promise of further stock-price increases enticed investors worldwide to find ways to get in on the Tokyo exchange's growth. A convertible bond issued by a Japanese firm on world markets was one way. In return, the Japanese firms were able to sell their equity-linked bonds with very low coupon interest rates due to the strong demand. But the Tokyo exchange fell in 1990, and with it, the equity-linked market.

International Equity Markets

Firms are financed with both debt and equity. Although the debt markets have been the center of activity in the international financial markets over the past three decades, there are signs that international equity capital is becoming more popular.

Again using the same categories of international financial activities, the Category 2 transaction of a foreign borrower in a domestic market in local currency is the predominant international equity activity. Foreign firms often issue new shares in foreign markets and list their stock on major stock exchanges such as those in New York, Tokyo, or London. The purpose of foreign issues and listings is to expand the investor base, hopefully gaining access to capital markets in which the demand for shares of equity ownership is strong.

A foreign firm that wants to list its shares on an exchange in the United States does so through American Depositary Receipts. These are the receipts to bank accounts that hold shares of the foreign firm's stock in that firm's country. Because the equities are actually in a foreign currency, by holding them in a bank account and listing the receipt on the account on the American exchange, the shares can be revalued in dollars and redivided so that the price per share is more typical of that of the U.S. equity markets ($20 to $60 per share being the frequently desired range).

Although listing on a multitude of foreign exchanges is quite common among the world's largest multinational corporations, the degree of success achieved to date is debatable. There is evidence that most foreign listings do little more than react to price movements of the stock on its home exchange and with little additional investor appeal other than simple international diversification. In fact, a number of large multinationals based in the United States have been delisting their stock on exchanges in Europe and particularly Tokyo in recent years.

There has been considerable growth, however, in the Euro-equity markets. A Euro-equity issue is the simultaneous sale of a firm's shares in several different countries, with or without listing the shares on an exchange in that country. The sales take place through investment banks. Once issued, most Euro-equities are listed at least on the computer-screen quoting system of the International Stock Exchange (ISE) in London, the SEAQ. Between 1986 and 1989, the SEAQ increased the number of listed equities from 444 to more than 700. There is, however, substantial doubt regarding the future of Euro-equities and international equities in general. The sale of equities outside the country of the firm's operations and denominated in foreign currencies is argued to constitute little more than a mail-order form of stock ownership. Since the market is still in its infancy, it is still too early to conclude anything about its long-term prospects as a source of equity capital for the world's corporations.

Private Placements

One of the largest and largely unpublicized capital markets is the **private placement** market. A private placement is the sale of debt or equity to a large investor. The sale is normally a one-time-only transaction in which the buyer of the bond or stock purchases the investment and intends to hold it until maturity (if debt) or until repurchased by the firm (if equity). How does this differ from normal bond and stock sales? The answer is that the securities are not resold on a secondary market like the domestic bond market or the New York or American stock exchanges. If the security was intended to be publicly traded, the issuing firm would have to meet a number of disclosure and registration requirements with the regulatory authorities. In the United States this would be the Securities and Exchange Commission.

Historically much of the volume of private placements of securities occurred in Europe, with a large volume being placed with large Swiss financial institutions and large private investors. But in recent years the market has grown substantially across all countries as the world's financial markets have grown and as large institutional investors (particularly pension funds and insurance firms) have gained control over increasing shares of investment capital. The United States recently passed new legislation to encourage private placement. The legislation, entitled Rule 144A, allows limited trading of privately placed debt and equity between "qualified buyers." "Qualified buyers" are defined as institutions holding $100 million or more in securities. By allowing limited trading, the regulatory authorities believed that more institutions would be willing to accept privately placed debt and equity, both domestic and international in origin, because the market would be more liquid. Time will tell whether the rule will actually increase this type of financial activity.

Accessing International Financial Markets

Although these international markets are large and growing, this does not mean they are for everyone. For many years only the largest of the world's multinational firms could enter another country's capital markets and find acceptance. The reasons are information and reputation.

Financial markets are by definition risk-averse. This means they are very reluctant to make loans to or buy debt issued by firms that they know little about. Therefore, the ability to access the international markets is dependent on a firm's reputation, its ability to educate the markets about what it does, how successful it has been, and its patience. The firm must in the end be willing to expend the resources and effort required to build a credit reputation in the international markets. If successful, the firm may enjoy the benefits of new, larger, and more diversified sources of the capital it needs.

The individual firm, whether it be a chili-dog stand serving the international tastes of office workers at the United Nations Plaza or a major multinational firm like Honda of Japan (as illustrated in Global Perspective 5.2) is impacted by exchange rates and international financial markets. Although the owner of the chili-dog stand probably has more important and immediate problems to deal with, it is clear that firms such as Honda see the movements in these markets as critically important to their long-term competitiveness.

Global Perspective

5.2

Honda Says Stronger Yen to Hurt Sales and Weak Market Will Curb Car Prices

Special to The Wall Street Journal

TOKYO—A stronger yen will shave 3%–4% off Honda Motor Co.'s sales during the coming fiscal year and weak market conditions will stop the Japanese company from covering the loss by raising car prices, a Honda official said.

Takashi Matsuda, Honda's managing director in charge of finance, said soft auto market conditions will limit any potential price boosts during the fiscal year starting April 1 to around 1%.

The yen's rise in currency markets makes Japanese products more expensive overseas and lowers the value of overseas earnings when translated into yen terms.

Mr. Matsuda said the dollar is likely to average between 115 yen and under 120 yen during the coming fiscal year, down from an average of 125 yen for the current year.

But the Honda official, who spoke with a reporter Wednesday when the dollar was trading just below 119 yen, said the company isn't rushing to lock in the U.S. currency around 117–118 yen. Mr. Matsuda said the company will look to enter the forward currency market when the dollar moves to around 120 yen.

Mr. Matsuda said Honda will continue to boost the local content of its overseas production as a means of guarding against foreign-exchange risk. At present, the local content of Honda's U.S. production is roughly 75%.

The official said his company isn't planning to boost the number of U.S.-made Hondas sold in Japan. The number of U.S. "reverse import" sales in Japan during the coming fiscal year should be around 20,000, little changed from the current fiscal year.

Separately, Honda's consolidated capital outlays for the current fiscal year will come to 170 billion yen ($1.46 billion), down 8.1% from the company's previous estimate of 185 billion yen, Mr. Matsuda said. He said capital outlays for the coming fiscal year beginning April 1 are likely to remain at roughly 170 billion yen.

Mr. Matsuda said the company's capital outlay plans already take into account needed expenditures for equipment to make new-vehicle models over the coming year.

Honda is using loans from banks and funds on hand to pay for 80 billion yen of equity warrant bonds maturing this month.

Moreover, while banks are eager to lend and interest rates are sufficiently low, Honda currently has no plans to raise funds in the capital markets, Mr. Matsuda said.

Honda borrowed 40 billion yen from Mitsubishi Bank and other domestic banks to refinance expiring paper, with the balance of the maturing bonds to be paid from the company's own funds, he added. After this month's maturation, Honda won't have any more equity-linked bonds outstanding.

SUMMARY

This chapter has spanned the breadth of the international financial markets from currencies to capital markets. The world's currency markets have expanded threefold in only the past six years, and there is no reason to believe this growth will end. It is estimated that more than $1 trillion worth of currencies changes hands daily, and the majority of it is either U.S. dollars, German marks, or Japanese yen. These are the world's major floating currencies.

But the world's financial markets are much more than currency exchanges. The rapid growth in the international financial markets—both on their own and as linkages between domestic markets—has resulted in the creation of a large and legitimate source of finance for the world's multinational firms. The recent expansion of market economics to more and more of the world's countries and economies sets the stage for further growth for the world's currency and capital markets.

Key Terms and Concepts

direct quotation	selling forward
indirect quotation	offshore banking
spot rates	securitization
forward rates	correspondent banks
cross rates	representative office
spread	International Banking Facility (IBF)
European Monetary System	syndicated loan
Eurocurrency	Euronote
Eurodollars	international bond
Eurocurrency interest rates	Euro-commercial paper (ECP)
LIBOR	Eurobond
Euromarkets	private placement

Questions for Discussion

1. How and where are currencies traded?
2. Does it matter whether a currency is quoted as DEM/USD or USD/DEM?
3. What is a forward rate? How do banks set forward rates?
4. What is a Eurocurrency?
5. What is a Eurocurrency interest rate? Is it different from LIBOR?
6. Are all currencies freely floating on world markets?
7. How does the European Monetary System work?
8. Are fixed exchange rates preferable to floating exchange rates?
9. Why have international financial markets grown so fast in the past decade?
10. What are the major types of securities traded on the international financial markets?

Recommended Readings

Bank for International Settlements, *Annual Report,* Basle, Switzerland, annually.

Eiteman, David, Arthur Stonehill, and Michael H. Moffett, *Multinational Business Finance,* sixth edition. Reading, Mass.: Addison-Wesley, 1992.

Federal Reserve Bank of New York, *Summary of Results of the U.S. Foreign Exchange Market Turnover Survey,* April 1992.

Giddy, Ian, *Global Financial Markets.* Heath, 1993.

Goodhart, C.A.E., and L. Figliuoli, "Every Minute Counts in Financial Markets," *Journal of International Money and Finance,* 10, 1991, 23-52.

Grabbe, J. Orlin, *International Financial Markets,* second edition. New York: Elsevier, 1991.

International Monetary Fund, *International Financial Statistics,* Washington, D.C., monthly.

The Wall Street Journal, Foreign Exchange Rates, Monday, January 11, 1993.

Tran, Hung Q., Larry Anderson, and Ernst-Ludwig Drayss, "Chapter 8: Eurocapital Markets," in *International Finance and Investing,* The Library of Investment Banking, edited by Robert Lawrence Kuhn. Homewood, Ill.: Dow Jones–Irwin, 1990, 129-160.

Notes

1. Rounding errors are solved quite simply with exchange rates. With a few notable exceptions, all active trading takes place using direct quotations on foreign currencies versus the U.S. dollar (DEM 1.5390/USD, YEN 123.21/USD) and for a conventional number of decimal places. These are the base rates that are then used for the calculation of the inverse indirect quotes on the foreign currencies if needed.

2. A currency trader once remarked to the authors that the spot quotes listed on such a screen were no more and no less accurate to the "true price" than the sticker price on a showroom automobile. Of course, this may no longer be true since the introduction of the Saturn, which sells at sticker price only!

3. Exchange rate "basis points" should not be confused with interest-rate basis points, where a single basis point is 1/100th of a percent.

4. There are, of course, exceptions. At different points in time different currencies have been allowed wider ranges. For example, at the time of the EMS grid depicted, the British pound was allowed a band of +/−6 percent, as were the Spanish peseta, Portuguese escudo, and Greek drachma. At this time the Greek drachma was not a member of the ERM.

5. Actual intervention is required when the currency value reaches 75 percent of the allowable movement from the central rate. This is termed the intervention indicator.

6. The federal government of Brazil was a prime example of this large borrowing capability. In the 1980-1982 period prior to the debt crisis, Brazil was the recipient of a number of what were termed "jumbo loans," which on occasion totaled several billion U.S. dollars.

7. Bearer bonds were issued by the U.S. government up until the early 1980s, when discontinued. Even though they were called bearer bonds, a list of bond registration numbers was still kept and recorded in order to tax investors holding the bearer instruments.

8. The standard and probably fictitious tale of bearer bond ownership is that of the "Belgian dentist" who earns so much money that he will purchase bearer bonds and keep them in a safe-deposit box in a relatively unregulated banking market country. Once a year, the Belgian dentist boards the train to Luxembourg. He clips his coupon, redeems it, redeposits the proceeds in his Luxembourg bank account, and returns home. The Belgian tax authorities are none the wiser.

Economic Integration

LEARNING OBJECTIVES

1. To review types of economic integration among countries.

2. To examine the costs and benefits of integrative arrangements.

3. To understand the structure of the European Community and its implications for firms within and outside Europe.

4. To explore the emergence of other integration agreements, especially the North American Free Trade Agreement.

A World of Trading Blocs

Regional groupings based on economics will become increasingly important in the 1990s. Countries around the globe are making efforts to give regional interests priority over national interests. There are at least 32 such groupings: three in Europe, four in the Middle East, five in Asia, and ten each in Africa and the Americas. With respect to the three major blocs, the North American, western European, and Asian, trade inside these blocs has grown at a rapid pace, while trading between these blocs or with outsiders is either declining or growing far more slowly.

Some of these groupings around the world have the superstructure of nation states (such as the European Community); some (like AFTA) are multinational agreements that may be more political arrangements than cohesive trading blocs at present. Some arrangements are not trading blocs per se, but work to further them. The Enterprise for the Americas Initiative is a foreign policy initiative designed to further democracy in the region through incentives to capitalistic development and trade liberalization. The Andean Common Market and Mercosur have both indicated an intention to negotiate with the North American Free Trade Agreement (NAFTA) to create a hemispheric market. Regional economic integration in Asia has been driven more by market forces than by treaties and by a need to maintain balance in negotiations with Europe and North America. Broader formal agreements are in formative stages: Malaysia, for instance, has led a move to form the East Asian Economic Group of AFTA countries plus Hong Kong, Japan, South Korea, and Taiwan.

Regional groupings will mean that companies are facing ever-intensifying competition and trading difficulties for sales inside a bloc. In the long term, firms will come under pressure to globalize and source locally. Actions of these global companies may also allay fears that regional blocs are nothing but protectionism on a grander scale.

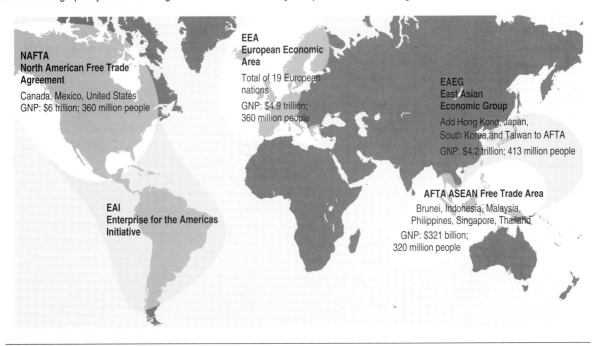

NAFTA
North American Free Trade Agreement

Canada, Mexico, United States
GNP: $6 trillion; 360 million people

EEA
European Economic Area

Total of 19 European nations
GNP: $4.9 trillion; 360 million people

EAEG
East Asian Economic Group

Add Hong Kong, Japan, South Korea, and Taiwan to AFTA
GNP: $4.2 trillion; 413 million people

EAI
Enterprise for the Americas Initiative

AFTA ASEAN Free Trade Area

Brunei, Indonesia, Malaysia, Philippines, Singapore, Thailand
GNP: $321 billion; 320 million people

Source: Ilkka A. Ronkainen, "Trading Blocs: Opportunity or Demise for International Trade?" *Multinational Business Review* 1(Spring 1993): 1–9; Paivi Vihma, "Gatt Kituu, Kauppablokit Nousevat," *Talouselama,* number 11, 1992, 42–43; and Joseph L. Brand, "The New World Order," *Vital Speeches of the Day* 58 (December 1991): 155–160.

The benefits of free trade and stable exchange rates are available only if nation-states are willing to give up some measure of independence and autonomy. This has resulted in increased economic integration around the world with agreements among countries to establish links through movement of goods, services, capital, and labor across borders. Some predict, however, that the regional **trading blocs** of the new economic world order will divide into a handful of protectionist superstates that, although liberalizing trade among members, may raise barriers to external trade.

Economic integration is best viewed as a spectrum. At one extreme we might envision a truly global economy in which all countries shared a common currency and agreed to free flows of goods, services, and factors of production. At the other extreme would be a number of closed economies, each independent and self-sufficient. The various integrative agreements in effect today lie along the middle of the spectrum. The most striking example of successful integration is the historic economic unification that is taking place in Europe and elsewhere today. These developments were discussed in the chapter's opening vignette. Some countries, however, give priority to maintaining economic self-sufficiency and independence. Examples of this latter strategy include the policies of North Korea, Vietnam, and Albania.

This chapter will begin with an explanation of the various levels of economic integration. The level of integration defines the nature and degree of economic links among countries. Next, major arguments both for and against economic integration will be reviewed. Finally, the European Community, the North American Free Trade Agreement, and other economic alliances will be discussed.

LEVELS OF ECONOMIC INTEGRATION

A trading bloc is a preferential economic arrangement among a group of countries. The forms it may take are provided in Table 6.1. From least to most integrative, they are the free trade area, the customs union, the common market, and the economic union.[1]

The Free Trade Area

The **free trade area** is the least restrictive and loosest form of economic integration among countries. In a free trade area, all barriers to trade among member countries are removed. Therefore, goods and services are freely traded among member countries in much the same way that they flow freely between, for example, South Carolina and New York. No discriminatory taxes, quotas, tariffs, or other trade barriers are allowed. Sometimes a free trade area is formed only for certain classes of goods and services. An agricultural free trade area, for example, implies the absence of restrictions on the trade of agricultural products only. The most notable feature

TABLE 6.1
Forms of International Economic Integration

Stage of Integration	Abolition of Tariffs and Quotas among Members	Common Tariff and Quota System	Abolition of Restrictions on Factor Movements	Harmonization and Unification of Economic Policies and Institutions
Free trade area	Yes	No	No	No
Customs union	Yes	Yes	No	No
Common market	Yes	Yes	Yes	No
Economic union	Yes	Yes	Yes	Yes

Source: Franklin R. Root, *International Trade and Investment,* Cincinnati, Ohio: South-Western Publishing Company, 1992, 254.

of a free trade area is that each country continues to set its own policies in relation to nonmembers. In other words, each member is free to set any tariffs, quotas, or other restrictions that it chooses for trade with countries outside the free trade area.

The most well-known free trade area is the European Free Trade Area (EFTA). The EFTA was formed in 1960 with an agreement by eight European countries. Barriers to trade among countries were dismantled, although each country maintained its own policies with nonmember countries. the EFTA, however, has lost much of its original significance due to the higher levels of integration in the European Community. Furthermore, many of the EFTA's members are seeking to join the EC or cooperate with it within the European Economic Area (EEA) arrangement.

A more recent example of a free trade agreement is that between the United States and Canada that went into effect in 1989. Plans call for the addition of Mexico to the existing arrangement to form the North American Free Trade Agreement by 1994. These agreements will be discussed in detail later in the chapter.

The Customs Union

The **customs union** is one step further along the spectrum of economic integration. Like members of a free trade area, members of a customs union dismantle barriers to trade in goods and services among themselves. In addition, however, the customs union establishes a common trade policy with respect to nonmembers. Typically, this takes the form of a common external tariff, whereby imports from nonmembers are subject to the same tariff when sold to any member country. Tariff revenues are then shared among members according to a prespecified formula.

The Common Market

Further still along the spectrum of economic integration is the **common market.** Like the customs union, a common market has no barriers to trade among members and has a common external trade policy. In addition, however, factors of production are also mobile among members. Factors of production include labor, capital, and technology. Thus restrictions on immigration, emigration, and cross-border investment are abolished. The importance of **factor mobility** for economic growth cannot be overstated. When factors of production are freely mobile, then capital, labor, and technology may be employed in their most productive uses. To see the importance of factor mobility, imagine the state of the U.S. economy if unemployed steelworkers in Pittsburgh were prevented from migrating to the growing Sunbelt in search of better opportunities. Alternatively, imagine that savings in New York banks could not be invested in profitable opportunities in Chicago.

Despite the obvious benefits, members of a common market must be prepared to cooperate closely in monetary, fiscal, and employment policies. Furthermore, while a common market will enhance the productivity of members in the aggregate, it is by no means clear that individual member countries will always benefit. Because of these difficulties, the goals of common markets have proved to be elusive in many areas of the world, notably Central America and Asia. However, the objective of the **Single European Act** and the 1992 process was to have a full common market in effect within the EC at the end of 1992. While many of the directives aimed at opening borders and markets are being implemented on schedule, major exceptions do still exist.

The Economic Union

The creation of a true **economic union** requires integration of economic policies in addition to the free movement of goods, services, and factors of production across borders. Under an economic union, members would harmonize monetary policies, taxation, and government spending. In addition, a common currency would be used by all members. This could be accomplished de facto, or in effect, by a system of fixed exchange rates. Clearly, the formation of an economic union requires nations to surrender a large measure of their national sovereignty. Needless to say, the barriers to full economic union are quite strong. Our global political system is built on the autonomy and supreme power of the nation-state, and attempts to undermine the authority of the state will undoubtedly always encounter opposition. As a result, no true economic unions are in effect today.

ARGUMENTS SURROUNDING ECONOMIC INTEGRATION

A number of arguments surround economic integration. They center on (1) trade creation and diversion; (2) the effects of integration on import prices, competition, economies of scale, and factor productivity; and (3) the benefits of regionalism versus nationalism.

Trade Creation and Trade Diversion

Economist Jacob Viner first formalized the economic costs and benefits of economic integration.[2] Chapter 2 illustrated that the classical theory of trade predicts a win-win result for countries participating in free trade. The question is whether similar benefits accrue when free trade is limited to one group of countries. The case examined by Viner was the customs union. The conclusion of Viner's analysis was that either negative or positive effects may result when a group of countries trade freely among themselves but maintain common barriers to trade with nonmembers.

Viner's arguments can be highlighted with a simple illustration. In 1986 Spain formally entered the European Community (EC) as a member. Prior to membership, Spain—like all nonmembers such as the United States, Canada, and Japan—traded with the EC and suffered the common external tariff. Imports of agricultural products from Spain or the United States had the same tariff applied to their products, for example, 20 percent. During this period, the United States was a lower-cost producer of wheat compared to Spain. U.S. exports to EC members may have cost $3.00 per bushel, plus a 20 percent tariff of $0.60, for a total of $3.60 per bushel. If Spain at the same time produced wheat at $3.20 per bushel, plus a 20 percent tariff of $0.64 for a total cost to EC customers of $3.84 per bushel, its wheat was more expensive and therefore less competitive.

But when Spain joined the EC as a member, its products were no longer subject to the common external tariffs; Spain had become a member of the "club" and therefore enjoyed its benefits. Spain was now the low-cost producer of wheat at $3.20 per bushel, compared to the price of $3.60 from the United States. Trade flows changed as a result. The increased export of wheat and other products by Spain to the EC as a result of its membership is termed **trade creation.** The elimination of the tariff literally created more trade between Spain and the EC. At the same time, because the United States is still outside of the EC, its products suffer the higher price as a result of tariff application. U.S. exports to the EC fall. When the source of trading competitiveness is shifted in this manner from one country to another, it is termed **trade diversion.**

Whereas trade creation is distinctly positive in moving toward freer trade, and therefore lower prices for consumers within the EC, the impact of trade diversion is negative. Trade diversion is inherently negative because the competitive advantage has shifted away from the lower-cost producer to the higher-cost producer. The benefits of Spain's membership are enjoyed by Spanish farmers (greater export sales) and EC consumers (lower prices). The two major costs are reduced tariff revenues collected and costs borne by the United States and its exports as a result of lost sales.

From the perspective of nonmembers like the United States, the formation or expansion of a customs union is obviously negative. Most damaged will naturally be countries that may need to have trade to build their economies, such as the countries of the Third World. As Viner shows, from the perspective of members of the customs union, the formation or expansion is only beneficial if the trade-creation benefits exceed trade-diversion costs.

Reduced Import Prices

When a small country imposes a tariff on imports, the price of the goods will typically rise because sellers will increase prices to cover the cost of the tariff. This increase in price, in turn, will result in lower demand for the imported goods. If a bloc of countries imposes the tariff, however, the fall in demand for the imported goods will be substantial. The exporting country may then be forced to reduce the price of the goods. The possibility of lower prices for imports results from the greater market power of the bloc relative to that of a single country. The result may then be an improvement in the trade position of the bloc countries. Any gain in the trade position of bloc members, however, is offset by a deteriorating trade position for the exporting country. Again, unlike the win-win situation resulting from free trade, the scenario involving a trade bloc is instead win-lose.

Increased Competition and Economies of Scale

Integration increases market size and therefore may result in a lower degree of monopoly in the production of certain goods and services.[3] This is because a larger market will tend to increase the number of competing firms, resulting in greater efficiency and lower prices for consumers. Moreover, less energetic and productive economies may be spurred into action by competition from the more industrious bloc members.

Many industries, such as steel and automobiles, require large-scale production in order to obtain economies of scale in production. Therefore, certain industries may simply not be economically viable in smaller, trade-protected countries. However, the formation of a trading bloc enlarges the market so that large-scale production is justified. The lower per-unit costs resulting from scale economies may then be obtained. These lower production costs resulting from greater production for an enlarged market are called **internal economies of scale.**

In a common market, **external economies of scale** may also be present. Because a common market allows factors of production to flow freely across borders, the firm may now have access to cheaper capital, more highly skilled labor, or superior technology. These factors will improve the quality of the firm's product or service or will lower costs or both.

Higher Factor Productivity

When factors of production are freely mobile, the wealth of the common market countries, in aggregate, will likely increase. The theory behind this contention is straightforward: Factor mobility will lead to the movement of labor and capital from areas of low productivity to areas of high productivity. In addition to the economic gains from factor mobility, there are other benefits not so easily quantified. The free movement of labor fosters a higher level of communication across cultures. This, in turn, leads to a higher degree of cross-cultural understanding; as people move, their ideas, skills, and ethnicity move with them.

Again, however, factor mobility will not necessarily benefit each country in the common market. A poorer country, for example, may lose badly needed investment capital to a richer country, where opportunities are perceived to be more profitable. Another disadvantage of factor mobility that is often cited is the brain-drain phenomenon. A poorer country may lose its most talented workers when they are free to search out better opportunities.

Regionalism versus Nationalism

Economists have composed elegant and compelling arguments in favor of the various levels of economic integration. It is difficult, however, to turn these arguments into reality in the face of intense nationalism. The biggest impediment to economic integration remains in the reluctance of nations to surrender a measure of their autonomy. Integration, by its very nature, requires the surrender of national power and self-determinism. An example of this can be seen in Global Perspective 6.1.

THE EUROPEAN COMMUNITY

Economic Integration in Europe from 1948 to the Mid-1980s

The period of the Great Depression from the late 1920s through World War II was characterized by isolationism, protectionism, and fierce nationalism. Because of the economic chaos and political difficulties of the period, no serious attempts at economic integration were made until the end of the war. From the devastation of the war, however, a spirit of cooperation gradually emerged in Europe.

The first step in this regional cooperative effort was the establishment of the Organization for European Economic Cooperation (OEEC) in 1948 to administer Marshall Plan aid from the United States. Although the objective of the OEEC was limited to economic reconstruction following the war, its success set the stage for more ambitious integration programs.

In 1952, six European countries (West Germany, France, Italy, Belgium, the Netherlands, and Luxembourg) joined in establishing the European Coal and Steel Community (ECSC). The objective of the ECSC was the formation of a common market in coal, steel, and iron ore for member countries. These basic industries were rapidly revitalized into competitive and efficient producers. The stage was again set for further cooperative efforts.

In 1957, the European Economic Community (now called the European Community, or EC) was formally established by the **Treaty of Rome.** Table 6.2 shows the founding members of the community in 1957, the members in 1993 as well as likely members by 1996. The Treaty of Rome is a monumental document, composed of more than 200 articles. The main provisions of the treaty are summarized in Table 6.3. The document was (and is) quite ambitious. The cooperative spirit apparent throughout the treaty was based on the premise that the mobility of goods, services, labor, and capital (the "four freedoms") was of paramount importance for the economic prosperity of the region. Founding members envisioned that the successful integration of the European economies would result in an economic power to rival that of the United States.

Global Perspective

6.1
Labor Pains of Integration

Economic integration, despite promises of great benefits from the free flow of people, goods, services, and money, is not making everyone happy. Rich nations, such as Germany and France, fear that a deepening recession will be compounded by a hemorrhage of jobs as companies shift their operations to less-prosperous regions in Europe where wages are lower.

A decision made by the U.S. vacuum-cleaner maker Hoover to relocate its production facilities from France's Burgundy region to Scotland, axing 600 jobs in the process, has sparked a controversy whether the single European market will strip France of jobs. France has revived accusations that Britain is engaged in "social dumping"— eroding workers' rights in a bid to attract foreign investment. As part of the Hoover deal, the firm's Scottish workforce has agreed to accept new working practices, including limits on strike action.

Yet Hoover has done nothing wrong. To remain competitive in what is fast becoming a global business, the company feels it must concentrate vacuum-cleaner production in Europe in a single plant. It also needs a flexible workforce, which is a big competitive advantage in many industries. The employees at Hoover's Scottish plant were simply more willing to change their ways than their French counterparts. By shifting its production to Scotland, Hoover is estimated to cut its costs by a quarter. Part of this saving will come from economies of scale, the rest from lower wages.

Such hard-headed economics will not stop Europe's politicians from complaining when jobs are lost in their own backyard. Other companies, such as the German television maker, Grundig are considering moves. As long as politicians complain every time a company makes such a move, integration decisions are challenged.

Source: "French Say United Europe Promotes 'Job Poaching,'" *The Washington Post,* February 10, 1993, A23, A27; "Labour Pains," *The Economist,* February 6, 1993, 71.

TABLE 6.2 Membership of the European Community	1957	1993	1996
	France West Germany Italy Belgium Netherlands Luxembourg	Great Britain (1973) Ireland (1973) Denmark (1973) Greece (1981) Spain (1986) Portugal (1986)	Austria (1996) Finland (1996) Norway (1996) Sweden (1996)

TABLE 6.3 Main Provisions of the Treaty of Rome	1. Formation of a free trade area: the gradual elimination of tariffs, quotas, and other barriers to trade among members 2. Formation of a customs union: the creation of a uniform tariff schedule applicable to imports from the rest of the world 3. Formation of a common market: the removal of barriers to the movement of labor, capital, and business enterprises 4. The adoption of common agricultural policies 5. The creation of an investment fund to channel capital from the more-advanced to the less-developed regions of the community

Some countries, however, were reluctant to embrace the ambitious integrative effort of the treaty. In 1960 a looser, less-integrated philosophy was endorsed with the formation of the European Free Trade Association (EFTA). The members of the

EFTA were the United Kingdom, Norway, Denmark, Sweden, Austria, Finland, Portugal, and Switzerland. As the name implies, the goal of the EFTA was to dismantle trade barriers among members. Since 1960, however, the distinctions between the EC and the EFTA have blurred considerably. Great Britain, Portugal, and Denmark have since joined the EC, and other EFTA members have formed free trade agreements with the community. For those EFTA countries not wanting to join the EC, the European Economic Area agreement will give them most of the benefits of Europe's single market.

Many believe that a move away from the spirit and intent of the Treaty of Rome was taken in 1966 with the passage of the Luxembourg Compromise. The Luxembourg Compromise granted member countries the right to veto any EC decision if they felt their "vital interests" were threatened. In fact, however, "the governments invoked 'vital interests' each time the slightest segment of their population risked a social or economic disadvantage. . . . As EC membership expanded it became more and more difficult to reach any decisions at all. The Luxembourg Compromise virtually paralyzed the EC."[4]

A conflict that intensified throughout the 1980s was between the richer and more industrialized countries and the poorer countries of the Mediterranean region. The power of the bloc of poorer countries was strengthened in the 1980s when Greece, Spain, and Portugal became EC members. Many argue that the dismantling of barriers between the richer and poorer countries will benefit the poorer countries by spurring them to become competitive. However, it may also be argued that the richer countries have an unfair advantage and therefore should accord protection to the poorer members before all barriers are dismantled.

Another source of difficulty that intensified in the 1980s was the administration of the community's **common agricultural policy (CAP).** Most industrialized countries, including the United States, Canada, and Japan, have adopted wide-scale government intervention and subsidization schemes for the agriculture industry. In the case of the EC, however, these policies have been implemented on a community-wide, rather than national, level. The CAP includes (1) a price-support system whereby EC agriculture officials intervene in the market to keep farm-product prices within a specified range, (2) direct subsidies to farmers, and (3) rebates to farmers who export or agree to store farm products rather than sell them within the community. The implementation of these policies absorbs about two-thirds of the annual EC budget.

The CAP has caused problems both within the EC and in relationships with nonmembers. Within the EC, the richer, more industrialized countries resent the extensive subsidization of the more agrarian economies. Outside trading partners, especially the United States, have repeatedly charged the EC with unfair trade practices in agriculture.

The European Community since the Mid-1980s

By the mid-1980s, a sense of "Europessimism" permeated most discussions of European integration. Although the members remained committed in principle to the "four freedoms," literally hundreds of obstacles to the free movement of goods, services, people, and capital remained. For example, there were cumbersome border restrictions on trade in many goods, and although labor was theoretically mobile, the professional certifications granted in one country were often not recognized in others.

Growing dissatisfaction with the progress of integration, as well as threats of global competition from Japan and the United States, prompted the European Community to take action. An EC policy paper published in 1985 (now known as the **1992 White Paper**) exhaustively identified the remaining barriers to the four freedoms and proposed means of dismantling them.[5] It listed 279 specific measures designed to make the four freedoms a reality. Illustrative proposals are shown in Table 6.4. Although nearly 90 percent of the single-market directives have already been approved by the member countries, enforcement is lax in fields such as the environment. Some sections have faded away, including plans for Europe-wide corporate law and the creation of EC organizations, such as a food and drug agency and a patent center.[6]

The implementation of the White Paper proposals began formally in 1987 with the passage of the Single European Act, which stated that "the community shall adopt measures with the aim of progressively establishing the internal market over a period expiring on 31 December 1992." The Single European Act envisaged a true common market where goods, people, and money move between Germany and France with the same ease that they move between Wisconsin and Illinois.

Progress toward the goal of free movement of goods has been achieved largely due to the move from a "common-standards approach" to a "mutual-recognition approach." Under the common-standards approach, EC members were forced to negotiate the specifications for literally thousands of products, often unsuccessfully. For example, because of differences in tastes, agreement was never reached on specifications for beer, sausage, or mayonnaise. Global Perspective 6.2 discusses the difficulties associated with obtaining free trade in strawberry jam. Under the mutual-recognition approach, the laborious quest for common standards is in most cases no longer necessary. Instead, as long as a product meets legal and specification requirements in one member country, it may be freely exported to any other.

Less progress toward free movement of people in Europe has been made than toward free movement of goods. The primary difficulty is that EC members have been unable to agree on a common immigration policy. As long as this disagreement persists, travelers between countries must pass through border checkpoints. Some countries—notably Germany—have relatively lax immigration policies, while others—especially those with higher unemployment rates—favor strict controls on immigration. A second issue concerning the free movement of people is the acceptability of professional certifications across countries. In 1993, the largest EC member countries passed all of the professional worker directives. This means that workers' professional qualifications will be recognized throughout the EC guaranteeing them equal treatment in terms of employment, working conditions, and social protection in the host country.

Attaining free movement of capital within the EC entails several measures. First, citizens will be free to trade in EC currencies without restrictions. Second, the regulations governing banks and other financial institutions will be harmonized. In addition, mergers and acquisitions will be regulated by the EC rather than by national governments. Finally, securities will be freely tradable across countries.

A key aspect of free trade in services is the right to compete fairly to obtain government contracts. Under the 1992 guidelines, a government should not give preference to its own citizens in awarding government contracts. However, little progress has been made in this regard.

Project 1992 has always been part of a larger plan and a process more so than a deadline.[7] Many in the EC bureaucracy argued that the 1992 campaign required a commitment to **economic and monetary union (EMU)** and subsequently to

TABLE 6.4 Progress Report on Project 1992

Area	Rating	Goal	Progress report	Comment
Airlines		Totally open skies, including freedom of pricing, entry of new airlines, and access by foreign carriers to routes within individual countries (known as cabotage).	Free pricing and licensing of new airlines began January 1, 1993. Cabotage will be phased in between then and April 1997.	The ambitious plan should fully deregulate air travel—and reduce fares—by 2000. In the next few years, though, EC members will use loopholes to protect their own carriers.
Banks		Freedom to provide financial services in any member country, including checking accounts, mortgages, and business loans.	The final changes took effect January 1, 1993.	Banks have begun moving into other countries, but customers are sometimes cautious about trusting their money to foreigners. Many banks are looking for strong local partners.
Insurance		Freedom to sell insurance in all member countries.	The final changes took effect January 1, 1993.	Big insurance companies have begun to move into neighboring markets. But they also are finding it better to operate with partners.
Stock Markets		Investors in any member country should be able to buy and sell shares and bonds in any other.	The last restrictions were lifted January 1, 1993.	Cross-border investing is steaming ahead across Europe, though much of the action remains in London.
Capital Movement		Abolish all restrictions on movement across borders of capital owned by EC residents.	Member states have approved all directives.	Cross-border capital flows are increasing, but tax laws can still impede them in some countries.
Mobility		European residents should be able to cross borders without passports, and workers should be allowed to move to any EC country, based on Europe-wide recognition of professional or other qualifications.	By January 1, 1993, all professional worker directives were passed by six states. No agreement on movement of individuals yet	In theory, very exciting. In practice, language barriers and nationalism could delay free movement of workers for a generation. And no sensible European is throwing away his passport.
Pharmaceuticals		Deregulate prices and bring standards and test procedures of all EC countries into line with each other and with the United States and Japan.	Half of all directives have been adopted. Approval on the rest was expected by January 1, 1993.	Harmonization of procedures is going well, but there has been no progress on deregulating prices.
Technical Standards		An end to restriction of foreign manufacturers on safety and technical grounds, assuming those manufacturers meet minimum standards.	Implementation so far in toys, pressure vessels, and safety clothing, among other areas.	Many small companies that can't meet the new standards, particularly in Greece and Portugal, will go out of business. But it will be some years before all barriers fall.
Automobiles		Removal of all quotas and tariffs by the mid-1990s.	Original aim scrapped in 1991 when European car makers asked for barriers against the Japanese until 1999.	Cars in Europe, already the most expensive in the world, aren't getting any cheaper. Those built by the Japanese in Europe are not subject to quotas, but even that could change.
Television		Satellite broadcasters should be allowed to transmit anywhere in the EC.	Although this goal was adopted by the EC, no country has officially adopted it into national law.	Put that dish purchase on hold. Individual governments have been unable to reach agreement on decency standards, advertising regulations, and national program quotas.
Public Procurement		Open all bidding for public projects, including transportation and telecommunication.	Adopted by the EC, but no country has passed it into local law.	Though EC law in theory supersedes national law, it is hard to enforce. Fewer than 20 percent of public projects have been open to bidding.

All measures agreed on by all 12 countries   Progressing satisfactorily   Not progressing at all

Source: Carla Rapoport, "Europe Looks Ahead to Hard Choices," *FORTUNE*, December 14, 1992, pp. 144–149. © 1992 Time Inc. All rights reserved.

Global Perspective

6.2
What Is Jam?

The Dutch prefer their strawberry jam smooth because they typically use it as a spread. The French, however, like it lumpy, because they often eat it straight from the jar on a spoon. Europeans also differ over how much sugar and how many preservatives jam should contain. It fact, Europeans disagree over the very definition of jam, so regulations governing its composition differ from country to country.

The problem may seem trivial, but EC members spent 25 years arguing over the definition of jam in pursuit of a common standard. The debate was complicated in 1973 when Britain joined the community and disagreed vehemently with EC standards for marmalade. It is easy to see that if it had taken 25 years to agree on jam, it could take centuries to agree on specifications for the thousands of products involved in European trade.

In the mid-1980s, a simple solution to this bureaucratic nightmare emerged: Why not let the market decide? Under "mutual recognition," as long as a product was lawfully manufactured in one member country and clearly labeled, it could be sold throughout the community. If Italians wanted to sell their oily mayonnaise in Denmark—where they like it creamy—or the French wanted to sell their weak beer in Germany—where they like it strong—or the Dutch wanted to sell smooth jam in France—where they like it lumpy—they were free to do so, as long as the contents were clearly labeled.

The deceptively simple move from common standards to mutual recognition represented a giant leap forward toward a single market for Europe.

Source: E. S. Browning, "Sticky Solutions," *The Wall Street Journal,* September 22, 1989.

political union. The summit in Maastricht in December 1991, which produced recommendations for a single European currency and a single, independent central bank, did not meet unanimous approval. The Danes rejected it in the spring of 1992, the British delayed decision on it, and the French approved it by the narrowest of margins because many feel that it would create an unresponsive, supranational body in Brussels. As the undesirable elements are being reassessed, work continues on some of its dimensions as shown in Global Perspective 6.3. (The European Monetary System, its history, and future are discussed in detail in Chapter 4.)

Despite the uncertainties about the future of the EC, new members are wanting to join. Most EFTA countries want to join in spite of the fact that the European Economic Area treaty gives them most of the benefits of the single market. They also want to have a say in making EC laws. Although many experts believe that it will be 20 years or more before the EC includes any central European countries, cooperation is essential.[8] Access to the EC is essential for growth in central Europe. It could also create investment opportunities for Western firms and provide cheaper goods for EC consumers.

Organization of the EC

The executive body of the EC is the European Commission, headquartered in Brussels. The commission may be likened to the executive branch of the U.S. government. It is composed of 17 commissioners (two from each larger member country

Global Perspective

6.3
Preparing for EMU

Although the future of European monetary union is not certain, preparation for it has started. Its scale is such that the central banks of Europe need to get work started on Europe's future bank notes. The Maastricht Treaty requires the European Monetary Institute, an institution that should come to life in 1994 as a forerunner of the European central bank, to "supervise the technical preparation of ECU banknotes." The start of monetary union could be as early as 1997, latest by 1999.

Using all Europe's note-printing capacity, it will take two years just to print the 16 billion notes needed to replace the national monies. Before the presses can roll, many politically sensitive decisions have to be made. Among them are the following:

- **Denominations** These must reconcile note habits that vary a lot from country to country: for in-

stance, Belgium's BFr100 note ($3) to Germany's DM1,000 ($620) note.
- **Languages** The EC's nine languages should, in theory, be featured in each note.
- **National vs. European** The planners are working on six varieties ranging from pure, pan-European ECU notes to national-currency notes with discreet references to their ECU value.
- **Heads** Each member will insist on having its illuminaries on a note.
- **Paper or plastic** Plastic would be more durable.
- **Big bang or phase in** As an example, it took Britain four years just to decimalize its coinage.

Source: "EMU in Note Form," *The Economist,* February 27, 1993, 54; Commission of the European Communities, *The European Community 1992 and Beyond* (Luxembourg: Office for Official Publications of the European Communities, 1991), 21–22.

The EC Parliament, which can veto membership applications and trade agreements with non-EC countries, is the weakest of the European Community's governing bodies. Most power is concentrated in the Council of Ministers.
Source: © St. Ellie/REA/SABA.

and one from each smaller member). The commissioners oversee 23 directorates (or departments), such as agriculture, transportation, and external relations. The commissioners are appointed by the member states, but according to the Treaty of Rome, their allegiance is to the community, not to their home country.

The Council of Ministers has the final power to decide EC actions. There are a total of 76 votes in the council. The votes are allocated to the representatives of member countries on the basis of country size. Some of the most important provisions of the Single European Act expanded the ability of the council to pass legislation. The number of matters requiring unanimity was reduced, and countries' ability to veto legislation was weakened substantially.

The Court of Justice is somewhat analogous to the judicial branch of the U.S. government. The court is composed of 13 judges and is based in Luxembourg. The court adjudicates matters related to the European Constitution, especially trade and business disputes. Judicial proceedings may be initiated by member countries, as well as by firms and individuals.

The European Parliament is composed of 518 members elected by popular vote in member countries. The Parliament is essentially an advisory body with relatively little power. The fact that the only elected body of the EC has little policymaking power has led many to charge that the EC suffers from a "democratic deficit." In other words, decisions are made bureaucratically rather than democratically. However, the Single European Act empowered the Parliament to veto EC membership

FIGURE 6.1   **Organization and Decision Making of the EC**

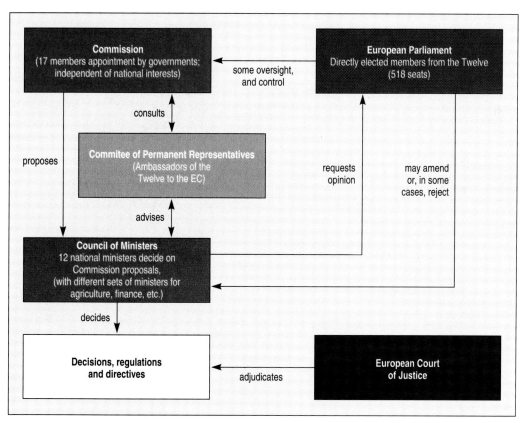

Source: "My, How You've Grown," *The Economist*, January 25, 1992, 31–32.

applications as well as trade agreements with non–EC countries. Many observers believe that the Parliament will gain new powers as European integration proceeds.

The entities and the process of decision making are summarized in Figure 6.1.

Implications of Europe 1992

Perhaps the most important implication of the four freedoms for Europe is the economic growth that is expected to result.[9] Several specific sources of increased growth have been identified. First, there will be gains from eliminating the transaction costs associated with border patrols, customs procedures, and so forth. Second, economic growth will be spurred by the economies of scale that will be achieved when production facilities become more concentrated. Third, there will be gains from more intense competition among EC companies. Firms that were monopolists in one country will now be subject to competition from firms in other EC countries. Economists have estimated that the 1992 reforms will cause an increase in European gross domestic product of about 5 percent over the medium term. In addition, perhaps 2 million new jobs will be created.

The 1992 proposals have important implications for firms within and outside Europe because 1992 poses both threats and opportunities, benefits and costs. There will be substantial benefits for those firms already operating in Europe. These firms will gain because their operations in one country can now be freely expanded into others, and their products may be freely sold across borders. In a borderless Europe, firms will have access to approximately 320 million consumers. In addition, the free movement of capital will allow these firms to sell securities, raise capital, and recruit labor throughout Europe. Substantial economies of scale in production and marketing will also result.

For firms from nonmember countries, 1992 presents various possibilities depending on the firm's position within the EC.[10] Table 6.5 provides four different scenarios with proposed courses of action. Well-established U.S.–based multinational marketers such as H.J. Heinz and Colgate-Palmolive will be able to take advantage of the new economies of scale. For example, 3M plants earlier turned out different versions of the company's products for various markets. Now, the 3M plant in Wales,

**TABLE 6.5
Proposed Company
Responses to 1992**

Company Status	Challenges	Response
Established multinational market/multiple markets	Exploit opportunities from improved productivity	
	Meet challenge of competitors	Pan-European strategy
	Cater to customers/ intermediaries doing same	
Firm with one European subsidiary	Competition	Expansion
	Loss of niche	Strategic alliances
		Rationalization
		Divestment
Exporter to Europe	Competition	European branch
	Access	Selective acquisition
		Strategic alliance
No interest	Competition at home	Entry
	Lost opportunity	

Source: John F. Magee, "1992: Moves Americans Must Make," *Harvard Business Review* 67 (May–June 1989): 78–84.

for example, makes videotapes and videocasettes for all of Europe.[11] Colgate-Palmolive has to watch out for competitors, like Germany's Henkel, in the brutally competitive detergent market. At the same time, large-scale retailers, such as France's Carrefour and Germany's Aldi group, are undertaking their own efforts to exploit the situation with hypermarkets supplied by central warehouses with computerized inventories. Their procurement policies have to be met by companies like Heinz. Many multinationals are developing pan-European strategies to exploit the emerging situation; that is, they are standardizing their products and processes to the greatest extent possible without compromising local input and implementation.

A company with a foothold in only one European market is faced with the danger of competitors who can use the strength of multiple markets. Furthermore, the elimination of barriers may do away with the company's competitive advantage. For example, more than half of the 45 major European food companies are in just one or two of the individual European markets and seriously lag behind broader-based U.S. and Swiss firms. Similarly, automakers PSA and Fiat are nowhere close to the cross-manufacturing presence of Ford and GM. The courses of action include expansion through acquisitions or mergers, formation of strategic alliances (for example, AT&T's joint venture with Spain's Telefonica to produce state-of-the-art microchips), rationalization by concentrating only on business segments in which the company can be a pan-European leader, and finally, divestment.

Exporters will need to worry about maintaining their competitive position and continued access to the market. Companies with a physical presence may be in a better position to assess and to take advantage of the developments. Some firms, like Filament Fiber Technology Inc. of New Jersey, have established production units in Europe. Digital Microwave Corporation of California decided to defend its market share in Europe by joining two British communications companies and setting up a digital microwave radio and optical-fiber plant in Scotland.[12] In some industries, marketers do not see a reason either to be in Europe at all or to change from exporting to more involved modes of entry. Machinery and machine tools, for example, are in great demand in Europe, and marketers in these companies say they have little reason to manufacture there.

The term **Fortress Europe** has been used to describe the fears of many U.S. firms about a unified Europe. The concern is that while Europe dismantles internal barriers, it will raise external ones, making access to the European market difficult for U.S. and other non-EC firms. In a move designed to protect European farmers, for example, the EC has recently banned the import of certain agricultural goods from the United States. The EC has also called on members to limit the number of American television programs broadcast in Europe. Finally, many U.S. firms are concerned about the relatively strict domestic-content rules recently passed by the EC. These rules require certain products sold in Europe to be manufactured with European inputs. One effect of the perceived threat of Fortress Europe has been increased direct investment in Europe by U.S. firms. Fears that the EC will erect barriers to U.S. exports and of the domestic-content rules governing many goods have led many U.S. firms to initiate or expand European direct investment.

NORTH AMERICAN ECONOMIC INTEGRATION

Although the EC is undoubtedly the most successful and well-known integrative effort, integration efforts in North America, although only a few years old, have gained momentum and attention. What started as a trading pact between two close and economically well-developed allies has already been expanded conceptually to include

Mexico, and long-term plans call for further additions. However, in North American integration the interest is purely economic; there are no constituencies for political integration.

U.S.–Canada Free Trade Agreement

After three failed tries this century, the United States and Canada signed a free-trade agreement that went into effect January 1, 1989. The agreement created a $5 trillion continental economy, 10 percent bigger than the United States on its own and 15 percent larger than the EC.[13] The two countries had already had sectoral free-trade arrangements; for example, one for automotive products has existed for 23 years. Even before the agreement, however, the United States and Canada were the world's largest trading partners, and there were relatively few trade barriers. The new arrangement eliminates duties selectively in three stages over the 1989–1999 period: (1) immediately, (2) five equal cuts of 20 percent beginning January 1, 1989, and (3) ten equal cuts of 10 percent beginning January 1, 1989.[14] For example, the first round eliminated a 3.9 percent tariff on U.S. computers shipped to Canada as well as 4.9–22 percent duties on trade in whiskey, skates, furs, and unprocessed fish. The sensitive sectors, such as textiles, steel, and agricultural products, will not be liberalized until the latter part of the transitionary period. Both countries see the free-trade agreement as an important path to world competitiveness. Although there will be some dislocations, due to production consolidation, for example, the pact is expected to create 750,000 jobs in the United States and 150,000 in Canada. It is also expected to add as much as 1 percent in growth to both countries' economies as it takes effect in various stages.

North American Free Trade Agreement

Negotiations on a North American Free Trade Agreement (NAFTA) began in 1991 to create the world's largest free market, with 364 million consumers and a total output of $6 trillion, 25 percent larger than the EC.[15] The pact would mark a bold departure: never before have industrialized countries created such a massive free-trade area with a developing-country neighbor. The deadline for wrapping up the negotiations is January 1, 1994, but before that politicians in all of the three countries have to persuade constituents that for the country as a whole, NAFTA has more to offer than to fear.

Since Canada stands to gain very little from NAFTA (its trade with Mexico is 1 percent of its trade with the United States), much of the controversy has centered on the gains and losses for the United States and Mexico. Proponents argue that the agreement will give U.S. firms access to a huge pool of relatively low-cost Mexican labor at a time when demographic trends are indicating labor shortages in many parts of the United States. At the same time, many new jobs are created in Mexico. The agreement will give firms in both countries access to millions of additional consumers, and the liberalized trade flows will result in faster economic growth in both countries. Overall, the corporate view toward NAFTA is overwhelmingly positive, as can be seen in Global Perspective 6.4.

Reforms have turned Mexico into an attractive market in its own right. Mexico's gross domestic product has been expanding by more than 3 percent every year since 1989, and exports to the United States have risen 72 percent since 1986. Inflation has dropped from 131 percent in 1987 to 22 percent in 1991. By institutionalizing the nation's turn to open markets, the free-trade agreement will likely attract considerable new foreign investment. The United States has benefitted from Mexico's

Debate over the North American Free Trade Agreement in 1992 was complicated by difficulties associated with the existing Canadian-U.S. Free Trade Agreement. Detractors in the United States have accused Canada of subsidizing its lumber exports in order to gain an unfair advantage over the U.S. lumber industry. Disputes of this type undermine efforts toward the kind of trading partnership advocated by proponents of NAFTA.

Source: © Robert Semeniuk/FIRST LIGHT, Toronto.

Global Perspective

6.4
Heading South

Most U.S. companies see themselves as winners with the North American Free Trade Agreement; 81 percent of corporate executives strongly or mostly favor the agreement. A full 40 percent indicate that they are inclined to move some manufacturing to Mexico in the next few years.

At the same time, more than one-third of U.S. companies think that a regional trade accord will be at least somewhat unfavorable for American workers. The origins of new jobs created in Mexico are likely to be contentious; some are likely to be ones that otherwise might have gone to Southeast Asia or other low-wage areas; others may represent a transfer of work from the United States.

Based on a survey of 455 top U.S. executives conducted by the Roper Organization:

- Support for NAFTA is strongest among large companies. Apprehensions are higher for executives at small companies, particularly those who say they do not know much about the accord.

- Telecommunications, banking, and high technology are the U.S. industries that are expected to benefit the most from the trade accord. No industry is rated a victim, but more than one-third of respondents think the textile industry will suffer.

- The development of regional trading blocs is endorsed by a two-to-one margin, with executives saying they want a North American alliance that competes with similar groupings in Europe and Asia.

- About one-quarter say they are likely to make a capital investment in Canada in the next few years, significantly fewer than the percentage targeting Mexico.

- By a three-to-two margin, executives say they would support an even wider trade agreement that would cover all of Latin America.

Of those companies wanting to invest in Mexico, the eagerness is highest among those with sales over $1 billion, 55 percent of the total. Some caution against moving production to Mexico just for the lower wages. Pay scales for skilled workers in Mexico and in the United States are already closer than many people realize. And as Mexico gets more prosperous, wages are likely to rise further. About one-quarter of the executives surveyed say that they are likely to use the trade accord as a bargaining chip to try to hold down wages in the United States.

While Mexico is the main area of interest, executives signal increased interest in Canada as well. Overall, 23 percent say the 1989 agreement led them to increase exports to Canada. Some 9 percent say they invested more in Canada, and 7 percent say they faced increased competition from Canadian companies. But nearly two-thirds say that the agreement has not affected their business. Looking ahead, 27 percent of the respondents say that they are very likely to make capital investment in Canada in the next few years. The current recession in Canada has muted some interest in expanding there. Once Canada's economy picks up, companies are more likely to take advantage of any opportunities presented by liberalized trade.

Many actually see NAFTA as a first step toward a tariff-free common market that would cover all of the Western Hemisphere. Some 56 percent of all executives (70 percent from large companies) favor a trade accord that would cover all of Latin America.

Source: "One America," *The Wall Street Journal Reports,* September 24, 1992, R1–R28.

success. The U.S. trade deficit with Mexico shrank from $4.9 billion in 1986 to $1.4 billion in 1991 due to doubling of exports during that period. This has resulted in 264,000 jobs.[16] Among the U.S. industries to benefit are computers, autos, petrochemicals, and financial services. In 1990, Mexico opened its computer market by eliminating many burdensome licensing requirements and cutting the tariff from 50 percent to 20 percent. As a result, exports surged 23 percent in that year alone. IBM, which makes personal and mid-size computers in Mexico, anticipates sales growth to about $1 billion from that country by the mid-1990s. In Mexico's growth toward a more advanced society, manufacturers of consumer goods will also stand to benefit.

Free trade does produce both winners and losers. Although opponents concede that the agreement is likely to spur economic growth, they point out that segments of the U.S. economy will be harmed by the agreement. It is likely that wages and employment for unskilled workers in the United States will fall because of Mexico's low-cost labor pool. U.S. companies have been moving operations to Mexico since the 1960s. The door was opened when Mexico liberalized export restrictions to allow for more so-called **maquiladoras,** plants that make goods and parts or process food for export back to the United States. The supply of labor is plentiful, the pay and benefits are low, and the work regulations are lax by U.S. standards. The average maquiladora wage equals $1.73 per hour, compared with $2.17 an hour for Mexican manufacturers.[17] U.S. labor leaders also charge that Mexico's inadequate environmental and worker protections will encourage U.S. companies to move there to evade tougher standards at home. In fact, Mexican laws are just as strict as U.S. regulations, but until recently nobody enforced them. A 1993 International Trade Commission assessment estimates that while NAFTA would create a net gain of 35,000 to 93,500 U.S. jobs by 1995, it would also cause U.S. companies to shed as many as 170,000 jobs.[18] The good news is that free trade will create higher-skilled and better-paying jobs in the United States as a result of growth in exports. Potential losers are going to be U.S. manufacturers of auto parts, furniture, and household glass; sugar, peanut, and citrus growers; and seafood and vegetable producers.

Countries dependent on trade with NAFTA countries are concerned that the agreement would divert trade and impose significant losses on their economies. Asia's continuing economic success depends largely on easy access to the North American markets, which account for more than 25 percent of annual export revenue for many Asian countries. Lower-cost producers in Asia are likely to lose some exports to the United States if they are subject to tariffs while Mexican firms are not.[19] Similarly, many in the Caribbean and Central America fear that the apparel industries of these regions will be threatened, as would much-needed investments.[20]

NAFTA may be the first step toward a hemispheric bloc, but nobody expects it to happen any time soon. It took more than three years of tough bargaining to reach an agreement between the United States and Canada, two countries with parallel economic, industrial, and social systems.[21] The challenges of expanding free trade throughout Latin America will be significant. However, many of Latin America's groupings are making provisions to join in the 1990s.

OTHER ECONOMIC ALLIANCES

Perhaps the world's developing countries have the most to gain from successful integrative efforts. Because many of these countries are also quite small, economic growth is difficult to generate internally. Many of these countries have adopted policies of **import substitution** to foster economic growth. With an import-substitution policy, new domestic industries produce goods that were formerly imported. Many of these industries, however, can be efficient producers only with a higher level of production than can be consumed by the domestic economy. Their success, therefore, depends on accessible export markets made possible by integrative efforts.

Integration in Latin America

Before the signing of the U.S.–Canada Free Trade Agreement, all of the major trading-bloc activity in the Americas had taken place in Latin America. One of the longest-lived integrative efforts among developing countries was the Latin America Free Trade Association (LAFTA), formed in 1961. As the name suggests, the primary objective of LAFTA was the elimination of trade barriers. The 1961 agreement called for trade barriers to be gradually dismantled, leading to completely free trade by 1973. By 1969, however, it was clear that a pervasive protectionist ideology would keep LAFTA from meeting this objective, and the target date was extended to 1980. In the meantime, however, the global debt crisis, the energy crisis, and the collapse of the Bretton Woods system prevented the achievement of LAFTA objectives. Dissatisfied with LAFTA, the group made a new start as the Latin American Integration Association (LAIA) in 1980. The objective is a higher level of integration than that envisioned by LAFTA; however, the dismantling of trade barriers remains a necessary and elusive first step.

The Central American Common Market (CACM) was formed by the Treaty of Managua in 1960. The CACM has often been cited as a model integrative effort for other developing countries. By the end of the 1960s, the CACM had succeeded in eliminating restrictions on 80 percent of trade among members. A continuing source of difficulty, however, is that the benefits of integration have fallen disproportionately to the richer and more developed members. Political difficulties in the area have also hampered progress. However, the member countries renewed their commitment to integration in 1990.

Integration efforts in the Caribbean have focused on the Caribbean Community and Common Market formed in 1968. These Caribbean nations (as well as Central American nations) have benefitted from the **Caribbean Basin Initiative (CBI),** which, since 1983, has extended trade preferences and granted access to the markets of the United States. Under NAFTA these preferences are lost, which means that these countries have to cooperate more closely among each other. Mexico and CACM have already started planning for a free-trade arrangement.

None of the activity in Latin America has been hemispheric; the Central Americans have had their structures, the Caribbean nations theirs, and the South Americans had their own different forms. However, in a dramatic transformation, these nations are now looking for free trade as a salvation from stagnation, inflation, and debt.[22] Recent foreign policy of the United States has also responded to Latin American regionalism. The **Enterprise for the Americas Initiative (EAI)** was designed to further democracy in the region by providing incentives to capitalistic development and trade liberalization. Frameworks have already been signed under the EAI. In response to the recent developments, Brazil, Argentina, Uruguay, and Paraguay set up a common market with completion by the end of 1994 called Mercosur.[23] Bolivia, Colombia, Ecuador, Peru, and Venezuela have formed the Andean Common Market (ANCOM). Many Latin nations are realizing that if they do not unite, they will become decreasingly important in the global market.

The ultimate goal is a free-trade zone from Point Barrow, Alaska, to Patagonia. The argument is that free trade throughout the Americas would channel investment and technology to Latin nations and give U.S. firms a head start in those markets. If Latin America grows, as estimated, at an average of 4 percent annually during the 1990s under trade liberalization, imports will increase by $170 billion, of which U.S. firms can capture as much as 40 percent. However, before it can become a reality, many political (such as democratization) and economic (such as market-oriented policies) changes have to take place.

Integration in Asia

The development in Asia has been quite different from that in Europe and in the Americas. While European and North American arrangements have been driven by political will, market forces may compel politicians in Asia to move toward formal integration. While Japan is the dominant force in the area to take leadership in such an endeavor, neither the Japanese themselves nor the other nations want Japan to do it. The concept of a "Co-Prosperity Sphere" of 50 years ago has made nations wary of Japan's influence.[24] Also, in terms of economic and political distance, the potential member countries are far from each other, especially compared to the EC. However, Asian interest in regional integration is increasing for pragmatic reasons. First, European and American markets are significant for the Asian producers and some type of organization or bloc may be needed to maintain leverage and balance against the two other blocs. Secondly, given that much of the growth in trade for the nations in the region is from intra-Asian trade, having a common understanding and policies will become necessary. A future arrangement will most likely be using the frame of the most established arrangement in the region, the Association of Southeast Asian Nations (ASEAN). Before late 1991, ASEAN had no real structures, and consensus was reached through information consultations. In October 1991, ASEAN members (Brunei, Indonesia, Malaysia, Philippines, Singapore, and Thailand) announced the formation of a customs union called ASEAN Free Trade Area (AFTA). The Malaysians have pushed for the formation of the East Asia Economic Group (EAEG), which would add Hong Kong, Japan, South Korea, and Taiwan to the list. This proposal makes sense; without Japan and the rapidly industrializing countries of the region, such as South Korea and Taiwan, the effect of the arrangement would be small. Japan's reaction has been generally negative toward all types of regionalization efforts, mainly because it has had the most to gain from free-trade efforts. However, part of what has been driving regionalization has been Japan's reluctance to foster some of the elements that promote free trade, like reciprocity.[25] Should the other trading blocs turn against Japan, her only resort may be to work toward a more formal trade arrangement in Pacific Asia.

Another formal proposal for cooperation would start building bridges between two emerging trade blocs. Some individuals have publicly called for a U.S.–Japan common market. Given the differences on all fronts between the two, the proposal may be quite unrealistic at this time. Negotiated trade liberalization will not open Japanese markets due to major institutional differences, as seen in many rounds of successful negotiations but totally unsatisfactory results. The only solution for the U.S. government is to forge better cooperation between the government and the private sector to improve competitiveness.[26]

In 1988, Australia proposed the Asia Pacific Economic Cooperation (APEC) as an annual forum. The proposal calls for ASEAN members to be joined by Australia, New Zealand, Japan, China, Hong Kong, Taiwan, South Korea, Canada, and the United States. The model for APEC would not be the EC with its Brussels bureaucracy but the Organization for Economic Cooperation and Development (OECD), which is a center for research and high-level discussion. This development is discussed further in Global Perspective 6.5.

However, the future actions of the other two blocs will determine how quickly and in what manner the Asian bloc, whatever it is, will respond. Also, the stakes are the highest for the Asian nations in the present round of GATT negotiations since their traditional export markets have been in Europe and in North America and, in this sense, very dependent on free access.

Economic integration has also taken place on the Indian subcontinent. In 1985, seven nations of the region (India, Pakistan, Bangladesh, Sri Lanka, Nepal, Bhutan, and the Maldives) launched the South Asian Association for Regional Cooperation (SAARC). Cooperation is limited to relatively noncontroversial areas, such as agriculture and regional development. Elements such as the formation of a common market have not been included.

Global Perspective

6.5
A New Cooperative Effort for the Pacific Century

In 1990, the newly formed Asia Pacific Economic Cooperation (APEC) forum met in Singapore to discuss the region's growing integration in the world's economy. APEC's members include most of the countries that produced the Asian economic miracle of the 1980s and that many believe will make the 21st century the "Pacific Century."

However, political progress in the region lags far behind the economic progress, and political reforms and development are needed before many Asian countries can join the ranks of the true economic powers. For example, the citizens of Indonesia, Singapore, and Malaysia do not yet have the political liberties necessary for the free flow of information, a critical aspect of a market economy. Even freedom of the press is an elusive goal for some of these countries.

APEC may be able to help keep Asia on track for the Pacific Century. The forum will need to find ways for the governments of Pacific Rim countries to keep pace with their economies. Political freedoms have already followed economic success in many Asian countries. For example, citizens of some Asian countries were effectively denied access to many imported goods until recently. However, many of the region's biggest exporters found that their successes left them with so much cash that they could no longer keep their borders closed to French champagne and Swiss chocolates. APEC, it is hoped, can help sustain the Pacific miracle through economic integration from which political freedom and development will follow.

Source: Emily Thorton, "Will Japan Rule a New Trade Bloc?" *Fortune,* October 5, 1992, 131–132; and "The Asian Connection," *The Wall Street Journal,* July 7, 1990, A8.

Integration in Africa and the Middle East

Africa's economic groupings range from currency unions among European nations and their former colonies to customs unions between neighboring states. In 1975, 16 west African nations attempted to create a megamarket large enough to interest investors from the industrialized world and reduce hardship through economic integration. The objective of the Economic Community of West African States (ECOWAS) was to form a customs union and eventual common market. Although many of its objectives have not been reached, its combined population of 160 million represents the largest economic entity in sub-Saharan Africa. Other entities in Africa include the Afro-Malagasy Economic Union, the East Africa Customs Union, the West African Economic Community, and the Maghreb Economic Community. Many of these, however, have not been successful due to the small size of the members and lack of economic infrastructure to produce goods to be traded inside the blocs.

Countries in the Arab world have made some progress in economic integration. The Gulf Cooperation Council (GCC) is one of the most powerful, economically speaking, of any trade groups. The per-capita income of its six member states (Bahrain, Kuwait, Oman, Qatar, Saudi Arabia, and the United Arab Emirates) is $7,690. The GCC was formed in 1980 mainly as a defensive measure due to the perceived threat from the Iran-Iraq war. Its aim is to achieve free-trade arrangements with the EC and EFTA as well as bilateral trade agreements with western European nations.

A listing of the major regional trade agreements is provided in Table 6.6.

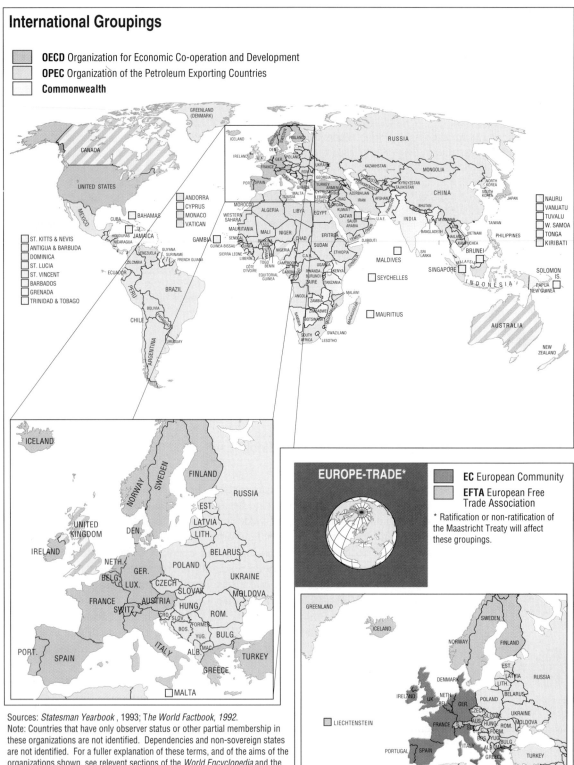

International Groupings

OECD Organization for Economic Co-operation and Development
OPEC Organization of the Petroleum Exporting Countries
Commonwealth

EUROPE-TRADE*

EC European Community
EFTA European Free Trade Association

* Ratification or non-ratification of the Maastricht Treaty will affect these groupings.

Sources: *Statesman Yearbook*, 1993; *The World Factbook, 1992*.
Note: Countries that have only observer status or other partial membership in these organizations are not identified. Dependencies and non-sovereign states are not identified. For a fuller explanation of these terms, and of the aims of the organizations shown, see relevent sections of the *World Encyclopedia* and the *Statesman Yearbook*.

PACIFIC BASIN

ASEAN Association of South East Asian Nations

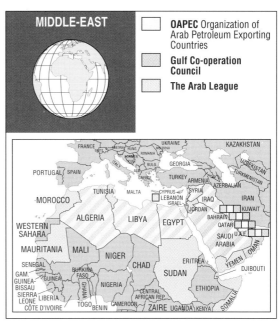

MIDDLE-EAST

OAPEC Organization of Arab Petroleum Exporting Countries

Gulf Co-operation Council

The Arab League

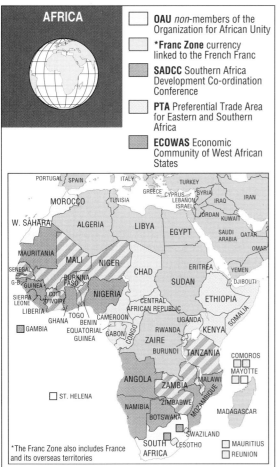

AFRICA

OAU *non*-members of the Organization for African Unity

***Franc Zone** currency linked to the French Franc

SADCC Southern Africa Development Co-ordination Conference

PTA Preferential Trade Area for Eastern and Southern Africa

ECOWAS Economic Community of West African States

*The Franc Zone also includes France and its overseas territories

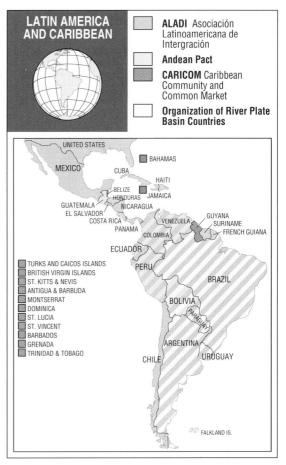

LATIN AMERICA AND CARIBBEAN

ALADI Asociación Latinoamericana de Intergración

Andean Pact

CARICOM Caribbean Community and Common Market

Organization of River Plate Basin Countries

Cartels and Commodity Price Agreements

An important characteristic that distinguishes developing countries from industrialized countries is the nature of their export earnings. While industrialized countries rely heavily on the export of manufactured goods, technology, and services, the developing countries rely chiefly on the export of primary products and raw materials—for example, copper, iron ore, and agricultural products. This distinction is important for several reason. First, the level of price competition is higher among sellers of primary products, because of the typically larger number of sellers and also because primary products are homogeneous. This can be seen by comparing the sale of computers with, for example, copper. Only three or four countries are a competitive force in the computer market, whereas at least a dozen compete in the sale of copper. Furthermore, while product differentiation and therefore brand loyalty are likely to exist in the market for computers, buyers of copper are likely to purchase on the basis of price alone. A second distinguishing factor is that supply variability will be greater in the market for primary products because production often depends on uncontrollable factors such as weather. For these reasons, market prices of primary products—and therefore developing country export earnings—are highly volatile.

Responses to this problem have included cartels and commodity price agreements. A **cartel** is an association of producers of a particular good. While a cartel may consist of an association of private firms, our interest is in the cartels formed by nations. The objective of a cartel is to suppress the market forces affecting its product in order to gain greater control over sales revenues. A cartel may accomplish this objective in several ways. First, members may engage in price fix

TABLE 6.6 **Major Regional Trade Associations**	**AFTA**	**ASEAN Free Trade Area** Brunei, Indonesia, Malaysia, Philippines, Singapore, Thailand
	ANCOM	**Andean Common Market** Bolivia, Colombia, Ecuador, Peru, Venezuela
	CACM	**Central American Common Market** Costa Rica, El Salvador, Guatemala, Honduras, Nicaragua
	CARICOM	**Caribbean Community** Antigua, Bahamas, Barbados, Belize, Dominica, Grenada, Guyana, Jamaica, Montserrat, St. Kitts-Nevis-Anguilla, St. Lucia, St. Vincent and the Grenadines, Trinidad-Tobago
	ECOWAS	**Economic Community of West African States** Benin, Berkina Faso, Cape Verde, Gambia, Ghana, Guinea, Guinea-Bissau, Ivory Coast, Liberia, Mali, Mauritania, Niger, Nigeria, Senegal, Sierra Leone, Togo
	EC	**European Community** Belgium, Denmark, France, Germany, Greece, Ireland, Italy, Luxembourg, Netherlands, Portugal, Spain, United Kingdom
	EFTA	**European Free Trade Association** Austria, Finland, Iceland, Liechtenstein, Norway, Sweden, Switzerland
	GCC	**Gulf Cooperation Council** Bahrain, Kuwait, Oman, Qatar, Saudi Arabia, United Arab Emirates
	LAIA	**Latin American Integration Association** Argentina, Bolivia, Brazil, Chile, Colombia, Ecuador, Mexico, Paraguay, Peru, Uruguay, Venezuela
	MERCOSUR	**Southern Common Market** Argentina, Brazil, Paraguay, Uruguay
	NAFTA	**North American Free Trade Agreement** Canada, Mexico, United States

ing. This entails an agreement by producers to sell at a certain price, eliminating price competition among sellers. Second, the cartel may allocate sales territories among its members, again suppressing competition. A third tactic calls for members to agree to restrict production, and therefore supplies, resulting in artificially higher prices.

The most widely known cartel is the Organization of Petroleum Exporting Countries (OPEC). OPEC became a significant force in the world economy in the 1970s. In 1973, the Arab members of OPEC were angered by U.S. support for Israel in the war in the Mideast. In response, the Arab members declared an embargo on the shipment of oil to the United States and quadrupled the price of oil—from approximately $3 to $12 per barrel. OPEC tactics included both price fixing and production quotas. Continued price increases brought the average price per barrel to nearly $35 by 1981. The cartel experienced severe problems during the 1980s, however. First, the demand for OPEC oil declined considerably as the result of conservation, the use of alternative sources, and increased oil production by nonmembers. All of these factors also contributed to sharp declines in the price of oil. Second, the cohesiveness among members diminished. Sales often occurred at less than the agreed-upon price, and production quotas have been repeatedly violated. The members of OPEC convened following the Persian Gulf war in early 1991 in an attempt to regain control over oil prices, but it remains to be seen whether OPEC will regain its influence as a major force in the world economy.

International **commodity price agreements** involve both buyers and sellers in an agreement to manage the price of a certain commodity. Often, the free market is allowed to determine the price of the commodity over a certain range. However, if demand and supply pressures cause the commodity's price to move outside that range, an elected or appointed manager will enter the market to buy or sell the commodity to bring the price back into the range. The manager controls the **buffer stock** of the commodity. If prices float downward, the manager purchases the commodity and adds to the buffer stock. Under upward pressure, the manager sells the commodity from the buffer stock. This system is somewhat analogous to a managed exchange rate system such as the EMS, in which authorities buy and sell to influence exchange rates. International commodity agreements are currently in effect for sugar, tin, rubber, cocoa, and coffee.

SUMMARY

Economic integration involves agreements among countries to establish links through the movements of goods, services, and factors of production across borders. These links may be weak or strong depending on the level of integration. Levels of integration include the free trade area, customs union, common market, and full economic union.

The benefits derived from economic integration include trade creation, economies of scale, improved terms of trade, the reduction of monopoly power, and improved cross-cultural communication. However, a number of disadvantages may also exist. Most importantly, economic integration may work to the detriment of nonmembers by causing deteriorating terms of trade and trade diversion. In addition, no guarantee exists that all members will share the gains from integration. The biggest impediment to economic integration is nationalism. There is strong resistance to surrendering autonomy and self-determinism to cooperative agreements.

The most successful example of economic integration is the European Community. The EC has succeeded in eliminating most barriers to the free flow of goods, services, and factors of production. In addition, the EC has made progress toward the evolution of a common currency and central bank, which are fundamental requirements of an economic union. In the Americas, NAFTA is paving the way for a hemispheric trade bloc.

A number of regional economic alliances exist in Africa, Latin America, and Asia, but they have achieved only low levels of integration. Political difficulties, low levels of development, and problems with cohesiveness have impeded integrative progress among many developing countries. However, many nations in these areas are seeing economic integration as the only way to prosperity in the future.

International commodity price agreements and cartels represent attempts by producers of primary products to control sales revenues and export earnings. The former involves an agreement to buy or sell a commodity to influence prices. The latter is an agreement by suppliers to fix prices, set production quotas, or allocate sales territories. OPEC had inestimable influence on the global economy during the 1970s, but its importance has since diminished.

Key Terms and Concepts

trading bloc	common agricultural policy (CAP)
free trade area	1992 White Paper
customs union	economic and monetary union (EMU)
common market	Fortress Europe
factor mobility	maquiladoras
Single European Act	import substitution
economic union	Caribbean Basin Initiative (CBI)
trade creation	Enterprise for the Americas Initiative (EAI)
trade diversion	cartel
internal economies of scale	commodity price agreement
external economies of scale	buffer stock
Treaty of Rome	

Questions for Discussion

1. Explain the difference between a free trade area and a customs union. Speculate why negotiations are being held for a North American Free Trade Agreement rather than for a North American Common Market.
2. What problems might a member country of a common market be concerned about?
3. Construct an example of a customs union arrangement resulting in both trade creation and trade diversion.
4. Distinguish between external and internal economies of scale resulting from economic integration.
5. What are the main provisions of the Single European Act?
6. Discuss the relationship between import substitution and economic integration among developing countries.
7. Suppose that you work for a medium-sized manufacturing firm in the Midwest. Approximately 20 percent of your sales are to European customers. What threats and opportunities does your firm face as a result of Europe 1992?

8. What type of adjustments will U.S. firms make as a result of NAFTA?

Recommended Readings

Buiter, William, and Richard Marston. *International Economic Policy Coordination.* Cambridge, England: Cambridge University Press, 1987.

Cooper, Richard. *Economic Policy in an Interdependent World.* Cambridge, Mass.: MIT Press, 1987.

EC Commission. *Completing the Internal Market: White Paper from the Commission to the European Council.* Luxembourg: EC Commission, 1985.

Fair, D. E., and C. de Boissieu, eds. *International Monetary and Financial Integration—The European Dimension.* Norwell, Mass.: Kluwer, 1987.

Ryans, Jr., John K., and Pradeep A. Rau. *Marketing Strategies for the New Europe: A North American Perspective on 1992.* Chicago, Ill.: American Marketing Association, 1990.

Sapir, André, and Alexis Jacquemin, eds. *The European Internal Market.* Oxford, England: Oxford University Press, 1990.

Schott, Jeffrey. *United States–Canada Free Trade: An Evaluation of the Agreement.* Washington, D.C.: Institute for International Economics, 1988.

Stoeckel, Andrew, David Pearce, and Gary Banks. *Western Trade Blocs.* Canberra, Australia: Centre for International Economics, 1990.

Suriyamongkol, Marjorie L. *Politics of ASEAN Economic Cooperation.* Oxford, England: Oxford University Press, 1988.

United Nations. *From the Common Market to EC92: Integration in the European Community and Transnational Corporations.* New York: United Nations Publications, 1992.

Notes

1. The discussion of economic integration is based on the pioneering work by Bela Balassa, *The Theory of Economic Integration* (Homewood, Ill.: Richard D. Irwin, 1961).
2. Jacob Viner, *The Customs Union Issue* (New York: Carnegie Endowment for International Peace, 1950).
3. J. Waelbroeck, "Measuring Degrees of Progress in Economic Integration," in *Economic Integration, Worldwide, Regional, Sectoral,* ed. F. Machlop (London: Macmillan, 1980).
4. Paul Belien, "Bitter Birthday for Europe's Common Market," *The Wall Street Journal,* March 25, 1987, 31.
5. EC Commission, *Completing the Internal Market: White Paper from the Commission to the European Council* (Luxembourg: EC Commission, 1985).
6. Carla Rapoport, "Europe Looks Ahead to Hard Choices," *Fortune,* December 14, 1992, 144-149.
7. Various aspects of the 1992 Common Market are addressed in André Sapir and Alexis Jacquemin, eds., *The European Internal Market* (Oxford, England: Oxford University Press, 1990).

8. "Will More Be Merrier?" *The Economist,* October 17, 1992, 75.
9. Economic growth effects are discussed in Richard Baldwin, "The Growth Effects of 1992," *Economic Policy* (October 1989): 248-281; or Rudiger Dornbusch, "Europe 1992: Macroeconomic Implications," *Brookings Papers on Economic Activity* 2 (1989): 341-362.
10. John F. Magee, "1992: Moves Americans Must Make," *Harvard Business Review* 67 (May-June 1989), 72-84.
11. Richard I. Kirkland, "Outsider's Guide to Europe in 1992," *Fortune,* October 24, 1988, 121-127.
12. "Should Small U.S. Exporters Take the Plunge?" *Business Week,* November 14, 1988, 64-68.
13. "Getting Ready for the Great American Shakeout," *Business Week,* April 4, 1988, 44-46.
14. "Summary of the U.S.-Canada Free Trade Agreement," *Export Today* 4 (November-December 1988), 57-61.

15. See *The Likely Impact on the United States of a Free Trade Agreement with Mexico* (Washington, D.C.: United States International Trade Commission, 1991).

16. Ann Reilly Dowd, "Viva Free Trade with Mexico," *Fortune,* June 17, 1991, 97-100.

17. Jim Carlton, "The Lure of Cheap Labor," *The Wall Street Journal,* September 14, 1992, R16.

18. "A Noose Around NAFTA," *Business Week,* February 22, 1993, 37.

19. Andrew Stoeckel, David Pearce, and Gary Banks, *Western Trade Blocs* (Canberra, Australia: Centre for International Economics, 1990).

20. Jose De Cordoba, "Alarm Bells in the Caribbean," *The Wall Street Journal,* September 24, 1992, R8.

21. "A Giant Step Closer to North America Inc.," *Business Week,* December 5, 1988, 44-45.

22. Thomas Kamm, "Latin Links," *The Wall Street Journal,* September 24, 1992, R6.

23. "The World's Newest Trading Bloc," *Business Week,* May 4, 1992, 50-51.

24. Emily Thornton, "Will Japan Rule a New Trade Bloc?" *Fortune,* October 5, 1992, 131-132.

25. Paul Krugman, "A Global Economy Is Not the Wave of the Future," *Financial Executive* 8 (March/April 1992): 10-13.

26. Michael R. Czinkota and Masaaki Kotabe, "America's New World Trade Order," *Marketing Management* 1 (Summer 1992): 49-56.

National Trade and
Investment Policies

LEARNING OBJECTIVES

1. To see how trade and investment policies have historically been a subset of domestic policies.

2. To examine how historical attitudes toward trade and investment policies are changing.

3. To see how global linkages in trade and investment have made policymakers less able to focus solely on domestic issues.

4. To understand that nations must cooperate closely in the future to maintain a viable global trade and investment environment.

A Rover Is a Rover Is a Rover

In order to stem the increasing tide of imports, the U.S. Customs Service ruled that multipurpose vehicles (MPVs) are light trucks and therefore subject to the 25 percent tariff on trucks and not the 2.5 percent levied on cars.

Britain's Land Rover, maker of four-wheel-drive vehicles, was exporting its $40,000 Range Rover to the United States. The firm protested that its luxury vehicle (favored transport by the royal family) was definitely not a truck. The complaints paid off in that the U.S. Treasury reclassified the Range Rover as a car, subject to the low import levy.

When the luxury tax was introduced in 1991, it covered 10 percent of the part of a car's price that exceeded $30,000. The tax did not apply to trucks. Land Rover worked closely with the U.S. Internal Revenue Service to establish that four-wheel-drive utility vehicles are trucks. Since the IRS definition of trucks requires a gross vehicle weight of more than 6,000 pounds, some slight adjustments in the U.S. model Range Rover increased its weight to a total of 6,019 pounds. Maybe there is such a thing as eating your cake and having it too.

"What's in a Name?" *The Economist,* February 2, 1991, 60.

This concluding chapter of Part 2 will discuss the policy actions taken by countries. All nations have international trade and investment policies. These policies may be publicly pronounced or kept secret, they may be disjointed or coordinated, they may be applied consciously or determined by a laissez-faire attitude. In any case, they are manifest when measures taken by governments affect the flow of trade and investment across national borders. As the opening vignette illustrates, nations can and will target their actions to achieve particular policy goals. In the instance of U.S. import tariffs on trucks, clearly Japanese manufacturers were the key target. Therefore it was possible for Land Rover to circumvent these tariffs.

RATIONALE AND GOALS OF TRADE AND INVESTMENT POLICIES

Government policies are designed to regulate, stimulate, direct, and protect national activities. The exercise of these policies is the result of **national sovereignty,** which provides a government with the right and burden to shape the environment of the country and its citizens. Because they are "border bound," governments focus mainly on domestic policies. Most actions taken, even if they have an international impact, are a subset of domestic policies. Nevertheless, many policy actions have repercussions on other nations, firms, and individuals abroad and are therefore a component of a nation's trade and investment policy.

Government policy can be subdivided into two groups of policy actions that affect trade and investment. One of them affects trade and investment indirectly, the other directly. The domestic policy actions of most governments aim to increase—or at least maintain—the **standard of living** of the country's citizens; maintain or improve the **quality of life;** stimulate national development; and achieve full employment. Clearly, all of these goals are closely intertwined. For example, an improved standard of living is likely to contribute to national development. Similarly, quality of life and standard of living are closely interlinked. Also, a high level of employment will play a major role in determining the standard of living. Yet all of these policy goals will also have international impact. For example, if foreign industries become more competitive and rapidly increase their exports, employment in the importing countries may suffer. Likewise, if a country accumulates large quantities of debt, which at some time must be repaid, the present and future standard of living will be threatened.

A country may also pursue policies of increased development that mandate either technology transfer from abroad or the exclusion of foreign industries to the benefit of domestic infant firms. Also, government officials may believe that imports threaten the culture, health, or standards of the country's citizens and thus the quality of life. As a result, officials are likely to develop regulations to protect the citizens.

In more direct ways, nations institute **foreign policy** measures. They are designed with domestic concerns in mind but explicitly aim to exercise influence abroad. One major goal of foreign policy measures is often national security. For example, nations may develop alliances, coalitions, and agreements in order to protect their borders or their spheres of interest. Similarly, nations may take measures to enhance their national security preparedness in case of international conflict. Governments also wish to improve trade and investment opportunities and to contribute to the security and safety of their own firms abroad.

All of these policy aims may be approached in various ways. For example, in order to develop new markets abroad and to increase their sphere of influence, nations may give foreign aid to other countries. This was the case when the United States generously awarded Marshall Plan funds for the reconstruction of Europe. Similarly, Japan provides development aid to nations in Asia. Governments may also feel a need to restrict or encourage trade and investment flows in order to preserve or enhance the capability of industries that are important to national security.

Not all of these measures necessarily work in favor of international trade and investment flows. Some argue, for example, that foreign policy concerns of the United States have led to consistently destructive trade-offs in U.S. trade policy. They point out that the U.S. government frequently accommodates or even bails out foreign nations for foreign-policy purposes and this in turn results in detrimental repercussions for U.S. producers and workers.[1] U.S. willingness to permit Chinese textile imports is often cited as an example, even though the Chinese government may feel that its exports are strangled by U.S. quotas.

Because each country develops its own domestic policies, policy aims will vary from nation to nation. Inevitably, conflicts arise. For example, full employment policies in one country may directly affect employment policies in another. Similarly, the development aims of one country may reduce the development capability of another. Even when health issues are concerned, disputes may arise. One nation may argue that its regulations are in place to protect its citizens, whereas other nations may interpret these regulations as market barriers. An example for the latter situation is the celebrated hormone dispute between the United States and the European Community. U.S. cattle are treated with growth hormones. While the United States claims that these hormones are harmless to humans, many Europeans find them scary. Given these differences in perspectives, there is much room for conflict when it comes to trade policies, particularly when the United States wants to export more beef and the European Community attempts to restrict such beef imports.[2]

Conflicts among nations are also likely to emerge when foreign-policy goals lead to trade and investment measures. Such conflicts can even involve international aid. For example, because of its vast current account surplus, Japan is able to grant generous **developmental aid** to countries in Asia. While few governments would criticize altruistic aid, many of them dispute the use of aid funds for purposes of trade distortions. Japanese aid payments are seen as linked to the purchases of Japanese products. Even if such linkages are not overt, the simple fact that Japanese engineers and designers may assess a project and contribute to its development can have major repercussions on trade flows. The reason is that the design determines the specifications of machines, computers, and materials that will be purchased. Obviously, if influences in the design phase come from only one nation, they will provide significant direction for future purchases.

Conflicts among national policies have always existed but have only recently come to prominence. The reason lies in the changes that have taken place in the world trade and investment climate. A brief review of the global developments that led to the current environment will be useful here.

GLOBAL DEVELOPMENTS SINCE 1945

In 1945, the United States led in the belief that international trade and investment flows were a key to worldwide prosperity. Many months of international negotiations in London, Geneva, and Lake Success (New York) culminated on March 24, 1948, in Havana, Cuba, with the signing of the Havana Charter for the **International Trade Organization (ITO).** This charter represented a series of agreements among 53 countries. It was designed to cover international commercial policies, restrictive business practices, commodity agreements, employment and reconstruction, economic development and international investment, and a constitution for a new United Nations agency to administer the whole.[3]

Even though the International Trade Organization incorporated many farsighted notions, most nations refused to ratify its provisions. They feared the power and bureaucratic size of the new organization—and the consequent threats to national sovereignty. As a result, this most forward-looking approach to international trade and investment was never implemented. However, other organizations conceived at the time have made major contributions toward improving international business. An agreement was initiated for the purpose of reducing tariffs and therefore facilitating trade. In addition, international institutions such as the United Nations, the World Bank, and the International Monetary Fund were negotiated.

The **General Agreement on Tariffs and Trade (GATT)** has been called a "remarkable success story of a postwar international organization that was never intended to become one."[4] It started out in 1947 as a set of rules to ensure nondiscrimination, transparent procedures, the settlement of disputes, and the participation of the lesser-developed countries in international trade. The main tools GATT uses to increase trade consist of tariff concessions, through which member countries agree to limit the level of tariffs they will impose on imports from other GATT members, and the **Most-Favored Nation (MFN)** clause, which calls for each member country to grant every other member country the most favorable treatment it accords to any country with respect to imports and exports.[5]

The GATT was not originally intended to be an international organization. Rather, it was to be a multilateral treaty designed to operate under the International Trade Organization (ITO), which was to be chartered in 1948. However, because the ITO never came into being, the GATT became the governing body for settling international trade disputes. Gradually it evolved into an institution that sponsored various successful rounds of international trade negotiations. Headquartered in Geneva, Switzerland, the GATT Secretariat conducts its work as instructed by the representatives of its member nations. Even though the GATT has no independent enforcement mechanism and relies entirely on moral suasion and on frequently wavering membership adherence to its rules, it has achieved major progress for world trade.

Early in its history, the GATT achieved the reduction of duties for trade in 50,000 products, amounting to two-thirds of the value of the trade among its participants.[6] In subsequent years, special GATT negotiations such as the Kennedy Round, named after John Kennedy, and the Tokyo Round, named after the location where the negotiations were agreed upon, further reduced trade barriers and improved dispute-settlement mechanisms. The GATT also developed better provisions for dealing with subsidies and more explicit definitions of roles for import controls. Table 7.1 provides an overview of the different GATT rounds.

The International Monetary Fund (IMF), another major international institution, was conceived in 1944 at Bretton Woods in New Hampshire and was designed to provide stability for the international monetary framework and to maintain fixed exchange rates between countries. The use of the dollar as the main world currency resulted in a glut of dollar supplies in the 1960s. This forced the United States to abandon the gold standard and to devalue the dollar, leading to flexible, or floating, exchange rates in 1971. In spite of this major change, the IMF has continued to contribute to international liquidity and thus facilitated international trade.

Like the GATT and the IMF, the World Bank is a third major international institution that has had major successes. Formed in 1944 to aid countries suffering from the destruction of war, it later took on the task of aiding world development. As more and more new nations have emerged, the bank has played a major role in assisting fledgling economies to participate in the modern economic-trade framework.

The success of these institutions and the resulting increase in welfare, particularly in the Western nations, has refuted the old postulate that "the strong is most powerful alone." Nations have increasingly come to recognize that international trade and investment activities are important to their own economic well-being.

Nations have also come to accept that they must generate sufficient outgoing export and investment activities to compensate for the inflow of imports and investment taking place. In the medium and long term, the Balance of Payments must be maintained. For short periods of time, gold or capital transfers can be used to finance a deficit. Such financing, however, can continue only while gold and foreign assets last or while foreign countries will accept the IOUs of the deficit countries, permitting them to pile up foreign liabilities.[7] This willingness, of course, will vary. Some countries, such as the United States, can run up deficits of hundreds of billions of dollars because of political stability, acceptable rates of return, and perceived economic security. Yet, over the long term, all nations are subject to the same economic rules.

TABLE 7.1 Negotiations in the GATT

Round	Dates	Numbers of Countries	Value of Trade Covered	Average Tariff Cut	Average Tariffs Afterward
Geneva	1947	23	$10 billion	35%	n/a
Annecy	1949	33	Unavailable		n/a
Torquay	1950	34	Unavailable		n/a
Geneva	1956	22	$2.5 billion		n/a
Dillon	1960–1961	45	$4.9 billion		n/a
Kennedy	1962–1967	48	$40 billion	35%	8.7%
Tokyo	1973–1979	99	$155 billion	34%	4.7%
Uruguay	1986–1993				n/a

Source: John H. Jackson, *The World Trading System* (Cambridge, Mass.: MIT Press, 1989).

CHANGES IN THE GLOBAL POLICY ENVIRONMENT

Three major changes have occurred over time in the global policy environment: a reduction of domestic policy influence, a weakening of traditional international institutions, and a sharpening of the conflict between industrialized and developing nations. These three changes in turn have had a major effect on policy responses in the international trade and investment field.

Reduction of Domestic Policy Influences

The effects of growing global linkages on the U.S. economy have been significant. Policymakers have increasingly come to recognize that it is very difficult to isolate domestic economic activity from international market events. Again and again, domestic policy measures are vetoed or counteracted by the activities of global market forces. Decisions that were once clearly in the domestic purview now have to be revised due to influences from abroad. Occasionally one can even see how international factors begin to shape or direct domestic economic policy.

Agricultural policies, for example—historically a major domestic issue—have been thrust into the international realm. Any industrial policy consideration must now be seen in light of international repercussions due to increased reliance on trade. The following examples highlight the penetration of U.S. society by foreign-trade considerations:

- One of every four U.S. farm acres is producing for export.
- One of every six U.S. manufacturing jobs is producing for export.
- One of every seven dollars of U.S. sales is to someone abroad.
- One of every three cars, nine of every ten television sets, two of every three suits, and every video recorder sold in the United States is imported.
- One of every four dollars' worth of U.S. bonds and notes is issued to foreigners.[8]

To some extent, the economic world as we knew it has been turned upside down. For example, trade flows used to determine currency flows and therefore the exchange rate. In the more recent past, **currency flows** took on a life of their own, increasing from an average daily trading volume of $18 billion in 1980 to hundreds of billions in the 1990s. As a result, they have begun to set the value of exchange rates independent of trade. These exchange rates in turn have now begun to determine the level of trade. Governments that wish to counteract these developments with monetary policies find that currency flows outnumber trade flows by ten to one. Also, private-sector financial flows vastly outnumber the financial flows that can be marshaled by governments, even when acting in concert. Financial flows influence interest rates, and interest rates are increasingly determined by the activity of international financial markets, not by governmental financial institutions. Similarly, constant, rapid technological change and vast advances in communication permit firms and countries to quickly emulate innovation and counteract carefully designed plans. As a result, governments are often powerless to implement effective policy measures, even when they know what to do.

Governments also find that domestic regulations, which used to be established and implemented without regard for international effects, often have major international repercussions for domestic firms and industries. In the United States, for example, the breakup of AT&T resulted in significant changes in the purchasing practices of the newly formed Bell companies. Overnight, competitive bids became decisive in a process that previously was entirely within the firm. This change opened up the U.S. market for foreign suppliers of telecommunications equipment, with only limited commensurate market developments abroad for U.S. firms. Similarly, policy measures such as grazing rights on federal lands or subsidized water prices in dry-land areas, which may appear to be only domestically focused, may bring counter-action from other nations.[9] Global Perspective 7.1 provides an example of how domestic environmental legislation may affect business activities around the world.

Throughout the world, legislation has a profound impact on the ability of firms to compete abroad. Legislators often ignore the side-effects in the international marketplace because countries view it as their sovereign right to set domestic policies. Yet, given the linkages between economies, this is an unwarranted and often dangerous view. It threatens to place firms at a competitive disadvantage in the international marketplace and may make it easier for foreign firms to compete in the domestic market.

Global Perspective

7.1
Green Reach

A little-noticed federal appeals court ruling issued in early 1993 in Washington, D.C., may lead to the expansion overseas of one of the United States' toughest environmental laws. Since 1970, the National Environmental Policy Act has required federal agencies to consider the impact on soil, water, air, people, and wildlife of any federally financed project—from damming rivers and building highways to poisoning agricultural pests and mining gold on public land.

The ruling, prompted by an Environmental Defense Fund lawsuit, requires the National Science Foundation to prepare an environmental impact statement before it builds two incinerators in Antarctica. The potential implications beyond the NSF case are significant. The United States finances thousands of projects and programs abroad every year, some of which are environmentally damaging. If the NEPA ruling is broadly interpreted, U.S. military efforts to downsize overseas, for example, may require cleaning up polluted bases—at a cost of hundreds of millions of dollars.

Source: Michael Satchell, "Green Reach," *U.S. News and World Report,* February 15, 1993, 26. © February 15, 1993. *U.S. News & World Report.*
Photo source: Gordon Wiltsie/Black Star.

Even when policymakers want to take decisive steps, they are often unable to do so. In the late 1980s, for example, the United States decided to impose **punitive tariffs** of 100 percent on selected Japanese imports to retaliate for Japanese non-adherence to a previously reached semiconductor agreement. The initial goal was clear. Yet the task became increasingly difficult as the U.S. government identified specific imports as targets. In many instances, the U.S. market was heavily dependent on the Japanese imports, which meant that U.S. manufacturers and consumers would be severely affected by punitive tariffs. As Figure 7.1 shows, many Japanese products are actually assembled in the United States. To halt the importing of components would throw Americans out of work.

Other targeted products were not actually produced in Japan. Rather, Japanese firms had opened plants in third countries, such as Mexico. Penalizing these product imports would therefore punish Mexican workers and affect Mexican employment, an undesirable result.

More and more products were eliminated from the list before it was published. In two days of hearings, additional linkages emerged. For example, law-enforcement agencies testified that if certain fingerprinting equipment from Japan were sanctioned, law-enforcement efforts would suffer significantly. Of the $1.8 billion worth of products initially considered for the sanctions list, the government was barely able to scrape together $300 million worth. Figure 7.2 illustrates how far such linkages have progressed in the aircraft industry. With so many product components being sourced from different countries around the world, it becomes increasingly difficult to decide what constitutes a domestic product.

FIGURE 7.1
Examples of Japanese Products Assembled in the United States

FIGURE 7.2   **Who Builds the Boeing 777?**

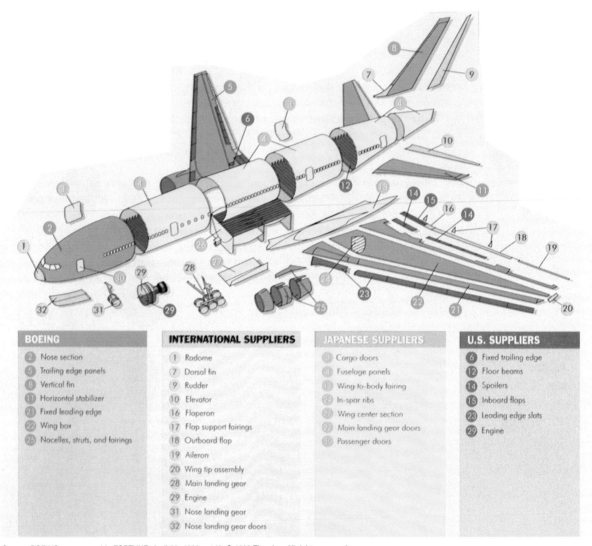

BOEING	INTERNATIONAL SUPPLIERS	JAPANESE SUPPLIERS	U.S. SUPPLIERS
2 Nose section	1 Radome	3 Cargo doors	6 Fixed trailing edge
5 Trailing edge panels	7 Dorsal fin	4 Fuselage panels	12 Floor beams
8 Vertical fin	9 Rudder	13 Wing-to-body fairing	14 Spoilers
11 Horizontal stabilizer	10 Elevator	24 In-spar ribs	15 Inboard flaps
21 Fixed leading edge	16 Flaperon	26 Wing center section	23 Leading edge slats
22 Wing box	17 Flap support fairings	27 Main landing gear doors	29 Engine
26 Nacelles, struts, and fairings	18 Outboard flap	30 Passenger doors	
	19 Aileron		
	20 Wing tip assembly		
	28 Main landing gear		
	29 Engine		
	31 Nose landing gear		
	32 Nose landing gear doors		

Policymakers find themselves with increasing responsibilities, yet with fewer and less-effective tools to carry them out. More segments of the domestic economy are vulnerable to international shifts at the same time that they are becoming less controllable. To regain some power to influence policies, some governments have sought to restrict the influence of world trade by erecting barriers, charging tariffs, and implementing import regulations. However, these measures too have been restrained by the existence of international agreements forged through institutions such as the GATT or bilateral negotiations. World trade has therefore changed many previously held notions about the sovereignty of nation-states and extraterritoriality. The same interdependence that made us all more affluent has left us more vulnerable.

Weakening of Traditional International Institutions

One institution losing influence is the GATT. Many nations have developed new tools for managing and distorting trade flows that are not covered by the GATT rules. Examples are **voluntary agreements** to restrain trade; bilateral or multilateral special trade arrangements such as the Multifibre Accord, which restricts trade in textiles and apparel; and nontariff barriers such as licensing requirements, customs inspection rules, standards, or other bureaucratic obstacles. GATT also does not cover certain types of trade, such as trade in services or in military goods. Because these types of trade comprise an increasing portion of world trade, the impact of GATT is shrinking even more.

In addition, the GATT agreement provides "escape clauses" that nations can use to avoid abiding by GATT rules. Even though these escape clauses are to be used only in emergency cases, nations increasingly take advantage of them. Finally, the GATT was founded by 24 like-minded governments to operate by consensus. With a current GATT membership of 110 countries, this consensus rule often leads to a stalemate on many proposals.

In order to restore the importance of the GATT, a new set of negotiations, called the Uruguay Round, commenced in 1986. The discussions in this round still addressed the issue of tariffs. However, since tariffs had already been reduced greatly in earlier negotiations, any further reduction would do little to encourage trade. Therefore, the main thrust of the Uruguay Round was to sharpen the use of existing rules by strengthening the dispute-settlement procedures and to integrate into the treaty the trade areas that were outside of the GATT. Several key areas emerged: **Nontariff barriers** were to be reduced or eliminated; trade areas such as textiles, agriculture, and services were to become subject to GATT rules; intellectual property rights rules were to be developed to protect patents and trademarks; and trade-related investment measures were to be agreed upon to avoid rules that would distort trade flows.

As was to be expected, key disagreements developed between the GATT members in many of these areas. The discussions on agricultural and services produced particular disharmony. Some countries wanted to reduce agricultural subsidies rapidly and achieve major liberalization of services trade. Other nations believed agriculture to be politically far too sensitive for sharp reductions in subsidies. Similarly, the services discussions resulted in clashes due to different service dependency of the various members.

Even though it has become clear that major changes are necessary for the GATT to function effectively, no agreement was reached by the negotiation deadline in 1990. Continued negotiations in 1993 aimed to achieve a better meeting of the minds. Until major progress is made in a new agreement, however, the GATT continues to be substantially weakened.

Similar problems have befallen international financial institutions. For example, although the IMF has functioned well so far, it is currently under severe challenge by the substantial debts incurred by less-developed countries. These debts, which are the result of overextended development credits and changes in the cost of energy, increasingly hamper trade and investment flows worldwide. This debt crisis has existed since 1982, but the IMF has been able only to smooth over the most difficult problems. It has not found ways to solve them. Similarly, the World Bank successfully met its goal of aiding the reconstruction of Europe but has been less successful in furthering the economic goals of the developing world and the newly

The Global Environment: A Source of Conflict Between Developed and Less-Developed Nations

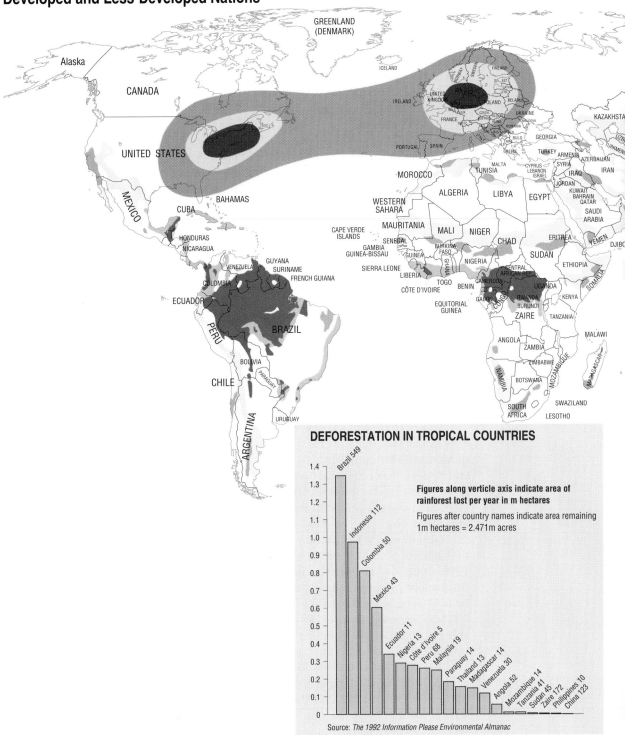

DEFORESTATION IN TROPICAL COUNTRIES

Figures along verticle axis indicate area of rainforest lost per year in m hectares

Figures after country names indicate area remaining
1m hectares = 2.471m acres

Source: *The 1992 Information Please Environmental Almanac*

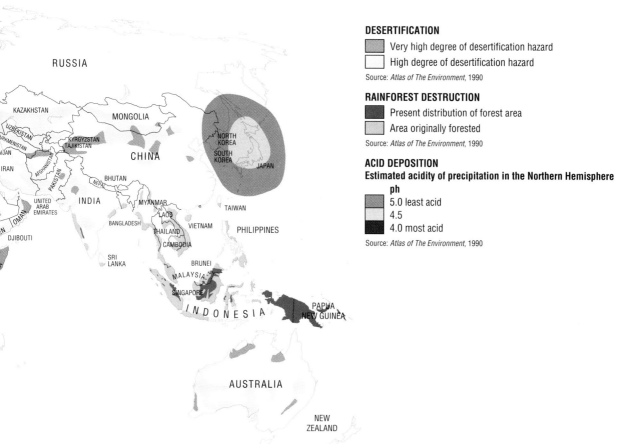

DESERTIFICATION

Very high degree of desertification hazard

High degree of desertification hazard

Source: *Atlas of The Environment*, 1990

RAINFOREST DESTRUCTION

Present distribution of forest area

Area originally forested

Source: *Atlas of The Environment*, 1990

ACID DEPOSITION
Estimated acidity of precipitation in the Northern Hemisphere
ph

5.0 least acid

4.5

4.0 most acid

Source: *Atlas of The Environment*, 1990

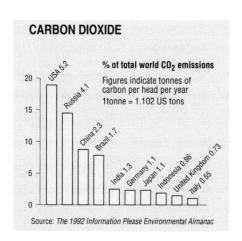

CARBON DIOXIDE

% of total world CO₂ emissions

Figures indicate tonnes of
carbon per head per year
1tonne = 1.102 US tons

USA 5.2
Russia 4.1
China 2.3
Brazil 1.7
India 1.3
Germany 1.1
Japan 1.1
Indonesia 0.86
United Kingdom 0.73
Italy 0.55

Source: *The 1992 Information Please Environmental Almanac*

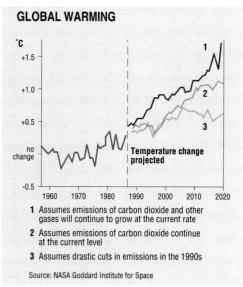

GLOBAL WARMING

°C

+1.5

+1.0

+0.5

no change

-0.5

1960 1970 1980 1990 2000 2010 2020

Temperature change projected

1 Assumes emissions of carbon dioxide and other gases will continue to grow at the current rate

2 Assumes emissions of carbon dioxide continue at the current level

3 Assumes drastic cuts in emissions in the 1990s

Source: NASA Goddard Institute for Space

emerging market economies in the former Soviet bloc. Therefore, at the same time when domestic policy measures have become less effective, international institutions that could help to develop substitute international policy measures have been weakened.

Sharpening of the Conflict between Industrialized and Developing Nations

In the 1960s and 1970s it was hoped that the developmental gap between industrialized nations and many countries in the less-developed world could gradually be closed. This goal was to be achieved with the transfer of technology and the infusion of major funds. Even though the 1970s saw vast quantities of petrodollars available for recycling and major growth in the borrowing by some developing nations, the results have not been as expected. Since the Mexican debt crisis of 1982, the Western world has recognized that the goals envisioned have not been achieved. Even though several less-developed nations have gradually emerged as newly industrialized countries (NICs), even more nations are faced with a grim economic future.

Particularly in Latin America, nations such as Brazil are saddled with enormous amounts of debt, rapidly increasing populations, and very fragile economies. The newly emerging democracies in central Europe and the former Soviet Union also face major debt and employment problems. In view of their shattered dreams, policymakers in these nations have become increasingly aggressive in their attempts to reshape the ground rules of the world trade and investment flows. Even though many other nations share the view that major changes are necessary to resolve the difficulties that exist, no clear-cut solutions have emerged.

Lately, an increase in environmental awareness has contributed to a further sharpening of the conflict. As Global Perspective 7.2 shows, developing countries may place different emphasis on environmental protection. If they are to take measures that will assist the industrialized nations in their environmental goals, they expect to be assisted and rewarded in these efforts. Yet, many in the industrialized world view environmental issues as "global obligation," rather than as a matter of choice.

POLICY RESPONSES TO CHANGING CONDITIONS

The word *policy* conjures up an image of a well-coordinated set of governmental activities. Unfortunately, in the trade and investment sector, as in most of the domestic policy areas, this is rarely the case. Policymakers need to respond too often to short-term problems, need to worry too much about what is politically salable to multiple constituencies, and in some countries, are in office too short a time to formulate a guiding set of long-term strategies. All too often, because of public and media pressures, policymakers must be concerned with current events—such as monthly trade deficit numbers and investment flow figures—that may not be very meaningful in the larger picture. In such an environment, actions may lead to extraordinarily good tactical measures but fail to achieve long-term realignments.

Policy responses in the trade and investment area tend to consist mainly of political ad hoc reactions, which over the years have changed from concern to protectionism. This is particularly true in the United States. While in the mid-1970s most lawmakers and administration officials simply regretted the poor U.S. performance in international markets, industry pressures have forced increasing action in more recent times.

Global Perspective

7.2
North versus South at the Earth Summit

At the Earth Summit in Rio de Janeiro, the developing world essentially wanted two things: money and technology. The industrialized nations in turn focused primarily on the environment, wanting to do something about potential threats like global warming.

The two viewpoints often clashed. Said Jessica Ocaya-Lakidi of Uganda: "We don't yet have the big industries. We are lagging so far behind that we don't talk of industrial pollution." Maximo Kalaw, Jr., from Manila added: "The message is, if you cannot help us on debt, forget about the environmental conservation of our forests, because it is too much of a burden to handle." In essence, the developing countries are suggesting a straightforward bargain: If we get money, they say to the industrialized world, we will protect the environmental resources you claim to value so highly.

By contrast, the developed world sees a common responsibility of mankind that developing nations have to help fulfill. For example, the rosy periwinkle, a pink shrub found only in Madagascar, can be used to make drugs that have proved effective in fighting childhood leukemia and Hodgkin's disease. Plant genes found in Africa can also be used to improve varieties of wheat, corn, rice, and tomatoes. Therefore, it is important to maintain as much biodiversity as possible, a goal that requires the protection of natural resources. Some companies have already taken action to help. BankAmerica Corp., for example, forgave $6 million of its outstanding loans to Latin American countries in exchange for the debtor nations' promise to conserve ecologically critical rain forests.

In spite of the wide praise for such debt-for-nature swaps, many developing nations see them as a potential threat to their sovereignty. There is concern that these swaps are an attempt to put areas of sovereign territory somehow off-limits.

Based on: Eugene Robinson, "At Earth Summit, South Aims to Send Bill North," *The Washington Post,* June 1, 1992, A1, A14; Martha M. Hamilton, "BankAmerica to Forgive Loans in Deal to Aid Rain Forests," *The Washington Post,* June 12, 1991: C1.

Restrictions of Imports

The U.S. Congress in recent years has increasingly been ready to provide the president with additional powers to restrict trade and investment flows. Many resolutions have also been passed and much legislation enacted admonishing the president to pay closer attention to such policy issues. However, most of these admonitions provided only for an increasing threat against foreign importers and investors, not for better conditions for U.S. exporters of goods, services, or capital. The power of the executive branch of government to improve international trade and investment opportunities for U.S. firms through international negotiations and the relaxation of rules, regulations, and laws has become increasingly restricted over time.

A tendency has existed to disregard the achievements of past international negotiations. For example, members of the 98th Congress attempted to amend protectionist legislation by stipulating that U.S. international trade legislation, when not in conformity with internationally negotiated rules, should not take effect. The amendment was voted down by an overwhelming majority, demonstrating a legislative lack of concern for such international trade agreements.

Worldwide, most countries maintain at least a surface-level conformity with international principles. However, many exert substantial restraints on free trade through import controls and barriers. Some of the more frequently encountered barriers are listed in Table 7.2. They are found particularly in countries that suffer from

TABLE 7.2
Trade Barriers

There are literally hundreds of ways to build a barrier. The following list provides just a few of the trade barriers that exporters face.

- Restrictive licensing
- Special import authorization
- Global quotas
- Voluntary export restraints
- Temporary prohibitions
- Advance import deposits
- Taxes on foreign exchange deals
- Preferential licensing applications
- Excise duties
- Licensing fees
- Statistical taxes
- Sales taxes
- Consumption taxes
- Discretionary licensing

- Licenses for selected purchases
- Country quotas
- Seasonal prohibitions
- Health and sanitary prohibitions
- Foreign exchange licensing
- Licenses subject to barter and countertrade
- Customs surcharges
- Stamp taxes
- Consular invoice fees
- Taxes on transport
- Service charges
- Value-added taxes
- Turnover taxes
- Internal taxes

Source: Mark Magnier, "Blockades to Food Exports Hide Behind Invisible Shields," *The Journal of Commerce* (September 18, 1989): 5A. Reprinted with permission.

major trade deficits or major infrastructure problems, causing them to enter into voluntary restraint agreements with trading partners or to selectively apply trade-restricting measures such as tariffs, quotas, or nontariff barriers against trading partners.

Tariffs are taxes based primarily on the value of imported goods and services. Quotas are restrictions on the number of foreign products that can be imported. Nontariff barriers consist of a variety of measures such as testing, certification, or simply bureaucratic hurdles that have the effect of restricting imports. All of these measures tend to raise the price of imported goods. They therefore constitute a transfer of funds from the buyers (or, if absorbed by them, the sellers) of imports to the government, and—if accompanied by price increases of competing domestic products—to the domestic producers of such products.

Voluntary-restraint agreements are designed to help domestic industries reorganize, restructure, and recapture production prominence. Even though officially "voluntary," these agreements are usually implemented through severe threats against trading partners. Due to this "voluntary" nature, these agreements are not subject to any previously negotiated bilateral or multilateral trade accords.

When nations do not resort to the subtle mechanism of voluntary agreements to affect trade flows, they often impose tariffs and quotas. For example, in 1983 the International Trade Commission imposed a five-year tariff on Japanese heavy motorcycles imported into the United States. The 49.4 percent duty was granted at the request of Harley-Davidson, which could no longer compete with the heavily discounted bikes being imported by companies such as Honda and Kawasaki. The gradually declining tariff gave Harley-Davidson the time to enact new management strategies without worrying about the pressure of the Japanese imports. Within four years, Harley-Davidson was back on its feet and again had the highest market share in the heavyweight class of bikes. In 1987, Harley-Davidson officials requested that the tariff be lifted a year early. As a result, the policy was labeled a success. However, at no time were the costs of these measures to U.S. consumers even considered.

Similarly, quotas were discussed for tuna fish packaged in water. U.S. producers complained that Japanese processors took away their market share for the product.

However, U.S. firms had forced Japanese processors to concentrate on water-packed tuna by preventing them in the early 1970s from entering the U.S. market with tuna fish packed in oil. At that time, the majority of canned tuna sold in the United States was packed in oil. Only 7 percent of all canned tuna sold was water-packed. Eventually the situation was reversed; most canned tuna purchased was packed in water. The Japanese firms that had been forced to concentrate on this small market niche had grown quite successful in penetrating it. They became even more successful as it became larger. However, the market share situation changed not because of Japanese ingenuity but because of changing consumer tastes. The Japanese adapted, whereas many U.S. firms did not.

The third major method by which imports have been restricted is nontariff barriers. These consist of buy-domestic campaigns, preferential treatment for domestic bidders compared with foreign bidders, national standards that are not comparable to international standards, and an emphasis on the design rather than the performance of products. Global Perspective 7.3 gives an example of a buy-domestic campaign. As can be seen, such campaigns do not need to be implemented by governments (even though some governments may encourage them). At the same times, these campaigns may encounter great difficulty in differentiating between domestic and foreign products, particularly when many product components come from different countries.

One other way in which imports are sometimes reduced is by tightening market access and entry of foreign products through involved procedures and inspections. Probably the most famous are the measures implemented by France. In order to stop or at least reduce the importation of foreign video recorders, the French gov-

Global Perspective

7.3
Buy American—The Job You Save May Be Your Own

In 1992, Monsanto Chemical Company became the first Fortune 500 company to offer a $1,000 incentive for employees to buy cars made in America. With one-fourth of the firm's annual sales coming from U.S. and foreign car makers, the program covers all cars made or assembled in the United States, Canada, or Mexico, including those made by Japanese companies.

Other U.S. companies offering car incentives typically are more selective in their programs and confine them to cars carrying the nameplates of the traditional Big Three American automakers: Chrysler, Ford, and General Motors. John Henry Foster Co., a St. Louis distributor of industrial pumps and compressors, for example, offers $1,500 to any employee who buys a car sold by the Big Three. It doesn't

matter if the American-brand car is made overseas, as some are. A gas station in Edwardsville offers a 2-cents-a-gallon discount to drivers of American cars. American Bank offers car loans with an interest one-half percent below its regular rate to buyers of Ford, Chrysler, or GM cars. St. Louise barber Bob Fuhrmann charges $1 less on an $8 haircut to customers who drive to his shop in an American car.

Oliver Dulle, executive director of the Japan-American Society of St. Louis, takes a dim view of the buy-American movement: "It is a simplistic response to a complicated problem that could lead to bigotry or a break in relations between the American and Japanese people."

Source: Stuart Auerbach, "Spirit in St. Louis: 'Buy American,'" *The Washington Post,* February 2, 1992, H1, H4.

ernment ruled in 1983 that all of them had to be sent to the customs station at Poitiers. This customshouse was located away from major transport routes, woefully understaffed, and open only a few days each week. In addition, the few customs agents at Poitiers insisted on opening each package separately to inspect the merchandise. Within a few weeks, imports of video recorders came to a halt. Members of the French government, however, were able to point to the fact that they had fully adhered to the letter of international law.

The discussion of import restrictions has focused thus far on merchandise trade. Similar restrictions are applicable to investment flows and, by extension, to international trade in services. In order to protect ownership, control, and development of domestic industries, many countries impose varying restrictions on investment capital flows. Most frequently, they are in the form of investment-screening agencies that decide whether any particular foreign investment project is sufficiently meritorious to warrant execution. Canada, for example, has a Foreign Investment Review Agency (FIRA) that scrutinizes foreign investments.[10] So do most developing nations, where special government permission must be obtained for investment projects. This permission frequently carries with it certain conditions, such as levels of ownership permitted, levels of dividends that can be repatriated, number of jobs that must be created, or the extent to which management can be carried out by individuals from abroad.

The United States restricts foreign investment in instances where national security or related concerns are at stake. Major foreign investments may be reviewed by the **Committee for Foreign Investments in the United States (CFIUS).** CFIUS became active, for example, during the intended purchase of Fairchild Semiconductor Industries by Fujitsu of Japan. The review precipitated a major national discussion and resulted in the withdrawal of the Fujitsu purchase offer. Prior to that, national attention was focused on investment strategies of Arab firms, governments, and individuals in the United States. The concern was that, because of their increased oil income in the 1970s, Arab countries and nationals would be able to take over significant portions of U.S. industry and real estate. Yet the fears of being bought out were never justified, because investor perceptions of the potential political backlash resulted in a self-regulatory mechanism.

Foreign direct investment in the United States has steadily increased in recent years. Americans are again becoming concerned about the level of foreign direct investment in the United States. Legislators have been proposing, debating, and in some instances implementing foreign investment controls in an effort to curb "the sale of America." However, the bottom line is that although the restriction of investments may permit more domestic control over industries, it also denies access to foreign capital. This in turn can result in a tightening up of credit markets, higher interest rates, and less impetus for innovation.

The Effects of Import Restrictions   Policymakers are faced with several problems when trying to administer import controls. First, most of the time such controls exact a huge price from domestic consumers. Import controls may mean that the most efficient sources of supply are not available. The result is either second-best products or higher costs for restricted supplies, which in turn cause customer-service standards to drop and consumers to pay significantly higher prices. Even though these costs may be widely distributed among many consumers and so less obvious, the social cost of these controls may be damaging to the economy and subject to severe attack from individuals. However, these attacks are countered by pressure from protected groups that benefit from import restrictions. For example, while citizens of the

European Community may be forced by import controls to pay an elevated price for all the agricultural products they consume, agricultural producers in the region benefit from higher incomes. Achieving a proper trade-off is often difficult, if not impossible, for the policymaker.

A second major problem resulting from import controls is the downstream change in the composition of imports that may result. For example, if the importation of copper ore is restricted, through either voluntary restraints or quotas, producing countries may opt to shift their production systems and produce copper wire instead, which they can export. As a result, initially narrowly defined protectionistic measures may snowball in order to protect one downstream industry after another.

A final major problem that confronts the policymaker is that of efficiency. Import controls designed to provide breathing room to a domestic industry so it can either grow or recapture its competitive position often do not work. Rather than improve the productivity of an industry, such controls may provide it with a level of safety and a cushion of increased income, subsequently causing it to lag behind in technological advancements.

Restrictions of Exports

In addition to imposing restraints on imports, nations also control their exports. The reasons are short supply, foreign policy purposes, or the desire to retain capital.

The United States, for example, places major emphasis on export controls because it regards trade as a privilege of the firm, granted by the state, rather than a right or a necessity. As will be explained in more detail in Chapter 8, U.S. legislation to control exports focuses on **national security** controls—that is, the control of weapons exports or high-technology exports that might adversely affect the safety of the nation. In addition, U.S. exports are controlled for reasons of foreign policy and short supply. These controls restrict the international business opportunities of firms if an administration feels that such a restriction would send a necessary foreign policy message to another country. Such action may be undertaken regardless of whether the message will have any impact or whether similar products can easily be supplied by companies in other nations. Although perhaps valuable as a tool of international relations, such policies give U.S. firms the reputation of being unreliable suppliers and may divert orders to firms in other countries.

Many nations restrict exports, particularly of capital, because **capital flight** is a major problem for them. Citizens who accumulate funds often believe that the return on investment or the safety of the capital is not sufficiently ensured in their own countries. The reason may be governmental measure or domestic economic factors such as inflation. These holders of capital want to invest abroad. By doing so, however, they deprive their domestic economy of much-needed investment funds.

Once governments impose restrictions on the export of funds, the desire to transfer capital abroad only increases. Because companies and individuals are ingenious in their efforts to achieve capital flight, governments, particularly in developing countries, continue to suffer. In addition, few new investment funds will enter the country because potential investors fear that dividends and profits will not be remitted easily.

Export-Promotion Efforts

The desire to increase participation in international trade and investment flows has led nations to implement export-promotion programs. These programs are designed primarily to help domestic firms enter and maintain their position in international markets and to match or counteract similar export promotion efforts by other nations.

Most governments supply some support to their firms participating or planning to participate in international trade. Typically, this support falls into one of four categories: export information and advice, production support, marketing support, or finance and guarantees.[11] Such export promotion raises several questions. One concerns the justification of the expenditure of public funds for what is essentially an activity that should be driven by profits. It appears, however, that the start-up cost for international operations, particularly for smaller firms, may be sufficiently high to warrant some kind of government support.[12] A second question focuses on the capability of government to provide such support. Both for the selection and reach of firms as well as the distribution of support, government is not necessarily better equipped than the private sector to do a good job. A third issue concerns competitive export promotion. If countries provide such support to their firms, they may well distort the flow of trade. If other countries then increase their support of firms in order to counteract the effects, all that results is the same volume of trade activity, but at subsidized rates. It is therefore important to carefully evaluate export-promotion activities as to their effectiveness and competitive impact. Perhaps such promotion is only beneficial when it addresses existing market gaps.

Given the deterioration of the U.S. trade balance, U.S. government trade policy is focusing on export programs to improve the international trade performance of U.S. firms. The Department of Commerce has added new information services that provide data on foreign trade and market developments. The Foreign Commercial Service was reformed and is now under the aegis of the U.S. Department of Commerce; it was formerly part of the Department of State. Many new professionals were hired to provide an inward and outward link for U.S. business in terms of information flow and marketing assistance.

Another new area of interest is export financing. Although many efforts were made in the past to reduce the activities of the Export-Import Bank of the United States (Exim Bank), U.S. policymakers have increasingly recognized that U.S. business may be placed at a disadvantage if it cannot meet the subsidized financing rates of foreign suppliers. The bank, charged with a new mission of aggressively meeting foreign export financing conditions, has in recent years even resorted to offering **mixed aid credits.** These credits, which take the form of loans composed partially of commercial interest rates and partially of highly subsidized developmental aid interest rates, result in very-low-interest loans.

Tax legislation that inhibited the employment of Americans by U.S. firms abroad has also been altered. In the past, U.S. nationals living abroad were, with some minor exclusions, fully subject to U.S. federal taxation. Because the cost of living abroad can often be quite high—for example, rent for a small apartment can approach $2,000 per month—this tax structure often imposed a significant burden on U.S. firms and citizens abroad. As a result, companies frequently were not able to send U.S. employees to their foreign subsidiaries. However, a revision of the tax code now allows a substantial amount of income (up to $70,000) to remain tax free. More Americans can now be posted abroad. In their work they may specify the use of U.S. products, thus enhancing the competitive position of U.S. firms.

A major U.S. export promotion effort consisted of the passage of the Export Trading Company Act of 1982. Intended to be the American response to the *sogoshosha,* the giant Japanese trading companies, this legislation permits firms to work together to form export consortia. The basic idea is to provide the foreign buyer with one-stop shopping centers in which a group of U.S. firms offers a variety of complementary and competitive products. The act exempted U.S. firms from current antitrust statutes. It also permitted banks to cooperate in the formation of the consortia through direct capital participation in the financing of trading activities. It was hoped that the legislation would enable more firms to participate in the international marketplace. Although the legislation was originally hailed as a masterstroke, so far it has not attracted a large number of successful firms. Perhaps the desire of U.S. firms to be independent is so strong that collaborative efforts are unacceptable for many companies.

Import-Promotion Efforts

Increasingly, policymakers resort to import-promotion measures. The measures are implemented primarily by nations that have accumulated and maintained large Balance-of-Trade surpluses. They hope to allay other nations' fears of continued imbalances and to gradually redirect trade flows.

Japan, for example, has completely refurbished the operations of the Japan External Trade Organization (JETRO). This organization, which initially was formed to encourage Japanese exports, has now begun to focus on the promotion of imports to Japan. It organizes trade missions of foreign firms coming to Japan, hosts special exhibits and fairs within Japan, and provides assistance and encouragement to potential importers. Global Perspective 7.4 provides some details on the newest Japanese import-promotion measures.

Countries such as South Korea and Taiwan sponsor buying missions to countries with which they have major trade surpluses. For example, representatives of several

Global Perspective

7.4
Import and Investment Promotion in Japan

In order to help alleviate concerns about ongoing and mushrooming trade surpluses, Japan is developing measures to facilitate both imports and foreign direct investment. On the import side, the steps include $250 million for government procurement of imports, lower rates on import-related loans from government financial institutions, the providing of international business consulting and training services to the management and staff of foreign firms, and the posting of Japanese trade advisers abroad. To encourage direct foreign investment in Japan, the government offers low-interest loans for constructing offices for the use of foreign affiliates, loan guarantees to foreign affiliates, and office space for up to three months without charge. In addition, a new program will invite potential foreign investors to Japan and offer to introduce prospective joint-venture partners and merger and acquisition opportunities. Yet, many foreign business executives and even some private Japanese economists question the sufficiency of these provisions.

Adapted from: Ai Nakajima, "Import-promotion efforts diversifying," *The Nikkei Weekly,* September 12, 1992:3; Yas Idei, "MITI plans venture to support foreign firms in Japan," *The Nikkei Weekly,* September 12, 1992:3; *Measures for Promoting Foreign Direct Investment in Japan.* (Tokyo: Ministry of International Trade and Industry), February 1992.

Korean firms, under the sponsorship of Korean government, periodically visit the United States to sign highly visible purchasing contracts. Through these measures, governments attempt to demonstrate their willingness to reduce trade imbalances.

Many countries are also implementing policy measures to attract foreign direct investment. These policies are the result of the needs of poorer countries to attract additional foreign capital to fuel economic growth without taking out more loans that call for fixed schedules of repayment.[13] Industrialized nations also participate in these efforts since governments are under pressure to provide jobs for their citizens and have come to recognize that foreign direct investment can serve as a major means to increase employment and income. Increasingly, even state and local governments are participating in investment promotion. Some U.S. states, for example, are sending out "Invest in the USA" missions on a regular basis. Others have opened offices abroad to inform local businesses about the beneficial investment climate at home. Many countries and states also advertise widely to let the world know about the investment advantages they have to offer. One such advertisement is reproduced as Figure 7.3.

Incentives used by policymakers to facilitate such investments are mainly of three types: fiscal, financial, and nonfinancial. **Fiscal incentives** are specific tax measures designed to attract the foreign investor. They typically consist of special depreciation allowances, tax credits or rebates, special deductions for capital expenditures, tax holidays, and the reduction of tax burdens on the investor. **Financial incentives** offer special funding for the investor by providing, for example, land or buildings, loans, and loan guarantees. Finally, **nonfinancial incentives**

**FIGURE 7.3
An Invitation to
Business Travelers as
Well as Tourists to
"Come to Calgary."**

Source: *World Trade*, May 1993, p.59.

can consist of guaranteed government purchases; special protection from competition through tariffs, import quotas, and local content requirements; and investments in infrastructure facilities.

All of these incentives are designed primarily to attract more industry and therefore create more jobs. They may slightly alter the advantage of a region and therefore make it more palatable for the investor to choose to invest in that region. By themselves, they are unlikely to spur an investment decision if proper market conditions do not exist.

Such policies have several drawbacks. For example, when countries compete for foreign investment, several of them may offer more or less the same investment package. The slight advantage that the incentives of one country may have over another's package generally makes little difference in the investment site selected.[14] Moreover, investment policies aimed at attracting foreign direct investment may on occasion place established domestic firms at a disadvantage if they do not receive any support.

A STRATEGIC OUTLOOK FOR U.S. TRADE AND INVESTMENT POLICIES

All countries have international trade and investment policies. The importance and visibility of these policies have grown dramatically as international trade and investment flows have become more relevant to the well-being of most nations. Given the growing linkages between nations, it will be increasingly difficult to consider domestic policy without looking at international repercussions.

The U.S. need is for a positive trade policy rather than reactive, ad hoc responses to specific situations. Protectionistic legislation can be helpful, provided it is not enacted. Proposals in Congress, for example, can be quite useful as bargaining chips in international negotiations. If passed and signed into law, however, protectionistic legislation can result in the destruction of the international trade and investment framework.

It has been suggested that a variety of regulatory agencies could become involved in administering U.S. trade policy. Although such agencies would be useful from the standpoint of addressing narrowly defined grievances, they carry the danger that commercial policy will be determined by a new chorus of discordant voices. Shifting the power of setting trade and investment policy from the executive branch to agencies or even states could give the term *New Federalism* a quite unexpected meaning and might cause progress at the international negotiation level to grind to a halt. No U.S. negotiator can expect to retain the goodwill of foreign counterparts if he or she cannot place issues on the table that can be negotiated without constantly having to check back with various authorities.

In light of continuing large U.S. trade deficits, there is much disenchantment with past trade policies. This disappointment with past policy measures, particularly trade negotiations, is mainly the result of overblown expectations. Too often, the public has mistakenly expected successful trade negotiations to affect the domestic economy in a major way, even though the issue addressed or resolved was only of minor economic impact. Yet, in light of global changes, U.S. trade policy does need to change. Rather than treating trade policy as a strictly "foreign" phenomenon, it must be recognized that it is mainly domestic economic performance that determines global competitiveness. Therefore, trade policy must become more domestically oriented at the same time as domestic policy must become more international in vision. Such a new approach should pursue at least four key objectives. The nation must improve the quality and amount of information government and business share to facilitate competitiveness. Policy must encourage collaboration among companies in such areas as product and process technologies. Collectively, American industry must overcome its export reluctance and its short-term financial orientation. And, fourth, America must invest in its people, providing education and training suited to the competitive challenges of the next century.[15]

From an international perspective, negotiations must continue. In doing so, trade and investment policy can also take either a multilateral or bilateral approach. **Bilateral negotiations** are carried out mainly between two nations, while **multilateral negotiations** are carried out among a number of nations. The approach can also be broad, covering a wide variety of products, services, or investments, or it can be narrow in that it focuses on specific problems.

In order to address narrowly defined trade issues, bilateral negotiations and a specific approach seem quite appealing. Very specific problems can be discussed and resolved expediently, as demonstrated by the U.S.–Canada Free Trade Agreement. However, to be successful on a global scale, negotiations need to produce winners. Narrow-based bilateral negotiations require that there be, for each issue, a clearly identified winner and loser. Therefore, such negotiations have less chance for long-term success, because no one wants to be the loser. This points toward multilateral negotiations on a broad scale. Here concessions can be traded off among countries, thus making it possible for all participants to emerge and declare themselves as winners. The difficulty lies in devising enough incentives to bring the appropriate and desirable partners to the bargaining table.

Policymakers must be willing to trade off short-term achievements for long-term goals. All too often, measures that would be beneficial in the long term are sacrificed to short-term expediency to avoid temporary pain and the resulting political cost. Given the increasing linkages between nations and their economies, however, such adjustments are inevitable. In the recent past, trade and investment volume continued to grow for everyone. Conflicts were minimized and adjustment possibilities were increased manyfold. As trade and investment policies must be implemented in an increasingly competitive environment, however, conflicts are likely to increase significantly. Thoughtful economic coordination will therefore be required among the leading trading nations. Such coordination will result to some degree in the loss of national sovereignty.

New mechanisms to evaluate restraint measures will also need to be designed. Because the beneficiaries of trade and investment restraints are usually clearly defined and have much to gain, whereas the losers are much less visible, a key issue will be coalition building. The total cost of policy measures affecting trade and investment flows must be assessed, must be communicated, and must be taken into consideration before such measures are implemented.[16]

The affected parties need to be concerned and join forces. The voices of retailers, consumers, wholesalers, and manufacturers all need to be heard. Only then will policymakers be sufficiently responsive in setting policy objectives.

SUMMARY

Trade and investment policies historically have been a subset of domestic policies. Domestic policies in turn have aimed primarily at maintaining and improving the standard of living, the developmental level, and the employment level within a nation. Occasionally, foreign-policy concerns also played a role. Increasingly, however, this view of trade and investment policies is undergoing change. While the view was appropriate for global developments that took place following World War II, changes in the world environment require changes in policies.

Increasingly, the capability of policymakers simply to focus on domestic issues is reduced because of global linkages in trade and investment. In addition, traditional international institutions concerned with these policies have been weakened, and the developmental conflict among nations has been sharpened.

In the future, nations must cooperate closely. They must view domestic policymaking in the global context in order to maintain a viable and growing global trade and investment environment. Policies must be long term in order to ensure the well-being of nations and individuals.

Key Terms and Concepts

national sovereignty

standard of living

quality of life

foreign policy

developmental aid

International Trade Organization (ITO)

General Agreement on Tariffs and Trade (GATT)

Most-Favored Nation (MFN)

currency flows

punitive tariff

voluntary agreements

nontariff barriers

Committee for Foreign Investments in the United States (CFIUS)

national security

capital flight

mixed aid credits

fiscal incentives

financial incentives

nonfinancial incentives

bilateral negotiations

multilateral negotiations

Questions for Discussion

1. Discuss the role of voluntary import restraints in international business.
2. What is meant by multilateral negotiations?
3. Discuss the impact of import restrictions on consumers.
4. Why would policymakers sacrifice major international progress for minor domestic-policy gains?
5. Discuss the varying inputs to trade and investment restrictions of beneficiaries and of losers.
6. Why are policymakers often oriented to the short term?
7. Discuss the effect of foreign direct investment on trade.

Recommended Readings

Cavusgil, S. Tamer, and Michael R. Czinkota, editors, *International Perspectives on Trade Promotion and Assistance.* New York: Quorum, 1990.

Cohen, Stephen D. *The Making of United States Economic Policy.* 3d ed. New York: Praeger, 1988.

Conybeare, John A. C. *Trade Wars.* New York: Columbia University Press, 1987.

Czinkota, Michael R., ed. *Improving U.S. Competitiveness.* Washington, D.C.: Government Printing Office, 1988.

Frazier, Michael, *Implementing State Government Export Programs.* New York: Praeger, 1992.

Goldberg, Ellen S., and Dan Haendel. *On Edge: International Banking and Country Risk.* New York: Praeger, 1987.

Guide to the Evaluation of Trade Promotion Programmes. Geneva, Switzerland: International Trade Centre, UNCTAD/GATT, 1987.

Howell, Thomas R., Alan William Wolff, Brent L. Bartlett, and R. Michael Gadbaw, *Conflict Among Nations: Trade Policies in the 1990's.* Boulder, Colo.: Westview Press, 1992.

Jackson, John H. *The World Trading System.* Cambridge, Mass.: MIT Press, 1989.

McKibbin, Warwick J., and Jeffrey D. Sachs, *Global Linkages: Macroeconomic Interdependence and Cooperation in the World Economy.* Washington, D.C.: Brookings Institution, 1991.

Ramdas, Ganga Persaud, *U.S. Export Incentives and Investment Behavior.* Boulder, Colo.: Westview Press, 1991.

U.S. Department of Commerce. International Trade Administration. *United States Trade Performance Report.* Washington, D.C.: Government Printing Office, 1991.

Waldmann, Raymond J. *Managed Trade.* Cambridge, Mass.: Ballinger, 1986.

Wolf, Charles, Jr., *Linking Economic Policy and Foreign Policy.* New Brunswick, N.J.: Transaction Publishers, 1991.

Notes

1. D. Quinn Mills, "Destructive Tradeoffs in U.S. Trade Policy," *Harvard Business Review* 64 (November-December 1986): 199-124.
2. Peter Passell, "Tuna and Trade: Whose Rules?" *The New York Times,* February 19, 1992, D2.
3. Edwin L. Barber III, "Investment-Trade Nexus," in *U.S. International Economic Policy,* ed. Gary Clyde Hufbauer (Washington, D.C.: The International Law Institute, 1982), 9-4.
4. Thomas R. Graham, "Global Trade: War and Peace," *Foreign Policy* 50 (Spring 1983): 124-127.
5. Barber, "Investment-Trade Nexus," 9-5.
6. Mordechai E. Kreinin, *International Economics: A Policy Approach* (New York: Harcourt Brace Jovanovich, 1971), 12.
7. Raymond J. Waldmann, *Managed Trade: The Competition between Nations* (Cambridge, Mass.: Ballinger, 1986); and *Ward's Automotive Report,* January 9, 1989.
8. Tobey, "Currency Trading," *Washington Post,* September 14, 1989, E1.
9. John H. Jackson, *The World Trading System* (Cambridge, Mass.: MIT Press, 1989).

10. The U.S-Canada Free Trade Agreement of 1988 provides for a significant downscaling of these screening activities.
11. Lisa A. Elvey, "Export Promotion and Assistance: A Comparative Analysis," in *International Perspectives on Trade Promotion and Assistance,* (S.T. Cavusgil and M.R. Czinkota, editors). Quorum, New York, 1990, 133-146.
12. Masaaki Kotabe and Michael R. Czinkota, "State Government Promotion of Manufacturing Exports: A Gap Analysis," *Journal of International Business Studies,* Winter 1992, 637-658.
13. Stephen Guisinger, "Attracting and Controlling Foreign Investment," *Economic Impact* (Washington, D.C.: United States Information Agency, 1987), 18.
14. Ibid., 20.
15. Michael R. Czinkota and Masaaki Kotabe, "America's New World Trade Order," *Marketing Management,* 1, 3, 1992, 46-54.
16. Michael R. Czinkota, ed., *Proceedings of the Conference on the Feasibility of a Protection Cost Index,* August 6, 1987 (Washington, D.C.: Department of Commerce, 1987), 7.

P A R T

2

Cases

Debt-for-Nature Swaps: A Green Solution to LDC Debt

Around the world, major companies are hailing the 1990s as the "decade of the environment."[1] As concern for the environment grows from a radical idea championed by Greenpeace to a mainstream political and social reform movement, businesses are beginning to take notice. The Green movement is more than a new craze. For example, in 1990 a group of environmentalists, along with institutional investors controlling $150 billion in assets, proclaimed the Valdez Principles. Crafted as a combative response to the 1989 *Valdez* oil spill in Alaska, these principles outline environmentally responsible actions and policies for corporations. The group has implied that future investments may hinge on corporations' complying with the principles. Some of the requirements specified include reducing waste and taking responsibility for past environmental harm. Shareholders at a number of large firms, including General Electric and Union Pacific, have introduced resolutions calling for the companies to subscribe to the principles.

In addition, most industrialized countries are passing more stringent environmental legislation. Some new laws hold lenders responsible for environmental damage caused by borrowers. A bank found lending to polluting borrowers can find itself in trouble. As a result, financial institutions are examining whether their loans and investments are environmentally responsible. Such examinations are known as "Green audits."

Financial institutions can benefit from "Green marketing"—selling their image as environmentally responsible. One form of Green marketing introduced in the 1980s was the debt-for-nature swap. In order to obtain desperately needed dollars to service immense debt obligations, many developing countries have witnessed the devastation of their environments in the name of progress. By using debt-for-nature swaps, indebted countries are able to cultivate their natural resources for future growth while paying off part of the billions of dollars owed to foreign lenders.

Debt-for-nature swaps work as follows: First, concerned individuals and institutions make tax-deductible contributions to nonprofit organizations with a debt-for-nature swap program. Next, the nonprofit organization contacts a commercial or investment bank and buys some of the developing country's debt at a discount. For example, in early 1991, Mexico's debt was selling for approximately 47 cents per

Source: This case was written by Janet G. Farley and Pietra Rivoli.
[1]David Kirkpatrick, "Environmentalism: The New Crusade," *Fortune*, February 12, 1990, 44–55.

dollar of face value. Then, the developing country repays the face value of the debt in local currency. At early 1991 exchange rates, Mexico could repay one dollar (face value) in debt for about 2,500 Mexican pesos. These funds are then channeled to a local conservation organization that finances environmental projects. Because the debt is purchased at a discount, the value of the original contribution is multiplied. In one instance, a debt-for-nature swap in Ecuador increased the value of contributions eightfold. For every 12.5 cents contributed, the Ecuadoran government committed one dollar worth of local currency to finance conservation projects.

Dr. Thomas Lovejoy, now at the Smithsonian Institution, developed the debt-for-nature swap tool in 1984. In a joint program with Fidelity Investments, Dr. Lovejoy and his team are currently working to save the Latin American rain forest (see Figure 1). Fidelity Investment customers are given the opportunity to contribute to the project without subsidizing Fidelity's management expenses. Since its inception, the program has worked in 10 countries on such projects as reforestation of buffer zones, training of conservation professionals, and preservation of one million acres of remote parklands. Fidelity's involvement in the program is a direct result of its customers' concern for the environment. Fidelity has given its customers an opportunity to contribute to global conservation efforts that they may not have had otherwise. More than just Green marketing, Fidelity's program is a social response to a global concern.

The debt-for-nature swaps have reduced Third World debt by approximately $40 million while funding conservancy projects. However, total debt in these countries is well over $1,000 billion. Can debt-for-nature swaps make a dent in the Third World debt crisis? Many experts believe that the success of these swaps rests with the involvement of government and multilateral lenders such as the World Bank and the International Monetary Fund (IMF). Tax incentives that encourage institutions to swap debt for cash or equity need to be carried over to debt-for-nature swaps. IMF and World Bank endorsement will ensure debtor countries that debt-for-nature swaps are not just another form of foreign intervention, but rather a Green solution to their debt problem—a solution the world can live with.

FIGURE 1   **Why Is Fidelity Involved in Saving Rainforests?**

In our surveys, our customers rank the environment as their highest social priority.

Traditionally, we have built Fidelity's business by giving customers access to investment diversification and professional money management. What's more, we pride ourselves on creating new and interesting opportunities for investors.

Now, Fidelity customers have an opportunity to contribute to protecting the environment through the novel debt-for-nature swap. And our customers can support a conservation effort that they may not find on their own: a rainforest protection project, sponsored by the prestigious Smithsonian Institution.

100% of the money contributed by Fidelity customers will go to the Smithsonian Rainforest Project. None of the costs of soliciting for or arranging the debt-for-nature swap comes out of your contributions to the Smithsonian, nor from money invested in Fidelity funds.

Please consider this excellent opportunity to meet one of the global environment's most urgent challenges by helping to improve the future of the rainforests.

Source: "The Smithsonian Rainforest Project," *Investment Vision*, September/October 1990, 35–40.

Questions for Discussion

1. What are the benefits and costs of debt-for-nature swaps for (a) the banks and (b) the citizens of the developing countries?
2. Do you think that banks should be encouraged through tax incentives or other legislative assistance to participate in the swap programs? Why or why not?

Who Owns Hollywood?

During the 1980s, foreign direct investment in the United States increased by more than 250 percent. For the first time in decades, U.S. direct investment abroad fell below foreign investment in the United States. As foreign firms increased their holdings of U.S. assets, foreign direct investment in the United States became a controversial political and economic issue.

Foreign investment has been particularly strong in the U.S. entertainment industry. By early 1991, foreigners had purchased four of the seven major U.S. film companies (see Table 1). In addition, foreign firms now own four of the five major U.S. record companies, several U.S. publishing companies, and several large U.S. music publishers. The entire entertainment industry is consolidating into a few large—and mostly foreign—firms. With the latest acquisition of MCA by Matsushita in December 1990, Americans are wondering, "Who owns Hollywood?"

The entertainment industry is becoming globally integrated. Cultural barriers have diminished, and the United States—until recently the undisputed leader in the industry—no longer goes unchallenged. In addition to global competition, film studios are facing soaring production costs. The estimated industry average expenditure per film is $27 million. Sheer size and financial strength will dictate whether or not a studio will survive the 1990s. Gordon Crawford, senior vice president of the Capital Research Company, notes that "global and vertical integration in the production and distribution of entertainment is a dominant theme that is going to continue."[1]

Source: This case was written by Janet G. Farley and Pietra Rivoli.

[1]Richard W. Stevenson, "Move Reflects a Belief in Role of Sheer Size," *The New York Times*, November 27, 1990, D7.

TABLE 1 Ownership in the U.S. Movie Industry	Company	Owner
	Columbia Pictures	Sony (Japan)
	Universal Pictures (MCA)	Matsushita (Japan)
	20th Century Fox	News Corp. (Australia)
	MGM–UA	Pathe Communications (Italy)
	Warner Brothers	Time Warner (United States)
	Walt Disney Pictures	Walt Disney Company (United States)
	Paramount Pictures	Paramount Communications (United States)

Source: *The Washington Post*, November 27, 1990, C1.

As of early 1991, Walt Disney Pictures and Paramount Pictures were the only two major movie studios that had not been acquired by another company. Walt Disney is avoiding takeover activity by generating cash through joint projects with Japanese investors. Industry experts believe that Paramount is a prime acquisition target.

It is in this increasingly competitive and rapidly changing environment that MCA started to look for the capital required to compete against other industry giants. Matsushita of Japan appeared to be the perfect provider.

MCA, founded in 1923 as Music Corporation of America, owned Universal Studios, Universal Pictures, MCA Records, several theme parks, WWOR-TV, and Putnam publishing house. In 1989, MCA's television and movie productions accounted for $1.69 billion, or half of the company's revenues. Universal Studios produced such movies as *Back to the Future* and *E.T.: The Extraterrestrial,* directed by Steven Spielberg, and the Sidney Pollack film *Out of Africa.* Universal's television production, originally specializing in one-hour television series, started to diversify into half-hour comedy shows with the TV hits "Major Dad" and "Coach."

Matsushita, a $38 billion Japanese giant, manufactures consumer electronics, including such brands as Panasonic, Quasar, and Technics. Sony, Matsushita's biggest competitor, purchased Columbia Pictures in late 1989 to protect its prominent position in consumer electronics. Hardware (television, VCR, laser disc player) superiority is partially dependent on controlling the software (movies, videos, music). Sony discovered the relationship between hardware and software the hard way: Without a library of videos in the Beta format, Sony was forced to abandon its Betamax VCR. To avoid a similar fate with its compact disc player, Sony purchased CBS Records, ensuring that CDs were available for the players. Similar logic motivated Sony's purchase of Columbia Pictures in 1989.

With the acquisition of Columbia Pictures, Sony made a strong move toward controlling emerging standards for the next generation of hardware, the high-definition television (HDTV)—a move Matsushita could not ignore. Akio Tanii, president of Matsushita, recognized that "software and hardware have been developing simultaneously. They are like wheels of the same car."[2] The company that owns movie and television production studios and therefore controls the production format will have an advantage in developing and selling the televisions and VCRs of the future.

To maintain a competitive position in consumer electronics against Sony and other Japanese manufacturers, Matsushita—in the largest purchase of a U.S. company by a Japanese firm—bought MCA on December 28, 1990, for a total of $6.13 billion in cash and $1.37 billion in shares of an MCA subsidiary for the New York area television station WWOR-TV. (Federal Communications Commission regulations prohibit foreign ownership of U.S. television networks.)

In addition to its studios and other interests, MCA owned the Yosemite Park and Curry Company, a hotel and concession business in Yosemite National Park. To appease growing public concern over a Japanese company's owning an interest in one of America's national park concessions, and under increasing pressure from Secretary of the Interior Manuel Lujan, Jr., Matsushita agreed to sell the Yosemite interests to the National Park Foundation for $49.5 million, $50.5 million below their estimated $100 billion value. Under the agreement, the National Park Foundation, a nonprofit organization, will gain control of the concessions on September 30, 1993. Matsushita, under its MCA subsidiary, will continue to operate the concession and receive profits until 1993.

---

[2]Paul Farhi, "Matsushita Seeking Synergy," *The Washington Post,* November 28, 1990, C1.

Many Americans have voiced concern over the foreign purchases of high-profile U.S. entertainment companies. Along with their resentment over American culture's being "sold out" to foreign investors, many Americans fear foreign owners will influence public opinion and U.S. politics. The recent purchases in the entertainment industry have many Americans worried about who chooses what Americans will watch in the theaters or on television. There is also concern over the impact of FCC regulations on U.S. companies' competitiveness and over the future of proposed technology standards for such media as HDTV.

Some observers of the film industry fear censorship by the new Japanese owners. The manipulation of Bernardo Bertolucci's movie *The Last Emperor* by a Japanese distributor is cited as an example of foreign intervention in movie contents. A scene in the movie showing activities of Japanese troops in China during World War II was cut from the version shown in Japan. Only after Bertolucci protested was the scene replaced. Tanii would not guarantee that Matsushita would not interfere with the contents of MCA's movies, records, or books. However, he pointed out that this area of concern was not raised when Australian and Italian companies purchased Hollywood studios.

With or without a guarantee, Jeff Faux, president of the Economic Policy Institute, a Washington think tank, suggests that foreign ownership could lead to a change in programming through a process of self-censorship. Faux believes that "it's inevitable that producers and directors will be sensitive to Japanese interests and sensibilities, and things that criticize the Japanese may get a second look. It's simply a fact of life that he who pays the piper calls the tune."[3]

In addition to the movie industry, the U.S. television networks are also crying foul. Foreign companies do not fall under the FCC regulations prohibiting television networks from syndicating television programs both in the United States and abroad and from purchasing Hollywood studios. These FCC regulations prevented General Electric from purchasing MCA because it owns the NBC network. U.S. Representative John D. Dingell, chairman of the Energy and Commerce Committee, does not want the FCC to "protect foreign-owned companies at the expense of American enterprise."[4] The networks are using these latest Hollywood acquisitions as ammunition in their 20-year battle with the FCC to change these regulations.

The U.S. electronics industry is also unhappy with the recent purchases of movie studios by the Japanese. The future U.S. role in defining the standards for the next generation of television, HDTV, is greatly affected by who owns the companies that produce movies and television shows. As J. Richard Iverson, president of the American Electronics Association, points out, foreign investors are "picking up everything from womb to tomb in the communications field. If you control the production of material, the display of material, and the manufacturing of equipment, you have a significant advantage in the future information age."[5] Many worry that the United States is losing control over one more of its successful industries, an industry described as an "export powerhouse." As one electronics industry insider points out, "The U.S. library of motion pictures is a nonrenewable resource. It seems obvious that the value of this resource, plus the control of the studios and their production

---

[3]Paul Farhi and John Burgess, "Buyout Expected to Get Tough Reviews in U.S.," *The Washington Post,* November 27, 1990, A6

[4]Martin Tolchin, "Acquisition May Benefit the TV Networks," *The New York Times*, November 27, 1990, D6.

[5]Geraldine Fabrikant, "$6.13 Billion MCA Sale to Japanese," *The New York Times,* November 27, 1990, D1.

facilities, is significantly higher than the price paid by the Japanese to purchase this heritage."[6]

Despite these concerns, the United States continues to welcome foreign investment. In an increasingly global economy, the market for firms must also be global. In the case of the entertainment industry, the foreign investment has brought much-needed capital that will allow the firms to compete more effectively. In fact, if the choice is between a strong industry that is foreign owned or a weak industry owned by Americans, then perhaps there is no choice at all.

Questions for Discussion

1. Are you concerned about foreign company purchases in the U.S. film industry? Why or why not?
2. Suppose the U.S. government prohibited foreign ownership of U.S. film companies. What would be the effect of this prohibition on the industry and the economy?

---

[6]Gene Parrott, "Japan's Studio Buyouts Will Hurt U.S. Long Term," *San Jose Mercury News,* December 17, 1990.

One Afternoon at the United States International Trade Commission

Chairwoman Stern: We turn now to investigation TA–201–55 regarding nonrubber footwear. Staff has assembled. Are there any questions? Vice Chairman Liebeler has a question. Please proceed.

Vice Chairman Liebeler: My questions are for the Office of Economics, Mr. Benedick. Do foreign countries have a comparative advantage in producing footwear?

Mr. Benedick: Yes, foreign producers generally have a comparative advantage vis-a-vis the domestic producers in producing footwear. Footwear production generally involves labor-intensive processes which favor the low-wage countries such as Taiwan, Korea, and Brazil, which are the three largest foreign suppliers by volume. For instance, the hourly rate for foreign footwear workers in these countries ranges from about one-twelfth to one-fourth of the rate for U.S. footwear workers.

Vice Chairman Liebeler: Is it likely that this comparative advantage will shift in favor of the domestic industries over the next several years?

Mr. Benedick: It is not very likely. There seems to be little evidence that supports this. The domestic industry's generally poor productivity performance over the last several years, which includes the period 1977 to 1981, roughly corresponding to the period of OMAs (Orderly Marketing Arrangements) for Taiwan and Korea, suggests that U.S. producers must significantly increase their modernization efforts to reduce the competitive advantage of the imported footwear.

Source: *Official Transcript Proceedings before the U.S. International Trade Commission,* meeting of the Commission, June 12, 1985, Washington, D.C.

Vice Chairman Liebeler: Have you calculated the benefits and costs of import relief using various assumptions about the responsiveness of supply and demand to changes in price?

Mr. Benedick: Yes. On the benefit side, we estimated benefits of import restrictions to U.S. producers, which included both increased domestic production and higher domestic prices. We also estimated the terms of trade benefits resulting from import restrictions. These latter benefits result from an appreciation of the U.S. dollar as a result of the import restrictions.

On the cost side, we estimated cost to consumers of the increase in average prices on total footwear purchases under the import restrictions and the consumer costs associated with the drop in total consumption due to the higher prices.

Vice Chairman Liebeler: In your work, did you take into account any retaliation by our trading partners?

Mr. Benedick: No.

Vice Chairman Liebeler: What was the 1984 level of imports?

Mr. Benedick: In 1984, imports of nonrubber footwear were approximately 276 million pairs.

Vice Chairman Liebeler: If a six hundred million pair quota were imposed, what would the effect on price of domestic and foreign shoes be, and what would the market share of imports be?

Mr. Benedick: At your request, the Office of Economics estimated the effects of the six hundred million pair quota. We estimate that prices of domestic footwear would increase by about 11 percent, and prices of imported footwear would increase by about 19 percent.

The import share, however, would drop to about 59 percent of the market in the first year of the quota.

Vice Chairman Liebeler: What would aggregate cost to consumers be of that kind of quota?

Mr. Benedick: Total consumer cost would approach 1.3 billion dollars in each year of such a quota.

Vice Chairman Liebeler: What would be the benefit to the domestic industry of this quota?

Mr. Benedick: Domestic footwear production would increase from about 299 million pairs for 1984, to about 367 million pairs, or by about 23 percent. Domestic sales would increase from about $3.8 billion to about $5.2 billion, an increase of about 37 percent.

Vice Chairman Liebeler: How many jobs would be saved?

Mr. Benedick: As a result of this quota, domestic employment would rise by about 26,000 workers over the 1984 level.

Vice Chairman Liebeler: What is the average paid to those workers?

Mr. Benedick: Based on questionnaire responses, each worker would earn approximately $11,900 per year in wages and another $2,100 in fringe benefits, for a total of about $14,000 per year.

Vice Chairman Liebeler: So what then would be the cost to consumers of each of these $14,000-a-year jobs?

Mr. Benedick: It would cost consumers approximately $49,800 annually for each of these jobs.

Vice Chairman Liebeler: Thank you very much, Mr. Benedick.

Commissioner Eckes: I have a question for the General Counsel's Representative. I heard an interesting phrase a few moments ago, "comparative advantage." I don't recall seeing that phrase in Section 201. Could you tell me whether it is there and whether it is defined?

Ms. Jacobs: It is not.

Chairwoman Stern: I would like to ask about cost/benefit analysis. Perhaps the General Counsel's Office again might be the best place to direct this question. It is my understanding that the purpose of Section 201 is to determine whether a domestic industry is being injured, the requisite level for requisite reasons, imports being at least as important a cause of the serious injury as any other cause, and then to recommend a remedy which we are given kind of a short menu to select from to remedy the industry's serious injury.

Are we to take into account the impact on the consumer?

Are we to do a cost/benefit analysis when coming up with the remedy which best relieves the domestic industry's serious injury?

Ms. Jacobs: As the law currently stands, it is the responsibility of the Commission to determine that relief which is a duty or import restriction which is necessary to prevent or remedy the injury that the Commission has determined to exist. The President is to weigh such considerations as consumer impact, etc. The Commission is not necessarily responsible for doing that. Of course, the Commission may want to realize that, knowing the President is going to consider those factors, they might want to also consider them, but in fact, that it is not the responsibility of the Commission. It is the responsibility of the Commission only to determine that relief which is necessary to remedy the injury they have found.

Chairwoman Stern: I can understand our reporting to the President other materials which aren't part of our consideration, but nevertheless necessary for the President in his consideration, but having that information and providing it to the President is different from its being part of the Commission's consideration in its recommendations.

Ms. Jacobs: That's right. Your roles are quite different in that respect.

Vice Chairman Liebeler: Nations will and should specialize in production of those commodities in which they have a comparative advantage. Fortunately, our country has a large capital stock which tends to provide labor with many productive employments. Our comparative advantage is in the production of goods that use a high ratio of capital to labor. Shoes, however, are produced with a low ratio of capital to labor.

Therefore, American footwear cannot be produced as cheaply as foreign footwear. The availability of inexpensive imports permits consumers to purchase less-expensive shoes and it allows the valuable capital and labor used in this footwear industry to shift to more-productive pursuits.

This situation is not unique to the footwear industry. The classic example is agriculture, where the share of the labor force engaged in farming declined from 50 percent to 3 percent over the last 100 years. This shift did not produce a 47 percent unemployment rate. It freed that labor to produce cars, housing, and computers.

The decline of the American footwear industry is part of this dynamic process. This process is sometimes very painful. Congress, by only providing for temporary relief, has recognized that our continued prosperity depends on our willingness to accept such adjustments.

The industry has sought this so-called "temporary import relief" before. The ITC has conducted approximately 170 investigations relating to this industry. This is the fourth footwear case under Section 201, and so far the industry has gotten relief twice. The 1975 petition resulted in adjustment assistance. The 1976 case resulted in orderly marketing agreements with Taiwan and Korea.

In spite of the efforts of the domestic industry to suppress imports, the industry has been shrinking. Between 1981 and 1984, 207 plants closed; 94 of these closings occurred just last year. The closing of unprofitable plants is a necessary adjustment. Import relief at this stage will retard this process and encourage entry into a dying industry.

Because there is no temporary trade restriction that would facilitate the industry's adjustment to foreign competition, I cannot recommend any import barrier.

Chairwoman Stern: The intent of the General Import Relief law is to allow a seriously injured industry to adjust to global competition. The Commission must devise a remedy which corresponds to the industry and the market forces it must face.

No other manufacturing sector of our economy faces stiffer competition from abroad than the U.S. shoe industry. Imports have captured three-fourths of our market. No relief program can change the basic conditions of competition that this industry must ultimately face on its own. The best that we as a Commission can do—and under Section 201 that the President can do—is to give the industry a short, predictable period of relief to allow both large and small firms to adjust, coexist, and hopefully prosper.

I am proposing to the President an overall quota on imports of 474 million pairs of shoes in the first year. Shoes with a customs value below $2.50 would not be subject to this quota. The relief would extend for a full five years.

Commissioner Lodwick: Section 201 is designed to afford the domestic industry a temporary respite in order to assist it in making an orderly adjustment to import competition. The fact that the law limits import relief to an initial period of up to five years, to be phased down after three years to the extent feasible, indicates that Congress did not intend domestic producers to find permanent shelter from import competition under the statute.

Accordingly, I intend to recommend to the President a five-year quota plan which affords the domestic nonrubber footwear industry ample opportunity to implement feasible adjustment plans which will facilitate, as the case may be, either the orderly transfer of resources to alternative uses or adjustments to new conditions of competition.

Commissioner Rohr: In making my recommendation, I emphasize the two responsibilities which are placed on the Commission by statute. First, it must provide a remedy which it believes will effectively remedy the injury which is found to exist.

Secondly, Congress has stated that we, as Commissioners, should attempt, to the extent possible, to develop a remedy that can be recommended to the President by a majority of the Commission. I have taken seriously my obligations to attempt to fashion a remedy with which at least a majority of my colleagues can agree. Such remedy is a compromise.

I am concurring in the remedy proposal which is being presented today by a majority of the Commission. This majority recommendation provides for an overall limit on imports of 474 million pairs; an exclusion from such limitation of shoes entering the United States with a value of less than $2.50 per pair; a growth in such limitation over a five-year period of zero percent, three percent, and nine percent; and the sale of import licenses through an auctioning system.

Commissioner Eckes: It is my understanding that a majority of the Commission has agreed on these points. I subscribe to that and will provide a complete description of my views in my report to the President.

Questions for Discussion

1. What are your views of the ITC recommendation?
2. Should the principle of comparative advantage always dictate trade flows?

3. Why are the consumer costs of quotas so often neglected?
4. Discuss alternative solutions to the job displacement problem.
5. How would you structure a "temporary relief program?"

Imposing Trade Restrictions on Brazil

In October 1986, President Reagan determined that certain Brazilian policies were unreasonable and a burden and restriction on U.S. commerce. In particular he was concerned about administrative burdens on imports, prohibitions on foreign investment, and the lack of copyright protection for computer software.

After more than a year of negotiations, Brazil still had not rectified its unfair trade practices. As a result, President Reagan decided to impose sanctions on selected Brazilian exports to the United States. A notice was placed in the Federal Register listing products upon which sanctions might be imposed in the form of increased tariffs. As required by statute, the Commerce Department scheduled public hearings in order to take U.S. industry concerns into consideration before finalizing the sanctions. During these hearings various industry positions emerged.

The position of the American Electronics Association was that the electronics industry already suffered from Brazil's information policies; therefore any sanctions the administration finally decided on should not further hurt that industry. The acting president of the Computer and Business Equipment Manufacturer's Association testified that products manufactured by overseas subsidiaries and affiliates of U.S. firms should not be subject to sanctions because of U.S. investment in Brazil. His reasons were that the sanctions would add to the burden already exerted on these firms by Brazil's policies and that high-technology companies were already hurt by trade sanctions.

The Computer Software and Services Industry Association supported the sanctions. An association representative said the message "must be sent" that other countries cannot build their export industries at the expense of U.S. firms.

The Footwear Group of the American Association of Exporters and Importers objected to sanctions on leather footwear for men and boys. Sanctions would hurt lower-income U.S. consumers by raising prices of Brazilian shoes since no competing products were available from domestic firms. The International Footwear Association also opposed sanctions in the belief that they would hurt its members—importers, wholesalers, and domestic manufacturers. The Footwear Industries of America Inc. favored sanctions on nonrubber footwear, however, believing that they would restrain Brazilian trade and encourage a change in its trade-restraining policies. In addition, sanctions would help the U.S. footwear industry.

The president of the Ferroalloy Association said that inclusion of ferrosilicon and silicon metal on the sanctions list would be appropriate because they are important exports from Brazil. Moreover, Brazil's "very lax" pollution and safety regulations give

Source: This case, written by Michael R. Czinkota, draws on public secondary source materials: "Tariff on Brazilian Exports," White House Fact Sheet, November 13, 1987; "Industry Testifies on Brazil Retaliation as Administration Moves toward Sanctions," *International Trade Reports*, December 23, 1987, 1590-1591; and various newspaper articles and press releases.

that country an unfair advantage over U.S. industry. He added that U.S. imports have cost jobs and that Brazil accounts for more than 25 percent of the imports. However, the American Iron and Steel Institute disagreed, citing negative consequences for U.S. specialty steel producers.

According to the American Restaurant China Council Inc., restrictions on all Brazilian commercial chinaware would be an effective and appropriate response to Brazil's trade policies. The council was in favor of including imports of all Brazilian chinaware on the list of sanctioned products.

Following the hearings, administration officials met to determine the most appropriate products for sanctioning. Shortly before sanctions were announced, Brazilian officials suggested that the view being taken in the trade dispute was far too narrow, because Brazilian exports were directly linked to Brazil's ability to service and repay its international debt. Should exports be curtailed, payments would probably be affected. In addition, the Brazilian government was working hard at resolving the issue but simply needed more time. The U.S. Department of the Treasury promised to raise that concern on the interagency level.

As a result of the subsequent interagency consultations, the Office of the United States Trade Representative announced on February 29, 1988, that the imposition of sanctions against Brazil would be postponed.

Questions for Discussion

1. How would you characterize the positions taken by the various industries?
2. How should policymakers resolve such conflicting advice?
3. Should overseas subsidiaries of U.S. firms be exempt from trade policy actions by the U.S. government?
4. If debt repayment is the reason for not imposing sanctions, does that not give preferential treatment to banks over service providers and manufacturers?

Harley-Davidson (A): Protecting Hogs

On September 1, 1982, Harley-Davidson Motor Company and Harley-Davidson York, Inc., filed a petition for "relief" or protection with the U.S. International Trade Commission (ITC). The filing, a request under Section 201 of the U.S. Trade Act of 1974, was a request for escape clause relief from the damaging imports of heavyweight motorcycles into the United States. Harley-Davidson Motor Company, and more specifically its traditional large engine motorcycle, the hog,[1] was facing dwindling domestic market share. This was a last desperate act for survival.

Source: This case was written by Michael H. Moffett, March 1993. This case is intended for class-discussion purposes only and does not represent either efficient or inefficient management practices.

[1]The motorcycles produced and sold by Harley-Davidson have traditionally been known as hogs. The nickname is primarily in reference to their tradional large size, weight, and power.

IMPORT PENETRATION

Throughout most of the first half of the 20th century, there were more than 150 different manufacturers of motorcycles in the United States. By 1978, however, there were only three, and only one, Harley-Davidson, was U.S.–owned. The other two U.S. manufacturers were Japanese-owned, Kawasaki and Honda America.

By the early 1980s, Harley-Davidson was in trouble. Imports held a 60 percent share of the total heavyweight motorcycle market by 1980, and they continued to grow. Harley's difficulties worsened as its products suffered increasing quality problems, with labor and management facing off against one another instead of against the competition. By the end of 1982, in a total domestic market that had seen no growth in three years, import market share rose to 69 percent.

The declining market share of domestic producers in a flat market translated into a fight of Harley against all competitors, because Harley was up against two domestic competitors who were really not "domestic." Kawasaki and Honda America were producing in the U.S. essentially the same products as those being imported. In fact, Harley argued that the two domestic competitors were only assembling foreign-made parts in the United States and were therefore not domestic producers at all.

THE HARLEY LAW

What has become known as the "Harley Law" was the resulting finding of the ITC that imports were a contributing cause of injury to the domestic heavyweight motorcycle industry. The ITC recommended to then President Ronald Reagan that import duties be increased for a period of five years. Duties were to be raised to 45 percent the first year (1983), with the duty declining steadily over each following year until reaching 10 percent in the fifth and final year of protection (1988).

The President and his staff agreed with the finding but wanted a Tariff Rate Quota (TRQ) instead of a straight tariff increase. A TRQ is a combination of tariffs and quotas; in this case, the increased tariff rates would be imposed only on imports (by volume) above a specific number per year. This was intended to allow specific small foreign producers to have continued access to the U.S. markets while still providing Harley with protection from the large-volume importers who were rapidly gaining domestic market share. Table 1 provides a listing of the major tariff rate quotas as specified by the ITC.

[2]Hufbauer, 1986, 263.

TABLE 1
Tariff Rate Quotas for Heavyweight Motorcycles

Country	Pre-1983 Share[2]	1983 Quota[1]	1983 Share	1988 Quota[3]
West Germany	.4%	5,000	33.3%	10,000
Japan	93.0%	6,000	40.0%	11,000
Others	6.6%	4,000	26.7%	9,000

Notes:

[1]These quotas and tariff schedules applicable to motorcycles with engine displacement of 700 cubic centimeters and greater, only. Volume quotas are per engine.

[2]Pre-1983 shares are percentage of total imports into the United States originating from that country.

[3]All quota shares rise 1,000 units per year after 1983, with the terminal quotas of 1988 being effective only for that final year (after which there would be no further Tariff Rate Quotas).

Source: Adapted from *Trade Protection in the United States: 31 Case Studies,* Institute for International Economics, Washington, D.C., 1986, 263–264.

The domestic industry that was to be protected was defined as those motorcycles "with a total piston displacement of over 700 cc."[2] This was strategic success for Harley in that most of its motorcycle sales were actually 1000 cc and higher. This meant Harley was able to hinder competitor sales in product categories other than those reflecting the head-to-head competition. Harley had also requested that the imported parts that were being used by its two domestic competitors also be subject to tariff restrictions. Harley argued that the lower-cost product that was damaging the domestic industry was composed of the same parts, whether assembled in Japan or in the United States by Kawasaki and Honda America. On this last point, however, they were unsuccessful. Domestic producers would be protected against final product sales only, and no restrictions would be placed on imported parts.

COMPETITIVE RESPONSE: COMPETITORS	TRQs were implemented for the 1983 through 1988 period. As seen in Table 2, the first two years of protection did have the desired result: import market share fell precipitously. Imports fell from a high of 69 percent in 1982 to just 24 percent in 1984. It is also interesting to note, however, that total market sales fell dramatically over this same period. After two years of significant protection, domestic production had increased only 20 percent (from 100 to 121 thousand units per year), although the total market had fallen by 130 thousand from 1982 to 1983 alone (and 1983 was a year of rapid economic growth in the United States following the severe recession of 1981–1982).

The response of Harley's major competitors to the TRQs was rapid and predictable. First, the two major domestic producers, Kawasaki and Honda America, immediately stepped up production of heavyweight motorcycles within the United States. The ITC estimates that imports of parts other than engines increased 82 percent in the first year of protection (1983) and more than 200 percent in the second year (1984). The ITC also estimates that between 50 and 70 percent of the final value of the domestically produced Kawasaki and Honda America motorcycles was imported as parts. Secondly, these same Japanese-owned producers altered the product manufactured outside the United States, primarily in Japan, to reduce engine displacement from the designed 750 cc to between 690 and 700 cc in order to fall below the TRQ coverage. Third, the Japanese government, on behalf of its own producers, filed a complaint under Article XIII of the General Agreement on Tariffs and Trade (GATT) that the European competitors (Germany) were receiving discriminatory treatment (although filed, there were no formal findings ever made on this complaint).

TABLE 2 **Import and Domestic Heavyweight Motorcycle Market Shares** **(thousands of units)**	Year	Total Sales[1]	Domestic Share (%)	Import Share (%)
	1980	326 (100%)	130 (40%)	196 (60%)
	1981	327 (100%)	125 (38%)	202 (62%)
	1982	324 (100%)	100 (31%)	224 (69%)
	1983 (TRQ)	194 (100%)	100 (52%)	94 (48%)
	1984 (TRQ)	159 (100%)	121 (76%)	38 (24%)

Source: Adapted from *Trade Protection in the United States: 31 Case Studies,* Institute for International Economics, Washington, D.C., 1986, and various publications of the U.S. International Trade Commission.

[1]Total sales is the sum of domestic production and imports; exports were negligible over the subject period.

COMPETITIVE RESPONSE: HARLEY

Harley-Davidson used the period of import relief to restructure, retool, and retrain. Two specific actions were taken to strengthen Harley to once again be a competitive firm.

1. **A rededication to quality.** Although Harley had instituted quality circles in manufacturing as early as 1976, renewed efforts in quality monitoring and labor involvement improved the quality of the product dramatically.[3] By 1988 Harley had 117 quality circles in operation with more than 50 percent of all employees involved in the improvement of their own product. The implementation of a just-in-time materials-management program, which Harley termed "materials as needed," also aided greatly in reducing costs of production.

2. **Diversification of earnings.** In 1986 Harley purchased Holiday Rambler Corporation of Wakarusa, Indiana. Holiday Rambler is a recreational vehicle manufacturer that was expected to provide Harley with broadened earnings flows as the domestic motorcycle industry was increasingly stagnant in growth. Harley has also continued to increase production and sales of other products, such as metal bomb casings and liquid-fuel rocket engines for the U.S. Department of Defense.

Harley's measures were indeed effective in returning the company to profitability and competitiveness. In 1987, a year ahead of schedule, Harley requested that the Tariff Rate Quotas be removed from imported motorcycles.

Questions for Discussion

1. Were the Tariff Rate Quotas (TRQs) really effective in protecting Harley-Davidson against Japanese manufacturer import penetration? What was the role of imported parts in this effectiveness of protection?

2. Did Harley-Davidson "adjust" to changing market conditions during the period in which the U.S. government afforded them protection from foreign competition? Do you believe they responded to the expectations of public policy makers to reattain competitiveness on world markets?

References

Beals, Vaughn, "Harley-Davidson: An American Success Story," *Journal for Quality & Participation,*" Vol. 11, Issue 2, June 1988, A19–A23.

Fortune, "How Harley Beat Back the Japanese," September 25, 1989, 155–164.

Gelb, Thomas, "Overhauling Corporate Engine Drives Winning Strategy," *Journal of Business Strategy,* Vol. 10, Issue 6, November/December 1989, 8–12.

Grant, Robert M., R. Krishnan, Abraham B. Shani, and Ron Baer, "Appropriate Manufacturing Technology: A Strategic Approach," *Sloan Management Review,* Vol. 33, Issue 1, Fall 1991, 43–54.

Hackney, Holt, "Easy Rider," *Financial World,* Vol. 159, Issue 18, September 4, 1990, 48–49.

---

[3]When the first quality circles were created in 1976, it was estimated that the first 100 motorcycles off the production line were costing an additional $100,000 to "repair" before they were up to standards for sale. This had to change.

Hufbauer, Gary Clyde, Diane T. Berliner, and Kimberly An Elliot, *Trade Protection in the United States:* 31 Case Studies, The Institute for International Economics, Washington, D.C., 1986.

Manufacturing Engineering, "Mounting the Drive for Quality," Vol. 108, Issue 1, January 1992, 92, 94.

Muller, E.J., "Harley's Got the Handle on Inbound," *Distribution,* Vol. 88, Issue 3, March 1989, 70, 74.

Pruzin, Daniel R., "Born to Be Verrucht," *World Trade,* Vol. 5, Issue 4, May 1992, 112–117.

Reid, Peter C., *Well-Made in America,* McGraw-Hill, New York, 1989.

Rudin, Brad, "Harley Revs Up Image Through Diversifying," *Pensions & Investment Age,* Vol. 15, Issue 3, February 9, 1987, 21–23.

Sepehri, Mehran, "Manufacturing Revitalization at Harley-Davidson Motor Co.," *Industrial Engineering,* Vol. 19, Issue 8, August 1987, 86–93.

Funding from Eximbank

The Export-Import Bank of the United States (Eximbank) is an independent federal agency that provides financing support for the export sale or lease of U.S. goods and services. Its programs include:

- Loans to foreign buyers at the fixed interest rate set by the Organization for Economic Cooperation and Development (OECD). These are typically used for large export transactions of $10 million or more involving capital equipment or projects with a repayment period of seven years or more.

- Standby loans, called intermediary credits, to other lenders on export sales of less than $10 million with repayment periods of less than seven years. These are also typically used for transactions involving capital equipment or projects.

- Guarantees of repayment on medium- to long-term loans made by other lenders on export sales involving capital equipment or projects, or on U.S. bank to foreign bank credit lines for the sale of capital equipment.

- Guarantees of repayment on short-term working capital loans made by banks to U.S. exporters in support of export transactions. This program can be used in conjunction with the U.S. Small Business Administration's exporter's revolving line of credit, which has a limit of $750,000.

- Export credit insurance against commercial and specific political risks that a foreign obligor may not pay a U.S. exporter, or bank financing for an export transaction involving the sale or lease of capital equipment with a repayment period of up to five years, or the sale of services, consumables, spare parts, or raw materials with a repayment period of up to 180 days.

Source: This case was written by Daniel V. Dowd, Export-Import Bank of the United States. Reprinted with permission.

The program is administered by Eximbank's agent, the Foreign Credit Insurance Association (FCIA).

Any responsible party (exporter, U.S. bank, foreign bank, foreign buyer) may receive a preliminary commitment from Eximbank for its support on an export transaction. All transactions must present a reasonable assurance of repayment; that is, the buyer must be creditworthy. In the case of Eximbank's working capital loan guarantee, the exporter must provide collateral for the loan. Eximbank only supports exports of products of U.S. origin. When the repayment period is short term, insurance may be used and the product must be at least 50 percent of U.S. origin, exclusive of markup. For longer repayment periods, insurance, guarantees, or loans may be used, and Eximbank will allow up to 15 percent foreign content. However, a 15 percent cash payment by the buyer is required for the longer repayment period. Guarantees and insurance make it easier for the exporter or other lenders to provide financing by protecting against credit risks. The "other" lender is often the Private Export Funding Corporation (PEFCO), which will make long-term export loans when guaranteed by Eximbank. PEFCO also purchases foreign notes when guaranteed by Eximbank. Eximbank loans are used when other lenders are unwilling to provide financing or the foreign competition is offering low-interest and/or fixed-interest rate financing supported by other export credit agencies.

The American Drill Company provides design, assembly, and installation of irrigation well drilling rigs. It also sells parts and makes repairs. American Drill has its design and assembly operations in the United States. Repair work is done by its own personnel, sent to the site. Installation is done under the supervision of its personnel using local labor and construction materials. It sources virtually all its components in the United States, although electronic sensors are sourced in Switzerland. Due to a decline in the domestic agriculture market, it has started to pursue foreign orders, initially as a subcontractor to larger firms doing business overseas. Thus far, it has been able to get advance payments and finance its operations internally. Midwest Bank has provided financial services to American Drill in the form of working capital loans, secured by inventory, and the confirmation of foreign letters of credit. American Drill's president is anxious to expand and has been made aware of potential overseas contracts for building, repairing, and providing spare parts. The company has the personnel and expertise to fulfill such contracts; however, the overseas buyers are demanding credit and have indicated that French competitors are providing credit as part of their contract with the support of France's Export Credit Agency (COFACE).

American Drill is now faced with several problems. It will need additional working capital to acquire components if it is to expand by accepting foreign orders. Midwest is reluctant to provide additional working capital to fund an expansion based on foreign sales. The potential overseas buyers are requesting a financing proposal as part of the bid on larger contracts to build and install rigs. American Drill's personnel are neither familiar with how to structure such a proposal nor certain that the company can offer medium- or long-term financing on its own. In fact, the company's controller believes that it may even have difficulty offering short-term open account credit to potential foreign purchasers of spare parts or repair services because American Drill must pay cash to its suppliers.

Questions for Discussion

1. Should the U.S. government help American Drill to expand sales overseas?
2. Discuss the benefits and drawbacks of government involvement in competitive export financing.

3. What Eximbank programs might be of use to American Drill for the various aspects of its potential foreign sales financing needs? Who may apply?

4. How might Midwest Bank become involved in American Drill's expansion plans while minimizing its exposure to foreign credit risks?

Republica de Centroica

The Republica de Centroica (pronounced cen TRO ee ca) is a small, poor Latin American country with per capita income around $300 per year. Its transport and communications facilities are poor, and the labor force is largely semiskilled or unskilled. Only about half the people are literate at or above the sixth grade level, and about a quarter are unemployed or underemployed.

Starting in the 1960s the country had attempted several industrialization programs, mostly based on import substitution schemes. It had set up a number of state-owned enterprises (SOEs) to manufacture chemicals, certain metals, basic tools, and automotive equipment. However, these had proven to be politically driven, over-staffed, inefficient, and incapable of producing quality goods at competitive prices. It had also given incentives to local entrepreneurs and foreign companies to establish plants to manufacture or assemble products for the local market and, eventually, for export. These too were largely unsuccessful because their products were more expensive and lower quality than competing products available on the world market. Indeed, Centroica had to erect high tariff walls to protect these infant industries. The ventures had often caused a substantial drain of foreign exchange to pay for imports of materials and components, while producing relatively small foreign exchange savings and virtually no exports. They had created some jobs, but not as many as had originally been expected. The main beneficiaries of the industrialization program turned out to be scions of the Forty Families who had dominated Centroican government, landholdings, and banking for generations. They had been able to gain ownership interests and favored positions in most of the new industrial ventures through their wealth and political influence.

Centroica, like many countries that attempted economic development through import substitution, imposes high tariffs against many imports. Its currency is over-valued; the black market rate (pesos/$) is about double the official exchange rate. Consequently it has had to impose exchange controls. It has enacted a minimum wage for factory workers and other urban employees that is significantly above the prevailing wages in the informal sector. In the past in order to prevent profit abuses by foreign investors, it attempted to restrict dividend remittances to 12% or 15% of invested capital. Eventually it gave up on this policy, but it restricted most foreign companies to minority ownership. (Members of the Forty Families often acquired the majority ownership holdings.) Then in order to overcome the disincentives to investment created by these laws and policies, it enacted tax holidays and other sub-

Prepared by William A. Stoever, Keating-Crawford Professor of International Business at Seton Hall University, South Orange, New Jersey 07079. Copyright 1993 by William A. Stoever. Reprinted by permission.

The author appreciates the helpful comments of Elias Groviyannis, Chander Kant, Anthony Loviscek, Balu Swaminathan and Jason Z. Yin on this case.

sidies for domestic and foreign investors. Some local companies prospered with the subsidies and protected market.

In the past Centroica experienced frequent coups and military dictatorships. However, it conducted a relatively democratic election 6 years ago in which General Alberto Colon Silves was elected president. He had had a creditable military career and had earned an M.B.A. from the University of Chicago. Although descended from three of the Forty Families, he seemed to have a genuine concern for the welfare of his country and of its poorest citizens. His government has been attempting to institute pragmatic, reformist economic policies.

Presidente Colon has noted that locales such as Hong Kong, Taiwan, Singapore, and Mexican border cities prospered in the early stages of their development by selling their most abundant asset, cheap labor. If Centroica invited in Japanese, European, and American firms to produce labor-intensive products for export, then perhaps laborers' incomes might rise more rapidly and some basic industrial skills be imparted. The average peasant in Centroica now earns less than $1 per day; he might make the equivalent of $1 an hour in a foreign-owned factory. The scheme would work only if Centroica could find some goods that it could produce efficiently and sell on world markets. Foreign technical skills, management, marketing, and capital would be essential.

Presidente Colon and his more sophisticated advisors realize that Centroica would have to liberalize some of its investment and trade restrictions if it were to attract any significant amount of export-oriented investment. Several foreign businessmen have said they would not risk their capital in the country if they didn't exercise enough control to make their operations profitable. Thus this strategy would make his country even more dependent on the affluent industrial countries' companies and economies and might involve a significant loss of national control and autonomy. The government also realizes that labor unions and local manufacturers might object if their privileged positions were threatened.

Some of the president's advisors have noted the apparent success of export-processing zones (EPZs) in creating jobs and increasing their countries' manufactured exports in such countries as China, Taiwan, Mauritius, Indonesia, and India, and have wondered whether Centroica could establish similar zones. They argued that setting up such zones would not entail the economic disruptions and political problems that would accompany a more general economic liberalization. Other advisors noted, however, that these zones are not always successful in attracting desirable investments and at best are only a short-term, small-scale measure that avoids confronting the country's real problems.

Presidente Colon is aware that he can learn from other countries' experiences in increasing export-oriented investment and that he will need expert advice before initiating any such changes in his country.

Questions for Discussion

Suppose you were a consultant hired by the United Nations Centre on Transnational Corporations (UN-CTC) to go to Centroica and make recommendations on the following questions:

1. Should Presidente Colon try to remove his country's tariff barriers, open its economy to the world, privatize the state-owned enterprises, and shift towards a development strategy based on exports? Why or why not?

2. What problems would the Colon administration be likely to encounter if it tried to implement these changes? How should it attempt to handle these problems?

3. Should Centroica set up an Export-Processing Zone (EPZ) with improved transportation and communications infrastructure and with laws providing for 100% foreign ownership, tax holidays, and other incentives to attract foreign companies to set up labor-intensive export-oriented plants?

4. From another perspective, suppose you were managing a company producing microchips or inexpensive dolls in Los Angeles or Osaka. Would you consider moving your operations to Centroica? Why or why not? What risks would you worry about in making such an investment?

The Banana War

The European Community is the main market in the world for bananas, constituting 37.5 percent of all world trade (see Figure 1). That is why a decision by the EC Farm Council in December of 1992 attracted attention among banana-producing nations. Up until the decision, different EC countries had different policies regarding imports of bananas. While Germany, for example, had no restrictions at all, countries such as the United Kingdom, France, and Spain restricted their imports to favor those from their current and former African, Caribbean, and Pacific (ACP) colonies. (This preferential trading agreement is known as the Lome Convention.) The decision calls for a quota of two million tons with a 20 percent tariff for all banana imports from Latin America ($126 per ton), rising to 170 percent for quantities over that limit ($1,150 per ton). Since Latin American exports to Europe were approximately 2.7 million tons in 1992, the quota would cut almost 25 percent of these countries' exports to the EC.

The main stated reason for imposing the quota and the tariffs is to protect former colonies by allowing them to enjoy preferential access to the EC market. Other reasons implied have been the $260 million in tariff revenue resulting from the measures as well as moving against the "banana dollar" (reference to the U.S. control of the Latin American banana trade through its multinationals). Belgium, Germany, and Holland object to the measures not only because of the preference given to higher-cost, lower-quality bananas from current and former colonies, but also because of the economic impact. The Belgians, who want the issue to be taken up by GATT, estimate an immediate loss of 500 jobs in its port cities, which have, up to now, handled substantial amounts of Latin American banana imports. Even in the United Kingdom, where the preferential treatment has enjoyed widespread support, there has been criticism of the decision.

THE LATIN AMERICAN POSITION

The presidents of Colombia, Costa Rica, Ecuador, Guatemala, Honduras, Nicaragua, Panama, and Venezuela held a summit February 11, 1993, in Ecuador and issued a declaration rejecting the EC banana-marketing guidelines as a violation of GATT and

Source: This case was prepared by Gladys Navarro and Ilkka A. Ronkainen. It is based on: Joseph L. Brand, "The New World Order," *Vital Speeches of the Day* 58 (December 1991): 155–160; "The Banana War," *International Business Chronicle* 4 (February 1-15, 1993): 22; and Organization of American States, "OAS Takes Note of Regional Statements on the Marketing of Bananas in Europe," *Report on the OAS Permanent Council Meeting,* February 24, 1993.

FIGURE 1   **Trade In Bananas: EC Country Imports by Source**

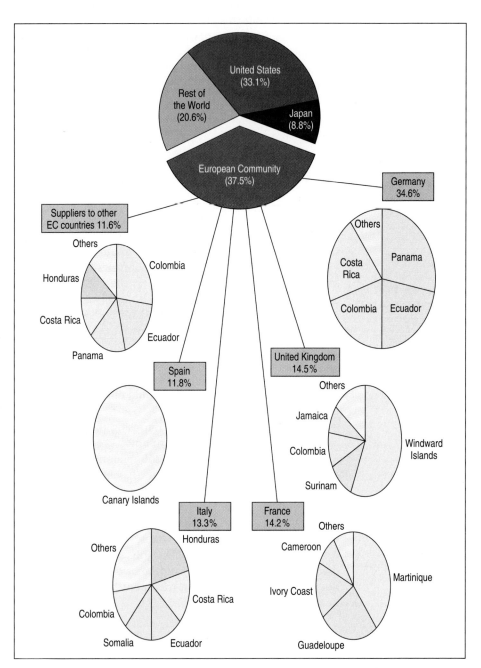

Source: Brent Borrell and Sandy Cuthbertson, *EC Banana Policy 1992*, Center for International Economics, Sydney, Australia, 1991, chart 2.1.

principles of trade liberalization. The effect on the Latin American economies is reduction in the needed growth at a time when many of them are relatively weak.

The economics of production are clearly in favor of the Latin producers. The
unit cost of production in the Caribbean is nearly 2.5 times what it is for Latin Amer-

ican producers. For some producers, such as Martinique and Guadeloupe, the cost difference is even higher. The EC quota therefore results in major trade diversion.

The affected Latin nations are using various means at the international level to get the EC to modify its position. In addition to the summit, many are engaged in lobbying in Brussels as well as the individual EC-member capitals. They have also sought the support of the United States, given its interests both in terms of U.S. multinational corporations' involvement in the banana trade as well as its investment in encouraging economic growth in the developing democracies of Latin America. The State Department issued the following statement:

> The United States Government will continue to encourage Latin banana producers as they work for fair market access to the EC. We will also provide suggestions on how to best make their own case to the GATT and EC member states. The United States cannot intervene directly in the GATT on behalf of Latin banana exporters, as we are not a banana producer. We believe that continuation of previous Latin American efforts in Geneva, Brussels, and EC member state capitals provides a sound and effective diplomatic strategy for advancing producer interests in the coming months.

THE CARIBBEAN POSITION

Heads of government of the 13-member Caribbean Community (CARICOM) approved a resolution February 24, 1993, supporting the EC guidelines. "No one country in this hemisphere is as dependent on bananas for its economic survival as the Windward Islands," declared Ambassador Joseph Edsel Edmunds of Saint Lucia. Referring to the criticism of the EC decision by the Latin nations, he added: "Are we being told that, in the interest of free trade all past international agreements between the Caribbean and friendly nations are to be dissolved, leaving us at the mercy of Latin American states and megablocs?" He noted that Latin American banana producers command 95 percent of the world market and more than two-thirds of the EC market.

Ambassador Kingsley A. Layne of Saint Vincent and the Grenadines asserted that the issue at stake "is nothing short of a consideration of the right of small states to exist with a decent and acceptable standard of living, self-determination, and independence. The same flexibility and understanding being sought by other powerful partners in the GATT in respect of their specific national interests must also be extended to the small island developing states."

Questions for Discussion

1. Should you be a member of the Organization of American States (of which all of the Caribbean and Latin American countries mentioned in the case are members) and its Permanent Council, which must react to two opposing statements concerning the EC decision, which one would you side with?

2. What can the EC do to alleviate the impact of its decision on the Latin American banana producers?

3. What types of strategic moves will an international marketing manager of a Latin American banana exporter have to take in light of the quota and the tariffs?

North American Free Trade Agreement

The benefits of trade among nations are only available if countries are willing to relinquish some independence and autonomy. There are four basic levels of economic integration: the free-trade area, the customs union, the common market and the economic union. This case, which looks at a trade pact being developed between the United States and Mexico, is an example of the first level of integration, the free-trade area.

Under a free-trade area, considered the least restrictive form of economic integration, all barriers to trade among members are removed. Goods and services are freely traded among members. The United States and Mexico began negotiating a free-trade agreement in late 1990. The pact, the North America Free Trade Agreement, also will include Canada. The Bush Administration began talks with Mexico on the belief that free trade with Mexico is crucial, and it pushed for quick approval by Congress. The fast-track approach means that when the negotiating on the agreement is done, Congress can only vote the bill up or down, it cannot amend the agreement and cannot hold it up. The negotiations are underway, and the agreement faces formidable opposition in the United States.

One concern raised by opponents is whether Mexico's lower wages will make it an unfair competitor. The worry is that Mexican goods and services will be priced much lower than those of Canada and the United States because Mexico's costs are so much lower. Lower wages also are viewed as a threat to U.S. jobs.

"If you take the United States, an average manufacturing worker earns about $10.57 an hour, thereabouts," said U.S. Sen. Donald Riegle, D-Mich. "And down in Mexico it's a tiny fraction of that, about 57 cents an hour. So I think with those huge differentials, if you have a free trade agreement, what's going to happen is the manufacturing jobs are going to run out of the United States and go down to Mexico," he said.

Former U.S. Trade Representative Carla Hills disagrees. Jobs could have tumbled down south without a free-trade agreement, she counters. "What a free-trade agreement will do is to reduce the barriers to our exports to Mexico."

Meanwhile, European countries are working to create economic integration through the European Community, designed to sweep away all trade barriers. Advocates of the North American Free Trade Agreement say its members, particularly the United States, need it to compete globally.

"It isn't the United States alone that's trying to produce," said U.S. Sen. John Chafee, R-R.I. "We're in a competitive position, whether we like it or not, with the European Community and with the Asian rim countries."

According to Hills, Japan has been enormously successful in developing collaborative arrangements with lower-wage countries in east Asia. Germany has created successful collaborations with Spain and Portugal, she said. "And I can't imagine why the United States would not want to have a close, collaborative arrangement with a neighbor with whom we share a 2,000-mile border."

This case was drawn from the Public Broadcasting System's television program "Adam Smith," which aired in 1991. Producer: Alvin H. Perlmutter, Inc.

In addition to the wage differential, treatment of the environment along the U.S.–Mexico border is another major concern of opponents. John O'Connor of the National Toxics Campaign said manufacturers are "turning the border into a 2,000-mile Love Canal, the largest toxic lagoon ever known to humankind."

Treasury Secretary Lloyd Bentsen of Texas, formerly a U.S. senator and chairman of the Senate Finance Committee, said he has seen enormous improvements in the way business is conducted along the border, especially with regard to environmental protection. "I was born and reared on that Mexican border, and I have never seen the kinds of changes that are happening there, such as the privatizing of industry and the lowering of tariffs," Bentsen said. "I've seen moves made on environmental improvement that I have not seen in any other developing country." But Bentsen, who led the fight on Capitol Hill for fast-track consideration of the free-trade agreement, concedes some environmental problems remain in that area.

"We've got a serious problem so far as the environment along the border," Bentsen said. "We've got a situation where in one of those towns they've been dumping 26 million gallons of raw sewage every day into the Rio Grande River. Well, that's a real problem. It creates problems of cholera and of water contamination generally. But now you're having a joint effort between the United States and Mexico to build the sewage plants, the treatment plants there. That's real progress."

Bentsen, the Democratic candidate for vice president in 1988, was asked what he says to labor unions, traditional supporters of the Democratic Party that typically oppose the free-trade accord. "I stated repeatedly during these debates for the fast track that it would depend on what came back, whether I supported it or not," Bentsen said. He would support an agreement that produces a net increase in jobs on both sides. "But if we don't get that, I'll fight it just as strongly as I worked to see that we got the fast track, he said.

Questions for Discussion

1. Compare and contrast the other three levels of economic integration with that of NAFTA.
2. What are the central arguments for and against adopting NAFTA, as outlined in the case? Are there any non-economic arguments for or against adopting NAFTA?
3. Should the United States adopt NAFTA? Why or why not? Be prepared to explain your position.
4. How has NAFTA developed since this video was aired? Has former Sen. Bentsen's position changed since he has become secretary of the Treasury?

Foreign Currency Traders

What's a dollar worth? This question is a priority on the agenda every year at the joint annual meeting of the World Bank and the International Monetary Fund (IMF). The dollar and other currency exchange rates used to be regulated by governments. Today they bounce around, and there is a growing array of speculators, hedgers, and investors who gamble that the dollar will move up or down. This activity can severely affect the profitability of firms that compete internationally. Financial leaders from around the world continue to debate exchange rates long after the World Bank and the IMF Annual Meeting adjourns. Meanwhile, exchange rate traders continue to affect financial markets and government policies.

In the 1930s at Bretton Woods, New Hampshire, world leaders fixed the dollar to gold and pegged other currencies to the dollar. Many countries were content to simply trade their dollars and leave the real gold in Fort Knox. But in the 1960s, the United States struggled with a chronic deficit in its Balance of Payments. The United States was buying more goods than it was selling, and with dollars overseas convertible to gold, it was building up a stack of worrisome IOUs. By the late 1960s, people were losing confidence. That stack of IOUs was a lot bigger than the pile of gold in Fort Knox. In fact, U.S. gold reserves dropped by almost $13 billion between 1957 and 1971. That's when it all came to a head. Faced with a run on the dollar and the expense of the Vietnam War, President Nixon cut the dollar's ties to gold. He suspended convertibility and left the world's currencies to float. Since then, currency exchange rates have fluctuated dramatically. The same dollar that was worth $1\frac{1}{2}$ Deutschemarks in 1971 was worth 1.8 Deutschemarks in 1980, and 3 Deutschemarks in 1984. Today, no one knows at breakfast what the dollar will be worth at dinner.

Governments may want their currencies to be higher or lower for trading purposes, and markets may have their own opinions. In 1985, the dollar was high and American consumers enjoyed good prices on Japanese cars and VCRs, but American exporters such as Caterpillar and Boeing suffered. To get the American trade deficit down, James Baker, former treasury secretary, needed a cure for the growing trade deficit. Imports were flooding into the country and dollars were flowing back to foreign countries threatening the U.S. economy. Baker called together the top financial officials of the five major nations in a gathering called the Group of Five. They designed a formula that could solve the world's trade imbalances. The United States would have to cut its huge federal budget deficit. The Germans and Japanese would have to stimulate their weak economies, but the key ingredient was a lower dollar. The high dollar had made imports cheap and exports uncompetitive, so the G-5 leaders agreed to reduce the dollar.

According to Geoffrey Bell, an alumnus of both the Bank of England and the Federal Reserve, "Most people want to have a more stable environment. The only people that really don't want stable exchange rates are those who make money by speculating one way or another, and so the central banks usually prefer to have stable exchange rates for as long a period as they can get them. When they become

This case was drawn from the Public Broadcasting System's television program "Adam Smith," which aired September 29, 1988. Producer: Alvin H. Perlmutter, Inc.

obviously overvalued like in 1985, with the dollar, then they want them to change. But really they want stability, and what they've tried to do is persuade the markets by using their own moneys to be in and out and to go counter to the market so they can, in a sense, push the exchange rates in the right direction."

The primary factors that determine currency fluctuation include interest rates, domestic government policies, the domestic inflation rate, the psychology that follows the direction of those rates, and the trade flows. Governments may wish their currency in one direction or another, but a growing number of traders and speculators have their own opinions.

According to Bell, foreign exchange turnover around the world is about $400 billion a day, which is approximately 40 times the level of imports and exports across continents. According to Bell, "It has very little to do with the physical volume of trade." To many it is the excitement that motivates traders to pursue their enterprise.

According to Tim Leitch, head of the Foreign Options Trading Desk at Manufacturers Hanover, "I believe I got into trading because of the excitement and the intrigue and the glamorous side of the business—talking to various different centers around the world, then dealing in the middle of the night. I have dealing systems in my apartment and we are always getting phone calls in the middle of the night from the various branches of our own bank. There are great stories of young traders in the market who plan to have one of their overseas offices call them late at night so they can impress a new girlfriend."

Traders like Tim Leitch have a spot position limit of about $25 million. If they exceed their limit they either do a trade to pull inside the limit, or go to their supervisors and have their belief in a position approved.

According to Jim Hohorst, Leitch's supervisor at Manufacturers Hanover, "We run fairly good sized positions, but if we go out and take a position that's the wrong way, we're going to get rolled over and I often tell young traders it's like rolling a stone on a hill. You get behind the stone and you push it down the hill and it rolls and it looks great. You think, gee, aren't I very strong? You get on the other side of the stone and you're trying to roll it up, you loosen it and it rolls right over you."

In this business the rules are simple. According to Hohorst, "the trend is your friend," or "Run your profits and cut your losses." And then you'll hear the same guy look at the other guy and say, "Bulls make money, bears make money, but pigs never make money." And what you're talking about is one guy saying, "Take your profit," and another guy who's saying, "Let your profits run."

Currency traders in the spot market, the immediate market, watch their screens and then decide to buy or sell within minutes. Options traders have more time. Some traders are conservative and some even challenge market stability. One such trader was Andrew Krieger.

Andrew Krieger came to Wall Street equipped with three degrees from the University of Pennsylvania. As a currency trader for Bankers Trust, he made over $300 million for the bank in 1987. The bank gave him a bonus of $3 million. Krieger took his bonus and left Bankers Trust and went to work for George Soros. At his trading desk, Krieger spotted an opportunity. The German Bundesbank was trying to keep the Deutschemark from rising to keep German exports competitive. The Bank of England wanted to keep the pound in line with the Deutschemark, so it was selling pounds. Krieger's bet was that the market forces would push the pound higher, even though the Bank of England was trying to hold it down. Krieger's purchases totaled more than a billion pounds. Krieger later left Soros to open Krieger and Associates, but the billion pound bet will probably remain as a benchmark in the chronicles of foreign exchange. Some worry that Krieger could be the beginning of a trend in the market.

According to John Williamson, Institute for International Economics, it is not a trend. Said Williamson, "I think it's the sort of thing that can happen from time to time and probably happened on this occasion because of the particular set of policies that were being followed in Britain. The government had, more or less, fixed an exchange rate ceiling in terms of the Deutschemark, and at the same time it had introduced a budget which increased demand by cutting taxes. There was really no other way to fight inflation but to let the exchange rate go through that ceiling, and so that would have been an invitation to a trader to bet large sums on the fact that the pound was going to go up."

What Krieger identified as an opportunity was the anomaly of Britain's fiscal policy not matching its monetary policy. Most traders didn't see the anomaly in the market. When asked why, one trader replied, "Why didn't we see it? I suppose we weren't focusing on the issue. It wasn't our job to look for those market opportunities." So how did Krieger, the maverick, manage to upset the market so effectively?

According to Stephen Axilrod, Rikko Securities, "Markets run day to day on psychology to a great extent. The basic trend of the market is certainly going to go with the economics, the underlying economics, which are partly unknown at any moment in time, of course. And so on a day-to-day basis, you could have someone pushing up rates, pushing down rates very substantially through very aggressive activities, and people will sort of go with it. Now when that proves to be unsustainable, then the market might just reverse itself terribly, and then you could get kind of a panic situation developing. And we've had these things in the foreign exchange markets. We've had it in the credit markets. We've had it in the stock markets at various times."

Fortunately the market has certain rules that are agreed to when traders become primary dealers. However, although it is possible to be reprimanded by central banking institutions, it is usually only a slap on the wrist. According to Axilrod, the institutions are "reluctant, because no central bank wants to interfere with anyone's business decisions."

Foreign exchange rates continue to bounce around in the market. Should governments reduce any volatility? The question remains unanswered and strongly debated. If the answer is yes, how do they do it? Some say we need a certain amount of volatility in the markets.

According to Axilrod, "without volatility, in my experience, markets tend to die. People, traders, don't take positions; you don't get any sense of movement. So you need a decent amount of volatility."

Some conservative traders continue to lament fixed rates, some dream of a gold-backed currency, and others are content with the current market's volatility. Although change may make conducting international business more confusing, for the trader it is also more profitable at the margin.

Questions for Discussion

1. How does the videocase illustrate the linkage between exchange rates and international strategy? What factors affect currency fluctuations? Explain.

2. Should government control exchange rates or let them float? Provide arguments for fixed and floating exchange rate systems. Discuss.

3. What are some of the implications of monetary systems on policy makers and strategic planners? What is the current monetary policy in the United States?

4. What is a dollar worth today? How has the nature of foreign exchange markets changed since the program aired?

International Business
and the Nation-State

The successful international manager understands the political, legal, and cultural environments of countries in which the firm does business. Part 3 therefore begins with a discussion of the effect of politics and laws on business from the perspective of both the home country and the host country. It then outlines the agreements, treaties, and laws that govern the relationships between home and host countries.

Managing conflicts between cultures requires an understanding of cultural differences in language, religion, values, customs, and education. This knowledge is the key to developing cross-cultural competence.

Part 3 concludes with a chapter on doing business with emerging market economies and state-owned enterprises. The manager must become accustomed to significant differences in outlook, plans, and operations when dealing with the economies of the former Soviet Union, Central and Eastern Europe, and China.

Politics and Laws

LEARNING OBJECTIVES

1. To understand the importance of the political and legal environments in both the home and host countries to the international business executive.

2. To learn how governments affect business through legislation and regulations.

3. To see how the political actions of countries expose firms to international risks.

4. To examine the differing laws regulating international trade found in different countries.

5. To understand how international political relations, agreements, and treaties can affect international business.

The Use of Economic Sanctions

Economic sanctions have been used by nations as a foreign-policy tool for centuries. Sanctions were imposed in ancient Greece in 432 B.C. during events leading to the Peloponnesian War between Athens and Sparta. The United States used sanctions against the British and French from 1808 to 1809 to try to get them to make concessions on the rights of neutral states. Since the late 1950s, the use of sanctions has been particularly widespread. The most recent episodes of sanctions include multilateral measures against South Africa imposed in 1985 and 1986 in response to its politics of racial segregation, U.S. financial sanctions against Panama in 1988 to destabilize the government of General Manuel Noriega, selected embargoes on China in 1989 after its repression of political dissent, most visible in Tiananmen Square, and the comprehensive United Nations trade quarantine against Iraq in 1990 after it invaded Kuwait.

Economic sanctions used for foreign-policy purposes are economic penalties, such as prohibiting trade, stopping financial transactions, or barring economic and military assistance, used to achieve the goal of influencing the target nation. Sanctions can be imposed selectively, stopping only certain trade and financial transactions or aid programs, or comprehensively, halting all economic relations with the target nation. Sanctions often are imposed when domestic pressure for action exists, but diplomacy or propaganda would be too mild a response, yet the most severe responses, covert action or military action, would be too severe.

Sanctions can be imposed to serve multiple goals. The measures are more successful in achieving the less ambitious and often unarticulated goals of (1) upholding international norms by punishing the target nation for unacceptable behavior and (2) deterring future objectionable actions. However, they are usually less successful in achieving the most prominently stated goal of making the target country comply with the sanctioning nation's stated wishes. Thus, inflated expectations are often formed about what sanctions can achieve.

Source: *Economic Sanctions: Effectiveness as Tools of Foreign Policy,* United States General Accounting Office, GAO/NSAID 92-106, Washington, D.C. 1992.

Politics and laws often play a critical role in international business. Even the best plans can go awry as a result of unexpected political or legal influences, and the failure to anticipate these factors can be the undoing of an otherwise successful business venture.

Of course, a single international political and legal environment does not exist. The business executive has to be aware of political and legal factors on a variety of levels. For example, while it is useful to understand the complexities of the host country's legal system, such knowledge may not protect against sanctions imposed by the home country, as we saw in the example that opened the chapter.

This chapter will examine politics and laws from the manager's point of view. The two subjects are considered together because laws generally are the result of political decisions. The chapter discussion will break down the study of the international political and legal environment into three segments: the politics and laws of the home country; those of the host country; and the bilateral and multilateral agreements, treaties, and laws governing the relations between host and home countries.

THE HOME-COUNTRY PERSPECTIVE

No manager can afford to ignore the rules and regulations of the country from which he or she conducts international business transactions. Many of these laws and regulations may not specifically address international business issues, yet they can have a major impact on a firm's opportunities abroad. Minimum-wage legislation, for example, has a bearing on the **international competitiveness** of a firm using production processes that are highly labor intensive. The cost of domestic safety regulations may significantly affect the pricing policies of firms. For example, U.S.

legislation creating the Environmental Superfund requires payment by chemical firms based on their production volume, regardless of whether the production is sold domestically or exported. As a result, these firms are at a disadvantage internationally when exporting their commodity-type products. They are required to compete against firms that have a cost advantage because their home countries do not require payment into an environmental fund.

Other legal and regulatory measures, however, are clearly aimed at international business. Some may be designed to help firms in their international efforts. For example, governments may attempt to aid and protect the business efforts of domestic companies facing competition from abroad by setting standards for product content and quality.

The political environment in most countries tends to provide general support for the international business efforts of firms headquartered within the country. For example, a government may work to reduce trade barriers or to increase trade opportunities through bilateral and multilateral negotiations. Such actions will affect individual firms to the extent that they improve international climate for free trade.

Often, however, governments also have specific rules and regulations that restrict international business. Such regulations are frequently political in nature and are based on governmental objectives that override commercial concerns. These restrictions are particularly sensitive when they address activities outside the country. Such measures challenge the territorial sovereignty of other governments and raise the issue of **extraterritoriality**—meaning a nation's attempt to set policy outside its territorial limits. Yet actions implying such extraterritorial reach are common, because nations often argue that their citizens and products maintain their nationality wherever they may be, and they therefore continue to be subject to the rules and laws of their home country.

Three main areas of governmental activity are of major concern to the international business manager. They are embargoes or trade sanctions, export controls, and the regulation of international business behavior.

Embargoes and Sanctions

The terms **sanction** and **embargo** as used here refer to governmental actions that distort free flows of trade in goods, services, or ideas for decidedly adversarial and political, rather than economic, purposes. Sanctions tend to consist of specific coercive trade measures such as the cancellation of trade financing or the prohibition

The United Nations trade sanctions devastated Iraq's economy following Iraq's invasion of Kuwait because most Iraqi trading partners, including many Arab nations, honored the sanctions. However, the sanctions did not prove effective in averting the Gulf War.
Source: © Reuters/Bettmann.

of high-technology trade, while embargoes are usually much broader in that they prohibit trade entirely. To understand them better, it is useful to examine the auspices and legal justifications under which they are imposed.[1]

After World War I, the League of Nations set a precedent for the legal justification of economic sanctions by subscribing to a covenant that contained penalties or sanctions for breaching its provisions. The members of the League of Nations did not intend to use military or economic measures separately, but the success of the blockades of World War I fostered the opinion that "the economic weapon, conceived not as an instrument of war but as a means of peaceful pressure, is the greatest discovery and most precious possession of the League."[2] The basic idea was that economic sanctions could force countries to behave peacefully in the international community.

The idea of multilateral use of economic sanctions was again incorporated into international law under the charter of the United Nations, but greater emphasis was placed on the enforcement process. Sanctions decided on are mandatory, even though each permanent member of the Security Council can veto efforts to impose them. The charter also allows for sanctions as enforcement actions by regional agencies, such as the Organization of American States, the Arab League, and the Organization of African Unity, but only with the Security Council's authorization.

The apparent strength of the United Nations' enforcement system was soon revealed to be flawed. Stalemates in the Security Council and vetoes by permanent members often led to a shift of discussions to the General Assembly, where sanctions are not enforceable. Also, concepts such as "peace" and "breach of peace" were seldom perceived in the same context by all members, and thus no systematic sanctioning policy developed under the United Nations.[3]

Over the years, economic sanctions and embargoes have become a principal tool of foreign policy for many countries. Often, they are imposed unilaterally in the hope of changing a country's government or at least changing its policies. Between 1914 and 1983, there were 99 incidents in which sanctions were used to pursue political goals, 46 of which occurred after 1970.[4] Reasons for the impositions have varied, ranging from the upholding of human rights to attempts to promote nuclear nonproliferation or antiterrorism.

The problem with sanctions, however, is that frequently their unilateral imposition has not produced the desired result. Sanctions may make the obtaining of goods more difficult or expensive for the sanctioned country, yet their purported objective is almost never achieved. In order to work, sanctions need to be imposed multilaterally—a goal that is clear, yet difficult to implement. On rare occasions, however, global cooperation can be achieved. For example, when Iraq invaded Kuwait in August of 1990, virtually all members of the United Nations condemned this hostile action and joined a trade embargo against Iraq. Typically, individual countries have different relationships with the country subject to the sanctions and cannot or do not wish to terminate trade relations. In this instance, however, both major and minor Iraqi trading partners—including many Arab nations—honored the United Nations trade sanctions and ceased trade with Iraq in the attempt to force it to withdraw its troops from Kuwait. Agreements were made to financially compensate those countries most adversely affected by trade sanctions.

Sanctions imposed by governments normally mean significant loss of business, and the issue of compensating the domestic firms and industries affected by these sanctions is always raised. Yet, trying to impose sanctions slowly or making them less expensive to ease the burden on these firms undercuts their ultimate chance for success. The international business manager is often caught in this political web and loses business as a result. Frequently, firms try to anticipate sanctions based on their evaluations of the international political climate. Nevertheless, even when substantial precautions are taken, firms may still suffer substantial losses.

One case in which sanctions had a major impact on a wide variety of firms involved the efforts by the U.S. government to block the construction of the Yamal pipeline, which was supposed to carry natural gas from the Soviet Union to western Europe. The U.S. government opposed the project on the grounds that it would make Europeans too dependent on Soviet gas and would provide the Soviets with large amounts of hard currency. Despite this opposition, several U.S. and European firms bid successfully for contracts to work on the pipeline. Following the imposition of martial law in Poland in December 1981, however, the United States imposed an embargo on the export of all U.S.–origin oil and gas transmission equipment, services, and technology to the Soviet Union. The international business efforts of many firms were damaged by the deterioration in the political relationship between the two countries, even though some of them were operating outside the United States. More recently, firms doing business in Libya, Iran, Nicaragua, and Iraq experienced major financial losses when the U.S. government ordered the severing of trade ties.

Export Controls

Many nations have **export-control systems,** which are designed to deny or at least delay the acquisition of strategically important goods to adversaries. In the United States, the export-control system is based on the Export Administration Act and the Munitions Control Act. These laws control all exports of goods, services, and ideas from the United States. The determinants for controls are national security, foreign policy, short supply, and nuclear nonproliferation.

In order for any export from the United States to take place, the exporter needs to obtain an **export license** from the Department of Commerce, which administers the Export Administration Act.[5] In consultation with other government agencies—particularly the Departments of State, Defense, and Energy—the Commerce Department has drawn up a list of commodities whose export is considered particularly sensitive. In addition, a list of countries differentiates nations according to their political relationship with the United States. Finally, a list of individual firms that are considered to be unreliable trading partners because of past trade-diversion activities exists for each country.

After an export license application has been filed, specialists in the Department of Commerce match the commodity to be exported with the **critical commodities list,** a file containing information about products that are either particularly sensitive to national security or controlled for other purposes. The product is then matched with the country of destination and the recipient company. If no concerns regarding any of the three exist, an export license is issued. Control determinants and the steps in the decision process are summarized in Figure 8.1.

This process may sound overly cumbersome, but it does not apply in equal measure to all exports. Many international business activities can be carried out with a **general license,** which provides blanket permission to export. Under such a license, which is not even a piece of paper, exports can be freely shipped to most trading partners provided that neither the product nor the country involved is considered sensitive. However, the process becomes more complicated and cumbersome when products incorporating high-level technologies and countries not friendly to the United States are involved. The exporter must then apply for a **validated export**

**FIGURE 8.1
U.S. Export-Control
System**

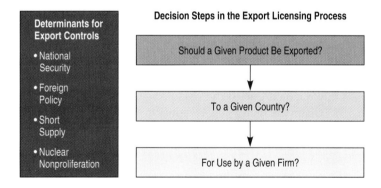

Determinants for Export Controls

• National Security

• Foreign Policy

• Short Supply

• Nuclear Nonproliferation

Decision Steps in the Export Licensing Process

Should a Given Product Be Exported?

To a Given Country?

For Use by a Given Firm?

license, which consists of written authorization to send a product abroad. Due to changes in world politics, the need to obtain these licenses is, however, decreasing. In 1991, the Bureau of Export Administration of the U.S. Department of Commerce received 29,955 license applications (down from more that 96,000 applications in 1988), of which only 4,264 were either returned without action or rejected.[6]

Still, export controls make time delays inevitable and are burdensome to firms. They complicate international business because firms trying to close a sale often do not know whether they will be permitted to ship abroad. Delays are especially long if a license application must be referred to another U.S. government agency or, more troublesome yet, to the **Coordinating Committee for Multilateral Export Controls (COCOM),** an international organization that coordinates export controls among Japan, Australia, and all NATO countries with the exception of Iceland.

The international business repercussions of export controls have become increasingly important. It is one thing to design an export-control system that is effective and that restricts those international business activities subject to important national concerns. It is, however, quite another when controls lose their effectiveness and when one country's firms are placed at a competitive disadvantage with firms in other countries whose control systems are less extensive or even nonexistent.

Export controls are increasingly difficult to implement and enforce for several reasons. First, the number of countries able to manufacture products of strategic importance has increased. Industrializing nations, which only a decade ago were seen as poor imitators at best, are now at the forefront of cutting-edge technology. Their products can have a significant impact on the balance of power in the world. Second, products that are in need of control are developed and disseminated very quickly. Product life cycles have been shortened to such an extent that even temporary delays in distribution may result in a significant setback for a firm. Third, because of advances in miniaturization, products that are in need of control are shrinking in size. The smuggling and diversion of such products have become easier because they are easier to conceal. Finally, the transfer of technology and know-how has increasingly taken on major strategic significance because such services are often invisible, performed by individuals, and highly personalized. They are easy to transship and therefore difficult to trace and control.

In order for the control process to work to any meaningful extent, alliances must be forged between nations that possess and can export strategic goods and knowledge. The United States has pursued such alliances by harmonizing export-control systems in the Western world. COCOM attempts to continuously determine which items need to be controlled or decontrolled and how national policies can be structured to create a unified international export-control system. In addition, neutral countries have been brought into the fold by joining in the overall export-control aims of COCOM. To encourage participation by these countries, they are given access to high technology if their control system works. However, if they are unwilling to forge effective export controls, the flow of high technology is necessarily reduced due to the risk of diversion.

Given the increasing advances in technology and the recent changes in the global strategic and political environment, substantial efforts are under way to streamline the licensing system, control only those commodities truly in need of control, and ease the licensing burden through automation. COCOM members have recognized the need to revamp the export-control list so that only the most strategic goods and technologies are restricted. With the official end of the Cold War and the disintegration of the Soviet bloc, countries of the former Soviet Union and former Eastern bloc countries are no longer seen as adversaries. Controls on exports of computers, machine tools, and telecommunications to former Eastern bloc countries have already been relaxed.

As Global Perspective 8.1 shows, the goals of COCOM are beginning to shift, and there is an increasing desire to use technology to assist the former Eastern bloc countries. Export controls to these nations can therefore be expected to be relaxed further as long as the countries develop systems that safeguard technology. At the same time, the shift away from the traditional East-West orientation is likely to be accompanied by an increased North-South orientation. Export controls will be more specific and even more targeted when it comes to nations that contribute to international turbulence.[7] Therefore, it may well be that in spite of the current decrease in controls, over time, firms must be even more sensitive to control issues in the future.

Global Perspective

8.1
A New Role for COCOM

In late 1992, the adversaries of the Cold War joined forces to transform the Coordinating Committee for Multilateral Export Controls (COCOM). Founded in 1949, COCOM was designed to stop the Soviet Union from acquiring Western technology. Now, the same organization is to become a tool to bring high technology and economic prosperity to the 25 newly independent nations of the old Soviet empire.

A new consensus recognizes the importance of speeding the flow of computers, machine tools, telecommunications systems, and other technology to help those countries develop vibrant, market-driven economies. Yet, there is also agreement that these products must be safeguarded to ensure that the technology will be used only for peaceful civilian purposes. Said Joan McEntee, U.S. Under Secretary of Commerce: "The world is still not a safe place," and there are "people that we are going to want to keep this technology from." In particular, there is concern that technology not fall into the hands of nations that are building nuclear, chemical, or biological weapons. As a result, major efforts will be directed toward development of a system to safeguard advanced technology. As nations develop such systems, their access to technology from the West will increase.

Stuart Auerbach and John Mintz, "COCOM Becomes Agency to Promote Technology Transfers," *The Washington Post,* November 24, 1992, D1,D3.

Regulating International Business Behavior Home countries may implement special laws and regulations to ensure that the international business behavior of firms headquartered within them is conducted within moral and ethical boundaries considered appropriate. The definition of appropriateness may vary from country to country and from government to government. Therefore, the content of such regulations, their enforcement, and their impact on firms may vary substantially between nations.

A major area in which the United States attempts to govern international business activities involves **boycotts.** As an example, Arab nations have developed a blacklist of companies that deal with Israel. Further, Arab customers frequently demand assurance that products they purchase are not manufactured in Israel and that the supplier company does not do any business with Israel. The goal of these actions clearly is to impose a boycott on business with Israel. Because of U.S. political ties to Israel, the U.S. government has adopted in response to these Arab actions a variety of laws to prevent U.S. firms from complying with the boycott. These laws include a provision to deny foreign income tax benefits to companies that comply with the boycott, and they also require notifying the U.S. government if boycott requests are received. U.S. firms that comply with the boycott are subject to heavy fines and to denial of export privileges.

Caught in a web of governmental activity, U.S. firms may be forced either to lose business or to pay substantial fines. This is especially true if the firm's products are competitive yet not unique, so that the supplier can opt to purchase them elsewhere. The heightening of such conflict can sometimes force companies to search for new ways to circumvent the law, which may be very risky, or to totally withdraw operations from a country.

Another area of regulatory activity affecting the international business efforts of U.S. firms is U.S. **antitrust laws.** These laws apply to international operations as well as to domestic business. The Justice Department watches closely when a U.S. firm buys an overseas company, engages in a joint venture with a foreign firm, or makes an agreement abroad with a competing firm in order to ensure that the action does not result in restraint of competition.

Given the increase in worldwide cooperation among companies, however, the wisdom of extending U.S. antitrust legislation to international activities is being questioned. Some limitations to these tough antitrust provisions were already implemented decades ago. For example, the **Webb-Pomerene Act** of 1918 excludes from antitrust prosecution firms cooperating to develop foreign markets. This law was passed as part of an effort to aid U.S. export efforts in the face of strong foreign competition by oligopolies and monopolies. The exclusion of international activities from antitrust regulation was further enhanced by the Export Trading Company Act of 1982, which ensures that cooperating firms are not exposed to the threat of treble damages. The law was designed specifically to assist small and medium-sized firms in their export efforts by permitting them to join forces. Further steps to loosen the application of U.S. antitrust laws to international business are under consideration because of increased competition from state-supported enterprises, strategic alliances, and mega-corporations from abroad.

U.S. firms operating overseas are also affected by U.S. laws against **bribery** and corruption. In many countries, payments or favors are a way of life, and "a greasing of the wheels" is expected in return for government services. As a result, many U.S. companies doing business internationally had routinely paid bribes or done favors for foreign officials in order to gain contracts. In the 1970s, a major national debate erupted about these business practices, led by arguments that U.S. firms have an ethical and moral leadership obligation and that contracts won through bribes do not reflect competitive market activity. As a result, the **Foreign Corrupt Practices Act** was passed in 1977, making it a crime for U.S. executives of publicly traded firms to bribe a foreign official in order to obtain business.

A number of U.S. firms have complained about the act, arguing that it hinders their efforts to compete internationally against companies whose home countries have no such antibribery laws. The problem is one of ethics versus practical needs and, to some extent, of the amounts involved. For example, it may be hard to draw the line between providing a generous tip and paying a bribe in order to speed up a business transaction. Many business executives believe that the United States should not apply its moral principles to other societies and cultures in which bribery and corruption are endemic. To compete internationally, executives argue, they must be free to use the most common methods of competition in the host country.

On the other hand, applying different standards to executives and firms based on whether they do business abroad or domestically is difficult to do. Also, bribes may open the way for shoddy performance and loose moral standards among executives and employees and may result in a spreading of general unethical business practices. Unrestricted bribery could result in firms concentrating on how to bribe best rather than on how to best produce and market their products.

The international manager must carefully distinguish between reasonable ways of doing business internationally—that is, complying with foreign expectations—and outright bribery and corruption. To assist the manager in this task, the 1988 Trade Act clarifies the applicability of the Foreign Corrupt Practices legislation. These revisions outline when a manager is expected to know about violation of the act, and they draw a distinction between the facilitation of routine governmental actions and governmental policy decisions. Routine actions concern issues such as the obtaining of permits and licenses, the processing of governmental papers (such as visas and work orders), the providing of mail and phone service, and the loading and unloading of cargo. Policy decisions refer mainly to situations in which the obtaining or retaining of a contract is at stake. While the facilitation of routine actions is not prohibited, the illegal influencing of policy decisions can result in the imposition of severe fines and penalties.

All of these issues of governmental regulation pose difficult and complex problems, for they place managers in the position of having to choose between home-country regulations and foreign business practices. This choice is made even more difficult because diverging standards of behavior are applied to businesses in different countries.

A final, major issue that is critical for international business managers is that of general standards of behavior and ethics. Increasingly, public concerns are raised about such issues as environmental protection, global warming, pollution, and moral behavior. However, these issues are not of the same importance in every country. What may be frowned upon or even illegal in one nation may be customary or at least acceptable in others. For example, the cutting down of the Brazilian rain forest may be acceptable to the government of Brazil, but scientists and concerned consumers may object vehemently because of the effect on global warming and other climatic changes. The export of U.S. tobacco products may be legal but results in accusations of exporting death to developing nations. China may use prison labor in producing products for export, but U.S. law prohibits the importation of such products. Mexico may permit the use of low safety standards for workers, but the buyers of Mexican products may object to the resulting dangers.

International firms must understand these conflicts and should assert leadership in implementing change. Not everything that is legally possible should be exploited for profit. Although companies need to return a profit on their investments, these issues must be seen in the context of time. By acting on existing, leading-edge knowledge and standards, firms will be able to benefit in the long term through consumer goodwill and the avoidance of later recriminations.

HOST COUNTRY POLITICAL AND LEGAL ENVIRONMENT

Politics and laws of a host country affect international business operations in a variety of ways. The good manager will understand the country in which the firm operates so that he or she can work within existing parameters and can anticipate and plan for changes that may occur.

Political Action and Risk

Firms usually prefer to conduct business in a country with a stable and friendly government, but such governments are not always easy to find. Managers must therefore continually monitor the government, its policies, and its stability to determine the potential for political change that could adversely affect corporate operations.

There is **political risk** in every nation, but the range of risks varies widely from country to country. In general, political risk is lowest in countries that have a history of stability and consistency. Political risk tends to be highest in nations that do not have this sort of history. In a number of countries, however, consistency and stability that were apparent on the surface have been quickly swept away by major popular movements that drew on the bottled-up frustrations of the population. Three major types of political risk can be encountered: **ownership risk,** which exposes property and life; **operating risk,** which refers to interference with the ongoing operations of a firm; and **transfer risk,** which is mainly encountered when attempts are made to shift funds between countries. Firms can be exposed to political risk due to government actions or even outside the control of governments. The type of actions and their effects are classified in Figure 8.2.

A major political risk in many countries is that of conflict and violent change. A manager will want to think twice before conducting business in a country in which the likelihood of such change is high. To begin with, if conflict breaks out, violence directed toward the firm's property and employees is a strong possibility. Guerrilla warfare, civil disturbances, and terrorism often take an anti-industry bent, making companies and their employees potential targets. U.S. corporations or firms linked to the United States are often subject to major threats, even in countries that boast of great political stability. For example, in the spring of 1991, Detlev Rohwedder, chairman of the German Treuhand (the institution in charge of privatizing the state-owned firms of the former East Germany), was assassinated at his home in Germany by the Red Army Faction because of his "representation of capitalism."

International terrorists have frequently targeted U.S. corporate facilities, operations, and personnel abroad for attack in order to strike a blow against the United States and capitalism. U.S. firms are prominent symbols of the U.S. presence abroad, and by their nature they cannot have the elaborate security and restricted access of U.S. diplomatic offices and military bases. The methods used by terrorists against business facilities include bombing, arson, hijacking, and sabotage. To obtain funds, the terrorists resort to kidnapping executives, armed robbery, and extortion.[8]

FIGURE 8.2
Exposure to
Political Risk

Contingencies May Include:	Loss May Be the Result of:	
	The actions of legitimate government authorities	Events caused by factors outside the control of government
The involuntary loss of control over specific assets without adequate compensation	• Total or partial expropriation • Forced divestiture • Confiscation • Cancellation or unfair calling of performance bonds	• War • Revolution • Terrorism • Strikes • Extortion
A reduction in the value of a stream of benefits expected from the foreign-controlled affiliate	• Nonapplicability of "national treatment" • Restriction in access to financial, labor, or material markets • Controls on prices, outputs, or activities • Currency and remittance restrictions • Value-added and export performance requirements	• Nationalistic buyers or suppliers • Threats and disruption to operations by hostile groups • Externally induced financial constraints • Externally imposed limits on imports or exports

Source: José de la Torre and David H. Neckar, "Forecasting Political Risks for International Operations," in H. Vernon-Wortzel and L. Wortzel, *Global Strategic Management: The Essentials,* 2nd ed. (New York: John Wiley and Sons, 1990), 195.

In many countries, particularly in the developing world, coups d'état can result in drastic changes in government. The new government often will attack foreign firms as remnants of a Western-dominated colonial past, as has happened in Cuba, Nicaragua, and Iran. Even if such changes do not represent an immediate physical threat, they can lead to policy changes that may have a drastic effect. The past few decades have seen coups in Ghana, Ethiopia, Iraq, and Kuwait, for example, that have seriously impeded the conduct of international business.

Less drastic, but still worrisome, are changes in government policies that are not caused by changes in the government itself. These occur when, for one reason or another, a government feels pressured to change its policies toward foreign businesses. The pressure may be the result of nationalist or religious factions or widespread anti-Western feeling. In any case, the aware manager will work to anticipate such changes and plan for ways to cope with them.

A broad range of policy changes is possible as a result of political unrest. All of the changes can affect the company's international operations, but not all of them are equal in weight. Except for extreme cases, companies do not usually have to fear violence against their employees, although violence against company property is quite common. Also common are changes in policy that result from a new government or a strong new stance that is nationalist and opposed to foreign investment. The most drastic public steps resulting from such policy changes are usually expropriation and confiscation.

Expropriation is the transfer of ownership by the host government to a domestic entity. According to the World Bank, from the early 1960s through the 1970s, a total of 1,535 firms from 22 different countries were expropriated in 511 separate actions by 76 nations.[9] Expropriation was an appealing action to many countries

The Risk of Terrorist Activity: A Factor in International Business Decisions

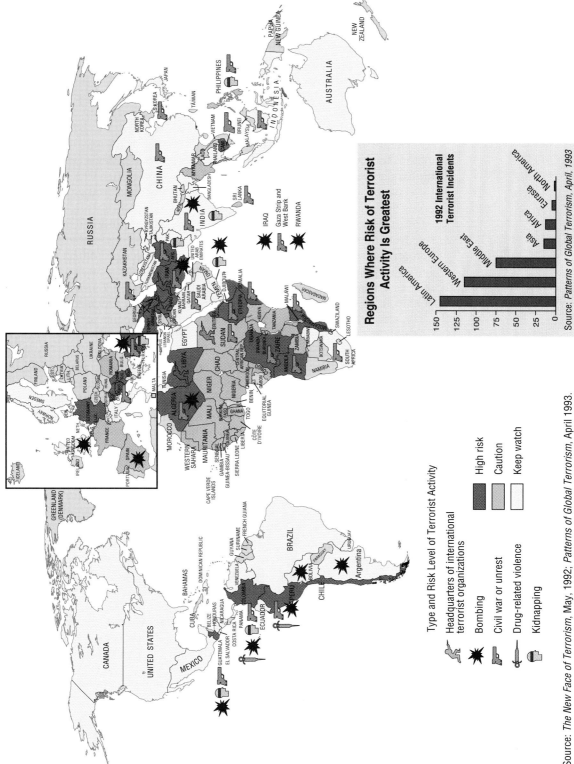

Regions Where Risk of Terrorist Activity Is Greatest

1992 International Terrorist Incidents

Source: *Patterns of Global Terrorism, April, 1993*

Type and Risk Level of Terrorist Activity

Headquarters of international terrorist organizations

Bombing

Civil war or unrest

Drug-related violence

Kidnapping

High risk

Caution

Keep watch

Source: *The New Face of Terrorism*, May, 1992; *Patterns of Global Terrorism*, April 1993.

because it demonstrated their nationalism and transferred a certain amount of wealth and resources from foreign companies to the host country immediately. It did have costs to the host country, however, to the extent that it made other firms more hesitant to invest there. Expropriation does not relieve the host government of providing compensation to the former owners. However, these compensation negotiations are often protracted and frequently result in settlements that are unsatisfactory to the owners. For example, governments may offer compensation in the form of local, nontransferable currency or may base compensation on the book value of the firm. Even though firms that are expropriated may deplore the low levels of payment obtained, they frequently accept them in the absence of better alternatives.

The use of expropriation as a policy tool has sharply decreased over time. In the mid-1970s, more than 83 expropriations took place in a single year. By the 1980s, the annual average had declined to fewer than 3. Apparently, governments have come to recognize that the damage they inflict on themselves through expropriation exceeds the benefits they receive.[10]

Confiscation is similar to expropriation in that it results in a transfer of ownership from the firm to the host country. It differs in that it does not involve compensation for the firm. Some industries are more vulnerable than others to confiscation and expropriation because of their importance to the host country's economy and their lack of agility to shift operations. For this reason, sectors such as mining, energy, public utilities, and banking have frequently been targets of such government actions.

Confiscation and expropriation constitute major political risk for foreign investors. Other government actions, however, are equally detrimental to foreign firms. Many countries are turning from confiscation and expropriation to more subtle forms of control, such as **domestication.** The goal of domestication is the same—that is, to gain control over foreign investment—but the method is different. Through domestication, the government demands transfer of ownership and management responsibility. It can impose **local-content** regulations to ensure that a large share of the product is locally produced or demand that a larger share of the profit is retained in the country. Changes in labor laws, patent protection, and tax regulations are also used for purposes of domestication.

Domestication can have profound effects on an international business operation for a number of reasons. If a firm is forced to hire nationals as managers, poor cooperation and communication can result. If domestication is imposed within a very short time span, corporate operations overseas may have to be headed by poorly trained and inexperienced local managers. Domestic-content requirements may force a firm to purchase its supplies and parts locally. This can result in increased costs, higher inefficiency, and lower-quality products. Export requirements imposed on companies may create havoc for their international distribution plans and force them to change or even shut down operations in third countries. If government action consists of weakening or not enforcing **intellectual property right** protection, companies run the risk of losing their core competitive edge. Such steps may temporarily permit domestic firms to become quick imitators. Yet, in the longer term, they will not only discourage the ongoing transfer of technology and knowledge by multinational firms, but also reduce the incentive for local firms to invest in innovation and progress. Finally, domestication usually will shield an industry within one country from foreign competition. As a result, inefficiencies will be allowed to thrive due to a lack of market discipline. This will affect the long-run international competitiveness of an operation abroad and may turn into a major problem when, years later, domestication is discontinued by the government.

Most businesses operating abroad face a number of other risks that are less dangerous, but probably more common, than the drastic ones already described. A host government's political situation or desires may lead it to impose regulations or laws to restrict or control the international activities of firms.

Nations that face a shortage of foreign currency sometimes will impose controls on the movement of capital in and out of the country. Such controls may make it difficult for a firm to remove its profits or investments from the host country. Sometimes **exchange controls** are also levied selectively against certain products or companies in an effort to reduce the importation of goods that are considered to be a luxury or to be sufficiently available through domestic production. Such regulations are often difficult for the international manager to deal with because they may affect the importation of parts, components, or supplies that are vital to production operations in the country. Frequently, restrictions on such imports may force a firm either to alter its production program or, worse yet, to shut down its entire plant. Prolonged negotiations with government officials may be necessary to reach a compromise on what constitutes a "valid" expenditure of foreign-currency resources. Because the goals of government officials and corporate managers are often quite different, such compromises, even when they can be reached, may result in substantial damage to the international operations of the firm.

Countries may also raise tax rates applied to foreign investors in an effort to control multinational corporations and their capital. Such tax increases may raise much-needed revenue for the host country, but they can severely damage the operations of foreign investors. This damage, in turn, will frequently result in decreased income for the host country in the long run. The raising of tax rates needs to be carefully differentiated from increased tax scrutiny of foreign investors. Many governments believe that multinational firms may be tempted to shift tax burdens to lower-tax countries by using artificial pricing schemes between subsidiaries. In such instances, governments are likely to take measures to obtain their fair contribution from multinational operations. In the United States, for example, increased focus on the taxation of multinational firms demanded by President Clinton has resulted in various back-tax payments by foreign firms and the development of pricing policies jointly with the Internal Revenue Service.[11]

The international executive also has to worry about **price controls.** In many countries, domestic political pressures can force governments to control the prices of imported products or services, particularly in sectors considered highly sensitive from a political perspective, such as food or health care. A foreign firm involved in these areas is vulnerable to price controls because the government can play on citizens' nationalistic tendencies to enforce the controls. Particularly in countries that suffer from high inflation, frequent devaluations, or sharply rising costs, the international executive may be forced to choose between shutting down the operation or continuing production at a loss in the hope of recouping profits when the government loosens or removes its price restrictions. Price controls can also be administered to prevent prices from being too low. As explained in more detail in Chapter 16, governments have enacted antidumping laws, which prevent foreign competitors from pricing their imports unfairly low in order to drive domestic competitors out of the market. Since dumping charges depend heavily on the definition of "fair" price, a firm can sometimes become the target of such accusations quite unexpectedly. Proving that no dumping took place can become quite onerous in terms of time, money, and information disclosure.

Managers face the risk of confiscation, expropriation, domestication, or other government interference whenever they conduct business overseas, but ways exist to lessen the risk. Obviously, if a new government comes into power that is dedicated to the removal of all foreign influences, there is little a firm can do. In less extreme cases, however, managers can take actions that will reduce the risk, provided they understand the root causes of the host country's policies.

Adverse governmental actions are usually the result of nationalism, the desire for independence, or opposition to colonial remnants. If a host country's citizens feel exploited by foreign investors, government officials are more likely to take anti-foreign action. To reduce the risk of government intervention, the international firm needs to demonstrate that it is concerned with the host country's society and that it considers itself an integral part of the host country, rather than simply an exploitative foreign corporation. Ways of doing this include intensive local hiring and training practices, better pay, contributions to charity, and societally useful investments. In addition, the company can form joint ventures with local partners to demonstrate that it is willing to share its gains with nationals. Although such actions will not guarantee freedom from political risk, they will certainly lessen the exposure.

Another action that can be taken by corporations to protect against political risk is the close monitoring of political developments. Increasingly, private-sector firms offer such monitoring assistance, permitting the overseas corporation to discover potential trouble spots as early as possible and to react quickly to prevent major losses. Firms can also take out insurance to cover losses due to political risk. In the United States, for example, the Overseas Private Investment Corporation (OPIC) offers such insurance. The cost of coverage varies by country and type of activity, but it averages $0.30 for $100 of coverage per year to protect against inconvertibility, $0.60 to protect against expropriation, and $1.05 to compensate for damage to business income and assets from political violence.[12] Usually the policies do not cover commercial risks and, in the event of a claim, cover only the actual loss—not lost profits. Even though settling a claim can be quite cumbersome and consume a lot of resources, risk insurance can be critical to a firm's survival.

Despite the risks, the international business executive should not feel overwhelmed. Many research groups and publications—such as the Economist Intelligence Unit and Global Risk Assessments Inc.—devote major efforts to the assessment of country risk. Figure 8.3 shows an advertisement for such advisory services. Risks in international business will always exist. Rather than react negatively, the manager may be aware of the existence of international risk and take steps to keep informed.

The discussion to this point has focused primarily on the political environment. Laws have been mentioned only as they appear to be the direct result of political change. However, the laws of host countries need to be considered on their own to some extent, for the basic system of law is important to the conduct of international business.

Legal Differences and Restraints

Countries differ in their laws as well as in their use of the law. For example, over the past decade the United States has become an increasingly litigious society in which institutions and individuals are quick to initiate lawsuits. Court battles are often protracted and costly, and even the threat of a court case can reduce business

**FIGURE 8.3
Advertisement for an
Advisory Service**

We are the world's leading source of analysis and advice for international business.

Any questions?

We cover 192 countries and a full range of management and industry topics. For a free catalogue call 800 938 4685 or 212 460 0600.

The Economist Intelligence Unit
215 Park Avenue South
New York, New York 10003
Fax 212 995 8837

E·I·U

**The Economist
Intelligence Unit**
Incorporating
BUSINESS INTERNATIONAL

opportunities. Interestingly, Japan has only about 12,500 fully licensed lawyers, compared with some 650,000 in the United States. Whether the number of lawyers is cause or effect, the Japanese tend not to litigate.[13] Litigation in Japan means that the parties have failed to compromise, which is contrary to Japanese tradition and results in loss of face. A cultural predisposition therefore exists to settle conflicts outside the court system, as shown in Global Perspective 8.2. Over the millenia of civilization, many different laws and legal systems emerged. King Hammurabi of Babylon codified a series of decisions by judges into a body of laws. Hebrew law was the result of the dictates of God. Legal issues in many African tribes were settled through the verdicts of clansmen.

A key legal perspective that survives today is that of theocracy. For example, Islamic law, or the sharia, is the result of scripture, prophetic utterances and practices, and scholarly interpretations.[14] Together with Hebrew law, these legal systems have faith and belief as their key focus and are a mix of societal, legal, and spiritual guidelines.

While these legal systems are important to society, from an international business perspective, the two major legal systems worldwide can be categorized into common law and code law. Common law is based on tradition and depends less on written statutes and codes than on precedent and custom. Common law originated in England and is the system of law in the United States. Code law, on the other hand, is based on a comprehensive set of written statutes. Countries with code law try to spell out all possible legal rules explicitly. Code law is based on Roman law and is found in the majority of the nations of the world.

Global Perspective

8.2

Two Air Disasters, Two Cultures, Two Remedies

When two jumbo jets crashed 10 days apart in Dallas and in the mountains near Tokyo, Americans and Japanese shared a common bond of shock and grief. Soon, however, all parties in Japan—from the airline to the employers of victims—moved to put the tragedy behind them. In the United States, legal tremors will continue for years.

Lawyers hustled to the scene of the Delta Air Lines accident at Dallas–Ft. Worth Airport and set up shop at an airport hotel. Proclaimed San Francisco attorney Melvin Belli: "I'm not an ambulance chaser—I get there before the ambulance." "We always file the first suit," bragged Richard Brown, a Melvin Belli associate who flew to Dallas "to get to the bottom of this and to make ourselves available." But he adds: "We never solicited anyone directly. We were called to Texas by California residents who lost their loved ones." Within 72 hours, the first suit against Delta was filed. Insurance adjusters working for Delta went quickly to work as well.

Seven thousand miles away, Japan Air Lines (JAL) President Yasumoto Takagi humbly bowed to families of the 520 victims and apologized "from the bottom of our hearts." He vowed to resign once the investigation was complete. Next of kin received "condolence payments" and negotiated settlements with the airline. Traditionally, few if any lawsuits are filed following such accidents.

Behind these differences lie standards of behavior and corporate responsibility that are worlds apart. "There is a general Japanese inclination to try to settle any disputes through negotiations between the parties before going to court," said Koichiro Fujikura, Tokyo University law professor. Added Carl Green, a Washington, D.C., attorney and specialist on Japanese law, "There is an assumption of responsibility. In our adversarial society, we don't admit responsibility. It would be admitting liability."

After a JAL jet crashed into Tokyo Bay in 1982, killing 24, JAL President Takagi visited victims' families, offered gifts, and knelt before funeral altars. JAL offered families about $2,000 each in condolence payments, then negotiated settlements reported to be worth between $166,000 and $450,000, depending on the age and earning power of each victim. Only one family sued.

Japanese legal experts expected settlements in the 1985 crash to be as high as 500 million yen—about $2.1 million—apiece. Negotiations may be prolonged. But if families believe that JAL is sincerely sorry, "I think their feelings will be soothed," predicted attorney Takeshi Odagi.

Japan's legal system encourages these traditions. "Lawyers don't descend in droves on accident scenes because they barely have enough time to handle the suits they have," says John Haley, a law professor at the University of Washington who has studied and worked in Japan. "There are fewer judges per capita than there were in 1890," Haley added. Only 500 lawyers are admitted to the bar each year.

Source: Clemens P. Work, Sarah Peterson, and Hidehiro Tanakadate, "Two Air Disasters, Two Cultures, Two Remedies," *U.S. News and World Report*, August 26, 1985, 25–26.

In general, countries with the code law system have much more rigid laws than those with the common law system. In the latter, courts adopt precedents and customs to fit cases, allowing a better idea of basic judgment likely to be rendered in new situations. The differences between code law and common law and their impact on international business, while wide in theory, are not as broad in practice. One reason is that many common law countries, including the United States, have adopted commercial codes to govern the conduct of business.

Host countries may adopt a number of laws that affect the firm's ability to do business, as discussed in Chapter 7. Tariffs and quotas, for example, can affect the entry of goods. Special licenses for foreign goods may be required.

Other laws may restrict entrepreneurial activities. In Argentina, for example, pharmacies must be owned by the pharmacist. This legislation prevents an ambitious businessperson from hiring druggists and starting a pharmacy chain. Similarly, the law prevents the addition of a drug counter to an existing business such as a supermarket and thus the broadening of the product offering to consumers.[15]

Specific legislation may also exist regulating what does and does not constitute deceptive advertising. Many countries prohibit specific claims that compare products to the competition, or they restrict the use of promotional devices. Even when no laws exist, regulations may hamper business operations. For example, in some countries, firms are required to join the local chamber of commerce or become a member of the national trade association. These institutions in turn may have internal sets of regulations that specify standards for the conduct of business that may be quite confining.

Finally, seemingly innocuous local regulations that may easily be overlooked can have a major impact on the firm's success. For example, Japan has an intricate process regulating the building of new department stores or supermarkets. Because of the government's desire to protect smaller merchants, these regulations brought the opening of new, large stores to a virtual standstill. As department stores and supermarkets serve as the major conduit for the sale of imported consumer products, the lack of new stores severely affected opportunities for market penetration of imported merchandise.[16] Only after intense pressure from the outside did the Japanese government decide in early 1991 to reconsider these regulations.

The Influencing of Politics and Laws

To succeed in a market, the international manager needs much more than business know-how. He or she must also deal with the intricacies of national politics and laws. Although to fully understand another country's legal political system will rarely be possible, the good manager will be aware of its importance and will work with people who do understand how to operate within the system.

Many areas of politics and law are not immutable. Viewpoints can be modified or even reversed, and new laws can supersede old ones. Therefore, existing political and legal restraints do not always need to be accepted. To achieve change, however, some impetus for it—such as the clamors of a constituency—must occur. Otherwise, systemic inertia is likely to allow the status quo to prevail.

The international manager has various options. One is to simply ignore prevailing rules and expect to get away with it. Pursuing this option is a high-risk strategy because the possibility of objection and even prosecution exists. A second, traditional option is to provide input to trade negotiators and expect any problem areas to be resolved in multilateral negotiations. The drawbacks to this option are, of course, the quite time-consuming process involved and the lack of control by the firm.

A third option involves the development of coalitions and constituencies that can motivate legislators and politicians to consider and ultimately implement change. This option can be pursued in various ways. First of all, direct linkages and their costs and benefits can be explained to legislators and politicians. For example, a manager can explain the employment and economic effects of certain laws and regulations and demonstrate the benefits of change. The picture can be enlarged by including indirect linkages. For example, suppliers, customers, and distributors can be asked to help explain to decision makers the benefit of change. In addition, the public at large can be involved through public statements or advertisements. Figure 8.4 provides an example of such an explanatory effort by the U.S. steel industry.

FIGURE 8.4
Lobbying by the U.S.
Steel Industry

Have you heard about the country whose steel industry has invested more than $22.5 billion in modernization since 1980 and is now the world's most efficient steel producer?

The country is America. But even with our modern facilities and productivity leadership, our steel industry is in danger of losing jobs. Over $100 billion in foreign government subsidies to their steel industries and steel dumped in the U.S. market at artificially low prices are hurting American steel.

Surprised? There's even more we can tell you about the new American steel industry. Call 1-800-STEEL WORKS.

American Steel.
It's not business as usual anymore.

This state-of-the-art coil storage and retrieval facility helps ensure steel quality and on-time delivery.

Source: Courtesy of American Iron and Steel Institute.

Developing such coalitions is not an easy task. Companies often seek assistance in effectively influencing the government decision-making process. Such assistance is particularly beneficial when narrow economic objectives or single-issue campaigns are involved. Typically, **lobbyists** provide this assistance. Usually, there are well-connected individuals and firms that can provide access to policymakers and legislators in order to communicate new and pertinent information.

Many U.S. firms have representatives in Washington, D.C., as well as in state capitals and are quite successful at influencing domestic policies. Often, however, they are less adept at ensuring proper representation abroad. For example, a survey of U.S. international marketing executives found that knowledge and information about foreign trade and government officials was ranked lowest among critical international business information needs. This low ranking appears to reflect the fact that many U.S. firms are far less successful in their interactions with governments abroad and far less intensive in their lobbying efforts than are foreign entities in the United States.[17]

Foreign countries and companies have been particularly effective in their lobbying in the United States. As an example, Brazil has retained nearly a dozen U.S. firms to cover and influence trade issues. Brazilian citrus exporters and computer manufacturers have hired U.S. legal and public relations firms to provide them with

Global Perspective

8.3
Washington: Under the Influence?

Peter Wallison, who served both the Treasury Department and the White House as legal counsel, took a lot of heat when he turned lobbyist. He was accused on the Senate floor by Sen. Donald Riegle of Michigan of serving as an intermediary between Honda Motor Co. and the U.S. Treasury Department when the U.S. Customs Service ruled that Canadian-built Honda Civic automobiles do not qualify for duty-free entry into the United States as stipulated by the free-trade agreement with Canada.

Many were also unhappy when Timothy MacCarthy moved from a 16-year job at the U.S. Motor Vehicle Manufacturers Association to head Nissan North America's Washington corporate office. "I don't think I represent the Japanese company," says MacCarthy, insisting that he works for Nissan North America, a U.S. firm that employs some 6,000 workers. He sees lobbying as a corporate right in America. "If a company is not active in lobbying, that could even represent a failure to fulfill its responsibility toward its employees," says MacCarthy.

Source: Waichi Sekiguchi, "Washington: Under the Influence?" *The Nikkei Weekly,* September 12, 1992, 11.

information on relevant U.S. legislative activity. The Banco do Brasil also successfully lobbied for the restructuring of Brazilian debt and favorable U.S. banking regulations.

Although representation of the firm's interests to government decision makers and legislators is entirely appropriate, the international manager must also consider any potential side-effects. Major questions can be raised if such representation becomes very overt. Short-term gains may be far outweighed by long-term negative repercussions if the international firm is perceived as exerting too much political influence.

As Global Perspective 8.3 shows, there are major public concerns about the representation of foreign firms in Washington, D.C. Particularly the issue of representation by former government officials has come under public scrutiny, and many complaints have been voiced about the "revolving door." Legislation has therefore been passed that provides for cooling off periods during which former policymakers cannot return to their agencies and represent clients. The ethics provisions implemented by President Clinton have tightened the restrictions even more, with a focus on the representation of foreign firms. Yet, some opponents have argued that these provisions are overly harsh since they deprive former policymakers of employment, discriminate against foreign firms, and prevent individuals from seeking to serve in government.

INTERNATIONAL RELATIONS AND LAWS

In addition to understanding the politics and laws of both home and host countries, the international manager must also consider the overall international political and legal environment. This is important because policies and events occurring between countries can have a profound impact on firms trying to do business internationally.

The International Political Environment

The effect of politics on international business is determined by both the bilateral political relations between home and host countries and by multilateral agreements governing the relations among groups of countries.

The government-to-government relationship can have a profound influence in a number of ways, particularly if it becomes hostile. Among numerous examples in recent years of the relationship between international politics and international business, perhaps the most notable involves U.S.-Iranian relations following the 1979 Iranian revolution. Although the internal political and legal changes in the aftermath of that revolution certainly would have affected anyone doing international business in Iran, the deterioration in U.S.-Iranian political relations that resulted from the revolution had a significant additional impact on U.S. firms. Following the revolution, U.S. firms were injured not only by the physical damage caused by the violence, but also by the anti-American feelings of the Iranian people and their government. The resulting clashes between the two governments subsequently destroyed business relationships, regardless of corporate feelings or agreements on either side.

International political relations do not always have harmful effects. If bilateral political relations between countries improve, business can benefit. One example is the improvement in U.S. relations with eastern Europe following the official end of the Cold War. The political warming opened the potentially lucrative former Eastern bloc markets to U.S. businesses. For example, the IBM Corporation is now able to develop actively the market for computers, particularly personal computers, in eastern Europe.

The overall international political environment has effects, whether good or bad, on international business. For this reason, the good manager will strive to remain aware of political currents worldwide and will attempt to anticipate changes in the international political environment so that his or her firm can plan for them.

International Law

International law plays an important role in the conduct of international business. Although no enforceable body of international law exists, certain treaties and agreements are respected by a number of countries and profoundly influence international business operations. For example, the General Agreement on Tariffs and Trade (GATT) defines internationally acceptable economic practices for its member nations. Although it does not directly deal with individual firms, it does affect them indirectly by providing some predictability in the international environment.

International law also plays a major role in protecting intellectual property rights. Rights to intellectual property involve rights to inventions, **patents, trademarks,** and industrial designs, and copyrights for literary, musical, artistic, photographic, and cinematographic works. Currently, these types of intellectual property are not completely defined by any international treaty, and the laws differ from country to country on several important points. Thus the rights granted by a U.S. patent, trademark, or copyright extend only through the United States and confer no protection in a foreign country.

Some international agreements exist to ease the task of filing for intellectual property rights in those countries in which a firm wishes to conduct business or ensure protection. The **Paris Convention for the Protection of Industrial Property,** to which the United States and 95 other countries are party, sets minimum standards of protection and provides the right of national treatment and the right of priority. This means that members will not discriminate against foreigners and that firms have one year (six months for a design or trademark) in which to file an application.

The Patent Cooperation Treaty (PCT) provides procedures for filing one international application designating countries in which a patent is sought, which has the same effect as filing national applications in each of those countries. Similarly, the European Patent Office examines applications and issues national patents in any of its member countries. Other regional offices include the African Industrial Property Office (ARIPO), the French-speaking African Intellectual Property Organization (OAPI), and one in Saudi Arabia for six countries in the Gulf region.[18]

Much more needs to be done to protect intellectual property. Because so many disparate regulations exist worldwide, intellectual-property issues constituted a significant portion of the Uruguay Round negotiations. Knowledge is often the firm's most precious competitive advantage, and violation of these rights can have significant financial repercussions.

In addition to multilateral agreements, firms are affected by bilateral treaties and conventions between the countries in which they do business. For example, the United States has signed bilateral Treaties of Friendship, Commerce, and Navigation (FCN) with a number of countries. These agreements generally define the rights of U.S. firms doing business in the host country. They normally guarantee that U.S. firms will be treated by the host country in the same manner in which domestic firms are treated. While these treaties provide for some sort of stability, they can also be canceled, as the withdrawal of the United States from its FCN agreement with Nicaragua demonstrated.

The international legal environment also affects the manager to the extent that firms must concern themselves with jurisdictional disputes. Because no single body of international law exists, firms usually are restricted by both home and host country laws. If a conflict occurs between contracting parties in two different countries, a question arises concerning which country's laws are to be used and in which court the dispute is to be settled. Sometimes the contract will contain a jurisdictional clause, which settles the matter with little problem. If the contract does not contain such a clause, however, the parties to the dispute have a few choices. They can settle the dispute by following the laws of the country in which the agreement was made, or they can resolve it by obeying the laws of the country in which the contract will have to be fulfilled. Which laws to use and in which location to settle the dispute are two different decisions. As a result, a dispute between a U.S. exporter and a French importer could be resolved in Paris but be based on New York State law. The importance of such provisions was highlighted by the lengthy jurisdictional disputes surrounding the Bhopal incident in India.

In cases of disagreement, the parties can choose either **arbitration** or litigation. Litigation is usually avoided for several reasons. It often involves extensive delays and is very costly. In addition, firms may fear discrimination in foreign countries. Therefore, companies tend to prefer conciliation and arbitration, because these processes result in much quicker decisions. Arbitration procedures are often spelled out in the original contract and usually provide for an intermediary who is judged to be impartial by both parties. Frequently, intermediaries will be representatives of chambers of commerce, trade associations, or third-country institutions.

SUMMARY

The political and legal environment in the home and host countries and the laws and agreements governing relationships between nations are important to the international business executive. Compliance is mandatory in order to do business successfully abroad. To avoid the problems that can result from changes in the political and legal environment, it is essential to anticipate changes and to develop strategies for coping with them. Whenever possible, the manager must avoid being taken by surprise and letting events control business decisions.

Governments affect international business through legislation and regulations, which can support or hinder business transactions. An example is when export sanctions or embargoes are imposed to enhance foreign-policy objectives. Similarly, export controls are used to preserve national security. Nations also regulate the international business behavior of firms by setting standards that relate to bribery and corruption, boycotts, and restraint of competition.

Through political actions such as expropriation, confiscation, or domestication, countries expose firms to international risk. Management therefore needs to be aware of the possibility of such risk and alert to new developments. Many private sector services are available to track international risk situations. In the event of a loss, firms may rely on insurance for political risk or they may seek redress in court. International legal action, however, may be quite slow and may compensate for only part of the loss.

Managers need to be aware that different countries have different laws. One clearly pronounced difference is between code-law countries, where all possible legal rules are spelled out, and common-law countries such as the United States, where the law is based on tradition, precedent, and custom.

Managers must also pay attention to international political relations, agreements, and treaties. Changes in relations or rules can mean major new opportunities and occasional threats to international business.

Key Terms and Concepts

international competitiveness	operating risk
extraterritoriality	transfer risk
sanction	expropriation
embargo	confiscation
export-control system	domestication
export license	local content
critical commodities list	intellectual property rights
general license	exchange controls
validated export license	price controls
Coordinating Committee for Multilateral Export Controls (COCOM)	common law
	code law
boycott	lobbyist
antitrust laws	international law
Webb-Pomerene Act	patent
bribery	trademark
Foreign Corrupt Practices Act	Paris Convention for the Protection of Industrial Property
political risk	
ownership risk	arbitration

Questions for Discussion

1. Discuss this potential dilemma: "High political risk requires companies to seek a quick payback on their investments. Striving for a quick payback, however, exposes firms to charges of exploitation and results in increased political risk."

2. How appropriate is it for governments to help drum up business for their companies abroad? Shouldn't commerce be completely separate from politics?

3. Discuss this statement: "The national security that our export-control laws seek to protect may be threatened by the resulting lack of international competitiveness of U.S. firms."

4. Discuss the advantages and disadvantages of common law and code law.

5. Research some examples of multinational corporations that have remained untouched by waves of expropriation. What was their secret to success?

6. The United States has been described as a litigious society. How does frequent litigation affect international business?

7. After you hand your passport to the immigration officer in country X, he misplaces it. A small "donation" would certainly help him find it again. Should you give him the money? Is this a business expense to be charged to your company? Should it be tax deductible?

8. What are your views on lobbying efforts by foreign firms?

Recommended Readings

Bertsch, G.K., and S.E. Gowen, editors. *Export Controls in Transition: Perspectives, Problems, and Prospects.* Durham, N.C.: Duke University Press, 1992.

Carter, Barry E. *International Economic Sanctions.* New York: Cambridge University Press, 1988.

Choate, Pat. *Agents of Influence.* New York: Knopf, 1990.

Czinkota, Michael R., editor. *Export Controls.* New York: Praeger, 1984.

De la Torre, José and David H. Neckar, "Forecasting Political Risks for International Operations," in *Global Strategic Management: The Essentials* (2nd ed.) H. Vernon-Wortzel and L. Wortzel, editors. New York: John Wiley and Sons, 1990.

Export Controls: Multilateral Efforts to Improve Enforcement, United States General Accounting Office, GAO/NSIAD-92-167, Washington, D.C., 1992.

Finding Common Ground: U.S. Export Controls in a Changed Global Environment. Washington, D.C.: National Academy Press, 1991.

Heinz, John, *U.S. Strategic Trade: Export Control Systems for the 1990's.* Boulder, Colo.: Westview Press, 1991.

Hufbauer, Gary Clyde, Diane T. Berlinger, and Kimberly Ann Elliott. *Trade Protection in the United States.* Washington, D.C.: Institute for International Economics, 1986.

Hufbauer, Gary Clyde, and Jeffrey J. Schott. *Economic Sanctions Reconsidered: A History and Current Policy.* Washington, D.C.: Institute for International Economics, 1985.

Jeffries, Francis M. *American Business and International Risk: Past, Present, and Future.* Poolesville, Md.: Jeffries and Associates, 1985.

Notes

1. This section draws from Michael R. Czinkota, "International Economic Sanctions and Trade Controls: A Taxonomic Analysis," in *Export Controls,* ed. M. Czinkota (New York: Praeger, 1984), 3–17.

2. Robin Renwick, *Economic Sanctions* (Cambridge, Mass.: Harvard University Press, 1981), 11.

3. Margaret P. Doxey, *Economic Sanctions and International Enforcement* (New York: Oxford University Press, 1980), 10.

4. Gary Clyde Hufbauer and Jeffrey J. Schott, "Economic Sanctions: An Often Used and Occasionally Effective Tool of Foreign Policy," in *Export Controls,* ed. Michael R. Czinkota (New York: Praeger, 1984), 18–33.

5. Robert M. Springer, Jr., "New Export Law an Aid to International Marketers," *Marketing News,* January 3, 1986, 10, 67.

6. Bureau of Export Administration, U.S. Department of Commerce, Washington, D.C., March 1992.

7. Dan Haendel and Amy L. Rothstein, "The Shifting Focus of Dual Use Export Controls: An Overview of Recent Developments and a Forecast for the Future," *The International Lawyer,* 25, 1, Spring 1991, 267–276.

8. Harvey J. Iglarsh, "Terrorism and Corporate Costs," *Terrorism* 10 (1987): 227–230.

9. Joseph V. Miscallef, "Political Risk Assessment," *Columbia Journal of World Business* 16 (January 1981): 47.

10. Michael Minor, "LDCs, TNCs, and Expropriations in the 1980s," *The CYC Reporter,* Spring 1988, 53.

11. Paul Blustein, "Kawasaki to Pay Additional Taxes to U.S.," *The Washington Post,* December 11, 1992, D1.

12. Personal communication with Overseas Private Investment Corporation, Washington, D.C., 1989.

13. "Japan Still Has Only 12,500 Lawyers," *The Exporter* 6 (September 1986): 18.

14. Surya Prakash Sinha, *What Is Law? The Differing Theories of Jurisprudence* (New York, Paragon House), 1989.

15. James L. Rowe, Jr., "Inflation Slowed, Argentina's Alfonsin Now Tackling Economic Stagnation," *The Washington Post*, July 13, 1986, Gl, G8.

16. Michael R. Czinkota and Jon Woronoff, *Unlocking Japan's Market* (Chicago: Probus Publishing, 1991).

17. Michael R. Czinkota, "International Information Needs for U.S. Competitiveness," *Business Horizons,* 34, 6, November/December 1991, 86–91.

18. Judy Winegar Goans, "Protecting American Intellectual Property Abroad," *Business America,* U.S. Department of Commerce, International Trade Administration, October 27, 1986, 2–7.

The Cultural Challenge

LEARNING OBJECTIVES

1. To define and demonstrate the effect of culture's various dimensions on international business.

2. To examine ways in which cultural knowledge can be acquired and individuals and organizations prepared for cross-cultural interaction.

3. To illustrate ways in which cultural risk poses a challenge to the effective conduct of business communications and transactions.

4. To suggest ways in which international businesses act as change agents in the diverse cultural environments in which they operate.

Business Is Business Around the World, or Is It?

Mr. Smith, the head of a U.S. beverage firm, is involved in negotiations with a Japanese food company to export beer to Japan. Exploratory discussions have already been held with the U.S. representative for the Japanese company. Now Mr. Smith is flying to Japan to discuss details and, preferably, secure an agreement that can be drawn up for signature.

In the United States, he has usually concluded similar deals successfully in a day or two. His habit is to get down to business as soon as possible and not spend a lot of time on preliminaries. He would like to adopt the same approach in Tokyo, so he has allowed only three days for his stay. "Business is business," he says, and, he has been briefed, his Japanese partners are just as interested in the planned cooperation as he is.

Once in Tokyo, Mr. Smith takes the opportunity to begin discussions on the main points of the projected transaction over dinner the first night of his stay. However, instead of definite statements, Mr. Smith hears nothing but friendly and noncommittal conversation. The following day, at his first meeting with the heads of the Japanese company, the situation remains unchanged. In spite of several attempts by Mr. Smith to begin discussions, his counterparts say nothing about the project but instead concentrate on talking about the history, traditions, and ethos of their company. He is also frustrated that only one member of the Japanese group speaks English.

Mr. Smith is irritated. After all, the principle that "time is money" surely must apply everywhere. He finally loses patience when he learns that the afternoon is not devoted to business discussions but has instead been reserved for sightseeing. In despair, he turns to the Japanese with a stern request that they get down to business. After a brief consultation among themselves, the Japanese finally agree to his request. However, contrary to his expectations, the negotiations do not progress as anticipated. They proceed without any definite statements, let alone promises, and no conclusions are reached. The fact that he puts forward specific proposals makes no difference. After three days of frustration and little progress, Mr. Smith flies home without having achieved anything, or so he feels. He feels he was well prepared to discuss any aspect of the business deal, and yet nothing happened.

Preparation, however, is needed not only in the business sense but in a cultural sense as well. Just a few of the potential areas in which Mr. Smith was not prepared include: (1) insufficient understanding of different ways of thinking; (2) insufficient attention to the necessity to save face; (3) insufficient knowledge and appreciation of the host country—history, culture, government, and image of foreigners; (4) insufficient recognition of the decision-making process and the role of personal relations and personalities; and (5) insufficient allocation of time for negotiations.

Source: Sergey Frank, "Global Negotiations: Vive Les Differences!" *Sales & Marketing Management* 144 (May 1992): 64–69; and Sergey Frank, "Avoiding the Pitfalls of Business Abroad," *Sales & Marketing Management* 144 (March 1992): 48–52.

As seen in the opening vignette, the world has become smaller as a result of improvements in transportation and information systems, but the behavioral patterns, values, and attitudes that govern human interaction may still remain relatively unchanged. Technological innovation is bringing about the internationalization of business, and individuals at all levels of the firm are becoming involved in cross-cultural interaction. Firms expanding internationally acquire foreign clients as well as foreign personnel with whom regular communication is necessary, with the result that day-to-day operations require significant cross-cultural competence. As the distinction between domestic and international activities diminishes, cultural sensitivity in varying degrees is required from every employee.

In the past, business managers who did not want to worry about the cultural challenge could simply decide not to do so and concentrate on domestic markets. In today's business environment, a company has no choice but to face international competition. In this new environment, believing that concern about cultural elements is a waste of time often proves to be disastrous.

Cultural differences often are the subject of anecdotes, and business blunders may provide a good laugh. Cultural incompetence, however, can easily jeopardize millions of dollars through wasted negotiations, lost purchases, sales, and contracts, and poor customer relations. Furthermore, the internal efficiency of a multinational corporation may be weakened if managers and workers are not "on the same wavelength." **Cultural risk** is just as real as political risk in the international business arena.

The intent of this chapter is first to analyze the concept of culture and its various elements and then to provide suggestions for meeting the cultural challenge. Culture does, after all, affect each and every aspect of business.

CULTURE DEFINED

Culture gives an individual an anchoring point, an identity, as well as codes of conduct. Of the more than 160 definitions of culture analyzed by Kroeber and Kluckhohn, some conceive of culture as separating humans from nonhumans, some define it as communicable knowledge, and some as the sum of historical achievements produced by man's social life.[1] All of the definitions have common elements: Culture is learned, shared, and transmitted from one generation to the next. Culture is primarily passed on from parents to their children but also transmitted by social organizations, special interest groups, the government, the schools, and the church. Common ways of thinking and behaving that are developed are then reinforced through social pressure. Hofstede calls this the "collective programming of the mind."[2] Culture is also multidimensional, consisting of a number of common elements that are interdependent. Changes occurring in one of the dimensions will affect the others as well.

For the purposes of this text, culture is defined as an integrated system of learned behavior patterns that are characteristic of the members of any given society. It includes everything that a group thinks, says, does, and makes—its customs, language, material artifacts, and shared systems of attitudes and feelings.[3] The definition, therefore, encompasses a wide variety of elements from the materialistic to the spiritual. Culture is inherently conservative, resisting change and fostering continuity. Every person is encultured into a particular culture, learning the "right way" of doing things. Problems may arise when a person encultured in one culture has to adjust to another one. The process of **acculturation**—adjusting and adapting to a specific culture other than one's own—is one of the keys to success in international operations.

Edward T. Hall, who has made some of the most valuable studies on the effects of culture on business, makes a distinction between high- and low-context cultures.[4] In **high-context cultures,** such as Japan and Saudi Arabia, context is at least as important as what is actually said. The speaker and the listener rely on a common understanding of the context. In the **low-context cultures,** however, most of the information is contained explicitly in the words. North American cultures engage in low-context communications. Unless one is aware of this basic difference, messages and intentions can easily be misunderstood. As an example, performance appraisals are typically a human resources function. If performance appraisals are to be centrally guided or conducted in a multinational corporation, those involved must be acutely aware of cultural nuances. One of the interesting differences is that the U.S. system emphasizes the individual's development, whereas the Japanese system focuses on the group within which the individual works. In the United States, criticism is more direct and recorded formally, whereas in Japan it is more subtle and verbal. What is not being said can carry more meaning than what is said.

Few cultures today are as homogeneous as those of Japan and Saudi Arabia. Elsewhere intracultural differences based on nationality, religion, race, or geographic areas have resulted in the emergence of distinct subcultures. The international manager's task is to distinguish relevant cross-cultural and intracultural differences and then to isolate potential opportunities and problems. Good examples are the Hispanic subculture in the United States and the Flemish and the Walloons in Belgium. On the other hand, borrowing and interaction between national cultures may lead to narrowing gaps between cultures. Here the international business entity will act as a **change agent** by introducing new products or ideas and practices. Although this may consist of no more than shifting consumption from one product brand to another, it may lead to massive social change in the manner of consumption, the type of products consumed, and social organization. Consider, for example, that in a 10-year period the international portion of McDonald's annual sales grew from 13 percent to 23 percent. In markets such as Taiwan, the entry of McDonald's and other fast food entities dramatically changed eating habits, especially of the younger generation.

In bringing about change or in trying to cater to increasingly homogeneous demand across markets, the international business entity may be accused of "cultural imperialism," especially if the changes brought about are dramatic or if culture-specific adaptations are not made in management or marketing programs. This is highlighted by the experience of Disney's expansion into Europe in Global Perspective 9.1.

THE ELEMENTS OF CULTURE

The study of culture has led to generalizations that may apply to all cultures. Such characteristics are called **cultural universals,** which are manifestations of the total way of life of any group of people. These include such elements as bodily adornments, courtship rituals, etiquette, concept of family, gestures, joking, mealtime customs, music, personal names, status differentiation, and trade customs.[5] These activities occur across cultures, but they may be uniquely manifested in a particular society, bringing about cultural diversity. Common denominators can indeed be found across cultures, but cultures may vary dramatically in how they perform the same activities.[6]

Observation of the major cultural elements summarized in Table 9.1 suggests that these elements are both material (such as tools) and abstract (such as attitudes). The sensitivity and adaptation to these elements by an international firm depends on the firm's level of involvement in the market—for example, licensing versus direct investment—and the product or service marketed. Naturally, some products and services or management practices require very little adjustment, while some have to be adapted dramatically.

TABLE 9.1
Elements of Culture

Language
    Verbal
    Nonverbal
Religion
Values and attitudes
Manners and customs
Material elements
Aesthetics
Education
Social institutions

Global Perspective

9.1
An American Park in Paris

EuroDisneyland, the world's biggest and splashiest theme park, opened April 12, 1992, about 20 miles east of Paris. There, tourists from throughout Europe can greet Mickey Mouse, explore Adventure Island, and have an all-American good time. According to Robert J. Fitzpatrick, chairman of Euro-Disneyland, the park will "help change Europe's chemistry."

Not everyone is as excited about the park's prospects. Many critics in France, which is viewed as half the theme park's market, are downright hostile. The criticisms have ranged from "not Europe's cup of tea" to a "cultural Chernobyl." Besides criticizing the cultural imperialism of the venture, many doubt that Europeans will seek an entertainment experience in the suburbs of Paris. The diversity of European tastes and the grim winter weather in Paris also are expected to cut into EuroDisneyland's projected attendance and sales.

In an effort to overcome some of these obstacles, Disney is seeking to maintain a high profile on television. The company has fixed weekly slots for such series as "Adventures of the Gummi Bears," "Duck Tales," and "Rescue Rangers." The "Disney Club" has become a staple of Sunday-morning viewing in most of continental Europe. The company is also addressing the climate problem with such adaptations as a glass dome to cover the teacup ride, and it plans to advertise the park as the "warmest place in Paris."

One adaptation Disney has refrained from making is to serve liquor in the park. However, admit Disney officials, if customers are insistent, the park will probably serve wine and beer. The company has already made a few concessions in its strict grooming code. For example, women employees may wear redder nail polish than is permitted in the United States. However, men must abide by the company's prohibition of facial hair.

Other cultural challenges have arisen in the training of the 12,000 employees, half of them French, who are to serve as Disney "cast members." Disney emphasized that a central part of employees' role is to make each visitor to the park feel like a VIP. Thus, Disney University (which operates in each Disney park) provides a course in Disney culture as well as specific job training. According to trainers, those in the EuroDisneyland classes need more explanations. For example, a group of French students spent 20 minutes discussing how to define "efficiency."

Whereas opening a theme park in France involves much concern about French reluctance to embrace American popular culture, the experience in Japan has been much different. Tokyo Disneyland reflects the Japanese fascination with things American. All the signs are in English, most of the food is American style, and the attractions are identical to those in Disney's U.S. parks. "Everything we imported that worked in the U.S. works here," reports Ronald D. Pogue, managing director of Walt Disney Attractions Japan Ltd.

But even the Japanese park had to make adjustments to accommodate local tastes. The park includes a Japanese restaurant, which caters to the park's older visitors. And even though Tokyo Disneyland is a thoroughly American creation, its cleanliness, order, outstanding service, and technological marvels appeal to Japanese values.

Industry experts observe that the U.S. market for theme parks is already saturated, but Disney's international ventures are building interest in this type of entertainment in other countries, particularly in Europe and the Far East. These international theme parks may help cultivate—and benefit from—a global popular culture among young people.

Source: "Disneyn Eurohiirenloukku," *Helsingin Sanomat,* March 21, 1992, 6–7; Sara Khalili, "Is This Another Japanese 'Goofy' Investment?" *North American International Business,* February 1991, 74–75, 78; "An American in Paris," *Business Week,* March 12, 1990, 60–64; John Huey, "America's Hottest Export: Pop Culture," *Fortune,* December 31, 1990, 50–60; "In Japan, They're Goofy about Disney," *Business Week,* March 12, 1990, 64.

Language

Language has been described as the mirror of culture. Language itself is multidimensional by nature. This is true not only of the spoken word but also of what can be called the nonverbal language of international business. Messages are conveyed by the words used, by how the words are spoken (for example, tone of voice), and through nonverbal means such as gestures, body position, and eye contact.

Very often mastery of the language is required before a person is accultured to a culture other than his or her own. Language mastery must go beyond technical competency because every language has words and phrases that can be readily understood only in context. Such phrases are carriers of culture; they represent special ways a culture has developed to view some aspect of human existence.

Language capability serves four distinct roles in international business.[7] Language is important in information gathering and evaluation. Rather than rely completely on the opinions of others, the manager is able to see and hear personally what is going on. People are far more comfortable speaking their own language, and this should be treated as an advantage. The best intelligence on a market is gathered by becoming part of the market rather than observing it from the outside. For example, local managers of a multinational corporation should be the firm's primary source of political information to assess potential risk. Second, language provides access to local society. Although English may be widely spoken and may even be the official company language, speaking the local language may make a dramatic difference. Third, language capability is increasingly important in company communications, whether within the corporate family or with channel members. Imagine the difficulties encountered by a country manager who must communicate with employees through an interpreter. Finally, language provides more than the ability to communicate. It extends beyond mechanics to the interpretation of contexts.

The manager's command of the national language(s) in a market must be greater than simple word recognition. Consider, for example, how dramatically different English terms can be when used in Australia, the United Kingdom, or the United States. In negotiations, U.S. delegates "tabling a proposal" mean that they want to delay a decision, while their British counterparts understand the expression to mean that immediate action is to be taken. If the British promise something "by the end of the day," this does not mean within 24 hours, but rather when they have completed the job. Additionally, they may say that negotiations "bombed," meaning that they were a success, which to an American could convey exactly the opposite message.

An example of this separation of Americans and British by the same language is provided in Figure 9.1. Electrolux's theme in marketing its vacuum cleaners is interpreted in the United Kingdom without connotations, while in the United States the slang implications would earn the campaign blunder honors. Similar problems occur with other languages and markets. Swedish is spoken as a mother tongue by 8 percent of the population in Finland, where it has idioms that are not well understood by Swedes.

Difficulties with language usually arise through carelessness, which is manifested in a number of translation blunders. The old saying, "If you want to kill a message, translate it," is true. A classic example involves GM and its "Body by Fisher" theme; when translated into Flemish, this became "Corpse by Fisher."[8] Braniff Airlines' "Fly in Leather" was translated as "Fly Naked" for the company's Latin American campaign. There is also the danger of sound-alikes. For example, Chanel No. 5 would have fared poorly in Japan had it been called Chanel No. 4, because the Japanese word for four (shih) also sounds like the word for death. This is the reason that IBM's series 44 computers had a different number classification in Japan than in any other market. The danger of using a translingual homonym also exists; that is, an innocent English word may have strong aural resemblance to a word not used in polite company in another country. Examples in French-speaking areas include Pet milk products and a toothpaste called Cue. A French firm trying to sell pâté to a Baltimore importer experienced a prob-

FIGURE 9.1
Example of an Ad That Will Transfer Poorly

Source: "Viewpoint: Letters," *Advertising Age,* June 29, 1987, 20.

lem with the brand name Tartex, which sounded like shoe polish. Kellogg renamed Bran Buds in Sweden, where the brand name translated roughly to "burned farmer."

Another consideration is the capability of language to convey different shades of meaning. As an example, a one-word equivalent to "aftertaste" does not exist in many languages and in others is far-fetched at best. To communicate the idea may require a lengthy translation of "the taste that remains in your mouth after you have finished eating or drinking."

The role of language extends beyond that of a communications medium. Linguistic diversity often is an indicator of other types of diversity. In Quebec, the French language has always been a major consideration of most francophone governments, because it is one of the clear manifestations of the identity of the province vis-à-vis the English-speaking provinces. The Charter of the French Language states that the rights of the francophone collectivity are (1) the right of every person to have the civil administration, semipublic agencies, and business firms communicate with him or her in French; (2) the right of workers to carry on their activities in French; and (3) the right of consumers to be informed and served in French. The Bay, a major Quebec retailer, spends $8 million annually on its translation operations. It has even changed its name to La Baie in appropriate areas.

If a brand name or an advertising theme is to be extended, care has to be taken to make sure of a comfortable fit. Kellogg's Rice Krispies snap, crackle, and pop in most markets; the Japanese, who have trouble pronouncing these words, watch the caricatures "patchy, pitchy, putchy" in their commercials.

Dealing with the language problem invariably requires local assistance. A good local advertising agency and a good local market-research firm can prevent many problems. When translation is required, as when communicating with suppliers or customers, care should be taken in selecting the translator. One of the simplest methods of control is **backtranslation**—the translating of a foreign-language version back to the original language by a different person than the one who made the first translation.

Nonverbal Language

Managers also must analyze and become familiar with the hidden language of foreign cultures.[9] Five key topics—time, space, material possessions, friendship patterns, and business agreements—offer a starting point from which managers can begin to acquire the understanding necessary to do business in foreign countries. In many parts of the world, time is flexible and not seen as a limited commodity; people come late to appointments or may not come at all. In Hong Kong, for example, it is futile to set exact meeting times, because getting from one place to another may take minutes or hours depending on the traffic situation. Showing indignation or impatience at such behavior would astonish an Arab, Latin American, or Asian. Understanding national and cultural differences in the concept of time is critical for the international business manager, as seen in the opening vignette of this chapter.

In some countries, extended social acquaintance and the establishment of appropriate personal rapport are essential to conducting business. The feeling is that one should know one's business partner on a personal level before transactions can occur. Therefore, rushing straight to business will not be rewarded, because deals are made on the basis of not only the best product or price but also the entity or person deemed most trustworthy. Contracts may be bound on handshakes, not lengthy and complex agreements—a fact that makes some, especially Western, businesspeople uneasy.

Individuals vary in the amount of space they want separating them from others. Arabs and Latin Americans like to stand close to people they are talking with. If an American, who may not be comfortable at such close range, backs away from an Arab, this might incorrectly be taken as a negative reaction. Also, Westerners are often taken aback by the more physical nature of affection between Slavs—for example, being kissed squarely on the lips by a business partner, regardless of sex.

International body language must be included in the nonverbal language of international business. For example, an American manager may, after successful completion of negotiations, impulsively give a finger-and-thumb OK sign. In southern France, the manager will have indicated that the sale is worthless, and in Japan, that a little bribe has been asked for, while the gesture is grossly insulting to Brazilians. An interesting exercise is to compare and contrast the conversation styles of different nationalities. Northern Europeans are quite reserved in using their hands and maintain a good amount of personal space, whereas southern Europeans involve their bodies to a far greater degree in making a point.

Religion

Every culture finds its legitimacy in being part of a larger context. Most cultures find in religion a reason for being. To define religion requires the inclusion of the supernatural and the existence of a higher being.

Religion can provide the basis for transcultural similarities under shared beliefs in Islam, Buddhism, or Christianity, for example. An obvious example of the effect on international business of religious beliefs is the prohibition of pork products and alcoholic beverages in the Middle East. When beef or poultry is exported to a Muslim country, the animal must be killed in the "halal" method. Currently 12 Islamic centers slaughter and certify meat for export. Recognition of religious restrictions can reveal opportunities as well as liabilities, as evidenced by the recent successful launch of several nonalcoholic beverages in some Middle Eastern countries. Islam requires extensive fasting during the holy month of Ramadan, the start and duration of which vary because the lunar year is 11 to 12 days shorter than that based on the Gregorian calendar. The impact of religion may vary from one country to another in a given region, on the other hand. One of the Muslim countries, Tunisia, has discouraged its people from too diligent an observance to avoid marked drops in productivity. Another major characteristic is the pilgrimage to Mecca, which has required the Saudi Arabian government to improve its transportation system. A problem of the Swedish firm that had primary responsibility for building a traffic system to Mecca was that non-Muslims are not allowed access to the sacred place. The solution was to use closed-circuit television to supervise the work.

Major holidays are often tied to religion. These holidays will be observed differently from one culture to the next, to the extent that the same holiday may have different connotations. Most Western cultures, because they are predominantly Christian, observe Christmas and exchange gifts on either December 24 or December 25. However, the Dutch exchange gifts on St. Nicholas Day (December 6) and the Russians on Frost Man's Day (January 1). Tandy Corporation, in its first year in Holland, targeted its major advertising campaign for the third week of December, with disastrous results. The international manager must see to it that local holidays are taken into account in the scheduling of events ranging from fact-finding missions to marketing programs and in preparing local work schedules.

The role of women in business is tied to religion, especially in the Middle East, where they are not able to function as they would in the West. This affects management in two ways: The firm may not be able to use women managers or personnel in certain countries, and women's role as consumers and influencers in the consumption process may be altogether different. Access to women in Islamic countries, for example, may only be possible through the use of female sales personnel, direct marketing, and women's specialty shops.[10]

International human resource managers must be aware of religious divisions in the countries of operation. The impact of these divisions may range from hostilities, as in Sri Lanka, to below-the-surface suspicion—for example, in many European markets where Protestant and Catholic are the main religious divisions.

Values and Attitudes

Values are shared beliefs or group norms that have been internalized by individuals.[11] Attitudes are evaluations of alternatives based on these values. The Japanese culture raises an almost invisible—yet often unscalable—wall against all *gaijin* (foreigners). Many middle-aged bureaucrats and company officials, for example, feel that buying foreign products is downright unpatriotic. The resistance therefore is not so much to foreign products as to those who produce and market them. Similarly, foreign-based corporations have had difficulty in hiring university graduates or mid-career personnel because of bias against foreign employers.

Even under these adverse conditions, the race can be run and won through tenacity, patience, and drive. As an example, Procter & Gamble has made impressive inroads with its products by adopting a long-term, Japanese-style view of profits. Since the mid-1970s, the company has gained some 20 percent of the detergent market and made Pampers a household word among Japanese mothers. The struggle toward such rewards can require foreign companies to take big losses for five years or more.

Religions of the World: A Part of Culture

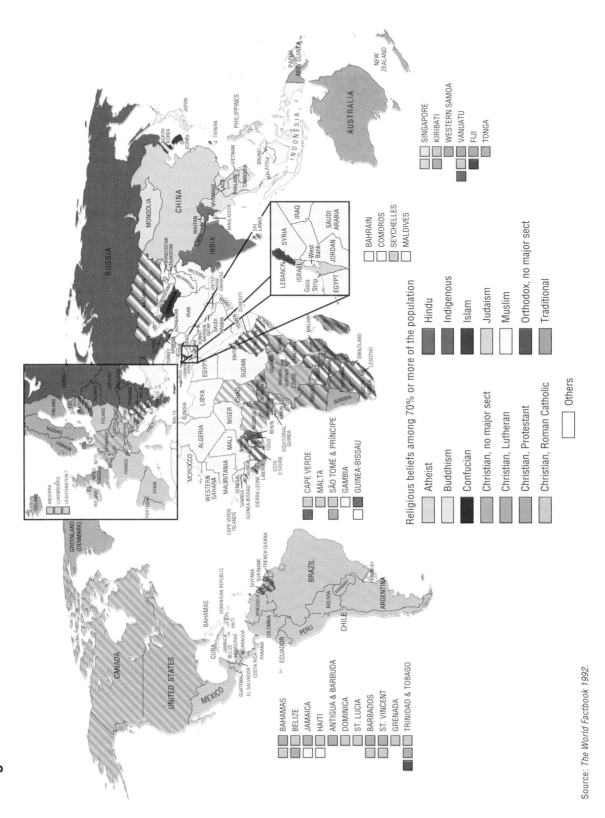

Source: *The World Factbook 1992.*

The more rooted that values and attitudes are in central beliefs (such as religion), the more cautiously the international business manager has to move. Attitudes toward change are basically positive in industrialized countries, whereas in more tradition-bound societies, change is viewed with great suspicion—especially when it comes from a foreign entity. These situations call for thorough research, most likely a localized approach, and a major commitment at the top level for a considerable period of time.

Cultural differences in themselves can be a selling point suggesting luxury, prestige, or status. Sometimes U.S. companies use domestic-marketing approaches when selling abroad because they believe the American look will sell the product. In Japan, Borden sells Lady Borden ice cream and Borden cheese deliberately packaged and labeled in English, exactly as they are in the United States. Similarly, in France, General Foods sells a chewing gum called Hollywood with an accompanying Pepsi-generation type of ad campaign that pictures teenagers riding bicycles on the beach.

Occasionally, U.S. firms successfully use American themes abroad that would not succeed at home. In Japan, Levi Strauss promoted its popular jeans with a television campaign featuring James Dean and Marilyn Monroe, who represent the epitome of Japanese youth's fantasy of freedom from a staid, traditional society. The commercials helped to establish Levi's as *the* prestige jeans, and status-seeking Japanese youth now willingly pay 40 percent more for them than for local brands. Their authentic Levi's, however, are designed and mostly made in Japan, where buyers like a tighter fit than do Americans.[12] At the same time, in the U.S. market many companies have been quite successful emphasizing their foreign, imported image.

Manners and Customs

Changes occurring in manners and customs must be carefully monitored, especially in cases that seem to indicate a narrowing of cultural differences between peoples. Phenomena such as McDonald's and Coke have met with success around the world, but this does not mean that the world is becoming Westernized. Modernization and Westernization are not at all the same, as can be seen in Saudi Arabia, for example.

Understanding manners and customs is especially important in negotiations, because interpretations based on one's own frame of reference may lead to a totally incorrect conclusion. To negotiate effectively abroad, all types of communication should be read correctly. Americans often interpret inaction and silence as negative signs. As a result, Japanese executives tend to expect that their silence can get Americans to lower prices or sweeten the deal. Even a simple agreement may take days to negotiate in the Middle East because the Arab party may want to talk about unrelated issues or do something else for a while. The abrasive style of Russian negotiators and their usual last-minute change requests may cause astonishment and concern on the part of ill-prepared negotiators. As another example, consider the reaction of an American businessperson if a Finnish counterpart were to propose the continuing of negotiations in the sauna.

In many cultures, certain basic customs must be observed by the foreign businessperson. One of them concerns use of the right and left hands. In so-called right-hand societies, the left hand is the "toilet hand," and using it to eat, for example, is considered impolite. While many managers have caught on to cultural differences in the past decade or so, continued attention to details when approaching companies or when negotiating with their officials is necessary.

Campbell Soup positioned Swanson Chicken Broth as a base for Chinese meals in order to gain consumer acceptance in Hong Kong, Taiwan, and mainland China.

Source: Courtesy of Campbell Soup Company.

Managers must be concerned with differences in the ways products are used. For example, General Food's Tang is positioned as a breakfast drink in the United States; in France, where orange juice usually is not consumed at breakfast, Tang is positioned as a refreshment. The questions that the international manager must ask are: "What are we selling?" and "What are the use benefits we should be providing?"

Usage differences have to be translated into product form and promotional decisions. Maxwell House coffee is a worldwide brand name. It is used to sell coffee in both ground and instant form in the United States. In the United Kingdom, Maxwell House is available only in instant form. In France and Germany, it is sold in freeze-dried form only, while in the Scandinavian countries Maxwell House is positioned as the top-of-the-line entry. As a matter of fact, Maxwell House is called simply Maxwell in France and Japan, because "House" is confusing to consumers in those countries. In one South American market, a shampoo maker was concerned about poor sales of the entire product class. Research uncovered the fact that many women wash their hair with bars of soap and use shampoo only as a brief rinse or topper.

Many Western companies have stumbled in Japan because they did not learn enough about the distinctive habits of Japanese consumers. Purveyors of soup should know that the Japanese drink it mainly for breakfast. Johnson & Johnson had relatively little success in selling baby powder until research was conducted on the use conditions of the product. In their small homes, mothers fear that powder will fly around and get into their spotlessly clean kitchens. The company now sells baby powder in flat boxes with powder puffs so that mothers can apply it sparingly. Adults will not use it at all. They wash and rinse themselves before soaking in hot baths; powder would make them feel dirty again. Another classic case involves General Mills' Betty Crocker cake mix. The company designed a mix to be prepared in electric rice cookers. After the product's costly flop, the company found that the Japanese take pride in the purity of their rice, which they thought would be contaminated by cake flavors. General Mills' mistake was comparable to asking an English housewife to make coffee in her teapot.

Package sizes and labels must be adapted in many countries to suit the needs of the particular culture. In Mexico, for example, Campbell's sells soup in cans large enough to serve four or five because families are generally large. In Britain, where con-

Global Perspective

9.2
Bad Chemistry

It's out! The Hotel Conrad's trademark structure, the giant bronze sculpture 'Hong Kong People' (picture below) was removed from the hotel's lobby—on the orders of a fung shui man. The Conrad in Hong Kong is part of the Hilton Hotels' international operations. (Hilton has not been able to use the Hilton name in its international facilities after selling Hilton International in 1972). The reason hotel management brought in the traditional "consultant" was that occupancy rates were at unsatisfactory levels.

Fung shui men are foretellers of future events and the unknown through occult means, and they are used extensively by Hong Kong businesses when plans for new buildings are being made, for example. The fees that these individuals charge are considerable.

In this case, the 16-figure statue, which includes a replica of former governor Lord Wilson, is being taken away because it is "not good" for business, according to the sage. In fact, it is "too busy" for the lobby, and the final character, a man racing off the end of the tableau, looks like he is trying to "run out of the hotel." 'Hong Kong People' also includes life-sized depictions of a businessman on his mobile phone, a woman shopping, and an old man with a caged bird.

So the sculpture was placed outside of the building. "The fung shui man told us it would create more activity outside the hotel, which would be good for business," said the Hotel Conrad spokesperson. A new painting was unveiled inside the foyer the same day the statue was removed.

If the predictions hold true, the hotel should be in for a boom time. The latter half of 1992 the hotel ran at a high occupancy level.

Source: "Fung Shui Man Orders Sculpture Out of Hotel," *South China Morning Post,* July 27, 1992, 4. Photo © South China Morning Post, Ltd.

sumers are more accustomed to ready-to-serve soups, Campbell's prints "one can makes two" on its condensed soup labels to ensure that shoppers understand how to use it.

Managers must be careful of myths and legends. One candy company had almost decided to launch a new peanut-packed chocolate bar in Japan, aimed at giving teenagers quick energy during the cramming for exams. The company then found out about the Japanese old wives' tale that eating chocolate with peanuts can cause a nosebleed. The launch never took place. Similarly, approaches that would not be considered in the United States or Europe might be recommended in other regions, as shown in Global Perspective 9.2.

Meticulous research plays a major role in avoiding these types of problems. Concept tests determine the potential acceptance and proper understanding of a proposed new product. **Focus groups,** each consisting of 8 to 12 consumers representative of the proposed target audience, can be interviewed and their responses used as disaster checks and to fine-tune research findings. The most sensitive types of products, such as consumer packaged goods, require consumer usage and attitude studies as well as retail distribution studies and audits to analyze the movement of the product to retailers and eventually to households.

Material Elements

Material culture refers to the results of technology and is directly related to how a society organizes its economic activity. It is manifested in the availability and adequacy of the basic economic, social, financial, and marketing infrastructure for the international business in a market. The basic **economic infrastructure** consists of transportation, energy, and communications systems. **Social infrastructure** refers to housing, health, and educational systems prevailing in the country of interest. **Financial** and **marketing infrastructures** provide the facilitating agencies for the international firm's operation in a given market—for example, banks and research firms. In some parts of the world, the international firm may have to be an integral partner in developing the various infrastructures before it can operate, whereas in others it may greatly benefit from their high level of sophistication.

The level of material culture can aid segmentation efforts if the degree of industrialization is used as a basis. For companies selling industrial goods, such as General Electric, this can provide a convenient starting point. In developing countries, demand may be highest for basic energy-generating products. In fully developed markets, time-saving home appliances may be more in demand.

Technological advances have probably been the major cause of cultural change in many countries. For example, the increase in leisure time so characteristic in Western cultures has been a direct result of technological development. With technological advancement comes also **cultural convergence.** Black-and-white television sets extensively penetrated U.S. households more than a decade before similar levels occurred in Europe and Japan. With color television, the lag was reduced to five years. With video-cassette recorders, the difference was only three years, but this time the Europeans and the Japanese led the way while the United States was concentrating on cable systems. With the compact disc, penetration rates were equal in only one year. Today, with MTV available by satellite across Europe, no lag exists.[13]

Material culture—mainly the degree to which it exists and how it is esteemed—will have an impact on business decisions. Many exporters do not understand the degree to which Americans are package conscious; for example, cans must be shiny and beautiful. In foreign markets, packaging problems may arise due to the lack of certain materials, different specifications when the material is available, and immense differences in quality and consistency of printing ink, especially in South America and the Third World. Ownership levels of television sets and radios will have an impact on the ability of media to reach target audiences.

Aesthetics

Each culture makes a clear statement concerning good taste, as expressed in the arts and in the particular symbolism of colors, form, and music. What is and what is not acceptable may vary dramatically even in otherwise highly similar markets. Sex, for example, is a big selling point in many countries. In an apparent attempt to preserve the purity of Japanese womanhood, however, advertisers frequently turn to blond, blue-eyed foreign models to make the point. In the same vein, Commodore International, the U.S.-based personal computer manufacturer, chose to sell computers in Germany by showing a naked young man in ads that ran in the German version of *Cosmopolitan.* Needless to say, approaches of this kind would not be possible in the United States because of regulations and opposition from consumer groups.

Color is often used as a mechanism for brand identification, feature reinforcement, and differentiation. In international markets, colors have more symbolic value than in domestic markets. Black, for instance, is considered the color of mourning in the United States and Europe, whereas white has the same symbolic meaning in Japan and most of the Far East. A British bank was interested in expanding its operations to Singapore and wanted to use blue and green as its identification colors. A consulting firm was quick to tell the client that green is associated with death in that country. Although the bank insisted on its original choice of colors, the green was changed to an acceptable shade.[14] Similarly, music used in broadcast advertisements is often adjusted to reflect regional differences.

International firms, such as McDonald's, have to take into consideration local tastes and concerns in designing their facilities. They may have a general policy of uniformity in building or office space design, but local tastes often warrant modifications.

Education

Education, either formal or informal, plays a major role in the passing on and sharing of culture. Educational levels of a culture can be assessed using literacy rates, enrollment in secondary education, or enrollment in higher education available from secondary data sources. International firms also need to know about the qualitative aspects of education, namely varying emphases on particular skills and the overall level of the education provided. Japan and South Korea, for example, emphasize the sciences, especially engineering, to a greater degree than do Western countries.

Educational levels will have an impact on various business functions. Training programs for a production facility will have to take the educational backgrounds of trainees into account. For example, a high level of illiteracy will suggest the use of visual aids rather than printed manuals. Local recruiting for sales jobs will be affected by the availability of suitably trained personnel. In some cases, international firms routinely send locally recruited personnel to headquarters for training.

The international manager may also have to be prepared to overcome obstacles in recruiting a suitable sales force or support personnel. For example, the Japanese culture places a premium on loyalty, and employees consider themselves members of the corporate family. If a foreign firm decides to leave Japan, its employees may find themselves stranded in mid-career, unable to find their place in the Japanese business system. Therefore, university graduates are reluctant to join any but the largest and most well known of foreign firms.[15]

If technology is marketed, the level of sophistication of the product will depend on the educational level of future users. Product-adaptation decisions are often influenced by the extent to which targeted customers are able to use the product or service properly.

Social Institutions

Social institutions affect the ways people relate to each other. The family unit, which in Western industrialized countries consists of parents and children, in a number of cultures is extended to include grandparents and other relatives. This will have an impact on consumption patterns and must be taken into account, for example, when conducting market research.

The concept of kinship, or blood relations between individuals, is defined in a very broad way in societies such as those in sub-Saharan Africa. Family relations and a strong obligation to family are important factors to be considered in human-resource management in those regions. Understanding tribal politics in countries such as Nigeria may help the manager avoid unnecessary complications in executing business transactions.

The division of a particular population into classes is termed **social stratification.** Stratification ranges from the situation in northern Europe, where most people are members of the middle class, to highly stratified societies in which the higher strata control most of the buying power and decision-making positions.

An important part of the socialization process of consumers worldwide is **reference groups.**[16] These groups provide the values and attitudes that influence and shape behavior. Primary reference groups include the family and coworkers and other intimate acquaintances, while secondary groups are social organizations where less-continuous interaction takes place, such as professional associations and trade organizations. In addition to providing socialization, reference groups develop a person's concept of self, which is manifested, for example, through the choice of products used. Reference groups also provide a baseline for compliance with group norms, giving the individual the option of conforming to or avoiding certain behaviors.

Social organization also determines the roles of managers and subordinates and how they relate to one another. In some cultures, managers and subordinates are separated explicitly and implicitly by various boundaries ranging from social-class differences to separate office facilities. In others, cooperation is elicited through equality. For example, Nissan USA has no privileged parking spaces and no private dining rooms, everyone wears the same type of white coveralls, and the president sits in the same room with a hundred other white-collar workers.[17] The fitting of an organizational culture to the larger context of a national culture has to be executed with care. Changes that are too dramatic may cause disruption of productivity or, at the minimum, suspicion.

SOURCES OF CULTURAL KNOWLEDGE

The concept of cultural knowledge is broad and multifaceted. Cultural knowledge can be defined by the way it is acquired. Objective or factual information is obtained from others through communication, research, and education. **Experiential knowledge,** on the other hand, can be acquired only by being involved in a culture other than one's own.[18] A summary of the types of knowledge needed by the international manager is provided in Table 9.2. Both factual and experiential information can be general or country-specific. In fact, the more a manager becomes involved in the international arena, the more he or she is able to develop a metaknowledge; that is, ground rules that apply to a great extent whether in Kuala Lumpur, Malaysia, or Asunción, Paraguay. Market-specific knowledge does not necessarily travel well; the general variables on which the information is based, do.

In a survey of managers on how to acquire international expertise, they ranked eight factors in terms of their importance, as shown in Table 9.3. These managers emphasized the experiential acquisition of knowledge. Written materials were indicated to play an important but supplementary role, very often providing general or country-specific information before operational decisions must be made. Interest-

TABLE 9.2
Types of International Information

Source of Information	Type of Information	
	General	Country Specific
Objective	Examples: Impact of GDP Regional integration	Examples: Tariff barriers Government regulations
Experiential	Example: Corporate adjustment to internationalization	Examples: Product acceptance Program appropriateness

TABLE 9.3
Managers' Ranking of Factors Involved in Acquiring International Expertise

Factor	Considered Critical	Considered Important
1. Business travel	60.8%	92.0%
2. Assignments overseas	48.8	71.2
3. Reading/Television	16.0	63.2
4. Training programs	6.4	28.8
5. Precareer activities	4.0	16.0
6. Graduate course	2.4	15.2
7. Nonbusiness travel	0.8	12.8
8. Undergraduate courses	0.8	12.0

Source: Stephen J. Kobrin, *International Expertise in American Business* (New York: Institute of International Education, 1984), 38.

ingly, many of today's international managers have precareer experience in government, the Peace Corps, the armed forces, or missionary service. Although the survey emphasized travel, a one-time trip to London with a stay at a very large hotel and scheduled sightseeing tours does not contribute to cultural knowledge in a significant way. Travel that involves meetings with company personnel, intermediaries, facilitating agents, customers, and government officials, on the other hand, does contribute.[19]

A variety of sources and methods are available to the manager for extending his or her knowledge of specific cultures. Most of these sources deal with factual information that provides a necessary basis for market studies. Beyond the normal business literature and its anecdotal information, specific-country studies are published by the U.S. government, private companies, and universities. *Country Studies* are available for 108 countries from the U.S. Government Printing Office, while *Country Updates,* produced by Overseas Briefing Associates, feature 22 countries. *Information Guide for Doing Business in X* is the basic title for a series of publications produced by Price Waterhouse and Co.; so far, 48 countries are included. *Brief Culturegrams* for 63 countries and the more extensive *Building Bridges for Understanding with the People of X* are published by the Language and Intercultural Research Center of Brigham Young University.[20] Many facilitating agencies—such as banks, advertising agencies, and transportation companies—provide background information for their clients on the markets they serve. One of the more attractive sources is provided by the Hong Kong and Shanghai Banking Corporation, which has a *Business Profile Series* that is especially good for the Middle East.

Blunders in foreign markets that could have been avoided with factual information are generally inexcusable. A manager who travels to Taipei without first obtaining a visa and is therefore turned back has no one else to blame. Other oversights may lead to more costly mistakes. For example, Brazilians are several inches shorter than the average American, but this was not taken into account when Sears erected American-height shelves that block Brazilian shoppers' view of the rest of the store.

International business success requires not only comprehensive fact finding and preparation but also an ability to understand and appreciate fully the nuances of different cultural traits and patterns. Gaining this readiness requires "getting one's feet wet" over a sufficient length of time.

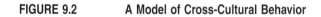

CULTURAL ANALYSIS

To try to understand and explain differences among cultures and subsequently in cross-cultural behavior, checklists and models showing pertinent variables and their interaction can be developed. An example of such a model is provided in Figure 9.2. Developed by Sheth and Sethi, this model is based on the premise that all international business activity should be viewed as innovation and as producing change processes.[21] After all, multinational corporations introduce management practices as well as products and services from one country to other cultures, where they are

FIGURE 9.2   A Model of Cross-Cultural Behavior

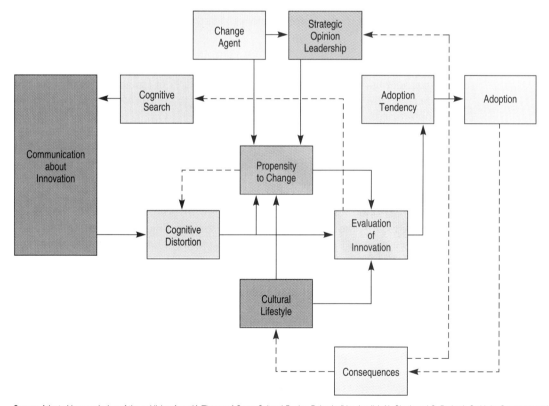

Source: Adapted by permission of the publisher from "A Theory of Cross-Cultural Buying Behavior," by Jagdish N. Sheth and S. Prakash Sethi, in *Consumer and Industrial Buyer Behavior,* eds. Arch G. Woodside, Jagdish N. Sheth, and Peter D. Bennett, 1977, 373. Copyright 1977 by Elsevier Science Publishing Co., Inc.

perceived to be new and different. Although many question the usefulness of such models, they do bring together, into one presentation, all or most of the relevant variables that have an impact on how consumers in different cultures may perceive, evaluate, and adopt new behaviors. However, any manager using such a tool should periodically cross-check its results with reality and experience.

The key variable of the model is propensity to change, which is a function of three constructs: (1) cultural lifestyle of individuals in terms of how deeply held their traditional beliefs and attitudes are, and also which elements of culture are dominant; (2) change agents (such as multinational corporations and their practices) and strategic-opinion leaders (for example, social elites); and (3) communication about the innovation from commercial sources, neutral sources (such as government), and social sources, such as friends and relatives.

It has been argued that differences in cultural lifestyle can be accounted for by four dimensions of culture.[22] These dimensions consist of (1) individualism ("I" consciousness versus "we" consciousness), (2) power distance (levels of equality in society), (3) uncertainty avoidance (need for formal rules and regulations), and (4) masculinity (attitude toward achievement, roles of men and women).[23] Understanding the implications of these dimensions will help prepare for international business encounters. For example, in negotiating in Germany one can expect a counterpart who is thorough, systematic, very well prepared, but also rather dogmatic and therefore lacking in flexibility and compromise. Great emphasis is placed on efficiency. In Mexico, however, the counterpart may prefer to address problems on a personal and private basis rather than on a business level. This means more emphasis on socializing and conveying one's humanity, sincerity, loyalty, and friendship. Also, the differences in pace and business practices of the region have to be accepted.[24]

Communication about the innovation takes place through the physical product itself (samples) or through experiencing a new policy in the company. If a new personnel practice, such as quality circles or flextime, is in question, results may be communicated in reports or through word of mouth by the participating employees. Communication content depends on the following factors: the product's or policy's relative advantage over existing alternatives; compatibility with established behavioral patterns; complexity, or the degree to which the product or process is perceived as difficult to understand and use; trialability, or the degree to which it may be experimented with without incurring major risk; and observability, which is the extent to which the consequences of the innovation are visible.

Before the product or policy is evaluated, information about it will be compared with existing beliefs about the circumstances surrounding the situation. Distortion will occur as a result of selective attention, exposure, and retention. As examples, anything foreign may be seen in a negative light, another multinational company's efforts may have failed, or the government may implicitly discourage the proposed activity. Additional information may then be sought from any of the input sources or from opinion leaders in the market.

Adoption tendency refers to the likelihood that the product or process will be accepted. Examples are advertising in the People's Republic of China and equity joint ventures with Western participants in Russia, both of them unheard of a decade ago. If an innovation clears the hurdles, it may be adopted and slowly diffused into the entire market. An international manager has two basic choices: to adapt company offerings and methods to those in the market or to try to change market conditions to fit company programs. In Japan, a number of Western companies have run into obstructions in the Japanese distribution system, where great value is placed on established relationships; everything is done on the basis of favoring the familiar and fearing the unfamiliar. In most cases, this problem is solved by joint venturing with a major Japanese entity that has established contacts. On occasion, when the company's approach is compatible with the central beliefs of a culture, the company may be able to change existing customs rather than adjust to them. Initially, Procter & Gamble's traditional hard-selling style in television commercials jolted most Japanese viewers accustomed to more subtle approaches. Now the ads are being imitated by Japanese competitors.

Although models like the one in Figure 9.2 may aid in strategy planning by making sure that all variables and their interlinkages are considered, any analysis is incomplete without the basic recognition of cultural differences. Adjusting to differences requires putting one's own cultural values aside. James A. Lee proposes that the natural **self-reference criterion**—the unconscious reference to one's own cultural values—is the root of most international business problems.[25] However, recognizing and admitting this are often quite difficult. The following analytical approach is recommended to reduce the influence of one's own cultural values:

1. Define the problem or goal in terms of the domestic cultural traits, habits, or norms.
2. Define the problem or goal in terms of the foreign cultural traits, habits, or norms. Make no value judgments.
3. Isolate the self-reference criterion influence in the problem, and examine it carefully to see how it complicates the problem.
4. Redefine the problem without the self-reference criterion influence, and solve for the optimum-goal situation.

This approach can be applied to product introduction. If Kellogg's wants to introduce breakfast cereals into markets where breakfast is traditionally not eaten or where consumers drink very little milk, managers must consider very carefully how to instill this new habit. The traits, habits, and norms concerning the importance of breakfast are quite different in the United States, France, and Brazil, and they have to be outlined before the product can be introduced. In France, Kellogg's commercials are aimed as much at providing nutrition lessons as they are at promoting the product. In Brazil, the company advertised on a soap opera to gain entry into the market, because Brazilians often emulate the characters of these television shows.

Analytical procedures require constant monitoring of changes caused by outside events as well as the changes caused by the business entity itself. Controlling **ethnocentrism**—the tendency to consider one's own culture superior to others—can be achieved only by acknowledging it and properly adjusting to its possible effects in managerial decision making. The international manager needs to be prepared and able to put that preparedness to effective use.[26]

THE TRAINING CHALLENGE

International managers face a dilemma in terms of international and intercultural competence. The lack of adequate foreign language and international business skills has cost U.S. firms lost contracts, weak negotiations, and ineffectual management. A UNESCO study of 10- and 14-year-old students in nine countries placed Americans next to last in their comprehension of foreign cultures. A sad 61 percent of U.S. business schools offer few or no courses in international business.[27] Although the types of jobs for which cross-cultural training has been deemed most important—mainly expatriate positions—are on the decline, the increase in the overall international activity of firms has increased the need for cultural sensitivity training at all levels of the organization. Further, today's training must take into consideration not only outsiders to the firm but interaction within the corporate family as well. However inconsequential the degree of interaction may seem, it can still cause problems if proper understanding is lacking. Consider, for example, the date 11/12/93 on a telex; a European will interpret this as the 11th of December, an American as the 12th of November.

Some companies try to avoid the training problem by hiring only nationals or well-traveled Americans for their international operations. This makes sense for the management of overseas operations but will not solve the training need, especially if transfers to a culture unfamiliar to the manager are likely. International experience may not necessarily transfer from one market to another.

To foster cultural sensitivity and acceptance of new ways of doing things within the organization, management must institute internal-education programs. These programs may include (1) culture-specific information (data covering other countries, such as videopacks and culturegrams), (2) cultural-general information (values, practices, and assumptions of countries other than one's own), and (3) self-specific information (identifying one's own cultural paradigm, including values, assumptions, and perceptions about others).[28] One study found that Japanese assigned to the United States get mainly language training as preparation for the task. In addition, many companies use mentoring, whereby an individual is assigned to someone who is experienced and who will spend the required time squiring and explaining. Talks given by returnees and by visiting lecturers hired specifically for the task round out the formal part of training.[29]

The objective of formal training programs is to foster the four critical characteristics of preparedness, sensitivity, patience, and flexibility in managers and other

**FIGURE 9.3
Cross-Cultural
Training Methods**

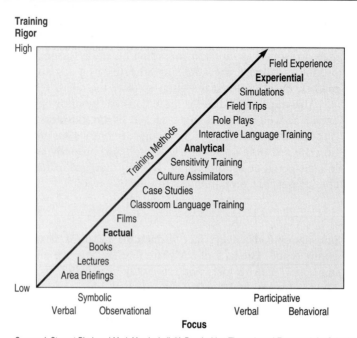

Source: J. Stewart Black and Mark Mendenhall, "A Practical but Theory-based Framework for Selecting Cross-Cultural Training Methods," in *International Human Resource Management*, eds. Mark Mendenhall and Gary Oddou (Boston: PWS-Kent, 1991), 188.

personnel. These programs vary dramatically in terms of their rigor, involvement, and, of course, cost.[30] A summary of these programs is provided in Figure 9.3.

Environmental briefings and cultural-orientation programs are types of **area studies** programs. These programs provide factual preparation for a manager to operate in, or work with people from, a particular country. Area studies should be a basic prerequisite for other types of training programs. Alone, area studies serve little practical purpose because they do not really get the manager's feet wet. Other, more involved, programs contribute the context in which to put facts so that they can be properly understood.

The **cultural assimilator** is a program in which trainees must respond to scenarios of specific situations in a particular country. These programs have been developed for the Arab countries, Iran, Thailand, Central America, and Greece.[31] The results of the trainees' assimilator experience are evaluated by a panel of judges. This type of program has been used in particular in cases of transfers abroad on short notice.

When more time is available, managers can be trained extensively in language. This may be required if an exotic language is involved. **Sensitivity training** focuses on enhancing a manager's flexibility in situations that are quite different from those

Global Perspective

9.3
Learning the Strange Foreign Ways

Samsung, Korea's largest conglomerate, has launched an internationalization campaign. The company wants to be culturally more sensitive, and not just to avoid gaffes. It believes that learning more about foreign countries can make its products more competitive. And it is not alone in these activities. A generation of Korean managers came of age thinking that if they built it, they could sell it. Today's international competitive environment requires more.

These programs have taken various forms. At Kumho Group, the chairman has ordered all employees of the airline and tire maker to spend an hour each morning learning a language or learning more about foreign cultures. Cards taped up in bathrooms teach a phrase a day of English or Japanese. At Samsung, overseas-bound managers attend a month-long boot camp where they are awakened at 5:50 a.m. for a job, meditation, and then lessons on issues such as table manners or avoiding sexual harassment. For example, students are taught not to ask female job applicants whether they are married or when they intend to marry, nor their age or religion.

Samsung is sending 400 of its brightest junior employees overseas for a year. Their mission is not 100 percent business either. "International exposure is important,

but you have to develop an appreciation of the foreign environment as well. You have to goof off at the mall, watch people, and develop international tastes," say Samsung officials. The program costs about $80,000 a year per person and takes key people out of circulation. But Samsung is convinced that cultural immersion will pay off in more astute judgments about what customers want. One concrete result is that the company is tailoring more products for specific overseas markets despite resistance of engineers in Seoul. "They want one model to sell to everyone. But they are accepting the concept now," state Samsung marketers. Much of that change has been attributed to people like Park Sang Jin, who had been overseas for 15 years, mostly in the United States. "If we do not do this type of concept, we will never catch up with our competitors," he states.

Samsung employees coming back from overseas see much work to be done. After five years in Paris, Kim Jeong Kyu recognizes that time abroad has changed him. Now back in Seoul, he is trying to change Samsung—and having problems. "Even if I have a good idea, I will not suggest it too fast," Kim says. "They will say, 'He doesn't know the Korean situation. Maybe it will work in France, but not here.'"

Source: "Sensitivity Kick" *The Wall Street Journal*, December 30, 1992, 1, 4.

at home. The approach is based on the assumption that understanding and accepting oneself is critical to understanding a person from another culture. Finally, training may involve **field experience,** which exposes a manager to a different cultural environment for a limited amount of time. While this approach is expensive, it is used by some companies, as seen in Global Perspective 9.3.

One field experience technique that has been suggested when the training process needs to be rigorous is the host-family surrogate. This technique places a trainee (and possibly his or her family) in a domestically located family of the nationality to which they are assigned.[32]

Regardless of the degree of training, preparation, and positive personal characteristics, a manager will always remain foreign. A manager should never rely on his or her own judgment when local managers can be consulted. In many instances, a manager should have an interpreter present at negotiations, especially if the manager is not completely bilingual. Overconfidence in one's language capabilities can create problems.

SUMMARY

Culture is one of the most challenging elements of the international marketplace. This system of learned behavior patterns characteristic of the members of a given society is constantly shaped by a set of dynamic variables: language, religion, values and attitudes, manners and customs, aesthetics, technology, education, and social institutions. To cope with this system, an international manager needs both factual and interpretive knowledge of culture. To some extent, the factual knowledge can be learned; its interpretation comes only through experience.

The most complicated problems in dealing with the cultural environment stem from the fact that one cannot learn culture—one has to live it. Two schools of thought exist in the business world on how to deal with cultural diversity. One is that business is business the world around, following the model of Pepsi and McDonald's. In some cases, globalization is a fact of life; however, cultural differences are still far from converging.

The other school proposes that companies must tailor business approaches to individual cultures. Setting up policies and procedures in each country has been compared to an organ transplant; the critical question centers around acceptance or rejection. The major challenge to the international manager is to make sure that rejection is not a result of cultural myopia or even blindness.

Fortune examined the international performance of a dozen large companies that earn 20 percent or more of their revenue overseas.[33] The internationally successful companies all share an important quality: patience. They have not rushed into situations but rather built their operations carefully by following the most basic business principles. These principles are to know your adversary, know your audience, and know your customer.

Key Terms and Concepts

cultural risk	change agent
acculturation	cultural universals
high-context cultures	backtranslation
low-context cultures	focus groups

economic infrastructure

social infrastructure

financial infrastructure

marketing infrastructure

cultural convergence

social stratification

reference groups

experiential knowledge

self-reference criterion

ethnocentrism

area studies

cultural assimilator

sensitivity training

field experience

Questions for Discussion

1. Comment on the assumption, "If people are serious about doing business with you, they will speak English."

2. You are on your first business visit to Germany. You feel confident about your ability to speak the language (you studied German in school and have taken a refresher course), and you decide to use it. During introductions, you want to break the ice by asking "Wie geht's?" and insisting that everyone call you by first name. Speculate as to the reaction.

3. Q: "What do you call a person who can speak two languages?"
   A: "Bilingual."
   Q: "How about three?"
   A: "Trilingual."
   Q: "Excellent. How about one?"
   A: "Hmmmmm. . . . American!"
   Is this joke malicious, or is there something to be learned from it?

4. What can be learned about a culture from reading and attending to factual materials?

5. Given the tremendous increase in international business, where will companies in a relatively early stage of the internationalization process find the personnel to handle the new challenges?

6. Management at a U.S. company trying to market tomato paste in the Middle East did not know that, translated into Arabic, "tomato paste" is "tomato glue." How could it have known in time to avoid problems?

7. Provide examples of how the self-reference criterion might manifest itself.

8. Is any international business entity not a cultural imperialist? How else could one explain the phenomenon of multinational corporations?

Recommended Readings

Bache, Ellyn. *Culture Clash*. Yarmouth, Maine: Intercultural Press, 1990.

Brislin, R. W., Kenneth Cushner, Craig Cherrie, and Mahealani Yong. *Intercultural Interactions*. San Francisco: Sage Publications, 1986.

Brislin, R. W., W. J. Lonner, and R. M. Thorndike. *Cross-Cultural Research Methods*. New York: Wiley, 1973.

Copeland, Lennie, and Lewis Griggs. *Going International: How to Make Friends and Deal Effectively in the Global Marketplace*. New York: Random House, 1985.

Fisher, Glen. *International Negotiation.* Yarmouth, Maine: Intercultural Press, 1986.

Hall, Edward T., and Mildred Reed Hall. *Understanding Cultural Differences.* Yarmouth, Maine: Intercultural Press, 1990.

Storti, Craig. *The Art of Crossing Cultures.* Yarmouth, Maine: International Press, 1990.

Terpstra, Vern, and Keith David. *The Cultural Environment of International Business.* Cincinnati: Southwestern, 1991.

Weiss, Joseph. *Regional Cultures, Managerial Behavior, and Entrepreneurship.* Westport, Conn.: Quorum Books, 1988.

Notes

1. Alfred Kroeber and Clyde Kluckhohn, *Culture: A Critical Review of Concepts and Definitions* (New York: Random House, 1985), 11.
2. Geert Hofstede, "National Cultures Revisited," *Asia-Pacific Journal of Management* 1 (September 1984): 22-24.
3. Robert L. Kohls, *Survival Kit for Overseas Living* (Chicago: Intercultural Press, 1979), 3.
4. Edward T. Hall, *Beyond Culture* (Garden City, N.Y.: Anchor Press, 1976), 15.
5. George P. Mundak, "The Common Denominator of Cultures," in *The Science of Man in the World,* ed. Ralph Linton (New York: Columbia University Press, 1945), 123-142.
6. Philip R. Harris and Robert T. Moran, *Managing Cultural Differences* (Houston: Gulf, 1987), 201.
7. David A. Ricks, *Big Business Blunders* (Homewood, Ill.: Irwin, 1983), 4.
8. Ibid., 24-28.
9. Edward T. Hall, "The Silent Language of Overseas Business," *Harvard Business Review* 38 (May–June 1960): 87-96.
10. Mushtaq Luqmami, Zahir A. Quraeshi, and Linda Delene, "Marketing in Islamic Countries: A Viewpoint," *MSU Business Topics* 23 (Summer 1980): 17-24.
11. James F. Engel, Roger D. Blackwell, and Paul W. Miniard, *Consumer Behavior* (Hinsdale, Ill.: Dryden, 1986), 223.
12. "Learning How to Please the Baffling Japanese," *Fortune,* October 5, 1981, 122.
13. Kenichi Ohmae, "Managing in a Borderless World," *Harvard Business Review* 67 (May-June 1989): 152-161.
14. Joe Agnew, "Cultural Differences Probed to Create Product Identity," *Marketing News,* October 24, 1986, 22.
15. Joseph A. McKinney, "Joint Ventures of United States Firms in Japan: A Survey," *Venture Japan* 1 (1988): 14-19.
16. Engel, Blackwell, and Miniard, *Consumer Behavior,* 318-324.
17. "The Difference That Japanese Management Makes," *Business Week,* July 14, 1986, 47-50.
18. James H. Sood and Patrick Adams, "Model of Management Learning Styles as a Predictor of Export Behavior and Performance," *Journal of Business Research* 12 (June 1984): 169-182.
19. Stephen J. Kobrin, *International Expertise in American Business* (New York: Institute of International Education, 1984), 36.
20. Lennie Copeland, "Training Americans to Do Business Overseas," *Training,* July 1984, 22-23.
21. Jagdish N. Sheth and S. Prakash Sethi, "A Theory of Cross-Cultural Buying Behavior," in *Consumer and Industrial Buying Behavior,* eds. Arch G. Woodside, Jagdish N. Sheth, and Peter D. Bennett (New York: Elsevier North-Holland, 1977), 369-386.
22. Geert Hofstede, *Culture's Consequences: International Differences in Work-Related Values* (Beverly Hills, Calif.: Sage Publications, 1984), Chapter 1.
23. For applications of the framework, see Sudhir H. Kale, "Culture-Specific Marketing Communications," *International Marketing Review* 8, no. 2 (1991): 18-30; and Sudhir H. Kale, "Distribution Channel Relationships in Diverse Cultures," *International Marketing Review* 8, no. 3 (1991): 31-45.
24. Sergey Frank, "Global Negotiations: Vive Les Differences!" *Sales and Marketing Management* 144 (May 1992): 64-69.
25. James A. Lee, "Cultural Analysis in Overseas Operations," *Harvard Business Review* 44 (March-April 1966): 106-114.
26. Peter D. Fitzpatrick and Alan S. Zimmerman, *Essentials of Export Marketing* (New York: American Management Organization, 1985), 16.
27. Copeland, "Training Americans to Do Business Overseas," 22-33.
28. W. Chan Kim and R. A. Mauborgne, "Cross-Cultural

Strategies," *Journal of Business Strategy* 7 (Spring 1987): 28-37.

29. Mauricio Lorence, "Assignment USA: The Japanese Solution," *Sales & Marketing Management* 144 (October 1992): 60-66.

30. Rosalie Tung, "Selection and Training of Personnel for Overseas Assignments," *Columbia Journal of World Business* 16 (Spring 1981): 68-78.

31. Harris and Moran, *Managing Cultural Differences,* 267-295.

32. Simcha Ronen, "Training the International Assignee," in *Training and Career Development,* ed. I. Goldstein (San Francisco: Jossey-Bass, 1989), 426-440.

33. Kenneth Labich, "America's International Winners," *Fortune,* April 14, 1986, 34-46.

Emerging Market Economies and State-Owned Enterprises

LEARNING OBJECTIVES

1. To understand the special concerns that must be considered by the international manager when dealing with emerging market economies.

2. To survey the vast opportunities for trade offered by emerging market economies.

3. To understand why economic change is difficult and requires much adjustment.

4. To become aware that state-owned enterprises are major players in international business and require adaptive corporate strategies.

A New May Day

Dancing children, billboard advertisements, and an evangelist from Lakeview, Missouri, replaced the rolling tanks, rockets, and Lenin banners in the 1992 May Day celebrations in Moscow's Red Square. Instead of the customary review of the troops and long speeches by the party hierarchy focusing on the goals of world communism, two stages for dancing and folk music were set up in front of St. Basil's Cathedral. The background did not consist in the usual flags of hammer and sickle, Lenin and Marx, but rather reflected the arrival of capitalism through paid advertisements.

The Spanish Ministry of Tourism had rented a sign urging would-be tourists to "enjoy 320 days of sun a year in the Canary Islands." Another big sign, erected on behalf of the Freedom Forum, a journalism foundation based in Arlington, Virginia, proclaimed in English and Russian "Freedom Works, Free press, free speech and free spirit."

In the early afternoon, the Rev. Cecil Todd, founder of Revival Fires Ministries in Lakeview, Missouri, preached to teenagers—right before the disco started.

Source: Carole Landry, "May Day Takes Turn to Capitalism," *USA Today,* May 1, 1992:8A.

This chapter addresses the major societal and ideological shifts that have occurred in the global economy. The focus is on the emerging democracies of central Europe and the Commonwealth of Independent States (CIS), which has replaced the former Soviet Union. In addition, the role of state-owned enterprises will be discussed. The former centrally planned economies are singled out due to the significant shifts in economic thinking that have taken place there. As this chapter's opening vignette showed, the economies and the thinking in these countries has been transformed, a change that has important implications for the international business manager, both in terms of opportunities and risks. State-owned enterprises are discussed because, even though many of them exist in market economies, they reflect to a significant extent the desires of their governments. Yet, in many instances, a shift in ideology and a new economic pragmatism is leading governments to take the road toward privatization.

The chapter begins with a brief description of the historical economic structures in the emerging democracies. Subsequently, we will explore the realities of economic change and the challenges and opportunities facing the international manager. Joint ventures between Western firms and emerging market economies are proliferating and are therefore an important part of the future trade relationship between countries and firms. This subject will be discussed in greater detail in Chapter. 12.

DOING BUSINESS WITH EMERGING MARKET ECONOMIES

The major emerging market economies are the Commonwealth of Independent States, East Germany (now unified with West Germany), the eastern and central European nations (Albania, Bulgaria, The Czech and Slovak Republics, Hungary, Poland, and Romania), and the People's Republic of China.

It is a common belief that business ties between the Western world and these nations are a new phenomenon. That is not the case. In the 1920s, for example, General Electric and RCA helped to develop the Soviet electrical and communications industries. Ford constructed a huge facility in Gorky to build Model A cars and buses. DuPont introduced its technology to Russia's chemical industry. Conversely, Tungsram in Hungary conducted research and development for General Electric. However, by the mid-1930s most American companies had withdrawn from the scene

Prague, Czech Republic, is coming alive with business opportunities in its newly freed economy.

Source: © 1992 Filip Horvat/SABA.

or were forced to leave. Since then, former centrally planned economies and Western corporations engaged in international business have had rather limited contact.[1]

To a large extent, this limited contact has been the result of an ideological wariness on both sides. Socialist countries often perceived international corporations as "aggressive business organizations developed to further the imperialistic aims of Western, especially American, capitalists the world over."[2] Furthermore, many aspects of capitalism, such as the private ownership of the means of production, were seen as exploitative and antithetical to communist ideology.[3] Western managers, in turn, often saw socialism as a threat to the Western world and the capitalist system in general.

Over time, these rigid stances were modified on both sides. Decision makers in former centrally planned economies recognized the need to purchase products and technology that were unavailable domestically or that could be produced only at a substantial comparative disadvantage. They were determined to achieve economic growth and improve the very much neglected standard of living in their society, deciding that the potential benefits of cooperation in many instances outweighed the risks of decentralized economic power and reduced reliance on plans. As a result, government planners in former socialist economies began to include some market considerations in their activities and opened up their countries to Western businesses.

At the same time, the greater openness on the part of these governments resulted in more flexibility of Western government control of East-West trade. The drive toward modernization of production and growing consumer demand greatly raised the attractiveness of doing business with the newly emerging democracies (NEDs). Furthermore, many Western firms experienced a need to diversify their international business activities from traditional markets because of current trade imbalances and were searching for new opportunities. The large populations and pent-up demand of the NEDs offered those opportunities.

A Brief Historic Review

Due to differing politics and ideology, the trade history of socialist countries is quite different from that of the United States and the West. The former Soviet system of foreign trade dates to a decree signed by Lenin on April 22, 1918. It established that the state would have a monopoly on foreign trade and that all foreign-trade operations were to be concentrated in the hands of organizations specifically authorized

Central Europe and Asia: The Location of Major Emerging Market Economies

Major Emerging Market Economies

ICELAND

IRELAND

UNITED KINGDOM

PORTUGAL

SPAIN

NORWAY

SWEDEN

FINLAND

DEN.

NETH.
BELG.
LUX.
FRANCE

GERMANY
SWZ.

ITALY

AUSTRIA
SLO.
CRO.
BOS.

EST.
LATVIA
LITH.

POLAND

CZECH
HUNG.

YUG.
ALB.
GREECE

BULG.
ROMANIA

MACE.
SER.

BELARUS

UKRAINE

MOLDOVA

CYPRUS

TURKEY

GEORGIA

ARMENIA

AZERBAIJAN

LEBANON

ISRAEL

SYRIA

JORDAN

IRAQ

KUWAIT

BAHRAIN
QATAR

SAUDI
ARABIA

YEMEN

OMAN

UNITED
ARAB
EMIRATES

IRAN

TURKMENISTAN

UZBEKISTAN

KAZAKHSTAN

RUSSIA

MONGOLIA

KYRGYZSTAN

TAJIKISTAN

AFGHANISTAN

PAKISTAN

INDIA

NEPAL

BHUTAN

CHINA

BANGLADESH

MYANMAR

SRI
LANKA

LAOS

THAILAND

CAMBODIA

VIETNAM

BRUNEI

MALAYSIA

NORTH
KOREA

SOUTH
KOREA

JAPAN

TAIWAN

PHILIPPINES

by the state. These organizations served as the basis for all trade, economic, scientific, and technical transactions with foreign countries.[4] This system of a state-controlled monopoly was also adopted by the East European satellites of the Soviet Union and by the People's Republic of China.

In effect, this trade structure isolated the firms and consumers in socialist economies from the West and unlinked demand from supply. Any international transaction was cumbersomely reviewed by **foreign trade organizations (FTOs),** ministries, and a multitude of state committees. In addition, rigid state bureaucracies regulated the entire economy. Over time, domestic economic problems emerged. In spite of some top-down and bottom-up planning interaction, the lack of attention to market forces resulted in misallocated resources, and the lack of competition promoted inefficiency. Centralized allocation prevented the emergence of effective channels of distribution. Managers of plants were more concerned with producing the quantities stipulated by a rigid **central plan** (often five-year plans, one following another) than with producing the products and the quality desired. Overfulfillment of the plan was discouraged because it would result in a quota increase for the following year. Entrepreneurship was disdained, innovation risky. Consequently, socialist economies achieved only lackluster growth, and their citizens fell far behind the West in their standard of living.

In the early 1980s, the economic orientation of centrally planned economies began to shift. Hungary and Poland started to cautiously encourage their firms to develop an export-oriented strategy. Exporting itself was nothing new, because much trade took place among the countries belonging to the communist bloc. What was new was the fact that government policy emphasized trade with the West and increasingly exposed domestic enterprises to the pressure of international competitions.[5] In addition, socialist countries began to import more equipment from the West and started to encourage direct investment from foreign firms.

In the mid-1980s, the Soviet Union developed two new political and economic programs: **perestroika** and **glasnost.** Perestroika was to fundamentally reform the Soviet economy by improving the overall technological and industrial base as well as the quality of life for Soviet citizens through increased availability of food, housing, and consumer goods. Glasnost was to complement these efforts by encouraging the free exchange of ideas and discussion of problems, pluralistic participation in decision making, and increased availability of information.[6]

These major domestic steps were followed shortly by legislative measures that thoroughly reformed the Soviet foreign-trade apparatus. In a major move away from previous trade centralization through the channels of the Ministry of Foreign Trade, organizations such as national agencies, large enterprises, and research institutes were authorized to handle their own foreign transactions directly. A 1987 decree asserted that it was essential to develop economic ties with the capitalist world in order to consistently move along the strategic course of using the advantages of the world division of labor, to strengthen the position of the USSR in international trade, and to introduce the achievements of world science and technology into the national economy.[7] By 1989, all Soviet enterprises that could compete in foreign markets were permitted to apply for independent trading rights.

Concurrent with the steps taken in the Soviet Union, other socialist countries also initiated major reforms affecting international business. China began to launch major programs of modernization and developed multinational corporations of its own. Virtually all socialist countries began to invite foreign investors to form joint ventures in their countries to help satisfy both domestic and international demand and started to privatize state enterprises.

THE DEMISE OF THE SOCIALIST SYSTEM

By late 1989, all the individual small shifts so far discussed resulted in the emergence of a new economic and geopolitical picture. With an unexpected suddenness, the Iron Curtain disappeared, and, within less than three years, the communist empire ceased to exist. Virtually overnight eastern Europe and the former Soviet Union, with their total population of 400 million and a combined GNP of $3 trillion,[8] shifted their political and economic orientation toward a market economy. The former socialist satellites shed their communist governments. Newly elected democratic governments decided to let market forces shape their economies. East Germany was unified with West Germany. In March 1992, Hungary was admitted as an associate member of the European Community. The Czech Republic, Slovakia, and Poland announced their desire to achieve full convertibility of their currencies and to join the GATT system. By 1992, the entire Soviet Union had disappeared. Individual regions within the Commonwealth of Independent States reasserted their independence and autonomy, resulting in a host of emerging nations, often heavily dependent on one another, but now separated by nationalistic feelings and political realities.

The political changes were accompanied by major economic action. Externally, trade flows were redirected from the former Soviet Union toward the European Community. Internally, austerity programs were introduced and prices of subsidized products were adjusted upwards to avoid distorted trade flows due to distorted prices. Wages were kept in check to reduce inflation. Entire industries were either privatized or closed down. As Figure 10.1 shows, these steps led to a significant decrease in the standard of living of the population. Yet the support for the internal economic transformation continued, demonstrating the great desire on the part of individuals and governments to participate in the world marketplace, and the hope that these transformations would achieve a better standard of living over time.

While China did not undergo the radical political shifts of Europe, its economic changes were of similar significance. New enterprise zones were opened, designed to produce products targeted for export. Foreign investors were invited. Individuals were permitted to translate their entrepreneurial skills into action and keep the profits. As Global Perspective 10.1 shows, a new perspective has begun to permeate business and the economy.

From a Western perspective, all these changes indicated the end of the Cold War and a resultant significant decrease in the need to withhold economic benefits and technology from an entire world region. It was also understood that the shouts for democracy were, to a large degree, driven not only by political but also by economic desires. Freedom meant not only the right to free elections but also the expectation of an increased standard of living in the form of color televisions, cars, and the many benefits of a consumer society. To sustain the drive toward democracy, these economic desires had to appear attainable. Therefore, it was in the interest of the Western world as a whole to contribute toward the democratization of the former communist nations by searching for ways to bring them "the good life."

The Realities of Economic Change

For Western firms, all these shifts resulted in the conversion of what had been a latent market into a market offering very real and vast opportunities. Yet these shifts are only the beginning of a process. The announcement of an intention to change does not automatically result in change itself. For example, the abolition of a centrally planned economy does not create a market economy. Laws permitting the

FIGURE 10.1   **Signs of Spring**

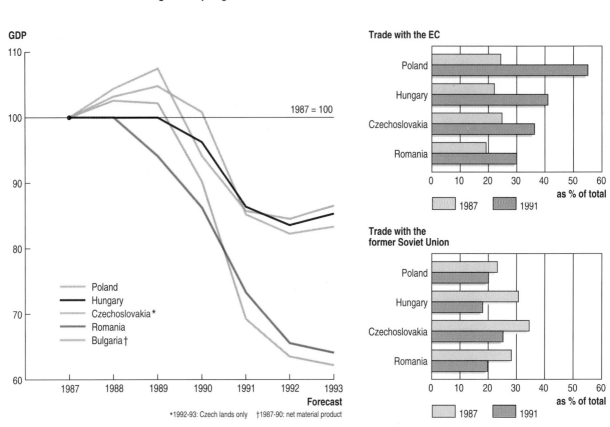

Source: *The Economist,* December 19, 1992, 50. Copyright © 1992, The Economist, Ltd. Distributed by The New York Times/Special Features.

Global Perspective

10.1
Consumer Orientation in China

"Consumer" has traditionally been a dirty word in Communist China. Society was geared toward producers, and consumers had to take what they were offered. Department stores were gloomy warehouses where poor merchandise was stacked on dusty counters. But no longer.

In front of the Beijing Department Store in the city's bustling Wang Fu Jing Street, people line up three deep to gawk at bright red cars. The store is giving away three Chinese brand autos and a minivan to lucky customers who win a drawing. At the counter of Beijing's Xidan Department Store, whose motto is "We sell cheaper," a fast-talking young woman demonstrates a kitchen tool that slices, dices, and shreds vegetables. Sending carrots and sweet potatoes flying, she keeps up a constant sales patter while her assistants press the plastic gadgets, selling for the equivalent of 75 cents, into the hands of shoppers.

The new watchword today is competition. Department stores are advertising, renovating, and putting foreign brand-name products in the forefront. Counters are stacked with Head and Shoulders shampoo, Johnson & Johnson baby products, and Lux soap. Says Yu Cai Xiang, head of the marketing division at the Ministry of Commerce: "The producers have to satisfy the consumers now. The aim is to invigorate the entire market, and it seems to be working."

Source: "Of Lotteries, Giveaways and the Hard Sell," *The New York Times,* October 11, 1992:6.

emergence of private-sector entrepreneurs do not create entrepreneurship. The reduction of price controls does not immediately make goods available or affordable. Deeply ingrained systemic differences between the emerging democracies and Western firms continue. Highly prized, fully accepted fundamentals of the market economy, such as the reliance on competition, support of the profit motive, and the willingness to live with risk on a corporate and personal level, are not yet fully accepted. It is therefore useful to review the major economic and structural dimensions of the emerging democracies to identify major shortcomings and opportunities for international business.

The elected democratic governments in central Europe are a completely new phenomenon. While full of good intentions, these governments are new to the tasks of governing and have either very limited experience or none at all. At the same time, they face major legal uncertainties and the existence of old, entrenched bureaucracies, whose members are still deeply suspicious of any change and less than helpful or forthcoming. These governments have precipitated the disappearance of the previous trading system but have yet to replace the old, imperfect set of trading relationships with a new one. As a result, their ability to successfully shape the competitive environment of their nations is limited.

Many of the NEDs also face major infrastructure shortages. Transportation systems, particularly those leading to the West, are either nonexistent or in disrepair. The housing stock is in need of total overhaul. Communication systems will take years to improve. Market intermediaries often do not exist. Payments and funds-transfer systems are inadequate. Even though major efforts are under way to improve the infrastructure—evidenced, for example, by the former Soviet Union's desire to obtain fiber-optic telephone lines or by Hungary's success in installing a cellular telephone system—infrastructure shortcomings will inhibit economic growth for years to come.

Capital shortages are also a major constraint. Catching up with the West in virtually all industrial areas will require major capital infusions. In addition, a new environmental consciousness will require large investments in environmentally sound energy-generation and production facilities. Even though major programs are being designed to attract hidden personal savings into the economies, NEDs must rely to a large degree on attracting capital from abroad. Continued domestic uncertainties and high demand for capital around the world make this difficult.

Firms doing business with the emerging democracies encounter very interesting demand conditions. Clearly, the pent-up demand from the past bodes well for sales. Yet buyers, in many instances, have never been exposed to the problem of decision making; their preferences are vague and undefined, and they are therefore poorly trained in making market choices.[9] As a result, buyers are unlikely to demand high levels of quality or service. Rather, their demand is driven much more by product availability than by product sophistication. Yet little accurate market information is available. For example, knowledge about pricing, advertising, research, and trading is virtually nonexistent, and few institutions are able to accurately assess demand and channel supply. As a result, corporate responsiveness to demand is quite difficult.

To the surprise of many investors, the emerging democracies have substantial knowledge resources to offer. For example, it is claimed that the former USSR and eastern former Europe possess about 35 to 40 percent of all researchers and engineers working in the world.[10] At the same time, however, these nations suffer from the drawback imposed by a lack of management skills. In the past, management mainly consisted of skillful maneuvering within the allocation process. Central planning, for example, required firms to request tools seven years in advance; material requirements needed to be submitted two years in advance. Ordering was done haphazardly, since requested quantities were always reduced, and surplus allocations could always be traded with other firms. The driving mechanism for management was therefore not responsiveness to existing needs, but rather plan fulfillment through the development of a finely honed allocation mentality.

Commitment by managers and employees to hard work is similarly nonexistent. Employees are to a large degree still caught up in old work habits, which consisted of never having to work a full shift. The notion that "they pretend to pay us, and we pretend to work" is still very strong. The current dismantling of the past policy of the "Iron Rice Bowl," which made layoffs virtually impossible, is further reducing rather than increasing such commitment.

The new environment also complicates managerial decision making. Because of the total lack of prior market orientation, even simple reforms require an almost unimaginable array of decisions about business licenses, the setting of optimal tax rates, rules of business operation, definitions of business expense for taxation purposes, safety standards, and rules concerning nondiscrimination and consumer protection.[11] All new market economies experience a gap in management skills. Improved managerial training is therefore a key building block in developing the international competitiveness of the region. Recognizing the importance of such training, a variety of universities, firms, and governments are beginning to offer programs. Global Perspective 10.2 explains some efforts made by U.S. and European universities.

Global Perspective

10.2
Education Is Key to Market Success

Five of the most influential business schools in the United States—Harvard, Wharton, Stanford, Northwestern, and MIT—try to make a difference in the management skills of eastern European countries. The schools jointly launched a $3.5 million program designed to teach business basics to professors from universities and management in central and eastern Europe and to give them "an advanced management perspective on a market economy." The effort is concentrated on 120 of eastern Europe's best professors of management, economics, and technology. While attending classes in the United States, the participants will be exposed to such unfamiliar fields as competitor analysis and marketing. The goal is to train them as multipliers so that they can lead the march to a market economy when they return home.

But eastern Europe does not have to rely on the United States alone. France's INSEAD, the London Business School (LBS), and Switzerland's IMD also intend to educate Eastern professors in Western ways. LBS, INSEAD, and Spain's IESE have raised $4.4 million to help the former Soviet Union to bring its management education up to capitalist scratch. In addition, many schools are working with individual institutions. For example, Georgetown University is developing an executive-management program in the Czech Republic.

There is some concern that many East-West projects will fail if Western schools simply force-feed eastern Europe with Western management theory. Says Bruno Dufour, of ESC in Lyon, France: "We have to remember that management is largely a cultural activity."

Adapted from "Educating Milos," *The Economist*, May 16, 1992:86.

Adjusting to Rapid Change

Both institutions and individuals tend to display some resistance to change. The resistance grows if the speed of change increases. It does not necessarily indicate a preference for the earlier conditions but rather concern about the effects of adjustment and fear of the unknown. In light of the major shifts that have occurred both politically and economically in central Europe and the CIS and the accompanying substantial dislocations, resistance should be expected. Deeply entrenched interests and traditions are not easily dislocated by the tender and shallow root of market-oriented thinking. The understanding of linkages and interactions cannot be expected to grow overnight. For example, greater financial latitude for firms also requires that inefficient firms be permitted to go into bankruptcy—a concept not cherished by many. The need for increased efficiency and productivity will cause sharp reductions in employment—a painful step for the workers affected. The growing ranks of unemployed are swelled by the members of the military who have been brought home or demobilized. Concurrently, wage reforms threaten to relegate blue-collar workers, who were traditionally favored by the socialist system, to second-class status while permitting the emergence of a new entrepreneurial class of the rich, an undesirable result for those not participating in the upswing. Retail-price reforms may endanger the safety net of large population segments, and widespread price changes may introduce inflation. It is difficult to accept a system where there are winners and losers, particularly for those on the losing side. As a result, an increase in ambivalence and uncertainty may well produce rapid shifts in economic and political thinking, which in turn may produce another set of unexpected results.

But it is not just in the emerging democracies that major changes have come about. The shifts experienced there also have a major impact on the established market economies of the West. Initially, the immediate changes in the West were confined to the reduction of the threat of war and a redefinition of military and political strategy. Over time, however, Western governments are discovering that the formation of new linkages and dismantling of old ones will also cause major dislocations at home. For example, the change in military threat is likely to have an effect on military budgets, which for the United States alone was $300 billion annually. Budget changes in turn will affect the production of military goods and the employment level in the defense sector. A declining size of armies will only reinforce the resulting employment needs.

Over the long term, major changes will also result from the reorientation of trade flows. With traditional and "forced" trade relationships vanishing and the need for income from abroad increasing, most of the former socialist countries will exert major efforts to become partners in global trade. They will attempt to export much more of their domestic production. Many of these exports will be in product categories such as agriculture and basic manufacturing, which are precisely the economic sectors in which the Western nations are already experiencing surpluses. As a result, the threat of displacement will be high for traditional producers.

The immediate consequence of these shifts will likely be resistance to change. Typical of such resistance is government action that attempts to contain the effect of change abroad and limit its effect at home. Such governmental restrictions to trade flows from the emerging market economies are dangerous. Figure 10.2 provides various scenarios for Western economic relations with the emerging democracies. The two main dimensions guiding these scenarios are government restrictions to trade and the competitive gap between the two areas. In Scenario 1, Western governments attempt to reduce the inflow of trade from these new regions. Concurrently, increases

**FIGURE 10.2
Scenarios for Western
Economic Relations
with the Emerging
Democracies**

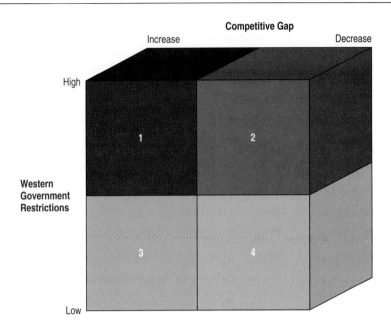

in economic integration in the West combined with the significant competitive advantages of Western firms will lead to a widening of the competitive gap between the two regions. In Scenario 2, government restrictions remain high, but the competitive gap is diminishing, a result that would heavily depend on quick adjustment by the NEDs and sufficient resources to improve their competitive standing. Scenario 3 decreases government restrictions, but the competitive gap continues to increase. In Scenario 4, government restrictions decrease together with a closing of the competitive gap.

An analysis of these four possibilities shows that Scenario 1 is likely to lead to major economic and political instability in the NEDS due to individual hardships and disappointed expectations. Scenario 2 is unlikely to materialize, since the investments required for a decrease in the competitive gap will not occur unless market opportunities for the exports generated by such investment exist in the West. Scenario 3 indicates that the lowering of government restrictions is a necessary but insufficient condition for the improvement of the competitive standing of the NEDs. Scenario 4 is the most desirable because it offers long-term change and economic improvement to the NEDS. Yet this scenario will result in the highest internal-adjustment needs by Western governments and firms and will require significant transfers of resources to close the competitive gap. This scenario will also depend on close collaboration between the public and the private sector. Private-sector investment will be required in order to transfer and generate the domestic resources necessary for economic competitiveness. Even with low government restrictions, private capital flows will need encouragement. Such encouragement will, to a large degree, depend on the domestic governmental actions of the NEDs. The providing of open markets and of governmental assistance on the part of the West, however, will also be instrumental. One could argue that governmental expenditures assisting the recovery of the economies of the NEDs should be minimized. This argument is substantially weakened if such expenditures are seen as investment or even as insurance. In light of the more than $500 billion in annual military expenses that the

Western world imposed on itself during Cold War days, protection against future instability may well be worth a small percentage of the armament expenditures of the past.

Disappointment and disenchantment in the NEDs brings with it the potential for social upheaval and chaos. One must recognize that economic borders can be just as divisive and perhaps even more painful than political ones.[12] Instability and confrontation result not only from tanks but also from poverty-driven countries' knowledge that the next-door neighbor lives in wealth and amplitude. To avoid conflict and increase opportunity, it is therefore in the long-term interest of Western governments and citizens to lower their restrictions to trade and assist in building up the competitive capabilities of the East. There is an urgent need to collaborate now to encourage the formulation of joint approaches and inhibit the advancement of disjointed, incompatible policies. Such collaboration will bring painful economic shifts in the West. Although governments and individuals may not be prepared for such pain, the burden must be borne in order to increase the likelihood of survival for market-oriented thinking and democracy in the NEDs and, in the longer term, to create new targets of opportunity abroad.

International Business Challenges and Opportunities

The pressure of change in the NEDs also presents vast opportunities for the expansion of international business activities. Their large populations offer potential consumer demand and production supply unmatched by any other region in the world. Furthermore, the knowledge of the international manager may be particularly useful to these economies where business skills are only rudimentary. These countries need assistance and contacts to reshape their domestic economies and penetrate foreign markets. For example, Russia is asking for help in areas such as business and personnel training, marketing, banking, auditing, and compilation of statistics.[13]

Of major concern are the limitations placed on goods that can be sold to emerging market economies. Although export restrictions have been eased in light of political developments, the international manager needs to consider the current and future political environments when planning long-term business commitments. A second major challenge is the lack of information about end users. Business strives to satisfy the needs and wants of individuals and organizations. Unable to ascertain

The fall of the Berlin Wall signaled the opening of Eastern Europe, providing vast opportunities for the expansion of international marketing activities.
Source:Filip Horvat/SABA.

their desires directly, the international manager must use secondary information such as hearsay, educated guesses, and the opinions of intermediaries.

Another major difficulty encountered in conducting business with these countries is the frequent unavailability of hard currency. Products, however necessary, often cannot be purchased by emerging market economies because no funds are available to pay for them. As a result, many of these countries resort to barter and countertrade. This places an additional burden on the international manager, who must not only market products to the clients but must also market the products received in return to other consumers and institutions.

Similar problems are encountered when attempting to source products from emerging market economies. Many firms have found that selling is not part of the economic culture of these countries. The available descriptive materials are often poorly written and devoid of useful information. Obtaining additional information about a product may be difficult and time consuming.

The quality of the products obtained can also be a major problem. In spite of their great desire to participate in the global marketplace, the NEDs still tend to place primary emphasis on product performance and, to a large extent, to neglect style and product presentation. The result is "a willingness to leave equipment rough and unfinished when a lack of finishing does not significantly affect function."[14] Therefore, the international manager needs to forge agreements that require the manufacturer to improve quality, provide for technical control, and ensure prompt delivery before sourcing products from emerging market economies.

Even when satisfactory products are obtained from emerging market economies, the marketing of these products elsewhere can be a major problem. One study revealed negative attitudes toward products sourced from emerging market economies—particularly consumer products. International managers may well "find a portion of the population [in the United States] hesitant to purchase [such] goods."[15]

Nevertheless, sufficient opportunities exist to make consideration of these international business activities worthwhile. Emerging market economies do have products that can be of use in free-market economies and that are often unique in performance. In most instances, these tend to be industrial rather than consumer products, reflecting the past orientation of centrally planned research and development.

Consumer products may in time play a larger role. Lower labor costs and, in some instances, the greater availability of labor may enable emerging market economies to offer consumers in free-market economies a variety of products at a lower cost. Due to their low cost, existing service capabilities may also present interesting international business possibilities. As Global Perspective 10.3 shows, already U.S. companies are beginning to develop collaborative arrangements in the research field, at a cost well below home-country levels.

STATE-OWNED ENTERPRISES AND PRIVATIZATION

One phenomenon that plays a major role in international business is **state-owned enterprise.** State-owned enterprises represent a formidable pool of international suppliers, customers, and competitors for the international business executive. Currently, however, many of these firms are gradually being converted into privately owned enterprises through the privatization process. This transition also presents new opportunities for the international manager.

Global Perspective

10.3
Russia's Top Scientists Work for U.S. Firms

AT&T Bell Laboratories, the research and development arm of AT&T, announced that it had hired about 100 scientists of the General Physics Institute of the Russian Academy of Sciences in Moscow to work with Bell Labs researchers. In addition, the two sides agreed to let AT&T control international patents that may come from the joint research, while the Russian institute will own patents within Russia. This move represents one of the largest efforts by U.S. companies to glean expertise form the sophisticated research community in Russia. The scientists will work on finding stronger glass for fiber; better doping methods for making fiber amplifiers; and cutting-edge projects such as soliton propagation, which if perfected will allow communications companies to send vast amounts of voice, data, and video traffic through optical fiber over tremendous distances with little amplification.

AT&T is getting this top-level scientific talent at bargain rates, by Western standards. Kumar Patel, executive director of Bell Labs, stated that the company will pay each scientist the equivalent of $60 a month, or $720 annually. He said that the Russian scientists requested that their wages be kept down to avoid significant distortion with other workers' pay scales. Including lab supplies, equipment, and infrequent travel, the whole deal will cost in the low six figures.

By contrast, holders of doctoral degrees who are on the corporate "fast track" with similar experience at Bell Labs earn $60,000 to $70,000 annually.

John J. Keller, "AT&T Bell Labs and Corning Inc. Hire Over 200 Top Scientists in Russia," *The Wall Street Journal*, May 27, 1992:B5.

Reasons for the Emergence of State-Owned Enterprises

A variety of economic and noneconomic factors have contributed to the existence of state-owned enterprises. Two primary ones are national security and economic security. Many countries believe that, for national-security purposes, certain industrial sectors must be under state control. Typically, these sectors include telecommunications, airlines, banking, and energy.

Economic-security reasons are primarily cited in countries that are heavily dependent on specific industries for their economic performance. This may be the case when countries are heavily commodity dependent. For example, in 18 African countries, one commodity contributes more than half of export revenues.[16] Governments frequently believe that, given such heavy national dependence on a particular industrial sector, government control is necessary to ensure national economic health.

Other reasons have also contributed to the development of state-owned enterprises. On occasion, the sizable investment required for the development of an industry is too large to come from the private sector. Therefore, governments close the gap between national needs and private-sector resources by developing industries themselves. In addition, governments often decide to rescue failing private enterprises by placing them in government ownership. In doing so, they fulfill important policy objectives such as the maintenance of employment, the development of depressed areas, or the increase of exports.

Some governments have also maintained that state-owned firms may be better for the country than privately held companies because they may be more societally oriented and therefore contribute more to the greater good. This is particularly the case in areas such as telecommunications and transportation, where profit maximization, at least from a governmental perspective, may not always be the appropriate primary objective.

Relevance of State-Owned Enterprises to International Business

Three types of activities in which the international manager is likely to encounter state-owned enterprises are market entry, the sourcing or marketing process, and international competition. On occasion, the very existence of a state-owned enterprise may inhibit or prohibit foreign-market entry. For reasons of development and growth, governments frequently make market entry from the outside quite difficult so that the state-owned enterprise can perform according to plan. Even if market entry is permitted, the conditions under which a foreign firm can conduct business are often substantially less favorable than the conditions under which state-owned enterprises operate. Therefore, the international firm may be placed at a competitive disadvantage and may not be able to perform successfully even though economic factors would indicate success.

The international manager also faces a unique situation when sourcing from or marketing to state-owned enterprises. Even though the state-owned firm may appear to be simply another business partner, it is ultimately an extension of the government and its activities. Quite often this may mean that a state-owned enterprise conducts its transactions according to the overall foreign policy of the country rather than according to economic rationale. For example, political considerations can play a decisive role in purchasing decisions. Contracts may be concluded for noneconomic reasons rather than based on product offering and performance. Contract conditions may depend on foreign policy outlook, prices may be altered to reflect government displeasure, and delivery performance may change to "send a signal." Exports and imports may be delayed or encouraged depending on the current needs of government. Even though an economic rationale appears to exist within a state-owned enterprise, the interests and concerns of the owner—the state—may lead it to be driven by politics.[17]

This also holds true when the international firm encounters international competition from state-owned enterprises. Very often, the concentration of these firms is not in areas of comparative advantage, but rather in areas that at the time are most beneficial for the government owning the firm. Input costs often are much less important than policy objectives. Sometimes, state-owned enterprises may not even know the value of the products they buy and sell because prices in themselves have such a low priority. As a result, the international manager may be confronted with competition that is very tough to beat.

The Strategic Response to the State-Owned Enterprise

Given the problems that state-owned enterprises can represent for the international firm and its management, various strategic alternatives for dealing with this challenge should be considered.

One major alternative is to demonstrate the benefits of working through private-sector and free-market activities rather than government control. If results can show that the benefits gained from government control are far outweighed by its cost, foreign policymakers may reconsider the value of creating state-owned enterprises. The United States, for example, has taken an international lead by deregulating some industries that were tightly controlled or regulated. As a result of the U.S. activity, a philosophical realignment has taken place in other countries, reversing the trend toward state ownership and resulting in increased privatization of such enterprises.

A second response to the state-owned enterprise is international negotiation and government intervention to "level the playing field." Whenever discriminatory market conditions are encountered, complaints can be launched to the home government. These complaints in turn can be accumulated and aired at meetings of international trade negotiators, with the goal of eliminating the discrimination. Alternatively, particularly in the United States, lawsuits can be initiated against unfair competition from abroad. If the findings are favorable, penalties for subsidization or dumping are frequently imposed against foreign firms.

A third response lies in the antitrust area, particularly for firms or industries in which economies of scale play a major role. To provide relief for firms that are subject to pressures by large-scale, state-owned enterprises, governments can consider relaxing antitrust provisions. In the United States, for example, antitrust laws were originally written with domestic rather than global competition in mind. Their relaxation permits domestic firms to cooperate in domestic and international activities through measures such as joint research and development efforts.

The strategic responses just described may be valuable in the medium and long term. For the short term, the international firm needs to persevere in the marketplace in spite of the existence of state-owned enterprises. This means that dealings with such enterprises are often necessary. In doing so, the international manager must be wary of policy objectives and policy changes. Business proposals for either sourcing or selling must be structured with not only the economic rationale in mind, but also the policy imperative under which the state-owned enterprise operates. Managers may decide to license only older technology to state-owned enterprises. Moreover, to be at least partially insulated from sudden policy actions by state-owned enterprises, they must develop alternative sources of supply and contingency plans in case of rapid shifts in demand.

The international manager can also seek opportunities that are created by the very existence of state-owned enterprises. For example, there may be room for joint ventures or cooperation agreements. Alternatively, the international firm may be able to provide services such as distribution agreements or management training.

State-owned enterprises often originate very large projects. Because domestic supply is frequently insufficient for the needs of such projects, there may be room for the participation of foreign firms, particularly when new technology or sophisticated project-management techniques are required. Yet proper caution must be exercised so that the firm can be assured of participating in a successful venture.

In many instances, large-scale projects are cofinanced by international institutions such as the World Bank or by regional institutions such as the Interamerican Development Bank. Even though these organizations make allowances for the policy aims of the borrower, they also impose stringent requirements regarding the efficiency of the project. They may therefore permit a domestic sourcing preference but insist on limits to its extent. Cofinanced projects therefore offer interesting opportunities to the international firm, particularly because their contracting requirements are reasonably tightly defined and easily available internationally through the financing institutions.

Privatization

Governments are increasingly recognizing that it is possible to reduce the cost of governing by changing their role and involvement in the economy. Through privatization, governments can cut their budget costs and still ensure that more efficient services—not fewer services—are provided to the people. In addition, the product or service may also become more productive and more innovative and may expand choices for the private sector.

In the mid-1970s, the United States took the lead in reducing government involvement with industry by deregulating domestic industries such as telephone service and airlines, which had been tightly controlled or regulated. Britain pioneered the concept of privatization in 1979 by converting 20 state firms into privately owned companies. In the 1980s Chile privatized 470 enterprises, which had produced 24 percent of the country's value added.[18] By the 1990s, privatization had become a key element in governmental economic strategy around the world. In addition to Asia, Africa, Latin America, and the eastern European nations, even western Europe entered the privatization field on a large scale, as Global Perspective 10.4 shows.

The methods of privatization vary from country to country. Some nations come up with a master plan for privatization, whereas others deal with it on a case-by-case basis. The Treuhandanstalt of Germany, for example, which has been charged with disposing of most East German state property, aims to sell firms but maximize the number of jobs retained. In other countries, ownership shares are distributed to citizens and employees. Some nations simply sell to the highest bidder in order to maximize the proceeds. For example, Mexico has used most of its privatization proceeds to amortize its internal debt, resulting in savings of nearly $1 billion a year in interest payments.

The purpose of many privatization programs is to improve productivity, profitability, and product quality and to shrink the size of government. It is expected that as companies are exposed to market forces and competition, they will have to produce better goods at lower costs. In most instances, privatization also intends to attract new capital for these firms so that they can carry out necessary adjustments

Global Perspective

10.4
Privatization Sweeps the Globe

After record privatization in eastern Europe, Russia, Latin America, and Asia, privatization is now sweeping across western Europe like a tidal wave. Italy is selling off giant industries that have been part of the government since the Mussolini era. State-owned industrial conglomerates have been turned into public-stock companies in fields such as oil, banking, food, power, and aerospace. France is cutting loose control over everything from computer companies to giant insurers. Even Germany is getting into the act by putting its national airline, Lufthansa, and Deutsche Bundespost Telekom on the block.

This is not an easy step to take. Says Daniel Gros of the Brussels-based Center for European Policy Studies: "Some diehards don't want to sell their state firms." They give the power to government to "give people hundreds of thousands of jobs. That's where they get their power from."

Why all the privatization? First of all, state enterprises were not very successful. Under state ownership, both managers and workers have strong incentives to "decapitalize" the enterprises that employ them by extracting as much wealth as they can for themselves. They have little or no incentive to increase the value of the firm through wise investments, increasing productivity, or restraining wages and employment, because they have little chance of sharing in the firm's future prosperity. But new rules in the European Community also helped. These rules have banned billions in state subsidies that uncompetitive state firms have relied on for decades to stay afloat. Finally, many countries see privatization as an opportunity to trim massive budget deficits and national debt.

Sources: Patrick Oster, "Europe Dashes to Jettison State-Owned Businesses," *The Washington Post*, July 23, 1992: D10,D14; "Owners Are the Only Answer," *The Economist*, September 21, 1991: 10.

and improvements. Since local capital is often scarce, and government budgets tight, privatization efforts increasingly aim at attracting foreign capital. Therefore, the trend toward privatization offers unique opportunities for international managers. Existing firms, both large and small, can be acquired at low cost, often with governmental support through tax exemptions, investment grants, special depreciation allowances, and low interest rate credits. The purchase of such firms enables the international firm to expand operations without having to start from scratch. In addition, since wages are often low in the countries where privatization takes place, there is a major opportunity to build low-cost manufacturing and sourcing bases. Furthermore, the international firm can also act as a catalyst by accelerating the pace of transferring business skills and technology and by boosting trade prospects. In short, the very process of change offers new opportunities to the adept manager.

SUMMARY

Special concerns must be considered by the international manager when dealing with emerging market economies or with state-owned enterprises. Although the former centrally planned economies offer vast opportunities for trade, business practices may be significantly different from those to which the executive is accustomed.

In the emerging market economies, the key to international business success will be an understanding of the fact that societies in transition require special adaptation of business skills and time to complete the transformation. It must also be recognized that the changes in these economies will in turn precipitate changes in the West, particularly in the trade sector. Adapting early to these changes can offer new opportunities to the international firm.

Often the international manager is also faced with state-owned enterprises that have been formed in noncommunist nations for reasons of national or economic security. These firms may inhibit foreign-market entry, and they frequently reflect in their transactions the overall domestic and foreign policy of the country rather than any economic rationale.

The current global trend toward privatization offers new opportunities to the international firm, either through investment or by offering business skills and knowledge to assist in the success of privatization.

Key Terms and Concepts

foreign trade organizations (FTOs)	glasnost
central plan	state-owned enterprise
perestroika	

Questions for Discussion

1. Planning is necessary, yet central planning is inefficient. Why?
2. Discuss the observation that "Russian products do what they are supposed to do—but only that."
3. How can U.S. consumer acceptance of Russian products be improved?
4. How can and should the West help eastern European countries?
5. How can central European managers be trained to be market oriented?

6. Under what circumstances would you be in favor of state-owned enterprises?

7. Where do you see the greatest potential in future trade between emerging market economies and the West?

8. What are the benefits of privatization?

Recommended Readings

Boecker, Paul M. (ed.) *Latin America's Turnaround: The Paths to Privatization and Foreign Investment.* San Francisco: ICS Press, 1993.

Carvounis, Chris, and Brinda Z. Carvounis. *U.S. Commercial Opportunities in the Soviet Union.* Westport, Conn.: Quorum Books, 1989.

Czinkota, Michael, "The EC '92 and Eastern Europe: Effects of Integration vs. Disintegration," *Columbia Journal of World Business* 26, no. 1 (1991): 20–27.

Gatti, Charles, "East-Central Europe: The Morning After," *Foreign Affairs* 69 (Winter 1990/91).

Goldman, Marshall, *What Went Wrong with Perestroika.* New York: W.W. Norton, 1992.

Hachette, Dominique and Rolf Luders, *Privatization in Chile: An Economic Appraisal.* San Francisco: ICS Press, 1992.

Puffer, Sheila M. (ed.) *The Russian Management Revolution.* Armonk, N.Y.: M.E. Sharpe, 1992.

Silverman, Bertram, Robert Vogt, and Murray Yanowitch (eds.) *Labor and Democracy in the Transition to a Market System.* Armonk, N.Y.: M.E. Sharpe, 1992.

Simai, Mihaly. *East-West Cooperation at the End of the 1980s: Global Issues, Foreign Direct Investments and Debts.* Budapest, Hungarian Scientific Council for World Economy, 1989.

Notes

1. Richard M. Hammer, "Dramatic Winds of Change," *Price Waterhouse Review* 33 (1989): 23–27.

2. Peter G. Lauter and Paul M. Dickie, "Multinational Corporations in Eastern European Socialist Economies," *Journal of Marketing* 25 (Fall 1975): 40–46.

3. Alan B. Sherr, "Joint Ventures in the USSR: Soviet and Western Interests with Considerations for Negotiations," *Columbia Journal of World Business* 23 (Summer 1988): 25–37.

4. Raymond J. Waldmann, *Managed Trade: The New Competition Among Nations* (Cambridge, Mass.: Ballinger Press, 1986), 136.

5. Mihaly Simai, "Problems, Conditions, and Possibilities for an Export-Oriented Economic Policy in Hungary," in *Export Policy: A Global Assessment,* eds. M. Czinkota and G. Tesar (New York: Praeger, 1982), 20–30.

6. Eugene Theroux and Arthur L. George, *Joint Ventures in the Soviet Union: Law and Practice,* rev. ed. (Washington, D.C.: Baker & McKenzie, 1989), 1.

7. Sherr, "Joint Ventures in the USSR," 27.

8. *The World Factbook 1992* (Washington, D.C.: Central Intelligence Agency, 1992).

9. Johny K. Johansson, *Marketing, Free Choice and the New International Order* (Washington, D.C.: Georgetown University, March 2, 1990), 10.

10. Mihaly Simai, *East-West Cooperation at the End of the 1980s: Global Issues, Foreign Direct Investments, and Debts* (Budapest: Hungarian Scientific Council for World Economy, 1989), 21.

11. Jerry F. Hough, *Opening Up the Soviet Economy* (Washington, D.C.: The Brookings Institution, 1988), 46.

12. Michael R. Czinkota, "The EC '92 and Eastern Europe: Effects of Integration vs. Disintegration,"

Columbia Journal of World Business 26 (1991): 20-27.

13. Janet Porter, "Western Consultants Benefits as Soviets Restructure Business," *The Journal of Commerce* (July 12, 1988): 1A, 3A.

14. John W. Kiser, "Tapping Soviet Technology," in *Common Sense in U.S.-Soviet Trade,* eds. M. Chapman and C. Marcy (Washington, D.C.: American Committee on East-West Accord, 1983), 104.

15. Robert D. Hisrich, Michael P. Peters, and Arnold K. Weinstein, "East-West Trade: The View from the United States," *Journal of International Business Studies* 12 (Winter 1981): 109-121.

16. Martin C. Schnitzer, Marilyn L. Liebrenz, and Connard W. Kubin, *International Business* (Cincinnati: South-Western Publishing, 1985), 421.

17. Renato Mazzolini, "European Government-Controlled Enterprises: An Organizational Politics View," *Journal of International Business Studies* 11 (Spring-Summer 1980): 48-58.

18. "Owners Are the Only Answer," *The Economist,* September 21, 1991: 10.

Cases

Promoting U.S. Tobacco Exports:
A Conflict between Trade and Health

Tobacco and its related products have traditionally played an important role in the U.S. economy. Tobacco represents the sixth largest cash crop in the United States. Twenty-one states and more than two million people are engaged in tobacco growing, manufacturing, and marketing.

On January 11, 1964, the *Surgeon General's Report* documented the adverse health effects of smoking. Since then, the Surgeon General and other medical experts have determined that smoking may cause lung cancer and low birth weights, as well as other health problems. Concurrent with these findings, U.S. cigarette consumption, as well as other forms of tobacco use, has been gradually decreasing. While health considerations definitely played an important role in discouraging smoking, other factors such as higher cigarette prices, steeper federal and local taxes, and governmental restrictions on where smoking is permitted also contributed to the decline in U.S. cigarette consumption.

Although the use of tobacco products is no longer as socially acceptable as before, tobacco use is still tolerated and even welcomed by the government as a source of tax revenues. Apart from the desire to discourage smoking, a major rationale behind raising taxes on tobacco products continues to be the positive revenue impact for the government. Even though many people have quit smoking, about 550 billion cigarettes were consumed in the United States in 1989. With a 16-cent federal excise tax per pack, the amount of taxes collected is very meaningful to a deficit-constrained budget process.

THE IMPORTANCE OF EXPORTS FOR U.S. TOBACCO COMPANIES

In the face of higher domestic taxes, greater governmental restrictions on smoking in public places, and the growing unpopularity of tobacco use, U.S. tobacco companies are vigorously promoting cigarette exports overseas in order to compensate

Source: This case was written by Michael R. Czinkota with the assistance of Homer Teng, using the following background material: United States General Accounting Office, "Trade and Health Issues: Dichotomy between U.S. Tobacco Export Policy and Antismoking Initiatives," May 1990; Andrew Copenhaver, Statement on behalf of the United States Cigarette Export Association before the Subcommittee on Health and the Environment Committee on Energy and Commerce, United States House of Representatives, May 17, 1990.

for their diminishing domestic market. Due to the high quality of American tobacco and the determination of U.S. tobacco companies to sell their products overseas, U.S. tobacco firms have been increasing their export shipments steadily since 1985.

The chief lobbyist for the tobacco industry, the United States Cigarette Export Association (USCEA), claims that the export of tobacco is beneficial to the U.S. economy. It contributes substantially to the lowering of the country's enormous trade deficit, and it generates hundreds of thousands of jobs for Americans. According to U.S. Department of Commerce statistics, U.S. net exports of unmanufactured tobacco in the first half of 1990 amounted to $362.9 million. During the same period, the trade surplus in cigarettes amounted to $2,021.3 million. More than 125,000 people were directly involved in tobacco exports in 1989, and many others were employed in the derivative areas of the tobacco industry.

U.S. TRADE POLICY

This recent boom in U.S. exports is the direct result of the opening of new overseas markets in Asia to American tobacco products. The opening was achieved due to the success of the United States Trade Representative (USTR) in negotiating the elimination of unfair trade barriers in Asia. The USTR is the governmental organization charged with the promotion of U.S. trade interests abroad. In the name of free trade, the USTR acts on behalf of U.S. companies in negotiating for the removal of unfair trade barriers and any discriminatory trade practices directed against U.S. products. Under Section 301 of the Trade Act of 1974, the United States Trade Representative is obligated to investigate cases of trade discrimination faced by U.S. companies abroad.

Throughout the 1980s, the USCEA filed several petitions under Section 301 of the Trade Act of 1974 aimed at removing unfair foreign trade barriers in Japan, South Korea, Taiwan, and Thailand, which restricted the export of American tobacco products. U.S. cigarette exporters had long been experiencing trade discrimination in these potentially lucrative Asian countries. In Thailand, for instance, more than 60 percent of the adult males smoke. According to figures from the mid-1980s, approximately 40 percent of the people of both Japan and South Korea smoke. The governments of these countries had restricted the sale of foreign tobacco products because tobacco production and manufacturing play a significant part in their national economies. For example, Japan and Taiwan are ranked 18th and 36th in terms of tobacco production, respectively, out of a total of 94 tobacco-growing countries worldwide. The estimated green-weight tobacco production figures are 71,000 tons for Japan and 20,100 tons for Taiwan.

Realizing the importance of tobacco to their agricultural sector and to their financial coffers, the governments of the aforementioned countries had set up monopolies to protect their tobacco industries from foreign competition. The following statement in the 1989 annual report of the Thailand Tobacco Monopoly (TTM) illustrates clearly the function of such a government-controlled monopoly:

> The outcome of operation of TTM not only creates income to the government to be used to develop the country, but also benefits many tobacco ranchers in the northern and northeastern regions whose major income is derived from tobacco plantations.

Japan, Taiwan, South Korea, and Thailand traditionally blocked the import of American cigarettes by imposing high import tariffs, discriminatory taxes, and unfair marketing and distribution restrictions. These trade practices caused outrage among the U.S. tobacco companies and led to the intervention of the USTR. The following are examples of USTR successes in opening the previously closed tobacco markets.

Following the discovery of evidence that Japan imposed high tariffs and severe restrictions on the import and manufacturing of foreign cigarettes, the president of the United States instructed the USTR to initiate a Section 301 action against the country on September 16, 1985. This led Japan to remove cigarette tariffs, as well as other discriminatory barriers directed against imported cigarettes. Similarly, on December 12, 1986, Taiwan lifted its restrictions on the distribution and sale of U.S. tobacco products following the threat of retaliatory measures from the United States. After prolonged negotiations with the USTR, the South Korean Monopoly Corporation, the government tobacco monopoly in that country, agreed to allow U.S. cigarettes to enter the Korean market without discrimination on February 16, 1988.

PROMOTION OF TOBACCO EXPORTS

Besides ensuring fair treatment for U.S. cigarettes overseas, the U.S. government actively supports the export of tobacco by funding three export-promotion programs. These are the Department of Agriculture's Cooperator Market Development Program, the Targeted Export Assistance Program, and the Export Credit Guarantee programs.

The Department of Agriculture's cooperator program aims at expanding and seeking overseas markets for U.S. agricultural products through the efforts of private, nonprofit organizations. The Department of Agriculture allocates $150,000 to Tobacco Associates, the tobacco cooperator, to promote market-development activities for U.S. tobacco products.

The Targeted Export Assistance Program's purpose is to counteract the adverse effects of subsidies, import quotas, or other unfair trade practices in foreign countries on U.S. agricultural products. Again, Tobacco Associates is the private organization entrusted to carry out this endeavor. In 1990, Tobacco Associates received $5 million in U.S. government funding to provide certain countries with the technical know-how, training, and equipment to manufacture cigarettes that use U.S. flue-cured and burley tobacco products.

Finally, the Department of Agriculture's Export Credit Guarantee programs, GSM 102 and 103, help U.S. farm export sales by stimulating U.S. bank financing of foreign purchases on credit terms. The GSM 102 program guarantees the repayment of loans extended up to three years, while the GSM 103 program guarantees loans of up to ten years. During the period between October 1985 and September 1989, 66 companies received GSM guarantee credits for the sale of 127 million pounds of tobacco, which had a market value of $214 million.

CONFLICTING OBJECTIVES

The involvement of the U.S. government in furthering the export of tobacco has generated controversy within the United States. This controversy centers on the dilemma of simultaneously pursuing policies that are obviously at odds with each other.

On one hand, the U.S. government, spearheaded by the Department of Health and Human Services, has been actively discouraging smoking on the domestic scene. Also, the United States is a strong supporter of the worldwide antismoking movement. The Department of Health and Human Services serves as a collaborating headquarters for the United Nations World Health Organization and maintains close relationships with other health organizations around the world in sharing information on the detrimental health effects of smoking. On the other hand, a different part of the government, the USTR, has been helping tobacco companies expand their export sales by opening up previously closed markets. In addition, the government is actively promoting tobacco exports overseas by funding three export-market-development programs. The U.S. trade policy that aims to boost the exports of tobacco products is clearly in conflict with the U.S. health policy aimed at reducing the use of tobacco.

THE CURRENT SITUATION

U.S. production of tobacco has risen in the last four years because of an increase in foreign demand for high-quality U.S. tobacco leaves. The Tobacco Merchants Association concluded in a 1989 report:

> As U.S. cigarette exports gain an even greater foothold in Asia, one would expect that the foreign monopoly demand for direct burley shipments, along with high-quality U.S. flue-cured, will grow as the monopolies compete head-to-head against U.S. cigarette blends.

These economic benefits, together with the fact that Asian countries such as Japan and Thailand are permitting tobacco advertisements, lead many members of Congress, such as Rep. Thomas J. Bliley of Virginia, to support U.S. tobacco exports. However, the health and moral questions surrounding tobacco exports continue to generate congressional and public opposition to tobacco exports. A vocal opponent of tobacco exports is Rep. Henry A. Waxman, who considers U.S. tobacco export policies morally offensive and comparable to the British exports of opium to China in the 19th century.

Questions for Discussion

1. Should U.S. exports of tobacco products be permitted in light of the domestic campaign against smoking?
2. Should the U.S. government get involved in tearing down foreign trade barriers to U.S. tobacco?
3. Should export promotion support be provided to U.S. tobacco producers?
4. To what degree should ethics influence government policy or corporate decision making in the case of tobacco exports?
5. Will your answers change if you differentiate between the short and the long term?

Union Carbide at Bhopal

On Sunday, December 3, 1984, the peaceful life of a U.S. corporate giant was joltingly disrupted. The Union Carbide plant at Bhopal, a city less than 400 miles from New Delhi, India, had leaked poisonous gas into the air. Within one week over 2,000

Source: This case study was written by Michael R. Czinkota by adapting secondary source materials from: Alan Hall, "The Bhopal Tragedy Has Union Carbide Reeling," Business Week, December 17, 1984, 32; Clemens P. Work, "Inside Story of Union Carbide's India Nightmare," U.S. News & World Report, January 21, 1985, 51–52; Armin Rosencranz, "Bhopal, Transnational Corporations, and Hazardous Technologies," Ambio 17, no. 5 (1988): 336–341; and Sanjoy Hazarika, "Carbide Plant Closed by India Unrest," The New York Times, Monday, May 13, 1991, D12.

people died and more remained critically ill. Over 100,000 people were treated for nausea, blindness, and bronchial problems. It was one of history's worst industrial accidents.

Union Carbide is America's 37th largest industrial corporation, with more than 100,000 employees, and annual sales of more than $9 billion. The firm is active in petrochemicals, industrial gases, metals and carbon products, consumer products, and technology transfers.

Union Carbide operated 14 plants in India. Total Indian operations accounted for less than 2 percent of corporate sales. In spite of a policy by the Indian government to restrict foreign majority ownership of plants, Union Carbide owned 50.9 percent of the Bhopal plant. This special arrangement was granted by the government because the plant served as a major technology transfer project. In order to achieve the goal of technology transfer, management of the plant was mostly carried out by Indian nationals. General corporate safety guidelines applied to the plant, but local regulatory agencies were charged with enforcing Indian environmental laws. Only three weeks before the accident, the plant had received an "environmental clearance certificate" from the Indian State Pollution Board.

The accident resulted in wide public awareness in the United States. A poll showed that 47 percent of those questioned linked Union Carbide's name to the Bhopal disaster. The direct impact of this awareness on Union Carbide's business remains uncertain. Most U.S. consumers do not connect the Union Carbide name to its line of consumer products, which consists of brands such as Energizer, Glad, and Presto. Industrial users, on the other hand, are highly aware of Union Carbide's products. One area that could be particularly affected is that of technology transfer, which in 1983 accounted for 24 percent of Union Carbide's revenues. The firm has concentrated increasingly on that sector, selling mainly its know-how in the fields of engineering, manufacturing, and personnel training.

THE PUBLIC REACTION

Internationally, the reaction was one of widespread consumer hostility. Environmentalists demonstrated at Union Carbide plants in West Germany and Australia. Some facilities were firebombed; most were spray painted. Plans for plants in Scotland had to be frozen. The operation of a plant in France was called into question by the French government.

Major financial repercussions occurred as well. Within a week of the accident, Union Carbide stock dropped by $10, a loss in market value of nearly $900 million. A $1.2 billion line of credit was frozen. Profits of Union Carbide India Ltd., which in 1984 had been about 8.2 million rupees, or about $480,000, dropped by 1985 to 1.3 million rupees, or $78,000. By 1990, the company reported a loss of 132 million rupees, about $7.8 million.

In the ensuing debate of the Bhopal disaster, three basic issues were highlighted—responsible industrial planning, adequate industrial-safety measures, and corporate accountability. In terms of industrial planning, both Union Carbide and the Indian government were said to have failed. The Indian subsidiary of Union Carbide did little to inform workers about the highly toxic methyl isocyanate (MIC) the plant was producing and the potential health threat to neighboring regions. When the accident occurred, the subsidiary's management team reportedly resisted the parent company's instructions to apply first aid to victims for fear of generating widespread panic within the corporation and the region. The Indian government, on the other hand, seemed to regard technology transfer to be a higher priority than public safety. The local government approved construction of the plant with little med-ical and scientific investigation into its biological effects on the environment and on people.

The second issue was the absence of a "culture of safety" among Indian techni-cians, engineers, and management. From the very beginning, the project lacked a team of experienced maintenance personnel who would have recognized the need for higher safety measures and, more important, a different choice of technology. When the entire Indian government wholeheartedly approved the import of the most advanced chemical production facility in any developing country without qualified personnel to handle the material and without insight into appropriate precautionary measures in case of an accident, the seeds were sown for potential disaster.

The third area of interest in the Bhopal incident is that of corporate account-ability. There are three general norms of international law concerning the jurispru-dence of the home government over the foreign subsidiary:

1. Both state and nonstate entities are liable to pay compensation to the victims of environmental pollution and accidents.

2. The corporation is responsible for notifying and consulting the involved offi-cials of actual and potential harm involved in the production and transport of hazardous technologies and materials.

3. The causer or originator of environmental damage is liable to pay compensa-tion to the victims.

These and other developing norms of international law serve to make transnational corporations more responsible for their operations.

COMPENSATION TO VICTIMS

Five days after the incident the first damage suit, asking for $15 billion, was filed in U.S. Federal District Court. Since then more than 130 suits have been filed in the United States and more than 2,700 in India. Union Carbide offered to pay $300 mil-lion over a period of 30 years to settle the cases before the courts in the United States and India. The Indian government rejected the offer, claiming that the amount was far below its original request of $615 million. By 1986 most U.S. lawsuits had been consolidated in the New York Federal Court. In May 1986, however, the judge presiding over the collective Bhopal cases ruled that all suits arising out of the ac-cident should be heard in the Indian judicial system, claiming that "India is where the accident occurred, and where the victims, witnesses and documents are located." While this decision appeared to benefit Union Carbide because of lower damage awards in India, the judge explicitly stated that (1) Union Carbide (USA) and its In-dian affiliate will have to submit to the jurisdiction of the Indian court system, (2) Union Carbide must turn over all relevant documents to the plaintiffs' lawyers in In-dia as they would if in the United States, and (3) Union Carbide must agree to what-ever judgment is rendered in India. This decision had a major effect on Union Car-bide (USA) because (1) both Union Carbide (USA) and its Indian subsidiary now had to answer to the Indian court and (2) the entire company's assets had become in-volved.

In India, the class suit traveled from the Bhopal district court to the Madhya Pradesh High Court and finally to the Indian Supreme Court, where it stood as of May 1991. Although a settlement agreement was reached between Union Car-bide and the Indian government, the descendents of the 2,000 victims were not satis-fied. Several victims' consumer groups and public-interest lawyers filed petitions contesting the authority of the government to handle the lawsuit on behalf of the victims' descendents. The petitions claim that the government has no right to represent the victims because governmental negligence caused the accident in the first place and the government should be as much a target as Union Carbide in the suit itself. If the Indian Supreme Court were to uphold this rationale, then the government would be unable to settle on the victims' behalf, thereby nullifying the agreed amount. As a result of the internal debate in India, the $421 million paid in settlement by Union Carbide was frozen. Instead, the Indian government itself is disbursing 200 rupees, about $10, a month to all persons who lived in the neighborhoods affected by the gas leak. The government plans to get these expenses back when the case is completed.

The lessons learned? Several chemical companies have reduced the size of their storage tanks of toxic materials while others have cut their inventories by as much as 50 percent. Many have provided information to the communities in which they manufacture. Some have even invested in risk-assessment studies of their operations of hazardous materials.

Questions for Discussion

1. How could Union Carbide have planned for an event such as Bhopal?
2. How would such planning have improved corporate response to the disaster?
3. Does it make sense to base corporate strategy on worst-case scenarios?
4. Which other firms are exposed to similar risks?
5. What are the future implications for the management of Union Carbide?
6. What are the future implications for the government of India?
7. What are your views on the delay of compensation paid to the victims?
8. In general, should joint venture partners absorb part of the blame and cost when accidents occur?

IKEA: "It's a Big Country; Someone Has to Furnish It"

IKEA, the world's largest home furnishings retail chain, was founded in Sweden in 1943 as a mail-order company and opened its first showroom 10 years later. From its headquarters in Almhult, IKEA has since expanded to worldwide sales of more than $3 billion from 119 outlets in 24 countries (see Table 1). In fact, the second

Source: This case, prepared by Ilkka A. Ronkainen, is based on: Bill Saporito, "IKEA's Got 'Em Lining Up," Fortune, March 11, 1991, 72; Rita Martenson, "Is Standardization of Marketing Feasible in Culture-Bound Industries? A European Case Study," International Marketing Review 4 (Autumn 1987): 7-17; Eleanor Johnson Tracy, "Shopping Swedish Style Comes to the U.S.," Fortune, January 27, 1986, 63-67; Mary Krienke, "IKEA—Simple Good Taste," Stores, April 1986, 58; Jennifer Lin, "IKEA's U.S. Translation," Stores, April 1986, 63; "Furniture Chain Has a Global View," Advertising Age, October 26, 1987, 58; and Bill Kelley, "The New Wave from Europe," Sales and Marketing Management, November 1987, 46-48. Updated information provided directly by IKEA U.S., Inc.

store that IKEA built was in Oslo, Norway. Today, IKEA operates large warehouse showrooms in Sweden, Norway, Denmark, Holland, France, Belgium, Germany, Switzerland, Austria, Canada, the United States, Saudi Arabia, and the United Kingdom. It has smaller stores in Kuwait, Australia, Hong Kong, Singapore, the Canary Islands, and Iceland. A store near Budapest opened in 1990.

The international expansion of IKEA has progressed in three phases, all of them continuing at the present time: Scandinavian expansion, begun in 1963; west European expansion, begun in 1973; and North American expansion, begun in 1974. Of the individual markets, Germany is the largest, accounting for 27.5 percent of company sales. The phases of expansion are detectable in the worldwide sales shares depicted in Figure 1. "We want to bring the IKEA concept to as many people as possible," IKEA officials have said.

TABLE 1.1
IKEA's International Expansion

Year	Outlets[a]	Countries[a]	Coworkers[b]	Catalog Circulation[c]	Turnover in Swedish Kronor[d]
1954	1	1	15	285,000	3,000,000
1964	2	2	250	1,200,000	79,000,000
1974	10	5	1,500	13,000,000	616,000,000
1984	66	17	8,300	45,000,000	6,770,000,000
1988	75	19	13,400	50,535,000	14,500,000,000
1990	95	23	16,850	N/A	19,400,000,000
1992	119	24	23,200	N/A	24,275,000,000

[a]Stores/countries being opened by end of 1993.

[b]23,200 coworkers are equivalent to 18,500 full-time workers.

[c]13 languages, 29 editions; exact number no longer made available.

[d]Corresponding to net sales of the IKEA group of companies.

Source: IKEA U.S., Inc.

FIGURE 1
IKEA Worldwide Sales Expressed as Percentages of Turnover

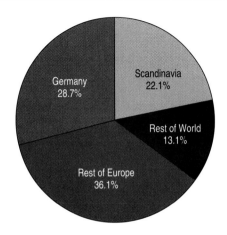

THE IKEA CONCEPT

Ingvar Kamprad, the founder, formulated as IKEA's mission to "offer a wide range of home furnishings of good design and function at prices so low that the majority of people can afford to buy them." The principal target market of IKEA, which is similar across countries and regions in which IKEA has a presence, is composed of people who are young, highly educated, liberal in their cultural values, white-collar workers, and not especially concerned with status symbols.

IKEA follows a standardized product strategy with an identical assortment around the world. Today, IKEA carries an assortment of thousands of different home furnishings that range from plants to pots, sofas to soup spoons, and wine glasses to wallpaper. The smaller items are carried to complement the bigger ones. IKEA does not have its own manufacturing facilities but designs all of its furniture. The network of subcontracted manufacturers numbers nearly 2,100 in 63 countries. IKEA shoppers have to become "prosumers"—half producers, half consumers—because most products must be assembled.

Manufacturers are responsible for shipping the components to large warehouses, for example, to the central one in Almhult. These warehouses then supply the various stores, which are in effect miniwarehouses. The final distribution is the customer's responsibility. IKEA does cooperate with car-rental companies to offer vans and small trucks at reasonable rates for customers needing delivery service.

Although IKEA has concentrated on company-owned, larger-scale outlets, franchising has been used in areas in which the market is relatively small or where uncertainty may exist as to the response to the IKEA concept. IKEA uses mail order in Europe and Canada but has resisted expansion into it in the United States, mainly because of capacity constraints.

IKEA offers prices that are 30 to 50 percent lower than fully assembled competing products. This is a result of large-quantity purchasing, low-cost logistics, store location in suburban areas, and the do-it-yourself approach to marketing. IKEA's prices do vary from market to market, largely because of fluctuations in exchange rates and differences in taxation regimes, but price positioning is kept as standardized as possible.

IKEA's promotion is centered on the catalog. The IKEA catalog is printed in 13 languages and has a worldwide circulation of well over 50 million copies. The catalogs are uniform in layout except for minor regional differences. The company's advertising goal is to generate word-of-mouth publicity through innovative approaches.

The IKEA concept is summarized in Table 2.

TABLE 2
The IKEA Concept

Target market:	"Young people of all ages"
Product:	IKEA offers the same products worldwide. The countries of origin of these products are: Nordic countries (39 percent), western Europe (31 percent), eastern Europe (15 percent), and others (15 percent). Most items have to be assembled by the customer. The furniture design is modern and light. Textiles and pastels.
Distribution:	IKEA has built its own distribution network. Outlets are outside the city limits of major metropolitan areas. Products are not delivered, but IKEA cooperates with car-rental companies that offer small trucks. IKEA offers mail order in Europe and Canada.
Pricing:	The IKEA concept is based on low price. The firm tries to keep its price image constant.
Promotion:	IKEA's promotional efforts are mainly through its catalogs. IKEA has developed a prototype communications model that must be followed by all stores. Its advertising is attention getting and provocative. Media choices vary by market.

IKEA IN THE COMPETITIVE ENVIRONMENT

IKEA's strategic positioning is unique. As Figure 2 illustrates, few furniture retailers anywhere have engaged in long-term planning or achieved scale economies in production. European furniture retailers, especially those in Sweden, Switzerland, Germany, and Austria, are much smaller than IKEA. Even when companies have joined forces as buying groups, their heterogeneous operations have made it difficult for them to achieve the same degree of coordination and concentration as IKEA. Because customers are usually content to wait for the delivery of furniture, retailers have not been forced to take purchasing risks.

The value-added dimension differentiates IKEA from its competition. IKEA offers limited customer assistance but creates opportunities for consumers to choose (for example, through informational signage), transport, and assemble units of furniture. The best summary of the competitive situation was provided by a manager at another firm: "We can't do what IKEA does, and IKEA doesn't want to do what we do."

IKEA IN THE UNITED STATES

After careful study and assessment of its Canadian experience, IKEA decided to enter the U.S. market in 1985 by establishing outlets on the East Coast and, later, one in Burbank, California. IKEA's six stores on the East Coast (Philadelphia; Woodbridge near Washington, D.C.; Baltimore; Pittsburgh; Elizabeth, New Jersey; and Hicksville, New York) generated $337 million in 1992. The overwhelming level of success in 1987 led the company to invest in a warehousing facility near Philadelphia that receives goods from Sweden as well as directly from suppliers around the world. Plans call for two to three additional stores annually over the next 25 years, concentrating on the northeastern United States and California.

FIGURE 2
Competition in Furniture Retailing

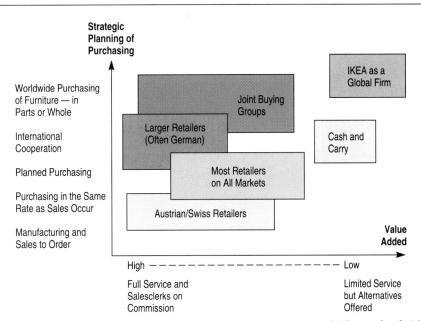

Source: Rita Martenson, "Is Standardization of Marketing Feasible in Culture-Bound Industries? A European Case Study," *International Marketing Review* 4 (Autumn 1987): 14.

Questions for Discussion

1. What accounts for IKEA's success with a standardized product and strategy in a business that is usually described as having some of the strongest cultural influences? Consider, for example, that an American buying IKEA beds will also have to buy IKEA sheets, because the beds are in European sizes.

2. Which features of the "young people of all ages" are universal and can be exploited by a global/regional strategy?

3. Is IKEA destined to succeed everywhere it cares to establish itself?

Poland's Dramatic Gamble: From Marx to Markets

Over the last few years scholars, policymakers, and international business executives have studied the dramatic developments in eastern Europe. Poland was one of the first countries to attempt a move from a planned, centrally run economy to a market economy. Many still ask: Can the Poles do it? What happens if they fail? And what's the impact on us?

Poland's troubles began at the end of World War II when the Russians liberated the country from the Germans. The communists implemented Stalinist Central Planning. Production was determined by state decree, not by markets. Huge state-run monopolies, such as Lenin Steel, dominated the economy. Prices and wages were set by the state. There was a saying in Poland, "We pretend to work, and the state pretends to pay us."

To achieve the communist goal of full employment, everyone was given a job, whether or not it was necessary. To employ so many people, wages had to be kept low. Therefore, subsidies were put in place for farmers and factories. This plan resulted in government budget deficits, a nonconvertible currency, low productivity, and shortages of almost everything.

According to one Polish citizen, "There was no food. We were lucky if we could find a kilogram of sausage . . . many times the last two kilograms of sausage were bought by the person in front of us in line."

By 1989, coping with continuing shortages and inflation running at more than 500 percent, the communists were forced to negotiate with Lech Walesa and the Solidarity Trade Union. The result was a Solidarity-led coalition government.

The new leaders did not choose a path of gradual reform. Instead, Finance Minister Leszek Balcerowicz, with the assistance of western economists, came up with a radical plan of economic reform that would move Poland from central planning to free markets virtually overnight. The government reduced its budget deficit by slashing government subsidies. Enterprises had to show a profit, or face the possibility of bankruptcy. Many state-run enterprises were privatized, sold to investors. Prices were allowed to rise to whatever the market would bear, but wages were held in check. And the Polish currency, the zloty, was devalued as the first step toward making it compatible with western currencies.

To eliminate long lines and shortages, the new plan allowed prices to rise so that producers would produce more. Prices went up for almost everything including gasoline. With gas prices and insurance so high, thousands of Poles stopped driving. Bread prices went up, electric bills quadrupled. Meanwhile, salaries only went up slightly, held in check to fight inflation. As a result of these events, the country was forced into recession. Fortunately, many enterprising Poles figured out ways to beat the old system. People sold goods from their cars and trucks, circumventing the state distribution system to lower prices on their products.

This case was drawn from the Public Broadcasting System's television program, "Adam Smith," which aired May 1, 1990. Producer: Alvin H. Perlmutter, Inc.

In the new free markets, farmers sell directly to customers. And industrious entrepreneurs have gone into business to bring products to market. One woman buys wheat from farmers, brings it to a mill to be ground, and sells the flour in Warsaw. Even students have gone into business for themselves. According to a Warsaw student, "It's great! We have a lot of customers, the business is growing. This is how it should be. This is a different market. And I'm sure, you know, in the United States it's the same. The market should be for the customer. If there is a demand, then we provide everything."

The profit motive is also one of the new laws at large state-run enterprises throughout Poland. Under the old communist system, factories sold as many products as the Central Committee told it to. Managers didn't actually know how much each product cost, and they didn't have control of costs. At the end of each fiscal year, managers would determine the loss, send it to the government, and the government would print the money to pay for it.

Under that system, line workers and managers had little or no incentive to be efficient in their work. There was little motivation for them to work harder because they were all paid the same wage. Employees who worked less got the same money as those who worked hard. Qualifications weren't important. It was more important to have a communist party card. Many party members were given jobs as directors at the factories. The general rule was that managers were "mediocre, but trustworthy."

Factories have been learning to operate under new rules. According to Jan Buczkowski, a production director, "now we have more problems than we had in the past. There are different troubles. We have to think about costs of our production. We have to think about the costs of spare parts. And we must think about our customers. It is a new market."

In the old days, workers didn't care if a line shut down for lack of parts, their jobs were guaranteed. Now if the factory doesn't turn a profit, it will be allowed to lay off workers, or worse, go bankrupt. In spite of personal hardship, many Poles seem to support the government's program.

According to Konstanty Gebert, a political analyst, the Polish people "reason in terms of a national emergency and are willing to accept sacrifices as long as they think that these sacrifices serve a general national cause. As long as they have trust and confidence in their leaders, who for the first time since the war they could democratically elect."

Privatization has been an important step on the road to reform. Laws for selling state enterprises to private investors were enacted. One of the first privatized firms was Omig, a maker of electronic components. As a private company, Omig operates more efficiently than it did before. According to Omig's Marek Ogradzki, "I think that the only way for Poland is privatization. In the future I think it will be 80 percent private sector and 20 percent state or government sector. Right now, it's the opposite way."

Privatization also includes ways of allowing workers and the public to buy shares in these companies, such as a stock exchange.

However, not all Poles are eager to buy into the reforms. Zbigniew Holdys is one of Poland's most famous rock stars. In the early 1980s his band, Perfect, filled stadiums until it was banned by the government. In spite of his position as a progressive artist, he is uneasy about life in the new Poland.

Holdys stated that, "In my generation—I am 38 years old right now—even people who are a little bit younger than me, I mean, about 30 years old feel that we are a loss for this country. I don't think anyone from our generation is ready to stand this situation. You have to learn to work in a different way, in a capitalist way."

According to Holdys, "there are hundreds, thousands, maybe even millions of people who were working in the old system. To take a man who worked in the Ministry of Culture and tell him that he must now be a manager—it's impossible. People are afraid. I don't think older generations are ready to change everything in a very short time. Probably this kind of Eden—this beautiful picture—will belong to my 2-year-old son when he is older."

Many Poles have not waited. They are learning the ways of capitalism and markets through another growth industry in eastern Europe—entrepreneurship education. For example, young managers are attending courses at the International School of Management in Warsaw that are taught by visiting professors from the United States. The school teaches English and western management skills, but the most important training is in developing an entrepreneurial mindset. Many institutions in Poland such as Solidarity have established links with universities in the United States to promote entrepreneurship and trade.

Poland needs western management skills, modern western technology, and, above all, western capital to succeed with its dramatic transformation. Official U.S. investment has increased through U.S. congressional legislation called the S.E.E.D. Act. However, new private investment is the key to long-term development.

According to Dr. Jeffrey Sachs, a Harvard economist, "If the plan fails, I think there could be a terrible calamity, not only for the Poles, but for the West. There would be an explosion of political unrest and a loss of faith that moving toward a market economy is the right direction. It could lead to a rise in populism and an explosion of new hyperinflation in Poland and in the rest of the region. The crisis could become very deep and ugly, given all the ethnic and national tension in the region. And eastern Europe and the former Soviet union could be thrown into a cauldron of violence and nationalist conflict because they've lost a clear way out. I think their hope and belief—creating a market economy and integrating with western Europe—is the direction for the future. If they lost heart in that strategy, what comes next? All sorts of terrible things could happen."

It's hard for Americans to comprehend a society in which you have to stand in line to buy everything, where the waiting time is 21 years for a telephone and 30 years for an apartment. In Poland, the lines are gone now, and so are the secret police and some of the communist apparatus. But it takes time to change the habits and the thinking of a people.

Poland's national anthem begins, "Poland has not yet perished." After surviving more than 50 years of oppression by Hitler, Stalin, and the Soviet Communist party, the Polish people clearly have the courage and commitment to rebuild and prosper. It may, however, take a generation to change the collective consciousness of the people. Do Polish people still have the patience to survive? Will the rest of the world invest for the long term?

Questions for Discussion

1. Explain the Polish expression, "We pretend to work and the state pretends to pay us." How have the Polish people adapted to market reforms and unemployment?

2. How did the old system of controlled management affect productivity and motivation in Poland's factories.

3. What have been the benefits of privatizing state-owned enterprises in Poland?

4. How had the Polish economy evolved since this program aired? Have the rapid reform programs succeeded in creating a free-market economy?

McDonald's Goes to Moscow

In the mid-1980s, a bold new program called "perestroika" was developed in the Soviet Union. Perestroika was to fundamentally reform the Soviet economy by improving the overall technological and industrial base as well as improving the quality of life for Soviet citizens through increased availability of food, housing, and consumer goods. It was hoped that this program would stimulate the entrepreneurial spirit of Soviet citizens and help the country and its government overcome crucial shortcomings. These shortcomings were the result of decades of communist orientation, which had led to significant capital and management shortages and to the lack of a market orientation and of consumer-oriented technology.

In subsequent years, a number of joint ventures between Western firms and Soviet institutions were either contemplated or even formed. However, many of these ventures, due to internal difficulties, met with only limited success. Nevertheless, the efforts of one firm, McDonald's—an icon of free enterprise—were hailed as a spectacular success.

The January 31, 1990, grand opening of McDonald's in the center of Moscow represents an important milestone for McDonald's Corporation and for the food service industry in the Soviet Union. The state-of-the art renovated building, formerly a cafe and a cultural gathering place, has indoor seating for over 700 people, has outside seating for 200, and is fully accessible to the handicapped. It currently employs over 1,000 people—the largest McDonald's crew in the world—and has served over 30,000 people per day. The original plans were to serve between 10,000 and 15,000 customers per day. The Soviet Union has become the 52nd country to host the world's largest quick-service food restaurant company, and the Russian language is the 28th working language in which the company operates. McDonald's Corporation, based in Oak Brook, Illinois, serves over 22 million people daily in 11,000 restaurants in 52 countries. The Soviet population of over 291 million represents the largest potential market of new customers for McDonald's.

THE NEGOTIATIONS	George A. Cohon, vice chairman of Moscow McDonald's and president and chief executive officer of McDonald's Restaurants of Canada, Limited, provided the leadership for the company's successful venture. His personal commitment and energy were irreplaceable during the long period of joint venture discussions with the Soviet Union. Cohon's Canadian team spent over 12 years negotiating the agreement for McDonald's to enter into the Soviet market. In April 1988, agreement was reached on the largest joint venture ever made between a food company and the Soviet Union. This concluded the longest new-territory negotiations by the company since it was founded in 1955.

Sources: "A Month Later, Moscow McDonald's Is Still Drawing Long and Hungry Lines," *Houston Post,* March 1, 1990; background information from McDonald's Restaurants of Canada, Ltd.; Tannenbaum, Jeffrey A., "Franchisers See a Future in East Bloc," *The Wall Street Journal,* June 5, 1990, B1; Maney, Kevin, and Diane Rinehart, "McDonald's in Moscow Opens Today," *USA Today*, January 31, 1990, B1; "McDonald's on the Volga," *Employment Review,* vol. 3, no. 10, 1990; Moscow McDonald's videotape produced for Dryden Press, 1990; Wates, Oliver, "Crowds Still Gather at Lenin's Tomb, but Lineups are Longer at McDonald's," *The London Free Press,* June 9, 1990.

Cohon and his Canadian team had spent thousands of hours in Moscow making presentations to hundreds of senior trade officials, staff at various ministries, and countless other groups within the Soviet Union. Despite numerous setbacks and requests for endless submissions of and revisions to their proposals, Cohon persisted because many Soviets appeared to genuinely want to establish closer ties with the West. According to Cohon, McDonald's negotiations "outlived three Soviet premiers."

The historic joint venture contract provides for an initial 20 McDonald's restaurants in Moscow and a state-of-the-art food production and distribution center to supply the restaurants. The first McDonald's accepts only rubles; the next restaurants will accept only hard currency. McDonald's Canada is managing the new venture in partnership with the Food Service Administration of the Moscow City Council in a 51 to 49 percent Soviet-Canadian partnership.

INTERNATIONAL TECHNOLOGY TRANSFER

Cohon stated that what ultimately sold the Soviets on McDonald's was the food technology it had to offer. In addition, the company's emphasis on quality, service, cleanliness, and value convinced the Moscow city officials that McDonald's could work in their city. Vladimir Malyshkov, chairman of the board of Moscow McDonald's, stated that McDonald's "created a restaurant experience like no other in the Soviet Union. It demonstrates what can be achieved when people work together."

Moscow McDonald's was clearly an international venture. McDonald's personnel from around the world helped prepare for the opening. Dutch agricultural consultants assisted in improving agricultural production. For example, they helped plant and harvest a variety of potato needed to make french fries that met McDonald's quality standards. Other international consultants assisted in negotiating contracts with farmers throughout the country to provide quality beef and other food supplies, including onions, lettuce, pickles, milk, flour, and butter. Once the Soviet farmers learned to trust the consultants, they became eager to learn about the new Western production technologies.

This technology transfer provided important long-term benefits to the Soviet citizenry. For example, through the transfer of agricultural technology and equipment, the Soviet potato farm Kishira increased its yield by 100 percent. According to the Kishira chairman, farmers from all over the Soviet Union have requested technical training in production methods to increase their crop yields. Also, since the Soviet machinery lagged 15 to 20 years behind Western technology, new machinery from Holland was used to harvest the potatoes used to make french fries. However, according to a Dutch agricultural consultant, because of the McDonald's venture, it may not take the Soviets 20 years to catch up to Western production methods.

The development of a 10,000-square-meter food production and distribution center, located in the Moscow suburb of Solntsevo, was also an international effort involving equipment and furnishings from Austria, Canada, Denmark, Finland, Holland, Italy, Japan, Spain, Sweden, Switzerland, Taiwan, Turkey, the United Kingdom, the United States, Germany, and Yugoslavia. The center provides a state-of-the-art food processing environment that meets McDonald's rigid standards.

At full capacity, the center will employ over 250 workers from the Soviet Union. Also at full capacity, the meat line will produce 10,000 patties per hour from locally acquired beef. Milk will be delivered in McDonald's refrigerated dairy trucks from a local Soviet farm and will be pasteurized and processed at the center. Flour, yeast, sugar, and shortening from sources in the Soviet Union will be used to produce over 14,000 buns per hour on the center's bakery line. Storage space at the center will hold 3,000 tons of potatoes, and the pie line will produce 5,000 apple pies per hour, made from fruit from local farmers.

MANAGEMENT TRAINING

Training for McDonald's crew and managers is essential to the customer service that the company provides. According to Bob Hissink, vice president of operations for Moscow McDonald's, hiring was just the beginning of assembling the largest McDonald's crew in the world. Over 25,000 applications were sorted, and 5,000 of the most qualified candidates were interviewed. Finally, the 630 new members of the first Moscow McDonald's team were selected. Initial training sessions were compressed into a four-week period with four or five shifts 12 hours a day. Seasoned McDonald's staff from around the world assisted the Soviet managers with crew training. The new crew of 353 women and 277 men was trained to work in several different capacities at the restaurant and had accumulated over 15,000 hours of skills development by opening day. During restaurant operating hours, about 200 crew members at a time are on duty.

The training requirements were more extensive for McDonald's managers. Four Soviets selected as managers of Moscow McDonald's spent more than nine months in North American training programs that must be completed by any McDonald's manager in the world. The Soviets graduated from the Canadian Institute of Hamburgerology after completing over 1,000 hours of training. Their studies included classroom instruction, equipment maintenance techniques, and on-the-job restaurant management.

Their training also included a two-week, in-depth study program at Hamburger University, McDonald's international training center in Oak Brook, Illinois. With more than 200 other managers from around the world, they completed advanced restaurant operations studies in senior management techniques and operating procedures. The Soviet managers are qualified to manage any McDonald's restaurant in the world.

LONG-TERM EXPECTATIONS

According to Cohon, "McDonald's is a business, but also is a responsible member of the communities it serves. The joint venture with the Soviet Union should help foster cooperation between nations and a better understanding among people. When individuals from around the world work shoulder-to-shoulder, they learn to communicate, to get along, and to be part of a team. That's what we call burger diplomacy." There is a Soviet expression that says that you must eat many meals with a person before you come to know him. At 30,000 meals per day, it may not take long for the Soviets to better understand the West through its corporate ambassador, McDonald's.

Questions for Discussion

1. Was Cohon's negotiation effort worth the success? Why or why not?
2. Discuss the extent of infrastructural investment necessary to start the first McDonald's restaurant in Moscow.
3. What effect is the "ruble only" policy going to have in light of the future "hard currency" restaurants?
4. How can McDonald's use the acquired rubles?

International Business Strategy and Operations

The initial focus in Part 4 is on small and medium-sized companies that are only beginning to enter into international markets. The focus then shifts to the activities of multinational corporations, taking into account their large resources and capabilities. Full chapters are devoted to the important strategic dimensions of business research, services, logistics, and countertrade—as well as the traditional functional areas of marketing, finance, accounting and taxation, human resources, and management.

Throughout Part 4, the differentiation between small or medium-sized firms and multinational corporations is maintained. Each chapter begins by describing a low-cost, low-risk approach appropriate for firms with little international experience. Chapters then assume a globally oriented perspective and present major international strategies.

International Business Entry

LEARNING OBJECTIVES

1. To see how firms gradually progress through an internationalization process.

2. To examine the differing reasons why firms may internationalize.

3. To study the various modes of entering the international market.

4. To understand the role and functions of international intermediaries.

5. To learn about the multiple problems and challenges of export trading.

Some Keys to Export Success

Since 1985, the United States has experienced an export boom unprecedented in history. Never before had a developed nation accomplished such rapid export growth of manufactured goods. Considering that in 1985 the United States was already the world's top exporter, the growth is extremely impressive. This success seems in stark contrast to the recent domestic recession. Although the volume of annual export growth has slowed down during the past couple years, unless the world economy takes a significant slump, exports of U.S. manufactured goods are expected to continue to do well.

What factors account for the success of U.S. exporters? Peter Drucker identifies characteristics consistent across many of the successful U.S. exporters.

1. Don't compete based on price:

All of the export powerhouses sold a high-value-added product in the foreign market. In only very few cases is the product sold primarily on price competition. Instead, the product is often unique and occupies a distinct niche position in the marketplace. One clear example is 3-M's Post-its.

2. Know your foreign customers:

Successful exporters know their customers well. Drucker argues that even with the huge geographical separation, this intimacy is easy to achieve. Take the example of Boeing, for instance, whose business is to know and track all the world's airlines. When Boeing enters a foreign market, it has good insight into the customer's marketplace, needs, and resources. Similarly, a U.S. rock-and-roll producer, after performing some market research, is likely to have good insight into whether or not a hit U.S. tape will also be a hit in Germany. Says Drucker: "The world market is a 'foreign' market only in terms of trade statistics. For successful businesspeople, these are all 'familiar' markets, at least for knowledge-intensive products." This proposition is supported by an exporting heart-valve manufacturer who said: "I do not sell to the world market. I sell to cardiac surgeons."

3. Bigness is not an advantage:

Many of the winners of the U.S. export boom are mid-size or small companies boasting a particular expertise in a specific field. Even the large companies doing business abroad often create independent business units responsible for exporting and marketing a specific product abroad. General Electric is an example. Although GE is engaged in a variety of businesses, its European medical electronics division only sells medical electronics, and its European jet engine division only sells jet engines.

Source: Drucker, Peter. "Secrets of the U.S. Export Boom", *The Wall Street Journal*, August 1, 1991. p.A12. (E)

International business holds out the promise of large new market areas, yet firms cannot simply jump into the international marketplace and expect to be successful. They must adjust to needs and opportunities abroad, have quality products, understand their customers, and do their homework, as this chapter's opening vignette shows. The rapid globalization of markets, however, reduces the time available to adjust to new market realities.[1]

This chapter is concerned with the activities of firms preparing to enter international markets. Primary emphasis is placed on export activities. The chapter focuses on the role of management in starting up international operations and describes the basic stimuli for international activities. Entry modes for the international arena are highlighted, and the problems and benefits of each mode are discussed. Finally, the role of facilitators and intermediaries in international business is described.

THE ROLE OF MANAGEMENT

The type and quality of its management are the keys to whether or not a firm will enter the international marketplace. Researchers have found that management dynamism and commitment are crucial in the first steps toward international operations.[2] The management of firms that have been successful internationally is usually described as active rather than passive [3,4] or as aggressive rather than nonaggressive.[5] Conversely, the managers of firms that are unsuccessful or inactive internationally usually exhibit a lack of determination or devotion to international business. The issue of managerial commitment is a critical one because foreign-market penetration requires a vast amount of market-development activity, sensitivity toward foreign environments, research, and innovation.

Initiating international business activities takes the firm in an entirely new direction, quite different from adding a product line or hiring a few more people. Going international means that a fundamental strategic change is taking place. Research has shown that the decision to export, for example, usually comes from the highest levels of management. Typically, the president, chairman, or vice president of marketing is the chief decision maker.[6] A survey of the fastest growing mid-sized companies in the United States showed that for all international operations, the personal commitment and vision of the chief executive officer played a forceful role.[7]

The carrying out of the decision—that is, the initiation of international business transactions and their implementation—is then the primary responsibility of marketing personnel. However, in the final decision stage of evaluating international activities, the responsibility again rests with senior management. It therefore appears that, in order to influence a firm to go international, the president first needs to be convinced. Once the decision to internationalize is made, the marketing department becomes active in international business.

The first step in acquiring international commitment is to become aware of international business opportunities. Management may then decide to enter the international marketplace on a limited basis and evaluate the results of the initial activities. An international business orientation develops over time.

Management in the majority of firms is much too preoccupied with short-term, immediate problems to engage in sophisticated long-run planning. As a result, most firms are simply not interested in international business. Yet certain situations may lead a manager to discover and understand the value of going international and to decide to pursue international business activities. Trigger factors frequently are foreign travel, during which new business opportunities are discovered, or the receipt of information that leads management to believe that such opportunities exist. Managers who have lived abroad and have learned foreign languages or are particularly interested in foreign cultures are more likely to investigate whether international business opportunities would be appropriate for their firms.

New management or new employees can also bring about an international orientation. For example, managers entering a firm may already have had some international business experience and may try to use this experience to further the business activities of the firm where they are currently employed.

MOTIVATIONS TO GO ABROAD

Normally, management will consider international activities only when stimulated to do so. A variety of motivations can push and pull individuals and firms along the international path.[8] An overview of the major motivations that have been found to make firms go international is provided in Table 11.1. Proactive motivations represent stimuli for firm-initiated strategic change. Reactive motivations describe stimuli that result in a firm's response and adaptation to changes imposed by the outside environment.

TABLE 11.1	

TABLE 11.1
Major Motivations to
Internationalize Small
and Medium-Sized
Firms
	Proactive
	    Profit advantage
	    Unique products
	    Technological advantage
	    Exclusive information
	    Managerial commitment
	    Tax benefit
	    Economies of scale
	Reactive
	    Competitive pressures
	    Overproduction
	    Declining domestic sales
	    Excess capacity
	    Saturated domestic markets
	    Proximity to customers and ports

Proactive Motivations

Profits are the major proactive motivation for international business. Management may perceive international sales as a potential source of higher profit margins or of more added-on profits. Of course, the profitability perceived when planning to go international is often quite different from the profitability actually obtained. Recent research has indicated that, particularly in international start-up operations, initial profitability may be quite low.[9] The gap between perception and reality may be particularly large when the firm has not previously engaged in international business. Despite thorough planning, unexpected influences often shift the profit picture substantially. Shifts in exchange rates, for example, may drastically affect profit forecasts.

Unique products or a technological advantage can be another major stimulus. A firm may produce goods or services that are not widely available from international competitors. Again, real and perceived advantages must be differentiated. Many firms believe that they offer unique products or services, even though this may not be the case internationally. If products or technologies are unique, however, they certainly can provide a competitive edge. What needs to be considered is how long such an advantage will last. The length of time is a function of the product, its technology, and the creativity of competitors. In the past, a firm with a competitive edge could often count on being the sole supplier to foreign markets for years to come. This type of advantage has shrunk dramatically because of competing technologies and the frequent lack of international patent protection.

Special knowledge about foreign customers or market situations may be another proactive stimulus. Such knowledge may result from particular insights by a firm, special contacts an individual may have, in-depth research, or simply from being in the right place at the right time (for example, recognizing a good business situation during a vacation trip). Although such exclusivity can serve well as an initial stimulus for international business, it will rarely provide prolonged motivation because competitors—at least in the medium run—can be expected to catch up with the information advantage. Only if firms build up international information advantage as an ongoing process, through, for example, broad market scanning or assured informational exclusivity, can prolonged corporate strategy be based on this motivation.

Another motivation reflects the desire, drive, and enthusiasm of management toward international business activities. This **managerial commitment** can exist

simply because managers like to be part of a firm that engages in international business. (It sounds impressive.) Further, such activity can often provide a good reason
for international travel—for example, to call on a major customer in the Bahamas
during the cold winter months. Often, however, the managerial commitment to internationalize is simply the reflection of a general entrepreneurial motivation, that
is, a desire for continuous growth and market expansion.[10]

Tax benefits can also play a major motivating role. In the United States, for example, a tax mechanism called a foreign sales corporation (FSC) provides firms with
certain tax deferrals and makes international business activities more profitable.
(More detail on the FSC is presented in Chapter 19.) As a result of the tax benefits,
firms either can offer their product at a lower cost in foreign markets or can accumulate a higher profit.

A final major proactive motivation involves economies of scale. International activities may enable the firm to increase its output and therefore climb more rapidly
on the learning curve. The Boston Consulting Group has shown that the doubling
of output can reduce production costs up to 30 percent. Increased production for
international markets can therefore help to reduce the cost of production for domestic sales and make the firm more competitive domestically as well.[11]

Reactive Motivations

A second set of motivations, primarily characterized as reactive, influences firms to
respond to environmental changes and pressures rather than to attempt to blaze
trails. Competitive pressures are one example. A company may fear losing domestic
market share to competing firms that have benefitted from the economies of scale
gained through international business activities. Further, it may fear losing foreign
markets permanently to competitors that have decided to focus on these markets.
Because market share usually is most easily retained by firms that obtained it initially,
companies frequently enter the international market head over heels. Quick entry,
however, may result in similarly quick withdrawal once the firm recognizes that its
preparation has been inadequate.

Similarly, overprotection can result in a major reactive motivation. During down-
turns in the domestic business cycle, foreign markets have historically provided an
ideal outlet for excess inventories. International business expansion motivated by

overproduction usually does not represent full commitment by management, but rather a safety-valve activity.[12] As soon as domestic demand returns to previous levels, international business activities are curtailed or even terminated. Firms that have used such a strategy once may encounter difficulties when trying to employ it again because many foreign customers are not interested in temporary or sporadic business relationships.

Declining domestic sales, whether measured in sales volume or market share, have a similar motivating effect. Products marketed domestically may be at the declining stage of their product life cycle. Instead of attempting to push back the life cycle process domestically, or in addition to such an effort, firms may opt to prolong the product life cycle by expanding the market. In the past, such efforts by firms in industrialized countries often met with success because customers in less-developed countries only gradually reached the level of need and sophistication already obtained by customers in the developed countries. Increasingly, however, because of the more rapid diffusion of technology, these lags are shrinking.

Excess capacity can also be a powerful motivator. If equipment for production is not fully utilized, firms may see expansion abroad as an ideal way to achieve broader distribution of fixed costs. Alternatively, if all fixed costs are assigned to domestic production, the firm can penetrate foreign markets with a pricing scheme that focuses mainly on variable cost. Yet such a view is feasible only for market entry. A market-penetration strategy based on variable cost alone is unrealistic because, in the long run, fixed costs have to be recovered to replace production equipment.

The reactive motivation of a saturated domestic market has similar results to that of declining domestic sales. Again, firms in this situation can use the international market to prolong the life cycle of their product and even of their organization.

A final major reactive motivation is that of proximity to customers and ports. Physical and psychological closeness to the international market can often play a major role in the international business activities of the firm. For example, a firm established near a border may not even perceive itself as going abroad if it does business in the neighboring country. Except for some firms close to the Canadian or Mexican border, however, this factor is much less prevalent in the United States than in many other nations. Most European firms automatically go abroad simply because their neighbors are so close.

In general, firms that are most successful in international business are usually motivated by proactive—that is, firm internal—factors. Proactive firms are also frequently more service oriented than reactive firms. Further, proactive firms are more marketing and strategy oriented than reactive firms, which have as their major concern operational issues. The clearest differentiation between the two types of firms can probably be made ex post facto by determining how they initially entered international markets. Proactive firms are more likely to have solicited their first international order, whereas reactive firms frequently begin international activities after receiving an unsolicited order from abroad.

ALTERNATIVE ENTRY STRATEGIES

Conceivably, a new firm could create large-scale subsidiaries abroad or could even be formed for international business purposes. However, four forms of entry strategies are used by the majority of firms that initiate international business activities: indirect exporting and importing, direct exporting and importing, licensing, and franchising.[13] These alternatives are discussed in this chapter in more detail. Other modes of entry, such as direct foreign investment, management contracts, contract manufacturing, and turnkey operations, are mostly used by larger and more experienced firms and are therefore addressed in Chapter 12.

Indirect and Direct Exporting and Importing

Firms can be involved in exporting and importing in an indirect or direct way. Indirect involvement means that the firm participates in international business through an intermediary and does not deal with foreign customers or firms. Direct involvement means that the firm works with foreign customers or markets with the opportunity to develop a relationship. The end result of exporting and importing is similar whether the activities are direct or indirect. In both cases, goods and services either go abroad or come to the domestic market from abroad, and goods may have to be adapted to suit the targeted market.

Many firms are indirect exporters and importers, often without their knowledge. As an example, merchandise can be sold to a domestic firm that in turn sells it abroad. This is most frequently the case when smaller suppliers deliver products to large multinational corporations, which use them as input to their foreign sales.

Similarly, firms may sell products to a government agency, for example, the Department of Defense, and they may ultimately be shipped to military outposts abroad. Or foreign buyers purchase products locally and then send them immediately to their home country. More examples of "exporting in your own backyard" are given in Table 11.2. While indirect exports may be the result of unwitting participation, many firms also choose this method of international entry as a strategic alternative that conserves effort and resources while still taking advantage of foreign opportunities.

At the same time, many firms that perceive themselves as buying domestically may in reality buy imported products. They may have long-standing relations with a domestic supplier who, because of cost and competitive pressures, has begun to source products from abroad rather than produce them domestically. In this case, the buyer firm has become an indirect importer.

Firms that participate indirectly in international business rarely are able to gather much experience and knowledge about how to do business abroad. Therefore, while indirect activities represent a form of international market entry, they are unlikely to result in growing management commitment to international markets or increased capabilities in serving them.

TABLE 11.2 Exporting in Your Own Backyard: A Dozen Segments of the United States for Export Markets

1. Large U.S. companies purchasing U.S. goods for their own foreign affiliates
2. Large design and construction firms purchasing U.S. goods for foreign projects awarded to them
3. U.S. branches of gigantic foreign trading companies purchasing U.S. goods for their affiliates
4. Export merchants buying for their own account
5. Large foreign companies purchasing U.S. goods through their U.S. buying office or agents
6. U.S. military purchasing for use abroad
7. U.S. exporters seeking U.S. goods to round out their own lines
8. United Nations members purchasing for development projects
9. Foreign governments purchasing U.S. goods
10. Foreign department stores purchasing U.S. goods through U.S. buying offices
11. Foreign buyers on purchasing trips
12. AID-financed transactions requiring U.S. goods

Source: Nelson Joyner, Georgetown University, teaching notes, 1993.

Firms that opt to export or import directly have more opportunities ahead of them. As Global Perspective 11.1 shows, they learn much quicker the competitive advantages of their products and can therefore expand more rapidly. They also have the ability to control their international activities better and can forge relationships with their trading partners, which can lead to further international growth and success.

However, these firms also are faced with obstacles that those who access international markets indirectly avoid. These hurdles include identifying and targeting foreign suppliers and/or customers and finding retail space, which can be very costly and time consuming. Some firms are overcoming these barriers through the use of mail-order catalogs ("storeless" distribution networks) or video brochures, as seen in Global Perspective 11.2. In Japan, for example, "high-cost rents, crowded shelves, and an intricate distribution system have made launching new products via conventional methods an increasingly difficult and expensive proposition. Direct marketing via catalog short-circuits the distribution train and eliminates the need for high-priced shop space."[14] Entrepreneurs are becoming creative in other ways to avoid the high cost of land and labor in Japan. Taking advantage of the fact that the Japanese are used to vending machines (there are over 5.4 million machines in the country), a San Diego meat-packing firm is thinking of entering the Japanese market by selling steaks in vending machines located outside train stations and convenience stores.[15]

Direct importers and exporters frequently make use of intermediaries who can assist with troublesome yet important details such as documentation, financing, and

Global Perspective

11.1
No Pig in a Poke

Mike Kane, owner of Kane Manufacturing Co. of Des Moines, Iowa, manufactures products for farrow-to-finish operations in the pig industry. Products include nursery feeders for piglets, as well as other types of feeders that will handle pigs from 40 pounds to 250 pounds; baby pig waterers; and heat mats. Kane's wife, Donna, took charge of the firm's export operations four years ago and started an aggressive international program.

The export potential of their products became apparent to the Kanes when they received numerous replies to advertisements placed in the U.S. Department of Commerce catalog-magazine, *Commercial News USA,* and the magazine *Pig International.* Says Mike Kane: "The style of our feeders had never been introduced in most other countries. Our feeders are made of tough polyethylene; they don't rust, crack, break, or draw moisture. Once the pig industry overseas saw that we had something more rugged

and durable than any feeding equipment they had ever seen, we found a good demand for our product."

Initially the firm showed its products to foreign customers mainly at trade shows in the United States, starting with International Pig America in Atlanta, Georgia, and the World Pork Expo. Later on, the company also participated in overseas trade shows, including Huhn & Schwein in Hannover, Germany, and Expo Aviga in Barcelona, Spain. Explains Kane: "Distributors and other businesspeople from all over the world come to these trade shows looking for new products, and we had some that caught their eye."

In just three years, Kane's exports have increased from 10 percent of sales to 33 percent. To help fill the growing demand in Europe, the company just opened a warehouse in Germany. In addition, the firm exports to Japan, Canada, Mexico, Taiwan, Korea, New Zealand, Australia, Cyprus, and the Philippines.

"Exporting Pays Off," *Business America,* June 29, 1992:21.

Global Perspective

11.2
Use Technology When Marketing Abroad

Wealthy Japanese are buying million-dollar properties in Beverly Hills, fast-food companies have found franchise clients overseas, and exporters are marketing high-tech products in several languages—all through a relatively new medium known as the video brochure.

Video brochures are professional, television-quality messages, normally five to seven minutes in length, that describe a product or service with the visual impact of a TV commercial but the targetability of direct-mail advertising. The new tool is particularly useful when selling abroad. It saves costly sales trips, surmounts language barriers, and allows customers to see what products, such as real estate, look like.

Video brochures don't come cheap, though. A video company will charge from $5,000 to more than $100,000 to produce one, but when hundreds or even thousands of videos are involved, the unit cost can be quite reasonable.

Robert Parker, a producer at Direct Impact Video Associates in Venice, California, said DIVA distributed 175,000 video brochures for Toyota Motor Co., and the unit cost worked out to about $5 a cassette. Most accounts, of course, require a fraction of the Toyota mailings, so the unit costs are higher, and the price of the product being marketed takes on greater significance.

Homes in Beverly Hills that sell for $1 million and up have been marketed effectively in Tokyo and Hong Kong. High-tech products that require detailed explanation and visual imagery are also likely candidates, as are high-end consumer items such as yachts and sports cars.

Jeff Goddard, founder and president of the Video Agency, a Hollywood, California, video marketing firm that specializes in Asian-language videos, said video brochures are popular in trans-Pacific marketing because of the distances that separate sellers and buyers.

The Video Agency has 55 clients, about 70 percent of them international. At least half of its business is in real estate, although Goddard hopes to increase the number of manufacturing clients to about 75 percent. "I will feel better if I can help Americans become more competitive," he said.

The key to producing a successful Asian-language video, Goddard says, is to make it not only professional in every detail but culturally correct as well.

Source: Bill Mongelluzzo, "Selling Overseas? Try Sending a Video Brochure," *The Journal of Commerce* (July 13, 1990):5A. Reprinted with permission.

transportation. The intermediaries may also identify foreign suppliers or customers. Facilitators in this process will be discussed later in this chapter. After firms have acquired some experience, however, they may carry out all export and import transactions on their own.

Licensing

Under a **licensing agreement,** one firm permits another to use its intellectual property for compensation designated as **royalty.** The recipient firm is the licensee. The property licensed might include patents, trademarks, copyrights, technology, technical know-how, or specific business skills. For example, a firm that has developed a bag-in-the-box packaging process for milk can permit other firms abroad to use the same process. Licensing therefore amounts to exporting intangibles.

Assessment of Licensing Licensing has intuitive appeal to many would-be international managers. As an entry strategy, it requires neither capital investment nor detailed involvement with foreign customers. By generating royalty income, licensing provides an opportunity to exploit research and development already conducted. After initial costs, the licensor can reap benefits until the end of the license contract period. Licensing also reduces the risk of expropriation because the licensee is a local company that can provide leverage against government action.

Licensing may help to avoid host-country regulations that are more prevalent in equity ventures. Licensing also may provide a means by which foreign markets can be tested without major involvement of capital or management time. Similarly, licensing can be used as a strategy to preempt a market before the entry of competition, especially if the licensor's resources permit full-scale involvement only in selected markets.

Licensing is not without disadvantages. It is the most limited form of foreign market participation and does not in any way guarantee a basis for future expansion. As a matter of fact, quite the opposite may take place. In exchange for the royalty, the licensor may create its own competitor not only in the market for which the agreement was made but for third-country markets as well.

Licensing has also come under criticism from many governments and supranational organizations. They have alleged that licensing provides a mechanism for corporations in industrialized countries to capitalize on older technology. These accusations have been made even though licensing offers a foreign entity the opportunity for immediate market entry with a proven concept. It therefore eliminates the risk of R&D failure, the cost of designing around the licensor's patents, or the fear of patent-infringement litigation.

Some companies are increasingly hesitant to enter licensing agreements. For example, Japanese firms are delighted to sell goods to China but are unwilling to license the Chinese to produce the goods themselves. They fear that, because of the low wage structure in China, such licenses could create a powerful future competitor in markets presently held by Japan.

Principal Issues in Negotiating Licensing Agreements   The key issues in negotiating licensing agreements include the scope of the rights conveyed, compensation, licensee compliance, dispute resolution, and the term and termination of the agreement.[16] The more clearly these are spelled out, the more trouble free the association between the two parties can be.

The rights conveyed are product and/or patent rights. Defining their scope involves specifying the technology, know-how, or show-how to be included. In addition, the transfer process must be negotiated. For example, an agreement should specify whether or not manuals will be translated into the licensee's language.

Compensation for the license is a second major issue. The licensor will want the agreement to cover (1) **transfer costs,** namely all variable costs incurred in transferring technology to a licensee and all ongoing costs of maintaining the agreement; (2) **R&D costs** incurred in developing the licensed technology; and (3) **opportunity costs** incurred in the foreclosure of other sources of profit, such as exports or direct investment. The licensor wants a share of the profits generated from the use of the license.

Licensees usually do not want to include allowances for opportunity costs and often argue that the R&D costs have already been covered by the licensor. License payments, or royalties, are therefore a function both of the licensor's minimum necessary return and the cost of the licensee's next best alternative. The methods of compensating the licensor typically take the form of running royalties—such as five percent of license sales—and/or up-front payments, service fees, and disclosure fees (for proprietary data).

Licensee compliance should be stipulated in the agreement. Some areas of compliance are technology-transfer regulations, confidentiality of information provided, record keeping and audit provisions, and quality standards. Provisions for dispute resolution center on the choice of law for contract interpretation and conflict resolution. Often these provisions include arbitration clauses that allow a third, neutral party to resolve any disputes that arise.

Finally, the term, termination, and survival rights of licenses must be specified. Government regulations in the licensee's market must be studied. If the conditions are not favorable (for example, in terms of the maximum allowed duration), a waiver should be applied for.

A special form of licensing is **trademark licensing,** which has become a substantial source of worldwide revenue for companies that can trade on well-known names and characters. Trademark licensing permits the names or logos of designers, literary characters, sports teams, or movie stars to appear on clothing, games, foods and beverages, gift and novelties, toys, and home furnishings. Licensors can make millions of dollars with little effort, while licensees can produce a brand or product that consumers will recognize immediately. Trademark licensing is possible, however, only if the trademark name indeed conveys instant recognition. The total volume of trademark licensing was $62 billion in 1989 and is expected to grow by 8.5 percent in the 1990s.[17]

Franchising

A fourth international entry strategy, **franchising,** is the granting of the right by a parent company (the franchisor) to another, independent entity (the franchisee) to do business in a prescribed manner. This right can take the form of selling the franchisor's products; using its name, production, and marketing techniques; or using its general business approach.[18] Usually franchising involves a combination of many of these elements. The major forms of franchising are manufacturer-retailer systems (such as a car dealership), manufacturer-wholesaler systems (such as soft drink companies), and service firm–retailer systems (such as lodging services and fast-food outlets).

Typically, to be successful in international franchising, the firm must be able to offer unique products or unique selling propositions. If such uniqueness can be of-

Franchising is one way to expand into international markets. The Dunkin´ Donuts franchise in Thailand operates some 50 stores like this one.

Source: Courtesy of Allied Lyons.

fered, growth can be rapid and sustained. Global Perspective 11.3 provides an example of combining unique cosmetics products with an environmental and ethical appeal.

International franchising has grown strongly in the past decade. In 1990, more than 350 franchising companies in the United States operated about 31,000 outlets in international markets.[19] Foreign franchisors are penetrating international markets as well. Examples include Holiday Rent-a-Car of Canada and Descamps, a French firm selling linens and tablecloths.

The reasons for international expansion of franchise systems are market potential, financial gain, and saturated domestic markets. U.S. franchisors expanded dramatically in 1984, taking advantage of the strong U.S. dollar. Foreign market demand was also very high for franchises. For example, the initial impetus for ComputerLand's expansion into the Asia/Pacific region was that "Asian entrepreneurs [were] coming knocking on our door asking for franchises."[20] From a franchisee's perspective, the franchise is beneficial because it reduces risk by implementing a proven concept. From a governmental perspective, there are also major benefits. The source country does not see a replacement of exports or export jobs. The recipient country sees franchising as requiring little outflow of foreign exchange, since the bulk of the profits generated remains within the country.[21]

Franchising by its very nature calls for a great degree of standardization. In most cases, this does not mean 100 percent uniformity but, rather, international **recog-**

Global Perspective

11.3
The Body Shop: Franchisor with an Ethics Message

Building a global chain of cosmetics stores would be ambition enough for most people. But British entrepreneur Anita Roddick was never one to settle for mere success. Since opening her first Body Shop in 1976 in the English resort town of Brighton, Roddick has been committed to improving minds as well as complexions. With 560 outlets in 38 countries, the Body Shop has become a global business with a message, espousing a variety of environmental and social causes from recycling to animal and human rights. Its more staid competitors may be horrified, but consumers seem to love the Body Shop for being different.

In 1991, the Body Shop moved into Japan, with its first franchise outlet opening in Tokyo, and far surpassed its first-year revenue target of 215 million yen. Plans are to open 50 more stores in Japan. The store's success owes a lot to Japan's globe-trotting young women. Authenticity is important to this group, and the first concern for many visitors is whether they can receive the same range of products as in Body Shops abroad. They are not disappointed. Product and presentation are the same. All 350 toiletry products are made from natural sources, like pineapples, aloe vera, bananas, and seaweed. The accent on ethics is equally strong worldwide. The Body Shop only sells products developed without animal testing, and, whenever possible, products are dispensed in simple, recyclable plastic containers. In line with the Body Shop's community orientation, staff at all outlets must also devote two hours a week to charitable activities. While a good thing in itself, this kind of idealism also helps attract intelligent, self-motivated staff. Says Miyako Ando, spokesperson for the company: "I think many Japanese companies are too preoccupied with profits, and they don't give enough thought to helping society. We are a new type of enterprise which aims at returning its profits to society."

"The Body Shop: Marketer with a Message," *Focus Japan,* July 1991: 8.

International Locations of U.S. Franchising Operations

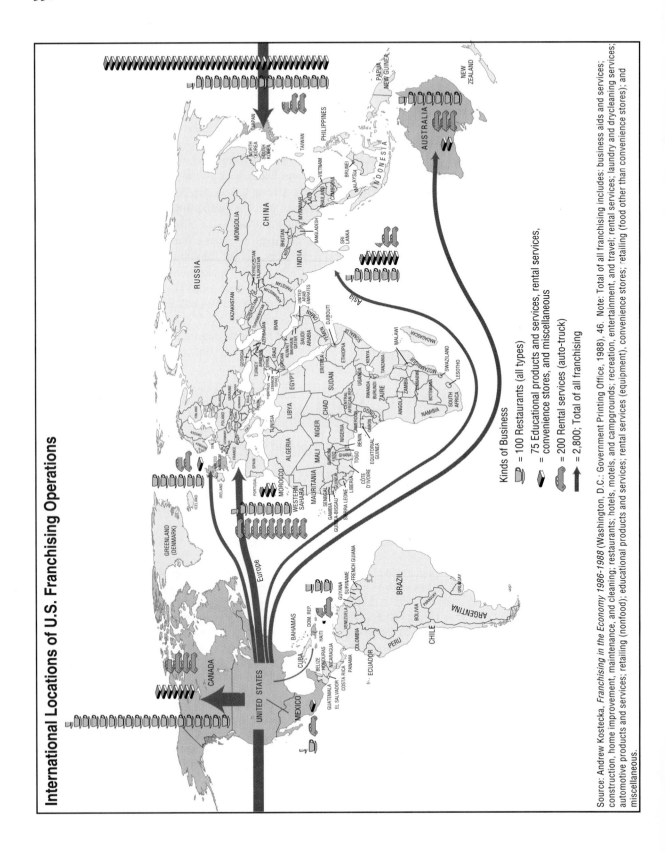

Kinds of Business

= 100 Restaurants (all types)

= 75 Educational products and services, rental services, convenience stores, and miscellaneous

= 200 Rental services (auto-truck)

= 2,800; Total of all franchising

Source: Andrew Kostecka, *Franchising in the Economy 1986-1988* (Washington, D.C.: Government Printing Office, 1988), 46. Note: Total of all franchising includes: business aids and services; construction, home improvement, maintenance, and cleaning; restaurants; hotels, motels, and campgrounds; recreation, entertainment, and travel; rental services; laundry and drycleaning services; automotive products and services; retailing (nonfood); educational products and services; rental services (equipment), convenience stores; retailing (food other than convenience stores); and miscellaneous.

TABLE 11.3
Rank Order of Problems Encountered in International Markets by U.S. Franchise Systems

1. Host government regulations and red tape
2. High import duties and taxes in foreign environment
3. Monetary uncertainties and royalty remission to franchisor
4. Logistical problems in operation of international franchise system
5. Control of franchisees
6. Location problems and real estate costs
7. Patent, trademark, and copyright protection
8. Recruitment of franchisees
9. Training of foreign franchisee personnel
10. Language and cultural barriers
11. Availability of raw materials for company product
12. Foreign ownership limitations
13. Competition in foreign market areas
14. Adaptation of franchise package to local markets

Source: Donald W. Hackett, "The International Expansion of U.S. Franchise Systems," in *Multinational Product Management,* eds. Warren Keegan and Charles Mayer (Chicago: American Marketing Association, 1979), 78.

nizability. Fast-food franchisors, for example, will vary the products and product lines offered depending on local market conditions and tastes.

Even though franchising has been growing rapidly, problems are often encountered in international markets. Some of them are summarized in Table 11.3. A major problem is foreign government intervention. In the Philippines, for example, government restrictions on franchising and royalties hindered ComputerLand's Manila store from offering a broader range of services, leading to a separation between the company and its franchisee. Selection and training of franchisees represents another problem area. The lag of McDonald's behind Burger King in France was the result of the company's suing to revoke the license of its largest franchisee for failure to operate 14 stores according to McDonald's standards.

Many franchise systems have run into difficulty by expanding too quickly and granting franchises to unqualified entities. Although the local franchisee knows the market best, the franchisor still needs to understand the market for product adaptation and operational purposes. The franchisor, in order to remain viable in the long term, needs to coordinate the efforts of individual franchisees—for example, to share ideas and engage in joint undertakings, such as cooperative advertising.

CONCERNS AND PROBLEMS IN GOING INTERNATIONAL

Going international presents the firm with new environments, entirely new ways of doing business, and a host of new problems. The problems have a wide range. They can consist of strategic considerations, such as service delivery and compliance with long-term government regulations, or focus on start-up issues, such as how to find customers and communicate with them effectively. In addition, firms must worry about operational matters, such as information flows and the mechanics of carrying out an international business transaction. This involves a variety of new documents, including commercial invoices, bills of lading, consular invoices, inspection certificates, and shipper's export declarations. This paperwork is necessary to comply with various domestic, international, or foreign regulations. The regulations may be designed to control international business activities, to streamline the individual transaction, or, as in the case of the shipper's export declaration, to compile trade statistics. In order to fill out these forms, the exporter often needs to obtain specialized information—for example, the tariff schedule number for the product. By signing these forms, exporters warrant that their declarations are correct, and they can be prosecuted if that is not the case. A sample export declaration is provided in Figure 11.1.

In going international, managers learn that a new body of knowledge and expertise is needed. In most cases, however, major internal constraints restrict the ability of the firm to fully respond to the new problems and concerns. Even one person assigned part time to the exploration of international business opportunities can make a major difference, but there are limits to what one person can do. The firm should therefore make use of available forms of assistance provided by international intermediaries and facilitators.

FIGURE 11.1
Shipper's Export Declaration

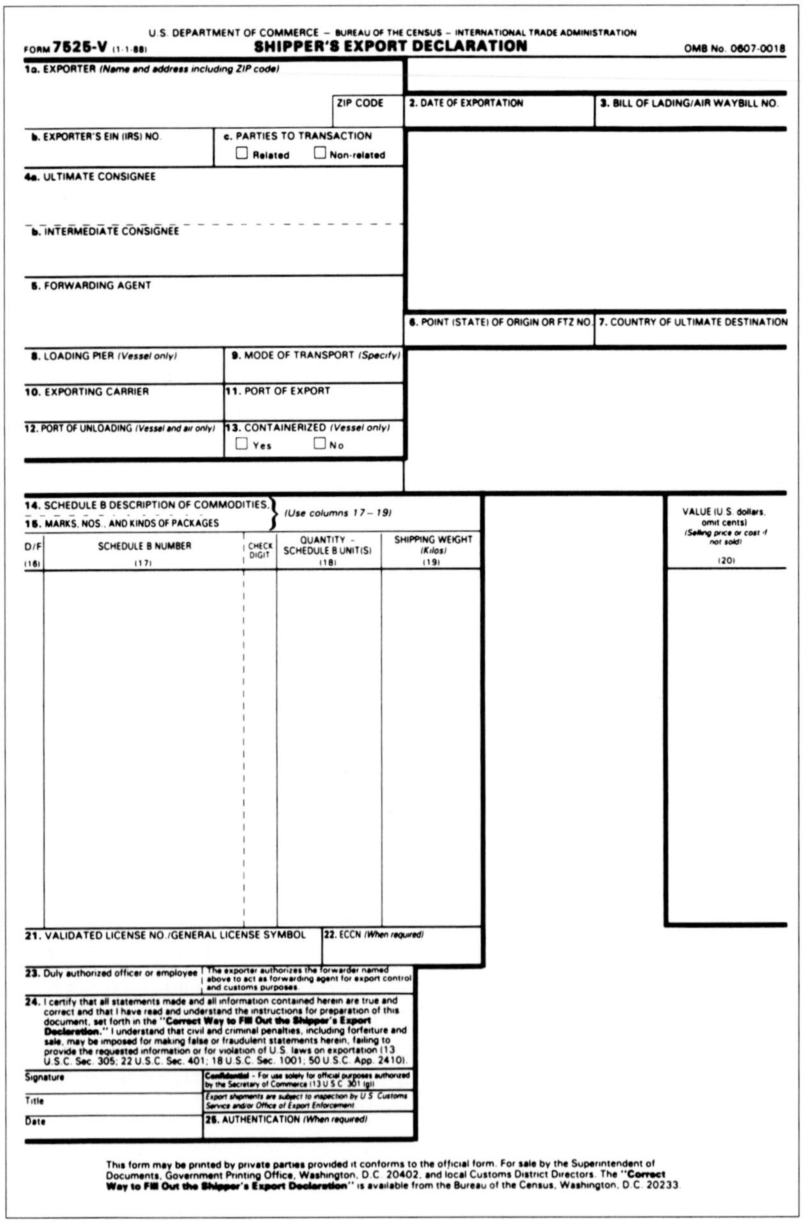

U.S. DEPARTMENT OF COMMERCE – BUREAU OF THE CENSUS – INTERNATIONAL TRADE ADMINISTRATION

FORM 7525-V (1-1-88) **SHIPPER'S EXPORT DECLARATION** OMB No. 0607-0018

1a. EXPORTER (Name and address including ZIP code)

ZIP CODE

2. DATE OF EXPORTATION

3. BILL OF LADING/AIR WAYBILL NO.

b. EXPORTER'S EIN (IRS) NO.

c. PARTIES TO TRANSACTION ☐ Related ☐ Non-related

4a. ULTIMATE CONSIGNEE

b. INTERMEDIATE CONSIGNEE

5. FORWARDING AGENT

6. POINT (STATE) OF ORIGIN OR FTZ NO.

7. COUNTRY OF ULTIMATE DESTINATION

8. LOADING PIER (Vessel only)

9. MODE OF TRANSPORT (Specify)

10. EXPORTING CARRIER

11. PORT OF EXPORT

12. PORT OF UNLOADING (Vessel and air only)

13. CONTAINERIZED (Vessel only) ☐ Yes ☐ No

14. SCHEDULE B DESCRIPTION OF COMMODITIES,
15. MARKS, NOS., AND KINDS OF PACKAGES
(Use columns 17–19)

D/F (16)	SCHEDULE B NUMBER (17)	CHECK DIGIT	QUANTITY - SCHEDULE B UNIT(S) (18)	SHIPPING WEIGHT (Kilos) (19)	VALUE (U.S. dollars, omit cents) (Selling price or cost if not sold) (20)

21. VALIDATED LICENSE NO./GENERAL LICENSE SYMBOL

22. ECCN (When required)

23. Duly authorized officer or employee

The exporter authorizes the forwarder named above to act as forwarding agent for export control and customs purposes.

24. I certify that all statements made and all information contained herein are true and correct and that I have read and understand the instructions for preparation of this document, set forth in the "**Correct Way to Fill Out the Shipper's Export Declaration.**" I understand that civil and criminal penalties, including forfeiture and sale, may be imposed for making false or fraudulent statements herein, failing to provide the requested information or for violation of U.S. laws on exportation (13 U.S.C. Sec. 305; 22 U.S.C. Sec. 401; 18 U.S.C. Sec. 1001; 50 U.S.C. App. 2410).

Signature

Confidential - For use solely for official purposes authorized by the Secretary of Commerce (13 U.S.C. 301 (g))

Title

Export shipments are subject to inspection by U.S. Customs Service and/or Office of Export Enforcement

Date

25. AUTHENTICATION (When required)

This form may be printed by private parties provided it conforms to the official form. For sale by the Superintendent of Documents, Government Printing Office, Washington, D.C. 20402, and local Customs District Directors. The "**Correct Way to Fill Out the Shipper's Export Declaration**" is available from the Bureau of the Census, Washington, D.C. 20233.

INTERNATIONAL INTERMEDIARIES

Intermediaries can provide significant assistance to firms engaged in international business. Three major types of international intermediaries are export management companies, Webb-Pomerene associations, and export trading companies.

Export Management Companies

Domestic firms that specialize in performing international business services as commission representatives or as distributors are known as **export management companies (EMCs).** Although few directories listing EMCs are available, more than 1,000 of these firms are estimated to be operating in the United States. A study conducted by the National Federation of Independent Businesses found that more than 20 percent of all manufactured-goods exporters in the United States are EMCs.[22] Most EMCs are quite small. Many were formed by one or two principals with experience in international business or in a particular geographic area. Their expertise enables them to offer specialized services to domestic corporations.

EMCs have two primary forms of operation: They either take title to goods and operate internationally on their own account, or they perform services as agents. Because they often serve a variety of clients, their mode of operation may vary from client to client and from transaction to transaction. An EMC may act as an agent for one client and as a distributor for another. It may even act as both for the same client on different occasions.

The EMC as an Agent   When working as an agent, the EMC is primarily responsible for developing foreign business and sales strategies and establishing contact abroad. Because the EMC does not share in the profits from a sale, it depends heavily on a high sales volume, on which it charges commission. The EMC may therefore be tempted to take on as many products and as many clients as possible in order to obtain a high sales volume. As a result, the EMC may spread itself too thin and may be unable to adequately represent all the clients and products it carries. The risk is particularly great with small EMCs.

In addition to its international activities, this type of EMC must concentrate a substantial amount of effort on the development of domestic clients. These clients often are exactly the firms that are unwilling to commit major resources to the international business effort. They must be convinced that it is worthwhile to consider international business. In order to develop and expand its clientele, the EMC must divert some of its limited resources to that task.

EMCs that have specific expertise in selecting markets because of language capabilities, previous exposure, or specialized contacts appear to be the ones most successful and useful in aiding client firms in their international business efforts. For example, they can cooperate with firms that are already successful in international business but have been unable to penetrate a specific region. By sticking to their area of expertise and representing only a limited number of clients, such agents can provide quite valuable services.

The EMC as a Distributor   When operating as a distributor, the EMC purchases products from the domestic firm, takes title, and assumes the trading risk. Selling in its own name, it has the opportunity to reap greater profits than when acting as an agent. The potential for greater profit is appropriate, because the EMC has drastically reduced the risk for the domestic firm while increasing its own risk. The burden of the merchandise acquired provides a major motivation to complete an international sale successfully. The domestic firm selling to the EMC is in the comfortable position of having sold its merchandise and received its money without having to deal with the complexities of the international market. On the other hand, it is less likely to gather much international business expertise.

Compensation of EMCs   The mechanism of an EMC may be very useful to the domestic firm if such activities produce additional sales abroad. However, certain services must be performed that demand resources for which someone must pay. As an example, in order for a firm to enter foreign markets, it must incur market-development expenses. At the very least, products must be shown abroad, visits must be arranged, or contacts must be established. Even though it may often not be discussed, the funding for these activities must be found.

One possibility is a fee charged to the manufacturer by the EMC for market development, sometimes in the form of a retainer and often on an annual basis. These retainers vary and are dependent on the number of products represented and the difficulty of foreign-market penetration. Frequently, manufacturers are also expected to pay all or part of the direct expenses associated with foreign-market penetration. Some of these expenses may involve the production and translation of promotional product brochures. Others may be related to the rental of booth space at foreign trade shows, the provision of product samples, or trade advertising.[23]

Alternatively, the EMC may demand a price break for international sales. Because it will take on many of the business activities for the manufacturer, the EMC wants the price discounted for these activities. Therefore, sales to EMCs may occur only at a reduced price.

In one way or another, the firm that uses an EMC must pay the EMC for the international business effort. This compensation can be in the form of fees and/or cost sharing or in terms of lower prices and resulting higher profits for the EMC. Otherwise, despite promises, the EMC may simply add the firm and product in name only to its product offering and do nothing to achieve international success. Management needs to be aware of this cost and the fact that EMCs do not offer a free ride. Depending on the complexity of a product and the necessity to carry out developmental research, promotion, and services, management must be prepared to part with some portion of the potential international profitability to compensate the EMC for its efforts.

Power Conflicts between EMCs and Clients   The EMC in turn faces the continuous problem of retaining a client once foreign-market penetration is achieved. Many firms use an EMC's services mainly to test the international arena, with the clear desire to become a direct participant once successful operations have been established. Of course, this is particularly true if foreign demand turns out to be strong and profit levels are high. The conflict between the EMC and its clients, with one side wanting to retain market power by not sharing too much international business information, and the other side wanting to obtain that power, often results in short-term relationships and a lack of cooperation. Because international business development is based on long-term efforts, however, this conflict frequently leads to a lack of success.

For the concept of an export management company to work, both parties must fully recognize the delegation of responsibilities; the costs associated with these activities; and the need for information sharing, cooperation, and mutual reliance. Use of an EMC should be viewed just like domestic channel commitment. This requires a thorough investigation of the intermediary and the advisability of relying on its efforts, a willingness to cooperate on a relationship rather than on a transaction basis, and a willingness to properly reward its efforts. The EMC in turn must adopt a flexible approach to managing the export relationship. It must continue to upgrade the levels of services offered, constantly highlighting for the client the dimensions of post-sales service and providing in-depth information, since these are its biggest sources of differential advantage.[24] By doing so, the EMC lets the client know that the cost charted is worth the service and thereby reduces the desire for circumvention.

Webb-Pomerene Associations

Legislation enacted in 1918 that led to **Webb-Pomerene associations** permits firms to cooperate in terms of international sales allocation, financing, and pricing information. The associations must take care not to engage in activities that would reduce compensation within the United States. To more successfully penetrate international markets, however, they can allocate markets, fix quotas, and select exclusive distributors or brokers.

In spite of this early effort to encourage joint activities by firms in the international market, the effectiveness of Webb-Pomerene associations has not been substantial. At their peak, from 1930 to 1934, 50 Webb-Pomerene associations accounted for about 12 percent of U.S. exports. By 1991 only 22 associations were active and accounted for less than 2 percent of U.S. exports.[25] In addition, it appears that most of the users of this particular form of export intermediary are not the small and medium-sized firms the act was initially intended to assist, but rather the dominant firms in their respective industries.

The lack of success of this particular intermediary has mainly been ascribed to the fact that the antitrust exemption granted was not sufficiently ironclad. Further, specialized export firms are thought to have more to offer to a domestic firm than does an association, which may be particularly true if the association is dominated by one or two major competitors in an industry. This makes joining the association undesirable for smaller firms.

Trading Companies

A third major intermediary is the trading company. The most famous ones are the general trading companies, or **sogoshosha,** of Japan. Names like Mitsubishi, Mitsui, and C. Itoh have become household words in the United States. The nine trading company giants of Japan in 1991 acted as intermediaries for about half of the country's exports and two-thirds of its imports.[26] These general trading companies play a unique role in world commerce by importing, exporting, countertrading, investing, and manufacturing. Because of their vast size, they can benefit from economies of scale and perform their operations at high rates of return even though their profit margins are in the range of two percent.[27]

Four major reasons have been given for the success of the Japanese sogoshosha. First, by concentrating on obtaining and disseminating information about market opportunities and by investing huge funds in the development of information systems, these firms now have the mechanisms and organizations in place to gather, evaluate, and translate market information into business opportunities. Second, economies of scale permit the firms to take advantage of their vast transaction volume to obtain preferential treatment by, for example, negotiating transportation rates or even opening up new transportation routes and distribution systems. Third, these firms serve large internal markets, not only in Japan but also around the world, and can benefit from opportunities for countertrade. Finally, sogoshosha have access to vast quantities of capital, both within Japan and in the international capital markets. They can therefore carry out transactions that are too large or risky to be palatable or feasible for other firms.[28]

For many decades the emergence of trading companies was commonly believed to be a Japan-specific phenomenon. Particularly, Japanese cultural factors were cited as the reason that such intermediaries could operate successfully only from that country. In 1975, however, trading companies were established by government declaration in Korea. The intent was to continue Korea's export-led growth in a more efficient fashion. With the new legislation, the Korean government tied access to financing and government contracts to the formation of trading companies. Less than a decade later, the major trading companies of Korea (such as Hyundai, Samsung, and Daewoo) were handling 43 percent of Korea's total exports.[29] They were considered to be a major success. Similarly, the Brazilian government stimulated the creation of trading companies by offering preferential financing arrangements. Within several years, these Brazilian firms increased their activities dramatically and accounted for almost 20 percent of total Brazilian exports.[30]

In the United States, **export trading company (ETC)** legislation designed to improve the export performance of small and medium-sized firms was implemented in 1982. In order to improve export performance, bank participation in trading companies was permitted and the antitrust threat to joint-export efforts was reduced through precertification of planned activities by the U.S. Department of Commerce. Businesses were encouraged to join together to export or offer export services.

Permitting banks to participate in ETCs was intended to allow ETCs better access to capital and therefore permit more trading transactions and easier receipt of title to goods. The relaxation of antitrust provisions in turn was meant to enable firms to form joint ventures more easily. The cost of developing and penetrating international markets would then be shared, with the proportional share being, for many small and medium-sized firms, much easier to bear. As an example, in case a warehouse is needed in order to secure foreign-market penetration, one firm alone does not have to bear all the costs. A consortium of firms can jointly rent a foreign warehouse. Similarly, each firm need not station a service technician abroad at substantial cost. Joint funding of a service center by several firms makes the cost less prohibitive for each one. The trading-company concept also offers a one-stop shopping center for both the firm and its foreign customers. The firm can be assured that all international functions will be performed efficiently by the trading company, and at the same time, the foreign customer will have to deal with few individual firms.

The legislation permits a wide variety of possible structures for an ETC. General trading companies may handle many commodities, perform import and export services, countertrade, and work closely with foreign distributors. Regional trading companies may handle commodities produced in only one region, specializing in products in which that region possesses a comparative advantage. Product-oriented trading companies may concentrate on a limited number of products and offer their market-penetration services for only these products. Trading companies may also be geographically oriented, targeting one particular foreign nation, or may be focused on certain types of projects such as turnkey operations and joint ventures with foreign investors. Finally, trading companies may develop an industry-oriented focus, handling only goods of specific industry groups, such as metals, chemicals, or pharmaceuticals.[31]

Independent of its form of operation, an ETC can engage in a wide variety of activities. It can purchase products, act as a distributor abroad, or offer services. It can provide information on distribution costs and even handle domestic and international distribution and transportation. This can range from identifying distribution costs to booking space on ocean or air carriers and handling shipping contracts.

Although ETCs seem to offer major benefits to many U.S. firms wishing to go abroad, they have not been very extensively used. By 1992 only 130 individual ETC certificates had been issued by the U.S. Department of Commerce. Since some of these certificates covered all the members of trade associations, a total of 4,800 companies were part of an ETC.[32]

This lack of acceptance requires the examination of several potential shortcomings in the export-trading-company concept. Banks need to consider whether the mentalities of bankers and traders can be made compatible. Traders, for example, are known for rapidly seizing the opportune moment, whereas bankers often appear to move more slowly. A key challenge will be to find ways to successfully blend business entrepreneurship with banking regulations.

Banks also need to understand the benefits they can derive from working with small or medium-sized exporters. The first impression may be that an ETC offers only added risk and cost. Yet involvement with an ETC may provide the bank with a broader client base, profitable use of its extensive international information system and network of corresponding institutions, and a stepping-stone toward the internationalization of its own banking services. Because of the international debt situation, many banks have been hesitant to increase the volume of their international activities. In the long run, however, an improved understanding of this type and profitability of such transactions and the increasing pressures of a highly competitive deregulated home market will lead to more international involvement by U.S. banks.

The antitrust protection offered by the ETC Act may also not be very important to many firms, particularly the small and medium-sized ones. There may even be a clash with the offered protection and the corporate goals of firms. Companies, due to reasons of independence or the fear of losing marketing information and control, may not want to band together with their competitors.

Yet, given the current market structure, in which most exporters are small and fragmented and unable to avail themselves of international markets due to a lack of resources and information, the opportunity for collaboration is still useful. However, several cautionary remarks are in order if the ETC concept is to be applied successfully.

Firms participating in trading companies by joining or forming them should be aware of the difference between product- and market-driven ETCs. Firms may have a strong tendency to use the trading company primarily to dispose of their merchandise. Successful foreign sales, however, depend on foreign demand and the foreign market. A blend of demand-driven activities and existing product lines needs to be achieved in order for a trading company to be successful.

The trading company itself must solicit continuous feedback on foreign-market demands and changes in these demands so that its members will be able to maintain a winning international product mix. Substantial attention must be paid to gathering information on the needs and wants of foreign customers and disseminating this information to participating U.S. producers. Otherwise, lack of responsiveness to foreign-market demands will result in a decline of the ETC's effectiveness.[33] The ETC should also determine the activities on which to concentrate, basing this determination on the types of suppliers represented and the types of products exported. One possible differentiation for such service requirements is provided in Figure 11.2.

FIGURE 11.2
Service Requirements for American Export Trading Companies

Suppliers Represented	Products Exported	
	Undifferentiated	Differentiated
Low Export Volume	Requires a Less Than Average Capability in Promotion, Market Contact, and Consolidation	Requires an Above Average Capability in Promotion, but an Average Capability in Market Contact and Consolidation
High Export Volume	Requires a Less Than Average Capability in Promotion, but an Average Capability in Market Contact and Consolidation	Requires an Above Average Capability in Promotion, Market Contact, and Consolidation

Source: Reprinted with permission from *Journal of Marketing* 49 (Fall 1985): 67, Daniel C. Bello and Nicholas C. Williamson, "The American Export Trading Company: Designing a New International Marketing Institution," published by the American Marketing Association, Chicago, IL 60606.

Depending on whether products are differentiated or undifferentiated, the ETC should place varying degrees of emphasis on developing its capability for international promotion. At the same time, undifferentiated products require greater price competitiveness, which may be precisely the major advantage offered by an ETC as a result of economies of scale. For differentiated products, an ETC may be able to place emphasis on promotion and have greater flexibility in price determination.

ETCs may still become the major vehicle for the generation of new international business entry activities by small and medium-sized firms. The concepts of synergism and cooperation certainly make sense in terms of enhancing the international competitiveness of firms. Yet the focus of ETCs should perhaps not be pure exporting. Importing and third-country trading may also generate substantial activity and profit. Through the carrying out of a wide variety of business transactions, international-market knowledge is obtained. This management and consulting expertise may in itself be a salable service.

INTERNATIONAL FACILITATORS

Facilitators are entities outside the firm that assist in the process of going international by supplying knowledge and information but not participating in the transaction. A major facilitator consists of the statements and actions of other firms in the same industry. Information that would be considered proprietary if it involved domestic operations is often freely shared by competing firms when it concerns international business. This information not only has source credibility but is viewed with a certain amount of fear, because a too-successful competitor may eventually infringe on the firm's domestic business.

A second, quite influential group of facilitators is distributors. Often a firm's distributors are engaged, through some of their business activities, in international business. In order to increase their international distribution volume, they encourage purely domestic firms to participate in the international market. This is true not only for exports but also for imports. For example, a major customer of a manufacturing firm may find that materials available from abroad, if used in the domestic-production process, would make the product available to him or her at lower cost. In such instances, the customer may approach the supplier and strongly encourage foreign sourcing.

Banks and other service firms, such as accounting and consulting firms, can serve as major facilitators by alerting their clients to international opportunities. While these service providers historically follow their major multinational clients abroad, increasingly they are establishing a foreign presence on their own. Frequently, they work with domestic clients on expanding market reach in the hope that their service will be used for any international transaction that results. Given the extensive information network of many service providers—banks, for example, often have a wide variety of correspondence relationships—the role of these facilitators can be major. Like a mother hen, they can take firms under their wings and be pathfinders in foreign markets.

Chambers of commerce and other business associations that interact with firms can frequently heighten their interest in international business. Yet, in most instances, these organizations function only as secondary intermediaries, because true change is brought about by the presence and encouragement of other managers. Increasingly, however, associations recognize the importance of international business, and they produce and disseminate materials that can be useful in the development of entry strategies.

Government offices, such as the U.S. Department of Commerce, can also serve as major facilitators. The Commerce Department has district offices across the coun-

Global Perspective

11.4
Incubator Helps Export Effort

Many companies, especially small ones, lack the expertise and the financing to expand into the international marketplace. In the United States, the financial issue is a particularly tricky one. U.S. banks are reluctant to finance international deals because they are seldom familiar with international business, and the U.S. government is less involved in helping exporters than are governments in other nations. At the same time, financing is critical because collecting payment for goods shipped overseas typically takes almost four months.

For a number of Long Island manufacturers, help has come in the form of a business incubator, the National Institute for World Trade. The goal of this nonprofit corporation is to promote and expand international trade. The Lloyd Harbor (Long Island), New York–based organization considers the products of small manufacturers in the area, looking for items that should be able to compete effectively because they have a technological advantage. Of special interest to the National Institute are laboratory equipment,

laser technology, aerospace, and biotechnology businesses.

Spencer Ross, president of the National Institute, worked with four students of international marketing from the State University of New York at Stony Brook to select about a dozen firms to participate in the institute's program. The program will spread out the risks and costs of exporting so that the participating companies can afford to go international. Once the companies have been launched into the international marketplace, they are expected to eventually operate on their own.

Drawing on his foreign trade experience in the corporate and public sectors, Ross says international success hinges on three characteristics. First, the company's chief executive officer must be dedicated to the concept of global operations. Second, the firm must be strong enough to properly organize an international division. Finally, the company must have good products with a stable track record.

Source: Martha E. Mangelsdorf, "Unfair Trade," *Inc.,* April 1991, 28ff; and Peter Troiano, "Going Global," *Economic World,* November 1989, 26.

try that are charged with increasing the international business activities of U.S. firms. District officers, with the help of voluntary groups such as export councils, visit firms in the district and attempt to analyze their international business opportunities. Such activities raise questions about market and product knowledge. Only rarely will government employees have expertise in all areas. However, they can draw on the vast resources of their agency to provide more information to an interested firm.

Increasingly, nonfederal entities—primarily at the state and local level—also are active in encouraging firms to participate in international business. Global Perspective 11.4 provides an example. Many states have formed agencies for economic development that provide information, display products abroad, conduct trade missions, and sometimes even offer financing. Similar services can also be offered by state and local port authorities and by some of the larger cities. Most of these efforts are too recent to evaluate; however, it appears that, because of their closeness to firms, state and local authorities can become a major factor in facilitating international activities.

Finally, universities increasingly are launching internship programs, short-term consultancies, and course projects that are useful to firms interested in international business. As an example, students may visit a firm and examine its potential in the international market as a fulfillment of a course requirement. Because the skill and supervision of faculty members help to form the final report, student projects can be very useful.

FIGURE 11.3   **A Model for Going International**

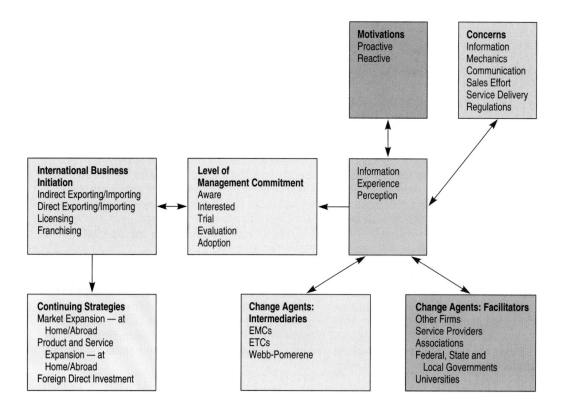

THE PROGRESS OF INTERNATIONAL EXPANSION

The central driver of internationalization is the level of managerial commitment. This commitment will grow gradually from an awareness of international potential to the adaptation of international business as a strategic-business direction. It will be influenced by the information, experience, and perception of management, which in turn is shaped by motivations, concerns, and the activities of change agents.

Management's commitment and its view of the capabilities of the firm will then trigger various international business activities, which can range from indirect exporting and importing to more direct involvement in the global market. Eventually, the firm may then expand further through measures such as joint ventures, strategic alliances, or foreign direct investment. These latter activities are the subject of the next chapter.

All of the developments, processes, and factors involved in the overall process of going international are presented schematically in Figure 11.3.

SUMMARY

Firms do not become experienced in international business overnight, but rather progress gradually through an internationalization process. This process is triggered by different motivations to go abroad. These motivations can be proactive or reactive. Proactive motivations are initiated by aggressive management, whereas reactive motivations are the defensive response of management to environmental changes and pressures. Firms that are primarily stimulated by proactive motivations are more likely to enter international business and succeed.

Apart from indirect and direct exporting and importing, alternatives for international business entry are licensing and franchising. The basic advantage of licensing is that it does not involve capital investment or knowledge of foreign markets. Its major disadvantage is that licensing agreements typically have time limits, are often proscribed by foreign governments, and may result in creating a competitor. The use of franchising as a means of expansion into foreign markets has increased dramatically. Franchisors must learn to strike a balance between, on the one hand, adapting to local environments and, on the other, standardizing to the degree necessary to maintain international recognizability.

In going abroad, firms encounter multiple problems and challenges. These range from a lack of information to mechanics and documentation. In order to gain assistance in its initial international experience, the firm can make use of either intermediaries or facilitators. Intermediaries are outside companies that actively participate in an international transaction. They are export management companies, Webb-Pomerene associations, or export trading companies. In order for these intermediaries to perform international business functions properly, however, they must be compensated. This will result in a reduction of profits.

International facilitators do not participate in an international business transaction, but they contribute knowledge and information. Increasingly, facilitating roles are played by private-sector groups, such as industry associations, banks, accountants, or consultants and by federal, state, and local government authorities.

Key Terms and Concepts

managerial commitment	transfer cost
licensing agreement	R&D cost
royalty	opportunity cost

trademark licensing

franchising

recognizability

export management companies (EMCs)

Webb-Pomerene association

sogoshosha

export trading company (ETC)

Questions for Discussion

1. Discuss the difference between a proactive and a reactive firm, focusing your answer on international business.
2. Why is management commitment so important to export success?
3. Explain the benefits that international sales can have for domestic business activities.
4. Discuss the benefits and the drawbacks of treating international market activities as a safety-valve mechanism.
5. Give some of the reasons why distributors would want to help a firm gain a greater foothold in the international market.
6. Comment on the stance that "licensing is really not a form of international involvement because it requires no substantial additional effort on the part of the licensor."
7. Suggest reasons for the explosive international expansion of U.S.–based franchise systems.
8. What is the purpose of export intermediaries?
9. How can an export intermediary avoid circumvention by a client or customer?
10. What makes an export agent different from any other channel member?
11. Is there a need for export trading companies?
12. What makes a U.S. export trading company different from Japanese trading companies?
13. How can the discrepancy between product-driven and market-driven orientations within export trading companies be resolved?

Recommended Readings

Contractor, Farok J. *Licensing in International Strategy: A Guide for Planning and Negotiations.* Westport, Conn.: Quorum Books, 1985.

Czinkota, Michael R. *Export Development Strategies: U.S. Promotion Policy.* New York: Praeger, 1982.

Czinkota, Michael R., and George Tesar, eds. *Export Management: An International Context.* New York: Praeger, 1982.

Directory of Leading U.S. EMC's, 3rd ed. Fairfield, Conn.: Bergano Book Co., 1990.

The Export Yellow Pages, Washington, D.C.: Venture Publishing, 1991.

Joyner, Nelson, and Richard G. Lurie. *How to Build an Export Business.* Washington, D.C: U.S. Department of Commerce, Office of Minority Business Enterprise, n.d.

Kunio, Yoshihara. *Sogoshosha, The Vanguard of the Japanese Economy.* Tokyo: Oxford University Press, 1982.

Mamis, Robert A. "Global Start-Up." *Inc.,* August 1989, 38.

Perry, Anne C. "The Evolution of Selected U.S. Trade Intermediaries in the International Environment of the 1980's," Doctoral Dissertation, George Washington University, Washington, D.C., 1990.

Root, Franklin. *Entry Strategies for International Markets.* Lexington, Mass.: Lexington Books, 1987.

Rosson, Philip J. and Stanley D. Reid. *Managing Export Entry and Expansion.* New York: Praeger, 1987.

Yip, George S., Pierre M. Loewe, and Michael Y. Yoshino. "How to Take Your Company to the Global Market." *Columbia Journal of World Business* 23 (Winter 1988).

Notes

1. Theodore Levitt, "The Globalization of Markets," *Harvard Business Review* 61 (May–June 1983): 92-102.
2. Warren J. Bilkey and George Tesar, "The Export Behavior of Smaller Sized Wisconsin Manufacturing Firms," *Journal of International Business Studies* 8 (Spring–Summer 1977): 93-98.
3. William C. Pavord and Raymond G. Bogart, "The Dynamics of the Decision to Export," *Akron Business and Economic Review* 6 (Spring 1975): 6-11.
4. Finn Wiedersheim-Paul, H.C. Olson, and L.S. Welch, "Pre-Export Activity: The First Step in Internationalization," *Journal of International Business Studies* 9 (Spring–Summer 1978): 47-58.
5. George Tesar and Jesse S. Tarleton, "Comparison of Wisconsin and Virginia Small and Medium-Sized Exporters: Aggressive and Passive Exporters," in *Export Management,* eds. Michael R. Czinkota and George Tesar (New York: Praeger, 1982), 85-112.
6. Michael R. Czinkota, *Export Development Strategies* (New York: Praeger, 1982), 10.
7. *Winning in the World Market* (Washington, D.C.: American Business Conference Inc., November 1987), 20.
8. S. Tamer Cavusgil, "Global Dimensions of Marketing," in *Marketing,* eds. Patrick E. Murphy and Ben M. Enis (Glenview, Ill.: Scott, Foresman, 1985), 577-599.
9. Masaaki Kotabe and Michael R. Czinkota, "State Government Promotion of Manufacturing Exports: A Gap Analysis," *Journal of International Business Studies,* Winter, 1992.
10. Yoo S. Yang, Robert P. Leone, and Dana L. Alden, "A Market Expansion Ability Approach to Identify Potential Exporters," *Journal of Marketing* 56 (January 1992): 84-96.
11. Michael R. Czinkota and Michael L. Ursic, "An Experience Curve Explanation of Export Expansion," *Journal of Business Research* 12 (Spring 1984), 159-168.
12. Wesley J. Johnston and Michael R. Czinkota, "Managerial Motivations as Determinants of Industrial Export Behavior," in *Export Management: An International Context,* eds. Michael R. Czinkota and George Tesar (New York: Praeger, 1982), 3-7.
13. *Winning in the World Market,* 3-7.
14. "New 'Storeless' Market Gateways," *Focus Japan,* August 1989, 3.
15. Fred Hiatt, "Vending U.S. Steak on Japanese Corners," *International Herald Tribune,* April 5, 1990, 13.
16. Martin F. Connor, "International Technology Licensing" (Washington, D.C.: Seminars in International Trade, National Center for Export-Import Studies, 1985), Teaching Notes.
17. Kate Fitzgerald and Julie Liesse, "Jetsons Fly into Hot Licensing Year," *Advertising Age* 61, (July 16, 1990): 43.
18. Donald W. Hackett, "The International Expansion of U.S. Franchise Systems," in *Multinational Product Management,* eds. Warren J. Keegan and Charles S. Mayer (Chicago: American Marketing Association, 1979), 61-81.
19. Peng S. Chan and Robert T. Justis, "Franchise Management in East Asia," *Academy of Management Executives* 4 (1990): 75-85.
20. "ComputerLand Debugs Its Franchising Program for Asia/Pacific Region," *Business International,* September 13, 1985, 294-295.
21. Nizamettin Aydin and Madhav Kacker, "International Outlook of U.S.-based Franchisers," *International Marketing Review,* 7, 1990:43-53.
22. Economic Consulting Services, *A Study of the Feasibility of Using Export Associations to Promote Increased Exports by Small Businesses* (Washington, D.C.: Economic Consulting Services, 1982), 29.
23. John J. Brasch, "Export Management Companies," *Journal of International Business Studies* (Spring–Summer 1978), 69.
24. Daniel C. Bello, David J. Urban, and Bronislaw J. Verhage, "Evaluating Export Middlemen in Alternative Channel Structures," *International Marketing Review,* 8, 1991: 49-64.
25. Carl Hevener, Federal Trade Commission, Washington, D.C., 1992.
26. "The Giants that Refused to Die," *Economist,* June 1, 1991: 72-73.
27. Kiyoshi Kojima and Ozawa Terutomo, *Japan's General Trading Companies: Merchants of Economic*

Development (Paris: Organization for Economic Co-operation and Development, 1984), 88.

28. Yoshi Tsurumi, *Sogoshosha: Engines of Export Based Growth* (Montreal: The Institute for Research on Public Policy, 1980).

29. Chang-Kyun Shin, "Korean General Trading Companies: A Study of Their Development and Strategies," unpublished doctoral dissertation, George Washington University, Washington, D.C., 1984, 236.

30. Umberto Costa Pinto, "Trading Companies: The Brazilian Experience," in *U.S.—Latin American Trade Relations,* ed. Michael R. Czinkota (New York: Praeger, 1983), 251.

31. *The Export Trading Company Act of 1982* (Washington, D.C.: Chamber of Commerce of the United States of America, 1983), 4.

32. Don Stowe, Office of Export Trading Companies, U.S. Department of Commerce, Washington, D.C., 1992.

33. Michael R. Czinkota, "The Business Response to the Export Trading Company Act of 1982," *The Columbia Journal of World Business* 19 (Fall 1984): 111.

Multinational Corporations

LEARNING OBJECTIVES

1. To define the concept of a multinational corporation and assess its various dimensions.

2. To compare arguments for and against foreign direct investment from the viewpoints of firms, nation-states, and other interest groups.

3. To examine the role of technology transfer in foreign direct investment and the operations of the multinational corporation.

4. To analyze the various modes of operation and co-operation available to a multinational corporation.

The Stateless Corporation

As cross-border trade and investment flows reach new heights, big global companies are effectively making decisions with little regard to national boundaries. The European, U.S., and Japanese giants heading in this direction are learning how to juggle multiple identities and multiple loyalties. Worried by the emergence of regional trading blocs in Europe, North America, and east Asia, these world corporations are building insider capabilities no matter where they operate. At the same time, factories and laboratories are moved around the world freely. Given the wave of mergers, acquisitions, and strategic alliances, the question of national control has become even more unclear.

A fitting example of such a corporation is ABB (Asea Brown Boveri), a $28 billion electrical engineering giant. From headquarters in Zurich, Swedish, German, and Swiss managers shuffle assets around the globe, keep the books in dollars, and conduct most of their business in English. Yet the companies that make up their far-flung operations tailor ABB's turbines, transformers, robots, and high-speed trains to local markets so successfully that ABB looks like an established domestic player everywhere.

Statelessness does provide certain environmental advantages. Among the benefits are the ability to avoid trade and political problems, to sidestep regulatory hurdles, to achieve labor concessions, to balance costs, and to win technology breakthroughs.

The Canadian telecommunications giant, Northern Telecom, has moved so many of its manufacturing functions to the United States that it can win Japanese contracts on the basis of being a U.S. company. Japan favors U.S. over Canadian telecommunications companies because of the politically sensitive U.S.–Japanese trade gap.

When Germany's BASF launched biotechnology research at home, it confronted legal and political challenges from the environmentally conscious Green movement. As a result, the company moved its cancer and immune-system research to Cambridge, Massachusetts, because of the availability of engineers and scientists and because the state has better resolved controversies involving safety, animal rights, and the environment.

One of the main factors that prompted U.S. pharmaceutical maker SmithKline and Britain's Beecham to merge was that they needed to guarantee that they could avoid licensing and regulatory hassles in their largest markets, western Europe and the United States. The new company can now identify itself as an inside player on both sides of the Atlantic.

When Xerox Corp. started moving copier rebuilding work to Mexico, its union in Rochester, New York, objected. The risk of job loss was clear, and the union agreed to undertake the changes in work style and productivity needed to keep the jobs.

Some world companies make almost daily decisions on where to shift production. When Dow Chemical saw European demand for a certain solvent decline recently, the company scaled back its production in Germany and shifted to producing another chemical there, one previously imported from Louisiana and Texas.

Otis Elevator Inc.'s latest product, the Elevonic 411, benefited from the company's global operations. The elevator was developed by six research centers in five countries. Otis's group in Farmington, Connecticut, handled the systems integration, Japan designed the special motor drives that make the elevators ride smoothly, France perfected the door systems, Germany handled the electronics, and Spain took care of the small-geared components. The international process saved more than $10 million in design costs and cut the development cycle from four years to two.

Some analysts have suggested that today's global firms will be superseded by a new form, the "relationship enterprise." These are networks of strategic alliances among big firms, spanning different industries and countries, but held together by common goals that encourage them to act almost as a single firm. For example, early in the 21st century, Boeing, British Airways, Siemens, TNT (an Australian parcel-delivery firm), and SNECMA (a French aircraft-engine maker) might together win a deal to build new airports in China. British Airways and TNT would receive preferential routes and landing slots, Boeing and SNECMA would win aircraft contracts, and Siemens would provide the air-traffic-control systems.

Source: "The Global Firm: R.I.P.," *The Economist,* February 6, 1993, 69; "Cooperation Worth Copying," *The Washington Post,* December 13, 1992, H1, H6; "The Euro-Gospel According to Percy Barnevik," *Business Week,* July 23, 1990, 64–66; and "The Stateless Corporation," *Business Week,* May 14, 1990, 98–106.

Once a firm establishes a production facility abroad, its international operations take on new meaning. The firm has typically evolved to this stage through exporting and/or licensing, which no longer can satisfy its growth objectives. Many companies have found their exports dramatically curtailed because of unfavorable changes in exchange rates or trade barriers. Moreover, for firms in small domestic markets, physical presence through manufacturing is a must in the world's largest markets if the firm is to survive in the long term. Direct investment makes the firm's commitment to the international marketplace more permanent.

At the same time, the firm also becomes a corporate citizen in another nation-state, subject to its laws and regulations as well as its overall environmental influences. To remain effective and efficient as an entity, the firm has to coordinate and control its activities in multiple environments, making decisions that may not be optimal for one or more of the markets in which it operates. As a result, the firm may come under scrutiny by private and public organizations, ranging from consumer groups to supranational organizations such as the United Nations.

In today's environment—with no single country dominating the world economy or holding a monopoly on innovation—technologies, capital, and talents flow in many different directions, driving the trend toward a form of "stateless" corporation, as seen in the chapter's opening vignette.

This chapter will outline the basics of the multinational corporate phenomenon. It will compare the arguments for and against foreign direct investment from the viewpoints of firms, nation-states, and other interest groups. Further, it will analyze alternative arrangements available to multinational corporations in their operations in the world marketplace.

THE MULTINATIONAL CORPORATE PHENOMENON

Multinational entities have played a role in international trade for more than 300 years. The beginnings of these operations can be traced to the British and Dutch trading companies and, after their decline, to European overseas investments, mainly in the extractive industries. The phenomenon as it is known today is the result of the lead taken by U.S.-based companies in the post–World War II period and later followed by western European and Japanese entities.[1] By 1990 the total number of multinationals exceeded 35,000 with 150,000 affiliates around the world.[2] They are engaged in activities from the extractive to the manufacturing sectors, and they account for a significant share of the world's output. The global sales of foreign affiliates of multinationals are estimated to be $4.4 trillion, far greater than world exports at $2.5 trillion. The largest 600 multinationals are estimated to generate between one-fifth and one-fourth of the value added in the production of goods and services.[3]

The Multinational Corporation Defined

Different terms abound for the multinational corporation. They include global, world, transnational, international, supernational, and supranational corporation. The term *multinational enterprise* is used by some when referring to internationally involved entities that may not be using a corporate form. In this text, the term *multinational corporation (MNC)* will be used throughout.

Similarly, there is an abundance of definitions. The United Nations defines multinational corporations as "enterprises which own or control production or service facilities outside the country in which they are based."[4] Although this definition has been criticized as being oriented too much to the economist,[5] it nevertheless captures the quantitative and qualitative dimensions of many of the other definitions proposed.

Quantitatively, certain minimal criteria have been proposed that firms must satisfy before they can be regarded as multinational. The number of countries of operation is typically two, although the Harvard multinational enterprise project required subsidiaries in six or more nations.[6] Another measure is the proportion of overall revenue generated from foreign operations. Although no agreement exists over the exact percentage to be used, 25 to 30 percent is the one most often cited.[7] One proposal is that the degree of involvement in foreign markets has to be substantial enough to make a difference in decision making. Another study proposed that several nations should be owners of the corporation, as is the case with Royal Dutch Shell Group and Unilever or, more recently, as in the merger between Swiss Brown Boveri and Swedish Asea to form ABB.[8]

However, production abroad does not necessarily indicate a multinational corporation. Qualitatively, the behavior of the firm is the determining factor. If the firm is to be categorized as a multinational corporation, its management must consider it to be multinational and must act accordingly. In terms of management philosophies, firms can be categorized as **ethnocentric** (home-market oriented), **polycentric** (oriented toward individual foreign markets), or **regiocentric** or **geocentric** (oriented toward larger areas, even the global marketplace).[9] Even ethnocentric firms would qualify as multinational corporations if production were the sole criterion. However, the term should be reserved for firms that view their domestic operation as a part of worldwide (or regionwide) operations and direct an integrated business system. The definition excludes polycentric firms, which may be comparable to holding companies.

Both quantitative and qualitative criteria are important in the defining task. Regardless of the definition, the key criteria are that the firm controls its production facilities abroad and manages them (and its domestic operations) in an integrated fashion in pursuit of global opportunities.

The World's Multinational Corporations

Many of the world's largest corporate entities, listed in Table 12.1, are larger economically than most of their host nations. Some operate in well over 100 countries; for example, IBM has operations in 132 nations. Of the 25 firms listed, 10 are headquartered in the United States, 10 in western Europe, and 5 in east Asia. The economic power they command is enormous; according to one estimate, the 500 largest industrial corporations account for 80 percent of the world's direct investment and ownership of foreign affiliates.[10]

Although dominated by certain countries, the multinational corporate phenomenon has spread worldwide. For example, corporate headquarters for the 500 largest industrial corporations are in 32 different nations. Direct investment by firms from Africa, Asia, and Latin America has increased dramatically, especially by firms from more industrialized nations such as the Republic of Korea, Mexico, and Brazil.[11] Samsung, Korea's largest company, has assets of $16 billion and operations in 55 countries.[12]

The impact of multinationals varies by industry sector and by country. In oil, multinational corporations still command 30 percent of production, despite strong national efforts by some countries.[13] Their share in refining and marketing is still 45 percent. In several agribusiness sectors, such as pineapples, multinationals account for approximately 60 percent of the world output. Similarly, the contribution of multi-

TABLE 12.1
The 25 Largest
Industrial Corporations
Ranked by Sales (1992)

		Sales (in millions of dollars)	Foreign Revenue (as a percentage of total)	Foreign Profits (as a percentage of total)
1	General Motors/United States	123,780	31.8	P-D
2	Royal Dutch-Shell/U.K.-Holland	103,834	55.1*	37.6*
3	Exxon/United States	103,242	75.9	84.2
4	Ford Motor/United States	88,962	39.1	35.9
5	Toyota Motor/Japan	78,061	42.0	N/A
6	IBM/United States	65,394	62.3	P-D
7	IRI/Italy	64,095	N/A	N/A
8	General Electric/United States	60,236	14.4	10.0
9	British Petroleum/U.K.	58,355	65.5	80.3
10	Daimler-Benz/Germany	57,321	61.0	N/A
11	Mobil/United States	56,910	68.1	86.3
12	Hitachi/Japan	56,053	21.0	N/A
13	Matsushita Electric/Japan	48,595	40.0	N/A
14	Philip Morris/United States	48,109	27.4	25.4
15	Fiat/Italy	46,812	33.0	N/A
16	Volkswagen/Germany	46,042	65.0	N/A
17	Siemens/Germany	44,859	40.0	N/A
18	Samsung Group/South Korea	43,701	N/A	N/A
19	Nissan Motor/Japan	42,905	N/A	N/A
20	Unilever/U.K.-Holland	41,262	42.0*	N/A
21	ENI/Italy	41,047	19.0	N/A
22	E.I. DuPont/United States	38,031	44.8	52.7
23	Texaco/United States	37,551	49.9	57.6
24	Chevron/United States	36,795	38.2	87.4
25	Elf Aquitane/France	36,315	38.0	N/A

P-D Profit to deficit
* Non-European revenues and profits

Sources: "Everybody's Favourite Monsters," *The Economist*, March 27, 1993, S6–S7; "The Global 500," *Fortune*, July 27, 1992, 273; "U.S. Corporations with the Biggest Foreign Revenues," *Forbes*, July 20, 1992, 298–300; and various 1991 and 1992 corporate annual reports.

national corporations' affiliates may account for more than one-third of the output of the marketing sector in certain countries.[14] For example, U.S. companies owned 32 percent of the paper and pulp industry, 36 percent of the mining and smelting industry, and 39 percent of manufacturing overall in Canada before the foreign direct investment climate changed in the early 1980s.[15] Despite a tightening of investment regulations, 40 percent of Canadian manufacturing was foreign owned in 1990, with U.S. firms accounting for 80 percent of that share.

The importance of the world marketplace to multinational corporations also varies. The foreign-sales share of total sales for the world's largest industrial corporations has increased steadily. The percentage will naturally vary by industry (for example, oil company ratios are well over half) and by the country of origin. For many European-based companies, domestic sales may be less than 10 percent of overall sales. In 1992, for example, as a percentage of total worldwide sales, Philips's sales in Holland were 4 percent, SKF's sales in Sweden were 4 percent, and Sandoz's sales in Switzerland were a mere 2 percent. Comparable figures for U.S.–based companies, such as Johnson & Johnson and 3M, are about 50 percent.

The 1980s saw an increasing multinationalization of service companies, mainly in the finance and trade-related services, although other service MNCs such as accounting and advertising firms established considerable numbers of affiliates abroad.

FOREIGN DIRECT INVESTMENT

To understand the multinational corporate phenomenon, one must analyze the rationale for foreign direct investment. Foreign direct investment represents one component of the international business flow and includes start-ups of new operations as well as purchases of more than 10 percent of existing companies. The other component is portfolio investment—that is, the purchase of stocks and bonds internationally—which was discussed in Chapter 5.

Foreign direct investment has only recently received adequate attention. In 1974, for example, no comprehensive list of foreign firms investing in the United States was available, no one knew which firms were indeed foreign owned, and major shortcomings existed in the foreign direct investment data available.[16] In view of the fact that the U.S. data gathering system is highly sophisticated, much less information about foreign direct investment was probably available in other countries.

Recent concerted data gathering and estimation efforts by organizations such as the Organization for Economic Cooperation and Development (OECD) and the International Monetary Fund (IMF) indicate that foreign direct investments have grown tremendously. The total value of such global investment, which in 1967 was estimated at $105 billion, had climbed to an estimated $596 billion by 1984[17] and $1.809 trillion by 1991.[18] Foreign direct investment has clearly become a major avenue for foreign market entry and expansion. Foreign direct investment in the United States, for example, totaled $408 billion in 1991, up from a meager $6.9 billion in 1970.[19] Examples of this investment in terms of industries and locations are provided in Figure 12.1. At the same time, U.S. direct investment abroad totaled $421 billion.

Reasons for Foreign Direct Investment

Firms expand internationally for a variety of reasons. An overview of the major determinants of foreign direct investment is provided in Table 12.2.

Marketing Factors   Marketing considerations and the corporate desire for growth are major causes of the increase in foreign direct investment. Even a sizable domestic market may present limitations to growth. Firms therefore need to seek wider market access in order to maintain and increase their sales. Laidlaw Transportation Ltd., the biggest school bus operator in Canada, moved south of the border, where it saw considerably more room to grow. Business has quadrupled, and the company now draws 60 percent of its revenue from the United States.[20] Some firms make investments in order to be closer to and better serve some of their major clients, such as Siemens with its $4.3 billion investment in the U.S. market. The growth objective can be achieved most quickly through the acquisition of foreign firms. One of the companies that has made the largest acquisitions in the U.S. market in recent years is Nestlé, which has acquired companies such as Carnation and Alcon Laboratories. Other reasons for foreign direct investment include the desire to gain know-how and the need to add to existing sales-force strength.

A major cause for the recent growth in foreign direct investment is derived demand. Often, as large multinational firms move abroad, they are quite interested in maintaining their established business relationships with other firms. Therefore, they frequently encourage their suppliers to follow them and continue to supply them from the new foreign location. For example, advertising agencies often move abroad in order to service foreign affiliates of their domestic clients. Similarly, engineering firms, insurance companies, and law firms often are invited to provide their services abroad. Yet not all of these developments come about from co-optation by client

FIGURE 12.1   A Sampler of Foreign Investment in the United States

U.S. INVESTMENT   FOREIGN INVESTOR

Rydell Labs/Lion Corp. drugs (*Lion Corp., Japan*)
Allis Chalmers Agricultural Equipment (*Klöckner-Humboldt Deutz, Germany*)
SMC Pneumatic Inc. temperature control devices (*Shoketsu Kinzoku Koygo CO., Japan*)
BASF Wyandotte Corp. chemicals (*BASF AG, Germany*)
Detroit Race Course (*Ladbroke Group, Britain*)
White Consolidated (*Electrolux, Sweden*)
Inotek International fertilizers (*Sempernoval, Britain*)
Pennsylvania Glass Sand Corp. (*Rio Tinto-Zinc Corp., Britain*)
Bver Environmental refuse systems (*Haniel Umweltschutz, Germany*)

PMP malt beverages (*Fujisawa Pharmaceutical Co., Japan*)
Wilson Sporting Goods (*Amer Group, Finland*)
Lawyers Medical Digest (*Thomson family, Canada*)
Streptococcus Lab animal feed (*Bonnierforetagen AB, Sweden*)
Keidon Oil (*Rushden Investments, Britain*)
Alumax aluminum manufacturing (*Mitsui & Co., Japan*)
Dale Electronics (*Mezzanine Capital Corp., Britain*)
Montana Tunnel Minings Project (*Centennial Minerals, Canada*)
Grant Gold Mine (*Marubeni Corp., Japan*)
PVC Lines water transportation (*PV Christensen, Denmark*)
Kuparuk Transportation pipelines (*Government of Britain*)
Coal Mine Development (*Hyundai Group, S. Korea*)
Japan Forest Industry sporting equipment (*Kudo Trading, Japan*)

Real Robin International restaurant (*Skylard Co., Japan*)
Silver Dollar Mining (*Faisal Abu-Khadra, Saudi Arabia*)
Amfac nurseries (*Agrogen Biotechnologies, Canada*)
Publishers paper Co. (*Smurfit family, Ireland*)
Epson Portland computers (*Shinshu Seiki Co., Japan*)
Cheyenne's Aero Tech School (*BOC, Britain*)
Davis Oil Properties (*Hiram Walker-Consumers Home, Canada*)
Tom Brown Inc.'s Oil Properties (*Pan Canadian Petroleum, Canada*)
Airport Inn (*Chaudry family, Pakistan*)
Greystone Office Complex (*Hudson's Bay Co., Canada*)
Marathon Gold Corp. (*Hampton Gold Mining Areas, Britain*)
Bioximetry Technology (*BOC International, Britain*)
Carnation Co. (*Nestle SA, Switzerland*)
Crown Zellerback (*James Goldsmith, Britain*)
Elite Software Systems (*Moore Corp., Canada*)
Fireman's Fund (*Allianz, Germany*)
McCracken Silver Mine (*Arizona Silver Corp., Canada*)
Baxter's Surgical Glove Plant (*Dunlop Olympic, Austalia*)

Potash Producers Inc.'s Assets mineral mining (*Rayrock Resources, Canada*)
Medico Industries drug manufacturer (*Wellcome Foudation, Britain*)
Breddo Food Products Corp. (*Centrale Suikermaatschappij NY, Netherlands*)
International American Ceramics (*Keramik Holding AG, Switzerland*)
Big Three Industries chemicals (*L'Air Liquide, France*)
Southland Corporation (*Ito-Yokado, Japan*)
Two Pershing Square real estate (*Trizec Corp., Canada*)
Purina Mills pet food (*British Petroleum, Britain*)
Airco Energy pipeline (*BOC International, Britain*)
National Old Line Insurance (*Ennia NV, Netherlands*)
Kentucky Horse Center Inc. (*Hagopian, Erika, Germany*)
Louisville Cement Co. (*Pollet, France*)
Copper Range Co. (*Echo Bay Mines Ltd., Canada*)
Mississippi River Alcohol Co. (*Ferruzzi family, Italy*)

Stangewald Bldg. (*Robert Jones Investments, New Zealand*)
Innovative Media Inc. typesetting (*Cotbridge Co., Hong Kong*)

Geo-Con Inc. construction (*Taisei Corp., Japan*)
Marsteller advertising (*Government of France*)
Celanese (*Hoechst, Germany*)
SCM Corp. (*Hanson Trust, Britain*)
Northland Products sporting equipment (*Pearson Forest Products, Canada*)
Green Mountain Inn (*Gameroff, Simon and David, Canada*)
New Hampshire Ball Bearings (*Takahashi family, Japan*)
Hannaford Bros. grocery stores (*Sobey family, Canada*)
Scott Paper Co. (*Bronfman family, Canada*)
Compo Industries coated fabric (*Gemina SPA, Italy*)
Pixley-Richards plastic products (*DSM-Dutch State Mines, Netherlands*)
Trea Industries plastics (*Toray Industries, Japan*)
Pawtuxet Valley Daily Times (*Independent Newspaper, New Zealand*)
Thatcher Glass Corp. (*Power Corp. of America, Canada*)
Atlantic Cement Co. (*Blue Circle Industries, Britain*)
Inmont paint and ink (*BASF AG, Germany*)
Johanna Farms milk processing (*John Labatt, Canada*)
Monmouth Plastics (*Cookson Group, Britain*)
Hercules Commercial Explosive Div. (*Dyno Industries AS, Norway*)
Litton Bionetics research laboratory (*Akzo NV, Netherlands*)
Peoples Drug Inc. (*BAT Industries PLC, Britain*)
Government Research Co. consulting and public relations (*Public Affairs Resource Group, Canada*)

Diesel Marine Norship shipbuilding (*Torday & Carlisle, Britain*)
Clarita's Cos. computer software (*V NU BV, Netherlands*)
Food Lion (*Delhaize "Le Lion", Belgium*)
Hamilton Beach/Moulinex Inc. housewares and fans (*Moulinex SA, France*)
Santee Portland Cement Co. (*Holderbank financiere Glaris, Switzerland*)
Carolina Formed Fabrics Corp. (*Low & Bonar, Britain*)
Atlantic Center real estate (*Cadillac Fairview, Canada*)
Elsons newsstands (*Smith Wh & Sons Holding, Britain*)
Austell Packaging (*Smurfit family, Ireland*)
Country Sanitation Inc. (*Attwoods Group, Britain*)

Probat US roasted coffee (*Probat-Werke Von Gimborn, Germany*)
Gulf of Mexico Oil/Gas Leases (*Royal Dutch Shell, Netherlands*)
Goldstar of America refrigeration machines (*Lucky Group, S. Korea*)
Michelin Tire Corp. (*Michelin, France*)

TABLE 12.2
Major Determinants of Direct Foreign Investment

Marketing Factors
1. Size of market
2. Market growth
3. Desire to maintain share of market
4. Desire to advance exports of parent company
5. Need to maintain close customer contact
6. Dissatisfaction with existing market arrangements
7. Export base
8. Desire to follow customers
9. Desire to follow competition

Barriers to Trade
1. Government-erected barriers to trade
2. Preference of local customers for local products

Cost Factors
1. Desire to be near source of supply
2. Availability of labor
3. Availability of raw materials
4. Availability of capital/technology
5. Lower labor costs
6. Lower other production costs
7. Lower transport costs
8. Financial (and other) inducements by government
9. More favorable cost levels

Investment Climate
1. General attitude toward foreign investment
2. Political stability
3. Limitation on ownership
4. Currency exchange regulations
5. Stability of foreign exchange
6. Tax structure
7. Familiarity with country

General
1. Expected higher profits
2. Other

Source: Adapted from Organizations for Economic Cooperation and Development, *International Investment and Multinational Enterprises* (Paris: OECD, 1983), 41.

firms. Often firms invest abroad for defensive reasons, out of fear that their clients may find other sources abroad, and this eventually might jeopardize their status even in the domestic market. To preserve quality, Japanese automakers have urged more than 40 of their suppliers from Japan to establish production in the United States.[21]

For similar reasons, firms follow their competitors abroad. Competitive firms influence not only their engaging in foreign direct investment, but even where the investments are made.[22] Many firms have found that even their competitive position at home is affected by their ability to effectively compete in foreign markets.

Barriers to Trade   Foreign direct investment permits firms to circumvent barriers to trade and operate abroad as domestic firms, unaffected by duties, tariffs, or other import restrictions. The enormous amount of U.S. investment would not have been attracted to Canada had it not been for the barriers to trade erected by the Canadian government to support domestic industry.

In addition to government-erected barriers, barriers may also be imposed by customers through their insistence on domestic goods and services, either as a result of nationalistic tendencies or as a function of cultural differences. Furthermore, local buyers may wish to buy from sources that they perceive to be reliable in their supply, which means buying from local producers. For some products, country-of-origin effects may force a firm to establish a plant in a country that has a built-in positive stereotype for product quality.[23]

Cost Factors   Servicing markets at sizable geographic distances and with sizable tariff barriers has made many exporters' offerings in foreign markets prohibitively expensive. Many manufacturing multinationals have established plants overseas to gain cost advantages in terms of labor and raw materials. For example, many of the border plants in Mexico provide their U.S. parents with low-cost inputs and components through the maquiladora program.

Foreign direct investment occurs not only horizontally, by firms acquiring or establishing similar firms abroad, but also vertically. Some firms engage in foreign direct investment to secure their sources of supply for raw materials and other intermediary goods. This usually secures supply and may provide it at a lower cost as well.

All in all, cost factors are not necessarily the primary attraction for manufacturers to make foreign direct investments, as seen in Global Perspective 12.1.

Investment Climate   Foreign direct investment by definition implies a degree of control over the enterprise.[24] Yet this may be unavailable because of environmental constraints, even if the firm owns 100 percent of the subsidiary. The general attitude toward foreign investment and its development over time may be indicative of the long-term prospects for investment. For example, if asked to choose, 48 percent of Americans would discourage Japanese investment and only 18 percent would encourage it.[25] In many countries, foreign direct investment tends to arouse nationalistic feelings. Political risk has to be defined broadly to include not only the threat of political upheaval but also the likelihood of arbitrary or discriminatory government action that will result in financial loss. This could take the form of tax increases, price controls, or measures directed specifically at foreign firms such as partial divestment of ownership, local-content requirements, remittance restrictions, export requirements, and limits on expatriate employment.[26] The investment climate is also measured in terms of foreign-currency risk. The evaluations will typically focus on possible accounting translation exposure levels and cashflows in foreign currency.

In a survey of 108 U.S.–based multinational corporations, foreign direct investment was found to be profit and growth driven.[27] The influence of the other variables will vary depending on the characteristics of the firm and its management, on its objectives, and on external conditions. Firms can be divided into three categories according to their orientations: resource seekers, market seekers, and efficiency seekers.[28] **Resource seekers** are after either natural or human resources. Natural resources are typically based on mineral, agricultural, or oceanographic advantages and result in firms locating in areas where they are available. The availability of choices is therefore tied to the availability of the resources sought. If human resources are sought for reasons of cost or skill level, the decision can be altered over time if the labor advantage or environmental conditions change.

Firms primarily in search of better opportunities to enter and expand within markets are **market seekers.** Particularly when markets are closed or access is restricted, firms have a major incentive to locate in them. **Efficiency seekers,** for their part, attempt to obtain the most economical sources of production. They frequently have affiliates in various markets that are highly specialized in product lines or com-

Global Perspective

12.1
U.S. Producers Shun Low-Wage Countries

A study by Ernst & Young finds that only one-third of 650 projects announced by U.S. public companies during 1991 went to countries with low-cost labor and that the majority were placed in targeted industrialized markets.

Just two of the ten countries that attracted the most U.S. investments, Mexico and the former Soviet Union, have cheap labor (defined by the U.S. Labor Department as less than 25 percent of U.S. wages). Altogether, only 196 new projects (30 percent) were destined for low-cost-labor nations. The most popular sites for new projects were Canada, the United Kingdom, Germany, and France.

The main reasons U.S. manufacturers locate overseas is to gain footholds in prime markets. Many U.S. companies are looking to build market share in industrialized countries by accessing customers, technology, and skills, as opposed to choosing a country due to the availability of cheap labor. Other important factors, particularly for first-time investors, are financial incentives and low corporate tax rates.

Europe, mainly the EC, was the most popular site for U.S. investment (357 projects). Asia attracted 20 percent of all the projects, and four-fifths of the projects in Asia were joint ventures. Only 22 projects were announced for South America and the Caribbean, 6 for the Middle East, and only 1 for Africa.

Top U.S. Investment Locations

Country*	Number of Projects
Canada	84
United Kingdom	72
Germany	60
France	59
MEXICO	56
Japan	43
USSR	20
Australia	17
Italy	17
Netherlands	16
Spain	16
Ireland	15
CHINA	14
HUNGARY	14
POLAND	12
INDIA	11
Belgium	10
South Korea	10
Brazil	8
INDONESIA	8

*Upper case indicates countries with low rates for hourly labor.

Source: Gregory Sandler, "NAFTA Aims Spotlight at Border Sites," *Export Today* 8 (November/December 1992): 19.

ponents and engage in major intrafirm transfers in order to maximize the benefits to the entire firm.

The Host Country Perspective

The host government is caught in a love-hate relationship with foreign direct investment.[29] On the one hand, the host country has to appreciate the various contributions, especially economic, that the foreign direct investment will make. On the other hand, fears of dominance, interference, and dependence are often voiced and acted upon. The major positive and negative impacts are summarized in Table 12.3.

The Positive Impact Foreign direct investment has contributed greatly to world development in the past 40 years. Said Lord Lever, a British businessman who served in the cabinets of Harold Wilson and James Callaghan, "Europe got 20 times more out of American investment after the war than the multinationals did; every country gains by productive investment.[30]

TABLE 12.3 Positive and Negative Impacts of Foreign Direct Investment on Host Countries	**Positive Impact** 1. Capital formation 2. Technology and management skills transfer 3. Regional and sectoral development 4. Internal competition and entrepreneurship 5. Favorable effect on Balance of Payments 6. Increased employment **Negative Impact** 1. Industrial dominance 2. Technological dependence 3. Disturbance of economic plans 4. Cultural change 5. Interference by home government of multinational corporation

Source: Jack N. Behrman, *National Interests and the Multinational Enterprise* (Englewood Cliffs, N.J.: Prentice-Hall, 1970), chapters 2 through 5; Jack N. Behrman, *Industrial Policies: International Restructuring and Transnationals* (Lexington, Mass.: Lexington Books, 1984), chapter 5; and Christopher M. Korth, *International Business* (Englewood Cliffs, N.J.: Prentice-Hall, 1985), chapters 12 and 13.

Capital flows are especially beneficial to countries with limited domestic sources and restricted opportunities to raise funds in the world's capital markets. In addition, foreign direct investment may attract local capital to a project for which local capital alone would not have sufficed.

The role of foreign direct investment has been seen as that of **technology transfer.**[31] Technology transfer includes the introduction of not only new hardware to the market but also the techniques and skills to operate it. In industries where the role of intellectual property is substantial, such as pharmaceuticals or software development, access to parent companies' research and development provides benefits that may be far greater than those gained through infusion of capital. This explains the interest that many governments have expressed in having multinational corporations establish R&D facilities in their countries.

An integral part of technology transfer is managerial skills, which are the most significant labor component of foreign direct investment. With the growth of the service sector, many economies need skills rather than expatriate personnel to perform the tasks.

Foreign direct investment can be used effectively in developing a geographical region or a particular industry sector. Foreign direct investment is one of the most expedient ways in which unemployment can be reduced in chosen regions of a country. Furthermore, the costs of establishing an industry are often too prohibitive and the time needed too excessive for the domestic industry, even with governmental help, to try it on its own. In many developing countries, foreign direct investment may be a way to diversify the industrial base and thereby reduce the country's dependence on one or a few sectors.

At the company level, foreign direct investment may intensify competition and result in benefits to the economy as a whole as well as to consumers through increased productivity and possibly lower prices. Competition typically introduces new techniques, products and services, and ideas to the markets. It may improve existing patterns of how business is done.

The major impact of foreign direct investment on the Balance of Payments is long term. Import substitution, export earnings, and subsidized imports of technology and management all assist the host nation on the trade account side of the Balance of Payments. Not only may a new production facility substantially decrease the need to import the type of products manufactured, but it may start earning export revenue as well. Several countries, such as Brazil, have imposed export requirements as a precondition for foreign direct investment. On the capital account side, foreign direct investment may have short-term impact in lowering a deficit as well as long-term impact in keeping capital at home that could have otherwise been invested or transferred abroad. However, measurement is difficult because significant portions of the flows may miss—or evade—the usual government reporting channels. In 1990, more than half of foreign investment was "unidentified," in that experts could not figure out what type it was or where it came from.[32]

Jobs are often the most obvious reason to cheer about foreign direct investment. Foreign companies directly employ three million Americans, or about 3 percent of the workforce, and indirectly create opportunities for millions more. The benefits reach far beyond mere employment. Salaries paid by multinational corporations are usually higher than those paid by domestic firms. The creation of jobs translates also into the training and development of a skilled workforce. Consider, for example, the situation of many Caribbean states that are dependent on tourism for their well-being. In most cases, multinational hotel chains have been instrumental in establishing a pool of trained hospitality workers and managers.

All of the benefits discussed are indeed possible advantages of foreign direct investment. Their combined effect can lead to an overall enhancement in the standard of living in the market as well as an increase in the host country's access to the world market and its international competitiveness. It is equally possible, however, that the impact can be negative rather than positive.

The Negative Impact   In 1971, Herb Gray attributed Canada's economic plight largely to the extensive foreign ownership of its industries. Gray in 1980 was industry minister in Pierre Trudeau's cabinet, which cracked down on foreign—especially U.S.—investment. Canada had a branch-plant economy, the characteristics of which included stunted economic development and low levels of research and development. Gray argued that foreign-owned companies did not provide their host countries with benefits equal to those provided by indigenous companies.[33]

Although some of the threats posed by multinational corporations and foreign direct investment are exaggerated, in many countries some industrial sectors are dominated by foreign-owned entities. In France, for example, three-fourths of the computer and data-processing equipment sector was dominated by foreign affiliates in 1980.[34] In Belgium, oil refining (78 percent) and electrical engineering (87 percent) showed the highest rates of foreign participation.[35]

Because foreign direct investment in most cases is concentrated in technology-intensive industries, research and development account for another area of tension. Multinational corporations usually want to concentrate their R&D efforts, especially their basic research. With its technology transfer, the multinational corporation can assist the host country's economic development, but it may leave the host country dependent on flows of new and updated technology. Furthermore, the multinational firm may contribute to the **brain drain** by attracting scientists from host countries to its central research facility. Many countries have demanded, and won, research facilities on their soil, the results of which they can control to a better extent. Many countries are weary of the technological dominance of the United States and Japan and see this as a long-term threat. Western European nations, for example, are joining forces in basic research and development under the auspices of the so-called EUREKA project, which is a pan-European pooling of resources to develop new technologies with both governmental and private-sector help.

Growth In Employment: A Sign of Economic Vitality

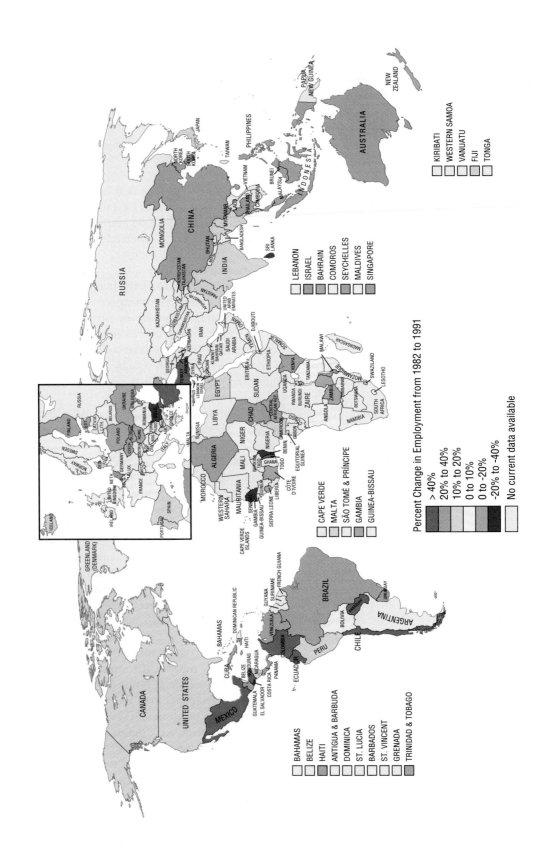

Percent Change in Employment from 1982 to 1991

- \> 40%
- 20% to 40%
- 10% to 20%
- 0 to 10%
- 0 to -20%
- -20% to -40%
- No current data available

Source: Yearbook of Labour Statistics, 1992.

Foreign direct investment creates jobs. Even developed nations such as the United States benefit from additional employment opportunities provided by foreign investment in production facilities such as the Toyota–GM plant in California.

Source: Courtesy of New United Motor Manufacturing, Inc.

Many of the economic benefits of foreign direct investment are controversial as well. Capital inflows may be accompanied by outflows in a higher degree and over a longer term than is satisfactory to the host government. For example, many of the hotels built in the Caribbean by multinational chains were unable to find local suppliers and have had to import supplies and thus spend much-needed foreign currency. Many officials also complain that the promised training of local personnel, especially for management positions, has never taken place. Rather than stimulate local competition and encourage entrepreneurship, multinationals with their often superior product offering and marketing skills have stifled competition. Many countries, including the United States, have found that multinational companies do not necessarily want to rely on local suppliers but rather bring along their own from the domestic market.

Many governments see multinationals as a disturbance to their economic planning. Decisions are made concerning their economy over which they have little or no control. Host countries do not look favorably on a multinational that may want to keep the import content in a product high, especially when local suppliers may be available.

Multinational companies are, by definition, change agents. They bring about change not only in the way business may be conducted but also, through the products and services they generate and the way they are marketed, cause change in the lifestyles of the consumers in the market. The extent to which this is welcomed or accepted varies by country. For example, the introduction of fast-food restaurants to Taiwan dramatically altered eating patterns, especially of teenagers, who made these outlets extremely popular and profitable. Concern has been expressed about the apparent change in eating patterns and the higher relative cost of eating in these establishments.

The multinational corporation will also have an impact on business practices. Although multinationals usually pay a higher salary, they may also engage in practices that are alien to the local workforce, such as greater work-rule flexibility. Older operators in Japan, for example, may be removed from production lines to make room for more productive employees. In another country where the Japanese firm establishes a plant, tradition and union rules may prevent this.[36]

Some host nations have expressed concern over the possibility of interference, economically and politically, by the home government of the multinational corporation; that is, they fear that the multinational may be used as an instrument of influence.[37] The United States has used U.S–based corporations to extend its foreign policy in areas of capital flows, technology controls, and competition. Foreign direct investment regulations were introduced in the United States in the 1960s to diminish capital outflows from the country and thus to strengthen the country's Balance-of-Payment situation. If the actions of affiliates of U.S.-based companies are seen to have a negative impact on competition in the U.S. market, antitrust decrees may be used to change the situation. Increasingly, major foreign direct investments are screened by the Committee for Foreign Investments in the United States (CFIUS). Concerns have been raised mainly in terms of national security and the large numbers of investors from a particular country; for example, in the 1970s, Arabs were seen by some to wield too much influence through their investments in this country, and in the late 1980s, the same was true of the Japanese.

Of course, the multinational is available not only to the home government as a political or economic instrument but to the host government and other groups as well. Fixed investments by multinationals can be held hostage by a host country in trying to win concessions from other governments. In an increasing number of cases, host governments insist on quid pro quo deals in which foreign direct investment is contingent on adherence to specified requirements, such as export targets. Many United Nations sanctions, although approved by governments, have to be carried out through the compliance of multinational companies, as was the case with the divestment that took place to force the South African government to abandon the policy of apartheid.

Countries engage in formal evaluation of foreign direct investment, both outbound and inbound. Canada, for example, uses the Foreign Investment Review Agency to determine whether foreign-owned companies are good corporate citizens. Sweden reviews outbound foreign direct investment in terms of its impact on the home country, especially employment.

The Home Country Perspective

Most of the aspects of foreign direct investment that concern host countries apply to the home country as well. Foreign direct investment means addition to the home country's gross national product from profits, royalties, and fees remitted by affiliates.[38] In many cases, intracompany transfers bring about additional export possibilities.[38] Many countries, in promoting foreign direct investment, see it as a means to stimulate economic growth—an end that would expand export markets and serve other goals, such as political motives, as well. For example, the **Overseas Private Investment Corporation** provides insurance for new U.S. foreign direct investment in friendly developing countries against currency inconvertibility, expropriation, and political violence.[39] Some countries, such as Japan, have tried to gain preferential access to raw materials through firms that owned the deposits. Other factors of production can be obtained through foreign direct investment as well. Companies today may not have the luxury of establishing R&D facilities wherever they choose but must locate them where human power is available. This explains, for example, why Northern Telecom, the Canadian telecommunications giant, has more than 500 of its roughly 2,000 R&D people based in the United States, mostly in California.

The major negative issue centers on employment. Many unions point not only to outright job loss but also to the effect on imports and exports. The most controversial have been investments in plants in developing countries that export back to the home countries. Multinationals such as electronics manufacturers, who have moved plants to southeast Asia and Mexico, have justified this as a necessary cost-cutting competitive measure.

Another critical issue is that of technological advantage. Some critics state that, by establishing plants abroad or forming joint ventures with foreign entities, the country may be giving away its competitive position in the world marketplace. This is especially true when the recipients may be able to avoid the time and expense involved in developing new technologies.

The U.S. government has also taken a position on the behavior of U.S.-based firms overseas. The Foreign Corrupt Practices Act was passed in 1977, and a section of it deals with bribery. It is a form of the extraterritoriality concept discussed earlier; in this case, the concern is the ethics of business practices. Although clear-cut bribery of elected officials is universally banned, the United States is the only country in the world that has legislation as extensive as the FCPA guiding the conduct of its firms. Many firms have indeed complained about the negative impact that compliance has in some markets of the world where facilitating payments are common.[40]

Management of the Relationship

Arguments for and against foreign direct investment are endless. Costs and benefits must be weighed. Only the multinational corporation itself can assess expected gains against perceived risks in its overseas commitments. At the same time, only the host and home countries can assess benefits realized against costs in terms of their national priorities. If these entities cannot agree on objectives because their most basic interests are in conflict, they cannot agree on the means either. In most cases, the relationship between the parties is not necessarily based on logic, fairness, or equity, but on the relative bargaining power of each.[41] Furthermore, political changes may cause rapid changes in host government–MNC relations, as seen in Global Perspective 12.2.

The bargaining positions of the multinational corporation and the host country change over time. The course of these changes is summarized in Figure 12.2. The multinational wields its greatest power before the investment is actually made; in the negotiation period, it can require a number of incentives over a period of time. Whether or not the full cycle of events takes place depends on developments in the market as well as the continued bargaining strength of the multinational.

The multinational corporation can maintain its bargaining strength by developing a local support system through local financing, procurement, and business contacts as well as by maintaining control over access to technology and markets. The first approach attempts to gain support from local market entities if discriminating actions by the government take place. The second approach aims to make the operation of the affiliate impossible without the contribution of the parent.

Host countries, on the other hand, try to enhance their role by instituting control policies and performance requirements. Governments attempt to prevent the integration of activities among affiliates and control by the parent. In this effort, they exclude or limit foreign participation in certain sectors of the economy and require local participation in the ownership and management of the entities established. The extent of this participation will vary by industry, depending on how much the investment is needed by the host economy. Performance requirements typically are programs aimed at established foreign investors in an economy. These often are such discriminatory policies as local content requirements, export requirements, limits on foreign payments (especially profit repatriation), and demands concerning the type

Global Perspective

12.2
From Gung Ho to Uh-Oh

Business people from around the world have flocked to Moscow since 1986, when Soviet President Mikhail Gorbachev encouraged them to seek joint ventures with Soviet partners. Gorbachev's strategy was to revitalize the Soviet economy by introducing modern technology and Western business methods. The foreign companies were attracted by the prospect of getting an early toehold in a largely untapped market of nearly 300 million consumers.

Especially since the breakup of the Soviet Union in December 1991, reality has failed to match expectations for both parties. Western investment has totaled almost $1.5 billion ($500 million in 1992) in Russia, and those already in continue to feel confident about the country's long-term potential. Conoco has invested $75 million on pipeline and infrastructure projects in three Russian oil and gas regions. Says James Tilley, head of Conoco's Moscow office: "There will be ups and downs; it is just a matter of how far those downs are going to be." Michael Adams, CEO of Young & Rubicam/Sovero (an advertising joint venture) states: "This is a lousy business environment, but there is great growth potential. Right now, most people are happy if they aren't bleeding to death." Many companies have concluded that not investing poses the greater risk.

However, once there a company has to live with a befuddling array of legal, economic, and political uncertainties in Russia, the Ukraine, or Kazakhstan. The struggle to introduce capitalism has produced a hodgepodge of commercial laws and regulations that are often vague, bizarre, or contradictory. Rules may change overnight. And it is frequently impossible to know which official is responsible for what decision. On the territory of some countries, companies have to face more or less independent 'substates' that decide independently which laws of the republic are accepted and which are not.

Among the biggest pitfalls is the uncertainty over property rights. Power struggles as to who controls buildings may emerge and leave the Western entity in limbo. Otis Elevator Co., which is setting up joint ventures in both Russia and the Ukraine, obtains written statements from the highest public officials and then hopes for the best. "If a company needs a cast-iron guarantee that everything is in compliance with all laws and regulations, the company will find it very difficult to get things done."

Other Western investors cut through legal tangles by persuading political leaders to issue decrees on their behalf. For example, a decree from President Boris Yeltsin helped France's Elf Aquitane set up an oil-exploration venture in Russia. Other constituents may have to be dealt with as well. Coca-Cola's counterpart in Moscow wanted to show residents the benefits of dealing with a foreign entity. Thus, as part of the payment, Coca-Cola shipped $650,000 of medical supplies for a local hospital. In some cases only tougher measures will help. When a $5-a-barrel surcharge was imposed on Conoco after the deal was signed, the company managed to get an exemption from the surcharge by threatening to cancel its plans to help develop a 150-million-barrel field in Arkhangelsk.

Sources: "Aliens," *ABC Nightly News,* February 8, 1993; Paul Hofheinz, "Russia 1993: Europe's Timebomb," *Fortune,* January 25, 1993 106–108; "Russia, Ukraine Brim with Quirky Laws," *The Wall Street Journal,* October 19, 1992, A10; and "From Gung Ho to Uh-Oh," *Business Week,* February 11, 1991, 43–46.

of technology transferred or the sophistication and level of operation engaged in. In some cases, demands of this type have led to firms' packing their bags. For example, Coca-Cola left India when the government demanded access to what the firm considered to be confidential intellectual property. Cadbury Schweppes sold its plant in Kenya because price controls made its operation unprofitable.[42] On their part, governments can, as a last resort, expropriate the affiliate, especially if they see that the benefits are greater than the cost.[43]

The approaches and procedures that have been discussed are quite negative by nature. However, relations between the firm and its host country, or the home country for that matter, by no means need to be adversarial. The multinational corporation can satisfy its own objectives and find local acceptability by implementing activities that contribute to the following six goals: (1) efficiency, by applying ap-

**FIGURE 12.2
Bargaining Position of
Multinational
Corporation (MNC) and
Host Country**

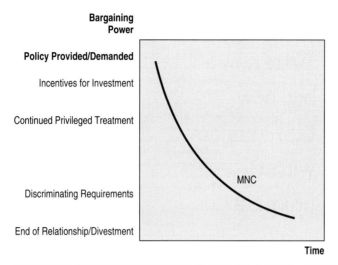

Sources: Christopher M. Korth, *International Business* (Englewood Cliffs, N.J.: Prentice-Hall, 1985), 350; and Thomas A. Poynter, "Managing Government Intervention: A Strategy for Defending the Subsidiary," *Columbia Journal of World Business* 21 (Winter 1986): 55–65.

propriate technologies to different markets; (2) equity, by reinvesting earnings; (3) participation, by establishing local training programs; (4) creativity, by introducing indigenous R&D capabilities in local affiliates; (5) stability, by consistently and openly explaining behavior; and (6) diversity, by developing product lines specifically for local demand.[44] An example of such an approach is provided in Figure 12.3.

Environmental concerns are emerging as an important part of a multinational's normal business operations. Multinationals have extensive involvement in many pollution-intensive industries and have, by definition, mobility to seek attractive locations for production sites. However, multinationals give rise to higher expectations and often are expected to assume leadership roles in environmental protection due to their financial, managerial, and technological strength. Studies have found that although multinationals may have adopted lower environmental standards in their developing-country operations, they maintain overall a better record than their local counterparts.[45]

A number of efforts have been made in the past 25 years to establish guidelines for the conduct of multinational corporations. The major ones are those drafted by the Organization of Economic Cooperation and Development and by the United Nations. Most multinationals have drafted their own versions of codes of conduct as well as value systems.[46]

Dealing with Other Constituents

Multinational corporations also have to manage their relations with various other constituencies. This is crucial because even small, organized groups of stockholders may influence control of the firm, particularly if the ownership base is wide. Companies must, therefore, adopt policies that will allow them to effectively respond to pressure and criticism, which will continue to surface. Oliver Williams suggests that these policies have the following traits: (1) openness about corporate activities with a focus on how these activities enhance social and economic performance; (2) preparedness to utilize the tremendous power of the multinational corporation in a responsible manner and, in the case of pressure, to counter criticisms swiftly; (3) in-

**FIGURE 12.3
Developing a Local
Image**

We're now a big, new U.S. company with a unique focus.

This is because we've now brought together the complementary strengths of Asea Brown Boveri, the Westinghouse transmission and distribution business and, most recently, Combustion Engineering. As a result, we're now the most complete electrical engineering company. And, with annual sales in the U.S. now approaching $7 billion, we're also the largest American company to focus on the application of electrical power. This includes power generation; transmission and distribution; industrial systems and process automation; transportation; robotics; environmental protection and the full gamut of related services, from engineering to financial.

With over 40,000 employees at facilities in nearly every state, ABB is now in a unique position to address five of America's most important economic needs: (1) a growing supply of energy (2) a more competitive industrial sector (3) improved mass transportation (4) environmental protection and (5) reliable product and system services. In reality, we're the only company with the commitment and the combined research, engineering and financial resources appropriate to this undertaking.

This is because, in addition to our U.S. strengths, we're able to draw on our worldwide resources, $25 billion in sales, 215,000 employees in 140 countries. And a $1.5 billion R&D commitment to environmentally compatible and cost-efficient technology in our core areas.

No other company has this particular focus, or these resources. This puts us in a unique position to serve markets which will show strong growth in the '90s.

ASEA BROWN BOVERI

Asea Brown Boveri Inc., 900 Long Ridge Road, Stamford, Connecticut 06904. Copyright 1990.

tegrity, which very often means that the corporation must avoid not only actual wrong-doing but the mere appearance of it; and (4) clarity, because it will help ameliorate hostility if a common language is used with those pressuring the corporation.[47] He proposes that the corporation's role is one of enlightened self-interest: Reasonable critics understand that the business cannot compromise the bottom line.

Complicating the situation very often is the fact that groups in one market criticize what the marketer is doing in another market. For example, the Interfaith Center on Corporate Responsibility urged Colgate-Palmolive to stop marketing Darkie toothpaste under that brand name in Asia because of the term's offensiveness elsewhere in the world. Darkie toothpaste has been sold in Thailand, Hong Kong, Singapore, Malaysia, and Taiwan, packaged in a box that features a likeness of Al Jolson in blackface.[48]

TRANSFER OF TECHNOLOGY

To a great extent, the role of foreign direct investment is that of technology transfer. Technology transfer is the transfer of systematic knowledge for the manufacture of a product, for the application of a process, or for the rendering of a service and does not extend to the mere sale or lease of goods.[49] Multinational corporations are one of the major vehicles for channeling technology to other countries.

The Basics of Technology Transfer

The essential requirements for the transfer of technology are: (1) the availability of suitable technology, (2) social and economic conditions favoring transfer, and (3) the willingness and ability of the receiving party to use and adapt the technology. In industrialized countries, sophisticated processes can be applied economically, with specialists available to solve problems and develop techniques. The problems arise in smaller developing countries with little industrial experience. Production facilities must be scaled down for small series; machinery and procedures must be simplified to cope with the lack of skill and training. Yet, in most cases, the quality has yet to meet worldwide standards. To overcome these kinds of problems, the Dutch electronics giant Philips created a special pilot plant. The plant sees to it that the many elements constituting an industrial activity are properly adapted to local circumstances and that the necessary know-how and other elements are transferred to developing countries. The elements of the transfer are summarized in Table 12.4. Through people and capital, the necessary human ware, software, and hardware are combined for the transfer of appropriate manufacturing technology. The transfer cannot be accomplished by sending machinery and manuals; it is achieved as technicians show the recipients what should be done and how.

Technology transfer can occur both formally and informally. Formal channels include licensing, foreign direct investment, and joint ventures. Informal channels include reverse engineering, diversions, and industrial espionage. Most of the technology trade has traditionally taken place between developed countries. A significant proportion of the trade has also been effected through traditional equity interactions (subsidiaries or joint ventures) and nonequity interactions, such as licensing agreements between nonaffiliated entities.[50] The informal channels' share of the market, although difficult to determine, is of concern to both the governments and the entities generating technology.

Technology transfer is likely to increase considerably with increased industrialization, which will generate not only new technological needs but also more sophisticated processes and technologies in existing sectors. Many countries are no longer satisfied to receive as much know-how as possible as quickly as possible; they want to possess technology themselves and to generate technology indigenously.

Adapting Technology to Local Conditions

Technology has to be adapted to factors that are often contradictory. For example, three standards for color television are in use in the world: NTSC in the Americas (except for Brazil) and Japan; PAL in Europe, British Commonwealth Countries, the Middle East, and Brazil; and SECAM in France, former French colonies, and eastern and central Europe. These standards differ from each other in terms of the numbers

---

**TABLE 12.4
Elements of
Technology Transfer**

Human Ware	Software	Hardware
Product know-how	Manuals	Buildings
Manufacturing know-how	Procedures	Assembly lines
Equipment know-how	Documentation	Equipment
Training	Information	Tools
		Components
		Raw materials

Source: J. C. Ramaer and P. H. Pijs, "Adapting Technology," undated working paper, Utrecht, The Netherlands: Philips.

of fields and lines in the picture. Videotapes from the NTSC standard cannot be played on PAL or SECAM machines and vice versa. In some cases, performance requirements at the transfer location may even be more demanding; for example, machinery may have to be operated in a facility where it is not completely protected from the elements. If the multinational corporation has multiple production bases, technology may have to be adjusted at each one and still meet worldwide quality standards. Often the quantities to be produced are a factor in technology transfer. For example, producing 7,000 sets in Thailand is considerably different from producing 700,000 in Holland.

Of critical concern in preparing the transfer are the strengths and weaknesses of the people who will be involved in production: their practical knowledge, experience, abilities, and attitudes. Machinery may need to be simplified and on-site maintenance provided for. Moreover, technology from countries such as the United States and Japan may be inappropriate if the recipient wants labor-intensive technology in order to create employment and income-earning opportunities. In these cases, the adjustment may consist of backward invention whereby a technically simplified version of the product is developed. Technology transfer also involves providing management and staff with advance information about conditions they will find in the transfer location. Costs of the various input elements for the production process such as labor, energy, materials, and components will vary from one market to the next and thus call for differing specifications in the technology transferred.

The quality of the infrastructure requires special attention. For example, frequent power outages may be characteristic of the area in which machinery is to be used; this would indicate the need for features in the technology to avoid variations in output and quality. Some industries, such as home electronics, spend as much as 50 percent of each dollar earned on the purchase of component parts. Yet, in smaller developing countries, the few existing suppliers may need extensive technical assistance in order to produce what is needed. The designs for components often must be simplified to allow for local production. This assistance may be critical because of government regulation of component imports. Other government policies may affect payment for technology, types of technology that can be transferred, and foreign involvement in the process through, for example, work permits for foreigners.

MODES OF OPERATION

In carrying out its foreign direct investment, a multinational corporation has a variety of ownership choices, ranging from 100 percent ownership to a minority interest. With international competition intensifying, risks in market entry and product development escalating, and the need for global strategy increasing, many companies rely on interfirm cooperation as a means of survival. When the investment alternative is not attractive or feasible, management contracts provide a mode of foreign market participation.

Full Ownership

For many firms, the foreign direct investment decision is, initially at least, considered in the context of 100 percent ownership. The reason may have an ethnocentric basis; that is, management may feel that no outside entity should have an impact on corporate decision making. Alternatively, it may be based on financial concerns. For example, the management of IBM believes that by relinquishing a portion of its ownership abroad, it would be setting a precedent for shared control with local partners that would cost more than could possibly be gained.[51] In some cases, IBM has withdrawn operation from a country rather than agree to government demands for local ownership.

In order to make a rational decision about the extent of ownership, management must evaluate the extent to which total control is important to the success of its international marketing activities. Often full ownership may be a desirable, but not a necessary, prerequisite for international success. At other times it may be essential, particularly when strong linkages exist within the corporation. Interdependencies between and among local operations and headquarters may be so strong that nothing short of total coordination will result in an acceptable benefit to the firm as a whole.[52]

Increasingly, however, the international environment is hostile to full ownership by multinational firms. Government action through outright legal restrictions or discriminatory actions is making the option less attractive. The choice is either to abide by existing restraints and accept a reduction in control or to lose the opportunity to operation in the country. In addition to formal action by the government, the general conditions in the market may make it advisable for the firm to join forces with local entities.

Interfirm Cooperation

The world is too large and the competition too strong for even the largest multinational corporations to do everything independently. Technologies are converging and markets becoming integrated, thus making the costs and risks of both product and market development ever greater. Partly as a reaction to and partly to exploit these developments, management in multinational corporations has become more pragmatic about what it takes to be successful in global markets.[53] The result has been the formation of **strategic alliances** with suppliers, customers, competitors, and companies in other industries to achieve multiple goals.

A strategic alliance (or partnership) is an informal or formal arrangement between two or more companies with a common business objective. It is something more than the traditional customer-vendor relationship but something less than an outright acquisition. These alliances can take forms ranging from informal cooperation to joint ownership of worldwide operations. For example, Texas Instruments has reported agreements with companies such as IBM, Hyundai, Fujitsu, Alcatel, and L. M. Ericsson using such terms as "joint development agreement," "cooperative technical effort," "joint program for development," "alternative sourcing agreement," and "design/exchange agreement for cooperative product development and exchange of technical data."[54]

Reasons for Interfirm Cooperation   Strategic alliances are being used for many different purposes by the partners involved. Market development is one common focus. Penetrating foreign markets is a primary objective of many companies. In Japan, Motorola is sharing chip designs and manufacturing facilities with Toshiba to gain greater access to the Japanese market. Some alliances are aimed at defending home markets. With no orders coming in for nuclear power plants, Bechtel Group has teamed up with Germany's Siemens to service existing U.S. plants.[55] Another focus is the spreading of the cost and risk inherent in production and development efforts. Texas Instruments and Hitachi have teamed up to develop the next generation of memory chips. The costs of developing new jet engines are so vast that they force aerospace companies into collaboration; one such consortium was formed by United

Technologies' Pratt & Whitney division, Britain's Rolls-Royce, Motoren-und-Turbinen Union from Germany, Fiat of Italy, and Japanese Aero Engines (made up of Ishikawa-jima Heavy Industries and Kawasaki Heavy Industries).[56] Finally, some alliances are formed to block and co-opt competitors.[57] For example, Caterpillar formed a heavy equipment joint venture with Mitsubishi in Japan to strike back at its main global rival, Komatsu, in its home market. In many cases, companies have used most of these rationales to justify their alliances, as seen in James River's case in Global Perspective 12.3.

Types of Interfirm Cooperation   The types of strategic alliances are summarized in Figure 12.4, using the extent of equity involved and the number of partners in the endeavor as defining characteristics. Each form of alliance is distinct in terms of the amount of commitment required and the degree of control each partner has. The

Global Perspective

12.3
Joining Forces to Cast Net across Europe

The pan-European papermaking joint venture called Jamont is the second largest paper producer in Europe. This venture is owned by James River Corporation from the United States, Oy Nokia Ab from Finland, and an Italian merchant bank Cragnotti & Partners Capital Investment. It got its start in 1987, when James River looked at the European markets and found them to be growing at twice the U.S. rate. It also saw a need to challenge its main worldwide competitor, Scott Paper Co., which in its 30 years in the European market had emerged as the largest paper producer there.

Papermaking then was highly fragmented, like every other industry in Europe. James River saw the chance to develop a pan-European manufacturing and marketing strategy. After acquiring 13 companies in 10 countries with its partners, efforts were combined into Jamont in 1990. By the end of 1994, Jamont plans to have finished its capital-investment program, overhauled manufacturing, developed consistent quality, and become the low-cost producer in each country in which it operates. Some efforts will be consolidated for cost savings. For example, before becoming part of Jamont, each company made its own deep-colored napkins (a complex process because dye changing takes a lot of time). Now, Jamont produces all such products at one plant in Finland.

The goal in the production of tissues is softness, strength, and absorbency at minimum cost. Although it sounds simple, getting 10 cultures to cooperate makes it tough. To produce efficiently Jamont needs to make napkins the same size throughout its operations. But some countries wanted to make them 30 cm by 30 cm and others 35 cm by 35 cm. Similar problems arose with computer systems and ways of measuring production efficiency. Finding the common ground that everyone respects proved to be difficult. On most issues, Jamont forms a committee to solve issues. This method is successful 80 percent of the time. When it is not, the CEO and his staff—four Frenchmen, two Americans, two Italians, a Finn, a Spaniard, and a Dutchman—take over. However, tension between decentralization and the drive to move in a common European direction will continue. And as tastes converge, so will the products Jamont sells.

The recent currency alignments are also a headache for Jamont. The company figured that since European currencies had been fixed for the last five years, such stability would continue. Then the United Kingdom and Italy pulled out of the Exchange Rate Mechanism, which raised costs to those markets by 10–15 percent. Not only will more time be spent hedging the balance sheet, but Jamont will also probably invest in new manufacturing facilities in the United Kingdom and Italy sooner than it would have otherwise.

Source: "A Joint-Venture Papermaker Casts Net Across Europe." *The Wall Street Journal,* December 7, 1992, B4.

**FIGURE 12.4
Forms of Interfirm
Cooperation**

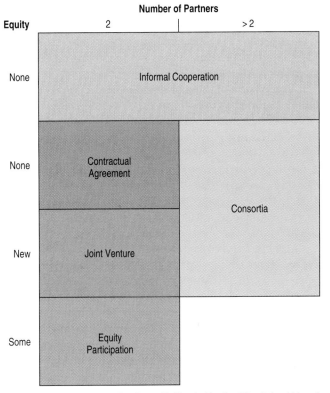

Source: Adapted with permission from Bernard L. Simonin, *Transfer of Knowledge of International Strategic Alliances: A Structural Approach,* unpublished dissertation, The University of Michigan, Ann Arbor, 1991.

equity alliances—minority ownership, joint ventures, and consortia—feature the most extensive commitment and shared control.

Informal Cooperation   In informal cooperative deals, partners work together without a binding agreement. This arrangement often takes the form of visits to exchange information about new products, processes, and technologies or may take the more formal form of the exchange of personnel for limited amounts of time. Often such partners are of no real threat in each other's markets and of modest size in comparison to the competition, making collaboration necessary.[58] The relationships are based on mutual trust and friendship, and they may lead to more formal arrangements, such as contractual agreements or joint projects.

Contractual Agreements   Strategic-alliance partners may join forces for joint R&D, joint marketing, or joint production. Similarly, their joint efforts might include licensing, cross-licensing, or cross-marketing activities. Nestlé and General Mills have signed an agreement whereby Honey Nut Cheerios and Golden Grahams are made in General Mills's U.S. plants, shipped in bulk to Europe for packaging at a Nestlé plant, and then marketed in France, Spain, and Portugal by Nestlé.[59] This arrangement—complementary marketing (also known as piggybacking)—allows firms to reach objectives that they cannot reach efficiently by themselves.[60] Firms also can have a reciprocal arrangement whereby each partner provides the other access to its markets for a product. AT&T and Olivetti have had such a cross-marketing agreement covering the United States and Europe. In the service sector, international airlines have started to share hubs, coordinate schedules, and simplify ticketing. SAS has entered into joint-marketing deals with All Nippon Airways, Lan-Chile, and Canadian Airlines International to provide links to routes and hubs in Tokyo, Latin America, and Toronto.[61] Contractual agreements also exist for out-sourcing; for example, General Motors buys cars and components from Korea's Daewoo, and Siemens buys computers from Fujitsu.

In some parts of the world and in certain industries, governments insist on complete or majority ownership of firms, which has caused multinational companies to turn to an alternative method of enlarging their overseas business.[62] The alternative is a **management contract,** in which the firm sells its expertise in running a company while avoiding the risk or benefit of ownership. Depending on the extensiveness of the contract, it may even permit some measure of control. As an example, the manufacturing process may have to be relinquished to foreign firms, yet international distribution may be required for the product. A management contract could serve to maintain a strong hold on the operation by ensuring that all distribution channels remain firmly controlled.

Management contracts may be more than a defensive measure. Although they are used to protect existing investment interests when they have been partly expropriated by the local government, an increasing number of companies are using them as a profitable opportunity to sell valuable skills and resources. For example, companies in the service sector often have independent entities with the sole task of seeking out opportunities and operating management contracts.[63]

Often a management contract is the critical element in the success of a project. For example, financial institutions may gain confidence in a project because of the existence of a management contract and may sometimes even make it a precondition for funding.[64]

One specialized form of management contract is the **turnkey operation.** Here, the arrangement permits a client to acquire a complete international system, together with skills investment sufficient to allow unassisted maintenance and operation of the system following its completion.[65] The client need not search for individual contractors or subcontractors or deal with scheduling conflicts or with difficulties in assigning responsibilities or blame. Instead, a package arrangement permits the accumulation of responsibility in one entity, thus greatly easing the negotiation and supervision requirements and subsequent accountability. When the project is on line, the system will be totally owned, controlled, and operated by the customer. An example of such an arrangement is the Kama River truck plant in Russia, built mainly by U.S. firms.

Management contracts have clear benefits for the client. They provide organizational skills not available locally, expertise that is immediately available rather than built up, and management assistance in the form of support services that would be difficult and costly to replicate locally. For example, hotels managed by the Sheraton Corporation have access to Sheraton's worldwide reservation system. Management contracts today typically involve training of locals to take over the operation after a given period.

Similar advantages exist for the supplier. The risk of participating in an international venture is substantially lowered, while significant amounts of control are still exercised. Existing know-how that has been built up through substantial investment can be commercialized, and frequently the impact of fluctuations in business volume can be reduced by making use of experienced personnel who otherwise would have to be laid off. In industrialized countries such as the United States, with economies that are increasingly service based, accumulated service knowledge and comparative advantage should be used internationally. Management contracts permit firms to do so.

Management contracts require an attitude change on two accounts: Control must be shared, and the time involvement may be limited. Establishing a working relationship with the owner in which both understand and respect their roles is essential. Even though the management contractor may be training local personnel to eventually take over, this by no means signifies the end of the relationship. For example, the hotel once managed by Sheraton may well remain in the system to buy reservation services, thus providing Sheraton with additional revenue.

From the client's perspective, the main drawbacks to consider are overdependence and potential loss of some essential control. For example, if the management contractor maintains all of the international relationships, little if any experience may be passed on to the local operation. Instead of gradual transfer of skills leading to increasing independence, the client may have to rely more and more on the performance of the contractor.

Equity Participation   Many multinational corporations have acquired minority ownerships in companies that have strategic importance for them to ensure supplier viability and build formal and informal working relationships. Examples include IBM's 12 percent share of Intel and Ford Motor Company's 25 percent share of Mazda. The partners continue operating as distinctly separate entities, but each enjoys the strengths the other partner provides. For example, thanks to Mazda, Ford has excellent support in the design and manufacture of subcompact cars, while Mazda has improved access to the global marketplace. Similar arrangements abound in the automotive sector: Mitsubishi Motors owns 10.2 percent of Chrysler, while Honda owns 20 percent of Britain's Rover.[66]

Joint Ventures   A joint venture can be defined as the participation of two or more companies in an enterprise in which each party contributes assets, owns the entity to some degree, and shares risk.[67] The venture is also considered long term.[68] The reasons for establishing a joint venture can be divided into three groups: (1) government suasion or legislation, (2) one partner's needs for other partners' skills, and (3) one partner's needs for other partners' attributes or assets.[69] Equality of the partners is not necessary. In some joint ventures, each partner holds an equal share; in others, one partner has the majority of shares. The partners' contributions—typically consisting of funds, technology, plant, or labor—also vary.

The key to a joint venture is the sharing of a common business objective, which makes the arrangement more than a customer-vendor relationship but less than an outright acquisition. The partners' rationales for entering into the arrangement may vary. An example is New United Motor Manufacturing Inc. (NUMMI), the joint venture between Toyota and GM. Toyota needed direct access to the U.S. market, while GM benefited from the technology and management approaches provided by the Japanese partner.

Joint ventures may be the only way in which a firm can profitably participate in a particular market. For example, India restricts equity participation in local operations by foreigners to 40 percent. Other entry modes may limit the scale of operation substantially; for example, exports may be restricted because of tariff barriers. Many Western firms are using joint ventures to gain access to eastern and central European markets.

Joint ventures are valuable when the pooling of resources results in a better outcome for each partner than if each were to conduct its activities individually. This is particularly the case when each partner has a specialized advantage in areas that benefit the venture. For example, a firm may have new technology yet lack sufficient capital to carry out foreign direct investment on its own. Through a joint venture,

A joint venture with Sterch Controls enabled Honeywell to enter the potentially vast markets of central Europe and the former Soviet Union.
Source: © Jim Sims for Honeywell.

the technology can be used more quickly and market penetration achieved more easily. Similarly, one of the partners may have a distribution system already established or have better access to local suppliers, either of which permits a greater volume of sales in a shorter period of time.

Joint ventures also permit better relationships with local government and other organizations such as labor unions. Government-related reasons are the major rationale for joint ventures in less-developed countries four times more frequently than in developed countries.[70] Particularly if the local partner is the government, or the local partner is politically influential, the new venture may be eligible for tax incentives, grants, and government support. Negotiations for certifications or licenses may be easier because authorities may not perceive themselves as dealing with a foreign firm. Relationships between the local partner and the local financial establishment may enable the joint venture to tap local capital markets. The greater experience (and therefore greater familiarity) with the local culture and environment of the local partner may enable the joint venture to benefit from greater insights into changing market conditions and needs.

A final major commercial reason to participate in joint ventures is the desire to minimize the risk of exposing long-term investment capital, while at the same time maximizing the leverage on the capital that is invested.[71] Economic and political conditions in many countries are increasingly volatile. At the same time, corporations tend to shorten their investment planning time span more and more. This financial rationale therefore takes on more importance.

Seven out of ten joint ventures have been found to fall short of expectations and/or are disbanded.[72] The reasons typically relate to conflicts of interest, problems with disclosure of sensitive information, and disagreement over how profits are to be shared—in general—to lack of communication before, during, and after formation of the venture. In some cases, managers have been more interested in the launching of the venture than the actual running of the enterprise. Many of the problems stem from a lack of careful consideration in advance of how to manage the new endeavor. A partnership works on the basis of trust and commitment or not at all. Actually, if either or both partners insist on voting on critical matters, the venture has already failed.

Typical disagreements cover the whole range of business decisions, including strategy, management style, accounting and control, marketing policies and strategies, research and development, and personnel. The joint venture may, for example, identify a particular market as a target only to find that one of the partners already has individual plans for it. U.S. partners have frequently complained that their Japanese counterparts do not send their most competent personnel to the joint venture; instead, because of their lifetime employment practice, they get rid of less-competent managers by sending them to the new entities.

Similarly, the issue of profit accumulation and distribution may cause discontent. If one partner supplies the joint venture with a product, the partner will prefer that any profits accumulate at headquarters and accrue 100 percent to one firm rather than at the joint venture, where profits are divided according to equity participation. Such a decision may not be greeted with enthusiasm by the other partner. Further, once profits are accumulated, their distribution may lead to dispute. For example, one partner may insist on a high payout of dividends because of financial needs, whereas the other may prefer the reinvestment of profits into a growing operation.

Consortia   A new drug can cost $200 million to develop and bring to market; a mainframe computer or a telecommunications switch can require $1 billion. Some $4 billion will go into creating the generation of computer chips due out in the early

1990s; up to $7 billion will be needed to develop the next generation.[73] To combat the high costs and risks of research and development, research consortia have emerged in the United States, Japan, and Europe. Since the passage of the **Joint Research and Development Act** of 1984 (which allows both domestic and foreign firms to participate in joint basic research efforts without the fear of antitrust action), well over 100 consortia have been registered in the United States. These consortia pool their resources for research into technologies ranging from artificial intelligence to those needed to overtake the Japanese lead in semiconductor manufacturing. (The major consortia in those fields are MCC and Sematech.)[74] The Europeans have five megaprojects to develop new technologies registered under the names EUREKA, ESPRIT, BRITE, RACE, and COMET. The Japanese consortia have worked on producing the world's highest-capacity memory chip and advanced computer technologies. On the manufacturing side, the formation of Airbus Industrie secured European production of commercial jets. The consortium, backed by France's Aerospatiale, German's Messerschmitt Bolkow Blohm, British Aerospace, and Spain's Construcciones Aeronauticas, has become a prime global competitor.

Recommendations   The first requirement of interfirm cooperation is to find the right partner. Partners should have an orientation and goals in common and should bring complementary and relevant benefits to the endeavor. The venture makes little sense if the expertise of both partners is in the same area; for example, if both have production expertise but neither has distribution know-how. Patience should be exercised; a deal should not be rushed into, nor should the partners expect immediate results. Learning should be paramount in the endeavor, while at the same time, partners must try not to give away core secrets to each other.[75]

Second, the more formal the arrangement, the greater care that needs to be taken in negotiating the agreement. In joint-venture negotiations, for example, extensive provisions must be made for contingencies. The points to be explored should include, depending on the partner and the venture: (1) a clear definition of the venture and its duration; (2) ownership, control, and management; (3) financial structure and policies; (4) taxation and fiscal obligation; (5) employment and training; (6) production; (7) government assistance; (8) transfer of technology; (9) marketing arrangements; (10) environmental protection; (11) record keeping and inspection; and (12) settlement of disputes.[76] They have to be addressed before the formation of the venture; otherwise, they will eventually surface as points of contention. A joint venture agreement, although comparable to a marriage agreement, should contain the elements of a divorce contract. In case the joint venture cannot be maintained to the satisfaction of partners, plans must exist for the dissolution of the agreement and for the allocation of profits and costs. Typically, however, one of the partners buys out the other partner(s) when partners decide to part ways.

A strategic alliance, by definition, also means a joining of two corporate cultures, which can often be quite different. To meet this challenge, partners must have frequent communication and interaction at three levels of the organization: the top management, operational leaders, and workforce levels. Trust and relinquishing control are difficult not only at the top but also at levels where the future of the venture is determined. A dominant partner may determine the corporate culture, but even then the other partners should be consulted.

Strategic alliances operate in a dynamic business environment and must therefore adjust to changing market conditions. The agreement between partners should provide for changes in the original concept so that the venture can flourish and grow. The trick is to have an a priori understanding as to which party will take care of which pains and problems so that a common goal is reached.

SUMMARY

Multinational corporations are probably among the most powerful economic institutions of all time. They not only have production facilities in multiple countries but also look beyond their own domestic markets for opportunities. They scan the globe to expand their operations. Multinational corporations are no longer the monopoly of the United States, western Europe, and Japan; many developing countries have a growing amount of foreign direct investment.

Foreign direct investment is sought by nations and firms alike. Nations are looking to foreign direct investment for economic development and employment, firms for new markets, resources, and increased efficiency. The relationship between the entities involved—the firm, the host government, and the home government—has to be managed to make it mutually beneficial. The critical role of foreign direct investment is technology transfer, which means the transfer of a combination of hardware, software, and skills for production processes.

Different operational modes are possible for the multinational corporation. Full ownership is becoming more unlikely in many markets as well as industries, and the firm has to look at alternative approaches. The main alternative is interfirm cooperation, in which the firm joins forces with other business entities, possibly even a foreign government. In some cases, when the firm may not want to make a direct investment, it will offer its management expertise for sale in the form of management contracts.

Key Terms and Concepts

ethnocentric	technology transfer
polycentric	brain drain
regiocentric	Overseas Private Investment Corporation
geocentric	strategic alliances
resource seekers	management contract
market seekers	turnkey operation
efficiency seekers	Joint Research and Development Act

Questions for Discussion

1. Of the quantitative and qualitative criteria that a firm has to satisfy to be considered a multinational corporation, which should be the major determinants?
2. Foreigners claim 5 percent of corporate earnings in the United States, yet there is concern about the selling off of corporate America. Is it justified?
3. Should every country have guidelines or a code of behavior for foreign companies to follow if they wish to be viewed as good corporate citizens?
4. The Middle East is an attractive market for technology transfer. How would Saudi Arabia, Egypt, and Iran differ in the type of technology they seek?
5. Discuss possible reasons why IBM withdrew from India's computer market rather than share ownership, yet Burroughs and International Computer entered the market at the same time as minority owners.
6. The rate of expropriation has been 10 times greater for a joint venture with the host government than for a 100 percent U.S.–owned subsidiary, according to a study on expropriation since 1960. Is this not contrary to logic?

7. Comment on the observation that "a joint venture may be a combination of Leonardo da Vinci's brain and Carl Lewis's legs; one wants to fly, the other insists on running."

8. Why would an internationalizing company opt for a management contract over other modes of operation? Relate your answer especially to the case of hospitality companies such as Hyatt, Marriott, and Sheraton.

Recommended Readings

Badaracoo, Joseph L. *The Knowledge Link: Competing Through Strategic Alliances.* Boston: Harvard Business School Press, 1991.

Casson, Mark. *Multinational Corporations.* New York: Stockton Press, 1989.

Collins, Timothy, and Thomas Doorley. *A Guide to International Joint Ventures and Strategic Alliances.* Homewood, Ill.: Richard D. Irwin, 1990.

Culpan, Refik, ed. *Multinational Strategic Alliances.* Binghamton, N.Y.: International Business Press, 1993.

Dunning, John H., ed. *The United Nations Library on Transnational Corporations.* Volumes 1–20. New York: Routledge, 1993.

Lewis, Jordan D. *Partnerships for Profit: Structuring and Managing Strategic Alliances.* New York: The Free Press, 1990.

Luostarinen, Reijo, and Lawrence Welch. *International Business Operations.* Helsinki, Finland: Kyriiri Oy, 1990.

Prahalad, C.K. *The Multinational Mission: Balancing Local and Global Vision.* New York: The Free Press, 1987.

Robinson, Richard D. *The International Transfer of Technology: Theory, Issues, and Practice.* Cambridge, Mass.: Ballinger, 1988.

Rubner, Alex. *The Might of the Multinationals.* Westport, Conn.: Quorum Books, 1990.

Strafford, David C., and Richard H. A. Purkis. *Director of Multinationals.* New York: Stockton Press, 1989.

Tolchin, Martin, and Susan Tolchin. *Buying into America.* New York: Times Books, 1988.

Walmsley, John. *The Development of International Markets.* Higham, Mass: Graham & Trotman, 1990.

Notes

1. Mark Casson, *Alternatives to the Multinational Enterprise* (London: Macmillan, 1979), 1.
2. United Nations, *World Investment Report: An Executive Summary* (New York: United Nations, 1993), 1.
3. United Nations, *Transnational Corporations in World Development* (New York: United Nations, 1988), 16.
4. United Nations, *Multinational Corporation in World Development* (New York: United Nations, 1973), 23.

5. Alan M. Rugman, *Inside the Multinationals* (London: Croom Helm, 1981), 31.
6. Raymond Vernon, *Sovereignty at Bay: The Multinational Spread of United States Enterprises* (New York: Basic Books, 1971), 11.
7. Alan M. Rugman, "Risk Reduction by International Diversification," *Journal of International Business Studies* 7 (Fall 1976): 75–80.
8. Donald Kircher, "Now the Transnational Enterprise," *Harvard Business Review* 42 (March–April 1964): 6–10, 172–176.

9. Howard V. Perlmutter, "The Tortuous Evolution of the Multinational Corporation," *Columbia Journal of World Business* 4 (January-February 1969): 9-18; Howard V. Perlmutter and David A. Heenan, "How Multinational Should Your Top Managers Be?" *Harvard Business Review* 52 (November-December 1974): 121-132; and Yoram Wind, Susan P. Douglas, and Howard V. Perlmutter, "Guidelines for Developing International Marketing Strategies," *Journal of Marketing* 37 (April 1973): 14-23.

10. John M. Stopford, *The World Directory of Multinational Enterprises* (London: Macmillan, 1982), xii.

11. Krishna Kumar and Maxwell G. McLeod, *Multinationals from Developing Countries* (Lexington, Mass.: Lexington Books, 1981), xv-xxv.

12. "Korea's Biggest Firm Teaches Junior Execs Strange Foreign Ways," *The Wall Street Journal,* December 30, 1992, 1.

13. George Chandler, "The Innocence of Oil Companies," *Foreign Policy* 27 (Summer 1977), 60.

14. United Nations Economic and Social Council, *Transnational Corporations in World Development: A Re-examination* (New York: United Nations, 1978), 13.

15. Herbert E. Meyer, "Trudeau's War on U.S. Business," *Fortune,* April 6, 1981, 74-82.

16. Jeffrey Arpan and David A. Ricks, "Foreign Direct Investments in the U.S. and Some Attendant Research Problems," *Journal of International Business Studies* 5 (Spring 1974): 1-7.

17. Harvey A. Poniachek, *Direct Foreign Investment in the United States* (Lexington, Mass.: Lexington Books, 1986), 2.

18. U.S. Department of Commerce, Office of Trade and Investment Analysis, estimate provided, February 16, 1993.

19. U.S. Department of Commerce, Office of Trade and Investment Analysis, estimate provided, February 16, 1993.

20. Jaclyn Fierman, "The Selling Off of America," *Fortune,* December 22, 1986, 34-43.

21. "The Difference Japanese Management Makes," *Business Week,* July 14, 1986, 47-50.

22. Edward B. Flowers, "Oligopolistic Reactions in European and Canadian Direct Investment in the United States," *Journal of International Business Studies* 7 (Fall-Winter 1976): 43-55.

23. Philip D. White and Edward W. Cundiff, "Assessing the Quality of Industrial Products," *Journal of Marketing* 42 (January 1978): 80-86.

24. Frank G. Vukmanic, Michael R. Czinkota, and David A. Ricks, "National and International Data Problems and Solutions in the Empirical Analysis of Intra-Industry Direct Foreign Investment," ed. A. Erdilek (Beckenham, Kent: Croom Helm Ltd., 1985), 160-184.

25. "Japan, U.S.A.," *Business Week,* July 14, 1986, 45-46.

26. Stephen Kobrin, "Assessing Political Risk Overseas," *The Wharton Magazine* 6 (No. 2, 1981): 6-14.

27. Marie E. Wicks Kelly and George C. Philippatos, "Comparative Analysis of the Foreign Investment Evaluation Practices by U.S.-based Manufacturing Multinational Companies," *Journal of International Business Studies* 13 (Winter 1982): 19-42.

28. Jack N. Behrman, "Transnational Corporations in the New International Economic Order," *Journal of International Business Studies* 12 (Spring-Summer 1981): 29-42.

29. Jack N. Behrman, *National Interests and the Multinational Enterprise* (Englewood Cliffs, N.J.: Prentice-Hall, 1970), 7.

30. Fierman, "The Selling Off of America," 35.

31. Casson, *Alternatives to the Multinational Enterprise,* 4.

32. Vivian Brownstein, "The Credit Crunch Myth," *Fortune,* December 17, 1990, 59-69.

33. Meyer, "Trudeau's War on U.S. Business," 76.

34. Charles Albert Michalet and Therese Chevallier, "France," in *Multinational Enterprises, Economic Structure and International Competitiveness,* ed. John H. Dunning (Chichester, England: Wiley, 1985), 91-125.

35. Daniel Van Den Bulcke, "Belgium," in *Multinational Enterprise, Economic Structure and International Competitiveness,* ed. John H. Dunning (Chichester, England: Wiley, 1985), 249-280.

36. "At Sanyo's Arkansas Plant the Magic Isn't Working," *Business Week,* July 14, 1986, 51-52.

37. Joseph S. Nye, "Multinational Corporations in World Politics," *Foreign Affairs* 53 (October 1974): 153-175.

38. Lawrence Franko, "Foreign Direct Investment in Less Developed Countries: Impact on Home Countries," *Journal of International Business Studies* 9 (Winter 1978): 55-65.

39. Paul S. Haar, "U.S. Government Political Risk Insurance Program" (Paper delivered at International Insurance and Political Risk Seminar, March 25, 1985, Washington, D.C.), 2.

40. Michael G. Harvey and Ilkka A. Ronkainen, "The Three Faces of the Foreign Corrupt Practices Act," *1984 AMA Educators' Proceedings* (Chicago: American Marketing Association, 1984), 230-235.

41. Peter P. Gabriel, "MNCs in the Third World: Is Conflict Unavoidable?" *Harvard Business Review* 50 (July-August 1972): 91-102.

42. Victor H. Frank, "Living with Price Control Abroad," *Harvard Business Review* 62 (March-April 1984): 137-142.

43. Thomas W. Shreeve, "Be Prepared for Political Changes Abroad," *Harvard Business Review* 62 (July-August 1984): 111-118.

44. Jack N. Behrman, *Industrial Policies: International Restructuring and Transnationals* (Lexington, Mass.: Lexington Books, 1984), 114-115.

45. William C. Frederick, "The Moral Authority of Transnational Corporations," *Journal of Business Ethics* 10 (March 1991): 165-178; and United Nations, *World Investment Report: An Executive Summary* (New York: United Nations, 1993), 11-12.

46. John M. Kline, *International Codes and Multinational Business: Setting Guidelines for International Business Operations* (Westport, Conn.: Quorum Books, 1985), Chapter 1.

47. Oliver Williams, "Who Cast the First Stone?" *Harvard Business Review* 62 (September–October 1984): 151-160.

48. "Church Group Gnashes Colgate-Palmolive," *Advertising Age,* March 24, 1986, 46.

49. United Nations, *Draft International Code of Conduct on the Transfer of Technology* (New York: United Nations, 1981), 3.

50. Asim Erdilek, "International Technology Transfer in the Middle East," in *International Business with the Middle East,* ed. Erdener Kaynak (New York: Praeger, 1984), 85-99.

51. Dennis J. Encarnation and Sushil Vachani, "Foreign Ownership: When Hosts Change the Rules," *Harvard Business Review* 63 (September–October 1985): 152-160.

52. Richard H. Holton, "Making International Joint Ventures Work" (Paper presented at the seminar on the Management of Headquarters/Subsidiary Relationships in Transnational Corporations, Stockholm School of Economics, June 2-4, 1980), 4.

53. *Collaborative Ventures: An Emerging Phenomenon in the Information Industry* (New York: Coopers & Lybrand, 1984), 3.

54. Thomas Gross and John Neuman, "Strategic Alliances Vital in Global Marketing," *Marketing News,* June 19, 1989, 1-2.

55. Louis Kraar, "Your Rivals Can Be Your Allies," *Fortune,* March 27, 1989, 66-76.

56. "MD-90 Airliner Unveiled by McDonnell Douglas," *The Washington Post,* February 14, 1993, A4.

57. Jordan D. Lewis, *Partnerships for Profit: Structuring and Managing Strategic Alliances* (New York: The Free Press, 1990), 85-87.

58. Gary Hamel, Yves L. Doz, and C. K. Prahalad, "Collaborate with Your Competitors—and Win," *Harvard Business Review* 67 (January-February 1989): 133-139.

59. Richard Gibson, "Cereal Venture Is Planning Honey of a Battle in Europe," *The Wall Street Journal,* November 14, 1990, B1, B8.

60. Vern Terpstra and Chwo-Ming J. Yu, "Piggybacking: A Quick Road to Internationalization," *International Marketing Review* 7 (Number 4, 1990): 52-63.

61. "Can SAS Keep Flying with the Big Birds?" *Business Week,* November 27, 1989, 142-146.

62. Lawrence S. Welch and Anubis Pacifico, "Management Contracts: A Role in Internationalization?" *International Marketing Review* 7 (Number 4, 1990): 64-74.

63. Richard Ellison, "An Alternative to Direct Investment Abroad," *International Management* 31 (June 1976): 25-27.

64. Michael Z. Brooke, *Selling Management Services Contracts in International Business* (London: Holt, Rinehart and Winston, 1985), 7.

65. Richard W. Wright and Colin S. Russel, "Joint Ventures in Developing Countries: Realities and Responses," *Columbia Journal of World Business* 10 (Spring 1975): 74-80.

66. "Mitsubishi Is Taking a Back Road into Europe," *Business Week,* November 19, 1990, 64.

67. Kathryn Rudie Harrigan, "Joint Ventures and Global Strategies," *Columbia Journal of World Business* 19 (Summer 1984): 7-16.

68. W. G. Friedman and G. Kalmanoff, *Joint International Business Ventures* (New York: Columbia University Press, 1961), 5.

69. J. Peter Killing, *Strategies for Joint Venture Success* (New York: Praeger, 1983), 11-12.

70. Paul W. Beamish, "The Characteristics of Joint Ventures in Developed and Developing Countries," *Columbia Journal of World Business* 20 (Fall 1985), 13-19.

71. Charles Oman, *New Forms of International Investment in Developing Countries* (Paris: Organization for Economic Cooperation and Development, 1984), 79.

72. Yankelovich, Skelly and White, Inc., *Collaborative Ventures: A Pragmatic Approach to Business Expansion in the Eighties* (New York: Coopers and Lybrand, 1984), 10.

73. "Can Europe Catch Up in the High-Tech Race?" *Business Week,* October 23, 1989, 142-154.

74. Lee Smith, "Can Consortiums Defeat Japan?" *Fortune,* June 5, 1989, 245-254.

75. Jeremy Main, "Making Global Alliances Work," *Fortune,* December 17, 1990, 121-126.

76. United Nations, *Guidelines for Foreign Direct Investment* (New York: United Nations, 1975), 65-76.

International Business Research

LEARNING OBJECTIVES

1. To gain an understanding of the need for research.

2. To explore the differences between domestic and international research.

3. To learn where to find sources of secondary information.

4. To gain insight into the gathering of primary data.

5. To examine different international management information systems.

Some First Steps in International Research

Most company executives know that they need to conduct careful research before they prepare to market abroad. But knowing what to do is not the same as knowing how to get it done. Because many small and medium-sized firms are looking at international markets for the first time these days, they frequently go charging off in the wrong direction or spend tremendous sums on research. In reality, a great deal of international research can be accomplished for very little money, if you know where to look.

When my firm is asked to help answer international research questions, we try very hard not to reinvent the wheel or redo research that is already available. One of the first things we do is check established sources of information. Typically that involves several steps.

First, we check reference information on countries, products, markets, and competitors. We look at reference guides, country directories, and publications of industrial development organizations. We also use international sources, including the United Nations, the World Bank, and the Food and Agriculture Organization, where the right kind of digging can pay off with useful information. The same is true of U.S. government agencies.

Next we conduct secondary research on-line and in the library. Here we check all secondary information that may help answer client questions regarding products, markets, opportunities, competitors, and the wisdom of alternative business strategies. Typically we conduct on-line research through Dialog, Nexis, and other services. The trick here is knowing which of the hundreds of databases to check for appropriate questions, key words, and subjects. After appropriate articles and published references have been identified, we spend time in the library reviewing abstracts and getting copies of pertinent articles and other references.

A third step then consists of identifying multiclient studies that have already been conducted that answer some of the questions we have. At this point, we know what is available. However, it is not cost efficient or wise to purchase every possible study, so some additional research is necessary. This involves contacting the publishers of the studies, requesting copies of the contents page and the prospectus for each study of interest.

Only after reviewing all the material obtained will we start developing a plan for proprietary primary research.

Souce: Ian MacFarlane, "Do-It-Yourself Marketing Research," *Management Review,* May 1991: 34–37.

The single most important cause for failure in international business is insufficient preparation and information. The failure of managers to comprehend cultural disparities, the failure to remember that customers differ from country to country, and the lack of investigation into whether or not a market exists prior to market entry has made international business a high risk activity.[1] International business research is therefore instrumental to international business success. As we saw in the opening vignette, research does not always have to consist of packing one's bags and traveling to foreign countries at great cost in time and money. A library nearby or simply access to good databases can be very useful in starting up the research process.

This chapter discusses data collection and provides a comprehensive overview of how to obtain general screening information on international markets, to evaluate business potential, and to assess current or potential opportunities and problems. Data sources that are low cost and that take little time to accumulate—in short, secondary data—are considered first. The balance of the chapter is devoted to more sophisticated forms of international research, including primary data collection and the development of an information system.

INTERNATIONAL AND DOMESTIC RESEARCH

The tools and techniques of international research are the same as those of domestic research. The difference is in the environment to which the tools are applied. However, the environment determines how well the tools, techniques, and concepts work. Although the objectives of research may be the same, the execution of international research may differ substantially from that of domestic research. The four primary reasons for this difference are new parameters, new environmental factors, an increase in the number of factors involved, and a broader definition of competition.

New Parameters

In crossing national borders, a firm encounters parameters not found in domestic business. Examples include duties, foreign currencies and changes in their value, different modes of transportation, and international documentation. New parameters also emerge because of differing modes of operating internationally. For example, the firm can export, it can license its products, it can engage in a joint venture, or it can carry out foreign direct investment. The firm that has done business only domestically will have had little or no experience with the requirements and conditions of these types of operations. Managers must therefore obtain information about them in order to make good business decisions.

New Environmental Factors

When going international, a firm is exposed to an unfamiliar environment. Many of the domestic assumptions on which the firm and its activities were founded may not hold true internationally. Management needs to learn the culture of the host country, understand its political systems and its level of stability, and comprehend the existing differences in societal structures and language. In addition, it must understand pertinent legal issues in order to avoid violating local laws. The technological level of the society must also be incorporated in the business plan. In short, all the assumptions that were formulated over the years based on domestic business activities must be reevaluated. This crucial point is often neglected because most managers are born in the environment of their domestic operations and only subconsciously learn to understand the constraints and opportunities of their business activities. The situation is analogous to learning one's native language. Speakers with little knowledge of rules of grammar may use the language correctly. Only when attempting to learn a foreign language will they begin to appreciate the structure of language and the need for grammatical rules.

The Number of Factors Involved

Environmental relationships need to be relearned whenever a firm enters a new international market. The number of changing dimensions increases geometrically. Because of their sheer number, coordination of interaction among the dimensions becomes increasingly difficult. The international-research process can help in this undertaking.

Broader Definition of Competition

The international market exposes the firm to a much greater variety of competition than found in the home market. For example, a firm may find that seafood competes not only against other seafood but also against meat or even vegetarian substitutes. Similarly, firms that offer labor-saving devices domestically may suddenly be exposed to competition from cheap manual labor. As a result, the firms must determine the breadth of the competition, track competitive activities, and evaluate their actual and potential impact on its own operations.

RECOGNIZING THE NEED FOR INTERNATIONAL RESEARCH

Many firms do little research before they enter a foreign market. Often, decisions concerning entry and expansion in overseas markets and selection and appointment of distributors are made after a cursory, subjective assessment of the situation. The research done is less rigorous, less formal, less quantitative than for domestic activities. Furthermore, once a firm has entered a foreign market, it is likely to discontinue researching that market.[2,3] Many business executives appear to view foreign research as relatively unimportant.

A major reason why managers are reluctant to engage in international research is their lack of sensitivity to differences in culture, consumer tastes, and market demands. Often managers assume that their methods are both best and acceptable to all others. Fortunately, this is not true. What a boring place the world would be if it were!

A second reason is limited appreciation for the different environments abroad. Often firms are not prepared to accept that labor rules, distribution systems, the availability of media, or advertising regulations may be entirely different from those in the home market. Because of the pressure to satisfy short-term financial goals, managers are unwilling to spend money to find out about the differences.

A third reason is lack of familiarity with national and international data sources and inability to use international data once they are obtained. As a result, the cost of conducting international research is seen as prohibitively high and therefore not a worthwhile investment relative to the benefits to be gained.[4]

Finally, firms often build up their international business activities gradually, frequently based on unsolicited orders. Over time, actual business experience in a country or with a specific firm may then be used as a substitute for organized research.[5]

Despite the reservations firms have, research is as important internationally as it is domestically. Firms must learn where the opportunities are, what customers want, why they want it, and how they satisfy their needs and wants so that the firm can serve them efficiently. Firms must obtain information about the local infrastructure, labor market, and tax rules before making a plant-location decision. Doing business abroad without the benefit of research places firms, their assets, and their entire international future at risk.

Research allows management to identify and develop international strategies. This task includes the identification, evaluation, and comparison of potential foreign business opportunities and the subsequent target-market selection. In addition, research is necessary for the development of a business plan that identifies all the requirements necessary for market entry, market penetration, and expansion. On a continuing basis, research provides the feedback needed to fine-tune various business activities. Finally, research can provide management with the intelligence to help anticipate events, take appropriate action, and adequately prepare for global changes.

DETERMINING RESEARCH OBJECTIVES

Before research can be undertaken, research objectives must be determined. They will vary depending on the views of management, the corporate mission of the firm, the firm's level of internationalization, and its competitive situation.

Going International—Exporting

A frequent objective of international research is that of foreign-market opportunity analysis. When a firm launches its international activities, it will usually find the world to be uncharted territory. Fortunately, information can be accumulated to provide basic guidelines. The aim is not to conduct a painstaking and detailed analysis of the world on a market-by-market basis, but instead to utilize a broadbrush approach. Accomplished quickly and at low cost, this approach will narrow the possibilities for international business activities.

Such an approach should begin with a cursory analysis of general variables of a country, including total and per capita GNP, mortality rates, and population figures. Although these factors in themselves will not provide any detailed information, they will enable the researcher to determine whether corporate objectives might be met in the market. For example, high-priced consumer products are unlikely to be successful in the People's Republic of China, as their price may be equal to a significant proportion of the annual salary of the customer, the benefit to the customer may be minimal, and the government is likely to prohibit their importation. Similarly, the offering of computer-software services may be of little value in a country where there is very limited use of computers. Such a cursory evaluation will help reduce the number of markets to be considered to a more manageable number—for example, from 147 to 25.

As a next step, the researcher will require information on each individual country for a preliminary evaluation. Information typically desired will highlight the fastest-growing markets, the largest markets for a particular product or service, demand trends, and business restrictions. Although precise and detailed information may not be obtainable, information is available for general product categories or service industries. Again, this overview will be cursory but will serve to quickly evaluate markets and further reduce their number.

At this stage, the researcher must select appropriate markets for in-depth evaluation. The focus will now be on opportunities for a specific type of service, product, or brand, and will include an assessment as to whether demand already exists or can be stimulated. Even though aggregate industry data have been obtained previously, this general information is insufficient to make company-specific decisions. For example, the demand for medical equipment should not be confused with the potential demand for a specific brand.[6] Now, the research should identify demand and supply patterns and evaluate any regulation and standards. Finally, a **competitive assessment** needs to be made, matching markets to corporate strengths and providing an analysis of the best potential for specific offerings. A summary of the various stages in the determination of market potential is provided in Figure 13.1.

Going International—Importing

When importing, the major focus shifts from supplying to sourcing. Management must identify markets that produce supplies or materials desired or that have the potential to do so. Foreign firms must be evaluated in terms of their capabilities and competitive standing.

Just as management would wish to have some details on a domestic supplier, the importer needs to know, for example, about the reliability of a foreign supplier, the consistency of its product or service quality, and the length of delivery time. Information obtained through the subsidiary office of a bank or an embassy can prove very helpful.

FIGURE 13.1
A Sequential Process of Researching Foreign Market Potentials

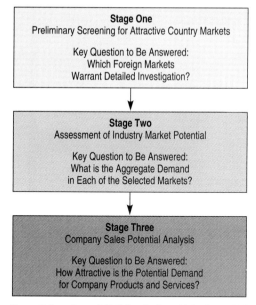

Stage One
Preliminary Screening for Attractive Country Markets

Key Question to Be Answered:
Which Foreign Markets
Warrant Detailed Investigation?

Stage Two
Assessment of Industry Market Potential

Key Question to Be Answered:
What is the Aggregate Demand
in Each of the Selected Markets?

Stage Three
Company Sales Potential Analysis

Key Question to Be Answered:
How Attractive is the Potential Demand
for Company Products and Services?

Source: S. Tamer Cavusgil, "Guidelines for Export Market Research," *Business Horizons* 28 (November–December 1985): 29. Copyright 1985 by the foundation for the School of Business at Indiana University. Reprinted by permission.

In addition, foreign rules must be scrutinized as to whether exportation is possible. As examples, India may set limits on the cobra handbags it allows to be exported, and laws protecting a nation's cultural heritage may prevent the exportation of pre-Columbian artifacts from Latin American countries.

The international manager must also analyze domestic restrictions and legislation that may prohibit the importation of certain goods into the home country. Even though a market may exist in the United States for foreign umbrella handles, for example, quotas may restrict their importation in order to protect domestic industries. Similarly, even though domestic demand may exist for ivory, its importation may be illegal because of legislation enacted to protect wildlife worldwide.

Market Expansion

Research objectives include the obtaining of more detailed information for business expansion or the monitoring of the political climate so that the firm can maintain its international operation successfully. Information may be needed to enable the international manager to evaluate new business partners or assess the impact of a technological breakthrough on future business operations. The better defined the research objective is, the better able the researcher will be to determine information requirements and thus conserve the time and financial resources of the firm.

CONDUCTING SECONDARY RESEARCH

Identifying Sources of Data

Typically, the information requirements of firms will cover both macro information about countries and trade, as well as micro information specific to the firm's activities. Table 13.1 provides an overview of the types of information that, according to a survey of U.S. executives, is most crucial for international business.

Tyson Foods customizes more than 5,000 products to satisfy local taste preferences in 57 countries. Targeted research helps Tyson identify opportunities globally.

Souce: Courtesy of Tyson Foods.

TABLE 13.1 Most Critical International Information for U.S. Firms	**Macro Data** ● Tariff information ● U.S. export/import data ● Nontariff measures ● Foreign export/import data ● Data on government trade policy **Micro Data** ● Local laws and regulations ● Size of market ● Local standards and specifications ● Distribution system ● Competitive activity

Source: Michael R. Czinkota, "International Information Needs for U.S. Competitiveness," *Business Horizons* 34, 6 (November–December 1991): 86–91.

As we saw in this chapter's opening vignette, a wide variety of sources present **secondary data.** The principal ones are the U.S. government, other governments, international institutions, service organizations, trade associations, directories, and other firms. This section provides a brief review of major data sources. Details on selected monitors of international issues are presented in Appendix 13A at the end of the chapter.

U.S. Government   The U.S. government has a great variety of data available. Most of them are collected by the Department of Commerce, the Department of Agriculture, the Department of State, the Department of the Treasury, and by U.S. embassies abroad.

Typically, the information provided by the U.S. government addresses either macro or micro issues or offers specific data services. Macro information includes data on population trends, general trade flows between countries, and world agricultural production. Micro information in turn includes materials on specific industries in a country, their growth prospects, and their foreign-trade activities. Increasingly, a public debate is shaping up regarding the role of government in collecting international business information. As Global Perspective 13.1 shows, some argue that the intelligence capabilities of government ought to be used to provide more information relevant to the successful and competitive conduct of international business since economic rather than national-security concerns should shape government intelligence in the future. Yet, there are also many who are quite uneasy about such a use of government resources.

Other Governments   Most countries have a wide array of national and international trade data available. Unfortunately, the data are often published only in their home countries and in their native languages. These publications mainly present numerical data, however, and so the translation task is relatively easy. In addition, these information sources are often available at embassies and consulates, whose mission includes the enhancement of trade activities. The commercial counselor or commercial attaché can provide the information available from these sources. The user should be cautioned, however, that the information is often dated and that the industry categories used abroad may not be compatible with industry categories used at home.

International Organizations   Some international organizations provide useful data for the researcher. The *Statistical Yearbook* produced by the United Nations (UN) contains international trade data on products and provides information on exports and imports by country. However, because of the time needed for worldwide data

Global Perspective

13.1
Economic Intelligence from the CIA?

The Clinton Administration will review whether economic intelligence gathered by U.S. spy agencies should be shared with private companies or individuals. CIA Director R. James Woolsey told a Senate committee: This issue is "the hottest current topic in intelligence policy." The Review will examine the complexities, legal difficulties, and foreign-policy difficulties of passing along to private firms important commercial secrets learned in the course of routine intelligence work.

Analysts expect that the review will fuel the debate about the CIA's potential role in helping American companies combat foreign competition. The previous director of central intelligence, Robert M. Gates, had strongly opposed authorizing the sharing of commercial secrets with private firms, stating that "the U.S. intelligence community does not, should not, and will not engage in industrial espionage."

Some business organizations have since urged the government to reverse that decision, citing increased efforts by foreign intelligence organizations to obtain industrial secrets from U.S. corporations. Others feel strongly about setting an international example, keeping spying and business separate, and avoiding what would surely become special and preferential treatment of individual firms.

Source: Adapted from R. Jeffrey Smith, "Administration to Consider giving Spy Data to Business," *The Washington Post*, February 3, 1993: 1.

collection, the information is often quite dated. Additional information is compiled and made available by specialized substructures of the United Nations. Some of these are the United Nations Conference on Trade and Development (UNCTAD), which concentrates primarily on international issues surrounding developing nations, such as debt and market access, and the United Nations Center on Transnational Corporations. The *World Atlas* published by the World Bank provides useful general data on population, growth trends, and GNP figures. The Organization for Economic Cooperation and Development (OECD) also publishes quarterly and annual trade data on its member countries. Finally, organizations such as the International Monetary Fund (IMF) and the World Bank publish summary economic data and occasional staff papers that evaluate region- or country-specific issues in depth.

Service Organizations   A wide variety of service organizations that provide information include banks, accounting firms, freight forwarders, airlines, international trade consultants, foreign research firms, and publishing houses located abroad. Frequently they are able to provide information on business practices, legislative or regulatory requirements, and political stability, as well as basic trade and financial data. Although this information is available without charge, its basic intent is to serve as an "appetizer." Much of the initial information is quite general in nature, as Figure 13.2 suggests. More detailed and up-to-date answers are also available from these sources, but they will require payment of an appropriate fee.

Trade Associations   Associations such as world trade clubs and domestic and international chambers of commerce (such as the American Chamber of Commerce abroad) can provide good information on local markets. Often files are maintained on international trade flows and trends affecting international managers. Valuable information can also be obtained from industry associations. These groups, formed to represent entire industry segments, often collect from their members a wide variety of data that are then published in an aggregate form. Because most of these associations represent the viewpoints of their member firms to the federal government, they usually have one or more publicly listed representatives in Washington. The information provided is often quite general, however, because of the wide variety of clientele served.

Directories and Newsletters   A large number of industry directories are available on local, national, and international levels. These directories primarily serve to identify firms and to provide very general background information, such as the name of the chief executive officer, the level of capitalization of the firm, the location, the address and telephone number, and some description of a firm's products. In the past few years, a host of newsletters have sprung up discussing specific international business issues, such as international trade finance, legislative activities, countertrade, international payment flows, and customs news. Usually these newsletters cater to narrow audiences but can provide important information to the firm interested in a specific area.

Databases   Increasingly, electronic databases also provide international business information. For example, information can be found on financial markets, the latest in trade press and academic writings, and political developments, among other topics. Information services are provided through various media, including on-line interac-

**FIGURE 13.2
Advertisement Offering
International Services**

Source: *Forbes*, June 21, 1993.

tive delivery, compact disc read-only memory, magnetic tape, floppy disk, interactive voice/audiotext, and on-line broadcast. The United States is the largest producer and consumer of electronic information services. In 1992, this $12 billion industry had more than 6,000 on-line services available, with a projected annual growth of 16 percent.[7] The information found in these databases is usually available for a subscription fee, often in addition to payments on an as-used basis.

Other Firms   Often home-country competitors can provide useful information for international business purposes. Firms appear to be more open about their international than about their domestic business activities. On some occasions, valuable information can also be obtained from foreign firms and distributors.

Selection of Secondary Data

Just because secondary information has been found to exist does not mean that it has to be used. Even though one key advantage of secondary data over primary research is that they are available relatively quickly and inexpensively, the researcher should still assess the effort and benefit of using them. Secondary data should be evaluated regarding the quality of their source, their recency, and their relevance to the task at hand. Clearly, since the information was collected without the current research requirements in mind, there may well be difficulties in coverage, categorization, and comparability. For example, an "engineer" in one country may differ substantially in terms of training and responsibilities from a person in another country holding the same title. It is therefore important to use such data carefully when getting ready to interpret and analyze them.

Interpretation and Analysis of Secondary Data

Once secondary data have been obtained, the researcher must creatively convert them into information. Secondary data were originally collected to serve another purpose than the one in which the researcher is currently interested. Therefore, they can often be used only as **proxy information** in order to arrive at conclusions that address the research objectives. For example, the market penetration of television sets may be used as a proxy variable for the potential demand for video recorders. Similarly, in an industrial setting, information about plans for new port facilities may be useful in determining future containerization requirements. The researcher should proceed with caution when comparing secondary data across borders.

The researcher must use creative inferences, and such creativity brings risks. Therefore, once interpretation and analysis have taken place, a consistency check must be conducted. The researcher should always cross-check the results with other possible sources of information or with experts. Yet, if properly implemented, such creativity can open up one's eyes to new market potential, as Global Perspective 13.2 shows.

CONDUCTING PRIMARY RESEARCH

Even though secondary data are useful to the researcher, on many occasions primary information will be required. **Primary data** are obtained by a firm to fill specific information needs. Firms do specialize in primary international research, even under difficult circumstances as indicated in Figure 13.3. Although the research may not be conducted by the company with the need, the work must be carried out for a specific research purpose in order to qualify as primary research. Typically, primary research intends to answer such clear-cut questions as:

- What is our sales potential in Market X?
- How skilled is the labor force in this region?
- What will happen to demand if we raise the price by 10 percent?
- What effect will a new type of packaging have on our sales?

When extending his or her efforts abroad, the researcher must determine the specific country or region to be investigated. Conducting research in an entire country may not be necessary if, for example, only urban centers are to be penetrated. Multiple regions of a country need to be investigated, however, if a lack of homogeneity exists because of different economic, geographic, or behavioral factors. The researcher must of course have a clear idea of what the population under study should be and where it is located before deciding on the country or region to investigate.

Industrial versus Consumer Sources of Data

The researcher must decide whether research is to be conducted in the consumer or the industrial product area, which in turn determines the size of the universe and

Global Perspective

13.2
Creative Research

When American entrepreneur Peter Johns went to Mexico to do business, he couldn't buy what he needed most: information. So he dug it up himself. Johns wanted to distribute mail-order catalogs for upscale U.S. companies to consumers in Mexico. He thought that a large market was there just waiting to be tapped. However, when he tried to test his theory against hard data, he ran into a big blank.

Johns, who has spent 30 years in international marketing, couldn't find a useful marketing study for Mexico City. Government census reports weren't much help because they stop breaking down income levels at about $35,000, and they give ranges, rather than precise numbers, on family size.

So Johns embarked on some primary research. He went into the affluent neighborhoods and found just what he had suspected: satellite dishes, imported sports cars, and women carrying Louis Vuitton handbags. He reached his own conclusions about the target market for his catalogs. "There is no question there is a sense of consumer deprivation in the luxury market of Mexico City," says Johns.

After deciding to pursue his new enterprise, Johns reached another obstacle. His new enterprise, Choices Unlimited, had gotten rights from about 20 U.S. companies to distribute their catalogs in Mexico City. Now, he needed mailing lists, and he couldn't find them. Owners of mailing lists do not like to sell them because buyers tend to recycle the lists without authorization. Some of those that are available are expensive and may not include information like zip codes, important barometers of household wealth.

Johns asked his local investors for membership lists of the city's exclusive golf clubs. He also obtained directories of the parents of students at some of the city's exclusive private schools. Johns received these lists for free. "That's called grass-roots marketing intelligence," says Johns.

Down the road, Johns hopes to have a Mexican customer base of 7,500 families spending an average of $600 a year on his products. By then, he should have another product to sell: his customer list.

Source: Dianna Solis, "Grass-Roots Marketing Yields Clients in Mexico City," *The Wall Street Journal,* October 24, 1991, B2.

respondent accessibility. Consumers usually are a very large group, whereas the total population of industrial users may be fairly limited. Cooperation by respondents may also vary, ranging from very helpful to very limited. In the industrial setting, differentiation between users and decision makers may be important because their personalities, their outlooks, and their evaluative criteria may differ widely. Determining the proper focus of the research is therefore of major importance to its successful completion.

Determining the Research Technique

Selection of the research technique depends on a variety of factors. First, the objectivity of the data sought must be determined. Standardized techniques are more useful in the collection of objective data than of subjective data. Also, the degree of structure sought in the data collection needs to be determined. Unstructured data will require more open-ended questions and more time than structured data. Whether the data are to be collected in the real world or in a controlled environment must be determined. Finally, it must be decided whether to collect historical facts or information about future developments. This is particularly important for consumer research, because firms frequently want to determine the future intention of consumers to purchase a certain product.

Once the structure of the type of data sought is determined, the researcher must choose a research technique. As in domestic research, the types available are inter-

**FIGURE 13.3
An Example of Primary
Research Under
Difficult Conditions**

**THE INTERVIEWING IS EASY...
IF THIS MAN DOESN'T SHOOT YOU FIRST**

TASK :

Interview Afghans who fled across the border into Pakistan to see if they're listening to the BBC. Problem: you have to get past the local warlords who control the area.

Hand this problem to any old research company claiming to do international research, and you're in trouble. The BBC turned to Research International.

KNOWING WHAT WORKS

In today's competitive world, companies are increasingly looking toward off-shore markets. And that means good information is essential, even in developed markets.

But international research isn't just a case of taking what you do here and transplanting it there.

A national probability sample in Brazil will have you climbing a palm tree. "I will buy" on a scale in Japan doesn't mean the same thing in Spain. In tax-shy Italy, quota sampling on the basis of income won't get you very far!

**GLOBAL PERSPECTIVE
+ LOCAL INSIGHT**

We have Research International offices on the ground in 38 of the world's most important markets, from France to Argentina, the USA to Russia, London to Singapore. All our companies are leaders in their markets.

Our professional staff know their markets because they live there—not through visits or by reading the statistics.

We have conducted more than 4,000 international projects. In the last two years alone, we've worked in over 100 countries.

We know what works. And what doesn't. We know what

research should cost. We know how to insure comparable high quality standards worldwide.

**RESEARCH INTERNATIONAL
IN NORTH AMERICA**

You may be surprised to know that Research International has 6 companies and 9 offices in this region. Whether it's large scale survey work, product testing, customer satisfaction research, qualitative or observational research, we can help.

We can put together an unrivaled team drawing on Research International resources in place in New York, Boston, San Francisco, Chicago, Toronto, Mexico City and in San Juan.

**COMMITMENT TO
INNOVATION WORLDWIDE**

Being on the ground all around the world also means that we have access to the best brains and the best thinking around the globe. Which means that we can offer our clients innovative, powerful techniques regardless of place of origin.

Our commitment to R. & D. runs very deep. Each year, we spend more of our own money on basic research than most of our competitors bring to the bottom line.

FREE OFFER

We've prepared a paper to help avoid some of the traps. Called "8 Common Pitfalls of International Research," it's free to marketers. Simply fax Daphne Chandler at—212-889-0487.

For specific help right now—call Daphne at 212-679-2500.

RESEARCH INTERNATIONAL

Source: Reprinted by permission of Research International, The Leading Worldwide Research Company.

views, focus groups, observation, surveys, and experimentation. Each one provides a different depth of information and has its unique strengths and weaknesses.

Interviews   Often interviews with knowledgeable people can be of great value for the corporation desiring international information. Because bias from the individual may be part of the findings, the intent should be to obtain not a wide variety of data, but rather in-depth information. Particularly when specific answers are sought to very narrow questions, interviews can be most useful.

Focus Groups   Focus groups are a useful research tool resulting in interactive interviews. A group of knowledgeable people is gathered for a limited period of time (two to four hours). Usually, seven to ten participants is the ideal size for a focus group. A specific topic is introduced and thoroughly discussed by all group members. Because of the interaction, hidden issues are sometimes raised that would not have been detected in an individual interview. The skill of the group leader in stimulating discussion is crucial to the success of a focus group. Focus groups, like in-depth interviews, do not provide statistically significant information; however, they can be helpful in providing information about perceptions, emotions, and attitudinal factors. In addition, once individuals have been gathered, focus groups are highly efficient means of rapidly accumulating a substantial amount of information.

When planning international research using focus groups, the researcher must be aware of the importance of language and culture in the discussion process. Not all societies encourage frank and open exchange and disagreement among individuals. Status consciousness may result in the opinion of one participant being reflected by all others. Disagreement may be seen as impolite, or certain topics may be taboo. Unless a native focus group leader is used, it also is possible to completely misread the interactions among group participants and to miss out on nuances and constraints participants feel when commenting in the group situation. Before deciding on a focus group in an international setting, the researcher must be fully aware of these issues.

Observation   Observation requires the researcher to play the role of a nonpartici-pating observer of activity and behavior. In an international setting, observation can be extremely useful in shedding light on practices not previously encountered or understood. This aspect is especially valuable to the researcher who has no knowledge of a particular market or market situation. It can help in understanding phenomena that would have been difficult to assess with other techniques. For example, Toyota sent a group of its engineers and designers to southern California to nonchalantly "observe" how women get into and operate their cars. They found that women with long fingernails have trouble opening the door and operating various knobs on the dashboard. Toyota engineers and designers were able to "understand" the women's plight and redesign some of their automobile exterior and interior, producing more desirable cars.[8]

All the research instruments discussed so far are useful primarily for the gathering of qualitative information. The intent is not to amass data or to search for statistical significance, but rather to obtain a better understanding of given situations, behavioral patterns, or underlying dimensions. The researcher using these instruments must be cautioned that even frequent repetition of the measurements will not lead to a statically valid result. However, statistical validity often may not be the major focus of corporate research. Rather, it may be the better understanding, description, and prediction of events that have an impact on decision making. When quantitative data are desired, surveys and experimentation are more appropriate research instruments.

Surveys   Survey research is useful in quantifying concepts. In the social sciences, it is generally accepted that the cross-cultural survey is scientifically the most powerful method of hypothesis testing.[9] Surveys are usually conducted via questionnaires that are administered personally, by mail, or by telephone. Use of the survey technique presupposes that the population under study is accessible—able to comprehend and respond to the question posed through the chosen medium. Particularly for mail and telephone surveys, a major precondition is the feasibility of using the postal system or the widespread availability of telephones. Obviously, this is not a given in all countries. In many nations only limited records about dwellings, their location, and their occupants are available. In Venezuela, for example, most houses are not numbered but rather are given individual names like Casa Rosa or El Retiro. In some countries, street maps are not even available. As a result, reaching respondents by mail is virtually impossible. In other countries, obtaining a correct address may be easy, but the postal system may not function well. The Italian postal service, for example, repeatedly has suffered from scandals that exposed such practices as selling undelivered mail to paper mills for recycling.

Telephone surveys may also be inappropriate if telephone ownership is rare. In such instances, any information obtained would be highly biased even if the researcher randomized the calls. In some cases, inadequate telephone networks and systems, frequent line congestion, and a lack of telephone directories may also prevent the researcher from conducting surveys. Yet, as Figure 13.4 shows, with today's communication capabilities, research firms are able to conduct telephone research around the world from a single location.

Since surveys deal with people, who in an international setting are likely to display major differences in culture, preference, education, and attitude, just to mention a few factors, the use of the survey technique must be carefully examined. For example, in some regions of the world, recipients of letters may be illiterate.[10] Others may be very literate, but totally unaccustomed to some of the standard research scaling techniques used in the United States and therefore unable to respond to the instrument. Other recipients of a survey may be reluctant to respond in writing, particularly when sensitive questions are asked. This sensitivity, of course, also varies by country. In some nations, any questions about income, even in categorical form, are considered highly proprietary; in others the purchasing behavior of individuals is not easily divulged.

The researcher needs to understand these constraints and prepare a survey that is responsive to them. For example, surveys can incorporate drawings or even cartoons to communicate better. Personal administration or collaboration with locally accepted intermediaries may improve the response rate. Indirect questions may need to substitute for direct ones in sensitive areas. Questions may have to be reworded to ensure proper communication. Figure 13.5 provides an example of a rating scale developed by researchers in order to work with a diverse population with relatively little education. In its use, however, it was found that the same scale aroused negative reactions among better-educated respondents, who considered the scale childish and insulting to their intelligence.

**FIGURE 13.4
An Advertisement for
International Data
Collection**

**INTERNATIONAL
DATA COLLECTION
BY TELEPHONE
FROM LOS ANGELES**

*Over Fifty Languages
24 Hours, 7 Days A Week
Data Processing
Residential And Business Sample
Translations (Cultural/Idiomatic)
Data Processing*

Conducting International Market Research can be extremely expensive and discouraging. It's less expensive and frustrating to conduct your international telephone studies with ISA International. For the past two years we've been saving our clients 10-15% by utilizing our capabilities in over 50 languages. All interviewers are foreign born nationals currently residing in the USA.

Get rid of your headaches. Call ISA International for a bid on your next project.

Call for a bid or to discuss your next project.

Michael Halberstam at 818-989-1044

Spanish	Hebrew	Korean
Vietnamese	Japanese	Tagalog
French	German	Armenian
German	Mandarin	Cantonese
Russian	Italian	Portuguese
	Plus Many More	

Source: *Marketing News*, November 23, 1992.

FIGURE 13.5
The Funny Faces Scale

Very Happy

Happy

Not Happy But
Also Not Unhappy

Unhappy

Very Unhappy

Source: C. K. Corder, "Problems and Pitfalls in Conducting Marketing Research in Africa," in Betsy Gelb (ed.), *Marketing Expansion in a Shrinking World,* Proceedings of American Marketing Association Business Conference (Chicago: AMA, 1978), pp. 86–90.

In spite of all the potential difficulties, the survey technique remains a useful one because it allows the researcher to rapidly accumulate a large quantity of data amenable to statistical analysis. With constantly expanding technological capabilities, international researchers will be able to use this technique even more in the future.

Experimentation   Experimental techniques determine the effect of an intervening variable and help establish precise cause-and-effect relationships. However, they are difficult to implement in international research. The researcher faces the task of designing an experiment in which most variables are held constant or are comparable across cultures. For example, an experiment to determine a causal effect within the distribution system of one country may be very difficult to transfer to another country because the distribution system may be quite different. For this reason, experimental techniques are only rarely used, even though their potential value to their international researcher is recognized.

THE INTERNATIONAL INFORMATION SYSTEM

Many organizations have data needs that go beyond specific international research projects. Most of the time, daily decisions must be made for which there is neither time nor money for special research. An information system can provide the decision maker with basic data for most ongoing decisions. Separation in time and space, as well as wide differences in culture and technological environments, makes information and data management more complex internationally than domestically.[11] These same factors, however, highlight the increased need for an international information system. Corporations have responded by developing systems such as the one shown in Table 13.2. Defined as "the systematic and continuous gathering, analysis, and reporting of data for decision-making purposes,"[12] such a system serves as a mechanism to coordinate the flow of information to corporate managers.

In order to be useful to the decision maker, the system must have certain attributes. First of all, the information must be *relevant.* The data gathered must have meaning for the manager's decision-making process. Only rarely can corporations afford to spend large amounts of money on information that is simply "nice to know." Any information system will have to continuously address the balance to be struck between the expense of the research design and process and the value of the information to ongoing business activities. Second, the information must be *timely.* Managers derive little benefit if decision information needed today does not become available until a month from now. Third, information must be *flexible*—that is, it must be available in the form needed by management. An information system must therefore permit manipulation of the format and combination of the data. Fourth, information contained in the system must be *accurate.* This is especially important in international research because information quickly becomes outdated as a result of major environmental changes. Fifth, the system's information bank must be reasonably *exhaustive.* Because of the interrelationship between variables, factors that may influence a particular decision must be appropriately represented in the information system. This means that the information system must be based on a wide variety of factors. Finally, to be useful to managers, the system must be *convenient* to both use and access. Systems that are cumbersome and time consuming to reach and to use will not be used enough to justify corporate expenditures to build and maintain them.

To build an information system, corporations use the internal data that area available from divisions such as accounting and finance and also from various subsidiaries. In addition, many organizations put mechanisms in place to enrich the basic data flow to information systems. Three such mechanisms are environmental scanning, Delphi studies, and scenario building.

Environmental Scanning

Any changes in the environment, whether domestic or foreign, may have serious repercussions on the activities of the firm. Corporations therefore understand the necessity for tracking developments in the environment. Although this can be done

---

TABLE 13.2 **An Example of an** **International Marketing** **Information System**	**RJR Tobacco International, Inc.** This multinational cigarette manufacturer utilizes various methods of operation—exporting, licensing, wholly owned subsidiary—in major geographic markets around the world. Examples of subsystems of its marketing information system might be: a. Central databank on customers from different regions regarding demographic, psychological, sociological, and behavioral characteristics and sales data on each region. Tools from the statistical bank, like experimental design, can be used to measure the impact of competitive actions on company's sales. b. Shipment reports data system to provide information regarding export shipments. Control data would be provided to management to measure program results against forecast goals. c. Subsidiary operations subsystem to provide financial and accounting information flows. d. Econometric modeling procedures to be applied to forecasting economic and other trends affecting the cigarette industry around the world.

Source: Sayeste Daser, "International Marketing Information Systems: A Neglected Prerequisite for Foreign Market Planning," in *International Marketing Management,* ed. Erdener Kaynak (New York: Praeger Publishers, 1984), 143.

Advances in Telephone and Data Transmission Technology Facilitate the Collection of Data for International Business Research

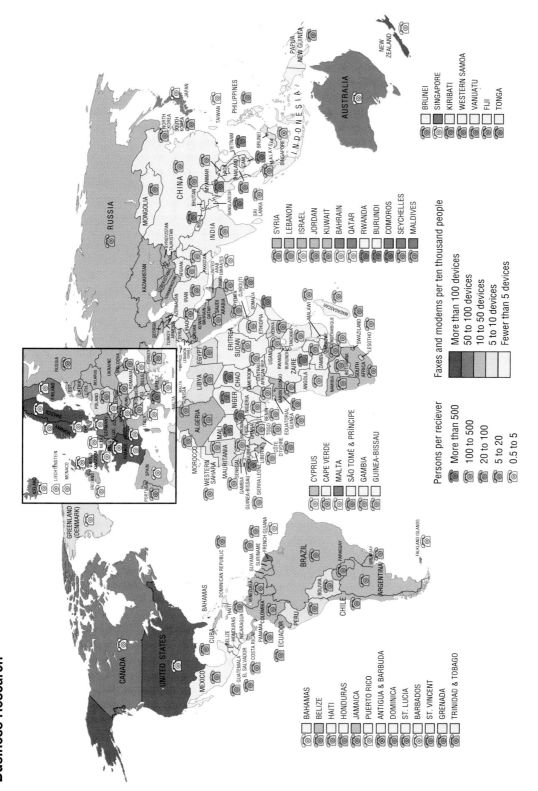

Persons per reciever

- More than 500
- 100 to 500
- 20 to 100
- 5 to 20
- 0.5 to 5

Faxes and modems per ten thousand people

- More than 100 devices
- 50 to 100 devices
- 10 to 50 devices
- 5 to 10 devices
- Fewer than 5 devices

Sources: *Peters Atlas of the World, 1990; The New Book of World Rankings, 1991.*

implicitly in the domestic environment, the remoteness of international markets necessitates continuous informational updates. For this purpose, some large multinational organizations have formed environmental-scanning groups.

Environmental-scanning activities provide continuous information on political, social, and economic affairs internationally; on changes of attitudes of public institutions, and private citizens; and on possible upcoming alterations. Environmental-scanning models are used for a variety of purposes, some of which are:

1. The development of broad strategies and long-term policies.
2. The development of action plans and operating programs.
3. The development of a frame of reference for the annual budget.
4. The provision of a mind-stretching or educational experience for management.[13]

Obviously, the precision required for environmental scanning varies with its purpose. For example, whether information is to serve for mind stretching or for budgeting must be taken into account when constructing the framework for the scanning process. The more immediate and precise the application will be within the corporation, the greater the need for detailed information. On the other hand, heightened precision may reduce the usefulness of environmental scanning in strategic planning, which is long term.

Environmental scanning can be performed in various ways. One consists of obtaining factual input regarding many variables. For example, the International Data Base (IDB) of the U.S. Census Bureau collects, evaluates, and adjusts a wide variety of demographic, social, and economic characteristics of foreign countries. Estimates are provided for all countries of the world, particularly on economic variables such as labor force statistics, GNP, and income statistics. Health and nutritional variables are also covered.[14] Similar factual information can be obtained from international organizations, such as the World Bank or the United Nations.

Frequently, managers believe that factual data alone are insufficient for their information needs. Particularly for forecasting future developments, other methods are used to capture underlying dimensions of social change. One significant method is that of media analysis. A wide array of newspapers, magazines, and other publications are scanned worldwide in order to pinpoint over time the gradual evolution of new views or trends. Corporations also use the technique of media analysis to pinpoint upcoming changes in their line of business. For example, the Alaskan oil spill by the Exxon *Valdez* and the rash of oil spills that followed resulted in entirely new international concern about environmental protection and safety, reaching far beyond the actual incidents and participants.

With the current heightened awareness of environmental and ethical issues such as pollution, preservation of natural resources, and animal testing, firms are increasingly looking for new opportunities to expand their operations while remaining within changing moral and environmental boundaries. Global Perspective 13.3 provides an example.

Environmental scanning is conducted by a variety of groups within and outside the corporation. Quite frequently, small corporate staffs are created at headquarters to coordinate the information flow. In addition, subsidiary staff can be used to provide occasional intelligence reports. Groups of volunteers are also formed to gather and analyze information worldwide and feed their individual analyses back to corporate headquarters, where the "big picture" can then be constructed. Increasingly, large corporations also services in environmental scanning to outsiders. In this way, profits can be made from an in-house activity that has to be carried out anyway.

Global Perspective

13.3
Ethics and Profits Do Mix!

Washington's World Resources Institute estimates that Brazil's Amazon forest is disappearing at a rate of almost 20 million acres, or 2.2 percent, a year, according to Chuck Lee, a WRI economic analyst. U.S. importers who buy everything from buttons to nuts from the sprawling Amazon basin are discovering that it can be profitable to support the ethical standards of rain forest conservationists.

By paying far more than world market prices for the products and donating a hefty portion of their profits to organizations that work to preserve the forest, importers can market their goods to consumers as environmentally sound. Despite a modest start involving only a few small companies, more and larger companies are expected to use rain forest imagery in launching "green" versions of such mundane products as breakfast cereals.

Companies that are active now are pioneering capitalists with a social conscience. For example, John Curtis, California lumber retailer and president of Healdsburg-based Luthier's Mercantile, soon will import his second container of Peruvian hardwood from a small cooperative in the remote Palcazu Valley. Rather than concentrating on mahogany imports like his Japanese competitors, Curtis is marketing relatively unknown species of wood to U.S. customers, who are taking a "leap of faith" in buying the products. His customers try out the wood knowing that the timber was harvested under so-called "sustained yield" management practices that minimize damage to the forest.

Similarly, Ben & Jerry's Homemade Inc. of Waterbury, Vermont, has been making money since late 1989 with its "Rainforest Crunch" ice cream, made with Brazil nuts that are harvested by a local cooperative opposed to lumbering. Rob Michelak, who describes himself as Ben & Jerry's "PR czar," commented, "Rainforest Crunch is an expensive ice cream to make, but business can be profitable and still do good." Ben & Jerry's is formulating other ice creams flavored with a variety of Amazon fruits.

Patagonia Inc. of Ventura, California, and Smith and Hawken of Mill Valley, California, are buying a million buttons made from tagua palm to help minimize commercial lumbering in the Esmeraldas province of Ecuador, just over the Andes mounts from the Amazon basin but still part of the same forest. Their purchase has been arranged through Conservation International, a Washington-based group working to preserve the rain forest.

A more esoteric interest in Amazonian products has motivated The Body Shop of Little Hampton, England, which operates 22 retail stores in the United States. The company hopes to launch a line of rain forest–based skin- and hair-care products next year. According to Rob Forster, the company's environmental research manager, The Body Shop has short-listed 10 products for potential development out of hundreds of herbs, oils, and other forest substances it has examined.

Source: Charles W. Thurston, "Importing from the Amazon Can Be Profitable and Ethical," *The Journal of Commerce,* September 20, 1990, 4A. Reprinted with permission.

Typically, environmental scanning is designed primarily to aid the strategic-planning process rather than the tactical activities of the corporation. A survey of corporate environmental-scanning activities found that "the futurity of the scanning exercise ranges from the medium term (say, about 5 years) to the truly long term (around 20 years) with the mode being about 10 years."[15] Environmental scanning, therefore, primarily addresses the future in order to complement the continuous flow of factual data to the corporation.

Not all managers perceive environmental scanning as important to the corporate planning process. For example, researchers have noted "that in those constructs and frameworks where the environment has been given primary consideration, there has been a tendency for the approach to become so global that studies tend to become shallow and diffuse, or impractical if pursued in sufficient depth."[16] Obviously, this presents one of the major continuous challenges corporations face in their international environmental scanning. The trade-off still exists between the breadth and depth of information. However, the continuous evolution of manipulative power through the ever-increasing capabilities of data processing may reduce at least the scope of the problem. Nevertheless, the cost of data acquisition and the issue of actual data use will continue to form major restraints on the development of environmental-scanning systems.

Delphi Studies

To enrich the information obtained from factual data, corporations frequently resort to the use of creative and highly qualitative data-gathering methods. One approach is through Delphi studies. These studies are particularly useful in the international environment because they are "a means for aggregating the judgments of a number of . . . experts . . . who cannot come together physically."[17] This type of research clearly aims at qualitative rather than quantitative measures by aggregating the information of a group of experts. It seeks to obtain a consensus from those who know, rather than average responses from many people with only limited knowledge.

Typically, Delphi studies are carried out with groups of about 30 well-chosen participants who possess expertise in an area of concern, such as future developments of the international trade environment. The participants are asked, most frequently by mail, to identify the major issues in the given area of concern. They are also requested to rank order their statements according to importance and explain the rationale behind the order. The aggregated information and comments are then sent to all participants in the Delphi group. Group members are encouraged to agree or disagree with the various rank orders and the comments. This allows statements to be challenged. In another round, the challenges can be responded to. Several rounds of challenges and responses result in a reasonably coherent consensus.

The Delphi technique is particularly valuable because it uses mail to bridge large distances and therefore makes experts quite accessible. It avoids the drawback of ordinary mail investigations, which lack interaction among participants. Because several rounds may be required, however, months may elapse before the information is obtained. Also, substantial effort must be expended in selecting the appropriate participants and in motivating them to participate in the exercise with enthusiasm and continuity. When carried out on a regular basis, Delphi studies can provide crucial augmentation of the factual data available for the information system.

Scenario Building

The information obtained through environmental scanning or Delphi studies can then be used to conduct a scenario analysis. One approach involves the development of a series of plausible scenarios that are constructed from trends observed in the environment. Another method consists of formally reviewing assumptions built into existing business plans and positions.[18] Subsequently, some of these key assumptions such as economic growth rates, import penetration, population growth, and political stability can be varied. By projecting variations for medium- to long-term periods, completely new environmental conditions can emerge. These conditions can then be analyzed for their potential domestic and international impact on corporate strategy.

The identification of crucial variables and the degree of variation are of major importance in scenario building. Frequently key experts are used to gain information about potential variations and about the viability of certain scenarios. An example of input from such experts is provided in Global Perspective 13.4.

Global Perspective

13.4
Advice from Kissinger Associates

Kissinger Associates is a New York–based consulting firm established in 1982 by former Secretary of State Henry Kissinger, former Undersecretary of State Lawrence S. Eagleburger, and former National Security Advisor Brent Scowcroft. For its corporate clients, the firm offers broadbrush pictures of political and economic conditions in particular countries or regions along with analyses of political and economic trends. Because none of the founders is particularly known for his business or economic expertise, an investment banker and an economist were brought on board.

Some have argued that the pointing out of political trends is an insufficient base from which to make a living. Kissinger himself stated that to provide only abstract information on the political condition in a foreign country is not fair to the client. The firm sees its primary strength to be its sensitivity to the international political situation and its continued closeness to information sources. Although Kissinger Associates offers no voluminous country reports, the principals believe that by correctly assessing, for example, the political outlook in Greece for the next five years,

they can help a client decide whether to make new investments there or preparations to leave in anticipation of a hostile socialist government. Similarly, the firm might help a U.S. oil company with limited Middle East experience in its first attempts to negotiate and work with a government in the region. Although this type of work does not involve Kissinger Associates deeply in specific business decisions, it does require a good understanding of clients' businesses and goals.

One practical reason for using high-powered consulting input was explained by a former member of Kissinger Associates: "These days, in case an investment goes sour, it is useful for [management] to be able to say, 'We got this expert advice and acted on that basis.' They have to show due diligence in exercising their fiduciary duties."

Even though client identities and fees are well-guarded secrets, congressional confirmation hearings for former employees of Kissinger Associates revealed that clients such as Union Carbide, Coca-Cola, Volvo, Fiat, and Daewoo pay between $150,000 and $400,000 per year for the firm's services.

Sources: Christopher Madison, "Kissinger Firm Hopes to Make Its Mark as Risk Advisors to Corporate Chiefs," *National Journal*, June 22, 1985, 1452–1456; and "The Out-of-Office Reign of Henry I," *U.S. News and World Report*, March 27, 1989, 10.

A wide variety of scenarios must be built in order to expose corporate executives to a number of potential occurrences. Ideally, even farfetched scenarios deserve some consideration, if only to address worst-case possibilities. A scenario for Union Carbide Corporation, for example, could have included the possibility of a disaster as it occurred in Bhopal.

Scenario builders also need to recognize the nonlinearity of factors. To simply extrapolate from currently existing situations is insufficient, since extraneous factors often enter the picture with significant impact. Finally, in scenario building, the possibility of **joint occurrences** must be recognized because changes may not come about in isolated fashion but instead may spread over wide regions. An example of such a joint occurrence is the indebtedness of Latin American nations. Although the inability of any one country to pay its debts would not have presented a major problem for the international banking community, large and simultaneous indebtedness posed a problem of major severity. Similarly, given large technological advances, the possibility of wholesale obsolescence of current technology must also be considered. For example, quantum leaps in computer development and new generations of computers may render obsolete the entire technological investment of a corporation.

In order for scenarios to be useful, management must analyze and respond to them by formulating contingency plans. such planning will broaden horizons and may prepare managers for unexpected situations. Through the anticipation of possible problems, managers hone their response capability and in turn shorten response times to actual problems.

The development of an international information system is of major importance to the multinational corporation. It aids the ongoing decision process and becomes a vital tool in performing the strategic-planning task. Only by observing global trends and changes will the firm be able to maintain and improve its competitive position. Much of the data available are quantitative in nature, but researchers must also pay attention to qualitative dimensions. Quantitative analysis will continue to improve as the ability to collect, store, analyze, and retrieve data increases as a result of computer development. Nevertheless, the qualitative dimension will remain a major component for corporate research and planning activities.

SUMMARY

Constraints of time, resources, and expertise are the major inhibitors to international research. Nevertheless, firms need to carry out planned and organized research in order to explore foreign market opportunities and challenges successfully. Such research must be linked closely to the decision-making process.

International research differs from domestic research in that the environment—which determines how well tools, techniques, and concepts apply—is different abroad. In addition, the international manager must deal with duties, exchange rates, and international documentation; a greater number of interacting factors; and a much broader definition of the concept of competition.

The research process starts by recognizing the need for research, which is often not well understood. When the firm is uninformed about international differences in consumer tastes and preferences or about foreign-market environments, the need for international research is particularly great. Research objectives need to be determined based on the corporate mission, the level of international expertise, and the business plan. These objectives will enable the research to identify the information requirements.

Given the scarcity of resources, companies beginning their international effort must rely on data that have already been collected. These secondary data are available from sources such as governments, international organizations, directors, or trade associations.

To fulfill specific information requirements, the researcher may need to collect primary data. An appropriate research technique must be selected to collect the information. Sensitivity to different international environments and cultures will aid the researcher in deciding whether to use interviews, focus groups, observation, surveys, or experimentation as data-collection techniques.

To provide ongoing information to management, an information system is useful. Such a system will provide for the continuous gathering, analysis, and reporting of data for decision-making purposes. Data gathered through environmental scanning, Delphi studies, or scenario building enable management to prepare for the future and hone its decision-making abilities.

Key Terms and Concepts

competitive assessment	primary data
secondary data	joint occurrence
proxy information	

Questions for Discussion

1. What is the difference between domestic and international research?
2. How does "going international" affect the environmental perspective of a firm?
3. You are employed by National Engineering, a U.S. firm that designs subways. Because you have had a course in international business, your boss asks you to spend the next week exploring international possibilities for the company. How will you go about this task?
4. Discuss the possible shortcomings of secondary data.
5. Why should a firm collect primary data in its international research?
6. How is international research affected by differences in language?
7. Is highly priced personalized advice from an individual really worth the money?
8. What type of data would you enter into your international information system?

Recommended Readings

Barnard, Philip. "Conducting and Co-ordinating Multicountry Quantitative Studies across Europe." In: *Global Marketing Perspectives,* edited by Jagdish Sheth and Abdolreza Eshghi. Cincinnati: South-Western, 1989: 56–73.

Davidson, James Dale, and Sir William Rees-Mogg. *Blood in the Streets.* New York: Summit Books, 1987.

Delphos, William S. (ed.). *International Direct Marketing Guide: Regional Markets and Selected Countries.* Alexandria, Va.: Braddock Communications, 1992.

Douglas, Susan P., and C. Samuel Craig. *International Marketing Research.* Englewood Cliffs, N.J.: Prentice-Hall, 1983.

Exporter's Guide to Federal Resources for Small Business. Washington, D.C.: Interagency Task Force on Trade, 1988.

Naisbitt, John, *Megatrends: Ten New Directions Transforming Our Lives.* New York: Warner Books, 1982.

Sheth, Jagdish N., ed. *Research in Marketing,* vol. 7. Greenwich, Conn.: JAI Press, 1984.

Smith, Craig N., and Paul Dainty. *The Management Research Handbook.* London: Routledge, 1991.

Notes

1. David A. Ricks, *Blunders in International Business* (Cambridge, Mass.: Blackwell, 1993).
2. Vinay Kothari, "Researching for Export Marketing," in *Export Promotion: The Public and Private Sector Interaction,* ed. M. Czinkota (New York: Praeger, 1983), 155.
3. S. Tamer Cavusgil, "International Marketing Research: Insights into Company Practices," in *Research in Marketing,* vol. 7, ed. J. N. Sheth (Greenwich, Conn.: JAI Press, 1984), 261–288.
4. Susan P. Douglas and C. Samuel Craig, *International Marketing Research* (Englewood Cliffs, N.J.: Prentice-Hall, 1983), 2.
5. Cavusgil, "International Marketing Research," 261–288.
6. S. Tamer Cavusgil, "Guidelines for Export Market Research," *Business Horizons* 28 (November–December 1985): 27–33.

7. Mary C. Inoussa, "Information Services," *U.S. Industrial Outlook 1993* (Washington, D.C.: U.S. Department of Commerce, 1993), 25-1–25-4.

8. Michael R. Czinkota and Masaaki Kotabe, "Product Development the Japanese Way," *The Journal of Business Strategy,* 11(6) (November/December 1990): 31–36.

9. Lothar G. Winter and Charles R. Prohaska, "Methodological Problems in the Comparative Analysis of International Marketing Systems," *Journal of the Academy of Marketing Science* 11 (Fall 1983): 421.

10. Douglas and Craig, *International Marketing Research,* 200.

11. Sayeste Daser, "International Marketing Information Systems: A Neglected Prerequisite for Foreign Market Planning," in *International Marketing Management,* ed. E. Kaynak (New York: Praeger, 1984), 139–154.

12. Thomas C. Kinnear and James R. Taylor, *Marketing Research: An Applied approach,* 2d ed. (New York: McGraw-Hill, 1983), 120.

13. Robert N. Anthony, John Dearden, and Richard F. Vancio, *Management Control Systems,* 5th ed. (Homewood, Ill.: Richard D. Irwin, 1984).

14. "IDB Provides Demographics of Foreign Markets," *Marketing News,* May 24, 1985, 14.

15. Phillip S. Thomas, "Environmental Scanning—The State of the Art," *Long Range Planning* 13 (February 1980): 24.

16. Winter and Prohaska, "Methodological Problems," 429.

17. Andrel Delbecq, Andrew H. Van de Ven, and David H. Gustafson, *Group Techniques for Program Planning* (Glenview, Ill.: Scott Foresman, 1975), 83.

18. William H. Davidson, "The Role of Global Scanning in Business Planning," *Organizational Dynamics,* Winter 1991: 5–16.

Selected Organizations

American Bankers Association
1120 Connecticut Avenue N.W.
Washington, D.C. 20036

American Bar Association
750 N. Lake Shore Drive
Chicago, IL 60611
and
1800 M Street N.W.
Washington, D.C. 20036

American Management Association
440 First Street N.W.
Washington, D.C. 20001

American Marketing Association
250 S. Wacker Drive Suite 200
Chicago, IL 60606

American Petroleum Institute
1220 L Street N.W.
Washington, D.C. 20005

Asian Development Bank
2330 Roxas Boulevard
Pasay City, Philippines

Chamber of Commerce of the
United States
1615 H Street N.W.
Washington, D.C. 20062

Commission of the European
Communities to the United States
2100 M Street N.W. Suite 707
Washington, D.C. 20037

Conference Board
845 Third Avenue
New York, NY 10022
and
1755 Massachusetts Avenue N.W.
Suite 312
Washington, D.C. 20036

Electronic Industries Association
2001 Pennsylvania Avenue N.W.
Washington, D.C. 20004

European Community Information
Service
200 Rue de la Loi
1049 Brussels, Belgium
and
2100 M Street N.W. 7th Floor
Washington, D.C. 20037

Export-Import Bank of the United
States
811 Vermont Avenue N.W.
Washington, D.C. 20571

Federal Reserve Bank of New York
33 Liberty Street
New York, NY 10045

Inter-American Development Bank
1300 New York Avenue N.W.
Washington, D.C. 20577

International Bank for
Reconstruction and Development
(World Bank)
1818 H Street N.W.
Washington, D.C. 20433

International Monetary Fund
700 19th Street N.W.
Washington, D.C. 20431

Marketing Research Society
111 E. Wacker Drive Suite 600
Chicago, IL 60601

National Association of
Manufacturers
1331 Pennsylvania Avenue Suite 1500
Washington, D.C. 20004

National Federation of
Independent Business
600 Maryland Avenue S.W.
Suite 700
Washington, D.C. 20024

Organization for Economic
Cooperation and Development
2 rue Andre Pascal
75775 Paris Cedex Ko, France
and
2001 L Street N.W. Suite 700
Washington, D.C. 20036

Organization of American States
17th and Constitution Avenue
N.W.
Washington, D.C. 20006

Society for International
Development
1401 New York Avenue N.W.
Suite 1100
Washington, D.C. 20005

United Nations

Conference of Trade and
  Development
Palais des Nations
1211 Geneva 10
Switzerland

Department of Economic and
  Social Affairs
1 United Nations Plaza
New York, NY 10017

Industrial Development
  Organization
1660 L Street N.W.
Washington, D.C. 20036
and
Post Office Box 300
Vienna International Center
A-1400 Vienna, Austria

Publications
Room 1194
1 United Nations Plaza
New York, NY 10017

Statistical Yearbook
1 United Nations Plaza
New York, NY 10017

U.S. Government

Agency for International
  Development
Office of Business Relations
Washington, D.C. 20523

Customs Service
1301 Constitution Avenue N.W.
Washington, D.C. 20229

Department of Agriculture
12th Street and Jefferson Drive
  S.W.
Washington, D.C. 20250

Department of Commerce
Herbert C. Hoover Building
14th Street and Constitution
  Avenue N.W.
Washington, D.C. 20230

Department of State
2201 C Street N.W.
Washington, D.C. 20520

Department of the Treasury
15th Street and Pennsylvania
  Avenue N.W.
Washington, D.C. 20220

Federal Trade Commission
6th Street and Pennsylvania
  Avenue N.W.
Washington, D.C. 20580

International Trade Commission
500 E Street N.W.
Washington, D.C. 20436

Small Business Administration
409 Third Street S.W.
Washington, D.C. 20416

Trade Development Program
1621 North Kent Street
Rosslyn, VA 22209

World Trade Centers Association
1 World Trade Center Suite 7701
New York, NY 10048

Indexes to Literature

Business Periodical Index
H.W. Wilson Co.
950 University Avenue
Bronx, NY 10452

New York Times Index
University Microfilms
  International
300 N. Zeeb Road
Ann Arbor, MI 48106

Public Affairs Information Service
  Bulletin
11 W. 40th Street
New York, NY 10018

Readers' Guide to Periodical
  Literature
H.W. Wilson Co.
950 University Avenue
Bronx, NY 10452

Wall Street Journal Index
University Microfilms
  International
300 N. Zeeb Rd.
Ann Arbor, MI 48106

Periodic Reports, Newspapers, Magazines

Advertising Age
Crain Communications Inc.
740 N. Rush Street
Chicago, IL 60611

Advertising World
Directories International Inc.
150 Fifth Avenue Suite 610
New York, NY 10011

Arab Report and Record
84 Chancery Lane
London WC2A 1DL, England

Barron's
University Microfilms
    International
300 N. Zeeb Road
Ann Arbor, MI 48106

Business America
U.S. Department of Commerce
14th Street and Constitution
    Avenue N.W.
Washington, D.C. 20230

Business International
Business International Corp.
One Dag Hammarskjold Plaza
New York, NY 10017

Business Week
McGraw-Hill Publications Co.
1221 Avenue of the Americas
New York, NY 10020

Commodity Trade Statistics
United Nations Publications
1 United Nations Plaza
Room DC2-853
New York, NY 10017

Conference Board Record
Conference Board Inc.
845 Third Avenue
New York, NY 10022

Customs Bulletin
U.S. Customs Service
1301 Constitution Avenue N.W.
Washington, D.C. 20229

Dun's Business Month
Goldhirsh Group
38 Commercial Wharf
Boston, MA 02109

The Economist
Economist Newspaper Ltd.
25 St. James Street
London SW1A 1HG, England

Europe Magazine
2100 M Street N.W. Suite 707
Washington, D.C. 20037

The Financial Times
Bracken House
10 Cannon Street
London EC4P 4BY, England

Forbes
Forbes, Inc.
60 Fifth Avenue
New York, NY 10011

Fortune
Time, Inc.
Time & Life Building
1271 Avenue of the Americas
New York, NY 10020

Global Trade
North American Publishing Co.
401 N. Broad Street
Philadelphia, PA 19108

Industrial Marketing
Crain Communications, Inc.
740 N. Rush Street
Chicago, IL 60611

International Financial Statistics
International Monetary Fund
Publications Unit
700 19th Street N.W.
Washington, D.C. 20431

Investor's Daily
Box 25970
Los Angeles, CA 90025

Journal of Commerce
110 Wall Street
New York, NY 10005

Sales and Marketing Management
Bill Communications Inc.
633 Third Avenue
New York, NY 10017

Wall Street Journal
Dow Jones & Company
200 Liberty Street
New York, NY 10281

World Agriculture Situation
U.S. Department of Agriculture
Economics Management Staff
Information Division
1301 New York Avenue N.W.
Washington, D.C. 20005

World Development
Pergamon Press Inc.
Journals Division
Maxwell House
Fairview Park
Elmsford, NY 10523

World Trade Center Association
    (WTCA) Directory
World Trade Centers Association
1 World Trade Center
New York, NY 10048

Directories

American Register of Exporters
   and Importers
38 Park Row
New York, NY 10038

Arabian Year Book
Dar Al-Seuassam Est. Box 42480
Shuwakh, Kuwait

Directories of American Firms
   Operating in Foreign Countries
World Trade Academy Press
Uniworld Business Publications Inc.
50 E. 42nd Street
New York, NY 10017

Encyclopedia of Associations
Galel Research Co.
Book Tower
Detroit, MI 48226

Polk's World Bank Director
R.C. Polk & Co.
2001 Elm Hill Pike
P. O. Box 1340
Nashville, TN 37202

Verified Directory of
   Manufacturers' Representatives
MacRae's Blue Book Inc.
817 Broadway
New York, NY 10003

World Guide to Trade
   Associations
K.G. Saur & Co.
175 Fifth Avenue
New York, NY 10010

Encyclopedias, Handbooks, and Miscellaneous

A Basic Guide to Exporting
U.S. Government Printing Office
Superintendent of Documents
Washington, D.C. 20402

Doing business in . . . Series
Price Waterhouse
1251 Avenue of the Americas
New York, NY 10020

Economic Survey of Europe
The United Nations
United Nations Publishing
   Division
1 United Nations Plaza
Room DC2-0853
New York, NY 10017

Economic Survey of Latin
   America
United Nations
United Nations Publishing
   Division
1 United Nations Plaza
Room DC2-0853
New York, NY 10017

Encyclopedia Americana,
   International Edition
Grolier Inc.
Danbury, CT 06816

Encyclopedia of Business
   Information Sources
Gale Research Co.
Book Tower
Detroit, MI 48226

Europa Year Book
Europa Publications Ltd.
18 Bedford Square
London WC1B 3JN, England

Export Administration Regulations
U.S. Government Printing Office
Superintendent of Documents
Washington, D.C. 20402

Exporters' Encyclopedia–World
   Marketing Guide
Dun's Marketing Services
49 Old Bloomfield Rd.
Mountain Lake, NJ 07046

Export-Import Bank of the United
   States Annual Report
U.S. Government Printing Office
Superintendent of Documents
Washington, D.C. 20402

Exporting for the Small Business
U.S. Government Printing Office
Superintendent of Documents
Washington, D.C. 20402

Exporting to the United States
U.S. Government Printing Office
Superintendent of Documents
Washington, D.C. 20402

Export Shipping Manual
U.S. Government Printing Office
Superintendent of Documents
Washington, D.C. 20402

Foreign Business Practices:
   Materials on Practical Aspects
   of Exporting, International
   Licensing, and Investing
U.S. Government Printing Office
Superintendent of Documents
Washington, D.C. 20402

A Guide to Financing Exports
U.S. Government Printing Office
Superintendent of Documents
Washington, D.C. 20402

Handbook of Marketing Research
McGraw-Hill Book Co.
1221 Avenue of the Americas
New York, NY 10020

International Encyclopedia of the
    Social Sciences
Macmillan and the Free Press
866 Third Avenue
New York, NY 10022

Marketing and Communications
    Media Dictionary
Media Horizons Inc.
50 W. 25th Street
New York, NY 10010

Market Share Reports
U.S. Government Printing Office
Superintendent of Documents
Washington, D.C. 20402

Media Guide International:
    Business/Professional
    Publications
Directories International Inc.
150 Fifth Avenue Suite 610
New York, NY 10011

Overseas Business Reports
U.S. Government Printing Office
Superintendent of Documents
Washington, D.C. 20402

Trade Finance
U.S. Department of Commerce
International Trade Administration
Washington, D.C. 20230

World Economic Conditions in
    Relation to Agricultural Trade
U.S. Government Printing Office
Superintendent of Documents
Washington, D.C. 20402

Yearbook of International Trade
    Statistics
United Nations
United Nations Publishing
    Division
1 United Nations Plaza
Room DC2-0853
New York, NY 10017

13B

Selected U.S. Government Publications and Services

Macrodata

World Population is issued by the U.S. Bureau of the Census, which collects and analyzes worldwide demographic data. Information is provided about total population, fertility, mortality, urban population, growth rate, and life expectancy. Also published are detailed demographic profiles, including an analysis of the labor force structure of individual countries.

Foreign Trade Highlights are annual reports published by the Department of Commerce. They provide basic data on U.S. merchandise trade with major trading partners and regions. They also contain brief analyses of recent U.S. trade developments.

Foreign Trade Report FT410 provides a monthly statistical record of shipments of all merchandise from the United States to foreign countries, including both the quantity and dollar value of exports to each country. It also contains cumulative export statistics from the first of the calendar year.

World Agriculture, a publication of the U.S. Department of Agriculture, provides production information, data, and analyzes by country along with a review of recent economic conditions and changes in agricultural and trade policies. Frequent supplements provide an outlook of anticipated developments for the coming year.

Country Information

National Trade Data Bank, a key product of the U.S. Department of Commerce, provides monthly CD-ROM disks that contain overseas market research, trade statistics, contact information, and other reports that may assist U.S. exporters in their international marketing efforts.

Country Marketing Plan reports on commercial activities and climate in a country and is prepared by the Foreign Commercial Service staffs abroad. It also contains an action plan for the coming year, including a list of trade events and research to be conducted.

Industry SubSector Analyses are market research reports, ranging from 5 to 20 pages, on specific product categories, for example, electromedical equipment in one country.

Overseas Business Reports (OBR) present economic and commercial profiles on specific countries and provide background statistics. Selected information on the direction and the volume and nature of U.S. foreign trade is also provided.

Background Notes, prepared by the Department of State, present a survey of a country's people, geography, economy, government, and foreign policy. The reports also include important national economic and trade information.

Foreign Economic Trends presents recent business and economic developments and the latest economic indicators of more than 100 countries.

Product Information

Export Statistics Profiles analyze exports for a single industry, product by product, country by country, over a five-year period. Data are rank-ordered by dollar value for quick identification of the leading products and industries. Tables show the sales of each product to each country as well as competitive information, growth, and future trends. Each profile also contains a narrative analysis that highlights the industry's prospects, performance, and leading products.

U.S. Industrial Outlook, an annual publication of the U.S. Department of Commerce, provides an overview of the domestic and international performance of all major U.S. industries, complete with employment and shipment information and a forecast of future developments.

Export Information System Data Reports, available from the U.S. Small Business Administration, provide small businesses with a list of the 25 largest importing markets for their products and the 10 best markets for U.S. exporters of the products. Trends within those markets and the major sources of foreign competition are also discussed.

Services

Agent Distributor Service (ADS): The Foreign Commercial Service (FCS) provides a customized search for interested and qualified foreign representatives for a firm's product.

Aglink: Collaborative effort between the Foreign Agricultural Service and the Small Business Administration to match foreign buyers with U.S. agribusiness firms.

Catalog Exhibitions: The Department of Commerce organizes displays of product literature and videotape presentations overseas.

Comparison Shopping Service: The FCS provides a custom foreign market survey on a product's overall marketability, names of competitors, comparative prices, and customary business practices.

Economic Bulletin Board: The Department of Commerce provides access to the latest economic data releases, including trade opportunities, for on-line users.

Foreign Agricultural Service: Employees of the U.S. Department of Agriculture, stationed both abroad and in the U.S. with the mission to facilitate agricultural exports from the United States. Provides counseling, research, general market information, and market introduction services.

Foreign Buyer Program: The FCS brings foreign buyers to U.S. trade shows for industries with high export potential.

Going Global: A computerized, on-line information system which lists market opportunities, information on foreign countries, and export intermediaries. Primarily focused on agricultural firms.

Matchmaker Events: The Department of Commerce introduces U.S. companies to new markets through short visits abroad to match the U.S. firm with a representative or prospective partner.

Seminar Missions: The Department of Commerce sponsors technical seminars abroad designed to promote sales of sophisticated products and technology.

Trade Missions: Groups of U.S. business executives, led by Commerce Department staff, meet with potential foreign buyers, agents, and distributors.

Trade Opportunity Program: The FCS daily collection of trade opportunities worldwide is published and electronically distributed to subscribers.

World Traders Data Reports: The FCS publishes background research conducted by FCS officers abroad on potential trading partners, such as agents, distributors, and licensees.

International Logistics

LEARNING OBJECTIVES

1. To examine the escalating importance of international logistics as competitiveness becomes increasingly dependent on cost efficiency.

2. To learn about materials management and physical distribution, both part of international logistics.

3. To learn why international logistics is more complex than domestic logistics.

4. To see how the transportation infrastructure in host countries often dictates the options open to the international manager.

5. To learn why inventory management is crucial for international success.

Trade Depends on Logistics

Africa jumped into the global perishable market when world prices for its traditional foreign currency earners (such as cocoa, coffee, tea, and tobacco) began to decline. Now, African countries are becoming major exporters of fresh fruit, vegetables, and flowers. Yet shipments of these perishable goods are getting locked out of the U.S. market for lack of adequate transportation.

"There's no transportation from Africa for fresh fruit. I don't think you're going to find anything of importance in fruit from Africa for a long time," said Peter Kopke, president of Kopke Inc., an importer of fresh fruit and vegetables based in Lake Success, New York.

The biggest buyers of African fruits, vegetables, and flowers are in Europe, the Middle East, and Japan. Kenya is now the world's fourth-largest exporter of flowers—particularly carnations, roses, and orchids—but sells barely $300,000 worth of flowers in the United States each year.

"It's simply a matter of logistics. Freight economics do not permit [perishables] being brought into the United States from Africa," said Larry Ladutko, president of First Flower Corp. in Miami.

"I'm sure those who do export to Europe have looked at the U.S. market," said Phillip Michelini, who tracks U.S. commercial relations with a number of West African countries for the Commerce Department. "But so far, there's no produce sold to the United States in any quantity. There's a basic problem of keeping such perishables as bananas and pineapples refrigerated."

Whether African producers will begin to rival Latin American, European, and Asian suppliers in the U.S. perishable market depends on whether they can solve the problem of cold storage facilities and air cargo space.

African exporters depend on national airlines. According to most U.S. and European cargo carriers and charter operators, there is still not enough African trade to fill flights.

Source: Rosalind Rachid, "African Exporters Find U.S. Tough," *The Journal of Commerce* (September 21, 1990): 1A. Reprinted with permission.

For the international firm, customer locations and sourcing opportunities are widely dispersed. The physical distribution and logistics aspects of international business therefore have great importance. To obtain and maintain favorable results from the complex international environment, the international manager must coordinate activities and gain the cooperation of all departments. The firm can attain a strategically advantageous position only if system synergism exists. Neglect of distribution and logistics issues brings not only higher costs but eventual noncompetitiveness, which will result in diminished market share, more expensive supplies, or lower profits. As we saw in the opening vignette, logistics problems can prevent exporters from fully exploiting a potentially profitable market overseas. Worse yet, different logistics regulations based on environmental concerns may even preclude any market participation.

This chapter will focus on international logistics activities. Primary areas of concern are transportation, inventory, packaging, storage, and logistics management. The logistics problems and opportunities that are peculiar to international business will also be highlighted.

THE FIELD OF INTERNATIONAL LOGISTICS

The concept of business logistics is relatively new. Although some aspects were discussed as early as 1951, John F. Magee is generally credited with publishing the first article on logistics theory in 1960.[1] The theoretical development of international logistics is even more recent, probably originating in a 1966 article by Robert E. McGarrah on "Logistics for the International Manufacturer."[2] The importance of international logistics has quickly been recognized by practitioners of international business.

Logistics costs currently comprise between 10 and 25 percent of the total landed cost of an international order, and they continue to increase.[3] International firms have already achieved many of the cost reductions that are possible in financing, communication, and production, and they are now beginning to look at international logistics as a competitive tool. Managers realize that "competition is the name of the game" in international business and that logistics "is key to making—and keeping—customers."[4] They also believe that future sales growth in the international market will come mainly from the development of wider and better logistics systems.[5]

A Definition of International Logistics

International logistics is defined as the designing and managing of a system that controls the flow of materials into, through, and out of the international corporation. It encompasses the total movement concept by covering the entire range of operations concerned with product movement, including therefore both exports and imports simultaneously. An overview of the logistics function is provided in Figure 14.1.

Two major phases in the movement of materials are of logistical importance. The first phase is **materials management,** or the timely movement of raw materials, parts, and supplies into and through the firm. The second phase is **physical distribution,** which involves the movement of the firm's finished product to its customers. In both phases, movement is seen within the context of the entire process. Stationary periods (storage and inventory) are therefore included. The basic goal of logistics management is the effective coordination of both phases and their various components to result in maximum cost effectiveness while maintaining service goals and requirements. In the words of the director of international logistics operations of General Motors Corporation, the purpose of international logistics is "to plan cost-effective systems for future use, attempt to eliminate duplication of effort, and determine where distribution policy is lacking or inappropriate. Emphasis is placed on

FIGURE 14.1   **The Logistics Function**

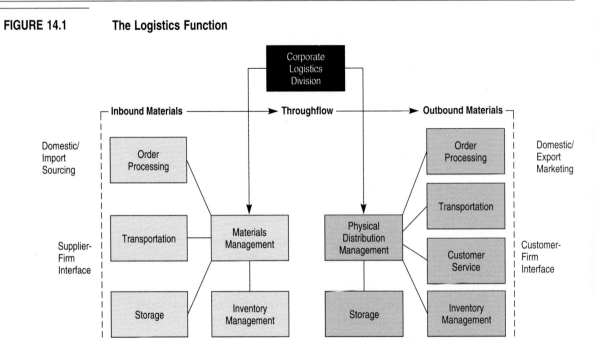

consolidating existing movements, planning new systems, identifying useful ideas, techniques, or experiences, and working with various divisions toward implementation of beneficial changes."[6]

The growth of logistics as a field has brought to the forefront three major new concepts: the systems concept, the total cost concept, and the trade-off concept. The **systems concept** is based on the notion that materials-flow activities within and outside the firm are so extensive and complex that they can be considered only in the context of their interaction. Instead of each corporate function, supplier, and customer operating with the goal of individual optimization, the systems concept stipulates that some components may have to work suboptimally in order to maximize the benefits of the system as a whole. Clearly, the systems concept intends to provide the firm, its suppliers, and its customers, both domestic and foreign, with the benefits of synergism expected from size.

A logical outgrowth of the systems concept is the development of the **total cost concept.** In order to evaluate and optimize logistical activities, cost is used as a basis for measurement. The purpose of the total cost concept is to minimize the firm's overall logistics cost by implementing the systems concept appropriately. Increasingly, however, the total cost concept is being partially supplanted by a **total after-tax profit concept.** This takes into account the impact of national tax policies on the logistics function and has the objective of maximizing after-tax profits rather than minimizing total cost. Because tax variations in the international arena often have major consequences, this new focus appears quite appropriate.[7]

The **trade-off concept,** finally, recognizes the linkages within logistics systems that result from the interaction of their components. For example, locating a warehouse near the customer may reduce the cost of transportation. However, additional costs are associated with new warehouses. Similarly, a reduction of inventories will save money but may increase the need for costly emergency shipments. Managers can maximize performance of logistics systems only by formulating decisions based on the recognition and analysis of these trade-offs.

Differences between Domestic and International Logistics

In the domestic environment, logistics decisions are guided by the experience of the manager, possible industry comparisons, an intimate knowledge of trends, and discovered heuristics—or rules of thumb. The logistics manager in the international firm, on the other hand, frequently has to depend on educated guesses to determine the steps required to obtain a desired service level. Variations in locale mean variations in environment. Lack of familiarity with these variations leads to uncertainty in the decision-making process. By applying decision rules based only on the environment encountered at home, the firm will be unable to adapt well to new circumstances and the result will be inadequate profit performance. The long-term survival of international activities depends on an understanding of the differences inherent in the international logistics field. These variations can be classified as basic differences and country-specific differences.[8]

Basic Differences   Basic differences in international logistics emerge because the corporation is active in more than one country. One example of a basic difference is distance. International business activities frequently require goods to be shipped farther to reach final customers. These distances in turn result in longer lead times, more opportunities for things to go wrong, more inventories—in short, greater complexity. Currency variation is a second basic difference in international logistics. The corporation must adjust its planning to incorporate the existence of different currencies and changes in exchange rates. The border-crossing process brings with it the need for conformity with national regulations, an inspection at customs, and proper documentation. As a result, additional intermediaries participate in the international logistics process. They include freight forwarders, customs agents, customs brokers, banks, and other financial intermediaries. Finally, the **transportation modes** may also be different. Most transportation within the United States is either by truck or by rail, whereas the multinational corporation quite frequently ships its products by air or by sea. Airfreight and ocean freight have their own stipulations and rules that require new knowledge and skills.

Country-Specific Differences   Within each country, the multinational corporation faces specific logistical attributes that may be quite different from those experienced at home. Transportation systems and intermediaries may vary. The computation of freight rates may be unfamiliar. Packaging and labeling requirements differ from country to country. Management must consider all of these factors in order to develop an efficient international logistics operation.

INTERNATIONAL TRANSPORTATION ISSUES

International transportation is of major concern to the international firm because transportation determines how and when goods will be received. Further, transportation costs represent 7 to 15 percent of the total landed cost of an international order[9] and therefore deserve special attention. The transportation issue can be divided into three components: infrastructure, the availability of modes, and the choice of modes among the given alternatives.

Transportation Infrastructure

In the United States, firms can count on an established transportation network. Internationally, however, major infrastructural variations may be encountered. Some countries may have excellent inbound and outbound transportation systems but weak

This Sea-Land container ship approaching Dubai exemplifies the primary difference between the transportation modes of national and international trade. Ocean freight and air freight are essential to international trade.
Source: © 1991 Charles Crowell/Black Star.

internal transportation links. This is particularly true in former colonies, where the original transportation systems were designed to maximize the extractive potential of the countries. In such instances, shipping to the market may be easy, but distribution within the market may represent a very difficult and time-consuming task. This lack of infrastructure can also be found in colonizing countries, where most transportation networks were established between major ports and cities in past centuries. Those areas lying outside the major transportation networks will encounter problems in bringing their goods to market.

Due to the political changes that have occurred in the recent past, new routes of commerce have also opened up, particularly between the former East and West political blocs. Yet, as Global Perspective 14.1 shows, without the proper infrastructure the opening of markets is mainly accompanied by major new bottlenecks. On the part of the firm, it is crucial to have wide market access in order to be able to appeal to sufficient customers. The firm's **logistics platform,** which is determined by a location's ease and convenience of market reach under favorable cost circumstances, is a key component of a firm's competitive position. Since different countries and regions may offer alternative logistics platforms, the firm must recognize that such alternatives can decide the difference between success and failure.

The logistics manager must therefore learn about existing and planned infrastructures abroad and at home and factor them into the firm's strategy. In some countries, for example, railroads may be an excellent transportation mode, far surpassing the performance of trucking, while in others the use of railroads for freight distribution may be a gamble at best. The future routing of pipelines must be determined before any major commitments are made to a particular location if the product is amenable to pipeline transportation. The transportation methods used to carry cargo to seaports or airports must be investigated.

Extreme variations also exist in the frequency of transportation services. For example, a particular port may not be visited by a ship for weeks or even months.

Global Perspective

14.1
Traffic Jams Halt Free Trade

In Frankfurt an der Oder, a German city near the Polish border, the line of trucks stretches farther than the eye can see. For the drivers, it stretches from today until tomorrow.

Since the fall of communism in eastern Europe, German-Polish trade has exploded. What was state-directed trade between the former German Democratic Republic and the People's Republic of Poland has become liberalized and market-oriented. But free trade comes to a screeching halt at the border.

Typical waits at the frontier are 25 to 35 hours. The truckers blame the Polish border authorities, claiming that there are only two customs workers on duty, and there is no 24-hour service, so no trucks are processed at night. They think that perhaps the Polish government is intentionally slowing down the border procedures to dampen the strong rise in imports and smuggled goods. The German Transportation Ministry states that the rise in trade has simply overtaken the ability of border agents to handle it. The border infrastructure in many places dates to before World War II. New roads, bridges, and border crossings are planned, but they take time.

Source: Miriam Widman, "German-Polish Border Is Trucker Traffic Jam," *The Journal of Commerce*, December 24, 1992, 1A, 3A.

Sometimes only carriers with particular characteristics, such as small size, will serve a given location. All of these infrastructural concerns must be taken into account in the initial planning of the firm's location and transportation framework.

Availability of Modes

Even though some goods are shipped abroad by rail or truck, international transportation frequently requires ocean or airfreight modes, which many U.S. corporations only rarely use domestically. In addition, combinations such as **land bridges** or **sea bridges** frequently permit the transfer of freight among various modes of transportation, resulting in **intermodal movements.** The international logistics manager must understand the specific properties of the different modes in order to use them intelligently.

Ocean Shipping   Three types of vessels operating in **ocean shipping** can be distinguished by their service: liner service, bulk service, and tramp or charter service. **Liner service** offers regularly scheduled passage on established routes. **Bulk service** mainly provides contractual services for individual voyages or for prolonged periods of time. **Tramp service** is available for irregular routes and scheduled only on demand.

In addition to the services offered by ocean carriers, the type of cargo a vessel can carry is also important. Most common are conventional (break bulk) cargo vessels, container ships, and roll-on-roll-off vessels. Conventional cargo vessels are useful for oversized and unusual cargoes but may be less efficient in their port operations. **Container ships** carry standardized containers that greatly facilitate the loading and unloading of cargo and intermodal transfers. As a result, the time the ship has to spend in port is reduced. Roll-on-roll-off (RORO) vessels are essentially oceangoing ferries. Trucks can drive onto built-in ramps and roll off at the destination. Another vessel similar to the RORO vessel is the LASH (lighter aboard ship) vessel. LASH vessels consist of barges stored on the ship and lowered at the point of destination. These individual barges can then operate on inland waterways, a feature that is particularly useful in shallow water.

The availability of a certain type of vessel, however, does not automatically mean that it can be used. The greatest constraint in international ocean shipping is the lack of ports and port services. For example, modern container ships cannot serve some ports because the local equipment cannot handle the resulting traffic. This problem is often found in developing countries, where local authorities lack the funds to develop facilities. In some instances, nations may purposely limit the development of **ports** to impede the inflow of imports. Increasingly, however, governments have begun to recognize the importance of an appropriate port facility structure and are developing such facilities in spite of the large investments necessary. If such investments are accompanied by concurrent changes in the overall infrastructure, transportation efficiency should, in the long run, more than recoup the original investment. The investment may be even more profitable if ports of neighboring countries are not adequate. Merchants may opt to use neighboring ports with port facilities that are up to their standards and then transport the goods over land to their final destination. For example, with the opening of the east European markets, the German ports of Hamburg, Bremen, and Bremerhaven are in an ideal location. Because larger vessels would have to sail around Denmark to reach eastern European ports, thereby adding at least a couple of days of voyage time, the German ports expect to snare a good portion of the anticipated increases in trade.[10]

Large investments in infrastructure are always necessary to produce results. Selective allocation of funds to transportation usually results only in the shifting of bottlenecks to some other point in the infrastructure. If these bottlenecks are not removed, the consequences may be felt in the overall economic performance of the nation.

Air Shipping To and from most countries, **airfreight** is available. This includes the developing world, where it is often a matter of national prestige to operate a national airline. The tremendous growth in international airfreight over past decades is shown in Table 14.1. However, the total volume of airfreight in relation to total shipping volume in international business remains quite small. It accounts for less than 1 percent of the total volume of international shipments, although it often represents more than 20 percent of the value shipped by industrialized countries.[11] Clearly, high-value items are more likely to be shipped by air, particularly if they have a high **density**, that is, a high weight-to-volume ratio.

Over the years, airlines have made major efforts to increase the volume of airfreight. Many of these activities have concentrated on developing better, more efficient ground facilities, automating air waybills, introducing airfreight containers, and providing and marketing a wide variety of special services to shippers. In addition, some airfreight companies and ports have specialized and become partners in the international logistics effort.

Changes have also taken place within the aircraft. As an example, 30 years ago, the holds of large propeller aircraft could take only about 10 tons of cargo. Today's jumbo jets can hold more than 30 tons and can therefore transport bulky products. In addition, aircraft manufacturers have responded to industry demands by developing both jumbo cargo planes and combination passenger and cargo aircraft. The latter carry passengers in one section of the main deck and freight in another. These

	Year	Ton-kilometers (billions)
TABLE 14.1 **International Airfreight, 1960–1992**[a]	1960	1.0
	1965	2.6
	1970	6.4
	1975	11.7
	1980	20.3
	1985	39.8
	1990	46.4
	1992[b]	49.2

[a]Based on data supplied by member states of the International Civil Aviation Organization (ICAO). As the number of member states increased from 116 in 1970 to 150 in 1983, there is some upward bias in the data, particularly from 1970 on, when data for the USSR were included for the first time.
[b]Preliminary figure.
Source: *Civil Aviation Statistics of the World* (Montreal: ICAO, 1993).

hybrids can be used by carriers on routes that would be uneconomical for passengers or freight alone.[12]

From the shipper's perspective, the products involved must be appropriate for air shipment in terms of their size. In addition, the market situation for any given product must be evaluated. Airfreight may be needed if a product is perishable or if, for other reasons, it requires a short transit time. The level of customer service needs and expectations can also play a decisive role. For example, the shipment of an industrial product that is vital to the ongoing operations of a customer is usually much more urgent than the shipment of most consumer products.

Choice of Modes

The international logistics manager must make the appropriate selection from the available modes of transportation. This decision, of course, will be heavily influenced by the needs of the firm and its customers. The manager must consider the performance of each mode on four dimensions: transit time, predictability, cost, and noneconomic factors.

Transit Time   The period between departure and arrival of the carrier varies significantly between ocean freight and airfreight. For example, the 45-day **transit time** of an ocean shipment can be reduced to 24 hours if the firm chooses airfreight. The length of transit time will have a major impact on the overall logistical operations of the firm. As an example, a short transit time may reduce or even eliminate the need for an overseas depot. Also, inventories can be significantly reduced if they are replenished frequently. As a result, capital can be freed up and used to finance other corporate opportunities. Transit time can also play a major role in emergency situations. For example, if the shipper is about to miss an important delivery date because of production delays, a shipment normally made by ocean freight can be made by air.

Perishable products require shorter transit times. Transporting them rapidly prolongs the shelf life in the foreign market. As shown in Figure 14.2, air delivery may be the only way to successfully enter foreign markets with products that have a short life span. International sales of cut flowers have reached their current volume only as a result of airfreight.

This interaction between selling price, market distance, and form of transportation is not new. Centuries ago, Johann von Thünen, a noted German economist, developed models for the market reach of agricultural products that incorporated these factors. Yet, given the forms of transportation available today, these factors no longer pose the rigid constraints postulated by von Thünen, but rather offer new opportunities in international business.

Predictability   Providers of both ocean freight and airfreight service wrestle with the issue of reliability. Both modes are subject to the vagaries of nature, which may impose delays. Yet, because **reliability** is a relative measure, the delay of one day for airfreight tends to be seen as much more severe and "unreliable" than the same delay for ocean freight. However, delays tend to be shorter in absolute time for air shipments. As a result, arrival time via air is more predictable. This attribute has a major influence on corporate strategy. For example, because of the higher predictability of airfreight, inventory safety stock can be kept at lower levels. Greater predictability also can serve as a useful sales tool for foreign distributors, which can make more precise delivery promises to their customers. If inadequate port facili-

FIGURE 14.2
Advertisement for Cut Flowers

How to ship tulips by air and come up smelling like a rose.

Cut flowers are almost as ephemeral as dreams. Beautiful, fragile, fragrant, they have a life span of mere days under the best of circumstances. So the challenge of shipping tulips from a field in Holland to a table in Ohio, still in their glorious prime, is a major one.

That's why so many tulip growers in Holland choose The New York & New Jersey Air Cargo Center through which to ship their flowers. Last year, more than $55 million worth of tulips were shipped through our airports.

The Dutch shippers know that time, coordination and connections are of the essence. They know that our Federal inspectors and import brokers are available when needed to meet their shipments as they arrive and to help expedite the flowers through the airport and on their way to market. And, they know we have the best air and surface connections to protect their flowers' freshness in transport and to meet tight delivery schedules.

We really care about the life of your product. We want you to come up smelling like a rose, whatever you ship.

Whether it's tulips or tubas, if it's going through the NY/NJ Air Cargo System, we'll get it there fast, fresh and—if it began that way—still fragrant.

For more information on air cargo services at the New York/New Jersey Airports, write to:

Manager, Air Cargo Market Development
Port Authority of New York and New Jersey
One World Trade Center, Suite 64N
New York, NY 10048

NEW YORK/NEW JERSEY AIRPORTS
Kennedy Newark LaGuardia
THE PORT AUTHORITY OF NY & NJ

Source: Courtesy of Customer and Marketing Services Division, Aviation Department, Port Authority of New York and New Jersey.

ties exist, airfreight may again be the better alternative. Unloading operations from oceangoing vessels are more cumbersome and time consuming than for planes. Finally, merchandise shipped via air is likely to suffer less loss and damage from exposure of the cargo to movement. Therefore, once the merchandise arrives, it is more likely to be ready for immediate delivery—a facet that also enhances predictability.

Cost of Transportation A major consideration in choosing international transportation modes is the cost factor. International transportation services are usually priced on the basis of both cost of the service provided and value of the service to the shipper. Because of the high value of the products shipped by air, airfreight is often priced according to the value of the service. In this instance, of course, price becomes a function of market demand and the monopolistic power of the carrier.

The manager must decide whether the clearly higher cost of airfreight can be justified. In part, this will depend on the cargo's properties. For example, the physical density and the value of the cargo will affect the decision. Bulky products may be too expensive to ship by air, whereas very compact products may be more appropriate for airfreight transportation. High-priced items can absorb transportation costs more easily than low-priced goods because the cost of transportation as a percentage of total product cost will be lower. As a result, sending diamonds by airfreight is easier to justify than sending coal.

Most important, however, are the overall logistical considerations of the firm. The manager must determine how important it is for merchandise to arrive on time. The need to reduce or increase international inventory must be carefully measured. Related to these considerations are the effect of transportation cost on price and the need for product availability abroad. For example, some firms may wish to use airfreight as a new tool for aggressive market expansion. Airfreight may also be considered a good way to begin operations in new markets without making sizable investments.

Although costs are the major consideration in modal choice, the overall cost perspective must be explored. Simply comparing transportation modes on the basis of price alone is insuffficient. The manager must factor in all corporate activities that are affected by the modal choice and explore the total cost effects of each alternative.

Noneconomic Factors   Often noneconomic dimensions will enter into the selection process for a proper form of transportation. The transportation sector, nationally and internationally, both benefits and suffers from government involvement. Carriers may be owned or heavily subsidized by governments. As a result, governmental pressure is exerted on shippers to use national carriers, even if more economical alternatives exist. Such **preferential policies** are most often enforced when government cargo is being transported. Restrictions are not limited to developing countries. For example, in the United States, the federal government requires that all cargo and official travelers use national flag carriers when available.

For Balance of Payments reasons, international quota systems of transportation have been proposed. The United Nations Conference on Trade and Development (UNCTAD), for example, has recommended that 40 percent of the traffic between two nations be allocated to vessels of the exporting country, 40 percent to vessels of the importing country, and 20 percent to third-country vessels. However, stiff international competition among carriers and the price sensitivity of customers frequently render such proposals ineffective, particularly for trade between industrialized countries.

Although many justifications are possible for such national policies, ranging from prestige to national security, they may distort the economic choices of the international corporation. Yet, these policies are a reflection of the international environment within which the firm must operate. Proper adaptation is necessary.

Export Documentation

A firm must have numerous forms and documents when exporting to ensure that all goods meet local and foreign laws and regulations.

A **bill of lading** is a contract between the exporter and the carrier indicating that the carrier has accepted responsibility for the goods and will provide transportation in return for payment. The bill of lading can also be used as a receipt and to prove ownership of the merchandise. There are two types of bills, negotiable and nonnegotiable. **Straight bills of lading** are nonnegotiable and are usually used in prepaid transactions. The goods are delivered to a specific individual or company. **Shipper's order** bills of lading are negotiable; can be bought, sold, or traded while the goods are still in transit; and are used for letter-of-credit transactions. The customer usually needs the original or a copy of the bill of lading as proof of ownership to take possession of the goods.[13]

A **commercial invoice** is a bill for the goods stating basic information about the transaction, including a description of the merchandise, total cost of the goods sold, addresses of the shipper and seller, and delivery and payment terms. The buyer needs the invoice to prove ownership and to arrange payment. Some governments use the commercial invoice to assess customs duties.

Other export documentation that may be required includes export licenses, consular invoices (used to control and identify goods and obtained from the country to which the goods are being shipped), certificates of origin, inspection certification, dock and/or warehouse receipts, destination control statements (serve to notify the carrier and all foreign parties that the item may only be exported to certain destinations), insurance certificates, shipper's export declarations (used to control exports and compile trade statistics), and export packaging lists.[14]

The documentation required depends on the merchandise in the shipment and its destination. The number of documents required can be quite cumbersome and costly, creating a deterrent to trade. For example, it was estimated that the border-related red tape and controls within the European Community cost European companies $9.2 billion in extra administrative costs and delays annually.[15] In order to eliminate the barriers posed by all this required documentation, the EC introduced the Single Administrative Document (SAD) in 1988. The SAD led to the elimination of nearly 200 customs forms required of truckers throughout the EC when traveling from one member country to another.

To ensure that all documentation required is accurately completed and to minimize potential problems, firms entering the international market should consider using **freight forwarders,** specialists in handling export documentation.

Terms of Shipment and Sale   The responsibilities of the buyer and the seller should be spelled out as they relate to what is and what is not included in the price quotation and when ownership of goods passes from seller to buyer, **Incoterms** are the internationally accepted standard definitions for terms of sale by the International Chamber of Commerce (ICC). The Incoterms 1990 went into effect on July 1, 1990, with significant revisions to better reflect changing transportation technologies and to facilitate electronic data interchange.[16] Although the same terms may be used in domestic transactions, they gain new meaning in the international arena. The most common of the 13 Incoterms used in international marketing are summarized in Figure 14.3.

Prices quoted **ex-works (EXW)** apply only at the point of orgin, and the seller agrees to place the goods at the disposal of the buyer at the specified place on the date or within the fixed period. All other charges are for the account of the buyer.

One of the new Incoterms is **free carrier (FCA),** which replaced a variety of FOB terms for all modes of transportation except vessel. FCA (named inland point) applies only at a designated inland shipping point. The seller is responsible for loading goods into the means of transportation; the buyer is responsible for all subsequent expenses. If a port of exportation is named, the costs of transporting the goods to the named port are included in the price.

Free alongside ship (FAS) at a named U.S. port of export means that the exporter quotes a price for the goods, including charges for delivery of the goods alongside a vessel at the port. The seller handles the cost of unloading and wharfage; loading, ocean transportation, and insurance are left to the buyer.

Free on board (FOB) applies only to vessel shipments. The seller quotes a price covering all expenses up to and including delivery of goods on an overseas vessel provided by or for the buyer.

FIGURE 14.3   Selected Trade Terms

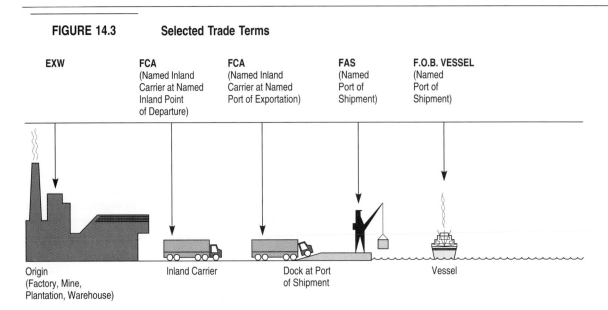

Source: Ann Dwyer Maffry, *Foreign Commerce Handbook* (Washington, D.C.: Chamber of Commerce of the United States,1981), 128–129.

Under **cost and freight (CFR)** to a named overseas port of import, the seller quotes a price for the goods, including the cost of transportation to the named port of debarkation. The cost of insurance and the choice of insurer are left to the buyer.

With **cost, insurance, and freight (CIF)** to a named overseas port of import, the seller quotes a price including insurance, all transportation, and miscellaneous charges to the point of debarkation from the vessel or aircraft. Items that may enter into the calculation of the CIF cost are (1) port charges: unloading, wharfage (terminal use) handling, storage, cartage, heavy lift, and demurrage; (2) documentation charges: certification of invoice, certificate of orgin, weight certificate, and consular forms; and (3) other charges, such as fees of the freight forwarder and freight (inland and ocean) insurance premiums (marine, war, credit).

With **delivery duty paid (DDP),** the seller delivers the goods, with import duties paid, including inland transportation from import point to the buyer's premises. With **delivered duty unpaid (DDU),** only the destination customs duty and taxes are paid by the consignee. Ex-works signifies the maximum obligation for the buyer; delivered duty paid puts the maximum burden on the seller.

The careful determination and clear understanding of terms used and their acceptance by the parties involved are vital if subsequent misunderstandings and disputes are to be avoided.

These terms are also powerful competitive tools. The exporter should therefore learn what importers usually prefer in the particular market and what the specific transaction may require. An exporter should quote CIF whenever possible because it clearly shows the buyer the cost to get the product to a port in or near a desired country.

An inexperienced importer might be discouraged from further action by a quote such as ex-plant Jessup, Maryland, whereas CIF Kotka will enable the Finnish importer to handle the remaining costs because they are incurred at home.

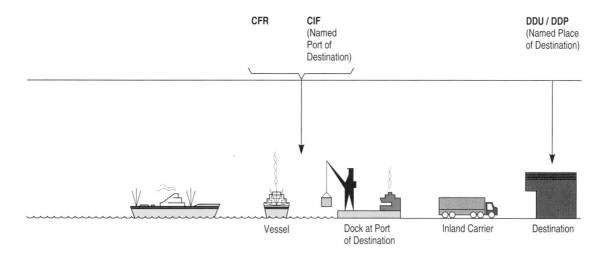

| CFR | CIF | | DDU / DDP |
| | (Named Port of Destination) | | (Named Place of Destination) |

Vessel   Dock at Port   Inland Carrier   Destination
                of Destination

Country of Destination

INTERNATIONAL INVENTORY ISSUES

Inventories tie up a major portion of corporate funds. Capital used for inventory is not available for other corporate opportunities. Because annual **inventory carrying costs** (the expense of maintaining inventories) can easily account for 25 percent or more of the value of the inventories themselves,[17] proper inventory policies should be of major concern to the international logistician. In addition, **just-in-time inventory** policies are increasingly being adopted by multinational manufacturers. These policies minimize the volume of inventory by making it available only when it is needed for the production process. Firms using such a policy will choose suppliers on the basis of their delivery and inventory performance. Proper inventory management may therefore become a determining variable in obtaining a sale.

Although inventories are closely monitored domestically, this is often not the case internationally. One observer wrote, "As the risk of foreign operations increases, companies are less likely to follow prescribed procedures for optimizing models related to inventory management."[18] This lack of preoccupation, however, does not reduce the importance of the issue. In its international inventory management, the multinational corporation is faced not only with new situations that affect inventories negatively but also with new opportunities and alternatives.

The purpose of establishing **inventory** systems—to maintain product movement in the delivery pipeline—is the same for domestic and international operations. The international environment, however, includes unique factors such as currency exchange rates, greater distances, and duties. At the same time, international operations provide the corporation with an opportunity to explore alternatives not available in a domestic setting, such as new sourcing or location alternatives. In international operations, the firm can make use of currency fluctuations by placing varying degrees of emphasis on inventory operations, depending on the stability of the currency of a specific country. Entire operations can be shifted to different nations to take advantage of new opportunities. International inventory management can therefore be much more flexible in its response to environmental changes.

In deciding the level of inventory to be maintained, the international manager must consider three factors: the order cycle time, desired customer service levels, and use of inventories as a strategic tool.

Order Cycle Time   The total time that passes between the placement of an order and the receipt of the merchandise is referred to as **order cycle time.** Two dimensions are of major importance to inventory management: the length of the total order cycle and its consistency. In international business, the order cycle is frequently longer than in domestic business. It comprises the time involved in order transmission, order filling, packing and preparation for shipment, and transportation. Order transmission time varies greatly internationally depending on whether facsimile, telex, telephone, or mail is used in communicating. The order-filling time may also be increased because lack of familiarity with a foreign market makes the anticipation of new orders more difficult. Packing and shipment preparation require more detailed attention. Finally, of course, transportation time increases with the distances involved. As a result, total order cycle time frequently approaches 100 days or more.[19] Larger inventories may have to be maintained both domestically and internationally in order to bridge these time gaps.

Consistency, the second dimension of order cycle time, is also more difficult to maintain in international business. Depending on the choice of transportation mode, delivery times may vary considerably from shipment to shipment. This variation requires the maintenance of larger safety stocks in order to be able to fill demand in periods when delays occur.

The international inventory manager should attempt to reduce order cycle time and increase its consistency without an increase in total costs. This can be accomplished by altering methods of transportation, changing inventory locations, or improving any of the other components of the order cycle time, such as the way orders are transmitted. Shifting order placement from a mail to a facsimile system can significantly reduce the order cycle time. Yet, because such a shift is likely to increase the cost of order transmittal, offsetting savings in other inventory areas must be achieved.

Customer Service Levels   The level of **customer service** denotes the responsiveness that inventory policies permit to any given situation. A customer service level of 100 percent would be defined as the ability to fill all orders within a set time—for example, three days. If within the same three days only 70 percent of the orders can be filled, the customer service level is 70 percent. The choice of customer service level for the firm has a major impact on the inventories needed. In their domestic operations, U.S. companies frequently aim to achieve customer service levels of 90 to 95 percent. Often such "homegrown" rules of thumb are then used in international inventory operations as well.

Many managers do not realize that standards determined heuristically and based on competitive activity in the home market are often inappropriate abroad. Different locales have country-specific customer service needs and requirements. Service levels should not be oriented primarily around cost or customary domestic standards. Rather, the level chosen for use internationally should be based on expectations encountered in each market. These expectations are dependent on past performance, product desirability, customer sophistication, and the competitive status of the firm.

Because high customer service levels are costly, the goal should not be the highest customer service level possible, but rather an acceptable level. If, for example, foreign customers expect to receive their merchandise within 30 days, for the international corporation to promise delivery within 10 or 15 days does not make sense. Customers may not demand or expect such quick delivery. Indeed, such delivery may result in storage problems. In addition, the higher prices associated with higher customer service levels may reduce the competitiveness of a firm's product.

Inventory as a Strategic Tool International inventories can be used by the international corporation as a strategic tool in dealing with currency valuation changes or hedging against inflation. By increasing inventories before an imminent devaluation of a currency instead of holding cash, the corporation may reduce its exposure to devaluation losses. Similarly, in the case of high inflation, large inventories can provide an important inflation hedge. In such circumstances, the international inventory manager must balance the cost of maintaining high levels of inventories with the benefits accruing to the firm from hedging against inflation or devaluation. Many countries, for example, charge a property tax on stored goods. If the increase in tax payments outweighs the hedging benefits to the corporation, it would be unwise to increase inventories before a devaluation.

Despite the benefits of reducing the firm's financial risk, inventory management must still fall in line with the overall corporate market strategy. Only by recognizing the trade-offs, which may result in less than optimal inventory policies, can the overall benefit to the corporation be maximized. Operations-research models can be very helpful in modeling such trade-offs.

INTERNATIONAL PACKAGING ISSUE

Packaging is of particular importance in international logistics because it is instrumental in getting the merchandise to the ultimate destination in a safe, maintainable, and presentable condition. Packaging that is adequate for domestic shipping may be inadequate for international transportation because the shipment will be subject to the motions of the vessel on which it is carried. Added stress in international shipping also arises from the transfer of goods among different modes of transportation. Figure 14.4 provides examples of some sources of stress in intermodal movement that are most frequently found in international transportation.

The responsibility for appropriate packaging rests with the shipper of goods. The U.S. Carriage of Goods by Sea Act of 1936 states: "Neither the carrier nor the ship shall be responsible for loss or damage arising or resulting from insufficiency of packing." The shipper must therefore ensure that the goods are prepared appropriately for international shipping. This is important because it has been found that "the losses that occur as a result of breakage, pilferage, and theft exceed the losses caused by major maritime casualties, which include fires, sinkings, and collision of vessels. Thus the largest of these losses is a preventable loss."[20]

FIGURE 14.4   **Stresses in Intermodal Movement**

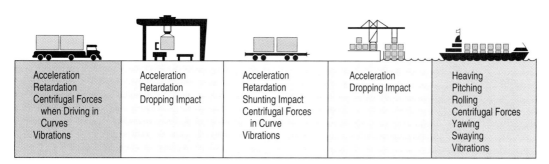

Note: Each transportation mode exerts a different set of stresses and strains on containerized cargoes. The most commonly overlooked are those associated with ocean transport.
Source: David Greenfield, "Perfect Packing for Export," from *Handling and Shipping Management,* September 1980 (Cleveland, Ohio: Penton Publishing), 47.

Trade and Travel Networks

Civilization depends on trade for growth and travel makes this possible. Shipping is the most important method of world transport but economic progress and mobility are constantly being improved by the development of new routes and new methods of transport.

Road and Rail

Integrated road and rail networks are the basis of industrial society. Containerization and the extension of modern highway systems have increased flexibility and reduced the emphasis on railways transporting freight.

Roads

Bar length equals the total road network in log scale.
Number next to country name is the total road network in thousands of kilometers.

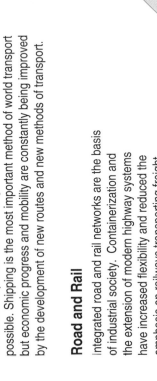

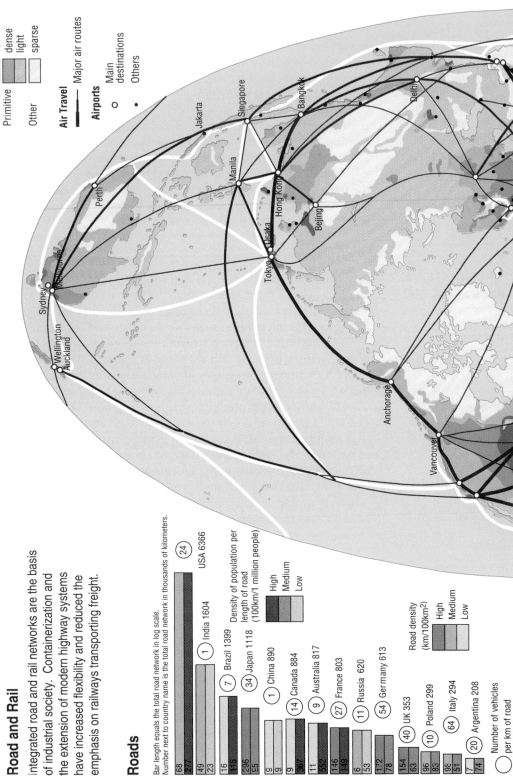

Sea travel
- Major sea lanes
- ○ Seaports

Road / rail network
Modern
- dense
- medium
- light

Primitive
- dense
- light

Other
- sparse

Air Travel
- Major air routes

Airports
- ○ Main destinations
- • Others

Density of population per length of road (100km/1 million people)
- High
- Medium
- Low

Road density (km/100km²)
- High
- Medium
- Low

○ Number of vehicles per km of road

USA 6366
① India 1604
⑦ Brazil 1399
㉞ Japan 1118
① China 890
⑭ Canada 884
⑨ Australia 817
㉗ France 803
⑪ Russia 620
㊱ Germany 613
㊵ UK 353
⑩ Poland 299
㊽ Italy 294
⑳ Argentina 208

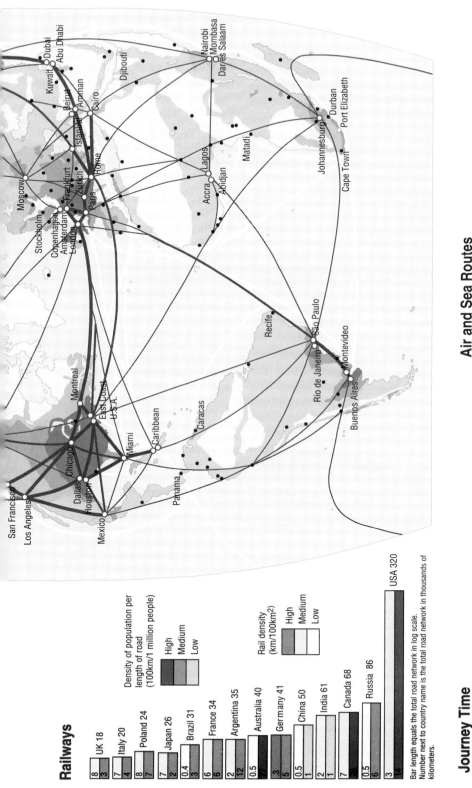

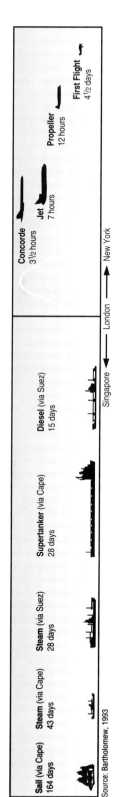

Railways

UK 18
Italy 20
Poland 24
Japan 26
Brazil 31
France 34
Argentina 35
Australia 40
Germany 41
China 50
India 61
Canada 68
Russia 86
USA 320

Density of population per
length of road
(100km/1 million people)

High
Medium
Low

Rail density
(km/100km²)

High
Medium
Low

Bar length equals the total road network in log scale.
Number next to country name is the total road network in thousands of
kilometers.

Durban
Port Elizabeth
Johannesburg
Cape Town
Nairobi
Mombasa
Dar es Salaam
Djibouti
Matadi
Accra
Lagos
Abidjan
Cairo
Beirut
Amman
Istanbul
Kuwait
Dubai
Abu Dhabi
Rome
Frankfurt
Zürich
Paris
Moscow
Stockholm
Copenhagen
Amsterdam
London
Recife
São Paulo
Rio de Janeiro
Montevideo
Buenos Aires
Caracas
Panama
Mexico
Houston
Dallas
Chicago
San Francisco
Los Angeles
Montreal
East Coast
U.S.A.
Miami
Caribbean

Air and Sea Routes

A complex network of primary air routes centered on the Northern Hemisphere provides rapid transit across the world for mass travel, mail, and urgent freight.

Ships also follow these principal routes, plying the oceans between major ports and transporting the commodities of world trade in bulk.

Journey Time

The Suez Canal cuts 3600 nautical miles off the London–Singapore route, while the Concorde halves the London–New York journey time.

Concorde 3½ hours
Jet 7 hours
Propeller 12 hours
First Flight 4½ days

Singapore ⟷ London ⟷ New York

Sail (via Cape) 164 days
Steam (via Cape) 43 days
Steam (via Suez) 28 days
Supertanker (via Cape) 28 days
Diesel (via Suez) 15 days

Source: Bartholomew, 1993

Packaging decisions must also take into account differences in environmental conditions—for example, climate. When the ultimate destination is very humid or particularly cold, special provisions must be made to prevent damage to the product. The task becomes even more challenging when one considers that, in the course of long-distance transportation, dramatic changes in climate can take place. Global Perspective 14.2 shows how some of these difficulties can be overcome.

The weight of packaging must also be considered, particularly when airfreight is used, as the cost of shipping is often based on weight. At the same time, packaging material must be suffficiently strong to permit stacking in international transportation. Another consideration is that, in some countries, duties are assessed according to the gross weight of shipments, which includes the weight of packaging. Obviously, the heavier the packaging, the higher the duties will be.

The shipper must pay suffficient attention to instructions provided by the customer for packaging. For example, requests by the customer that the weight of any one package should not exceed a certain limit, or that specific package dimensions should be adhered to, usually are made for a reason. Often they reflect limitations in transportation or handling facilities at the point of destination.

Although the packaging of a product is often used as a form of display abroad, international packaging can rarely serve the dual purpose of protection and display. Therefore double packaging may be necessary. The display package is for future use at the point of destination; another package surrounds it for protective purposes.

One solution to the packaging problem in international logistics has been the development of intermodal containers—large metal boxes that fit on trucks, ships, railroad cars, and airplanes and ease the frequent transfer of goods in international shipments. In addition, containers offer greater safety from pilferage and damage. Of course, if merchandise from a containerized shipment is lost, frequently the entire container has been removed. Developed in different forms for both sea and air trans-

Global Perspective

14.2
Quilting for Profit

With Australian wine exports to the United States increasing sharply, shipping lines have discovered a new tool for competitiveness, the insulating quilt. The service, first introduced by Australia–New Zealand Direct Line, is designed to protect wine shipments from freezing on shipments arriving in bitter U.S. East Coast winters. The shipping line licensed its quilt from Chicago-based Unicargo Corporation, which developed the insulator so that food could remain in dry rail cars during the coldest months, rather than going by more expensive refrigerated trucks. (Refrigerated trucks are used to keep products from getting too cold as well as too warm).

Apart from protecting the product, the quilt offers other benefits as well. Because importers are now able to ship all year rather than being forced to stockpile before the November–February period, they can ease bottlenecks and reduce inventory carrying costs.

The insulators also offer potential for other shipments like canned fruit and beer. The shipping line has already been approached by a specialty metals company interested in reducing rust damage on the coatings of shipments that cross the equator.

Source: Mark Magnier, "Ocean Carriers find 'Quilt' a Cozy Way to Protect Wine," *The Journal of Commerce*, Nov. 12, 1992, p. B8.

portation, containers also offer better utilization of carrier space because of standardization of size. The shipper therefore may benefit from lower transportation rates.

Container traffic is heavily dependent on the existence of appropriate handling facilities, both domestically and internationally. In addition, the quality of inland transportation must be considered. If transportation for containers is not available and the merchandise must be removed, the expected cost reductions may not materialize.

In some countries, rules for the handling of containers may be designed to maintain employment. For example, U.S. union rules obligate shippers to withhold containers from firms that do not employ members of the International Longshoremen's Association for the loading or unloading of containers within a 50-mile radius of Atlantic or Gulf ports. Such restrictions can result in an onerous cost burden. Packaging issues also need to be closely linked to overall strategic plans. The international logistician should focus on the total delivery picture to ensure customer satisfaction: The type of packaging, method of transportation, route, country of destination, port facilities, customs procedures, identification markings, final destination, and customer specifications all need to be taken into consideration when packing goods for export.

Overall, close attention must be paid to international packaging. The customer who ordered and paid for the merchandise expects it to arrive on time and in good condition. Even with replacements and insurance, the customer will not be satisfied if there are delays. This dissatisfaction will usually translate directly into lost sales.

INTERNATIONAL STORAGE ISSUES

Although international logistics is discussed as a movement or flow of goods, a stationary period is involved when merchandise becomes inventory stored in warehouses. Heated arguments can arise within a firm over the need for and utility of warehousing internationally. On the one hand, customers may expect quick responses to orders and rapid delivery. Accommodating the customer's expectations may require locating many distribution centers around the world. On the other hand, warehousing space is expensive. In addition, the larger volume of inventory increases the inventory carrying cost. The international logistician must consider the trade-offs between service and cost to determine the appropriate levels of warehousing. Other trade-offs also exist within the logistics function. As an example, fewer warehouses will allow for consolidation of transportation and therefore lower transportation rates to the warehouse. However, if the warehouses are located far from customers, the cost of outgoing transportation from them will increase.

Storage Facilities

The international logistician is faced with the **location decision** of how many distribution centers to have and where to locate them. The availability of facilities abroad will differ from the domestic situation. For example, while public storage is widely available in the United States, such facilities may be scarce or entirely lacking abroad. Also, the standards and quality of facilities abroad are often not comparable to those available in the United States. As a result, the storage decision of the firm is often accompanied by the need for large-scale, long-term investments. An example of the possible costs encountered by a firm seeking warehouse space internationally is given in Global Perspective 14.3. Despite the high cost, international storage facilities

Global Perspective

14.3
The Cost of Warehousing in Japan

One of the major shortcomings of the Japanese distribution system is its lack of warehousing facilities. Even though the Japanese government has begun to introduce change by making warehousing facilities more widely available and by legislating the building of distribution centers, the cost of storage space is quite high. In order to obtain space in an existing distribution center, tenants often must pay a number of charges. Some of these are:

- Construction contribution fund: Participation in this fund consists of a one-time payment, which is refundable only after 10 years, with no interest payment.

- Security deposit: This deposit is refundable only at the end of the lease, with no interest payment.
- Monthly rent.
- Administrative charges: These charges are paid for administrative support that is rendered by the management of the distribution center.

Leases typically need to be signed for a minimum of 10 years. Despite these substantial costs, vacancy rates at existing distribution centers are extremely low, with outside turnover often lower than two percent.

Source: Michael R. Czinkota and Jon Woronoff, *Unlocking Japan's Market* (Chicago: Probus Publishing, 1991), 90.

should be established if they support the overall logistics effort. In many markets, adequate storage facilities are imperative in order to satisfy customer demands and to compete successfully.

Once the decision is made to utilize storage facilities abroad, the warehouses must be carefully analyzed. As an example, in some countries warehouses have low ceilings. Packaging developed for the high stacking of products is therefore unnecessary. In other countries, automated warehousing is available. Proper bar coding of products and the use of package dimensions acceptable to the warehousing system are basic requirements. In contrast, in warehouses still stocked manually, weight limitations will be of major concern.

To optimize the logistics system, the logistician should analyze international product sales and then rank order products according to warehousing needs. Products that are most sensitive to delivery time may be classified as "A" products. "A" products would be stocked in all distribution centers, and safety stock levels would be kept high. Products for which immediate delivery is not urgent may be classified as "B" products. They would be stored only at selected distribution centers around the world. Finally, products for which short delivery time is not important, or for which there is little demand, would be stocked only at headquarters. Should an urgent need for delivery arise, airfreight could be considered for rapid shipment. Classifying products enables the international logistician to substantially reduce total international warehousing requirements and still maintain acceptable service levels.

Special Trade Zones

Areas where foreign goods may be held or processed and then reexported without incurring duties are called **foreign trade zones.**[21] These zones can be found at major ports of entry and also at inland locations near major production facilities. For example, Kansas City, Missouri, has one of the largest foreign trade zones in the United States.

The existence of trade zones can be quite useful to the international firm. For example, in a particular country the benefits derived from lower factor costs, such as labor, may be offset by high duties and tariffs. As a result, location of manufacturing and storage facilities in that country may prove uneconomical. Foreign trade zones are designed to exclude the impact of duties from the location decision. This is done by exempting merchandise in the foreign trade zone from duty payment. The international firm can therefore import merchandise; store it in the foreign trade zone; and process, alter, test, or demonstrate it—all without paying duties. If the merchandise is subsequently shipped abroad (that is, reexported), no duty payments are ever due. Duty payments become due only if the merchandise is shipped into the country from the foreign trade zone.

All parties to the arrangement benefit from foreign trade zones. The government maintaining the trade zone achieves increased employment and investment. The firm using the trade zone obtains a spearhead in the foreign market without incurring all of the costs customarily associated with such an activity. As a result, goods can be reassembled, and large shipments can be broken down into smaller units. Also, goods can be repackaged when packaging weight becomes part of the duty assessment. Finally, goods can be given domestic "made-in" status if assembled in the foreign trade zone. Thus, duties may be payable only on the imported materials and component parts rather than on the labor that is used to finish the product.

In addition to foreign trade zones, governments also have established export-processing zones and special economic areas. The common dimensions for all these zones are that special rules apply to them, when compared with other regions of the country, and that the purpose of these special rules lies in the government's desire to stimulate the economy, particularly the export side of international trade.

Export-processing zones usually provide tax- and duty-free treatment for production facilities whose output is destined abroad. The maquiladoras of Mexico are one example. Special economic zones in turn provide an "environmental" incentive and are primarily designed to attract foreign investors who will produce for export. Such zones may be treated preferentially by government in terms of infrastructure, such as roads, energy, or ports. Special tax provisions and employment contracts may also be possible in such zones. In the international setting, China has made particular efforts in establishing such special economic zones.

For the logistician, the decision whether to use such zones is mainly framed by the overall benefit for the logistics system. Clearly, often transport and retransport are required, warehousing facilities need to be constructed, and material handling frequency will increase. However, these costs may well be balanced by the preferential government treatment or by lower labor cost.

MANAGEMENT OF INTERNATIONAL LOGISTICS

Because the very purpose of a multinational firm is to benefit from system synergism, a persuasive argument can be made for the coordination of international logistics at corporate headquarters. Without coordination, subsidiaries will tend to optimize their individual efficiency but jeopardize the overall performance of the firm.

Centralized Logistics Management

A significant characteristic of the centralized approach to international logistics is the existence of headquarters staff that retains decision-making power over logistics activities affecting international subsidiaries. If headquarters exerts control, it must also take the primary responsibility for its decisions. Clearly, ill will may arise if local managers are appraised and rewarded on the basis of a performance they do not control. This may be particularly problematic if headquarters staff suffers from a lack of information or expertise.

To avoid internal problems, both headquarters staff and local management should report to one person. This person, whether the vice president for international logistics or the president of the firm, can then become the final arbiter to decide the firm's priorities. Of course, this individual should also be in charge of determining appropriate rewards for managers, both at headquarters and abroad, so that corporate decisions that alter a manager's performance level will not affect the manager's appraisal and evaluation. Further, this individual can contribute an objective view when inevitable conflicts arise in international logistics coordination. The internationally centralized decision-making process leads to an overall logistics management perspective that can dramatically improve profitability.

Decentralized Logistics Management

An alternative to the centralized international logistics system is the "decentralized full profit center model."[22] The main rationale for such decentralization is the fact that "when an organization attempts to deal with markets on a global scale, there are problems of coordination."[23] Particularly when the firm serves many international markets that are diverse in nature, total centralization would leave the firm unresponsive to local-adaptation needs.

If each subsidiary is made a profit center in itself, each one carries the full responsibility for its performance, which can lead to greater local management satisfaction and to better adaptation to local market conditions. Yet often such decentralization deprives the logistics function of the benefits of coordination. For example, while headquarters, referring to its large volume of overall international shipments, may be able to extract bottom rates from transportation firms, individual subsidiaries by themselves may not have similar bargaining power.

Once products are within a specific market, however, increased input from local logistics operations should be expected and encouraged. At the very least, local managers should be able to provide input into the logistics decisions generated by headquarters. Ideally, within a frequent planning cycle, local managers can identify the logistics benefits and constraints existing in their particular market and communicate them to headquarters. Headquarters can then either adjust its international logistics strategy accordingly or explain to the manager why system optimization requires actions different from the ones recommended. Such a justification process will help greatly in reducing the potential for animosity between local and headquarters operations.

Outsourcing Logistics Services

A third option, used by some corporations, is the systematic outsourcing of logistics capabilities. By collaborating with transportation firms, private warehouses, or other specialists, corporate resources can be concentrated on the firm's core product. Global Perspective 14.4 provides an example. While the cost savings and specialization benefits of such a strategy seem clear, one must also consider the loss of control both for the firm and its customers that may result from such outsourcing.

Global Perspective

14.4
Logistics Collaboration

Federal Express Corporation and National Semiconductor have signed a logistics agreement under which Federal Express will be responsible for shipping all of National Semiconductor's global air express shipments. According to the agreement, Business Logistics Services, a unit of Federal Express, will handle all facets of National Semiconductor's air distribution operation, including pickup, line-haul, customs clearance, and delivery to the customer's dock. All deliveries will be made in two business days, regardless of destination.

Business Logistics Services, which has annual revenues between $500 million and $600 million, has been one of the fastest-growing divisions within Federal Express. The unit focuses on providing logistics and distribution services to customers who find it more economical to contract out the work rather than perform it in-house. In return, the logistics provider is guaranteed a set level of freight from the shipping customer. While the system can be more efficient, it does reduce the options of customers who wish to choose their own air express carriers.

Source: Mark B. Solomon, "National Semiconductor, FedEX Unit Ink Pact," *The Journal of Commerce*, October 23, 1992, p. B3

LOGISTICS AND THE ENVIRONMENT

Apart from the structure of the logistics function, major changes are also occurring in the strategic orientation of the function. The logistician plays an increasingly important role in allowing the firm to operate in an environmentally conscious way. Environmental laws, expectations, and self-imposed goals set by firms are difficult to adhere to without a logistics orientation that systematically takes these concerns into account. Since laws and regulations differ across the world, the firm's efforts need to be responsive to a wide variety of requirements. One new logistics orientation that has grown in importance due to environmental concerns is the development of **reverse distribution** systems. Such systems are instrumental in ensuring that the firm not only delivers the product to the market, but also can retrieve it from the market for subsequent use, recycling, or disposal. As Global Perspective 14.5 shows, to a growing degree, the ability to develop such reverse logistics is a key determinant for market acceptance and profitability.

Society is also beginning to recognize that retrieval should not be restricted to short-term consumer goods, such as bottles. Rather, it may be even more important to devise systems that enable the retrieval and disposal of long-term capital goods, such as cars, refrigerators, air conditioners, and industrial goods, with the least possible burden on the environment. The design of such long-term systems across the world may well be one of the key challenges and opportunities for the logistician and will require close collaboration with all other functions in the firm, such as design, production, and marketing.

On the transportation side, logistics managers will need to expand their involvement in carrier and routing selection. For example, for shippers of oil or other potentially hazardous materials, it will be increasingly expected to ensure that the carriers used have excellent safety records and use only double-hulled ships. Society may even expect corporate involvement in choosing the route that the shipment will travel, preferring routes that are far from ecologically important and sensitive zones.

Global Perspective

14.5
Environmental Impact on Logistics

Increasingly, countries pass laws that create environmental standards. A recent German law regulates packaging, a U.S. law levies taxes on certain chemicals destined for toxic-waste dumps, a law in Denmark requires that drinks be sold in refillable bottles, and a Canadian regulation requires deposits on beer bottles.

On the surface, it appears that these laws are a necessary and appropriate response to growing world concerns about the environment. Yet, these environmental standards may have been motivated at least in part by protectionistic reasons. For example, a provision of Germany's packaging law requires that at most, 28 percent of all beer and soft-drink containers can be "one-trip" (disposable). Importers suspect the provision was designed to benefit small German brewers who will find it easier to collect and refill the empties. Packagers also dislike the law's insistence that companies collect their used packaging for recycling. The fact that this will be easier for local manufacturers may prejudice retailers in favor of domestically produced goods.

Sources: "Free Trade's Green Hurdle," *Economist*, June 15, 1991, 61–62, and "Should Trade Go Green?" *Economist*, January 26, 1991, 13–14.

The logistics function will also need to consider trade-offs between firm-specific performance and the resulting environmental burden. For example, even though a just-in-time inventory system may connote highly desirable inventory savings, the resulting cost of frequent delivery, additional highway congestion, and incremental air pollution also need to be factored into the planning horizon. Despite the difficulty, firms will need to assert leadership in such trade-off considerations in order to provide society with a better quality of life.

SUMMARY

The relevance of international logistics was not widely recognized in the past. As competitiveness is becoming increasingly dependent on cost efficiency, however, the field is emerging as one of major importance, because international distribution accounts for between 10 and 25 percent of the total landed cost of an international order.

International logistics is concerned with the flow of materials into, through, and out of the international corporation and therefore includes materials management as well as physical distribution. The logistician must recognize the total systems demands of the firm in order to develop trade-offs between various logistics components.

International logistics differs from domestic activities in that it deals with greater distances, new variables, and greater complexity because of national differences. One major factor to consider is transportation. The international manager needs to understand transportation infrastructures in other countries and modes of transportation such as ocean shipping and airfreight. The choice among these modes will depend on the customer's demands and the firm's transit time, predictability, and cost requirements. In addition, noneconomic factors such as government regulations weigh heavily in this decision.

Inventory management is another major consideration. Inventories abroad are expensive to maintain yet often crucial for international success. The logistician must evaluate requirements for order cycle times and customer service levels in order to develop an international inventory policy that can also serve as a strategic management tool.

International packaging is important because it ensures arrival of the merchandise at the ultimate destination in safe condition. In developing packaging requirements, environmental conditions such as climate and handling conditions must be considered.

The logistics manager must also deal with international storage issues and determine where to locate inventories. International warehouse space will have to be leased or purchased and decisions made about utilizing foreign trade zones.

International logistics management is increasing in importance. Connecting the logistics function with overall corporate strategic concerns will increasingly be a requirement for successful global competitveness.

Key Terms and Concepts

materials management

physical distribution

systems concept

total cost concept

total after-tax profit concept

trade-off concept

transportation modes

logistics platforms

land bridges

sea bridges

intermodal movements

ocean shipping

liner service

bulk service

tramp service

container ships

ports

airfreight

density

transit time

reliability

preferential policies

bill of lading

straight bill of lading

shipper's order

commercial invoice

freight forwarders

Incoterms

ex-works (EXW)

free carrier (FCA)

free alongside ship (FAS)

free on board (FOB)

cost and freight (CFR)

cost, insurance, and freight (CIF)

delivery duty paid (DDP)

delivery duty unpaid (DDU)

inventory carrying costs

just-in-time inventory

inventory

order cycle time

customer service

location decision

foreign trade zones

reverse distribution

Questions for Discussion

1. Why do international firms pay so little attention to international logistics issues?

2. Contrast the use of ocean shipping and airfreight.

3. Explain the meaning and impact of transit time in international logistics.

4. How and why do governments interfere in "rational" freight carrier selection?

5. What is your view of the 40/40/20 freight allocation rule of the United Nations Conference on Trade and Development?

6. How can an international firm reduce its order cycle time?

7. Why should customer service levels differ internationally? Is it, for example, ethical to offer a lower customer service level in developing countries than in industrialized countries?

8. Given all the uncertainties in the international environment, is it worthwhile to attempt to model international logistics?

9. What role can the international logistician play in improving the environmental performance of the firm?

Recommended Readings

Ballou, Ronald H. *Business Logistics Management.* Englewood Cliffs, N.J.: Prentice-Hall, 1992.

Blanding, Warren. *Practical Handbook of Distribution/Customer Service, A Management Perspective.* Oakbrook, Ill.: Council of Logistics Management, 1988.

Christopher, Martin. *Logistics: The Strategic Issues.* New York, Chapman and Hall, 1992.

Kotabe, Masaaki. *Global Sourcing Strategy: R&D, Manufacturing and Marketing Interfaces.* New York: Quorum Books, 1992.

LaLonde, Bernard, Martha Cooper, and Thomas Noordewier. *Customer Service: A Third Party Perspective.* Oakbrook, Ill.: Council of Logistics Management, 1989.

Owen, Wilfried. *Transportation and World Development.* Baltimore, Md.: Johns Hopkins University Press, 1987.

Shapiro, Roy D., and James L. Heskett. *Logistics Strategy: Cases and Concepts.* St. Paul, Minn.: West, 1985.

Stephenson, Frederick J., Jr. *Transportation USA.* Reading, Mass.: Addison-Wesley, 1987.

Notes

1. John F. Magee, "The Logistics of Distribution," *Harvard Business Review* 38 (July–August 1960).
2. Robert E. McGarrah, "Logistics for the International Manufacturer," *Harvard Business Review* 44 (March–April 1966).
3. "Distribution's Vital Role," *Distribution* 79 (October 1980).
4. Dennis Davis, "New Involvement in the Orient," *Distribution* 78 (October 1979).
5. U.S. Department of Commerce, *Survey of Export Management Companies on the Export Trading Company Concept* (Washington, D.C.: Government Printing Office, 1977).
6. Rex R. Williams, "International Physical Distribution Management," in *Contemporary Physical Distribution and Logistics,* 4th ed., ed. James C. Johnson and Donald F. Wood (Tulsa, Okla.: Penwell Books, 1981), 150.

7. Paul T. Nelson and Gadi Toledano, "Challenges for International Logistics Management," *Journal of Business Logistics* 1 (No. 2, 1979): 7.
8. Ibid., 2.
9. Robert L. Vidrick, "Transportation Cost Control—The Key to Successful Exporting," *Distribution* 79 (March 1980).
10. William Armbruster, "W. German Ports Hope to Win East Bloc Trade," *The Journal of Commerce* (December 27, 1989): 1A.
11. Gunnar K. Sletmo and Jacques Picard, "International Distribution Policies and the Role of Air Freight," *Journal of Business Logistics* 6 (No. 1, 1984): 35-52.
12. Klaus Wittkamp, "Rickshaws for Taiwan or Cattle for China, It's All Air Freight," *The German Tribune,* June 26, 1983, 10.

13. *A Basic Guide to Exporting* (Washington, D.C.: U.S. Department of Commerce, 1986), 64.

14. Ibid.

15. Julie Wolf, "Help for Distribution in Europe," *Northeast International Business,* January 1989, 52,

16. Kevin Maloney, "Incoterms: Clarity at the Profit Margin," *Export Today* 6 (November–December 1990): 45–46.

17. Bernard J. LaLonde and Paul H. Zinszer, *Customer Service: Meaning and Measurement* (Chicago: National Council of Physical Distribution Management, 1976).

18. David A. Ricks, *International Dimensions of Corporate Finance* (Englewood Cliffs, N.J.: Prentice-Hall, 1978). '

19. Michael R. Czinkota, Harvey J. Iglarsh, Richard L. Seeley, and James Sood, "The Role of Order Cycle Time for the Latin American Exporting Firm" (presentation at the Annual Meeting of the Academy of International Business, New Orleans, La., October 21, 1980), 9.

20. Charles A. Taft, *Management of Physical Distribution and Transportation,* 7th ed. (Homewood, Ill.: Irwin, 1984), 324.

21. Ronald H. Ballou, *Basic Business Logistics* (Englewood Cliffs, N.J.: Prentice-Hall, 1978), 445.

22. Jacques Picard, "Physical Distribution Organization in Multinationals: The Position of Authority," *International Journal of Physical Distribution and Materials Management* 13 (No. 2, 1983): 24.

23. Philip B. Schary, *Logistics Decisions* (Hinsdale, Ill.: Dryden, 1984), 407.

International Marketing

LEARNING OBJECTIVES

1. To suggest how markets for international expansion can be selected, their demand assessed, and appropriate strategies for their development devised.

2. To describe how environmental differences generate new challenges for the international marketing manager.

3. To compare and contrast the merits of standardization versus localization strategies for country markets and of regional versus global marketing efforts.

4. To discuss market-specific and global challenges within each of the marketing functions: product, price, distribution, and promotion.

Thinking Globally, Profiting Locally

Constantly seeking out new international markets and waiting patiently for them to mature has always been the Loctite way. As far back as 1960, the company was generating some 20 percent of its sales abroad. Today its products are sold in more than 80 countries, and it has subsidiaries and joint ventures in more than 32 international locales. Nearly 60 percent of Loctite's $561 million in 1991 sales came from overseas, and foreign operations accounted for 80 percent of profits.

Loctite's international strategy is straightforward: it seeks out local partners, provides them with good margins, and commits itself to the long haul. Its Chinese operations, for example, took 10 years to turn a profit. Ideally, Loctite runs its foreign businesses as wholly owned subsidiaries, as it is doing in Argentina, Brazil, and Venezuela. Much depends on local custom and law. Some countries, such as India and Thailand, demand local ownership. In those cases, Loctite sets up a joint venture, often buying out its partner when the law changes. France is a good example. In the mid-1960s, with its British operations growing rapidly, Loctite joined forces with a French distributor, Francois Baur. As sales increased, Loctite bought a 50 percent interest in the company in 1986, and in 1990 it bought the rest to form what is today Loctite France. Baur continues to run the operation.

While its products are no different from one country to the next, Loctite lets local managers run their own shows. In controlling the marketing implementation, most of the headaches of doing business overseas are eliminated. Since the managers are local, they know the language and their way around their country's customs and laws. Product-related adjustments can also be handled. With labeling, for example, Loctite's plant in Ireland can just as easily produce tubes of adhesives for Britain or Israel, thanks to a computerized labeling system.

The company's philosophy is "not to have a huge headquarters staff—but to provide all the support and expertise possible on the local scene." The major role of headquarters is to provide strong strategic direction in international operations. Staff functions at headquarters are bolstered to promote a global flow of product information. One of these staff functions is the New Business Development group responsible for all research and new-product development. Loctite has divided the world outside the United States into three regions—Europe, Latin America, and the Pacific—each of which is managed by a regional vice president. Managers responsible for country operations report to their respective regional heads. The primary responsibilities of each country manager are to satisfy local customer needs, manage the growth of country-specific businesses, help cross-fertilize ideas, and execute global strategies.

Source: "Why Ignore 95% of the World's Market?" *Business Week/Reinventing America,* Fall 1992, 64; "How Loctite Prospers with 3-man Global HQ, Strong Country Managers," *Business International,* May 2, 1988, 129–130.

M arketing is the process of planning and executing the conception, pricing, promotion, and distribution of ideas, goods, and services to create exchanges that satisfy individual and organizational objectives.[1] The concepts of satisfaction and exchange are at the core of marketing. For an exchange to take place, two or more parties have to come together physically, through the mails, or through technology, and they must communicate and deliver things of perceived value. Customers should be perceived as information seekers who evaluate marketers' offerings in terms of their own drives and needs. When the offering is consistent with their needs, they tend to choose the product or service; if it is not, other alternatives are chosen. A key task of the marketer is to recognize the ever-changing nature of needs and wants. Marketing techniques apply not only to products but to ideas and services as well. Further, well over 50 percent of all marketing activities are business marketing—directed at other businesses, governmental entities, and various types of institutions.

The marketing manager's task is to plan and execute programs that will ensure a long-term competitive advantage for the company. This task has two integral parts: (1) the determining of specific target markets and (2) marketing management, which consists of manipulating marketing-mix elements to best satisfy the needs of the individual target markets. Regardless of geographic markets, these basic tasks do not vary; they have been called the technical universals of marketing.[2]

This chapter will focus on the formulation of marketing strategy for international operations. The first section describes target-market selection and how to identify pertinent characteristics of the various markets. The balance of the chapter is devoted to adjusting the elements of the marketing program to a particular market for maximum effectiveness and efficiency, while attempting to exploit global and regional similarities. The goal is to have the type of success Loctite has had in recent years, as described in the opening vignette.

TARGET-MARKET SELECTION

The process of target-market selection involves narrowing down potential country markets to a feasible number of countries and market segments within them. Rather than try to appeal to everyone, firms best utilize their resources by (1) identifying potential markets for entry and (2) expanding selectively over time to those deemed attractive.

Identification and Screening

A four-stage process for screening and analyzing foreign markets is presented in Figure 15.1. It begins with very general criteria and ends with product-specific market analyses. The data and the methods needed for decision making change from secondary to primary as the steps are taken in sequence. Although presented here as a screening process for choosing target markets, the process is also applicable to change of entry mode or even divestment.

If markets were similar in their characteristics, the international marketer could enter any one of the potential markets. However, differences between markets exist in three dimensions: physical, psychic, and economic.[3] Physical distance is the geographic distance between home and target countries; its impact has decreased as a result of recent technological developments. Psychic, or cultural, distance refers to differences in language, tradition, and customs between the two countries. Economic distance is created by differences in the economic environments of the host country and the target market. Generally, the greater the overall distance—or difference—between the two countries, the less knowledge the marketer has about the target market. The amount of information that is available varies dramatically. For example, although the marketer can easily learn about the economic environment from secondary sources, invaluable interpretive information may not be available until the firm actually operates in the market.

The four stages in the screening process are: preliminary screening, estimation of market potential, estimation of sales potential, and identification of segments.[4] Each stage should be given careful attention. The first stage, for example, should not merely reduce the number of alternatives to a manageable few for the sake of reduction, even though the expense of analyzing markets in depth is great. Unless care is taken, attractive alternatives may be eliminated.

Preliminary Screening   The preliminary screening process must rely chiefly on secondary data for country-specific factors as well as product- and industry-specific factors. Country-specific factors typically include those that would indicate the market's overall buying power; for example, population, gross national product in total and per capita, total exports and imports, and production of cement, electricity, and steel.[5] Product-specific factors narrow the analysis to the firm's specific areas of operation. A company such as Motorola, manufacturing for the automotive aftermarket, is interested in the number of passenger cars, trucks, and buses in use. These

FIGURE 15.1
The Screening Process
in Target-Market Choice

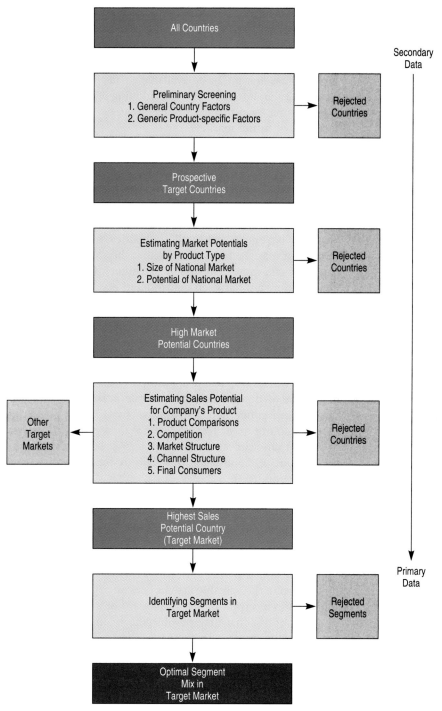

Source: Reprinted by permission of the publisher from *Entry Strategies for International Markets*, p. 34, by Franklin R. Root (Lexington, Mass.: Lexington Books, D.C. Heath & Co., Copyright 1990, D.C. Heath & Co.).

statistical analyses must be accompanied by qualitative assessments of the impact of cultural elements and the overall climate for foreign firms and products. A market that satisfies the levels set becomes a prospective target country.

Estimating Market Potential   Total market potential is the sales, in physical or monetary units, that might be available to all firms in an industry during a given period under a given level in industry-marketing effort and given environmental conditions.[6] The international marketer needs to assess the size of existing markets and forecast the size of future markets.

Because of the lack of resources, and frequently the lack of data, market potentials are often estimated using secondary data–based analytical techniques.[7] These techniques focus on or utilize demand patterns, income-elasticity measurements, multiple-factor indexes, estimation by analogy, and input-output analysis.

Demand pattern analysis indicates typical patterns of growth and decline in manufacturing. At early stages of growth, for example, manufacturing is concentrated in food, beverage, and textile industries, and some light industry. An awareness of trends in manufacturing will enable the marketer to estimate potential markets for input, such as raw materials or machinery. **Income elasticity of demand** describes the relationship between demand and economic progress as indicated by growth in income. The share of income spent on necessities will provide both an estimate of the market's level of development and an approximation of how much money is left for other purchases.

Multiple-factor indexes measure market potential indirectly by using proxy variables that have been shown (either through research or intuition) to correlate closely with the demand for the particular product. An index for consumer goods might involve population, disposable personal income, and retail sales in the market or area concerned. **Estimation by analogy** is used when data for a particular market do not exist. The market size for a product in country A is estimated by comparing a ratio for an available indicator (such as disposable income) for country A and country B, and using this ratio in conjunction with detailed market data available for country B.

Finally, **input-output analysis** provides a method of estimating market potentials, especially in the industrial sector. Input-output tables provide a summary of the structure of an economy by showing the impact of changes in the demand for one industry's products on other industries' products. Using these tables and combining them with economic projections, the international marketer can estimate the volume demanded by the various sectors of the economy.

Despite the valuable insight generated through these techniques, caution should be used in interpreting the results. All of these quantitative techniques are based on historical data that may be obsolete or inapplicable because of differences in cultural and geographic traits of the market. Further, with today's technological developments, lags between markets are no longer at a level that would make all of the measurements valid. Moreover, the measurements look at a market as an aggregate; that is, no regional differences are taken into account. In an industrialized country like Sweden, the richest 10 percent of the population receives 20 percent of the income, while the respective income figures for the richest 10 percent in the middle-income countries such as Brazil (46 percent) and low-income countries such as Sri-Lanka (43 percent) are much higher.[8] Therefore, even in the developing countries with low GNP figures, segments exist with buying power rivaled only in the richest developed countries.

In addition to these quantitative techniques that rely on secondary data, international marketers can use various survey techniques. They are especially useful

Income Distribution: A Factor in Evaluating Market Potential

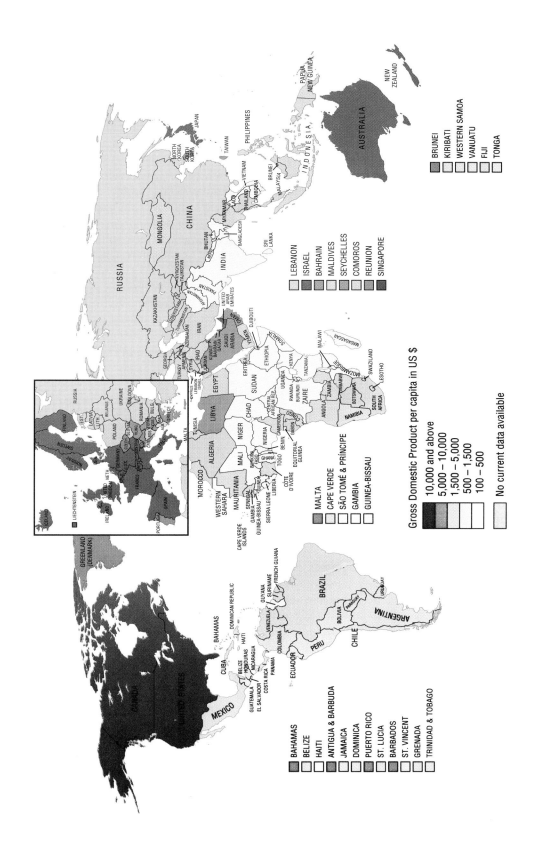

Gross Domestic Product per capita in US $

10,000 and above
5,000 – 10,000
1,500 – 5,000
500 – 1,500
100 – 500

No current data available

Source: *The World Factbook 1992.*

when marketing new technologies. A survey of end-user interest and responses may provide a relatively clear picture of the possibilities in a new market.

Comparing figures for market potential with actual sales will provide the international marketer with further understanding of his or her firm's chances in the market. If the difference between potential and reality is substantial, the reasons can be evaluated using **gap analysis.** The differences can be the result of usage, distribution, or product-line gaps.[9] If the firm is already in the market, part of the difference between its sales and the market potential can be explained through the competitive gap. Usage gaps indicate that not all potential users are using the product or that those using it are not using as much as they could, which suggests mainly a promotional task. Distribution gaps indicate coverage problems, which may be vertical (not enough regions) or horizontal (if the product is not marketed as well as it could be). Product-line gaps typically suggest latent demand. An emerging trend in which Japanese consumers want to acquire an American look will help drive sales for companies like Ralph Lauren, L. L. Bean, and Northeastern Log Homes.

Estimating Sales Potential   Even when the international marketer has gained an understanding of markets with the greatest overall promise, the firm's own possibilities in those markets are still not known. Sales potential is the share of the market potential that the firm can reasonably expect to get over the longer term. To arrive at an estimate, the marketer needs to collect product- and market-specific data. These will have to do with:

1. Competition—strength, likely reaction to entry.
2. Market—strength of barriers.
3. Consumers—ability and willingness to buy.
4. Product—degree of relative advantage, compatibility, complexity, trialability, and communicability.
5. Channel structure—access to retail level.

The marketer's questions can never be fully answered until the firm has made a commitment to enter the market and is operational. The mode of entry has special significance in determining the firm's sales potential.[10]

Identifying Segments   Within the markets selected, individuals and organizations will vary in their wants, resources, geographical locations, buying attitudes, and buying practices. Initially, the firm may cater to one or only a few segments and later expand to others, especially if the product is innovative. Segmentation is indicated when segments are indeed different enough to warrant individualized attention, are large enough for profit potential, and can be reached through the methods that the international marketer wants to use.

Once the process is complete for a market or group of markets, the international marketer may begin again for another one. When growth potential is no longer in market development, the firm may opt for market penetration.

Concentration versus Diversification

Choosing a market expansion policy involves the allocation of effort among various markets. The major alternatives are **concentration** on a small number of markets or **diversification,** which is characterized by growth in a relatively large number of markets in the early stages of international market expansion.[11]

	Factor	Diversification	Concentration
TABLE 15.1 Factors Affecting the Choice between Concentration and Diversification Strategies	Market growth rate	Low	High
	Sales stability	Low	High
	Sales response function	Concave	S Curve
	Competitive lead time	Short	Long
	Spillover effects	High	Low
	Need for product adaptation	Low	High
	Need for communication adaption	Low	High
	Economics of scale in distribution	Low	High
	Extent of constraints	Low	High
	Program control requirements	Low	High

Source: Igal Ayal and Jehiel Zif, "Marketing Expansion Strategies in Multinational Marketing," *Journal of Marketing* 43 (Spring 1979): 89.

Expansion Alternatives   Either concentration or diversification is applicable to market segments or to total markets, depending on the resource commitment the international marketer is willing and able to make. One option is a dual-concentration strategy, in which efforts are focused on a few segments in a limited number of countries. Another is a dual-diversification strategy, in which entry is to most segments in most available markets. The first is a likely strategy for small firms or firms that market specialized products to clearly definable markets, for example, ocean-capable sailing boats. The second is typical for large consumer-oriented companies that have sufficient resources for broad coverage. Market concentration/segment diversification opts for a limited number of markets but for wide coverage within them, putting emphasis on company acceptance. Market diversification/segment concentration usually involves the identification of a segment, possibly worldwide, to which the company can market without major changes in its marketing mix.

Factors Affecting Expansion Strategy   Expansion strategy is determined by the market-, mix-, and company-related factors listed in Table 15.1. In most cases, the factors are interrelated.

Market-Related Factors   These factors are the ones that were influential in determining the attractiveness of the market in the first place. In the choice of expansion strategy, demand for the firm's products is a critical factor. With high and stable growth rates in certain markets, the firm will most likely opt for a concentration strategy. If the demand is strong worldwide, diversification may be attractive.

A forecast of the sales response function can be used to predict sales at various levels of marketing expenditure. Two general response functions exist: concave and S curve. When the function is concave, sales will increase at a decreasing rate because of competition and a lowering adoption rate. This function might involve a unique, innovative product or marketing program. An S-curve function assumes that viable market share can be achieved only through sizable marketing efforts. This is typical for new entrants to well-established markets.

The uniqueness of the firm's offering with respect to competition is also a factor in the expansion strategy. If lead time over competition is considerable, the decision to diversify may not seem urgent. Complacency can be a mistake in today's competitive environment, however; competitors can rush new products into the market in a matter of days.

Global Perspective

15.1
American Takes on the World

By the year 2000, American Airlines aims to generate about 30 percent of its revenues from foreign routes, up from virtually nothing in 1980. To reach this ambitious goal, a total of $11 billion—more than half of American's capital-spending budget—has been committed to expanding and upgrading international operations.

To stay on top, company executives believe that now is the time to accelerate expansion into overseas markets. The most compelling reason is that air traffic in the U.S. market is expected to grow merely 3 percent to 4 percent over the next decade compared with much quicker increases abroad—6 percent to 7 percent in Europe and Latin America and 8 percent to 9 percent in Asia. It is also quite evident that entry into foreign markets, already a tortuous process, will become harder as time goes by. Carriers from the EC may exert more pressure to keep out U.S. airlines after the unified market is forged in 1992. In addition, air traffic congestion will limit opportunities for newcomers in Japan and key European cities.

Since permission to fly between countries is granted only after bilateral negotiations, some of the hotly contested markets, such as New York–London, are difficult to penetrate. Although American has purchased some prime routes from other carriers (such as the Chicago-to-London route from TWA), the airline is breaking up the traditional system of flying big planes across the Atlantic from one international city, like New York, to another, like London or Paris. Instead, it gathers a smaller number of passengers from cities like Des Moines and Indianapolis and funnels them through hubs such as Chicago to less-congested cities like Glasgow or Brussels. The trans-Atlantic flights are on more fuel-efficient planes, such as the Boeing 767–300ER.

American's entry into Latin America was made possible through the purchase of Eastern's Latin American route system, which connects 20 cities in 15 Central and South American countries—a move that made American a major player in that market overnight. Entry into the lucrative markets of the Pacific Basin has been far more tentative. The problem is that about half of all trans-Pacific traffic is destined for Japan, and American has been able to secure only a very few of these routes.

Strategic alliances form an integral part of American's effort to be more competitive. In early 1993, American announced a joint marketing pact with America West Airlines which will result in America West feeding passengers into American's trans-Pacific and transcontinental routes. Similarly, American is spending $191 million for a share in Canadian Airlines.

Just as critical is the internal marketing adjustment of the internationalization effort. This calls for flexibility in coping with brand new situations in places like Latin America and Asia and retraining to provide the better service demanded by international fliers. Some changes are universal, such as providing quick, simple executive meals for business fliers, who want to eat soon after takeoff and then sleep or work undisturbed the rest of the way. Some services are adjusted to national preferences. German passengers, for example, are very particular about the use of formal titles when addressed by attendants. Japanese customers abhor being touched. On flights carrying Latin American passengers, the main course is likely to be beef, and the wines better be French.

AMR, American's parent, is also poised to take advantage of international markets. AMR has agreed to manage the Warsaw airport for the Polish government, train computer programmers at Aeroflot (the major Russian airline), and teach English among other things to employees of Turkish Airlines. Furthermore, AMR's greatest opportunities come from exploiting its powerful SABRE computer reservations system, which is the world's largest privately owned, real-time network.

Sources: "Course Correction," *The Wall Street Journal,* February 18, 1993, 1, 6; Carla Rapoport, "Hard Choices," *Fortune,* December 14, 1992, 144–149; Michael Oneal, "Dog Fight: United and American Battle for Global Supremacy," *Business Week,* January 21, 1991, 56–60; and Kenneth Labich, "American Takes on the World," *Fortune,* September 24, 1990, 68–73.

In many product categories marketers will be, knowingly or unknowingly, affected by spillover effects. Consider, for example, the impact that satellite channels have had on advertising in Europe, where ads for a product now reach most of the western European market. Where geographic (and psychic) distances are short, spillover is likely, and marketers are most likely to diversify.

Governmental constraints—or the threat of them—can be a powerful motivator in a firm's expansion. As seen in Global Perspective 15.1, anticipated restrictions both in Europe and in Japan are accelerating American Airlines' entry into new markets.

Mix-Related Factors These factors relate to the degree to which marketing-mix elements—primarily product, promotion, and distribution—can be standardized. The more that standardization is possible, the more diversification is indicated. Overall savings through economies of scale can then be utilized in marketing efforts.

Depending on the product, each market will have its own challenges. Whether constraints are apparent (such as tariffs) or hidden (such as tests or standards), they will complicate all of the other factors. Nevertheless, regional integration has allowed many marketers to diversify their efforts.

Company-Related Factors These include the objectives set by the company for its international operations and the policies it adopts in those markets. As an example, the firm may require—either by stated policy or because of its products—extensive interaction with intermediaries and clients. When this is the case, the firm's efforts will likely be concentrated because of resource constraints.

MARKETING MANAGEMENT	After target markets are selected, the next step is the determination of marketing efforts at appropriate levels. A key question in international marketing concerns the extent to which the elements of the marketing mix—product, price, place, and distribution—should be standardized. The marketer also faces the specific challenges of adjusting each of the mix elements in the international marketplace.

Standardization versus Adaptation

The international marketer must first decide what modifications in the mix policy are needed or warranted. Three basic alternatives in approaching international markets are available:

1. Make no special provisions for the international marketplace but, rather, identify potential target markets and then choose products that can easily be marketed with little or no modification.
2. Adapt to local conditions in each and every target market (the multidomestic approach).
3. Incorporate differences into a regional or global strategy that will allow for local differences in implementation (globalization approach).

In today's environment, standardization usually means cross-national strategies rather than a policy of viewing foreign markets as secondary and therefore not important enough to have products adapted for them. Ideally, the international marketer should think globally and act locally,[12] focusing on neither extreme: full standardization or full localization. Global thinking requires flexibility in exploiting good ideas and products on a worldwide basis.

The question of whether to standardize or to custom tailor marketing programs in each country has continued to trouble practitioners and academics alike and has produced many and varied opinions. In the 1960s, Robert Buzzell stated that it depends on the strengths of the barriers to standardization, such as national differences in consumer preferences and legal restrictions, and on the potential payoffs of standardizing marketing strategy.[13] Studies on how firms view standardization have found that arguments in favor of standardizing whenever possible fall into two categories: better marketing performance and lower marketing cost.[14] Factors that encourage standardization or adaptation are summarized in Table 15.2

The World-Customer Controversy   The world customer[15] identified by Ernest Dichter more than 20 years ago has gained new meaning with Theodore Levitt's suggestion that inexpensive air travel and new technologies have led consumers the world over to think and shop increasingly alike.[16] In addition, Kenichi Ohmae has identified a new group of consumers that is emerging in a triad composed of the United States, Japan, and western Europe. Marketers can treat the triad as a single market with the same spending habits.[17] Approximately 600 million in number, these consumers have similar educational backgrounds, income levels, lifestyles, use of leisure time, and aspirations. One reason given for the similarities in their consumer demand is a level of purchasing power that is ten times greater than that of less developed countries (LDCs) or newly industrialized countries (NICs). This translates into higher diffusion rates for certain products. Another reason is that developed infrastructures—ownership of telephones and an abundance of paved roads—lead to attractive markets for other products. Products can be designed to meet similar demand conditions throughout the triad. Whirlpool, after conducting consumer research throughout Europe, entered the fast-growing microwave market with a product that offered various product features with different appeal in different countries clearly targeted at the Euroconsumer.[18]

Even companies that are famous for following the same methods worldwide that they follow domestically have made numerous changes in their marketing programs, however. For instance, McDonald's serves abroad the same menu of hamburgers, soft drinks, and other foods it does in the United States, and the restaurants look the same. But in Japan, Ronald McDonald is called Donald McDonald because it is easier to pronounce. Menu adjustments include beer in Germany and wine in France. Of course, similar situations may occur in domestic markets; for example, U.S. fast-food restaurants in the South offer iced tea, but those in the Northeast do not.

Globalization   Globalization is a business initiative based on the belief that the world is becoming more homogenous; further, distinctions between national markets are not only fading but, for some products, will eventually disappear. As a result, com-

---

**TABLE 15.2
Standardization versus
Adaptation**

Factors Encouraging Standardization
- Economies in product R & D
- Economies of scale in production
- Economies in marketing
- Control of marketing programs
- "Shrinking" of the world marketplace

Factors Encouraging Adaptation
- Differing use conditions
- Government and regulatory influences
- Differing buyer behavior patterns
- Local initiative and motivation in implementation
- Adherence to the marketing concept

panies need to globalize their international strategy by formulating it across country markets to take advantage of underlying market, cost, environmental, and competitive factors.[19]

About 20 percent of large U.S. corporations now consider themselves global marketers.[20] Companies such as Coca-Cola and Levi Strauss have proven that universal appeal exists. Coke's "one sight, one sound, one sell" approach is a legend among global marketers. Other companies have some "world products" and some products that are not. If cultural and competitive differences are less important than similarities, a single advertising approach can exploit the similarities to stimulate sales everywhere. This can be done at far lower cost than if campaigns were developed for each market.

Globalization differs from the multidomestic approach in these three basic ways:

1. The global approach looks for similarities between markets. The multidomestic approach ignores similarities.

2. The global approach actively seeks homogeneity in products, image, marketing, and advertising message. The multidomestic approach results in unnecessary differences from market to market.

3. The global approach asks, "Is this product or process suitable for world consumption?" The multidomestic approach, relying solely on local autonomy, never asks the question.[21]

In a globalization strategy, marketing is typically the most "localized" of the business functions. Even within marketing, however, differences exist in mix elements and between companies. Elements that are strategic—such as positioning—are more easily globalized, while tactical elements—such as sales promotions—are typically determined locally. A comparison of the marketing-mix elements of two multinational companies is given in Table 15.3. Notice that adaptation is present even at Coca-Cola, which is acknowledged to be one of the world's most global marketers. The key is the worldwide use of good ideas rather than absolute standardization of all facets of the marketing programs, as seen in Global Perspective 15.2.

Globalization, by definition, means the centralization of decision making. Changes in philosophy concerning local autonomy are delicate issues, and the "not invented here" syndrome may become a problem. It can be solved by utilizing various motivational policies:

TABLE 15.3
Globalization of the Marketing Mix by Two Multinational Companies—Coca-Cola and Nestlé

Marketing Mix Elements	Adaptation		Standardization	
	Full	Partial	Partial	Full
Product design			N	C
Brand name			N	C
Product positioning		N		C
Packaging			C/N	
Advertising theme		N		C
Pricing		N	C	
Advertising copy	N			C
Distribution	N	C		
Sales promotion	N	C		
Customer service	N	C		

Key: C = Coca-Cola; N = Nestlé

Source: John A. Quelch and Edward J. Hoff, "Customizing Global Marketing," *Harvard Business Review,* May–June 1986 (Boston: Harvard Business School Publishing Division), 61.

Global Perspective

15.2
It Played in Phon Phaeng . . . and Peoria, Too

Executing an advertising campaign in multiple markets requires a balance between conveying the message and allowing for local nuances. The localization of global ideas can be achieved by using a modular approach, localizing international symbols, and using international advertising agencies.

In 1989, McCann-Erickson Worldwide developed a dozen global ads, of which half were adapted for domestic TV. An estimated two billion people in nearly 100 nations saw the ads. To adapt the global ads to the U.S. market, some shots of bottles (which are more popular overseas) were replaced by shots of cans. And "Coke," the name the original formula carries in most countries, was changed to "Coke Classic."

Language differences present a challenge to global campaigns. Translation is rarely used; what copywriters in individual markets try to do is convey the common idea in the message. The worldwide theme, "Can't Beat the Feeling," was "I Feel Coke," in Japan, "Unique Sensation," in Italy, and "Feeling of Life" in Chile. In Germany, where no translation really worked, the original English-language theme was used.

Blueprint advertising, which uses the same theme throughout the world but adjusts to local variations, is a major factor in global advertising strategy. The frames displayed are from a set of 14 developed by McCann for its client. The U.S. set featured former Pittsburgh Steeler "Mean Joe" Greene, while local sports celebrities were used elsewhere. They included soccer stars Niwat in Thailand (shown) and Diego Maradona in many Latin American markets.

Source: Maj-Lis Tanner, "Pan-Eurooppalainen Mainonta Lisaantyy," *Optio,* March 26, 1992; "Coke Spins the Same Sell All Around the World," *USA Today,* December 29, 1988; "Global Marketing Campaigns with a Local Touch," *Business International,* July 4, 1988, 205–210; and Anne B. Fisher, "The Ad Biz Gloms onto 'Global,'" *Fortune,* November 12, 1984, 77. Photos courtesy of The Coca-Cola Company/McCann-Erickson Worldwide.

1. Encourage local managers to generate ideas.
2. Ensure that local managers participate in the development of marketing strategies and programs for global brands.
3. Maintain a product portfolio that includes local as well as regional and global brands.
4. Allow local managers control over their marketing budgets so they can respond to local consumer needs and counter local competition.[22]

Finding the balance between overglobalizing and underglobalizing is indeed difficult. While the benefits of cost reduction and improved quality and competitiveness of products and programs are attractive, there are pitfalls that can leave the marketing effort catering to no one.[23] For example, Lego A/S, the Danish toy manufacturer, tried American-style consumer promotions, which had proven highly successful in North America, unaltered in Japan. Subsequent research showed that Japanese consumers considered them wasteful, expensive, and not very appealing.

Some firms approach markets regionally, and some have bridged local and global strategies through a regionalization policy.[24] As an example, Colgate-Palmolive considered using a "one sight, one sound" approach and hiring one advertising agency for all brands. Eventually management settled on a regional approach, with one agency in Europe, another in Asia, and another for Latin America.

Factors Affecting Adaptation   Even when marketing programs are based on highly standardized ideas and strategies, they depend on three sets of variables: (1) the market(s) targeted, (2) the product and its characteristics, and (3) company characteristics, including factors such as resources and policy.[25]

Questions of adaptation have no easy answers. Marketers in many firms rely on decision-support systems to aid in program adaptation, while others consider every situation independently. All products must, of course, conform to environmental conditions over which the marketer has no control. Further, the international marketer may use adaptation to enhance its competitiveness in the marketplace.

Product Policy

Products or services form the core of the firm's international operations. Its success depends on how well products satisfy needs and wants and how well they are differentiated from those of the competition. This section will focus on product and product-line adaptation to foreign markets as well as product counterfeiting as a current problem facing international marketers.

Factors in Product Adaptation   Factors affecting product adaptation to foreign market conditions are summarized in Figure 15.2. The changes vary from minor ones, such as translation of a user's manual, to major ones, such as a more economical version of the product. Many of the factors have an impact on product selection as well as product adaptation for a given market.

A detailed examination of 174 consumer-packaged goods destined for developing countries showed that, on the average, 4.1 changes per product were made in terms of brand name, packaging, measurement units, labeling, constituents, product features, and usage instructions. Only one out of ten products was transferred without modification. Some of the changes were mandatory, some discretionary.[26]

Regional, Country, or Local Characteristics   Typically, the market environment mandates the majority of product modifications. However, the most stringent requirements often result from government regulations. Some of the requirements may serve no purpose other than a political one (such as protection of domestic industry or response to political pressures). Because of the sovereignty of nations, individual firms must comply, but they can influence the situation by lobbying directly or through industry associations to have the issue raised during trade negotiations. Government regulations may be spelled out, but firms need to be ever vigilant for

FIGURE 15.2   Factors Affecting Product-Adaptation Decisions

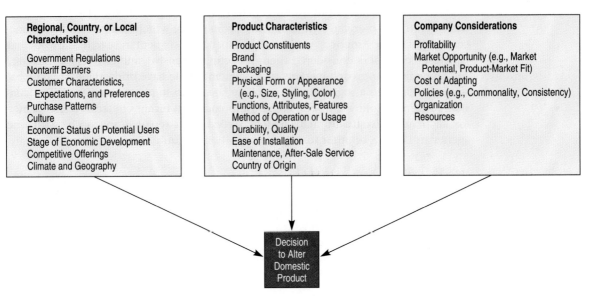

Source: V. Yorio, *Adapting Products for Export* (New York: The Conference Board, 1983), 7.

changes and exceptions. The 19 member countries of the European Economic Area are imposing standards in more than 10,000 product categories ranging from toys to tractor seats. While companies like Murray Manufacturing have had to change their products to comply with these standards (in Murray's case making its lawn-mowers quieter), they will be able to produce one European product in the future. Overall, U.S. producers may be forced to improve quality of all their products be-cause some product rules require adoption of an overall system approved by the In-ternational Standards Organization (ISO).[27]

Product decisions made by marketers of consumer products are especially af-fected by local behavior, tastes, attitudes, and traditions—all reflecting the marketer's need to gain the customer's approval. A knowledge of cultural and psychological dif-ferences may be the key to success. For example, Brazilians rarely eat breakfast; there-fore Dunkin' Donuts markets doughnuts as snacks, as dessert, and for parties. To fur-ther appeal to Brazilians, doughnuts are made with local fruit fillings like papaya and guava.

Often no concrete product changes are needed, only a change in the product's **positioning.** Positioning in the perception by consumers of the firm's brand in re-lation to competitor's brands; that is, the mental image a brand, or the company as a whole, evokes. Coca-Cola took a risk in marketing Diet Coke in Japan because the population in not overweight by Western standards. Further, Japanese women do not like to drink anything clearly labeled as a diet product. The company changed the name to Coke Light and subtly shifted the promotional theme from "weight loss" to "figure maintenance."

Nontariff barriers include product standards, testing or approval procedures, sub-sidies for local products, and bureaucratic red tape. The nontariff barriers affecting product adjustments usually concern elements outside the core product. For example, France requires the use of the French language "in any offer, presentation, advertisement, written or spoken, instructions for use, specification or guarantee terms for goods or services, as well as for invoices and receipts." Because nontariff barriers are usually in place to keep foreign products out or to protect domestic producers, getting around them may be the single toughest problem for the international marketer.

The monitoring of competitors' product features, as well as determining what has to be done to meet and beat them, is critical to product-adaptation decisions. Competitive offerings may provide a baseline against which resources can be measured—for example, they may help to determine what it takes to reach a critical market share in a given competitive situation. American Hospital Supply, a Chicago-based producer of medical equipment, adjusts its product in a preemptive way by making products that are hard to duplicate. As a result, the firm increased sales and earnings in Japan about 40 percent a year over a 10-year period.

Product decisions are affected by cultural variables discussed in Chapter 9. Reflecting the social, political, and religious heritage of the country, culture often presents the most difficult variable for any company to change. An example is the experience of the Coca-Cola Company when it introduced Mellow Yellow in Thailand. Because "yellow" in Thai means "pus," the name was shortened to Mello.[28]

Management must take into account the stage of economic development of the overseas market. As a country's economy advances, buyers are in a better position to buy and to demand more sophisticated products and product versions. On the other hand, the situation in some developing markets may require **backward innovation;** that is, the market may require a drastically simplified version of the firm's product because of lack of purchasing power or of usage conditions. Economic conditions may affect packaging decisions. For example, Pillsbury packages its products in six- and eight-serving sizes for developing-country markets, while the most popular size in the North American market is two servings.[29]

The target market's physical separation from the host country and its climatic conditions will usually have an effect on the total product offering: the core product; tangible elements, mainly packaging; and the augmented features. The international marketer must consider two sometimes-contradictory aspects of packaging. On the one hand, the product itself has to be protected against longer transit times and possibly longer shelf life. On the other hand, care has to be taken not to use proscribed preservatives. Initial attempts to sell Colombian guava paste in the United States were not successful because the original packaging could not withstand the longer distribution channels and the longer time required for distribution.

Product Characteristics   Product characteristics are the inherent features of the product offering, whether actual or perceived. The inherent characteristics of products, and the benefits they provide to consumers in the various markets in which they are marketed, make certain products good candidates for standardization—and others not.

The international marketer has to make sure that products do not contain ingredients that might violate legal requirements or religious or social customs. DEP Corporation, a Los Angeles manufacturer with $19 million in annual sales of hair and skin products, takes particular pains to make sure that no Japan-bound products contain formaldehyde, an ingredient commonly used in the United States, but illegal in Japan.[30] Where religion or custom determines consumption, ingredients may have to be replaced for the product to be acceptable. In Islamic countries, for example, vegetable shortening has to be substituted for animal fats.

Packaging is an area where firms generally do make modifications.[31] Because of the longer time that products spend in channels of distribution, international companies, especially those marketing food products, have used more expensive packaging materials and/or more expensive transportation modes for export shipments. Food processors have solved the problem by using airtight, reclosable containers that seal out moisture and other contaminants.

The promotional aspect of packaging relates primarily to labeling. The major adjustments concern legally required bilinguality, as in Canada (French and English), Belgium (French and Flemish), and Finland (Finnish and Swedish). Other governmental requirements include more informative labeling of products for consumer protection and education. Inadequate identification, failure to use the required languages, or inadequate or incorrect descriptions printed on the labels may all cause problems. Increasingly, environmental concerns are impacting on packaging decisions, as seen in Global Perspective 15.3.

Brand names convey the image of the product or service. The term *brand* refers to a name, term, symbol, sign, or design used by a firm to differentiate its offerings from those of its competitors. Offhand, brands may seem to be one of the most standardizable items in the product offering. However, the establishment of worldwide brands is difficult; how can a marketer of consumer products establish world brands when the firm sells 800 products in more than 200 countries and most of them under different names? This is the situation of Gillette. A typical example is Silkience hair conditioner, which is sold as Soyance in France, Sientel in Italy, and Silkience in Germany. Standardizing the name to reap promotional benefits is difficult because

Global Perspective

15.3
Thinking Green in Packaging

Pan-European marketers are keeping a watchful eye on a European directive that is expected to be approved of by the EC Council of Ministers. Under the EC directive, within five years 60 percent of packaging waste by weight has to be recoverable for recycling or other uses and 90 percent within 10 years. In anticipation, marketers are repackaging and launching more environmentally friendly line extensions of their brands. For example, Procter & Gamble is selling its Ariel liquid detergent in plastic bottles and refill pouches containing 25 percent recycled material in some European markets.

Germany has already enacted an even tougher law that has marketers scrambling to set up a national recycling program to avoid triggering a provision that would require all consumer-goods packages to be returned to the source. Germany's consumer-goods marketers, retailers, and the packaging industry have banded together to form a com-

pany to collect, sort, and recycle empty packaging throughout the country. Members, including Procter & Gamble and Unilever, will display Green Dot emblems on their recyclable packaging.

Each German household will be issued a special yellow garbage can to dispose of packaging from Green Dot products. To fund the nonprofit system's waste-disposal activities, all companies using the Green Dot will pay a volume-based levy amounting to, for example, less than 2 cents for a small 200-to-300-milliliter bottle. The program aims to be nationwide by 1995.

To aid environmentally aware consumers and encourage producers to cater to them, the World Wildlife Fund has certified a variety of products as "environmentally safe," among them Wonder low-mercury batteries, LeChat machine detergent from Henkel, and recyclable yogurt containers from Dany and Danone.

Source: Dagmar Mussey and Juliana Koranteng, "Packaging Strict Green Rules," *Advertising Age,* December 2, 1991, S-4; and Alain Laufenburger, "The Greening of Western Europe," *Export Today* 7(January 1991): 9.

names have become established in each market, and the action would lead to objections from local managers.

In some markets, brand-name changes are required by the government. In Korea, unnecessary foreign words are barred from use; for example, Sprite has been renamed Kin. The same situation has emerged in Mexico, where the reason for local branding is primarily to control the marketing leverage that foreign companies would have with a universal brand.

Adjustments in product styling, color, size, and other appearance features are more common in consumer marketing than in industrial marketing. Color plays an important role in how consumers perceive a product, and marketers must be aware of what signal their product's color is sending. Color can be used for brand identification—for example, the yellow of Hertz, red of Avis, and green of National. It can be used for feature reinforcement; for example, Rolls-Royce uses a dazzling silver paint that spells luxury. Colors communicate in a subtle way in developed societies, whereas they have direct meaning in more traditional societies.

The product offered in the domestic market may not be operable in the foreign market. One of the major differences faced by appliance manufacturers is electrical power systems. In some cases, variations may exist within a country, such as Brazil. An exporter can find out about these differences through local government regulations or various trade publications such as *Electric Current Abroad,* published by the U.S. Department of Commerce. Some companies have adjusted their products to operate in different systems; for example, VCR equipment can be adjusted to record and play back on different color systems.

When a product that is sold internationally requires repairs, parts, or service, the problems of obtaining, training, and holding a sophisticated engineering or repair staff are not easy to solve. If the product breaks down, and the repair arrangements are not up to standard, the product image will suffer. In some cases, products abroad may not even be used for their intended purpose and may thus require not only modifications in product configuration but also in service frequency. For instance, snowplows exported from the United States are used to remove sand from driveways in Saudi Arabia.

The country of origin of a product, typically communicated by the phrase "made in (country)," has considerable influence on quality perceptions. The perception of products manufactured in certain countries is affected by a built-in positive or negative assumption about quality. One study of machine-tool buyers found that the United States and Germany were rated higher than Japan, with Brazil rated below all three of them.[32] These types of findings indicate that steps must be taken by the international marketer to overcome or at least neutralize biases. This issue is especially important to developing countries, which need to increase exports, and for importers who source products from countries different from where they are sold.[33]

Company Considerations   Company policy will often determine the presence and degree of adaptation. Discussions of product adaptation often end with the question, "Is it worth it?" The answer depends on the company's ability to control costs, to correctly estimate market potential and, finally, to secure profitability. The decision to adapt should be preceded by a thorough analysis of the market. Formal market research with primary data collection and/or testing is warranted. From the financial standpoint, some companies have specific return-on-investment levels (for example, 25 percent) to be satisfied before adaptation. Others let the requirement vary as a function of the market considered and also the time in the market—that is, profitability may be initially compromised for proper market entry.

Most companies aim for consistency in their market efforts. This means that all products must fit in terms of quality, price, and user perceptions. Consistency may be difficult to attain in, for example, the area of warranties. Warranties can be uniform only if use conditions do not vary drastically and if the company is able to deliver equally on its promise anywhere it has a presence.

Product-Line Management   International marketers' product lines consist of local, regional, and global brands. In a given market an exporter's product line, typically shorter than domestically, concentrates on the most profitable products. Product lines may vary dramatically from one market to another depending on the extent of the firm's operations. Some firms at first cater only to a particular market segment and eventually expand to cover an entire market. For example, Japanese auto manufacturers moved into the highly profitable luxury car segment after establishing a strong position in the world small-car segment.[34]

The domestic market is not the only source of new-product ideas for the international marketer, nor is it the only place where they are developed.[35] Some products may be developed elsewhere for worldwide consumption because of an advantage in skills, for example. Mazda, which is 25 percent owned by Ford, has designed and engineered cars to be produced by others in the Ford empire. Ford Motor Co. of Australia Ltd. developed a two-seater, sports-style specialty car because of its expertise in low-volume production.[36] In fact, many firms have benefited greatly from subsidiaries' local or regional product lines when demand conditions changed in the domestic market to favor new product characteristics. U.S. car manufacturers, for example, have used products from their European operations to compete in the small-sized and sports-style segments.

Sensitivity to local tastes has to also be reflected in the company's product line. In Brazil, Levi Strauss developed the Femina line of jeans exclusively for women there, who prefer ultratight jeans. However, what is learned in one market can often be adopted in another. Levi's line of chino pants and casual wear originated in the company's Argentine unit and was applied to loosely cut pants by its Japanese subsidiary. The company's U.S. operation adopted both in 1986, and the line generated $550 million in North American revenues in 1990.[37]

Product Counterfeiting   About $20 billion in domestic and export sales are estimated to be lost by U.S. companies annually because of product counterfeiting and trademark patent infringement of consumer and industrial products. Counterfeit goods are any goods bearing an unauthorized representation of a trademark, patented invention, or copyrighted work that is legally protected in the country where it is marketed.

The practice of product counterfeiting has spread to high technology and services from the traditionally counterfeited products: high-visibility, strong-brand-name consumer goods. In addition, a new dimension has emerged to complicate the situation. Previously, the only concern was whether a firm's product was being counterfeited; now, management has to worry about whether raw materials and components purchased for production are themselves real.[38]

Four types of action against counterfeiting are legislative action, bilateral and multilateral negotiations, joint private-sector action, and measures taken by individual firms. Governments have enacted special legislation and set country-specific negotiation objectives for reciprocity and retaliatory options for intellectual property protection.

In today's environment, firms are taking more aggressive steps to protect themselves. Victimized firms are losing not only sales. They are also losing goodwill in the longer term if customers, believing they are getting the real product, unknowingly end up with a copy of inferior quality. In addition to the normal measures of registering trademarks and copyrights, firms are taking steps in product development to prevent copying of trademarked goods. For example, new authentication materials in labeling are virtually impossible to duplicate. Jointly, companies have formed organizations to lobby for legislation and to act as information clearinghouses.

Pricing Policy

Pricing is the only element in the marketing mix that is revenue generating; all of the others are costs. It should therefore be used as an active instrument of strategy in the major areas of marketing decision making. Pricing in the international environment is more complicated than in the domestic market, however, because of such factors as government influence, different currencies, and additional costs. International pricing situations can be divided into three general categories: export pricing, foreign-market pricing, and intracompany, or transfer, pricing.[39]

Export Pricing   Three general price-setting strategies in international marketing are a standard worldwide price; dual pricing, which differentiates between domestic and export prices; and market-differentiated pricing.[40] The first two are cost-oriented pricing methods that are relatively simple to establish, easy to understand, and cover all of the necessary costs. **Standard worldwide pricing** is based on average unit costs of fixed, variable, and export-related costs.

In **dual pricing,** the export price is often based on marginal cost pricing, resulting in a lower export price than the domestic price. This method, based on incremental costs, considers the direct costs of producing and selling products for export as the floor beneath which prices cannot be set, while the firm considers other fixed costs (such as basic R&D) to have been recaptured by domestic operations. This may open the company to dumping charges, because determination of dumping has generally been based on average total costs, which can be considerably higher. Lower export prices are common, especially among western European companies, which have a heavier tax burden (value-added tax) on their domestically sold products than on exported products because the tax is refunded for exported products. Cost-oriented pricing creates some major problems because it (1) is based on arbitrary cost allocations, (2) does not take into consideration highly differing market conditions, and (3) is subject to differing internal conditions in the various markets, such as entry mode and stage of the product's life cycle in the respective markets.

On the other hand, **market-differentiated pricing** is based on a demand-oriented strategy and is thus more consistent with the marketing concept. This method also allows consideration of competitive forces in setting export price. The major problem is the exporter's perennial dilemma: lack of information. Therefore, in most cases, marginal costs provide a basis for competitive comparisons, on which the export price is set.

In preparing a quotation, the exporter must be careful to take into account unique export-related costs and, if possible, include them. They are in addition to the normal costs shared with the domestic side. They include:

1. The cost incurred in modifying the product for foreign markets.
2. Operational costs of the export operation. Examples are personnel, market research, additional shipping and insurance costs, communications costs with foreign customers, and overseas promotional costs.

3. Costs incurred in entering foreign markets. These include tariffs and taxes; risks associated with a buyer in a different market (mainly commercial credit risks and political risks); and dealing in other than the exporter's domestic currency—that is, foreign exchange risk.

The combined effect of both clear-cut and hidden costs results in export prices far in excess of domestic prices. This is called **price escalation.**

Export credit and terms add another dimension to the profitability of an export transaction. Before the transaction, the exporter has in all likelihood formulated a credit policy that determines the degree of risk the firm is willing to assume and the preferred selling terms. The main objective is to meet the importer's requirements without jeopardizing the firm's financial goals. The exporter will be concerned about being paid for the goods shipped and will, therefore, consider the following factors in negotiating terms of payment: (1) the amount of payment and the need for protection, (2) terms offered by competitors, (3) practices in the industry, (4) capacity for financing international transactions, and (5) relative strength of the parties involved.[41] If the exporter is well established in the market with a unique product and accompanying service, price and terms of trade can be set according to the exporter's preferences. If, on the other hand, the exporter is breaking into a new market, or if competitive pressures exist, pricing and selling terms should be used as major competitive tools.

Inexpensive imports often trigger accusations of **dumping**—that is, selling goods overseas for less than in the exporter's home market, or at a price below the cost of production, or both. Cases that have been reported include charges by Florida tomato growers that Mexican vegetables were being dumped across the border and the ruling of the Canadian Anti-Dumping Tribunal that U.S. firms were dumping radioactive diagnostic reagents in Canada.[42]

Dumping ranges from predatory to unintentional. Predatory dumping is the tactic of a foreign firm that intentionally sells at a loss in another country in order to increase its market share at the expense of domestic producers. This amounts to an international price war. Unintentional dumping is the result of time lags between the date of sales transactions, shipment, and arrival. Prices, including exchange rates, can change in such a way that the final sales price is below the cost of production or below the price prevailing in the exporter's home market.

In the United States, domestic producers may petition the government to impose antidumping duties on imports alleged to be dumped. The remedy is a duty equal to the dumping margin. International agreements and U.S. law provide for countervailing duties. They may be imposed on imports that are found to be subsidized by foreign governments. They are designed to offset the advantages imports would otherwise receive from the subsidy.

Foreign-Market Pricing   Pricing within the individual markets in which the firm operates is determined by (1) corporate objectives, (2) costs, (3) customer behavior and market conditions, (4) market structure, and (5) environmental constraints. Because all of these factors vary from country to country, pricing policies of the multinational corporation must vary as well. Despite arguments in favor of uniform pricing in multinational markets, price discrimination is an essential characteristic of the pricing policies of firms conducting business in differing markets.[43] In a study of 42 U.S.-based multinational corporations, the major problem areas they reported in making pricing decisions were meeting competition, cost, lack of competitive information, distribution and channel factors, and governmental barriers.[44]

The issue of standard worldwide pricing may be mostly a theoretical one because of the influence of a variety of factors. However, coordination of the pricing function is necessary, especially in larger, regional markets such as the European Community. Standardization efforts usually address price levels and the use of pricing as a positioning tool.

Of great importance to multinational corporations is the control and coordination of pricing to intermediaries. When currency-exchange-rate discrepancies widen, **gray markets** emerge. The term refers to brand-name imports that enter a country legally but outside regular, authorized distribution channels. The gray market is fueled by companies that sell goods in foreign markets at prices that are far lower than prices charged to, for example, U.S. distributors, and by one strong currency, such as the dollar or the yen. The gray market in the United States has flourished in cars, watches, and even baby powder, cameras, and chewing gum. The retail value of gray markets in the United States has been estimated at $6 billion to $10 billion. This phenomenon not only harms the company financially but also may harm its reputation, because authorized distributors often refuse to honor warranties on items bought through the gray market. Cars bought through the gray market, for example, may not pass EPA inspections and thus may cause major expense to the unsuspecting buyer.[45]

The proponents of gray marketing argue for their right to "free trade" by pointing to manufacturers who are both overproducing and overpricing in some markets. The main beneficiaries are consumers, who benefit from lower prices, and discount distributors, who now have access to the product.

Transfer Pricing   Transfer, or intracompany, pricing is the pricing of sales to members of the corporate family. The overall competitive and financial position of the firm forms the basis of any pricing policy. In this, transfer pricing plays a key role. Intracorporate sales can easily change consolidated global results because they often are one of the most important ongoing decision areas in a company. Transfer prices are usually set by the firm's major financial officer—the financial vice president or comptroller—and parent company executives are uniformly unwilling to allow much participation by other department or subsidiary executives.[46]

Four main transfer-pricing possibilities have merged over time: (1) transfer at direct cost, (2) transfer at direct cost plus additional expenses, (3) transfer at a price derived from end-market prices, and (4) transfer at an **arm's length price,** or the price that unrelated parties would have reached on the same transaction. Doing business overseas requires coping with complexities of environmental peculiarities, the effect of which can be alleviated by manipulating transfer prices. Factors that call for adjustments include taxes, import duties, inflationary tendencies, unstable governments, and other regulations.[47] For example, high transfer prices on goods shipped to a subsidiary and low ones on goods imported from it will result in minimizing the tax liability of a subsidiary operating in a country with a high income tax. Tax liability thus results not only from the absolute tax rate but also from differences in how income is computed. On the other hand, a higher transfer price may have an effect on the import duty, especially if it is assessed on an ad valorem basis. Exceeding a certain threshold may boost the duty substantially and thus have a negative impact on the subsidiary's posture.

The main concerns with transfer pricing are both internal and external to the multinational corporation. Manipulating intracorporate prices complicates internal control measures and, without proper documentation, will cause major problems. If the firm operates on a profit-center basis, some consideration must be given to the effect of transfer pricing on the subsidiary's apparent profit and its actual performance. To judge a subsidiary's profit performance as not satisfactory when it was targeted to be a net source of funds can easily create morale problems. The situation may be further complicated by cultural differences among subsidiaries, especially if the need to subsidize less-efficient members of the corporate family is not made clear. An adjustment in the control mechanism is called for to give appropriate credit to the divisions for their actual contributions. The method called for may range from dual bookkeeping to compensation in budgets and profit plans. Regardless of the method, proper organizational communication is required to avoid unnecessary conflict between subsidiaries and headquarters.

Transfer prices will by definition involve tax and regulatory jurisdiction of the countries in which the company does business. Sales and transfers of tangible properties and transfers of intangibles such as patent rights and manufacturing know-how are subject to close review and to determinations about the adequacy of compensation received. Typically, authorities try to establish or approximate an arm's length level. Quite often the multinational corporation is put in a difficult position. U.S. authorities may think the transfer price is too low, whereas the foreign entity (especially a less-developed country) may perceive it to be too high.

In the host environments, the concern of the multinational corporation is to maintain its status as a good corporate citizen. Many corporations, in drafting multinational codes of conduct, have specified that intracorporate pricing will follow the arm's length principle. Multinationals have also been found to closely abide by tax regulations governing transfer pricing.[48]

Distribution Policy

Channels of distribution provide the essential linkages that connect producers and customers. The channel decision is the longest term of the marketing-mix decisions in that it cannot be readily changed. In addition, it involves relinquishing some of the control the firm has over the marketing of its products. These two factors make choosing the right channel structure a crucial decision. Properly structured and staffed, the distribution system will function more as one rather than as a collection of often quite different units.

Channel Design   The term *channel design* refers to the length and width of the channel employed. **Channel design** is determined by factors that can be summarized as the 11 Cs: customer, culture, competition, company, character, capital, cost, coverage, control, continuity, and communication. The international marketer can use the 11 Cs as a checklist to determine the proper approach to reach target audiences before selecting channel members to fill the roles. The first 3 factors are givens in that the company must adjust its approach to the existing structures. The other 8 are controllable to a certain extent by the marketer.

The demographic and psychographic characteristics of targeted customers will form the basis for channel-design decisions. Answers to questions such as what customers need as well as why, when, and how they buy are used to determine ways in which products should be made available in order to generate a competitive advantage. Anheuser-Busch's success in Japan began in 1981, for example, when Suntory, one of the country's largest liquor distillers, acquired the importing rights. One important aspect of Suntory's marketing plan was to stress distribution of Budweiser in discos, pubs, and other night spots where Japan's affluent, well-traveled youth gather. Young people in Japan are influenced by American culture and adapt more readily to new products than do older Japanese. Taking advantage of this fact, Suntory concentrated its efforts on one generation. The result was that on-premise sales led to major off-premise (retail outlet) sales as well.

Customer characteristics may cause one product to be distributed through two different types of channels. All sales of Caterpillar's earthmoving equipment are handled by independent dealers, except that sales are direct to the U.S. government and the People's Republic of China.

The marketer must analyze existing channel structures, or what might be called the distribution culture of a market. For example, the general nature of the Japanese distribution system presents one of the major reasons for the apparent failure of foreign companies to penetrate the market.[49] In most cases, the international marketer must adjust to existing structures. In Finland, for example, 92 percent of all distribution of nondurable consumer goods is through four wholesale chains. In the United Kingdom, major retail chains control markets. Without their support, no significant penetration of the market is possible.

Foreign legislation affecting distributors and agents is an essential part of the distribution culture of a market. For example, legislation may require foreign companies to be represented only by firms that are 100 percent locally owned. Some countries have prohibited the use of dealers so as to protect consumers from abuses in which intermediaries have engaged.

Channels used by competitors form another basis for plans. First, channels utilized by the competition may make up the only distribution system that is accepted both by the trade and by consumers. In this case, the international marketer's task is to use the structure more effectively and efficiently. An alternate strategy is to use a totally different distribution approach from the competition and hope to develop a competitive advantage in that manner. A new approach will have to be carefully analyzed and tested against the cultural, political, and legal environments in which it is to be introduced. In some cases, all feasible channels may be blocked by domestic competitors through contractual agreements or other means.

No channel of distribution can be properly selected unless it meets the requirements set by overall company objectives for market share and profitability. Sometimes management may simply want to use a particular channel of distribution, even though no sound business basis exists for the decision. Some management goals may have conflicting results. When investment in the restaurant business in Japan was liberalized, a number of U.S. fast-food chains rushed in to capitalize on the development. The companies attempted to establish mass sales as soon as possible by opening numerous restaurants in the busiest sections of several Japanese cities. Unfortunately, control proved to be quite difficult because of the sheer number of openings over a relatively short period of time. The individual stores changed the product as they grew, ruining the major asset—standardization—that the U.S. companies were advocating.[50]

The character of the product will have an impact on the design of the channel. Generally, the more specialized, expensive, bulky, or perishable the product and the more it may require after-sale service, the more likely the channel is to be relatively short. Staple items, such as soap, tend to have longer channels. The type of channel chosen has to match the overall positioning of the product in the market. Changes in overall market conditions, such as currency fluctuations, may require changes in distribution as well. An increase in the value of the dollar may cause a repositioning of the marketed product as a luxury item, necessitating an appropriate channel (such as an upscale department store) for its distribution.

The term *capital* is used to describe the financial requirements in setting up a channel system. The international marketer's financial strength will determine the type of channel and the basis on which channel relationships will be built. The stronger the marketer's finances, the more able the firm is to establish channels it either owns or controls. Intermediaries' requirements for beginning inventories, selling on a consignment basis, preferential loans, and need for training all will have an impact on the type of approach chosen by the international marketer.

Closely related to the capital dimension is cost—that is, the expenditure incurred in maintaining a channel once it is established. Costs will naturally vary over the life cycle of the relationship as well as over the life cycle of the products marketed. An example of the costs involved is promotional monies spent by a distributor for the marketer's product. Costs may also be incurred in protecting the company's distributors against adverse market conditions. A number of U.S. manufacturers helped their distributors maintain competitive prices through subsidies when the exchange rate for the U.S. dollar caused pricing problems.

The term *coverage* is used to describe both the number of areas in which the marketer's products are represented and the quality of that representation. Coverage, therefore, is two dimensional in that horizontal and vertical coverage need to be considered in channel design. The number of areas to be covered depends on the dispersion of demand in the market and also the time elapsed since the product's introduction to the market. A company typically enters a market with one local distributor, but, as volume expands, the distribution base often has to be adjusted.

The use of intermediaries will automatically lead to loss of some control over the marketing of the firm's products. The looser the relationship is between the marketer and the intermediaries, the less control can be exerted. The longer the channel, the more difficult it becomes for the marketer to have a final say over pricing, promotion, and the types of outlets in which the product will be made available.

Nurturing continuity rests heavily on the marketer because foreign distributors may have a more short-term view of the relationship. For example, Japanese wholesalers believe that it is important for manufacturers to follow up initial success with continuous improvement of the product. If such improvements are not forthcoming, competitors are likely to enter the market with similar, but lower priced, products and the wholesalers of the imported product will turn to the Japanese suppliers.[51]

Communication provides the exchange of information that is essential to the functioning of the channel. Proper communication will perform important roles for the international marketer. It will help convey the marketer's goals to the distributors, help solve conflict situations, and aid in the overall marketing of the product. Communication is a two-way process that does not permit the marketer to dictate to intermediaries. Sometimes the planned program may not work because of a lack of communication. Prices may not be competitive; promotional materials may be obsolete or inaccurate and not well received overall.[52]

Selection and Screening of Intermediaries

Once the basic design of the channel has been determined, the international marketer must begin a search to fill the roles defined with the best available candidates. Choices will have to be made within the framework of the company's overall philosophy on distributors versus agents, as well as whether the company will use an indirect or direct approach to foreign markets.

Firms that have successful international distribution attest to the importance of finding top representatives. The undertaking should be held in the same regard as recruiting and hiring within the company because "an ineffective foreign distributor can set you back years; it is almost better to have no distributor than a bad one in a major market."[53]

Various sources exist to assist the marketer in locating intermediary candidates. One of the easiest and most economical ways is to use the services of governmental agencies. The U.S. Department of Commerce has various services that can assist firms in identifying suitable representatives abroad; some have been designed specifically for that purpose. A number of private sources are also available to the international marketer. Trade directories, many of them published by Dun & Bradstreet, usually list foreign representatives geographically and by product classification. Telephone directories, especially the yellow page sections or editions, can provide distributor lists. Although not detailed, these listings will give addresses and an indication of the products sold. The firm can solicit the support of some of its facilitating agencies, such as banks, advertising agencies, shipping lines, and airlines. The marketer can take an even more direct approach by buying advertising space to solicit representation. These advertisements typically indicate the type of support the marketer will be able to give to its distributor.

Intermediaries can be screened on their performance and professionalism. An intermediary's performance can be evaluated on the basis of financial standing and sales as well as the likely fit it would provide in terms of its existing product lines and coverage. Professionalism can be assessed through reputation and overall standing in the business community.

Managing the Channel Relationship   A channel relationship can be likened to a marriage in that it brings together two independent entities that have shared goals. For the relationship to work, each party has to be open about its expectations and openly communicate changes perceived in the other's behavior that might be contrary to the agreement. An excellent framework for managing channel relationships is provided in Table 15.4.

The complicating factors that separate the two parties fall into three categories: ownership, geographic and cultural distance, and different rules of law. Rather than lament their existence, both parties must take strong action to remedy them. Often the first major step is for both parties to acknowledge that differences exist.

TABLE 15.4
Managing Relations with Overseas Distributors

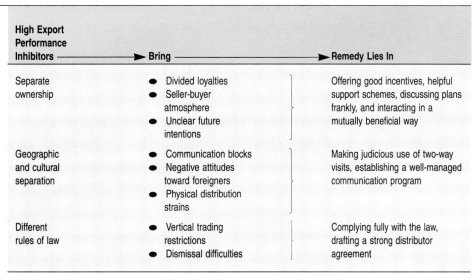

High Export Performance Inhibitors ⟶	Bring ⟶	Remedy Lies In
Separate ownership	• Divided loyalties • Seller-buyer atmosphere • Unclear future intentions	Offering good incentives, helpful support schemes, discussing plans frankly, and interacting in a mutually beneficial way
Geographic and cultural separation	• Communication blocks • Negative attitudes toward foreigners • Physical distribution strains	Making judicious use of two-way visits, establishing a well-managed communication program
Different rules of law	• Vertical trading restrictions • Dismissal difficulties	Complying fully with the law, drafting a strong distributor agreement

Source: Philip J. Rosson,. "Source Factors in Manufacturer–Overseas Distributor Relationships in International Marketing," in *International Marketing Management,* ed. Erdener Kaynak (New York: Praeger, 1984), 95.

Promotional Policy

The international marketer must choose a proper combination of the various promotional tools—advertising, personal selling, sales promotion, and publicity—to create images among the intended target audience. The choice will depend on the target audience, company objectives, the product or service marketed, the resources available for the endeavor, and the availability of the tool in a particular market.

Advertising   The key decision-making areas in advertising are (1) media strategy, (2) the promotional message, and (3) the organization of the promotional program.

Media strategy is applied to the selection of media vehicles and the development of a media schedule. In some cases, the international marketer may find that the choice is limited. For example, the J. Walter Thompson advertising agency has estimated that advertising expenditures on western European television would be $2.4 to $3.3 billion more if regulations were completely eased.[54] Some of the regulations include limits on the amount of time available for advertisements, ranging from complete prohibition (as in Sweden) to 15 to 20 minutes per day in blocks of 3 to 5 minutes (as in Germany). France and Italy limit the percentage of revenues that the state monopoly systems can derive from advertising. Strict separation between programs and commercials is almost a universal requirement, preventing U.S.-style sponsored programs. Restrictions on items such as comparative claims and gender stereotypes are prevalent; for example, Germany prohibits the use of superlatives such as "best."

Consumer protection dominated the regulatory scene of the 1980s and is expected to continue in the 1990s.[55] Tobacco products and alcoholic beverages are the most heavily regulated products in terms of promotion; however, the manufacturers of these products have not abandoned their promotional efforts. Philip Morris engages in corporate image advertising via its cowboy-spokesperson. John Player sponsors sports events, especially Formula-One car racing. What is and is not allowable is very much a reflection of the country imposing the rules.

Some media vehicles have been developed that have target audiences on at least three continents and for which the media buying takes place through a centralized office. Global media have traditionally been publications that, in addition to the worldwide edition, have provided advertisers the option of using regional editions. For example, *Time* provides 133 editions, enabling advertising to reach a particular country, continent, or the world. Other global publications include *The International Herald Tribune, The Wall Street Journal,* and *National Geographic.*

In broadcast media, pan-regional radio stations have been joined in Europe by television as a result of satellite technology. By the end of the 1990s, approximately half of the households in Europe will have access to additional television broadcasts either through cable or direct satellite, and television will no longer be restricted by national boundaries. As a result, marketers need to make sure that advertising works not only within markets but across countries as well.[56]

Developing the **promotional message** is referred to as creative strategy. The marketer must determine what the consumer is really buying—that is, the consumer's motivations. They will vary, depending on:

1. The diffusion of the product into the market. For example, to penetrate Third World markets with business computers is difficult when potential customers may not be able to type.
2. The criteria on which the consumer will evaluate the product. For example, in traditional societies, the time-saving qualities of a product may not

be the best ones to feature, as Campbell Soups learned in Italy and in Brazil, where housewives felt inadequate as homemakers if they did not make soups from scratch.

3. The product's positioning. For example, Parker Pen's upscale image around the world may not be profitable enough in a market that is more or less a commodity business. The solution is to create an image for a commodity product and make the public pay for it—for example, the positioning of Perrier in the United States as a premium mineral water.

The ideal situation in developing message strategy is to have a world brand—a product that is manufactured, packaged, and positioned the same around the world. However, a number of factors will force companies to abandon identical campaigns in favor of recognizable campaigns. These factors are culture, of which language is the main manifestation, economic development, and lifestyles. Consider, for example, the campaign for Conner Peripherals presented in Figure 15.3. The images in the southeast Asia and Japanese versions of the company's "Unique Ideas" ad differ in subtle but important ways. The southeast Asian execution pictures bone Chinese chopsticks on black cloth; the Japanese version shows enameled pointed chopsticks on a marble slab to appeal to a different aesthetic.[57]

Many multinational corporations are staffed and equipped to perform the full range of promotional activities. In most cases, however, they rely on the outside expertise of advertising agencies and other promotions-related companies such as media-buying companies and specialty marketing firms. According to a Grey Advertising survey of 50 multinational marketers, 76 percent believe the ideal situation is to use the same agency worldwide, with some local deviation as necessary. The same percentage believes an ad agency should be centrally run, and 72 percent believe in using the same advertising strategy worldwide.[58] Local agencies will survive, however, because of governmental regulations. In Peru, for example, a law mandates that any commercial aired on Peruvian television must be 100 percent nationally produced. Local agencies tend to forge ties with foreign ad agencies for better coverage and customer service and thus become part of the general globalization effort.

Personal Selling   Although advertising is often equated with the promotional effort, in many cases promotional efforts consist of personal selling. In the early stages of internationalization, exporters rely heavily on personal contact. The marketing of industrial goods, especially of high-priced items, requires strong personal selling efforts. In some cases, personal selling may be truly international; for example, Boeing or Northrop salespeople engage in sales efforts around the world. However, in most cases, personal selling takes place at the local level. The best interests of any company in the industrial area lie in establishing a solid base of dealerships staffed by local people. Personal selling efforts can be developed in the same fashion as advertising. For the multinational company, the primary goal again is the enhancement and standardization of personal selling efforts, especially if the product offering is standardized.

As an example, Eastman Kodak has developed a line-of-business approach to allow for standardized strategy throughout a region.[59] In Europe, one person is placed in charge of the entire copier-duplicator program in each country. That person is responsible for all sales and service teams within the country. Typically, each customer is served by three representatives, each with a different responsibility. Sales representatives maintain ultimate responsibility for the account; they conduct demonstrations, analyze customer requirements, determine the right type of equipment for each installation, and obtain orders. Service representatives install and maintain the

FIGURE 15.3
A Campaign Adapted to
Local Conditions

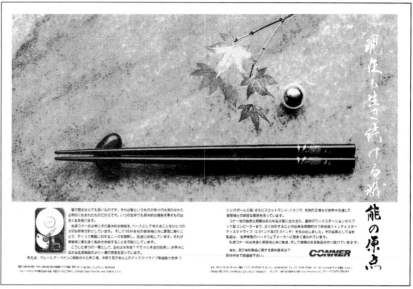

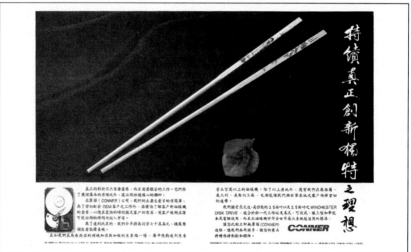

equipment and retrofit new-product improvements to existing equipment. Customer service representatives are the liaison between sales and service. They provide operator training on a continuing basis and handle routine questions and complaints. Each team is positioned to respond to any European customer within four hours.

Sales Promotion   Sales promotion has been used as the catchall term for promotion that is not advertising, personal selling, or publicity. Sales promotion directed at consumers involves such activities as couponing, sampling, premiums, consumer education and demonstration activities, cents-off packages, point-of-purchase materials, and direct mail. The success in Latin America of Tang, General Foods' presweetened powder juice substitute, is for the most part traceable to successful sales promotion efforts. One promotion involved trading Tang pouches for free popsicles from Kibon (General Foods' Brazilian subsidiary). Kibon also placed coupons for free groceries in Tang pouches. In Puerto Rico, General Foods ran Tang sweepstakes. In Argentina, in-store sampling featured Tang poured from Tang pitchers by girls in orange Tang dresses. Decorative Tang pitchers were a hit throughout Latin America.

For sales promotion to work, the campaigns planned by manufacturers or their agencies have to gain the support of the local retailer population. As an example, retailers must redeem coupons presented by consumers and forward them to the manufacturer or to the company handling the promotion. A. C. Nielsen tried to introduce cents-off coupons in Chile and ran into trouble with the nation's supermarket union, which notified its members that it opposed the project and recommended that coupons not be accepted. The main complaint was that an intermediary, like Nielsen, would unnecessarily raise costs and thus the prices to be charged to consumers. Also, some critics felt that coupons would limit individual negotiations, because Chileans often bargain for their purchases.

Sales promotion directed at intermediaries, also known as trade promotion, includes activities such as trade shows and exhibits, trade discounts, and cooperative advertising. For example, attendance at an appropriate trade show is one of the best ways to make contacts with government officials and decision makers, work with present intermediaries, or attract new ones.

Public Relations   Public relations is the marketing communications function charged with executing programs to earn public understanding and acceptance, which means both internal and external communication. Internal communication is important, especially in multinational companies, to create an appropriate corporate culture. External campaigns can be achieved through the use of corporate symbols, corporate advertising, customer relations programs, and the generation of publicity. Some material on the firm is produced for special audiences to assist in personal selling.

A significant part of public relations activity focuses on portraying multinational corporations as good citizens of their host markets. Examples of these "social investments" are provided in Global Perspective 15.4.

Public relations activity includes anticipating and countering criticism. The criticisms range from general ones against all multinational corporations to specific complaints. They may be based on a market; for example, a company's presence in China. They may concern a product; for example, Nestlé's practices in advertising and promoting infant formula in developing countries where infant mortality is unacceptably high. They may center on the company's conduct in a given situation; for example, Union Carbide's perceived lack of response in the Bhopal disaster. If not addressed, these criticisms can lead to more significant problems, such as an internationally orchestrated boycott of products. The six-year boycott of Nestlé did not so much harm earnings as it harmed image and employee morale.

SUMMARY   The task of the international marketer is to seek new opportunities in the world marketplace and satisfy emerging needs through creative management of the firm's product, pricing, distribution, and promotional policies. By its very nature, marketing is the most sensitive of business functions to environmental effects and influences.

The analysis of target markets is the first of the international marketer's challenges. Potential and existing markets need to be evaluated and priorities established

Global Perspective

15.4
Expanding the Social Vision: Global Community Relations

At the time when many companies are making more money overseas than in their home countries, executives are realizing that they should devote substantial attention to community relations. This attention should not be developed only as a reaction to a crisis, nor should it be a fuzzy, piecemeal effort, but corporations should have a social vision and a planned long-term social policy.

IBM's policy of good corporate citizenship means accepting responsibility as a participant in community and national affairs and striving to be among the most-admired companies in its host countries. In Thailand, for example, IBM provides equipment and personnel to universities and donates money to the nation's wildlife fund and environmental protection agency. In 1986, the firm became one of only two companies with a U.S.–based parent to win the Garuda Award, which recognizes significant contributions to Thailand's social and economic development. In 1989, IBM introduced Worldwide Initiatives in Volunteerism, a $1 million–plus program to fund projects worldwide and promote employee volunteerism.

Ford Motor Company's commitment to community relations extends to 30 countries where Ford has manufacturing, assembly, or sales facilities. The community affairs department at world headquarters in Dearborn, Michigan, has functional responsibility for all corporate community relations around the globe. However, in practical terms, managers at each overseas facility have the day-to-day job of cultivating and maintaining close ties with the local community. Headquarters also supplies every Ford operation with the *Community Relations Handbook,* a 100-plus-page guide to community involvement that is updated annually.

Increased privatization and government cutbacks in social services in many countries offer numerous opportunities for companies to make substantive contributions to solving various global, regional, and local problems. Conservative governments in Europe are welcoming private-sector programs to provide job training for inner city youth, to meet the needs of immigrants, and to solve massive pollution problems. And in eastern and central Europe, where the lines between the private and public sectors are just now being drawn, corporations have a unique opportunity to take a leadership role in shaping new societies.

James Parkel, director of IBM's Office of Corporate Support Programs, summarizes the new expectations in the following way: "Employees don't want to work for companies that have no social conscience, customers don't want to do business with companies that pollute the environment or are notorious for shoddy products and practices, and communities don't welcome companies that aren't good corporate citizens. Mary shareholder issues are socially driven."

Source: "Corporate Generosity Is Greatly Appreciated," *Business Week,* November 2, 1992, 118–120; "Achieving Success in Asia: IBM Sees 'Localization' as a Critical Element," *Business International,* November 11, 1991, 379–383; "Global Community Relations: Expanding the Social Vision," *Business International,* September 16, 1991, 313–314; "How Corporate Activism Can Spread Your Message," *Business International,* June 10, 1991, 199.

for each, ranging from rejection to a temporary holding position to entry. Decisions at the level of the overall marketing effort must be made with respect to the selected markets, and a plan for future expansion must be formulated. The closer that potential target markets are in terms of their geographical, cultural, and economic distance, the more attractive they typically are to the international marketer.

A critical decision in international marketing concerns the degree to which the overall marketing program should be standardized or localized. The ideal is to standardize as much as possible without compromising the basic task of marketing: satisfying the needs and wants of the target market. Many multinational marketers are adopting globalization strategies that involve the standardization of good ideas, while leaving the implementation to local entities.

The technical side of marketing management is universal, but environments require adaptation within all of the mix elements. The degree of adaptation will vary by market, product or service marketed, and overall company objectives.

Key Terms and Concepts

demand pattern analysis

income elasticity of demand

multiple-factor indexes

estimation by analogy

input-output analysis

gap analysis

concentration

diversification

positioning

backward innovation

standard worldwide pricing

dual pricing

market-differentiated pricing

price escalation

dumping

gray markets

arm's length price

channel design

media strategy

promotional message

Questions for Discussion

1. Many rational reasons exist for rejecting a particular market in the early stages of screening. Because such decisions are made by humans, some irrational reasons must exist as well. Suggest some.

2. If, indeed, the three dimensions of distance are valid, to which countries would U.S. companies initially expand? Consider the interrelationships of the distance concepts.

3. Is globalization ever a serious possibility, or is the regional approach the closest the international marketer can ever hope to get to standardization?

4. Is a "world car" a possibility?

5. What are the possible exporter reactions to extreme foreign-exchange-rate fluctuations?

6. Argue for and against gray marketing.

7. What courses of action are open to an international marketer who finds all attractive intermediaries already under contract to competitors?

8. You are planning a pan-European advertising campaign for calculators with a back-to-school theme. The guideline specifies illustrating the various models sold in the market along the margins of the advertisement and using a title that suggests calculators help students to do better in school and college. What type of local adjustments do you expect to make to the campaign?

Recommended Readings

Abdallah, Wagdy. *International Transfer Pricing Policy.* Westport, Conn.: Quorum Books, 1989.

Baudot, Barbara. *International Advertising Handbook.* Lexington, Mass.: Lexington Books, 1990.

Czinkota, Michael R., and Ilkka A. Ronkainen. *International Marketing.* Ft. Worth, Texas: Dryden, 1993.

Czinkota, Michael R., and Jon Woronoff. *Unlocking Japan's Market.* Chicago: Probus Publishers, 1991.

Douglas, Susan P., and C. Samuel Craig. *International Marketing Research.* Englewood Cliffs, N.J.: Prentice-Hall, 1983.

Ohmae, Kenichi. *Triad Power: The Coming Shape of Global Competition.* New York: The Free Press, 1985.

Root, Franklin. *Entry Strategies for International Markets.* Lexington, Mass.: Lexington Books, 1990.

Smith, N. Craig, and John A. Quelch. *Ethics in Marketing.* Homewood, Ill.: Irwin, 1993.

U.S. Department of Commerce. *A Basic Guide to Exporting.* Washington, D.C.: U.S. Government Printing Office, 1989.

Walmsley, James. *The Development of International Markets.* Hingham, Mass.: Graham & Trotman, 1990.

Webber, Robert. *The Marketer's Guide to Selling Products Abroad.* Westport, Conn.: Quorum Books, 1989.

Yip, George S. *Total Global Strategy.* Englewood Cliffs, N.J.: Prentice-Hall, 1992.

Notes

1. "AMA Board Approves New Marketing Definition," *Marketing News,* March 1, 1985, 1.
2. Robert Bartels, "Are Domestic and International Marketing Dissimilar?" *Journal of Marketing* 36 (July 1968): 56-61.
3. Reijo Luostarinen, *Internationalization of the Firm* (Helsinki, Finland: The Helsinki School of Economics, 1979), 124-33.
4. Franklin R. Root, *Entry Strategies for Foreign Markets: From Domestic to International Business* (Lexington, Mass.: Lexington Books, 1990), 15-20.
5. For one of the best summaries, see Business International, *Indicators of Market Size for 117 Countries* (New York: Business International, 1992).
6. Philip Kotler, *Marketing Management: Analysis, Planning and Control* (Englewood Cliffs, N.J.: Prentice-Hall, 1984), 234.
7. Reed Moyer, "International Market Analysis," *Journal of Marketing Research* 16 (November 1968): 353-360.
8. The World Bank, *World Development Report* (Oxford, England: Oxford University Press, 1990), 236-237.
9. J. A. Weber, "Comparing Growth Opportunities in the International Marketplace," *Management International Review* 19 (Winter 1979): 47-54.
10. Root, *Entry Strategies for Foreign Markets,* 19.
11. Igal Ayal and Jehiel Zif, "Marketing Expansion Strategies in Multinational Marketing," *Journal of Marketing* 43 (Spring 1979): 84-94.
12. Alice Rudolph, "Standardization Not Standard for Global Marketers," *Marketing News,* September 27, 1985, 3-4.
13. Robert Buzzell, "Can You Standardize Multinational Marketing?" *Journal of Marketing* 46 (November-December 1968): 98-104.
14. Ralph Z. Sorenson and Ulrich E. Wiechmann, "How Multinationals View Marketing Standardization," *Harvard Business Review* 53 (May-June 1975): 38-56.
15. Ernest Dichter, "The World Customer," *Harvard Business Review* 40 (July-August 1962): 113-122.
16. Theodore Levitt, *The Marketing Imagination* (New York: The Free Press, 1983), 20-49.
17. Kenichi Ohmae, *Triad Power—The Coming Shape of Global Competition* (New York: The Free Press, 1985), 22-27.
18. Warren Strugatch, "Make Way for the Euroconsumer," *World Trade,* February 1993, 46-50.
19. George Yip, "Global Strategy . . . In a World of Nations," *Sloan Management Review* 31 (Fall 1989): 29-41.
20. Anne B. Fisher, "The Ad Biz Gloms onto 'Global,'" *Fortune,* November 12, 1984, 77-80.
21. Laurence Farley, "Going Global: Choices and Challenges" (paper presented at the American Management Association Conference, Chicago, Ill., June 10, 1985).
22. John A. Quelch and Edward J. Hoff, "Customizing Global Marketing," *Harvard Business Review* 64 (May-June 1986): 59-68.

23. Kamran Kashani, "Beware the Pitfalls of Global Marketing," *Harvard Business Review* 67 (September-October 1989): 91-98.

24. John Daniels, "Bridging National and Global Marketing Strategies through Regional Operations," *International Marketing Review* 4 (Autumn 1987): 29-44.

25. V. Yorio, *Adapting Products for Export* (New York: The Conference Board, 1983), 1.

26. John S. Hill and Richard R. Still, "Adapting Products to LDC Tastes," *Harvard Business Review* 62 (March-April 1984): 92-101.

27. Cyndee Miller, "U.S. Firms Lag in Meeting Global Quality Standards," *Marketing News,* February 15, 1993, 1, 6; and "Europe's Standards Blitz Has Firms Scrambling," *The Washington Post,* October 18, 1992, H1, H4.

28. "One Mello, Please," *Advertising Age,* August 1, 1983, 26.

29. Hill and Still, "Adapting Products to LDC Tastes," 92-101.

30. "Going through Customs," *Inc.,* December 1984, 180-184.

31. Bruce Seifert and John Ford, "Are Exporting Firms Modifying Their Product, Pricing and Promotion Policies?" *International Marketing Review* 6 (Number 6, 1989): 53-68.

32. Phillip D. White and Edward W. Cundiff, "Assessing the Quality of Industrial Products," *Journal of Marketing* 42 (January 1978): 80-86.

33. Warren J. Bilkey and Erik Nes, "Country-of-Origin Effects on Product Evaluations," *Journal of International Business Studies* 13 (Spring-Summer 1982): 89-99.

34. "Detroit Beware: Japan Is Ready to Sell Luxury," *Business Week,* December 9, 1985, 114-118.

35. Ilkka A. Ronkainen, "Product Development in the Multinational Firm," *International Marketing Review* 1 (Winter 1983): 24-30.

36. "Can Ford Stay on Top?" *Business Week,* September 28, 1987, 78-88.

37. "For Levi's, a Flattering Fit Overseas," *Business Week,* November 5, 1990, 76-77.

38. Michael G. Harvey and Ilkka A. Ronkainen, "International Counterfeiters: Marketing Success without the Cost or Risk," *Columbia Journal of World Business* 20 (Fall 1985): 37-46.

39. Helmut Becker, "Pricing: An International Marketing Challenge," in *International Marketing Strategy,* eds. Hans Thorelli and Helmut Becker (New York: Pergamon Press, 1980), 201-215.

40. Richard D. Robinson, *Internationalization of Business: An Introduction* (Hinsdale, Ill.: Dryden, 1984), 49-54.

41. Chase Manhattan Bank, *Dynamics of Trade Finance* (New York: Chase Manhattan Bank, 1984), 10-11.

42. Steven Plaut, "Why Dumping Is Good for Us," *Fortune,* May 5, 1980, 212-222.

43. Peter Kessler, "Is Uniform Pricing Desirable in Multinational Markets?" *Akron Business and Economic Review* 2 (Winter 1971): 3-8.

44. James C. Baker and John K. Ryans, "Some Aspects of International Pricing: A Neglected Area of Management Policy," *Management Decisions* (Summer 1973): 177-182.

45. Ilkka A. Ronkainen and Linda Van de Gucht, "Making a Case for Gray Markets," *Journal of Commerce,* January 6, 1987, 13A.

46. Jeffrey Arpan, "Multinational Firm Pricing in International Markets," *Sloan Management Review* 15 (Winter 1973): 1-9.

47. James Shulman, "When the Price Is Wrong—By Design," *Columbia Journal of World Business* 4 (May-June 1967): 69-76.

48. Mohammad F. Al-Eryani, Pervaiz Alam, and Syed H. Akhter, "Transfer Pricing Determinants of U.S. Multinationals," *Journal of International Business Studies* 21 (Fall 1990): 409-425.

49. Randolph Ross, "Understanding the Japanese Distribution System: An Explanatory Framework," *European Journal of Marketing* 17 (Winter 1983): 5-15.

50. Robert H. Luke, "Successful Marketing in Japan: Guidelines and Recommendations," in *Contemporary Perspectives in International Business,* eds. Harold W. Berkman and Ivan R. Vernon (Chicago, Ill.: Rand McNally, 1979), 307-315.

51. Michael R. Czinkota, "Distribution of Consumer Products in Japan," *International Marketing Review* 2 (Autumn 1985): 39-51.

52. Philip J. Rosson, "Success Factors in Manufacturer-Overseas Distributor Relationships in International Marketing," in *International Marketing Management,* ed. Erdener Kaynak (New York: Praeger, 1984), 91-107.

53. "How to Evaluate Foreign Distributors: A *BI* Checklist," *Business International,* May 10, 1985, 145-149.

54. D. Pridgen, "Satellite Television Advertising and Regulatory Conflict in Western Europe," *Journal of Advertising* 14 (Winter 1985): 23-29.

55. Jean J. Boddewyn, "Advertising Regulation in the 1980s," *Journal of Marketing* 46 (Winter 1982): 22-28.

56. John Clemens, "Television Advertising in Europe," *Columbia Journal of World Business* 22 (Fall 1987): 35-41.

57. Kate Bertrand, "Conner's Japanese Success Drive," *Business Marketing,* December 1991, 18-20.

58. Dennis Chase, "Global Marketing: The New Wave," *Advertising Age,* June 25, 1984, 49, 74.

59. Joseph A. Lawton, "Kodak Penetrates the European Copier Market with Customized Marketing Strategy and Product Changes," *Marketing News,* August 3, 1984, 1, 6.

International Services

LEARNING OBJECTIVES

1. To examine the increasingly important role of services in international business.

2. To understand why international trade in services is more complex than international trade in goods.

3. To appreciate the heightened sensitivity required for international service success.

4. To learn that stand-alone services are becoming more important to world trade.

5. To examine the competitive advantage U.S. firms have in some service sectors.

U.S. Education: A Product in Demand—in Japan

With only mixed success in selling widgets to Japan, the United States has turned to selling a service there: Yankee education. About 30 U.S. colleges and universities now have programs in Japan, and nearly 100 U.S. institutions have sent delegations to Japan to explore the possibility of establishing campuses there.

Even though the Japanese have criticized America's educational system as the core reason for its flagging economic performance, they have little doubt about the quality of U.S. post-secondary education. And the Japanese, as they so often say to U.S. producers, want quality.

Enrollments in U.S. programs are substantial. Temple University, which has the oldest and largest program in Japan, has about 2,200 students. Southern Illinois University has about 600. Texas A & M is planning for between 650 and 700 students. Thunderbird, the American Graduate School of International Business, has begun to offer graduate programs. After finishing two years on the U.S. universities' campus in Japan, students generally transfer to the United States to complete their American education. For students, this means high-performance demands at the university level, learning a new culture, and learning English.

For American colleges and universities, which are facing declining enrollments, the prospect of foreign students arriving by the hundreds is a welcome one. Even for state schools, which typically charge nonresident students more than twice the tuition residents pay, Japanese students can be a good source of income. As one university administrator said: "We have 125 Japanese students coming this year. That's the same as 300 to 400 Illinois students in terms of tuition."

But the benefit does not have to end at the doors of the university. Growing ties with Japan may well translate into better times economically. Perhaps the exposure to the United States will eventually result in a better foothold for U.S. products in Japan or in investment flows into the United States.

Source: Chuck Freadhoff, "A U.S. Product that Japan Wants: Education," *Investor's Daily*, May 3, 1991, 1.

International services are becoming a major component of world trade. To reflect this development, this chapter will highlight business dimensions that are specific to services, with particular attention given to their international aspects. A definition of services will be provided, and trade in services and in products will be differentiated. The role of services in the U.S. economy and in the world economy will then be explained. The chapter will discuss the opportunities and new problems that have arisen because of increasing service trade. This discussion will focus particularly on the worldwide transformations of industries as a result of profound changes in the environment and in technology. The strategic responses to these transformations by both governments and firms will be explained. Finally, the chapter will outline the initial steps that firms need to undertake in order to offer services internationally and will look at the future of international service trade.

DIFFERENCES BETWEEN SERVICES AND PRODUCTS

We rarely contemplate or analyze the precise role of services in our lives. Services often accompany products, but they are also, by themselves, an increasingly important part of our economy. One author has contrasted services and products by stating that "a good is an object, a device, a thing; a service is a deed, a performance, an effort."[1] This definition, although quite general, captures the essence of the difference between products and services. Services tend to be more intangible, personalized, and custom made than products. In addition, services are the fastest-growing sector in world trade. These major differences bring with them the need for a major differentiation, because they add dimensions to services that are not present in products.

Linkage between Services and Products

Services may complement products; at other times, products may complement services. The offering of products that are in need of substantial technological support and maintenance may be useless if no proper assurance for service can be provided. For this reason, the initial contract of sale often includes the service dimension. This practice is frequent in aircraft sales. When an aircraft is purchased, the buyer contracts not only for the physical product—namely, the plane—but often for the training of personnel, maintenance service, and the promise of continuous technological updates. Similarly, the sale of computer hardware depends on the availability of proper servicing and software. In an international setting, the proper service support can often be crucial. Particularly for newly opening markets or for products new to market, the provision of the product alone may be insufficient. Rather, to be successful, communication services need to accompany the product in order to inform and prepare the potential market.

The linkage between products and services often makes international business efforts quite difficult. A foreign buyer, for example, may wish to purchase helicopters and contract for service support over a period of 10 years. If the sale involves a U.S. firm, both the product and the service sale will require an export license. Such licenses are issued only for an immediate sale. Therefore, over the 10 years, the seller will have to apply for an export license each time service is to be provided. Because the issuance of a license is often dependent on the political climate, the buyer and the seller are haunted by uncertainty. As a result, sales may be lost to firms in countries that can unconditionally guarantee the long-term supply of product-supporting services.

Services can be just as dependent on products. For example, an airline that prides itself on providing an efficient reservation system and excellent linkups with rental cars and hotel reservations could not survive if it were not for its airplanes. As a result, many offerings in the marketplace consist of a combination of products and services. A graphic illustration of the tangible and intangible elements in the market offering of an airline is provided in Figure 16.1.

The simple knowledge that services and products interact, however, is not enough. Successful managers must recognize that different customer groups will frequently view the service-product combination differently. The type of use and the usage conditions will also affect evaluations of the market offering. For example, the intangible dimension of "on-time arrival" by airlines may be valued differently by college students than by business executives. Similarly, a 20-minute delay will be judged differently by a passenger arriving at his or her final destination than by one who has just missed an overseas connection. As a result, adjustment possibilities in both the service and the product areas emerge that can be used as a strategic tool to stimulate demand and increase profitability. As Figure 16.2 shows, service and product elements may vary substantially. The manager must identify the role of each and adjust all of them to meet the desires of the target customer group. By rating the offerings on a scale ranging from dominant tangibility to dominant intangibility, the manager can compare offerings and also generate information for subsequent market-positioning strategies.

Stand-Alone Services

Services do not always come in unison with products. Increasingly, they compete against products and become an alternative offering. For example, rather than buy an in-house computer, the business executive can contract computing work to a lo-

**FIGURE 16.1
Tangible and Intangible
Offerings of Airlines**

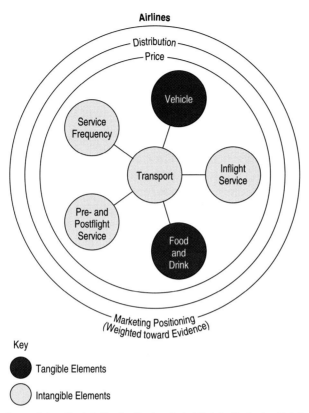

Source: G. Lynn Shostack, "Breaking Free from Product Marketing," in *Services Marketing: Text, Cases, and Readings,* ed. Christopher H. Lovelock (Englewood Cliffs, N.J.: Prentice-Hall, Inc., 1984), 40.

**FIGURE 16.2
Scale of Elemental
Dominance**

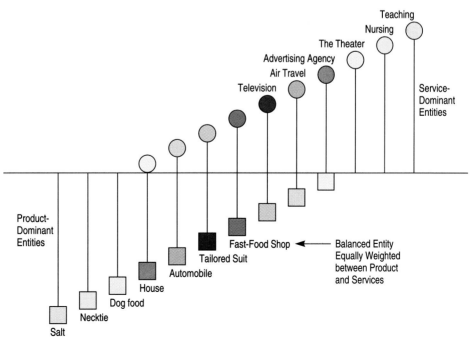

Source: Reprinted with permission from *Marketing of Services,* eds. J. Donnelly and W. George; G. Lynn Shostack, "How to Design a Service," 1981, p. 222, published by the American Marketing Association, Chicago, IL 60606.

cal or foreign service firm. Similarly, the purchase of a car (a product) can be converted into the purchase of a service by leasing the car from an agency.

Services may also compete against one another. As an example, a store may have the option of offering full service to customers or of converting to the self-service format. The store may provide only checkout services, with customers engaging in other activities such as selection, transportation, and sometimes even packaging and pricing.

Services differ from products most strongly in their **intangibility:** They are frequently consumed rather than possessed. Even though the intangibility of services is a primary differentiating criterion, it is not always present. For example, publishing services ultimately result in a tangible product—namely, a book or a computer disk. Similarly, construction services eventually result in a building, a subway, or a bridge. Even in those instances, however, the intangible component that leads to the final product is of major concern to both the producer of the service and the recipient of the ultimate output, because it brings with it major considerations that are nontraditional to products.

One major difference concerns the storing of services. Because of their nature, services are difficult to inventory. If they are not used, the "brown around the edges" syndrome tends to result in high **perishability.** Unused capacity in the form of an empty seat on an airplane, for example, becomes nonsalable quickly. Once the plane has taken off, selling an empty seat is virtually impossible—except for an in-flight upgrade from coach to first class—and the capacity cannot be stored for future usage. Similarly, the difficulty of inventorying services makes it troublesome to provide service backup for peak demand. To maintain **service capacity** constantly at levels necessary to satisfy peak demand would be very expensive. The business manager must therefore attempt to smooth out demand levels in order to optimize overall use of capacity.

For the services offering, the time of production is usually very close to or even simultaneous with the time of consumption. This frequently means close **customer involvement** in the production of services. Customers frequently either service themselves or cooperate in the delivery of services. As a result, the service provider often needs to be physically present when the service is delivered. This physical presence creates both problems and opportunities, and it introduces a new constraint that is seldom present in the marketing of products. For example, close interaction with the customer requires a much greater understanding of and emphasis on the cultural dimension of each market. A good service delivered in a culturally unacceptable fashion is doomed to failure. A common pattern of internationalization for service businesses is therefore to develop stand-alone business systems in each country.[2] Yet, at the same time, cultural diversity in a home market may assist greatly in succeeding abroad since firms may already be much more aware of cultural differences and willing to adjust to them. Figure 16.3 provides an example of such sensitivity.

At the same time, however, some services have become "delocalized" as advances in modern technology have made it possible for firms to unlink production and service processes and move labor-intensive service performance to areas where qualified, low-cost labor is plentiful. Global Perspective 16.1 provides some examples.

The close interaction with customers also points to the fact that services often are custom made. This contradicts the desire of the firm to standardize its offering; yet at the same time, it offers the service provider an opportunity to differentiate the service. The concomitant problem is that, in order to fulfill customer expectations, **service consistency** is required. For anything offered on-line, however, con-

**FIGURE 16.3
A Culturally Sensitive
Telephone Number**

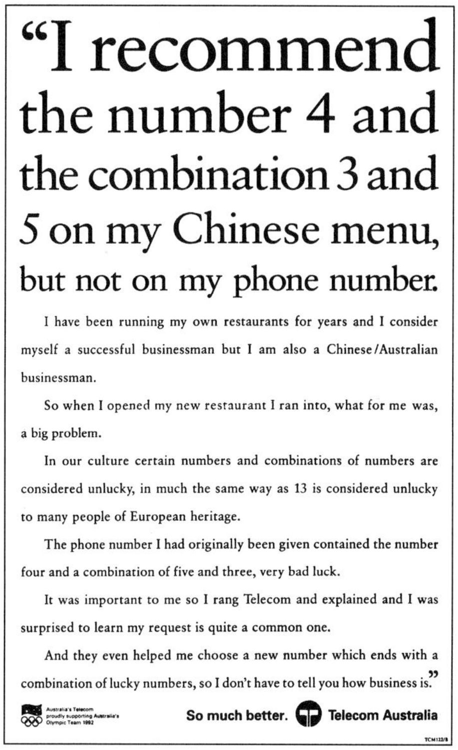

> **"I recommend the number 4 and the combination 3 and 5 on my Chinese menu, but not on my phone number.**
>
> I have been running my own restaurants for years and I consider myself a successful businessman but I am also a Chinese/Australian businessman.
>
> So when I opened my new restaurant I ran into, what for me was, a big problem.
>
> In our culture certain numbers and combinations of numbers are considered unlucky, in much the same way as 13 is considered unlucky to many people of European heritage.
>
> The phone number I had originally been given contained the number four and a combination of five and three, very bad luck.
>
> It was important to me so I rang Telecom and explained and I was surprised to learn my request is quite a common one.
>
> And they even helped me choose a new number which ends with a combination of lucky numbers, so I don't have to tell you how business is."
>
> Australia's Telecom proudly supporting Australia's Olympic Team 1992   **So much better.** ☎ **Telecom Australia**

Source: *The Sydney Morning Herald,* Tuesday, June 16, 1992.

sistency is difficult to maintain over the long run. Therefore, the human element in the service offering takes on a much greater role than in the product offering. Errors may enter the system, and unpredictable individual influences may affect the outcome of the service delivery. The issue of quality control affects the provider as well as the recipient of services because efforts to increase control through uniform service may sometimes be perceived by customers as the limiting of options. It may therefore have a negative market effect.[3]

Buyers have more difficulty observing and evaluating services than products. This is particularly true when the shopper tries to choose intelligently among service providers. Even when sellers of services are willing and able to provide more **market transparency,** the buyer's problem is complicated: Customers receiving the same service may use it differently, service quality may vary for each delivery, and service offerings are not directly comparable. Services therefore often defy quality measurement and transparency efforts. As a result, the reputation of the service provider plays an overwhelming role in the customer's choice process.

Services often require entirely new forms of distribution. Traditional channels frequently have multiple levels and are therefore long and slow. They often cannot be used at all because of the perishability of services. A weather news service, for example, either reaches its audience quickly or rapidly loses value. As a result, direct delivery and short distribution channels are required. When they do not exist, which is often the case domestically and even more so internationally, service providers need to be distribution innovators in order to reach their market.

The unique dimensions of services exist in both international and domestic settings, but their impact has greater importance for the international manager. For ex-

Global Perspective

16.1
White-Collar Jobs Move Abroad

If you dial the toll-free reservation number for Jamaica's Wexford Court Hotel, you'll find yourself speaking to an agent with a Jamaican accent. Your call will have automatically become an international one, because the hotel's booking office for American guests is located on Jamaica, and calls are routed there by satellite. Previously, the work has been done by a Miami reservation center.

Tom Kelly, who heads a $70 million Eastman Kodak research laboratory, can see Mount Fuji from the lab. He works in Yokohama, where his job requires him to hire Japanese researchers to develop new technology for Kodak. According to Kelly, "If you're serious about staying competitive globally, you've got to be on the ground [in Japan]."

If the buzzword in the 1980s was the "global factory," with U.S.–owned factories operating in lower-cost nations, the more current trend is the "global office." Thanks to advances in communications technology and a more-sophisticated work force in many countries, white-collar jobs are increasingly moving out of the United States.

Companies in many industries have taken advantage of the global office. Cigna Corporation, the huge insurer, plans to open in the Irish town of Loughrea a $5 million center for processing medical claims. A software development facility set up by Texas Instruments in Bangalore, India, is linked by satellite to TI's Dallas headquarters. Editors in Barbados prepare manuscripts for Chicago publisher R. R. Donnelley & Sons to print in the United States. And many companies, including Texas Instruments, Dow Corning, and IBM, have set up research laboratories in Japan.

In response to the exodus of blue-collar jobs to low-wage countries, many economists have downplayed the importance of manufacturing to the U.S. economy's long-term vitality. The enormous growth in the service sector, they say, is more than adequate to make up the difference. However, as white-collar jobs move overseas, they seem a less dependable part of America's economic future.

Many developing countries are offering tax incentives and start-up assistance to woo U.S. service companies to their shores. In addition, workers in these countries earn only one-third the rate paid to comparable U.S. workers. With these advantages, businesses in developing countries are hopeful that they will be able to handle such operations as software development, telemarketing, and data entry.

The trend has caused some concern among U.S. labor unions. According to Dennis Chamot, who works for the AFL-CIO's department for professional employees, "As office work becomes more electronic, it becomes easier to move."

Sources: John Burgess, "Global Offices on Rise as Firms Shift Service Jobs Abroad," *The Washington Post*, April 20, 1990, E1; and Susan Moffat, "Picking Japan's Research Brains," *Fortune*, March 25, 1991, 84–86.

ample, the perishability of a service, which may be an obstacle in domestic business, may become a barrier internationally because of the longer distances involved. Similarly, quality control for international services may be much more difficult because of different service uses, changing expectations, and varying national regulations.

Because services are delivered directly to the user, they are frequently much more sensitive to cultural factors than are products. Their influence on the individual abroad may be welcomed or greeted with hostility. For example, Walt Disney, the first studio guaranteed a time slot on Polish television, began broadcasting Disney animated shows and live-action features in September 1990.[4] On the other hand, countries that place a strong emphasis on cultural identity have set barriers inhibiting market penetration by foreign films. For instance, Brazil imposed the CONCINE Resolution 98, which, among other restrictions, requires all Brazilian home video distributors and outlets to carry a minimum inventory of 25 percent Brazilian titles. As Brazil is the 10th largest foreign market in revenue for all media, this barrier severely restricts the number of foreign film titles imported into the country.[5]

THE ROLE OF SERVICES IN THE U.S. ECONOMY

Since the Industrial Revolution, the United States has seen itself as a primary international competitor in the production of goods. In the past few decades, however, the U.S. economy has increasingly become a service economy, as Figure 16.4 shows. The service sector now produces 68 percent of the GNP and employs 76 percent of the workforce.[6] The major segments that compose the service sector are communications, transportation, public utilities, finance, insurance and real estate, wholesale and retail businesses, government, and "services" (a diverse category including business services, personal services, and professional and health services). The service sector accounts for most of the growth in total nonfarm employment: Out of the approximately 19 million new workers added to the total U.S. employment payroll during the period from 1982 to 1989, for example, the service sector employed roughly 17.1 million, compared with approximately 1.9 million for the manufacturing sector. Within the service sector, retail trade, services, and state and local government employed almost 75 percent of the increase.[7]

Of course, only a limited segment of the total range of services is sold internationally. Federal, state, and local government employees, for example, sell few of their services to foreigners. U.S. laundries and restaurants only occasionally service foreign tourists. Many service industries that do sell abroad often have at their disposal large organizations, specialized technology, or advanced professional expertise. Strength in these characteristics has enabled the United States to become the world's largest exporter of services. Total U.S. services exported grew from $6 billion in 1958 to over $178.3 billion in 1992.[8] For a long time, this growth of services trade enabled the United States to maintain a favorable Balance of Payments, even though the U.S. merchandise trade account was in deficit. The contribution of services to

**FIGURE 16.4
Employment in Industrial Sectors as a Percentage of the Total Labor Force**

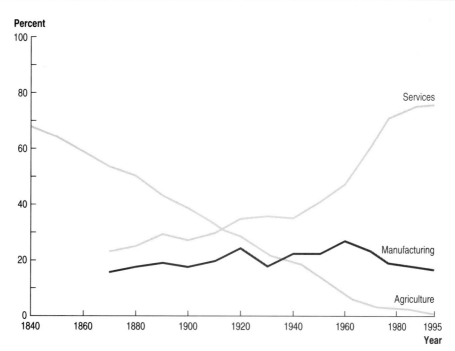

Source: J.B. Quinn, "The Impacts of Technology on the Services Sector," *Technology and Global Industry: Companies and Nations in the World Economy* (Washington, D.C.: National Academy of Sciences, 1987).

This driver's mobile radio equipment operates on Motorola's Japan Specialized Mobile Radio System, which is among the world's most advanced services of its type.

Source: Courtesy of Motorola, Inc.

the Balance of Payments is highlighted in Table 16.1. It shows that even though the U.S. services trade balance is still producing a substantial surplus, it can no longer make up for the huge deficits in merchandise trade.

International service trade has had very beneficial results for many U.S. firms. Citibank, for example, receives 65 percent of its total revenues from foreign operations; the world's top 10 advertising agencies obtain most of their gross revenue from abroad, as Table 16.2 shows. The top 10 U.S. construction contractors derive more than 40 percent of their revenues from overseas. These facts demonstrate that many service firms have become truly international and formidable in size.

However, dramatic international growth is not confined to U.S. firms. The import of services into the United States is also increasing dramatically. In 1992, the United States imported more than $123.4 billion worth of services.[9] Competition in international services is rising rapidly at all levels. Hong Kong, Singapore, and western Europe are increasingly active in service industries such as banking, insurance, and advertising. Years ago, U.S. construction firms could count on a virtual monopoly on large-scale construction projects. Today, firms from South Korea, Italy, and other countries are taking a major share of the international construction business. Furthermore, the United States has long been recognized as the leader in software development, yet, as Global Perspective 16.2 indicates, this lead may be challenged soon. The overall result of these developments is that the U.S. share of international service trade is estimated to have declined in relative terms—from 25 to 20 percent of the world market—within a decade.

THE ROLE OF INTERNATIONAL SERVICES IN THE WORLD ECONOMY

The United States is not unique in its conversion to a service economy. Similar changes have taken place internationally, and several developed countries have service sectors that produce more than 50 percent of their gross domestic products. At the present time, services trade is taking place mainly among the industrialized countries. However, this trend appears to be changing.

The economies of developing countries have traditionally first established a strong agricultural and then a manufacturing sector to meet basic needs such as food and shelter before venturing into the services sector. Some developing countries, such as Mexico, Singapore, Hong Kong, Bermuda, and the Bahamas, are steering away from the traditional economic development pattern and are concentrating on developing strong service sectors.[10] The reasons vary from a lack of natural resources with which to develop agricultural and/or manufacturing sectors to recognition of

**TABLE 16.1
Balance of Trade in
Goods and Services,
1992 (in billions)**

Exports of goods and services:		$617.6
Goods	$439.3	
Services	178.3	
Services as a percentage of goods: 41%		
Imports of goods and services:		$659.0
Goods	$535.6	
Services	123.4	
Services as a percentage of goods: 23%		
Balance on goods trade	−96.3	
Balance on services	54.9	
Balance on goods and services		−41.4

Sources: U.S. Department of Commerce, *National Trade Data Bank;* U.S. Department of Commerce, Office of International Investment.

**TABLE 16.2
The World's Top 10
Advertising Agencies
by Gross Income, 1991
(in millions of dollars)**

Firm	Worldwide	United States
1. WPP Group	$2,661.80	$1,303.90
2. Interpublic Group of Cos.	1,798.90	558.20
3. Saatchi & Saatchi Co.	1,705.50	698.90
4. Omnicom Group	1,471.20	678.40
5. Dentsu	1,451.00	23.90
6. Young & Rubicam	1,057.10	980.80
7. Euro RSCG	1,016.30	140.00
8. Grey Advertising	659.30	292.90
9. Hakuhodo	655.60	7.10
10. Foote, Cone and Belding	616.00	299.60

Source: Compiled from "World's Top 30 Advertising Organizations," *Advertising Age,* April 13, 1992.

the strong demand for services and the ability to provide them through tourism and a willing, skilled, and inexpensive labor force. As a result, it is anticipated that services trade will continue to grow. However, as more countries enter the sector, the international services business will become more competitive.

GLOBAL TRANSFORMATIONS IN THE SERVICES SECTOR

What changes account for the dramatic rise in services trade? Two major factors that seem to be responsible are environmental and technological change.

One primary environmental change is reduced governmental regulation of services, particularly within the United States. In the mid-1970s, a philosophical decision was made to reduce government interference in the marketplace in the hope of enhancing competition. The primary deregulated industries in the United States have been transportation, banking, and telecommunications. As a result of regulatory changes, new competitors participate in the marketplace. Some service sectors have benefited and others have suffered from this withdrawal of government intervention. Regulatory changes were initially thought to have primarily domestic effects, but they have rapidly spread internationally. For example, the 1984 **deregulation** of AT&T has given rise to competition not only in the United States. Japan's telecommunication monopoly, NT&T, was deregulated in 1985. Today, domestic and international competition in the telecommunications sector has increased dramatically. Growth for all U.S. long-distance carriers typically has been stronger interna-

Global Perspective

16.2
Indian Exports: Not Just Carpets but Software

Tata Consultancy Services, the leading software maker in India, sold in just one year 11,000 copies of a $140 accounting program for personal computers. That is remarkable because it shows that the world's second most populous nation may be beginning to build a viable domestic software market. Such a development may well put India in a position to compete in global software markets.

India's domestic software market grew by 45 percent in 1992. This growth is helping the 500 local software houses to hone their development and marketing skills at home so they can sell abroad. Software exports jumped by 67 percent, to $144 million. If the growth keeps up, it will mean that India's 2.5 million computer and software professionals can advance their careers without relocating abroad.

In 1991, the World Bank surveyed 150 prominent U.S. and European hardware and software manufacturers. The respondents ranked India's programmers first out of eight countries for both on-site and offshore software development, ahead of Ireland, Israel, Mexico, and Singapore. With average annual programmer salaries of about $3,000, quality software production in India costs much less than what it would cost in the United States.

Source: Sunita Wadekar Bhargava, "Software from India? Yet, it's for real," *Business Week,* January 18, 1993, p. 77.

tionally than domestically. Apart from AT&T, firms such as MCI and Sprint now offer their services worldwide. As MCI President Bert C. Roberts stated: "I can't overemphasize the importance of the international market to the growth of this business."[11]

Similarly, deregulatory efforts in the transportation sector have had international repercussions. New air carriers have entered the market to compete against established truck carriers and have done so successfully by pricing their services differently both nationally and internationally. Deregulatory efforts therefore have also affected international regulations, such as **conference pricing,** and have caused deregulation in foreign countries. Obviously, a British airline can count only to a limited extent on government support in order to remain competitive with new, low-priced fares offered by other carriers also serving the British market. The deregulatory movement that originated in the United States has spread internationally, particularly to Europe, and fostered new competition and new competitive practices. Because many of these changes resulted in lower prices, demand has been stimulated, leading to a rise in the volume of international services trade.

Another major environmental change in the United States has been the decreased regulation of service industries by their service groups. For example, business practices in fields such as health care, law, and accounting are becoming increasingly competitive and aggressive. New economic realities require firms in these industries to search for new ways to attract market share and expand their markets. International markets are one frequently untapped possibility for market expansion and have therefore become a prime target for such firms.

Technological advancement is the second major change that has taken place. Increasingly, progress in technology is offering new ways of doing business and is permitting businesses to expand their horizons internationally. Through computerization, for instance, service exchanges that previously would have been prohibitively expensive are now feasible. As an example, Ford Motor Company uses one major computer system to carry out its new car designs in both the United States and Europe. This practice not only lowers expenditures on hardware but also permits better utilization of existing equipment by allowing design groups in different time zones to use the equipment around the clock. Of course, this development could take place only after advances in data-transmission procedures. Similarly, more rapid data transmission also enabled financial institutions to expand their service delivery through a worldwide network.

Another result of technological advancement is that service industry expansion is not confined to those services that are labor intensive and therefore better performed in areas of the world where labor possesses a comparative advantage. Rather, technology-intensive services are becoming the sunrise industries of the 1990s.

PROBLEMS IN INTERNATIONAL SERVICE TRADE

Together with the increase in the importance of service trade, new problems have emerged in the service sector. Many of these problems have been characterized as affecting mainly the negotiations between nations, but they are of sufficient importance to firms engaged in international activities to merit a brief review.

Data-Collection Problems

The data collected on service trade are quite poor. Service transactions are often invisible statistically as well as physically. For example, the trip abroad of a consultant for business purposes may be hard to track and measure. The fact that the U.S. Department of Commerce has precise data on the number of trucks exported down to the last bolt but has little information on reinsurance flows reflects past governmental inattention to services. Only recently has it been recognized that the income generated and the jobs created through the sale of services abroad are just as important as income and jobs resulting from the production and exportation of goods. In spite of increased attention paid to the issue, official government sources have stated that "we don't really know how much is being earned from service exports, but we do know that service exports are growing substantially."[12] Consequently, estimates of services trade vary widely. Total actual volume of U.S. exports of services is believed to be almost double the amount shown by official statistics.[13]

When considering the dimension of the problem of data collection on services in the United States, with its sophisticated data gathering and information system, it is easy to imagine how many more problems are encountered in countries lacking such elaborate systems and unwilling to allocate funds for them. The gathering of information is of course made substantially more difficult because services are intangible and therefore more difficult to measure and to trace than products. Insufficient knowledge and information have led to a lack of transparency, making it difficult for nations either to gauge or to influence services trade. As a result, regulations are often put into place without precise information as to their repercussions on actual trade performance.

U.S. Disincentives to the Offering of International Services

Despite its commitment to free trade, the United States has erected and maintained major barriers to international services. These disincentives affect both inbound and

Services as a Portion of Gross Domestic Product

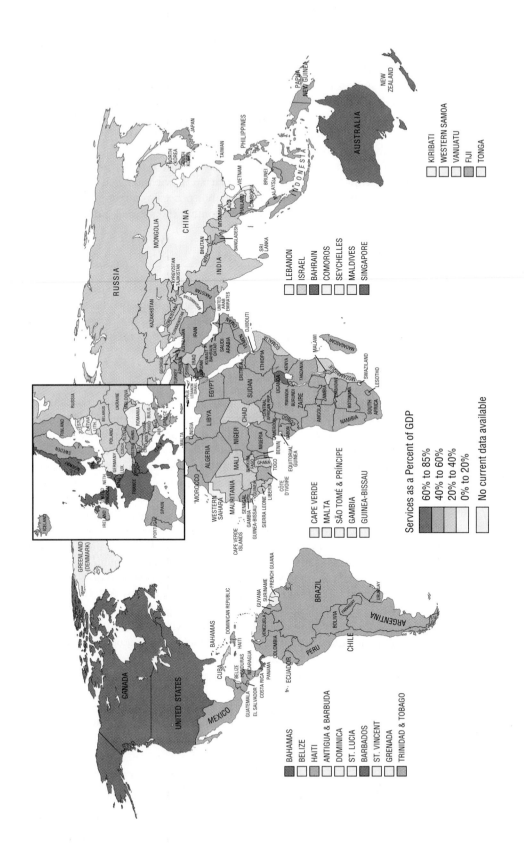

Source: *Book of Vital World Statistics*, 1990.

492

outbound services. Barriers to services destined for the U.S. market result mainly from regulatory practices. The fields of banking, insurance, and accounting provide some examples. These industries are regulated at both federal and state levels, and the regulations often pose a formidable barrier to potential entrants from abroad.

The chief complaint of foreign countries is not that the United States discriminates against foreign service providers, but rather that the United States places more severe restrictions on them than do foreign countries. In addition, the entire U.S. regulatory process gives little weight to international policy issues and often operates in isolation from executive branch direction.[14] These barriers are, of course, a reflection of the decision-making process within the U.S. domestic economy and are unlikely to change in the near future. A coherent approach toward international commerce in services is hardly likely to emerge from the disparate decisions of agencies such as the Interstate Commerce Commission (ICC), the Federal Communications Commission (FCC), the Securities and Exchange Commission (SEC), and the many licensing agencies at the state level.

Various domestic laws and regulations also often impede the export of U.S. services. One disincentive frequently mentioned in the past is the Foreign Corrupt Practices Act, which arguably discourages U.S. businesses and particularly service industries from competing overseas. Similarly, export-control legislation increasingly has been extended to the services sector and limits the possibility of services exports.

National Regulations of Services Abroad

Obstacles to service trade abroad can be categorized into two major types: barriers to entry and problems in performing services abroad.

Barriers to entry are often justified by reference to "national security" and "economic security." For example, the impact of banking on domestic economic activity is given as a reason why banking should be carried out only by nationals or indeed should be operated entirely under government control. Sometimes the protection of service users is cited, particularly of bank depositors and insurance policyholders. Another justification for barriers is the frequently used infant-industry argument: "With sufficient time to develop on our own, we can compete in world markets." Often, however, this argument is used simply to prolong the ample licensing profits generated by restricted entry. Yet, defining a barrier to service marketing is not always easy. For example, Taiwan gives an extensive written examination to prospective accountants (as do most countries) to ensure that licensed accountants are qualified to practice. Naturally, the examination is given in Chinese. The fact that few U.S. accountants read and write Chinese and hence are unable to pass the examination does not necessarily constitute a barrier to trade in accountancy services.[15]

Even if barriers to entry are nonexistent or can be overcome, service companies have difficulty performing abroad effectively once they have achieved access to the local market. One reason is that rules and regulations based on tradition may inhibit innovation. A more important reason is that governments pursue social objectives through national regulations. The distinction between discriminatory and nondiscriminatory regulations is of primary importance here. Regulations that impose larger operating costs on foreign service providers than on the local competitors, that provide subsidies to local firms only, or that deny competitive opportunities to foreign suppliers are a proper cause for international concern. The problem of discrimination becomes even more acute when foreign firms face competition from government-owned or government-controlled enterprises. On the other hand, nondiscriminatory regulations may be inconvenient and may hamper business operations, but they offer less cause for international criticism.

All of these regulations make it difficult for international services to penetrate world markets. At the governmental level, services frequently are not recognized as a major facet of world trade or are viewed with suspicion because of a lack of understanding, and barriers to entry often result. To make progress in tearing them down, much educational work needs to be done.

MACRO RESPONSES TO PROBLEMS IN INTERNATIONAL SERVICE TRADE

U.S. Developments

Greater experience and know-how give the United States a major comparative advantage in service trade. As a result, the United States has been the country most concerned with international problems in the providing of services. This concern originated in the private sector in the 1960s. International insurance companies began to organize into advisory committees, shortly to be joined by companies in the banking and transportation sectors.

A major boost to this effort occurred when the **Trade Act of 1974** pointedly expanded the definition of international trade to include trade in services, gave the president a mandate to negotiate reduced services barriers, and made provision for presidential retaliation against countries that discriminate against U.S. service companies. In 1976, a White House study made a series of recommendations on services issues, including suggestions for international negotiations and government reorganization.[16] In 1978, the U.S. Chamber of Commerce founded its International Services Industry Committee to influence the formulation of policy.

The recommendation to reorganize resulted in 1978 in the creation of an international services division within the U.S. Department of Commerce. However, responsibility for services issues remained far-flung and dispersed across departments such as State, Treasury, and Transportation. The Trade Act of 1979 and trade reorganization plan assigned policy leadership in the area of services trade to the office of the **United States Trade Representative** and created a Services Policy Advisory Committee.

In its international efforts to improve the climate for international service trade, the United States has had some success with bilateral negotiations. For many decades, selected services were given general coverage in bilateral treaties of Friendship, Commerce, and Navigation. Since 1980, however, specific services negotiations and agreements have been concluded with major trading partners. For example, bilateral negotiations resulted in Japan's lifting of restrictions on U.S. computer service sales. The Korean insurance market began to open to foreign firms in 1983. The banking sector in Japan was opened in 1984 to foreign participation in offering financial services and syndicated loans. U.S. lawyers were permitted to begin operations in Japan in 1987.

In addition, the United States has taken various steps to strengthen its hand in future international negotiations. Most of them consist of threatening retaliation in the event that other nations refuse to liberalize services trade. The **International Banking Act of 1978,** for example, which established a comprehensive federal government role in the regulation of foreign bank participation, directed the government to submit a report to Congress on "the extent to which U.S. banks are denied, whether by law or practice, national treatment in conducting bank operations in foreign countries."[17] Congress has also added **reciprocity provisions** for services in various fields, with the general thrust that reciprocity should be a significant factor in determining whether and to what extent foreign firms would be able to participate in regulated industries in the United States. Usually this approach requires that, in order for foreign firms to participate in the U.S. market, U.S. firms must have access to the foreign market.

International Developments

Less progress has been made on the global level. Although the GATT provides a framework for disciplining national restraint of trade in goods, no similar framework exists for trade in services. Even though the original ITO incorporated services considerations, they were not part of the subsequently implemented GATT framework.

An early postwar multilateral effort to liberalize international trade in services was the OECD code on invisible transactions, which in the 1950s removed some barriers to service trade. Within the GATT, the United States attempted in the late 1970s, near the end of the **Tokyo Round,** to add service issues to the agenda. However, this move was greeted with international suspicion because the United States has the largest service economy and the most service exports, and other nations suspected that any liberalization would principally benefit the United States. Moreover, some of the negotiating partners were as lacking in knowledge about services trade as U.S. negotiators had been a few years earlier. As a result, services were addressed only to a very limited extent in the Tokyo Round.

Services are therefore covered in the international trade framework only by the **Government Procurement Code** and the **Subsidies and Countervailing Measures Code.** The former covers services only to the extent that they are ancillary to purchases of goods and do not exceed the goods in value. The latter is restricted to services that are ancillary to trade in goods.

Currently, the United States is pushing hard to have services included in international trade negotiations. As part of this effort, the United States has obtained agreement on the establishment of a study group on services trade barriers within the OECD. The information produced may eventually improve the climate for a services trade agreement.

In a major breakthrough in Punta del Este in 1986, the United States also obtained agreement from the major GATT participants to conduct services trade negotiations parallel with product negotiations in the Uruguay Round. However, many developing nations, particularly Brazil and India, continue to oppose such negotiation because they believe that product issues should be resolved first and that any agreement on services trade would restrict their future international competitiveness. Talks on services trade have continued in the Uruguay Round, focusing attention on the vast benefits of expanded trade in services. Although fundamental differences still exist between the United States and several other countries, a marker has been established for any future negotiations of services trade.[18]

| CORPORATE INVOLVEMENT IN INTERNATIONAL SERVICE TRADE | ## Typical International Services |

CORPORATE INVOLVEMENT IN INTERNATIONAL SERVICE TRADE

Typical International Services

Although many firms are active in the international service arena, others do not perceive their existing competitive advantage. Numerous services that are efficiently performed in the home market may have great potential for internationalization.

U.S. financial institutions, for example, are very competitive internationally in providing banking services. In particular, banks possess an advantage in areas such as credit-card operations, customer service, and collection management. In the general area of international finance, however, U.S. banks need to expend major efforts in order to remain competitive. Increasingly, the leadership role has been taken by banks in Japan and Europe, which are boosted by large assets and a solid income performance, as seen in Table 16.3.

Construction, design, and engineering services also have great international potential. Because of vast U.S. experience, providers of these services can achieve economies of scale not only for machinery and material but also in areas such as personnel management and the overall management of projects. Particularly for international projects that are large scale and long term, the experience advantage could weigh heavily in favor of U.S. firms.

Because of their long history in the United States, insurance services sold internationally are backed by substantial knowledge about underwriting, risk evaluation, and operations. Firms offering legal and accounting services can aid U.S. firms abroad through support activities; they can also help foreign firms and countries improve business and governmental operations.

In the field of computer and data services, the United States has more experience than most other countries. Knowledge of computer operations, data manipulations, data transmission, and data analysis is insufficiently exploited internationally by many small and medium-sized firms.

Similarly, U.S. communication services may have substantial future international opportunities. For example, U.S. experience in the areas of videotext, home banking, and home shopping may be valuable abroad, particularly where geographic obstacles make the establishment of retail outlets cumbersome and expensive. Alternatively, global communication services, as shown in Figure 16.5, can greatly expand the reach of U.S. corporations.

Many U.S. organizations have vast experience in the field of teaching services. Both the educational and the corporate sector, which largely have concentrated their work in the domestic market, have expertise in management motivation as well as the teaching of operational, managerial, and theoretical issues. As this chapter's opening vignette has shown, major growth opportunities may exist both for U.S. educational efforts abroad and the education of non–U.S. individuals at home, both of which result in services exports. In the same vein, management consulting services can be provided by U.S. firms and individuals to the many foreign countries and corporations in need of them. Of particular value could be management expertise in areas where U.S. firms maintain global leadership, such as transportation and logistics. Major opportunities also exist abroad for U.S. industries that deal with societal problems. For example, U.S. firms that develop environmentally safe products or produce pollution-control equipment may be able to exploit new markets as other nations increase their awareness of and concern about the environment and tighten their laws. Similarly, advances in health care or new knowledge in combatting AIDS will offer major opportunities for foreign-market penetration.

Because all service expenditures funded from abroad by foreign citizens also represent a service export, tourism plays an increasingly vital role in U.S. services trade. Every foreign visitor who spends foreign currency in the United States contributes to an improvement in the current account. With the value of the dollar declining, tourism services may well be destined to become a key national export. Tourism is already the largest employer in 13 states, headed by Nevada and Hawaii, where 33 percent and 21 percent of all jobs are attributable to tourism.[19] The same holds true for U.S. health services offered to citizens from abroad and U.S. education provided to foreign students. Yet, in order to be even more effective exporters, firms in these service industries need to properly promote their offerings to such new clients.

TABLE 16.3   International Bank Scoreboard

			Assets		Capital	Performance			Market Value
			Millions of Dollars	Change from 1990 %	Millions of Dollars	Net Income $ Mil	Change from 1990 %	Return on Equity %	Millions of Dollars 5/31/92
1	Dai-Ichi Kangyo Bank	Japan	446,881.4	−1.36	15,459.5	689.5	−7.57	4.52	34,677
2	Sumitomo Bank	Japan	428,226.6	−1.09	17,203.6	909.3	−19.31	5.39	37,119
3	Sakura Bank	Japan	421,455.0	−2.55	13,427.2	609.7	−5.92	4.75	29,047
4	Fuji Bank	Japan	420,059.5	−0.64	14,679.7	715.1	−9.61	4.92	33,991
5	Sanwa Bank	Japan	412,788.9	−3.12	14,470.5	805.4	−5.39	5.69	30,408
6	Mitsubishi Bank	Japan	401,327.8	−3.13	13,216.4	467.4	−31.23	3.58	39,839
7	Norinchukin Bank	Japan	307,741.8	16.49	1,905.2	304.9	−11.96	16.70	NT
8	Credit Agricole	France	307,203.5	2.40	15,042.1	986.5	6.64	7.02	NT
9	Credit Lyonnais	France	306,334.9	8.46	9,651.5	787.3	−10.61	8.57	4,109
10	Industrial Bank of Japan	Japan	303,214.9	−1.21	10,420.0	448.6	−10.38	4.36	34,045
11	Deutsche Bank	Germany	288,879.4	12.86	11,497.7	930.3	32.11	8.42	20,158
12	Banque Nationale de Paris	France	275,876.3	−3.84	9,366.6	660.6	58.65	7.56	5,193
13	Tokai Bank	Japan	252,877.7	−4.31	8,170.1	384.6	16.40	4.79	14,590
14	Barclays	Britain	251,052.7	2.39	11,461.2	538.1	−30.84	4.50	10,979
15	ABN AMRO Holding	Netherlands	242,685.9	5.55	9,344.0	912.1	12.07	10.02	6,466
16	Long-Term Credit Bank of Japan	Japan	241,007.9	6.00	8,187.4	475.7	69.44	5.94	14,607
17	Societe Generale	France	234,748.3	8.56	6,860.4	711.6	25.63	11.16	7,544
18	National Westminster Bank	Britain	222,805.9	1.21	10,328.7	94.5	−75.47	0.88	10,498
19	Bank of Tokyo	Japan	219,105.8	−7.22	7,733.5	332.0	−19.67	4.35	17,322
20	Citicorp	U.S.	216,922.0	−0.03	9,489.0	−457.0	NM	−4.50	6,449
21	Kyowa Saitama Bank	Japan	212,940.0	−8.24	7,820.9	285.3	−25.10	3.69	13,147
22	Paribas	France	199,973.9	9.62	11,279.0	211.8	−73.16	2.06	NT
23	Mitsubishi Trust & Banking	Japan	194,243.9	−3.09	6,417.8	264.2	−14.81	4.18	9,896
24	Dresdner Bank	Germany	189,444.5	3.92	6,500.6	430.0	−29.23	6.67	7,717
25	Union Bank of Switzerland	Switzerland	181,905.6	6.59	13,266.0	911.8	35.08	6.99	12,257
26	Sumitomo Trust & Banking	Japan	178,325.9	−0.44	6,304.9	243.1	−29.48	3.91	9,050
27	Instituto Bancario San Paolo di Torino	Italy	178,078.7	38.38	6,890.4	773.7	8.11	12.88	5,857
28	Caisses d'Epargne	France	172,973.0	1.13	7,072.2	482.6	−10.87	7.17	NT
29	Mitsui Trust & Banking	Japan	168,975.5	−0.86	5,238.2	186.7	−26.84	3.61	8,102
30	Bank of China	China	162,987.4	33.85	9,837.1	1,533.4	35.25	17.32	NT
31	HSBC Holdings	Hong Kong	160,354.9	7.82	10,405.8	1,321.1	85.74	13.27	10,052
32	Swiss Bank Corp.	Switzerland	152,484.8	8.50	9,579.3	796.0	29.83	8.65	6,391
33	Bayerische Vereinsbank	Germany	147,306.3	9.80	3,848.5	242.5	2.08	6.85	4,925
34	Westdeutsche Landesbank	Germany	146,741.1	11.29	3,360.0	148.2	298.93	4.45	NT
35	Commerzbank	Germany	146,661.1	5.01	4,493.5	360.9	−1.81	8.21	4,161
36	Daiwa Bank	Japan	142,289.0	1.96	4,564.5	237.9	−14.82	5.31	10,631
37	Chemical Banking	U.S.	138,930.0	1.97	7,281.0	154.0	−65.00	2.02	8,761
38	DG Bank	Germany	135,670.2	3.30	3,470.3	195.3	0.00	5.81	NT
39	Nippon Credit Bank	Japan	134,098.6	−1.24	4,137.7	313.1	84.89	7.79	9,236
40	Yasuda Trust & Banking	Japan	130,472.0	−5.03	4,158.8	174.6	−12.78	4.26	7,399
41	Rabobank	Netherlands	126,900.7	7.50	7,612.8	594.0	4.31	8.12	NT
42	Hypo-Bank	Germany	125,539.8	10.29	3,155.7	238.1	15.19	7.61	4,732
43	Banca Nazionale del Lavoro	Italy	122,929.4	−4.45	5,580.7	73.8	−24.78	1.55	NT
44	Shoko Chunkin Bank	Japan	115,999.2	6.78	3,026.7	208.5	1.47	7.25	NT
45	Bankamerica	U.S.	115,509.0	4.32	8,063.0	1,123.7	0.78	15.78	15,578
46	Credit Suisse	Switzerland	114,116.6	4.07	6,689.0	689.8	70.31	10.68	5,855
47	Bayerische Landesbank	Germany	111,635.3	10.24	2,830.9	192.5	66.04	7.77	NT
48	Royal Bank of Canada (10)	Canada	111,445.4	8.28	6,977.4	889.9	2.62	14.28	5,984
49	Nationsbank	U.S.	110,319.0	−2.19	6,518.0	201.9	−66.06	3.06	11,034
50	Toyo Trust & Banking	Japan	110,236.4	−1.45	3,534.1	136.2	−16.59	3.91	5,555

Japanese data are for fiscal year ended March 31, 1992. Data for all other banks are for fiscal year ended December 31, 1991, unless otherwise designated. Stock market data are for CS Holding. NT = not traded.

**FIGURE 16.5
An Advertisement for
an International
Communication Service**

International services should be seen not only from the U.S. perspective, how-ever. Many other countries possess factor advantages that make some of their ser-vices very competitive. In Japan, for example, because of the lack of privacy legis-lation, retailers can obtain a substantial amount of information about their customer groups and usage habits that can be useful to foreign firms. Firms in other nations may have developed a specific expertise due to their environment. As Global Per-spective 16.3 shows, Israeli knowledge in arid agriculture has already been converted into very successful services exports.

A proper mix in international services might also be achieved by pairing the strengths of different partners. For example, U.S. information technology could be combined with the financial resources of individuals and countries abroad. The strengths of both partners would be used to obtain maximum benefits.

Combining international advantages in services may ultimately result in the de-velopment of an even more drastic comparative lead. For example, the United States has an international head start in such areas as high technology, information gath-ering, information processing, information analysis, and teaching. Ultimately, the ma-jor thrust of U.S. international services might not be to provide these service com-ponents individually but rather to ensure that, based on all U.S. resources, better decisions are made. If better decision making is transferable to a wide variety of in-ternational situations, this in itself might become the overriding future comparative advantage of the United States in the international market.

Global Perspective

16.3
Israel Provides Services in Central Asia

After a long day's work in the blistering sun, young Israeli kibbutz members return to their spartan quarters. Yet, this is not a scene from the Jordan Valley but takes place in central Asia, where kibbutz members are helping economic advancement and seeking a bit of profit as well.

A rapidly growing number of Israeli enterprises have begun to plow the distant fields of the Moslem republics of the former Soviet Union, which only a short time ago were unlikely to do business with the Jewish state. Says Shoul Eisenberg, an Israeli entrepreneur: "The key to the operation is the kibbutz members willing to live in harsh conditions." One of his projects aims to improve cotton growth in Uzbekistan. He offers Israeli drip irrigation, which requires much less water, as well as other Israeli-developed farming techniques. Even though the Uzbekis had been growing cotton for over 2,000 years, they were astonished by the results. Cotton production increased by 40 percent, water usage was reduced by 66 percent, and there was 10–20 percent less use of fertilizers and pesticides. Thousands of officials and agriculturists flocked to the site from all over central Asia to look at the spectacular size of the cotton and hear the statistics. Contracts for similar projects were subsequently signed with Kazakhstan and Tadzhikistan.

Source: Adapted from Abraham Rabinovich, "A benign, business-oriented march into Central Asia," *The Jerusalem Post International Edition,* September 5, 1992, B3.

Starting to Offer Services Internationally

For services that are delivered mainly in support of or in conjunction with products, the most sensible approach for the international novice is to follow the path of the product. For years, many large accounting and banking firms have done this by determining where their major multinational clients have set up new operations and then following them. Smaller service providers who cooperate closely with manufacturing firms can determine where the manufacturing firms are operating internationally. Ideally, of course, it would be possible to follow clusters of manufacturers abroad in order to obtain economies of scale internationally while simultaneously looking for entirely new client groups.

Service providers whose activities are independent from products need a different strategy. These individuals and firms must search for market situations abroad that are similar to the domestic market. Such a search should be concentrated in their area of expertise. For example, a design firm learning about construction projects abroad can investigate the possibility of rendering its design services. Similarly, a management consultant learning about the plans of a foreign country or firm to computerize can explore the possibility of overseeing a smooth transition from manual to computerized activities. What is required is the understanding that similar problems are likely to occur in similar situations.

Another opportunity consists of identifying and understanding points of transition abroad. Just as U.S. society has undergone change, foreign societies are subject to a changing domestic environment. If, for example, new transportation services are introduced, an expert in containerization may wish to consider whether to offer his or her service to improve the efficiency of the new system.

Leads for international service opportunities can also be gained by keeping informed about international projects sponsored by domestic organizations such as the

U.S. Agency for International Development or the Trade Development Program as well as international organizations such as the United Nations, the International Finance Corporation, or the World Bank. Frequently such projects are in need of support through services. Overall, the international service provider needs to search for similar situations, similar problems, or scenarios requiring similar solutions in order to formulate an effective international-expansion strategy.

Strategic Indications

To be successful in the international service offering, the manager must first determine the nature and the aim of the services-offering core—that is, whether the service will be aimed at people or at things and whether the service act in itself will result in tangible or intangible actions. Table 16.4 provides examples of such a classification strategy that will help the manager to better determine the position of the services effort.

During this determination, the manager must consider other tactical variables that have an impact on the preparation of the service offering. For example, in the field of research, the measurement of capacity and delivery efficiency often remains highly qualitative rather than quantitative. In the field of communications, the intangibility of the service reduces the manager's ability to provide samples. This makes communicating the service offered much more difficult than communicating a product offer. Brochures or catalogs explaining services often must show a proxy for the service in order to provide the prospective customer with tangible clues. A cleaning service, for instance, can show a picture of an individual removing trash or clean-

TABLE 16.4 Understanding the Nature of the Service Act

Nature of the Service Act	Direct Recipient of the Service	
	People	**Things**
Tangible Actions	Services directed at people's bodies:	Services directed at goods and other physical possessions:
	Health care Passenger transportation Beauty salons Exercise clinics Restaurants Haircutting	Freight transportation Industrial equipment repair and maintenance Janitorial services Laundry and dry cleaning services Landscaping/lawn care Veterinary care
Intangible Actions	Services directed at people's minds:	Services directed at intangible assets:
	Education Broadcasting Information services Theaters Museums	Banking Legal services Accounting Securities Insurance

Source: Christopher H. Lovelock, *Managing Services: Marketing, Operations, and Human Resources* (Englewood Cliffs, N.J.: Prentice-Hall, Inc., 1988), 47.

ing a window. However, the picture will not fully communicate the performance of the service. Because of the different needs and requirements of individual consumers, the manager must pay attention to the two-way flow of communication. Mass communication must be supported by intimate one-on-one follow-up.

The role of personnel deserves special consideration in international service delivery. Because the customer interface is intense, proper provisions need to be made for training of personnel both domestically and internationally. Major emphasis must be placed on appearance. Most of the time the person delivering the service—rather than the service itself—will communicate the spirit, value, and attitudes of the service corporation.

This close interaction with the consumer will also have organizational implications. For example, while tight control over personnel may be desired, the individual interaction that is required points toward the need for an international decentralization of service delivery. This, in turn, requires delegation of large amounts of responsibility to individuals and service "subsidiaries" and requires a great deal of trust in all organizational units. This trust, of course, can be greatly enhanced through proper methods of training and supervision.

The areas of pricing and financing require special attention. Because services cannot be stored, much greater responsiveness to demand fluctuation must exist, and therefore much greater pricing flexibility must be maintained. At the same time, flexibility is countered by the desire to provide transparency for both the seller and the buyer of services in order to foster an ongoing relationship. The intangibility of services also makes financing more difficult. Frequently, even financial institutions with large amounts of international experience are less willing to provide financial support for international services than for products. The reasons are that the value of services is more difficult to assess, service performance is more difficult to monitor, and services are difficult to repossess. Therefore, customer complaints and difficulties in receiving payments are much more troublesome for a lender to evaluate in the area of services than for products.

Finally, the distribution implications of international services must be considered. Usually, short and direct channels are required. Within these channels, closeness to the customer is of overriding importance in order to understand what the customer really wants, to trace the use of the service, and to aid the customer in obtaining a truly tailor-made service.

SUMMARY   Services are taking on an increasing importance in international trade. They need to be considered separately from trade in merchandise because they no longer simply complement products. Often, products complement services or are in competition with them. Because of service attributes such as their intangibility, their perishability, their custom design, and their cultural sensitivity, international trade in services is frequently more complex than trade in goods.

Services play an increasing role in the economies of the United States and of other industrialized nations. As a result, international growth and competition in this sector have begun to outstrip that of merchandise trade and are likely to intensify in the future. Even though services are unlikely to replace production, the sector will account for the shaping of new competitive advantages internationally.

The many service firms now operating domestically need to investigate the possibility of going global. Historical patterns of service providers following manufacturers abroad have become obsolete as stand-alone services become more important to world trade. Management must therefore assess its vulnerability to service competition from abroad and explore opportunities to provide its services internationally.

Key Terms and Concepts

intangibility	Trade Act of 1974
perishability	United States Trade Representative
service capacity	International Banking Act of 1978
customer involvement	reciprocity provisions
service consistency	Tokyo Round
market transparency	Government Procurement Code
deregulation	Subsidies and Countervailing Measures Code
conference pricing	

Questions for Discussion

1. Discuss the major reasons for the growth of international services.
2. Why has the U.S. world market share in trade in services declined?
3. Why does the United States have a comparative advantage in many services sectors?
4. How does the international sale of services differ from the sale of goods?
5. What are some of the international business implications of service intangibility?
6. What are some ways for a firm to expand its services internationally?
7. Some predict that "the main future U.S. international service will be to offer better decisions." Do you agree? Why or why not?
8. How can a firm in a developing country participate in the international services boom?
9. Which services would you expect to migrate abroad in the next decade? Why?

Recommended Readings

Bateson, John E. G. *Managing Services Marketing.* Hinsdale, Ill.: Dryden Press, 1992.

Berry, Leonard L., David R. Bennett, and Carter W. Brown. *Service Quality.* Homewood, Ill.: Dow Jones-Irwin, 1989.

Blum, Julius M. "World Trade in Services: Opportunities and Obstacles." *1985 Proceedings of the Southwestern Marketing Association.* Denton, Tex.: March 1985.

Czepiel, John, et al., eds. *The Service Encounter.* Lexington, Mass.: Lexington Books, 1985.

Daniels, P. W., ed. *Services and Metropolitan Development: International Perspectives.* London: Routledge, 1991.

Feketekuty, Geza. *International Trade in Services.* Cambridge, Mass.: Ballinger, 1988.

Giersch, Herbert. *Services in World Economic Growth.* Boulder, Colo.: Westview Press, 1989.

Lovelock, Christopher H. *Managing Services: Marketing, Operations and Human Resources.* Englewood Cliffs, N.J.: Prentice-Hall, 1988.

——————. *Services Marketing.* 2d ed. Englewood Cliffs, N.J.: Prentice-Hall, 1990.

Robinson, Peter. *Electronic Highways for World Trade.* Boulder, Colo.: Westview Press, 1989.

Shames, Germaine W., and W. Gerald Glover. *World-Class Service.* Yarmouth, Maine: Intercultural Press, 1989.

United States Congress. *International Competition in Services.* Washington, D.C.: Congress of the United States, Office of Technology Assessment, undated.

Weisman, Ethan. *Trade in Services and Imperfect Competition: Applications to International Aviation.* Boston: Kluwer Academic, 1990.

Notes

1. Leonard L. Berry, "Services Marketing Is Different," in *Services Marketing,* ed. Christopher H. Lovelock (Englewood Cliffs, N.J.: Prentice-Hall, 1984), 30.
2. *Winning in the World Market* (Washington, D.C.: American Business Conference, November 1987), 17.
3. G. Lynn Shostack, "Service Positioning through Structural Change," *Journal of Marketing* 51 (January 1987): 38.
4. "Mickey and Co. Go to Poland," *Journal of Commerce* (July 20, 1990): 5A.
5. *1989 National Trade Estimate Report on Foreign Trade Barriers* (Washington, D.C.: Office of the United States Representative, 1989), 21–22.
6. "Service Economic Highlights," *The Service Economy,* July 1990.
7. Samuel D. Kahan, "The Service Economy—At Present, Employment Tells the Whole Story," *The Service Economy,* April 1990, 1.
8. U.S. Department of Commerce, *Survey of Current Business*, March 1991.
9. Ibid.
10. Allen Sinai and Zaharo Sofianou, "Service Sectors in Developing Countries: Some Exceptions to the Rule," *The Service Economy,* July 1990, 13.
11. Cindy Skrzycki, "China Answers a Ringing Need," *The Washington Post,* July 30, 1991, E1, E4.

12. *Current Developments in the U.S. International Service Industries* (Washington, D.C.: U.S. Department of Commerce, March 1980).
13. "The Problem of Data on Services," *International Services Newsletter* 1 (January–June 1981): 11.
14. Gary C. Hufbauer, remarks, Seminar on Services in the World Economy, organized by the United States Council of the International Chamber of Commerce, New York, May 5, 1980, 3.
15. Dorothy I. Riddle, *Key LDCs: Trade in Services,* American Graduate School of International Studies, Glendale, Ariz., March 1987, 346–347.
16. "U.S. Service Industries in World Markets," *Current Problems in Future Policy Development,* White House Interagency Study, December 1976.
17. Geza Feketekuty, "International Trade in Banking Services: The Negotiation Agenda," draft, prepared for the International Law Institute conference on the International Framework for Money and Banking in the 1980s, Washington, D.C., April 30–May 1, 1981, 8.
18. "CSI Special Report on the Uruguay Round," *CSI Newsletter,* December 1990.
19. Ilkka A. Ronkainen and Richard J. Farano, "United States' Travel and Tourism Policy," *Journal of Travel Research* 25 (Spring 1987): 2–8.

CHAPTER 17

Countertrade

LEARNING OBJECTIVES

1. To examine why countertrade transactions are becoming increasingly common.

2. To see how countertrade transactions are becoming more sophisticated and creative.

3. To discover some of the problems and dislocations caused by countertrade.

4. To understand that corporations increasingly use countertrade as a competitive tool to maintain or increase market share.

5. To learn about the new intermediaries that have emerged to facilitate countertrade transactions.

Crabs for Cars: A Winning Proposition

Nemuro, a Japanese fishing town in eastern Hokkaido, has become the site of a bustling border trade. Every Tuesday and Friday at 8 a.m. Russian fishing boats pull into Hanasaki Harbor hauling tons of crab. While some of the crew members conduct sales at the fish market, others walk to the wharf to strike bargains for used cars, which they buy with the proceeds from the crab exports. Later on in the day, the ships are loaded with cars, which are lowered with wooden beams running through window spaces, and depart for Sakhalin or Vladivostok.

With the ruble in daily decline, crab has effectively become a stable unit of currency in regional commerce. The going rate for a used car is 50,000 yen or five king crabs or 10 kegani crabs. The used cars in turn can be resold in Russia for 150,000 rubles. The crab trade has benefitted some and disadvantaged others. Some workers in Nemuro's fishing industry grumble that Russian crabs are squeezing profits. Consumers are clear winners, enjoying the world's most delicious crab at bargain prices thanks to the increased supply. Retailers and recycling shops gain from export sales to their Russian visitors. The flourishing trade has already affected the landscape of Nemuro. Signs in Russian have begun to appear in hotels, public buildings, and some shops. The Japan-Russian Information Center opened in August 1992 and is run by two Russian-speaking Japanese. There are even plans to arrange special "home stays" for Russian schoolchildren in Nemuro.

Source: Adapted from Bill Clifford, "Meeting Russia at the front line," *The Nikkei Weekly,* September 12, 1992, 1, 4.

General Motors exchanged automobiles for a trainload of strawberries. Control Data swapped a computer for a package of Polish furniture, Hungarian carpet backing, and Russian greeting cards. Ford traded cars for sheepskins from Uruguay, potatoes from Spain, toilet seats from Finland, cranes from Norway, and coffee from Colombia.[1] These are all examples of countertrade activities carried out around the world. As we saw in the chapter's opening vignette, countertrade can even lead to the emergence of new "currency" units.

This chapter will focus on the ancient, yet new, forms of barter and countertrade that are reemerging in world trade. The types of countertrade that currently exist and the reasons why these types of transactions are reemerging will be discussed. Policy issues associated with countertrade will be explored by examining the attitudes held toward countertrade by both national governments and international bodies such as the GATT, the OECD, and the U.N. Corporate countertrade practices will be reviewed, as we examine what firms do and why they do it. Finally, information will be provided on how to organize for countertrade, what problems to look out for, and how countertrade can be used as an effective international business tool.

A DEFINITION OF COUNTERTRADE

Countertrade is a sale that encompasses more than an exchange of goods, services, or ideas for money. In the international market, countertrade transactions "are those transactions which have as a basic characteristic a linkage, legal or otherwise, between exports and imports of goods or services in addition to, or in place of, financial settlements."[2] Historically, countertrade was mainly conducted in the form of **barter,** which is a direct exchange of goods of approximately equal value between parties, with no money involved. Such transactions were the very essence of business at times during which no money—that is, no common medium of exchange—existed or was available. Over time, money emerged as a convenient medium that unlinked transactions from individual parties and their joint timing and therefore permitted greater flexibility in trading activities. Repeatedly, however, we can see returns to the barter system as a result of environmental circumstances. For example, because of the tight financial constraints of both students and the institution, Georgetown University during its initial years of operation after 1789 charged part of its tuition in foodstuffs and required students to participate in the construction of university buildings. During periods of high inflation in Europe in the 1920s, goods such as bread, meat, and gold were seen as much more useful and secure than paper money, which decreased in real value by the minute. Even more recently, in the late 1940s, American cigarettes were an acceptable medium of exchange in most European countries, much more so than any particular currency except for the dollar.

Countertrade transactions have therefore always arisen when economic circumstances made it more acceptable to exchange goods directly rather than to use money as an intermediary. Conditions that encourage such business activities are lack of money, lack of value of or faith in money, lack of acceptability of money as an exchange medium, or greater ease of transaction by using goods.

These same reasons prevail in today's resurgence of countertrade. Beginning in the 1950s, countertrade and barter transactions were mainly carried out with Eastern bloc countries. The currencies of these countries were not acceptable elsewhere, because they were not freely convertible. At the same time, these countries did not want their currencies distributed outside of their economic bloc, and they did not possess sufficient foreign "hard" currency to make purchases of Western goods that were not available within COMECON countries but were crucial for further economic development. To some extent, these countries solved their currency problem by depleting their gold reserves—which, indirectly, because of the world market price for gold, was a financial transaction. However, these measures did not generate sufficient funds. Many Eastern bloc countries therefore insisted in their dealings with Western nations that the goods they produced be taken in exchange for imports so as to reduce their need for foreign currencies.

Throughout the 1980s, the official use of countertrade steadily increased. In 1972, countertrade was used by only 15 countries. By 1979, the countries conducting countertrade transactions numbered 27, and by 1989, the number was 94. Figure 17.1 lists the countries that currently request countertrade transactions from their trading partners. Estimates as to the total volume of global countertrade vary widely. A consensus of experts has put the percentage of world trade financed through countertrade transactions between 20 and 25 percent.[3] Such an estimate conflicts with IMF figures, which attribute only a very small percentage of world trade to countertrade. Yet, if all business transactions in which countertrade plays some kind of role are considered, the estimate of 20 to 25 percent could be reasonable.

Increasingly, countries are deciding that countertrade transactions are more beneficial to them than transactions based on financial exchange alone. A primary reason is that the world debt crisis has made ordinary trade financing very risky. Many countries, particularly in the developing world, simply cannot obtain the trade credit or financial assistance necessary to pay for desired imports. Heavily indebted countries, faced with the possibility of not being able to afford imports at all, hasten to use countertrade in order to maintain at least a trickle of product inflow. Furthermore, the use of countertrade permits the covert reduction of prices and therefore allows the circumvention of price and exchange controls.[4] Particularly in commodity markets with operative cartel arrangements, such as oil or agriculture, this benefit may be very useful to a producer. For example, by using oil as a countertraded

**FIGURE 17.1
Countries Requesting
Countertrade**

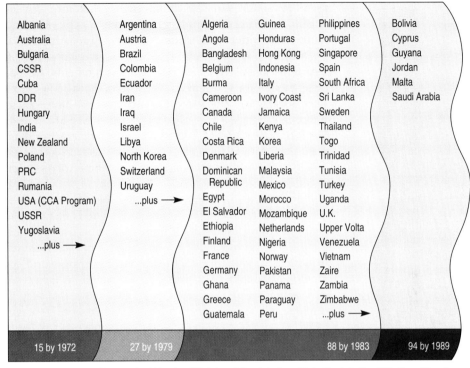

Albania	Argentina	Algeria	Guinea	Philippines	Bolivia
Australia	Austria	Angola	Honduras	Portugal	Cyprus
Bulgaria	Brazil	Bangladesh	Hong Kong	Singapore	Guyana
CSSR	Colombia	Belgium	Indonesia	Spain	Jordan
Cuba	Ecuador	Burma	Italy	South Africa	Malta
DDR	Iran	Cameroon	Ivory Coast	Sri Lanka	Saudi Arabia
Hungary	Iraq	Canada	Jamaica	Sweden	
India	Israel	Chile	Kenya	Thailand	
New Zealand	Libya	Costa Rica	Korea	Togo	
Poland	North Korea	Denmark	Liberia	Trinidad	
PRC	Switzerland	Dominican	Malaysia	Tunisia	
Rumania	Uruguay	Republic	Mexico	Turkey	
USA (CCA Program)	...plus →	Egypt	Morocco	Uganda	
USSR		El Salvador	Mozambique	U.K.	
Yugoslavia		Ethiopia	Netherlands	Upper Volta	
...plus →		Finland	Nigeria	Venezuela	
		France	Norway	Vietnam	
		Germany	Pakistan	Zaire	
		Ghana	Panama	Zambia	
		Greece	Paraguay	Zimbabwe	
		Guatemala	Peru	...plus →	

| 15 by 1972 | 27 by 1979 | 88 by 1983 | 94 by 1989 |

Source: Willis A. Bussard, "Countertrade: A View from U.S. Industry," *Countertrade and Barter Quarterly,* May 1984, 54; and Pompiliu Verzariu, Office of Barter and Countertrade, U.S. Department of Commerce, May 1989.

product for industrial equipment, a surreptitious discount (by using a higher price for the acquired products) may expand market share.

A second reason for the increase in countertrade is that many countries are again responding favorably to the notion of bilateralism. Thinking along the lines of "you scratch my back and I'll scratch yours," they prefer to exchange goods with countries that are their major business partners.

Countertrade is also often viewed by firms and nations alike as an excellent mechanism to gain entry into new markets. When a producer believes that marketing is not its strong suit, particularly in product areas that face strong international competition, it often sees countertrade as useful. The producer often hopes that the party receiving the goods will serve as a new distributor, opening up new international marketing channels and ultimately expanding the original market.

Conversely, because countertrade is highly sought after in many enormous, but hard-currency poor emerging market economies such as China, the CIS, and the former Eastern bloc countries, as well as in other cash-strapped countries in South America and the Third World, engaging in such transactions can provide major growth opportunities for firms. In increasingly competitive world markets, countertrade can be a good way to attract new buyers. By providing countertrade services, the seller is in effect differentiating its product from those of its competitors.[5]

Finally, countertrade can provide stability for long-term sales. For example, if a firm is tied to a countertrade agreement, it will need to source the product from a particular supplier, whether it wishes to do so or not. This stability is often valued very highly because it eliminates, or at least reduces, vast swings in demand and thus allows for better planning. Countertrade, therefore, can serve as a major mechanism to shift risk from the producer to another party. In that sense one can argue that countertrade offers a substitute for missing forward markets.[6]

In spite of all these apparent benefits of countertrade, there are strong economic arguments against this activity. These arguments are based mainly on efficiency grounds. As Samuelson stated, "Instead of there being a double coincidence of wants, there is likely to be a want of coincidence; so that, unless a hungry tailor happens to find an undraped farmer, who has both food and a desire for a pair of pants, neither can make a trade."[7] Clearly, countertrade ensures that instead of balances being settled on a multilateral basis, with surpluses from one country being balanced by deficits with another, accounts must now be settled on a country-by-country or even transaction-by-transaction basis. Trade then results only from the ability of two parties or countries to purchase specified goods from one another rather than from competition. As a result, uncompetitive goods may be traded. In consequence, the ability of countries and their industries to adjust structurally to more efficient production may be restricted. Countertrade can therefore be seen as eroding the quality and efficiency of production and as lowering world consumption.

These economic arguments notwithstanding, however, countries and companies increasingly see countertrade as an alternative that may be flawed but worthwhile to undertake.

TYPES OF COUNTERTRADE

Under the traditional types of barter arrangements, goods are exchanged directly for other goods of approximately equal value. As Table 17.1 shows, such transactions can encompass the exchange of a wide variety of goods—for example, bananas for cars or airplane parts for training—and are carried out both in developing and industrialized countries. However, such straightforward barter transactions, which were quite frequent in the 1950s, are less often used today "because it is difficult to find two parties prepared to make a simultaneous or near-simultaneous exchange of goods of equivalent value."[8]

Increasingly, participants in countertrade have resorted to more sophisticated versions of exchanging goods that often also include some use of money. Figure 17.2 provides an overview of the different forms of countertrade. One such refinement of simple barter is the **counterpurchase,** or **parallel barter,** agreement. In order to unlink the timing of contract performance, the participating parties sign two separate contracts that specify the goods and services to be exchanged. In this way, one transaction can go forward even though the second transaction needs more time. Such an arrangement can be particularly advantageous if delivery performance is dependent on a future event—for example, the harvest. Frequently, the exchange is not of precisely equal value; therefore some amount of cash will be involved. However, despite the lack of linkage in terms of timing, an exchange of goods for goods does take place. A special case of parallel barter is that of reverse reciprocity, "whereby parallel contracts are signed, granting each party access to needed resources (for example, oil in exchange for nuclear power plants)."[9] Such contracts are useful when long-term exchange relationships are desired.

Another common form of countertrade is the **buy-back,** or **compensation arrangement.** One party agrees to supply technology or equipment that enables the other party to produce goods with which the price of the supplied products or technology is repaid. These arrangements often "include larger amounts of time, money,

**TABLE 17.1
A Sample of Barter
Agreements**

Country		Exported Commodity	
A	B	A	B
China	Morocco	Plant protection chemicals valued at U.S. $260 million	Equivalent value of Moroccan phosphate products
China	U.S.	100 Chinese-made tail fins for 737 jetliner	Assist in qualifying personnel and machinery to meet FAA standards. Contracts valued at U.S. $39 million
U.S. (Chrysler)	Jamaica	200 pickup trucks	Equivalent value in iron ore
U.S. (General Electric)	Rumania	Two nuclear steam-generating turbines worth $121 million	Equal value of miscellaneous Rumanian goods
(U.S. (Pierre Cardin)	China	Technical advice	Silks and cashmeres
U.K. (Raleigh Bicycle)	CIS	Training CIS scientists in mountain-bike production	Titanium. Enough for 30,000 bike frames per year.
Brazil	Mexico	Foodstuff: Soybeans Sunflower seeds Petrochemicals Oil Chemicals Oil-drilling equipment Total, $3 billion	Oil at 80,000 barrels a day
Russia	Ecuador	LADA cars NIVA cars SKM pickup trucks	Bananas

Sources: Aspy P. Palia and Oded Shenkar, "Countertrade Practices in China," *Industrial Marketing Management,* 1991, 58; Raj Aggarwal, "International Business through Barter and Countertrade," *Long Range Planning,* 1989; James Ferguson, "Sputnik Experts Tackle High-flying Bikes," *European,* July 12–14, 1991, 11; Donna Vogt, *U.S. Government International Barter,* Report No. 83–211 ENR (Washington, D.C.: Congressional Research Service, 1983).

and products than straight barter arrangements."[10] They originally evolved "in response to the reluctance of communist countries to permit ownership of productive resources by the private sector—especially by foreign private sectors."[11] One example of such a buy-back arrangement is an agreement entered into by Levi Strauss and Hungary. The company transferred know-how and the Levi's trademark to Hungary. A Hungarian firm began to produce Levi's products. Some of the output was sold domestically, and the rest was marketed in western Europe by Levi Strauss, in compensation for the know-how. In the past decade, buy-back arrangements have been extended to encompass many developing and newly industrialized nations.

Another form of more refined barter, which tries to reduce the effect of bilateralism and the immediacy of the transaction, is called **clearing account barter.** Here, clearing accounts are established to track debits and credits of trades. These entries merely represent purchasing power, however, and are not directly withdrawable in cash. As a result, each party can agree in a single contract to purchase goods or services of a specified value. Although the account may be out of balance on a transaction-by-transaction basis, the agreement stipulates that over the long term a balance in the account will be restored. Frequently, the goods available for purchase with clearing account funds are tightly stipulated. In fact, funds have on occasion been labeled "apple clearing dollars" or "horseradish clearing funds." Sometimes, additional flexibility is given to the clearing account by permitting

510

Preferred Items for Export in Countertrade Transactions

Preferred Items for Export in Countertrade Transactions

Copper
Iron ore
Refined silver
Lead
Zinc
Coal
Natural gas
Petroleum
Petroleum products
Crude oil

Fruits & vegetables
Agriculture
Coffee
Sugar
Cotton
Shrimp
Bauxite
Gold
Alumina

Fish Meal
Grain
Rice
Wool
Salt
Oil Seeds
Rum
Molasses

Industrial goods
Industrial machinery
Equipment
Manufactured goods
Construction
Engineering goods
Computer software
Plastic products
Sporting goods
Hides, skins & leather

Textiles
Animals
Foodstuffs
Timber & wood products
Minerals
Gems & jewelry
Metals
Chemicals & allied products
Tobacco

Source: International Countertrade, Individual Country Practices, August 1992.

FIGURE 17.2   **Classification of Forms of Countertrade**

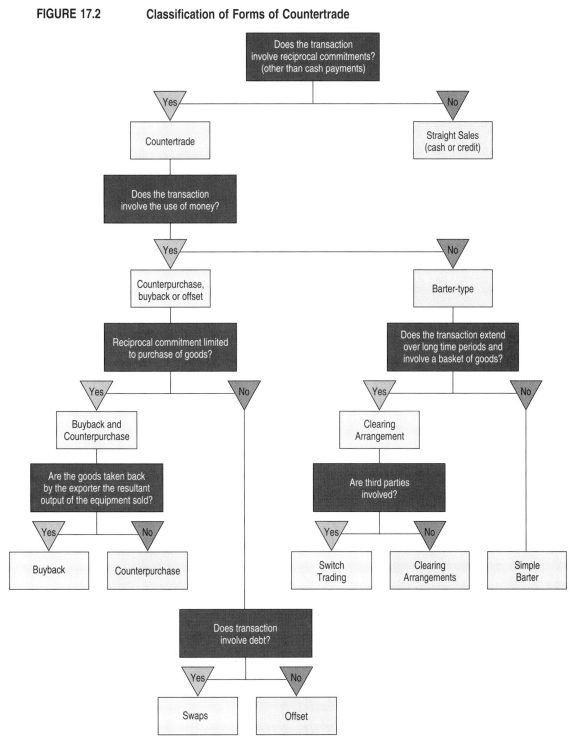

Source: Adapted from Jean-François Hennart, "Some Empirical Dimensions of Countertrade," *Journal of International Business Studies,* 21(2) 1990, 245.

switch-trading, in which credits in the account can be sold or transferred to a third party. Doing so can provide creative intermediaries with opportunities for deal making by identifying clearing account relationships with major imbalances and structuring business transactions to reduce them.

Another major form of countertrade arrangement is called **offset.** These arrangements are most frequently found in the defense-related sector and in sales of large-scale, high-priced items such as aircraft and were designed to "offset" the negative effects of large purchases from abroad on the the current account of a country. For example, a country purchasing aircraft from the United States might require that certain portions of the aircraft be produced and assembled in the purchasing country. Such a requirement is often a condition for awarding the contract or is used as the determining factor in contract decisions. Offset arrangements can take on many forms, such as coproduction, licensing, subcontracting, or joint ventures, and they are typically long term. Global Perspective 17.1 provides examples of offsets and explains some of the dangers associated with that practice. Table 17.2 lists some of the already incurred offset obligations by U.S. firms.

A final, newly emerging form of countertrade, chiefly used as a financial tool, consists of **debt swaps.** These swaps are carried out particularly with less-developed countries in which both the government and the private sector face large debt burdens. Because the debtors are unable to repay the debt anytime soon, debt holders have increasingly grown amenable to exchange of the debt for something else. Five types of swaps are most prevalent: debt-for-debt swaps, debt-for-equity swaps, debt-for-product swaps, debt-for-nature swaps, and debt-for-education swaps.

A **debt-for-debt swap** is when a loan held by one creditor is simply exchanged for a loan held by another creditor. For example, a U.S. bank may swap Argentine debt for Chilean debt with a European bank. Through this mechanism, debt holders are able to consolidate their outstanding loans and concentrate on particular countries or regions.

Debt-for-equity swaps arise when debt is converted into foreign equity in a domestic firm. The swap therefore serves as the vehicle for foreign direct investment. Although the equity itself is denominated in local currency, the terms of the conversion may allow the investor future access to foreign exchange for dividend remittances and capital repatriation.[12] In some countries, these debt-for-equity swaps have been very successful. For example, investments in Chile have so far retired

TABLE 17.2
The High Obligation from Offsets

Country	Value of Export Sales Contracts	Value of Offset Obligations	Offset Obligations as Percentage of Sales
Britain	$ 1,800.8	$ 1,896.5	105.3%
Canada	3,874.1	3,024.2	78.1
Egypt	383.0	87.8	22.9
Israel	6,083.7	1,384.2	22.8
NATO group	667.4	320.4	48.0
South Korea	1,055.8	488.0	46.2
Spain	2,151.3	2,851.1	132.5
Sweden	381.7	663.3	173.8
Switzerland	370.9	248.5	67.0
World total	**$34,816.9**	**$19,929.1**	**57.2%**

U.S. Military Export-Sales Contracts, with Associated Offset Obligations (in millions of dollars)

Note: Figures are for 1980–1987.
Basic data: U.S. Dept of Defense.
Source: *U.S. News & World Report*, April 23, 1990, p. 53.

Global Perspective

17.1
Are Offsets Offsetting U.S. Profits?

General Dynamics, a defense contractor based in St. Louis, makes F-16 fighter planes, Trident submarines, and Stinger missiles. Some people would be surprised to know that the company is also involved in hotel and tourism ventures. Why such a diverse product mix? The reason is offsets. For example, to get a multibillion-dollar contract to sell F-16s to Turkey, General Dynamics agreed to buy a number of Turkish products, to invest in Hilton hotels there, to set up a joint venture to coproduce the planes, and to build housing, a school, and a mosque for 4,000 workers in Turkey.

More and more often, such arrangements are becoming a part of international arms deals. In the 1970s, only a few countries required offsets in order to create jobs and learn new technology. Today, in contrast, about 100 countries insist on offsets from defense contractors, and the resulting agreements are becoming increasingly complex and expensive. Furthermore, the use of offsets is expected to grow as cash-poor countries in eastern Europe convert to capitalism and forge economic links with the West.

The concept extends beyond arms sales. For example, PepsiCo and the Soviet Union signed a $3 billion deal, the largest between a U.S. company and the Soviet Union. Under this contract, PepsiCo will construct 26 new factories in the Soviet Union and sell Pepsi-Cola to the Soviets; in exchange, the company will purchase Stolichnaya vodka to sell in the United States, as well as a minimum of 10 Soviet freighters.

Critics say these deals can have harmful economic consequences. For example, people in the shipbuilding industry worry that Pepsi's arrangement with the Soviets could result in excess capacity of ships because the Soviet ships are being built to generate a contract to sell beverages, not to satisfy market demand for ships.

Offsets also are criticized for adding to the amount of imports into the United States at a time when the country already has a trade deficit. According to a survey by the Office of Management and Budget, between 1980 and 1987 companies made $19.9 billion in offset commitments to generate sales of $34.8 billion—that is, offsets accounted for 57 percent of revenues. Among those most worried about these figures are domestic subcontractors to the defense industry, who fear that they are losing business.

Another criticism is that offset arrangements involving transfers of technology may enable foreign businesses to become future competitors. For example, South Korea, which is seeking to develop capabilities in the aerospace industry, is signing deals that will enable it to assemble planes with parts imported from the United States and to manufacture additional planes itself. In this way, the U.S. contractor working with Seoul is giving that country the technology to continue on its own.

Despite such worries, companies in the United States see no alternative. A defense contractor that rejects offsets risks losing business to more accommodating competitors from Israel, Europe, or Brazil.

Sources: Gregory Sandler, "Bringing Back Barter," *World Trade,* December 1990–January 1991, 88–92; and Jim Impoco, "The New Global Game: Let's Make a Deal," *U.S. News and World Report,* April 23, 1990, 53–54.

about $2.9 billion of external debt, representing more than 10 percent of the country's foreign debt.[13]

A third form of debt swap consists of **debt-for-product swaps.** Here, debt is exchanged for products. Usually, these transactions require that an additional cash payment be made for the product. For example, First Interstate Bank of California concluded an arrangement with Peruvian authorities whereby a commitment was made to purchase $3 worth of Peruvian products for every $1 of products paid for by Peru against debt.[14]

An emerging form of debt swap is that of the **debt-for-nature swap.** Firms or entities buy what are otherwise considered to be nonperforming loans at substantial discounts and return the debt to the country in exchange for the preservation of natural resources. The banks like these deals because they recoup some of the money they had written off; some countries like them, as they are able to retire debt, but others do not because they believe they are selling their natural resources. However, pressing environmental concerns can be addressed by applying debt-for-nature swaps. As an example, Conservation International, an American environmental group, paid Citicorp $100,000 for $650,000 of Bolivian debt, then returned the debt to Bolivia in exchange for an agreement to turn a 4-million-acre stretch of the Amazon Basin into a wildlife sanctuary and pay for its upkeep.[15] As repayment of debt becomes more and more difficult for an increasing number of nations, the swap of debt for social causes is likely to increase.

Debt-for-education swaps have been suggested in the U.S. government by one of the authors as a means to reduce the debt burden and to enable more U.S. students to study abroad, which could greatly enhance the international orientation, foreign language training, and cultural sensitivity of the U.S. education system.[16] As Global Perspective 17.2 shows, some universities are already taking advantage of this form of countertrade.

With the increasing sophistication of countertrade, the original form of straight barter is less used today. Most frequently used is the counterpurchase agreement. Because of high military expenditures, offsets are the second most frequently used form. Figure 17.3 presents the results of a survey of U. S. firms that showed—for U.S. firms at least—the relatively low use of barter, findings confirmed by other research.[17]

Global Perspective

17.2
Debt Funds Study Abroad

Harvard University recently agreed to extend a helping hand to the debt-burdened government of Ecuador in South America. In an unprecedented agreement, the university will help convert a portion of Ecuador's $11 billion debt into scholarships for Ecuadorean students to attend Harvard.

The debt-for-scholarship agreement exchanges foreign debt for educational opportunities. Ecuador has passed special legislation making the agreement possible. "Harvard is putting up the original money to purchase the debt, and then the Ecuadorean government is basically financing the rest through the debt swap," says Ned Strong, area director of the Harvard-based Latin American Scholarship Program of American Universities (LASPAU). Harvard will buy $5 million in Ecuadorean debt at the market price. The current rate is 15 percent of face value; therefore, the school will invest $750,000.

That debt will be given to Fundacion Capacitar, an educational foundation in Ecuador that will exchange the debt for Ecuadorean government bonds worth 50 percent of the debt's face value, or $2.5 million.

"The national government obviously much prefers to have half as much debt outstanding," says Robert Scott, vice president for finance at Harvard.

The government bonds, issued in *sucres,* the local currency, will be sold in Ecuador by the foundation. Income from the sale will be converted to dollars and invested in the United States to create an endowment providing scholarship funds for the Ecuadorean students.

The arrangement also provides funds for Harvard students and professors to conduct research and internships in Ecuador. For the Ecuadoreans, the debt-reduction agreement is simply a mechanism to bring educational opportunities to their citizens. "The main purpose is the capacity for studying at Harvard," says Miguel Falconi, president of Fundacion Capacitar.

"It's definitely a two-way street," says Strong of LASPAU. The foreign student gets advanced training and enriches the university community, he says.

OFFICIAL ATTITUDES TOWARD COUNTERTRADE

Official U.S. Policy

When trying to ascertain official U.S. government attitudes, one must investigate the various departments within the executive, legislative, and judicial branches. On occasion, a coherent policy view can be identified. More often than not, discrepancies among the different groups become visible because they have different outlooks and serve different constituencies. Such discrepancies are particularly obvious when looking at the issue of countertrade.

A government report on U.S. competitiveness made a strong statement against countertrade. The report briefly examined the incidence of countertrade, its growth, and the incentives for its practice. The report concluded "that the transactions are purely bilateral in nature and are not competitive since they squeeze out competition from a third market or specify the export market. Trade is formulated on the basis of the willingness to countertrade and not on economic considerations."[18]

The Department of the Treasury tends to take a similarly dim view of countertrade. Treasury officials stated with regard to offsets and coproduction that they "suspect that offset and coproduction agreements mandated by governments [do not] promote . . . economic . . . efficiency. They may constitute implicit subsidies to the industry of the purchasing countries. They may result in diversion of business away from efficient U.S. producers . . . thus causing economic inefficiency and dislocations. . . . Since these practices appear to involve spillover effects on nondefense production and trade, they may have adverse effects on future U.S. production, trade, employment, and tax revenue."[19]

The Office of the U.S. Trade Representative, which is the chief U.S. trade negotiator, is somewhat more flexible. At a House of Representatives hearing, a negotiator testified that "our position is that countertrade is a second-best option for international trade transactions. It represents a distortion of international trade and is contrary to an open, free trading system. It is not in the long-run interest of the United States or the U.S. business community. Nevertheless, as a matter of policy, the U.S. government does not oppose U.S. companies' participating in countertrade arrangements unless such actions could have a negative impact on national security. If a company believes a countertrade transaction is in its interest, the company is in a better position than we are to make that business decision."[20]

**FIGURE 17.3
Countertrade Usage—
By Types**

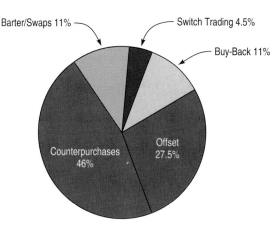

Barter/Swaps 11%
Switch Trading 4.5%
Buy-Back 11%
Counterpurchases 46%
Offset 27.5%

Source: Laura B. Forker, *Countertrade: Purchasing's Perceptions and Involvement* (Tempe: Center for Advanced Purchasing Studies, Arizona State University, 1991), 29.

The Department of Defense is concerned with enhancing its principles of RSI—rationalization, standardization, and interoperability. This means that the department strongly encourages other nations allied with the United States to use similar equipment that can be interchanged in case of an armed conflict. For this reason, the Department of Defense tries to encourage foreign acquisitions of U.S. military hardware. Because such acquisition is only likely to come about through promises of offsets and coproduction, the department tends to display a policy of "positive neutrality" toward these countertrade methods.

This attitude makes a lot of sense from the perspective of production cost. Given the economies of scale and the learning curve effects inherent in the manufacture of arms, more international sales result in longer production runs, which in turn permit weapons manufacturers to offer their products at a lower price. If the Department of Defense can encourage more international sales, it can either buy a given number of products for less money or purchase more products with a given budget. From that perspective, one could argue that countertrade transactions contribute to U.S. national security.

The Department of Commerce displays the most supportive view of countertrade in the official community. Given its mandate to help U.S. firms compete internationally, the department has its own Office of Barter and Countertrade, which provides advice to firms interested in such transactions. However, this office was established only after significant congressional pressure.

While all these different views exist within the departments of the administration, Congress repeatedly has passed bills that permit or even encourage countertrade transactions. This legislation has primarily focused on barter possibilities for U.S. agricultural commodities or stockpiling purposes. As a result, the Commodities Credit Corporation and the General Services Administration have been carrying out countertrade transactions for years. An example is the swap of U.S. agricultural commodities for Jamaican bauxite. This large-scale transaction was designed to reduce the U.S. surplus of agricultural products while increasing national stockpiles of a strategic material. Global Perspective 17.3 provides an example of congressional views.

In the judicial branch, countertrade involvement stems mostly from the enforcement activities of the Internal Revenue Service. The IRS is, of course, primarily concerned with the valuation of countertrade transactions and with ensuring that

The Department of Defense encourages nations allied with the United States to use similar equipment to facilitate repairs in the event of an armed conflict. Here, a Luftwaffe flight-test team checks a Hughes-built radar on a German F-4F aircraft.
Source: Courtesy of Hughes Aircraft Company.

Global Perspective

17.3
Barter Deals Will Bring Trade Growth

Senator James Exon of Nebraska is a leading proponent of barter and authored legislation that created an Office of Barter and Countertrade in the U.S. Department of Commerce. He believes that "barter now constitutes about 20 percent of all international trade. If we want to deal with the republics of the former Soviet Union, we need to be creative and think of alternative ways to do business besides direct cash for goods. The capitalist system has a preoccupation with worshiping the almighty dollar. Unfortunately, the former Soviet Union doesn't have many dollars for us to worship. There are more possibilities for trade between our countries if we barter, especially in commodities in which we both have an abundance, such as oil for U.S. wheat. A barrel of oil purchased or bartered with the former Soviet Union could facilitate additional American sales of food and products, whereas a barrel of oil from a Persian Gulf nation would simply add to a bilateral trade deficit. In other words, oil from the former Soviet Union could equal new American exports."

In the senator's view, the federal government should undertake a much more active role in promoting barter. Otherwise, nations that are more agreeable to bartering will get ahead of the United States. He thinks that the federal role could include the establishment of a national database of U.S. and CIS companies interested in barter opportunities, or a barter insurance program to guarantee some percentage of the barter arrangement. When confronted with arguments from U.S. Treasury Department officials, "Why barter when dealing in money is better?" he responds: "Well, one side doesn't have any money."

Source: Adapted from Bill Pietrucha, *WE/Mbl*, August 10–23, 1992, 7.

proper tax payments are made. A proper **assessment of taxes,** however, usually requires a painstaking determination of all facets of the transaction. Difficulties are often encountered in ascertaining the exact vale of the countertraded goods, the time when the income has been received, and the profitability of the entire transaction. As a result of these problems, tax authorities are not in favor of countertrade. Other judicial activities are mainly concerned with valuation issues for import purposes. One major issue is the threat of dumping, whereby goods obtained through countertrade transactions may be disposed of cheaply in the domestic market and therefore harm domestic competitors, who do not benefit from the sales end of a countertrade transaction.

One can conclude that as a nation the United States is ambivalent toward countertrade. There are differing views within the administration and in the legislative and the judicial branches. Countertrade is partially encouraged, as long as no major negative effects on nonparticipants are visible within the domestic economy.

Foreign Government Views

Most industrialized countries, including western European countries, Japan, New Zealand, and Australia, have participated actively in the growing countertrade phenomenon. Frequently, they are catalysts for countertrade transactions. The emerging market economies have continued to favor countertrade because of their ongoing need to preserve hard currencies. Countries in the developing world have taken varied positions. Indonesia, for example, cited two choices it faced as its export revenues declined dramatically: One was to drastically limit its imports, the other was to liberalize its trade with alternative measures such as countertrade. As a result, the government officially instituted a mandatory countertrade requirement for any transaction exceeding a value of $500,000.

In a similar vein, Mexico created a countertrade office in the Ministry of Foreign Trade. Several U.S. companies were told that they could increase their exports to Mexico only if the new sales were linked to exports from Mexico. Other developing countries have more subtle policies but are implementing and supporting countertrade nonetheless. Brazil, for example, keeps quite a low profile. Although the country "has issued no countertrade regulations and does not officially sanction its practice, . . . awards of import licenses and export performance are linked at the level of the firm."[21] This is a position taken more and more frequently by less-developed countries. Although officially they abhor the use of countertrade, unofficially they have made it clear that, in order to do business, countertrade transactions are mandatory.

Attitudes of International Organizations

International organizations almost uniformly condemn countertrade. Public statements by both the IMF and the GATT indicate that their opposition "is based on broad considerations of macroeconomic efficiency." These authorities complain that instead of a rational system of exchange, based on product quality and price, countertrade introduces extraneous elements into the sales equation.[22] Arthur Dunkel, director general of the GATT, went so far as to warn that the very viability of GATT is threatened by the proliferation of countertrade. He cautioned that if the trend continued, world trade practices would become inconsistent with the GATT principle of nondiscriminatory, most-favored-nation treatment in international trade. In addition, he warned that government-mandated bilateral arrangements could politicize international trade and diminish the purely commercial considerations that are now the cornerstone of multilateral, liberalized trade and its related institutions.[23]

Officials from the OECD (Organization for Economic Cooperation and Development) also deplore countertrade arrangements. They think that such arrangements would lead to an increase in trade conflicts as competitive suppliers, unwilling to undertake countertrade arrangements, are displaced by less competitive suppliers who are willing to do so.[24]

The international organization most neutral toward countertrade is the United Nations. A report of the secretary general stated only that there appeared to be some economic and financial problems with countertrade transactions and that any global, uniform regulation of countertrade may be difficult to implement because of the complexity and variety of transactions. The report lacks any kind of general conclusion, because such conclusions "may be somewhat hazardous in the absence of a sufficient volume of contracts that are easily available."[25]

This statement highlights one of the major problems faced by policymakers interested in countertrade. Corporations and executives consider the subject of countertrade to be sensitive, because public discussion of such practices could imply that a product line may be difficult to sell or indicate that the corporation is willing to conduct countertrade. Because such knowledge would result in a weakening of the corporation's international negotiation position, executives are usually tight-lipped about their firm's countertrade transactions.[26] At the same time, rumors about countertrade deals are often rampant, even though many of the transactions gossiped about may never materialize. To some extent, therefore, the public view of countertrade may represent an inverted iceberg: Much more is on the surface than be-low. Policymakers are therefore uncertain about the precise volume and impact of countertrade, a fact that makes taking proper policy actions all the more difficult.

Countertrade does appear to be on the increase. The main reason for that conclusion is the fact that countertrade may perhaps be the only practical solution to the fundamental difficulties in the world economy, of which it is a symptom. Access to developed markets for the less-developed countries has become increasingly limited. Balance-of-Payment crises, debt problems, and other financial difficulties have hurt their ability to import needed products. In the face of limited trade opportunities, both less-developed countries and industrialized nations appear to regard countertrade as an alternative solution to no trade at all.[27]

THE CORPORATE SITUATION

A few years ago, most executives claimed both in public and in private that countertrade was a hindrance to international business and was avoided by their firms. More recently, however, changes in corporate thinking have taken place. Even though most companies may not like countertrade transactions, if they refuse to engage in them, business will be lost to foreign rivals who are willing to participate in countertrade. Increasingly, companies forced to take countertraded goods are altering their perspective from a reactive to a proactive one. In the past, U.S. corporations frequently resorted to countertrade only because they were compelled by circumstances to do so. However, times have changed, and companies have begun to use countertrade as a tool to improve their market position. Rockwell International Corporation, for example, uses its own internal barter capabilities through its trading subsidiary, which Rockwell created several years ago. As a result, Rockwell's products have a special appeal abroad because of the company's willingness to engage in countertrade. Rather than simply react to requirements, "Rockwell is going at it in an active way in suggesting countertrade possibilities."[28]

Increasingly, companies are formulating international business strategies and are planning to acquire market share from their competition by seeking out countertrade opportunities, provided they lead to an expansion of their own product sales. These companies go beyond the traditional view that some sales, even those subject to countertrade, are better than no sales. They are using countertrade systematically as a strategic tool that brings with it favorable government consideration and greater pricing flexibility. Yet, as Global Perspective 17.4 shows, it is not easy to develop such new corporate direction.

Particularly for longer-range countertrade transactions, executives may not be as risk averse as for shorter-range transactions. By the time the countertrade requirements fall due, which may be five to ten years in the future, they may not be around to take the blame if problems arise because they may have been promoted, changed positions, or retired. On the other hand, for these long-term risks, many companies make it clear that the preferred compensation is cash, preferably in dollars, and that any kind of countertrade transaction is not acceptable. However, the number of stalwart opponents of all countertrade deals is decreasing.

Companies and countries imposing countertrade requirements believe that there are more merits to these transactions than purely conserving foreign currency. For example, the countertrade partner can be used as a marketing arm to explore new markets. Long-term countertrade requirements can ensure markets for future output; these are particularly important to producers in industries highly sensitive to capacity

Global Perspective

17.4
Coping with Offsets

Many governments of countries that experience trade deficits view imports as a problem. As a result, they may limit imports through the use of tariffs, quotas, or other nontariff barriers. A small but growing number of governments restrict imports, and simultaneously encourage exports, by requiring firms to offset import sales with export spending. The rationale behind such actions is to restrict imports, increase exports, and create jobs.

One way governments offset a negative impact on the trade or current account is through offset purchasing. This means that a company that desires to import products must prove to the government that it is purchasing an agreed-upon percentage of these imports in local goods or services, which in turn are exported. The thought is that if the importer purchases local products for export, local companies will be strengthened, and export volume will grow.

The Business Development Group at a U.S. computer firm faces offset regulations every day. In its drive to open new markets around the globe, the firm is increasingly confronted with government demands to offset the trade balance effect of its computer imports. The Business Development Group works with the Procurement Group, third-party suppliers, and governments to comply with offset regulations. For example, the Business Development Group will attempt to source components that are required to build computers, printers, and peripherals from firms in those

countries to which computers are exported. Often, the goals of the Business Development Group and the procurement organization within the firm tend to clash. Procurement favors suppliers that offer the best combination of cost, quality, and delivery. Business Development, in turn, prefers sourcing from those suppliers that enable the company to fulfill offset requirements, since doing so will increase sales volume abroad. Unfortunately, these suppliers often do not offer lowest cost, highest quality, or fastest delivery. To reduce the intraorganizational conflict, Business Development has begun to work with foreign suppliers to give them the tools necessary to compete with other suppliers. As a result, technology transfer, training, and quality instructions are often provided abroad.

One concurrent problem faced by the Business Development Group is the fact that it is very difficult to count the dollar volume of purchases from countries. Today, international trade is so complex that it is difficult to tell from which country a good or service originated. Goods are often transshipped before arriving at their final destination. Distributors often do not know from where a certain shipment came. Goods and services often have component parts from a number of countries. In consequence, the Business Development Group is in the process of revamping the firm's entire sourcing system in order to track country of origin more carefully.

Source: Scott Ciener, Georgetown University.

utilization. Security and stability of purchasing and sales arrangements can also play a major role. Some countries also see counterpurchases as a major way of ensuring that technology transfer is carried out as promised, because the transferor will have to take back the product produced and will therefore ensure that the repayment will be of high quality.

Other reasons for engaging in countertrade can be more effective introduction of new products, the desire to more easily enter new markets, and the goal of expanding the company's market share. Countertrade has been found to provide "outlets for integrative growth in addition to market penetration and development."[29] Finally, countertrade can provide markets and open up new trade channels for surplus products that could not be sold otherwise.[30] Particularly in instances when a world market glut exists for commodities that are in ample supply in some countries yet scarce in others, countertrade transactions may be an appealing trade mechanism.

THE EMERGENCE OF NEW INTERMEDIARIES

The rise in countertrade transactions has resulted in the emergence of new specialists to handle such transactions. These intermediaries can be either in-house or outside the corporation. Some companies have been founded to facilitate countertrade transactions for other firms. By purchasing unwanted inventories from companies at a steep discount, sometimes very high profit margins can be obtained. For example, Fred Tarter of Deerfield Communications founded his company on this principle and made $17 million when he sold it in 1984 to Integrated Barter International of New York. He took on inventory from companies and paid for it in cash or advertising time or both. When he paid in advertising, he exchanged bartered goods for other bartered commodities that were more desirable.

FIGURE 17.4
Advertisement Offering
Countertrade Services

Other intermediaries that have benefited from the rise of countertrade are trading companies or trading houses that act frequently as third-party intermediaries. Some of them are subsidiaries of large corporations that seek to supplement the trading volume generated by their corporation with business from other firms. An example of such multinational activity is provided in Figure 17.4. Because of their widespread connections around the world, trading companies or trading houses can dispose of countertraded goods more easily than can corporations that only infrequently consummate countertrade transactions. They are also more capable of evaluating the risks of such transactions and can benefit from both the discount and the markup portion of the exchange.

Firms that deal with trading houses in order to receive assistance in their countertrade transactions need to be aware that the fees charged are often quite steep and may increase cumulatively. For example, there may be an initial consulting fee when the transaction is contemplated, a fee for the consummation of the acquisition, and a subsequent steep discount for the disposal of the acquired products. Also, these trading houses frequently refuse to take countertraded goods on a nonrecourse basis, which means that the company that has obtained countertraded goods still shares some of the risks inherent in their disposal.

International banks also have some involvement in countertrade in order to serve their clients better and to increase their own profitability. Banks may be able to use their experience in international trade finance and apply it to the financial aspects of countertrade transactions. Banks may also have a comparative advantage over trading firms by having more knowledge and expertise about financial risk management and more information about and contacts with the global market.

Countertrade intermediaries need not be large. Smaller firms can successfully compete with a niche strategy. By exploiting specialized geographic or product knowledge and developing countertrade transactions that may be too small for the multinational firm, an entrepreneur can conduct trades with little capital, yet receive sound profit margins.

Another new type of intermediary, mostly smaller, is represented by countertrade information service providers. These institutions are exemplified by Batis Ltd. in London and ACECO in France. They provide databases on countertrade products and countertrade regulations in various countries, which subscribers may tap. They are beginning also to provide computerized matchmaking services between companies in debit to some country's counterpurchase system and those in credit, or those willing to buy counterpurchase items.[31]

PREPARING FOR COUNTERTRADE

The majority of countertrade transactions in the United States are consummated by countertrade specialists who are outside the corporation, as Figure 17.5 shows. However, increasingly companies consider carrying out countertrade transactions in-house. If this can be done, the need for steep discounts may decrease, and the profitability of countertrade may improve.

Developing an in-house capability for handling countertrade should be done with great caution. First, the company should determine the import priorities of its products to the country or firm to which it is trying to sell. Goods that are highly desirable and/or necessary for a country mandating countertrade are less likely to be subject to countertrade requirements or may be subject to less stringent requirements than goods considered luxurious and unnecessary. Next, the firm needs to identify the countertrade arrangements and regulations that exist in the country to which it

FIGURE 17.5
Countertrade Services
Employed by U.S. Firms

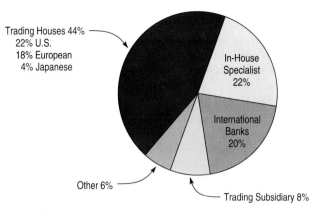

Trading Houses 44%
22% U.S.
18% European
4% Japanese

In-House Specialist 22%

International Banks 20%

Other 6%

Trading Subsidiary 8%

Source: Willis A. Bussard, "An Overview of Countertrade Practices of Corporations and Individual Nations," in *International Countertrade*, ed. C. Korth (Westport, Conn.: Quorum Books, a division of Greenwood Press, Inc., 1987), 21.

exports. An awareness of the alternatives available and of the various countertrade percentages demanded will strengthen the company's bargaining position at the pre-contract stage. Obtaining this information is also important in order to incorporate possible countertrade costs into the pricing scheme. Once a "cash deal" price has been quoted, increasing the price is difficult if a subsequent countertrade demand is made.

At this stage, the most favored countertrade arrangement from the buyer's perspective should be identified. The company should find out why this particular arrangement is the most favored one and explore whether other forms of transactions would similarly meet the objectives of the countertrading partner. In order to do this, the goals and objectives of the countertrading parties need to be determined. As discussed earlier, they can consist of import substitution, a preservation of hard currency, export promotion, and so on.

The next step is to match the strengths of the firm with current and potential countertrade situations. This requires an assessment of corporate capabilities and resources. Any internal sourcing needs that might be used to fulfill a countertrade contract should be determined—that is, raw materials or intermediate products that could be obtained from the countertrade partner rather than current suppliers. However, this assessment should not be restricted to the internal corporate use of a countertraded product. The company should also determine whether it can use, for example, its distribution capabilities or its contacts with other customers and suppliers to help in its countertrade transactions.

At this point, the company can decide whether it should engage in countertrade transactions. The accounting and taxation aspects of the countertrade transactions should be considered, because they are often quite different from usual procedures. The use of an accounting or tax professional is essential in order to comply with difficult and obscure IRS regulations in this area.

Next, all of the risks involved in countertrade must be considered. This means that the goods to be obtained need to be specified, that the delivery time for these goods needs to be determined, and that the reliability of the supplier and the quality and consistency of the goods need to be assessed. It is also useful to explore the impact of countertrade on future prices, both for the specific goods obtained and for the world market price for the category of goods. For example, a countertrade transaction may appear to be quite profitable at the time of agreement. Because several months or even years may pass before the transaction is actually consummated, however, a change in world market prices may severely affect its profitability. The effect of a countertrade transaction on the world market price should also be considered. In cases of large-volume transactions, the established price may be affected because of a glut of supply. Such a situation may not only affect the profitability of a transaction but can also result in possible legal actions by other suppliers of similar products.

In conjunction with the evaluation of the countertraded products, which as a general requirement should be specified in as much detail as possible rather than left open, the corporation needs to explore the market for these products. This includes forecasting future market developments, paying particular attention to competitive reaction and price fluctuations. It is also useful at this stage to determine the impact of the countertraded products on the sales and profits of other complementary product lines currently marketed by the firm. Possible repercussions from outside groups should be investigated. Such repercussions may consist of antidumping actions brought about by competitors or reactions from totally unsuspected quarters. For example, McDonnell-Douglas ran into strong opposition when it used bartered Yugoslavian ham in its employees' cafeteria and as Christmas gifts. The local meat-packers' union complained vociferously that McDonnell-Douglas was threatening the jobs of its members.

Using all the information obtained, the company can finally evaluate the length of the intended relationship with the countertrading partner and the importance of this relationship for its future plans and goals. These parameters will be decisive for the final action, because they may form constraints overriding short-term economic effects. Overall, management needs to remember that, in most instances, a countertrade transaction should remain a means for successful international business and not become an end in itself.

SUMMARY

Countertrades are business transactions in which the sale of goods is linked to other goods or performance rather than only to money. In spite of their inefficiency, such transactions are emerging with increasing frequency due to hard currency shortfalls in many nations around the world.

Concurrent with their increased use, countertrade transactions have also become more sophisticated. Rather than exchange goods for goods in a straight barter deal, companies and countries now structure counterpurchase agreements, compensation arrangements, clearing accounts, offset agreements and debt swaps to promote their industrial policies and encourage development.

Governments worldwide and internal organizations are concerned about the trend toward countertrade, yet in light of existing competition and the need to find creative ways of financing trade, they exercise very little interference with countertrade.

Corporations are increasingly using countertrade as a competitive tool in order to maintain or increase market share. The complexity of these transactions requires careful planning in order to avoid major corporate losses. Management must consider how the acquired merchandise will be disposed of, what the potential for market disruptions is, and to what extent countertraded goods fit in with the corporate mission.

New intermediaries have emerged to facilitate countertrade transactions, yet their services can be very expensive. However, they can enable firms without countertrade experience to participate in this growing business practice. In addition, the development of intermediary skills may offer profitable opportunities for small business entrepreneurs.

Key terms and Concepts

barter	debt swaps
counterpurchase	debt-for-debt swap
parallel barter	debt-for-equity swap
buy-back	debt-for-product swap
compensation arrangement	debt-for-nature swap
clearing account barter	debt-for-education swap
switch-trading	assessment of taxes
offset	

Questions for Discussion

1. What are some of the major causes for the resurgence of countertrade?
2. What forms of countertrade exist and how do they differ?
3. Discuss the advantages and drawbacks of countertrade.
4. Discuss the benefits and drawbacks of swaps.
5. How would you characterize the U.S. government's position toward countertrade?
6. How consistent is countertrade with the international trade framework?
7. Why would a firm take goods rather than cash?
8. Why would a buyer insist on countertrade transactions?
9. What particular benefits can an outside countertrade intermediary offer to a firm engaged in such transactions?
10. How would you prepare your firm for countertrade?
11. Discuss some of the possible accounting and taxation ramifications of countertrade.
12. Develop a corporate goals statement that uses countertrade as a proactive tool for international expansion.
13. Explain why countertrade may be encouraged by the increasing technology transfer taking place.
14. What are some of the dangers of using countertraded goods in-house?
15. What is your view of the future of countertrade?

Recommended Readings

Alexandrides, C.G., and B.L. Bowers, *Countertrade*. New York: Wiley, 1987

Countertrade and Barter. A magazine published by Metal Bulletin Inc., New York, N.Y.

Countertrade Outlook, a biweekly update.

Elderkin, Kenton W., and Warren E. Norquist. *Creative Countertrade.* Cambridge, Mass.: Ballinger, 1987.

Hennart, Jean-François. "Some Empirical Dimensions of Countertrade." *Journal of International Business Studies* (Second Quarter 1990): 243–270.

Kopinski, Thaddeus C. *Negotiating Countertrade and Offsets: Avoiding Legal and Contractual Pitfalls.* Arlington, Va.: Asian Press, 1987.

Korth, Christopher M., ed. *International Countertrade.* Westport, Conn.: Quorum Books, 1987.

Palia, Aspy P., and Oded Shenkar. "Countertrade Practices in China." *Industrial Marketing Management,* 20, 1991, 57–65.

Schaffer, Matt. *Winning the Countertrade War: New Export Strategies for America.* New York: Wiley, 1989.

Verzariu, Pompiliu. *International Countertrade, A Guide for Managers and Executives.* Washington, D.C.: U.S. Department of Commerce, 1992.

Verzariu, Pompiliu, and Paula Mitchell. *International Countertrade, Individual Country Practices.* Washington, D.C.: U.S. Department of Commerce, 1992.

Zurawicki, Leon, and Louis Suichmezian. *Global Countertrade, An Annotated Bibliography.* New York: Garland Publishers, 1991.

Notes

1. Raj Aggarwal, "International Business through Barter and Countertrade," *Long Range Planning,* June 1989, 75–81.
2. "Current Activities of International Organizations in the Field of Barter and Barter-like Transactions," *Report of the Secretary General,* United Nations, General Assembly, 1984, 4.
3. Sam Okoroafo, "Determinants of LDC Mandated Countertrade," *International Marketing Review,* Winter 1989, 16–24.
4. Jean-François Hennart, "Some Empirical Dimensions of Countertrade," *Journal of International Business Studies,* 21(2) (Second Quarter, 1990): 243–270.
5. Jong H. Park, "Is Countertrade Merely a Passing Phenomenon? Some Public Policy Implications," in *Proceedings of the 1988 Conference,* ed. R. King (Charleston, S.C.: Academy of International Business, Southeast Region, 1988), 67–71.
6. Hennart, "Some Empirical Dimensions of Countertrade."
7. Paul Samuelson, *Economics,* 11th ed. (New York: McGraw Hill, 1980), 260.
8. "Current Activities of International Organizations," 4.
9. Christopher M. Korth, "The Promotion of Exports with Barter," in *Export Promotion,* ed. M. Czinkota (New York: Praeger, 1983), 42.
10. Donna U. Vogt, *U.S. Government International Barter,* Congressional Research Service, Report No. 83-211ENR (Washington, D.C.: Government Printing Office, 1983), 65.
11. Korth, "The Promotion of Exports with Barter," 42.
12. Richard A. Debts, David L. Roberts, and Eli M. Remolona, *Finance for Developing Countries* (New York: Group of 30, 1987), 18.
13. Pompiliu Verzariu, "An Overview of Nontraditional Finance Techniques in International Commerce," in *Trade Finance: Current Issues and Developments* (Washington, D.C. : Government Printing Office, 1988), 48.
14. Ibid., 50.
15. "Greensback-Debt," *The Economist,* August 6, 1988, 62–63.
16. Michael R. Czinkota and Martin J. Kohn, *A Report to the Secretary of Commerce: Improving U.S. Competitiveness—Swapping Debt for Education* (Washington, D.C.: Government Printing Office, 1988).
17. Donald J. Lecraw, "The Management of Countertrade: Factors Influencing Success," *Journal of International Business Studies* 20 (Spring 1989): 41–59.
18. *Report of the President on U.S. Competitiveness* (transmitted to Congress in September, 1980), V-45.

19. John D. Lange, Jr., Director, Office of Trade Finance, U.S. Department of the Treasury, testimony before the House Economic Stabilization Subcommittee, Committee on Banking, Finance, and Urban Affairs, 97th Congress, 1st session, September 24, 1981.

20. Donald W. Eiss, statement before the Subcommittee on Arms Control, International Security and Science and the Subcommittee on International Economic Policy and Trade, Committee on Foreign Affairs, U.S. House of Representatives, July 1, 1987, 4–5.

21. Steven M. Rubin, "Countertrade Controversies Stirring Global Economy," *The Journal of Commerce*, September 24, 1984, 14.

22. Ibid.

23. "GATT Director Dunkel Criticizes Trend toward Unilateral Trade Law Interpretations," *U.S. Export Weekly*, July 20, 1982, 557.

24. Jacques de Miramon, "Countertrade: A Modern Form of Barter," *OECD Observer*, January 1982, 12.

25. "Current Activities of International Organizations," 5.

26. Michael R. Czinkota, "New Challenges in U.S.–Soviet Trade," *Journal of the Academy of Marketing Science* 5 (Special Issue, Summer 1977): 17–20.

27. Michael R. Czinkota and Anne Talbot, "Countertrade and GATT: Prospects for Regulation," *International Trade Journal* 1 (Fall 1986): 173.

28. Patrick N. Hall, quoted in "New Restrictions on World Trade," *Business Week*, July 19, 1982, 118.

29. Sandra M. Huszagh and Hiram C. Barksdale, "International Barter and Countertrade: An Exploratory Study," *Journal of the Academy of Marketing Science* 14 (Spring 1986): 21–28.

30. Lynn G. Reiling, "Countertrade Revives 'Dead Goods,'" *Marketing News*, August 29, 1986, 1, 22.

31. Kate Mortimer, "Countertrade in Western Europe," in *International Countertrade*, ed. Christopher M. Korth (Westport, Conn.: Quorum Books, 1987), 41.

International Financial Management

LEARNING OBJECTIVES

1. To understand how international business and investment activity alters the traditional financial management activities of the firm.

2. To explore how the very value of all firms, even those with no direct international business activity, changes with exchange rate movements.

3. To examine the three exposures of multinational firms to exchange rate changes over time.

4. To understand which strategies and financial techniques are used to manage the currency risks of the modern multinational firm.

The Way We Were: The Return of Capital Controls

On September 23, with the peseta under ferocious selling pressure within the European exchange-rate mechanism (ERM), the Spanish government announced new controls on banks' foreign-exchange transactions. The next day Ireland's government tried to shore up its pound in the same way. Both governments hoped to slow the selling of their currencies on the foreign-exchange market, and thus to defend their exchange rates.

These, you might say, were panic measures. Under such circumstances, it is hardly surprising that the markets voted against capital controls. But this does not prove that all such controls are folly.

Increasingly, the case for a return to (explicit or implicit) restrictions on capital flows is likely to be put, and on both sides of the Atlantic. Recent turbulence in the currency markets has not been confirmed to the ERM—witness the dollar's continuing slide against the yen, which America's policymakers are likely to describe before long as a "problem" needing a solution.

Capital controls—restrictions on the convertibility of domestic currency into foreign currency—come in many shapes and sizes. They range from the relatively unobtrusive (eg, taxes on holdings of foreign-currency assets) to the burdensomely bureaucratic (eg, detailed rules on the uses to which foreign currency can be put, with more favorable treatment for currency obtained in certain ways).

Given that capital controls were so popular for so long, you might expect rich-country governments to embrace them again willingly. Not so. In recent years controls have been out of favour, for two main reasons. The first is simply the view that, by and large, economic openness is desirable. Second, most governments came to believe that, in any case, making new controls effective was no longer possible. This is undoubtedly true for many sorts of restrictions. Financial innovation and cheap, rapid communication have made it much easier than before to evade controls, especially those of the clumsy bureaucratic sort.

Financial management is a broad term that covers all business decisions regarding cash flows. These cash flows extend from the funding of the entire enterprise to the preservation of firm liquidity given the gaps in time between when products are produced, sold, and shipped, to when payment is received. International financial management is the extension of this same set of concerns to the cross-border activities of the enterprise.

OVERVIEW OF INTERNATIONAL FINANCIAL MANAGEMENT

International financial management is not a separate set of issues from domestic or traditional financial management, but the additional levels of risk and complexity introduced by the conduct of business across borders. Business across borders introduces different laws, different methods, different markets, different interest rates, and most of all, different currencies.

The many dimensions of international financial management are most easily explained in the context of a firm's financial decision-making process of evaluating a potential foreign investment.

- Capital Budgeting: the process of evaluating the financial feasibility of an individual investment, whether it be the purchase of a stock, real estate, or a firm.
- Capital Structure: the determination of the relative quantities of debt capital and equity capital that will constitute the funding of the investment.

- Raising Long-Term Capital: the acquisition of equity or debt for the investment. This requires the selection of the exact form of capital, its maturity, its reward or repayment structure, its currency of denomination, and its source.
- Working Capital and Cash-Flow Management: the management of operating and financial cash flows passing in and out of a specific investment project.

International financial management means that all the above financial activities will be complicated by the differences in markets, laws, and especially currencies. This is the field of financial risk management. Firms may intentionally borrow foreign currencies, buy forward contracts, or price their products in different currencies in order to manage their cash flows which are denominated in foreign currencies.

Changes in interest and exchange rates will affect each of the above steps in the international investment process. All firms, no matter how "domestic" they may seem in structure, are influenced by exchange-rate changes. The financial managers of a firm that has any dimension of international activity, imports or exports, foreign subsidiaries or affiliates, must pay special attention to these issues if the firm is to succeed in its international endeavors.

INTERNATIONAL CAPITAL BUDGETING

Any investment, whether it be the purchase of stock, the acquisition of real estate, or the construction of a manufacturing facility in another country, is financially justified if the present value of expected cash inflows is greater than the present value of expected cash outflows, in other words, if it has a positive **net present value (NPV).** The construction of a **capital budget** is the process of projecting the net operating cash flows of the potential investment in order to determine if it is indeed a good investment or not.

Capital Budget Components and Decision Criteria

All capital budgets, either domestic or international, are only as good as the accuracy of the cost and revenue assumptions. Adequately anticipating all of the incremental expenses that the individual project imposes on the firm is critical to a proper analysis. The critical term here is incremental. If the undertaking of a new project in a foreign country requires the establishment of a new office in the parent firm for handling shipments of people and materials, this needs to be added in to the incremental cash flows of the project. Only after all these values are estimated for the entire life span of the investment would the necessary information exist for financial analysis.

A capital budget is composed of three primary cash flow components:

1. Initial expenses and capital outlays. The initial capital outlays are normally the largest net cash outflow occurring over the life of a proposed investment. Because these cash flows occur up-front, they have a substantial impact on the net present value of the project.
2. Operating cash flows. The operating cash flows are the net cash flows the project is expected to yield once production is under way. The primary positive net cash flows of the project are realized in this stage; net operating cash flows will determine the success or failure of the proposed investment.

3. Terminal cash flows. This final component of the capital budget is composed of the salvage value or resale value of the project at its end. The terminal value will include whatever working capital balances can be recaptured once the project is no longer in operation (at least by this owner).

The financial-decision criterion for an individual investment is whether the net present value of the project is positive or negative.[1] The net cash flows in the future are discounted by the average cost of capital for the firm (the average of debt and equity costs). The purpose of discounting is to capture the fact that the firm has acquired investment capital at a cost (interest). This same capital could have been used for other projects or other investments. It is therefore necessary to discount the future cash flows to account for this forgone income of the capital, its opportunity cost. If NPV is positive, then the project is an acceptable investment. If the project's NPV is negative, then the cash flows expected to result from the investment are insufficient to provide an acceptable rate of return, and the project should be rejected.

A Proposed Project Evaluation

The capital budget for a manufacturing plant in Singapore serves as a basic example. ACME, a U.S. manufacturer of household consumer products, is considering the construction of a plant in Singapore in 1994. It would cost US$1,660,000 to build and would be ready for operation on January 1, 1995. ACME would operate the plant for three years, after which it would sell the plant to the Singapore government.

To analyze the proposed investment, ACME must estimate what the sales revenues would be per year, the costs of production, the overhead expenses of operating the plant per year, the depreciation allowances for the new plant and equipment, and the Singapore tax rate on corporate income. The estimation of all net operating cash flows is very important to the analysis of the project. Often the entire acceptability of a foreign investment may depend on the sales forecast for the foreign project.

But ACME needs U.S. dollars, not Singapore dollars. The only way the stockholders of ACME would be willing to undertake this investment is if it would be profitable in terms of their own currency, the U.S. dollar. This is the primary theoretical distinction between a domestic capital budget and a multinational capital budget. The evaluation of the project in the viewpoint of the parent will focus on whatever cash flows, either operational or financial, will find their way back to the parent firm in U.S. dollars.

ACME must therefore forecast the movement of the Singapore dollar (S$) over the four-year period as well. The spot rate on January 1, 1994, is S$1.6600/US$. ACME concludes that the rate of inflation will be roughly 5 percent higher per year in Singapore than in the United States. If the theory of purchasing power parity holds, as described in Chapter 5, it should take roughly 5 percent more Singapore dollars to buy a U.S. dollar per year. Using this assumption, ACME forecasts the exchange rate from 1994 to 1997.

After considerable study and analysis, ACME estimates that the net cash flows of the Singapore project, in Singapore dollars, would be those on line 1 in Table 18.1. Line 2 lists the expected exchange rate between Singapore dollars and U.S. dollars over the four-year period, assuming it takes 5 percent more Singapore dollars per U.S. dollar each year (the Singapore dollar is therefore expected to depreciate versus the U.S. dollar). Combining the net cash flow forecast in Singapore dollars with

Inflation Rates: One Factor in Forecasting Exchange Rates

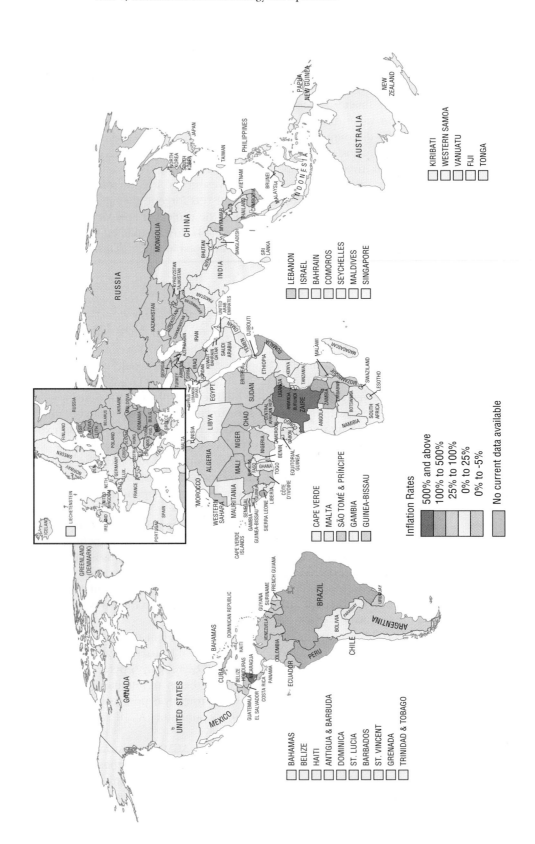

Inflation Rates

500% and above
100% to 500%
25% to 100%
0% to 25%
0% to -5%

No current data available

Source: *The World Factbook 1992.*

TABLE 18.1 Preliminary Capital Budget: Singapore Manufacturing Facility	Line #	1994	1995	1996	1997
	1 Net cash flow in S$	(1,660,000)	300,000	600,000	1,500,000
	2 Exchange rate, S$/US$	1.6600	1.7430	1.8302	1.9217
	3 Net cash flow in US$	(1,000,000)	172,117	327,833	780,559
	4 Present value factor	1.0000	.8475	.7182	.6086
	5 Present value in US$	(1,000,000)	145,869	235,450	475,048
	6 Net Present Value (NPV)	US$ 85,628			

Notes:

a. The spot exchange rate of S$1.6600/US$ is assumed to change by 5 percent per year; $1.6600 \times 1.05 = 1.7430$.

b. The present value factor assumes a weighted average cost of capital, the discount rate, of 18 percent. The present value factor is then found using the standard formula of $1/(1+.18)^t$, where t is the number of years in the future (1, 2, or 3).

the expected exchange rates, ACME can now calculate the net cash flow per year in U.S. dollars. ACME notes that although the initial expense is sizable, S$1,660,000 or US$1,000,000, the project produces net cash flows in its very first year of operations, (1995) of US$172,117, and every year after.

Acme estimates that its cost of capital, both debt and equity combined (the weighted average cost of capital), is about 18 percent per year. Using this as the rate of discount, the discount factor for each of the future years is found. Finally, the net cash flow in U.S. dollars multiplied by the present value factor yields the present values of each net cash flow. The net present value of the Singapore project is a positive ($85,628); ACME may now decide to proceed with the project since it is financially acceptable.

Risks in International Investments

How is this capital budget different from a similar project constructed in Phoenix, Arizona? It is riskier, at least from the standpoint of cross-border risk. The higher risk of an international investment arises from the different countries, their laws, regulations, potential for interference with the normal operations of the investment project, and obviously currencies, all of which are unique to international investment.

The risk of international investment is considered greater because the proposed investment will lie within the jurisdiction of a different government. Governments have the ability to pass new laws, including the potential nationalization of the entire project. The typical problems that may arise from operating in a different country are changes in foreign tax laws, restrictions placed on when or how much in profits may be repatriated to the parent company, and other types of restrictions that hinder the free movement of merchandise and capital between the proposed project, the parent, and any other country relevant to its material inputs or sales.

The other major distinction between a domestic investment and a foreign investment is that the viewpoint or perspective of the parent and the project are no longer the same. The two perspectives differ because the parent only values cash flows it derives from the project. So, for example, in Table 18.1 the project generates sufficient net cash flows in Singapore dollars that the project is acceptable both from the project's viewpoint and the parent's viewpoint. But what if the spot exchange rate were to deteriorate much more rapidly, at 10 percent or even 20 percent per year? The cash flows in U.S. dollars that find their way back to the parent would no longer justify the investment. Or, what if the Singapore government were to restrict the payment of dividends back to the U.S. parent firm, or somehow prohibit the Sin-

Although projects may be similar, the capital budgeting process must include an assessment of the higher risks associated with international projects, such as Mobil Corporation's expanded oil production platforms in the British sector of the North Sea.
Source: © Larry Lee 1992.

gapore subsidiary from exchanging Singapore dollars for U.S. dollars (capital controls)? Without cash flows in U.S. dollars, the parent would have no way of justifying the investment. And all of this could occur while the project itself is sufficiently profitable when measured in local currency. This split between project and parent viewpoint is a critical difference in international-investment analysis. Any individual investment can be judged only on the basis of the future cash flows that it will generate in the investor's own currency.

CAPITAL STRUCTURE: INTERNATIONAL DIMENSIONS

The choice of how to fund the firm is called capital structure. Capital is needed to open a factory, build an amusement park, or even start a hot-dog stand. If capital is provided by owners of the firm, it is called equity. If capital is obtained by borrowing from others, like commercial banking institutions, it is termed debt. Debt must be repaid with interest over some specified schedule. Equity capital, however, is kept in the firm. Because owners are risking their own capital in the enterprise, they are entitled to a proportion of the profits.

The Capital Structure of the Firm

The trade-offs between debt and equity are easily seen by looking at extreme examples of capital structures. If a firm had no debt, all capital would have to come from the owners. This may limit the size of the firm, as the owners do not have bottomless pockets. The primary benefit is that all net operating revenues are kept. There are no principal or interest payments to make. A firm with a large debt (highly leveraged), however, would have the capital of others with which to work. The scale of the firm could be larger, and all net profits would still accrue to the equity holders alone. The primary disadvantage of debt is the increasing expense of making principal and interest payments. This could prove to be an ever-increasing proportion of net cash flows at the extreme.

Any firm's ability to grow and expand is dependent on its ability to acquire additional capital as it grows. The net profits generated over previous periods may be valuable but are rarely enough to provide needed capital expansion. Firms therefore need access to capital markets, both debt and equity. Chapter 5 provided an overview of the major debt and equity markets available internationally, but it is important to remember that the firm must have access to these markets in order to enjoy their fruits. Smaller firms operating in the smaller markets are generally unable to tap these larger international capital markets. These markets are still the domains of the multinational firms, the behemoths of multinational business.

The Capital Structure of Foreign Subsidiaries

The choice of what proportions of debt and equity to use in international investments is usually dictated by either the debt-equity structure of the parent firm or the debt-equity structure of the competitive firms in the country where the investment is to be made. The parent firm sees equity investment as capital at risk; it, therefore, would normally prefer to provide as little equity capital as possible. Although funding the foreign subsidiary primarily with debt would still put the parent's capital at risk, debt-service provides a strict schedule for cash-flow repatriation to the lender—regular principal and interest payments according to the debt agreement. Equity capital's return, dividends from profits, depends on managerial discretion. It is this discretion, the proportion of profits returned to the parent versus profits retained and reinvested in the project or firm, that often leads to conflict between host-country authorities and the multinational firm.

The sources of debt for a foreign subsidiary are theoretically quite large, but in reality they are often quite limited. The alternatives listed in Table 18.2 are often reduced radically in practice because many countries have relatively small capital markets. These countries often either officially restrict the borrowing by foreign-owned firms in their countries or simply do not have affordable capital available for the foreign firm's use. The parent firm is then often forced to provide not only the equity but also a large proportion of the debt to its foreign subsidiaries. If the project or subsidiary is a new project, it has no existing line of business or credit standing. The parent must then represent the subsidiary's credit worth, and provide the debt capital at least until the project is operating and showing (hopefully) positive net cash flows.

The larger firms internationally will often have their own financial subsidiaries, companies purely for the purpose of acquiring the capital needed for the entire company's continuing growth needs. These financial subsidiaries will often be the actual unit extending the debt or equity capital to the foreign project or subsidiary. Hopefully, with time and success, the foreign investment will grow sufficiently to establish its own credit standing and acquire more and more of its capital needs from the

TABLE 18.2 **Financing Alternatives** **for Foreign Affiliates**	Foreign affiliate can raise equity capital:	Foreign affiliate can raise debt capital:
	1. From the parent 2. From a joint-venture partner in the parent's country, a joint-venture partner in the host country, or a share issue in the host country 3. From a third-country market such as a share issue in the Euro-equity market	1. From the parent 2. From a bank loan or bond issue in the host country or the parent firm's home country 3. From a third-country bank loan, bond issue, Euro-syndicated credit or Euro-bond issue

local markets in which it operates, or even from the international markets which become aware of its growth.

Working-capital management is the financing of short-term or current assets, but the term is used here to describe all short-term financing and financial management of the firm. Even a small multinational firm will have a number of different cash flows moving throughout its system at one time. The maintenance of proper liquidity, the monitoring of payments, and the acquisition of additional capital when needed require a great degree of organization and planning in international operations.

Operating and Financial Cash Flows

Firms have both operating cash flows and financial cash flows. Operating cash flows arise from the everyday business activities of the firm, such as paying for materials or resources (accounts payable) or receiving payments for items sold (accounts receivable). In addition to the direct cost and revenue cash flows from operations, there are a number of indirect cash flows. These indirect cash flows are primarily license fees paid to the owners of particular technological processes and royalties to the holders of patents or copyrights. Many multinational firms also spread their overhead and management expenses incurred at the parent over their foreign affiliates and subsidiaries that are utilizing the parent's administrative services.

Financial cash flows arise from the funding activities of the firm. The servicing of funding sources, interest on debt, and dividend payments to shareholders constitute potentially large and frequent cash flows. Periodic additions to debt or equity through new bank loans, new bond issuances, or supplemental stock sales may constitute additional financial cash flows in the international firm.

A Sample Cash-Flow Mapping

Figure 18.1 provides an overview of how these operational and financial cash flows may appear for a U.S.-based multinational firm. In addition to having some export sales in Canada, it may import some materials from Mexico. The firm accesses several different European markets by first selling its product to its German subsidiary, which then provides the final touches necessary for sales in Germany, France, and Switzerland. Sales and purchases by the parent with Canada and Mexico give rise to a continuing series of accounts receivable and accounts payable, which may be denominated in Canadian dollars, Mexican pesos, or U.S. dollars.

Cash flows between the U.S. parent and the German subsidiary will be both operational and financial in nature. The sale of the major product line to the German subsidiary creates intrafirm accounts receivable and payable. These payments may be denominated in either U.S. dollars or German marks. And these intrafirm transfers may in fact be two way if the German subsidiary is actually producing a form of the product not made in the United States but needed there. The German subsidiary may also be utilizing techniques, machinery, or processes that are owned or patented by the parent firm and so must pay royalties and license fees. These cash flows are usually calculated as a percentage of the sales price in Germany.

There are also a number of financial cash flows between the U.S. parent and the German subsidiary. If the subsidiary is partially financed by loans extended by the

FIGURE 18.1
The Operational and
Financial Cash Flows of
a U.S. Multinational with
a German Subsidiary

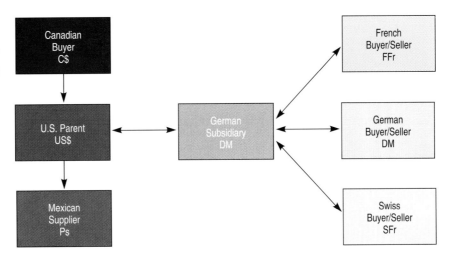

parent, the subsidiary needs to make regular principal and interest payments to the parent. If the German subsidiary is successful in its operations and generates a profit, that portion of the profits not reinvested in the subsidiary is sent to the parent as dividends.[2] If at some point the German subsidiary needs more capital than it can retain from its own profits, it may need additional debt or equity capital (from any of the potential sources listed in Table 18.2). These would obviously add to the financial cash flow volume.

The subsidiary in turn is dependent on its sales in Germany (German mark revenues), France (French franc revenues), and Switzerland (Swiss franc revenues) to generate the needed cash flows for paying everyone else. This "map" of operating and financial cash flows does not even attempt to describe the frequency of these various foreign currency cash flows or to assign the responsibility for managing the currency risks. The management of cash flows in a larger multinational firm, one with possibly 10 or 20 subsidiaries, is obviously complex. The proper management of these cash flows is, however, critical to the success or failure of the international business.

Cash-Flow Management

The structure of the firm dictates the ways cash flows and financial resources can be managed. The trend in the past decade has been for the increasing centralization of most financial and treasury operations. The centralized treasury is often responsible for both funding operations and cash-flow management. The centralized treasury may often enjoy significant economies of scale, offering more services and expertise to the various units of the firm worldwide than the individual units themselves could support. However, regardless of whether the firm follows a centralized or decentralized approach, there are a number of operating structures that aid the multinational firm in managing its cash flows.

Cash Pooling   A large firm with a number of units operating within an individual country and across countries may be able to economize on the amount of firm assets needed in cash if the cash holding is operated through one central pool. With one pool of capital and up-to-date information on the cash flows in and out of the various units, the firm spends much less in terms of lost interest on cash balances that are held in safe-keeping against unforeseen cash-flow shortfalls. A single large pool may also be able to negotiate better financial-service rates with banking institutions for clearing purposes.

Netting   As illustrated in Figure 18.1, many of the cash flows between units of a multinational firm are two-way and may result in unneeded transfer costs and transaction expenses. Coordination between units simply requires some planning and budgeting of intrafirm cash flows in order that two-way flows are "netted" against one another, with one smaller cash flow replacing two opposed flows. This is particularly helpful if the two-way flow is in two different currencies, as each would be suffering currency-exchange charges for intrafirm transfers.

Leads and Lags   The timing of payments between units of a multinational is somewhat flexible. This flexibility allows the firm to not only position cash flows where they are needed most, but may actually aid in currency-risk management. A foreign subsidiary that is expecting its local currency to fall in value relative to the U.S. dollar may try to speed up, or "lead," its payments to the parent. Similarly, if the local currency is expected to rise versus the dollar, the subsidiary may want to wait, or "lag," payments until exchange rates are more favorable.

Reinvoicing   Multinational firms with a variety of manufacturing and distribution subsidiaries scattered over a number of countries within a region may often find it more economical to have one office or subsidiary taking ownership of all invoices and payments between units. This subsidiary literally buys from one unit and sells to a second unit, therefore taking ownership of the goods and reinvoicing the sale to the next unit. Once ownership is taken, the transaction can be redenominated in a different currency, netted against other payments, hedged against specific currency exposures, or repriced in accordance with potential tax benefits of the reinvoicing center's host country. The additional flexibility achievable in cash-flow management, product pricing, and profit placement may be substantial.

Internal Banks   Some multinational firms have found that their financial resources and needs are becoming either too large or too sophisticated for the financial services that are available in many of their local subsidiary markets. One solution to this has been the establishment of an "internal bank" within the firm. This bank actually buys and sells payables and receivables from the various units. This frees the units of the firm from struggling for continual working-capital financing and allows them to focus on their primary business activities.

These structures and procedures are often combined in different ways to fit the needs of the individual multinational firm. Some techniques are encouraged or prohibited by laws and regulations, depending on the host country's government and stage of capital-market liberalization. In fact, it is not uncommon to find one system at work in one hemisphere of firm operations with a different system in use in the other hemisphere. Multinational-cash-flow management requires flexible thinking on the part of managers.

IMPORT/EXPORT TRADE FINANCING

Unlike most domestic business, international business often occurs between two parties that do not know each other very well. Yet, in order to conduct business, a large degree of financial trust must exist. This financial trust is basically the trust that the buyer of a product will actually pay for it on or after delivery. For example, if a furniture manufacturer in South Carolina receives an order from a distributor located in Cleveland, Ohio, the furniture maker will ordinarily fill the order, ship the furniture, and await payment. Payment terms are usually 30 to 60 days. This is trade on an "open-account basis." The furniture manufacturer has placed a considerable amount of financial trust in the buyer but normally is paid with little problem.

Internationally, however, this financial trust is pushed to its limit. An order from a foreign buyer may constitute a degree of credit risk (the risk of not being repaid) that the producer (the exporter) cannot afford to take. The exporter needs some guarantee that the importer will pay for the goods. Other factors that tend to intensify this problem include the increased lag times necessary for international shipments and the potential risks of payments in different currencies. For this reason, arrangements that provide guarantees for exports are important to countries and companies wanting to expand international sales. This is accomplished through a sequence of documents surrounding the letter of credit.

Trade-Financing Mechanics

A lumber manufacturer in the Pacific Northwest of the United States, Vanport, receives a large order from a Japanese construction company, Endaka, for a shipment of old-growth pine lumber. Vanport has not worked with Endaka before and therefore seeks some assurance that payment for the lumber will actually be made. Vanport ordinarily does not require any assurance of the buyer's ability to pay (sometimes a small down-payment or deposit is made as a sign of good faith), but an international sale of this size is too large to risk. If in the event Endaka could not or would not pay, the cost of returning the lumber products to the United States would be prohibitive. The following sequence of events will complete the transaction.

1. Endaka Construction (JAP) requests a letter of credit (L/C) to be issued by its bank, Yokohama Bank.

2. Yokohama Bank will determine whether Endaka is financially sound and capable of making the payments as required. This is a very important step because Yokohama Bank simply wants to guarantee the payment, not make the payment.

3. Yokohama Bank, once satisfied with Endaka's application, issues the L/C to a representative in the United States or to the exporter's bank, Pacific First Bank. The L/C guarantees payment for the merchandise if the goods are shipped as stipulated in accompanying documents. Customary documents include the commercial invoice, customs clearance and invoice, the packing list, certification of insurance, and a bill of lading.

4. The exporter's bank, Pacific First, assures Vanport that payment will be made after evaluating the letter of credit. At this point the credit standing of Yokohama Bank has been substituted for the credit standing of the importer itself, Endaka Construction.

5. When the lumber order is ready, it is loaded on-board the shipper (called a common carrier). When the exporter signs a contract with a shipper, the signed contract serves as the receipt that the common carrier has received the goods, and it is termed the bill of lading.

6. Vanport draws a draft against Yokohama Bank for payment. The draft is the document used in international trade to effect payment and explic-

itly requests payment for the merchandise, which is now shown to be shipped and insured consistent with all requirements of the previously issued L/C. (If the draft is issued to the bank issuing the L/C, Yokohama Bank, it is termed a bank draft. If the draft is issued against the importer, Endaka Construction, it is a trade draft.) The draft, L/C, and other appropriate documents are presented to Pacific First Bank for payment.

7. If Pacific First Bank (US) had confirmed the letter of credit from Yokohama Bank, it would immediately pay Vanport for the lumber and then collect from the issuing bank, Yokohama. If Pacific First Bank had not confirmed the letter of credit, it only passes the documents to Yokohama Bank for payment (to Vanport). The confirmed letter of credit obviously speeds up payment to the exporter as opposed to being unconfirmed.

Regardless, with the letter of credit as the financial assurance, the exporter or the exporter's bank is collecting payment from the importer's bank, not from the importer itself. It is up to the specific arrangements between the importer (Endaka) and the importer's bank (Yokohama) to arrange the final settlement on that end of the purchase.

If this trade relationship continues over time, both parties will gain faith and confidence in the other. With this strengthening of financial trust, a loosening of the trade-financing relationship will come. Sustained buyer-seller relations across borders eventually end up operating on an open-account basis similar to domestic commerce.

FINANCIAL RISK MANAGEMENT

All firms are in some way influenced by three financial prices; exchange rates, interest rates, and commodity prices. The management of these prices, these risks, is termed **financial risk management.** Interest rates have always received, deservedly, much of management's attention in business; it is only recently that many firms have chosen to acknowledge their financial health is also affected by exchange rates and commodity prices. The following analysis focuses on the exchange-rate risks suffered by firms operating internationally.

Financial Price Risk and Firm Value

Risk is a word that deserves more respect than is commonly afforded it. Most dictionaries will refer to risk as the possibility of suffering harm or loss, danger; or a factor or element involving uncertain danger or hazards. These are negative definitions. Yet in the field of finance, the word risk has a neutral definition: a value or result that is at present unknown. This means that risk can be either positive or negative in impact.

There are three categories of financial price risk: interest-rate risk, exchange-rate risk, and commodity-price risk. Each can have potentially positive or negative impacts on the profitability or value of the firm. For example, a U.S. exporter like Eastman Kodak pays specific attention to the value of the U.S. dollar. If the dollar were to appreciate against other major currencies like the Japanese yen, Kodak's products would be more expensive to foreign buyers, and it may lose market share to foreign competitors (like Fuji).

The negative relationship between Kodak's firm value and the yen-dollar exchange rate is illustrated in Figure 18.2. As the dollar appreciates versus the yen (for example, if the spot rate moved from ¥125/$ to ¥140/$), Kodak would suffer falling sales in Japan, and possibly also in the United States, because Fuji's comparable prod-

**FIGURE 18.2
Financial Price Risks
and the Value of the
Firm**

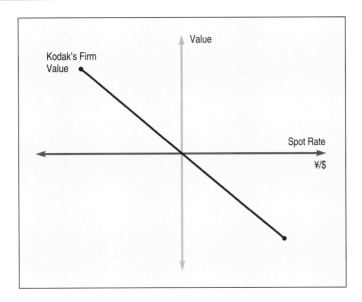

ucts would be relatively cheaper. The result is a fall in the value of Kodak. Corporate management expects financial managers to control these risks and protect the firm against exchange-rate risks as best they can.

But this same firm-value sensitivity also exists for interest rates and commodity prices. Most firms are at least partially financed with short-term floating-rate debt. Therefore, whenever interest rates rise, these firms suffer higher financing costs, reducing the value of the firms.

Similarly, an increase in the price of commodities like oil or coal, which are inputs into the production processes of many firms, will also reduce the value of those firms. But it does vary across firms. For example, a company like Kidder Peabody, which mines coal, will see rising profits and firm value when coal prices rise. Each firm is different. It simply depends on the markets and makeup of each company. Although the following sections will focus on the measurement and management of exchange-rate risk, it is important to remember that other financial price risks such as those of interest rates and commodity prices are fundamentally the same. They too can be measured and managed by firms.

Classification of Foreign-Currency Exposures

Companies today know the risks of international operations. They are aware of the substantial risks to balance-sheet values and annual earnings that interest rates and exchange rates may inflict on any firm at any time. And as is the case with most potential risks or problems to the firm, senior management expects junior management to do something about it. Financial managers, international treasurers, and financial officers of all kinds are expected to protect the firm from these risks. But before you can manage a risk, you must be able to measure it. There are three types of foreign-currency exposures that firms have in varying degrees:

1. **Transaction exposure.** This is the risk associated with a contractual payment of foreign currency. For example, a U.S. firm that exports products to France will receive a guaranteed (by contract) payment in French francs in the future. Firms that buy or sell internationally have **transaction exposures** if any of the cash flows are denominated in foreign currency.

2. **Economic exposure.** This is the risk to the firm that its long-term cash flows will be affected, positively or negatively, by unexpected future exchange-rate changes. Although many firms that consider themselves to be purely domestic may not realize it, all firms have some degree of **economic exposure.**

3. **Translation exposure.** This risk arises from the legal requirement that all firms consolidate their financial statements (balance sheets and income statements) of all worldwide operations annually. Therefore, any firm with operations outside its home country, operations that will be either earning foreign currency or valued in foreign currency, has **translation exposure.**

Transaction exposure and economic exposure are "true exposures" in the financial sense. This means they both present potential threats to the value of a firm's cash flows over time. The third exposure, translation, is a problem that arises from accounting. Under the present accounting principles in practice across most of the world's industrialized countries, translation exposure is not the problem it once was. For the most part, few real cash resources should be devoted to a purely accounting-based event.

TRANSACTION EXPOSURE

Transaction exposure is the most commonly observed type of exchange-rate risk. Only two conditions are necessary for a transaction exposure to exist: (1) a cash flow that is denominated in a foreign currency; (2) the cash flow to occur at a future date. Any contract, agreement, purchase or sale that is denominated in a foreign currency which will be settled in the future constitutes a transaction exposure.[3]

The risk of a transaction exposure is that the exchange rate might change between the present date and the settlement date. The change may be for the better or for the worse. For example, an American firm signs a contract to purchase heavy rolled-steel pipe from a South Korean steel producer for 21,000,000 Korean won. The payment is due in 30 days upon delivery. This 30-day account payable, so typical of international trade and commerce, is a transaction exposure for the U.S. firm. If the spot exchange rate on the date the contract is signed is Won 700/$, the U.S. firm would expect to pay

$$\frac{\text{Won } 21,000,000}{\text{Won } 700/\$} = \$30,000$$

But the firm is not assured of what the exchange rate will be in 30 days. If the spot rate at the end of 30 days is Won 720/$, the U.S. firm would actually pay less. The payment would then be $29,167. If, however, the exchange rate changed in the opposite direction, for example to Won 650/$, the payment could just as easily have increased to $32,308. This type of price risk, transaction exposure, is a major problem for international commerce.

Transaction-Exposure Management

Management of transaction exposures is usually accomplished by either **natural hedging** or **contractual hedging.** Natural hedging is the term used to describe how a firm might arrange to have foreign-currency cash flows coming in and going out at roughly the same times and same amounts. This is referred to as natural hedging because the management or hedging of the exposure is accomplished by matching offsetting foreign-currency cash flows and therefore does not require the firm to undertake unusual financial contracts or activities to manage the exposure. For example, a Canadian firm that generates a significant portion of its total sales in U.S. dollars may acquire U.S. dollar debt. The U.S. dollar earnings from sales could then be used to service the dollar debt as needed. In this way, regardless of whether the C$/US$ exchange rate goes up or down, the firm would be naturally hedged against the movement. If the U.S. dollar went up in value against the Canadian dollar, the U.S. dollars needed for debt service would be generated automatically by the export sales to the United States. U.S. dollar cash inflows would match U.S. dollar cash outflows.

Contractual hedging is when the firm uses financial contracts to hedge the transaction exposure. The most common foreign-currency contractual hedge is the **forward contract,** although other financial instruments and derivatives, such as currency futures and options, are also used. The forward contract (see Chapter 5) would allow the firm to be assured a fixed rate of exchange between the desired two currencies at the precise future date. The forward contract would also be for the exact amount of the exposure. Both natural hedging and contractual hedging are discussed in Global Perspective 18.1.

Before proceeding further into financial and currency risk management, it is important to be precise regarding the definition of hedging. A **hedge** is an asset or a position whose value moves in the equal but opposite direction of the exposure. This means that if an exposure experienced a loss in value of $50, the hedge asset would offset the loss with a gain in value of $50. The total value of the position would not change. This would be termed a perfect hedge.

But perfect hedges are hard to find. And many people would not use them if they were readily available. Why? Because the presence of a perfect hedge eliminates all down-side risk, but also eliminates all up-side potential. Many businesses accept this two-sided risk as part of doing business. However, it is generally best to accept risk in the line of business, not in the cash-payment process of settling the business. By hedging the value of the currency, the total value of the position will be protected against either good or bad exchange-rate changes.

Risk Management versus Speculation

The distinction between managing currency cash flows and speculating with currency cash flows is sometimes lost among those responsible for the safekeeping of the firm's treasury. If the previous description of currency hedging is followed closely (the selection of assets or positions only to counteract potential losses on existing exposures), few problems should arise. Problems arise when currency positions or financial instruments are purchased (or sold) with the expectation that a specific currency movement will result in a profit.

There are a number of major multinational firms that treat their international treasury centers as "service centers," but rarely do they consider financial management a "profit center." One of the most visible examples of what can go wrong when currency speculation is undertaken for corporate profit occurred in Great Britain in 1991. A large British food conglomerate, Allied-Lyons, suffered losses of £158 million ($268 million) on currency speculation after members of its international treasury staff suffered losses on currency positions at the start of the Persian Gulf War and then doubled-up on their positions in the following weeks in an attempt to recover previous losses. They of course lost even more.[4]

Global Perspective

18.1
"Lost in a Maze of Hedges"

Volatile exchange rates in recent weeks have sent many a nervous boss scurrying to his finance department to check up on its currency-hedging strategy. Few of them will emerge much the wiser, for the typical multinational's strategy can seem impenetrable.

Hedging is simple enough in theory. Just doing business exposes many firms to foreign-exchange risk: if an exchange rate moves the wrong way, profit or the balance sheet suffers. Suppose a British exporter sells goods that will be paid for in dollars three months later. If the dollar weakens against the pound, the exporter will get less in sterling than it expected. Hedging lets firms reduce or eliminate this risk by using a financial instrument that moves in the opposite way when exchange rates change. For the British exporter, that means one that is worth more pounds as the dollar falls.

The best way to hedge is to do it "naturally." Firms can design their trading, borrowing, and investment strategies to match their sales and assets in a particular currency with their purchases and liabilities in it. If, say, a British firm owns an asset valued in dollars, it can hedge by borrowing in dollars. No matter what happens to the pound-dollar exchange rate, there will be no net effect on the firm's balance sheet.

Few firms can hedge all, or even most, of their risk naturally. So many hedge actively in the financial markets, mainly using forward contracts and options. Forward contracts, agreements to buy or sell a given amount of a currency at an agreed exchange rate on a particular date,

get rid of all exchange-rate risk, and are often thought of as the perfect hedge. If the British exporter is going to be paid $1m in three months, it can make a forward contract to sell the $1m on that date and know exactly how many pounds it will get in return even if exchange rates fluctuate in the spot market.

The trouble with forward contracts is that they are irrevocable. If the dollar strengthens against sterling, the British exporter with a forward contract is worse off than it would have been with no hedge at all. Options, which give firms the right, but not the obligation, to use a particular forward contract, are more flexible. Imagine that the British exporter buys an option to sell dollars in three months at the forward rate. If the exchange rate moves against the firm, it can use its option and limit the damage; if the rate goes in its favor, it can let the option lapse and enjoy the windfall.

Firms seem to use forward contracts at least twice as much as options. One reason is cost. Forward contracts are no dearer than an ordinary trade in the spot market. Options, by contrast, are expensive and must be paid for whether or not they are used. Option prices can jump about wildly, depending on which currencies are involved and how volatile the market is. Prices have gone through the roof recently: on September 29 Swiss Bank Corporation priced a three-month option to sell dollars at 2.7 percent of the contract, a hefty $27,000 for a British exporter wanting to hedge $1 million.

Transaction Exposure Case: Lufthansa (1985)

In January 1985, the German airline Lufthansa purchased 20 Boeing 737 jet aircraft. The jets would be delivered to Lufthansa in one year, in January 1986. Upon delivery of the aircraft, Lufthansa would pay Boeing (U.S.) $500 million. This constituted a huge transaction exposure for Lufthansa. (Note that the exposure falls on Lufthansa, not Boeing. If the purchase agreement had been stated in deutschemarks, the transaction exposure would have been transferred to Boeing.)

The Exposure   The spot exchange rate in January 1985, when Lufthansa signed the agreement, was DM 3.2/$. The expected cost of the aircraft to Lufthansa was then

$$\$500,000,000 \times DM3.2/\$ = DM1,600,000,000.$$

Figure 18.3 illustrates how the expected total cost of $500 million changes to Lufthansa with the spot exchange rate. If the deutschemark continued to fall against the U.S. dollar as it had been doing for more than four years, the cost to Lufthansa of the Boeing jets could skyrocket to more than DM 2 billion easily.

But the most important word here is expected. There was no guarantee that the spot exchange rate in effect in January of the following year would be DM 3.2/$. The U.S. dollar had been appreciating against the deutschemark for more than four years at this point. Senior management of Lufthansa was afraid the appreciating dollar trend might continue. For example, if the U.S. dollar appreciated over the coming year from DM 3.2/$ to DM 3.4/$, the cost of the aircraft purchased from Boeing would rise by DM 100 million. Figure 18.4 shows how the DM/$ exchange rate had continued to trend upward for several years. By looking at graphics such as this, it was hard to believe that the U.S. dollar would do anything but continue to rise. It takes the truly brave to buck the trend.

But at the same time many senior members of Lufthansa's management believed that the U.S. dollar had risen as far as it would go. They argued that the dollar would fall over the coming year against the deutschemark (see Figure 18.4). If for example the spot rate fell to DM 3.0/$ by January 1986, Lufthansa would pay only DM 1,500 million, a savings of DM 100 million. This was true currency risk, in every sense of the word.

The Management Strategy   After much debate, Lufthansa's management decided to use forward contracts to hedge one-half of the $500 million exposure. This was obviously a compromise. First, because the exposure was a single large foreign currency payment, to occur one time only, natural hedging was not a realistic alternative. Secondly, although management believed the dollar would fall, the risk was too

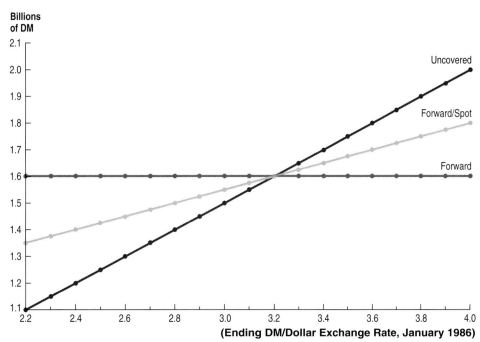

FIGURE 18.3
Lufthansa's Transaction Exposure: Alternatives for Managing the Purchase of $500 million in Boeing 737s

(Ending DM/Dollar Exchange Rate, January 1986)

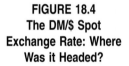

FIGURE 18.4
The DM/$ Spot
Exchange Rate: Where
Was it Headed?

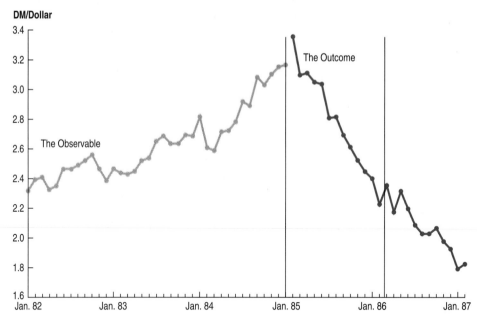

large to ignore. It was thought that by covering one-half of the exposure, Lufthansa would be protected against the U.S. dollar appreciating, yet still allow Lufthansa some opportunity to benefit from a fall in the dollar. Lufthansa signed a one-year forward contract (sold $250 million forward) at a forward rate of DM 3.2/$. The remaining $250 million owed Boeing was left unhedged.

The Outcome   By January 1986, the U.S. dollar not only fell, it plummeted versus the deutschemark. The spot rate fell from DM 3.2/$ in January 1985 to DM 2.3/$ in January 1986. Lufthansa had therefore benefited from leaving half the transaction exposure uncovered. But this meant that the half that was covered with forward contracts "cost" the firm DM 225 million!

The total cost to Lufthansa of delivering $250 million at the forward rate of DM 3.2/$ and $250 million at the ending spot rate of DM 2.3/$ was

$$[\$250,000,000 \times DM3.2/\$] + [\$250,000,000 \times DM2.3/\$] = DM\ 1,375,000,000.$$

Although this was DM 225 million less than the expected purchase price when the contract was signed in January 1985, Lufthansa's management was heavily criticized for covering any of the exposure. If the entire transaction exposure had been left uncovered, the final cost would have been only DM 1,150 million. The critics of course, had perfect hindsight.

Currency Risk Sharing

Firms that import and export on a continuing basis have constant transaction exposures. If a firm is interested in maintaining a good business relationship with one of its suppliers, it must work with that supplier to assure it that it will not force all currency risk or exposure off on the other party on a continual basis. Exchange-rate movements are inherently random; therefore some type of risk-sharing arrangement may prove useful.

If Ford (U.S.) imports automotive parts from Mazda (Japan) every month, year after year, major swings in exchange rates can benefit one party at the expense of the other. One solution would be for Ford and Mazda to agree that all purchases by Ford will be made in Japanese yen as long as the spot rate on the payment date is between ¥120/$ and ¥130/$. If the exchange rate is between these values on the payment dates, Ford agrees to accept whatever transaction exposure exists (because it is paying in a foreign currency). If, however, the exchange rate falls outside of this range on the payment date, Ford and Mazda will "share" the difference. If the spot rate on settlement date is ¥110/$, the Japanese yen would have appreciated versus the dollar, causing Ford's costs of purchasing automotive parts to rise. Since this rate falls outside the contractual range, Mazda would agree to accept a total payment in Japanese yen that would result from a "shared" difference of ¥10. Thus, Ford's total payment in Japanese yen would be calculated using an exchange rate of ¥115/$.

Risk-sharing agreements like these have been in use for nearly 50 years on world markets. They became something of a rarity during the 1950s and 1960s, when exchange rates were relatively stable (under the Bretton Woods Agreement). But with the return to floating exchange rates in the 1970s, firms with long-term customer-supplier relationships across borders returned to some old ways of keeping old friends. And sometimes old ways work very well.

ECONOMIC EXPOSURE

Economic exposure, also called operating exposure, is the change in the value of a firm arising from unexpected changes in exchange rates. Economic exposure emphasizes that there is a limit to a firm's ability to predict either cash flows or exchange-rate changes in the medium to long term. All firms, either directly or indirectly, have economic exposure.

It is customary to think of only firms that actively trade internationally as having any type of currency exposure (like Lufthansa or Eastman Kodak described previously). But actually all firms that operate in economies affected by international financial events such as exchange-rate changes are affected by these events. A barber in Ottumwa, Iowa, seemingly isolated from exchange-rate chaos, is still affected when the dollar rises as it did in the early 1980s. U.S. products become increasingly expensive to foreign buyers, American manufacturers like John Deere & Co. in Iowa are forced to cut back production and lay off workers, and businesses of all types decline. Even the business of barbers. The impacts are real, and they affect all firms, domestic or international alike.

But how exposed is an individual firm in terms of economic exposure? It is impossible to say. Measuring economic exposure is subjective, and for the most part it is dependent on the degree of internationalization present in the firm's cost and revenue structure, as well as potential changes over the long run. But simply because it is difficult to measure does not mean that management cannot take some steps to prepare the firm for the unexpected.

Impact of Economic Exposure

The impacts of economic exposure are as diverse as are firms in their international structure. Take the case of a U.S. corporation with a successful British subsidiary. The British subsidiary manufactured and then distributed the firm's products in Great Britain, Germany, and France. The profits of the British subsidiary are paid out annually to the American parent corporation. What would be the impact on the prof-

Establishing similar manufacturing operations in several countries is one way for a firm such as Corning Vitro Corporation to reduce the impact of unfavorable changes in exchange rates.
Source: Courtesy of Corning Incorporated.

itability of the British subsidiary and the entire U.S. firm if the British pound suddenly fell in value against all other major currencies (as it did in September and October 1992)?

If the British firm had been facing competition in Germany, France, and its own home market from firms from those other two continental countries, it would now be more competitive. If the British pound is cheaper, so are the products sold internationally by British-based firms. The British subsidiary of the American firm would, in all likelihood, see rising profits from increased sales.

But what of the value of the British subsidiary to the U.S. parent corporation? The same fall in the British pound that allowed the British subsidiary to gain profits would also result in substantially fewer U.S. dollars when the British pound earnings are converted to U.S. dollars at the end of the year. It seems that it is nearly impossible to win in this situation. Actually, from the perspective of economic-exposure management, the fact that the firm's total value, subsidiary and parent together, is roughly a wash as a result of the exchange-rate change is desirable. Sound financial management assumes that a firm will profit and bear risk in its line of business, not in the process of settling payments on business already completed.

Economic Exposure Management

Management of economic exposure is being prepared for the unexpected. A firm such as Hewlett Packard (HP), which is highly dependent on its ability to remain cost competitive in markets both at home and abroad, may choose to take actions now that would allow it to passively withstand any sudden unexpected rise of the dollar. This could be accomplished through diversification: diversification of operations and diversification of financing.

Diversification of operations would allow the firm to be desensitized to the impacts of any one pair of exchange-rate changes. For example, a multinational firm such as Hewlett Packard may produce the same product in manufacturing facilities in Singapore, the United States, Puerto Rico, and Europe. If a sudden and prolonged rise in the dollar made production in the United States prohibitively expensive and uncompetitive, HP is already positioned to shift production to a relatively cheaper currency environment. Although firms rarely diversify production location for the sole purpose of currency diversification, it is a substantial additional benefit from such global expansion.

Diversification of financing serves in hedging economic exposure much in the same way as it did with transaction exposures. A firm with debt denominated in many different currencies is sensitive to many different interest rates. If one country or currency experiences rapidly rising inflation rates and interest rates, a firm with diversified debt will not be subject to the full impact of such movements. Purely domestic firms, however, are actually somewhat captive to these local conditions and are unable to ride out such interest-rate storms as easily.

It should be noted that in both cases, diversification is a passive solution to the exposure problem. This means that without knowing when or where or what the problem may be, the firm simply spreads its operations and financial structure out over a variety of countries and currencies to be prepared.

TRANSLATION EXPOSURE

Translation or accounting exposure results from the conversion or translation of foreign currency-denominated financial statements of foreign subsidiaries and affiliates into the home currency of the parent. This is necessary in order to prepare consolidated financial statements for all firms as country-law requires. The purpose is to have all operations worldwide stated in the same-currency terms for comparison purposes. Management often uses these translated statements to judge the performance of foreign affiliates and their personnel on the same currency terms as the parent itself.

The problem, however, arises from the translation of balance sheets in foreign currencies into the domestic currency. Which assets and liabilities are to be translated at current exchange rates (at the current balance-sheet date) versus historical rates (those in effect on the date of the initial investment)? Or should all assets and liabilities be translated at the same rate? The answer is somewhere in between, and the process of translation is dictated by financial accounting standards.

The Current-Rate Method

At present in the United States, the proper method for translating foreign financial statements is given in Financial Accounting Standards Board statement No. 52 (FASB 52). According to FASB 52, if a foreign subsidiary is operating in a foreign currency functional environment,[5] most assets, liabilities, and income statement items of foreign affiliates are translated using current exchange rates (the exchange rate in effect on the balance-sheet date). For this reason, it is often referred to as the current-rate method. Table 18.3 provides an example of how this translation process might work.

A U.S. firm, Moab, established a Canadian subsidiary two years ago. The subsidiary, Moab-Can, is wholly owned and operated by Moab. The balance sheet of Moab-Can on December 31, 1992, is shown in Canadian dollars in Column (1) of Table 18.3. In order for Moab to construct a consolidated financial statement, all Moab-Can's assets and liabilities must be translated into U.S. dollars at the end-of-year exchange rate. This rate is C$1.20/$. All assets and liabilities are translated at the current rate except for equity capital, which is translated at the exchange rate in effect at the time of the Canadian subsidiary's establishment, C$1.10/$. The exchange rates used to translate each individual asset and liability of the Canadian subsidiary are listed in Column (2).

	(1) Canadian dollars (thousands)	(2) Current rate C$/$	(3) U.S. dollars (thousand)
Assets			
Cash	120	1.20	100
Accounts payable	240	1.20	200
Inventory	120	1.20	100
Net plant and equipment	480	1.20	400
Total	C$ 960		$ 800
Liabilities and Net Worth			
Accounts payable	120	1.20	100
Short-term debt	120	1.20	100
Long-term debt	240	1.20	200
Equity capital	480	1.10	436
Cumulative Translation Adjustment			(36)
Total	C$ 960		$ 800

TABLE 18.3 Translation of Foreign Affiliate's Balance Sheet: Canadian Subsidiary of a U.S. Firm

The U.S.–dollar value of all translated assets and liabilities is shown in Column (3). Because all assets and liabilities except equity capital were translated at the current rate, an imbalance results. A new account must be created in order for the translated balance sheet to balance. This new account, the Cumulative Translation Adjustment or CTA, takes on a gain or loss value necessary to maintain a balanced translation. Moab-Can, because the equity capital was invested when the Canadian dollar was stronger, now represents a CTA translation loss of US$36,000 to the parent company.

But what does this translation loss mean to the company? The CTA account is an accounting construction. It is created in order to produce a consolidated balance sheet. Neither the Canadian subsidiary nor the U.S. parent experiences any cash-flow impact as a result of the translation gain or loss. It is quite possible that consolidation in the following year or years could result in CTA translation gains that could reduce or even cancel this year's loss.

The translation of the income statement of Moab-Can offers no such problems under FASB 52, so that consolidated reporting results in no other surprises or problems. The CTA account remains a "paper-fiction" until the time the Canadian subsidiary is either sold or liquidated. On the sale or liquidation of the Canadian subsidiary, the CTA gains or losses attributed to Moab-Can must be realized by the parent company. The result is that these gains or losses are included with other current income of the parent for that period.[6]

Translation-Exposure Management

Translation exposure under FASB 52 results in no cash-flow impacts under normal circumstances. Although consolidated accounting does result in CTA translation losses or gains on the parent's consolidated balance sheet, these accounting entries are not ordinarily realized. Unless liquidation or sale of the subsidiary is anticipated, neither the subsidiary nor the parent firm should expend real resources on the management of an accounting convention.

In the event that the realization of the CTA translation gain or loss is imminent, traditional currency hedging instruments can be used. If Moab planned on liquidating Moab-Can this year, Moab could use a forward-contract hedge to protect the firm's income for the period. The value of the forward contract would make up for part of the expected loss if the firm believed the Canadian dollar would be lower than C$1.10/$ by the end of the year. Firms that are more concerned with their CTA position will structure their foreign subsidiaries to reduce the degree of net translation exposure. The primary method for this is the holding of some assets that are not denominated in the functional currency. For example, in the previous Moab-Can balance sheet shown in Table 18.3, if some portion of cash or accounts payable had been denominated in U.S. dollars rather than Canadian dollars, Moab-Can's net exposure, its translation loss in this case, would have been less. This restructuring of the foreign subsidiary's balance sheet is termed a balance sheet hedge. Although this will protect the parent against translation losses or gains, it is often difficult or costly to achieve in practice.

INTEREST RATE AND CURRENCY SWAPS

One of the most significant developments in international finance in the 1980s was the development of the interest rate and currency swap markets. Although markets of all kinds (goods, services, labor, and capital) have continued to open up across the world in the past two decades, there are still "paper walls" between many capital markets. Firms operating in their home markets are both helped and hindered; they are well known in their own capital markets but still may not be recognized in other potentially larger capital markets. The interest rate and currency swap markets have allowed firms to arbitrage the differences between markets, using their comparative advantage of borrowing in their home market and swapping for interest rates or currencies that are not as readily accessible.

Interest Rate Swaps

Firms that are considered to be better borrowers in financial markets borrow at lower rates. These lower rates may be lower fixed rates or lower spreads over floating-rate bases. In fact, lower quality borrowers often are limited in their choices to floating rates in many markets. The **interest rate swap,** often called the "plain vanilla swap," allows one firm to use its good credit standing to borrow capital at low fixed rates and exchange its interest payments with a slightly lower credit-rated borrower who has debt-service payments at floating rates. Each borrower ends up making net interest payments at rates below those it could have achieved on its own.

If Firm Alpha is considered an extremely sound borrower, it can borrow capital at lower interest rates, probably fixed rates, than a second firm, Zeta. Zeta, although profitable and sound, is simply not rated as highly as a borrower in the eyes of the financial markets, and it must borrow at higher rates, often only at floating rates. If each firm were to borrow where it is "well received," using its comparative advantages, they may then swap or exchange their debt-service payments. Alpha, which has taken on fixed-rate debt-service payments, will exchange these payments for Zeta's floating-rate payments. Both companies end up paying less interest in the form that they desired by negotiating rates between themselves that are better than what the markets had offered directly.

Currency Swaps

The **currency swap** is the equivalent of the interest-rate swap, only the currency of denomination of the debt is different. Many international and multinational firms need capital denominated in different currencies for international investments or even for the purpose of risk management (for natural hedging, as described previously). Foreign firms often find themselves at a disadvantage, however, when trying to enter new markets. The interest rates available to them in the necessary currencies may simply not be affordable.

Figure 18.5 illustrates how a currency swap arrangement would work for a Swedish firm desiring U.S. dollar debt, and a U.S. firm desiring Swedish krona debt. The mechanics of the swap are actually quite simple. The Swedish firm, Ericcsson, borrows capital in its home market, where it is well-known and can obtain capital at attractive interest rates. The U.S. firm, Sioux, also acquires local debt in its own advantaged-access market. Then, working through a swap dealer, each firm exchanges the debt-service payment schedule on its own debt for the debt-service payment schedule of the other firm's debt. The principal amounts borrowed must be equal at current exchange rates in order for the swap to be made. The U.S. firm, Sioux, now agrees to make interest payments in Swedish kronor, and the Swedish firm Ericcsson agrees to make U.S. dollar interest payments. The two firms have swapped payment schedules.

But what of the risk of nonpayment? If one of the swap parties does not make its agreed-upon payments, who is responsible in meeting the obligations of the original debt agreement? The answer is that the initial borrower is responsible for covering any shortfall or nonpayment by the swap party. This risk, termed counterparty risk, is an increasing concern in the interest rate and currency swap markets as more and more firms utilize these markets to manage their debt structures.

The currency swap market allows any firm to exchange its own comparative advantage in acquiring capital for the advantaged access of another firm in the foreign currency market. Both parties benefit from the free exchange of their comparative advantages. Although the swap market is not a source of capital, it is an important way to change the characteristics of capital.

The swap markets have grown rapidly over the past decade as more firms have sought to diversify their operations and their financing. In the early days of the market (early 1980s) most swaps were literally matched pairs of firms and debt issues as described above. The market has since grown and matured to the stage that most firms can now simply contact the swap desk of major international banks and arrange a swap directly with the bank. The bank is able to find the counterparty for the transaction on its own without involving the other firm. As more firms attempt to expand internationally, the swap market is expected to grow in significance as a means of managing the international financial risks and exposures of the firm.

FIGURE 18.5
Sample Currency Swap:
Arbitrage Between the
U.S. Dollar and Swedish
Krona Debt Markets

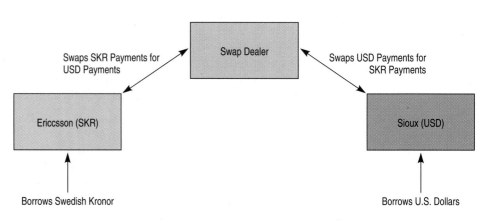

SUMMARY

International financial management is both complex and critical to the multinational firm. All traditional functional areas of financial management are affected by the internationalization of the firm. Capital budgeting, firm financing, capital structure, and working-capital and cash-flow management, all traditional functions, are made more difficult by business activities that cross borders and oceans, not to mention currencies and markets.

In addition to the traditional areas of financial management, international financial management must deal with the three types of currency exposure: (1) transaction exposure, (2) economic exposure, and (3) translation exposure. Each type of currency risk confronts a firm with serious choices regarding its exposure analysis and its degree of willingness to manage these inherent risks.

This chapter described not only the basic types of risk, but also outlined a number of the basic strategies employed in the management of these exposures. Some of the solutions available today have only arisen with the development of new types of international financial markets and instruments, such as the currency swap. Others, such as currency risk-sharing agreements, are as old as exchange rates themselves.

Key Terms and Concepts

net present value (NPV)

capital budget

working capital management

intrafirm transfers

multilateral netting

financial risk management

transaction exposure

economic exposure

translation exposure

natural hedging

hedge

forward contracts

money market hedges

interest rate swaps

currency swap

Questions for Discussion

1. Why is it important to identify the cash flows of a foreign investment from the perspective of the parent rather than from just the project?

2. Is currency risk unique to international firms? Is currency risk good or bad for the potential profitability of the multinational?

3. Which type of currency risk is the least important to the multinational firm? Should resources be expended in the management of this risk?

4. Are firms with no direct international business (imports and exports) subject to economic exposure?

5. What would you have recommended that Lufthansa do to manage its transaction exposure if you had been the airline's chief financial officer in January 1985?

6. Why do you think Lufthansa and Boeing did not use some form of "currency-risk sharing" in their 1985–1986 transaction?

7. Which type of firm do you believe is more "naturally hedged" against exchange rate exposure, the purely domestic firm (the barber) or the multinational firm (subsidiaries all over the world)?

8. Why have the currency-and-interest-rate-swap markets grown so rapidly in the past decade?

Recommended Readings

Ahn, Mark J., and William D. Falloon. *Strategic Risk Management: How Global Corporations Manage Financial Risk for Competitive Advantage.* Chicago: Probus Publishing, 1991.

Brigham, Eugene F., and Louis C. Gapenski. *Intermediate Financial Management.* New York: Dryden, 1993.

Eiteman, David K., Arthur I. Stonehill, and Michael H. Moffett. *Multinational Business Finance,* Sixth edition. Reading, Mass.: Addison-Wesley Publishing, 1992.

Howcroft, Barry, and Christopher Storey. *Management and Control of Currency and Interest Rate Risk.* Chicago: Probus Publishing, 1989.

Smith, Clifford W., Charles W. Smithson, and D. Sykes Wilford. *Managing Financial Risk,* The Institutional Investor Series in Finance. New York: Harper Business, 1990.

Smith, Roy C., and Ingo Walter. *Global Financial Services.* New York: Harper & Row Publishers, 1990.

Wunnicke, Diane B., David R. Wilson, and Brooke Wunnicke. *Corporate Financial Risk Management.* New York: John Wiley & Sons, 1992.

Notes

1. There are of course other traditional decision criteria used in capital budgeting, such as the internal rate of return, modified internal rate of return, payback period, and so forth. For the sake of simplicity, NPV is used throughout the analysis in this chapter. Under most conditions, NPV is also the most consistent criterion for selecting good projects, as well as selecting between projects.

2. One of the most difficult pricing decisions many multinational firms must make is the price at which they sell their own products to their subsidiaries and affiliates. These prices, called transfer prices, are theoretically equivalent to what the same product would cost if purchased on the open market. However, it is often impossible to find such a product on the open market; it is unique to this firm's product line. The result is a price that is set internally that may make the subsidiary more or less profitable. This, in turn, has impacts on taxes paid in host countries.

3. Many firms only acknowledge the existence of a transaction exposure when they "book" the receivable, when they ship the order to the customer and issue the account receivable. In fact, whether they realize it or not, when they accepted the order at a fixed price in terms of foreign currency, they gave birth to a transaction exposure.

4. A note of particular irony in this case was that the chief currency trader for Allied-Lyons had authored an article in the British trade journal *The Treasurer* only a few months before. The article had described the proper methods and strategies for careful corporate foreign-currency risk management. He had concluded with the caution to never confuse "good luck with skillful trading."

5. The distinction as to what the "functional currency" of a foreign subsidiary or affiliate operation is depends on a number of factors, including the currency that dominates expenses and revenues. If the foreign subsidiary's dominant currency is the local currency, the current-rate method of translation is used. If, however, the functional currency of the foreign subsidiary is identified as the currency of the parent, the U.S. dollar in the example, the temporal method of translation is used. The temporal method is the procedure that was used in the United States from 1975 to 1981 under FASB 8.

6. Prior to the passage of FASB 52, FASB 8 had been the primary directive on translation in the United States. FASB 8, often termed the monetary/non-monetary method, differed from FASB 52 in two important ways. First, it applied historical exchange rates to several of the long-term asset categories, resulting normally in a lower net exposed asset position. Secondly, all translation gains and losses were passed through the parent's consolidated income for the current period. This resulted in volatile swings in the critical earnings per share (EPS) reported by multinational firms. Although this was still only an accounting convention, the volatility introduced to EPS caused much concern among firms.

International Accounting and Taxation

1. To understand how accounting practices differ across countries, and how these differences may alter the competitiveness of firms in international markets.

2. To isolate which accounting practices are likely to constitute much of the competitiveness debate in the coming decade.

3. To examine the two basic philosophies of international taxation as practiced by governments, and how they in turn deal with foreign firms in their home markets and domestic firms in foreign markets.

4. To understand how the degree of ownership and control of a foreign enterprise alters the taxable income of a foreign enterprise in the eyes of U.S. tax authorities.

5. To understand the problems faced by many U.S.-based multinational firms in paying taxes both in foreign countries and in the United States.

The Prophet of Profit: British Accounting Practices

"The book they tried to ban," trumpets the cover. This time the forbidden topic is not the spooks of "Spycatcher" or the erotica of "Lady Chatterley's Lover," but the somewhat duller subject of massaging corporate results to make them look better. "Accounting for Growth" by Terry Smith, a top analyst at UBS Phillips & Drew, a London brokerage house, is the chilling tale of "creative" accounting in the boardrooms of Britain's 200 biggest firms. Published on August 18th, the book has made national headlines and won an unrepentant Mr. Smith suspension from his job.

The 12 techniques identified by Mr. Smith are perfectly legal but, he argues, can be used to mislead investors. They include the inconsistent use of extraordinary and exceptional items, some tricks of acquisition and disposal accounting, off-balance-sheet financing, disguising debt as equity, changing depreciation rules and capitalising costs. These practices all tend to do one of two things: increase reported profits or make a company's balance sheet look stronger. So the shares of companies using such ploys may be over-valued. As a crude rule of thumb, investors should steer clear of firms that use the criticised techniques, says Mr. Smith.

Many economists have a more fundamental objection to Mr. Smith's views. In an efficient market, they argue, accounting tricks should have no effect on share prices. Provided a handful of clever analysts can find a way through the accounting jungle to the firm's true financial position and there are big investors willing to trade on that information, share prices will reflect the firm's true value because the canny investors will continue to buy or sell the shares until the right price is reached. In other words, a few informed people can set the correct price for everyone, including investors who cannot tell a profit-and-loss account from a balance sheet.

Does this mean that the market sees through creative accounting? Most of these studies looked at large firms and well-publicized accounting changes. The market might take longer to spot subtler massaging of profits, especially by small and medium-sized firms.

When a firm uses accounting tricks to boost earnings, it usually means that there is a lot more bad news to come, says Mr. Lev (of the University of California at Berkeley). Mr. Smith's advice to avoid firms that practise creative accounting may not be so crude after all.

The methods used in the measurement of company operations, accounting principles and practices, vary across countries. These methods have a very large impact on how firms operate, how they compare against domestic and international competitors, and how governments view their respective place in society. Accounting principles are, however, moving toward more standardization across countries.

Taxation and accounting are fundamentally related. The principles by which a firm measures its sales and expenses, its assets and liabilities, all go into the formulation of profits, which are subject to taxation. The tax policies of more and more governments, in conjunction with accounting principles, are also becoming increasingly similar. Many of the tax issues specifically in the mind of officials, such as the avoidance of taxes in high-tax countries or by shielding income from taxation by holding profits in so-called tax havens, are slowly being eliminated by increasing cooperation between governments. Like the old expression of "death and taxes," they are today, more than ever, inevitable.

This chapter provides an overview of the major differences between accounting practices and corporate taxation philosophies among major industrial countries. Although the average business manager cannot be expected to have a detailed understanding (or recall) of the multitudes of tax laws and accounting principles across countries, a basic understanding of many of these issues aid in the understanding of why "certain things are done certain ways" in international business.

ACCOUNTING DIVERSITY

The fact that accounting principles differ across countries is not, by itself, a problem. The primary problem is that real economic decisions by lenders, investors, or government policymakers may be distorted by these differences. Table 19.1 provides a simple example of the potential problems that may arise if two identical firms were operating in similar or dissimilar economic and accounting environments.

First, if two identical firms (in terms of structure, products, and strategies) are operating in similar economic situations and are subject to similar accounting treatment (cell A), a comparison of their performance will be logical in practice and easily interpreted. The results of a competitive comparison or even an accounting audit (measurement and monitoring of their accounting practices) will lead to results that make sense. The two same firms operating in dissimilar economic situations will, when subject to the same accounting treatment, potentially look very different. And it may be that they should appear different if they are operating in totally different environments.

For example, one airline may depreciate its aircraft over five years, while another airline may depreciate over 10 years. Is this justified? It is if these two identical air carriers are in fundamentally different economic situations. If the first airline flies predominantly short commuter routes, which require thousands of takeoffs and landings, and the second airline flies only long intercontinental flights, which require many fewer takeoffs and landings, the first may be justified in depreciating its fixed assets much faster. The airline with more-frequent takeoffs and landings will wear out its aircraft more quickly, which is what the accounting principle of depreciation is attempting to capture.[1] The economic situations are different.

The most blatantly obvious mismatch of economic environments and accounting treatments is probably that of cell C. Two identical firms operating within the same economic environment that receive different accounting treatment are not comparable. These same firms, if placed in the same environment, would appear differently, with one potentially gaining competitive advantage over the other simply because of accounting treatment. This is inconsistent with most of the private and public goals of accounting in all countries.

Finally, cell D offers the mismatch of different environments and different accounting treatments. Although logical in premise, the results are most likely incomparable in outcome. Identical firms in differing economic environments require differing approaches to financial measurement. But the fact that the results of financial comparison may not be usable is not an error; it is simply a fact of the differing markets in which the firms operate. As firms expand internationally, as markets expand

TABLE 19.1 Accounting Diversity and Economic Environments	Accounting Treatment	Economic Situation of Two Identical Firms	
		Similar	Dissimilar
	Similar	Logical practice A Results are comparable	May/may not be logical B Results may/may not be comparable
	Dissimilar	Illogical practice C Results are not comparable	Logical practice D Results may not be comparable

Source: "International Accounting Diversity and Capital Market Decisions," Frederick D.S. Choi and Richard Levich, in *The Handbook of International Accounting*, Frederick D.S. Choi, editor, 1992.

across borders, as businesses diversify across currencies, cultures, and economies, the movement toward cell A continues from market forces rather than from government intention.

PRINCIPAL ACCOUNTING DIFFERENCES ACROSS COUNTRIES

International **accounting diversity** can lead to any of the following errors in international business conducted with the use of financial statements: (1) poor or improper business decision making; (2) hinder the ability of a firm or enterprise to raise capital in different or foreign markets; (3) hinder or prevent the monitoring of competitive factors across firms, industries, and countries. Examples of these problems abound in international business literature. For example, it is widely believed that much of the recent trend of British firms acquiring U.S. companies is primarily a result of their ability to completely expense "goodwill" (the added cost of a firm purchased over and above the fair market value of its constituent components).

Origins of Differences

Accounting standards and practices are in many ways no different from any other legislative or regulatory statutes in their origins. Laws reflect the people, places, and events of their time (see Global Perspective 19.1). Most accounting practices and

Global Perspective

19.1
The Father of Accounting: Luca Pacioli Who?

Doctors have Hippocrates and philosophers have Plato. But who is the father of accounting? Knowing that accountants have long had inferiority complexes, two Seattle University professors have decided that the profession should have a father and that he should be Luca Pacioli.

But their anointing of the Renaissance scholar occasions an identity crisis. Hardly anyone—accountants included—has ever heard of Pacioli (pronounced pot-CHEE-oh-lee).

Five centuries ago Pacioli published *"Summa de Arithmetica, Geometria, Proportioni et Proportionalita."* It contained a slender tract for merchants on double-entry bookkeeping, which had been in wide use in Venice for years. Because of that, some accounting historians including Professors Weis and Tinius credit Pacioli with codifying accounting principles for the first time. That would seem to establish paternity.

Professor Vangermeersch [University of Rhode Island] says the origins of double-entry bookkeeping are open to question. "If you're crediting people of past centuries for contributions to accounting, you should include Leonardo of Pisa, who brought Arabic numerals to the West; James Peele, who initiated journal-entry systems; and Emile Garcke and J.M. Fells, who applied accounting to factory use," he says. All these men have another thing in common, he adds: They are just as obscure as Luca Pacioli.

Even in literature, says Prof. Vangermeersch, the only famous accountant was Daniel Defoe, who wrote "Robinson Crusoe." Unfortunately, Defoe was a terrible businessman and failed in a series of ventures, the professor observes. "Even as a dissenter and pamphleteer, he was tarred and feathered by the public."

Source: Abstracted from "Father of Accounting Is a Bit of a Stranger To His Own Progeny," *The Wall Street Journal,* January 29, 1993, p. A1, A6. Reprinted by permission of The Wall Street Journal, © 1993 Dow Jones & Company, Inc. All Rights Reserved Worldwide.

laws are linked to the objectives of the parties who will use this financial information. These end-users are investors, lenders, and governments.

National accounting principles are also frequently affected by other environmental factors, such as the dominance of one country's trade and financial activity over the trade and financial activity of another country. Although there are substantial differences between U.S. and Canadian accounting practices, many of the recent changes forced on Canadian firms have their origins in U.S. practice.

Classification Systems

There are several ways to classify and group national accounting systems and practices. Figure 19.1 illustrates one such classification based on a statistically based clustering of practices across countries by C. W. Nobes. The systems are first subdivided into micro-based (characteristics of the firms and industries) and macro-uniform (following fundamental government or economic factors per country). The micro-based national accounting systems are then broken down into those that follow a theoretical principle or pragmatic concerns. The latter category includes the national accounting systems of countries as diverse as the United States, Canada, Japan, the United Kingdom, and Mexico.

The macro-uniform systems, according to Nobes, are primarily European countries. The continental Europeans are typified by accounting systems that are formu-

---

FIGURE 19.1   Nobes Classification of National Accounting Systems

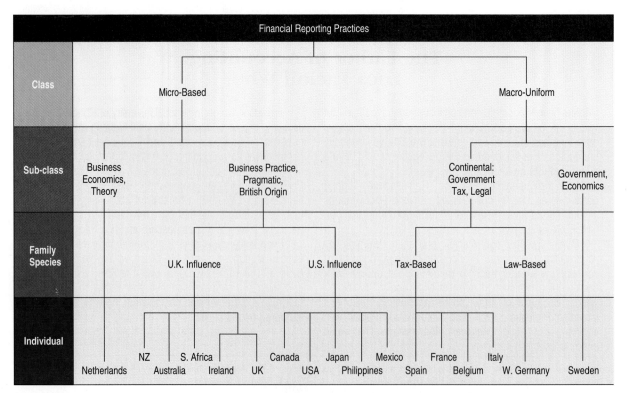

Source: C.W. Nobes, "International Classification of Accounting Systems," unpublished paper, April 1980, Table C, as cited in Choi and Mueller, 1992, p. 34.

lated in secondary importance to legal organizational forms (Germany) or for the apportionment and application of national tax laws (France, Spain, Italy), or the more pure forms of government and economic models (Sweden). An alternative approach to these in the European classification would be those such as Sweden and Germany, which have pushed their firms to adopt more widespread uniform standards. However, as with all classification systems, the subtle differences across countries can quickly make such classifications useless in practice. As the following sections will illustrate, slight differences can also yield significant competitive advantages or disadvantages to companies organized and measured under different financial reporting systems.

Principal Differences: The Issues

The resulting impact of accounting differences is to separate or segment international markets for investors and firms alike. Communicating the financial results of a foreign company operating in a foreign country and foreign currency is often a task that must be undertaken completely separately from the accounting duties of the firm. Actually, financial results must often be reinterpreted and presented in other markets like that of Figure 19.2, in which Cathay Pacific, a Hong Kong–based firm, must have its financial results presented in terms that are known to the larger U.S. dollar markets through a marketing presentation. As long as significant accounting practices differ across countries, markets will continue to be segmented (and accountants may be required to be interpreters and marketers as much as bookkeepers).

Table 19.2 provides an overview of nine major areas of significant differences in accounting practices across countries.[2] There are, of course, many more hundreds of differences, but these nine serve to highlight some of the fundamental philosophical differences across countries. Accounting differences are real and persistent, and there is still substantial question of competitive advantages and informational deficiencies that may result from these continuing differences across countries.

Accounting for Research and Development Expenses

Are research and development expenses capitalized or expensed as costs are incurred? Those who argue that there is no certainty that the R&D expenditures will lead to benefits in future periods would require immediate recognition of all expenses as in typical conservative practice. Alternatively, if R&D expenditures do lead to future benefits and revenues, the matching of expenses and revenues would be better served if the R&D expenditures were capitalized, and expenses therefore spread out over the future benefit periods.

Accounting for Fixed Assets

How are fixed assets (land, buildings, machinery, equipment) to be expensed and carried? These assets constitute large outlays of capital, result in assets that are held by the firm for many years, and yield benefits for many future years. All countries require companies to capitalize these fixed assets, so that they are depreciated over their future economic lives (once again spreading the costs out over periods roughly matching the revenue-earning useful life). There are, however, significant differences in depreciation methods used (straight-line, sum-of-years-digits, accelerated methods of cost recovery, and so forth), resulting in very different expensing schedules across countries.

FIGURE 19.2
Cathay Pacific Airways:
Communicating
Financial Results

The Swire Group
Cathay Pacific Airways Limited
1992 Interim Results – Highlights

Consolidated results — unaudited:

	Six months ended 30 June		
	1992 US$M	1991 US$M	
Turnover	1,420	1,262	
Operating profit	201	174	
Net finance charges	29	15	
Net operating profit	172	159	
Associated companies	15	10	
Profit before taxation	187	169	
Taxation	23	25	
Profit after taxation	164	144	
Minority interest	1	1	
Profit attributable to shareholders	163	143	
Dividend	39	39	
Retained profit	124	104	
Earnings per share	US5.7¢	US5.0¢	
Interim dividend per share	US1.3¢	US1.3¢	
	12 months ended		
	30/6/92	30/6/91	
Available tonne kilometres (millions)	5,963	5,525	+7.9%

Note: The results of the Company have been translated from Hong Kong dollars, its currency of account, into United States dollars at an exchange rate of HK$7.731 = US$1, the approximate free rate of exchange at 30th June 1992.

Prospects
The passenger revenue forecast for the full year suggests that the passenger load factor should exceed the 1991 level but there are concerns about yields caused by widespread fare wars. On the cargo front, Hong Kong revenue is expected to recover and there are encouraging signs for the new freighter service to Los Angeles.
    On the cost side, inflation is still the prime concern. The persistently high rate of inflation in Hong Kong, compared with major economies, continues to erode the competitive advantages of Hong Kong. "Operation Better Shape", which was introduced in 1991 to improve productivity, continues to be the main focus to mitigate the effects of rising costs.
    Provided that there is no worsening of an already difficult operating environment, we are looking for improved results for the full year.

Interim Dividend
The interim dividend will be paid on 2nd October 1992 to shareholders registered at the close of business on 25th September 1992, the share register will be closed from 21st September 1992 to 25th September 1992, both dates inclusive.

P D A Sutch
Chairman

Hong Kong, 26th August 1992

CATHAY PACIFIC

Source: *The Economist*, September 5, 1992, p. 22.

The primary issue related to the accounting of fixed assets is whether they are to be carried on company financial statements at historical cost or current value. The conservative approach, used for example in the United States, is to carry these fixed assets at historical cost and allow analysts to use their own methods and additional financial statement notes to ascertain current values of individual fixed assets. The alternative is to allow the values of fixed assets to be periodically revalued, up or down, depending on the latest appraised value. Countries such as the Netherlands argue that this is more appropriate, given that the balance sheet of a firm should present the present fair market value of all assets. There is no doubt, however, that with more flexibility in the valuation of fixed assets there is also more opportunity for abuse of the valuation methods, potentially giving firms the ability to manipulate the values of fixed assets carried on the balance sheet.

Inventory Accounting Treatment   How are inventories to be valued? For many companies inventories are the single largest asset. Therefore, the reconciliation of how goods are valued as sold (on the income statement) and valued as carried in inventory unsold (on the balance sheet) is important. The three typical inventory-valuation principles are last-in-first-out, **LIFO,** the average cost method, and first-in-first-out, **FIFO.**

The LIFO method assumes that the last goods purchased by the firm (last-in) are the first ones sold (first-out). This is considered conservative by accounting standards in that the remaining inventory goods were the first ones purchased. The resulting expenses of cost of goods sold is therefore higher. The only country listed in Table 19.2 that does not allow the use of LIFO is France, although Germany only allows its use in specific cases, making it rarely used. The use of FIFO is thought to

TABLE 19.2   Summary of Principal Accounting Differences Around the World

Accounting Principle	United States	Japan	United Kingdom	France	Germany	Netherlands	Switzerland	Canada	Italy	Brazil
1. Capitalization of R&D costs	Not Allowed	Allowed in Certain Cases	Allowed in Certain Cases	Allowed in Certain Cases	Not Allowed	Allowed in Certain Cases	Allowed in Certain Cases	Allowed in Certain Cases	Allowed in Certain Cases	Allowed in Certain Cases
2. Fixed-Asset Revaluations Stated at Amount in Excess of Cost	Not Allowed	Not Allowed	Allowed	Allowed	Not Allowed	Allowed in Certain Cases	Not Allowed	Not Allowed	Allowed in Certain Cases	Allowed
3. Inventory Valuation Using LIFO	Allowed	Allowed	Allowed but Rarely Done	Not Allowed	Allowed in Certain Cases	Allowed	Allowed	Allowed	Allowed	Allowed but Rarely Done
4. Finance Leases Capitalized	Required	Allowed in Certain Cases	Required	Not Allowed	Allowed in Certain Cases	Required	Allowed	Required	Not Allowed	Not Allowed
5. Pension Expense Accrued During Period of Service	Required	Allowed	Required	Allowed	Required	Required	Allowed	Required	Allowed	Allowed
6. Book and Tax Timing Differences on Balance Sheet as Deferred Tax	Required	Allowed in Certain Cases	Allowed	Allowed in Certain Cases	Allowed but Rarely Done	Required	Allowed	Allowed	Allowed but Rarely Done	Allowed
7. Current Rate Method of Currency Translation	Required	Allowed in Certain Cases	Required	Allowed	Allowed	Required	Required	Allowed in Certain Cases	Required	Required
8. Pooling Method Used for Mergers	Required in Certain Cases	Allowed in Certain Cases	Allowed in Certain Cases	Not Allowed	Allowed in Certain Cases	Allowed but Rarely Done	Allowed but Rarely Done	Allowed but Rarely Done	Not Allowed	Allowed but Rarely Done
9. Equity Method Used for 20–50% Ownership	Required	Required	Required	Allowed in Certain Cases	Allowed	Required	Required	Required	Allowed	Required

Source: Adapted from "A Summary of Accounting Principle Differences Around the World," Philip R. Peller and Frank J. Schwitter, 1991, p. 4.3.

Differences in depreciation methods used in accounting for fixed assets, such as this Arco chemical plant under construction in Marseille, France, result in different expensing schedules across countries.

be more consistent theoretically with the matching of costs and revenues of actual inventory flows. The use of FIFO is generally regarded as creating a more accurately measured balance sheet as inventory is stated at the most recent prices.

Capitalizing or Expensing Leases   Are financing leases to be capitalized? The recent growth in popularity of leasing for its financial and tax flexibility has created a substantial amount of accounting discussion across countries. The primary question is whether a leased item should actually be carried on the balance sheet of the firm at all, since a lease is essentially the purchase of an asset only for a specified period of time. If not carried on the books, should the lease payments be expenses as paid as if a rent payment?

Some argue that the lease results in the transfer of all risks and benefits of ownership to the firm (from the lessor to the lessee) and the lease contract should be accounted for as the purchase of an asset. This would be a capital lease, and if the lessee borrowed money in order to acquire this asset, the lease payments of principal and interest should be accounted for in the same manner as the purchase of any other capital asset. The Netherlands, the United Kingdom, Switzerland, the United States, and other countries require capital-lease payment if certain criteria are met.

The alternative is that the lessee has simply acquired the rental use of the services of the asset for a specified period of time, and payments on this **operating lease** should be treated only as rent. In this case the asset would remain on the books of the lessor. France, Italy, and Brazil require all leases to be treated as operating leases.

Pension Plan Accounting   The accounting treatment of private pension plans is one of the most recent and significant accounting developments. A private pension plan is the promise by an employer to provide a continuing income stream to employees after their retirement from the firm. The critical accounting question is whether the pension promise should be expensed and carried at the time the employee is working for the firm (providing a service to the firm that will not be fully paid for by the firm until all pension payments are completed) or expensed only as pension payments are made after retirement.

The primary problem with expensing the pension as services are provided is that the firm does not know the exact amount or timing of the eventual pension payments. If it is assumed that these eventual pension payments can be reasonably approximated, the conservative approach is to account for the expenses as employee services are provided and carry the **pension liabilities** on the books of the firm. In some countries if it is believed that these pension liabilities cannot be accurately estimated, they will be expensed only as they are incurred on payment.

Accounting for Income Taxes   All countries require the payment of income taxes on earnings, however, the definition and timing of earnings can constitute a problem. In many countries the definition of earnings for financial accounting purposes differs from earnings for tax purposes. The question then focuses on whether the tax effect should be recognized during the period in which the item appears on the income statement or during the period in which the item appears on the tax return.

If the expense is recognized during the period in which the item appears on the income statement, the tax gives rise to an associated asset or liability referred to as deferred tax. Some countries do not suffer this debate (whether this deferred tax should actually appear on the balance sheet of the firm) by having all financial reporting follow tax rules. Examples include Germany, France, and Japan. However, most countries must deal with the timing mismatch of the deferred tax.

Foreign Currency Translation   As discussed in Chapter 18, corporations that operate in more than one country and one currency must periodically **translate** and **consolidate** all financial statements for home-country reporting purposes. The primary issues in foreign currency translation are which exchange rates should be used in the translation of currencies (historical or current rates) and how gains or losses resulting from the translation should be handled in the consolidation. The critical handling issue is whether the gains or losses are recognized in current income or carried on the consolidated balance sheet as an item under equity capital.

The first method used is the **current rate method,** which translates assets and liabilities at the exchange rate in effect on the balance-sheet date, with adjustments charged or credited to the equity account. Equity and income statement items are translated at a weighted average exchange rate. This results in translation gains and losses that are carried as a direct adjustment to equity and avoids altering current net income. This is particularly attractive given the movement of exchange rates are clearly outside the control of the firm, and the gains and losses are resulting not from real cash flows but only from consolidation of foreign operations for reporting purposes.

The second translation method is the **temporal method.** This method translates assets and liabilities at the current exchange rate, with all fixed assets and common stock translated at historical exchange rates. This method is more consistent with the principle of how the company's balance sheet would have looked if the original assets and liabilities and continuing operations had all occurred in the one currency of the parent corporation. The primary disadvantage is that remaining gains and losses from the translation process under the temporal method are typically included within current income and may result in substantial exchange rate–induced earnings volatility as a result. Countries that encourage the use of the temporal method include Canada and France.

Figure 19.3 provides a simple decision-tree approach to translation of foreign affiliates for U.S. corporations. The mechanical details of the translation of foreign affiliate balance sheets are covered in Chapter 18.

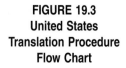

FIGURE 19.3
United States
Translation Procedure
Flow Chart

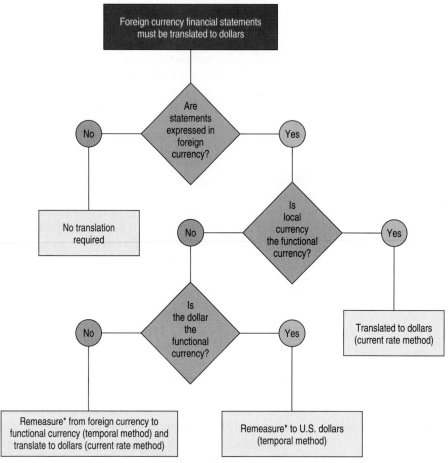

*The term *remeasure* means to translate so as to change the unit
of measure from a foreign currency to the functional currency.

Source: *International Accounting*, second edition, Frederick D.S. Choi and Gerhard G. Mueller, Prentice-Hall, Englewood Cliffs, N.J., 1992,
p. 169.

Accounting for Mergers and Acquisitions   This is obviously a relatively new issue in international accounting, given the sudden and rapid growth of merger and acquisition activity beginning in the United States and the United Kingdom in the 1980s. The primary accounting question is whether the assets and liabilities acquired should be carried at their original historic value or at the value at acquisition? In certain cases, however, it is believed that the shareholders of the acquired company end up owning shares of the acquirer, and accountants argue that their assets and liabilities should not be revalued, but simply merged or pooled. Accounting principles in the countries experiencing most mergers and acquisitions, the United States, the United Kingdom, Germany, and Japan, allow the use of pooling or merger accounting when certain criteria are met.

A second accounting issue of some concern is that often in the case of acquisitions, the price paid exceeds the fair value of the assets acquired. This is termed "goodwill" and constitutes a significant accounting problem. Many accountants argue that this is a true value that is purchased, and would not have been paid for if it did not exist. Even if goodwill is accepted as a legitimate economic value, the question remains as to how it is to be carried on the firm's balance sheet. The

United States, Japan, France, Canada, and Brazil all require that goodwill be accounted for as an asset, with amortization occurring over a maximum of anywhere from 5 to 40 years.

In other countries, accountants do not believe that goodwill is a real asset and therefore should not be carried on the books of the firm. In this case, such as in the United Kingdom, the firm is allowed to write off the entire amount against equity in the year of acquisition. It is also argued that this gives British firms a distinct advantage in their ability to make acquisitions and not suffer income-statement dilution impacts in the years following as the asset is amortized in the countries that capitalize goodwill. This is a classic example of the potential competitive benefits of a similar activity receiving dissimilar accounting treatment discussed at the beginning of this chapter and presented in Table 19.1.

Consolidation of Equity Securities Holdings   When one company purchases and holds an investment in another company, the question arises how these holdings are to be accounted for. There are two major methods of consolidation of equity holdings, the equity method and the consolidation method. The equity method requires that the holder list the security holdings as a line item on the firm's balance sheet. This is generally required when the firm holds substantial interest in the other firm, typically 20 to 50 percent of outstanding voting shares, such that it can exert substantial influence over the other firm but not necessarily dictate management or policy. The equity method is required in many countries, including the United States, Japan, Switzerland, Canada, and Brazil.

The second method of equity holdings, the consolidation method, requires the addition of all of the investee's individual assets and liabilities to the company's assets and liabilities. A minority interest is then subtracted out for all assets for the percentage of the net asset not owned. When an investor has controlling interest in the other firm, most countries require the use of the consolidation method. The remaining accounting debates focus on whether the individual assets and liabilities should be consolidated when the subsidiaries are very dissimilar, even if controlling interest is held. Countries like Italy and the United Kingdom believe that consolidation of dissimilar firms results in misleading information regarding the true financial status of the firms.

THE PROCESS OF ACCOUNTING STANDARDIZATION

One of the best indications as to the degree of success that has been achieved in international accounting standards is that there is still some conflict over the terminology of harmonization, standardization, or promulgation of uniform standards. As early as 1966 an Accountants International Study Group was formed by professional institutes in Canada, the United States, and the United Kingdom to begin the study of significant accounting differences across countries, but primarily only to aid in the understanding of foreign practices, not to form guidelines for more consistent or harmonious policies.

The establishment of the International Accounting Standards Committee (IASC) in 1973 was the first strong movement toward the establishment of international accounting standards. In the latter half of the 1970s other international institutions such as the United Nations, the Organization for Economic Cooperation and Development (OECD), and the European Community also began forming study groups and analyzing specific issues of confusion, such as corporate organization and varying degrees of disclosure required across countries.[3] The efforts of the European Community to harmonize standards between countries, not standardize, is particularly important in understanding how accounting principles and practices may be reformed to allow individual country differences but at the same time minimize the economic distortions. The recent completion of much of the Internal Financial Market of the Single European Program known as 1992 Europe has seen much progress along this harmonization front.

Two other recent developments merit special note concerning international standardization. In 1985 the General Electric Company became the first major U.S. corporation to acknowledge that the accounting principles underlying its 1984 financial statements "are generally accepted in the United States and are consistent with standards issued by the International Accounting Standards Committee."[4] Second, the Financial Accounting Standards Board (FASB), the organization in the United States charged with setting most standards for corporate accounting practices, committed itself to the full consideration of "an international perspective" to all its work in the future. And as other issues of international consequence arise—even environmentalism—accounting questions arise (see Global Perspective 19.2).

Global Perspective

19.2
The Cost of Being Green: Environmental Accounting

Like a staggering credit-card bill that arrives after a holiday spending spree, the tab for decades of pollution excesses is coming due—and sending shock waves through corporate accounting offices. The cleanup of the nation's known hazardous waste sites alone will cost $752 billion over 30 years under current environmental policies, according to a study by the University of Tennessee's Waste Management Research and Education Institute. And that's just a part of the bill. There are vapors to recover, underground storage tanks to replace, water recovery systems to install.

Because the accounting for environment-related expenses is still in its nascent stages, controversies are bound to emerge. When Longview Fibre, a $700 million-in-sales forest products company based in Longview, Washington, spent several million dollars on asbestos removal in the 1980s, it decided to take a conservative approach and charge the costs against income for both book and tax purposes. The company believed the accrual was suitable for the criteria set up in subsequent Financial Accounting Standards Board (FASB) Emerging Issues Task Force issues on the accounting treatment of asbestos abatement. But the Internal Revenue Service, upon audit, decided that such costs must be capitalized for taxes. The matter is now in the hands of the IRS chief counsel's office.

The FASB's Emerging Issues Task Force issue 90-8 provides guidance as to whether environmental contamination treatment costs should be capitalized or charged to expense. In general, such costs should be charged to expense, says Gregory Jones, a partner with Arthur Andersen who wrote the issue summary.

As environmental accounting develops, such issues will consume increasing amounts of a financial officer's time. In fact, the Clean Air Act of 1990 is a glimpse into the future, when the impact of environmental laws and of corporate efforts to deal with the physical world around them will be felt most heavily by accountants and CFOs. Suddenly, the power to clean up the environment is landing in their laps.

Source: Abstracted from "The Cost of Being Green," *Corporate Finance*, February 1993, 40–44.

INTERNATIONAL TAXATION

Governments alone have the power to tax. Each government wants to tax all companies within its jurisdiction without placing burdens on domestic or foreign companies that would restrain trade. Each country will state its jurisdictional approach formally in the tax treaties that it signs with other countries. One of the primary purposes of tax treaties is to establish the bounds of each country's jurisdiction to prevent double taxation of international income.

Tax Jurisdictions

Nations normally follow one of two basic approaches to international taxation: a residential approach or a territorial or source approach. The residential approach to international taxation taxes the international income of its residents without regard to where the income was earned. The territorial approach to transnational income taxes all parties, regardless of country of residency, within its territorial jurisdiction.

Most countries in practice must combine the two approaches to tax foreign and domestic firms equally. For example, the United States and Japan both apply the residential approach to their own resident corporations and the territorial approach to income earned by nonresidents within their territorial jurisdictions. Other countries, like Germany, apply the territorial approach to dividends paid to domestic firms from their foreign subsidiaries (such dividends are assumed taxed abroad and are exempt from further taxation).

Within the territorial jurisdiction of tax authorities, a foreign corporation is typically defined as any business that earns income within the host country's borders but is incorporated under the laws of another country. Normally the foreign corporation must surpass some minimum level of activity (gross income) before the host country assumes primary tax jurisdiction. However, if the foreign corporation owns income-producing assets or a permanent establishment, the threshold is automatically surpassed.

Tax Types

Taxes are generally classified as direct and indirect. **Direct taxes** are calculated on actual income, either individual or firm income. **Indirect taxes,** like sales taxes, sev-

Accounting practice for the costs of environmental contamination treatment and restoration, such as Amoco Corporation's reclamation of the dunes of Coatham Sands, Great Britain, is an evolving issue in international business.

Source: Courtesy of Amoco Corporation.

erance taxes, tariffs, and value-added taxes, are applied to purchase prices, material costs, quantities of natural resources mined, and so forth. Although most countries still rely on income taxes as the primary method of raising revenue, tax structures vary widely across countries.

The **value-added tax (VAT)** is the primary revenue source for the European Community. A value-added tax is applied to the amount of product value added by the production process. The tax is calculated as a percentage of the product price less the cost of materials and inputs used in its manufacture, which have been taxed previously. Through this process, tax revenues are collected literally on the value-added by that specific stage of the production process. Under the existing General Agreement on Tariffs and Trade (GATT), the legal framework under which international trade operates, value-added taxes may be levied on imports into a country or group of countries (like the European Community) in order to treat foreign producers entering the domestic markets equally with firms within the country paying the VAT. Similarly, the VAT may be refunded on export sales or sales to tourists who purchase products for consumption outside the country or community. For example, an American tourist leaving London may collect a refund on all value-added taxes paid on goods purchased within the United Kingdom. The refunding usually requires documentation of the actual purchase price and amount of tax paid.

Income Categories and Taxation

There are three primary methods used for the transfer of funds across tax jurisdictions: royalties, interest, and dividends. Royalties are under license for the use of intangible assets like patents, designs, trademarks, techniques, or copyrights. Interest is the payment for the use of capital lent for the financing of normal business activity. Dividends are income paid or deemed paid to the shareholders of the corporation from the residual earnings of operations. When a corporation declares the per-

TABLE 19.3 Comparison of Corporate Tax Rates: Japan, Germany, and the United States

Taxable Income Category	Japan	Germany	United States
Corporate income tax rates:			
Profits distributed to stockholders	42%	36%	34%
Undistributed profits	42%	50%	34%
Branches of foreign corporations	42%	46%	34%
Withholding taxes on dividends (portfolio):			
with Japan	—	15%	15%
with Germany	15%	—	15%
with United States	15%	10%	—
Withholding taxes on dividends (substantial holdings):			
with Japan	—	15%	10%
with Germany	10%	—	15%
with United States	10%	10%	—
Withholding taxes on interest:			
with Japan	—	10%	10%
with Germany	10%	—	0%
with United States	10%	0%	—
Withholding taxes on royalties:			
with Japan	—	10%	10%
with Germany	10%	—	0%
with United States	10%	0%	—

Source: *Corporate Taxes: A Worldwide Summary*, Price Waterhouse, 1990.

centage of residual earnings that is to go to shareholders, the dividend is declared and distributed.

Taxation of corporate income differs substantially across countries. Table 19.3 provides a summary comparison for Japan, Germany, and the United States. In some countries, for example the United States and Japan, there is one **corporate income tax** rate applied to all residual earnings, regardless of what is retained versus what is distributed as dividends. In other countries, for example Germany, separate tax rates apply to **distributed and undistributed earnings.** (Note that Germany lists a specific corporate income tax rate for the branches of foreign corporations operating within Germany.)

Royalty and interest payments to nonresidents are normally subject to **withholding taxes.** Corporate profits are typically double-taxed in most countries, through corporate and personal taxes. Corporate income is first taxed at the business level with corporate taxes, then a second time when the income of distributed earnings is taxed through personal income taxes. Withholding tax rates also differ by the degree of ownership that the corporation possesses in the foreign corporation. Minor ownership is termed portfolio, while major or controlling influence is categorized as substantial holdings. In the case of dividends, interest, or royalties paid to nonresidents, governments routinely apply withholding taxes to their payment in the reasonable expectation that these nonresidents will not report and declare such income with the host-country tax authorities. Withholding taxes are specified by income category in all bilateral tax treaties. Notice in Table 19.3 the differentials in withholding taxes across countries by bilateral tax treaties. The U.S. tax treaty with Germany results in a 0 percent withholding of interest or royalty payments earned by German corporations operating in the United States.

U.S. TAXATION OF FOREIGN OPERATIONS

The United States exercises its rights to tax U.S. residents' incomes regardless of where the income is earned. The two major categories for U.S. taxation of foreign-source income are foreign branches of U.S. corporations and foreign subsidiaries of U.S. corporations.

Taxation of Foreign Branches of U.S. Corporations

The income of a foreign branch of a U.S. corporation is treated the same as if the income was derived from sources within the United States. Because a foreign branch is an extension of the U.S. corporation and not independently capitalized and established, its profits are taxed with those of the parent whether actually remitted to the parent or not. Similarly, losses suffered by foreign branches of U.S. corporations are also fully and immediately deductible against U.S. taxable income.

As always, however, the U.S. tax authorities wish to prevent double taxation. The United States grants primary tax authority to the country in which the income is derived. If taxes are paid by the foreign branch to host-country tax authorities, these tax payments may be claimed as a tax credit toward U.S. tax liabilities on the same income.

Taxation of Foreign Subsidiaries of U.S. Corporations

Just as the United States taxes corporations from other countries operating within its borders, foreign countries tax the operations of U.S. corporations within their ju-

The Range of Corporate Tax Rates

Source: *1993 International Tax Summaries: A Guide for Planning and Decisions*
Note: **Angola:** Agriculture, silviculture, and cattle breeding are taxed 20%; an additional 10% tax is placed on profits over $10,000,000. **Bolivia**: Mining, smelting, and mineral trades are taxed 30%. **Brazil**: Agriculture is taxed 25%. **Ghana**: Mining, banking, and insurance companies are taxed 45%. **Mexico**: Book publishers have a 50% reduced rate; agriculture, cattle, forestry, and fishing have a 25% to 50% reduced tax rate. **United Arab Emirates**: 0% tax rate, except for banks and oil companies which are taxed a maximum of 55%. **United States**: Profits over $75,000 are are taxed 34%. **Serbia**: Large enterprises are taxed 40%; small enterprises are taxed 30%; free zones are taxed 25%. **Zambia**: Exports of goods manufactured from domestically produced agricultural raw products are exempted from taxes.

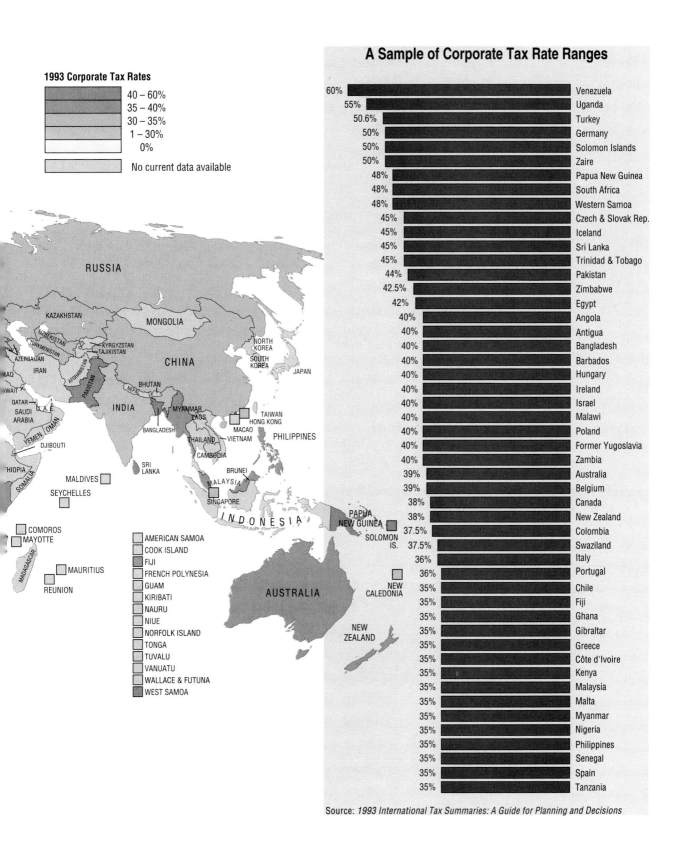

A Sample of Corporate Tax Rate Ranges

1993 Corporate Tax Rates

- 40 – 60%
- 35 – 40%
- 30 – 35%
- 1 – 30%
- 0%
- No current data available

60%	Venezuela
55%	Uganda
50.6%	Turkey
50%	Germany
50%	Solomon Islands
50%	Zaire
48%	Papua New Guinea
48%	South Africa
48%	Western Samoa
45%	Czech & Slovak Rep.
45%	Iceland
45%	Sri Lanka
45%	Trinidad & Tobago
44%	Pakistan
42.5%	Zimbabwe
42%	Egypt
40%	Angola
40%	Antigua
40%	Bangladesh
40%	Barbados
40%	Hungary
40%	Ireland
40%	Israel
40%	Malawi
40%	Poland
40%	Former Yugoslavia
40%	Zambia
39%	Australia
39%	Belgium
38%	Canada
38%	New Zealand
37.5%	Colombia
37.5%	Swaziland
36%	Italy
36%	Portugal
35%	Chile
35%	Fiji
35%	Ghana
35%	Gibraltar
35%	Greece
35%	Côte d'Ivoire
35%	Kenya
35%	Malaysia
35%	Malta
35%	Myanmar
35%	Nigeria
35%	Philippines
35%	Senegal
35%	Spain
35%	Tanzania

Source: *1993 International Tax Summaries: A Guide for Planning and Decisions* risdiction. Corporations operating in more than one country are therefore subject to double taxation. This double taxation could hinder the ability of U.S. corporations to operate and compete effectively abroad. The U.S. tax code removes this burden by reducing the U.S. taxes due on the foreign-source income by the amount of foreign taxes deemed paid.

The calculation of the foreign income taxes deemed paid and the additional U.S. taxes due, if any, is the result of the interaction of the following four components.

- Degree of Ownership and Control. The degree of ownership and control of the foreign corporation has a significant impact on the calculation of U.S. taxes payable on the foreign-source income. There are three basic ownership ranges applicable to taxation: (1) less than 10 percent; (2) 10–50 percent; (3) more than 50 percent. Figure 19.4 illustrates these three ownership classes under U.S. tax law. If the U.S. corporation owns more than 50 percent of the voting shares in the foreign corporation, the foreign corporation is classified as a Controlled Foreign Corporation (CFC).[5]

- Proportion of Income Distributed. The proportion of after-tax income that is distributed as profits to stockholders, dividends, is also important to the calculation of U.S. tax liability. Income that is retained by the foreign corporation and not distributed to shareholders, U.S. or other, will have the result of reducing the U.S. tax liability on the foreign corporation's income in certain cases.

- Active versus Passive Income. If a foreign subsidiary generates income through its own actions or activities (e.g., producing a product, selling a product, providing a service), the income is classified as *active*. If, however, the foreign subsidiary or affiliate earns income through its ownership in another firm, or by acting as a creditor to another firm and earning interest income, the income is classified as *passive*. It is quite common for a foreign subsidiary to have both active and passive income. Each is then treated separately for tax purposes.

**FIGURE 19.4
Classification of U.S.
Ownership of Foreign
Corporations for Tax
Uses**

Source: Adapted from *Multinational Business Finance* sixth edition, Eiteman, Stonehill, and Moffett, Addison-Wesley, Reading, 1992, Chapter 21.

● Relative Corporate Income Taxes. Whether foreign corporate income taxes are higher or lower than similar U.S. corporate income taxes will largely determine whether the U.S. shareholders will owe additional taxes in the United States on the foreign-source income, or whether the foreign tax credit will completely cover U.S. tax liabilities. If withholding taxes were applied to dividends paid to nonresidents (the U.S. corporation owner), this will also affect the U.S. tax liability.

Calculation of U.S. Taxes on Foreign-Source Earnings

Table 19.4 illustrates the complete calculation of foreign taxes, U.S. tax credits, additional U.S. taxes due on foreign income, and total worldwide tax burdens for four different potential cases. Each of the four cases is structured to highlight the different combinations of the three components discussed above, relative corporate income taxes (lines a, b, and c), degree of control or ownership of the U.S. corporation in the foreign corporation (line d), and the proportion of available income distributed to stockholders as dividends (line e).

TABLE 19.4	U.S. Taxation of Foreign-Source Income (in thousands of US$)			
	Case 1	Case 2	Case 3	Case 4
Baseline Values				
a Foreign corporate income tax rate	40%	20%	20%	20%
b U.S. corporate income tax rate	34%	34%	34%	34%
c Foreign dividend withholding tax rate	10%	10%	10%	10%
d Proportional ownership held by U.S. corporation in foreign corporation	30%	30%	30%	100%
e Payout rate (proportion of after-tax income declared as dividends)	100%	100%	50%	100%*
Foreign Affiliate Tax Computation				
1. Taxable income of foreign affiliate	$2,000	$2,000	$2,000	$2,000
2. Foreign corporate income taxes (@ rate a above)	−800	−400	−400	−400
3. Net income available for profit distribution	$1,200	$1,600	$1,600	$1,600
4. Retained earnings (1 − rate e above × line 3)	0	0	$800	0
5. Distributed earnings (rate e above × line 3)	$1,200	$1,600	$800	$1,600
6. Distributed earnings to U.S. corporation (rate d × line 5)	$360	$480	$240	$1,600
7. Withholding taxes on dividends to nonresidents (rate c × line 6)	−36	−48	−24	−160
8. Remittance of foreign income to U.S. corporation	$324	$432	$216	$1,440
U.S. Corporate Tax Computation on Foreign-Source Income				
9. Grossed-up U.S. income (rate d × rate e × line 1)	$600	$600	$300	$2,000
10. Tentative (theoretical) U.S. tax liability (rate b × line 9)	−204	−204	−102	−680
11. Foreign tax credit (rate d × rate e × line 2 + line 7)	+276	+168	+84	+560
12. Additional U.S. taxes due on foreign-source income (line 10 + line 11; if 11 > 10, U.S. tax liability is 0)	0	−36	−18	−120
13. After-tax dividends received by U.S. corporation (line 8 + line 12)	$324	$396	$198	$1,320
14. Total worldwide taxes paid (line 10 or line 11, whichever greater)	$276	$204	$102	$680
15. Effective tax rate on foreign income (line 14 ÷ line 9)	46%	34%	34%	34%

* When proportional ownership of the foreign corporation exceeds 50%, U.S. tax authorities classify it as a Controlled Foreign Corporation (CFC) and all passive income earned is taxed regardless of the payout rate or actual remittance to the U.S. corporation.

Case 1: Foreign Affiliate of a U.S. Corporation in a High-Tax Environment   This is a very common case. A U.S. corporation earns income in the form of distributed earnings (100 percent payout of available earnings to stockholders) from a foreign corporation in which it holds substantial interest (more than 10 percent) but does not control (less than 50 percent). The foreign corporate income tax rate (40 percent) is higher than the U.S. rate (34 percent). The foreign corporation has total taxable income of $2,000 (thousands of dollars), pays a 40 percent corporate income tax in the host country of $800, and distributes the entire after-tax income to stockholders. Total distributed earnings are therefore $1,200.

The foreign country imposes a 10 percent withholding tax on dividends paid to nonresidents. The U.S. corporation therefore receives its proportion of earnings (its 30 percent ownership entitles it to 30 percent of all dividends paid out) less the amount of the withholding taxes, $360 − $36, or $324. This is the net cash remittance actually received by the U.S. corporation on foreign earnings.

The calculation of U.S. taxes on foreign-source income requires first that the income be "grossed up," or reinflated to the amount of income the U.S. corporation has rights to prior to taxation by the foreign government. This is simply the percentage of ownership (30 percent) times the payout rate (100 percent) times the gross taxable income of the foreign affiliate ($2,000), or $600. A theoretical or **"tentative U.S. tax"** is calculated on this income to estimate U.S. tax payments that would be due on this income if it had been earned in the United States (or simply not taxed at all in the foreign country). U.S. taxes of 34 percent yield a tentative tax liability of $204.

Because taxes were paid abroad, however, U.S. tax law allows U.S. tax liabilities to be reduced by the amount of the foreign tax credit. The foreign tax credit is the proportion of foreign taxes deemed paid attributable to its ownership (30 percent ownership times the 100 percent payout rate of the foreign taxes paid, $800, plus the amount of withholding taxes imposed on the distributed dividends to the U.S. corporation, $36). The total foreign tax credit is then $240 + $36, or $276. Since the foreign tax credit exceeds the total tentative U.S. tax liability, no additional taxes are due the U.S. tax authorities on this foreign-source income. Special note should be made that the foreign tax credit may exceed the U.S. tax liabilities, but any excess cannot be applied toward other U.S. tax liabilities in the current period (it can be carried forward or back against this foreign-source income, however).

Finally, an additional calculation allows the estimation of the total taxes paid, both abroad and in the United States, on this income. In this first case, the $276 of total tax on gross income of $600 is an **effective tax rate** of 46 percent.

Case 2: Foreign Affiliate of a U.S. Corporation in a Low-Tax Environment   This case is exactly the same as the previous example, with the sole exception that the foreign tax rate (20 percent) is lower than the U.S. corporate tax rate (34 percent). All earnings, tax calculations, and dividends distributions are the same as before.

With lower foreign corporate income taxes, there is obviously more profit to be distributed, more income to the U.S. corporation's 30 percent share, and more withholding taxes to be paid on the larger dividends distributed. Yet the grossed-up income of the foreign-source income is the same as in the previous case, because grossed-up income is proportional ownership and distribution in the absence of taxes.

With lower foreign taxes, the foreign tax credit is significantly lower and is no longer sufficient to cover fully the tentative U.S. tax liability. The U.S. corporation will have an additional $36 due in taxes on the foreign-source income. After-tax dividends in total are still higher, however, rising to $396 from $324. Total worldwide taxes paid are now significantly less, $204 rather than $276.

Cases 1 and 2 point out the single most significant feature of the U.S. tax code's impact on foreign operations of U.S. corporations: the effective tax rate may be higher on foreign-source income but will never drop lower than the basic corporate income tax rate in effect in the United States (34 percent).

Case 3: Foreign Affiliate of a U.S. Corporation in a Low-Tax Environment, 50 percent Payout

The third case changes only one of the baseline values of the previous case, the proportion of income available for dividends that is paid out to stockholders. All distributed earnings and withholding taxes are therefore half what they were previously, as is grossed-up income and the additional U.S. tax liability (because the foreign tax credit has also been cut in half).

This third case illustrates that a reduced income distribution by the foreign subsidiary does reduce income received, and taxes due, in the United States on the foreign income. The effective tax rate is again at the minimum achievable, the rate of taxation that would be in effect if the income had been earned within the United States. As will be shown in the fourth and final case, this third case's results rely partially on the fact that the foreign corporation is only an affiliate (less than 50 percent ownership) of the U.S. corporation and is not controlled by the U.S. corporation.

Case 4: Foreign Subsidiary of a U.S. Corporation Is a CFC in a Low-Tax Environment

This final case highlights one of the critical components of U.S. taxation of foreign subsidiary earnings. If the foreign corporation is effectively controlled by the U.S. corporation, as indicated by its greater than 50 percent ownership, and all income is passive income, U.S. tax authorities calculate U.S. tax liabilities on the foreign income as if the entire income available for distribution to shareholders were remitted to the U.S. parent, regardless of what the actual payout rate is.

This tax policy, a result of the 1962 tax reform act, is referred to as Subpart F income. Subpart F income taxation is a reflection of the control component; it is assumed that the U.S. corporation exercises sufficient control over the management of the foreign subsidiary to determine the payout rate. If the subsidiary has chosen not to pay out all passive earnings, it is taken as a choice of the U.S. corporation and is deemed to be an effort at postponing U.S. tax liabilities on the income.

The 1962 tax act was largely aimed at eliminating the abuses of foreign affiliates of U.S. corporations paying dividends and other passive income flows out to subsidiaries in various tax havens (like Bermuda, the Bahamas, Panama, Luxembourg, the Cayman Islands), and not remitting the income back to the U.S. corporation. By placing the passive income in these tax havens, they were effectively postponing and evading taxation of the U.S. government.

Concluding Remarks Regarding U.S. Taxation of Foreign Income

The previous series of sample tax calculations highlights the interplay of ownership, distribution, and relative tax rates between countries in determining the tax liabilities of income earned by U.S. interests abroad. In many ways the case with the most long-term strategic significance was the first, the high-tax foreign environment. U.S.

Global Perspective

19.3
"All the President's Taxmen"

Bill Clinton's vow to make foreign businesses pay "their fair share" of U.S. taxes, set against the backdrop of the need to raise $300 billion of extra revenue between 1993 and 1996 to fund his domestic programs, could mean substantial new tax burdens on British businesses investing in the United States.

As part of a package of corporate "loophole closers," Clinton claims that he will raise $45 billion over four years by combating "tax avoidance" by foreign-owned corporations and branches that shift profits outside the United States, largely by juggling with transfer prices. Transfer prices are those charged within families of companies for goods, services, or intangibles. Clinton maintains that foreign-owned firms set these prices artificially high in order to reduce their U.S. taxable income.

The Treasury and U.S. Congress have provided Clinton with some statistical support for this perception, but not for the revenue estimate. President Bush's Commissioner of the Internal Revenue Service (IRS) stated in recent congressional hearings that 72 percent of foreign-controlled corporations operating in the United States pay no U.S. taxes. The U.S. Treasury released a study showing that in 1988 U.S.–controlled foreign corporations reported $890 billion in revenues and paid more than $25 billion in taxes to foreign governments. In contrast, in the same year foreign-controlled corporations in the United States had revenues of $825 billion but paid only $7 billion in U.S. taxes.

The draft transfer-pricing regulations the IRS issued earlier this year caused a storm of international protest; they are widely thought to introduce a different notion of what is "arm's length" from that generally accepted by other tax authorities. Although the draft rules may be toned down in theory, overseas tax authorities are well aware of their likely effect and Clinton's intended enforcement. The United States is not the only country with economic problems that is looking to transfer pricing to provide additional tax revenues. Japan, Australia, Korea, the U.K., and Germany have all introduced new rules, allocated extra resources to transfer pricing, or both.

Source: Abstracted from "All the President's Taxmen," Terry Symons, *Accountancy*, January 1993, p. 64. Reprinted by permission of the author.

corporate income tax rates are some of the lowest in the world. The normal result is the accumulation of substantial foreign tax credits by U.S. corporate interests, credits that increasingly cannot be applied to U.S. tax liabilities. The result is, as in Case 1, an effective tax rate that is significantly higher than if the income had been generated in the United States.

Recent accounting and tax rule changes may actually result in worsening this effective tax rate and excess foreign tax credit problem for U.S. corporations. Recent rule changes now require U.S. corporations to spread increasing amounts of parent-supplied overhead expenses to their foreign affiliates and subsidiaries, charging them for services provided. This results in increased costs for the foreign subsidiaries, reducing their profitability, reducing their taxable gross income, and subsequently reducing the foreign taxes, and tax credits, deemed paid. This is likely to increase the proportion of total taxes that are paid in the United States on the foreign-source income. Unfortunately, many of these overhead distributions are not recognized as a legitimate expense by many other governments (differing accounting practices in action), and the foreign units are paying a charge to the U.S. corporation that they are unable to expense against their local earnings. Recent concerns over the use of intrafirm sales, so-called transfer prices (see Chapter 16 and Global Perspective 19.3), to manipulate the profitability of foreign firms operating in the United States has also added fuel to the fires of governments and their individual shares of the world "tax pie." With that, the subject of accounting and taxation of international operations has completed a full circle.

SUMMARY

Accounting practices differ substantially across countries. The efforts of a number of international associates and agencies in the past two decades have, however, led to increasing cooperation and agreement among national accounting authorities. Real accounting differences remain, and many of these differences still contribute to the advantaged competitive position of some countries' firms over international competitors.

International taxation is a subject close to the pocketbook of every multinational firm. Although the tax policies of most countries are theoretically designed to not change or influence financial and business decision making by firms, they often do. The taxation of the foreign operations of U.S. multinational firms involves the elaborate process of crediting U.S. corporations for taxes paid to foreign governments. The combined influence of different corporate tax rates across countries, the degree of ownership and control a multinational may have or exercise in a foreign affiliate, and the proportion of profits distributed to stockholders at home and abroad all combine to determine the size of the parent's tax bill. As governments worldwide search for new ways to close their fiscal deficits and tax shortfalls, the pressures on international taxation and the reporting of foreign-source income will only increase.

Key Terms and Concepts

accounting diversity	capital or financial leases
expensing	direct taxes
capitalizing	indirect taxes
LIFO	value-added tax (VAT)
FIFO	distributed earnings
operating or service lease	undistributed earnings
pension liabilities	withholding taxes
current rate method	foreign tax credit
temporal method	effective tax rate

Questions for Discussion

1. Do you think all firms, in all economic environments, should operate under the same set of accounting principles?

2. What is the nature of the purported benefit that accounting principles provide British firms over American firms in the competition for mergers and acquisitions?

3. Why do most U.S. corporations prefer the current rate method of translation over the temporal method? How does each method affect reported earnings per share per period?

4. Name two major indications that progress is being made toward standardizing accounting principles across countries.

5. What is the distinction between harmonizing accounting rules and standardizing accounting procedures and practices across countries?

6. Why are foreign subsidiaries in which U.S. corporations hold more than 50 percent voting power classified and treated differently for U.S. tax purposes?

7. Why do the U.S. tax authorities want U.S. corporations to charge their foreign subsidiaries for general and administrative services? What does this mean for the creation of excess foreign tax credits by U.S. corporations with foreign operations?

8. What would be the tax implications of combining Cases 1 and 4 in the U.S. taxation of foreign-source income, a U.S. Controlled Foreign Corporation (CFC) that is operating in a high-tax environment?

Recommended Readings

Arpan, Jeffrey S., and Lee H. Radebaugh. *International Accounting and Multinational Enterprises.* New York: John Wiley & Sons, 1985.

BenDaniel, David J., and Arthur H. Rosenbloom. *The Handbook of International Mergers & Acquisitions.* Englewood Cliffs, N.J.: Prentice-Hall, 1990.

Bodner, Paul M. "International Taxation," in *The Handbook of International Accounting,* Frederick D.S. Choi, editor. New York: John Wiley & Sons, 1992.

Choi, Frederick D.S., editor. *Handbook of International Accounting.* New York: John Wiley & Sons, 1991.

Choi, Frederick D.S., and Richard Levich. "International Accounting Diversity and Capital Market Decisions," in *The Handbook of International Accounting,* Frederick D.S. Choi, editor. New York: John Wiley & Sons, 1992.

Choi, Frederick D.S., and Gerhard G. Mueller. *International Accounting,* second edition. Englewood Cliffs, N.J.: Prentice-Hall, 1992.

Dionne, Marylouise, and Stephen Orme. "Foreign Currency Transactions Under the Section 988 Regulations," *Taxes,* August 1992, 532–550.

Eiteman, David K., Arthur I. Stonehill, and Michael H. Moffett. *Multinational Business Finance,* sixth edition. Reading, Mass.: Addison-Wesley Publishing, 1992.

Goeltz, Richard K. "International Accounting Harmonization: The Impossible (and Unnecessary?) Dream," *Accounting Horizons,* March 1991, 85–88.

Hosseini, Ahmad, and Raj Aggarwal. "Evaluating Foreign Affiliates: The Impact of Alternative Foreign Currency Translation Methods," *International Journal of Accounting,* Fall 1983, 65–87.

Neuhausen, Benjamin. "Consolidated Financial Statements and Joint Venture Accounting," in *The Handbook of International Accounting,* Frederick D.S. Choi, editor. New York: John Wiley & Sons, 1992.

Nobes, Christopher, and Robert Parker. *Comparative International Accounting,* third edition. London: Prentice Hall International, Ltd., 1991.

Price Waterhouse, *Corporate Taxes: A Worldwide Summary.* 1990 International edition, New York, N.Y., 1990.

Notes

1. This example is borrowed from "International Accounting Diversity and Capital Market Decisions" by Choi and Levich, 1992.

2. This table and the following associated discussion draws heavily on the recent excellent study of this subject by Philip R. Peller and Frank J. Schwitter of Arthur Andersen & Company, "A Summary of Accounting Principle Differences Around the World," in *The Handbook of International Accounting,* Frederick D.S. Choi, editor, 1992, Chapter 4.

3. Disclosure has continued to be one of the largest sources of frustration between countries. The disclosure requirements of the Securities and Exchange Commission (SEC) in the United States for firms—foreign or domestic—in order to issue publicly traded securities are some of the strictest in the world. Many experts in the field have long been convinced that the depth of U.S. disclosure requirements has prevented many foreign firms from issuing securities in the United States. The SEC's approval of Rule 144A, selective secondary market trading of private placements, is an attempt to alleviate some of the pressure on foreign firms from U.S. disclosure.

4. Frederick D.S. Choi and Gerhard G. Mueller, *International Accounting,* second edition (Englewood Cliffs, N.J.: Prentice-Hall, 1992), 262.

5. A U.S. shareholder is a U.S. person (a citizen or resident of the United States, domestic partnership, domestic corporation, or any nonforeign trust or estate) owning 10 percent or more of the voting power of a controlled foreign corporation. A controlled foreign corporation (CFC) is any foreign corporation in which U.S. shareholders, including corporate parents, own more than 50 percent of the combined voting power or total value. The percentages are calculated on a constructive ownership basis, in which an individual is considered to own shares registered in the name of other family members, members of a trust, or any other related group.

International Human Resource Management[*]

LEARNING OBJECTIVES

1. To describe the challenges of managing managers and labor personnel both in individual international markets and in worldwide operations.

2. To examine the sources, qualifications, and compensation of international managers.

3. To assess the effects of culture on managers and management policies.

4. To illustrate the different roles of labor in international markets, especially that of labor participation in management.

---

[*]This chapter was contributed by Susan C. Ronkainen.

The Hunt for the Global Manager

The hunt for the global manager is on. From Amsterdam to Yokohama, recruiters are looking for a new breed of multilingual, multifaceted executives who can map strategy for the whole world.

One of the biggest challenges of the 1990s will be overcoming a severe shortage of Euromanagers. The problem is not the attitude of the available young executives, who are usually quite willing to move to new countries and cities even on short notice. Rather, it is that few companies—even those characterizing themselves as global—systematically develop international managers by rotating young executives through a series of foreign assignments. Finding and training the best cross-border managers will be crucial to reaping the benefits of 1992. To accomplish this, many companies have turned to executive-search firms when they need somebody immediately and have also started to change their traditional management structures.

According to headhunters, the best cross-border managers started out with U.S. multinationals. The new marketing manager for Cadbury-Schweppes PLC's European operation is Joost Pabst, a Dutchman recruited from Colgate-Palmolive Co. in New York City. Pabst, based in Barcelona, is charged with creating a single image for Schweppes in Europe—that of a classy but popular soft drink. "What sold me on this job was the chance to manage brands Europewide," says Pabst. And when CMB Packaging, an Anglo-French firm, decided to oust its French chief executive, it replaced him with a German-born American, Jurgen Hintz, from Procter & Gamble.

Restructuring and market-development efforts are driving the recruiting surge as well. In 1989, Whirlpool's acquisition of a 53 percent share of Philips's appliance business left the company without a manager to run the new unit. After a three-continent search, Jan Prising, a 21-year veteran of Sweden's Electrolux, was lured to the post by a salary and bonuses that could reach $500,000 a year. He now runs the U.S. company out of an office overlooking Lake Varese in Italy.

Major changes have also occurred at the Paris headquarters of Alcatel. Says Human Resource Manager Paul Claudell, "We don't want French domination." The joint venture of Cie Générale d'Electricité and ITT Corp. includes CGE's telephone businesses and ITT's European operations. The company is out to win a big share of the emerging pan-European market for telecommunications equipment. Of the 120 top executives in Paris, 60 percent are not French. For example, Alcatel's finance department includes managers from Italy, Sweden, Portugal, Holland, and Belgium, all recruited in the last two years. The Swede, Harald Bauer, was recruited from a top finance post at a Swedish trading company to become controller for Alcatel's subsidiaries in Scandinavia and part of France. "Having a Swede in this job definitely improves communications," says Bauer. "The management here is still very French and hierarchical. With the mix of nationalities, that should change quickly."

Experience with other companies is increasingly prized. Thorn EMI, the British music, software, and appliance rental company, transformed a management group accustomed to lifetime employment into a team of entrepreneurs. From 1983 to 1988, the company replaced about 130 of its 150 managers, at least half through executive search. Today, the average executive has had three previous jobs, versus none eight years ago. Given international expansion and the need to assign executives responsibility for more than one country, there is a desperate need for managers who understand foreign markets.

Not all are convinced about the need for Euromanagers. Some note that big differences remain between management systems in Europe, which executives may find hard to cope with no matter how culturally sensitive they are. Nationalism may continue to influence the choice of senior managers. Lastly, some companies are wary of shifting managers from one country to another and will have subsidiaries managed largely by locals who know their markets inside out.

Source: "The Elusive Euromanager," *The Economist,* November 7, 1992, 83; Shawn Tully, "The Hunt for the Global Manager," *Fortune,* May 21, 1990, 140–144; and Lester B. Korn, "How the Next CEO Will Be Different," *Fortune,* May 22, 1989, 157–161.

Organizations have two general human-resource objectives.[1] The first is the recruitment and retention of a workforce made up of the best people available for the jobs to be done. The recruiter in international operations will need to keep in mind both cross-cultural and cross-national differences in productivity and expectations when selecting employees. Once they are hired, the firm's best interest lies in maintaining a stable and experienced workforce.

The second objective is to increase the effectiveness of the workforce. This depends to a great extent on achieving the first objective. Competent managers or workers are likely to perform at a more effective level if proper attention is given to factors that motivate them.

To attain the two major objectives, the activities and skills needed include:

1. Personnel planning and staffing, the assessment of personnel needs, and recruitment.
2. Personnel training to achieve a perfect fit between the employee and the assignment.
3. Compensation of employees according to their effectiveness.
4. An understanding of labor-management relations in terms of how these two groups view each other and how their respective power positions are established.

This chapter will examine the management of human resources in international business from two points of view, first that of managers and then that of labor.

MANAGING MANAGERS

The importance of the quality of the workforce in international business cannot be overemphasized, regardless of the stage of internationalization of the firm. As seen in the chapter's opening vignette, international business systems are complex and dynamic and require competent people to develop and direct them.

Early Stages of Internationalization

The marketing or sales manager of the firm typically is responsible for beginning export activities. As foreign sales increase, an export manager will be appointed and given the responsibility for developing and maintaining customers, interacting with the firm's intermediaries, and planning for overall market expansion. The export manager also must champion the international effort within the company because the general attitude among employees may be to view the domestic market as more important. Another critical function is the supervision of export transactions, particularly documentation. The requirements are quite different for international transactions than for domestic ones, and sales or profits may be lost if documentation is not properly handled. The first task of the new export manager, in fact, often is to hire a staff to handle paperwork that typically had previously been done by a facilitating agent, such as a freight forwarder.

The firm starting international operations will usually hire an export manager from outside rather than promote from within. The reason is that knowledge of the product or industry is less important than international experience. The cost of learning through experience to manage an export department is simply too great from the firm's standpoint. Further, the inexperienced manager would be put in the position of having to demonstrate his or her effectiveness almost at once.

The manager who is hired will have obtained experience through Foreign Service duty or with another corporation. In the early stages, a highly entrepreneurial spirit with a heavy dose of trader mentality is required. Even then, management should not expect the new export department to earn a profit for the first year or so.

Advanced Stages of Internationalization

As the firm progresses from exporting to an international division to foreign direct involvement, manpower-planning activities will initially focus on need vis-à-vis various markets and functions. Existing personnel can be assessed and plans made to recruit, select, and train employees for positions that cannot be filled internally. The four major categories of overseas assignments are: (1) CEO, to oversee and direct the entire operation; (2) functional head, to establish and maintain departments and ensure their proper performance, (3) troubleshooters, who are utilized for their special expertise in analyzing, and thereby preventing or solving, particular problems; and (4) white- or blue-collar workers.[2] International oil companies typically assign a great many employees overseas when the available pool is small, such as in Saudi Arabia.

One of the major sources of competitive advantage of global corporations is their ability to attract talent around the world. These corporations need systematic management-development systems, with the objective of creating and carefully allocating management personnel. An example of this is provided in Figure 20.1. In global corporations, there is no such thing as a universal global manager, but a network of global specialists in four general groups of managers has to work together.[3] Global business (product) managers have the task to further the company's global-scale efficiency and competitiveness. Country managers have to be sensitive and responsive to local market needs and demands but, at the same time, be aware of global implications. Functional managers have to make sure that the corporation's capabilities in technical, manufacturing, marketing, human resource, and financial expertise are linked and can benefit from each other. Corporate executives at headquarters have to manage interactions between these three groups of managers as well as identify and develop the talent to fill these positions.

As an example of manpower planning, a management review of human resources is conducted twice a year with each general manager of Heineken operating companies, which are located in such countries as Canada, France, Ireland, and Spain. The meeting is attended by the general manager, the personnel manager, the regional coordinating director in whose region the operating company is located, and the corporate director of management development. Special attention is given to managers "in the fast lane," the extent to which they are mobile, what might be done to

---

FIGURE 20.1   **An Example of an International Management Development System**

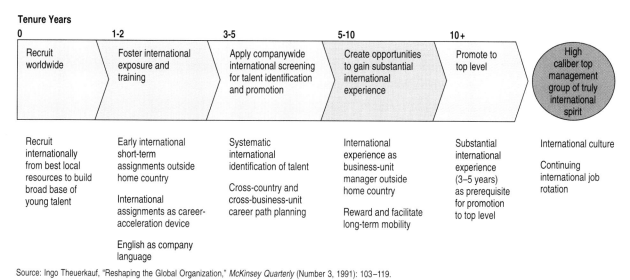

Source: Ingo Theuerkauf, "Reshaping the Global Organization," *McKinsey Quarterly* (Number 3, 1991): 103–119.

foster their development, and where they fit into succession planning.[4] Of course, any gaps must be filled by recruitment efforts.

International companies should show clear career paths for managers assigned overseas and develop the systems and the organization for promotion. This approach serves to eliminate many of the perceived problems and thus motivates managers to seek out foreign assignments. Foreign assignments can occur at various stages of the manager's tenure. In the early stages, assignments may be short-term, such as a membership in an international task force or 6–12 months at headquarters in a staff function. Later, an individual may serve as a business-unit manager overseas. Many companies use cross-postings to other countries or across product lines to further an individual's acculturation to the corporation.[5] A period in a head-office department or a subsidiary will not only provide an understanding of different national cultures and attitudes but also improve an individual's "know-who" and therefore establish unity and common sense of purpose necessary for the proper implementation of global programs.

Interfirm Cooperative Ventures

Global competition is forging new cooperative ties between firms from different countries, thereby adding a new management challenge for the firms involved. Although many of the reasons cited for these alliances (described in Chapter 12) are competitive and strategic, the human-resource function is critical to their implementation. As a matter of fact, some of the basic reasons so many of these ventures fail relate to human-resource management; for example, managers from disparate venture partners cannot work together, or managers within the venture cannot work with the owners' managers.[6]

While the ingredients for success of the human-resource function will differ with the type of cooperative venture, two basic types of tasks are needed.[7] The first task is to assign and motivate people in appropriate ways so that the venture will fulfill its set strategic tasks. This requires particular attention to such issues as job skills and compatibility of communication and other work styles. For example, some cooperative ventures have failed due to one of the partners' assigning relatively weak management resources to the venture or due to managers' finding themselves with conflicting loyalties to the parent organization and the cooperative venture organization. The second task is the strategic management of the human resources, that is, the appropriate use of managerial capabilities not only in the cooperative venture but in other later contexts, possibly back in the parent organization. An individual manager needs to see that an assignment in a cooperative venture is part of his or her overall career development.

Sources for Management Recruitment

The location and the nationality of candidates for a particular job are the key issues in recruitment, as shown in the example in Table 20.1. The table summarizes human-resource practices in the foreign operations of four Swedish multinational companies. The emphasis is on internal development. The advantage of internal recruitment is that candidates already know the corporate system and corporate culture. In fact, internal candidates may have been slated for certain positions when they entered the organization and have been trained accordingly.

When international operations are expanded, a management-development dilemma may result. Through internal recruitment, young managers will be offered

TABLE 20.1
Summary of
Recruitment Issues at
Four Swedish
Multinational
Companies: Source and
Nationality of Recruits

a) Recruitment of Managing Directors for Selected Subsidiaries as of 1981

Company	Local Promotion	Group Recruitment	External Recruitment
AGA	6	8	4
SKF	6	8	5
Sandvik	—	15	5
Ericsson	3	13	2

b) Nationality of Managing Directors for Selected Subsidiaries
(1981: Number of People)

Company	Local	Swedish	Third Country Nationals
AGA	7	9	2
SKF	10	6	3
Sandvik	4	11	5
Ericsson	5	12	1

c) Number of Expatriates per Thousand Employees

Company	Expatriates
AGA	5.0
SKF	3.6
Sandvik	7.5
Ericsson	10.1

Source: Anders Edstrom and Peter Lorange, "Matching Strategy and Human Resources in Multinational Corporations," *Journal of International Business Studies* (Fall 1984): 125–137.

interesting new opportunities. However, some senior managers may object to the constant drain of young talent from their units. Selective recruitment from the outside will help to maintain a desirable combination of inside talent and fresh blood. Furthermore, with dynamic market changes or new markets and new business development, outside recruitment may be the only available approach. Even in Japan, the taboo against hiring executives from other companies is breaking down. The practice of hiring from the top universities can no longer be depended on to provide the right people in all circumstances.[8]

A firm has three alternative sources for recruitment. All of them are typically used to some degree, depending on the characteristics of the firm and the industry. The first source is local, that is, citizens of the host country. The other two are home-country nationals and third-country nationals (citizens of countries other than the home or the host country). The factors that influence the choice are summarized in Table 20.2. They fall into three general categories: (1) the availability and quality of the local pool, (2) corporate policies and their cost, and (3) environmental constraints.

Currently, most managers in subsidiaries are host-country nationals. The reasons include an increase in availability of local talent, corporate relations in the particular market, and the economies realized by not having to maintain a corps of managers overseas. Local managers are generally more familiar with environmental conditions and how they should be interpreted. By employing local management, the multinational is responding to host-country demands for increased localization and providing advancement as an incentive to local managers. In this respect, however,

TABLE 20.2
Factors Determining the
Choice between Local
and Expatriate
Managers
	• Availability of managers
	• Competence
	   Market
	   Technical
		• Corporate objectives
		   Control
		   Management development
		   Corporate citizenship
			• Cost
			• Environment
			   Legal
			   Cultural

localization can be carried too far. If the firm does not subscribe to a global philosophy, the manager's development is tied to the local operation or to a particular level of management in that operation. This has been an issue of contention, especially with Japanese employers in the United States, as can be seen in Global Perspective 20.1. As a result, managers who outgrow the local operation may have nowhere to go except to another company.[9]

Local managers, if not properly trained and indoctrinated, may see things differently from the way they are viewed at headquarters. As a result, both control and the overall coordination of programs may be jeopardized. For the corporation to work effectively, of course, employees must first of all understand each other. Most corporations have adopted a common corporate language, with English as the **lingua franca;** that is, the language habitually used among people of diverse speech to facilitate communication. At Olivetti, all top-level meetings are conducted in English.[10] In some companies, two languages are officially in use; for example, at Nestlé both English and French are corporate languages. A second goal is to avoid overemphasis on localization, which would prevent the development of an internationalized group of managers with a proper understanding of the impact of the environment on operations. To develop language skills and promote an international outlook in their management pools, multinational corporations are increasingly recruiting among foreign students at business schools in the United States, western Europe, and the Far East. When these young managers return home, following an initial assignment at corporate headquarters, they will have a command of the basic philosophies of multinational operations.

Cultural differences that shape managerial attitudes must be considered when developing multinational management programs. For example, British managers place more emphasis than most other nationals on individual achievement and autonomy. French managers, however, value competent supervision, sound company policies, fringe benefits, security, and comfortable working conditions.[11]

The decision as to whether to use home-country nationals in a particular operation depends on such factors as the type of industry, the life-cycle stage of the product, the availability of managers from other sources, and the functional areas involved. The number of home-country managers is typically higher in the service sector than in the industrial sector. However, some overseas assignments, particularly in the service sector, may be quite short term. For example, many international hotel chains have established management contracts in the People's Republic of China with the understanding that home-country managers will train local successors within three to five years. In the start-up phase of an endeavor, headquarters involvement is generally substantial. This applies to all functions, including personnel. Especially if no significant pool of local managers is available or their competence levels are not satisfactory, home-country nationals may be used. For control and communication reasons, some companies always maintain a home-country national as manager in certain functional areas, such as accounting or finance.

The number of home-country nationals in an overseas operation rarely rises above 10 percent of the workforce and is typically only 1 percent. The reasons are

Global Perspective

20.1
Culture Shock at Home: Working for a Foreign Boss

Frank B. Ensign was hired in 1985 as chief financial officer of Fujitsu of America, Inc., and in subsequent years received glowing performance reviews and pay boosts that raised his annual earnings in salary and benefits to $210,000. But his career at Fujitsu suddenly ended on Good Friday, 1989. Ensign alleged that the parent company wanted to replace all American CFOs in all of its American subsidiaries with Japanese CFOs.

Many American managers believe that no amount of dedication to their Japanese employer can move them up in the company. One American senior vice president for marketing and sales left a Japanese company after seven years as its top U.S. manager despite a good salary, bonuses, and even a club membership. He wanted to be president. But the home office rotated Japanese executives in that post, and the American had to teach them the intricacies of the U.S. market. To the Japanese, his resignation confirmed that Americans are not loyal and cannot be trusted.

American managers have had greater upward mobility working for European companies. Both Japanese and American companies usually install executives from the home country in the chief executive post. But Europeans rely much more on Americans in middle- and upper-middle-management positions and give them more authority. If

Americans hold these positions in Japanese companies, they tend to lack decision-making power.

While the Americans and Europeans generally share cultural and political traditions, the Japanese have developed a unique managerial style and base working relationships on a tradition that emphasizes collective values over individualism. As one American manager put it: "The most difficult part of working for the Japanese is that you will always be working *with* the organization, but you will never be *of* the organization because you are not Japanese."

Although Japanese managers continue to express frustration in what they perceive to be disloyalty and opportunism on the part of U.S. employees, they are starting to change their practices so that they can retain talented U.S. nationals. For example, at Nippon Credit Bank, 70 percent of local employees have been promoted. At Nissan Motor Manufacturing, line managers are encouraged to apply for manager positions. These companies perceive that their success in building an international business depends on their ability to effectively manage and develop a truly global workforce. Human-resource management is finally seen as a critical factor in the globalization of Japanese companies.

Source: Elizabeth Klein, "The U.S./Japanese HR Culture Clash," *Personnel Journal* 71 (November 1992): 30–38; "Culture Shock at Home: Working for a Foreign Boss," *Business Week,* December 17, 1990, 80–84; and Susan Moffat, "Should You Work for the Japanese?" *Fortune,* December 3, 1990, 107–120.

both internal and external. In addition to the substantial cost of transfer, a manager may not fully adjust to foreign working and living conditions. Good corporate citizenship today requires multinational companies to develop the host country's workforce at the management level. Legal impediments to manager transfers may exist, or other difficulties may be encountered. Many U.S.-based hotel corporations, for example, have complained about delays in obtaining visas to the United States not only for managers but also for management trainees.

The use of third-country nationals is most often seen in large multinational companies that have adopted a global philosophy. The practice of some companies, such as the Dutch electronics giant N. V. Philips, is to employ third-country nationals as managing directors in subsidiaries. An advantage is that third-country nationals may contribute to the firm's overall international expertise. However, many third-country nationals are career international managers, and they may become targets for raids by competitors looking for high levels of talent. They may be a considerable

590   PART 4 / International Business Strategy and Operations

asset in regional expansion; for example, established subsidiary managers in Singapore might be used to start up a subsidiary in Malaysia. On the other hand, some transfers may be inadvisable for cultural or historical reasons, with transfers between Turkey and Greece as an example.

All firms use a similar pattern of recruitment during the internationalization process.[12] During the export stage, outside expertise is at first sought, but the firm then begins to develop its own personnel. Foreign entry through manufacture reverses this trend. The firm's reliance on home country personnel diminishes as host-country nationals are prepared for management positions. The use of home-country nationals and third-country nationals is increasingly restricted to special assignments, such as transfer of technology or expertise. They will continue to be used as a matter of corporate policy to internationalize management and to foster the infusion of a particular corporate culture.

Interesting differences are noted when recruitment is analyzed on the basis of the multinational corporation's home country. Table 20.3 gives a summary of the percentage of local managers in foreign-owned subsidiaries in Brazil. The reasons for the differences are sometimes cultural and sometimes related to the stage of development of the corporation. Japanese companies traditionally are more insistent than most on home-country managers. This has been evident in their expansion in the United States and western Europe. Especially in the case of European-based companies, differences in the numbers of local managers used may be explained by the fact that their internationalization may not be as advanced as that of U.S. companies.

The ability to recruit for international assignments is determined by the value an individual company places on international operations and the experience gained in working in them. Based on a survey of 1,500 senior executives around the world, U.S. executives still place less emphasis on international dimensions than their Japanese, western European, and Latin American counterparts. While most executives agree that an international outlook is essential for future executives, 70 percent of foreign executives think that experience outside one's home country is important, compared with only 35 percent of U.S. executives, and foreign language capability was seen as important by only 19 percent of U.S. respondents, compared with 64 percent of non–U.S. executives.[13]

Selection Criteria for Overseas Assignments

The traits that have been suggested as necessary for the international manager range from the ideal to the real. One characterization describes "a flexible personality, with

TABLE 20.3 Percentage of Local Managers in Foreign-Owned Subsidiaries in Brazil	Nationality of Parent	Local Managers		
		CEO	Marketing	All
	American	24%	52%	56%
	European*	8	68	38
	Japanese	0	13	16
	Total	13	53	40

*European subsidiaries in this study were headquartered in most western European countries, predominantly in the United Kingdom, Germany, and France.

Source: William K. Brandt and John M. Hulbert, *A Empresa Multinacional No Brasil* (Rio De Janeiro: Zahan Editors, 1977), 45.

In Tokyo, Merck representative Satomi Tomihari confers with Yasumasa Nakamura, M.D. Ms. Tomihari is one of 25 women recruited by Merck affiliate, Banyu Pharmaceutical, Ltd.

Source: Griffiths, Photographer for Magnum Photo. Courtesy of Merck & Co., Inc.

broad intellectual horizons, attitudinal values of cultural empathy, general friendliness, patience and prudence, impeccable educational and professional (or technical) credentials—all topped off with immaculate health, creative resourcefulness, and respect of peers. If the family is equally well endowed, all the better."[14] Although this would seem to describe a supermanager, a number of companies believe that the qualities that make a successful international manager are increasingly the traits needed at headquarters.[15] Traits typically mentioned in the choosing of managers for overseas assignments are listed in Table 20.4. Their relative importance may vary dramatically, of course, depending on the firm and the situation.

Competence Factors   An expatriate manager usually has far more responsibility than a manager in a comparable domestic position and must be far more self-sufficient in making decisions and conducting daily business. To be selected in the first place, the manager's technical competence level has to be superior to local candidates'; otherwise the firm would in most cases have chosen a local person. The manager's ability to do the job in the technical sense is one of the main determinants of ultimate success or failure in an overseas assignment.[16] However, management skills will not transfer from one culture to another without some degree of adaptation. This means that, regardless of the level of technical skills, the new environment still requires the ability to adapt them to local conditions. Technical competence must also be accompanied by the ability to lead subordinates in any situation or under any conditions.

Especially in global-minded enterprises, managers are selected for overseas assignments on the basis of solid experience and past performance. Many firms use the foreign tour as a step toward top management. By sending abroad internally recruited, experienced managers, the firm also ensures the continuation of corporate culture—a set of shared values, norms, and beliefs and an emphasis on a particular facet of performance. Two examples are IBM's concern with customer service and 3M's concentration on innovation.[17]

The role of **factual cultural knowledge** in the selection process has been widely debated. **Area expertise** includes a knowledge of the basic systems in the region or market for which the manager will be responsible—such as the roles of various ministries in international business, the significance of holidays, and the general way of doing business. None of these variables is as important as language, although lan-

TABLE 20.4 **Criteria for Selecting** **Managers for Overseas** **Assignment**	Competence	Adaptability	Personal Characteristics
	Technical knowledge	Interest in overseas work	Age
	Leadership ability	Relational abilities	Education
	Experience, Past performance	Cultural empathy	Sex
	Area expertise	Appreciation of new	Health
	Language	management styles	Marital relations
		Appreciation of environmental	Social acceptability
		constraints	
		Adaptability of family	

guage skill is not always highly ranked by firms themselves.[18] A manager who does not know the language of the country may get by with the help of associates and interpreters but is not in a position to assess the situation fully. Of the Japanese representing their companies in the United States, for example, almost all speak English. Of the Americans representing U.S. companies in Japan, however, few speak Japanese well.[19] Some companies place language skills or aptitude in a larger context; they see a strong correlation between language skill and adaptability. Another reason to look for language competence in managers considered for assignments overseas is that all managers spend most of their time communicating.

Adaptability Factors   The manager's own motivation to a great extent determines the viability of an overseas assignment and consequently its success. The manager's interest in the foreign culture must go well beyond that of the average tourist if he or she is to understand what an assignment abroad involves. In most cases, the manager will need counseling and training in order to comprehend the true nature of the undertaking.

Adaptability means a positive and flexible attitude toward change. The manager assigned overseas must progress from factual knowledge of culture to **interpretive cultural knowledge,** trying as much as possible to become part of the new scene. This scene may be quite different from the one at home. The work habits of middle-level managers may be more lax, productivity and attention to detail less, and overall environmental restrictions far greater. The manager on a foreign assignment is part of a multicultural team, in which both internal and external interactions determine the future of the firm's operations. For example, a manager from the United States may be used to an informal, democratic type of leadership that may not be applicable in countries such as Mexico or Japan, where employees expect more authoritarian leadership.[20]

Adaptability does not depend solely on the manager. Firms look carefully at the family situation because a foreign assignment often puts more strain on other family members than on the manager. As an example, a U.S. engineering firm had problems in Italy that were traced to the inability of one executive's wife to adapt. She complained to other wives, who began to feel that they too suffered hardships and then complained to their husbands. Morale became so low that the company, after missing important deadlines, replaced most of the Americans on the job.[21] This extreme case shows that spouses need to participate in the decision process throughout.

The characteristics of the family as a whole are important. Screeners look for family cohesiveness and check for marital instability or for behavioral difficulties in children. Abroad, the need to work together as a family often makes strong marriages stronger and causes the downfall of weak ones. Further, commitments or interests beyond the nuclear family affect the adjustment of family members to a new environment. Some firms use earlier transfers within the home country as an indicator of how a family will handle transfer abroad. With the dramatic increase in two-career households, foreign assignments usually call for one of the spouses to sacrifice a career or, at best, to put it on hold. As a result, a group of 38 corporations have formed a consortium to try to tackle this problem. Members of the group interview accompanying spouses and try to find them positions with other member companies.[22]

Personal Characteristics

Personal Characteristics   Despite all of the efforts made by multinational companies to recruit the best person available, demographics still play a role in the selection process. Because of either a minimum age requirement or the level of experience needed, many foreign assignments go to managers in their mid-30s or older. Normally, companies do not recruit candidates from graduating classes for immediate assignment overseas. They want their international people first to become experienced and familiar with the corporate culture, and this can best be done at the headquarters location.

Although the number of women in overseas assignments is only 3 percent according to one count, women are as interested as men are in these assignments.[23] Corporate hiring practices may be based on the myth that women will not be accepted in the host countries. Many of the relatively few women managers report being treated as foreign business people and not singled out as women.[24]

In the selection process, firms are concerned about the health of the people they may send abroad. Some assignments are in host countries with dramatically different environmental conditions from the home country, and they may aggravate existing health problems. Moreover, if the candidate selected is not properly prepared, foreign assignments may increase stress levels and contribute to the development of peptic ulcers, colitis, or other problems.

When candidates are screened, being married is usually considered a plus. Marriage brings stability and an inherent support system, provided family relations are in order. It may also facilitate adaptation to the local culture by increasing the number of social functions to which the manager is invited.

Social acceptability varies from one culture to another and can be a function of any of the other personal characteristics. Background, religion, race, and sex usually become critical only in extreme cases in which a host environment would clearly reject a candidate based on one or more of these variables. The Arab boycott of the state of Israel, for example, puts constraints on the use of managers of Jewish and Arab origin. Women cannot negotiate contracts in many Middle Eastern countries. This would hold true even if the woman were president of the company.

The Selection and Orientation Challenge

The Selection and Orientation Challenge   Because of the cost of transferring a manager overseas, many firms go beyond standard selection procedures and use **adaptability screening** as an integral part of the process. During the screening phase, the method most often used involves interviewing the candidate and the family. The interviews are conducted by senior executives, human-relations specialists within the firm, or outside firms. Interviewers ask the candidate and the family to consider the personal issues involved in the transfer; for example, what each will miss the

594

Organized Labor as a Percentage of the Labor Force

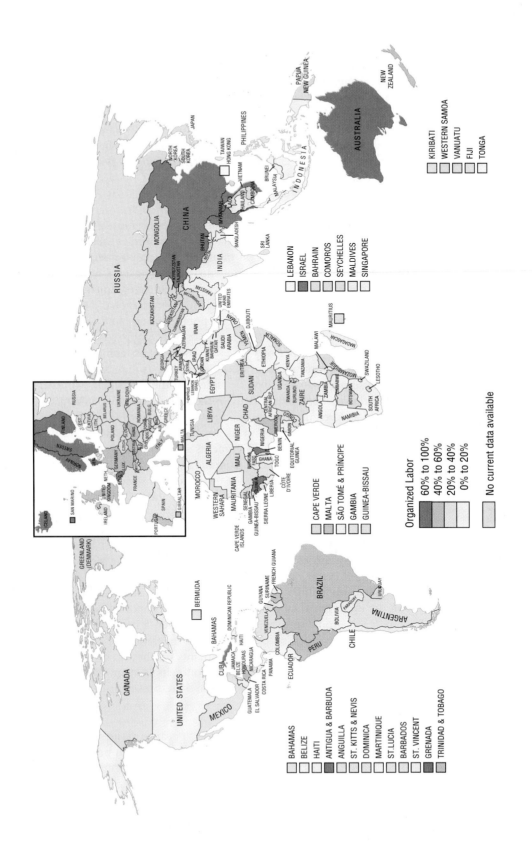

Organized Labor

- 60% to 100%
- 40% to 60%
- 20% to 40%
- 0% to 20%
- No current data available

Source: *The World Factbook 1992*.

most. In some cases, candidates themselves will refuse an assignment. In others, the firm will withhold the assignment on the basis of interviews that clearly show a degree of risk. For an example of such an approach, see Global Perspective 20.2.

The candidate selected will participate in an **orientation program** on internal and external aspects of the assignment. Internal aspects include issues such as compensation and reporting. External aspects are concerned with what to expect at the destination in terms of customs and culture. Typically these programs last from a few days to two weeks. Some last several months, especially when language training is involved. The emphasis is on enhancing the individual's capability to handle cross-cultural encounters. Methods vary from area studies to sensitivity training. For a discussion of these methods, see Chapter 9. Orientation for families is not as extensive; for example, the only orientation provided to the families of officers of the U.S. and Foreign Commercial Service is a half day devoted to terrorism.

The attrition rate in overseas assignments averages 40 percent among companies with neither adaptability screening nor orientation programs, 25 percent among companies with cultural orientation programs, and 5 to 10 percent among companies that use both kinds of programs.[25] Considering the cost of a transfer, catching

Global Perspective

20.2
Screening Candidates for Overseas Transfers

Eager to cut down on foreign transfers that fail, multinational corporations are selecting expatriates with greater care by asking them and their spouses to consider issues related to living abroad. American Telephone and Telegraph (AT&T) has long put prospective expatriates through management interviews and a written test. But recently it added a self-assessment checklist of "cultural adaptability" as well as interviews with a psychologist.

About three dozen families have run through the checklist and interviews, and a few have removed themselves from the running as a result. AT&T expects to expand the screening soon to cover most of the 125 to 150 employees it sends abroad each year. Among the questions posed are:

- Would your spouse be interrupting a career to accompany you on an international assignment? If so, how do you think this will [affect] your spouse and your relationship with each other?
- Do you enjoy the challenge of making your own way in new situations?

- Securing a job upon re-entry will be primarily your responsibility. How do you feel about networking and being your own advocate?
- How able are you in initiating new social contacts?
- Can you imagine living without television?
- How important is it for you to spend significant amounts of time with people of your own ethnic, racial, religious, and national background?
- As you look at your personal history, can you isolate any episodes that indicate a real interest in learning about other peoples and cultures?
- Has it been your habit to vacation in foreign countries?
- Do you enjoy sampling foreign cuisines?
- What is your tolerance for waiting for repairs?

Source: "As Costs of Expatriates Rise, Companies Select Them More Carefully," *The Wall Street Journal Europe*, January 10–11, 1992, 1, 20. Reprinted by permission of the *The Wall Street Journal*, © 1992 Dow Jones & Company, Inc. All Rights Reserved Worldwide.

even one potentially disastrous situation pays for the program for a full year. Most companies have no program at all, however, and others provide them for higher level management positions only. Companies that have the lowest failure rates typically employ a four-tiered approach to expatriate use: (1) clearly stated criteria, (2) rigorous procedures to determine the suitability of an individual across the criteria, (3) appropriate orientation, and (4) constant evaluation of the effectiveness of the procedures.[26]

Culture Shock

The effectiveness of orientation procedures can be measured only after managers are overseas. A unique phenomenon they face is **culture shock**. Although they all feel it, individuals differ widely in how they allow themselves to be affected by it.

Causes and Remedies　Culture shock is the term used for the more pronounced reactions to the psychological disorientation that most people experience when they move for an extended period of time into a culture markedly different from their own.[27] Culture shock and its severity may be a function of the individual's lack of adaptability but may equally be a result of the firm's lack of understanding of the situation into which the manager was sent. Often goals set for a subsidiary or a project may be unrealistic or the means by which they are to be reached may be totally inadequate. All of these lead to external manifestations of culture shock, such as bitterness and even physical illness. In extreme cases, they can lead to hostility toward anything in the host environment.

The culture shock cycle for an overseas assignment is presented in Figure 20.2. Four distinct stages of adjustment exist during a foreign assignment. The length of the stages is highly individual. The four stages are:

1. Initial euphoria: enjoying the novelty, largely from the perspective of a spectator.

**FIGURE 20.2
Culture Shock Cycle for
an Overseas
Assignment**

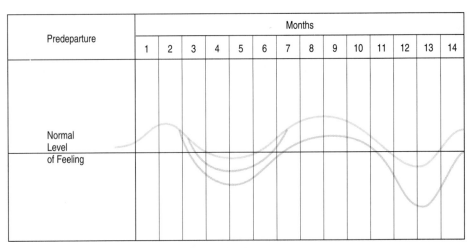

Note: Lines indicate the extreme severity with which culture shock may attack.
Source: L. Robert Kohls, *Survival Kit for Overseas Living* (Yarmouth, Maine: Intercultural Press, 1984), 68.

2. Irritation and hostility: experiencing cultural differences, such as the concept of time, through increased participation.

3. Adjustment: adapting to the situation, which in some cases leads to biculturalism and even accusations from corporate headquarters of "going native."

4. Reentry: returning home.

The manager may fare better at the second stage than other members of the family, especially if their opportunities for work and other activities are severely restricted. The fourth stage may actually cause a reverse culture shock when the adjustment phase has been highly successful and the return home is not desired.

Firms themselves must take responsibility for easing one of the causes of culture shock: isolation. By maintaining contact with the manager beyond business-related communication, some of the shock may be alleviated. Exxon, for example, assigns each expatriate a contact person at headquarters to share general information.

Terrorism: Tangible Culture Shock   International terrorists have frequently targeted for attack U.S. corporate facilities, operations, and personnel abroad.[28] Of the 166 incidents against U.S. interests abroad in 1992, 48 were attacks on businesses.[29] Corporate reactions have ranged from letting terrorism have little effect on operations to abandoning certain markets. Some companies try to protect their managers in various ways by fortifying their homes and using local-sounding names to do business in troubled parts of the world. Of course, insurance is available to cover key executives; the cost ranges from a few thousand dollars to hundreds of thousands a year depending on the extent and location of the company's operations.[30] Leading insurers include American International Underwriters, Chubb & Son, and Lloyd's of London.[31] The threat of terrorist activity may have an effect on the company's operations beyond the immediate geographic area of concern. For example, when hostilities between Iraq and the United States started in early 1991, many multinational companies restricted or completely banned foreign travel.

Repatriation

Returning home may evoke mixed feelings on the part of the **expatriate** and the family. Their concerns are both professional and personal. Even in two years, dramatic changes may have occurred not only at home but also in the way the individual and the family perceive the foreign environment. At worst, reverse culture shock may emerge.

The most important professional issue is finding a proper place in the corporate hierarchy. If no provisions have been made, a returning manager may be caught in a holding pattern for an intolerable length of time. For this reason Dow Chemical, for example, provides each manager embarking on an overseas assignment with a letter that promises a job at least equal in responsibility upon return. Furthermore, because of their isolation, assignments abroad mean greater autonomy and authority than similar domestic positions. Both financially and psychologically, many expatriates find the overseas position difficult to give up. Many executive perks, such as club memberships, will not be funded at home. Financial reasons, for example, make many officers of the U.S. and Foreign Commercial Service dread a summons for a two-year tour in the United States.

The family, too, may be reluctant to give up their special status. In India, for example, expatriate families have servants for most of the tasks they perform themselves at home. Many longer-term expatriates are shocked by increases in the prices of housing and education in the United States. For the many managers who want to stay abroad, this may mean a change of company or even career—from employee to independent business person. According to one study, 20 percent of the employees who complete overseas assignments want to leave the company upon their return.[32]

This alternative is not an attractive one for the company, which stands to lose valuable individuals who could become members of an international corps of managers. Therefore, planning for repatriation is necessary.[33] A four-step process can be used for this purpose. The first step involves an assessment of foreign assignments in terms of environmental constraints and corporate objectives, making sure that the latter are realistically defined. The second stage is preparation of the individual for an overseas assignment, which should include a clear understanding of when and how repatriation takes place. During the actual tour, the manager should be kept abreast of developments at headquarters, especially in terms of career paths. Finally, during the actual reentry, the manager should receive intensive organizational reorientation, reasonable professional adjustment time, and counseling for the entire family on matters of, for example, finance. A program of this type allows the expatriate to feel a close bond with headquarters regardless of geographical distance.

Compensation

A Japanese executive's salary in cash is quite modest by U.S. standards, but he is comfortable in the knowledge that the company will take care of him. Compensation is paternalistic; for example, a manager with two children in college and a sizable mortgage would be paid more than a childless manager in a comparable job. As this example suggests, Japanese compensation issues go beyond salary comparisons. They include exchange rates, local taxes, and what the money will buy in different countries. Many compensation packages include elements other than cash.[34]

A firm's international compensation program has to be effective in (1) providing an incentive to leave the home country on a foreign assignment, (2) maintaining a given standard of living, (3) taking into consideration career and family needs, and (4) facilitating reentry into the home country.[35] To achieve these objectives, firms pay a high premium beyond base salaries to induce managers to accept overseas assignments. The costs to the firm are 2 to 2.5 times the cost of maintaining a manager in a comparable position at home. For example, the average compensation package of a U.S. manager in Hong Kong is $225,500 (base salary is 47 percent of this figure) and for the British manager $170,500 (57 percent). U.S. firms traditionally offer their employees more high-value perks, such as bigger apartments.[36]

The compensation of the manager overseas can be divided into two general categories: (1) base salary and salary-related allowances and (2) nonsalary-related allowances. Although incentives to leave home are justifiable in both categories, they create administrative complications for the personnel department in tying them to packages at home and elsewhere. As the number of transfers increases, firms develop general policies for compensating the manager rather than negotiate individually on every aspect of the arrangement.

Base Salary and Salary-Related Allowances   A manager's **base salary** depends on qualifications, responsibilities, and duties, just as it would for a domestic position.

Furthermore, criteria applying to merit increases, promotions, and other increases are administered as they are domestically. Equity and comparability with domestic positions are important, especially in ensuring that repatriation will not cause cuts in base pay.[37] For administrative and control purposes, the compensation and benefits function in multinational corporations is most often centralized.[38]

The cost of living varies considerably around the world, as can be seen in Global Perspective 20.3. The purpose of the **cost of living allowance (COLA)** is to enable the manager to maintain as closely as possible the same standard of living that he or she would have at home. COLA is calculated by determining a percentage of base salary that would be spent on goods and services at the foreign location. (Figures around 50 percent are normal.) The ratios will naturally vary as a function of

Global Perspective

20.3
How Far Will Your Salary Go?

Living cost comparisons for Americans residing in foreign areas are developed four times a year by the U.S. Department of State Allowances Staff. For each post, two measures are computed: (1) a government index to establish post allowances for U.S. government employees and (2) a local index for use by private organizations. The government index takes into consideration prices of goods imported to posts and price advantages available only to U.S. government employees.

The local index is used by many business firms and private organizations to determine the cost of living allowance for their American employees assigned abroad. Local index measures for 12 key areas around the world are shown in the accompanying table. Maximum housing allowances, calculated separately, are also given.

The reports are issued four times annually under the title *U.S. Department of State Indexes of Living Costs Abroad, Quarters Allowances, and Hardship Differentials* by the U.S. Department of Labor.

Location	Cost of Living Index[a] (Washington, D.C. equals 100)		Maximum Annual Housing Allowance[b]	
	Survey Date	Index	Effective Date	Amount
Buenos Aires	May 1992	135		NA
Canberra, Australia	Nov. 1991	132		NA
Brussels, Belgium	Sep. 1991	146	Jan. 1993	$26,500
Rio de Janeiro, Brazil	Mar. 1990	127		NA
Paris, France	Sep. 1991	151	Dec. 1992	31,400
Frankfurt, Germany	Feb. 1992	134	Jan. 1993	20,500
Hong Kong	Mar. 1992	127		NA
Tokyo, Japan	Feb. 1992	192	Jan. 1993	61,900
Mexico City	Feb. 1992	105	Oct. 1991	32,800
The Hague, Netherlands	Feb. 1992	136	Jan. 1993	29,600
Geneva, Switzerland	Jun. 1992	166	Jan. 1993	38,200
London, U.K.	Jul. 1991	149	Jan. 1993	26,000

[a]Excluding housing and education.
[b]For a family of three to four members with an annual income of $55,000 and over. Allowances are computed and paid in U.S. dollars.
NA = not available.

income and family size. COLA tables for various U.S. cities (of which Washington, D.C., is the most often used) and locations worldwide are available through the U.S. State Department Allowances Staff and various consulting firms, such as Business International Corporation. Fluctuating exchange rates will of course have an effect on the COLA as well, and changes will call for reviews of the allowance. As an example, assume that living in Helsinki costs the manager 71 percent more than living in Washington, D.C. The manager's monthly pay is $4,000, and for his family of four, the disposable income is $2,150 (53.75 percent). Further assume that the dollar weakens from 5.9 Fmks to 5.7 Fmks. The COLA would be:

$$\$2,150 \times 171/100 \times 5.9/5.7 = \$3,805.$$

Similarly, if the local currency depreciated, the COLA would be less. When the cost of living is less than in the United States, no COLA is determined.

The **foreign service premium** is actually a bribe to encourage a manager to leave familiar conditions and adapt to new surroundings. Although the methods of paying the premium vary, as do its percentages, most firms pay it as a percentage of the base salary. The percentages range from 10 to 25 percent of base salary. One variation of the straightforward percentage is a sliding scale by amount—15 percent of the first $20,000, then 10 percent, and sometimes a ceiling beyond which a premium is not paid. Another variation is by duration, with the percentages decreasing with every year the manager spends abroad. Despite the controversial nature of foreign service premiums paid at some locations, they are a generally accepted competitive practice.

The environments in which a manager will work and the family will live vary dramatically. For example, consider being assigned to London or Brisbane versus Dar es Salaam or Port Moresby or even Bogota or Buenos Aires. Some locations may require little, if any, adjustment. Some call for major adaptation because of climatic differences; political instability; inadequacies in housing, education, shopping, or recreation; or overall isolation. For example, a family assigned to Beijing may find that schooling is difficult to arrange, with the result that younger children go to school in Tokyo and the older ones in the United States. To compensate for this type of expense and adjustment, firms pay **hardship allowances.** These allowances are based on U.S. State Department Foreign Post Differentials. The percentages vary from zero (for example, the manager in Helsinki) to 50 percent (as in Monrovia). The higher allowances typically include a danger pay extra added to any hardship allowance.[39]

Housing costs and related expenses are typically the largest expenditure in the expatriate manager's budget. Firms usually provide a **housing allowance** commensurate with the manager's salary level and position. When the expatriate is the country manager for the firm, the housing allowance will provide for suitable quarters in which to receive business associates. In most cases, firms set a range within which the manager must find housing. For common utilities, firms either provide an allowance or pay the costs outright.

One of the major determinants of the manager's lifestyle abroad is taxes. A U.S. manager earning $100,000 in Canada would pay nearly $40,000 in taxes—in excess of $10,000 more than in the United States. For this reason, 90 percent of U.S. multinational corporations have **tax-equalization** plans. When a manager's overseas taxes are higher than at home, the firm will make up the difference. However, in countries with a lower rate of taxation, the company simply keeps the difference. The firms' rationalization is that "it does not make any sense for the manager in Hong Kong to make more money than the guy who happened to land in Singapore."[40] Tax equalization is usually handled by accounting firms that make the needed calculations and prepare the proper forms. Managers can exclude a portion of their expatriate salary from U.S. tax; in 1993 the amount was $70,000, with the figure having steadily declined in the 1980s.

Nonsalary-Related Allowances   Other types of allowances are made available to ease the transition into the period of service abroad.[41] Typical allowances during the transition stage include (1) a relocation allowance to compensate for the additional expense of a move, such as purchase of electric converters; (2) a mobility allowance as an incentive to managers to go overseas, usually paid in a lump sum and as a substitute for the foreign service premium (some companies pay 50 percent at transfer, 50 percent at repatriation); (3) allowances related to housing, such as home sale or rental protection, shipment and storage of household goods, or provision of household furnishings in overseas locations; (4) automobile protection in terms of covering possible losses on the sale of a car or cars at transfer and having to buy others overseas, usually at a higher cost; (5) travel expenses, using economy-class transportation except for long flights (for example, from Washington to Taipei); and (6) temporary living expenses, which may become substantial if housing is not immediately available—as for the expatriate family that had to spend a year at a hotel in Beijing, for example.

Education for children is one of the major concerns of expatriate families. Free public schooling may not be available and the private alternatives expensive. In many cases, children may have to go to school in a different country. Firms will typically reimburse for such expenses in the form of an **education allowance.** In the case of college education, firms reimburse for one round-trip airfare every year, leaving tuition expenses to the family.

Finally, firms provide support for medical expenses, especially to provide medical services at a level comparable to the expatriate's home country. In some cases, this means traveling to another country for care; for example, from Malaysia to Singapore, where the medical system is the most advanced in southeast Asia.

Other issues should be covered by a clearly stated policy. Home leave is provided every year, typically after 11 months overseas, although some companies require a longer period. Home leaves are usually accompanied by consultation and training sessions at headquarters. Some hardship posts, such as Port Moresby, include rest and relaxation leaves to maintain morale. At some posts, club memberships are necessary because (1) the status of the manager requires them and (2) they provide family members with access to the type of recreation they are used to in the home environment. Because they are extremely expensive—for example, a "mandatory" golf club membership in Tokyo might cost thousands of dollars—the firm's assistance is needed.

Method of Payment   The method of payment, especially in terms of currency, is determined by a number of factors. The most usual method is to pay part of the salary in the local currency and part in the currency of the manager's home country. Host-country regulations, ranging from taxation to the availability of foreign currency, will influence the decision. Firms themselves look at the situation from the accounting and administrative point of view and would like, in most cases, to pay in local currencies to avoid burdening the subsidiary. The expatriate naturally will want to have some of the compensation in his or her own currency for various reasons; for example, if exchange controls are in effect, to get savings out of the country upon repatriation may be very difficult.

Compensation of Host-Country Nationals   The compensation packages paid to local managers—cash, benefits, and privileges—are largely determined as a function of internal equity and external competitiveness. Internal equity may be complicated because of cultural differences in compensation; for example, in Japan a year-end bonus of an additional month's salary is common. On the other hand, some incentive programs to increase productivity may be unknown to some nationals. Furthermore, in many countries, the state provides benefits that may be provided by the firm elsewhere. Because the firm and its employees contribute to these programs by law, the services need not be duplicated.

External competitiveness depends on the market price of trained individuals and their attraction to the firm. External competitiveness is best assessed through surveys of compensation and benefits levels for a particular market. The firm must keep its local managers informed of the survey results to help them realize the value of their compensation packages.

MANAGING LABOR PERSONNEL

None of the firm's objectives can be realized without a labor force, which can become one of the firm's major assets or its major problems depending on the relationship that is established. Because of local patterns and legislation, headquarters' role in shaping these relations is mainly advisory, limited to setting the overall tone for the interaction. However, as can be seen in Global Perspective 20.4, many of the practices adopted in one market or region may easily come under discussion in another, making it necessary for multinational corporations to set general policies concerning labor relations. Often multinational corporations have been instrumental in bringing about changes in the overall work environment in a country.

Labor strategy can be viewed from three perspectives: (1) the participation of labor in the affairs of the firm, especially as it affects performance and well-being; (2) the role and impact of unions in the relationship; and (3) specific human-resource policies in terms of recruitment, training, and compensation.

Team building at Avery Label Systems in the United Kingdom, a division of Avery Dennison Corporation, has created "work cell teams" that have full product responsibility throughout the production process. Each team member can perform every other team member's job.

Source: Courtesy of Avery Dennison Corporation.

Global Perspective

20.4
Labor's Blueprint for Unified Europe

For the most part, the idea of 1992 has been considered the brainchild of Europe's corporate and financial sectors eager to deregulate the Continent and design a single, efficient market. At the same time, however, labor has been crafting its own agenda for Europewide benefits and standards. Still awaiting passage, the proposed rules touch on everything from maternity leave to benefits for temporary workers, standardizing labor practices. Parts of the new package, officially called the Social Action Program, will pass easily because they mirror practices already in place in much of the EC.

Many employers, however, fear the higher costs and loss of flexibility will make it difficult for the Europeans to compete against the Americans and especially the Japanese. One of the toughest proposals would require worker representation on boards of directors of companies with more than 10,000 employees. German companies already have it in effect, but most European managers resist giving unions such a say in corporate decisions. And it is anathema to U.S. executives, who fear that workers in the United States could begin to demand similar access to companies' closely guarded strategic planning.

U.S. companies are balking at other restrictions as well. Caterpillar has 9,000 employees in Britain, Belgium, and France, each of which offers different ways to compensate for overtime. British workers, for example, can opt for overtime pay or compensatory time off. Under the new rules, they will have to take time off.

Some companies have already started Euro-lobbying efforts to turn things around. Led by the auto companies, U.S. businesses managed to win concessions on night work. However, if the executives were hoping that the moves toward a single market would pare down Europe's social programs to resemble the bare-bones U.S. system, they will be disappointed. In the tradition of Europe's social democracies, workers are almost certain to get their share although it may be less than they want. A visit to any truly competitive European company will reveal thousands of job cuts, plans for benefits reductions, and cost squeezing. And many expect these efforts to be only the beginning of the restructuring needed.

Source: Carla Rapoport, "Europe Looks Ahead to Hard Choices," *Fortune*, December 14, 1992, 144–149; and "Workers Want Their Piece of Europe Inc.," *Business Week*, October 22, 1990, 46–47.

Labor Participation in Management

Over the past quarter century, many changes have occurred in the traditional labor-management relationship as a result of dramatic changes in the economic environment and the actions of both firms and the labor force. The role of the worker is changing both at the level of the job performed and in terms of participation in the decision-making process. To enhance workers' role in decision making, various techniques have emerged: self-management, codetermination, minority board membership, and work councils. In striving for improvements in quality of work life, programs that have been initiated include flextime, quality circles, and work-flow reorganization. Furthermore, employee ownership has moved into the mainstream.

Labor Participation in Decision Making   The degree to which workers around the world can participate in corporate decision making varies considerably. Rights of information, consultation, and codetermination develop on three levels:

1. The shop-floor level, or direct involvement; for example, the right to be consulted in advance concerning transfers.

2. The management level, or through representative bodies; for example, work council participation in setting of new policies or changing of existing ones.

3. The board level; for example, labor membership on the board of directors.[42]

The extent of worker participation in decision making in 11 countries is summarized in Table 20.5. Yugoslavia, before its breakup, used to have the highest amount of worker participation in any country; **self-management** was standard through workers' councils, which decided all major issues including the choice of managing director and supervisory board.[43]

In some countries, employees are represented on the supervisory boards to facilitate communication between management and labor by giving labor a clearer picture of the financial limits of management and by providing management with new awareness of labor's point of view. This process is called **codetermination.** In Germany, companies have a two-tiered management system with a supervisory board and the board of managers, which actually runs the firm. In a firm with 20,000 employees, for example, labor would have 10 of the 20 supervisory board slots divided in the following way: 3 places for union officials and the balance to be elected from the workforce. At least one member must be a white-collar employee and one a managerial employee.[44] The supervisory board is legally responsible for the managing board. Reactions to codetermination vary. Six European nations—Sweden, the Netherlands, Norway, Luxembourg, Denmark, and France—have introduced their own versions and report lower levels of labor strife.[45] In some countries, labor has **minority participation.** In the Netherlands, for example, work councils can nominate (not appoint) board members and can veto the appointment of new members appointed by others. In other countries, such as the United States, codetermination has been opposed by unions as an undesirable means of cooperation, especially when management-labor relations are confrontational.

TABLE 20.5 Degree of Worker Involvement in Decision Making of Firms

	Direct Involvement of Workers[a]	Involvement of Representative Bodies[a]	Board Representation Standing[b]	Overall Standing[c]
Germany	3	1	1	A
Sweden	4	2	1	A
Norway	1	10	1	B
Netherlands	9	4	2	C
France	7	3	2	C
Belgium	5	6	3	D
Finland	2	9	3	D
Denmark	8	7	1	D
Israel	11	5	3	D
Italy	6	8	3	E
Great Britain	10	11	3	E

[a]Involvement is rated on an 11-point scale, where 1 stands for the greatest degree of involvement and 11 for almost no involvement.

[b]All cases without any kind of board participation are coded 3; the right to appoint two or more members, 1; the in-between category, 2.

[c]Rankings are from high (A) to low (E).

Source: Industrial Democracy in Europe International Research Group, *Industrial Democracy in Europe* (Oxford, England: Clarendon Press, 1981), 255.

A tradition in labor relations, especially in Britain, is **work councils.** These bodies provide labor a say in corporate decision making through a representative body, which may consist entirely of workers or of a combination of managers and workers. The councils participate in decisions on overall working conditions, training, transfers, work allocation, and compensation. In some countries, such as Finland and Belgium, workers' rights to direct involvement, especially as it involves their positions, are quite strong.

The countries described are unique in the world. In many countries and regions, workers have few if any of these rights. The result is long-term potential for labor strife. A good example is the Republic of Korea, where, during 1987, riots by workers demanding better overall work conditions disrupted an economy noted for its dependence on export trade.

Improvement of Quality of Work Life   The term **quality of work life** has come to encompass various efforts in the areas of personal and professional development. Its two clear objectives are to increase productivity and to increase the satisfaction of employees. Of course, programs leading to increased participation in corporate decision making are part of these programs; however, this section will concentrate on individual job-related programs: work redesign, team building, and work scheduling.[46]

By adding both horizontal and vertical dimensions to the work, **work redesign programs** attack undesirable features of jobs. Horizontally, task complexity is added by incorporating work stages normally done before and after the stage being redesigned. Vertically, each employee is given more responsibility for making the decisions that affect how the work is done.[47] Japanese car manufacturers have changed some of the work routines in their plants in the United States. For example, at Honda's unit in Marysville, Ohio, workers have reacted favorably to the responsibilities they have been given, such as inspecting their own work and instructing others.[48] On the other hand, work redesign may have significant costs attached, including wage increases, facility change costs, and training costs.

Closely related to work redesign are efforts aimed at **team building.** For example, at Volvo's Kalmar plant in Sweden, work is organized so that groups are responsible for a particular, identifiable portion of the car, such as interiors. Each group has its own areas in which to pace itself and to organize the work. The group must take responsibility for the work, including for inspection, whether it is performed individually or in groups. The group is informed about its performance through a computer system.[49] The team-building effort includes job rotation to enable workers to understand all facets of their jobs. Visiting American autoworkers were impressed with Volvo's physical working conditions, but they felt that teamwork would become tedious. Despite claims for increased worker participation, Americans expressed a preference for the more grass-roots unionism of the United States and its well-tested grievance procedure.[50] Another approach to team building makes use of **quality circles,** in which groups of workers regularly meet to discuss issues relating to their productivity. Although pioneered in Japan, quality circles began to appear in U.S. industry in the mid-1970s.

Flexibility in **work scheduling** has led to changes in when and how long workers are at the workplace. **Flextime** allows workers to determine their starting and ending hours in a given workday; for example, they might arrive between 7:00 and 9:30 A.M. and leave between 3:00 and 5:30 P.M. The idea spread from Germany, where it originated in 1967, to the European Community and to other countries such as

Switzerland, Japan, New Zealand, and the United States. In Switzerland, 40 percent of the labor force is said to be using the system.[51] Despite its advantages in reducing absenteeism, flextime is not applicable to industries using assembly lines. Flexible work scheduling has also led to compressed workweeks—for example, the four-day week—and job sharing, which allows a position to be filled by more than one person.

In addition to these programs, firms around the world have programs for personal and professional development, such as career counseling and health counseling. All of them are dependent on various factors external and internal to the firm. Of the external factors, the most important are the overall characteristics of the economy and the labor force. Internally, either the programs must fit into existing organizational structures or management must be inclined toward change. In many cases, labor unions have been one of the major resisting forces. Their view is that firms are trying to prevent workers from organizing by allowing them to participate in decision making and management.

The Role of Labor Unions

When two of the world's largest producers of electrotechnology, Swedish Asea and Switzerland's Brown Boveri, merged to remain internationally competitive in a market dominated by a few companies such as General Electric, Siemens, Hitachi, and Toshiba, not everyone reacted positively to the alliance. For tax reasons, headquarters would not be located in Sweden, and this caused the four main Swedish labor unions to oppose the merger. They demanded that the Swedish government exercise its right to veto the undertaking because Swedish workers would no longer have a say in their company's affairs if it were headquartered elsewhere. Furthermore, Swedes objected to Brown Boveri's four subsidiaries in South Africa.[52]

This incident is an example of the role labor unions play in the operation of a multinational corporation. It also points up the concerns of local labor unions when they must deal with organizations directed from outside their national borders.

The role of labor unions varies from country to country, often because of local traditions in management-labor relations. The variations include the extent of union power in negotiations and the activities of unions in general. In Europe, especially in the northern European countries, collective bargaining takes place between an employers' association and an umbrella organization of unions, on either a national or a regional basis, establishing the conditions for an entire industry. On the other end of the spectrum, negotiations in Japan are on the company level, and the role of larger scale unions is usually consultative. Another striking difference emerges in terms of the objectives of unions and the means by which they attempt to attain them. In the United Kingdom, for example, union activity tends to be politically motivated and identified with political ideology. In the United States, the emphasis has always been on improving workers' overall quality of life.

Internationalization of business has created a number of challenges for labor unions. The main concerns that have been voiced are: (1) the power of the firm to move production from one country to another if attractive terms are not reached in a particular market; (2) the availability of data, especially financial information, to support unions' bargaining positions; (3) insufficient attention to local issues and problems while focusing on global optimization; and (4) difficulty in being heard by those who eventually make the decisions.[53]

Although all of these concerns are valid, all of the problems anticipated may not develop. For example, transferring production from one country to another in the short term is impossible, and labor strife in the long term may well influence such moves. In order to maintain participation in corporate decision making, unions are taking action individually and across national boundaries as seen in Global Perspective 20.5. Individual unions refer to contracts signed elsewhere when setting the agenda for their own negotiations. Supranational organizations such as the International Trade Secretariats and industry-specific organizations such as the International Metal Workers' Federation exchange information and discuss bargaining tactics. The goal is also to coordinate bargaining with multinational corporations across national boundaries. The International Labor Organization, a specialized agency of the United Nations, has an information bank on multinational corporations' policies concerning wage structures, benefits packages, and overall working conditions.

Human-Resource Policies

The objectives of a human-resource policy pertaining to workers are the same as for management: to anticipate the demand for various skills and to have in place programs that will ensure the availability of employees when needed. For workers, however, the firm faces the problem on a larger scale and does not have, in most cases, an expatriate alternative. This means that, among other things, when technology is transferred for a plant, it has to be adapted to the local workforce.

Global Perspective

20.5
Cooperation Worth Copying

The southern shore of Lake Ontario seems an unlikely spot to fight a border war with Mexico. But it is here that Xerox Corp. and its union, the Amalgamated Clothing and Textile Workers Union of America (ACTWU), have fought the Mexicans to a standoff for more than a decade. Three times since 1982, the 200 workers who put together the wire harnesses for Xerox copiers have been forced to boost quality and cut costs to keep their jobs from going to Mexico, where wage rates are less than $1 an hour.

The result has been an alliance between labor and management that is an experiment in how to continue to provide well-paying factory jobs in the United States in the face of global competition. Working with its union, Xerox is developing what it sees as the factory of the future, the "focus factory," with equipment on wheels so that it can literally be rearranged over the weekend to deliver new products quickly and cheaper than its competitors without sacrificing quality.

By 1982, just before the ACTWU and Xerox began to explore seriously the idea of plant-floor cooperation, Xerox found that it could move this operation to an industrial park near Mexico City and eliminate further jobs in addition to cost savings and meet the competition presented by the

Japanese Canon and Ricoh. The union went to Xerox management and insisted that if employee involvement was to be a reality, the workers should be given a chance to develop a plan to squeeze enough costs (approximately $3 million) out of the operation to make it competitive with Mexico and save the jobs. This was accomplished. Furthermore, the workers argued that while their costs would be higher, the quality of their products was much higher.

The search for cost cuts continues. In late 1989, the company and the union formed the first of what they dubbed the "A-Delta-T" teams to study the actual performance of each work process to try to identify the best possible way that work can be performed in terms of cost. The work-study teams are trying to reduce inventories and streamline production for the just-in-time manufacturing process. The goal is to produce a quality product quicker and cheaper than anyone else in the world in a continuous effort to keep the manufacturing operation in the United States. So far it has been working well. While the efficiencies require fewer people to perform the job, expanding markets for the Xerox products have actually created new jobs.

Source: "Cooperation Worth Copying?" *The Washington Post,* December 13, 1992, H1, H6.

Although most countries have legislation and restrictions concerning the hiring of expatriates, many of them—for example some of the EC countries and some oil-rich Middle Eastern countries—have offset labor shortages by importing large numbers of workers from countries such as Turkey and Jordan. The EC by design allows free movement of labor. A mixture of backgrounds in the available labor pool of course puts a strain on personnel development. As an example, the firm may incur considerable expense to provide language training to employees. In Sweden, a certain minimum amount of language training must be provided for all "guest workers" at the firm's expense.

Bringing a local labor force to the level of competency desired by the firm may also call for changes. As an example, managers at Honda's plant in Ohio encountered a number of problems: Labor costs were 50 percent higher and productivity 10 percent lower than in Japan. Automobiles produced there cost $500 more than the same models made in Japan and then delivered to the United States. Before Honda began to produce the Accord in the United States, it flew 200 workers representing all areas of the factory to Japan to learn to build Hondas the Sayama way and then to teach their coworkers these skills.[54]

Compensation of the workforce is a controversial issue. Of course, payroll expenses must be controlled in order for the firm to remain competitive; on the other hand, the firm must attract in appropriate numbers the type of workers it needs. The compensation packages of U.S.-based multinational companies have come under criticism, especially when their level of compensation is lower in developing countries than the United States. Criticism has occurred even when the salaries or wages paid were substantially higher than the local average.[55]

Comparisons of compensation packages are difficult because of differences in the packages that are shaped by culture, legislation, collective bargaining, taxation, and individual characteristics of the job. In northern Europe, for example, new fathers can accompany their wives on a two-week paternity leave at the employer's expense.

SUMMARY

A business organization is the sum of its human resources. To recruit and retain a pool of effective people for each of its operations requires (1) personnel planning and staffing, (2) training activities, (3) compensation decisions, and (4) attention to labor-management relations.

Firms attract international managers from a number of sources, both internal and external. In the earlier stages of internationalization, recruitment must be external. Later, an internal pool often provides candidates for transfer. The decision then becomes whether to use home-country, host-country, or third-country nationals. If expatriate managers are used, selection policies should focus on competence, adaptability, and personal traits. Policies should also be set for the compensation and career progression of candidates selected for assignment overseas. At the same time, the firm must be attentive to the needs of local managers for training and development.

Labor can no longer be considered as simply services to be bought. Increasingly, workers are taking an active role in the decision making of the firm and in issues related to their own welfare. Various programs are causing dramatic organizational change, not only by enhancing the position of workers but by increasing the productivity of the workforce as well. Workers employed by the firm usually are local, as are the unions that represent them. Their primary concerns in working for a multinational firm are job security and benefits. Unions are therefore cooperating across national boundaries to equalize benefits for workers employed by the same firm in different countries.

Key Terms and Concepts

lingua franca	tax equalization
factual cultural knowledge	education allowance
area expertise	self-management
interpretive cultural knowledge	codetermination
adaptability screening	minority participation
orientation program	work councils
culture shock	quality of work life
expatriate	work redesign programs
base salary	team building
cost of living allowance (COLA)	quality circles
foreign service premium	work scheduling
hardship allowance	flextime
housing allowance	

Questions for Discussion

1. Is a "supranational executive corps," consisting of cosmopolitan individuals of multiple nationalities who would be an asset wherever utilized, a possibility for any corporation?

2. Comment on this statement by Lee Iacocca: "If a guy wants to be a chief executive 25 or 50 years from now, he will have to be well rounded. There will be no more of 'Is he a good lawyer, is he a good marketing guy, is he a good finance guy?' His education and his experience will make him a total entrepreneur in a world that has really turned into one huge market. He better speak Japanese or German, he better understand the history of both of those countries and how they got to where they are, and he better know their economics pretty cold."

3. What additional benefit is brought into the expatriate selection and training process by adaptability screening?

4. Develop general principles that firms could use in dealing with terrorism, apart from pulling out of a given market.

5. A manager with a current base salary of $100,000 is being assigned to Lagos, Nigeria. Assuming that you are that manager, develop a compensation and benefits package for yourself in terms of both salary-related and nonsalary-related items.

6. What accounts for the success of Japanese companies with both American unions and the more ferocious British unions? In terms of the changes that have come about, are there winners or losers among management and workers? Could both have gained?

7. How transferable are quality-of-work-life programs from one market to another? What internal and external variables determine their level of acceptance and success?

8. Develop general policies that the multinational corporation should follow in dealing (or choosing not to deal) with a local labor union.

Recommended Readings

Austin, James. *Managing in Developing Countries*. New York: Free Press, 1990.

Bamber, Greg J., and Russell D. Lansbury, eds. *International and Comparative Industrial Relations*. London, England: Allen & Unwin, 1989.

Black, J. Stewart, Hal B. Gregsen, and Mark E. Mendenhall. *Global Assignments*. San Francisco, CA: Jossey-Bass Publishers, 1992.

Casse, Pierre. *Training for the Multicultural Manager*. Washington, D.C.: SIETAR, 1987.

Dowling, Peter J., and Randall S. Schuler, *International Dimensions of Human Resource Management*. Boston: PWS–Kent, 1990.

Harris, Philip, and Robert T. Moran. *Managing Cultural Differences*. Houston, Tex.: Gulf, 1990.

Hodgetts, Richard, and Fred Luthans. *International Management*. New York: McGraw-Hill, 1991.

Katz, H. C., T. A. Kochum, and R. B. McKersie. *The Transformation of American Industrial Relations*. New York: Basic Books, 1986.

Lewis, Tom, and Robert Jungman, eds. *On Being Foreign: Culture Shock in Short Fiction*. Yarmouth, Maine: Intercultural Press, 1986.

Marquardt, Michael J., and Dean W. Engel. *Global Resource Development*. Englewood Cliffs, NJ: Prentice Hall, 1993.

Mendenhall, Mark, and Gary Oddou. *International Human Resource Management*. Boston: PWS–Kent, 1991.

Pucik, Vladimir, Noel M. Tichy, and Carole K. Barnett. *Globalizing Management: Creating and Leading the Competitive Organization*. New York: John Wiley, 1992.

Notes

1. Herbert G. Heneman and Donald P. Schwab, "Overview of the Personnel/Human Resource Function," in *Perspectives on Personnel/Human Resource Management*, eds. Herbert G. Heneman and Donald P. Schwab (Homewood, Ill.: Irwin, 1986), 3–11.

2. Richard D. Hays, "Expatriate Selection: Insuring Success and Avoiding Failure," *Journal of International Business Studies* 5 (Summer 1974): 25–37.

3. Christopher A. Bartlett and Sumantra Ghoshal, "What Is a Global Manager?" *Harvard Business Review* 70 (September–October 1992): 124–132.

4. Jan van Rosmalen, "Internationalising Heineken: Human Resource Policy in a Growing International Company," *International Management Development* (Summer 1985): 11–13.

5. Floris Majlers, "Inside Unilever: The Evolving Transnational Company," *Harvard Business Review* 70 (September–October 1992): 46–52.

6. Randall S. Schuler, Susan E. Jackson, Peter J. Dowling, and Denice E. Welch, "The Formation of an International Joint Venture: Davidson Instrument Panel," in *International Human Resource Management*, eds. Mark Mendenhall and Gary Oddou (Boston: PWS–Kent, 1991), 83–96.

7. Peter Lorange, "Human Resource Management in Multinational Cooperative Ventures," *Human Resources Management* 25 (Winter 1986): 133–148.

8. Carla Rapoport, "The Switch Is On in Japan," *Fortune*, May 21, 1990, 144.

9. Anders Edstrom and Peter Lorange, "Matching Strategy and Human Resources in Multinational Corporations," *Journal of International Business Studies* 16 (Fall 1985): 125–137.

10. "How Business Is Creating Europe Inc.," *Business Week*, September 7, 1987, 40–41.

11. Rabindra Kanungo and Richard W. Wright, "A Cross-Cultural Comparative Study of Managerial Job Attitudes," *Journal of International Business Studies* 14 (Fall 1983): 115–129.

12. Lawrence G. Franko, "Who Manages Multinational Enterprises?" *Columbia Journal of World Business* 8 (Summer 1973): 30-42.

13. Lester B. Korn, "How the Next CEO Will Be Different," *Fortune,* May 22, 1990, 157-161.

14. Jean E. Heller, "Criteria for Selecting an International Manager," *Personnel* (May-June 1980): 18-22.

15. Walter Kiechel, "Our Person in Pomparippu," *Fortune,* October 17, 1983, 213-218.

16. Richard D. Hays, "Ascribed Behavioral Determinants of Success-Failure among U.S. Expatriate Managers," *Journal of International Business Studies* 2 (Summer 1971): 40-46.

17. Richard Pascale, "Fitting New Employees into the Corporate Culture," *Fortune,* May 28, 1984, 28-40.

18. *Compensating International Executives* (New York: Business International, 1970), 35.

19. Lennie Copeland, "Training Americans to Do Business Overseas," *Training,* July 1984, 22-33.

20. Lee Smith, "Japan's Autocratic Managers," *Fortune,* January 7, 1985, 14-23.

21. "Gauging a Family's Suitability for a Stint Overseas," *Business Week,* April 16, 1979, 127-130.

22. "Global Managing," *The Wall Street Journal Europe,* January 10-11, 1992, 1, 20.

23. Nancy J. Adler, "Expecting International Success: Female Managers Overseas," *Columbia Journal of World Business* 19 (Fall 1984): 79-85.

24. Nancy J. Adler, "Pacific Basin Managers: A Gaijin, Not a Woman," *Human Resource Management* 26 (Summer 1987): 169-191.

25. "Gauging a Family's Suitability for a Stint Overseas."

26. Rosalie Tung, "Selection and Training of Personnel for Overseas Assignments," *Columbia Journal of World Business* 16 (Spring 1981): 68-78.

27. L. Robert Kohls, *Survival Kit for Overseas Living* (Yarmouth, Maine: Intercultural Press, 1979), 62-68.

28. Harvey Iglarsh, "Terrorism and Corporate Costs," *Terrorism* 10 (Fall 1987): 22-25.

29. Data provided by Pinkerton Risk Assessment Services, April 22, 1993.

30. Lynn Brenner, "How to Insure Against Political Risk," *Institutional Investor,* April 1981, 4-8.

31. Mary Helen Frederick, "Keeping Safe," *International Business,* October, 1992, 68-69.

32. Nancy J. Adler, *International Dimensions of Organizational Behavior* (Boston: PWS-Kent, 1990), Chapter 4.

33. Michael G. Harvey, "The Other Side of Foreign Assignments: Dealing with the Repatriation Dilemma," *Columbia Journal of World Business* 16 (Spring 1981): 79-85.

34. Lisa Miller Mesdag, "Are You Underpaid?" *Fortune,* March 19, 1984, 20-25.

35. Raymond J. Stone, "Compensation: Pay and Perks for Overseas Executives," *Personnel Journal* (January 1986): 64-69.

36. "Americans Lead the HK Perks Race," *Sunday Morning Post,* July 12, 1992, 14.

37. *1987 Professional Development Seminar: International Compensation* (Phoenix, Ariz.: American Compensation Association, 1987), module 1.

38. Brian Toyne and Robert J. Kuhne, "The Management of the International Executive Compensation and Benefits Process," *Journal of International Business Studies* 14 (Winter 1983): 37-49.

39. U.S. Department of State, *Indexes of Living Costs Abroad, Quarters Allowances, and Hardship Differentials,* January 1993, Table 1.

40. "How to Make a Foreign Job Pay," *Business Week,* December 23, 1985, 84-85.

41. *1987 Professional Development Seminar: International Compensation,* modules 4 and 5.

42. Industrial Democracy in Europe International Research Group, *Industrial Democracy in Europe* (Oxford, England: Clarendon Press, 1981), Chapter 14.

43. Osmo A. Wiio, *Yritysdemokratia ja Muuttuva Yhteiskunta* (Tapiola, Finland: Weilin+Goos, 1970), chapter 13.

44. E. B. Hoffman, "The German Way of Industrial Relations—Could We, Should We, Import It?" *Across the Board,* October 1977, 38-47.

45. Richard D. Robinson, *Internationalization of Business* (Hinsdale, Ill.: Dryden, 1986), Chapter 3.

46. Herman Gadon, "Making Sense of Quality of Work Life Programs," *Business Horizons* 27 (January-February 1984): 42-46.

47. Antone Alber, "The Costs of Job Enrichment," *Business Horizons* 22 (February 1984): 60-72.

48. Faye Rice, "America's New No. 4 Automaker—Honda," *Fortune,* October 28, 1985, 26-29.

49. Pehr G. Gyllenhammar, "How Volvo Adapts Work to People," *Harvard Business Review* 55 (July-August 1977): 24-28.

50. Joe Kelly and Kamran Khozan, "Participative Management: Can It Work?" *Business Horizons* 23 (August 1980): 74-79.

51. Robert J. Kuhne and Courtney O. Blair, "Flexitime," *Business Horizons* 21 (April 1978): 39-51.

52. *Helsingin Sanomat,* "Asean Ammattiliitot Vaativat Suuryhtyman Paapaikkaa Ruotsiin," September 16, 1987, 34.

53. S. B. Prasad and Y. Krishna Shetty, *An Introduction to Multinational Management* (Englewood Cliffs, N.J.: Prentice-Hall, 1976), Appendix 8-A.

54. Rice, "America's New No. 4 Automaker—Honda."

55. Oliver Williams, "Who Cast the First Stone?" *Harvard Business Review* 62 (September-October 1984): 151-160.

Organization and Control in International Operations

LEARNING OBJECTIVES

1. To describe alternative organizational structures for international operations.

2. To highlight factors affecting decisions about the structure of international organizations.

3. To indicate roles for country organizations in the development of strategy and implementation of programs.

4. To outline the need for and challenges of controls in international operations.

When Going Global Means "Move 'Em Out"

Going global has recently meant transferring world headquarters of important business units abroad. Multinational corporations are making these moves, despite some significant risks, because they want to operate near key customers and tough rivals in fast-changing markets far from home. More businesses recognize that they cannot manage worldwide operations from a single location, and experts predict that maybe 50 percent of Fortune 500 companies will be making such moves in the next 10 years. Relocated companies hope to gain power by acquiring an image of "a global firm with a global reach." Companies also hope that these moves help to break down parochialism and groom global managers. Some of the major moves are summarized in the table below.

In the fall of 1992, AT&T moved headquarters of its traditional corded-telephone business to France from Parsippany, N.J. It marked the first overseas move by a unit of AT&T, whose ranks of non–U.S. workers have jumped to 50,000 from 50 ten years ago. By 1995, several major AT&T units probably will have their headquarters abroad, according to the company.

Going the other direction, Hyundai Electronics Industries moved it personal computer division to San Jose, California, from Seoul, South Korea, so it could compete better in that industry's biggest market. The unit has complete autonomy in setting strategies and managing day-to-day operations, quite necessary if the unit is to respond to rapid changes in the U.S. market.

"The name of the game is to get closer to the customer and to understand the customer," says Jack Malloy, a DuPont senior vice president. In addition to having its agricultural-products division moved to Geneva, the company moved its worldwide electronics operations from the United States to Tokyo to be nearer its big base of Asian customers.

In some cases, however, the difficulty of overseeing units based thousands of miles away has led corporations to bring the business home. Cadbury Schweppes PLC moved the global headquarters of its beverage division back to London from Stamford, Connecticut. Cadbury officials say the return "allows our group chief executive to have his top managers around him; there were too many people commuting around the globe before."

Company	Home Country	New Location	Operation Shifted	Year Moved
AT&T	U.S.	France	Corded telephones	1992
DuPont	U.S.	Japan	Electronics	1992
Hyundai Electronics Industries	South Korea	U.S.	Personal computers	1992
IBM	U.S.	U.K.	Networking systems	1991
Siemens	Germany	U.K.	Air-traffic management	1991
Siemens	Germany	U.S.	Ultrasound equipment	
1991DuPont	U.S.	Switzerland	Agriculture products, and parts of fibers and polymers businesses	1991
Hewlett-Packard	U.S.	France	Desktop personal computers	1990
Siemens	Germany	U.S.	Nuclear-medicine products and radiation-therapy equipment	1989
Cadbury Schweppes	U.K.	U.S.	Beverages	1987*
DuPont	U.S.	Switzerland	Lycra business	1987

*Moved back to London in 1991.
Note: Every relocated operation previously had its headquarters in same country as parent company.

Source: "So Big," *Across the Board* 30 (January/February 1993): 16–21; "Firms Ship Unit Headquarters Abroad," *The Wall Street Journal*, December 9, 1992, B1, B8; "Made in the U.S.A. . . . By Hyundai," *Business Week*, October 26, 1992, 96; and "IBM Goes to Europe," *Fortune*, January 14, 1992, 107.

As companies evolve from purely domestic to multinational, their organizational structure and control systems must change to reflect new strategies. With growth comes diversity in terms of products and services, geographic markets, and people in the company itself, bringing along a set of challenges for the company. Two critical issues are basic to all of these challenges: (1) the type of organization that provides the best framework for developing worldwide strategies and maintaining flexibility with respect to individual markets and operations, and (2) the type and degree of control to be exercised from headquarters to maximize total effort. To achieve the optimum impact in these decision areas may result in dramatic decisions, such as transferring world headquarters abroad, as seen in the chapter's opening vignette.

This chapter will focus on the advantages and disadvantages of various organizational structures, as well as their appropriateness at different stages of internationalization. A determining factor is where decision-making authority within the organizational structure will be placed. Also, the roles of the different entities that make up the organization need to be defined. The chapter will also outline the need for devising a control system to oversee the international operations of the company, emphasizing the additional control instruments needed beyond those used in domestic business and the control strategies of multinational corporations. The appropriateness and eventual cost of the various control approaches will vary as the firm expands its international operations. The overall objective of the chapter is to study the intraorganizational relationships critical to the firm's attempt to optimize its competitiveness.

ORGANIZATIONAL STRUCTURE

The basic functions of an organization are to provide (1) a route and locus of decision making and coordination and (2) a system for reporting and communications. Authority and communication networks are typically depicted in the organizational chart.

Organizational Designs

The basic configurations of international organizations correspond to those of purely domestic ones; the greater the degree of internationalization, the more complex the structures can become. The types of structures that companies use to manage foreign activities can be divided into three categories, based on the degree of internationalization:

1. Little or no formal organizational recognition of international activities of the firm. This category ranges from domestic operations handling an occasional international transaction on an ad hoc basis to firms with separate export departments.
2. International division. Firms in this category recognize the ever-growing importance of the international involvement.
3. Global organizations. These can be structured by product, area, function, process, or customer.

Hybrid structures may exist as well, in which one market may be structured by product, another by areas. Matrix organizations have merged in large multinational corporations to combine products, regional, and functional expertise. As worldwide competition has increased dramatically in many industries, the latest organizational response is networked global organizations in which heavy flows of hardware, software, and human ware take place between strategically interdependent units to establish greater global integration.

Little or No Formal Organization

In the very early stages of international involvement, domestic operations assume responsibility for international activities. The role of international activities in the sales and profits of the corporation is initially so minor that no organizational adjustment takes place. No consolidation of information or authority over international sales is undertaken or is necessary. Transactions are conducted on a case-by-case basis, either by the resident expert or quite often with the help of facilitating agents, such as freight forwarders.

As demand from the international marketplace grows and interest within the firm expands, the organizational structure will reflect it. As shown in Figure 21.1, an export department appears as a separate entity. This may be an outside export management company—that is, an independent company that becomes the de facto export department of the firm. This is an indirect approach to international involvement in that very little experience is accumulated within the firm itself. Alternatively, a firm may establish its own export department, hiring a few seasoned individuals to take responsibility for international activities. Organizationally, the department may be a subdepartment of marketing (alternative b in Figure 21.1) or may have equal ranking with the various functional departments (alternative a). This choice will depend on the importance assigned to overseas activities by the firm. Because the export department is the first real step toward internationalizing the organizational structures, it should be a full-fledged marketing organization and not merely a sales organization.

Licensing as an international entry mode may be assigned to the R&D function despite its importance to the overall international strategy of the firm. A formal liaison among the export, marketing, production, and R&D functions has to be formed for the maximum utilization of licensing.[1] If licensing indeed becomes a major activity for the firm, a separate manager should be appointed.

The more the firm becomes involved in foreign markets, the more quickly the export department structure will become obsolete. For example, the firm may un-

FIGURE 21.1   **The Export Department Structure**

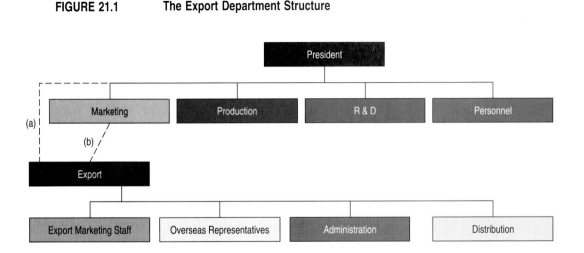

dertake joint ventures or direct foreign investment, which require those involved to have functional experience. The firm therefore typically establishes an international division.

Some firms that acquire foreign production facilities pass through an additional stage in which foreign subsidiaries report directly to the president or to a manager specifically assigned this duty.[2] However, the amount of coordination and control that are required quickly establish the need for a more formal international organization in the firm.

The International Division   The international division centralizes in one entity, with or without separate incorporation, all of the responsibility for international activities, as illustrated in Figure 21.2. The approach aims to eliminate a possible bias against international operations that may exist if domestic divisions are allowed to serve international customers independently. In some cases, international markets have been found to have been treated as secondary to domestic markets. The international division concentrates international expertise, information flows concerning foreign market opportunities, and authority over international activities. However, manufacturing and other related functions remain with the domestic divisions in order to take advantage of economies of scale.

To avoid putting the international division at a disadvantage in competing for products, personnel, and corporate services, coordination between domestic and international operations is necessary. Coordination can be achieved through a joint staff or by requiring domestic and international divisions to interact in strategic planning and to submit the plans to headquarters. Further, many corporations require and encourage frequent interaction between domestic and international personnel to discuss common problems in areas such as product planning. At Loctite Corporation, for example, coordination is also important because domestic operations are typically organized along product or functional lines, whereas international divisions are geographically oriented.

International divisions best serve firms with few products that do not vary significantly in terms of their environmental sensitivity and with international sales and profits that are still quite insignificant compared with those of the domestic divisions.[3] Companies may outgrow their international divisions as their international

FIGURE 21.2   **The International Division Structure**

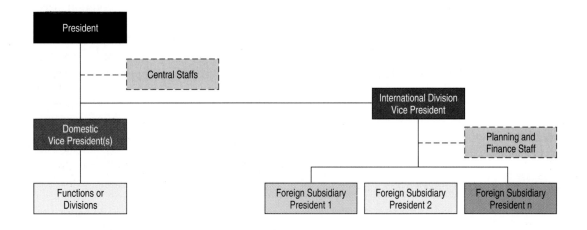

sales grow in significance, diversity, and complexity. A number of U.S.-based companies in the 1970s shifted from a traditional organizational structure with an independent international division to entities built around worldwide or global structures with no differentiation between "domestic" and "international" operations.[4]

Size in itself is not a limitation on the use of the international division structure. Some of the world's largest corporations rely on international divisions.[5] The management of these companies believes that specialization is needed, primarily in terms of the environment.

Global Organizational Structures

Global structures have grown out of competitive necessity. In many industries, competition is on a global basis, with the result that companies must have a high degree of reactive capability. European firms have traditionally had a global structure because of the relatively small size of their domestic markets. N.V. Philips, for example, never could have grown to its current prominence by relying on the Dutch market.

Six basic types of global structures are available:

1. Global product structure, in which product divisions are responsible for all manufacture and marketing worldwide.
2. Global area structure, in which geographic divisions are responsible for all manufacture and marketing in their respective areas.
3. Global functional structures, in which such functional areas as production, marketing, finance, and personnel are responsible for the worldwide operations of their own functional area.
4. Global customer structures, in which operations are structured based on distinct worldwide customer groups.
5. Mixed—or hybrid—structures, which may combine the other alternatives.
6. Matrix structures, in which operations have reporting responsibility to more than one group (typically, product, functions, or area).

Product Structure The **product structure** is the one most often used by multinational corporations.[6] This approach gives worldwide responsibility to strategic business units for the marketing of their product lines, as shown in Figure 21.3. Most consumer-product firms utilize some form of this approach, mainly because of the diversity of their products. One of the major benefits of the approach is improved cost efficiency through centralization of manufacturing facilities. This is crucial in industries in which competitive position is determined by world market share, which in turn is often determined by the degree to which manufacturing is rationalized.[7] Adaptation to this approach may cause problems because it is usually accompanied by consolidation of operations and plant closings. A good example is Black & Decker, which in the mid-1980s rationalized many of its operations in its worldwide competitive effort against Makita, the Japanese power-tool manufacturer. Similarly, Goodyear reorganized itself in 1988 into a single global organization with a complete business-team approach for tires and general products. The move was largely prompted by tightening worldwide competition.[8]

Other benefits of the product structure are the ability to balance the functional inputs needed for a product and the ability to react quickly to product-specific problems in the marketplace. Even smaller brands receive individual attention. Product-specific attention is important because products vary in terms of the adaptation they need for different foreign markets. All in all, the product approach is ideally suited to the development of a global strategic focus in response to global competition.

FIGURE 21.3   **The Global Product Structure**

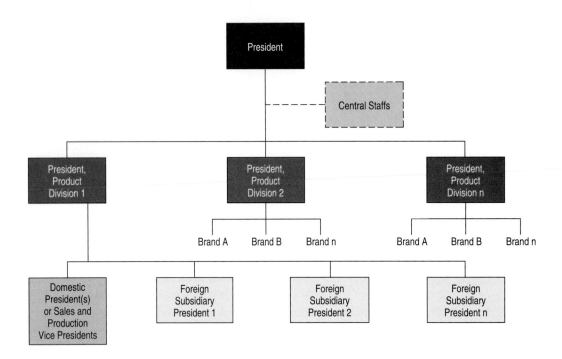

A truckload of tires from
Vienna arrives in Budapest,
site of Goodyear's first sales
office in central Europe.
Source: Peter Korniss/Black Star

At the same time, this structure fragments international expertise within the firm
because a central pool of international experience no longer exists. The structure
assumes that managers will have adequate regional experience or advice to allow
them to make balanced decisions. Coordination of activities among the various product groups operating in the same markets is crucial in order to avoid unnecessary
duplications of basic tasks. For some of these tasks, such as market research, special
staff functions may be created and then filled by the product divisions when needed.
If they lack an appreciation for the international dimension, product managers may

FIGURE 21.4   **The Global Area Structure**

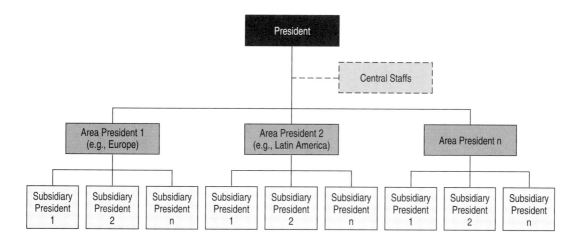

focus their attention only on the larger markets, or only on the domestic, and fail to take the long-term view.

Area Structure   The approach adopted second most frequently is the **area structure,** illustrated in Figure 21.4. Such firms are organized on the basis of geographical areas; for example, operations may be divided into those dealing with North America, the Far East, Latin America, and Europe. Regional aggregation may play a major role in this structuring; for example, many multinational corporations have located their European headquarters in Brussels, where the EC has its headquarters. In the case of Campbell Soup Co. the inevitability of a North American trading bloc led to the creation of the North American division in 1990, which replaced the U.S. operation as the power center of the company.[9] Similarly, many U.S. companies have their headquarters for Latin American operations in Miami. Ideally, no special preference is given to the region in which the headquarters is located—for example, North America or Europe. Central staffs are responsible for providing coordination support for worldwide planning and control activities performed at headquarters.

The area approach follows the marketing concept most closely because individual areas and markets are given concentrated attention. If market conditions with respect to product acceptance and operating conditions vary dramatically, the area approach is the one to choose. Companies opting for this alternative typically have relatively narrow product lines with similar end uses and end users. However, expertise is needed in adapting the product and its marketing to local market conditions. Once again, to avoid duplication of effort in product management and in functional areas, staff specialists—for product categories, for example—may be used.

Without appropriate coordination from the staff, essential information and experience may not be transferred from one regional entity to another. Also, if the company expands its product lines and if end markets begin to diversify, the area structure may become inappropriate.

Functional Structure   Of all the approaches, the **functional structure** is the simplest from the administrative viewpoint because it emphasizes the basic tasks of the firm—for example, manufacturing, sales, and research and development. This ap-

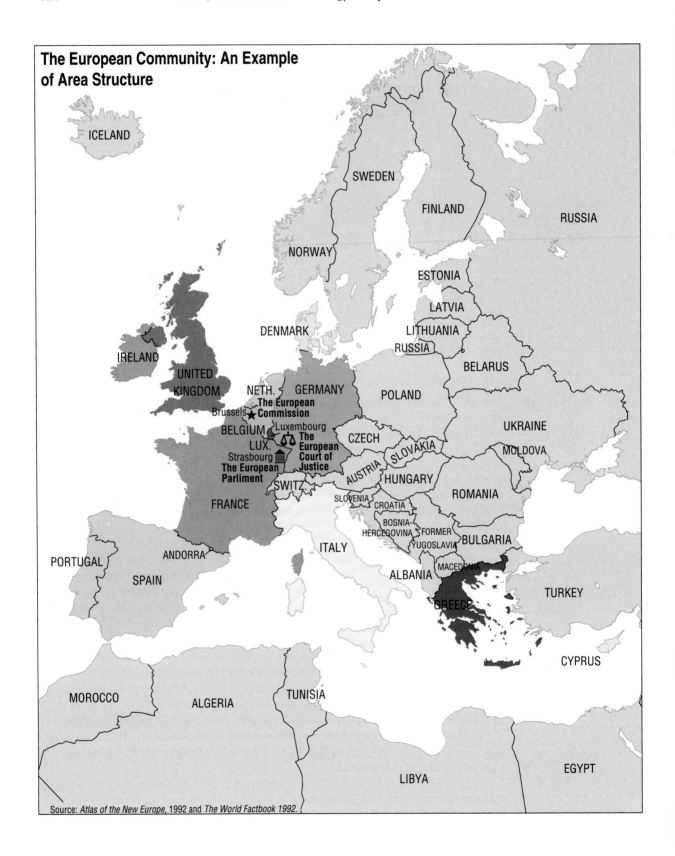

The European Community: An Example of Area Structure

Source: *Atlas of the New Europe*, 1992 and *The World Factbook 1992*.

FIGURE 21.5   **The Global Functional Structure**

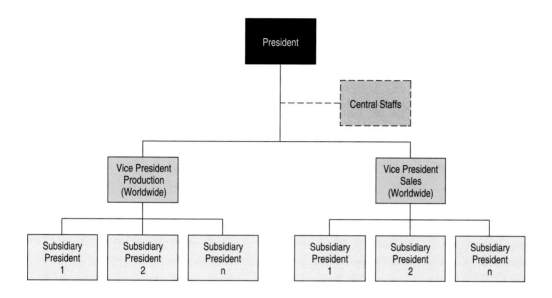

proach, illustrated in Figure 21.5, works best when both products and customers are relatively few and similar in nature. Because coordination is typically the key problem, staff functions have been created to interact between the functional areas. Otherwise, the company's marketing and regional expertise may not be exploited to the fullest extent possible.

A variation of this approach is one that uses processes as a basis for structure. The **process structure** is common in the energy and mining industries, where one corporate entity may be in charge of exploration worldwide and another may be responsible for the actual mining operation.

Customer Structure   Firms may also organize their operations using the **customer structure,** especially if the customer groups they serve are dramatically different—for example, consumers and businesses and governments. Catering to these diverse groups may require concentrating specialists in particular divisions. The product may be the same, but the buying processes of the various customer groups may differ. Governmental buying is characterized by bidding, in which price plays a larger role than when businesses are the buyers.

Mixed Structure   In some cases, mixed, or hybrid, organizations exist. A **mixed structure,** such as the one shown in Figure 21.6, combines two or more organizational dimensions simultaneously. It permits adequate attention to product, area, or functional needs as it is needed by the company. This approach may only be a result of a transitional period after a merger or an acquisition, or it may come about due to a unique customer group or product line (such as military hardware). It may also provide a useful structure before the implementation of the matrix structure.[10]

Naturally, organizational structures are never as clear-cut and simple as presented here. Whatever the basic format, product, functional, and area inputs are needed. Alternatives could include an initial product structure that would subsequently have regional groupings or an initial regional structure with subsequent product group-

FIGURE 21.6   **The Global Mixed Structure**

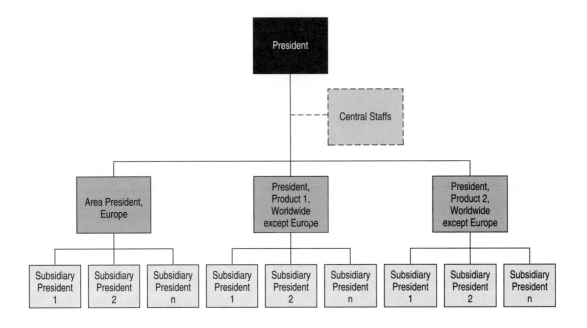

FIGURE 21.7   **The Global Matrix Structure at N.V. Philips**

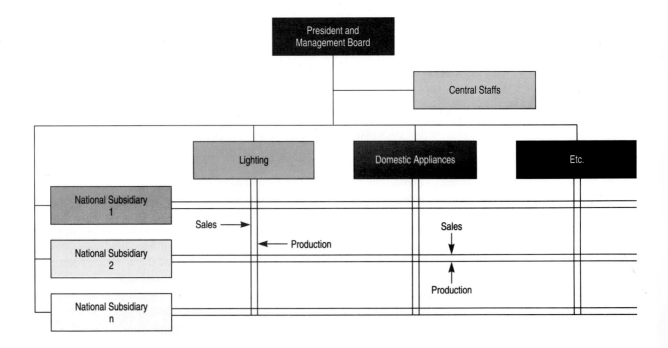

ings. However, in the long term, coordination and control across such structures become tedious.

Matrix Structure   Many multinational corporations, in an attempt to facilitate planning for, organizing, and controlling interdependent businesses, critical resources, strategies, and geographic regions, have adopted the **matrix structure.**[11] Eastman Kodak shifted from a functional organization to a matrix system based on business units. Business is driven by a worldwide business unit (for example, photographic products or commercial and information systems) and implemented by a geographic unit (for example, Europe or Latin America). The geographical units, as well as their country subsidiaries, serve as the "glue" between autonomous product operations.[12]

Organizational matrices integrate the various approaches already discussed, as the N.V. Philips example in Figure 21.7 indicates. The matrix manager will have functional, product, and resource managers reporting to him or her. The whole approach is based on team building and multiple command, with each manager specializing in his or her own area of expertise. The matrix approach will provide a mechanism for cooperation between country managers, business managers, and functional managers on a worldwide basis through increased communication, control, and attention to balance in the organization.

Matrices vary in terms of their number of dimensions. For example, Dow Chemical's three-dimensional matrix consists of five geographic areas, three major functions (marketing, manufacturing, and research), and more than 70 products. The matrix approach helps cut through enormous organizational complexities in making business managers, functional managers, and strategy managers cooperate. However, the matrix requires sensitive, well-trained middle managers who can cope with problems that arise from reporting to two bosses—for example, a product-line manager and an area manager. At 3M, for example, every management unit has some sort of multidimensional reporting relationship, which may cross functional, regional, or operational lines. On a regional basis, group managers in Europe, for example, report administratively to a vice president of operations for Europe. But functionally, they report to group vice presidents at headquarters in MinneapolisSt. Paul.[13] The functioning of the matrix structure at ABB is highlighted in Global Perspective 21.1.

Many companies have found the matrix arrangement problematic.[14] The dual reporting channel easily causes conflict, complex issues are forced into a two-dimensional decision framework, and even minor issues may have to be solved through committee discussion. Ideally, managers should solve these problems themselves through formal and informal communication; however, physical and psychic distance often make that impossible. The matrix structure, with its inherent complexity, may actually increase the reaction time of a company, a potentially serious problem when competitive conditions require quick responses.

Evolution of Organizational Structures   Companies have been shown to develop new structures in a pattern of stages as their products diversify and share of foreign sales increases.[15] At the first stage are autonomous subsidiaries reporting directly to top management; these are followed by the establishment of an international division. As product diversity and the importance of the foreign marketplace increase, companies develop global structures to coordinate subsidiary operations and rationalize worldwide production. As multinational corporations have been faced with simultaneous pressures to adapt to local market conditions and to rationalize production and globalize competitive reactions, many have opted for the matrix struc-

Global Perspective

21.1
The Organizing Logic of ABB

ABB Asea Brown Boveri is a global organization of staggering proportions. From the Zurich headquarters of this $25 billion electrical engineering giant, Swedish, German, and Swiss managers shuffle assets around the globe, keep the books in U.S. dollars, and conduct most of their business in English. Yet the companies that make up the far-flung operations tailor ABB's turbines, transformers, robots, and high-speed trains to local markets so successfully that ABB looks like an established domestic player everywhere.

To a large extent, this can be credited to the company's organization. Although ABB Asea Brown Boveri is a global organization of tremendous business diversity, its organizing principles are stark in their simplicity. Along one dimension, the company is a global network. Executives around the world make decisions on product strategy and performance without regard for national borders. Along a second dimension, it is a collection of traditionally organized national companies, each serving its home market as effectively as possible. ABB's global matrix holds the two dimensions together.

At the top of the company sit CEO Percy Barnevik and 12 colleagues on the executive committee. The group, which meets every three weeks, is responsible for ABB's global strategy and performance. The executive committee consists of Swedes, Swiss, Germans, and Americans. Several members of the executive committee are based outside Zurich, and their meetings are held around the world.

Reporting to the executive committee are leaders of the 50 or so business areas (BAs), located worldwide, into which the company's products and services are divided. The BAs are grouped into 8 business segments, for which different members of the executive committee are responsible. For example, the "industry" segment, which sells components, systems, and software to automate industrial processes, has 5 BAs, including metallurgy, drives, and process engineering. The BA leaders report to Gerhard Schulmeyer, a German member of the executive committee who works out of Stamford, Connecticut.

Each BA has a leader responsible for optimizing the business on a global basis. The BA leader devises and champions a global strategy, holds factories around the

world to cost and quality standards, allocates export markets to each factory, and shares expertise by rotating people across borders, creating mixed-nationality teams to solve problems, and building a culture of trust and communication. The BA leader for power transformers, who is responsible for 25 factories in 16 countries, is a Swede who works out of Mannheim, Germany. The BA leader for instrumentation is British. The BA leader for electric metering is an American based in North Carolina.

Similarly, country organizations may be assigned as worldwide centers of excellence for a particular product category, for example, ABB Strömberg in Finland for electric drives, a category in which it is a recognized world leader.

Alongside the BA structure sits a country structure. ABB's operations in the developed world are organized as national enterprises with presidents, balance sheets, income statements, and career ladders. In Germany, for example, Asea Brown Boveri Aktiengesellschaft, ABB's national company, employs 36,000 people and generates annual revenues of more than $4 billion. The managing director of ABB Germany, Eberhard von Koerber, plays a role comparable to that of a traditional German CEO. He reports to a supervisory board whose members include German bank representatives and trade union officials. His company produces financial statements comparable to those from any other German company and participates fully in the German apprenticeship program.

The BA structure meets the national structure at the level of ABB's member companies. Percy Barnevik advocates strict decentralization. Wherever possible, ABB creates separate companies to do the work of the 50 business areas in different countries. For example, ABB does not merely sell industrial robots in Norway. Norway has an ABB robotics company charged with manufacturing robots, selling to and servicing domestic customers, and exporting to markets allocated by the BA leader.

There are 1,100 such local companies around the world. Their presidents report to two bosses—the BA leader, who is usually located outside the country, and the president of the national company of which the local company is a subsidiary. Both global and local concerns have to be addressed at this intersection.

Sources: "The Euro-Gospel According to Percy Barnevik," *Business Week,* July 23, 1990, 64–66; "The Stateless Corporation," *Business Week,* May 14, 1990, 98–106; William Taylor, "The Logic of Global Business," *Harvard Business Review* 68 (March–April 1990): 91–105

ture.[16] The matrix structure probably allows a corporation to best meet the challenges of global markets (to be global and local, big and small, decentralized with centralized reporting) by allowing the optimizing of businesses globally and maximizing performance in every country of operation.[17] The evolutionary process is summarized in Figure 21.8.

Locus of Decision Making

Organizational structures themselves do not indicate where the authority for decision making and control rests within the organization. If subsidiaries are granted a high degree of autonomy, the system is called **decentralization.** In decentralized systems, controls are relatively loose and simple, and the flows between headquarters and subsidiaries are mainly financial; that is, each subsidiary operates as a profit center. On the other hand, if controls are tight and the strategic decision making concentrated at headquarters, the system is described as **centralization.** Firms are typically neither completely centralized nor decentralized; for example, some functions of the firm—such as finance—lend themselves to more centralized decision making; others—such as promotional decisions—do so far less. Research and development in organizations is typically centralized, especially in cases of basic research work. Some companies have, partly due to governmental pressures, added R&D functions on a regional or local basis. In many cases, however, variations are product and market based; for example, Corning Glass Work's TV tube marketing strategy requires global decision making for pricing and local decision making for service and delivery.

The basic advantage of allowing maximum flexibility at the subsidiary level is that subsidiary management knows its market and can react to changes more quickly. Problems of motivation and acceptance are avoided when decision makers are also the implementers of the strategy. On the other hand, many multinationals faced with global competitive threats and opportunities have adopted global strategy formulation, which by definition requires a higher degree of centralization. What has emerged as a result can be called **coordinated decentralization.** This means that overall

**FIGURE 21.8
Evolution of
International Structures**

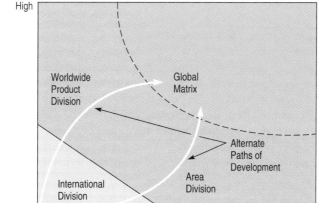

Source: From Christopher A. Bartlett, "Building and Managing the Transnational: The New Organizational Challenge," in *Competition in Global Industries*, ed. Michael E. Porter (Boston: Harvard Business School Press, 1986), 368

corporate strategy is provided from headquarters, while subsidiaries are free to implement it within the range agreed on in consultation with headquarters.

Factors Affecting Structure and Decision Making

The organizational structure and locus of decision making in a multinational corporation are determined by a number of factors, such as (1) its degree of involvement in international operations, (2) the products the firm markets, (3) the size and importance of the firm's markets, and (4) the human-resource capability of the firm.[18]

The effect of the degree of involvement on structure and decision making was discussed earlier in the chapter. With low degrees of involvement, subsidiaries can enjoy high degrees of autonomy as long as they meet their profit targets. The same situation can occur even with the most globally oriented companies, but within a different framework. Consider, for example, the North American Philips Corporation, a separate entity from the Dutch Philips, which enjoys independent status in terms of local policy-setting and managerial practices but is still, nevertheless, within the parent company's planning and control system.

The firm's country of origin and the political history of the area can also affect organizational structure and decision making. For example, Swiss-based Nestlé, with only 3 to 4 percent of its sales from its small domestic market, has traditionally had a highly decentralized organization. Moreover, European history for the past 75 years—particularly the two world wars—has often forced subsidiaries of European-based companies to act independently to survive.

The type and variety of products marketed will affect organizational decisions. Companies that market consumer products typically have product organizations with high degrees of decentralization, allowing for maximum local flexibility. On the other hand, companies that market technologically sophisticated products—such as GE, which markets turbines—display centralized organizations with worldwide product responsibilities. Even within matrix organizations, one of the dimensions may be granted more say in decisions; for example, at Dow Chemical, geographical managers have been granted more authority than other managers.

Apart from situations requiring the development of an area structure for an organization, the characteristics of certain markets or regions may require separate arrangements for the firm. For many Japanese and European companies, the North American market has been given priority, manifested by direct organizational links to top management at headquarters.

The human factor in any organization is critical. Management personnel both at headquarters and in the subsidiaries have to bridge the physical and psychic distances separating them. If subsidiaries have competent management that does not have to rely on headquarters consultation to solve the majority of its problems, they may be granted high degrees of autonomy. In the case of global organizations, subsidiary management has to understand the corporate culture of the firm to be an efficient part of the corporation, especially when decisions are called for that are not optimum for the local market but meet the long-term objectives of the firm as a whole.

The Networked Global Organization

There seems to be no ideal international structure, and some have challenged the wisdom of even looking for one. They have recommended attention to new processes that would, in a given structure, help to develop new perspectives and attitudes that reflect and respond to the complex, opposing demands of global integration and local responsiveness.[19] The question thus changes from which structural alternative is best to how the different perspectives of various corporate entities can better be taken into account when making decisions. In structural terms, nothing may change. As a matter of fact, Philips has not changed its basic matrix structure, although it has made major changes in how it conducts its internal relations.[20] It went from a decentralized federation model to a networked global organization, the effects of which are depicted in Figure 21.9. The term **glocal** has been coined to describe this approach.[21]

Companies that have adopted the approach have incorporated the following three dimensions into their organizations: (1) the development and communication of a clear corporate vision, (2) the effective management of human-resource tools to broaden individual perspectives and develop identification with corporate goals, and (3) the integration of individual thinking and activities into the broad corporate agenda.[22] The first dimension relates to a clear and consistent long-term corporate mission that guides individuals wherever they work in the organization. Examples of this are Johnson & Johnson's corporate credo of customer focus and NEC's C&C (= computers and communications). The second relates both to the development of global managers who can find opportunities in spite of environmental challenges as well as creating a global perspective among country managers. The last dimension relates to the development of a cooperative mindset among country organizations to ensure effective implementation of global strategies. Managers may feel that global strategies are intrusions on their operations if they do not have an understanding of the corporate vision, if they have not contributed to the global corporate agenda, or if they are not given direct responsibility for its implementation. Defensive, territorial attitudes can lead to the emergence of the **not-invented-here syndrome;** i.e., country organizations objecting to or rejecting an otherwise sound strategy.

The network avoids the problems of effort duplication, inefficiency of operations, and nonacceptance of ideas developed elsewhere by giving subsidiaries the latitude, encouragement, and tools to pursue local business development within the framework of the global strategy. Headquarters considers each unit a source of ideas, skills, capabilities, and knowledge that can be utilized for the benefit of the entire organization. This means that subsidiaries must be upgraded from mere implemen-

**FIGURE 21.9
The Networked Global
Organization**

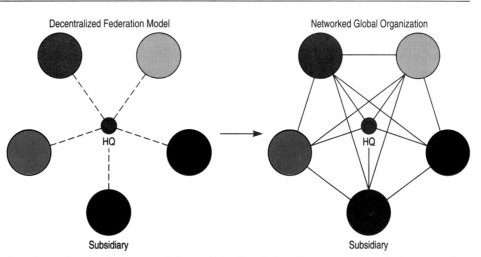

Source: Thomas Gross, Ernie Turner, and Lars Cederholm, "Building Teams for Global Operations," *Management Review*, June 1987 (New York: American Management Association), 34.

tors and adaptors to contributors and partners in the development and execution of worldwide strategies. Efficient plants may be converted into international production centers, innovative R&D units converted into centers of excellence (and thus role models), and leading subsidiary groups given the leadership role in developing new strategies for the entire corporation. At Ford Motor Company, development of a specific car or component is centralized in whichever Ford technical center worldwide has the greatest expertise in that product (see Global Perspective 21.2).

The main tool of implementation used in this approach is international teams of managers who meet regularly to develop strategy. While final direction may come from headquarters, it has been informed of local conditions, and implementation of the strategy is enhanced since local-country managers were involved in its development. This approach has worked even in cases involving seemingly impossible market differences. Both Procter & Gamble and Henkel have successfully introduced

Global Perspective

21.2
Ford's Centers of Excellence

To carry its momentum in the 1990s, Ford is organizing design and engineering teams into centers of excellence. The approach has two goals: to avoid duplicating efforts and to capitalize on the expertise of Ford's specialists.

Located in several countries, the centers will work on key components for cars. One will, for example, work on certain kinds of engines. Another will engineer and develop common platforms—the suspension and other undercarriage components—for similar-sized cars.

Designers in each market will then style exteriors and passenger compartments to appeal to local tastes. Each car will usually be built on the continent where it is to be sold. Ford of Europe is introducing the Mondeo which was designed to replace the 10-year-old Sierra line in Europe in 1993 and the Tempo/Topaz line in the United States in 1994. The U.S. and European versions will have 75 percent common parts, although the U.S. version will be slightly longer and have more chrome. Five Ford design studios had to compromise on design proposals that ranged from a soft and rounded body to a sharply angular one. Although European operations maintained the project leadership, key responsibilities were divided. The U.S. side took over automatic transmissions, with Europe handling the manual.

North America
Dearborn, Michigan
- Platform for cars to replace midsize Taurus, Sable, and Europe's Scorpio
- Six- and eight-cylinder engines
- Air-conditioning systems
- Automatic transmission

Mazda (25% owned by Ford)
Hiroshima, Japan
- Platform for replacement of Escort subcompact, the best-selling car in the world
- Cars smaller than Escort

Ford of Europe
Brentwood, England
- Platform for replacement of North American compacts Tempo and Topaz and Europe's Sierra
- Four-cylinder engines
- Manual transmissions

Asia; Pacific
Melbourne, Australia
- Specialty sports cars, beginning with two-seater Capri
- First introduced in the fall of 1988

Source: "Ford of Europe: Slimmer, But Maybe Not Luckier," *Business Week,* January 18, 1993, 44–46. "Can Ford Stay on Top?", reprinted from September 28, 1987, issue of *Business Week,* pp. 78–86, by special permission, copyright © 1987 by McGraw-Hill, Inc.

pan-European brands for which strategy was developed by European teams. These teams consisted of country managers and staff personnel to smooth eventual implementation and to avoid unnecessarily long and disruptive discussions about the fit of a new product to individual markets.

As can be seen from the discussion, the networked approach is not a structural adaptation but a procedural one, calling for a change in management mentality. It requires adjustment mainly in the coordination and control functions of the firm.

The Role of Country Organizations

Country organizations should be treated as a source of supply as much as a source of demand. Quite often, however, headquarters managers see their role as the coordinators of key decisions and controllers of resources and perceive subsidiaries as implementors and adaptors of global strategy in their respective local markets. Furthermore, they may see all country organizations as the same. This view severely limits utilization of the firm's resources and deprives country managers of the opportunity to exercise their creativity.[23]

The role that a particular country organization can play naturally depends on that market's overall strategic importance as well as its organizational competence. Using these criteria, four different roles emerge (see Figure 21.10).

The role of a **strategic leader** can be played by a highly competent national subsidiary located in a strategically critical market. Such a country organization serves as a partner of headquarters in developing and implementing strategy. Procter & Gamble's Eurobrand teams, which analyze opportunities for greater product and marketing program standardization, are chaired by a brand manager from a "lead country."[24]

**FIGURE 21.10
Roles for Country
Organizations**

Competence of Local Organization

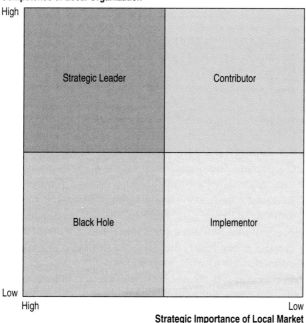

Source: Christopher Bartlett and Sumantra Ghoshal, "Tap Your Subsidiaries for Global Reach," *Harvard Business Review* 64, November–December 1986 (Boston: Harvard Business School Publishing Division), 87–94.

A **contributor** is a country organization with a distinctive competence, such as product development. Increasingly, country organizations are the source of new products. These range from IBM's recent breakthrough in superconductivity research, generated in its Zurich lab, to low-end innovations like Procter & Gamble's liquid Tide, made with a fabric-softening compound developed in Europe.[25]

Implementors provide the critical mass for the international marketing effort. These country organizations may exist in smaller, less-developed countries in which corporate commitment for market development is less. Although most entities are given this role, it should not be slighted, since the implementors provide the opportunity to capture economies of scale and scope that are the basis of a global strategy.

The **black hole** situation is one in which the international marketer has a low-competence country organization—or no organization at all—in a highly strategic market. In strategically important markets such as the European Community, a local presence is necessary to maintain the company's global position and, in some cases, to protect others. One of the major ways of remedying the black hole situation is to enter into strategic alliances. In the 1980s, AT&T, which had long restricted itself to its domestic market, needed to go global fast. Some of the alliances it formed were with Philips in telecommunications and Olivetti in computers and office automation.[26] In some cases, firms may use their presence in a major market as an observation post to keep up with developments before a major thrust for entry is executed.

Depending on the role of the country organization, its relationship with headquarters will vary from loose control based mostly on support to tighter control to ensure that strategies get implemented appropriately. Yet, in each of these cases, it is imperative that country organizations have enough operating independence to cater to local needs and to provide motivation to country managers. For example, an implementor's ideas concerning the development of a regional or global strategy or program should be heard. Strategy formulators should make sure that appropriate implementation can be achieved at the country level.

CONTROL

The function of the organizational structure is to provide a framework in which objectives can be met. A set of instruments and processes is needed, however, to influence the performance of organizational members so as to meet the goals. Controls focus on means to verify and correct actions that differ from established plans. Compliance needs to be secured from subordinates through different means of coordinating specialized and interdependent parts of the organization.[27] Within an organization, control serves as an integrating mechanism. Controls are designed to reduce uncertainty, increase predictability, and ensure that behaviors originating in separate parts of the organization are compatible and in support of common organizational goals despite physical, psychic, and temporal distances.[28]

The critical issue here is the same as with organizational structure: What is the ideal amount of control? On the one hand, headquarters needs controls to ensure that international activities contribute the greatest benefit to the overall organization. On the other hand, they should not be construed as a code of laws and subsequently allowed to stifle local initiative.

This section will focus on the design and functions of control instruments available for international business operations, along with an assessment of their appropriateness. Emphasis will be placed on the degree of formality of controls used by firms.

Types of Controls

Most organizations display some administrative flexibility, as demonstrated by variations in how they apply management directives, corporate objectives, or measurement systems. A distinction should be made, however, between variations that have emerged by design and those that are the result of autonomy. The first are the result of a management decision, whereas the second typically have grown without central direction and are based on emerging practices. In both instances, some type of control will be exercised. Here only controls that result from headquarters initiative rather than those that are the consequences of tolerated practices will be discussed. Firms that wait for self-emerging controls often experience rapid international growth but subsequent problems in product-line performance, program coordination, and strategic planning.[29]

Not all control systems evolve in the way originally envisioned. For example, shifts may be triggered by changes over time in the relative importance of headquarters when compared to the volume of international activity. Such a change was experienced by the Hoover Corporation in its European operations. Initially, the U.S. headquarters control capability was strong; over time, however, the European operations asserted an increasing role in overall corporate planning and control as they grew in importance.

In the design of the control systems, a major decision concerns the object of control. Two major objects are typically identified: output and behavior.[30] Output controls consist of balance sheets, sales data, production data, product-line growth, or a performance review of personnel. Measures of output are accumulated at regular intervals and forwarded from the foreign locale to headquarters, where they are evaluated and critiqued based on comparisons to the plan or budget. Behavioral controls require the exertion of influence over behavior after—or, ideally, before—it leads to action. These can be achieved through the preparation of manuals on such topics as sales techniques, to be made available to subsidiary personnel, or through efforts to fit new employees into the corporate culture.

In order to institute either of these measures, instruments of control have to be decided upon. The general alternatives are either bureaucratic/formalized control or cultural control.[31] Bureaucratic controls consist of a limited and explicit set of regulations and rules that outline the desired levels of performance. Cultural controls, on the other hand, are much less formal and are the results of shared beliefs and expectations among the members of an organization. Table 21.1 provides a schematic explanation of these types of controls and their objectives.

Bureaucratic/Formalized Control   The elements of a bureaucratic/formalized control system are (1) an international budget and planning system, (2) the functional reporting system, and (3) policy manuals used to direct functional performance.

Budgets refers to shorter-term guidelines regarding investment, cash, and personnel policies, while *plans* refers to formalized plans with more than a one-year horizon. The budget and planning process is the major control instrument in headquarters-subsidiary relationships. Although systems and their execution vary, the objective is to achieve as good a fit as possible with the objectives and characteristics of the firm and its environment.

The budgetary period is typically one year, since it is tied to the accounting systems of the multinational. The budget system is used for four main purposes: (1) allocation of funds among subsidiaries, (2) planning and coordination of global production capacity and supplies, (3) evaluation of subsidiary performance, and (4)

**TABLE 21.1
Comparison of
Bureaucratic and
Cultural Control
Mechanisms**

Object of Control	Type of Control	
	Pure Bureaucratic/ Formalized Control	Pure Cultural Control
Output	Formal performance reports	Shared norms of performance
Behavior	Company policies, manuals	Shared philosophy of management

Source: B.R. Baliga and Alfred M. Jaeger, "Multinational Corporations: Control Systems and Delegation Issues," *Journal of International*

**TABLE 21.2
Types of Functional
Reports in Multinational
Corporations**

Type of Report	U.S. MNCs (33)	German MNCs (44)	Japanese MNCs (40)
Balance sheet	97	49	42
Profit and loss statements	91	49	42
Production output	94	50	47
Market share	70	48	31
Cash and credit statement	100	41	39
Inventory levels	88	46	38
Sales per product	88	37	44
Performance review of personnel	9	15	2
Report on local economic and political conditions	33	32	12

Source: Anant R. Negandhi and Martin Welge, *Beyond Theory Z* (Greenwich, Conn.: JAI, 1984), 18.

communication and information exchange among subsidiaries, product organizations, and corporate headquarters.[32] Long-range plans vary dramatically, ranging from two years to ten years in length, and are more qualitative and judgmental in nature. However, shorter periods such as two years are the norm, considering the added uncertainty of diverse foreign environments.

Although firms strive for uniformity, achieving it may be as difficult as trying to design a suit to fit the average person. The processes themselves are very formalized in terms of the schedules to be followed.

Functional reports are another control instrument used by headquarters in managing subsidiary relations. These vary in number, complexity, and frequency. Table 21.2 summarizes the various types of functional reports in a total of 117 multinational corporations in three countries—the United States, Germany, and Japan. The structure and elements of these reports are typically highly standardized to allow for consolidation at the headquarters level.

Since the frequency of reports required from subsidiaries is likely to increase due to globalization trend, it is essential that subsidiaries see the rationale for this often time-consuming exercise. Two approaches, used in tandem, can facilitate this process: participation and feedback. The first refers to avoiding the perception at subsidiary levels that reports are "art for art's sake" by involving the preparers in the actual use of the reports. When this is not possible, feedback about their consequences is warranted. Through this process, communication is enhanced as well.

On the behavioral front, headquarters may want to guide the way in which subsidiaries make decisions and implement agreed-upon strategies. U.S.-based multinationals tend to be far more formalized than their Japanese and European counterparts, with a heavy reliance on manuals for all major functions.[33] These manuals discuss such items as recruitment, training, motivation, and dismissal policies. The use of manuals is in direct correlation with the required level of reports from subsidiaries, discussed in the previous section.

Cultural Control   As seen from the country comparisons, less emphasis is placed outside the United States on formal controls, as they are viewed as too rigid and too quantitatively oriented. Rather, MNCs in other countries emphasize corporate values and culture, and evaluations are based on the extent to which an individual or entity fits in with these norms. Cultural controls require an extensive socialization process to which informal, personal interaction is central. Substantial resources have to be spent to train the individual to share the corporate cultures, or "the way things are done at the company."[34] To build common vision and values, managers spend a substantial share of their first months at Matsushita in what the company calls "cultural and spiritual training." They study the company credo, the "Seven Spirits of Matsushita," and the philosophy of the founder, Konosuke Matsushita. Then they learn how to translate these internalized lessons into daily behavior and operational decisions. Although more prevalent in Japanese organizations, many Western entities have similar programs, such as Philips's "organization cohesion training" and Unilever's "indoctrination."[35]

The primary instruments of cultural control are the careful selection and training of corporate personnel and the institution of self-control. The choice of cultural controls can be justified if the company enjoys a low turnover rate; they are thus applied when companies can offer and expect lifetime or long-term employment, as many firms do in Japan.

In selecting home-country nationals and, to some extent, third-country nationals, MNCs are exercising cultural control. The assumption is that these managers have already internalized the norms and values of the company. For example, only 4 of 3M's 53 managing directors of overseas subsidiaries are local nationals. The company's experience is that nonnationals tend to run a country organization with a more global view. In some cases, the use of headquarters personnel to ensure uniformity in decision making may be advisable; for example, Volvo uses a home-country national for the position of chief financial officer. Expatriates are used in subsidiaries not only for control purposes but also to effect change processes. Companies control the efforts of management specifically through compensation and promotion policies, as well as through policies concerning replacement.

When the expatriate corps is small, headquarters can still exercise its control through other means. Management training programs for overseas managers as well as time at headquarters will indoctrinate individuals as to the company's ways of doing things. For instance, a Chinese executive selected to run Loctite's new operation in China spent two years at the company's headquarters before taking over in Beijing.[36] Similarly, formal visits by headquarters teams (say, for a strategy audit) or informal visits (perhaps to launch a new product) will enhance the feeling of belonging to the same corporate family.

Corporations rarely use one pure control mechanism. Rather, most use both quantitative and qualitative measures. Corporations are likely, however, to place different levels of emphasis on different types of performance measures and on how they are derived.

Exercising Control

Within most corporations, different functional areas are subject to different guidelines because they are subject to different constraints. For example, the marketing function has traditionally been seen as incorporating many more behavioral dimensions than manufacturing or finance. As a result, many multinational corporations employ control systems that are responsive to the needs of the function. Yet such differentiation is sometimes based less on appropriateness than on personalities. It has been hypothesized that manufacturing subsidiaries are controlled more intensively than sales subsidiaries because production more readily lends itself to centralized direction, and technicians and engineers adhere more firmly to standards and regulations than do salespeople.[37]

In their international operations, U.S.-based multinationals place major emphasis on obtaining quantitative data. Although this allows for good centralized comparisons against standards and benchmarks or cross-comparisons among different corporate units, it entails several drawbacks. In the international environment, new dimensions—such as inflation, differing rates of taxation, and exchange rate fluctuations—may distort the performance evaluation of any given individual or organizational unit. For the global corporation, measurement of whether a business unit in a particular country is earning a superior return on investment relative to risk may be irrelevant to the contribution an investment may make worldwide, or to the long-term results of the firm. In the short term, the return may even be negative.[38] Therefore, the control mechanism may quite inappropriately indicate reward or punishment. Standardizing the information received may be difficult if the various environments involved fluctuate and require frequent and major adaptations. Further complicating the issue is the fact that although quantitative information may be collected monthly, or at least quarterly, environmental data may be acquired annually or "now and then," especially when a crisis seems to loom on the horizon. In order to design a control system that is acceptable not only to headquarters but also to the organization and individuals abroad, great care must be taken to use only relevant data. Major concerns, therefore, are the data collection process and the analysis and utilization of data. Evaluators need management information systems that provide for greater comparability and equity in administering controls. The more behaviorally based and culture-oriented controls are, the more care needs to be taken.[39]

In designing a control system, management must consider the costs of establishing and maintaining it versus the benefits to be gained. Any control system will require investment in a management structure and in systems design. Consider, for example, costs associated with cultural controls: Personal interaction, use of expatriates, and training programs are all quite expensive. Yet these expenses may be justified by cost savings through lower employee turnover, an extensive worldwide information system, and an improved control system.[40] Moreover, the impact goes beyond the administrative component. If controls are misguided or too time consuming, they can slow or undermine the strategy implementation process and thus the overall capability of the firm. The result will be lost opportunities or, worse yet, increased threats. In addition, time spent on reporting takes time from everything else, and if the exercise is seen as mundane, results in lowered motivation. A parsimonious design is therefore imperative. The control system should collect all the information required and trigger all the intervention necessary; however, it should lead to the pulling of strings by a puppeteer.

The impact of the environment has to be taken into account as well, in two ways. First, the control system must measure only those dimensions over which the organization has actual control. Rewards or sanctions make little sense if they are based on dimensions that may be relevant to overall corporate performance but over which no influence can be exerted, such as price controls. Neglecting the factor of individual performance capability would send wrong signals and severely harm motivation. Second, control systems have to be in harmony with local regulations and customs. In some cases, however, corporate behavioral controls have to be exercised against local customs even though overall operations may be affected negatively. This type of situation occurs, for example, when a subsidiary operates in markets in which unauthorized facilitating payments are a common business practice.

Corporations are faced with major challenges in appropriate and adequate control systems in today's business environment. Given increased local-government demands for a share in companies established, controls can become tedious, especially if the MNC is a minority partner. Even if the new entity is a result of two companies' joining forces through a merger—such as the one between ASEA and Brown Boveri—or two companies' joining forces to form a new entity—such as NUMMI, established by Toyota and GM—the backgrounds of the partners may be different enough to cause problems in devising the required controls.

SUMMARY

This chapter discussed the structures and control mechanisms needed to operate in the international business field. These elements define relationships between the entities of the firm and provide the channels through which these relationships develop.

International firms can choose from a variety of organizational structures, ranging from a domestic organization that handles ad hoc export orders to a full-fledged global organization. The choice will depend heavily on the degree of internationalization of the firm, the diversity of international activities, and the relative importance of product, area, function, and customer variables in the process. A determining factor is also the degree to which headquarters wants to decide important issues concerning the whole corporation and the subsidiaries individually. Organizations that function effectively still need to be revisited periodically in order to ensure that they remain responsive to a changing environment. Some of this responsiveness is showing up not as structural changes, but rather in how the entities conduct their internal business.

In addition to organization, the control function takes on major importance for multinationals, due to the high variability in performance resulting from divergent local environments and the need to reconcile local objectives with the corporate goal of synergism. While it is important to grant autonomy to country organizations so that they can be responsive to local market needs, it is of equal importance to ensure close cooperation among units to optimize corporate effectiveness.

Control can be exercised through either bureaucratic means emphasizing formal reporting and evaluation of benchmark data or cultural means, in which norms and values are understood by the individuals and entities that make up the corporation. U.S. firms typically rely more on bureaucratic controls, while MNCs from other countries frequently run operations abroad through informal means and rely less on stringent measures.

The implementation of controls requires great sensitivity to behavioral dimensions and the environment. The measurements used must be appropriate and reflective of actual performance rather than marketplace vagaries. Similarly, entities should be judged only on factors over which they have some degree of control.

TABLE 21.3   Organizational and Control Characteristics of Selected Multinational Corporations

Company	Parent Company Characteristics	
	Dominant Organizational Concept	Planning and Control
American Cyanamid Company (U.S.)	Product divisions with global responsibility	Heavy reliance on strategic planning: under guidance of Corporate Planning and Development Department; plans prepared by designated business units; accompanied by annual profit plan: investment priority matrix to facilitate allocation of funds
Ciba-Geigy Limited (Switzerland)	Product divisions with global responsibility, but gradual strengthening of key regional organizations	Moderate reliance on strategic planning by global product divisions: gradual buildup of the role of key regional companies in the planning process; operational plans and capital budgets by country organizations and their product divisions, with the latter playing the more active role
The Dow Chemical Company (U.S.)	Decentralized geographically into five regional companies: central coordination through World Headquarters Group	Coordination of geographic regions through World Headquarters Group, particularly the Corporate Product Department; strategic planning at the corporate level on a product basis, and in the operating units on a regional basis; operational plans and capital budgets by geographic regions; control function at the corporate level
General Electric Company (U.S.)	Product-oriented strategic business units on a worldwide basis	Heavy reliance on strategic planning; under guidance of Corporate Planning and Development Department; plans prepared by designated strategic business units; investment priority matrix to facilitate allocation of funds
Imperial Chemical Industries Limited (U.K.)	Product divisions with global responsibility, but gradual strengthening of regional organizations	Coordination of planning through Central Planning Department; strategic planning and operational planning at the divisional and regional levels; tight financial reporting and control by headquarters
Nestlé S.A. (Switzerland)	Decentralized regional and country organizations	Increasing emphasis on strategic planning, with recent formation of Central Planning and Information Services Department; annual plans (budgets) by each major company; tight financial reporting and control by headquarters
N.V. Philips (The Netherlands)	Product divisions with global responsibility, but gradual strengthening of geographic organizations; U.S. company financially and legally separate from parent	Moderate to heavy reliance on strategic planning by planning units in product divisions, selected national organizations, and Central Planning Department; operational plans by division and national organizations, with initiative from the former; monthly review of performance

Parent Company Characteristics		
Research and/or Product Development	**U.S. Companies: Handling of International Business**	**European Companies: Handling of U.S. Business**
Research and product development activities carried out by product divisions at five separate centers, each concentrating on a particular technology and/or market	Separate international operating divisions organized into two geographic areas; limited authority, serving primarily in staff capacity	(not applicable)
Research and product development activities carried out by domestic product divisions and certain product divisions in key geographic areas	(not applicable)	Dual reporting relationship, with U.S. company reporting directly to headquarters and its local divisions also reporting to their counterpart domestic divisions
Research and development activities heavily process oriented and usually associated with manufacturing facilities reporting to geographic regions; central coordination by World Headquarters Group	Highly decentralized organization of five geographic areas, each with almost complete authority over planning and operations	(not applicable)
Centralized research, with supportive product-development activities at the operating level	International business sector, together with overseas activities in other sectors; nine country strategic business units, which prepare an international integration plan to coordinate activities with product SBUs	(not applicable)
Research and product development carried out by headquarters and selected regional organizations	(not applicable)	U.S. organizations oversees ICI activities in the Americas and reports directly to headquarters; U.S. board has considerable authority regarding local decisions and activities
Highly centralized research, but local product development by regional and country organizations	(not applicable)	U.S. activities divided among three main companies, each with special reporting relationship to headquarters
Highly centralized research, but with product development by product divisions and large national organizations; other research centers located in four key countries	(not applicable)	No formal chain of command between headquarters and U.S. organization; latter operating under direction of U.S. Philips Trust

Company	Parent Company Characteristics	
	Dominant Organizational Concept	Planning and Control
Rhône-Poulenc S.A. (France)	Product divisions with global responsibility, but major country organizations retain special status	Moderate reliance on strategic planning by Central Strategy and Planning Department; in addition, strategic planning at the operational level, primarily by product divisions; operational plans and capital budgets by divisions and country organizations; monthly review of performance
Solvay & Cie S.A. (Belgium)	Product divisions with global responsibility, but national subsidiary organizations allowed to exercise a reasonable degree of autonomy	Increasing emphasis on strategic planning with the recent formation of Central Planning Department; operational plans and capital budgets by country organizations

Source: Rodman Drake and Lee M. Caudill, "Management of the Large Multinational: Trends and Future Challenges," *Business Horizons* 24 (May–June 1981): 88–90. Reprinted with permission. Company information updated by interview, Fall 1990.

Table 21.3 shows how some of the world's most successful multinational corporations deal with the organizational and control issues discussed in this chapter. As can be seen in the table, they use widely varying approaches to achieve an overall balance between control and attention to local conditions.

Key Terms and Concepts

product structure	centralization
area structure	coordinated decentralization
functional structure	glocal
process structure	not-invented-here syndrome
customer structure	strategic leader
mixed structure	contributor
matrix structure	implementor
decentralization	black hole

Questions for Discussion

1. Firms differ, often substantially, in their organizational structures even within the same industry. What accounts for these differences in their approaches?
2. Discuss the benefits gained in adopting a matrix form of organizational structure.
3. What changes in the firm and/or in the environment might cause a firm to abandon the functional approach?
4. Is there more to the "not invented here" syndrome than simply hurt feelings on the part of those who believe they are being dictated to by headquarters?
5. If the purposes of the budget are in conflict, as is sometimes argued, what can be done about it?
6. Performance reviews of subsidiary managers and personnel are required rarely, if at all, by headquarters. Why?

Parent Company Characteristics		
Research and/or Product Development	**U.S. Companies: Handling of International Business**	**European Companies: Handling of U.S. Business**
Research and product development activities carried out by product divisions; several large centers, each focusing on different specializations	(not applicable)	Special reporting relationship directly to headquarters; U.S. company coordinates activities with product divisions at headquarters
Centralized research and product development activities; major national organizations also carry out product development	(not applicable)	U.S. organization functions as legal entity, overseeing Solvay's activities in the United States; however, several of the U.S. businesses report independently to headquarters

7. Why do European-based multinational corporations differ from U.S.–based corporations in the instruments they choose for exerting control?

8. One of the most efficient means of control is self-control. What type of program would you prepare for an incoming employee?

Recommended Readings

Bartlett, Christopher, and Sumantra Ghoshal. *Managing Across Borders.* Cambridge, Mass.: Harvard Business Press, 1989.

Davidson, William H., and José de la Torre. *Managing the Global Corporation.* New York: McGraw-Hill, 1989.

Deal, Terrence E., and Allen A. Kennedy. *Corporate Cultures: The Rights and Rituals of Corporate Life.* Boston: Addison-Wesley, 1982.

Goehle, Donna D. *Decision-Making in Multinational Corporations.* Ann Arbor, Mich.: UMI Research Press, 1980.

Hedlung, Gunar, and Per Aman. *Managing Relationships with Foreign Subsidiaries.* Stockholm, Sweden: Mekan, 1984.

Hulbert, John M., and William K. Brandt. *Managing the Multinational Subsidiary.* New York: Holt, Rinehart, and Winston, 1980.

Negandhi, Anant, and Martin Welge. *Beyond Theory Z.* Greenwich, Conn.: JAI Press, 1984.

Otterback, Lars, ed. *The Management of Headquarters-Subsidiary Relationships in Multinational Corporations.* Aldershot, England: Gower Publishing Company, 1981.

Porter, Michael E., ed. *Competition in Global Industries.* Boston: Harvard Business School Press, 1986.

Stopford, John M., and Louis T. Wells. *Managing the Multinational Enterprise: Organization of the Firm and Ownership of the Subsidiary.* New York: Basic Books, 1972.

Notes

1. Michael Z. Brooke, *International Management: A Review of Strategies and Operations* (London: Hutchinson, 1986), 173-174.

2. Stefan Robock and Kenneth Simmonds, *International Business and Multinational Enterprises* (Homewood, Ill.: Richard D. Irwin, 1973), 429.

3. Richard D. Robinson, *Internationalization of Business: An Introduction* (Hinsdale, Ill.: The Dryden Press, 1984).

4. William H. Davidson and Philippe Haspeslagh, "Shaping a Global Product Organization," *Harvard Business Review* 59 (March/April 1982): 69-76.

5. L. S. Walsh, *International Marketing* (Plymouth, England: MacDonald and Evans, 1981), 161.

6. See Joan P. Curhan, William H. Davidson, and Suri Rajan, *Tracing the Multinationals* (Cambridge, Mass.: Ballinger, 1977); M.E. Wicks, *A Comparative Analysis of the Foreign Investment Evaluation Practices of U.S.-based Multinational Corporations* (New York: McKinsey & Co., 1980); and Lawrence G. Franko, "Organizational Structures and Multinational Strategies of Continental European Enterprises," in *European Research in International Business*, eds. Michel Ghertman and James Leontiades (Amsterdam, Holland: North Holland Publishing Co., 1977).

7. Davidson and Haspeslagh, "Shaping a Global Product Organization."

8. "How Goodyear Sharpened Organization and Production for a Tough World Market," *Business International*, January 16, 1989, 11-14.

9. Bill Saporito, "Campbell Soup Gets Piping Hot," *Fortune*, September 9, 1991, 94-98.

10. Daniel Robey, *Designing Organizations: A Macro Perspective* (Homewood, Ill.: Richard D. Irwin, 1982), 327.

11. Thomas H. Naylor, "International Strategy Matrix," *Columbia Journal of World Business* 20 (Summer 1985): 11-19.

12. "Kodak's Matrix System Focuses on Product Business Units," *Business International*, July 18, 1988, 221-223.

13. "How 3M Develops Managers to Meet Global Strategic Objectives," *Business International*, March 21, 1988, 81-82.

14. Thomas J. Peters, "Beyond the Matrix Organization," *Business Horizons* 22 (October 1979): 15-27.

15. See John M. Stopford and Louis T. Wells, *Managing the Multinational Enterprise* (New York: Basic Books, 1972); also A. D. Chandler, *Strategy and Structure* (Cambridge, Mass.: MIT Press, 1962); and B. R. Scott, *Stages of Corporate Development* (Boston: ICCH, 1971).

16. Stanley M. Davis, "Trends in the Organization of Multinational Corporations," *Columbia Journal of World Business* 11 (Summer 1976): 59-71.

17. William Taylor, "The Logic of Global Business," *Harvard Business Review* 68 (March–April 1990): 91-105.

18. Rodman Drake and Lee M. Caudill, "Management of the Large Multinational: Trends and Future Challenges," *Business Horizons* 24 (May–June 1981): 83-91.

19. Christopher Bartlett, "MNCs: Get Off the Reorganization Merry-Go-Round," *Harvard Business Review* 60 (March/April 1983): 138-146.

20. Cheryll Barron, "Format Fears at Philips," *Management Today*, August 1978, 35-41, 101-102.

21. Thomas Gross, Ernie Turner, and Lars Cederholm, "Building Teams for Global Operations" *Management Review*, June 1987, 32-36.

22. Christopher A. Bartlett and Sumantra Ghoshal, "Matrix Management: Not a Structure, A Frame of Mind," *Harvard Business Review* 68 (July–August 1990): 138-145.

23. Christopher A. Bartlett and Sumantra Ghoshal, "Tap Your Subsidiaries for Global Reach," *Harvard Business Review* 64 (November–December 1986): 87-94.

24. John A. Quelch and Edward J. Hoff, "Customizing Global Marketing," *Harvard Business Review* 64 (May–June 1986): 59-68.

25. Richard I. Kirkland, Jr., "Entering a New World of Boundless Competition," *Fortune*, March 14, 1988, 18-22.

26. Louis Kraar, "Your Rivals Can Be Your Allies," *Fortune*, March 27, 1989, 66-76.

27. Amitai Etzioni, *A Comparative Analysis of Complex Organizations* (Glencoe, England: Free Press, 1961).

28. William G. Egelhoff, "Patterns of Control in U.S., U.K., and European Multinational Corporations," *Journal of International Business Studies* 15 (Fall 1984): 73-83.

29. William H. Davidson, "Administrative Orientation and International Performance," *Journal of International Business Studies* 15 (Fall 1984): 11-23.

30. William G. Ouchi, "The Relationship between Organizational Structure and Organizational Control," *Administrative Science Quarterly* 22 (March 1977): 95-112.

31. B. R. Baliga and Alfred M. Jaeger, "Multinational Corporations: Control Systems and Delegation Issues," *Journal of International Business Studies* 15 (Fall 1984): 25-40.

32. Laurent Leksell, *Headquarters-Subsidiary Relationships in Multinational Corporations* (Stockholm, Sweden: Stockholm School of Economics, 1981), Chapter 5.

33. Anant R. Negandhi and Martin Welge, *Beyond Theory Z* (Greenwich, Conn.: JAI Press, 1984), 16.

34. Richard Pascale, "Fitting New Employees into the Company Culture," *Fortune*, May 28, 1984, 28–40.

35. Bartlett and Ghoshal, "Matrix Management: Not a Structure, A Frame of Mind."

36. Nathaniel Gilbert, "How Middle-Sized Corporations Manage Global Operations," *Management Review*, October 1988, 46–50.

37. R. J. Alsegg, *Control Relationships between American Corporations and Their European Subsidiaries*, AMA Research Study No. 107 (New York: American Management Association, 1971), 7.

38. John J. Dyment, "Strategies and Management Controls for Global Corporations," *Journal of Business Strategy* 7 (Spring 1987): 20–26.

39. Hans Schoellhammer, "Decision-Making and Intraorganizational Conflicts in Multinational Companies," presentation at the Symposium on Management of Headquarter-Subsidiary Relationships in Transnational Corporations, Stockholm School of Economics, June 2–4, 1980.

40. Alfred M. Jaeger, "The Transfer of Organizational Culture Overseas: An Approach to Control in the Multinational Corporation," *Journal of International Business Studies* 14 (Fall 1983): 91–106.

The Future

LEARNING OBJECTIVES

1. To understand the many changing dimensions that shape international business.

2. To learn about and evaluate the international business forecasts made by a panel of experts.

3. To be informed about different career opportunities for the student of international business.

The Demise of the Global Firm?

Cyrus Freidheim, vice chairman of the consulting firm Booz, Allen & Hamilton, has a provocative perspective of the global firm. He predicts that current economic and political developments mean that global firms will be superseded by the "relationship-enterprise," a network of strategic alliances among big firms, spanning different industries and countries, but held together by common goals that encourage them to act almost as a single firm. He sees these enterprises to be corporate juggernauts, with total revenues approaching $1 trillion by early next century, larger than all but the world's six biggest economies.

He suggests that early in the 21st century, Boeing, British Airways, Siemens, TNT (an Australian parcel delivery firm), and SNECMA (a French aero-engine maker) might together win a deal to build ten new airports in China. As part of the deal, British Airways and TNT would receive preferential routes and landing slots, the Chinese government would buy all state aircraft from Boeing-SNECMA, and Siemens would provide the air-traffic control systems for all ten airports.

While this may sound far-fetched, consider that Boeing, members of the airbus consortium, McDonnell Douglas, Mitsubishi, Kawasaki, and Fuji are already talking about jointly developing a new super-jumbo jet. Mitsubishi and Daimler-Benz already share engineers. General Motors and Toyota are discussing the possibility of Toyota's building light trucks in a GM plant.

According to Mr. Freidheim, the conventional model of the global firm is flawed. Most so-called global companies are still perceived as having a home base. For example, in 1991, only 2 percent of the board members of big American companies were foreigners. In Japanese companies, foreign directors are as rare as British sumo wrestlers. Firms therefore have a natural home-country bias, with the big decisions kept firmly at home.

This bias, together with various other constraints, hinders companies' efforts to become truly global. For instance, when capital is limited, firms tend to protect their home market at the expense of developing untapped markets overseas. Second, antitrust laws limit the ability of global firms to expand through takeovers. But most important of all is the problem of nationalism. No country likes foreigners controlling its industries. By contrast, a relationship enterprise can sidestep these constraints. Such an alliance can draw on lots of money; it can dodge antitrust barriers; and with home bases in all the main markets, it has the political advantage of being a local firm almost everywhere.

Source: "The Global Firm: R.I.P." *The Economist*, February 6, 1993: 69.

All international businesses face constantly changing world economic conditions. This is not a new situation nor one to be feared, because change provides the opportunity for new market positions to emerge and for managerial talent to improve the competitive position of the firm. Recognizing the importance of change and adapting creatively to new situations are the most important tasks of the international business executive.

Recently, changes are occurring more frequently, more rapidly, and have a more severe impact. The past has lost much of its value as a predictor of the future. What occurs today may not only be altered in short order but be completely overturned or reversed. For example, some countries find their major exports, which have increased steadily over decades, shrinking markedly in a brief period. Political stability can be completely disrupted over the course of a few months. Countries that have been considered enemies for decades, and with which no executive would dream of doing business, suddenly become close allies and offer a wealth of business opportunities. A major, sudden decline in world stock markets leaves corporations, investors, and consumers with strong feelings of uncertainty. In all, international business managers today face complex and rapidly changing economic and political conditions.

This chapter will discuss possible future developments in the international business environment, highlight the implications of these changes for international business management, and offer suggestions for a creative response to the changes. The chapter will also explore the meaning of both environmental and strategic changes as they relate to career choice and career path alternatives in international business.

THE INTERNATIONAL BUSINESS ENVIRONMENT

This section analyzes the international business environment by looking at political, financial, societal, and technological conditions of change and providing a glimpse of possible future developments as envisioned by an international panel of experts.* The impact of these factors on doing business abroad, on international trade relations, and on government policy is of particular interest to the international manager.

The Political Environment

The international political environment is undergoing a substantial transformation characterized by the reshaping of existing political blocs, the formation of new groupings, and the breakup of old coalitions.

The East-West Relationship Since 1945, the relationship between the dominant powers in the East and the West has changed little. Due to political developments in the late 1980s, however, this relationship is now undergoing a major transformation. Within only a few years, the communist empire briefly reshaped itself into a socialist league, only to emerge shortly thereafter as individual, distinct entities. The former eastern European satellite nations of the Soviet Union have reasserted their independence and are beginning to implement market-oriented economies. The Soviet Union itself has been replaced by a loose confederation of independent states. Politically and economically, the repercussions of these changes have been far reaching. The key collaborative military mechanism in the East—the Warsaw Pact—has ceased to exist. The economic agreement among the socialist countries—the Council for Mutual Economic Assistance (CMEA or COMECON)—has been disbanded.

These rapid transformations will cause major internal adjustments and economic dislocations, which in turn are likely to have political repercussions. It is likely that there will be a rapid rise of inflation in these nations, accompanied by deepening individual dissatisfaction due to unmet expectations of economic progress. Domestic markets and trade volumes are likely to shrink in the near and medium terms due to necessary adjustments in production capabilities based on market forces. Both the countries and companies involved are likely to suffer from deteriorating liquidity positions and a growing number of insolvencies.

The former East, which today sees itself as central Europe, is already benefiting politically from the shedding of the communist system through increased collaboration with the West. The raising of the Iron Curtain has also brought two separate economic and business systems closer together. The elimination of export controls, direct linkages with economic blocs, and the desire to help on the part of the West are likely to transform the business relations of the past.

As a result of easing political tensions within the West, firms will be presented with new opportunities. Demand—particularly for consumer products, which had been repressed in the past—can now be met with goods from the West. Yet, due to very limited consumer choice skills and knowledge levels, firms entering these new markets need to develop demand from the ground up—a difficult task.

Concurrently, central Europe is likely to emerge as a significant source of products and services destined for export. An increase in the formation of international joint ventures and cooperative alliances is also highly likely, particularly if current

*The information presented here is based largely on an original 1991 Delphi study by Michael R. Czinkota and Ilkka A. Ronkainen utilizing an international panel of experts.

plans for privatization are implemented. Due to liquidity shortages, new trading and financing techniques will need to be developed in order to make business propositions viable.

Overall, many of these business activities will be subject to regional economic and political instability, increasing their riskiness for foreign business partners. Yet the attractiveness of large market potential, combined with the availability of a relatively cheap and well-trained labor force, may help offset this risk.

The North-South Relationship　　The distinction between developed and less-developed countries (LDCs) is unlikely to change. Some theoreticians argue that the economic gap between these two groups will diminish, whereas others hold that the gap will increase. Both arguments lead to the conclusion that a gap will endure for some time. The ongoing disparity between developed and developing nations is likely to be based, in part, on continuing debt burdens and problems with satisfying basic needs. As a result, political uncertainty may well result in increased polarization between the haves and have-nots, with growing potential for political and economic conflict. Demands for political solutions to economic and financial problems are likely to increase. Some countries may consider migration as a key solution to population-growth problems, yet many may encounter government barriers to such migration. As a result, there may well be more investment flows by firms bringing their labor and skill-intensive manufacturing operations to these countries.[1]

The issue of environmental protection will also be a major force shaping the relationship between the developed and the developing world. In light of the need and desire to grow their economies, however, there may be much disagreement on the part of the industrializing nations as to what approaches to take. In light of these issues, three possible scenarios emerge.

One alternative is that of continued international cooperation. The developed countries could relinquish part of their economic power to less-developed ones, thus contributing actively to their development through a sharing of resources and technology. Although such cross-subsidization will be useful and necessary for the development of LDCs, it may result in a declining rate of increase in the standard of living in the more developed countries. It would, however, increase trade flows between North and South and precipitate the emergence of new international business opportunities.

A second alternative is that of confrontation. Because of an unwillingness to share resources and technology sufficiently (or excessively, depending on the point of view), the developing and the developed areas of the world may become increasingly hostile toward one another. As a result, the volume of international business, both by mandate of governments and by choice of the private sector, could be severely reduced.

A third alternative is that of isolation. Although there may not be some cooperation between the two major blocs, both groups, in order to achieve their domestic and international goals, may choose to remain economically isolated. This alternative may be particularly attractive if the countries in each bloc believe that they face unique problems and therefore must seek their own solutions.

Emergence of New Political Blocs　　Some foresee the realignment of global strategic power through the emergence of new political blocs. One such bloc would consist of a reshaped Europe, which would include political and economic membership of the 12 European Community nations, the central European nations, and possibly even some of the former Soviet republics. A second bloc would be led by Japan and would be mainly trade based. Members here would come mainly from the Pacific

Rim. A third bloc then could emerge in the Western Hemisphere, led by the United States and including Canada, Mexico, and several Central and South American nations. Such a bloc would be primarily trade based, but could eventually also incorporate many political dimensions.

These bloc formations could result in heightened business stability and cooperation within each arrangement. Yet a concurrent danger might be the emergence of bloc-based competition and protectionism. Such a development could force global firms to choose a "home bloc" and could introduce new inefficiencies into global trade relations. On the positive side, however, due to their relative equality of power, these blocs could also be the precursors of global cooperation, resulting in an even more open and free global business environment.

New Orientations   The people of some nations may possibly decide to reprioritize their values. The aim for financial progress and an improved quantitative standard of living may well give way to priorities based on religion, the environment, social relations, or other factors. Such a reorientation may result in complete reversals of currently held business values and the consumption orientation and may require a major readjustment of the activities of the international corporation in these countries. A continuous scanning of newly emerging national values thus becomes even more imperative for the international executive.

The International Financial Environment

Even though the international debt problem of the developing world appears temporarily subdued, it will remain a major international trade and business issue throughout this century. Debt constraints and low commodity prices will continue to create slower growth prospects for many developing countries. They will be forced to reduce their levels of imports and to exert more pressure on industrialized nations to open up their markets. Even if these markets are opened, however, demand for most primary products will be far lower than supply. Ensuing competition for market share will therefore continue to depress prices.

A key issue in resolving the debt crisis will be how the indebted LDCs and newly industrialized countries can pursue necessary or imposed austerity policies and achieve reasonable development goals without seriously damaging the growth requirements and exports of other countries. Developed nations in turn will have a strong incentive to help the debtor nations. This incentive consists of the market opportunities that economically healthy developing countries can offer and of national-security concerns. As a result, industrialized nations may very well be in a situation in which a funds transfer to debtor nations, accompanied by debt-relief measures such as debt forgiveness, are necessary to achieve economic stimulation at home.

The dollar will remain a major international currency, with little probability of gold returning to its former status in the near future. However, international transactions in both trade and finance are increasingly likely to be denominated in nondollar terms, using regional currencies such as the European Currency Unit (ECU). The system of floating currencies will likely continue, with occasional attempts by nations to manage exchange-rate relationships or at least reduce the volatility of swings in currency values. However, given the vast flows of financial resources across borders, it would appear that market forces rather than government action will be the key determinant of a currency's value. Factors such as investor trust, economic conditions, earnings perceptions, and political stability are therefore likely to have a much greater effect on the international value of currencies than domestic monetary and fiscal experimentation.

Given the close linkages among financial markets, shocks in one market will quickly translate into rapid shifts in others and easily overpower the financial resources of individual governments. Even if there should be a decision by governments to pursue closely coordinated fiscal and monetary policies, they are unlikely to be able to negate long-term market effects in response to changes in economic fundamentals.

A looming concern in the international financial environment will be the **international debt load** of the United States. Both domestically and internationally, the United States is incurring debt that would have been inconceivable only a decade ago. For example, in the 1970s the accumulation of financial resources by the Arab nations was of major concern in the United States. Congressional hearings focused on whether Arab money was "buying out America." At that time, however, Arab holdings in the United States were $10 billion to $20 billion. Current rapid accumulation of dollars by foreigners in the United States is leading to much more significant shifts in foreign holdings.

In 1985, the United States became a net negative investor internationally. The United States entered the 1990s with an international debt burden of more than $800 billion, making it the largest debtor nation in the world, owing more to other nations than all the developing countries combined. Mitigating this burden are the facts that most of these debts are denominated in U.S. dollars and that, even at such a large debt volume, U.S. debt-service requirements are only a small portion of GNP. Yet this accumulation of foreign debt may very well introduce entirely new dimensions into the international business relationships of individuals and nations. Once debt has reached a certain level, the creditor as well as the debtor is hostage to the loans.

Because foreign creditors expect a return on their investment, a substantial portion of future U.S. international trade activity will have to be devoted to generating sufficient funds for such repayment. For example, at an assumed interest rate or rate of return of 10 percent, the international U.S. debt level—without any growth—would require the annual payment of $80 billion, which amounts to about 20 percent of current U.S. exports. Eventually, U.S. trade must therefore not only be in balance but must produce a surplus in order to service the international debt. Therefore, it seems highly likely that international business will become a greater priority than it is today and will serve as a source of major economic growth for firms in the United States.

To some degree, foreign holders of dollars may also choose to convert their financial holdings into real property and investments in the United States. This will result in an entirely new pluralism in U.S. society. It will become increasingly difficult and, perhaps, even unnecessary to distinguish between domestic and foreign products—as is already the case with Hondas made in Ohio. Senators and members of Congress, governors, municipalities, and unions will gradually be faced with conflicting concerns in trying to develop a national consensus on international trade and investment. National-security concerns may also be raised as major industries become majority owned by foreign firms.

At the same time, the U.S. international debt situation will, among other things, contribute to an increasingly tight money supply around the world. When combined with the financial needs of the emerging eastern European market economies, the money required for the reconstruction of Kuwait and Iraq, the fund flows to the former Soviet Union, and the aid requirements of many developing nations, a more heated competition for capital is likely to emerge, with continuing scarcity leading to relatively high real interest rates worldwide. Industrialized countries are likely to attempt to narrow the domestic gap between savings and investments through fiscal policies. Without concurrent restrictions on international capital flows, such policies are likely to be only of limited success. Lending institutions can be expected to become more conservative in their financing, a move which may hit smaller firms and developing countries the hardest. Comparatively easier access to better financial resources will become a key competitive determinant and perhaps even be critical to the survival of many companies. At the same time, firms must strive to become best in their class. Given the increasing competition worldwide, products and services that only offer me-too features and capabilities will be hard pressed to stay in the market.

The Technological Environment

The concept of the global village is commonly accepted today and indicates the importance of communication in the technological environment. It is already feasible to build satellite dishes out of easily obtainable components. The rapid growth of fax machines, portable telephones, and personal communication devices points to the evolution of unrestricted information flows. Concurrently, the availability of information to be communicated has increased dramatically. Because all this information includes details about lifestyles, opportunities, and aspirations, international communication will be a great equalizer in the future.

Changes in other technologies will be equally rapid and will have a major effect on business in general. For example, the appearance of superconductive materials and composite materials has made possible the development of new systems in fields such as transportation and electric power, pushing the frontiers of human activity into as yet unexplored areas such as outer space and the depths of the oceans. The development of biotechnology is already leading to revolutionary progress not only in agriculture, medicine, and chemistry but also in manufacturing systems within industry.[2]

High technology is expected to become one of the more volatile areas of economic activity. For example, order of magnitude changes in technology can totally wipe out private and public national investment in a high-technology sector. In the hard-hitting race toward technological primacy, some nations will inevitably fall behind, and others will be able to catch up only with extreme difficulty.

Even firms and countries that are at the leading edge of technology will find it increasingly difficult to marshal the funds necessary for further advancements. For example, investments in semiconductor technology are measured in billions rather than millions of dollars and do not bring any assurance of success. Not to engage in the race, however, will mean falling behind quickly in all areas of manufacturing when virtually every industrial and consumer product is "smart" due to its chip technology.

As this chapter's opening vignette showed, it is likely that firms will join forces through cooperative agreements, joint ventures, and strategic partnerings in order to compete for major projects, spread the necessary financial commitments, and reduce the risk of technology development. Concurrently, governments will increase their spending on research and development in order to further "technonationalism" through the creation of more sources of technological innovation within their boundaries. Government-sponsored collaborative research ventures are likely to increase across industries and country groupings. However, difficulties may emerge when global firms threaten to rapidly internationalize any gains from such regionalized research ventures.

**CHANGES IN
TRADE RELATIONS**

The international trade framework, consisting primarily of the General Agreement on Tariffs and Trade (GATT), will remain under siege in the years to come. The GATT is greatly strained already in attempting to cope with the complexities of international trade. Given ongoing major imbalances in international trade flows, it will be increasingly difficult to get the industrialized nations to adhere to existing GATT rules. In addition, the framework will need to incorporate newly industrialized and the former socialist countries into its structure, requiring these countries to play by the established rules, to remove preferential tariffs, and to reduce and eliminate government support and offer equal access to their markets. Such requirements are likely to be resisted by the new participants in international trade because many of them will believe that the rules inhibit their economic development. The GATT will therefore also need to shoulder greater responsibilities for poor participants by offering economic development alternatives in exchange for market access.

In addition, the GATT will need to devise and implement effective rules for the forms of international trade currently under discussion in the Uruguay Round, such as trade in services, intellectual property rights, trade in high technology, and international investment. Concurrently, better dispute resolution and enforcement procedures will need to be developed along with mechanisms to supervise activities currently not under GATT auspices, such as countertrade and new forms of government support. The GATT must also consider abolishing or regulating trade arrangements that now occur outside the GATT forum and substantially distort trade flows, such as orderly or voluntary market-restraint agreements.

A key question will be whether the GATT can be restructured to accommodate current challenges or whether a new organization will be the requisite and only feasible alternative. **Multilateral trade negotiations** are essential to the survival of the multilateral trade system. Given the diverging interests of the participants in trade negotiations, however, widespread interest and support are difficult to generate. If trade relations cannot be continued on a multilateral basis, bilateral agreements and treaties will become more prevalent. As a result, protectionism would increase on a global scale as individual industrial polices are followed, and the volume of international trade would decline.

The international consensus in support of GATT may also diminish in light of strengthened regional trading blocs. Disillusioned with the diversity of GATT members, some of the major trade players or blocs may form a new global trading system that will incorporate the largest portion of world trade volume. Smaller countries could then negotiate gradual access to such a new system. Such a scenario, while less desirable than the success of GATT, may still provide a bright outlook for international business in most developed nations, but it could cause major problems for firms in the developing world.

International trade relations will also be shaped by new participants bringing with them the potential to restructure the composition of trade. For example, new entrants with exceptionally large productive potential, such as the People's Republic of China and eastern Europe, may substantially alter world trade flows. The international firm may be required to change many trading practices as a result but may also benefit both in terms of market and sourcing opportunities.

Finally, the efforts of governments to achieve self-sufficiency in economic sectors, particularly in agriculture and heavy industries, have ensured the creation of long-term, worldwide oversupply of some commodities and products, many of which had historically been traded widely. As a result, after some period of intense market share competition aided by subsidies and governmental support, a gradual and painful restructuring of these economic sectors will have to take place. This will be particularly true for agricultural cash crops such as wheat, corn, and dairy products and industrial products such as steel, chemicals, and automobiles.

GOVERNMENTAL POLICY

A clear worldwide trend exists toward increased management of trade by governments.[3] International trade activity now affects domestic policy more than in the past. For example, trade flows can cause major structural shifts in employment. The U.S. footwear manufacturing industry has experienced an import penetration level of more than 70 percent. Similarly, the textile industry in the United States is under pressure from foreign imports. These industries are faced with a need to substantially restructure their employment outlook because of productivity gains and competitive pressures. Yet such restructuring is not necessarily negative. Since the turn of the century, farm employment in the United States has dropped from more than 40 percent of the population to less than 3 percent. At the same time, the farm industry feeds 250 million people in the United States and produces large surpluses. A restructuring of industries can therefore greatly increase productivity and competitiveness and provide the opportunity for resource allocation to emerging sectors of an economy.

Governments cannot be expected, for the sake of the theoretical ideal of "free trade," to sit back and watch the effects of deindustrialization on their countries. The most that can be expected is that they will permit an open-market orientation subject to the needs of domestic policy. Even an open-market orientation is maintainable only if governments can provide reasonable assurances to their own firms and citizens that this openness applies to foreign markets as well. Therefore, unfair trade practices such as governmental subsidization, dumping, and industrial targeting will be examined more closely, and retaliation for such activities is likely to be swift and harsh.

Increasingly, governments will need to coordinate policies that affect the international business environment. The development of international indexes and **trigger mechanisms,** which precipitate government action at predetermined intervention points, will be a useful step in that direction. Yet, in order for them to be effective, governments will need to muster the political fortitude to implement the policies necessary for cooperation. For example, international monetary cooperation will work in the long term only if domestic fiscal policies are responsive to the achievement of the coordinated goals.

Governmental policymakers must also understand the international repercussions of domestic legislation. For example, in imposing a special surcharge tax on the chemical industry designed to provide for the cleanup of toxic waste products, they need to consider its repercussions on the international competitiveness of the chemical industry. Similarly, current laws such as antitrust legislation need to be reviewed if these laws hinder the international competitiveness of domestic firms. Global Perspective 22.1 provides insight into how the imposition of an energy tax in the United States is interpreted by countries supplying much of that energy.

Policymakers also need a better understanding of the nature of the international trade issues confronting them. Most countries today face both short-term and long-term trade problems. Trade balance issues, for example, are short term in nature, while competitiveness issues are much more long term. All too often, however, short-term issues are attacked with long-term **trade policy mechanisms,** and vice versa. In the United States, for example, the desire to "level the international playing field" with mechanisms such as vigorous implementation of import restrictions or volun-

Global Perspective

22.1
U.S. Energy Tax Triggers
Saudi Warning

When President Clinton announced a new energy tax in the United States, he received a blunt message from Saudi Arabian Oil Minister Hisham Nazer: Don't solve your deficit problem by taxing oil or gasoline. "Oil is cheap, clean and safe," he said. "We have it. The world needs it. So why penalize this precious gift of God at the expense of the welfare of the people of the world?" Nazer argued that the taxation of fuels is selfish, because such a tax discourages use of a cheap, available fuel essential to economic progress. Furthermore, such a tax is unfair to producers, who have invested billions in wells and pipelines to keep the oil flowing. Such a tax is also environmentally misguided, Nazer continued, because it discourages the economic progress developing countries need to improve their own environmental protection. In his view, environmental activists have "hijacked" the global agenda in an effort to cut petroleum use by any means, an effort that he said threatens the economic growth of developing countries. Nazer complained that some foreign governments take in taxes three times as much revenue for each barrel of oil, as do the nations that produce it. He stated that Saudi Arabia is interested in catering to U.S. consumers and should not be made a victim of its own cooperative polices.

Source: Thomas W. Lippman, "Saudi Oil Minister Warns U.S. on New Oil, Gasoline Taxes," *The Washington Post*, February 11, 1993: B11, B13.

tary restraint agreements may serve long-term competitiveness well, but it does little to alleviate the publicly perceived problem of the trade deficit. Similarly, a further opening of Japan's market to foreign corporations will have only a minor immediate effect on that country's trade surplus or the trading partners' deficit. Yet it is the expectation and hope of many in both the public and the private sectors that such instant changes will occur. For the sake of the credibility of policymakers, it therefore becomes imperative to precisely identify the nature of the problem and to design and use policy measures that are appropriate for its resolution.

Any kind of official **industrial policy** in the United States appears unlikely in the immediate future. However, the accuracy of this statement lies only in the context of an official posture. The United States is opposed to any industrial policy because of the historical rationale that bureaucrats will be less successful than the free market in choosing winners. Historically, we can also see that some industrial policies were in fact implemented, although indirectly. For example, when transportation across the country was vital, railroads were built, later followed by highways. When education became a national priority, substantial government funding was provided to create and upgrade scientific studies in universities.

In the years to come, governments will be faced with an accelerating technological race and with emerging problems that seem insurmountable by individual firms alone, such as pollution of the environment and global warming. As market gaps emerge and time becomes crucial, both governments and the private sector will find that even if the private sector knows that a lighthouse is needed, it may still be hard, time consuming, and maybe even impossible to build one with private funds alone. As a result, it seems likely that the concepts of administrative guidance and government-corporate collaboration will increasingly become part of the policy behavior of governments. The international manager will in turn have to spend more time and effort dealing with governments and macro rather than micro issues.

THE FUTURE OF INTERNATIONAL BUSINESS MANAGEMENT

Environmental changes result in an increase in international risk. One shortsighted alternative for risk-averse managers would be the termination of international activities altogether. However, businesses will not achieve long-run success by engaging only in risk-free actions. Furthermore, other factors make the continuance of international business highly probable.

International markets remain a source of high profits, as a quick look at the list of Fortune 500 firms will show. International activities help cushion slack in domestic sales resulting from recessionary or adverse domestic conditions and may be crucial to the very survival of the firm. International markets also provide firms with foreign experience that helps them compete more successfully with foreign firms in the domestic market. Finally, international activities are necessary to compensate for foreign product and service inflows into the economy and at least to contribute to an equilibration of the balance of trade. As long as supply potential exceeds demand on an international level, an inherent economic motivation will exist for international business activities.

International Planning and Research

Firms must continue to serve customers well in order to be active participants in the international marketplace. One major change that will come about is that the international manager will need to respond to general governmental concerns to a greater degree when planning a business strategy. Furthermore, societal concern about macro problems—even if only sporadic at first—needs to be taken into account more directly and quickly because societies have come to expect more social responsibility from corporations. Taking on a leadership role regarding social causes may also benefit corporations' bottom line, since consumers appear more willing than ever to act as significant pressure points for policy changes and to pay for their social concerns.

Another trend consists of increased competition in international markets. This trend will create a need for more niches in which firms can create a distinct international competence. As a result, increased specialization and segmentation will let firms fill very narrow and specific demands or resolve very specific problems for their international customers.[4] Identifying and filling these niches will be easier in

Mobil Oil Corporation credits international activities, such as these liquefied natural gas operations in Indonesia, with offsetting normal periods of decline in sales and production.
Source: © Larry Lee 1991.

the future because of the greater availability of international research tools and information.

In spite of the frequent short-term orientation by corporations and investors, companies will need to learn to prepare for long-term horizons. Particularly in an environment of heated competition and technological battles, of large projects and slow payoffs, companies, their stakeholders, and governments will need to find avenues that not only permit but encourage the development of strategic perspectives. Figure 22.1 provides an example of such a long-term view.

Governments both at home and abroad will demand that private business practices not increase public costs and that businesses serve customers equally and nondiscriminately.[5] This concept runs directly counter to the desire to serve first the markets that are most profitable and least costly. International executives will therefore be torn in two directions and, in order to provide results that are acceptable both to customers and to the societies they serve, they must walk a fine line, balancing the public and the private good.

International Product Policy

Two major trends are emerging in the product policies of multinational corporations. On one hand, automation and the search for increasing economies of scale demand that firms serve more markets. Even large domestic markets such as the United States or Japan may be "too small to absorb the output of the world-class automated plants needed for economies of scale in many product areas."[6] Europe, Japan, and the United States harbor the greatest buying power and demand concentration in the world for many products. For example, these three regions account for nearly 85

FIGURE 22.1
Long-Term Planning

Source: *The Economist,* October 24, 1992, p. 29.

percent of the world's demand for consumer electronic goods; they also consumed 85 percent of the computers and 70 percent of the machine tools produced in the world.[7] According to these facts, production should be concentrated in one of these regions and output widely distributed.

Although this trend would argue for greater exports and greater standardization of products, a counterargument holds that, because of increasing protectionist policies and the desire of nations to obtain and develop their own technology, foreign direct investment and multiple plant locations will replace exports.[8] As long as firms have the flexibility of choice of location, managers will have substantial leverage over domestic legislation and regulations that would affect their international effort. Governments will run the risk of unemployment growth if domestic firms, because of an unsatisfactory **competitive platform,** move their operations abroad.

Regardless of which avenue firms use to take their products and services abroad, it appears certain that worldwide introduction of products will occur much more rapidly in the future. As a result of the ever-quickening pace of technological change, the life cycles of most products will be greatly shortened. To stay ahead of the competition, firms will need to constantly adapt, adjust, and incrementally improve their products.[9] As a result, new products will be developed based on a system-oriented integration within the firm, where management, marketing, research, and development are joint rather than separate activities. Due to a more rapid commercialization of new technology, firms will have to develop more efficient, faster, and better targeted marketing strategies around the world, accompanied by better and shorter distribution channels. The homogenization of patterns of consumption will assist these efforts through the emergence of global or regional consumer segments, which will accelerate the penetration of global brands. Overall, product introduction will grow more complex, more expensive, and riskier, yet the rewards to be reaped from a successful product will need to be accumulated more quickly.

Factor endowment advantages have a significant impact on the decisions of international managers. Given the acceleration of product life cycles, nations with low production costs will be able to develop and offer products more cheaply. Countries such as India, Israel, or the Philippines offer large pools of skilled people at labor rates much lower than in Europe, Japan, or the United States. For example, India has the third largest number of engineers after the United States and the CIS.[10] All this talent also results in a much wider dissemination of technological creativity, a factor that will affect the innovative capability of firms. For example, in 1992, nearly half of all the patents in the United States were granted to foreign inventors. Table 22.1 shows the countries of origin of patent recipients in 1992.

This indicates that firms need to make foreign knowledge and advantages part of their production strategies—or they need to develop consistent comparative advantages in production technology—in order to stay ahead of the game. Similarly, workers engaged in the productive process must attempt, through training and skill enhancement, to stay ahead of foreign workers who are willing to charge less for their time. This need to stay ahead highlights the importance, for governments, companies, and workers alike to invest in human capital so that the interest from such investment can be drawn on for competitive success. Furthermore, firms will need to evaluate the formation of collaborative arrangements between nominally competing companies and search for complementary strengths, be they in personnel availability, specialized skills, access to capital markets, or technical know-how.

International Communications

The advances made in international communications will also have a profound impact on international management. Entire industries are becoming more footloose

TABLE 22.1 **U.S. Patents Granted to** **Foreign Inventors in** **1992**	*(table at right)*

Country	Patents	Country	Patents
Argentina	21	Malaysia	8
Australia	550	Mauritius	1
Austria	424	Mexico	44
Bahamas	2	Monaco	6
Barbados	1	Morocco	1
Belgium	382	Netherlands	1,019
Brazil	55	Netherlands Antilles	1
British Virgin Isl.	1	New Zealand	58
Bulgaria	4	Nigeria	2
Canada	2,313	Norway	120
Cayman Islands	4	Pakistan	1
Chile	6	Panama	1
China	50	Peru	4
Colombia	5	Philippines	10
Costa Rica	5	Poland	8
Czechoslovakia	18	Portugal	9
Denmark	263	Saudi Arabia	7
Dominican Republic	1	Senegal	1
Egypt	3	Singapore	23
Finland	368	South Africa	113
France	3,332	South Korea	543
Germany	7,960	Soviet Union	89
Greece	10	Spain	177
Guatemala	3	Sri Lanka	2
Guyana	1	Sweden	747
Hong Kong	169	Switzerland	1,369
Hungary	84	Syria	2
Iceland	5	Taiwan	1,195
India	23	Thailand	1
Indonesia	6	Trinidad & Tobago	3
Iran	1	Tunisia	1
Ireland	61	Turkey	4
Israel	377	United Arab Emirates	1
Italy	1,455	United Kingdom	2,851
Jamaica	1	Uruguay	2
Japan	23,481	Venezuela	28
Jordan	1	Yugoslavia	20
Kenya	1	Zimbabwe	1
Kuwait	2	Total patents issued in U.S., 1992	109,728
Lebanon	1	Total patents issued to U.S. inventors	59,760
Liechtenstein	11	Total patents issued to foreign inventors	49,968
Luxembourg	36	Foreign patents as percentage of total	45.5%

Source: *Patents Issued to Residents of the United States and Patents Issued to Residents of Foreign Countries,* United States Department of Commerce, Patent and Trademark Office, January, 1993.

in their operations; that is, they are less tied to their current location in their interaction with markets. For example, Best Western Hotels in the United States has channeled its entire reservation system through a toll-free number that is being serviced out of the prison system in Utah. Companies could even concentrate their communications activities in other countries. Communications for worldwide operations, for example, could easily be located in Africa or Asia without impairing international corporate activities.

Staff in different countries can not only talk together but can also share pictures and data on their computer screens.[11] Worldwide rapid product development will therefore become technically feasible. Technology will also make it possible to merge the capabilities of computers, televisions, and telecommunications. Communication

Advances in telecommunications allow staff in different countries to talk together and share pictures and data on their computer screens. In the state-of-the-art video conference center at Hoffmann-LaRoche's U.S. headquarters in Nutley, N.J., scientists discuss research goals and results with Roche colleagues in Basel, Switzerland.

Source: Courtesy of Hoffmann-LaRoche, Inc.

costs are likely to decrease significantly at the same time that the capabilities of communication tools increase. As a result, firms will have the opportunity for worldwide data exchange and benefit from virtually unlimited availability of detailed market and customer data. The challenge will then be to see who can use and apply information technology best.

Distribution Strategies

Worldwide distribution systems are beginning to emerge. Currently, only a few integrated systems, labeled sea bridges or land bridges, are operational. However, major trading routes that offer substantial distribution economies of scale are being developed. The international manager will experience relative ease in planning distribution as long as he or she stays within established routes but will encounter difficulties when attempting to deviate from them. Customers who are on the routes will benefit in turn from the low cost of distribution and will see a widening in their choice of products. More-distant customers will probably have their product choices reduced and pay increased prices for foreign products. Market access is also a crucial component in determining a firm's capability to develop new products since lack of customers will sharply reduce the economic benefits derived from new products. Therefore, the distribution systems may often become the deciding factor in whether or not markets can be served and whether or not industry will develop. Because communications advances will ensure that the customers in different markets are informed about product availability, distribution limitations will become even more painful.

More sophisticated distribution systems will also offer new management opportunities to firms but, at the same time, introduce new uncertainties and fragilities into corporate planning. For example, the development of just-in-time delivery systems will make firms more efficient yet, on an international basis, also expose them to more risk due to distribution interruptions. A strike in a faraway country may therefore be newly significant for a company depending on the timely delivery of supplies.

International Pricing

International price competition will become increasingly heated. Many products, as their distribution spreads throughout the world, will take on commodity characteristics, as semiconductors did in the 1980s. Therefore, price differentials of one cent per unit may become crucial in making an international sale. However, since many new products and technologies will address completely new needs, forward pricing will become increasingly difficult and controversial as demand levels are impossible to predict with any kind of accuracy.

Even for consumer products, price competition will be substantial. Because of the increased dissemination of technology, the firm that introduces a product will no longer be able to justify higher prices for long; domestically produced products will soon be of similar quality. As a result, exchange-rate movements may play more significant roles in maintaining the competitiveness of the international firm. Firms can be expected to prevail on their governments to manage the country's currency in order to maintain a favorable exchange rate.

Through subsidization, targeting, government contracts, or other hidden forms of support, nations will attempt to stimulate their international competitiveness. Because of the price sensitivity of many products, the international manager will be forced to identify such unfair practices quickly, communicate them to his or her government, and insist on either similar benefits or government negotiation of an internationally level playing field.

At the same time, many firms will work hard to reduce the price sensitivity of their customers. By developing relationships with their markets rather than just carrying out transactions, other dimensions such as loyalty, consistency, the cost of shifting suppliers, and responsiveness to client needs may become much more important for future competition than price.

CAREERS IN INTERNATIONAL BUSINESS

The student reader of this book will, it is hoped, have learned about the intricacies, complexities, and thrills of international business. Of course, a career in international business is more than jet-set travel between Rome, London, and Paris. It is hard work and requires knowledge and expertise. To prepare, students may wish to be well versed in a specific functional business area and take summer internships abroad, take language courses, and travel not simply for pleasure but to observe business operations abroad and gain a greater understanding of different peoples and cultures. The following pages will provide an overview of principal further training and employment opportunities in the international business field.

Further Training

One option for the student on the road to more international involvement is to obtain further in-depth training by enrolling in graduate business school programs that specialize in international business education. Even though the international orientation of U.S. universities is relatively recent, a substantial number of schools have developed specific international programs. In addition, universities abroad specialize in developing international managers. INSEAD in France, the London Business School in England, the University of Western Ontario in Canada, IMEDE in Switzerland, and the Stockholm School of Economics are only a few examples of such universities.[12]

Cost of Living for Expatriates

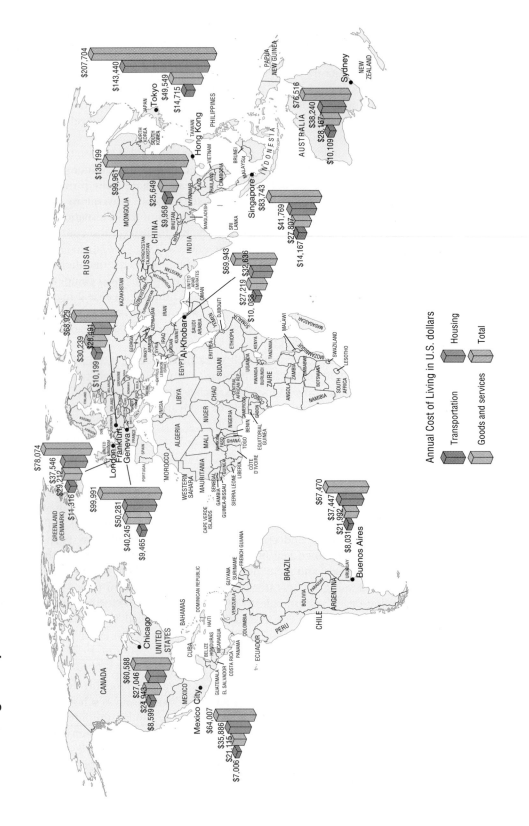

Annual Cost of Living in U.S. dollars

Transportation · Housing
Goods and services · Total

Source: Peter Van Pelt and Natalia Wolniansky, *Management Review*, July, 1990. Note: The data is based on a U.S. family of four with a base salary of $75,000. Housing costs are based on homes or apartments having six to nine rooms with annual expense for utilities and insurance included. Transportation costs include fixed and operating costs for one automobile. Costs of goods and services include the total amounts paid (including tax) for food, tobacco, alchohol, household furnishings and operations, clothing, domestic services, medical care, personal care, and recreation. Taxes are not included since they vary greatly.

Many organizations are able to assist students interested in studying abroad or in gathering foreign work experience. Apart from individual universities and their programs for study abroad, various nonprofit institutions stand ready to help and to provide informative materials.

For those ready to enter or rejoin the "real world," different employment opportunities need to be evaluated.

Employment with a Large Firm

One career alternative in international business is to work for a large multinational corporation. These firms constantly search for personnel to help them in their international operations. For example, a Procter & Gamble recruiting advertisement published in a university's student newspaper is reproduced in Figure 22.2.

Many multinational firms, while seeking specialized knowledge like languages, expect employees to be firmly grounded in the practice and management of business. Rarely, if ever, will a firm hire a new employee at the starting level and immediately place him or her in a position of international responsibility. Usually, a new employee is expected to become thoroughly familiar with the company's internal operations before being considered for an international position. The reason a manager is sent abroad is that the company expects him or her to reflect the corporate spirit, to be tightly wed to the corporate cultures, and to be able to communicate well with both local and corporate management personnel. In this liaison position, the manager will have to be exceptionally sensitive to both headquarters and local operations. As an intermediary, the expatriate must be empathetic, understanding, and yet fully prepared to implement the goals set by headquarters. However, as Global Perspective 22.2 shows, in light of growing globalization, firms increasingly are considering sending employees abroad at an earlier stage in their careers. But while the opportunities have grown, the demands and expectations have grown as well.

It is very expensive for companies to send an employee overseas. As Table 22.2 shows, the annual cost of maintaining a manager overseas is more than three times the cost of hiring a local manager. Companies want to be sure that the expenditure is worth the benefit they will receive, even though certainty is never possible.

Even if a position opens up in international operations, there is some truth in the saying that the best place to be in international business is on the same floor as the chairman at headquarters. Employees of firms that have taken the international route often come back to headquarters to find only a few positions available for them. After spending time in foreign operations, where independence is often high and authority significant, a return to a regular job at home, which sometimes may not even call on the many skills acquired abroad, may turn out to be a difficult and deflating experience. Such encounters lead to some disenchantment with international activities as well as to financial pressures and family problems, all of which may add up to significant executive stress during reentry.[13] Although many firms depend on their international operations for a substantial amount of sales volume and profits, less than 2 percent of U.S. companies have an overseas placement plan for rising young executives. Given the fact that management-development programs are scarce, it is not surprising that reentry programs are even scarcer and are often viewed as an unnecessary expense. The decision is difficult for the internationalist who wants to go abroad, make his or her mark, and return to an equivalent or even better position. However, as firms begin to recognize the importance of international operations, more efforts toward proper personnel management are likely to be made.

FIGURE 22.2
Advertisement
Recruiting New
Graduates for
Employment in
International Operations

EN BUSCA DE SU TALENTO

Procter & Gamble
División de Peru/Latino America

¤ Más de 40 productos de consumo en Latino America como Pampers, Ace, Ariel, Crest, Head & Shoulders, Camay y Vicks.

¤El area tiene el mayor volumen de ventas entre todas las divisiones Internacionales de P&G.

¤Oportunidades de desarrollar una carrera profesional en areas como Mercadeo, Finanzas, Computación, Ventas, etc.

Buscamos individuos con Talento, Empuje, Liderazgo, y continuo afán de superación para posiciones permanentes o practicas de verano en Peru, Puerto Rico, México, Colombia, Venezuela, Brazil, Chile, etc.

Es muy importante que envies tu RESUME pronto ya que estaremos visitando tu Universidad en la primera semana de Noviembre.

¿QUE DEBES HACER?
Envia tu resume tan pronto como sea posible a la atencion de Ms. Cynthia Huddleston (MBA Career Services) antes del 18 de Octubre.

Source: *The Hoya*, Georgetown University, October 6, 1989, 2.

Global Perspective

22.2
Go Global, Young Manager

Unless companies equip their best managers with global skills at younger ages, "they are going to come up short" in global competition, warns Michael Longua, Johnson & Johnson's director of international recruiting. In the summer of 1992, the health-care-products company sent six U.S. managers with an average tenure of 5 years, rather than the usual 7 to 10, abroad for up to 18 months.

A growing number of U.S. companies are giving fast-track managers a global orientation much sooner in their careers. General Electric Co. offers cross-cultural training and foreign-language lessons to people who may never live overseas. PepsiCo Inc., Raychem Corp., and other big concerns are moving Americans abroad or foreigners into the United States with only a few years' experience rather than waiting a decade.

Colgate-Palmolive has developed a program for recent college graduates. 'Globalites' undergo a 24-month training program and then become associate product managers in the United States or abroad. The program has become such a powerful recruiting tool that more than 15,000 people vie for the 15 slots every year.

Source: Joann S. Lublin, "Younger Managers Learn Global Skills," The *Wall Street Journal,* March 31, 1992: B1.

TABLE 22.2
The Price of an
Expatriate

An employer's typical first-year expenses of sending a U.S. executive to Britain, assuming a $100,000 salary and a family of four:

Direct Compensation Costs	
Base salary	$100,000
Foreign-service premium	15,000
Goods and services differential	21,000
Housing costs in London	39,000*
Transfer Costs	
Relocation allowance	$5,000
Air fare to London	2,000
Cost of moving household goods	25,000
Other Costs	
Company car	$15,000
Schooling (two children)	20,000
Annual home leave (four people)	4,000
U.K. personal income tax	56,000*
Total	$302,000

Note: Additional costs often incurred aren't listed above, including language and cross-cultural training for employee and family, and costs of selling home and cars in the United States before moving.

*Figures take into account payments by employee to company based on hypothetical U.S. income tax and housing costs.

Source: Joann S. Lublin, "Companies Try to Cut Subsidies for Employees," *The Wall Street Journal,* December 11, 1989, page B1; information provided by Organization Resource Counselors Inc.

Employment with a Small or Medium-Sized Firm

A second alternative is to begin work in a small or medium-sized firm. Very often, these firms have only recently developed an international outlook, and the new employee will arrive on the "ground floor." Initial involvement will normally be in the export field—evaluating potential foreign customers, preparing quotes, and dealing with activities such as shipping and transportation. With a very limited budget, the export manager will only occasionally visit foreign markets to discuss business strategies with foreign distributors. Most of the work will be done by mail, via telex, by fax, or by telephone. The hours are often long because of the need, for example, to reach a contact during business hours in Hong Kong. The main obstacle encountered in the small firm is the lack of an adequate budget—a phenomenon always found in business—yet the possibilities for implementing creative business transactions are virtually limitless. It is also gratifying and often rewarding that one's successful contribution will be visible directly through the firm's growing export volume.

Alternatively, international work in a small firm may involve importing; that is, finding low-cost sources that can be substituted for domestically sourced products. Decisions often must be based on limited information, and the manager is faced with many uncertainties. Often things do not work out as planned. Shipments are delayed, letters of credit are canceled, and products almost never arrive in exactly the form and shape anticipated. Yet the problems are always new and offer an ongoing challenge.

As a training ground for international activities, probably no better starting place exists than a small or medium-sized firm. Later on, the person with some experience may find work with an export-trading or export-management company, resolving other people's problems and concentrating almost exclusively on the international arena.

Self-Employment

A third alternative is to hang up a consultant's shingle or to establish a trading firm. Many companies are in need of help for their international business efforts and are prepared to part with a portion of their profits in order to receive it. Yet it requires in-depth knowledge and broad experience to make a major contribution from the outside or to successfully run a trading firm. Some of the initial expenses for an international business consulting service are listed in Table 22.3. The up-front costs are substantial and are not covered by turnover; rather, they have to be covered by profits.

Specialized services that might be offered by a consultant include international market research, international strategic planning, or, particularly desirable, beginning-to-end assistance for international entry or international negotiations. For an international business expert, the hourly billable rate typically is as high as $250 for principals and $100 for staff. Whenever international travel is required, overseas activities are often billed at the daily rate of $2,000 plus expenses. Even at these high rates, solid groundwork must be completed before all the overhead is paid. The advantage of this career option is the opportunity to become a true international entrepreneur. Consultants and those who conduct their own export-import or foreign direct investment activities work at a higher degree of risk than those who are not self-employed, but they have an opportunity for higher rewards.

SUMMARY

This final chapter has provided an overview of the environmental changes facing international managers and alternative managerial responses to these changes. International business is a complex and difficult activity, yet it affords many opportunities and challenges. Observing changes and analyzing how to best incorporate them in the international business mission is the most important task of the international manager. If the international environment were constant, there would be little challenge to international business. The frequent changes are precisely what make international business so fascinating and often highly profitable for those who are active in the field.

TABLE 22.3
Approximate Budget Requirements for an International Business Consulting Service

	Monthly	Annual
Rent (750 sq. ft. @ $25/sq.ft.)	$ 1,562.50	$ 18,750.00
Secretary/Receptionist	1,500.00	18,000.00
Administrative/Office manager	1,750.00	21,000.00
Withholding/Employer contributions	975.00	11,700.00
Employee health insurance	270.00	3,240.00
Computer (purchase)	—	4,500.00
Telex*	—	250.00
IBM Selectric II	—	850.00
Telephone (4 lines)		
Installation (one time)		250.00
Hardware (3 phones)		900.00
Computer box (lease)	70.00	840.00
C&P basic service	200.00	2,400.00
Copier		
Lease*	250.00	3,000.00
Supplies/Paper	100.00	1,180.00
Long-distance phone	600.00	7,200.00
FAX usage	800.00	9,600.00
Brochure, design & print (2,000)	—	10,000.00
Newsletter* copywriting (12 issues, 4 pages)	334.00	4,000.00
Printing charges*	200.00	2,400.00
Business stationery		
Layout/Design		300.00
Printing/Supply		1,000.00
Postage estimates*		
Leasing of meter (quarterly)	56.00	260.00
Postage	400.00	5,000.00
Business development		
Domestic travel and entertainment*	4,000.00	48,000.00
Total	$13,076.50	$174,620.00

*Denotes expenses partially recoverable from clients.

Source: Reprinted with permission from president, Robert D. Keezer & Associates, Washington, D.C.

Key Terms and Concepts

international debt load

multilateral trade negotiations

trigger mechanisms

trade policy mechanisms

industrial policy

competitive platform

Questions for Discussion

1. For many developing countries, debt repayment and trade are closely linked. What does protectionism mean to them?
2. Should we worry about the fact that the United States is a debtor nation?
3. How can a U.S. firm compete in light of low wages paid to workers abroad?
4. Is international segmentation ethical if it deprives poor countries of products?
5. How would our lives and our society change if imports were banned?

Recommended Readings

Academic Year Abroad 1991-1992. New York: Institute for International Education, 1991.

Czinkota, Michael R., and Ilkka Ronkainen. "Global Marketing 2000: A Marketing Survival Guide," *Marketing Management*, Winter 1992: 36–45.

Drucker, Peter F. "The Changed World Economy." *Foreign Affairs* 64 (Spring 1986): 768–791.

Judkins, David. *Study Abroad: The Astute Student's Guide*. Hawthorne, N.J.: Career Press, 1989.

Rossman, Marlene L. *The International Businesswoman of the 1990's: A Guide to Success in the Global Marketplace*. New York: Praeger, 1990.

Schwartz, Peter, and Jerry Saville. "Multinational Business in the 1990's—A Scenario." *Long Range Planning* 19 (December 1986): 31–37.

Sethi, S. Prakash. "Opportunities and Pitfalls for Multinational Corporations in a Changed Political Environment." *Long Range Planning* 20 (December 1987): 45–53.

Smith, Allen E., James M. MacLachlan, William Lazer, and Priscilla LaBarbera. *Marketing 2000: Future Perspectives on Marketing*. Chicago: American Marketing Association, 1989.

Thurow, Lester C. "A Weakness in Process Technology." *Science* 238 (December 1987): 1659–1663.

Win, David. *International Careers: An Insider's Guide*. Hawthorne, N.J.: Career Press, 1987.

Work Study Travel Abroad 1992–1993. 11th ed. New York: St. Martins Press, 1992.

Notes

1. William B. Johnston, "Global Workforce 2000: The New World Labor Market, " *Harvard Business Review*, March & April 1991: 115–127.
2. Shinji Fukukawa, *The Future of U.S.-Japan Relationship and Its Contribution to New Globalism* (Tokyo: Ministry of International Trade and Industry, 1989), 10–11.
3. Raymond J. Waldmann, *Managed Trade: The New Competition between Nations* (Cambridge, Mass.: Ballinger, 1986), 5.
4. Sudhir H. Kale and D. Sudharshan, "A Strategic Approach to International Segmentation," *International Marketing Review* 4 (Summer 1987): 60.
5. Robert Bartels, *Global Development and Marketing* (Columbus, Ohio: Grid, 1981), 111.
6. Kenichi Ohmae, "Only Triad Insiders Will Succeed," *The New York Times*, November 2, 1984, 2f.
7. Ibid.
8. Bartels, *Global Development and Marketing,* 112.
9. Michael R. Czinkota and Masaaki Kotabe, "Product Development in the Proper Context," *Product and Process Innovation,* November/December 1991: 33–37.
10. Vern Terpstra, "The Evolution of International Marketing," *International Marketing Review* 4 (Summer 1987): 60.
11. Ibid., 53.
12. Donald A. Ball and Wendell H. McCulloch, Jr., "International Business Education Programs in American and Non-American Schools: How They Are Ranked by the Academy of International Business," *Journal of International Business Studies* 19 (Summer 1988): 295–299.
13. Michael G. Harvey, "Repatriation of Corporate Executives: An Empirical Study," *Journal of International Business Studies* 20 (Spring 1989): 131–144.

Cases

Markked-Down: The Fall of the Finnish Markka

The Finnish markka, like Finland itself, was the subject of massive economic changes in the early 1990s. With the disintegration of the Soviet Union and the Eastern bloc economies, it was increasingly apparent to Finland that future economic survival lay in a closer relationship with western Europe. One of the major linkages between any country and its business partners is its currency. The Finnish markka was therefore the subject of a government-instituted policy of linking its value to the currencies of western Europe in 1991. The following case traces a number of the events, both in theory and as communicated through the popular press, of the markka's trials and tribulations.

Figure 1 provides a brief illustration of the markka's decline against the European Currency Unit (ECU), the weighted index of the currencies of the members of the European Monetary System (EMS). The rough road traveled by the markka during this period, being first fixed to the ECU, then devalued versus the ECU, and finally floated against the ECU, is a study in the dynamics of the workings of the international financial markets.

PEGGING THE MARKKA TO THE ECU

The Finnish parliament approved on June 7, 1991, the unilateral linkage of the markka to the European Currency Unit (ECU). Prior to this time the markka was managed against an index of major world currencies. The currencies included in the previous index constituted a cross-section of major Finnish trading partners, including the U.S. dollar and the Japanese yen. With the breakup of the Soviet bloc, and the newfound growth of the countries of the European Community (EC), Finland believed its economic future lay with increasing integration with the EC. Although not formalized at this time, if Finland were to consider eventual membership in the EC and be con-

Source: This was written by Michael H. Moffett, University of Michigan, March 1993. The author would like to thank Veikko Jaaskelainen and Ian Giddy for helpful materials and ideas.

FIGURE 1
Finnish Markka per
ECU Exchange Rate
(January 1991–March
1993)

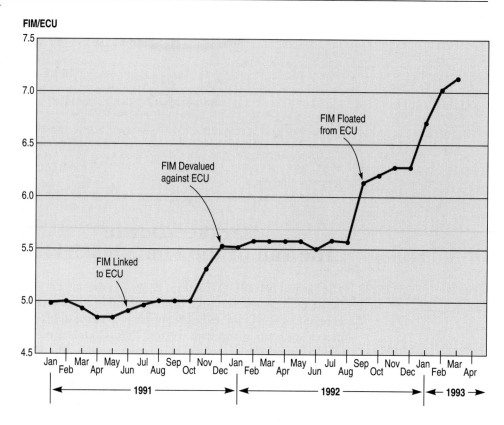

The pegging or fixing of the markka to the ECU was not without its controversy, however. As referred to in Figure 2, the controversy was focused more on the "no-devaluation policy" rather than the shifting focus of exchange-rate policy to the ECU. Many in and out of government argued that the Finnish export sector needed a boost, and a devaluation of the markka would provide that stimulus by making Finnish products relatively cheaper for Western buyers. The Finnish export sector had yet to recover from the devastating loss of exports to the Soviet Union, exports that had disappeared with the Communist Party. The trade deficit and Balance of Payments of Finland continued to worsen.

The Finnish government's stand, however, was that the reason for fixing the markka's value to the ECU was to demonstrate stability, and devaluing the markka at the same time would not be consistent with that goal. The government declared itself committed to the fixed value of the FIM/ECU and stood ready to defend its currency with whatever measures might be required. Markets, particularly international currency markets, often have their own ideas, however.

FIGURE 2
Finnish Markka Linked to ECU

Finland's new center-right government and the Bank of Finland decided in June to link the markka to the European Currency Unit (ECU) without devaluation. The decision was taken unilaterally by Finland. Sweden and Norway had earlier taken similar action.

Immediately after the government and the Bank of Finland had announced their intention to align themselves more and more closely with European monetary policy, domestic interest rates began falling. At the same time, the government banished the possibility of devaluation from the country's economic policy—at least momentarily.

The ECU is a notional currency unit, the value of which is composed of a basket of European Community countries' national currencies. The most important component in the basket, accounting for about 30 percent of the total weight, is the deutschemark. For Finland, the change in the currency system means that the markka's exchange rate will be more stable in relation to western European currencies.

The exclusion of the American dollar and the Japanese yen from the Finnish currency basket increases the exchange-rate risks with which Finnish companies must contend, because the markka will no longer follow the development of those currencies' exchange rates.

The strongest criticism of the ECU decision, especially the no-devaluation part of it, came from Finnish export industries and MTK, the organization representing farmers and forest owners. The chairman of Confederation of Finnish Industries, Casimir Ehrnrooth, later resigned in protest at the decision.

Finland's decision was welcomed in international circles. Both the Commission of the European Communities and individual EC countries expressed their satisfaction. One immediate effect of the ECU linkage was to reverse the outward flow of currency that had been a problem for Finland in recent months.

Source: *Blue Wings*, Finnair Inflight Magazine, August/September 1991, p. 30.

THE NOVEMBER SPECULATIVE ATTACK

The events of November 1991 serve as a classic example of the pressures that may accumulate versus a managed currency's value. Throughout October and early November, there were increasing concerns that the continuing Balance of Payments deficit signalled the need for the devaluation of the markka.[1]

As more and more currency speculators came to the conclusion that the markka would have to be devalued, they contributed to the devaluation pressures by speculating on its fall. By borrowing as much short-term capital as possible, the currency speculator could obtain additional markkas, which could then be converted into some other major currency. Once the expected devaluation occurred, the speculator could then use the foreign currency balances to convert back to markkas, repay the short-term markka debt obligation, and still possess a profit as a result of the devaluation.

THE NEW EXCHANGE RATE BAND

The Finnish markka, like most world currencies managed by their governments, was allowed to vary in a range in its exact exchange value versus the target rate or parity rate. These ranges are normally stated as a set percent change about a midpoint exchange rate. The Bank of Finland had originally established a midpoint exchange rate of the Finnish markka (FIM) versus its target the European Currency Unit (ECU) of FIM 4.8758/ECU.

---

[1]Note that this is termed a devaluation, not a depreciation. Because the Finmark's value is managed by the central bank to stay within an acceptable range versus the ECU, a governmental decision to alter the range is a devaluation. If the market was allowed to set the exchange rate without significant interference by the central bank (by way of interest-rate policy or currency-market intervention), it would be considered a floating rate, hence a fall in its value would be termed a depreciation .

FIGURE 3
Finmark Under Attack

STOCKHOLM—Finland's central bank caved in to a massive wave of currency speculation and allowed the markka to float in global foreign-exchange markets, presaging an imminent devaluation of as much as 20 percent, analysts said.

The decision to uncouple the markka from its fixed intervention range against the European currency unit came after the close of trading Thursday in Helsinki. Late Thursday evening, central bank officials huddled with parliamentary supervisors to discuss the nation's new exchange-rate policy.

In volatile international trading, the markka immediately plunged nearly 10 percent. London traders said the markka stabilized at about 5.5270 ECU, compared with about 5.0100 ECU at the close of trading in Helsinki. The weakest markka value allowed under the central bank's previous exchange-rate policy was 5.0220 ECU.

Source: "Finland Lets Markka Float; Devaluation Due," by Stephen D. Moore, *The Wall Street Journal Europe*, Friday–Saturday, November 15–16, 1991, page 15.

FIGURE 4
Devaluation of Markka

On November 14, 1991, the Bank of Finland decided to temporarily float the markka because of mounting pressure against the currency in the foreign exchange market. On the following day, November 15, the government decided on the basis of a proposal by the Parliamentary Supervisory Board of the Bank of Finland, to raise the limits of the markka's fluctuation range against the ECU by 14 percent, implying a 12.3 percent fall in the external value of the markka. The new midpoint is 5.55841 (FIM/ECU), and the markka may now fluctuate against the ECU in a range of 5.39166 to 5.72516.

Source: The Bank of Finland Bulletin, December 1991, Vol. 65 No. 12., p. 11.

The November devaluation of the Finnish markka noted in Figure 3 (the official announcement by the Bank of Finland is shown in Figure 4) provides an opportunity to demonstrate the quotation and calculation conventions used in currency markets. The exchange rate value of the Finnish markka for a Finnish investor can be stated either in FIM/ECU (a direct quote on the FIM) or as ECU/FIM (an indirect quote on the FIM).

The percentage change in the midpoint value of the markka, from the old value of FIM 4.87580/ECU to the new value of FIM 5.55841/ECU, would be calculated as follows using direct quotes:

$$\% \Delta = \frac{S_{midpt2} - S_{midpt1}}{S_{midpt1}} = \frac{\text{FIM } 5.55841/\text{ECU} - \text{FIM } 4.87580/\text{ECU}}{\text{FIM } 4.87580/\text{ECU}} = .139999 \approx 14\%.$$

This is the 14 percent increase in the midpoint rate noted in Figure 4 ("raise the limits . . by 14 percent"). If indirect quotes are used (where FIM 5.55841/ECU would be inverted to ECU 0.17990756/FIM), the calculation of the percentage change is:

$$\% \Delta = \frac{S_{midpt1} - S_{midpt2}}{S_{midpt2}} = \frac{\text{ECU } 0.20509455/\text{FIM} - \text{ECU } 0.17990756/\text{FIM}}{\text{ECU } 0.17990756/\text{FIM}}$$
$$= .139999 \approx 14\%.$$

Regardless of which quotation form is used, if the proper calculation formula is used, the percentage change in the value of the Finnish markka to Finnish investors (the internal value of the markka) is the same. The value of the Finnish markka to non-Finnish investors is what the Bank of Finland refers to in Figure 4 as the external value of the markka. The percent fall in the external value is found by reversing the preceding calculations.

$$\% \ \Delta = \frac{S_{midpt1} - S_{midpt2}}{S_{midpt2}} = \frac{\text{FIM } 4.87580/\text{ECU} - \text{FIM } 5.55841/\text{ECU}}{\text{FIM } 5.55841/\text{ECU}}$$

$$= -.1228067 \approx -12.3\%.$$

This is the same 12.3 percent fall in the external value referred to in Figure 4.

The new range over which the markka would be allowed to "freely move" would be $+/-3$ percent about this new midpoint of FIM 5.5841/ECU. The upper bound, S_{upper}, where the FIM/ECU exchange rate would be largest, and the markka would be weakest, is calculated as

$$S_{upper} = (.03)(5.55841) + 5.55841 = \text{FIM}5.72516/\text{ECU}.$$

The lower limit, S_{lower}, is found in the same way, such that the lower bound is

$$S_{lower} = (-.03)(5.55841) + 5.55841 = \text{FIM}5.39166/\text{ECU}.$$

The Bank of Finland's ability to preserve this range is aided by the expectations of market participants, if they believe that the new range of rates is appropriate and will be stable. (This often turns out to be a big "if." The Finnish markka was once again hit by speculative attacks in early April 1992. It was successful at this time, however, in "holding the fort.") If currency speculators, upon seeing the markka nearing either the upper or lower bounds, expect the Bank of Finland to intervene, they will buy or sell Finnish markkas. This expectation will lead speculative agents to undertake market trading that aids in moving the spot rate back toward the midpoint rate, aiding the bank in its task. These would be termed stabilizing expectations.

SAMPLE SPECULATION: FIM/USD

A short example of interest rates and exchange rates aids in the understanding of the events of mid-November 1991 in Helsinki. On Thursday, November 14, 1991, the markka was at the low end (meaning the markka was at the relatively weakest acceptable level) of the Finnish central bank's allowable exchange rate band, FIM 5.0220/ECU. Currency speculators may have believed a devaluation of the markka was imminent.

Although short-term interest rates were rising rapidly at this time (30-day markka borrowing rates were nearing 28 percent apr), any substantial devaluation of the markka would probably still make currency speculation profitable. A currency speculator, reading these signals, may have undertaken the following Finnish markka–U.S. dollar (USD) speculative positioning.[2]

Step 1: Borrow Finnish markka, even at the very high short-term interest rates.

 a. Borrow FIM 1,000,000 at 28 percent (apr).

 b. Which would then require repayment, in 30 days, of:

$$\text{FIM}1,000,000 \times \left[1 + \left(.28 \times \frac{30}{360} \right) \right] = \text{FIM}1,023,333.33.$$

---

[2]Exchange rates used in the numerical example are from *The Wall Street Journal,* November 15, 1991, and December 16, 1991, for the previous trading day. Eurodollar deposit rates are taken from *Harris Bank Weekly Bulletin,* Harris Bank of Chicago, November 22, 1991. Short-term Finmark interest is taken from *The New York Times,* Sunday November 17, 1991.

Step 2: Immediately exchange the markka borrowing's proceeds for U.S. dollars, deposit the dollars in a 30-day Eurodollar deposit, and calculate the proceeds of the Eurodollar deposit at the end of the 30 days.

   a. Converting the FIM 1,000,000 to USD:

$$\frac{FIM1,000,000}{FIM4.0025/USD} = USD\ 249,843.85$$

   b. Depositing the USDs in a 30-day Eurodollar deposit paying 4.8125 percent (apr).

   c. Calculating the total USD proceeds of the 30-day Eurodollar deposit:

$$USD249,843.85 \times \left[1 + \left(.048125 \times \frac{30}{360}\right)\right] = USD\ 250,845.83$$

Step 3: Convert the USD proceeds at the end of the 30-day period (Friday, December 13, 1991) back to FIM, repay the 30-day FIM borrowing (principal and interest), and pocket the rest as speculative profits.

   a. Converting the USD back to FIM at the spot rate on December 13, 1991:

$$USD250,845.83 \times FIM4.2940/USD = FIM1,077,131.99$$

   b. Repay the FIM loan and determine net speculative profits.

$$FIM1,077,131.99 - FIM1,023,333.33 = FIM53,798.66.$$

A sizeable profit for predicting the future accurately, Figure 5 provides an illustration of this currency–interest rate speculation. Note that this speculative strategy is intentionally "uncovered," meaning there was no forward contract purchased to re-exchange U.S. dollars into markkas. This is because the speculator wished to take advantage of the expected fall in the value of the markka and was willing to accept the currency risk of the exposed position. A position like this is termed self-insured.

    The above speculation leaves the end-of-period exchange rate open or uncovered, resulting in the above case of FIM4.2940/USD. If the speculation had been covered, meaning the speculator was simply trying to take advantage of differences in

---

FIGURE 5
Money Market
Speculation on the
Devaluation of the
Finmark

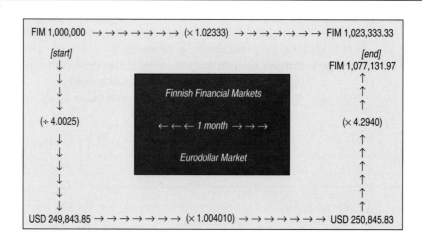

interest rates (Finnish markka and U.S. dollar interest rates in this case), the end-of-period exchange rate would have been a contractual forward rate. This forward rate would have been determined on November 14, 1991, rather than being left uncovered until December 13, 1991, as shown.

WORLD FINANCIAL MARKET REACTION

The devaluation of a currency has widespread impacts on world markets as noted in Figure 6. These impacts are increasingly spread over wider areas of the world's financial system as investors in all countries obtain increasing access to international investments. The benefits of international diversification, the potential to tap new markets and their expected higher returns, are combined with the potential for added risk as the exchange rate between the currencies of the investor and the investment differ, sometimes to the detriment of the investor.

International investing combines the expected returns of the asset itself, denominated in the home currency of the asset, and the change in the asset's currency value versus the investor's home currency. For example, a British-based investor's expected annual return on the purchase of a Finnish debt instrument would be

$$\left[(1 + r_{\text{FIM}}) \times (1 + e_{\text{FIM/STG}}) \right] - 1 = r_{\text{STG}}.$$

where r_{FIM} is the expected return on the Finnish debt, e is the expected change in the FIM/STG exchange rate, and r_{STG} is the resulting return to a foreign investor in London whose home currency is the British pound sterling (STG).

For example, consider the expectations of investment managers such as Thomas Berger, managing director for Lombard Odier International Portfolio Management in London. Berger had expected to earn the promised 12 percent (apr) return on three-year Finnish notes (r_{FIM}), because he assumed that the Finnish government would be able to maintain the stated exchange rate band versus the ECU. He was then not pleased to hear that the Finnish markka had been devalued by the Finnish government by 12.3 percent (annual percentage rate). His expected return, if nothing else changed before his Finnish debt instruments matured, would be

$$\left[(1 + .12) \times (1 + -.123) \right] - 1 = -.0178,$$

or a -1.8 percent return. This is particularly devastating for investment funds that are income/bond funds such as Berger's, for they often promise investors no losses on principal.

FIGURE 6
Finland Startles Investors

The Government of Finland suddenly let its currency float for one day last week. It was a jarring move that cost high-yield investors millions of dollars and provided a live reminder of the risk in betting that currencies will remain stable, even in the European Monetary System.

Mutual funds investing in short-term debt securities in Finland, which is not in the European Monetary System but had promised currency stability similar to that mandated by the E.M.S., were hurt by the surprise move that let the Finnish currency, the markka, plunge by about 12 percent.

Choosing markets with high interest rates is not hard. But if the high rates also signal economic problems that could lead to a sharp fall or devaluation of the currency, then they are not so attractive. But the promise of currency stability mitigates this risk and makes it hard to pass up rates that are two or more times rates in the United States.

Source: "World Markets: Finland Startles Its Investors," by Jonathan Fuerbringer, *The New York Times,* Sunday, November 17, 1991.

While Berger is more wary in the aftermath of the Finnish affair, he still sees it as just a bump on the road to yields that are good enough to absorb such shocks. Yet the episode should remind investors that this high-yield game carries more risk than some people might realize.

THE CRISIS OF SEPTEMBER 1992: THE MARKKA FLOATS

Although surviving a major speculative attack on its value in April of 1992, the markka once again reached a crisis in September. The markka was not simply devalued against the ECU this time, it was set free to float (see Figure 7). And float—or sink—it did. By March of 1993 the markka had depreciated from about FIM 6.2/ECU in September to FIM 7.1/ECU. (Against the U.S. dollar it was even worse. The markka fell from FIM 4.0/USD in August of 1992 to more than FIM 6.0/USD in March of 1993.)

If it is any consolation to the Finns, the currency crisis to which the markka fell victim in early September swept across the European Community in the second and third weeks of September. When it was all over, the British pound sterling and the Italian lira had both withdrawn from active participation in the European Monetary System and allowed their currencies to float. Continuing attacks on the Spanish peseta, Portuguese escudo, and Irish pound forced their devaluation within the EMS. And by November, the Swedish krona and Norwegian krone had both been devalued versus the ECU as well.

Although misery may love company, the falling values of other "satellite currencies" to the central currencies of Europe, the ECU and the German mark (DEM), was little comfort. The continuing deterioration of the Finnish markka in the fall of 1993 constituted an increasing source of concern to the Finnish government and Finnish industry. As described in Figure 8, the Finnish government has historically relied heavily on the international financial markets for the sale of much of its government debt, and that market was now in question. If the government of Finland states its intention to borrow a foreign currency such as the U.S. dollar and at the same time is experiencing rapid currency depreciation, foreign investors question the ability of the borrower to repay the debt.

FIGURE 7
Finland Lets Markka Float

STOCKHOLM—The Bank of Finland allowed the markka to float freely against all currencies, abandoning its attempts to maintain a fixed exchange rate policy and paving the way for the second devaluation of the markka in less than 10 months.

Sveriges Riksbank, the central bank in neighboring Sweden, responded to the spillover from the Finnish crisis by raising its marginal interest rate to 24 percent from 16 percent, the biggest single interest rate increase in the Riksbank's 324-year history.

In Brussels, a spokesman for the European Community Commission said it regretted Finland's decision to abandon the link with the EC's semi-fixed currency grid and allow the markka to float. He noted that any candidate country to join the EC's planned economic and monetary union must respect the membership rules for the European Monetary Union agreed to in the Maastricht Treaty.

With the markka down 17 percent to 18 percent against the dollar and major European currencies at the close of trade, Finnish traders speculated that the markka would eventually be devalued 10 percent to 20 percent. "It's very difficult to say how much the markka may fall in value. We have to see how the markets react," said Sirkka-Liisa Hamalainen, governor of [the] Bank of Finland.

Source: "Finland Lets Markka Float, Leading to Record Increase in Swedish Interest Rate," by Robert Flint, *The Wall Street Journal*, Wednesday, September 9, 1992.

FIGURE 8
The Republic of
Finland's Reception in
the International
Financial Markets

The Republic of Finland was in New York last Friday, presenting its economic policies and prospects to the local investment community. Finland has a US$3bn shelf filed with the US Securities and Exchange Commission and its officials are trying to take the temperature on what sort of pricing, structure and maturity US investors will find most appealing, once the markets begin to settle down.

Friday's meeting had been planned some time before the European currency crisis had started to build momentum, and it provided a useful lesson for US investors on what recent events will mean for those nations whose currencies were whipped senseless by the hurricane of speculation that swept through Europe last week.

Matti Vanhala, a member of the board of the Bank of Finland, assured his audience that the decision to float the Finnish markka was taken before, not after, the Bank had spent a high proportion of the national foreign currency reserves in supporting the currency. He said that Finland did not hope for depreciation of the currency, nor did it have a target level in mind. It is waiting for markets to stabilize before re-linking the markka to its European neighbors.

Central bank governor Sirkka Hamalainen was due to present a speech to the investors, but was unable to attend. In her prepared notes, she said that the markka would be "fixed against EC currencies again, but only when it is realistic to do so. Our ambitions concerning integration in Europe, including membership in the EC, have not changed." However, her speech added that it was "impossible to say how long it will take before a credible basis exists for fixing the exchange rate."

One of the big tasks facing the Republic, along with other European nations caught in the currency crossfire, is the rebuilding of foreign exchange reserves, which the central bank governor admitted to having been "insufficient" when the currency storm first started to brew up.

Partly as a result of this, estimated borrowings by the central government for the current year are estimated to rise to 30 percent of GDP, or around FIM150bn, and nearly 40 percent of GDP next year. These are historically high levels of borrowings for the Republic. 41 percent of Finnish government debt has been raised in the domestic markets, the rest in foreign ones.

Most European market professionals' view that there was no point in talking about what the currency crisis might have cost Finland, or any other issuer in terms of yield [price of debt]. Investors at the moment aren't buying at any price. "It is like the old Russian joke. The taxis in Moscow were very cheap, but you just couldn't get any."

Source: "Finland: Biding Time," *International Financing Review (IFR),* Issue 947, September 19, 1992, p. 7.

Access to international financial markets is critical for countries of all sizes, but most important for those that are small. Economic growth requires capital, and without access to international sources, government and industry may be forced to settle for slower growth and lower prospects. Only time will tell the degree to which the markka will eventually be "markked-down."

Damar International

Damar International, a fledgling firm importing handicrafts of chiefly Indonesian origin, was established in January 1984 in Burke, Virginia, a suburb of Washington, D.C. Organized as a general partnership, the firm is owned entirely by Dewi Soemantoro, its president, and Ronald I. Asche, its vice president. Their part-time, unsalaried efforts and those of Soemantoro's relatives in Indonesia constitute the entire labor base of the firm. Outside financing has been limited to borrowing from friends and relatives of the partners in Indonesia and the United States.

Source: This case was prepared by Michael R. Czinkota and Laura M. Gould.

Damar International imported its first shipment of handicrafts in April 1984 and estimates that its current annual sales revenues are between $20,000 and $30,000. Although the firm has yet to reach the break-even point, its sales revenues and customer base have expanded more rapidly than anticipated in Damar's original business plan. The partners are generally satisfied with results to date and plan to continue to broaden their operations.

Damar International was established in order to capitalize on Soemantoro's international experience and contacts. The daughter of an Indonesian Foreign Service officer, Soemantoro spent most of her youth and early adulthood in western Europe and has for the past 18 years resided in the United States. Her immediate family, including her mother, now resides in Indonesia. In addition to English and Malay, Soemantoro speaks French, German, and Italian. Although she has spent the past four years working in information management in the Washington area, first for MCI and currently for Records Management Inc., her interst in importing derives from about six years she previously spent as a management consultant. In this capacity, she was frequently called on to advise clients about importing clothing, furniture, and decoorative items from Indonesia. At the urging of family and friends, she decided to start her own business. While Soemantoro handles the purchasing and administrative aspects of the business, Asche is responsible for marketing and sales.

Damar International currently imports clothing, high-quality brassware, batik accessories, wood carvings, and furnishings from Indonesia. All of these items are handcrafted by village artisans working on a cottage-industry basis. Damar International estimates that 30 percent of its revenues from the sale of Indonesian imports are derived from clothing, 30 percent from batik accessories, and 30 prcent from wood carvings, with the remainder divided equally between brassware and furnishings. In addition, Damar markets in the eastern United States comparable Thai and Philippine handcrafted items imported by a small California firm. This firm in turn markets some of Damar's Indonesian imports on the West Coast.

Most of Damar's buyers are small shops and boutiques. Damar does not supply large department stores or retail chain outlets. By participating in gift shows, trade fairs, and handicraft exhibitions, the firm has expanded its customer base from the Washington area to many locations in the eastern United States.

In supplying small retail outlets with handcrafted Indonesian artifacts, Damar is pursuing a niche strategy. Although numerous importers market similar mass-produced, manufactured Indonesian items chiefly to department stores and chain retailers, Damar knows of no competitors that supply handcrafted artifacts to boutiques. Small retailers find it difficult to purchase in sufficient volume to order directly from large-scale importers of mass-produced items. More important, it is difficult to organize Indonesian artisans to produce handcrafted goods in sufficient quantity to supply the needs of large retailers.

Damar's policy is to carry little if any inventory. Orders from buyers are transmitted by Soemantoro to her family in Indonesia, who contract production to artisans in the rural villages of Java and Bali. Within broad parameters, buyers can specify modifications of traditional Indonesian wares. Frequently, Soemantoro cooperates with her mother in creating designs that adapt traditional products to American tastes and to the specifications of U.S. buyers. Soemantoro is in contact with her family in Indonesia at least once a week by telex or phone in order to report new orders and check on the progress of previous orders. In addition, Soemantoro makes an annual visit to Indonesia to coordinate policy with her family and maintain contacts with artisans.

Damar also fills orders placed by Soemantoro's family in Indonesia. The firm therefore in essence acts as both an importer and an exporter despite its extremely limited personnel base. In this, as well as in its source of financing, Damar is highly atypical. The firm's great strength, which allows it to fill a virtually vacant market niche with extremely limited capital and labor resources, is clearly the Soemantoro family's nexus of personal connections. Without the use of middlemen, this single bicultural family is capable of linking U.S. retailers and Indonesian village artisans and supplying products which, while unique and nonstandardized, are specifically oriented to the U.S. market.

Damar's principal weakness is its financing strucure. There are obvious limits to the amount of money that can be borrowed from family and friends for such an enterprise. Working capital is necessary because the Indonesian artisans must be paid before full payment is received from U.S. buyers. Although a 10 percent deposit is required from buyers when an order is placed, the remaining 90 percent is not due until 30 days from the date of shipment F.O.B. Washington, D.C. However, the simplicity of Damar's financing structure has advantages: To date, it has been able to operate without letters of credit and their concomitant paperwork burdens.

One major importing problem to date has been the paperwork and red tape involved in U.S. customs and quota regulations. Satisfying these regulations has occasionally delayed fulfillment of orders. Furthermore, because the Indonesian trade office in the United States is located in New York rather than Washington, assistance from the Indonesian government in expediting such problems has at times been difficult to obtain with Damar's limited personnel. For example, an order was once delayed in U.S. customs because of confusion between the U.S. Department of Commerce and Indonesian export authorities concerning import stamping and labeling. Several weeks were required to resolve this difficulty.

Although Damar received regulatory information directly from the U.S. Department of Commerce when it began importing, its routine contact with the government is minimal because regulatory paperwork is contracted to customs brokers.

One of the most important lessons that the firm has learned is the critical role of participating in gift shows, trade fairs, and craft exhibitions. Soemantoro believes that the firm's greatest mistake to date was not attending a trade show in New York. In connecting with potential buyers, both through trade shows and "walk-in scouting" of boutiques, Damar has benefited greatly from helpful references from existing customers. Buyers have been particularly helpful in identifying trade fairs that would be useful for Damar to attend. Here too, the importance of Damar's cultivation of personal contacts is apparent.

Similarly, personal contacts offer Damar the possibility of diversifying into new import lines. Through a contact established by a friend in France, Soemantoro is currently planning to import handmade French porcelain and silk blouses.

Damar is worried about sustained expansion of its Indonesian handicraft import business because the firm does not currently have the resources to organize large-scale cottage-industry production in Indonesia. Other major concerns are potential shipping delays and exchange-rate fluctuations.

Questions for Discussion

1. Evaluate alternative expansion strategies for Damar International in the United States.

2. Discuss Damar's expansion alternatives in Indonesia and France and their implications for the U.S. market.

3. How can Damar protect itself against exchange-rate fluctuations?

4. What are the likely effects of shipment delays on Damar? How can these effects be overcome?

Harley-Davidson (B) Hedging Hogs

Harley-Davidson's competitive comeback in the late 1980s is one of the few protectionist success stories. It is the story of a firm that used government protection in order to adjust to a changing competitive global market. But Harley's success in the late 1980s brought along new problems that threatened to undermine much of the progress already attained. Harley's primary problem was the same problem faced by many undiversified international firms: it produced its motorcycles, hogs[1], in only one country and exported its product to all foreign markets. But exchange rates change, and prices and earnings originally denominated in foreign currencies end up being worth very different amounts when finding their way back home to the dollar.[2]

EXPORTING HOGS

Harley's sales in 1990 were more than $864 million. Of total sales, $268 million, or 31 percent, were international sales. Harley had been exporting for a very long time: for 50 years to Japan and over 80 years to Germany. And new markets were growing in countries like Greece, Argentina, Brazil, and even the Virgin Islands. Although international sales were obviously very important to Harley's present profitability, they also represented its future. The domestic market in the United States for motorcycles—any firm's motorcycles—was beginning to decline. This was generally thought to be a result of changing consumer profiles and tastes. International market potential for Harley looked quite promising, but Harley had only 15 percent of the world market. It needed to do better, much better.

Harley's problem was that foreign distributors and dealers needed two things for continued growth and market share expansion: (1) local currency prices, and (2) stable prices. First, local currency pricing, whether it be Japanese yen, German marks, Australian dollars, or Canadian dollars, would allow the foreign dealers to compete on price in same currency terms with all competitors. And this competition would

Source: This case was written by Michael H. Moffett, The University of Michigan, March, 1993. This case is intended for class discussion purposes only and does not represent either efficient or inefficient financial management practices. Do not quote without prior permission.

[1]The motorcycles produced and sold by Harley-Davidson have traditionally been known as hogs. The nickname is primarily in reference to their traditional large size, weight, and power.

[2]This case draws upon several articles including "Harley Uses 'Risk Sharing' To Hedge Foreign Currencies," by Lawrence R. Quinn, *Business International Money Report,* March 16, 1992, 105–106; and "Harley: Wheeling and Dealing," by Lawrence Quinn, *Corporate Finance,* April 1992, 29–30.

not be hindered by the dealers and distributors adding currency surcharges to sticker prices as a result of their own need to cover currency exposure.[3] So Harley needed to sell its hogs to foreign dealers and distributorships in local currency. But this would not really solve the problems. First, Harley itself would now be responsible for managing the currency exposure. Second, it still did not assure the foreign dealers of stable prices, not unless Harley intended to absorb all exchange-rate changes itself.

Figure 1 illustrates this foreign currency pricing issue for sales of Harleys in Australia and Japan. Australian consumers shop, compare, and purchase in Australian dollars. Starting at the opposite end, however, is the fact that Harley hogs are produced and initially priced in U.S. dollars. Someone must bear the risk of currency exchange, either the parent, the distributor, or the consumer. And it will rarely be the consumer.

CURRENCY RISK SHARING AT HARLEY

John Hevey, manager of international finance, instituted a system that Harley calls "risk sharing." The idea is not new, but it has not been fashionable for some time. The idea is fairly simple: as long as the spot exchange rate does not move a great distance from the rate in effect when Harley quotes foreign currency prices to its foreign dealers, Harley will maintain that single price. This allows the foreign dealers and distributors, both those owned and not owned by Harley, to be assured of predictable and stable prices. And these stable prices needed to be denominated in the currency of the foreign dealer and distributor's operations. Harley would then be responsible for managing the currency exposures.

A typical currency risk-sharing arrangement specifies three bands or zones of exchanges: (1) Neutral Zone; (2) Sharing Zone; and (3) Renegotiation Zone. Figure 2 provides an example of how these currency zones may be constructed between a

---

[3]For example, an independent Australian dealer who sells and earns Australian dollar revenues but must pay for the Harley hogs shipped from the United States in U.S. dollars will be accepting currency risk. If the Australian dealer then adds a margin to the hog price to cover currency-hedging costs, the product is less competitive.

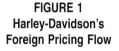

FIGURE 1
Harley-Davidson's Foreign Pricing Flow

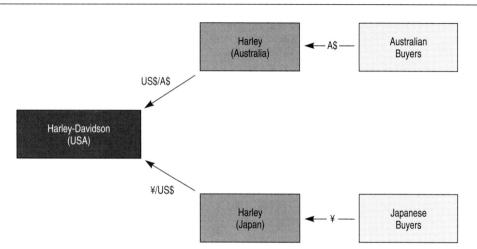

U.S. parent firm and its Japanese dealers or distributors. The Neutral Zone in Figure 2 is constructed as a band of $+/-5$ percent change about the central rate specified in the contract, ¥130.00/$. The central rate can be determined a number of ways, for example, the spot rate in effect on the date of the contract's consummation, the average rate for the past three-month period, a moving average of monthly rates, etc. In this case, the Neutral Zone's boundaries are ¥136.84/$ and ¥123.81/$.[4] As long as the spot exchange rate between the yen and dollar remains within this Neutral Zone, the U.S. parent assures the Japanese dealers of a constant price in yen. If a particular product line was priced in the United States at $4,000, the yen-denominated price would be ¥520,000. This assures the Japanese dealers a constant supply price in their own currency terms. This predictability of costs reduces the currency risks of the Japanese dealers and allows them to pass on these more predictable local-currency prices to their customers.

If, however, the spot rate moves out of the Neutral Zone into the Sharing Zone, the U.S. parent and the Japanese dealer will share the costs or benefits of the margin beyond the Neutral Zone rate. For example, if the Japanese yen depreciated against the dollar to ¥140.00/$, the spot rate will have moved into the upper Sharing Zone. If the contract specified that the sharing would be a 50/50 split, the new price to the Japanese dealer would be

$$\$4,000 \times \left[¥130.00/\$ + \frac{¥140.00/\$ - ¥136.84/\$}{2} \right] = \$4,000 \times ¥131.58/\$ = ¥526,320.$$

Although the supply costs have indeed risen to the Japanese dealers, from ¥520,000 to ¥526,320, the percentage increase is significantly less than the percentage change in the exchange rate.[5] The Japanese dealer is insulated against the constant fluctuations of the exchange rate and subsequent fluctuations on supply costs.

Finally, if the spot rate were to move drastically from the Neutral Zone into the Renegotiation Zone, the risk-sharing agreement calls for a renegotiation of the price to bring it more in line with current exchange rates and the economic and competitive realities of the market.

CURRENCY MANAGEMENT AT HARLEY

This risk-sharing program has allowed Harley to increase the stability of prices in foreign markets. But this stability has come about by the parent firm's accepting a larger proportion of the exchange-rate risk. Harley's approach to currency management is conservative, both in what it hedges and how it hedges.

The "what," the exposures that Harley actually manages, are primarily its sales, which are denominated in foreign currencies. Although Harley does import some inputs, the volume of imports denominated in foreign currencies (accounts payable)

---

[4]The upper and lower exchange rates of the band are calculated as:

$$\frac{¥130.00/\$ - ¥136.84/\$}{¥136.84/\$} \times 100 = -5.0\%.$$

and

$$\frac{¥130.00/\$ - ¥123.81/\$}{¥123.81\$} \times 100 = +5.0\%.$$

[5]The yen price has risen only 1.22 percent while the Japanese yen has depreciated 7.14 percent versus the U.S. dollar.

FIGURE 2
Currency Risk Sharing

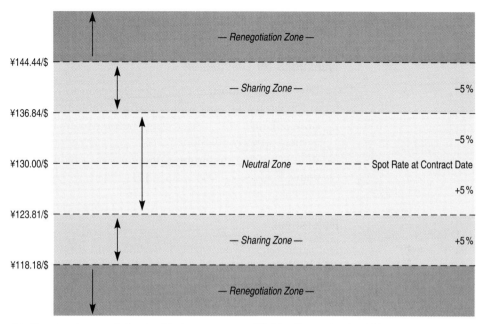

Note: Percentage changes are in the value of the Japanese yen versus U.S. dollar. For example, a "+ 5% " is a 5 percent appreciation in the value of the yen, from ¥130.00/$ to ¥123.81/$.

are relatively small compared to the export sales (the accounts receivable). Harley is a bit more aggressive in its exposure time frame than many other firms, however. Harley will hedge sales that will be made in the near future, anticipated sales, extending about 12 months out. The ability of the firm to hedge sales that have not yet been "booked" is a result of the firm's consistency and predictability of sales in the various markets. Like most firms that hedge future sales, however, Harley will intentionally leave itself a margin of error, therefore hedging less than 100 percent of the expected exposures.

Presently Harley is rather conservative in the "how," the instruments and methods used for currency hedging. Harley uses currency forward contracts for all hedging. Harley will estimate the amount of the various foreign-currency payments to be received per period and sell those foreign currency quantities forward (less the percentage margin for error). Like many other firms expanding international operations, Harley is now studying the use of additional currency-management approaches, such as the use of foreign-currency options. At present, however, Harley executives are happy with their currency management program in general.

FINANCIAL MANAGEMENT'S GROWING RESPONSIBILITIES

A third dimension of the new financial/currency management program at Harley is the increased role of financial management with sales. The finance staff keeps in touch with the sales and marketing staffs to work toward the most competitive combinations and packages of pricing. Financial staff also attempts to keep information lines open between its foreign dealers and distributors to help them maintain price competitiveness.

Harley-Davidson is a firm that continues to be unique in many ways. Not only is it one of the true "success stories" for American protectionism, but it has continued to work to improve its international competitiveness by responding to the needs of not only its customers, but its distributors and dealers.

Questions for Discussion

1. Why is it so important for Harley-Davidson to both price in foreign currencies in foreign markets, as well as provide stable prices?
2. How effective will "risk-sharing" be in actually achieving Harley's stated goals? Is there a better solution?
3. Who is bearing the brunt of the costs for this financial risk management program?

References

Hufbauer, Gary Clyde, Diane T. Berliner, and Kimberly Ann Elliot, *Trade Protection in the United States: 31 Case Studies,* The Institute for International Economics, Washington, D.C., 1986.

Pruzin, Daniel R., "Born to Be Verrucht," *World Trade,* Vol. 5, Issue 4, May 1992, 112–117.

Quinn, Lawrence R., "Harley Uses 'Risk Sharing' To Hedge Foreign Currencies," *Business International Money Report,* March 16, 1992, 105–106.

——— ,"Harley: Wheeling and Dealing," *Corporate Finance,* April 1992, 29–30.

Establishing an Overseas Law Office

Stuffim & Bacom is a 20-year-old, 125-member law firm based in St. Paul, Minnesota. Aside from its home office, the firm maintains offices in Washington, D.C.; Denver, Colorado; and Paris, France. As in any major firm, there are many areas of practice, but the firm's fastest growing section is its international business department. This department is headed by the firm's principal rainmaker and senior Washington partner, Harley Hambone, assisted by an aggressive junior partner, Sylvester Soupspoon, also based in Washington.

Stuffim & Bacom has just begun to acquire business on the African continent. Its biggest client, Safari Air Lines (SAL), is an international airfreight company with corporate headquarters in Abidjan, Ivory Coast. Last year, SAL was the major airfreight carrier for all of east, central, and west Africa. Recently, Hambone, an international finance expert and master salesman, persuaded SAL to drop the law firm of

Source: This case was written by William E. Casselman II, a senior attorney and shareholder in the law firm of Popham, Haik, Schnobrich & Kaufman, Ltd. (Washington office). Reprinted with permission. It is intended only to describe fictional business situations, and any resemblance to real individuals or business organizations is purely coincidental. The various economic, legal, political, and cultural conditions described in the case are for illustration only and do not necessarily reflect the actual conditions prevailing within the regions or countries mentioned.

Bend, Spindell & Mutilate, an old-line New York City firm, as the company's U.S. counsel and transfer all of SAL's business to the Stuffim firm. SAL is now almost a $1 million per year account for Stuffim & Bacom, which includes work with airline regulatory agencies in the United Sates, as well as general advice regarding international aviation matters.

In addition, Soupspoon, a transportation attorney, recently brought in Livingstone Tours Inc., a small but burgeoning U.S.–based travel agency specializing in three-month African safaris, as a new client. Livingstone maintains its only overseas office in Nairobi, Kenya. Stuffim bills Livingstone less than $500,000 per year, mainly for preparing and negotiating agreements with international charter airlines and local tour operators serving east Africa.

Due to their already substantial client obligations, as well as the sudden, unexpected growth in their business on the African continent and the impracticality of handling this work out of their Washington, D.C., office, Hambone and Soupspoon have decided to propose that the firm open an office in Africa to cover its growing client needs in that part of the world. This would not only enable the firm to better serve SAL and Livingstone Tours, but it would also help the firm garner more African business.

SAL and Livingstone Tours are each pressing Stuffim & Bacom to set up an African office as soon as possible, preferably close to their respective African operations. This will require the firm to invest $250,000 to start up an office, as well as yearly expenditures (including related overhead) of $125,000 per U.S. attorney and $75,000 per local attorney to staff it with qualified lawyers.

Establishing a foreign office is nothing new to Stuffim & Bacom. For almost 10 years the firm has maintained an office in Paris, France. As with many foreign branches of U.S. law firms, the Paris office generates very little profit and is regarded by the firm as something of a prestigious "foreign outpost." The firm continues to maintain the Paris office at a break-even level, mainly for the benefit of one major client, Ali Nord, an Arab- and French-owned freight forwarding company with extensive business in the United States, Central America, and the Middle East.

The Paris office's only attorney, Sylvia Souffle, a senior partner and member of the Colorado bar, is qualified under French law to advise clients, such as Ali Nord, on questions of foreign and international law but may not appear in French courts or advise clients regarding French law. After 10 years of general corporate practice in France, she has recently indicated her desire to leave the Paris office and head the proposed office in the Ivory Coast, a former French colony in West Africa. Souffle has many contacts in the Ivory Coast, where French is the official language.

The firm has also opened two other offices abroad, neither of which succeeded. The first office was opened six years ago in Saudi Arabia to represent U.S. engineering and construction firms doing business there. This branch closed after one year due to a lack of business stemming from a decline in the price of oil and threats from Middle East terrorists, who were upset over Stuffim's representation of Ali Nord, which they wrongly believed to be a CIA front. More recently, a heretofore unknown terrorist group announced in the Middle East that it would "go to the ends of the earth" to wreak revenge upon Ali Nord and its "yellow running dog lackeys of Yankee imperialism," including the Stuffim firm.

The second office was opened three years ago in Bangkok, Thailand, to service Torch & Glow Industries, a Colorado corporation and major provider of fire-resistant tiling and roofing materials. Torch & Glow had experienced an unanticipated boom in business in Southeast Asia. Therefore, Stuffim & Bacom opened a regional office in Bangkok with special permission of the Thai government to represent Torch &

Glow in Thailand, and then only on matters not requiring appearances in the courts of Thailand. Unfortunately, a massive class action suit was brought against Torch & Glow in both the United States and Thailand for damages caused by the unexplained flammability of the company's products when used in tropical climates. As a result, Torch & Glow recently went out of business, as did Stuffim's office in Bangkok. Both of these failures cost the firm a great deal of money in lost start-up expense and attorney and employee severance payments, and the firm's partners swore never again to open another overseas office.

Undaunted by these past failures, Hambone and Soupspoon wish to pursue the concept of a Stuffim & Bacom office in Africa. They have several options, which include but are not limited to the following: First, they could send a contingent of at least three Stuffim lawyers, possibly led by Souffle, to establish an Abidjan office. Unfortunately, none of the firm's current attorneys, other than Souffle, speaks adequate French. Second, they could recruit a group of SAL's in-house Ivory Coast lawyers from its headquarters in Abidjan, make them special partners in the Stuffim firm, and have them run Stuffim's office. Third, they could send one or more lawyers to open an office in Kenya, an English-speaking nation and former British colony, to work principally on the Livingstone account and secondarily on the SAL account. Fourth, they could form a joint venture with a Kenyan law firm to staff and run the Nairobi office.

Soupspoon, aware that Livingstone already employs a local law firm, Amen & Hadafly, to handle some of its legal needs in Kenya, approached that firm about its willingness to form a joint venture with Stuffim to run the Nairobi office. However, Amen & Hadafly, although personal friends of Soupspoon, would agree only on the condition that they receive full partnership status, not just a share of the local office profits to which special partners are entitled. In view of this demand, as well as Amen & Hadafly's somewhat questionable reputation in the Kenyan legal community, Hambone was reluctant to accept this offer. On the other hand, because Amen & Hadafly is well connected in the local legal establishment, it is unlikely that any other local firm would agree to such a joint venture. There are no joint venture possibilities in the Ivory Coast, owing to SAL's having its own in-house attorneys and preferring to work only with the Stuffim firm because of its expertise in international transportation law.

In addition to the differences in legal systems and languages, Kenya and the Ivory Coast also have different infrastructure conditions. For example, Nairobi has good telecommunications but a shortage of available office space. Abidjan is known for its modern office buildings but lacks the more up-to-date communications facilities found in Nairobi. Both countries enjoy roughly the same political and economic stability and have a generally favorable attitude toward foreign investment.

Further complicating matters, the laws of both the Ivory Coast and Kenya place serious restrictions on foreign law firms establishing local offices with foreign lawyers, requiring any foreign law firm to employ a majority of local lawyers or to ensure that their local office is managed by a local lawyer. Moreover, any foreign lawyer wishing to practice before the courts of either country has to be certified by the local bar association as being competent to do so (and no Stuffim lawyers are so certified in either the Ivory Coast or Kenya). There is one exception—any lawyer qualified in a comparable legal system can practice without satisfying the formal requirements. The United States common law system has not been recognized in the Ivory Coast, but, because of the Ivory Coast's close ties to France, the French code system has. Conversely, the Kenyan bar recognizes the English and U.S. systems, but not the French system. Of course, it might be possible to persuade either government to create an exception for a single Stuffim & Bacom client, as was done in Thailand for Torch & Glow.

Even if Hambone and Soupspoon could persuade the governments involved to permit them to practice locally without meeting local requirements, they would still have to persuade the rest of Stuffim & Bacom's partners that an African office is a good idea. In light of the two recent overseas office failures, the remaining partners, most of whom are in the St. Paul office, are not expected to enthusiastically embrace Hambone and Soupspoon's idea for an office in Africa.

The time has come for Hambone and Soupspoon to lay their idea on the line. Hambone has arranged meetings with government officials in the Ivory Coast and Kenya to negotiate an office in one of the two countries. Soupspoon must persuade the Stuffim & Bacom partners of the merits of establishing an African office in the country selected by Hambone. You have been asked by Hambone and Soupspoon to prepare them for these crucial meetings.

Questions for Discussion

1. Advise Hambone of the various business, legal, political, and cultural obstacles standing in the way of opening an office in each country and how he can best overcome them. Also make a recommendation as to where you think the office should be located and how (and by whom) it should be staffed and operated.

2. Advise Soupspoon as to how he can convince his fellow partners that an African office will be profitable for the firm, if not in the short term, then in the long term. This would include the type of representation arrangements that the Stuffim firm should make with its clients in Africa to minimize its financial risk.

3. How do you believe Stuffim & Bacom, as a growing international law firm, should respond to terrorist threats?

Anacron Pacific

Roger Dale, distribution manager for Anacron Pacific, had this to say when speculating on a possible future direction for the company's logistics operations: "We are in a different kind of business than the rest of the electronics industry. We are selling systems, not just hardware—and the hardware we do sell could be almost anybody's. I don't see why we have to put everything together at our location and ship to the customer. Why can't we tell our vendors to ship to our customer sites on precise schedules and assemble and test the systems there? After all, if you look at any large, technically complex construction project, isn't that exactly what the contractors do?"

Dale noted that the information requirements for doing business in a global market were continually increasing. At the same time, a profound change was starting

Source: This case was prepared for the Council of Logistics Management and contributed by Philip B. Schary, Ph.D., Professor of Marketing and Business Logistics at Oregon State University, Corvallis. Reprinted with permission.

to take place in the way that logistics information was being conveyed, that is, from paper documents to electronic data exchange. Discussion in the trade journals had expanded from establishment of data links between shipper and carrier and vendor to customer to the banks and customs agencies in almost every major country. The objective was ultimately to do business electronically around the world.

There were many potential advantages in riding the crest of the new technology if Anacron could move fast enough with a thoroughly developed plan for a global logistics information system. Faster data transmission and retrieval meant better customer service and better control over product movement.

Dealing with the carriers did not appear to Dale to be a problem. They too were pushing hard for electronic data interchange. The banks were interested, although they were caught up in the legal problems of electronic letters of credit. Customers would be able to place orders immediately, entering them either through terminals in the field sales offices or directly through their own computers. Even the U.S. Customs Service was moving toward an automated documentation system and had already established links to customshouse brokers. Surely it was only a matter of time before pressure would be placed on exporters like Anacron to change over as well.

Some major problems still existed, however. Would suppliers cooperate in implementing this new information system? The implications of the change extended far beyond electronic data exchange itself. Sharing of production and delivery schedules was a major issue. Some of Anacron's suppliers had not been able to meet promised delivery dates, forcing Anacron to delay shipments to its own customers. With electronic data exchange, Anacron could share its production schedules with suppliers and coordinate production and delivery to customers. If these suppliers would use the information, Anacron could plan its own deliveries precisely. However, suppliers resisted Anacron's efforts for better coordination. Unless this problem were solved, much of the advantage of rapid communication would be lost.

GENERAL BACKGROUND

Anacron Pacific is an electronics systems company located on the West Coast. It sells computer-aided engineering design work stations for developing and testing electronics equipment before it is built. The primary product in the line is software to be integrated into complete systems with hardware components including computers, hard disks, and peripheral equipment such as color printers, shipped as completely self-contained units, ready to install and operate at the customer's site. The company also manufactures special-purpose hardware as components of these systems.

TABLE 1
Summary of Financial Information for Anacron Pacific (in thousands)

	Year 1	Year 2	Year 3	Year 4	Year 5	Year 6
Net sales	$ 256	$5,311	$23,182	$45,678	$92,415	$144,918
Less: Cost of sales	524	4,112	14,673	23,769	43,728	75,641
Research and development	989	1,031	3,556	7,645	14,729	23,965
Marketing and administrative	564	2,197	4,396	6,896	12,371	21,786
Net operating income (loss)	(1,821)	(2,029)	557	7,368	21,587	23,526
Less: Provision for income taxes	0	0	201	3,241	10,011	11,285
Net income (loss)	(1,821)	(2,029)	356	4,127	11,576	12,241

The company grew rapidly in its first six years, reaching revenues of almost $145 million. However, net income has flattened out, as shown in Table 1.

Anacron Pacific markets its systems through a direct sales force to manufacturing customers in high-technology industries throughout the world, although the vast majority of sales are made in the North American, European, Japanese, and Southeast Asian markets. At present, there are few sales to other parts of the world, but Dale anticipated sales to these countries as their economies evolved.

The Anacron product line consists of 15 products, 7 of them introduced recently. The company began by producing specialized design, simulation, and testing units; these were the backbone of sales for the first four years. They were sold as complete systems, including terminal and display consoles, minicomputers, large disk drives, printers, and a special Anacron-designed circuit board that controlled the work station as a single unit.

Anacron is the dominant supplier of these systems in the world market. However, competitors are beginning to offer similar products. International sales were more than 35 percent of total revenue in Year 6, compared to 20 percent in Year 5, a trend that is likely to continue. Anacron has five sales offices in the Far East, in Singapore, Japan, Hong Kong, Seoul, and Taiwan. It has eight in Europe, in The Netherlands, England, Spain, Germany (2), France, Italy, and Sweden. The company's distribution centers in The Netherlands and Singapore serve not only as transshipment points but are also capable of performing some production operations: system assembly, testing, and calibration.

Anacron's own hardware production has been limited to circuit boards, special-purpose peripheral components, system assembly, and testing. The major manufacturing emphasis is on software. Anacron's own physical manufacturing activity itself is a relatively small part of the total product and for some models could be carried out at the distribution centers, bypassing the U.S. plant altogether. Anacron has preferred to do the complete system assembly and testing before shipping, primarily because of the erratic delivery performance of some suppliers.

One strategic option is to perform the actual system assembly, testing, and calibration at the customer's location instead of performing these operations in Anacron's facilities. This would place the distribution department in a new role, extending the production line to the customer's door. It would involve not only internal coordination of installation, assembly, and training teams, but also orchestrating a worldwide supply system. Could Anacron's suppliers be coordinated sufficiently well to make on-site assembly and testing possible?

PRODUCT FLOW

Material and product components flow from vendors to Anacron's West Coast location or to the overseas distribution centers. Orders to vendors are based for the most part on firm customer orders, although some standard units are purchased and kept in stock. The decision to stock inventory is a reflection of vendor delivery performance and the cost of the particular unit. This policy is monitored closely, and management has exerted pressure to reduce inventory because of the holding cost and capital commitment. Product components are normally shipped F.O.B. vendor, which permits Anacron in most cases to control inbound transportation.

All components are inspected and tested by the distribution department. Distribution also assembles the system, configured to the final design in accord with specific customer orders, in close coordination with the engineering department.

FIGURE 1   **Flowchart for Product Components Received at U.S. Locations**

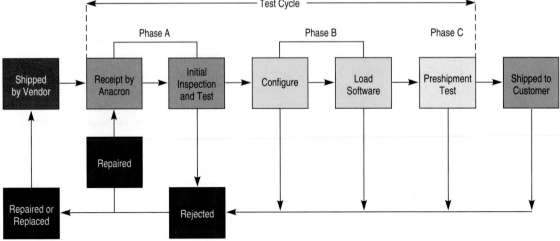

Anacron software is added, and the system is tested again. These operations are shown in Figure 1.

These operations are performed for the domestic market at the West Coast plant. Some components for overseas sales—for example, hard disks and computer processing units—are procured overseas and then moved under Anacron's control to distribution centers in the Netherlands and Singapore. This serves to avoid unnecessary transportation costs and long lead times to complete orders. A similar testing and assembly process to the U.S. operation then takes place before final shipment.

After the systems are assembled and tested, they are delivered to the customer-specified installation site, where Anacron arranges for site preparation, installation, and training of the customer's employees. Products are shipped to customers on a C.I.F. basis, allowing Anacron to achieve complete control over delivery. Domestic transportation includes normal airfreight, surface movement by van carriers, and small parcels express service. International movement is almost completely by air because of the extremely high value of the shipments. The final movements overseas are often by motor carrier.

Air transportation is normally coordinated through airfreight forwarders. One airfreight forwarder handles North American shipments. Two Japanese forwarders serve the Asian traffic—one to Japan, the other to other Asian points. An additional freight forwarder handles European shipments. Domestic surface transportation is negotiated directly with the carrier. In the case of beyond movement in international shipments, the responsibility is delegated to the forwarders.

MANUFACTURING POLICY

Anacron's unique competitive advantage has come from its proprietary software. Corporate policy has forbidden the manufacture of hardware components whenever possible. This has the effect of shifting responsibility to vendors for managing production operations for component units, including control over the bill of materials, process inventory control, and component lead times. Anacron's production and logistics operations therefore emphasize coordination of vendor operations delivery more than internal production process.

Anacron maintains only a "thin" bill of materials for production control and management operations because production involves major finished products as the building blocks. Component computers, disk drives, and peripherals from a number of vendors are considered to be potentially interchangeable. However, computers and color printers currently used have unique features that Anacron has utilized successfully in its system configurations. This has virtually ruled out the changing of vendors for the present. Otherwise, preference would be given to those demonstrating reliability in delivery schedules.

Product flow is managed as a make-to-order process. Customers may order with less than 30 days' notice or with lead times as long as six months, depending on their own internal procurement policies. Customer orders are often placed or cancelled on short notice, behavior that is characteristic of the industry as a whole. This volatility makes consistent production and distribution planning difficult to perform.

High service levels that is—precise delivery schedules in filling sales orders—are an important part of Anacron's strategy. The vice president of marketing has emphasized that Anacron must maintain its competitive advantage in delivery as well as product line, recognizing that a technological lead over competition is potentially transitory.

Dale interpreted this mandate as short order-cycle times and reliable "promise" dates. Logistics performance is limited, however, by the dual problem of erratic customer order practices and the unreliability of suppliers in delivery to Anacron. According to Dale, ideal performance would be achieved when suppliers deliver reliably within two weeks and customers order consistently on 30 days' notice. Neither of these is likely to occur under the present set of market conditions and vendor relationships.

The supply lead time is normally considerably longer than the normal customer order cycle time. This places heavy reliance on forecasting of demand by product, which has not been consistently accurate. The alternatives in response are either to make the customer wait or to hold more high-cost component inventories. Apart from the high capital cost of carrying expensive computer units and peripheral equipment as inventory, extremely rapid obsolescence is also a problem. Abacus, for example, made four major product changes within one and one-half years, requiring expensive modifications to computers held in stock.

Moving assembly operations overseas has distinct advantages. In some cases, it can result in lower taxes, depending on the location and the type of operation involved. Local procurement costs may also be lower than if the product were to be shipped from the United States. Lower labor costs at some locations can also be a factor, although this is not a governing reason. More important, however, are the marketing opportunities created by faster delivery times and local sourcing preferences.

Questions for Discussion

1. Shoud Anacron move its operations overseas?
2. Should Anacron products be assembled at the customer site? How would such a shift affect customer service levels?

3. How would Anacron's transportation be affected by the firm's shift to an ex-
electronic data exchange? How would this shift affect inventories?

4. How can Anacron change its vendor relationships?

Aston Systems Corporation

Gail Hartley, international regional manager of Aston Systems Corporation, briskly thumbed through the pile of fax transmittals on her desk as she finished her phone conversation and hung up. "I'm gong to have to cut this meeting short," she said as she glanced across her office apologetically, "our attorney is going out of town tonight, and I will be in Europe all next week. It's important that I meet with him to discuss the pending litigation."

As her coworkers left the room, Gail began to reflect on the recent problems she had faced at Aston. Realizing this wasn't the time for reflection, she gathered her papers and rushed out to make her appointment.

HISTORY

Aston Systems Corporation is a medium-sized computer software company with headquarters located in the eastern United States. The firm was founded in 1983 by a young software engineer named Roger McGuire and his wife, Cynthia Drake. The company's original focus was on marketing software that McGuire had developed to monitor and manage the performance of the IBM mainframe operating system. The initial product was the industry's first complete performance-management system running in CICS[1], one of IBM's smaller operating systems. By 1986 the company had branched out, developing software that managed a diverse group of larger operating-system platforms and subsystems.

Drake made the first sales, but within the first year, Aston hired Jeff Black as vice president of domestic sales. Black began hiring a sales force to meet the growing demand. By 1992 Aston had 230 employees, 95 percent of whom were based at its headquarters, with the other 5 percent based in its California sales office. From its headquarters, Aston's management oversaw domestic and international sales as well as product development and acquisition of other products and companies.

Aston has experienced remarkable growth, with gross revenues climbing from $56,000 in 1983 to more than $50 million in 1992 (see Figure 1). Aston management expects revenues to reach $100 million by 1994. To reach this goal, Aston has initiated an aggressive program to acquire complementary products and companies and plans to utilize its established distribution network to add value and thus increase profit.

Source: This case was developed by Professor Michael R. Czinkota and MBA candidate Marc S. Gross. Funding support by the U.S. Department of Education is gratefully acknowledged. Names have been disguised to protect proprietary interests.

[1]CICS stands for Customer Information Control System, which acts as transaction processing software. CICS is one of many operating systems for IBM mainframe computer systems.

FIGURE 1   **Aston Revenues**

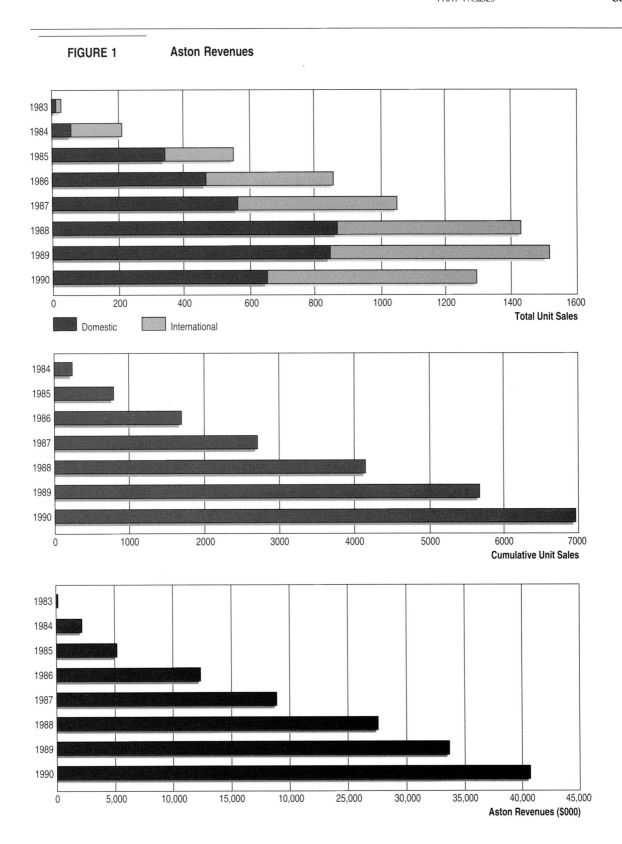

PRODUCTS

Aston sells system software tools for IBM mainframe computer users. These software packages operate in a number of IBM operating environments, including CICS, MVS, DB2, and VTAM. All Aston software products are easily integrated, menu driven, and share a common architecture and format. This means that once a customer has mastered the commands for an Aston software package, the same commands apply to all other Aston software. These user-friendly attributes encourage the purchase of multiple products.

Aston's complete performance-management software systems are designed to monitor IBM mainframe performance and diagnose information-system problems quickly, before they affect the user through costly system downtime. These performance-monitoring tools provide users with critical information about memory allocation, bottlenecks, and file utilization through full color charts, graphs, and real-time access. In addition, these tools provide upper management with an overview of the information system, its response times, number of tasks, and program and transaction codes. This helps users to optimize existing computer resources and plan for hardware upgrades.

The main Aston products as percent of sales both in units and revenues for the first half of 1992 were as follows: Monitor for CICS 45 percent of units sold, 49 percent of revenues; Monitor for MVS 17 percent of units sold, 23 percent of revenue; Monitor for DB2 14 percent of units sold, 17 percent of revenues; Monitor for VTAM 2 percent of units sold, 1 percent of revenues (see Figure 2). The monitor for the VTAM network communication systems was a new product that had been acquired from Cashwell Research, Inc., in 1990 and introduced only recently.

In addition to the software itself, much of the customer value came from Aston's after-sales service and support. Furthermore, Aston offered the finest in English-language brochures and reference manuals as part of the software package.

INTERNATIONAL EXPANSION

Aston was unique in its international expansion. Contrary to the normal patterns of expanding into international markets after establishing domestic sales, Aston had made its first sale to a company in the Netherlands. In 1983 Drake was attending a user group meeting for Oxford Software Company in Holland. At that meeting, she was introduced to Alex Nagle, one of Oxford's marketing representatives. As Drake told Nagle about Aston's product, he became increasingly enthusiastic about its market potential in Europe. Aston gave Nagle the opportunity to distribute the product, a relationship that proved to be long and prosperous.

As European sales grew, Aston authorized Nagle to establish agent relationships on its behalf. He then established distributorships in Sweden, Switzerland, the United Kingdom, France, Holland, and Germany. All distributors initially reported to Nagle, who maintained records and reported to Aston management.

In the software-production process at Aston, software engineers wrote commands to a master tape. In order to reduce overhead and administrative costs, Aston shipped master tapes directly to distributors and granted exclusive rights to reproduce and distribute the software and license to end users. End users received the software on floppy disks, which could be installed directly into their computer systems. In addition, the user received numerous English-language brochures and reference manuals.

FIGURE 2
Aston: Percent of Units
Sold First Half of 1992

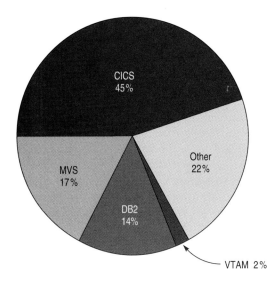

Aston: Percent of
Revenues First Half of
1992

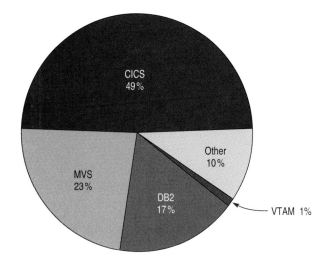

Sixty percent of sales revenue went to the distributor, who incurred production and marketing costs. Nagle received the remaining 40 percent, retaining 10 percent of gross sales revenue as a fee for managing the relationship with distributors and sending the remaining 30 percent to Aston.

For example, if a German distributor sold an Aston software package for DM 20,000, she would retain DM 12,000 to cover overhead expenses and sales commission. Nagle would receive DM 8,000, of which he would retain DM 2,000 for his management services and forward the dollar equivalent of the remaining DM 6,000 to Aston. Since Aston's distributors set prices in local currency, the dollar value of the revenue Aston received from its 30 percent margin varied as exchange rates fluctuated.

In 1989, a rapid increase in European sales caused Aston management to reconsider its relationship with Nagle. Aston management felt it had enough people employed in its headquarters to effectively manage distributors and wanted higher margins in order to continue its expansion. At the same time, Nagle no longer wanted to manage the effort, and Aston bought out the remainder of his contract. Aston retained all of its distributors and established direct communication and reporting channels and new contractual distributor agreements to replace the agreements distributors had with Nagle. These agreements granted distributors exclusive geographical marketing rights and provided them the same 60 percent of sales revenue. The remaining 40 percent went to Aston.

The nature of the distribution agreement provided Aston a built-in reporting system as a safeguard against unreported sales. Pursuant to the agreement, Aston provided sales support in terms of seminars, marketing materials and on-site client visits, as well as in-depth research support directly to clients. Most clients will at one time or another have a problem requiring direct contact with Aston technical-support staff. Having an unreported customer contact Aston for technical support could be very embarrassing and ultimately devastating for a distributor. Although Aston responded to both distributor and end-user inquiries from around the globe, there was no formal means of responding to inquiries made in languages other than English.

Currently, Aston has 21 international distributors marketing in more than 70 countries. International sales account for 51 percent of the total. In 1992, Aston's 12 largest distributors in Europe represented more than 60 percent of international income; Japan represented another 16 percent.

In late 1992 Hartley was in the process of finalizing an agreement to establish Aston's first subsidiary in the United Kingdom. Aston had recently acquired Integrated Software Group (ISG), which had developed a software product for the widely used UNIX operating platform. This subsidiary consisted of one full-time sales employee, formerly with ISG, a car, and a cellular telephone. Although Aston management was focused on minimization of overhead, it planned to launch the initial marketing phase of the product through this subsidiary. Although it had not yet been decided how to appoint distributors for this new product, Hartley did not plan to offer distributors exclusive marketing rights to this product as had been the case with other Aston products.

DISTRIBUTOR SELECTION

In selecting new distributors, Hartley relies heavily on referrals. She contacts current distributors for referrals as well as a variety of other vendors to find out whom they are using and if a candidate's performance has been satisfactory. After making contact with the prospective distributor, Hartley begins a formal interview process, much like that of hiring someone for a job within the company. Hartley looks to a distributor's financial backing, debt/equity structure, and business history, ensuring that there are sufficient assets to continue operations and sufficient business experience to minimize the risk of dissolution. In essence, Aston is looking to establish a long-term relationship with its distributors. On the administrative side, Aston analyzes credit reports provided by Dunn and Bradstreet to ensure that prospective distributors are paying creditors on time. In the final analysis, Hartley relies on her gut feeling of whether or not the distributor is hungry to get its hands on the product and sell it. Hartley travels abroad approximately two weeks out of each month to monitor distributor operations, interview potential distributors, and meet with large clients.

DECISION SITUATION

Despite this rigorous screening process, Aston has encountered problems with distributors. In 1990 Aston's Spanish distributor, Francisco Del Mar, decided to dissolve his company and establish a new company to sell a different range of products. Unbeknownst to Aston, Del Mar, who was based in the Netherlands Antilles, viewed his Spanish operation simply as a tax haven. Del Mar did not provide any advance notice of these intentions and thus left Aston without representation in Spain.

Recently, Hartley had also encountered problems with the Spanish distributor who replaced Del Mar. The individuals running this company had an excellent background and credentials. They were former Anderson Consulting partners who had been in management consulting for a long time. Despite having met all of Aston's rigorous selection criteria, the company overextended itself, hiring too large a staff too rapidly. After starting with only two employees, the company hired more than 150 within nine months. When the firm encountered difficulties in meeting overhead expense, it began using Aston's royalty share to finance other ventures and pay salaries. Aston had always been willing to work with distributors through legitimate short-term cash-flow problems. Normally Aston received payment in full within 30 days of a sale, as was stipulated in the distributor agreement, but it had occasionally extended the payment period. In this case, however, the problem seemed to go beyond the short term. Aston was in the process of terminating the distributor and as yet had no replacement.

ADDITIONAL UNCERTAINTIES

In addition to the uncertainties with the current Spanish distributor, the challenges associated with the launch of a foreign subsidiary and major exchange rate fluctuation significantly threaten revenues at Aston. Furthermore, a deepening global recession could severely impact cash flow and jeopardize Aston's stated goals of rapid expansion and product acquisition.

Questions for Discussion

1. How are Aston's revenues affected by fluctuations in currency exchange rates? Which is better for Aston, a strong or weak dollar? Why?

2. With such a large portion of revenues generated internationally, how should Aston handle inquiries and service requests made from abroad?

3. Should Aston actively pursue recovery of its money from its Spanish distributors?

4. How can Aston avoid distributor problems in the future without placing unreasonable constraints on distributors and market growth? How does the subsidiary relationship fit into Aston's stated long-term goals?

McDonnell Douglas: The F-18 Hornet Offset

When the Finnish government selected the F-18 Hornet over the Swedish JAS 39 Gripen, the French Mirage 2000-5, and fellow American F-16 to modernize the fighter arm of its air force, the sale of 67 aircraft worth more than $2 billion was a major boost to McDonnell Douglas in an otherwise quiet market. However, at the same time McDonnell Douglas and its main subcontractors (Northrop, General Electric, and Hughes), the "F-18 Team," obligated themselves to facilitate an equivalent amount of business for Finnish industry over the next 10 years.

THE FINNISH GOVERNMENT POSITION

Governments impose compensatory trade requirements especially when big-ticket items such as military equipment and transportation systems are being purchased. In some cases, governments may require "pre-deal counterpurchases" as a sign of commitment and ability to deliver should they be awarded the contract. In this case, for example, the Swedish bidder had arranged for deals worth $250 million for Finnish companies and the French for more than $100 million. While none of the bidders may like it, buyer's-market conditions give them very little choice to argue.

The rationale for the imposition has often to do with policy decisions to benefit certain targeted industries in addition to the concern over trade imbalance or foreign exchange. The required contracts can span a wide range of economic activity, from purchasing from a selected industry or industries, investing in or engaging in technology transfer with them, to coproduction and subcontracting parts of large projects.

Typically, the government sets up a committee to evaluate which sales qualify as part of the offset. In Finland's case, this committee consists of five members, with the Ministries of Defense, Foreign Affairs, Industry, and Trade represented. Their task is to advise the government which export contracts qualify and which do not. When the committee was established in 1977 in conjunction with a major military purchase, almost all contracts qualified until an export developmental role for offsets was outlined. The Finnish exporter is required to show that the offset agreement played a pivotal role in guaranteeing its particular contract.

The government takes two approaches to attain its developmental objective. First, the government will not make available (or give credit) for counterpurchasing goods that already have established market positions unless the counterpurchaser can show that the particular sale would not have materialized without its support (through distribution or financing). Secondly, the government will use compensation "multipliers" for the first time. While previous deals were executed on a one-on-one basis, the government wants now, through the use of multipliers, to direct purchases to certain industries or types of companies. For example, in the case of small or medium-sized companies, a multiplier of two may be used; that is, a purchase of $500,000 from such a firm will satisfy a $1 million share of the counterpurchaser's

Source: This case was prepared by Ilkka A. Ronkainen. It is based on: Keith Silverang, "Behind the Myth of Offset," *Style & Steel* 2 (Spring 1992): 28–29; Jukka Saastamoinen, "Jaita Vastakauppiaan Hattuun," *Optio*, May 21, 1992, 26-28; and Ron Matthews, "Countering or Countenancing Countertrade," *Management Accounting* 53 (October 1991): 42–44.

requirement. Attractive multipliers may also be used to generate long-term export opportunities or support Finland's indigenous arms industry.

THE F-18 TEAM'S POSITION	Offset deals are not barter, where the seller and the buyer swap products of equal value. The F-18 Team members complete offset programs through a number of different elements, including marketing assistance, export development, technology transfer, team purchases, and investment financing. The F-18 Team works with Finnish companies to develop exports for their products and services by identifying potential buyers and introducing the two parties to each other. Purchases can come from within the contractor companies, suppliers to the F-18 contractors, and third parties. The motivation for completing offset projects is financial penalties for the team members if they do not meet contract deadlines.

However, no one is obligated to engage in a given transaction just because Finland purchased fighters from McDonnell Douglas. The key point is that products must meet specifications, delivery dates, and price criteria to be sold in any market. After a sale has taken place, the F-18 Team receives offset credit based on the Finnish-manufactured content of the transaction value as approved by the Finnish offset committee.

Offset is not limited to the United States. The Team has offset partners all over the world because the members operate worldwide. Furthermore, given the long time frame involved, there are no time constraints on the members either.

The F-18 Team set up an office in Finland for its operations in 1992. Due to the worst recession in Finnish history, the response to the offset program has been unprecedented and the office has been inundated with requests for information.

ONE COMPANY'S EXPERIENCE	Hackman, one of Finland's leading exporters in the metal sector, started its cooperation with McDonnell Douglas by putting together a portfolio of Hackman products with the best offset potential. The proposal ended up covering a wide range of products, from tableware to turn-key cheese plants. Disinfecting machines and food processors created the most interest because of McDonnell Douglas's contacts in the hospital and construction sectors.

The first project identification came in July 1992, when word came from McDonnell Douglas that a $187 million hotel being planned for Denver, Colorado, was a potential offset target. The contractor was seeking export financing (through GE Finance) in exchange for sourcing products through offset from Finland. Ideally, the contractor would get attractive financing, the F-18 Team would get offset credits, and Finnish participants would get a shot at a deal worth up to $40 million.

Questions for Discussion

1. Why would the members of the F-18 Team, McDonnell Douglas, Northrop, General Electric, and Hughes, agree to such a deal rather than insist on a money-based transaction?

2. After the deal was signed, many Finnish companies expected that contracts and money would start rolling by merely calling up McDonnell Douglas. What are the fundamental flaws in this thinking?

3. Why do Western governments typically take an unsupportive stance on countertrade arrangements?

Norequip A/S

Norequip A/S, a Norwegian producer of fishing gear, markets net winches and related products in a host of northern European countries (Norway, Sweden, Denmark, the United Kingdom, Germany, Holland, and Iceland). It services two main segments in the market: (1) owners of existing fleets and (2) builders of new ships. Its sales have grown steadily (see Table 1), but at the same time its financial situation has deteriorated (see Table 2).

The market share varies from almost 40 percent in Norway to between 5 percent and 10 percent in the United Kingdom, Holland, and Germany. These figures vary, however, from one year to another. The company may well obtain 20 to 30 percent of all contracts concluded in the United Kingdom one year, whereas in Holland it is not awarded one single contract. This volatility of the market is detrimental to proper planning of operations.

Norequip operates mainly through agents in its export markets—except in Holland and Germany, where it is represented by distributors—and participates in the Fishing Gear Trade Fair arranged every second year in Aberdeen, Scotland. This exhibition is normally visited by customers not only from the United Kingdom but also from Scandinavia, Holland, Germany, and France. The agents mainly do local promotion, but they also very often conclude final contract negotiations. Norequip's three sales engineers concentrate mostly on Norway but occasionally take part in negotiations along with the agents, especially in Scandinavian markets. After some slack years in the fishing industry, the business of the shipyards and the fishing gear industry has become rather slow. The normal rate of capacity utilization was at one time between 50 and 60 percent. The slackening of business depressed prices and, in addition, caused agents to view the industry as less attractive. Many of them turned to the representation of offshore products to the oil industry.

Norwegian authorities tried to motivate the fishing gear industry to seek additional markets. They granted special credit insurance through NORAD (the Norwegian Agency for Development) and the Norwegian Export Credit Insurance Institute for projects in the Third World. At the same time the Export Council of Norway initiated market studies in North America and planned a major campaign there.

Source: This case was prepared by Professor C. A. Solberg of the Norwegian School of Management. Reprinted with permission.

TABLE 1 Norequip Sales, 1983–1985 (in millions of kroner)		1985	1984	1983
	Norway	24	22	21
	Sweden	1	3	2
	Denmark	4	3	3
	Netherlands	2	0.5	2.5
	United Kingdom	5	2	3
	Iceland	3	5	2
	Germany	1	2	0.5
	Others	—	0.5	—
		40	38	34

TABLE 2
Financial Statements

Balance Sheet at End of 1985 (in millions of kroner)

Assets		Liabilities	
Cash	1.2	Current liabilities	8.1
Receivables	3.1	Long-term liabilities	9.1
Inventory	3.6	Deferred taxes	1.3
Work in process	1.5	Equity capital	3.8
Fixed assets	12.9		
	22.3		22.3

Profit and Loss Statements, 1983–1985 (in millions of kroner)

	1985	1984	1983
Gross operating income	40.0	38.1	34.2
Less: Operating cost	35.5	33.5	29
Depreciation	3.0	2.5	2.5
Net operating income	1.5	2.1	2.7
Less: Interest expense	1.5	1.5	1.3
Exchange profit (loss)	(1.0)	0.1	(0.2)
Income (loss) from investments	0.2	0.2	0.3
Gross profit before extraordinary items	(0.8)	0.9	1.5

Exports, representing almost 40 percent of Norequip's sales, were increasingly crucial to profitability. Management therefore felt compelled to strengthen export activities. They were divided, however, on how to do it.

THE FINANCIAL DIRECTOR

Ingrid Johnsen thought that the greatest opportunity lay in strengthening marketing efforts in the company's traditional market (the northern countries of western Europe). In her opinion, the slack in business was temporary, mainly due to the financial problems in the fishing industry in western Europe. She stressed the principal conclusions of a five-year forecast made by the Export Council, predicting steady market growth. The European Community seemed especially interesting to her, mainly because of a major restructuring program financed by the EC. The main conclusions of the market survey are presented in Table 3.

As Johnsen explained, "I feel that we should take action now, reviving our activities in our traditional markets, so as to strengthen our overall market position. It is the least risky way out of our present impasse, and high-risk projects are the last thing we need right now." She alluded to the company's vulnerable cost position, adding that entering new markets was not only risky in itself, but also the exchange risks were unknown.

THE SALES DIRECTOR

Harald Opaas agreed that there was not great risk connected with the strategy proposed by Johnsen. However, he doubted whether market conditions in Europe really would improve, maintaining that the fishing resources in northern European waters had gradually eroded since the late 1960s. Although he agreed that the situation in the marketplace would improve, he claimed that demand would not be suf-

TABLE 3	Fish Catch, Fishing Vessels, and New Ships in Selected Countries, 1985			
	Fish Catch (million tons)	**Fishing Vessels**	**New Ships**	**Comments**
Norway	2.1 (14%)[a]	24,000[b]	19 plus 3 under construction	The parliament decided to condemn older vessels and support shipbuilding.
Sweden	0.2 (13%)	550	14	
Denmark	1.8 (±0)	3,300	131	EC subsidies to new building and repairs (7 million ECUs)
United Kingdom	0.8 (increasing)	7,600—mostly under 40'	130 (with subsidies)	EC subsidies to new building and repairs (50 million pounds)
Germany	0.2 (−30%)	990[b]	48	Subsidies to change structure of fleet (8 million German marks)
Netherlands	0.5 (+38%)	620	85	
Iceland	1.6 (+10%)	830	5 (mostly from Poland)	
United States	3.9 (+3%)	>5T 24,000 <5T 103,400	N/A	Expansion in New England and Alaska
Canada	1.4	39,000—mostly small	N/A	Expansion in industry was expected in 1986 through 1988
France	0.7 (+6%)	12,500 (2,000 > 10m)	46 small plus 1 large vessel	Subsidies to modernize the fleet (283 million francs)
Spain	0.9 (steadily reduced)	17,750 (4,300 > 20T) 2/3 older than 15 years	(51 in 1986; 103 in 1987)	Subsidies from EC
Portugal	0.3	7,123		Program under development to restructure fleet with EC aid
Poland	0.6 (stagnating)	1,450	Substantial exports	Navimore and Centromor exports to both Western and Third World countries

[a]Figures in parentheses indicate change since previous year.

[b]Number steadily declining.

Source: *Review of Fisheries in OECD Member Countries* (Paris: Organization for Economic Cooperation and Development, 1985), 1–6.

ficient to catch up with overcapacity in the foreseeable future. His main concern was the distribution network, which was reluctant to cooperate in overcoming difficulties when conditions were sluggish. He cited a telex from the British agent (Table 4). The situation was similar in most other countries. The only exception was Denmark, where market penetration had steadily improved in recent years and had reached 30 percent. Denmark was, in fact, the first export market that Norequip entered, and the company and its agent had long been recognized as reliable suppliers. Opaas saw little prospect of finding agents prepared to take over representation of Norequip's product line because the ones existing were already under contract to competitors. Moreover, he pointed out that changing agents is sometimes a more risky proposition than keeping the old ones, whose weaknesses and strengths are known.

Norequip could certainly establish its own sales subsidiary in key markets but, with the present negative results, Opaas could hardly see how the company could afford to invest in its own network.

I believe a good strategy is to entertain our present markets at the same level as today, with the hope of holding our position. We can then set up a project team to undertake market analysis in other markets, which have more interesting long-term prospects. I think one of my sales engineers, Hans Saleng, will be a good person to include in the team. He has traveled the most and is ripe for new tasks in the organization. One interesting area to be looked into more thoroughly is the Third World. In fact, the developing countries are increasingly emphasizing projects in this field, calling for new investment opportunities in the next five to ten years. It would therefore be worthwhile to take a closer look at the opportunities offered by NORAD in the Third World. In that part of the world, many new development projects are initiated in the fishing industry, and once we get some market experience, we could direct our marketing efforts toward other development agencies, such as the Regional Development Banks.

Opaas also assumed that prices in Third World countries were higher because competition was less acute. He was aware, however, that a new way of operating would require a change in attitude within the organization. Among other things, it might imply cooperating with other producers of fishing gear to set up total "project packages."

THE PRODUCTION MANAGER	Hans Pedersen was more attracted by the prospects on the North American continent than in the Third World. He assessed the market situation in Europe to be quite bleak and the Third World alternative to be much too risky. Therefore, he suggested that Norequip participate in the Fish Expo in Seattle together with a group of Norwegian companies under the Export Council umbrella. His main argument for entering Canada and the United States, however, was that the fishing industry in those countries supposedly was similar to that in Western Europe and therefore would require minimum adaptation in the production process. "Actually, we have a lot to gain

TABLE 4	Telex from: Sean Fisher, Aberdeen
	To: Harold Opaas, Norequip
	Re telecon last Friday. I certainly appreciate you would like us to sell more of your products and—I assure you—we try hard. Having a hard time, though, convincing potential customers to convert to your equipment. Both local British and other Norwegian companies seem to be well entrenched in the market, and seem to have managed to build lasting customer loyalty. My impression is that Norequip products are rated as being reliable and high quality, with features well in line with competition. But, as long as you don't have a local service network, it is hard to develop important customers. We are therefore restricted to a marginal market, where the main concern is price more than service reliability. The shipowners in this segment display a particular ability to play suppliers against one another in order to get bargains. The overcapacity in the industry does little other than exacerbate this situation. We have followed up some leads from last spring's trade fair and hope to achieve the same volume this year as last year. Look forward to hearing from you.
	Regards, Sean

TABLE 5
Cost Structure at Different Utilization Rates (millions of kroner)

Utilization as a percentage of capacity	60%	80%	95%
Materials	13.2	16.4	20.8
Labor	17.1	21.8	25.3
Direct costs	30.3	38.2	46.1
Overhead	5.2	6.6	7.9
	35.5	44.8	54.0
Depreciation	3.0	3.0	3.0
Total costs	38.5	47.8	57.0

FIGURE 1   **Organization Chart for Norequip A/S**

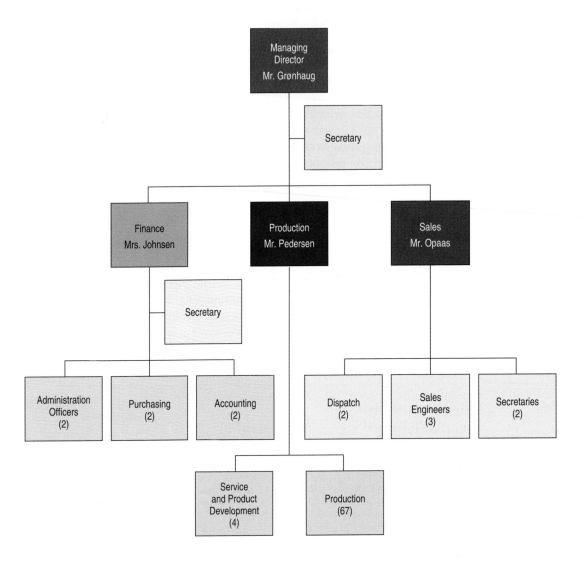

on scale—especially in the 60 to 80 percent capacity utilization bracket," he asserted, referring to the changing cost structure with increased production (Table 5). "If we produce to fill special orders, I'm afraid that part of the gains from increased production will be dissipated." He assumed (depending on the degree of adaptation) that special orders would increase labor costs by 5 to 10 percent, for example.

THE MANAGING DIRECTOR

Ove Grønhaug was aware that the company was too small to pursue more than one of the proposed strategies during the coming two to three years. Of the 90 employees (see chart in Figure 1), only 8 were in sales (sales director, 3 sales engineers, 2 secretaries, and 2 people in dispatch). In addition, 4 after-sales servicemen were available from the Production Department. The company could not possibly release more than 1 or 2 people to form a task force to look at the different opportunities. The financial situation was anything but promising. Grønhaug therefore invited the management team to discuss possible courses of action, pointing out that a decision had to be made within one month. At that time the application deadline for participation at the Fish Expo would expire, and he did not want to miss the deadline without having properly evaluated that opportunity.

Questions for Discussion

1. Evaluate the alternatives available to Norequip. What course of action would you recommend to Ove Grønhaug?
2. Do the managers' backgrounds contribute to their preferences for a course of action?
3. To what extend should Norequip consider working with governmental authorities? With other companies in the industry?

Finn-Vise Global

Finn-Vise Global, a Finnish construction company, was established in 1973 to meet the needs of the construction boom in the oil-rich developing countries. It successfully completed a few construction projects in Finland and Scandinavia during the 1970s before winning a contract to build a housing project for the Saudi Arabian government on a turnkey basis in December of 1975, followed later by similar projects.

Matti Lahti, a 50-year-old construction engineer, was selected in 1985 as the director responsible for the company's operation in Jeddah. Because Saudi Arabia was facing serious shortages of skilled labor at that time, Lahti had to recruit Finnish engineers, technicians, and skilled workers for numerous assignments. This met with the approval of top management and was in agreement with corporate guidelines and philosophy. Finn-Vise's aim was to train its workforce to work under different environmental conditions. In the Middle East, employees were required, in addition to being technically competent, to adjust to the unique circumstances of the sites, such as having to live in camps near the building sites and to refrain from alcohol consumption.

Largely based on the Saudi experience, the company had developed two basic personnel strategies for the Middle East: (1) differentiation based on recruiting Finnish personnel to establish a reputation for reliability and quality and (2) cost reduction by employing unskilled labor from local sources whenever possible. However, Matti Lahti noticed very early on that it was necessary to employ locals and third-country nationals. Headquarters in Finland allowed him some flexibility, provided that they were not employed in sensitive positions such as administration and accounting. Top management deemed it necessary that these positions be filled by Finns or expatriates of Arab origin who had lived or studied in Finland, and thus knew the Finnish language and Finnish culture. When he needed assistant managers for the various departments of the Saudi project, headquarters placed advertisements in the Helsinki

Source: This case was prepared by Zuhair Al-Obaidi, Training Manager, PRODEC, Helsinki School of Economics.

newspapers for university graduates with five years' working experience who were either Finns fluent in Arabic or Arabs fluent in Finnish. Among those chosen was Ahmed Hassan, an Iraqi business school graduate whose Finnish wife had a degree in Arabic from Helsinki University. Mr. Hassan was employed in the administration department, Mrs. Hassan as a translator.

In the autumn of 1987, Finn-Vise Global won another contract to build a hospital in Egypt. The contract obligated the company to train Egyptians to install, operate, and maintain the basic nonmedical facilities such as lifts, electrical appliances, energy equipment, and cooking and cleaning facilities. Matti Lahti was transferred to Egypt to run the project. He was assisted by two Finnish senior assistant managers. They were Kaarlo Savo, aged 55, and Ahti Peura, aged 54, who had worked on similar hospital projects in Finland. As managing director of the Egyptian project, he requested the head office to promote Ahmed Hassan to the rank of manager in charge of a new department devoted to recruitment and personnel development. He further recommended that Mrs. Hassan be trained for a market research and intelligence position. He argued that they would be assets to the firm in its possible future operations within the entire Arab region. His request was rejected. Instead, a Finnish manager was appointed, but the company promised to transfer the Hassans to Egypt with higher salaries. The Egyptian project was financially highly satisfactory for Finn-Vise. The company was able to recruit the necessary Egyptian engineers and technicians locally at reasonable salaries. Egyptian wages were lower compared with those in the region and the fact that most employment contracts were for one or two years helped lower the costs of operation. At the close of the project, headquarters advised Lahti to encourage the local personnel to seek jobs with the Egyptian Ministry of Health. The Hassans resigned at this time from Finn-Vise.

In 1989, the Iraqi government announced a development plan, which called for further utilization of oil revenues to transform the country into a modern industrial economy. Most oil-producing countries had been implementing similar plans, causing wages to soar and skilled labor to be in short supply. Finn-Vise targeted the Iraqi market, and the chief executive officer visited Baghdad on several occasions negotiating new projects. To show its commitment, the company established a branch office in Baghdad. Matti Lahti was again transferred to head the endeavor. During the first weeks it became apparent to him that the situation was dramatically different in Iraq. Most of the projects available were large, requiring long implementation times and strict adherence to rules. Furthermore, competition was fierce. Clear preference was given to local and Arab employees. Lahti met many engineers and technicians who had worked for Finn-Vise in Saudi Arabia and Egypt but were now working for Japanese firms on long-term contracts. He also learned that the Hassans were working for another Finnish company operating in Iraq. Both had managerial positions.

In August 1989, Matti Lahti flew back to Finland to brief top management on the situation. One of the proposed projects was a joint venture with the Iraqi State Organization for Contracting and Construction to build an entire university campus with appropriate teaching, administrative, and housing facilities. The project's duration was 10 years at a total cost of $500 million. Finn-Vise Global's share was to be 49 percent and to include, in addition to construction, training and maintenance services. To Lahti's disappointment, headquarters' management concentrated on the technical and financial aspects of the project. His requests to address the company's personnel policies were not met with enthusiasm. No change in policy was forthcoming because top management saw the present policies as adequate. Some managers pointed to the success in Egypt and saw no reason to change an apparently profitable formula.

Upon his return to Baghdad, Lahti contacted Mr. Hassan to offer him a commanding role in the project and to help him especially with the personnel challenge. Mr. Hassan refused the highly generous offer outright.

Questions for Discussion

1. What was basically wrong with Finn-Vise Global's policy regarding personnel?
2. If you were Matti Lahti, how would you recruit the necessary personnel for the Iraqi project should Finn-Vise secure it?
3. Should personnel issues play a secondary role to technical and financial aspects when a firm tries to develop a competitive advantage?
4. What effect would the 1991 war in the Persian Gulf have had on the case situation?

Spectrum Color Systems Inc.

Anthony Cordera, executive vice president of Spectrum Color Systems, sighed as he hung up the phone. The conversation still raced through his mind as he surveyed the fall foliage outside his office window. Cordera went over every nuance of the telephone conversation he had just completed with Roberto Cortez, vice president of European operations at BASF International. BASF had been a good customer for Spectrum, but today Cortez spoke with disdain, accusing Spectrum of questionable practices in its dealings with BASF. Cordera hated to see such a profitable relationship sour, but he saw no solution. As he turned back toward his desk, he wondered whether Spectrum might soon face similar sentiment from other large multinational clients. At the same time he wondered how to address this issue at the upcoming board meeting without alarming the company president and the board of directors.

HISTORY

Spectrum Color Systems is a medium-sized industrial firm with headquarters in the eastern United States. The firm was founded in 1952 when Daniel Clark, a government scientist working on techniques to measure aspects of color and appearance, was approached by Procter and Gamble (P&G).

Procter and Gamble recognized that customers held a perception of quality related to the color if its products. In order to offer consistency to its customers, and as part of its quality-control program, P&G sought a process to help it standardize the color and appearance of the products it manufactured. Clark balked at the request to work for P&G, building a machine that could quantify aspects of color, but as he recognized widespread commercial applications of such a machine, Clark went

Source: This case study was developed by Professor Michael R. Czinkota and MBA candidate Marc S. Gross. Funding support by the U.S. Department of Education is gratefully acknowledged. Some names have been disguised to protect proprietary interests.

into business for himself. Spectrum Color Systems started with the simple philosophy of providing solutions to customers' problems relating to measurement and control of color and appearance attributes. The first machines were developed under contract with P&G. As the quality-control movement developed throughout the industrialized world, the demand for Spectrum's products grew.

Spectrum Color Systems remains privately held; majority ownership and controlling voting rights remain in the Clark family. In 1990 Daniel Clark passed away. His son Paul is CEO and president; he runs domestic sales, finance, and human resources. Anthony Cordera joined Spectrum in 1985. As executive vice president, he is responsible for manufacturing, engineering, international sales, shipping, and receiving. He reports directly to Paul Clark.

The Clark family retains approximately 55 percent of company stock, including all voting stock. The executive and associate staff participate in an employee stock ownership plan and together own the remaining 45 percent of shares.

PRODUCT LINE

Spectrum Color Systems manufactures and sells an extensive array of colorimeters and spectrophotometers. These machines quantify aspects of color and appearance. As Appendix A discusses, such measurements are important, but no easy task. A colorimeter is the most basic instrument, with some models starting at $2,000. Most large manufacturers choose spectrophotometers, which are more exacting in their measurement ability, providing better performance and more options. These are generally integrated systems that can cost as much as $150,000.

Spectrum offers both on-line products and lab products. On-line products are designed for use on a production line, where products run under the instrument, which continuously monitors the product's appearance. These systems are manufactured in batch operations and customized to meet customer specifications. Typically, custom features are oriented to specific user applications and include hardware components such as moving optical scanners that measure lateral color variance as well as software components designed to meet the needs of specific industries. The first instruments built in the 1950s provided users with numerical values via a primitive screen and tape printer system with a 15- to 30-second lag between measurement and numerical output. Today, all of Spectrum's products are driven by user-friendly software that monitors color trends throughout a production run with real time output. Lab products are used when a customer takes a sample from a production line and brings it to the instrument for measurement.

Spectrum instruments are used in a wide variety of industries. Large food product companies measure the color of their products as well as packaging to ensure consistency. Paint companies purchase instruments to match colors and lease the machinery to paint stores. Automobile companies use Spectrum products to ensure that the color of interior cloth material, plastic molding, and exterior paint match. Some companies have forced suppliers to provide color-variance data sheets with all shipments. Spectrum recently supplied several instruments to a large bakery that produces buns for McDonald's. McDonald's had stipulated in its contract that buns be produced not only on time, but within certain color specifications. The bakery approached Spectrum to help meet these color standards.

A major manufacturer and supplier of denim uses Spectrum's "Color-Probe" spectrophotometer in its dye house to measure and grade the color of every strand of denim it produces. Color determines the value of the denim; it has a tremendous impact when millions of yards of denim are produced and the price fluctuates significantly depending on color.

THE COMPETITION   The color- and appearance-measurement market is considered a niche market with approximately $130 million to $140 million in annual sales worldwide. Spectrum has averaged $20 million annually in both retail and wholesale sales revenue over the last three years, placing it second in terms of market share. The industry became concentrated in 1990 when Color Value, a Swiss company with $5 million to $10 million in annual sales revenue, decided to dominate the color business. Color Value International, owned by a large Swiss brewery, purchased two competitors: Color Systems (CS), based in the United States and representing $35 million in annual sales, and International Color, based in the United Kingdom and representing $20 million in annual sales. Two smaller companies occupy third and fourth market share position; Speare accounts for approximately $12 million a year in sales, and Scientific Color generates about $9 million a year in sales (see Figure 1).

FIGURE 1
Color Industry
Concentration Before
1990

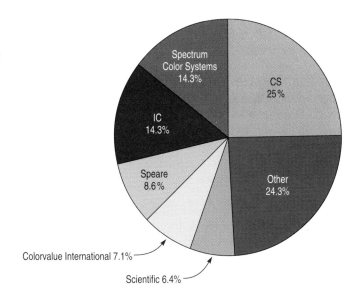

Color Industry
Concentration After
1990

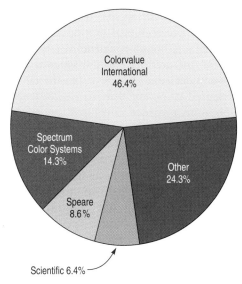

Although Color Value International holds almost 50 percent of world market share, Cordera believes that Spectrum now has a unique window of opportunity. The confusion associated with integrating three companies and the loss of goodwill caused by changing CS's company name, a well established and respected brand, to Color Value International gave Spectrum a sales advantage. In addition Spectrum entered the color matching and formulation market, one of Color Value's most profitable product lines. To gain market share in the United States, Spectrum's management decided to become the low-cost vendor and offered its new machines and color-matching software at prices of about one-half of the competition. Whereas the typical color-matching spectrophotometer by Color Value International was priced at $50,000, Spectrum offered a simpler $25,000 machine. In order to compete, Color Value International was forced to drastically reduce its prices to meet those of Spectrum, thus cutting deeply into profits.

INTERNATIONAL EXPANSION

In the 1950s and 1960s, Spectrum's management spent most of its time building the instruments and getting them out the door to meet the demand rather than developing a strategy to expand the company domestically or internationally. Spectrum's expansion into international markets succeeded despite its lack of strategic planning.

In the early days, Spectrum simply responded to requests from large companies such as Procter and Gamble to provide instruments to overseas subsidiaries. As the Clarks became more comfortable with this process, they decided to begin selling actively in Europe. By 1984 international sales comprised about one-fourth of total corporate sales. By 1992, the share had grown to more than one-third.

SALES FORCE

Spectrum Color Systems utilized independent sales agents domestically from its inception until 1986, when it developed an internal sales force. Cordera, drawing on his experience in marketing, set up the domestic sales force to provide more direct control over the marketing and sales strategies. After touring a number of agent offices, Cordera began to calculate the real cost of such a sales relationship. Working closely with Bob Holland, Spectrum's chief financial officer, Cordera tried to quantify some of the intangible and hidden costs of the agent relationship. Spectrum spent significant resources lobbying for agents' time and attention to sales of Spectrum products and provided all the technical support since few of the agents had technical expertise. Additionally, although Spectrum was responsible for billing customers and paid 15 percent of the sales price to the agent as commission, it had no access to lists of end users and decision makers within the client's organization. Spectrum is an application-oriented company, thus access to decision makers and end users within client organizations provides valuable information for product development and sales of transferable applications to current and future clients. A detailed financial analysis compared the true cost of using sales agents to the anticipated cost of an internal sales force. The analysis indicated that Spectrum could increase sales, reduce cost, and increase its control by developing is own sales force.

Internationally, Spectrum still relied mainly on independent distributors for its sales. Spectrum sold instruments outright to distributors at wholesale price. Spectrum billed the distributors 30-day net terms. Spectrum provided its distributors sales brochures and manuals in English. Distributors then translated these brochures as needed.

In the early days, distributors were selected largely through happenstance. Distributors of other products would hear about Spectrum and write a letter to the Clarks expressing interest in the distribution of their instruments. The Clarks would invite the distributor to the United States to see the products and get trained in their operation and thus become a Spectrum distributor. Spectrum now has distributors all over the world with extensive market penetration in Europe and the Far East. Although the company has encountered a steady international demand for its products, it continues to encounter problems with international distributors.

In 1984 Spectrum's sole French distributor, Gerard Bieux, abruptly closed his operation for medical reasons. Bieux had kept his sales operation close to his vest and thus maintained no customer lists or sales records. There was no one who could fill the void Bieux left, and Spectrum's management was forced to start over again building up its French distribution.

Cordera spent a great deal of time locating another French distributor and developing a profitable relationship. The relationship served Spectrum well until 1990, when a major competitor purchased the distributor. Again Cordera was left without a French representative for Spectrum instruments.

Cordera realized that the distributor-selection process was critical to Spectrum's international expansion and decided to become more proactive in selecting distributors. He worked closely with Holland to establish selection criteria for distributors based on financial stability, formal training programs, and financial goals. Additionally, Spectrum insisted that all distributors have service technicians trained at its U.S. facility. The distributor was responsible for paying the airfare for the technician, and Spectrum supplied food, lodging, and training. This strategy was not pursued so much for financial reasons, but to force the distributor to make both a financial and emotional investment in selling Spectrum products.

With the domestic direct sales force up and running, Cordera decided that if he was going to put the effort into forging an international presence, Spectrum should move toward an international direct sales force. In 1991 Spectrum opened its first European sales office in Paris. It opened an office in Germany in 1992.

DEVELOPMENT OF AN INTERNATIONAL DIRECT SALES FORCE

In spite of the detailed planning, financial budgeting, and strategy analysis that preceded the opening of both European offices, each showed a net loss in its first year of operation. Cordera consulted with large accounting firms in both France and Germany to gain insight into European business law and to develop first year budget projections. In addition, Spectrum management solicited information from its state Department of Economic Development on issues of taxation, international shipping, work permits, and visa restrictions for U.S. nationals working abroad. Despite such efforts, the combination of operating costs, which exceeded Spectrum's estimates, and slow sales associated with the European recession resulted in first-year losses in both France and Germany.

Cultural differences contributed to rising costs. Unlike the U.S. sales force where the majority of a sales representative's compensation consists of commission, European sales representatives are traditionally paid high salaries and relatively low commissions. In addition, employees are paid an annual salary bonus equivalent to one month's salary regardless of performance. Terminated employees can receive up to one year of severance pay based on the longevity of their relationship and position with the company. Middle managers and above expect to be provided with company cars, which was particularly difficult for Spectrum management to swallow since neither Cordera nor Clark was provided with a company car. Despite his uneasiness, Cordera agreed to provide these benefits since he felt it important to attract high-quality employees for the new offices. All of these benefits were stipulated in the long-term employment contracts required in Europe.

Difficulties soon became apparent with Spectrum's sales representative in Paris. In staffing the Paris office, Cordera, largely out of a desire to get someone out on the road in France, settled for an individual who, although the most qualified of the candidates, lacked the aggressiveness, sales orientation, and technical competence for the position. Cordera was disappointed by the sales representative's performance but found the process of terminating the employee a long and arduous one. Spectrum began working with an attorney in Paris, providing the employee with written documentation detailing the reasons for dissatisfaction, as well as sales goals that were to be met in order to retain the position. In the end, Spectrum was forced to negotiate an expensive severance package.

But now, the international activities seemed to be on track. Spectrum had two international offices abroad. The Paris office consists of the international sales director, one sales representative, one service technician, and two secretaries. From that office, Spectrum conducts marketing activities, sales, installation, and service for France. The German office employs two sales representatives, one secretary, and one service technician covering the German market.

To avoid future hiring difficulties, Cordera instituted a program that brings key individuals from European operations to its headquarters facility. The mission of this program is to integrate those individuals into Spectrum's corporate culture and create a team environment. On this point Cordera remarked, "the fax machine and telephone are great pieces of equipment, but nothing beats a face-to-face dinner or lunch where we can sit down and talk to each other."

COMMITMENT TO EUROPEAN CUSTOMERS

Spectrum management had historically marketed the same products throughout the world. Over time Spectrum recognized that the European market and the U.S. market had different needs and preferences in both hardware and software. For example, Spectrum sales representatives frequently found their sales efforts focusing on the software that accompanies the instruments, since that is the part the customer sees, feels, and touches.

To achieve market success, Spectrum management felt it had to design products to meet the needs of the European customers. There were two choices. The first was to translate existing software and then add the nuances the Europeans wanted. This proposition promised to be time consuming and very costly. The second option was to acquire a software company abroad.

In 1991 Cordera located a small software company in Switzerland that already had software written in German, French, Italian, and Spanish that was very applicable to the Spectrum system. Spectrum purchased the company for $275,000. Along with the company's assets and software copyrights, Spectrum also acquired the services of the company founder. This proved invaluable as he speaks five languages and can adapt Spectrum's software products to meet the needs of the European market.

Spectrum Color Systems paid for its acquisition out of the cash it had generated from operations. Spectrum management has historically taken a conservative view of financing. The focus is on cash management, trying to generate enough cash to finance any expansion. In fact, Spectrum would not have made the purchase unless it had the cash.

Spectrum does maintain a line of credit, but as yet it has not used loans to finance expansion. Occasionally, management borrows $500,000 on its credit line, invests in short-term CDs and repays the loan early just to show activity on its account.

DECISION SITUATION

In all remaining international markets, Spectrum still uses distributors. Recently this has resulted in significant problems. When BASF International in Germany purchased an instrument from Spectrum's German operation, it recommended that the BASF subsidiary in Spain buy the same instrument. When BASF received the invoice from Spectrum's Spanish distributor, the price was more than 50 percent higher than that paid in Germany. Cortez naturally felt that BASF was somehow being taken advantage of in Spain. However, there is little Spectrum can do about such disparities, since, pursuant to the distributor agreements, distributors purchase Spectrum products outright and determine the markup themselves. In addition, European Community antitrust regulations prevent Spectrum from setting a standardized price for its distributors.

This distributor arrangement is particularly advantageous in Italy and Spain. Given Spectrum's focus on cash management, the firm is leery about setting up direct operations in these countries. Cordera believes it is difficult to manage cash effectively in Italy and Spain, where vendors can wait six months to a year to receive payment from customers. There is an advantage to selling through distributors because Spectrum can collect cash on the sale in 30 or 45 days and the distributor has to wait for payment.

FUTURE STRATEGIES

By 1993, both European sales offices had become profitable. The emergence of the European Common Market could allow Spectrum to use its French and German operations as a base to expand into other countries without duplicating tasks. For example, the firm could place direct sales representatives throughout Europe with support provided by central office service technicians who would cross borders to perform installations and service. Yet Cordera still considered direct offices to be an expensive and somewhat risky proposition. His experience indicated that direct sales offices would not become self-sufficient for a least one year, and these types of financial losses caused friction with Spectrum's president and board of directors. Therefore, Cordera was not prepared for direct confrontation with distributors over markup. He dreaded the thought of being prematurely forced into opening other direct sales offices and repeating or even compounding the problems Spectrum had already endured.

In addition, recent changes in the exchange rates between the U.S. dollar and European currencies had tightened margins on export sales and decreased available cash. This pinch threatened to delay Cordera's planned expansion in the Far East.

Currently, Spectrum sells through distributors in the Pacific rim and China, but Cordera was in the process of negotiating a joint venture in China. Cordera thought that in order for Spectrum to continue its growth throughout the world and especially in the Pacific rim, it should establish a joint operation. The cultural differences in the Pacific rim seemed too great for Spectrum to overcome alone, so Cordera sought to marry Spectrum's technology and sales distribution with a company that has manufacturing capabilities similar to Spectrum's.

Questions for Discussion

1. Are current EC regulations beneficial or detrimental to Spectrum Color System's European operations in terms of distributor pricing and direct company sales?

2. How do fluctuations in the currency exchange rates affect Spectrum's revenues? Do you think Spectrum management would prefer to see a strong or weak dollar? Why?

3. How should Spectrum management respond to the BASF situation?

4. What has Spectrum done to meet the different needs of international customers? What more could be done to accommodate them?

APPENDIX A

THE BASICS OF COLOR AND APPEARANCE

What words would you use to describe a school bus? Yellow or slightly reddish yellow or perhaps orange? You might add the word shiny or maybe even glossy. But could the person on the other end of a telephone be expected to make a gallon of this paint for touch up based on these words? Most likely not.

To further complicate matters, is your color vision the same as the person making the paint? What about the lighting under which you made the initial judgment of color? Have you ever noticed how some colors appear quite different under the lamps used in your home or office compared to the outdoors?

Appearance characteristics are difficult to communicate objectively. Certainly a sample of the product could be sent to another person, but what is "close enough" when deciding if a match exists?

THE LANGUAGE OF COLOR

Color is a three-dimensional characteristic of appearance consisting of a lightness attribute, often called "Value," and two chromatic attributes, called "Hue" and "Chroma." Colors can be distinguished from one another by specifying these three visual attributes. Figure 1 shows a common arrangement of these three attributes often termed "color solid" or "color space."

Hue

Hue is often the first attribute of color that is mentioned. Consider the school bus. The most obvious thing about it is that it is a shade of yellow rather than blue or green. Hue is the attribute of color perception by which an object is judged to be red, yellow, green, blue, and so forth.

Chroma

A color specification requires more than just a designation of hue. How concentrated is the yellow? That is, how much color does there appear to be? Words such as depth, vividness, purity, and saturation have been used to convey how different the color is from gray. Chroma is the more accepted term and is used to specify the position of the color between gray and the pure hue.

Value

A third dimension is necessary to complete our specification. This is a luminous or lightness attribute, which distinguishes "light" colors from "dark" colors. Value is the term commonly used to express this attribute and is shown as the vertical axis in Figure 1.

FIGURE 1
Three-Dimensional
Color-Coordinate
System

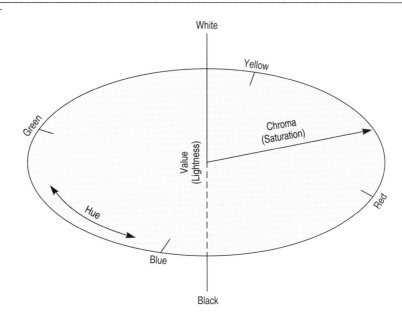

Encyclopaedia Britannica International: Exploring Emerging Market Opportunities

Laurence Maher, Executive Vice President of Encyclopaedia Britannica International, leaned back in his chair as another staff meeting concluded in his office at Britannica Centre on Chicago's Michigan Avenue. "Another meeting," he thought, "and still no proposal concerning a marketing strategy for the division in Europe now that the European Economic Community was established, the Berlin wall had fallen, Communism appeared doomed, and the Soviet Union had disintegrated." The major points of disagreement among the staff were assessing the level of opportunity in these new markets and determining the best marketing strategy to use to enter them.

Thomas Gies, president of the international division of the firm, had asked that another meeting on the same topic be scheduled for next week. Norman Wasz, Director of International Marketing Information, and Polly Sauer, Vice President of Marketing of the division, were also asked to attend.

CORPORATE AFFAIRS

Maher had concluded that the firm at the corporate level was in a good position for taking advantage of growth opportunities. He had witnessed a number of changes in the organizational structure, the opening of several new markets, the creation of many new products, and the start of several new business ventures in the company during the last 20 years.

Encyclopaedia Britannica International was a division of Encyclopaedia Britannica, Inc., an American firm which could trace its roots back to the publication of the first edition of the *Encyclopaedia Britannica* in Scotland on June 30, 1768. The company, a privately held organization, had its corporate offices in Britannica Centre at 310 S. Michigan Avenue, Chicago, Illinois.

Encyclopaedia Britannica, Inc., had a wide array of interests in the education field. In addition to the encyclopaedia, which appeared in the 15th edition as *The New Encyclopaedia Britannica*, the firm produced yearbooks, alternate reference works, and learning systems under a variety of names and formats.

Although the firm did not release exact figures, total annual sales were estimated at $650,000,000. Through wholly owned companies plus agreements with distributors, Britannica did business in more than 100 countries.

The corporate operating departments of Encyclopaedia Britannica, Inc., are shown in Figure 1. In addition to the departments of Corporate Finance, Editorial, Public Relations, Corporate Planning and Development and Human Resources, the division also contained the Department of Asia Product Development. This department coordinated product development and joint ventures for the firm in Japan and China. It also recently had assisted in the development of a Korean Britannica, was planning for expansion in other Asian countries, and was developing a new Italian language encyclopaedia.

FIGURE 1
Encyclopaedia
Britannica, Inc.,
Organizational Chart

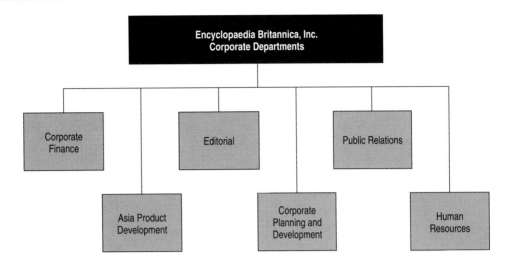

Encyclopaedia Britannica USA (EBUSA), one of the principal income producing divisions of the firm, as indicated in Figure 2, had the responsibility for sales of Encyclopaedia Britannica products in the United States, Puerto Rico, Guam, Virgin Islands, and U.S. Military. It was established in 1974 as a separate division consolidating the U.S. field sales organization and the company's support service departments.

Encyclopaedia Britannica products were traditionally sold door to door to consumers by a staff of independent contract salespeople. Although direct home sales by a highly motivated sales staff still accounted for a majority of sales, in the late 1970s, EBUSA expanded its methods of reaching the consumer. It established many more over-the-counter locations in which the product could be sold, including state fairs, shopping malls, theme parks such as Great America, and through large bookstore chains, such as Waldenbooks.

The sales field organization was backed by extensive public relations, national advertising on television and in print, special offers to groups, and direct mail programs which generated inquiries as sales leads. In a third-party program, mailings were made over the name of firms like American Express to reach potential customers at relatively high income levels. Prices in the product line in the United States were established in the Chicago office. Encyclopedia Britannica, Inc., had approximately 1,800 employees and more than 2,000 independent sales representatives in the United States.

The other principal income producing divisions of Encyclopaedia Britannica, Inc., were Encyclopaedia Britannica International which had responsibility for international interests; Merriam-Webster Inc. which published dictionaries and other reference works; Encyclopaedia Britannica Educational Corporation which was a major producer and distributor of educational films and multimedia audiovisual materials; American Learning Corporation which provided programs in individualized learning; and Britannica Software which specialized in business and financial planning simulation software.

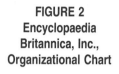

FIGURE 2
Encyclopaedia
Britannica, Inc.,
Organizational Chart

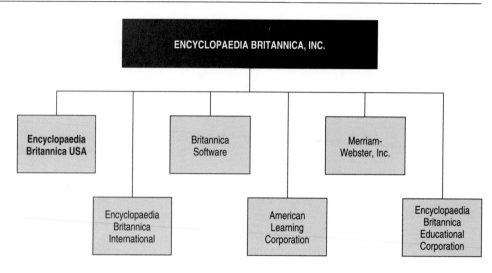

THE SPIRIT OF WILLIAM BENTON

Laurence Maher knew that the issues of maintaining control of the organization and planning for expansion had been perceived as problems in the organization for a considerable length of time. Much of the drive, determination, and creative practice of present management was attributed to the entrepreneurial spirit of William Benton who for 30 years had controlled the firm.

William Benton (1900–1973), a former advertising agency executive, was publisher and chairman of the board of Encyclopaedia Britannica, Inc., from 1943 until his death in 1973.

When the *Encyclopaedia Britannica* was offered as a gift to the University of Chicago by owner, Sears, Roebuck and Company, Benton offered to put up his own money as working capital. The university accepted the gift in 1943 and committed the management and the stock control to Benton, retaining a royalty arrangement providing for editorial assistance from the university.

As publisher and chairman, Benton made the corporate commitment of time, resources, and money to completely control and expand the company. He was responsible for producing the 15th Edition of *Encyclopaedia Britannica*. His longtime friend and colleague Robert M. Hutchins observed that "although he was under no pressure to publish a new edition, his own standards led him to conclude that he must do what he could to make *Britannica* better still." He was closely involved in every step of research, planning, design, and initial production of the 15th Edition while concurrently leading several other distinguished careers including that of U.S. Senator from Connecticut, 1945–1952.

Under Benton leadership the volume of Britannica's domestic business increased more than fiftyfold. Upon his death he was succeeded as publisher by his wife of 43 years, Helen Hemingway Benton. Robert P. Gwinn, then chairman of Sunbeam Corporation, became board chairman of Britannica in 1973. Under Gwinn's stewardship, Britannica experienced major growth at the international as well as at the domestic level. The William Benton Foundation, a not-for-profit organization, was the primary stockholder.

MARKETING IN THE INTERNATIONAL DIVISION

The international division, Encyclopaedia Britannica International, Inc., was head-quartered at Britannica Centre in Chicago. A small staff, consisting of the division's President, Thomas A. Gies; Executive Vice President, Laurence J. Maher; and Director of International Marketing Information, Norman Wasz, maintained offices there. The division's Vice President of Marketing, Polly Sauer, who traveled extensively on a worldwide basis, also operated out of the Chicago office. An order handling section, consisting of five people, handled merchandise orders from international subsidiary companies and independent distributors.

The division had primary responsibility for the management of wholly owned companies that sold Encyclopaedia Britannica and other products outside of the United States. These subsidiaries did business in 19 countries: Canada, Japan, Australia, New Zealand, the Philippines, Germany, Belgium, France, the Netherlands, Spain, Switzerland, Austria, South Korea, Italy, England, Scotland, Wales, Northern Ireland, and the Republic of Ireland. Each of these wholly owned companies was considered a profit center and was a complete self-contained unit. Each had its own president, chief financial officer, national sales manager, collection department, and sales forces. The products sold in each subsidiary were usually produced in the United States, but in some cases they were produced and manufactured in the local country. There were more than 230 offices staffed by 1,200 administrative employees and 2,000 independent sales representatives in the international division.

The division also had distribution agreements with a number of independent firms in more than 130 countries in the Middle East, Africa, Asia, Europe, and Latin America. An administrative center in Geneva, Switzerland, supervised the distributors in European countries where the firm did not have a subsidiary and in Africa. Asian and Latin American distributors were supervised from division offices in Britannica Centre in Chicago.

The international division was involved in a number of other endeavors such as a joint venture with Encyclopaedia Universalis in France. It also handled distribution of the concise Chinese-language version of the *Encyclopaedia Britannica* in all countries other than the United States and the People's Republic of China.

The product line of the international division consisted of a wide variety of encyclopedia, books, accessory products, yearbooks, dictionaries and language courses. The *Encyclopaedia Britannica,* published in English in a number of different bindings, was considered the cornerstone of the product mix. The EB international products are listed in Appendix A.

The International Division used a number of methods on the national and local level to obtain sales leads for the direct sales forces of subsidiaries. Management identified three types of these activities: (1) advertising, which was conducted on a national level through the various media to encourage response from potential consumers; (2) over the counter selling, which took place in high traffic locations like shopping malls, train stations and amusement parks to take advantage of "walkups"; and (3) "effort business," which involved leads and/or sales that salespeople created on their own without company support programs. The division Vice President of Marketing spent a considerable amount of her time traveling to plan, implement, and coordinate this part of the marketing program.

Management used a "Source of Order Report" to summarize and review the marketing activities which each subsidiary used to generate sales leads. The use of these tactics changed from country to country depending on trade tradition, custom, legality, interest, and other factors. The report was a complete listing of all of the tools that were used to generate leads for sales representatives. It represented the firm's effort in stimulating demand for the product line. As Maher noted, "In the old days, you went out on the street and knocked on the doors. We don't do that at all. Our salesperson has a name and an address and a place to go when he or she leaves the office." A list of the major items in the report appears in Appendix B.

For most products, prices were established through an annual agreement between the subsidiary president and the Chicago office. Once established in the operating plan for the fiscal year beginning on October 1, prices could not be changed without prior approval from Chicago. The corporate controlled pricing policy did not permit direct negotiation of the price of the product at the consumer level. Variations in price to the consumer would appear in the individual sales presentation as the sales representative suggested different types and styles of bindings or made special offer deals. The bindings ranged from a high quality platinum leather binding to a basic red one which was sold primarily to schools. The special offer deal included an extra book or free gift if the customer ordered at that time. Individual subsidiaries were provided considerable latitude in the operations provided they maintained their operating plan and did not make adjustments in prices. A similar program was established in maintaining sales commissions for sales representatives.

THE EXTERNAL ENVIRONMENT

Britannica management had identified two basic types of competition in the world market, international and local. International competition came from U.S. firms like World Book, Inc., and Grolier, Inc., which produced the *Encyclopedia Americana*. In the "direct to the consumer market," competition was considered negligible. In some countries, however, these firms had a fairly sizable presence in the mail order business selling a range of books including encyclopaedia. World Book, Inc., for instance, had scattered success in its operations in many countries such as Australia, Canada and the United Kingdom.

At the local level, competition was much more intense and varied from country to country. In Australia there was no significant local competition. In England there were a number of local competitors, but Britannica management did not consider the market saturated. In Japan, however, competition intensified because of the nature of the product line and sales force relationships. Britannica Japan Inc. was but one of many different companies that sold English language courses in Japan. In addition, at the sales level, loyalties were such that if competition hired away an influential sales manager, the manager typically would take the sales force to the new position. This proved to be extremely frustrating to management in the international division. The firm not only competed with firms that were selling similar products, but it competed for manpower to sell the product. Management had concluded that the situation was true worldwide, and it had become "a more important consideration from a competitive viewpoint than competition for the product."

In some countries, like in Italy, France, and South Korea, local firms produced an encyclopedia in the first language of the country. Also, in Europe, many companies produced sets of what were really encyclopedic dictionaries. They were labeled as encyclopedia and accepted by some consumers as substitutes in the marketplace.

A more recent development was the selling of pirated editions of the Chinese language *Encyclopaedia Britannica*. In Taiwan, for instance, several different companies duplicated the 20 volume Chinese [language] version of *Encyclopaedia Britannica*, rebound it, and sold it at a greatly reduced price. A similar situation also occurred with the English language version. The firm had some court convictions, but the practice continued.

Some companies like Amway, Mary Kay, and Encyclopaedia Britannica found that expansion into foreign markets met with mixed success. The concept of door-to-door selling was not equally accepted in all countries. Moreover, many cultures did not accept the concept of making a profit from selling to a friend, colleague at work, or a neighbor. As a result, alternative ways had to be found by marketing management to reach the consumer on an international level.

A EUROPEAN OPPORTUNITY

At the beginning of 1992, the drive for a unified market in Europe had converged with the fall of communism to make Europe a far bigger and more competitive place to do business. The result, according to *Fortune*, was "a new Europe with big risks and big opportunities." As Executive Vice President of the International Division, Maher had read a number of reports on the topic, had traveled extensively, and had recently discussed the issue with representatives of subsidiaries and other organizations that distribute the firm's product line.

The European Community (EC) provided a new free trade zone through the Single Europe Act (EC-92). The 12 original members were the countries of Belgium, Britain, Denmark, France, Germany, Greece, Ireland, Italy, Luxembourg, The Netherlands, Portugal, and Spain. The European Free Trade Association (EFTA) was comprised of the countries of Austria, Finland, Iceland, Norway, Sweden, and Switzerland. It was linked with the EC through a free-trade agreement. Industry analysts had predicted that this move to a single market in Europe in 1992 would stimulate a wealth of new regional business incentives.

The republics of the former Soviet Union and the other Eastern European nations of Poland, Hungary, Yugoslavia, Czechoslovakia, Romania, Albania, and Bulgaria were experiencing great political and economic change. The Communist Party was being replaced by democratic institutions in most of these countries. Czechoslovakia, Hungary, and Poland, Eastern Europe's three strongest economies, had agreed to open their markets to EC products within ten years. Albania, Bulgaria, and Romania, the least developed countries of Europe, had trade agreements with the Economic Community. They were expected to develop their home markets first. Yugoslavia had disintegrated in the turmoil of a civil war.

Challenges included a multitude of legal, fiscal and physical barriers to trade and exchange, as well as linguistic and cultural diversity. Because of the swift and uncontrolled nature of the changes taking place in Eastern Europe, marketing analysts had suggested that firms marketing their products in these countries should carefully monitor events and proceed cautiously. The nations were very different in terms of technology, infrastructure, foreign investment laws, and speed of change. As *Fortune* magazine noted as it described the opportunities and the challenges facing Europe in the decade ahead, "The risks are real, the problems deep."

Industry experts in 1992 were suggesting that the largest single market opportunity for U.S. firms would be in the developing nations of Eastern Europe. With the fall of Communism, Central Europe was expected to start growing slowly in 1993, then sprint ahead at up to an 8 percent annual rate toward the end of the decade, according to Scott Vicary, an analyst with the London investment firm of James Calpel. This promising growth was expected to lift the collective GNP of a number of Central European countries as well as the Economic Community and the European Free Trade Association.

Britannica management had already taken some steps to respond to the development of European Economic Community. A group had been formed at the division level to study the issues. The presidents of the existing European subsidiaries were brought in to corporate headquarters to compare how they did various things. They also discussed what they might be able to do better as a joint effort. Emphasis was placed upon improving the quality of the tasks that were performed as well as provisions for cost savings. One example of this effort was in the preparation of promotional material. Division management felt it could save money by using common art work and localizing it by putting it in different languages. The cost savings from this effort could be used to hire a better promotion staff and get a better product.

The computer was another area which was perceived as a source of saving and improved effectiveness. One computer was proposed for all of Europe to replace computer operations in Rome, Paris, Madrid, Geneva, and London. The division reasoned that it would have more control and get better service with a centralized staff, more capacity, and faster machines, if it could use one computer for all of Europe.

The fear of losing control became a major issue in this setting. "One thing we found out very quickly when we got into this," Maher noted, "everyone was protecting their own turf." Existing subsidiary management was reluctant to give up anything. "They wanted to maintain their own functions," Maher continued. "And of course, the five subsidiary presidents are afraid we'll end up with one company president in Europe."

THE PLANNING MEETING

Maher and Gies were well aware of how important expansion in the European marketplace was to upper level management of Encyclopaedia Britannica and to the International Division. For one thing, an increased demand for English language courses was predicted in the Eastern European countries as people sought ways to learn English. English courses sold by Britannica appeared to be too expensive for the individual consumer in most Eastern European countries.

A second problem concerned how to sell the product at the retail level. "It may be that the home-field sales force is not the avenue," Maher said. "Perhaps they'll have to go through bookstores. Perhaps newspaper stores or direct mail. It's not only creating the product, identifying the product need," he noted, "but it's also the distribution method and the restrictions on the amount of disposable income they have." He also suggested Eastern Europe as a source for manpower for a European operations sales force. Sales force expansion and retention had always been primary goals in direct selling activity.

The week had passed quickly. Senior management executives of the International Division assembled again in President Gies's office to consider the question of entry alternatives and market expansion opportunities in Eastern Europe. President Gies opened the meeting with a statement reflecting on one of the goals of the division: "to get quality educational products into the hands of people of all countries." Gies felt that it was absolutely necessary at the meeting to resolve the question of how this goal applied to developing strategies for Europe's new markets.

Maher knew that a detailed analysis of the cultural, social, economic, political, legal, and technological forces of the environment was essential before the company entered a foreign market. He suggested in his initial report that given its capital constraints, the firm should limit the number of markets it chose to enter. It should only select markets that have (1) low political risks, (2) few restrictions on business, and (3) high purchasing power. He felt that these factors should be considered when analyzing the relevant environments in each of the countries of Eastern Europe to assess market attractiveness.

Four possible Eastern Europe market entry strategies were identified by the executives of the International Division. Each of these possibilities involved an increasing amount of commitment or involvement on the firm's behalf and thus allowed management to have more control over marketing efforts. A fifth view favored consolidation of existing activity.

One viewpoint favored exporting selected products and selling them through an existing subsidiary. The executive supporting this view cited a number of factors favoring this approach. First, experience suggested that this would be a way to get into the market quickly. Second, using an existing subsidiary did not require a great deal of investment or risk-taking since it would use the expertise of established wholly owned companies that already sold Encyclopaedia Britannica and other products in Western Europe.

The second viewpoint suggested that an existing firm be given the right to market selected items in the product line for an agreed upon commission or fee. This type of licensing arrangement would be a low-investment form of market entry that would give the organization some form of control since the licensing arrangement could stipulate specific marketing methods. The firm already had contractual agreements with a number of firms worldwide to sell its products.

A third viewpoint called for entering into a joint venture with an existing foreign company. This proposal would also establish a legal presence in the European marketplace and position the firm for European expansion. Existing expertise would be used and market opportunities could be explored quicker. The partner would know the language, understand the culture, and be aware of the needs of the various markets. The executive that supported this approach acknowledged that it might be difficult to find a suitable partner since there was some question whether anyone would have expertise in how to take advantage of what was occurring in Eastern Europe. The operation of such a joint venture, if established, could be supervised from the administrative center in Geneva, Switzerland. It controlled agreements Encyclopaedia Britannica had with the independent distributors which operated in countries without wholly owned subsidiaries of the firm.

A fourth viewpoint suggested the direct ownership of a new subsidiary which would establish a separate legal presence within a selected country. This approach would not only meet potential regulations, but would establish a presence in countries like Germany to suggest that Encyclopaedia Britannica was a company that cared about different cultures and markets. It would also allow management to have control over service standard levels.

The alternative would require increased investment, the establishment of managerial and operational expertise and additional time to establish. The risk would therefore be greater.

A fifth proposal voiced by another executive was not to change. The executive believed that the international division could explore ways in which the existing subsidiaries could consolidate some of the functions to do a better job with the current marketing strategy. Hadn't they brought in the presidents of the European subsidiaries a little over a year ago to consider this very issue? Executive management at that time had concluded that this was an area where there might be a lot of cost savings while still maintaining the autonomy of existing subsidiaries.

The planning meeting adjourned without resolution. Tom Gies asked Laurence Maher to give the "opportunity" issue further consideration. He was to prepare recommendations for another meeting scheduled within the next 30 days.

Questions for Discussion

1. What differences and similarities do you see between domestic marketing and international marketing at Encyclopaedia Britannica, Inc.?

2. Identify and discuss the nature and scope of the problem confronting management of Encyclopaedia Britannica International., Inc. What factors did management consider as part of the process of choosing an Eastern European market entry strategy?

3. Once interested in international expansion, firms choose to customize their marketing strategies for different regions of the world or to standardize their marketing strategies for the entire world. What evidence is there to suggest that these alternatives are understood and applied by Encyclopaedia Britannica International management?

4. How much emphasis is placed on the management function of control by Encyclopaedia Britannica International management?

5. Review the changes in the external environment that affect the marketing strategy of Encyclopaedia Britannica International.

APPENDIX A

ENCYCLOPAEDIA BRITANNICA INTERNATIONAL PRODUCT LINE

Encyclopaedia Britannica
The Britannica Book of the Year
The Yearbook of Science and the Future
Medical and Health Annual
The Great Books of the Western World
The Great Ideas of Today
Webster's Third International Dictionary
Britannica Discovery Library
The Compton's Encyclopedia
Compton's Precyclopedia
Britannica Pre-Reading Readiness Program
Britannica Reading Achievement Program
Children's Britannica
Children's Britannica Work Cards
Australian Educational Products
Il Modulo
Anglotutor
Me Diverto Con Le Parole
Encounter English
Encyclopaedia Universalis
Encyclopaedia Universalis Yearbook
Atlas Universalis
Emile Littre Dictionary
Le Grand Atlas De L'Histoire Mondiale
Encyclopaedia Mirador International
The Mirador Atlas
Dicionario Brasileiro

Encyclopaedia Barsa Portuguese
Enciclopedia Barsa Spanish
New English Master Language Program
Gateway to the English Master
New English Master—Junior Course
New English Master—Senior Course
Effective Listening
Modern Business English
Let's Talk About Japan
Japan and I
The Children's Language Package
First Steps in English
Second Steps in English
Third Steps in English
Master Steps in English
The Canadian Encyclopedia
Encyclopedia of Visual Arts
Japanese Young Children's Encyclopedia
BIE-Britannica International Encyclopedia
BIE-Britannica Yearbook
Korean Young Children's Encyclopedia
Effective Listening
Deep-Rooted Tree
Korea Trade Books and Tea Company
Interfield Computer Based Language Course

APPENDIX B

ENCYCLOPAEDIA BRITANNICA SOURCE OF ORDER REPORT

Take-One Box
    Available Here Sign/Take One
    Counter Display
Untended Displays (large traffic area display)
Passouts (cards with sales message)
    Residences and Public Locations
    Retail Locations (bagging)
School Carding (literature handout)
School Lists (parents in area with children)
Local 3rd Party (Group Discounts)
Referrals (local sales office created)
Local Direct Mail (mail from sales office to customer)
Booklet Drop-off
Telephone Prospecting/Directory
    Special Lists
Inquiries/Call-in/Walk-in
    Direct Contact
Local/Free Standing Draw (free drawing)

SCAP (Small Community Appointment Plan)
    Retail Stores (counter)
    Special Functions (counter)
    Shopping Malls/Shopping Centers
    Others
    Free Draw Follow-up
OTC (Selling Product Over the Counter)
    Exhibition/Fairs
    Professional/Trade Shows
    Shopping Malls/Shopping Centers
    Theme Parks/Zoo
    Transportation Centers
    Home Appointment Plan (HAP)
    Others
    Free Draw Follow-up
Other Misc.—Local
National Advertising
National 3rd Party (home office leads)
Company Direct Mail
Other Misc.—National

Charting a Course in a Global Economy

The goal in the world of private, for-profit industry is simple: maximizing shareholder wealth. But some believe private businesses have other responsibilities as well, including the duty to be a good corporate citizen. After all, businesses do not exist in a vacuum, some argue. They are part of a larger community and draw from the resources of that community to exist and succeed. Therefore, they should act responsibly.

Say your organization decides to adopt an ethical approach to business, what then? Who is to say what is ethical in any given situation? Whose ethics? The dilemma becomes more complicated if your business is global in nature. What if your foreign customers and competitors have a different set of moral bearings? Consider the case of human-resource management in an international setting where cultural differences can complicate decision making.

A group from the Columbia University Business School was asked the following: What would you do if you were responsible for appointing a new director for your company's Asian office? The position is a key step on the fast track, and the most qualified candidate is a woman. However, you know that several important customers in the region will refuse to deal with a woman. You also expect some friction from the local staff. Do you go ahead with the appointment anyway?

Jennifer McVea is a manager in the international advertising group at AT&T. She is in Columbia's MBA program for mid-career executives. "I can speak from personal experience on this, having done business in the Far East," she said. "I think it would be difficult, especially in some countries perhaps more than others, to be in a leadership role as a woman. Some other cultures, and especially some Asian cultures, have not necessarily accepted women in that role yet. And while we Americans have, and perhaps as an American company operating in an Asian country, I don't believe that we can necessarily force our values on another culture."

McVea was then asked how she would respond if her company appointed her director of Asian affairs.

"I think if a company made the decision that it was going to offer the job to a woman, I would just hope that it would have taken into account, first of all, the cultural shock for the woman in terms that she may not get, will not get, the same level of acceptance that a man would," McVea said. "But also the possible business repercussions, in terms of other people either in that office, if they are nationals, who may not even be used to working for an American, let alone an American woman."

But given that condition, perhaps American companies should consider whether they have a role in influencing change in that condition, McVea was told.

Steve Markscheid, a vice president at First Chicago Bank and also a student in Columbia's executive MBA program, has some dealings with China through his work. Markscheid disagreed with McVea.

"I think we're working for American companies, and we have American values. And we don't let those fall by the wayside when we do our business overseas" recognizing, of course, that there could be a cost involved, he said.

Source: This case was drawn from the Public Broadcasting System's television program "Adam Smith," which aired on Oct. 5, 1990. Producer: Alvin H. Perlmutter, Inc.

The panel was asked what would happen if a woman who got the Asian appointment didn't do well on the job because she could not hurdle the cultural barriers.

Eric Guthrie, a law student who is studying ethics at the business school, replied. "I think Asian companies have to realize that the women in the corporations today are playing a major role. If they want to expand to the [West] and all around the globe, they have to consider that the woman is going to play a major part in the corporation," he said.

The panel was asked to consider the fact that competitors to the company might not have women in these roles and might thus find it easier to conduct business.

James Kuhn is a professor at Columbia who runs the school's teaching program in business ethics. "If you stop at women, where do we stop" he asked? "Because we have blacks, we have Hispanics, we have Filipinos. I don't think this country can afford to give up on that kind of value."

Markscheid added: "What sort of message are we sending to the people who work in our company back home, as well as to our customers? That we discriminate internally to take advantage of transient commercial opportunities overseas?"

Boors Yavitz, a former dean, also teaches in the Columbia business school. "I think that's an easy one," he said. "Assuming that the company has thought through and said, 'This is the right person,' and I assume they're not novices and they know the difficulties a woman will have, I think you clearly have to stick to your guns. Not only is it the right thing, but I think this is an interesting reversal of the Europeans, the Asians are always preaching to us to be sensitive to their cultural differences. We have to make it clear to our Asian customers that we operate in an American environment where this is not acceptable."

What do you do after a year if your company is losing ground, the panel was asked.

"Well, there is the short term and the long term," replied Guthrie. "And maybe in the short term you will lose some ground, but the adversity in the long term is very profitable. It will pay off in the long run, and the corporations that do practice those stringent procedures will eventually turn around—at least I would hope so," he said.

"We've got to be true to whatever our culture is, and its basic values—and we're talking about a very basic value here—and on this, I think we may be leaders in the world," said Kuhn. "If we pay a cost for that, then I think it is a short-term cost that will have a very high payoff in the long term."

Global standards are changing, are beginning to become more homogenized, said Yavitz. "I think they're moving to the more enlightened, liberal kind of view of life. Part of that is simply the sunlight, the fact that more and more is known, more and more is publicized. And my sense is that if we as American companies push our set of values and keep emphasizing those, that they do rub off, that you do get a change in the way global business is done."

Questions for Discussion

1. If U.S. companies can transmit their values abroad, should foreign firms be allowed to apply theirs in the United States?
2. Should personal characteristics, such as gender, nationality, or age, for example, be taken into consideration when selecting managers for overseas assignments? Why or why not? What could be the outcome of considering, or not considering, personal characteristics?

3. Other than personal characteristics, what are other selection criteria for overseas managers? Provide examples of each. Which are the most important criteria? Why?

4. Define culture shock. What are its four stages? What can be done to alleviate it?

Lakewood Forest Products

Since the 1970s the United States has had a merchandise trade deficit with the rest of the world. Up to 1982, this deficit mattered little because it was relatively small. As of 1983, however, the trade deficit increased rapidly and became, due to its size and future implications, an issue of major national concern. Suddenly, trade moved to the forefront of national debate. Concurrently, a debate ensued on the issue of the international competitiveness of U.S. firms. The onerous question here was whether U.S. firms could and would achieve sufficient improvements in areas such as productivity, quality, and price to remain long-term successful international marketing players.

The U.S.-Japanese trade relation took on particular significance, because it was between those two countries that the largest bilateral trade deficit existed. In spite of trade negotiations, market-opening measures, trade legislation, and other governmental efforts, it was clear that the impetus for a reversal of the deficit through more U.S. exports to Japan had to come from the private sector. Therefore, the activities of any U.S. firm that appeared successful in penetrating the Japanese market were widely hailed. One company whose effort to market in Japan aroused particular interest was Lakewood Forest Products, in Hibbing, Minnesota.

COMPANY BACKGROUND

In 1983, Ian J. Ward was an export merchant in difficulty. Throughout the 1970s his company, Ward, Bedas Canadian Ltd., had successfully sold Canadian lumber and salmon to countries in the Persian Gulf. Over time, the company had opened four offices worldwide. However, when the Iran–Iraq war erupted, most of Ward's long-term trading relationships disappeared within a matter of months. In addition, the international lumber market began to collapse. As a result, Ward, Bedas Canadian Ltd. went into a survivalist mode and sent employees all over the world to look for new markets and business opportunities. Late that year, the company received an interesting order. A firm in Korea urgently needed to purchase lumber for the production of chopsticks.

Learning about the Chopstick Market

In discussing the wood deal with the Koreans, Ward learned that in order to produce good chopsticks more than 60 percent of the wood fiber would be wasted. Given the high transportation cost involved, the large degree of wasted materials, and his need for new business, Ward decided to explore the Korean and Japanese chopstick industry in more detail.

Source: This case was written by Michael R. Czinkota based on the following sources: Mark Clayton, "Minnesota Chopstick Maker Finds Japanese Eager to Import His Quality Waribashi," *The Christian Science Monitor,* October 16, 1987, 11; Roger Worthington, "Improbable Chopstick Capitol of the World," *Chicago Tribune,* June 5, 1988, 39; Mark Gill, "The Great American Chopstick Master," *American Way,* August 1, 1987, 34, 78-79; "Perpich of Croatia," *The Economist,* April 20, 1991, 27; and personal interview with Ian J. Ward, president, Lakewood Forest Products.

He quickly determined that chopstick making in the Far East is a fragmented industry, working with old technology and suffering from a lack of natural resources. In Asia, chopsticks are produced in very small quantities, often by family organizations. Even the largest of the 450 chopstick factories in Japan turns out only 5 million chopsticks a month. This compares to an overall market size of 130 million pairs of disposable chopsticks a day. In addition, chopsticks represent a growing market. With increased wealth in Asia, people eat out more often and therefore have a greater demand for disposable chopsticks. The fear of communicable diseases has greatly reduced the utilization of reusable chopsticks. Renewable plastic chopsticks have been attacked by many groups as too newfangled and as causing future ecological problems.

From his research, Ward concluded that a competitive niche existed in the world chopstick market. He believed that, if he could use low-cost raw materials and ensure that the labor cost component would remain small, he could successfully compete in the world market.

The Founding of Lakewood Forest Products

In exploring opportunities afforded by the newly identified international marketing niche for chopsticks, Ward set four criteria for plant location:

1. Access to suitable raw materials
2. Proximity of other wood product users who could make use of the 60 percent waste for their production purposes
3. Proximity to a port that would facilitate shipment to the Far East
4. Availability of labor

In addition, Ward was aware of the importance of product quality. Because people use chopsticks on a daily basis and are accustomed to products that are visually inspected one by one, he would have to live up to high quality expectations in order to compete successfully. Chopsticks could not be bowed or misshapen, have blemishes in the wood, or splinter.

In order to implement his plan, Ward needed financing. Private lenders were skeptical and slow to provide funds. This skepticism resulted from the unusual direction of Ward's proposal. Far Eastern companies have generally held the cost advantage in a variety of industries, especially those as labor intensive as chopstick manufacturing. U.S. companies rarely have an advantage in producing low-cost items. Further, only a very small domestic market exists for chopsticks.

However, Ward found that the state of Minnesota was willing to participate in his new venture. Since the decline of the mining industry, regional unemployment had been rising rapidly in the state. In 1983, unemployment in Minnesota's Iron Range peaked at 22 percent. Therefore, state and local officials were anxious to attract new industries that would be independent of mining activities. Of particular help was the enthusiasm of Governor Rudy Perpich. The governor had been boosting Minnesota business on the international scene by traveling abroad and receiving many foreign visitors. He was excited about Ward's plans, which called for the creation of over 100 new jobs within a year.

Hibbing, Minnesota, turned out to be an ideal location for Ward's project. The area had an abundance of supply of aspen wood, which, because it grows in clay soil, tends to be unmarred. The fact that Hibbing was the hometown of the governor also did not hurt. In addition, Hibbing boasted an excellent labor pool, and both the city and the state were willing to make loans totaling $500,000. Further, the Iron Range Resources Rehabilitation Board was willing to sell $3.4 million in industrial revenue bonds for the project. Together with jobs and training wage subsidies, enterprise zone credits, and tax increment financing benefits, the initial public support of the project added up to about 30 percent of its start-up costs. The potential benefit of the new venture to the region was quite clear. When Lakewood Forest Products advertised its first 30 jobs, more than 3,000 people showed up to apply.

THE PRODUCTION AND SALE OF CHOPSTICKS

Ward insisted that in order to truly penetrate the international market, he would need to keep his labor cost low. As a result, he decided to automate as much of the production as possible. However, no equipment was readily available to produce chopsticks, because no one had automated the process before.

After much searching, Ward identified a European equipment manufacturer who produced machinery for making popsicle sticks. He purchased equipment from this Danish firm in order to better carry out the sorting and finishing processes. However, because aspen wood was quite different from the wood the machine was designed for, as was the final product, substantial design adjustments had to be made. Sophisticated equipment was also purchased to strip the bark from the wood and peel it into long, thin sheets. Finally, a computer vision system was acquired to detect defects in the chopsticks. This system rejected over 20 percent of the production, and yet some of the chopsticks that passed inspection were splintering. However, Ward firmly believed that further fine-tuning of the equipment and training of the new workforce would gradually take care of the problem.

Given this fully automated process, Lakewood Forest Products was able to develop capacity for up to 7 million chopsticks a day. With a unit manufacturing cost of $0.03 and an anticipated unit selling price of $0.057, Ward expected to earn a pretax profit of $4.7 million in 1988.

Due to intense marketing efforts in Japan and the fact that Japanese customers were struggling to obtain sufficient supplies of disposable chopsticks, Ward was able to presell the first five years of production quite quickly. By late 1987, Lakewood Forest Products was ready to enter the international market. With an ample supply of raw materials and an almost totally automated plant, Lakewood was positioned as the world's largest and least labor-intensive manufacturer of chopsticks. The first shipment of six containers with a load of 12 million pairs of chopsticks to Japan was made in October 1987.

Questions for Discussion

1. What are the future implications of continuing large U.S. trade deficits?
2. What are the important variables for the international marketing success of chopsticks?
3. Rank the variables in question 2 according to the priority you believe they have for foreign customers.
4. Why haven't Japanese firms thought of automating the chopstick production process?
5. How long will Lakewood Forest Products be able to maintain its competitive advantage?

ESPRIT

"Europe now has a position in technologies where we are no longer in danger of losing the pace." This statement by a European executive underlines the fact that Europe's experiment in cooperative research and development (R&D) is paying off. Since the mid-1980s, companies and research institutes from Denmark to Spain have pooled their resources in megaprojects ranging from genetic engineering to thermonuclear fusion. Roughly $20 billion will be spent in Europe from 1990 to 1994 on joint R&D. Although most projects are still in their early stages, ESPRIT (European Strategic Programs for Research in Information Technologies) claims contributions to 129 commercial products. This $6.7 billion European Commission–backed project of some 406 programs attempts to bolster Europe's information technologies, including creating a European multiprocessor computer.

BACKGROUND

The history of intra-European cooperation had a shaky beginning at best. The rising costs of research in aerospace, electronics, and chemicals, as well as the substantial technological gap between European and U.S. firms in the 1960s, provided the impetus for greater intra-European collaboration. In April 1970, the European Commission proposed the creation of an EC office to coordinate development contracts in advanced technology. Although the number of mergers did rise in the 1970s, the decade was marked by a series of failures in intra-European cooperation. Most prominent was the failure of UNIDATA, a computing resource venture by Bull, Philips, and Siemens.

In 1980, Étienne Daignon, then Commissioner of Industry in the EC, invited 12 of Europe's largest information technology firms (Siemens, AEG, and Nixdorf of Germany; Plessey, GEC, and STC of the United Kingdom; CGE, Thomson, and Bull of France; Philips of the Netherlands; and Olivetti and Stet of Italy) to help create a cooperative work program for their industry to be called ESPRIT. The objectives of the effort were (1) to promote intra-European industrial cooperation, (2) to furnish European industry with the basic technologies that it would need to bolster its competitiveness over the next five to ten years, and (3) to develop European norms and standards. Five major themes were agreed upon: advanced micro electronics, software technology, advanced information processing, office systems, and computer integrated manufacture. ESPRIT launched a pilot program in 1983 and began full-scale operations a year later.

Source: This case was compiled by Ilkka A. Ronkainen and Boyd J. Miller of Georgetown University. It is based on "Do Not Adjust Your Set Yet," *The Economist*, February 27, 1993, 65–66; "Sematech Claims Major Advance by Halving Size of Chip Circuits," *The Wall Street Journal*, January 22, 1992, B5; Lynn Krieger Mytelka and Michael Delapierre, "The Alliance Strategies of European Firms in the Information Technology Industry and the Role of ESPRIT," *Journal of Common Market Studies* 26 (December 1987): 231–251; Louis Kraar, "Your Rivals Can Be Your Allies," *Fortune*, March 27, 1989, 65–76; Lee Smith, "Can Consortiums Defeat Japan?" *Fortune*, June 5, 1989, 245–254; Thomas Gross and John Neuman, "Strategic Alliances Vital in Global Marketing," *Marketing News*, June 19, 1989; Jonathan B. Levine, "Hanging Tough by Teaming Up," *Business Week*, October 22, 1990, 121; and Jeremy Main, "Making Global Alliances Work," *Fortune*, December 17, 1990, 121–126.

Roughly half of ESPRIT's budget is paid for by the EC. The other half is provided by the participating companies. ESPRIT's project rules require that at least two firms located in two different EC countries be represented. This rule ensures that ESPRIT is an intercontinental program. Initially, the vast majority of programs included the big-12 firms. Over time, smaller firms, research institutes, and universities have become significant contributors. Since a significant amount of financing comes from taxpayers, officials must disperse funds equitably rather than to the strongest competitors. This has allowed smaller firms, such as IMEC, to collaborate with multinational giants such as Philips.

ESPRIT plays different roles for the participating entities. For firms already engaged in alliances, ESPRIT has helped complement them. Commitment levels to R&D and to individual projects have also improved. For example, European information technology companies increased their R&D and capital spending by five percentage points in the four years ended in 1990, to 19.2 percent of revenues from 14.5 percent, nearly matching the level of U.S. companies. Furthermore, ESPRIT has allowed participants to work together in the development of new European standards of technology to ensure, for example, that computer systems are able to work together.

By subsidizing the costs of R&D, facilitating the emergence of complementary technologies between firms, and promoting standardization, the ESPRIT program enhances interfirm cooperation without requiring explicit, formal, long-term contractual arrangements.

INDUSTRY CHALLENGES

Both the computer and telecommunications industries suffer from rising R&D costs, relatively short product life cycles, rapid product obsolescence, and extensive capital requirements. As product development costs soar, small and medium-sized firms especially come under considerable financial pressure to keep up with technological developments.

It is estimated that it takes nearly $1 billion to develop a new telecommunications switching system or a new generation of semiconductor. For this investment to be profitable, markets of nearly $14 billion are needed. New production lines also require considerable capital investment. In semiconductors, for example, the minimum investment for a new microelectronics production line is approaching the total value of annual output for that plant.

With rising R&D costs and shortened product life cycles, competition has intensified, and firms see little future in becoming national monopolies. Securing access to foreign markets and reducing costs and risks are essential to long-term survival in the industry.

COOPERATIVE EFFORTS IN JAPAN AND THE UNITED STATES

The success of the Ministry of International Trade and Industry (MITI) in Japan in including the private sector in public planning decisions was the inspiration for ESPRIT. In the late 1970s, a consortium of six companies, including NTT, Mitsubishi, and Matsushita, that was designed to overtake the United States in producing very large scale integrated (VLSI) circuits—high-powered memories-on-a-chip—functioned so well that the U.S. government pressured the Japanese government to stop giving the consortium money. It was too late; by the mid-1980s, Japanese companies dominated the market. Since then, the Japanese have launched other consortia. One of them consists of nine companies (including Hitachi, Toshiba, and NEC) whose mission is to develop advanced computer technologies such as artificial intelligence and parallel processing.

In the United States, well over 100 R&D consortia have registered with the Justice Department to pool their resources for research into technologies ranging from artificial intelligence to those needed to overtake the Japanese lead in semiconductor manufacturing. The major consortia are MCC (Microelectronics and Computer Technology Corp.) and Sematech, which boast as members the largest U.S. companies such as AT&T, GE, IBM, Motorola, and 3M. Sematech, founded in 1988, was formed to rescue an ailing U.S. computer chip industry. Funded jointly by the U.S. government and member companies, the consortium is credited with slowing the market-share drop of U.S. chip-equipment makers, who now control 53% of a $10 billion world market, up from less than 40% five years earlier. Although in theory most consortia have no real limitations on membership, barriers may exist. Sematech, for example, refuses to accept foreign firms, worrying that if Europeans were allowed to join, there would be no way to keep out the Japanese.

The race for developing the standard for high-definition television (HDTV) in the United States created interesting alliances. The government entity involved, the Federal Communications Commission (FCC), did not finance or participate actively in the choice of the standard; it formed a private sector advisory committee to pick the technically best system in an open contest. One company joined the U.S. subsidiaries of France's Thomson and Holland's Philips (backed by the EC to develop Europe's standard) as well as NBC, one of the major U.S. broadcast networks. The other two teams included Zenith and AT&T in one and General Instrument (a maker of cable-TV gear) and the Massachusetts Institute of Technology in the other one. In the spring of 1993, the FCC was encouraging all three teams to form a "grand alliance" combining all systems for a final round of testing. In late May of 1993, these three teams decided to join forces in a single approach, a move which was strongly supported by top federal officials. This agreement hastens the introduction of HDTV because it reduces the likelihood of protracted disputes and litigation and represents a broad technical consensus for the next generation of television sets.

MANAGEMENT OF COLLABORATIVE EFFORTS

Three factors have been shown to make collaborative efforts succeed: leaders who are inspired, angry, and even scared; goals that are limited and well defined; and a dependable source of revenue. Some never overcome inherent problems. As cooperative ventures, they are intrinsically anticompetitive, so they risk becoming sluggish and stifling.

The broader and more formal the collaborative effort, the greater the hazard that it will get bogged down in bureaucracy. Management by committee could be a problem if it results in a lack of responsiveness to the marketplace. Some also decry the participation of governments in these efforts, pointing to possible meddling in the choice of programs and the way they are run.

Culture clash can also threaten collaborative efforts, since they are often staffed at least partly by people on the payrolls of their members. Mixing corporate cultures may result in conflict. "Consortia are the wave of the future, but they sure are hard to manage," says a former consortium chief operating officer. Furthermore, if dominant companies refuse to join in an effort, and those participating remain aloof and suspicious of each other, the effort will not succeed.

The bottom line is that entities participating in collaborative efforts have to be as attentive to executing and maintaining them as they are to initiating them. Since working with former competitors is frequently a new experience, it requires new ground rules: from domestic market to a global economic and cultural perspective, from blanket secrecy and suspicion to judicious trust and openness, and from win-lose to win-win relationships.

Questions for Discussion

1. Can collaborative efforts, such as ESPRIT, really do things no single company could—or would—undertake?

2. What additional challenges are introduced when R&D collaboration is across national borders; i.e., will ESPRIT prove to be more problematic than Sematech (which does not allow non-U.S. members)?

3. How will ESPRIT's development of pan-European standards help Europe and European companies?

4. Will small and medium-sized firms benefit more from their participation in projects like ESPRIT than the large, multinational corporation?

GLOSSARY

absolute advantage   The ability to produce a good or service more cheaply than it can be produced elsewhere.

accounting diversity   The range of differences in national accounting practices.

acculturation   The process of adjusting and adapting to a specific culture other than one's own.

adaptability screening   A selection procedure that usually involves interviewing both the candidate for an overseas assignment and his or her family members to determine how well they are likely to adapt to another culture.

airfreight   Transport of goods by air; accounts for less than one percent of the total volume of international shipments.

antitrust laws   Laws that prohibit monopolies, restraint of trade, and conspiracies to inhibit competition.

arbitration   The procedure for settling a dispute in which an objective third party hears both sides and makes a decision; a procedure for resolving conflict in the international business arena through the use of intermediaries such as representatives of chambers of commerce, trade associations, or third-country institutions.

area expertise   A knowledge of the basic systems in a particular region or market.

area structure   An organizational structure in which geographic divisions are responsible for all manufacturing and marketing in their respective areas.

area studies   Training programs that provide factual preparation prior to an overseas assignment.

arm's length price   A price that unrelated parties would have reached.

assessment of taxes   The valuation of property or transactions for purposes of taxation; in countertrade, based on the exact value of the goods exchanged, the time when income was received, and the profitability of the transaction.

autarky   A country that is not participating in international trade.

backtranslation   The retranslation of text to the original language by a different person than the one who made the first translation.

backward innovation   The development of a drastically simplified version of a product.

Balance of Payments (BOP)   A statement of all transactions between one country and the rest of the world during a given period; a record of flows of goods, services, and investments across borders.

balance sheet hedge   The counterbalance of exposed assets with exposed liabilities to reduce translation or transaction exposure.

barter   A direct exchange of goods of approximately equal value, with no money involved.

base salary   Salary not including special payments such as allowances paid during overseas assignments.

basic balance   A summary measure of a country's Balance of Payments which is the sum of the current account and the long-term capital account.

bilateral negotiations   Negotiations carried out between two nations focusing only on their interests.

bill of lading   A contract between an exporter and a carrier indicating that the carrier has accepted responsibility for the goods and will provide transportation in return for payment.

black hole   The situation that arises when an international marketer has a low-competence subsidiary—or none at all—in a highly strategic market.

boycott   An organized effort to refrain from conducting business with a particular seller of goods or services; used in the international arena for political or economic reasons.

brain drain   A migration of professional people from one country to another, usually for the purpose of improving their incomes or living conditions.

Bretton Woods Agreement   An agreement reached in 1944 among finance ministers of 45 Western nations to establish a system of fixed exchange rates.

bribery   The use of payments or favors to obtain some right or benefit to which the briber has no legal right; a criminal offense in the United States but a way of life in many countries.

buffer stock   Stock of a commodity kept on hand to prevent a shortage in times of unexpectedly great demand; under international commodity and price agreements, the stock controlled by an elected or appointed manager for the purpose of managing the price of the commodity.

bulk service   Ocean shipping provided on contract either for individual voyages or for prolonged periods of time.

bureaucratic controls   A limited and explicit set of regulations and rules that outline desired levels of performance.

buy-back   A refinement of simple barter with one party supplying technology or equipment that enables the other party to produce goods, which are then used to pay for the technology or equipment that was supplied.

capital account   An account in the BOP statement that records transactions involving borrowing, lending, and investing across borders.

capital budget   The financial evaluation of a proposed investment to determine whether the expected returns are sufficient to justify the investment expenses.

capital flight   The flow of private funds abroad because investors believe that the return on investment or the safety of capital is not sufficiently ensured in their own countries.

capital or financial lease   A lease that transfers all substantial benefits and costs inherent in the ownership of the property to the lessee. The lessee accounts for the lease as if it is an acquisition of an asset or incurrence of a liability.

capital structure   The mix of debt and equity used in a corporation.

capitalizing   The accounting practice of charging a portion of the cost of a capital equipment purchase over a number of years, thus depreciating its useful life out over time.

Caribbean Basin Initiative (CBI)   Extended trade preferences to Caribbean countries and granted them access to the markets of the United States.

cartel   An association of producers of a particular good, consisting either of private firms or of nations, formed for the purpose of suppressing the market forces affecting the product.

central plan   The economic plan for the nation devised by the government of a socialist state; often a five-year plan that stipulated the quantities of industrial goods to be produced.

centralization   The concentrating of control and strategic decision making at headquarters.

change agent   A person or institution who facilitates change in a firm or in a host country.

channel design   The length and width of the distribution channel.

clearing account barter   A refinement of simple barter in which clearing accounts are established to track debits and credits. CAB permits barter transactions to take place over longer time periods.

code law   Law based on a comprehensive set of written statutes.

codetermination   A management approach in which employees are represented on supervisory boards to facilitate communication and collaboration between management and labor.

commercial invoice   A bill for transported goods that describes the merchandise and its total cost and lists the addresses of the shipper and seller and delivery and payment terms.

Committee for Foreign Investments in the United States (CFIUS)   A federal committee with the responsibility for reviewing major foreign investments to determine whether national security or related concerns are at stake.

commodity price agreement   An agreement involving both buyers and sellers to manage the price of a particular commodity, but often only when the price moves outside a predetermined range.

common agricultural policy (CAP)   An integrated system of subsidies and rebates applied to agricultural interests in the European Community.

common law   Law based on tradition and depending less on written statutes and codes than on precedent and custom—used in the United States.

common market   A group of countries that agree to remove all barriers to trade among members, to establish a common trade policy with respect to nonmembers, and also to allow mobility for factors of production—for example, labor, capital, and technology.

comparative advantage   The ability to produce a good or service more cheaply, relative to other goods and services, than is possible in other countries.

compensation arrangement   Another term for buyback.

competitive advantage   The ability to produce a good or service more cheaply than other countries due to favorable factor conditions and demand conditions, strong related and supporting industries, and favorable firm strategy, structure, and rivalry conditions.

competitive assessment   A research process that consists of matching markets to corporate strengths and providing an analysis of the best potential for specific offerings.

competitive devaluation   Reducing the value of one nation's currency in terms of other currencies to stimulate exports.

competitive platform   The business environment provided by a nation to its firms which affects their international competitiveness.

concentration   The market expansion policy that involves concentrating on a small number of markets.

conference pricing   The establishment of prices by a cartel; used in shipping.

confirmed letter of credit   A letter of credit confirmed by the recipient's bank.

confiscation   The forceful government seizure of a company without compensation for the assets seized.

container ships   Ships designed to carry standardized containers, which greatly facilitate loading and unloading as well as intermodal transfers.

contributor   A national subsidiary with a distinctive competence, such as product development.

convertibility   The ability to exchange a currency for any other currency without being subject to government restrictions, approvals, or government specified rates of exchange.

coordinated decentralization   The providing of headquarters of overall corporate strategy while granting subsidiaries the freedom to implement it within established ranges.

Coordinating Committee for Multilateral Export Controls (COCOM)   A body formed by NATO countries (including Japan, but not Iceland) that attempts to continually define those items for which exports need to be controlled, or decontrolled, and how national policies can be structured to result in a unified and effective export control system.

correspondent banks   Banks located in different countries and unrelated by ownership that have a reciprocal agreement to provide services to each other's customers.

cost and freight (CFR)   Seller quotes a price for the goods, including the cost of transportation to the named port of debarkation. Cost and choice of insurance are left to the buyer.

cost, insurance, and freight (CIF)   Seller quotes a price including insurance, all transportation, and miscellaneous charges to the point of debarkation from the vessel or aircraft.

cost of living allowance (COLA)   An allowance paid during assignment overseas to enable the employee to maintain the same standard of living as at home.

counterpurchase   A refinement of simple barter that unlinks the timing of the two transactions.

critical commodities list   A U.S. Department of Commerce file containing information about products that are either particularly sensitive to national security or controlled for other purposes.

cross rates   Exchange rate quotations which do not include the U.S. dollar as one of the two currencies quoted.

cultural assimilator   A program in which trainees for overseas assignments must respond to scenarios of specific situations in a particular country.

cultural convergence   Exposure to foreign cultures accelerated by technological advances.

cultural risk   The risk of business blunders, poor customer relations, and wasted negotiations that results when firms fail to understand and adapt to the cultural differences between their own and host countries' cultures.

cultural universals   Manifestations of the total way of life of any group of people.

culture shock   The more pronounced reactions to the psychological disorientation that most people feel when they move for an extended period of time in a markedly different culture.

currency flows   The flows of currency from nation to nation, which in turn determine exchange rates.

currency swap   An agreement by which a firm exchanges or swaps its debt service payments in one currency for debt service payments in a different currency. The equivalent of the interest rate swap, only the currency of denomination of the debt is different.

current account   An account in the BOP statement that records the results of transactions involving merchandise, services, and unilateral transfers between countries.

current rate method   A method for translating financial statements of a foreign subsidiary from the functional currency into the parent's reporting currency.

customer involvement   The active participation of customers; a characteristic of services in that customers often are actively involved in the provision of services they consume.

customer service   A total corporate effort aimed at customer satisfaction; customer service levels in terms of responsiveness that inventory policies permit for a given situation.

customer structure   An organizational structure in which divisions are formed on the basis of customer groups.

customs union   A union among trading countries in which members dismantle barriers to trade in goods and services and also establish a common trade policy with respect to nonmembers.

debt-for-debt swap   The exchange of a loan held by one creditor for a loan held by another creditor; allows debt holders to consolidate outstanding loans.

debt-for-education swap   The exchange of debt for educational opportunities in a foreign country.

debt-for-equity swap   An exchange of developing country debts for equity investments in the countries.

debt-for-nature swap   The purchase of nonperforming loans at substantial discounts and their subsequent return to the debtor country in exchange for the preservation of natural resources.

debt-for-product swap   An exchange of debt for products, often requiring an additional cash payment for the product.

debt swaps   An emerging form of countertrade in which debt holders exchange the debt of a less-developed country for some other good or service or financial instrument.

decentralization   The granting of a high degree of autonomy to subsidiaries.

delivery duty paid (DDP)   Seller delivers the goods, with import duties paid, including inland transportation from import point to the buyer's premises.

delivery duty unpaid (DDU)   Only the destination customs duty and taxes are paid by the consignee.

demand pattern analysis   Analysis that indicates typical patterns of growth and decline in manufacturing.

density   Weight-to-volume ratio; often used to determine shipping rates.

deregulation   Removal of government regulation.

developmental aid   International aid to developing countries.

direct investment   An account in the BOP statement that records investments with an expected maturity of more than one year and an investor's ownership position of at least 10 percent.

direct quotation   A foreign exchange quotation that specifies the amount of home country currency needed to purchase one unit of foreign currency.

direct taxes   Taxes applied directly to income.

distributed earnings   The proportion of a firm's net income after taxes which is paid out or distributed to the stockholders of the firm.

diversification   A market expansion policy characterized by growth in a relatively large number of markets or market segments.

division of labor   The premise of modern industrial production where each stage in the production of a good is performed by one individual separately, rather than one individual being responsible for the entire production of the good.

domestication   Government demand for partial transfer of ownership and management responsibility from a foreign company to local entities, with or without compensation.

double-entry bookkeeping   Accounting methodology where each transaction gives rise to both a debit and a credit of the same currency amount. It is used in the construction of the Balance of Payments.

double taxation   Taxing of the same income twice; taxing of multinational corporations by the home country and the host country.

dual pricing   Price-setting strategy in which the export price may be based on marginal cost pricing, resulting in a lower export price than domestic price; may open the company to dumping charges.

dumping   Selling goods overseas at a price lower than in the exporter's home market, or at a price below the cost of production, or both.

economic and monetary union (EMU)   The ideal among European leaders that economic integration should move beyond the four freedoms; specifically, it entails (1) closer coordination of economic policies to promote exchange rate stability and convergence of inflation rates and growth rates, (2) creation of a European central bank called the Eurofed, and (3) replacement of national monetary authorities by the Eurofed and adoption of the ECU as the European currency.

economic exposure   The potential for long-term effects on a firm's value as the result of changing currency values.

economic infrastructure   The transportation, energy, and communication systems in a country.

economic union   A union among trading countries that would have the characteristics of a common market and would also harmonize monetary policies, taxation, and government spending and use a common currency; none exists currently.

economies of scale   Production economies made possible by operating on a large scale.

education allowance   Reimbursement by the company for dependent educational expenses incurred while a parent is assigned overseas.

effective tax rate   Actual total tax burden after including all applicable tax liabilities and credits.

efficiency seekers   Firms attempting to obtain the most economical sources of production.

embargo   A governmental action, usually prohibiting trade entirely, for a decidedly adversarial or political rather than economic purpose.

Enterprise for the Americas Initiative (EAI)   An attempt by the United States to further democracy in Latin America by providing incentives for capitalistic development and trade liberalization.

equity method   An accounting method used for investments; a method used when a U.S. firm owns a substantial amount of voting stock in a foreign company, meaning more than 10 percent but less than 50 percent.

estimation by analogy   A method for estimating market potential when data for the particular market do not exist.

ethnocentric   Tending to regard one's own culture as superior; tending to be home-market oriented.

ethnocentrism   The regarding of one's own culture as superior to others'.

Eurobanks   Large international banks comprising the most active participants in the Eurocurrency markets.

Eurobond   A bond that is denominated in a currency other than the currency of the country in which the bond is sold.

Euro-commercial paper (ELP)   A short-term debt instrument, typically 30, 60, 90, or 180 days in maturity, sold in the Eurocurrency markets.

Eurocurrency   A bank deposit in a currency other than the currency of the country where the bank is located; not confined to banks in Europe.

Eurocurrency interest rates   Loan or deposit rates of interest on foreign currency denominated deposits.

Eurodollars   U.S. dollars deposited in banks outside the United States; not confined to banks in Europe.

Euromarkets   Money and capital markets in which transactions are denominated in a currency other than that of the place of the transaction; not confined to Europe.

Euronote   A short to medium-term debt instrument sold in the Eurocurrency markets. The three major classes of Euronotes are Euro-commercial paper, Euro-medium-term notes, and Euronotes.

European Monetary System (EMS)   An organization formed in 1979 by eight EC members committed to maintaining the values of their currencies within a 2 1/4 percent of each other's.

exchange controls   Controls on the movement of capital in and out of a country, sometimes imposed when the country faces a shortage of foreign currency.

exchange rate mechanism (ERM)   The acceptance of responsibility by a European Monetary System member to actively maintain its own currency within agreed-upon limits versus other member currencies established by the European Monetary System.

expatriate   One living in a foreign land; a corporate manager assigned to an overseas location.

expensing The accounting practice of claiming the entire cost of a purchase as a deductible expense from current income entirely in the present period.

experiential knowledge Knowledge acquired through involvement (as opposed to information, which is obtained through communication, research, and education).

export-control system A system designed to deny or at least delay the acquisition of strategically important goods to adversaries; in the United States, based on the Export Administration Act and the Munitions Control Act.

export license A license obtainable from the U.S. Department of Commerce Bureau of Export Administration, which is responsible for administering the Export Administration Act.

export management companies (EMCs) Domestic firms that specialize in performing international business services as commission representatives or as distributors.

export trading company (ETC) The result of 1982 legislation to improve the export performance of small and medium-sized firms, the export trading company allows businesses to band together to export or offer export services. Additionally, the law permits bank participation in trading companies and relaxes antitrust provisions.

expropriation The government takeover of a company with compensation frequently at a level lower than the investment value of the company's assets.

external economies of scale Lower production costs resulting from the free mobility of factors of production in a common market.

extraterritoriality An exemption from rules and regulations of one country that may challenge the national sovereignty of another. The application of one country's rules and regulations abroad.

ex-works (EXW) Price quotes that apply only at the point of origin; the seller agrees to place the goods at the disposal of the buyer at the specified place on the date or within the fixed period.

factor intensities The proportion of capital input to labor input used in the production of a good.

factor mobility The ability to freely move factors of production across borders, as among common market countries.

factor proportions theory Systematic explanation of the source of comparative advantage.

factors of production All inputs into the production process, including capital, labor, land, and technology.

factual cultural knowledge Knowledge obtainable from specific country studies published by governments, private companies, and universities and also available in the form of background information from facilitating agencies such as banks, advertising agencies, and transportation companies.

field experience Experience acquired in actual rather than laboratory settings; training that exposes a corporate manager to a different cultural environment for a limited amount of time.

FIFO Method of valuation of inventories for accounting purposes, meaning First-In-First-Out. The principle rests on the assumption that costs should be charged against revenue in the order in which they occur.

Financial Accounting Standards Board Statement No. 52 (FASB 52) A 1982 ruling governing accounting for international transactions and operations.

financial incentives Monetary offers intended to motivate; special funding designed to attract foreign direct investors that may take the form of land or buildings, loans, or loan guarantees, as examples.

financial infrastructure Facilitating financial agencies in a country; for example, banks.

financial risk management The management of a firm's cash flows associated with the three basic financial prices of interest rates, exchange rates, and commodity prices.

fiscal incentives Incentives used to attract foreign direct investment that provide specific tax measures to attract the investor.

flextime A modification of work scheduling that allows workers to determine their own starting and ending times within a broad range of available hours.

focus group A research technique in which representatives of a proposed target audience contribute to market research by participating in an unstructured discussion.

Foreign Corrupt Practices Act A 1977 act making it a crime for U.S. executives of publicly traded firms to bribe a foreign official in order to obtain business.

foreign direct investment The establishment or expansion of operations of a firm in a foreign country. Like all investments, it assumes a transfer of capital.

foreign policy The area of public policy concerned with relationships with other countries.

foreign service premium A financial incentive to accept an assignment overseas, usually paid as a percentage of the base salary.

foreign tax credit Credit applied to home-country tax payments due for taxes paid abroad.

foreign trade organizations (FTOs) Organizations authorized to make purchases and sales internationally as specified by the government; in the past, prevalent in the Soviet Union, Eastern Europe, and China.

foreign trade zones Special areas where foreign goods may be held or processed without incurring duties and taxes.

Fortress Europe Suspicion raised by trading partners of Western Europe, claiming that the integration of the European Community may result in increased restrictions on trade and investment by outsiders.

forward contracts　Agreements between firms and banks which assure the firm of either selling or buying a specific foreign currency at a future date at a known price.

forward rates　Contracts that provide for two parties to exchange currencies on a future date at an agreed-upon exchange rate.

franchising　A form of licensing that allows a distributor or retailer exclusive rights to sell a product or service in a specified area.

free alongside ship (FAS)　Exporter quotes a price for the goods, including charges for delivery of the goods alongside a vessel at a U.S. port. Seller handles cost of unloading and wharfage; loading, ocean transportation, and insurance are left to the buyer.

free carrier (FCA)　Applies only at a designated inland shipping point. Seller is responsible for loading goods into the means of transportation; buyer is responsible for all subsequent expenses.

free on board (FOB)　Applies only to vessel shipments. Seller quotes a price covering all expenses up to and including delivery of goods on an overseas vessel provided by or for the buyer.

free trade area　An area in which all barriers to trade among member countries are removed, although sometimes only for certain goods or services.

freight forwarders　Specialists in handling international transportation by contracting with carriers on behalf of shippers.

functional structure　An organizational structure in which departments are formed on the basis of functional areas such as production, marketing, and finance.

fundamental disequilibrium　A term commonly understood to mean persistent BOP imbalances that are unlikely to correct themselves.

gap analysis　Analysis of the difference between market potential and actual sales.

General Agreement on Tariffs and Trade (GATT)　An international code of tariffs and trade rules signed by 23 nations in 1947; headquartered in Geneva, Switzerland; 99 members currently.

general license　An export license that provides blanket permission to ship nonsensitive products to most trading partners.

geocentric　Tending to take a world view; tending to be oriented toward the global marketplace.

glasnost　The Soviet policy of encouraging the free exchange of ideas and discussion of problems, pluralistic participation in decision making, and increased availability of information.

global linkages　Worldwide interdependencies of financial markets, technology, and living standards.

glocal　A term coined to describe the networked global organization approach to an organizational structure.

gold standard　A standard for international currencies in which currency values were stated in terms of gold.

Government Procurement Code　A 1979 agreement among trading nations that opened government contracts to competitive bids from firms in other nations that were party to the agreement.

gray market　A market entered in a way not intended by the manufacturer of the goods.

Group of Five　The United States, Great Britain, Germany, France, and Japan.

Group of Seven　The United States, Great Britain, Germany, France, Japan, Italy, and Canada. The meeting of finance ministers of these seven countries in Jamaica in 1976 resulted in an agreement to allow their currencies to continue to float.

Group of Ten　The United States, Great Britain, Germany, France, Japan, Italy, Canada, Sweden, Netherlands, and Belgium.

hardship allowance　An allowance paid during an assignment to an overseas area that requires major adaptation.

hedge　To counterbalance a present sale or purchase with a sale or purchase for future delivery as a way to minimize loss due to price fluctuations; to make counterbalancing sales or purchases in the international market as protection against adverse movements in the exchange rate.

high-context cultures　Cultures in which cultural nuances are an important means of conveying information.

housing allowance　An allowance paid during assignment overseas to provide living quarters.

implementor　The typical subsidiary role, which involves implementing strategy that originates with headquarters.

import substitution　A policy for economic growth adopted by many developing countries that involves the systematic encouragement of domestic production of goods formerly imported.

income elasticity of demand　A means of describing change in demand in relative response to a change in income.

Incoterms　International Commerce Terms. Widely accepted terms used in quoting export prices.

indirect quotation　Foreign exchange quotation that specifies the units of foreign currency that could be purchased with one unit of the home currency.

indirect taxes　Taxes applied to non-income items, such as value-added taxes, excise taxes, tariffs, and so on.

industrial policy　Official planning for industry as a whole or for a particular industry; in the United States, occurs only indirectly.

input-output analysis　A method for estimating market potential that utilizes a combination of input-output tables and economic projections.

intangibility　The inability to be seen, tasted, or touched in a conventional sense; the characteristic of services that most strongly differentiates them from products.

intellectual property rights   Protects the technology and knowledge of multinational firms.

interest rate swap   A firm uses its credit standing to borrow capital at low fixed rates and exchange its interest payments with a slightly lower credit-rated borrower who has debt-service payments at floating rates.

intermodal movements   The transfer of freight from one mode or type of transportation to another.

internal economies of scale   Lower production costs resulting from greater production for an enlarged market.

internalization   Occurs when a firm establishes its own multinational operation, keeping information that is at the core of its competitiveness within the firm.

International Bank for Reconstruction and Development (World Bank)   An institution established in 1945 to make loans for reconstruction of war-ravaged countries; now focused on making loans to developing countries.

International Banking Act of 1978   An act that established a comprehensive federal government role in the regulation of foreign bank operations in the United States.

International Banking Facility (IBF)   Operations established by U.S. international banks that are free from a number of regulations restraining domestic banks, including deposit insurance and reserve requirements.

international bond   Bond issued in domestic capital markets by foreign borrowers, foreign bonds, or issued in the Eurocurrency markets in currency different from that of the home currency of the borrower, Eurobonds.

international competitiveness   The ability of a firm, an industry, or a country to compete in the international marketplace at a stable or rising standard of living.

international debt load   Total accumulated negative net investment of a nation.

international law   The body of rules governing relationships between sovereign states; also certain treaties and agreements respected by a number of countries.

International Monetary Fund (IMF)   A specialized agency of the United Nations established in 1944. An international financial institution for dealing with Balance of Payment problems; the first international monetary authority with at least some degree of power over national authorities.

international monetary system   The set of rules or procedures in place for making and receiving international payments.

International Trade Organization (ITO)   A forward-looking approach to international trade and investment embodied in the 1948 Havana Charter; due to disagreements among sponsoring nations, its provisions were never ratified.

interpretive cultural knowledge   An acquired ability to understand and fully appreciate the nuances of foreign cultural traits and patterns.

intrafirm transfers   The sale of goods or services between units of the same firm. For example, the sale of an unfinished product by the U.S. parent firm to its foreign subsidiary in the United Kingdom.

intraindustry trade   The simultaneous export and import of the same good by a country. It is of interest due to the traditional theory that a country will either export or import a good, but not do both at the same time.

inventory   Materials on hand for use in the production process; also finished goods on hand.

inventory carrying costs   The expense of maintaining inventories.

Jamaica Agreement   An agreement reached in 1976 by the Group of Seven to continue to allow their currencies to float in response to market pressures.

joint occurrence   Occurrence of a phenomenon affecting the business environment in several locations simultaneously.

Joint Research and Development Act   A 1984 act that allows both domestic and foreign firms to participate in joint basic-research efforts without fear of U.S. antitrust action.

just-in-time inventory   Materials scheduled to arrive precisely when they are needed on a production line.

land bridge   Transfer of ocean freight on land among various modes of transportation.

Law of One Price   The theory that the relative prices of any single good between countries, expressed in each country's currency, is representative of the proper or appropriate exchange rate value.

Leontief Paradox   Wassily Leontief's studies of U.S. trade indicated that the United States was a labor-abundant country, exporting labor-intensive products. This was a paradox because of the general belief that the United States was a capital-abundant country which should be exporting capital-intensive products.

letter of credit   Document issued by a bank promising to pay a specified amount of money to an exporter; the most common mechanism for financing international trade.

LIBOR   The London InterBank Offer Rate. The rate of interest charged by top-quality international banks on loans to similar quality banks in London. This interest rate is often used in both domestic and international markets as the rate of interest on loans and other financial agreements.

licensing agreement   An agreement in which one firm permits another to use its intellectual property for compensation.

LIFO   Method of valuation of inventories for accounting purposes, meaning Last-In-First-Out. The principle rests on the practice of recording inventory by "layer" of the cost at which it was incurred.

liner service   Ocean shipping characterized by regularly scheduled passage on established routes.

lingua franca   The language habitually used among people of diverse speech to facilitate communication.

lobbyist   Typically, a well-connected person or firm that is hired by a business to influence the decision making of policymakers and legislators.

local content   Regulations to gain control over foreign investment by ensuring that a large share of the product is locally produced or a larger share of the profit is retained in the country.

location decision   A decision concerning the number of facilities to establish and where they should be situated.

logistics platform   Vital to a firm's competitive position, it is determined by a location's ease and convenience of market reach under favorable cost circumstances.

London Interbank Offer Rate (LIBOR)   The rate at which large London banks will lend funds to each other in Eurodollars.

Louvre Accord   Another name for the Paris Pact.

low-context cultures   Cultures in which most information is conveyed explicitly rather than through cultural nuances.

Maastricht Treaty   The agreement signed in December 1991 in Maastricht, the Netherlands, in which European Community members agreed to a specific timetable and set of necessary conditions to create a single currency for the EC countries by the end of this century.

macroeconomic approach   An approach concerned with total output, income, and employment; an approach to accounting that gives government officials the information they need to take an active role in managing the economy, as occurs in centrally planned economies.

macroeconomic level   Level at which trading relationships affect individual markets.

management contract   An international business alternative in which the firm sells its expertise in running a company while avoiding the risk or benefit of ownership.

managerial commitment   The desire and drive on the part of management to act on an idea.

maquiladoras   Plants that make goods and parts or process food for export back to the United States.

market-differentiated pricing   Price-setting strategy based on demand rather than cost.

market imperfections   Depart from the strict assumptions of competitive economic theory; rationale for government intervention; for example, market gaps in long-term, high-volume export financing.

market seekers   Firms basing their growth strategy on better opportunities in foreign markets.

market transparency   Availability of full disclosure and information about key market factors such as supply, demand, quality, service, and prices.

marketing infrastructure   Facilitating marketing agencies in a country; for example, market research firms, channel members.

materials management   The timely movement of raw materials, parts, and supplies into and through the firm.

matrix structure   An organizational structure that uses functional and divisional structures simultaneously.

media strategy   Strategy applied to the selection of media vehicles and the development of a media schedule.

mercantilism   Political and economic policy in the 17th and early 18th centuries aimed at increasing a nation's wealth and power by encouraging the export of goods in return for gold.

merchandise trade   An account of the BOP statement that records funds used for merchandise imports and funds obtained from merchandise exports.

microeconomic level   Level of business concerns that affect an individual firm or industry.

minority participation   Participation by a group having less than the number of votes necessary for control.

mixed aid credits   Credits at rates composed partially of commercial interest rates and partially of highly subsidized developmental aid interest rates.

mixed structure   An organizational structure that combines two or more organizational dimensions; for example, products, areas, or functions.

money market hedge   The international equivalent of selling accounts receivable. A firm may wish to avoid currency risk by selling at a discount the foreign currency denominated receivable today to obtain the money now, eliminating the exposure.

Most-Favored Nation (MFN)   A term describing a GATT clause that calls for member countries to grant other member countries the most favorable treatment they accord any country concerning imports and exports.

multilateral negotiations   Negotiations carried out among a number of countries.

multilateral netting   The process of settling only the net difference in payments between units of a multinational firm.

multilateral trade negotiations   Trade negotiations among more than two parties; the intricate relationships among trading countries.

multiple factor indexes   Indexes that measure market potential indirectly by using proxy variables.

national security   The ability of a nation to protect its internal values from external threats.

national sovereignty   The supreme right of nations to determine national policies; freedom from external control.

natural hedging   The structuring of a firm's operations so that cash flows by currency, inflows against outflows, are matched.

net present value (NPV)   The sum of the present values of all cash inflows and outflows from an investment project discounted at the cost of capital.

1992 White Paper   A key document developed by the EC Commission to outline the further requirements necessary for a successful integration of the European Community.

nonfinancial incentives   Nonmonetary offers intended to motivate; special offers designed to attract foreign direct investors that may take the form of guaranteed government purchases, special protection from competition, or improved infrastructure facilities, as examples.

nontariff barriers   Barriers to trade, other than tariffs. Examples include buy-domestic campaigns, preferential treatment for domestic bidders, and restrictions on market entry of foreign products such as involved inspection procedures.

not-invented-here syndrome   A defensive, territorial attitude that, if held by managers, can frustrate effective implementation of global strategies.

ocean shipping   The forwarding of freight by ocean carrier.

official reserves account   An account in the BOP statement that shows (1) the change in the amount of funds immediately available to a country for making international payments and (2) the borrowing and lending that has taken place between the monetary authorities of different countries either directly or through the International Monetary Fund.

official settlements balance   A summary measure of a country's Balance of Payments which is the sum of the current account, long-term and short-term capital accounts, and the net balance on errors and omissions.

offset   A form of barter arrangement designed to reduce the Balance of Payment effect of an international transaction. Usually calls for portions of a purchased product to be produced or assembled in the purchasing country; may take the form of coproduction, licensing, subcontracting, or joint venture; mostly used in the context of military sales.

offshore banking   The use of banks or bank branches located in low-tax countries, often Caribbean islands, to raise and hold capital for multinational operations.

open account   A type of trade credit that allows buyers to purchase goods or services and pay for them within a specified period of time without charges or interest.

operating or service lease   A lease that transfers most but not all benefits and costs inherent in the ownership of the property to the lessee. Payments do not fully cover the cost of purchasing the asset or incurring the liability.

operating risk   The danger of interference by governments or other groups in one's corporate operations abroad.

opportunity cost   Cost incurred by a firm as the result of foreclosure of other sources of profit; for example, for the licenser in a licensing agreement, the cost of foregoing alternatives such as exports or direct investment.

order cycle time   The total time that passes between the placement of an order and the receipt of the merchandise.

orientation program   A program that familiarizes new workers with their roles; the preparation of employees for assignment overseas.

Overseas Private Investment Corporation   A federal agency that provides insurance to U.S. direct foreign investors.

ownership risk   The risk inherent in maintaining ownership of property abroad. The exposure of foreign owned assets to governmental intervention.

par value   The face value of a financial instrument.

parallel barter   Another term for counterpurchase.

Paris Convention for the Protection of Industrial Property   An agreement among 96 countries to set minimum standards of protection for patents, designs, and trademarks.

Paris Pact   Agreements reached in 1987 by the Group of Five plus Canada to cooperate closely to foster stability of exchange rates.

patent   A government grant to an inventor providing an exclusive right to the invention for 17 years.

pax Romana   Two relatively peaceful centuries in the Roman Empire.

pegging   Establishing and maintaining a par value for a currency.

pension liabilities   The accumulating obligations of employers to fund the retirement or pension plans of employees.

perestroika   A movement to fundamentally reform the Soviet economy by improving the overall technological and industrial base and the quality of life for Soviet citizens through increased availability of food, housing, and consumer goods.

perishability   Susceptibility to deterioration; the characteristic of services that makes them difficult to inventory.

physical distribution   The movement of finished products to customers.

Plaza Agreement   An accord reached in 1985 by the Group of Five that held that the major nations should join in a coordinated effort to bring down the value of the U.S. dollar.

political risk   The risk of loss by an international corporation of assets, earning power, or managerial control as a result of political actions by the host country.

polycentric   Tending to regard each culture as a separate entity; tending to be oriented toward individual foreign markets.

portfolio investment   An account in the BOP statement that records investments in assets with an original maturity of more than one year and where an investor's ownership position is less than 10 percent.

ports   Harbor towns or cities where ships may take on or discharge cargo; the lack of ports and port services is the greatest constraint in ocean shipping.

positioning   The perception by consumers of a firm's product in relation to competitors' products.

preferential policies   Government policies that favor certain (usually domestic) firms; for example, the use of national carriers for the transport of government freight even when more economical alternatives exist.

price controls   Government regulation of the prices of goods and services; control of the prices of imported goods or services as a result of domestic political pressures.

price escalation   The establishing of export prices far in excess of domestic prices—often due to a long distribution channel and frequent markups.

primary data   Data obtained directly for a specific research purpose through interviews, focus groups, surveys, observation, or experimentation.

private placement   The sale of debt securities to private or institutional investors without going through a public issuance like that of a bond issue or equity issue.

process structure   A variation of the functional structure in which departments are formed on the basis of production processes.

product cycle theory   A theory that views products as passing through four stages: introduction, growth, maturity, decline.

product differentiation   The effort to build unique differences or improvements into products.

product structure   An organizational structure in which product divisions are responsible for all manufacturing and marketing.

production possibilities frontier   A theoretical method of representing the total productive capabilities of a nation used in the formulation of classical and modern trade theory.

promotional message   The content of an advertisement or a publicity release.

proxy information   Data used as a substitute for more desirable data that are unobtainable.

punitive tariff   A tax on an imported good or service intended to punish a trading partner.

purchasing power parity (PPP)   A theory that the prices of tradable goods will tend to equalize across countries.

quality circles   Groups of workers who meet regularly to discuss issues related to productivity.

quality of life   The standard of living combined with environmental factors, it determines the level of well-being of individuals.

quality of work life   Various corporate efforts in the areas of personal and professional development undertaken with the objectives of increasing employee satisfaction and increasing productivity.

quotas   Legal restrictions on the import quantity of particular goods, imposed by governments as barriers to trade.

R&D cost Research and development cost; the costs incurred in developing technology.

reciprocity provisions   Provisions for the purchase of goods on a preferential basis with the expectation that the seller will in turn buy on a preferential basis.

recognizability   The characteristic of appearing to be previously known; the ability of a product to be recognized even though it has been adapted to local market conditions.

reference groups   Groups such as the family, co-workers, and professional and trade associations that provide the values and attitudes that influence and shape behavior, including consumer behavior.

reference zone   Another name for a managed float.

regiocentric   Tending to be oriented toward regions larger than individual countries as markets.

reliability   Dependability; the predictability of the outcome of an action. For example, the reliability of arrival time for ocean freight or airfreight.

representative office   An office of an international bank established in a foreign country to serve the bank's customers in the area in an advisory capacity; does not take deposits or make loans.

resource seekers   Firms looking for either natural or human resources.

reverse distribution   A system responding to environmental concerns that ensures a firm can retrieve a product from the market for subsequent use, recycling, or disposal.

royalty   The compensation paid by one firm to another under an agreement.

rules of the game   An expression symbolizing the unwritten rules of the gold standard—a country will allow gold to flow in and out in order to preserve currency values versus gold.

safe haven   The role played by the U.S. dollar as a currency which international investors may flock to during times of international crisis. The Japanese yen, however, is increasingly replacing the U.S. dollar as a safe haven.

sanction   A governmental action, usually consisting of a specific coercive trade measure, that distorts the free flow of trade for an adversarial or political purpose rather than an economic one.

sea bridge   The transfer of freight among various modes of transportation at sea.

secondary data   Data originally collected to serve another purpose than the one in which the researcher is currently interested.

securitization   The conversion of developing country bank debt into tradable securities.

self-management   Independent decision making; a high degree of worker involvement in corporate decision making.

self-reference criterion   The unconscious reference to one's own cultural values.

selling forward   A market transaction in which the seller promises to sell currency at a certain future date at a prespecified price.

sensitivity training   Training in human relations that focuses on personal and interpersonal interactions; training that focuses on enhancing an expatriate's flexibility in situations quite different from those at home.

service capacity   The maximum level at which a service provider is able to provide services to customers.

service consistency   Uniform quality of service.

service trade   The international exchange of personal or professional services, such as financial and banking services, construction, and tourism.

shipper's order   A negotiable bill of lading that can be bought, sold, or traded while the subject goods are still in transit and that is used for letter of credit transactions.

Single Europe Act   The legislative basis for the European Integration.

Smithsonian Agreement   An agreement reached by the Group of Ten in 1971 concerning changes in the Bretton Woods Agreement on currency values.

Smoot-Hawley Act   A 1930 act that raised import duties to the highest rates ever imposed by the United States; designed to promote domestic production, it resulted in the downfall of the world trading system.

social infrastructure   The housing, health, educational, and other social systems in a country.

social stratification   The division of a particular population into classes.

sogoshosha   A large Japanese general trading company.

Special Drawing Right (SDR)   International reserves created by the IMF to support growth in international trade and investment; essentially, a currency used only in transactions among central banks.

spot rates   Contracts that provide for two parties to exchange currencies with delivery in two business days.

spread   The difference between two amounts; a bank's profit on foreign exchange trading.

standard of living   The level of material affluence of a group or nation, measured as a composite of quantities and qualities of goods.

standard worldwide pricing   Price-setting strategy based on average unit costs of fixed, variable, and export-related costs.

state-owned enterprise   A corporate form that has emerged in non-Communist countries, primarily for reasons of national security and economic security.

straight bill of lading   A nonnegotiable bill of lading usually used in prepaid transactions in which the transported goods involved are delivered to a specific individual or company.

strategic alliances   A new term for collaboration among firms, often similar to joint ventures.

strategic leader   A highly competent national subsidiary located in a strategically critical market.

Subpart F income   Passive income as defined by the Tax Reform Act of 1986.

Subsidies and Countervailing Measures Code   An agreement reached during the Tokyo Round of negotiations that seeks to reduce the distortive effects of export subsidies on world trade.

switch-trading   A refinement of clearing account barter in which credits and debits can be sold or transferred to a third party.

syndicated loan   A loan which is arranged and managed by a small group of 2 to 5 banks and then sold in pieces to other banking institutions worldwide.

systems concept   A concept of logistics based on the notion that materials-flow activities are so complex that they can be considered only in the context of their interaction.

tariffs Taxes on imported goods and services, instituted by governments as a means to raise revenue and as barriers to trade.

tax equalization   Reimbursement by the company when an employee in an overseas assignment pays taxes at a higher rate than if he or she were at home.

team building   A process that enhances the cohesiveness of a department or group by helping members learn how to organize their work and assume responsibility for it.

technology transfer   The transfer of systematic knowledge for the manufacture of a product, the application of a process, or the rendering of a service.

temporal method   A method for translating the financial statements of a foreign subsidiary from the host country's currency to the functional currency.

Tokyo Round   One of a series of trade conferences sponsored by the General Agreement on Tariffs and Trade.

total after-tax profit concept   A decision concept that takes into account the impact of national tax policies on the logistics function.

total cost concept   A decision concept that uses cost as a basis for measurement in order to evaluate and optimize logistical activities.

Trade Act of 1974   An act that, among other provisions, expanded the definition of international trade to include trade in services.

trade creation   A benefit of economic integration; the benefit to a particular country when a group of countries trade a product freely among themselves but maintain common barriers to trade with nonmembers.

trade diversion   A cost of economic integration; the cost to a particular country when a group of countries trade a product freely among themselves but maintain common barriers to trade with nonmembers.

trade-off concept   A decision concept that recognizes linkages within the decision system.

trade policy mechanisms   Measures used to influence and alter trade relationships.

trademark The distinctive identification of a product or service in the form of a name, symbol, letter, picture, or other device to distinguish it from similar offerings.

trademark licensing A special form of licensing that permits the names or logos of recognizable individuals or groups to be used on products.

trading blocks Formed by agreements among countries to establish links through movement of goods, services, capital, and labor across borders.

tramp service Ocean shipping via irregular routes, scheduled only on demand.

transaction exposure The potential for losses or gains when a firm is engaged in a transaction denominated in a foreign currency.

transfer cost All variable costs incurred in transferring technology to a licensee and all ongoing costs of maintaining the licensing agreement.

transfer risk The danger of having one's ability to transfer profits or products in and out of a country inhibited by governmental rules and regulations.

transit time The period between departure and arrival of a carrier.

translation exposure The potential effect on a firm's financial statements of a change in currency values.

transportation modes Forms of transportation.

Treaty of Rome The original agreement that established the foundation for the formation of the European Economic Community.

trigger mechanisms Specific acts or stimuli that set off reactions.

tunnel A term describing the 1971 Smithsonian Agreement's allowance of a 2 1/4 percent variation from par value for currency exchange rates.

turnkey operation A specialized form of management contract between a customer and an organization to provide a complete operational system together with the skills investment needed for unassisted maintenance and operation.

undistributed earnings The proportion of a firm's net income after taxes which is retained within the firm for internal purposes.

uniform accounting A system of accounting that follows uniform standards prescribed by law, as in Germany and France.

unilateral transfer A current account on the Balance of Payments statement that records gifts from the residents of one country to the residents of another.

United States Trade Representative A U.S. cabinet position responsible for the area of trade negotiations, as designated in the Trade Act of 1979.

validated export license An export license from the Department of Commerce that authorizes shipment of a high-technology product.

value-added tax (VAT) A tax on the value added at each stage of the production and distribution process; a tax assessed in most European countries and also common among Latin American countries.

voluntary agreements Trade-restraint agreements resulting in self-imposed restrictions not covered by the GATT rules; used to manage or distort trade flows. For example, Japanese restraints on the export of cars to the United States.

Webb-Pomerene Act A 1918 statute that excludes from antitrust prosecution U.S. firms cooperating to develop foreign markets.

Webb-Pomerene association A group of U.S. firms cooperating to develop foreign markets, as permitted by the Webb-Pomerene Act.

withholding taxes Taxes applied to the payment of dividends, interest, or royalties by firms.

work councils Councils that provide labor a say in corporate decision making through a representative body that may consist entirely of workers or of a combination of managers and workers.

work redesign programs Programs that alter jobs to increase both the quality of the work experience and productivity.

work scheduling Preparing schedules of when and how long workers are at the workplace.

working capital management The management of a firm's current assets (cash, accounts receivable, inventories) and current liabilities (accounts payable, short-term debt).

NAME INDEX

SUBJECT INDEX